Collins

PORTUGUESE
DICTIONARY
ESSENTIAL EDITION

Published by Collins
An imprint of HarperCollins Publishers
Westerhill Road
Bishopbriggs
Glasgow G64 2QT

First Edition 2019

10 9 8 7 6 5 4 3 2 1

© HarperCollins Publishers 2019

ISBN 978-0-00-820088-6

Collins® is a registered trademark of
HarperCollins Publishers Limited

collinsdictionary.com
collins.co.uk/dictionaries

Typeset by Davidson Publishing
Solutions, Glasgow

Printed and bound by CPI Group (UK)
Ltd, Croydon, CR0 4YY

Entered words that we have reason to
believe constitute trademarks have
been designated as such. However,
neither the presence nor absence of
such designation should be regarded
as affecting the legal status of any
trademark.

The contents of this publication are
believed correct at the time of
printing. Nevertheless the Publisher
can accept no responsibility for errors
or omissions, changes in the detail
given or for any expense or loss
thereby caused.

HarperCollins does not warrant that
any website mentioned in this title will
be provided uninterrupted, that any
website will be error free, that defects
will be corrected, or that the website
or the server that makes it available
are free of viruses or bugs. For full
terms and conditions please refer to
the site terms provided on the website.

A catalogue record for this book is
available from the British Library.

If you would like to comment on any
aspect of this book, please contact us
at the given address or online.
E-mail: dictionaries@harpercollins.co.uk
 facebook.com/collinsdictionary
 @collinsdict

Acknowledgements
We would like to thank those authors
and publishers who kindly gave
permission for copyright material
to be used in the Collins Corpus.
We would also like to thank Times
Newspapers Ltd for providing
valuable data.

ÍNDICE

CONTENTS

MARCAS REGISTRADAS

As palavras que acreditamos
constituir marcas registradas
foram assim denominadas. Todavia,
não se deve supor que a presença ou
a ausência dessa denominação possa
afetar o status legal de qualquer
marca.

NOTE ON TRADEMARKS

Words which we have reason to
believe constitute trademarks have
been designated as such. However,
neither the presence nor the absence
of such designation should be
regarded as affecting the legal
status of any trademark.

INTRODUÇÃO

Ficamos felizes com a sua decisão de comprar o Dicionário Inglês-Português Collins e esperamos que ele lhe seja útil na escola, em casa, nas férias ou no trabalho.

Esta introdução fornece algumas sugestões de como utilizar da melhor maneira possível o seu dicionário – não somente a partir da ampla lista de palavras mas também a partir das informações fornecidas em cada verbete. Este dicionário visa a ajudá-lo a ler e a entender o inglês moderno, assim como a expressar-se corretamente.

No início do Dicionário Collins, aparecem as abreviaturas utilizadas, e a ilustração dos sons através de símbolos fonéticos. Você encontrará, a seguir, verbos irregulares ingleses e quadros com verbos em português, seguidos por uma seção com números, horas e datas.

COMO UTILIZAR O DICIONÁRIO COLLINS

Um grande número de informações pode ser encontrado neste dicionário. Foram utilizados vários tipos e tamanhos de letras, símbolos, abreviaturas e parênteses. As convenções e símbolos usados são explicados nas seções seguintes.

VERBETES

As palavras que você procurar no dicionário – os verbetes – estão em ordem alfabética. As palavras que aparecem no topo de cada página indicam o primeiro verbete (se for nas páginas pares) ou o último verbete (se for nas páginas ímpares) da página em questão. Informações sobre a utilização ou forma de certos verbetes são dadas entre parênteses e, em geral, aparecem em forma abreviada e em itálico (p. ex. (*fam*), (*Com*)).

Quando for apropriado, palavras derivadas aparecem agrupadas no mesmo verbete (**acento, acentuar**) num formato ligeiramente menor do que o verbete.

As expressões comuns nas quais o verbete aparece estão impressas em um tamanho diferente de negrito romano. O símbolo "~" usado nas expressões representa o verbete principal no começo de cada parágrafo. Por exemplo, na entrada "**cold**", a expressão "**to be ~**" equivale a "**to be cold**".

TRANSCRIÇÃO FONÉTICA

A transcrição fonética de cada palavra (indicando a sua pronúncia) encontra-se entre colchetes imediatamente a seguir ao verbete (p. ex. **big** [bɪg]). Há uma lista dos símbolos fonéticos utilizados nas páginas xii–xvii.

A tradução para o verbete aparece em letra normal e, quando há mais de um significado ou utilização, estes estão separados por um ponto e vírgula. Frequentemente, você encontrará outras palavras em itálico e entre parênteses antes da tradução, sugerindo contextos nos quais o verbete pode aparecer (p. ex. **rough** (*voice*) ou (*weather*)) ou fornecendo sinônimos (p. ex. **rush** (*hurry*)).

PALAVRAS-CHAVE

Foi dada atenção especial a certas palavras em inglês e em português consideradas "palavras-chave" em cada língua. Elas podem, por exemplo, ser usadas com muita frequência ou ter muitos tipos de utilização (p. ex., **be**, **get**). Verbetes destacados com números ajudam a distinguir as categorias gramaticais e diferentes significados. São fornecidas informações complementares entre parênteses e em itálico na língua relevante para o usuário.

INFORMAÇÃO GRAMATICAL

As categorias gramaticais são dadas em versalete e abreviadas após a ortografia fonética do verbete (p. ex., VT, ADJ, VI).

Os adjetivos aparecem em ambos os gêneros quando forem diferentes (**interno, -a**). Esta distinção também é feita quando os adjetivos têm uma forma irregular no feminino ou no plural (p. ex., **ateu**, **ateia**). As formas irregulares de substantivos feminino ou plural também são indicadas (p. ex., **child** (*pl* **children**)).

INTRODUCTION

We are delighted you have decided to buy the Collins Portuguese Dictionary and hope you will enjoy and benefit from using it at school, at home, on holiday or at work.

This introduction gives you a few tips on how to get the most out of your dictionary – not simply from its comprehensive wordlist but also from the information provided in each entry. This will help you to read and understand modern Portuguese, as well as communicate and express yourself in the language.

The Collins Portuguese Dictionary begins by listing the abbreviations used in the text and illustrating the sounds shown by the phonetic symbols. Next you will find English irregular verbs and Portuguese verb tables followed by a section on numbers, time, and dates.

USING YOUR COLLINS DICTIONARY

A wealth of information is presented in the dictionary, using various typefaces, sizes of type, symbols, abbreviations and brackets. The conventions and symbols used are explained in the following sections.

HEADWORDS

The words you look up in the dictionary – 'headwords' – are listed alphabetically. The headwords appearing at the top of each page indicate the first (if it appears on a left-hand page) and last word (if it appears on a right-hand page) dealt with on the page in question.

Information about the usage or form of certain headwords is given in brackets after the phonetic spelling. This usually appears in abbreviated form and in italics. (e.g. (*fam*), (*Comm*)).

Where appropriate, words related to headwords are grouped in the same entry (**produce, producer**) in a slightly smaller bold type than the headword. Common expressions in which the headword appears are shown in a different size of bold roman type. The swung dash, ~, represents the main headword at the start of each entry. For example, in the entry for '**caminho**', the phrase '**pôr-se a ~**' should be read '**pôr-se a caminho**'.

PHONETIC SPELLINGS

The phonetic spelling of each headword (indicating its pronunciation) is given in square brackets immediately after the headword (e.g. **grande** ['grãdʒi]). A guide to these spellings is given on pages xii–xvii.

MEANINGS

Headword translations are given in ordinary type and, where more than one meaning or usage exists, they are separated by a semicolon. You will often find other words in italics in brackets before the translations. These offer suggested contexts in which the headword might appear (e.g. **intenso** (*emoção*)) or provide synonyms (e.g. **cândido** (*inocente*)).

'KEY' WORDS

Special status is given to certain Portuguese and English words which are considered as 'key' words in each language. They may, for example, occur very frequently or have several types of usage (e.g. **bem**, **ficar**). A combination of lozenges and numbers helps you to distinguish different parts of speech and different meanings. Further helpful information is provided in brackets and in italics in the relevant language for the user.

GRAMMATICAL INFORMATION

Parts of speech are given in abbreviated form in small caps after the phonetic spellings of headwords (e.g. VT, ADJ, PREP).

Genders of Portuguese nouns are indicated as follows: *m* for a masculine and *f* for a feminine noun. Feminine and irregular plural forms of nouns are also shown next to the headword (**inglês, -esa**; **material** (*pl* **-ais**)). Adjectives are given in both masculine and feminine forms where these forms are different (**comilão, -lona**).

The gender of the Portuguese translation also appears in *italics* immediately following the key element of the translation, except where there is a regular masculine singular noun ending in 'o', or a regular feminine singular noun ending in 'a'.

ABREVIATURAS

ABBREVIATIONS

abreviatura	AB(B)R	abbreviation
adjetivo	ADJ	adjective
administração	Admin	administration
advérbio, locução adverbial	ADV	adverb, adverbial phrase
aeronáutica	Aer	flying, air travel
agricultura	Agr	agriculture
anatomia	Anat	anatomy
arquitetura	Arq, Arch	architecture
artigo definido	ART DEF	definite article
artigo indefinido	ART INDEF	indefinite article
uso atributivo do substantivo	ATR	compound element
Austrália	Aust	Australia
automobilismo	Aut(o)	the motor car and motoring
auxiliar	AUX	auxiliary
aeronáutica	Aviat	flying, air travel
biologia	Bio	biology
botânica, flores	Bot	botany
português do Brasil	br	Brazilian Portuguese
inglês britânico	brit	British English
química	Chem	chemistry
linguagem coloquial	col	colloquial
comércio, finanças, bancos	Com(m)	commerce, finance, banking
comparativo	compar	comparative
computação	Comput	computing
conjunção	CONJ	conjunction
construção	Constr	building
uso atributivo do substantivo	CPD	compound element
cozinha	Culin	cookery
artigo definido	DEF ART	definite article
economia	Econ	economics
educação, escola e universidade	Educ	schooling, schools and universities
eletricidade, eletrônica	Elet, Elec	electricity, electronics
especialmente	esp	especially
exclamação	excl	exclamation
feminino	f	feminine
ferrovia	Ferro	railways
uso figurado	fig	figurative use
física	Fís	physics

fotografia	*Foto*	photography
(verbo inglês) do qual a partícula é inseparável	FUS	(phrasal verb) where the particle is inseparable
geralmente	*gen*	generally
geografia, geologia	*Geo*	geography, geology
geralmente	*ger*	generally
impessoal	IMPESS, IMPERS	impersonal
artigo indefinido	INDEF ART	indefinite article
linguagem coloquial	*inf*	colloquial
infinitivo	*infin*	infinitive
invariável	INV	invariable
irregular	*irreg*	irregular
jurídico	*Jur*	law
gramática, linguística	*Ling*	grammar, linguistics
masculino	*m*	masculine
matemática	*Mat(h)*	mathematics
medicina	*Med*	medicine
masculino ou feminino	*m/f*	masculine/feminine militar,
exército	*Mil*	military matters
música	*Mús, Mus*	music
substantivo	N	noun
navegação, náutica	*Náut, Naut*	sailing, navigation
adjetivo ou substantivo numérico	NUM	numeral adjective or noun
	o.s.	oneself
pejorativo	*pej*	pejorative
fotografia	*Phot*	photography
física	*Phys*	physics
fisiologia	*Physiol*	physiology
plural	*pl*	plural
política	*Pol*	politics
particípio passado	PP	past participle
preposição	PREP	preposition
pronome	PRON	pronoun
português de Portugal	pt	European Portuguese
pretérito	*pt*	past tense
química	*Quím*	chemistry
religião e cultos	*Rel*	religion, worship
alguém	*sb*	somebody
educação, escola e universidade	*Sch*	schooling, schools and universities
singular	*sg*	singular

algo	*sth*	something
sujeito (gramatical)	*su(b)j*	(grammatical) subject
subjuntivo, conjuntivo	*sub(jun)*	subjunctive
superlativo	*superl*	superlative
também	*tb*	also
técnica, tecnologia	*Tec(h)*	technical term, technology
telecomunicações	*Tel*	telecommunications
tipografia, imprensa	*Tip*	typography, printing
televisão	*TV*	television
tipografia, imprensa	*Typ*	typography, printing
inglês americano	*us*	American English
verbo	VB	verb
verbo intransitivo	VI	intransitive verb
verbo reflexivo	VR	reflexive verb
verbo transitivo	VT	transitive verb
zoologia	*Zool*	zoology
marca registrada	®	registered trademark
equivalente cultural	≈	cultural equivalent
linguagem ofensiva	*!*	offensive

PRONÚNCIA EM INGLÊS

VOGAIS

	Exemplo em inglês	Explicação
[a:]	father	Entre o a de padre e o o de nó; como em fada
[√]	but, come	Aproximadamente como o primeiro a de cama
[æ]	man, cat	Som entre o a de lá e o e de pé
[ə]	father, ago	Som parecido com o e final de saudade na pronúncia de Portugal
[ə:]	bird, heard	Entre o e aberto e o o fechado
[ε]	get, bed	Como em pé
[ɪ]	it, big	Mais breve do que em si
[i:]	tea, see	Como em fino
[ɔ]	hot, wash	Como em pó
[ɔ:]	saw, all	Como o o de porte
[u]	put, book	Som breve e mais fechado do que em burro
[u:]	too, you	Som aberto como em juro

DITONGOS

	Exemplo em inglês	Explicação
[aɪ]	fly, high	Como em baile
[au]	how, house	Como em causa
[εə]	there, bear	Como o e de aeroporto
[eɪ]	day, obey	Como o ei de lei
[ɪə]	here, hear	Como ia de companhia
[əu]	go, note	[ə] seguido de um u breve
[ɔɪ]	boy, oil	Como em boia
[uə]	poor, sure	Como ua em sua

CONSOANTES

	Exemplo em inglês	Explicação
[d]	men**d**ed	Como em *da*do, an*d*ar
[g]	**g**et, bi**g**	Como em *g*rande
[dʒ]	**g**in, **j**udge	Como em i*d*ade
[˜]	si**ng**	Como em ci*n*co
[h]	**h**ouse, **h**e	*h* aspirado
[j]	**y**oung, **y**es	Como em *i*ogurte
[k]	**c**ome, mo**ck**	Como em *c*ama
[r]	**r**ed, t**r**ead	*r* como em po*r*que na pronúncia caipira
[s]	**s**and, ye**s**	Como em *s*ala
[z]	ro**s**e, **z**ebra	Como em *z*ebra
[ʃ]	**sh**e, ma**ch**ine	Como em *ch*apéu
[tʃ]	**ch**in, ri**ch**	Como *t* em *t*imbre
[w]	**w**ater, **wh**ich	Como o *u* em ág*u*a
[ʒ]	vi**s**ion	Como em *j*á
[θ]	**th**ink, my**th**	Sem equivalente, aproximadamente como um *s* pronunciado entre os dentes
[ð]	**th**is, **th**e	Sem equivalente, aproximadamente como um *z* pronunciado entre os dentes, e com vibração das cordas vocais

b, f, l, m, n, p, t, v pronunciam-se como em português.

O sinal [*] indica que o r final escrito pronuncia-se apenas em inglês britânico, exceto quando a palavra seguinte começa por uma vogal. O sinal [≠] indica a sílaba acentuada.

BRAZILIAN PORTUGUESE PRONUNCIATION

CONSONANTS

c	[k]	café	c before a, o, u is pronounced as in cat
ce, ci	[s]	cego	c before e or i, as in receive
ç	[s]	raça	ç is pronounced as in receive
ch	[ʃ]	chave	ch is pronounced as in shock
d	[d]	data	as in English *except*
de, di	[dʒ]	difícil cidade	d before an i sound or final unstressed e is pronounced as in judge
g	[g]	gado	g before a, o, u as in gap
ge, gi	[ʒ]	gíria	g before e or i, as s in leisure
h		humano	h is always silent in Portuguese
j	[ʒ]	jogo	j is pronounced as s in leisure
l	[l]	limpo, janela	as in English *except*
	[w]	falta, total	l after a vowel tends to become w
lh	[ʎ]	trabalho	lh is pronounced like the lli in million
m	[m]	animal, massa	as in English *except*
	[ãw]	cantam	m at the end of a syllable preceded by a
	[ĩ]	sim	vowel nasalizes the preceding vowel
n	[n]	nadar, penal	as in English *except*
	[ã]	cansar	n at the end of a syllable, preceded by a vowel
	[ẽ]	alento	and followed by a consonant, nasalizes the preceding vowel
nh	[˜]	tamanho	nh is pronounced like the ni in onion
q	[k]	queijo	qu before i or e is usually pronounced as in kick
q	[kw]	quanto cinquenta	qu before a or o, and sometimes before e or i, is pronounced as in queen
-r-	[r]	compra	r preceded by a consonant (except n) and followed by a vowel is pronounced with a single trill
r-, -r-	[h]	rato, arpão	inital r, r followed by a consonant and rr are
rr	[h]	borracha	pronounced like h in house
-r	[r]	pintar, dizer	word-final r can sometimes be heard as a single trill, but usually it is not pronounced at all in colloquial speech
s-	[s]	sol escada livros	as in English *except*

-s-	[z]	me**s**a	intervocalic *s* and *s* before *b, d, g, l, m, n, r,* and *v,* as in ro**s**e
		ra**s**gar, de**s**maio	
-ss-	[s]	no**ss**o	double *s* is always pronounced as in bo**ss**
t	[t]	**t**odo	as in English excep**t**
te, ti	[tʃ]	aman**te**	*t* followed by an *i* sound or final unstressed *e* is
		tipo	pronounced as *ch* in **ch**eer
x-	[ʃ]	**x**arope	initial *x* is pronounced like *sh* in **sh**ip
-x-	[s]	e**x**ceto	*x* before a consonant is pronounced like *s* in **s**ail
		e**x**plorar	
ex-	[z]	e**x**ame	*x* in the prefix *ex* before a vowel is pronounced as *z* in **s**queeze
-x-	[ʃ]	rela**x**ar	*x* in any other position may be pronounced as
	[ks]	fi**x**o	in **sh**ip, a**x**e or **s**ail
	[s]	au**x**iliar	
z	[z]	**z**angar	as in English
		carta**z**	

b, f, k, p, v, w are pronounced as in English.

VOWELS

a, á, à, â	[a]	m**a**ta	*a* is normally pronounced as in f**a**ther
ã	[ã]	irm**ã**	*ã* is pronounced approximately as in s**u**ng
e	[e]	v**e**jo	unstressed (except final) *e* is pronounced like *e* in th**ey**, stressed *e* is pronounced either as in th**ey** or as in b**e**t
-e	[i]	fom**e**	final *e* is pronounced as in mon**ey**
é	[ɛ]	mis**é**ria	*é* is pronounced as in b**e**t
ê	[e]	p**ê**lo	*ê* is pronounced as in th**ey**
i	[i]	v**i**da	*i* is pronounced as in m**ea**n
o	[o]	l**o**c**o**m**o**tiva	unstressed (except final) *o* is pronounced as in l**o**cal;
	[ɔ]	l**o**ja	stressed *o* is pronounced either as in l**o**cal or
	[o]	gl**o**bo	as in r**o**ck
-o	[u]	livr**o**	final *o* is pronounced as in f**oo**t
ó	[ɔ]	**ó**leo	*ó* is pronounced as in r**o**ck
ô	[o]	col**ô**nia	*ô* is pronounced as in l**o**cal
u	[u]	l**u**va	*u* is pronounced as in r**u**le
	[w]	ling**u**iça	it is usually silent as in *gue, gui, que, qui* but in
		freq**u**ente	some words it is pronounced as a *w* sound in this position

DIPHTHONGS

ãe	[ãj]	m**ãe**	nasalized, approximately as in fl*y*ing
ai	[aj]	v**ai**	as is r*i*de
ao, au	[aw]	**ao**s, **au**xílio	as is sh*ou*t
ão	[ãw]	v**ão**	nasalized, approximately as in r*ou*nd
ei	[ej]	f**ei**ra	as is th*ey*
eu	[ew]	d**eu**sa	both elements pronounced
oi	[oj]	b**oi**	as is t*oy*
ou	[o]	cen**ou**ra	as is l*o*cal
õe	[õj]	avi**õe**s	nasalized, approximately as in 'b*oi*ng!'

STRESS

The rules of stress in Portuguese are as follows:

(a) when a word ends in *a, e, o, m* (except *im, um* and their plural forms) or *s*, the second last syllable is stressed: cama*ra*da, cama*ra*das; *par*te, *par*tem

(b) when a word ends in *i, u, im* (and plural), *um* (and plural), *n* or a consonant other than *m* or *s*, the stress falls on the last syllable: ven*di*, al*gum*, al*guns*, fa*lar*

(c) when the rules set out in (a) and (b) are not applicable, an acute or circumflex accent appears over the stressed vowel: *ó*tica, *â*nimo, in*glês*

In the phonetic transcription, the symbol [≠] precedes the syllable on which the stress falls.

EUROPEAN PORTUGUESE PRONUNCIATION

The pronunciation of Brazilian Portuguese differs quite markedly from the Portuguese spoken in Portugal itself and in the African and island states. The more phonetic nature of Brazilian means that words nearly always retain their set pronunciation; in European Portuguese, on the other hand, vowels can often be unpronounced or weakened and consonants can change their sound, all depending on their position within a word or whether they are being elided with a following word. The major differences in pronunciation of European Portuguese are as follows:

CONSONANTS: as in Brazilian, except:

-b-	[β]	cu**b**a	*b* between vowels is a softer sound, closer to ha**v**e
d	[d]	**d**ança, **d**ifícil	as in English *except d* between vowels
-d-	[ð]	fa**d**o, ci**d**a**d**e	is softer, approximately as in **th**e
-g-	[ɣ]	sa**g**a	*g* between vowels is a softer sound, approximately as in la**g**er
gu	[ɣw]	a**gu**entar	in certain words *gu* is pronounced as in **Gw**ent
qu	[kw.]	tran**qu**ilo	in certain words *qu* is pronounced as in **qu**oits
r-, rr	[ʀ]		initial *r* and double *r* are pronounced either like
	[rr]		the French *r* or strongly trilled as in Scottish Rory; pronunciation varies according to region
-r-, -r	[ɾ]	**r**ato, a**r**ma	*r* in any other position is slightly trilled
t	[t]	**t**odo, aman**t**e	*t* is pronounced as in English
z	[ʒ]	**z**angar	as in English *except* final *z* is pronounced as *sh* in fla**sh**
	[ʃ]	carta**z**	

VOWELS: as in Brazilian, except:

a	[a]	fal**a**r	stressed *a* is pronounced either as in f**a**ther or as
	[ɐ]	c**a**ma	*u* in f**u**rther
-a-, -a	[ə]	f**a**lar, fal**a**	unstressed or final *a* is pronounced as *e* in furth**e**r
e	[ə]	m**e**dir	unstressed *e* is a very short *i* sound as in rabb**i**t
-e	[ə]	art**e**, regim**e**	final *e* is barely pronounced; these would sound like English *art* and *regime*
o	[u]	po**ç**o, p**o**der	unstressed or final *o* is pronounced as in f**oo**t

PORTUGUESE SPELLING

In 2009, a spelling reform was introduced in all the Portuguese-speaking countries with the aim of eliminating the differences which existed between Brazilian and European Portuguese spelling. The following table summarizes these differences, which you will come across in texts written before the 2009 reform:

Description	Brazilian spelling pre-2009	European Portuguese spelling pre-2009	Universal spelling post-2009
The combinations -gue-, -gui-, -que-, -qui- when u is pronounced	With trema, e.g. *lingüiça, freqüente* etc.	Without trema, e.g. *linguiça, frequente* etc.	Without trema, e.g. *linguiça, frequente* etc.
Stressed -ei- and -oi- in penultimate syllables	With acute accent, e.g. *idéia, heróico*	Without acute accent, e.g. *ideia, heroico*	Without acute accent, e.g. *ideia, heroico*
Stressed o followed by unstressed o	First o has circumflex accent, e.g *vôo, abençôo*	No written accent, e.g. *voo, abençoo*	No written accent, e.g. *voo, abençoo*
comum + mente	*comumente*	*comummente*	*comumente*
Latin consonant group -ct-	Simplified to -c-/-ç- or -t-, e.g. *acionar, ação, ator*	Silent -c- retained, e.g. *accionar, acção, actor*	Simplified spelling, e.g. *acionar, ação, ator*
Latin consonant group -pt-	Simplified to -ç- or -t-, e.g. *exceção, ótimo*	Silent -p- retained, e.g. *excepção, óptimo*	Simplified spelling, e.g. *exceção, ótimo*
Months of the year	e.g. *janeiro, dezembro*	e.g. *Janeiro, Dezembro*	e.g. *janeiro, dezembro*

One important difference between Brazilian and Portuguese spelling which still applies even after the reform is that, when a written accent is required on stressed e and o before m or n, Brazilian uses the circumflex while European uses the acute accent, reflecting the difference in the way the sounds are pronounced, e.g. *tênis* (BR), *ténis* (PT); *econômico* (BR), *económico* (PT).
In addition, there are cases where two different spellings are permitted in European Portuguese to reflect two possible pronunciations, e.g. *sutil/subtil, anistia/amnistia*.

VERBOS IRREGULARES EM INGLÊS

PRESENT	PT	PP	PRESENT	PT	PP
arise	arose	arisen	**find**	found	found
awake	awoke	awoken	**fling**	flung	flung
be (am, is,	was, were	been	**fly**	flew	flown
are; being)			**forbid**	forbad(e)	forbidden
bear	bore	born(e)	**forecast**	forecast	forecast
beat	beat	beaten	**forget**	forgot	forgotten
begin	began	begun	**forgive**	forgave	forgiven
bend	bent	bent	**freeze**	froze	frozen
bet	bet,	bet,	**get**	got	got,
	betted	betted			*(us)* gotten
bid *(at auction)*	bid	bid	**give**	gave	given
bind	bound	bound	**go** (goes)	went	gone
bite	bit	bitten	**grind**	ground	ground
bleed	bled	bled	**grow**	grew	grown
blow	blew	blown	**hang**	hung	hung
break	broke	broken	**hang** *(execute)*	hanged	hanged
breed	bred	bred	**have**	had	had
bring	brought	brought	**hear**	heard	heard
build	built	built	**hide**	hid	hidden
burn	burned,	burned,	**hit**	hit	hit
	burnt	burnt	**hold**	held	held
burst	burst	burst	**hurt**	hurt	hurt
buy	bought	bought	**keep**	kept	kept
can	could	(been able)	**kneel**	knelt,	knelt,
cast	cast	cast		kneeled	kneeled
catch	caught	caught	**know**	knew	known
choose	chose	chosen	**lay**	laid	laid
cling	clung	clung	**lead**	led	led
come	came	come	**lean**	leaned,	leaned,
cost	cost	cost		leant	leant
creep	crept	crept	**leap**	leaped,	leaped,
cut	cut	cut		leapt	leapt
deal	dealt	dealt	**learn**	learned,	learned,
dig	dug	dug		learnt	learnt
do (does)	did	done	**leave**	left	left
draw	drew	drawn	**lend**	lent	lent
dream	dreamed,	dreamed,	**let**	let	let
	dreamt	dreamt	**lie** (lying)	lay	lain
drink	drank	drunk	**light**	lit,	lit,
drive	drove	driven		lighted	lighted
eat	ate	eaten	**lose**	lost	lost
fall	fell	fallen	**make**	made	made
feed	fed	fed	**may**	might	–
feel	felt	felt	**mean**	meant	meant
fight	fought	fought	**meet**	met	met

PRESENT	PT	PP	PRESENT	PT	PP
mistake	mistook	mistaken	speed	sped,	sped,
mow	mowed	mown,		speeded	speeded
		mowed	spell	spelled,	spelled,
must	(had to)	(had to)		spelt	spelt
pay	paid	paid	spend	spent	spent
put	put	put	spill	spilled,	spilled,
quit	quit,	quit,		spilt	spilt
	quitted	quitted	spin	spun	spun
read	read	read	spit	spat	spat
rid	rid	rid	spoil	spoiled,	spoiled,
ride	rode	ridden		spoilt	spoilt
ring	rang	rung	spread	spread	spread
rise	rose	risen	spring	sprang	sprung
run	ran	run	stand	stood	stood
saw	sawed	sawed,	steal	stole	stolen
		sawn	stick	stuck	stuck
say	said	said	sting	stung	stung
see	saw	seen	stink	stank	stunk
sell	sold	sold	stride	strode	stridden
send	sent	sent	strike	struck	struck
set	set	set	swear	swore	sworn
sew	sewed	sewn	sweep	swept	swept
shake	shook	shaken	swell	swelled	swollen,
shear	sheared	shorn,			swelled
		sheared	swim	swam	swum
shed	shed	shed	swing	swung	swung
shine	shone	shone	take	took	taken
shoot	shot	shot	teach	taught	taught
show	showed	shown	tear	tore	torn
shrink	shrank	shrunk	tell	told	told
shut	shut	shut	think	thought	thought
sing	sang	sung	throw	threw	thrown
sink	sank	sunk	thrust	thrust	thrust
sit	sat	sat	tread	trod	trodden
sleep	slept	slept	wake	woke,	woken,
slide	slid	slid		waked	waked
sling	slung	slung	wear	wore	worn
slit	slit	slit	weave	wove	woven
smell	smelled,	smelled,	weep	wept	wept
	smelt	smelt	win	won	won
sow	sowed	sown,	wind	wound	wound
		sowed	wring	wrung	wrung
speak	spoke	spoken	write	wrote	written

PORTUGUESE VERB FORMS

1 Gerund. **2** Imperative. **3** Present. **4** Imperfect. **5** Preterite. **6** Future.
7 Present subjunctive. **8** Imperfect subjunctive. **9** Future subjunctive.
10 Past participle. **11** Pluperfect. **12** Personal infinitive.

etc indicates that the irregular root is used for all persons of the tense,
e.g. **ouvir 7** ouça, ouças, ouça, ouçamos, ouçais, ouçam.

abrir 10 aberto

acudir 2 acode **3** acudo, acodes, acode, acodem

aderir 3 adiro **7** adira

advertir 3 advirto **7** advirta *etc*

agir 3 ajo **7** aja *etc*

agradecer 3 agradeço **7** agradeça *etc*

agredir 2 agride **3** agrido, agrides, agride, agridem **7** agrida *etc*

AMAR 1 amando **2** ama, amai **3** amo, amas, ama, amamos, amais, amam **4** amava, amavas, amava, amávamos, amavéis, amavam **5** amei, amaste, amou, amamos amastes, amaram **6** amarei, amarás, amará, amaremos, amareis, amarão **7** ame, ames, ame, amemos, ameis, amem **8** amasse, amasses, amasse, amássemos, amásseis, amassem **9** amar, amares, amar, ámarmos, amardes, amarem **10** amado **11** amara, amaras, amara, amáramos, amáreis, amaram **12** amar, amares, amar, amarmos, amardes, amarem

ameaçar 5 ameacei **7** ameace *etc*

ansiar 2 anseia **3** anseio, anseias, anseia, anseiam **7** anseie *etc*

arrancar 7 arranque *etc*

arruinar 2 arruína **3** arruíno, arruínas, arruína, arruínam **7** arruíne, arruínes, arruíne, arruínem

atribuir 3 atribuo, atribuis, atribui, atribuímos, atribuís, atribuem

averiguar 7 averigúe, averigúes, averigúe, averigúem

bulir 2 bole **3** bulo, boles, bole, bolem

caber 3 caibo **5** coube *etc* **7** caiba *etc* **8** coubesse *etc* **9** couber *etc*

cair 2 cai **3** caio, cais, cai, caímos, caís, caem **4** caía *etc* **5** caí, caíste **7** caia *etc* **8** caisse *etc*

cobrir 3 cubro **7** cubra *etc* **10** coberto

compelir 3 compilo **7** compila *etc*

crer 2 crê **3** creio, crês, crê, cremos, credes, creem **5** cri, creste, creu, cremos, crestes, creram **7** creia *etc*

cuspir 2 cospe **3** cuspo, cospes, cospe, cospem

dar 2 dá **3** dou, dás, dá, damos, dais, dão **5** dei, deste, deu, demos, destes, deram **7** dê, dês, dê, demos, deis, deem **8** desse *etc* **9** der *etc* **11** dera *etc*

deduzir 2 deduz **3** deduzo, deduzes, deduz

denegrir 2 denigre **3** denigro, denigres, denigre, denigrem **7** denigre *etc*

despir 3 dispo **7** dispa *etc*

dizer 2 diz (dize) **3** digo, dizes, diz, dizemos, dizeis, dizem **5** disse *etc* **6** direi *etc* **7** diga *etc* **8** dissesse *etc* **9** disser *etc* **10** dito

doer 2 dói **3** doo, dóis, dói

dormir 3 durmo 7 durma *etc*

emergir 3 emirjo 7 emirja *etc*

escrever 10 escrito

ESTAR 2 está 3 estou, estás, está, estamos, estais, estão 4 estava *etc* 5 estive, estiveste, esteve, estivemos, estivestes, estiveram 7 esteja *etc* 8 estivesse *etc* 9 estiver *etc* 11 estivera *etc*

extorquir 3 exturco 7 exturca *etc*

FAZER 3 faço 5 fiz, fizeste, fez, fizemos, fizestes, fizeram 6 farei *etc* 7 faça *etc* 8 fizesse *etc* 9 fizer *etc* 10 feito 11 fizera *etc*

ferir 3 firo 7 fira *etc*

fluir 3 fluo, fluis, flui, fluímos, fluís, fluem

fugir 2 foge 3 fujo, foges, foge, fogem 7 fuja *etc*

ganhar 10 ganho

gastar 10 gasto

gerir 3 giro 7 gira *etc*

haver 2 há 3 hei, hás, há, havemos, haveis, hão 4 havia *etc* 5 houve, houveste, houve, houvemos, houvestes, houveram 7 haja *etc* 8 houvesse *etc* 9 houver *etc* 11 houvera *etc*

ir 1 indo 2 vai 3 vou, vais, vai, vamos, ides, vão 4 ia *etc* 5 fui, foste, foi, fomos, fostes, foram 7 vá, vás, vá, vamos, vades, vão 8 fosse, fosses, fosse, fôssemos, fôsseis, fossem 9 for *etc* 10 ido 11 fora *etc*

ler 2 lê 3 leio, lês, lê, lemos, ledes, leem 5 li, leste, leu, lemos, lestes, leram 7 leia *etc*

medir 3 meço, 7 meça *etc*

mentir 3 minto 7 minta *etc*

ouvir 3 ouço 7 ouça *etc*

pagar 10 pago

parar 2 pára 3 paro, paras, pára

parir 3 pairo 7 paira *etc*

pecar 7 peque *etc*

pedir 3 peço 7 peça *etc*

perder 3 perco 7 perca *etc*

poder 3 posso 5 pude, pudeste, pôde, pudemos, pudestes, puderam 7 possa 8 pudesse *etc* 9 puder *etc* 11 pudera *etc*

polir 2 pule 3 pulo, pules, pule, pulem 7 pula *etc*

pôr 1 pondo 2 põe 3 ponho, pões, põe, pomos, pondes, põem 4 punha *etc* 5 pus, puseste, pôs, pusemos, pusestes, puseram 6 porei *etc* 7 ponha *etc* 8 pusesse *etc* 9 puser *etc* 10 posto 11 pusera *etc*

preferir 3 prefiro 7 prefire *etc*

prevenir 2 previne 3 previno, prevines, previne, previnem 7 previna *etc*

prover 2 provê 3 provejo, provês, provê, provemos, provedes, proveem 5 provi, proveste, proveu, provemos, provestes, proveram 7 proveja *etc* 8 provesse *etc* 9 prover *etc*

querer 3 quero, queres, quer 5 quis, quiseste, quis, quisemos, quisestes, quiseram 7 queira *etc* 8 quisesse *etc* 9 quiser *etc* 11 quisera *etc*

refletir 3 reflito 7 reflita *etc*

repetir 3 repito 7 repita *etc*

requerer 3 requeiro, requeres, requer 7 requeira *etc*

reunir 2 reúne 3 reúno, reúnes, reúne, reúnem 7 reúna *etc*

rir 2 ri 3 rio, ris, ri, rimos, rides, ridem 5 ri, riste, riu, rimos, ristes, riram 7 ria *etc*

saber 3 sei, sabes, sabe, sabemos, sabeis, sabem 5 soube, soubeste, soube, soubemos, soubestes, souberam 7 saiba *etc* 8 soubesse *etc* 9 souber *etc* 11 soubera *etc*

seguir 3 sigo 7 siga *etc*

sentir 3 sinto 7 sinta *etc*

ser 2 sê 3 sou, és, é, somos, sois, são 4 era *etc* 5 fui, foste, foi, fomos, fostes, foram 7 seja *etc* 8 fosse *etc* 9 for *etc* 11 fora *etc*

servir 3 sirvo 7 sirva *etc*

subir 2 sobe 3 subo, sobes, sobe, sobem

suster 2 sustém 3 sustenho, sustens, sustém, sustendes, sustêm 5 sustive, sustiveste, susteve, sustivemos, sustivestes, sustiveram 7 sustenha *etc*

ter 2 tem 3 tenho, tens, tem, temos, tendes, têm 4 tinha *etc* 5 tive, tiveste, teve, tivemos, tivestes, tiveram 6 terei *etc* 7 tenha *etc* 8 tivesse *etc* 9 tiver *etc* 11 tivera *etc*

torcer 3 torço 7 torça *etc*

tossir 3 tusso 7 tussa *etc*

trair 2 trai 3 traio, trais, trai, traímos, traís, traem 7 traia *etc*

trazer 2 (traze) traz 3 trago, trazes, traz, 5 trouxe, trouxeste, trouxe, trouxemos, trouxestes, trouxeram 6 trarei *etc* 7 traga *etc* 8 trouxesse *etc* 9 trouxer *etc* 11 trouxera *etc*

UNIR 1 unindo 2 une, uni 3 uno, unes, une, unimos, unis, unem 4 unia, unias, uníamos, uníeis, uniam 5 uni, uniste, uniu, unimos, unistes, uniram 6 unirei, unirás, unirá, uniremos, unireis, unirão 7 una, unas, una, unamos, unais, unam 8 unisse, unisses, unisse, uníssemos, unísseis, unissem 9 unir, unires, unir, unirmos, unirdes, unirem 10 unido 11 unira, uniras, unira, uníramos, uníreis, uniram 12 unir, unires, unir, unirmos, unirdes, unirem

valer 3 valho 7 valha *etc*

ver 2 vê 3 vejo, vês, vê, vemos, vedes, veem 4 via *etc* 5 vi, viste, viu, vimos, vistes, viram 7 veja *etc* 8 visse *etc* 9 vir *etc* 10 visto 11 vira

vir 1 vindo, 2 vem 3 venho, vens, vem, vimos, vindes, vêm 4 vinha *etc* 5 vim, vieste, veio, viemos, viestes, vieram 7 venha *etc* 8 viesse *etc* 9 vier *etc* 10 vindo 11 viera *etc*

VIVER 1 vivendo 2 vive, vivei 3 vivo, vives, vive, vivemos, viveis, vivem 4 vivia, vivias, vivia, vivíamos, vivíeis, viviam 5 vivi, viveste, viveu, vivemos, vivestes, viveram 6 viverei, viverás, viverá, viveremos, vivereis, viverão 7 viva, vivas, viva, vivamos, vivais, vivam 8 vivesse, vivesses, vivesse, vivêssemos, vivêsseis, vivessem 9 viver, viveres, viver, vivermos, viverdes, viverem 10 vivido 11 vivera, viveras, vivera, vivêramos, vivêreis, viveram 12 viver, viveres, viver, vivermos, viverdes, viverem

DATAS

DATES

DIAS DA SEMANA

segunda(-feira)
terça(-feira)
quarta(-feira)
quinta(-feira)
sexta(-feira)
sábado
domingo

DAYS OF THE WEEK

Monday
Tuesday
Wednesday
Thursday
Friday
Saturday
Sunday

MESES

janeiro
fevereiro
março
abril
maio
junho
julho
agosto
setembro
outubro
novembro
dezembro

MONTHS

January
February
March
April
May
June
July
August
September
October
November
December

VOCABULÁRIO ÚTIL

Que dia é hoje?
Hoje é dia 28.
Quando?
hoje
amanhã
ontem
hoje de manhã/à tarde
em duas semanas
daqui a uma semana
o mês passado/que vem

USEFUL VOCABULARY

What day is it today?
Today is the 28th.
When?
today
tomorrow
yesterday
this morning/afternoon
in two weeks ou a fortnight
in a week's time
last/next month

HORAS

QUE HORAS SAO

É meio-dia/meia-noite.

It's noon (BRIT midday)/
midnight.

Faltam dez para as duas.
São duas menos dez (PT).

It's ten to two.

Faltam vinte para as oito.
São oito menos vinte (PT).

It's twenty to eight.

TIME

WHAT TIME IS IT?

É uma e quinze.
É uma e um quarto (PT).

It's a quarter past one.
(BRIT It's one fifteen.)

São três e meia.

It's three-thirty.
(BRIT It's half past three.)

São nove (horas) da
manhã/da noite.

It's nine o'clock in the
morning/at night.

NÚMEROS

NUMBERS

NÚMEROS CARDINAIS

CARDINAL NUMBERS

um (uma)	1	one
dois (duas)	2	two
três	3	three
quatro	4	four
cinco	5	five
seis	6	six
sete	7	seven
oito	8	eight
nove	9	nine
dez	10	ten
onze	11	eleven
doze	12	twelve
treze	13	thirteen
catorze	14	fourteen
quinze	15	fifteen
dezesseis (BR), dezasseis (PT)	16	sixteen
dezessete (BR), dezassete (PT)	17	seventeen
dezoito	18	eighteen
dezenove (BR), dezanove (PT)	19	nineteen
vinte	20	twenty
vinte e um (uma)	21	twenty-one
trinta	30	thirty
quarenta	40	forty
cinquenta	50	fifty
sessenta	60	sixty
setenta	70	seventy
oitenta	80	eighty
noventa	90	ninety
cem	100	a hundred
cento e um (uma)	101	a hundred and one
duzentos(-as)	200	two hundred
trezentos(-as)	300	three hundred
quinhentos(-as)	500	five hundred
mil	1.000/1,000	a thousand
um milhão	1.000.000/1,000,000	a million

FRAÇÕES ETC

zero vírgula cinco	0,5/0.5
três vírgula quatro	3,4/3.4
dez por cento	10%
cem por cento	100%

FRACTIONS ETC

zero point five
three point four
ten percent
(*BRIT* per cent)
a hundred percent
(*BRIT* per cent)

NÚMEROS ORDINAIS

primeiro	1º/1st
segundo	2º/2nd
terceiro	3º/3rd
quarto	4º/4th
quinto	5º/5th
sexto	6º/6th
sétimo	7º/7th
oitavo	8º/8th
nono	9º/9th
décimo	10º/10th
décimo primeiro	11º/11th
vigésimo	20º/20th
trigésimo	30º/30th
quadragésimo	40º/40th
quinquagésimo	50º/50th
centésimo	100º/100th
centésimo primeiro	101º/101st
milésimo	1000º/1000th

ORDINAL NUMBERS

first
second
third
fourth
fifth
sixth
seventh
eighth
ninth
tenth
eleventh
twentieth
thirtieth
fortieth
fiftieth
hundredth
hundred-and-first
thousandth

Inglês – Português

English – Portuguese

a

A [eɪ] N (*Mus*) lá *m*

(KEYWORD)

a [eɪ, ə] INDEF ART (*before vowel or silent h:
an*) **1** um(a); **a book/girl/mirror** um
livro/uma menina/um espelho; **an apple**
uma maçã; **she's a doctor** ela é médica
2 (*instead of the number "one"*) um(a);
a year ago há um ano, um ano atrás;
a hundred/thousand *etc* **pounds**
cem/mil *etc* libras
3 (*in expressing ratios, prices etc*): **3 a day/
week** 3 por dia/semana; **10 km an hour**
10 km por hora; **30p a kilo** 30p o quilo

aback [ə'bæk] ADV: **to be taken ~** ficar
surpreendido, sobressaltar-se
abandon [ə'bændən] VT abandonar ▶ N:
with ~ com desenfreio
abbey ['æbɪ] N abadia, mosteiro
abbreviation N abreviatura
abdomen ['æbdəmən] N abdômen *m*
abduct [æb'dʌkt] VT sequestrar
ability [ə'bɪlɪtɪ] N habilidade *f*,
capacidade *f*; (*talent*) talento
able ['eɪbl] ADJ capaz; (*skilled*) hábil,
competente; **to be ~ to do sth** poder
fazer algo
abnormal [æb'nɔːməl] ADJ anormal
aboard [ə'bɔːd] ADV a bordo ▶ PREP a
bordo de
abolish [ə'bɔlɪʃ] VT abolir
aborigine [æbə'rɪdʒɪnɪ] N aborígene *m/f*
abort [ə'bɔːt] VT (*Med*) abortar; (*plan*)
cancelar; **abortion** N aborto; **to have
an abortion** fazer um aborto

(KEYWORD)

about [ə'baut] ADV **1** (*approximately*)
aproximadamente; **it takes about**
10 hours leva mais ou menos 10 horas;
it's just about finished está quase
terminado
2 (*referring to place*) por toda parte, por
todo lado; **to run/walk** *etc* **about**
correr/andar *etc* por todos os lados
3: **to be about to do sth** estar a ponto
de fazer algo
▶ PREP **1** (*relating to*) acerca de, sobre;
what is it about? do que se trata?, é
sobre o quê?; **what** *or* **how about doing
this?** que tal se fizermos isso?
2 (*place*) em redor de, por

above [ə'bʌv] ADV em *or* por cima, acima
▶ PREP acima de, por cima de; **costing ~
£10** que custa mais de £10; **~ all**
sobretudo
abroad [ə'brɔːd] ADV (*be abroad*) no
estrangeiro; (*go abroad*) ao estrangeiro
abrupt [ə'brʌpt] ADJ (*sudden*) brusco;
(*curt*) ríspido
abscess ['æbsɪs] N abscesso (*BR*),
abcesso (*PT*)
absence ['æbsəns] N ausência
absent ['æbsənt] ADJ ausente;
absent-minded ADJ distraído
absolute ['æbsəluːt] ADJ absoluto;
absolutely [æbsə'luːtlɪ] ADV
absolutamente
absorb [əb'zɔːb] VT absorver; (*group,
business*) incorporar; (*changes*) assimilar;
(*information*) digerir; **absorbent cotton**
(*US*) N algodão *m* hidrófilo
abstain [əb'steɪn] VI: **to ~ (from)**
abster-se (de)
abstract ['æbstrækt] ADJ abstrato
absurd [əb'səːd] ADJ absurdo
abuse [n ə'bjuːs, vt ə'bjuːz] N (*insults*)
insultos *mpl*; (*misuse*) abuso; (*ill-treatment*)
maus tratos *mpl* ▶ VT insultar;
maltratar; abusar; **abusive** [ə'bjuːsɪv]
ADJ ofensivo
abysmal [ə'bɪzməl] ADJ (*ignorance*)
profundo, total; (*very bad*) péssimo
academic [ækə'dɛmɪk] ADJ acadêmico;
(*pej: issue*) teórico ▶ N universitário(-a)
academy [ə'kædəmɪ] N (*learned body*)
academia; **~ of music** conservatório
accelerate [æk'sɛləreɪt] VT, VI acelerar;
accelerator N acelerador *m*
accent ['æksɛnt] N (*written*) acento;
(*pronunciation*) sotaque *m*; (*fig: emphasis*)
ênfase *f*
accept [ək'sɛpt] VT aceitar;
(*responsibility*) assumir; **acceptable** ADJ
(*offer*) bem-vindo; (*risk*) aceitável;
acceptance N aceitação *f*

access ['ækses] N acesso; **accessible** [æk'sesəbl] ADJ acessível; (*available*) disponível

accessory [æk'sesərɪ] N acessório; (*Jur*): **~ to** cúmplice *m/f* de

accident ['æksɪdənt] N acidente *m*; (*chance*) casualidade *f*; **by ~** (*unintentionally*) sem querer; (*by coincidence*) por acaso; **accidental** [æksɪ'dɛntl] ADJ acidental; **accidentally** [æksɪ'dɛntəlɪ] ADV sem querer; **Accident and Emergency Department** N (*BRIT*) pronto-socorro

acclaim [ə'kleɪm] N aclamação *f*

accommodate [ə'kɔmədeɪt] VT alojar; (*subj: car, hotel, etc*) acomodar; (*oblige, help*) comprazer a; **accommodation** [əkɔmə'deɪʃən] N, (*US*) **accomodations** NPL alojamento

accompany [ə'kʌmpənɪ] VT acompanhar

accomplice [ə'kʌmplɪs] N cúmplice *m/f*

accomplish [ə'kʌmplɪʃ] VT (*task*) concluir; (*goal*) alcançar; **accomplishment** N realização *f*

accord [ə'kɔːd] N tratado ▶ VT conceder; **of his own ~** por sua iniciativa; **accordance** [ə'kɔːdəns] N: **in accordance with** de acordo com; **according** PREP: **according to** segundo; (*in accordance with*) conforme; **accordingly** ADV por conseguinte; (*appropriately*) do modo devido

account [ə'kaunt] N conta; (*report*) relato; **accounts** NPL (*books, department*) contabilidade *f*; **of no ~** sem importância; **on ~** por conta; **on no ~** de modo nenhum; **on ~ of** por causa de; **to take into ~, take ~ of** levar em conta; **account for** VT FUS (*explain*) explicar; (*represent*) representar; **accountant** N contador(a) *m/f*(BR), contabilista *m/f* (PT); **account number** N número de conta

accumulate [ə'kjuːmjuleɪt] VT acumular ▶ VI acumular-se

accuracy ['ækjurəsɪ] N exatidão *f*, precisão *f*

accurate ['ækjurɪt] ADJ (*description*) correto; (*person, device*) preciso; **accurately** ADV com precisão

accusation [ækju'zeɪʃən] N acusação *f*; (*instance*) incriminação *f*

accuse [ə'kjuːz] VT: **to ~ sb (of sth)** acusar alguém (de algo); **accused** N: **the accused** o/a acusado/a

ace [eɪs] N ás *m*

ache [eɪk] N dor *f* ▶ VI (*yearn*): **to ~ to do sth** ansiar por fazer algo; **my head ~s** dói-me a cabeça

achieve [ə'tʃiːv] VT alcançar; (*victory, success*) obter; **achievement** N realização *f*; (*success*) proeza

acid ['æsɪd] ADJ, N ácido

acknowledge [ək'nɔlɪdʒ] VT (*fact*) reconhecer; (*also*: **~ receipt of**) acusar o recebimento de (BR) *or* a receção de (PT); **acknowledgement** N notificação *f* de recebimento

acne ['æknɪ] N acne *f*

acorn ['eɪkɔːn] N bolota

acoustic [ə'kuːstɪk] ADJ acústico

acquire [ə'kwaɪə'] VT adquirir

acquit [ə'kwɪt] VT absolver; **to ~ o.s. well** desempenhar-se bem

acre ['eɪkə'] N acre *m* (= 4047m²)

across [ə'krɔs] PREP (*on the other side of*) no outro lado de; (*crosswise*) através de ▶ ADV: **to walk ~ (the road)** atravessar (a rua); **the lake is 12 km ~** o lago tem 12 km de largura; **~ from** em frente de

acrylic [ə'krɪlɪk] ADJ acrílico ▶ N acrílico

act [ækt] N ação *f*; (*Theatre*) ato; (*in show*) número; (*Jur*) lei *f* ▶ VI tomar ação; (*behave, have effect*) agir; (*Theatre*) representar; (*pretend*) fingir ▶ VT (*part*) representar; **in the ~ of** no ato de; **to ~ as** servir de; **acting** ADJ interino ▶ N: **to do some acting** fazer teatro

action ['ækʃən] N ação *f*, (*Mil*) batalha, combate *m*; (*Jur*) ação judicial; **out of ~** (*person*) fora de combate; (*thing*) com defeito; **to take ~** tomar atitude; **action replay** N (*TV*) replay *m*

activate ['æktɪveɪt] VT acionar

active ['æktɪv] ADJ ativo; (*volcano*) em atividade; **actively** ADV ativamente; **activity** [æk'tɪvɪtɪ] N atividade *f*

actor ['æktə'] N ator *m*

actress ['æktrɪs] N atriz *f*

actual ['æktjuəl] ADJ real; **actually** ADV realmente; (*in fact*) na verdade; (*even*) mesmo

acute [ə'kjuːt] ADJ agudo; (*person*) perspicaz

ad [æd] N ABBR = **advertisement**

A.D. ADV ABBR (= *Anno Domini*) d.C.

adamant ['ædəmənt] ADJ inflexível

adapt [ə'dæpt] VT adaptar ▶ VI: **to ~ (to)** adaptar-se (a)

add [æd] VT acrescentar; (*figures: also*: **~ up**) somar ▶ VI: **to ~ to** aumentar

addict ['ædɪkt] N viciado(-a); **drug ~** toxicômano(-a); **addicted** [ə'dɪktɪd] ADJ: **to be/become addicted to** ser/ficar viciado em; **addiction** N dependência; **addictive** ADJ que causa dependência

addition [ə'dɪʃən] N adição f; (thing added) acréscimo; **in ~** além disso; **in ~ to** além de; **additional** ADJ adicional

additive ['ædɪtɪv] N aditivo

address [ə'drɛs] N endereço; (speech) discurso ▶ VT (letter) endereçar; (speak to) dirigir-se a, dirigir a palavra a; **to ~ (o.s. to)** enfocar

adequate ['ædɪkwɪt] ADJ (enough) suficiente; (satisfactory) satisfatório

adhere [əd'hɪər] VI: **to ~ to** aderir a; (abide by) ater-se a

adhesive [əd'hi:zɪv] N adesivo

adjective ['ædʒɛktɪv] N adjetivo

adjoining [ə'dʒɔɪnɪŋ] ADJ adjacente

adjourn [ə'dʒə:n] VT (session) suspender ▶ VI encerrar a sessão; (go) deslocar-se

adjust [ə'dʒʌst] VT (change) ajustar; (clothes) arrumar; (machine) regular ▶ VI: **to ~ (to)** adaptar-se (a); **adjustment** N ajuste m; (of engine) regulagem f; (of prices, wages) reajuste m; (of person) adaptação f

administer [əd'mɪnɪstər] VT administrar; (justice) aplicar; (drug) ministrar; **administration** [ədmɪnɪs'treɪʃən] N administração f; (US: government) governo; **administrative** [əd'mɪnɪstrətɪv] ADJ administrativo

admiral ['ædmərəl] N almirante m

admire [əd'maɪər] VT (respect) respeitar; (appreciate) admirar

admission [əd'mɪʃən] N (admittance) entrada; (fee) ingresso; (confession) confissão f

admit [əd'mɪt] VT admitir; (accept) aceitar; (confess) confessar; **admit to** VT FUS confessar; **admittance** N entrada; **admittedly** ADV evidentemente

adolescent [ædəu'lɛsnt] ADJ, N adolescente m/f

adopt [ə'dɔpt] VT adotar; **adopted** ADJ adotivo; **adoption** N adoção f

adore [ə'dɔ:ʳ] VT adorar

Adriatic [eɪdrɪ'ætɪk], **Adriatic Sea** N (mar m) Adriático

adrift [ə'drɪft] ADV à deriva

ADSL N ABBR (= asymmetric digital subscriber line) ADSL m

adult ['ædʌlt] N adulto(-a) ▶ ADJ adulto; (literature, education) para adultos

adultery [ə'dʌltərɪ] N adultério

advance [əd'vɑ:ns] N avanço; (money) adiantamento ▶ ADJ antecipado ▶ VT (money) adiantar ▶ VI (move forward) avançar; (progress) progredir; **in ~** com antecedência; **to make ~s to sb** fazer propostas a alguém; **advanced** ADJ adiantado

advantage [əd'vɑ:ntɪdʒ] N vantagem f; (supremacy) supremacia; vantagem f; **to take ~ of** aproveitar-se de

adventure [əd'vɛntʃər] N aventura

adverb ['ædvə:b] N advérbio

adverse ['ædvə:s] ADJ (effect) contrário; (weather, publicity) desfavorável

advert ['ædvə:t] N ABBR = **advertisement**

advertise ['ædvətaɪz] VI anunciar ▶ VT (event, job) anunciar; (product) fazer a propaganda de; **to ~ for** (staff) procurar; **advertisement** [əd'və:tɪsmənt] N (classified) anúncio; (display, TV) propaganda, anúncio; **advertising** N publicidade f

advice [əd'vaɪs] N conselhos mpl; (notification) aviso; **piece of ~** conselho; **to take legal ~** consultar um advogado

advise [əd'vaɪz] VT aconselhar; (inform): **to ~ sb of sth** avisar alguém de algo; **to ~ sb against sth** desaconselhar algo a alguém; **to ~ sb against doing sth** aconselhar alguém a não fazer algo; **advisory** ADJ consultivo; **in an advisory capacity** na qualidade de assessor(a) or consultor(a)

advocate [VT 'ædvəkeɪt, n 'ædvəkɪt] VT defender; (recommend) advogar ▶ N advogado(-a); (supporter) defensor(a) m/f

Aegean [iː'dʒiːən] N: **the ~ (Sea)** o (mar) Egeu

aerial ['ɛərɪəl] N antena ▶ ADJ aéreo

aerobics [ɛə'rəubɪks] N ginástica

aeroplane ['ɛərəpleɪn] (BRIT) N avião m

aerosol ['ɛərəsɔl] N aerossol m

affair [ə'fɛər] N (matter) assunto; (business) negócio; (question) questão f; (also: **love ~**) caso

affect [ə'fɛkt] VT afetar; (move) comover; **affected** ADJ afetado

affection [ə'fɛkʃən] N afeto, afeição f; **affectionate** ADJ afetuoso

afflict [ə'flɪkt] VT afligir

affluent ['æfluənt] ADJ rico; **the ~ society** a sociedade de abundância

afford [ə'fɔ:d] VT (provide) fornecer; (goods etc) ter dinheiro suficiente para; (permit o.s.): **I can't ~ the time** não tenho tempo; **affordable** ADJ acessível

afraid [ə'freɪd] ADJ assustado; **to be ~ of/to** ter medo de; **I am ~ that** lamento que; **I'm ~ so/not** receio que sim/não

Africa ['æfrɪkə] N África; **African** ADJ, N africano(-a)

after ['ɑːftə^r] PREP depois de ▶ ADV depois ▶ CONJ depois que; **a quarter ~ two** (US) duas e quinze; **what are you ~?** o que você quer?; **who are you ~?** quem procura?; **~ having done** tendo feito; **to ask ~ sb** perguntar por alguém; **~ all** afinal (de contas); **~ you!** passe primeiro!; **aftermath** N consequências fpl; **afternoon** N tarde f; **after-shave, after-shave lotion** N loção f após-barba; **aftersun** ['ɑːftəsʌn] N loção f pós-sol; **afterwards** ADV depois

again [ə'gɛn] ADV (once more) outra vez; (repeatedly) de novo; **to do sth ~** voltar a fazer algo; **~ and ~** repetidas vezes

against [ə'gɛnst] PREP contra; (compared to) em contraste com

age [eɪdʒ] N idade f; (period) época ▶ VT, VI envelhecer; **he's 20 years of ~** ele tem 20 anos de idade; **to come of ~** atingir a maioridade; **it's been ~s since I saw him** faz muito tempo que eu não o vejo; **~d 10** de 10 anos de idade; **aged** ['eɪdʒɪd] ADJ idoso ▶ NPL: **the aged** os idosos; **age group** N faixa etária; **age limit** N idade f mínima/máxima

agency ['eɪdʒənsɪ] N agência; (government body) órgão m

agenda [ə'dʒɛndə] N ordem f do dia

agent ['eɪdʒənt] N agente m/f

aggravate ['ægrəveɪt] VT agravar; (annoy) irritar

aggressive [ə'grɛsɪv] ADJ agressivo

AGM N ABBR (= annual general meeting) AGO f

ago [ə'gəʊ] ADV: **2 days ~** há 2 dias (atrás); **not long ~** há pouco tempo; **how long ~?** há quanto tempo?

agony ['ægənɪ] N (pain) dor f; **to be in ~** sofrer dores terríveis

agree [ə'griː] VT combinar ▶ VI (correspond) corresponder; **to ~ (with)** concordar (com); **to ~ to do** aceitar fazer; **to ~ to sth** consentir algo; **to ~ that** concordar or admitir que; **agreeable** ADJ agradável; (willing) disposto; **agreed** ADJ combinado; **agreement** N acordo; (Comm) contrato; **in agreement** de acordo

agricultural [ægrɪ'kʌltʃərəl] ADJ (of crops) agrícola; (of crops and cattle) agropecuário

agriculture ['ægrɪkʌltʃə^r] N (of crops) agricultura; (of crops and cattle) agropecuária

ahead [ə'hɛd] ADV adiante; **go right** or **straight ~** siga em frente; **go ~!** (fig) vá em frente!; **~ of** na frente de

aid [eɪd] N ajuda ▶ VT ajudar; **in ~ of** em benefício de; **to ~ and abet** (Jur) ser cúmplice de

AIDS [eɪdz] N ABBR (= acquired immune deficiency syndrome) AIDS f (BR), SIDA f (PT)

aim [eɪm] VT: **to ~ sth (at)** apontar algo (para); (missile, remark) dirigir algo (a) ▶ VI (also: **take ~**) apontar ▶ N (skill) pontaria; (objective) objetivo; **to ~ at** mirar; **to ~ to do** pretender fazer

ain't [eɪnt] (inf) = **am not; aren't; isn't**

air [ɛə^r] N ar m; (appearance) aparência, aspecto ▶ VT arejar; (grievances, ideas) discutir ▶ CPD aéreo; **to throw sth into the ~** jogar algo para cima; **by ~** (travel) de avião; **to be on the ~** (Radio, TV) estar no ar; **air bed** ['ɛəbɛd] (BRIT) N colchão m de ar; **air conditioning** N ar-condicionado; **aircraft** N INV aeronave f; **airfield** N campo de aviação; **Air Force** N Força Aérea, Aeronáutica; **air hostess** (BRIT) N aeromoça (BR), hospedeira (PT); **airline** N linha aérea; **airliner** N avião m de passageiros; **airmail** N: **by airmail** por via aérea; **airplane** (US) N avião m; **airport** N aeroporto; **airsick** ADJ: **to be airsick** enjoar-se (no avião); **airtight** ADJ hermético; **airy** ADJ (room) arejado; (manner) leviano

aisle [aɪl] N (of church) nave f; (of theatre etc) corredor m

ajar [ə'dʒɑː^r] ADJ entreaberto

alarm [ə'lɑːm] N alarme m; (anxiety) inquietação f ▶ VT alarmar; **alarm clock** N despertador m

album ['ælbəm] N (for stamps etc) álbum m; (record) elepê m

alcohol ['ælkəhɔl] N álcool m; **alcohol-free** ADJ sem álcool; **alcoholic** [ælkə'hɔlɪk] ADJ alcoólico ▶ N alcoólatra m/f

ale [eɪl] N cerveja

alert [ə'ləːt] ADJ atento; (to danger, opportunity) alerta ▶ N alerta m ▶ VT: **to ~ sb (to sth)** alertar alguém (de or sobre algo); **to be on the ~** estar alerta; (Mil) ficar de prontidão

Algarve [æl'gɑːv] N: **the ~** o Algarve

algebra ['ældʒɪbrə] N álgebra

Algeria [æl'dʒɪərɪə] N Argélia

alias ['eɪlɪəs] ADV também chamado ▶ N (of criminal) alcunha; (of writer) pseudônimo

alibi ['ælɪbaɪ] N álibi m

alien ['eɪlɪən] N estrangeiro(-a); *(from space)* alienígena m/f ▶ ADJ: **~ to** alheio a

alight [ə'laɪt] ADJ em chamas; *(eyes)* aceso; *(expression)* intento ▶ VI *(passenger)* descer (de um veículo); *(bird)* pousar

alike [ə'laɪk] ADJ semelhante ▶ ADV similarmente, igualmente; **to look ~** parecer-se

alive [ə'laɪv] ADJ vivo; *(lively)* alegre

(KEYWORD)

all [ɔːl] ADJ *(singular)* todo(-a); *(plural)* todos(-as); **all day/night** o dia inteiro/a noite inteira; **all five came** todos os cinco vieram; **all the books/food** todos os livros/toda a comida
▶ PRON **1** tudo; **all of us/the boys went** todos nós fomos/todos os meninos foram; **is that all?** é só isso?; *(in shop)* mais alguma coisa?
2 *(in phrases)*: **above all** sobretudo; **after all** afinal (de contas); **not at all** *(in answer to question)* em absoluto, absolutamente não; **I'm not at all tired** não estou nada cansado; **anything at all will do** qualquer coisa serve; **all in all** ao todo
▶ ADV todo, completamente; **all alone** completamente só; **it's not as hard as all that** não é tão difícil assim; **all the more** ainda mais; **all the better** tanto melhor, melhor ainda; **all but** quase; **the score is 2 all** o jogo está empatado em 2 a 2

allegiance [ə'liːdʒəns] N lealdade f

allergic [ə'ləːdʒɪk] ADJ: **~ (to)** alérgico (a)

allergy ['ælədʒɪ] N alergia

alleviate [ə'liːvɪeɪt] VT *(pain)* aliviar; *(difficulty)* minorar

alley ['ælɪ] N viela

alliance [ə'laɪəns] N aliança

all-in (BRIT) ADJ, ADV *(charge)* tudo incluído

allocate ['æləkeɪt] VT destinar

allot [ə'lɔt] VT: **to ~ to** designar para

all-out ADJ *(effort etc)* máximo ▶ ADV: **all out** com toda a força

allow [ə'lau] VT permitir; *(claim, goal)* admitir; *(sum, time estimated)* calcular; *(concede)*: **to ~ that** reconhecer que; **to ~ sb to do** permitir a alguém fazer; **allow for** VT FUS levar em conta; **allowance** [ə'lauəns] N ajuda de custo; *(welfare, payment)* pensão f, auxílio; *(Tax)* abatimento; **to make allowances for** levar em consideração

all right ADV *(well)* bem; *(correctly)* corretamente; *(as answer)* está bem!

ally [n 'ælaɪ, vt ə'laɪ] N aliado ▶ VT: **to ~ o.s. with** aliar-se com

almighty [ɔːl'maɪtɪ] ADJ onipotente; *(row etc)* maior

almond ['ɑːmənd] N amêndoa

almost ['ɔːlməust] ADV quase

alone [ə'ləun] ADJ só, sozinho ▶ ADV só, somente; **to leave sb ~** deixar alguém em paz; **to leave sth ~** não tocar em algo; **let ~ ...** sem falar em ...

along [ə'lɔŋ] PREP por, ao longo de ▶ ADV: **is he coming ~?** ele vem conosco?; **he was hopping/limping ~** ele ia pulando/coxeando; **~ with** junto com; **all ~** o tempo todo; **alongside** PREP ao lado de ▶ ADV encostado

aloof [ə'luːf] ADJ afastado, altivo ▶ ADV: **to stand ~** afastar-se

aloud [ə'laud] ADV em voz alta

alphabet ['ælfəbɛt] N alfabeto

Alps [ælps] NPL: **the ~** os Alpes

already [ɔːl'rɛdɪ] ADV já

alright ['ɔːl'raɪt] (BRIT) ADV = **all right**

also ['ɔːlsəu] ADV também; *(moreover)* além disso

altar ['ɔltə'] N altar m

alter ['ɔltə'] VT alterar ▶ VI modificar-se

alternate [adj ɔl'təːnɪt, vi 'ɔltəːneɪt] ADJ alternado; *(us: alternative)* alternativo ▶ VI: **to ~ with** alternar-se (com)

alternative [ɔl'təːnətɪv] ADJ alternativo ▶ N alternativa; **alternatively** ADV: **alternatively one could ...** por outro lado se podia ...

although [ɔːl'ðəu] CONJ embora; *(given that)* se bem que

altitude ['æltɪtjuːd] N altitude f

altogether [ɔːltə'gɛðə'] ADV totalmente; *(on the whole)* no total

aluminium [ælju'mɪnɪəm] (BRIT) N alumínio

aluminum [ə'luːmɪnəm] (US) N = **aluminium**

always ['ɔːlweɪz] ADV sempre

Alzheimer's ['æltshaɪməz], **Alzheimer's disease** N mal m de Alzheimer

am [æm] VB *see* **be**

a.m. ADV ABBR (= *ante meridiem*) da manhã

amateur ['æmətə'] ADJ, N amador(a) m/f

amaze [ə'meɪz] VT pasmar; **to be ~d (at)** espantar-se (de or com); **amazement** N pasmo, espanto; **amazing** ADJ surpreendente; *(fantastic)* fantástico

Amazon ['æməzən] N Amazonas m

ambassador [æm'bæsədə^r] N embaixador/embaixatriz m/f

amber ['æmbə^r] N âmbar m; **at ~** (BRIT Aut) em amarelo

ambiguous [æm'bɪgjuəs] ADJ ambíguo

ambition [æm'bɪʃən] N ambição f; **ambitious** ADJ ambicioso

ambulance ['æmbjuləns] N ambulância

ambush ['æmbuʃ] N emboscada ▶ VT emboscar

amend [ə'mɛnd] VT emendar; **to make ~s (for)** compensar

America [ə'mɛrɪkə] N (continent) América; (USA) Estados Unidos mpl; **American** ADJ americano; (from USA) norte-americano, estadunidense ▶ N americano(-a); (from USA) norte-americano(-a)

amicable ['æmɪkəbl] ADJ amigável

ammunition [æmju'nɪʃən] N munição f

among [ə'mʌŋ], **amongst** [ə'mʌŋst] PREP entre, no meio de

amount [ə'maunt] N quantidade f; (of money etc) quantia ▶ VI: **to ~ to** (total) montar a; (be same as) equivaler a, significar

amp ['æmp], **ampere** ['æmpɛə^r] N ampère m

ample ['æmpl] ADJ amplo; (abundant) abundante; (enough) suficiente

amplifier ['æmplɪfaɪə^r] N amplificador m

amuse [ə'mju:z] VT divertir; (distract) distrair; **amusement** N diversão f; (pleasure) divertimento; (pastime) passatempo; **amusement park** N parque m de diversões

an [æn, ən, n] INDEF ART see **a**

anaesthetic [ænɪs'θɛtɪk], (US) **anesthetic** N anestésico

analyse ['ænəlaɪz], (US) **analyze** VT analisar; **analysis** [ə'næləsɪs] (pl **analyses**) N análise f; **analyst** ['ænəlɪst] N analista m/f; (psychoanalyst) psicanalista m/f

analyze ['ænəlaɪz] (US) VT = **analyse**

anarchy ['ænəkɪ] N anarquia

anatomy [ə'nætəmɪ] N anatomia

ancestor ['ænsɪstə^r] N antepassado

anchor ['æŋkə^r] N âncora ▶ VI (also: **to drop ~**) ancorar, fundear ▶ VT (fig): **to ~ sth to** firmar algo em; **to weigh ~** levantar âncoras

anchovy ['æntʃəvɪ] N enchova

ancient ['eɪnʃənt] ADJ antigo; (person, car) velho

and [ænd] CONJ e; **~ so on** e assim por diante; **try ~ come** tente vir; **he talked ~ talked** ele falou sem parar; **better ~ better** cada vez melhor

Andes ['ændi:z] NPL: **the ~** os Andes

angel ['eɪndʒəl] N anjo

anger ['æŋgə^r] N raiva

angina [æn'dʒaɪnə] N angina (de peito)

angle ['æŋgl] N ângulo; (viewpoint): **from their ~** do ponto de vista deles

Anglican ['æŋglɪkən] ADJ, N anglicano(-a)

angling ['æŋglɪŋ] N pesca à vara (BR) or à linha (PT)

angry ['æŋgrɪ] ADJ zangado; **to be ~ with sb/at sth** estar zangado com alguém/algo; **to get ~** zangar-se

anguish ['æŋgwɪʃ] N (physical) dor f, sofrimento; (mental) angústia

animal ['ænɪməl] N animal m, bicho ▶ ADJ animal

aniseed ['ænɪsi:d] N erva-doce f, anis f

ankle ['æŋkl] N tornozelo

annex [n'ænɛks, vt ə'nɛks] N (BRIT: building) anexo ▶ VT anexar

anniversary [ænɪ'və:sərɪ] N aniversário

announce [ə'nauns] VT anunciar; **announcement** N anúncio; (official) comunicação f; (in letter etc) aviso; **announcer** N (Radio, TV) locutor(a) m/f

annoy [ə'nɔɪ] VT aborrecer; **don't get ~ed!** não se aborreça!; **annoying** ADJ irritante

annual ['ænjuəl] ADJ anual ▶ N (Bot) anual f; (book) anuário

anonymous [ə'nɔnɪməs] ADJ anônimo

anorak ['ænəræk] N anoraque m (BR), anorak m (PT)

another [ə'nʌðə^r] ADJ: **~ book** (one more) outro livro, mais um livro; (a different one) um outro livro, um livro diferente ▶ PRON outro; see also **one**

answer ['ɑ:nsə^r] N resposta; (to problem) solução f ▶ VI responder ▶ VT (reply to) responder a; (problem) resolver; **in ~ to your letter** em resposta or respondendo à sua carta; **to ~ the phone** atender o telefone; **to ~ the bell** or **the door** atender à porta; **answer back** VI replicar, retrucar; **answer for** VT FUS responder por, responsabilizar-se por; **answer to** VT FUS (description) corresponder a; **answering machine** N secretária eletrônica; **answerphone** N (esp BRIT) secretária eletrônica

ant [ænt] N formiga

Antarctic [ænt'ɑ:ktɪk] N: **the ~** o Antártico

antenatal ['æntɪ'neɪtl] ADJ pré-natal

anthem ['ænθəm] N: **national ~** hino nacional

anticipate [æn'tɪsɪpeɪt] VT prever; (*expect*) esperar; (*look forward to*) aguardar, esperar; **anticipation** N expectativa; (*eagerness*) entusiasmo

anticlimax [æntɪ'klaɪmæks] N desapontamento

anticlockwise [æntɪ'klɔkwaɪz] (BRIT) ADV em sentido anti-horário

antics ['æntɪks] NPL bobices fpl; (*of child*) travessuras fpl

antifreeze ['æntɪfriːz] N anticongelante m

antihistamine [æntɪ'hɪstəmiːn] N anti-histamínico

antique [æn'tiːk] N antiguidade f ▶ ADJ antigo; **antique shop** N loja de antiguidades

antiseptic [æntɪ'sɛptɪk] N antisséptico

antisocial [æntɪ'səuʃəl] ADJ antissocial

antivirus ['æntɪvaɪərəs] ADJ antivírus m inv; **~ software** software antivírus

antlers ['æntləz] NPL esgalhos mpl, chifres mpl

anxiety [æŋ'zaɪətɪ] N (*worry*) inquietude f; (*eagerness*) ânsia; (*Med*) ansiedade f; **~ to do** ânsia de fazer

anxious ['æŋkʃəs] ADJ (*worried*) preocupado; (*worrying*) angustiante; (*keen*) ansioso; **~ to do/for sth** ansioso para fazer/por algo; **to be ~ that** desejar que

(KEYWORD)

any ['ɛnɪ] ADJ 1 (*in questions etc*) algum(a); **have you any butter/children?** você tem manteiga/filhos?; **if there are any tickets left** se houver alguns bilhetes sobrando

2 (*with negative*) nenhum(a); **I haven't any money/books** não tenho dinheiro/livros

3 (*no matter which*) qualquer; **choose any book you like** escolha qualquer livro que quiser

4 (*in phrases*): **in any case** em todo o caso; **any day now** qualquer dia desses; **at any moment** a qualquer momento; **at any rate** de qualquer modo; **any time** a qualquer momento; (*whenever*) quando quer que seja

▶ PRON 1 (*in questions etc*) algum(a); **have you got any?** tem algum?

2 (*with negative*) nenhum(a); **I haven't any (of them)** não tenho nenhum (deles)

3 (*no matter which one(s)*): **take any of those books (you like)** leve qualquer um desses livros (que você quiser)

▶ ADV 1 (*in questions etc*) algo; **do you want any more soup/sandwiches?** quer mais sopa/sanduíches?; **are you feeling any better?** você está se sentindo melhor?

2 (*with negative*) nada; **I can't hear him any more** não consigo mais ouvi-lo

anybody ['ɛnɪbɔdɪ] PRON qualquer um, qualquer pessoa; (*in interrogative sentences*) alguém

anyhow ['ɛnɪhau] ADV (*at any rate*) de qualquer modo, de qualquer maneira; **I shall go ~** eu irei de qualquer jeito; **do it ~ you like** faça do jeito que você quiser; **she leaves things just ~** ela deixa as coisas de qualquer maneira

anyone ['ɛnɪwʌn] PRON (*in questions etc*) alguém; (*with negative*) ninguém; (*no matter who*) quem quer que seja; **can you see ~?** você pode ver alguém?; **if ~ should phone …** se alguém telefonar; **~ could do it** qualquer um(a) poderia fazer isso

anything ['ɛnɪθɪŋ] PRON (*in questions etc*) alguma coisa; (*with negative*) nada; (*no matter what*) qualquer coisa; **can you see ~?** você pode ver alguma coisa?

anyway ['ɛnɪweɪ] ADV (*at any rate*) de qualquer modo; (*besides*) além disso; **I shall go ~** eu irei de qualquer jeito

anywhere ['ɛnɪwɛər] ADV (*in questions etc*) em algum lugar; (*with negative*) em parte nenhuma; (*no matter where*) não importa onde, onde quer que seja; **can you see him ~?** você pode vê-lo em algum lugar?; **I can't see him ~** não o vejo em parte nenhuma; **~ in the world** em qualquer lugar do mundo

apart [ə'paːt] ADV à parte, à distância; (*separately*) separado; **10 miles ~** a uma distância de 10 milhas um do outro; **to take ~** desmontar; **~ from** além de, à parte de

apartment [ə'paːtmənt] (US) N apartamento

ape [eɪp] N macaco ▶ VT macaquear, imitar

aperitif [ə'pɛrɪtɪf] N aperitivo

aperture ['æpətʃuər] N orifício; (*Phot*) abertura

APEX ['eɪpɛks] N (= *advance passenger excursion*) tarifa aérea com desconto por compra antecipada

apologize [ə'pɔlədʒaɪz] VI: **to ~ (for sth to sb)** desculpar-se or pedir desculpas (por or de algo a alguém); **apology** N desculpas fpl

apostrophe [ə'pɒstrəfɪ] N apóstrofo
app [æp] (inf) N ABBR (= application
program) aplicativo (BR), aplicação f (PT)
appalling [ə'pɔ:lɪŋ] ADJ (shocking)
chocante; (awful) terrível
apparatus [æpə'reɪtəs] N aparelho; (in
gym) aparelhos mpl; (organization)
aparato
apparent [ə'pærənt] ADJ aparente;
(obvious) claro, patente; **apparently** ADV
aparentemente, pelo(s) visto(s)
appeal [ə'pi:l] VI (Jur) apelar, recorrer ▶ N
(Jur) recurso, apelação f; (request) pedido;
(plea) súplica; (charm) atração f; **to ~ (to
sb) for** suplicar (a alguém); **to ~ to**
atrair; **to ~ to sb for mercy** pedir
misericórdia a alguém; **appealing** ADJ
atraente
appear [ə'pɪəʳ] VI aparecer; (Jur)
apresentar-se, comparecer; (publication)
ser publicado; (seem) parecer; **to ~ in
"Hamlet"** trabalhar em "Hamlet"; **to ~
on TV** (person, news item) sair na
televisão; (programme) passar na
televisão; **appearance** N aparecimento;
(presence) comparecimento; (look, aspect)
aparência
appendicitis [əpɛndɪ'saɪtɪs] N
apendicite f
appendix [ə'pɛndɪks] (pl **appendices**) N
apêndice m
appetite ['æpɪtaɪt] N apetite m; (fig)
desejo
appetizer ['æpɪtaɪzəʳ] N (food)
tira-gosto; (drink) aperitivo
applaud [ə'plɔ:d] VI aplaudir ▶ VT
aplaudir; (praise) admirar; **applause** N
aplausos mpl
apple ['æpl] N maçã f
appliance or [ə'plaɪəns] N aparelho;
electrical or **domestic ~s**
eletrodomésticos mpl
applicant ['æplɪkənt] N: **~ (for)** (for post)
candidato(-a) (a); (Admin: for benefit etc)
requerente m/f (de)
application [æplɪ'keɪʃən] N aplicação f;
(for a job, a grant etc) candidatura,
requerimento; (hard work) empenho;
application form N (formulário de)
requerimento
apply [ə'plaɪ] VT (paint etc) usar; (law etc)
pôr em prática ▶ VI: **to ~ to** (be suitable
for) ser aplicável a; (be relevant to) valer
para; (ask) pedir; **to ~ for** (permit, grant)
solicitar, pedir; (job) candidatar-se a; **to ~
o.s. to** aplicar-se a, dedicar-se a
appoint [ə'pɔɪnt] VT (to post) nomear;
appointment N (engagement) encontro,

compromisso; (at doctor's etc) hora
marcada; (act) nomeação f; (post) cargo;
to make an appointment (with sb)
marcar um encontro (com alguém)
appraisal [ə'preɪzl] N avaliação f
appreciate [ə'pri:ʃɪeɪt] VT (like) apreciar,
estimar; (be grateful for) agradecer;
(understand) compreender ▶ VI (Comm)
valorizar-se; **appreciation** N apreciação
f, estima; (understanding) compreensão f;
(gratitude) agradecimento; (Comm)
valorização f
apprehensive [æprɪ'hɛnsɪv] ADJ
apreensivo, receoso
apprentice [ə'prɛntɪs] N aprendiz m/f
approach [ə'prəʊtʃ] VI aproximar-se ▶ VT
aproximar-se de; (ask, apply to) dirigir-se
a; (subject, passer-by) abordar ▶ N
aproximação f; (access) acesso; (to
problem, situation) enfoque m
appropriate [adj ə'prəʊprɪɪt, vt
ə'prəʊprɪeɪt] ADJ (apt) apropriado;
(relevant) adequado ▶ VT apropriar-se de
approval [ə'pru:vəl] N aprovação f; **on ~**
(Comm) a contento
approve [ə'pru:v] VT (publication, product)
autorizar; (motion, decision) aprovar;
approve of VT FUS aprovar
approximate [ə'prɒksɪmɪt] ADJ
aproximado; **approximately** ADV
aproximadamente
apricot ['eɪprɪkɒt] N damasco
April ['eɪprəl] N abril m
apron ['eɪprən] N avental m
apt [æpt] ADJ (suitable) adequado;
(appropriate) apropriado; (likely): **~ to do**
sujeito a fazer
Aquarius [ə'kwɛərɪəs] N Aquário
Arab ['ærəb] ADJ, N árabe m/f
Arabian [ə'reɪbɪən] ADJ árabe
Arabic ['ærəbɪk] ADJ árabe; (numerals)
arábico ▶ N (Ling) árabe m
arbitrary ['ɑ:bɪtrərɪ] ADJ arbitrário
arbitration [ɑ:bɪ'treɪʃən] N arbitragem f
arcade [ɑ:'keɪd] N arcos mpl; (passage
with shops) galeria
arch [ɑ:tʃ] N arco; (of foot) curvatura ▶ VT
arquear, curvar
archaeology [ɑ:kɪ'ɔlədʒɪ], (US)
archeology N arqueologia
archbishop [ɑ:tʃ'bɪʃəp] N arcebispo
archeology [ɑ:kɪ'ɔlədʒɪ] (US) N =
archaeology
architect ['ɑ:kɪtɛkt] N arquiteto(-a);
architecture N arquitetura
Arctic ['ɑ:ktɪk] ADJ ártico ▶ N: **the ~** o
Ártico
are [ɑ:ʳ] VB see be

area ['ɛərɪə] N (zone) zona, região f; (part of place) região; (in room, of knowledge, experience) área; (Math) superfície f, extensão f ▶ **area code** (US) N (Tel) (código) DDD (BR), indicativo (PT)

aren't [ɑ:nt] = **are not**

Argentina [ɑ:dʒən'ti:nə] N Argentina

arguably ['ɑ:gjuəblɪ] ADV possivelmente

argue ['ɑ:gju:] VI (quarrel) discutir; (reason) argumentar; **to ~ that** sustentar que

argument ['ɑ:gjumənt] N (reasons) argumento; (quarrel) briga, discussão f

Aries ['ɛərɪz] N Áries m

arise [ə'raɪz] (pt **arose**, pp **arisen**) VI (emerge) surgir

arithmetic [ə'rɪθmətɪk] N aritmética

arm [ɑ:m] N braço; (of clothing) manga; (of organization etc) divisão f ▶ VT armar; **arms** NPL (weapons) armas fpl; (Heraldry) brasão m; **~ in ~** de braços dados

armchair N poltrona

armed ADJ armado

armour ['ɑ:məʳ], (US) **armor** N armadura

armpit ['ɑ:mpɪt] N sovaco

armrest ['ɑ:mrɛst] N braço (de poltrona)

army ['ɑ:mɪ] N exército

aroma [ə'rəumə] N aroma; **aromatherapy** N aromaterapia

arose [ə'rəuz] PT of **arise**

around [ə'raund] ADV em volta; (in the area) perto ▶ PREP em volta de; (near) perto de; (fig: about) cerca de

arouse [ə'rauz] VT despertar; (anger) provocar

arrange [ə'reɪndʒ] VT (organize) organizar; (put in order) arrumar ▶ VI: **to ~ to do sth** combinar em or ficar de fazer algo; **arrangement** N (agreement) acordo; (order, layout) disposição f; **arrangements** NPL (plans) planos mpl; (preparations) preparativos mpl; **home deliveries by arrangement** entregas a domicílio por convênio; **I'll make all the necessary arrangements** eu vou tomar todas as providências necessárias

array [ə'reɪ] N: **~ of** variedade f de

arrears [ə'rɪəz] NPL atrasos mpl; **to be in ~ with one's rent** estar atrasado com o aluguel

arrest [ə'rɛst] VT prender, deter; (sb's attention) chamar, prender ▶ N detenção f, prisão f; **under ~** preso

arrival [ə'raɪvəl] N chegada; **new ~** recém-chegado; (baby) recém-nascido

arrive [ə'raɪv] VI chegar

arrogant ['ærəgənt] ADJ arrogante

arrow ['ærəu] N flecha; (sign) seta

arse [ɑ:s] (BRIT!) N cu m (!)

arson ['ɑ:sn] N incêndio premeditado

art [ɑ:t] N arte f; (skill) habilidade f, jeito; **Arts** NPL (Sch) letras fpl

artery ['ɑ:tərɪ] N (Med) artéria; (fig) estrada principal

art gallery N museu m de belas artes; (small, private) galeria de arte

arthritis [ɑ:'θraɪtɪs] N artrite f

artichoke ['ɑ:tɪtʃəuk] N (globe artichoke) alcachofra; (also: **Jerusalem ~**) topinambo

article ['ɑ:tɪkl] N artigo; **articles** NPL (BRIT Jur: training) contrato de aprendizagem; **~s of clothing** peças fpl de vestuário

articulate [adj ɑ:'tɪkjulɪt, vt ɑ:'tɪkjuleɪt] ADJ (speech) bem articulado; (writing) bem escrito; (person) eloquente ▶ VT expressar

artificial [ɑ:tɪ'fɪʃəl] ADJ artificial; (person, manner) afetado

artist ['ɑ:tɪst] N artista m/f; (Mus) intérprete m/f; **artistic** [ɑ:'tɪstɪk] ADJ artístico

art school N ≈ escola de artes

(**KEYWORD**)

as [æz, əz] CONJ **1** (referring to time) quando; **as the years went by** no decorrer dos anos; **he came in as I was leaving** ele chegou quando eu estava saindo; **as from tomorrow** a partir de amanhã

2 (in comparisons) tão ... como, tanto(s) ... como; **as big as** tão grande como; **twice as big as** duas vezes maior que; **as much/many as** tanto/tantos como; **as much money/many books as** tanto dinheiro quanto/tantos livros quanto; **as soon as** logo que, assim que

3 (since, because) como

4 (referring to manner, way) como; **do as you wish** faça como quiser

5 (concerning): **as for** or **to that** quanto a isso

6: **as if** or **though** como se; **he looked as if he was ill** ele parecia doente ▶ PREP (in the capacity of): **he works as a driver** ele trabalha como motorista; **he gave it to me as a present** ele me deu isso de presente; see also **long**, **such**, **well**

a.s.a.p. ABBR = **as soon as possible**

asbestos [æz'bɛstəs] N asbesto, amianto

ash [æʃ] N cinza; (*tree, wood*) freixo

ashamed [ə'ʃeɪmd] ADJ envergonhado; **to be ~ of** ter vergonha de

ashore [ə'ʃɔːʳ] ADV em terra; **to go ~** descer à terra, desembarcar

ashtray ['æʃtreɪ] N cinzeiro

Asia ['eɪʃə] N Ásia; **Asian** ADJ, N asiático(-a)

aside [ə'saɪd] ADV à parte, de lado ▸ N aparte *m*

ask [ɑːsk] VT perguntar; (*invite*) convidar; **to ~ sb sth** perguntar algo a alguém; **to ~ sb to do sth** pedir para alguém fazer algo; **to ~ (sb) a question** fazer uma pergunta (a alguém); **to ~ sb out to dinner** convidar alguém para jantar; **ask after** VT FUS perguntar por; **ask for** VT FUS pedir; **it's just ~ing for it** or **trouble** é procurar encrenca

asleep [ə'sliːp] ADJ dormindo; **to fall ~** dormir, adormecer

asparagus [əs'pærəgəs] N aspargo (BR), espargo (PT)

aspect ['æspɛkt] N aspecto; (*direction in which a building etc faces*) direção *f*

aspire [əs'paɪəʳ] VI: **to ~ to** aspirar a

aspirin ['æsprɪn] N aspirina

ass [æs] N jumento, burro; (*inf*) imbecil *m/f*; (US!) cu *m* (!)

assassinate [ə'sæsɪneɪt] VT assassinar

assault [ə'sɔːlt] N assalto ▸ VT assaltar, atacar; (*sexually*) agredir, violar

assemble [ə'sɛmbl] VT (*people*) reunir; (*objects*) juntar; (*Tech*) montar ▸ VI reunir-se

assembly [ə'sɛmblɪ] N reunião *f*; (*institution*) assembleia

assert [ə'səːt] VT afirmar

assess [ə'sɛs] VT avaliar; **assessment** N avaliação *f*

asset ['æsɛt] N vantagem *f*, trunfo; **assets** NPL (*property, funds*) bens *mpl*

assign [ə'saɪn] VT (*date*) fixar; **to ~ (to)** (*task*) designar (a); (*resources*) destinar (a); **assignment** N tarefa

assist [ə'sɪst] VT ajudar; **assistance** N ajuda, auxílio; **assistant** N assistente *m/f*, auxiliar *m/f*; (BRIT: *also*: **shop assistant**) vendedor(a) *m/f*

associate [*adj* ə'səuʃiɪt, *vt, vi* ə'səuʃieɪt] ADJ associado; (*professor, director etc*) adjunto ▸ N sócio(-a) ▸ VI: **to ~ with sb** associar-se com alguém ▸ VT associar; **association** N associação *f*; (*link*) ligação *f*

assorted [ə'sɔːtɪd] ADJ sortido

assortment [ə'sɔːtmənt] N (*of shapes, colours*) sortimento; (*of books, people*) variedade *f*

assume [ə'sjuːm] VT (*suppose*) supor, presumir; (*responsibilities etc*) assumir; (*attitude, name*) adotar, tomar; **assumption** [ə'sʌmpʃən] N suposição *f*, presunção *f*

assurance [ə'ʃuərəns] N garantia; (*confidence*) confiança; (*insurance*) seguro

assure [ə'ʃuəʳ] VT assegurar; (*guarantee*) garantir

asthma ['æsmə] N asma

astonish [əs'tɔnɪʃ] VT assombrar, espantar; **astonishment** N assombro, espanto

astound [əs'staund] VT pasmar, estarrecer

astray [ə'streɪ] ADV: **to go ~** extraviar-se; **to lead ~** desencaminhar

astrology [əs'trɔlədʒɪ] N astrologia

astronaut ['æstrənɔːt] N astronauta *m/f*

astronomy [əs'trɔnəmɪ] N astronomia

asylum [ə'saɪləm] N (*refuge*) asilo; (*hospital*) manicômio; **asylum seeker** [-siː'kəʳ] N solicitante *m/f* de asilo

---

(KEYWORD)

at [æt] PREP **1** (*referring to position*) em; (*referring to direction*) a; **at the top** em cima; **at home/school** em casa/ na escola; **to look at sth** olhar para algo
2 (*referring to time*): **at 4 o'clock** às quatro horas; **at night** à noite; **at Christmas** no Natal; **at times** às vezes
3 (*referring to rates, speed etc*): **at £1 a kilo** a uma libra o quilo; **two at a time** de dois em dois
4 (*referring to manner*): **at a stroke** de um golpe; **at peace** em paz
5 (*referring to activity*): **to be at work** estar no trabalho; **to play at cowboys** brincar de mocinho
6 (*referring to cause*): **to be shocked/ surprised/annoyed at sth** ficar chocado/surpreso/chateado com algo; **I went at his suggestion** eu fui por causa da sugestão dele
▸ N (*symbol @*) arroba

ate [eɪt] PT *of* **eat**

atheist ['eɪθɪɪst] N ateu/ateia *m/f*

Athens ['æθɪnz] N Atenas

athlete ['æθliːt] N atleta *m/f*; **athletic** [æθ'lɛtɪk] ADJ atlético; **athletics** N atletismo

Atlantic [ət'læntɪk] ADJ atlântico ▸ N: **the ~ (Ocean)** o (oceano) Atlântico

atlas ['ætləs] N atlas m inv

ATM ABBR (= automated teller machine) caixa eletrônico m

atmosphere ['ætməsfɪəʳ] N atmosfera; (fig) ambiente m

atom ['ætəm] N átomo; **atomic** [ə'tɔmɪk] ADJ atômico

attach [ə'tætʃ] VT prender; (document, letter) juntar, anexar; (importance etc) dar; **to be ~ed to sb/sth** (like) ter afeição por alguém/algo; **to ~ a file to an email** anexar um arquivo a um e-mail

attachment [ə'tætʃmənt] N (tool) acessório; (to email) anexo; (love): **~ (to)** afeição f(por)

attack [ə'tæk] VT atacar; (subj: criminal) assaltar; (task etc) empreender ▶ N ataque m; (on sb's life) atentado; **heart ~** ataque cardíaco or de coração

attain [ə'teɪn] VT (also: **~ to**: happiness, results) alcançar, atingir; (: knowledge) obter

attempt [ə'tɛmpt] N tentativa ▶ VT tentar; **to make an ~ on sb's life** atentar contra a vida de alguém

attend [ə'tɛnd] VT (lectures) assistir a; (school) cursar; (church) ir a; (course) fazer; (patient) tratar; **attend to** VT FUS (matter) encarregar-se de; (needs, customer) atender a; (patient) tratar de; **attendance** N comparecimento; (people present) assistência; **attendant** N servidor(a) m/f ▶ ADJ concomitante

attention [ə'tɛnʃən] N atenção f; (care) cuidados mpl ▶ EXCL (Mil) sentido!; **for the ~ of ...** (Admin) atenção ...

attic ['ætɪk] N sótão m

attitude ['ætɪtjuːd] N atitude f

attorney [ə'təːnɪ] N (US: lawyer) advogado(-a)

attract [ə'trækt] VT atrair, chamar; **attraction** N atração f; **attractive** ADJ atraente; (idea, offer) interessante

attribute [n 'ætrɪbjuːt, vt ə'trɪbjuːt] N atributo ▶ VT: **to ~ sth to** atribuir algo a

aubergine ['əubəʒiːn] N beringela

auction ['ɔːkʃən] N (also: **sale by ~**) leilão m ▶ VT leiloar

audience ['ɔːdɪəns] N (in theatre, concert etc) plateia; (of writer, magazine) público

audit ['ɔːdɪt] VT fazer a auditoria de

audition [ɔː'dɪʃən] N audição f

August ['ɔːgəst] N agosto

aunt [ɑːnt] N tia; **auntie** N titia; **aunty** N titia

au pair ['əu'pɛəʳ] N (also: **~ girl**) au pair f

Australia [ɔs'treɪlɪə] N Austrália; **Australian** ADJ, N australiano(-a)

Austria ['ɔstrɪə] N Áustria; **Austrian** ADJ, N austríaco(-a)

authentic [ɔː'θɛntɪk] ADJ autêntico

author ['ɔːθəʳ] N autor(a) m/f

authority [ɔː'θɔrɪtɪ] N autoridade f; (government body) jurisdição f; (permission) autorização f; **the authorities** NPL (ruling body) as autoridades

authorize ['ɔːθəraɪz] VT autorizar

auto ['ɔːtəu] (US) N carro, automóvel m

autobiography [ɔːtəbaɪ'ɔgrəfɪ] N autobiografia

autograph ['ɔːtəgrɑːf] N autógrafo ▶ VT (photo etc) autografar

automatic [ɔːtə'mætɪk] ADJ automático ▶ N (gun) pistola automática; (washing machine) máquina de lavar roupa automática; (car) carro automático

automobile ['ɔːtəməbiːl] (US) N carro, automóvel m

autonomy [ɔː'tɔnəmɪ] N autonomia

autumn ['ɔːtəm] N outono

auxiliary [ɔːg'zɪlɪərɪ] ADJ, N auxiliar m/f

available [ə'veɪləbl] ADJ disponível; (time) livre

avalanche ['ævəlɑːnʃ] N avalanche f

avatar ['ævətɑː] N (Comput) avatar m

Ave. ABBR (= avenue) Av., Avda.

avenue ['ævənjuː] N avenida; (drive) caminho; (means) solução f

average ['ævərɪdʒ] N média ▶ ADJ (mean) médio; (ordinary) regular ▶ VT alcançar uma média de; **on ~** em média; **average out** VI: **to ~ out at** dar uma média de

avert [ə'vəːt] VT prevenir; (blow, one's eyes) desviar

avocado [ævə'kɑːdəu] N (BRIT: also: **~ pear**) abacate m

avoid [ə'vɔɪd] VT evitar

await [ə'weɪt] VT esperar, aguardar

awake [ə'weɪk] (pt awoke, pp awoken) ADJ acordado ▶ VT, VI despertar, acordar; **~ to** atento a

award [ə'wɔːd] N prêmio, condecoração f; (Jur: damages) sentença; (act) concessão f ▶ VT outorgar, conceder; (damages) determinar o pagamento de

aware [ə'wɛəʳ] ADJ: **~ of** (conscious) consciente de; (informed) informado de or sobre; **to become ~ of** reparar em, saber de; **awareness** N consciência

away [ə'weɪ] ADV fora; (faraway) muito longe; **two kilometres ~** a dois quilômetros de distância; **the holiday was two weeks ~** faltavam duas semanas para as férias; **he's ~ for a week** está ausente uma semana; **to**

take ~ levar; **to work/pedal** etc ~
trabalhar/pedalar etc sem parar; **to
fade ~** (colour) desbotar; (enthusiasm,
sound) diminuir
awe [ɔː] N temor m respeitoso
awful ['ɔːfəl] ADJ terrível, horrível;
(quantity): **an ~ lot of** um monte de;
awfully ADV (very) muito
awkward ['ɔːkwəd] ADJ (person,
movement) desajeitado; (shape)
incômodo; (problem) difícil; (situation)
embaraçoso, delicado
awoke [ə'wəuk] PT of **awake**; **awoken**
[ə'wəukən] PP of **awake**
axe [æks], (US) **ax** N machado ▶ VT
(project etc) abandonar; (jobs) reduzir
axle ['æksl] N (Aut) eixo

B [biː] N (Mus) si m
baby ['beɪbɪ] N neném m/f, nenê m/f,
bebê m/f; (US inf) querido(-a); **baby
carriage** (US) N carrinho de bebê; **baby
food** N papinha de bebê; **baby-sit** irreg VI
tomar conta da(s) criança(s);
baby-sitter N baby-sitter m/f; **baby
wipe** N lenço umedecido
bachelor ['bætʃələʳ] N solteiro; **B~ of
Arts** ≈ bacharel m em Letras; **B~ of
Science** ≈ bacharel m em Ciências
back [bæk] N (of person) costas fpl; (of
animal) lombo; (of hand) dorso; (of car,
train) parte f traseira; (of house) fundos
mpl; (of chair) encosto; (of page) verso;
(of book) lombada; (of crowd) fundo;
(Football) zagueiro (BR), defesa m (PT)
▶ VT (candidate: also: **~ up**) apoiar; (horse:
at races) apostar em; (car) dar ré com ▶ VI
(car etc: also: **~ up**) dar ré (BR), fazer
marcha atrás (PT) ▶ CPD (payment)
atrasado; (Aut: seats, wheels) de trás
▶ ADV (not forward) para trás; **he's ~** ele
voltou; **throw the ball ~** devolva a bola;
he called ~ (again) chamou de novo; **he
ran ~** voltou correndo; **back down** VI
desistir; **back out** VI (of promise) voltar
atrás, recuar; **back up** VT (support)
apoiar; (Comput) fazer um backup de;
backache N dor f nas costas; **backbone**
N coluna vertebral; (fig) esteio; **backfire**
VI (Aut) engasgar; (plan) sair pela culatra;
background N fundo; (of events)
antecedentes mpl; (basic knowledge)
bases fpl; (experience) conhecimentos
mpl, experiência; **family background**
antecedentes mpl familiares; **backing** N
(fig) apoio; **backlog** N: **backlog of work**
atrasos mpl; **backpack** N mochila; **back
pay** N salário atrasado; **backstage** ADV

nos bastidores; **backstroke** N nado de costas; **backup** ADJ (*train, plane*) reserva inv; (*Comput*) de backup ▶ N (*support*) apoio; (*Comput*: also: **backup file**) backup m; **backward** ADJ (*movement*) para trás; (*person, country*) atrasado; **backwards** ADV (*move, go*) para trás; (*read a list*) às avessas; (*fall*) de costas; **backyard** N quintal m

bacon ['beikən] N toucinho, bacon m

bacteria [bæk'tɪərɪə] NPL bactérias *fpl*

bad [bæd] ADJ mau/má, ruim; (*child*) levado; (*mistake, injury*) grave; (*meat, food*) estragado; **his ~ leg** sua perna machucada; **to go ~** estragar-se; **bad debt** N crédito duvidoso

badge [bædʒ] N (*of school etc*) emblema m; (*police officer's*) crachá m

badger ['bædʒəʳ] N texugo

badly ['bædlɪ] ADV mal; **~ wounded** gravemente ferido; **he needs it ~** faz-lhe grande falta; **to be ~ off (for money)** estar com pouco dinheiro

badminton ['bædmɪntən] N badminton m

bad-tempered ADJ mal humorado; (*temporary*) de mau humor

bag [bæg] N saco, bolsa; (*handbag*) bolsa; (*satchel, shopping bag*) sacola; (*case*) mala; **~s of ...** (*inf: lots of*) ... de sobra; **baggage** N bagagem f; **baggage allowance** N franquia de bagagem; **baggy** ADJ folgado, largo; **bagpipes** NPL gaita de foles

bail [beɪl] N (*payment*) fiança; (*release*) liberdade f sob fiança ▶ VT (*prisoner: grant bail to*) libertar sob fiança; (*boat: also*: **~ out**) baldear a água de; **on ~** sob fiança; **bail out** VT (*prisoner*) afiançar

bait [beɪt] N isca, engodo; (*for criminal etc*) atrativo, chamariz m ▶ VT iscar, cevar; (*person*) apoquentar

bake [beɪk] VT cozinhar ao forno; (*Tech: clay etc*) cozer ▶ VI assar; **baked beans** NPL feijão m cozido com molho de tomate; **baked potato** N batata assada com a casca; **baker** N padeiro(-a); **bakery** N (*for bread*) padaria; (*for cakes*) confeitaria; **baking** N (*act*) cozimento; (*batch*) fornada; **baking powder** N fermento em pó

balance ['bæləns] N equilíbrio; (*scales*) balança; (*Comm*) balanço; (*remainder*) resto, saldo ▶ VT equilibrar; (*budget*) nivelar; (*account*) fazer o balanço de; **~ of trade/payments** balança comercial/balanço de pagamentos; **balanced** ADJ (*report*) objetivo; (*personality, diet*) equilibrado; **balance sheet** N balanço geral

balcony ['bælkənɪ] N varanda; (*closed*) galeria; (*in theatre*) balcão m

bald [bɔːld] ADJ calvo, careca; (*tyre*) careca

ball [bɔːl] N bola; (*of wool, string*) novelo; (*dance*) baile m; **to play ~ with sb** jogar bola com alguém; (*fig*) fazer o jogo de alguém

ballerina [bælə'riːnə] N bailarina

ballet ['bæleɪ] N balé m; **ballet dancer** N bailarino(-a)

balloon [bə'luːn] N balão m

ballot ['bælət] N votação f

ballpoint ['bɔːlpɔɪnt], **ballpoint pen** N (*caneta*) esferográfica

ban [bæn] N proibição f, interdição f; (*suspension, exclusion*) exclusão f ▶ VT proibir, interditar; (*exclude*) excluir

banana [bə'nɑːnə] N banana

band [bænd] N orquestra; (*Mil*) banda; (*strip*) faixa, cinta; **band together** VI juntar-se, associar-se

bandage ['bændɪdʒ] N atadura (BR), ligadura (PT) ▶ VT enfaixar

B & B N ABBR = **bed and breakfast**

bang [bæŋ] N estalo; (*of door*) estrondo; (*of gun, exhaust*) explosão f; (*blow*) pancada ▶ EXCL bum!, bumba! ▶ VT bater com força; (*door*) fechar com violência ▶ VI produzir estrondo; (*door*) bater; (*fireworks*) soltar

bangs [bæŋz] (*US*) NPL (*fringe*) franja

banish ['bænɪʃ] VT banir

banister ['bænɪstəʳ] N, **banisters** ['bænɪstəz] NPL corrimão m

bank [bæŋk] N banco; (*of river, lake*) margem f; (*of earth*) rampa, ladeira ▶ VI (*Aviat*) ladear-se; **bank on** VT FUS contar com, apostar em; **bank account** N conta bancária; **bank card** N cartão m de garantia de cheques; **banker** N banqueiro(-a); **Bank holiday** (BRIT) N feriado nacional; **banking** N transações *fpl* bancárias; **banknote** N nota (bancária)

bankrupt ['bæŋkrʌpt] ADJ falido, quebrado; **to go ~** falir

bank statement N extrato bancário

banner ['bænəʳ] N faixa

baptism ['bæptɪzəm] N batismo

bar [bɑːʳ] N barra; (*rod*) vara; (*of window etc*) grade f; (*fig: hindrance*) obstáculo; (*prohibition*) impedimento; (*pub*) bar m; (*counter: in pub*) balcão m ▶ VT (*road*) obstruir; (*person*) excluir; (*activity*) proibir ▶ PREP **~ none** sem exceção; **behind ~s** (*prisoner*) atrás das grades; **the B~** (*Jur*) a advocacia

barbaric [bɑ:'bærɪk] ADJ bárbaro

barbecue ['bɑ:bɪkju:] N churrasco

barbed wire ['bɑ:bd-] N arame m farpado

barber ['bɑ:bəʳ] N barbeiro, cabeleireiro

bar code N código de barras

bare [bɛəʳ] ADJ despido; (*head*) descoberto; (*trees, vegetation*) sem vegetação; (*minimum*) básico ▶ VT mostrar; **barefoot** ADJ, ADV descalço; **barely** ADV apenas, mal

bargain ['bɑ:gɪn] N negócio; (*agreement*) acordo; (*good buy*) pechincha ▶ VI (*haggle*) regatear; (*negotiate*): **to ~ (with sb)** pechinchar (com alguém); **into the ~** ainda por cima; **bargain for** VT FUS: **he got more than he ~ed for** ele conseguiu mais do que pediu

barge [bɑ:dʒ] N barcaça; **barge in** VI irromper

bark [bɑ:k] N (*of tree*) casca; (*of dog*) latido ▶ VI latir

barley ['bɑ:lɪ] N cevada

barmaid ['bɑ:meɪd] N garçonete f (BR), empregada (de bar) (PT)

barman ['bɑ:mən] *irreg* N garçom m (BR), empregado (de bar) (PT)

barn [bɑ:n] N celeiro

barometer [bə'rɔmɪtəʳ] N barômetro

baron ['bærən] N barão m; (*of press, industry*) magnata m; **baroness** ['bærənɪs] N baronesa

barracks ['bærəks] NPL quartel m, caserna

barrage ['bærɑ:ʒ] N (*Mil*) fogo de barragem; (*dam*) barragem f; (*fig*): **a ~ of questions** uma saraivada de perguntas

barrel ['bærəl] N barril m; (*of gun*) cano

barren ['bærən] ADJ (*land*) árido

barricade [bærɪ'keɪd] N barricada

barrier ['bærɪəʳ] N barreira; (*fig: to progress etc*) obstáculo

barrister ['bærɪstəʳ] (BRIT) N advogado(-a), causídico(-a)

barrow ['bærəu] N (*wheelbarrow*) carrinho (de mão)

bartender ['bɑ:tɛndəʳ] (US) N garçom m (BR), empregado (de bar) (PT)

base [beɪs] N base f ▶ VT (*opinion, belief*): **to ~ sth on** basear or fundamentar algo em ▶ ADJ (*thoughts*) sujo; **baseball** N beisebol m

basement ['beɪsmənt] N porão m

bases¹ ['beɪsɪz] NPL *of* **base**

bases² ['beɪsɪz] NPL *of* **basis**

bash [bæʃ] (*inf*) VT (*with fist*) dar soco or murro em; (*with object*) bater em

basic ['beɪsɪk] ADJ básico; (*facilities*) mínimo; **basically** ADV basicamente;

(*really*) no fundo; **basics** NPL: **the basics** o essencial

basin ['beɪsn] N bacia; (*also*: **wash~**) pia

basis ['beɪsɪs] (*pl* **bases**) N base f; **on a part-time ~** num esquema de meio-expediente; **on a trial ~** em experiência

basket ['bɑ:skɪt] N cesto; (*with handle*) cesta; **basketball** N basquete(bol) m

bass [beɪs] N (*Mus*) baixo

bastard ['bɑ:stəd] N bastardo(-a); (!) filho da puta m (!)

bat [bæt] N (*Zool*) morcego; (*for ball games*) bastão m; (*BRIT: for table tennis*) raquete f ▶ VT: **he didn't ~ an eyelid** ele nem pestanejou

batch [bætʃ] N (*of bread*) fornada; (*of papers*) monte m

bath [bɑ:θ] N banho; (*bathtub*) banheira ▶ VT banhar; **to have a ~** tomar banho (de banheira); *see also* **baths**

bathe [beɪð] VI banhar-se; (*US: have a bath*) tomar um banho ▶ VT (*wound*) lavar; **bathing** N banho; **bathing costume**, (*US*) **bathing suit** N (*woman's*) maiô m (BR), fato de banho (PT)

bathrobe ['bɑ:θrəub] N roupão m de banho

bathroom ['bɑ:θrum] N banheiro (BR), casa de banho (PT)

baths [bɑ:θs] NPL banhos *mpl* públicos

baton ['bætən] N (*Mus*) batuta; (*Athletics*) bastão m; (*truncheon*) cassetete m

batter ['bætəʳ] VT espancar; (*subj: wind, rain*) castigar ▶ N massa (mole); **battered** ['bætəd] ADJ (*hat, pan*) amassado, surrado

battery ['bætərɪ] N bateria; (*of torch*) pilha

battle ['bætl] N batalha; (*fig*) luta ▶ VI lutar; **battlefield** N campo de batalha

bay [beɪ] N (*Geo*) baía; **to hold sb at ~** manter alguém a distância

bazaar [bə'zɑ:ʳ] N bazar m

BBC N ABBR (= *British Broadcasting Corporation*) companhia britânica de rádio e televisão

B.C. ADV ABBR (= *before Christ*) a.C. ▶ ABBR (CANADA) = **British Columbia**

(KEYWORD)

be [bi:] (*pt* **was, were**, *pp* **been**) AUX VB
1 (*with present participle, forming continuous tense*) estar; **what are you doing?** o que você está fazendo or a fazer (PT)?; **it is raining** está chovendo (BR) or a chover (PT); **I've been waiting**

for you for hours há horas que eu espero por você

2 (*with pp, forming passives*): **to be killed** ser morto; **the box had been opened** a caixa tinha sido aberta; **the thief was nowhere to be seen** tinha sumido o ladrão

3 (*in tag questions*): **it was fun, wasn't it?** foi divertido, não foi?; **she's back again, is she?** ela voltou novamente, é?

4 (+ *to* + *infin*): **the house is to be sold** a casa está para ser vendida; **you're to be congratulated for all your work** você devia ser cumprimentado pelo seu trabalho; **he's not to open it** ele não pode abrir isso

▶ VB + COMPLEMENT **1** (*gen*): **I'm English** sou inglês; **I'm tired** estou cansado; **2 and 2 are 4** dois e dois são quatro; **be careful!** tome cuidado!; **be quiet!** fique quieto!, fique calado!; **be good!** seja bonzinho!

2 (*of health*) estar; **how are you?** como está?

3 (*of age*): **how old are you?** quantos anos você tem?; **I'm twenty (years old)** tenho vinte anos

4 (*cost*) ser; **how much was the meal?** quanto foi a refeição?; **that'll be £5.75, please** são £5.75, por favor

▶ VI **1** (*exist, occur etc*) existir, haver; **the best singer that ever was** o maior cantor de todos os tempos; **is there a God?** Deus existe?; **be that as it may ...** de qualquer forma ...; **so be it** que seja assim

2 (*referring to place*) estar; **I won't be here tomorrow** eu não estarei aqui amanhã; **Edinburgh is in Scotland** Edinburgo é or fica na Escócia

3 (*referring to movement*) ir; **where have you been?** onde você foi?; **I've been in the garden** estava no quintal

▶ IMPERS VB **1** (*referring to time*) ser; **it's 8 o'clock** são 8 horas; **it's the 28th of April** é 28 de abril

2 (*referring to distance*) ficar; **it's 10 km to the village** o lugarejo fica a 10 km de distância

3 (*referring to the weather*) estar; **it's too hot/cold** está quente/frio demais

4 (*emphatic*): **it's only me** sou eu!; **it was Maria who paid the bill** foi Maria quem pagou a conta

beach [biːtʃ] N praia ▶ VT puxar para a terra or praia, encalhar

beacon ['biːkən] N (*lighthouse*) farol m; (*marker*) baliza

bead [biːd] N (*of necklace*) conta; (*of sweat*) gota

beak [biːk] N bico

beam [biːm] N (*Arch*) viga; (*of light*) raio ▶ VI (*smile*) sorrir

bean [biːn] N feijão m; (*of coffee*) grão m; **runner/broad ~** vagem f/fava

bear [bɛəʳ] (*pt* **bore**, *pp* **borne**) N urso ▶ VT (*carry, support*) arcar com; (*tolerate*) suportar ▶ VI: **to ~ right/left** virar à direita/à esquerda; **bear out** VT (*theory, suspicion*) confirmar, corroborar; **bear up** VI aguentar, resistir

beard [bɪəd] N barba

bearing ['bɛərɪŋ] N porte m, comportamento; (*connection*) relação f; **bearings** NPL (*also:* **ball ~s**) rolimã m; **to take a ~** fazer marcação

beast [biːst] N bicho; (*inf*) fera

beat [biːt] (*pt* **beat**, *pp* **beaten**) N (*of heart*) batida; (*Mus*) ritmo, compasso; (*of police officer*) ronda ▶ VT (*hit*) bater em; (*eggs*) bater; (*defeat*) vencer, derrotar ▶ VI (*heart*) bater; **to ~ it** (*inf*) cair fora; **off the ~en track** fora de mão; **beat off** VT repelir; **beat up** VT (*inf: person*) espancar; (*eggs*) bater; **beating** N (*thrashing*) surra

beautiful ['bjuːtɪful] ADJ belo, lindo, formoso

beauty ['bjuːtɪ] N beleza; (*person*) beldade f, beleza

beaver ['biːvəʳ] N castor m

because [bɪˈkɔz] CONJ porque; **~ of** por causa de

beckon ['bɛkən] VT (*also:* **~ to**) chamar com sinais, acenar para

become [bɪˈkʌm] (*irreg: like* **come**) VI (+ n) virar, fazer-se, tornar-se; (+ *adj*) tornar-se, ficar

bed [bɛd] N cama; (*of flowers*) canteiro; (*of coal, clay*) camada, base f; (*of sea, lake*) fundo; (*of river*) leito; **to go to ~** ir dormir, deitar(-se); **bed and breakfast** N (*place*) pensão f; (*terms*) cama e café da manhã (BR) or pequeno almoço (PT); **bedclothes** NPL roupa de cama; **bedding** N roupa de cama; **bedroom** N quarto, dormitório; **bedside** N: **at sb's bedside** à cabeceira de alguém ▶ CPD (*book, lamp*) de cabeceira; **bedsit** ['bɛdsɪt], **bedsitter** ['bɛdsɪtəʳ] (BRIT) N conjugado

> Um **bedsit** é um quarto mobiliado cujo aluguel inclui uso de cozinha e banheiro comuns. Esse sistema de alojamento é muito comum na Grã-Bretanha entre estudantes, jovens profissionais liberais etc.

bedspread ['bɛdsprɛd] N colcha
bedtime ['bɛdtaɪm] N hora de ir para cama
bee [bi:] N abelha
beech [bi:tʃ] N faia
beef [bi:f] N carne f de vaca; **roast ~** rosbife m; **beefburger** N hambúrguer m
been [bi:n] PP of **be**
beer [bɪə'] N cerveja
beetle ['bi:tl] N besouro
beetroot ['bi:tru:t] (BRIT) N beterraba
before [bɪ'fɔ:'] PREP (of time) antes de; (of space) diante de ▸ CONJ antes que ▸ ADV antes, anteriormente; à frente, na dianteira; **~ going** antes de ir; **the week ~** a semana anterior; **I've never seen it ~** nunca vi isso antes; **beforehand** ADV antes
beg [bɛg] VI mendigar, pedir esmola ▸ VT (also: **~ for**) mendigar; **to ~ sb to do sth** implorar a alguém para fazer algo; see also **pardon**
began [bɪ'gæn] PT of **begin**
beggar ['bɛgə'] N mendigo(-a)
begin [bɪ'gɪn] (pt **began**, pp **begun**) VT, VI começar, iniciar; **to ~ doing** or **to do sth** começar a fazer algo; **beginner** N principiante m/f; **beginning** N início, começo
behalf [bɪ'hɑ:f] N: **on** or **in** (US) **~ of** (as representative of) em nome de; (for benefit of) no interesse de
behave [bɪ'heɪv] VI comportar-se; (well: also: **~ o.s.**) comportar-se (bem); **behaviour**, (US) **behavior** N comportamento
behind [bɪ'haɪnd] PREP atrás de ▸ ADV atrás; (move) para trás ▸ N traseiro; **to be ~ (schedule) with sth** estar atrasado or com atraso em algo; **~ the scenes** nos bastidores
beige [beɪʒ] ADJ bege
Beijing [beɪ'ʒɪŋ] N Pequim
being ['bi:ɪŋ] N (state) existência; (entity) ser m
belated [bɪ'leɪtɪd] ADJ atrasado
belch [bɛltʃ] VI arrotar ▸ VT (also: **~ out**: smoke etc) vomitar
Belgian ['bɛldʒən] ADJ, N belga m/f
Belgium ['bɛldʒəm] N Bélgica
belief [bɪ'li:f] N (opinion) opinião f; (trust, faith) fé f
believe [bɪ'li:v] VT: **to ~ sth/sb** acreditar algo/em alguém ▸ VI: **to ~ in** (God, ghosts) crer em; (method, person) acreditar em; **believer** N (Rel) crente m/f, fiel m/f
bell [bɛl] N sino; (small, doorbell) campainha

bellow ['bɛləu] VI mugir; (person) bramar
bell pepper N (esp US) pimentão m
belly ['bɛlɪ] N barriga, ventre m
belong [bɪ'lɔŋ] VI: **to ~ to** pertencer a; (club etc) ser sócio de; **the book ~s here** o livro fica guardado aqui; **belongings** NPL pertences mpl
beloved [bɪ'lʌvɪd] ADJ querido, amado
below [bɪ'ləu] PREP (beneath) embaixo de; (lower than, less than) abaixo de ▸ ADV em baixo; **see ~** ver abaixo
belt [bɛlt] N cinto; (of land) faixa; (Tech) correia ▸ VT (thrash) surrar; **beltway** (US) N via circular
bemused [bɪ'mju:zd] ADJ bestificado, estupidificado
bench [bɛntʃ] N banco; (work bench) bancada (de carpinteiro); (BRIT Pol) assento num Parlamento; **the B~** (Jur) o tribunal; (people) os magistrados, o corpo de magistrados
bend [bɛnd] (pt **bent**, pp **bent**) VT (leg, arm) dobrar; (pipe) curvar ▸ VI dobrar-se, inclinar-se ▸ N curva; (in pipe) curvatura; **bend down** VI abaixar-se; **bend over** VI debruçar-se
beneath [bɪ'ni:θ] PREP abaixo de; (unworthy of) indigno de ▸ ADV em baixo
beneficial [bɛnɪ'fɪʃəl] ADJ: **~ (to)** benéfico (a)
benefit ['bɛnɪfɪt] N benefício, vantagem f; (money) subsídio, auxílio ▸ VT beneficiar ▸ VI: **to ~ from sth** beneficiar-se de algo
benign [bɪ'naɪn] ADJ (person, smile) afável, bondoso; (Med) benigno
bent [bɛnt] PT, PP of **bend** ▸ N inclinação f ▸ ADJ: **to be ~ on** estar empenhado em
bereaved [bɪ'ri:vd] NPL: **the ~** os enlutados
beret ['bɛreɪ] N boina
Berlin [bə:'lɪn] N Berlim
berry ['bɛrɪ] N baga
berth [bə:θ] N (bed) beliche m; (cabin) cabine f; (on train) leito; (for ship) ancoradouro ▸ VI (in harbour) atracar, encostar-se; (at anchor) ancorar
beside [bɪ'saɪd] PREP (next to) junto de, ao lado de, ao pé de; **to be ~ o.s. (with anger)** estar fora de si; **that's ~ the point** isso não tem nada a ver
besides [bɪ'saɪdz] ADV além disso ▸ PREP (as well as) além de
best [bɛst] ADJ melhor ▸ ADV (o) melhor; **the ~ part of** (quantity) a maior parte de; **at ~** na melhor das hipóteses; **to make the ~ of sth** tirar o maior partido possível de algo; **to do one's ~** fazer o

possível; **to the ~ of my knowledge** que eu saiba; **to the ~ of my ability** o melhor que eu puder; **best-before date** N validade f; **best man** N padrinho de casamento

bet [bɛt] (pt, pp **bet** or **betted**) N aposta ▶ VI: **to ~ (on)** apostar (em)

betray [bɪ'treɪ] VT trair; (denounce) delatar

better ['bɛtəʳ] ADJ, ADV melhor ▶ VT melhorar; (go above) superar ▶ N: **to get the ~ of sb** vencer alguém; **you had ~ do it** é melhor você fazer isso; **he thought ~ of it** pensou melhor, mudou de opinião; **to get ~** melhorar; **you'd be ~ off this way** seria melhor para você assim

betting ['bɛtɪŋ] N jogo; **betting shop** (BRIT) N agência de apostas

between [bɪ'twiːn] PREP no meio de, entre ▶ ADV no meio

beverage ['bɛvərɪdʒ] N bebida

beware [bɪ'wɛəʳ] VI: **to ~ (of)** precaver-se (de), ter cuidado (com); **"~ of the dog"** "cuidado com o cachorro"

bewildered [bɪ'wɪldəd] ADJ atordoado; (confused) confuso

beyond [bɪ'jɔnd] PREP (in space, exceeding) além de; (exceeding) acima de, fora de; (date) mais tarde que; (above) acima de ▶ ADV além; (in time) mais longe, mais adiante; **~ doubt** fora de qualquer dúvida; **to be ~ repair** não ter conserto

bias ['baɪəs] N parcialidade

bib [bɪb] N babadouro, babador m

Bible ['baɪbl] N Bíblia

bicycle ['baɪsɪkl] N bicicleta

bid [bɪd] (pt **bade** or **bid**, pp **bidden** or **bid**) N oferta; (at auction) lance m; (attempt) tentativa ▶ VI fazer lance ▶ VT oferecer; **to ~ sb good day** dar bom dia a alguém

big [bɪg] ADJ grande; (bulky) volumoso; **~ brother/sister** irmão/irmã mais velho/a

bigheaded ['bɪg'hɛdɪd] ADJ convencido

bike [baɪk] N bicicleta

bikini [bɪ'kiːnɪ] N biquíni m

bilingual [baɪ'lɪŋgwəl] ADJ bilíngue

bill [bɪl] N conta; (invoice) fatura; (Pol) projeto de lei; (US: banknote) bilhete m, nota; (in restaurant) conta, notinha; (notice) cartaz m; (of bird) bico; **to fit** or **fill the ~** (fig) servir; **billboard** N quadro para cartazes; **billfold** ['bɪlfəʊld] (US) N carteira

billiards ['bɪlɪədz] N bilhar m

billion ['bɪlɪən] N bilhão m (BR), mil milhão m (PT)

bin [bɪn] N caixa; (BRIT: also: **dust~**, **litter ~**) lata de lixo

bind [baɪnd] (pt, pp **bound**) VT atar, amarrar; (oblige) obrigar; (book) encadernar ▶ N (inf) saco

binge [bɪndʒ] (inf) N: **to go on a ~** tomar uma bebedeira; **binge-watch** ▶ VT (series, box set) fazer maratona de

bingo ['bɪŋgəʊ] N bingo

binoculars [bɪ'nɔkjuləz] NPL binóculo

bio ... [baɪəʊ] PREFIX bio ...; **biochemistry** N bioquímica; **biodiesel** ['baɪəʊdiːzl] N biodiesel m; **biodiversity** N biodiversidade f; **biofuel** N biocombustível m; **biography** N biografia; **biology** N biologia; **biometric** ADJ biométrico

bipolar [baɪ'pəʊlə] ADJ bipolar

birch [bəːtʃ] N bétula

bird [bəːd] N ave f, pássaro; (BRIT inf: girl) gatinha; **bird flu** N gripe f aviária

birth [bəːθ] N nascimento; **to give ~** dar à luz, parir; **birth certificate** N certidão f de nascimento; **birth control** N controle m de natalidade; (methods) métodos mpl anticoncepcionais; **birthday** N aniversário (BR), dia m de anos (PT) ▶ CPD de aniversário; see also **happy**

biscuit ['bɪskɪt] N (BRIT) bolacha, biscoito; (US) pão m doce

bishop ['bɪʃəp] N bispo

bit [bɪt] PT of **bite** ▶ N pedaço, bocado; (of horse) freio; (Comput) bit m; **a ~ of** (a little) um pouco de; **~ by ~** pouco a pouco

bitch [bɪtʃ] N (dog) cadela, cachorra; (!) cadela (!), vagabunda (!)

bite [baɪt] (pt **bit**, pp **bitten**) VT, VI morder; (insect etc) picar ▶ N (insect bite) picada; (mouthful) bocado; **to ~ one's nails** roer as unhas; **let's have a ~ (to eat)** (inf) vamos fazer uma boquinha

bitter ['bɪtəʳ] ADJ amargo; (wind, criticism) cortante, penetrante ▶ N (BRIT: beer) cerveja amarga

black [blæk] ADJ preto; (humour) negro ▶ N (colour) cor f preta ▶ VT (BRIT Industry) boicotar; **to give sb a ~ eye** esmurrar alguém e deixá-lo de olho roxo; **~ and blue** contuso, contundido; **to be in the ~** (in credit) estar com saldo credor; **blackberry** N amora(-preta) (BR), amora silvestre (PT); **blackbird** N melro; **blackboard** N quadro(-negro); **black coffee** N café m preto; **blackcurrant** N groselha negra; **blackmail** N chantagem f ▶ VT fazer chantagem a; **black market** N mercado or câmbio negro; **blackout** N blecaute m; (fainting) desmaio; (of radio signal) desvanecimento; **Black Sea** N: **the Black Sea** o mar Negro

bladder ['blædə'] N bexiga

blade [bleɪd] N lâmina; (of oar, rotor) pá f; **a ~ of grass** uma folha de relva

blame [bleɪm] N culpa ▶ VT: **to ~ sb for sth** culpar alguém por algo; **to be to ~** ter a culpa

bland [blænd] ADJ (taste) brando

blank [blæŋk] ADJ em branco; (look) sem expressão ▶ N (of memory): **to go ~** dar um branco; (on form) espaço em branco; (cartridge) bala de festim

blanket ['blæŋkɪt] N cobertor m

blast [blɑːst] N (of wind) rajada; (of explosive) explosão f ▶ VT fazer voar

blatant ['bleɪtənt] ADJ descarado

blaze [bleɪz] N (fire) fogo; (in building etc) incêndio; (fig: of colour) esplendor m; (: of glory, publicity) explosão f ▶ VI (fire) arder; (guns) descarregar; (eyes) brilhar ▶ VT: **to ~ a trail** (fig) abrir (um) caminho

blazer ['bleɪzə'] N casaco esportivo, blazer m

bleach [bliːtʃ] N (also: **household ~**) água sanitária ▶ VT (linen) branquear

bleak [bliːk] ADJ (countryside) desolado; (prospect) desanimador(a), sombrio; (weather) ruim

bleed [bliːd] (pt, pp **bled**) VI sangrar

blemish ['blemɪʃ] N mancha; (on reputation) mácula

blend [blend] N mistura ▶ VT misturar ▶ VI (colours etc: also: **~ in**) combinar-se, misturar-se; **blender** N liquidificador m

bless [bles] (pt, pp **blessed**) VT abençoar; **~ you!** (after sneeze) saúde!; **blessing** N bênção f; (godsend) graça, dádiva; (approval) aprovação f

blew [bluː] PT of **blow**

blind [blaɪnd] ADJ cego ▶ N (for window) persiana; (also: **Venetian ~**) veneziana ▶ VT cegar; (dazzle) deslumbrar; **~ people** os cegos; **blind alley** N beco sem saída m; **blindfold** N venda ▶ ADJ, ADV com os olhos vendados, às cegas ▶ VT vendar os olhos a

blink [blɪŋk] VI piscar

bliss [blɪs] N felicidade f

blister ['blɪstə'] N (on skin) bolha; (in paint, rubber) empola ▶ VI empolar-se

blizzard ['blɪzəd] N nevasca

bloated ['bləʊtɪd] ADJ (swollen) inchado; (full) empanturrado

blob [blɔb] N (drop) gota; (indistinct shape) ponto

block [blɔk] N (of wood) bloco; (of stone) laje f; (in pipes) entupimento; (of buildings) quarteirão m ▶ VT obstruir, bloquear; (progress) impedir; **~ of flats** (BRIT) prédio (de apartamentos); **mental ~** bloqueio; **blockade** [blɔ'keɪd] N bloqueio; **blockage** N obstrução f; **blockbuster** ['blɔkbʌstə'] N grande sucesso

blog ['blɔg] N blogue m ▶ VI blogar

blogger ['blɔgə'] N (person) blogueiro(-a); **blogosphere** ['blɔgəsfɪə'] N blogosfera; **blogpost** ['blɔgpəʊst] N post m de blog

bloke [bləʊk] (BRIT inf) N cara m (BR), gajo (PT)

blond, blonde [blɔnd] ADJ, N louro(-a)

blood [blʌd] N sangue m; **blood donor** N doador(a) m/f de sangue; **blood group** N grupo sanguíneo; **blood poisoning** N toxemia; **blood pressure** N pressão f arterial or sanguínea; **bloodshed** N matança, carnificina; **bloodshot** ADJ (eyes) injetado; **bloodstream** N corrente f sanguínea; **blood test** N exame m de sangue; **blood vessel** N vaso sanguíneo; **bloody** ADJ sangrento; (nose) ensanguentado; (BRIT !): **this bloody ...** essa droga de ..., esse maldito ...; **bloody strong/good** forte/bom pra burro (inf)

bloom [bluːm] N flor f ▶ VI florescer

blossom ['blɔsəm] N flor f ▶ VI florescer; **to ~ into** (fig) tornar-se

blot [blɔt] N borrão m; (fig) mancha ▶ VT borrar; **blot out** VT (view) tapar; (memory) apagar

blouse [blauz] N blusa

blow [bləʊ] (pt **blew**, pp **blown**) N golpe m; (punch) soco ▶ VI soprar ▶ VT (subj: wind) soprar; (instrument) tocar; (fuse) queimar; **to ~ one's nose** assoar o nariz; **blow away** VT levar, arrancar ▶ VI ser levado pelo vento; **blow down** VT derrubar; **blow off** VT levar; **blow out** VT (candle) apagar; **blow over** VI passar; **blow up** VI explodir ▶ VT explodir; (tyre) encher; (Phot) ampliar; **blow-dry** N escova; **blow-out** N (of tyre) furo

blue [bluː] ADJ azul; (depressed) deprimido; **blues** N (Mus): **the ~s** o blues; **out of the ~** (fig) de estalo, inesperadamente; **bluebell** N campainha

bluff [blʌf] VI blefar ▶ N blefe m; **to call sb's ~** pagar para ver alguém

blunder ['blʌndə'] N gafe f ▶ VI cometer or fazer uma gafe

blunt [blʌnt] ADJ (knife) cego; (pencil) rombudo; (person) franco, direto

blur [bləːʳ] N borrão m ▶ VT (vision) embaçar

blush [blʌʃ] VI corar, ruborizar-se ▶ N rubor m, vermelhidão f

board [bɔːd] N tábua; (blackboard) quadro; (notice board) quadro de avisos; (for chess etc) tabuleiro; (committee) junta, conselho; (in firm) diretoria, conselho administrativo; (Naut, Aviat): **on ~** a bordo ▶ VT embarcar em; **full ~** (BRIT) pensão f completa; **half ~** (BRIT) meia-pensão f; **~ and lodging** casa e comida; **to go by the ~** ficar abandonado, dançar (inf); **board up** VT entabuar; **boarding card** N = **boarding pass**; **boarding pass** (BRIT) N (Aviat, Naut) cartão m de embarque; **boarding school** N internato

boast [bəust] VI: **to ~ (about or of)** gabar-se (de), jactar-se (de)

boat [bəut] N barco m; (ship) navio

bob [bɔb] VI balouçar-se; **bob up** VI aparecer, surgir

body [ˈbɔdɪ] N corpo; (corpse) cadáver m; (of car) carroceria; (fig: group) grupo; (: organization) organização f; (: quantity) conjunto; (: of wine) corpo; **body-building** N musculação f; **bodyguard** N guarda-costas m inv; **bodywork** N lataria

bog [bɔg] N pântano, atoleiro ▶ VT: **to get ~ged down (in)** (fig) atolar-se (em)

bogus [ˈbəugəs] ADJ falso

boil [bɔɪl] VT ferver; (eggs) cozinhar ▶ VI ferver ▶ N (Med) furúnculo; **to come to the** (BRIT) **or a** (US) **~** começar a ferver; **boil down to** VT FUS (fig) reduzir-se a; **boil over** VI transbordar; **boiled egg** N ovo cozido; **boiled potatoes** NPL batatas fpl cozidas; **boiler** N caldeira; (for central heating) boiler m; **boiling point** N ponto de ebulição

bold [bəuld] ADJ corajoso; (pej) atrevido, insolente; (outline, colour) forte

Bolivia [bəˈlɪvɪə] N Bolívia

bollard [ˈbɔləd] (BRIT) N (Aut) poste m de sinalização

bolt [bəult] N (lock) trinco, ferrolho; (with nut) parafuso, cavilha ▶ ADV: **~ upright** direito como um fuso ▶ VT (door) fechar a ferrolho, trancar; (food) engolir às pressas ▶ VI fugir; (horse) disparar

bomb [bɔm] N bomba ▶ VT bombardear; **bomb scare** N ameaça de bomba

bond [bɔnd] N (binding promise) compromisso; (link) vínculo, laço; (Finance) obrigação f; (Comm): **in ~** (goods) retido sob caução na alfândega

bone [bəun] N osso; (of fish) espinha ▶ VT desossar; tirar as espinhas de

bonfire [ˈbɔnfaɪəʳ] N fogueira

bonnet [ˈbɔnɪt] N toucado; (BRIT: of car) capô m

bonus [ˈbəunəs] N (payment) bônus m; (fig) gratificação f

boo [buː] VT vaiar ▶ EXCL ruuh!, bu!

book [buk] N livro; (of stamps, tickets) talão m ▶ VT reservar; (driver) autuar; (football player) mostrar o cartão amarelo a; **books** NPL (Comm) contas fpl, contabilidade f; **bookcase** N estante f (para livros); **booking office** N (Rail, Theatre) bilheteria (BR), bilheteira (PT); **book-keeping** N escrituração f, contabilidade f; **booklet** N livrinho, brochura; **bookmark** N (for book) marcador m de livro; (Comput) favorito, bookmark m; **bookshop, bookstore** N livraria

boom [buːm] N (noise) barulho, estrondo; (in sales etc) aumento rápido ▶ VI retumbar; (business) tomar surto

boost [buːst] N estímulo ▶ VT estimular

boot [buːt] N bota; (for football) chuteira; (BRIT: of car) porta-malas m (BR), porta-bagagem m (PT) ▶ VT (Comput) iniciar; **to ~ ...** (in addition) ainda por cima ...

booth [buːð] N (at fair) barraca; (telephone booth, voting booth) cabine f

booze [buːz] (inf) N bebida alcoólica

border [ˈbɔːdəʳ] N margem f; (for flowers) borda; (of a country) fronteira; (on cloth etc) debrum m, remate m ▶ VT (also: **~ on**) limitar-se com; **border on** VT FUS (fig) chegar às raias de; **borderline** N fronteira

bore [bɔːʳ] PT of **bear** ▶ VT (hole) abrir; (well) cavar; (person) aborrecer ▶ N (person) chato(-a), maçante m/f; (of gun) calibre m; **to be ~d to tears** or **~d to death** or **~d stiff** estar muito entediado; **boredom** N tédio, aborrecimento; **boring** ADJ chato, maçante

born [bɔːn] ADJ: **to be ~** nascer

borne [bɔːn] PP of **bear**

borough [ˈbʌrə] N município

borrow [ˈbɔrəu] VT: **to ~ sth (from sb)** pedir algo emprestado a alguém

bosom [ˈbuzəm] N peito

boss [bɔs] N (employer) patrão(-troa) m/f ▶ VT (also: **~ about, ~ around**) mandar em; **bossy** ADJ mandão(-dona)

both [bəuθ] ADJ, PRON ambos(-as), os dois/as duas ▶ ADV: **~ A and B** tanto A como B; **~ of us went, we ~ went** nós dois fomos, ambos fomos

bother ['bɒðəʳ] VT (*worry*) preocupar; (*disturb*) atrapalhar ▶ VI (*also:* **~ o.s.**) preocupar-se ▶ N preocupação f; (*nuisance*) amolação f, inconveniente m

bottle ['bɒtl] N garrafa; (*of perfume, medicine*) frasco; (*baby's*) mamadeira (BR), biberão m (PT) ▶ VT engarrafar; **bottle up** VT conter, refrear; **bottle bank** N depósito de vidro para reciclagem, vidrão m (PT); **bottle-opener** N abridor m (de garrafas) (BR), abre-garrafas m inv (PT)

bottom ['bɒtəm] N fundo; (*buttocks*) traseiro; (*of page, list*) pé m; (*of class*) nível m mais baixo ▶ ADJ (*low*) inferior, mais baixo; (*last*) último

bought [bɔːt] PT, PP *of* **buy**

boulder ['bəʊldəʳ] N pedregulho, matacão m

bounce [bauns] VI saltar, quicar; (*cheque*) ser devolvido (*por insuficiência de fundos*) ▶ VT fazer saltar ▶ N (*rebound*) salto; **bouncer** (*inf*) N leão de chácara m

bound [baund] PT, PP *of* **bind** ▶ N (*leap*) pulo, salto; (*gen pl: limit*) limite m ▶ VI (*leap*) pular, saltar ▶ VT (*border*) demarcar ▶ ADJ: **~ by** limitado por; **to be ~ to do sth** (*obliged*) ter a obrigação de fazer algo; (*likely*) na certa ir fazer algo; **~ for** com destino a

boundary ['baundrı] N limite m, fronteira

bout [baut] N (*of malaria etc*) ataque m; (*of activity*) explosão f; (*Boxing etc*) combate m

bow¹ [bəu] N (*knot*) laço; (*weapon, Mus*) arco

bow² [bau] N (*of the body*) reverência; (*of the head*) inclinação f; (*Naut: also:* **~s**) proa ▶ VI curvar-se, fazer uma reverência; (*yield*) **to ~ to** *or* **before** ceder ante, submeter-se a

bowels ['bauəlz] NPL intestinos mpl, tripas fpl; (*fig*) entranhas fpl

bowl [bəul] N tigela; (*ball*) bola ▶ VI (*Cricket*) arremessar a bola

bowler ['bəuləʳ] N (*Cricket*) lançador m (da bola); (BRIT: *also:* **~ hat**) chapéu-coco m

bowling ['bəulıŋ] N (*game*) boliche m; **bowling alley** N boliche m; **bowling green** N gramado (BR) *or* relvado (PT) para jogo de bolas

bowls [bəulz] N jogo de bolas

bow tie ['bəu-] N gravata-borboleta

box [bɒks] N caixa; (*Theatre*) camarote m ▶ VT encaixotar; (*Sport*) boxear contra ▶ VI (*Sport*) boxear; **boxer** N (*person*) boxeador m, pugilista m; **boxer shorts** NPL cueca samba-canção; **boxing** N (*Sport*) boxe m, pugilismo; **Boxing Day** (BRIT) N *Dia de Santo Estevão* (26 de dezembro); **box office** N bilheteria (BR), bilheteira (PT)

boy [bɔı] N (*young*) menino, garoto; (*older*) moço, rapaz m; (*son*) filho

boycott ['bɔıkɒt] N boicote m, boicotagem f ▶ VT boicotar

boyfriend ['bɔıfrɛnd] N namorado

bra [braː] N sutiã m (BR), soutien m (PT)

brace [breıs] N (*on teeth*) aparelho; (*tool*) arco de pua ▶ VT retesar; **braces** NPL (BRIT) suspensórios mpl; **to ~ o.s.** (*for weight, fig*) preparar-se

bracelet ['breıslıt] N pulseira

bracket ['brækıt] N (*Tech*) suporte m; (*group*) classe f, categoria; (*range*) faixa; (*also:* **round ~**) parêntese m ▶ VT pôr entre parênteses; (*fig*) agrupar

brag [bræg] VI gabar-se, contar vantagem

braid [breıd] N (*trimming*) galão m; (*of hair*) trança

brain [breın] N cérebro; **brains** NPL (Culin) miolos mpl; (*intelligence*) inteligência, miolos

braise [breız] VT assar na panela

brake [breık] N freio (BR), travão m (PT) ▶ VT, VI frear (BR), travar (PT)

bran [bræn] N farelo

branch [braːntʃ] N ramo, galho; (Comm) sucursal f, filial f; **branch out** VI (*fig*) diversificar suas atividades; **to ~ out into** estender suas atividades a

brand [brænd] N marca; (*fig: type*) tipo ▶ VT (*cattle*) marcar com ferro quente; **brand-new** ADJ novo em folha, novinho

brandy ['brændı] N conhaque m

brash [bræʃ] ADJ (*forward*) descarado

brass [braːs] N latão m; **the ~** (Mus) os metais; **brass band** N banda de música

brat [bræt] (*pej*) N pirralho(-a), fedelho(-a)

brave [breıv] ADJ valente, corajoso ▶ VT (*face up to*) desafiar; **bravery** N coragem f, bravura

Brazil [brə'zıl] N Brasil m; **Brazilian** ADJ, N brasileiro(-a)

breach [briːtʃ] VT abrir brecha em ▶ N (*gap*) brecha; (*breaking*): **~ of contract** inadimplência (BR), inadimplemento (PT)

bread [brɛd] N pão m; **breadbin** (BRIT) N caixa de pão; **breadbox** (US) N caixa de pão; **breadcrumbs** NPL migalhas fpl; (Culin) farinha de rosca

breadth [brɛtθ] N largura; (*fig*) amplitude f

break [breɪk] (pt **broke**, pp **broken**) vт
quebrar (BR), partir (PT); (promise)
quebrar; (law) violar, transgredir; (record)
bater ▶ vı quebrar-se, partir-se; (storm)
estourar; (weather) mudar; (dawn)
amanhecer; (story, news) revelar ▶ N
(gap) abertura; (fracture) fratura; (rest)
descanso; (interval) intervalo; (at school)
recreio; (chance) oportunidade f; **to ~
the news to sb** dar a notícia a alguém;
to ~ even sair sem ganhar nem perder;
to ~ free or **loose** soltar-se; **to ~ open**
(door etc) arrombar; **break down** vт
(figures, data) analisar ▶ vı (machine, Aut)
enguiçar, pifar (inf); (Med) sofrer uma
crise nervosa; (person: cry) desatar a
chorar; (talks) fracassar; **break in** vт
(horse etc) domar ▶ vı (burglar) forçar uma
entrada; (interrupt) interromper; **break
into** vт FUS (house) arrombar; **break off**
vı (speaker) parar-se, deter-se; (branch)
partir; **break out** vı (war) estourar;
(prisoner) libertar-se; **to ~ out in spots/a
rash** aparecer coberto de manchas/
brotoejas; **break up** vı (ship) partir-se;
(partnership) acabar; (marriage)
desmanchar-se ▶ vт (rocks) partir;
(biscuit etc) quebrar; (journey) romper;
(fight) intervir em; **you're ~ing up** sua
voz está falhando; **breakdown** N (Aut)
enguiço, avaria; (in communications)
interrupção f; (of marriage) fracasso,
término; (Med: also: **nervous
breakdown**) esgotamento nervoso; (of
figures) discriminação f, desdobramento
breakfast ['brɛkfəst] N café m da manhã
(BR), pequeno-almoço (PT)
break-in N roubo com arrombamento
breakthrough ['breɪkθru:] N (fig)
avanço, novo progresso
breast [brɛst] N (of woman) peito, seio;
(chest, meat) peito; **breast-feed** (irreg:
like **feed**) vт, vı amamentar;
breaststroke N nado de peito
breath [brɛθ] N fôlego, respiração f; **out
of ~** ofegante, sem fôlego
breathe [bri:ð] vт, vı respirar; **breathe
in** vт, vı inspirar; **breathe out** vт, vı
expirar; **breathing** N respiração f
breathless ['brɛθlɪs] ADJ sem fôlego
breed [bri:d] (pt, pp **bred**) vт (animals) criar;
(plants) multiplicar ▶ vı acasalar-se ▶ N raça
breeze [bri:z] N brisa, aragem f; **breezy**
ADJ (person) despreocupado, animado;
(weather) ventoso
brew [bru:] vт (tea) fazer; (beer)
fermentar ▶ vı (storm, fig) armar-se;
brewery N cervejaria

Brexit ['brɛgzɪt] Brexit m
bribe [braɪb] N suborno ▶ vт subornar;
bribery N suborno
brick [brɪk] N tijolo; **bricklayer** N
pedreiro
bride [braɪd] N noiva; **bridegroom** N
noivo; **bridesmaid** N dama de honra
bridge [brɪdʒ] N ponte f; (Naut) ponte de
comando; (Cards) bridge m; (of nose)
cavalete m ▶ vт transpor
bridle ['braɪdl] N cabeçada, freio
brief [bri:f] ADJ breve ▶ N (Jur) causa;
(task) tarefa ▶ vт (inform) informar;
briefs NPL (for men) cueca (BR), cuecas fpl
(PT); (for women) calcinha (BR), cuecas fpl
(PT); **briefcase** N pasta; **briefly** ADV
(glance) rapidamente; (say) em poucas
palavras
bright [braɪt] ADJ claro, brilhante;
(weather) resplandecente; (person: clever)
inteligente; (: lively) alegre, animado;
(colour) vivo; (future) promissor(a),
favorável
brilliant ['brɪljənt] ADJ brilhante; (inf:
great) sensacional
brim [brɪm] N borda; (of hat) aba
brine [braɪn] N (Culin) salmoura
bring [brɪŋ] (pt, pp **brought**) vт trazer;
bring about vт ocasionar, produzir;
bring back vт restabelecer; (return)
devolver; **bring down** vт (price) abaixar;
(government, plane) derrubar; **bring
forward** vт adiantar; **bring off** vт (task,
plan) levar a cabo; **bring out** vт (object)
tirar; (meaning) salientar; (new product,
book) lançar; **bring round** vт fazer voltar
a si; **bring up** vт (person) educar, criar;
(carry up) subir; (question) introduzir;
(food) vomitar
brisk [brɪsk] ADJ vigoroso; (tone, person)
enérgico; (trade, business) ativo
bristle ['brɪsl] N (of animal) pelo rijo; (of
beard) pelo de barba curta; (of brush)
cerda ▶ vı (in anger) encolerizar-se
Britain ['brɪtən] N (also: **Great ~**)
Grã-Bretanha
British ['brɪtɪʃ] ADJ britânico ▶ NPL: **the ~**
os britânicos; **British Isles** NPL: **the
British Isles** as ilhas Britânicas
Briton ['brɪtən] N britânico(-a)
brittle ['brɪtl] ADJ quebradiço, frágil
broad [brɔːd] ADJ (street, range) amplo;
(shoulders, smile) largo; (distinction,
outline) geral; (accent) carregado; **in ~
daylight** em plena luz do dia;
broadband N banda larga; **broadcast**
(pt, pp **broadcast**) N transmissão f
▶ vт, vı transmitir; **broaden** vт alargar

▶ vi alargar-se; **to broaden one's mind** abrir os horizontes; **broadly** ADV em geral; **broad-minded** ADJ tolerante, liberal

broccoli ['brɒkəlɪ] N brócolis mpl (BR), brócolos mpl (PT)

brochure ['brəʊʃjʊəʳ] N folheto, brochura

broke [brəʊk] PT of **break** ▶ ADJ (inf) sem um vintém, duro; (: company): **to go ~** quebrar

broken ['brəʊkən] PP of **break** ▶ ADJ quebrado; **in ~ English** num inglês mascavado

broker ['brəʊkəʳ] N corretor(a) m/f

bronchitis [brɒŋ'kaɪtɪs] N bronquite f

bronze [brɒnz] N bronze m

brooch [brəʊtʃ] N broche m

brood [bruːd] N ninhada ▶ vi (person) cismar, remoer

broom [brum] N vassoura; (Bot) giesta-das-vassouras f

Bros. ABBR (Comm: = brothers) Irmãos

broth [brɒθ] N caldo

brothel ['brɒθl] N bordel m

brother ['brʌðəʳ] N irmão m; **brother-in-law** N cunhado

brought [brɔːt] PT, PP of **bring**

brow [braʊ] N (forehead) fronte f, testa; (eyebrow) sobrancelha; (of hill) cimo, cume m

brown [braʊn] ADJ marrom (BR), castanho (PT); (hair) castanho; (tanned) bronzeado, moreno ▶ N (colour) cor f marrom (BR) or castanha (PT) ▶ vT (Culin) dourar; **brown bread** N pão m integral; **Brownie** N (also: **Brownie Guide**) fadinha de bandeirante; **brown sugar** N açúcar m mascavo

browse [braʊz] vi (in shop) dar uma olhada; **to ~ through a book** folhear um livro; **browser** N (Comput) browser m

bruise [bruːz] N hematoma m, contusão f ▶ vT machucar

brunette [bruː'nɛt] N morena

brush [brʌʃ] N escova; (for painting, shaving etc) pincel m; (quarrel) bate-boca m ▶ vT varrer; (groom) escovar; (also: **~ against**) tocar ao passar, roçar; **brush aside** vT afastar, não fazer caso de; **brush up** vT retocar, revisar

Brussels ['brʌslz] N Bruxelas; **Brussels sprout** N couve-de-bruxelas f

brutal ['bruːtl] ADJ brutal

bubble ['bʌbl] N bolha (BR), borbulha (PT) ▶ vi borbulhar; **bubble bath** N banho de espuma; **bubble gum** N chiclete m (de bola) (BR), pastilha elástica (PT)

buck [bʌk] N (rabbit) macho; (deer) cervo; (US inf) dólar m ▶ vi corcovear; **to pass the ~** fazer o jogo de empurra; **buck up** vi (cheer up) animar-se, cobrar ânimo

bucket ['bʌkɪt] N balde m; **bucket list** N bucket list f (lista de coisas que se quer fazer antes de morrer)

buckle ['bʌkl] N fivela ▶ vT afivelar ▶ vi torcer-se, cambar-se

bud [bʌd] N broto; (of flower) botão m ▶ vi brotar, desabrochar

Buddhism ['budɪzəm] N budismo

buddy ['bʌdɪ] (US) N camarada m, companheiro

budge [bʌdʒ] vT mover ▶ vi mexer-se

budgerigar ['bʌdʒərɪgaːʳ] N periquito

budget ['bʌdʒɪt] N orçamento ▶ vi: **to ~ for sth** incluir algo no orçamento

budgie ['bʌdʒɪ] N = **budgerigar**

buff [bʌf] ADJ (colour) cor de camurça ▶ N (inf: enthusiast) aficionado(-a)

buffalo ['bʌfələʊ] (pl **buffalo** or **buffaloes**) N (BRIT) búfalo; (US: bison) bisão m

buffer ['bʌfəʳ] N para-choque m; (Comput) buffer m

buffet¹ ['bufeɪ] (BRIT) N (in station) bar m; (food) bufê m

buffet² ['bʌfɪt] vT fustigar

buffet car (BRIT) N vagão-restaurante m

bug [bʌg] N (esp US: insect) bicho; (fig: germ) micróbio; (spy device) microfone m oculto; escuta clandestina; (Comput: of program) erro; (: of equipment) defeito ▶ vT (inf: annoy) apoquentar, incomodar; (room) colocar microfones em; (phone) grampear

build [bɪld] (pt, pp **built**) N (of person) talhe m, estatura ▶ vT construir, edificar; **build up** vT acumular; **builder** N construtor(a) m/f, empreiteiro(-a); **building** N construção f; (residential, offices) edifício, prédio; **building society** (BRIT) N sociedade f de crédito imobiliário, financiadora

built [bɪlt] PT, PP of **build** ▶ ADJ: **~-in** (cupboard) embutido

bulb [bʌlb] N (Bot) bulbo; (Elec) lâmpada

Bulgaria [bʌl'gɛərɪə] N Bulgária

bulge [bʌldʒ] N saliência ▶ vi inchar-se; (pocket etc) fazer bojo

bulimia [buː'lɪmɪə] N bulimia

bulk [bʌlk] N volume m; **in ~** (Comm) a granel; **the ~ of** a maior parte de; **bulky** ADJ volumoso

bull [bʊl] N touro

bulldozer [ˈbuldəuzəʳ] N buldôzer m, escavadora
bullet [ˈbulɪt] N bala
bulletin [ˈbulɪtɪn] N noticiário; (*journal*) boletim m
bullfight [ˈbulfaɪt] N tourada; **bullfighter** N toureiro; **bullfighting** N tauromaquia
bully [ˈbulɪ] N fanfarrão m, valentão m ▶ VT intimidar, tiranizar
bum [bʌm] N (*inf: backside*) bumbum m; (*esp us: tramp*) vagabundo(-a), vadio(-a)
bumblebee [ˈbʌmblbi:] N mamangaba
bump [bʌmp] N (*in car*) batida; (*jolt*) sacudida; (*on head*) galo; (*on road*) elevação f ▶ VT bater contra, dar encontrão em ▶ VI dar sacudidas; **bump into** VT FUS chocar-se com or contra, colidir com; (*inf: person*) dar com, topar com; **bumper** N (BRIT) para-choque m ▶ ADJ: **bumper crop/harvest** supersafra; **bumpy** ADJ (*road*) acidentado, cheio de altos e baixos
bun [bʌn] N pão m doce (BR), pãozinho (PT); (*in hair*) coque m
bunch [bʌntʃ] N (*of flowers*) ramo; (*of keys*) molho; (*of bananas, grapes*) cacho; (*of people*) grupo; **bunches** NPL (*in hair*) cachos mpl
bundle [ˈbʌndl] N trouxa, embrulho; (*of sticks*) feixe m; (*of papers*) maço ▶ VT (*also: ~ up*) embrulhar, atar; (*put*): **to ~ sth/sb into** meter or enfiar algo/alguém correndo em
bungalow [ˈbʌŋgələu] N bangalô m, chalé m
bunion [ˈbʌnjən] N joanete m
bunk [bʌŋk] N beliche m; **bunk beds** NPL beliche m, cama-beliche f
bunker [ˈbʌŋkəʳ] N (*coal store*) carvoeira; (*Mil*) abrigo, casamata; (*Golf*) bunker m
buoy [bɔɪ] N boia; **buoy up** VT (*fig*) animar; **buoyant** ADJ flutuante; (*person*) alegre; (*market*) animado
burden [ˈbə:dn] N responsabilidade f, fardo; (*load*) carga ▶ VT sobrecarregar; (*trouble*): **to be a ~ to sb** ser um estorvo para alguém
bureau [bjuəˈrəu] (*pl* **bureaux**) N (BRIT: *desk*) secretária, escrivaninha; (*us: chest of drawers*) cômoda; (*office*) escritório, agência
bureaucracy [bjuəˈrɔkrəsɪ] N burocracia; **bureau de change** [-dəˈʃɑ̃ʒ] (*pl* **bureaux de change**) N casa de câmbio
burger [ˈbə:gəʳ] N hambúrguer m

burglar [ˈbə:gləʳ] N ladrão/ladrona m/f; **burglar alarm** N alarma de roubo; **burglary** N roubo
burial [ˈbɛrɪəl] N enterro
burn [bə:n] (*pt, pp* **burned** or **burnt**) VT queimar; (*house*) incendiar ▶ VI queimar-se, arder; (*sting*) arder, picar ▶ N queimadura; **burn down** VT incendiar; **burning** ADJ ardente; (*hot: sand etc*) abrasador(a); (*ambition*) grande
burrow [ˈbʌrəu] N toca, lura ▶ VI fazer uma toca, cavar; (*rummage*) esquadrinhar
burst [bə:st] (*pt, pp* **burst**) VT arrebentar; (*banks etc*) romper ▶ VI estourar; (*tyre*) furar ▶ N rajada; **to ~ into flames** incendiar-se de repente; **to ~ into tears** desatar a chorar; **to ~ out laughing** cair na gargalhada; **to be ~ing with** (*emotion*) estar tomado de; (*subj: room, container*) estar abarrotado de; **a ~ of energy/speed/enthusiasm** uma explosão de energia/velocidade/ entusiasmo; **burst into** VT FUS (*room etc*) irromper em
bury [ˈbɛrɪ] VT enterrar; (*at funeral*) sepultar; **to ~ one's head in one's hands** cobrir o rosto com as mãos; **to ~ one's head in the sand** (*fig*) bancar avestruz; **to ~ the hatchet** (*fig*) fazer as pazes
bus [bʌs] N ônibus m inv (BR), autocarro (PT); **bus conductor** N cobrador(a) m/f de ônibus
bush [buʃ] N arbusto, mata; (*scrubland*) sertão m; **to beat about the ~** ser evasivo
business [ˈbɪznɪs] N negócio; (*trading*) comércio, negócios mpl; (*firm*) empresa; (*occupation*) profissão f; **to be away on ~** estar fora a negócios; **it's my ~ to ...** encarrego-me de ...; **it's none of my ~** eu não tenho nada com isto; **he means ~** fala a sério; **business class** N (*on plane*) classe f executiva; **businesslike** ADJ eficiente, metódico; **businessman** irreg N homem m de negócios; **business trip** N viagem f de negócios; **businesswoman** irreg N mulher f de negócios
busker [ˈbʌskəʳ] (BRIT) N artista m/f de rua
bust [bʌst] N (*Anat*) busto ▶ ADJ (*inf: broken*) quebrado; **to go ~** falir
busy [ˈbɪzɪ] ADJ (*person*) ocupado, atarefado; (*shop, street*) animado, movimentado; (*us Tel*) ocupado (BR), impedido (PT) ▶ VT: **to ~ o.s. with** ocupar-se em or de

but [bʌt] CONJ **1** (*yet*) mas, porém; **he's tired but Paul isn't** ele está cansado mas Paul não; **the trip was enjoyable but tiring** a viagem foi agradável porém cansativa

2 (*however*) mas; **I'd love to come, but I'm busy** eu adoraria vir, mas estou ocupado

3 (*showing disagreement, surprise etc*) mas; **but that's far too expensive!** mas isso é caro demais!

▶ PREP (*apart from, except*) exceto, menos; **he was/we've had nothing but trouble** ele só deu problema/nós só tivemos problema; **no-one but him** só ele, ninguém a não ser ele; **but for** sem, se não fosse; **(I'll do) anything but that** (eu faria) qualquer coisa menos isso

▶ ADV (*just, only*) apenas; **had I but known** se eu soubesse; **I can but try** a única coisa que eu posso fazer é tentar; **all but finished** quase acabado

butcher ['bʊtʃə'] N açougueiro (BR), homem *m* do talho (PT) ▶ VT (*prisoners etc*) chacinar, massacrar; (*cattle etc for meat*) abater e carnear; **butcher's, butcher's shop** N açougue *m* (BR), talho (PT)

butler ['bʌtlə'] N mordomo

butt [bʌt] N (*cask*) tonel *m*; (*of gun*) coronha; (*of cigarette*) toco (BR), ponta (PT); (BRIT *fig: target*) alvo ▶ VT (*subj: goat*) marrar; (: *person*) dar uma cabeçada em; **butt in** VI (*interrupt*) interromper

butter ['bʌtə'] N manteiga ▶ VT untar com manteiga

butterfly ['bʌtəflaɪ] N borboleta; (*Swimming: also:* **~ stroke**) nado borboleta

buttocks ['bʌtəks] NPL nádegas *fpl*

button ['bʌtn] N botão *m*; (US: *badge*) emblema *m* ▶ VT (*also:* **~ up**) abotoar ▶ VI ter botões

buy [baɪ] (*pt, pp* **bought**) VT comprar ▶ N compra; **to ~ sb sth/sth from sb** comprar algo para alguém/algo a alguém; **to ~ sb a drink** pagar um drinque para alguém; **buyer** N comprador(a) *m/f*

buzz [bʌz] N zumbido; (*inf: phone call*): **to give sb a ~** dar uma ligada para alguém ▶ VI zumbir; **buzzer** N cigarra, vibrador *m*

by [baɪ] PREP **1** (*referring to cause, agent*) por, de; **killed by lightning** morto por um raio; **a painting by Picasso** um quadro de Picasso

2 (*referring to method, manner, means*) de, com; **by bus/car/train** de ônibus/carro/trem; **to pay by cheque** pagar com cheque; **by moonlight/candlelight** sob o luar/à luz de vela; **by saving hard, he ...** economizando muito, ele ...

3 (*via, through*) por, via; **we came by Dover** viemos por *or* via Dover

4 (*close to*) perto de, ao pé de; **a holiday by the sea** férias à beira-mar; **she sat by his bed** ela sentou-se ao lado de seu leito

5 (*past*) por; **she rushed by me** ela passou por mim correndo

6 (*not later than*): **by 4 o'clock** antes das quatro; **by this time tomorrow** esta mesma hora amanhã; **by the time I got here it was too late** quando eu cheguei aqui, já era tarde demais

7 (*during*): **by daylight** durante o dia

8 (*amount*) por; **by the kilometre** por quilômetro

9 (*Math, measure*) por; **it's broader by a metre** tem um metro a mais de largura

10 (*according to*) segundo, de acordo com; **it's all right by me** por mim tudo bem

11: **(all) by oneself** *etc* (completamente) só, sozinho; **he did it (all) by himself** ele fez tudo sozinho

12: **by the way** a propósito

▶ ADV **1** *see* **go, pass** *etc*

2: **by and by** logo, mais tarde; **by and large** em geral

bye ['baɪ], **bye-bye** ['baɪ'baɪ] EXCL até logo (BR), tchau (BR), adeus (PT)

bypass ['baɪpɑːs] N via secundária, desvio; (*Med*) ponte *f* de safena ▶ VT evitar

byte [baɪt] N (*Comput*) byte *m*

C

C [si:] N (*Mus*) dó *m*

cab [kæb] N táxi *m*; (*of truck etc*) boleia; (*of train*) cabina de maquinista

cabaret ['kæbəreɪ] N cabaré *m*

cabbage ['kæbɪdʒ] N repolho (*BR*), couve *f* (*PT*)

cabin ['kæbɪn] N cabana; (*on ship*) camarote *m*; (*on plane*) cabina de passageiros; **cabin crew** N (*Aviat*) tripulação *f*

cabinet ['kæbɪnɪt] N (*Pol*) gabinete *m*; (*furniture*) armário; (*also*: **display ~**) armário com vitrina

cable ['keɪbl] N cabo; (*telegram*) cabograma *m* ▶ VT enviar cabograma para; **cable television** N televisão *f* a cabo

cactus ['kæktəs] (*pl* **cacti**) N cacto

café ['kæfeɪ] N café *m*

cage [keɪdʒ] N (*bird cage*) gaiola; (*for large animals*) jaula; (*of lift*) cabina

cagoule [kə'gu:l] N casaco de náilon

Cairo ['kaɪərəu] N o Cairo

cake [keɪk] N (*large*) bolo; (*small*) doce *m*, bolinho; **cake of soap** N sabonete *m*

calculate ['kælkjuleɪt] VT calcular; (*estimate*) avaliar; **calculation** N cálculo; **calculator** N calculador *m*

calendar ['kæləndə'] N calendário; **calendar month** N mês *m* civil; **calendar year** N ano civil

calf [kɑ:f] (*pl* **calves**) N (*of cow*) bezerro, vitela; (*of other animals*) cria; (*also*: **~skin**) pele *f* or couro de bezerro; (*Anat*) barriga da perna

calibre ['kælɪbə'], (*US*) **caliber** N (*of person*) capacidade *f*, calibre *m*

call [kɔ:l] VT chamar; (*label*) qualificar, descrever; (*Tel*) telefonar a, ligar para; (*witness*) citar; (*meeting, strike*) convocar ▶ VI chamar; (*shout*) gritar; (*Tel*) telefonar; (*visit: also*: **~ in, ~ round**) dar um pulo ▶ N (*shout, announcement*) chamada; (*also*: **telephone ~**) chamada, telefonema *m*; (*of bird*) canto; **to be ~ed** chamar-se; **on ~** de plantão; **call back** VI (*return*) voltar, passar de novo; (*Tel*) ligar de volta; **call for** VT FUS (*demand*) requerer, exigir; (*fetch*) ir buscar; **call off** VT (*cancel*) cancelar; **call on** VT FUS (*visit*) visitar; (*appeal to*) pedir; **call out** VI gritar, bradar; **call up** VT (*Mil*) chamar às fileiras; (*Tel*) ligar para; **call box** (*BRIT*) N cabine *f* telefônica; **call centre** (*BRIT*) N (*Tel*) central *f* de chamadas; **caller** N visita *m/f*; (*Tel*) chamador(a) *m/f*

callous ['kæləs] ADJ cruel, insensível

calm [kɑ:m] ADJ calmo; (*peaceful*) tranquilo; (*weather*) estável ▶ N calma ▶ VT acalmar; (*fears, grief*) abrandar; **calm down** VT acalmar, tranquilizar ▶ VI acalmar-se

calorie ['kælərɪ] N caloria

calves [kɑ:vz] NPL *of* **calf**

Cambodia [kæm'bəudjə] N Camboja

camcorder ['kæmkɔ:də'] N filmadora, máquina de filmar

came [keɪm] PT *of* **come**

camel ['kæməl] N camelo

camera ['kæmərə] N máquina fotográfica; (*Cinema, TV*) câmera; **in ~** (*Jur*) em câmara; **camera phone** N celular *m* com câmera

camouflage ['kæməflɑ:ʒ] N camuflagem *f* ▶ VT camuflar

camp [kæmp] N campo, acampamento; (*Mil*) acampamento; (*for prisoners*) campo; (*faction*) facção *f* ▶ VI acampar ▶ ADJ afeminado

campaign [kæm'peɪn] N (*Mil, Pol etc*) campanha ▶ VI fazer campanha

camper ['kæmpə'] N campista *m/f*; (*vehicle*) reboque *m*

camping ['kæmpɪŋ] N camping *m* (*BR*), campismo (*PT*); **to go ~** acampar

campsite ['kæmpsaɪt] N camping *m* (*BR*), parque *m* de campismo (*PT*)

campus ['kæmpəs] N campus *m*, cidade *f* universitária

can[1] [kæn] N lata ▶ VT enlatar

can[2] [kæn] (*negative* **can't** *or* **cannot**, *pt, conditional* **could**) AUX VB **1** (*be able to*) poder; **you can do it if you try** se você tentar, você consegue fazê-lo; **I'll help you all I can** ajudarei você em tudo que eu puder; **she couldn't sleep that night**

ela não conseguiu dormir aquela noite; **can you hear me?** você está me ouvindo?
2 (know how to) saber; **I can swim** sei nadar; **can you speak Portuguese?** você fala português?
3 (may): **could I have a word with you?** será que eu podia falar com você?
4 (expressing disbelief, puzzlement): **it CAN'T be true!** não pode ser verdade!; **what CAN he want?** o que é que ele quer?
5 (expressing possibility, suggestion etc): **he could be in the library** ele talvez esteja na biblioteca; **they could have forgotten** eles podiam ter esquecido

Canada ['kænədə] N Canadá m; **Canadian** [kə'neɪdɪən] ADJ, N canadense m/f

canal [kə'næl] N canal m

canary [kə'neərɪ] N canário

cancel ['kænsəl] VT cancelar; (contract) anular; (cross out) riscar, invalidar; **cancellation** [kænsə'leɪʃən] N cancelamento

cancer ['kænsər] N câncer m (BR), cancro (PT); **C~** (Astrology) Câncer

candidate ['kændɪdeɪt] N candidato(-a)

candle ['kændl] N vela; (in church) círio; **candlestick** N (plain) castiçal m; (bigger, ornate) candelabro, lustre m

candy ['kændɪ] N (also: **sugar ~**) açúcar m cristalizado; (US) bala (BR), rebuçado (PT)

cane [keɪn] N (Bot) cana; (stick) bengala ▶ VT (BRIT Sch) castigar (com bengala)

canister ['kænɪstər] N lata

cannabis ['kænəbɪs] N maconha

canned [kænd] ADJ (food) em lata, enlatado

cannon ['kænən] (pl inv or **cannons**) N canhão m

cannot ['kænɔt] = **can not**

canoe [kə'nuː] N canoa

can't [kɑːnt] = **can not**

canteen [kæn'tiːn] N cantina; (BRIT: of cutlery) jogo (de talheres)

canter ['kæntər] VI ir a meio galope

canvas ['kænvəs] N (material) lona; (for painting) tela; (Naut) velas fpl

canvass ['kænvəs] VI (Pol): **to ~ for** fazer campanha por ▶ VT sondar

canyon ['kænjən] N canhão m, garganta, desfiladeiro

cap [kæp] N gorro; (of pen, bottle) tampa; (contraceptive: also: **Dutch ~**) diafragma m; (for toy gun) cartucho ▶ VT (outdo) superar; (put limit on) limitar

capable ['keɪpəbl] ADJ (of sth) capaz; (competent) competente, hábil

capacity [kə'pæsɪtɪ] N capacidade f; (of stadium etc) lotação f; (role) condição f, posição f

cape [keɪp] N capa; (Geo) cabo

caper ['keɪpər] N (Culin: gen pl) alcaparra; (prank) travessura

capital ['kæpɪtl] N (also: **~ city**) capital f; (money) capital m; (also: **~ letter**) maiúscula; **capitalism** N capitalismo; **capitalist** ADJ, N capitalista m/f; **capital punishment** N pena de morte

Capitol ['kæpɪtl] N ver nota

> O Capitólio (**Capitol**) é a sede do Congresso dos Estados Unidos, localizado no monte Capitólio (Capitol Hill), em Washington.

Capricorn ['kæprɪkɔːn] N Capricórnio

capsize [kæp'saɪz] VT, VI emborcar, virar

capsule ['kæpsjuːl] N cápsula

captain ['kæptɪn] N capitão m

caption ['kæpʃən] N legenda

capture ['kæptʃər] VT prender, aprisionar; (person) capturar; (place) tomar; (attention) atrair, chamar ▶ N captura; (of place) tomada

car [kɑː] N carro, automóvel m; (Rail) vagão m

caramel ['kærəməl] N (sweet) caramelo; (burnt sugar) caramelado

caravan ['kærəvæn] N reboque m (BR), trailer m (BR), rulote f (PT); (in desert) caravana

carb [kɑːb] (inf) N ABBR (= carbohydrate) carboidrato

carbohydrate [kɑːbəu'haɪdreɪt] N hidrato de carbono; (food) carboidrato

carbon ['kɑːbən] N carbono; **carbon copy** N cópia de papel carbono; **carbon dioxide** [-daɪ'ɔksaɪd] N dióxido de carbono; **carbon footprint** N pegada de carbono; **carbon monoxide** [-mə'nɔksaɪd] N monóxido de carbono; **carbon-neutral** ADJ sem emissão de carbono; **carbon offset** N compensação f de emissão de carbono

carburettor [kɑːbju'rɛtər], (US) **carburetor** N carburador m

card [kɑːd] N (also: **playing ~**) carta; (visiting card, postcard etc) cartão m; (thin cardboard) cartolina; **cardboard** N cartão m, papelão m

cardigan ['kɑːdɪgən] N casaco de lã, cardigã m

cardinal ['kɑːdɪnl] ADJ cardeal; (Math) cardinal ▶ N (Rel) cardeal m

care [kɛəʳ] N cuidado; (*worry*) preocupação f; (*charge*) encargo, custódia ▶ VI: **to ~ about** (*person, animal*) preocupar-se com; (*thing, idea*) ter interesse em; **~ of** (*on letter*) aos cuidados de; **in sb's ~** a cargo de alguém; **to take ~ (to do)** cuidar-se or ter o cuidado (de fazer); **to take ~ of** (*person*) cuidar de; (*situation*) encarregar-se de; **I don't ~** não me importa; **I couldn't ~ less** não dou a mínima; **care for** VT FUS cuidar de; (*like*) gostar de

career [kəˈrɪəʳ] N carreira ▶ VI (*also:* **~ along**) correr a toda velocidade

carefree [ˈkɛəfriː] ADJ despreocupado

careful [ˈkɛəful] ADJ (*thorough*) cuidadoso; (*cautious*) cauteloso; **(be) ~!** tenha cuidado!; **carefully** ADV cuidadosamente; cautelosamente

careless [ˈkɛəlɪs] ADJ descuidado; (*heedless*) desatento

carer [ˈkɛərəʳ] N (*professional*) acompanhante m/f; (*unpaid*) cuidador(a) m/f

caretaker [ˈkɛəteɪkəʳ] N zelador(a) m/f

car-ferry N barca para carros (BR), barco de passagem (PT)

cargo [ˈkɑːgəʊ] (*pl* **cargoes**) N carga

car hire (BRIT) N aluguel m (BR) or aluguer m (PT) de carros

Caribbean [kærɪˈbiːən] N: **the ~ (Sea)** o Caribe

caring [ˈkɛərɪŋ] ADJ (*person*) bondoso; (*society*) humanitário

carnation [kɑːˈneɪʃən] N cravo

carnival [ˈkɑːnɪvəl] N carnaval m; (US: *funfair*) parque de diversões

carol [ˈkærəl] N: **(Christmas) ~** cântico de Natal

car park (BRIT) N estacionamento

carpenter [ˈkɑːpɪntəʳ] N carpinteiro

carpet [ˈkɑːpɪt] N tapete m ▶ VT atapetar

carriage [ˈkærɪdʒ] N carruagem f; (BRIT *Rail*) vagão m; (*of goods*) transporte m; (: *cost*) porte m; **carriageway** (BRIT) N (*part of road*) pista

carrier [ˈkærɪəʳ] N transportador(a) m/f; (*company*) empresa de transportes, transportadora; (*Med*) portador(a) m/f; **carrier bag** (BRIT) N saco, sacola

carrot [ˈkærət] N cenoura

carry [ˈkærɪ] VT levar; (*transport*) transportar; (*involve: responsibilities etc*) implicar ▶ VI (*sound*) projetar-se; **to get carried away** (*fig*) exagerar; **carry on** VI seguir, continuar ▶ VT prosseguir, continuar; **carry out** VT (*orders*) cumprir; (*investigation*) levar a cabo, realizar

cart [kɑːt] N carroça, carreta ▶ VT transportar (em carroça)

carton [ˈkɑːtən] N (*box*) caixa (de papelão); (*of yogurt*) pote m; (*of milk*) caixa; (*packet*) pacote m

cartoon [kɑːˈtuːn] N (*drawing*) desenho; (BRIT: *comic strip*) história em quadrinhos (BR), banda desenhada (PT); (*film*) desenho animado

cartridge [ˈkɑːtrɪdʒ] N cartucho; (*of record player*) cápsula

carve [kɑːv] VT (*meat*) trinchar; (*wood, stone*) cinzelar, esculpir; (*initials, design*) gravar; **carve up** VT dividir, repartir; **carving** N (*object*) escultura; (*design*) talha, entalhe m

case [keɪs] N caso; (*for spectacles etc*) estojo; (*Jur*) causa; (BRIT: *also:* **suit~**) mala; (*of wine etc*) caixa; **in ~ (of)** em caso (de); **in any ~** em todo o caso; **just in ~** *conj* se por acaso; *adv* por via das dúvidas

cash [kæʃ] N dinheiro (em espécie) ▶ VT descontar; **to pay (in) ~** pagar em dinheiro; **~ on delivery** pagamento contra entrega; **cash card** (BRIT) N cartão m de saque; **cash desk** (BRIT) N caixa; **cash dispenser** N caixa automática or eletrônica

cashew [kæˈʃuː] N (*also:* **~ nut**) castanha de caju

cashier [kæˈʃɪəʳ] N caixa m/f

cashless [ˈkæʃlɪs] ADJ (*society, environment*) sem dinheiro

cash point N caixa m eletrônico

cash register N caixa registradora

casino [kəˈsiːnəʊ] N cassino

casket [ˈkɑːskɪt] N cofre m, porta-joias m inv; (US: *coffin*) caixão m

casserole [ˈkæsərəʊl] N panela de ir ao forno; (*food*) ensopado (BR) no forno, guisado (PT) no forno

cassette [kæˈsɛt] N fita-cassete f; **cassette player** N toca-fitas m inv

cast [kɑːst] (*pt, pp* **cast**) VT (*throw*) lançar, atirar; (*Theatre*): **to ~ sb as Hamlet** dar a alguém o papel de Hamlet ▶ N (*Theatre*) elenco; (*also:* **plaster ~**) gesso; **to ~ one's vote** votar; **cast off** VI (*Naut*) soltar o cabo; (*Knitting*) rematar os pontos; **cast on** VI montar os pontos

caster sugar [ˈkɑːstəʳ-] (BRIT) N açúcar m branco refinado

castle [ˈkɑːsl] N castelo; (*Chess*) torre f

casual [ˈkæʒjul] ADJ (*by chance*) fortuito; (*work etc*) eventual; (*unconcerned*) despreocupado; (*clothes etc*) descontraído, informal

casualty ['kæʒjʊltɪ] N ferido(-a); (*dead*) morto(-a); (*of situation*) vítima; (*department*) pronto-socorro

cat [kæt] N gato

catalogue ['kætəlɔg], (*US*) **catalog** N catálogo ▶ VT catalogar

catarrh [kə'tɑ:ʳ] N catarro

catastrophe [kə'tæstrəfɪ] N catástrofe f

catch [kætʃ] (*pt, pp* **caught**) VT pegar (*BR*), apanhar (*PT*); (*fish*) pescar; (*arrest*) prender, deter; (*person: by surprise*) flagrar, surpreender; (*attention*) atrair; (*hear*) ouvir; (*also:* **~ up**) alcançar ▶ VI (*fire*) pegar; (*in branches etc*) ficar preso, prender-se ▶ N (*fish etc*) pesca; (*game*) manha, armadilha; (*of lock*) trinco, lingueta; **to ~ fire** pegar fogo; (*building*) incendiar-se; **to ~ sight of** avistar; **catch on** VI (*understand*) entender (*BR*), perceber (*PT*); (*grow popular*) pegar; **catch up** VI equiparar-se ▶ VT (*also:* **~ up with**) alcançar; **catching** ADJ (*Med*) contagioso

category ['kætɪgərɪ] N categoria

cater ['keɪtəʳ] VI preparar comida; **cater for** VT FUS (*needs*) atender a; (*consumers*) satisfazer

caterpillar ['kætəpɪləʳ] N lagarta

cathedral [kə'θi:drəl] N catedral f; **Catholic** ADJ, N (*Rel*) católico(-a)

catholic ['kæθəlɪk] ADJ eclético

cattle ['kætl] NPL gado

catwalk ['kætwɔ:k] N passarela

caught [kɔ:t] PT, PP *of* **catch**

cauliflower ['kɔlɪflauəʳ] N couve-flor f

cause [kɔ:z] N causa; (*reason*) motivo, razão f ▶ VT causar, provocar

caution ['kɔ:ʃən] N cautela, prudência; (*warning*) aviso ▶ VT acautelar, avisar

cautious ['kɔ:ʃəs] ADJ cauteloso, prudente, precavido

cave [keɪv] N caverna, gruta; **cave in** VI ceder

cc ABBR (= *cubic centimetre*) cc; (*on letter etc*) = **carbon copy**

CCTV N ABBR (= *closed-circuit television*) CFTV; **CCTV camera** N câmera de segurança

CD N ABBR = **compact disc**; **CD burner**, **CD writer** N gravador m de CD; **CD-ROM** N ABBR (= *compact disc read-only memory*) CD-ROM m

cease [si:s] VT, VI cessar; **ceasefire** N cessar-fogo m

cedar ['si:dəʳ] N cedro

ceiling ['si:lɪŋ] N (*also fig*) teto

celebrate ['sɛlɪbreɪt] VT celebrar ▶ VI celebrar; (*birthday, anniversary etc*) festejar; (*Rel: mass*) rezar; **celebration** [sɛlɪ'breɪʃən] N (*party*) festa

celebrity [sɪ'lɛbrɪtɪ] N celebridade f

celery ['sɛlərɪ] N aipo

cell [sɛl] N cela; (*Bio*) célula; (*Elec*) pilha, elemento; (*US: cellphone*) celular m (*BR*), telemóvel m (*PT*)

cellar ['sɛləʳ] N porão m; (*for wine*) adega

cellphone ['sɛlfəun] N (telefone) celular m (*BR*), telemóvel m (*PT*)

cell tower (*US*) N (*Tel*) torre f de celular

cement [sə'mɛnt] N cimento

cemetery ['sɛmɪtrɪ] N cemitério

censor ['sɛnsəʳ] N censor(a) m/f ▶ VT censurar; **censorship** N censura

census ['sɛnsəs] N censo

cent [sɛnt] N cêntimo; *see also* **per cent**

centenary [sɛn'ti:nərɪ] N centenário

center ['sɛntəʳ] (*US*) = **centre**

centigrade ['sɛntɪgreɪd] ADJ centígrado

centimetre ['sɛntɪmi:təʳ], (*US*) **centimeter** N centímetro

central ['sɛntrəl] ADJ central; **Central America** N América Central; **central heating** N aquecimento central

centre ['sɛntəʳ], (*US*) **center** N centro; (*of room, circle etc*) meio ▶ VT centrar

century ['sɛntjʊrɪ] N século; **20th ~** século vinte

ceramic [sɪ'ræmɪk] ADJ cerâmico

cereal ['si:rɪəl] N cereal m

ceremony ['sɛrɪmənɪ] N cerimônia; (*ritual*) rito; **to stand on ~** fazer cerimônia

certain ['sə:tən] ADJ (*sure*) seguro; (*person*): **a ~ Mr Smith** um certo Sr. Smith; (*particular*): **~ days/places** certos dias/lugares; (*some*): **a ~ coldness/pleasure** uma certa frieza/ um certo prazer; **for ~** com certeza; **certainly** ADV certamente, com certeza; **certainty** N certeza

certificate [sə'tɪfɪkɪt] N certidão f

certify ['sə:tɪfaɪ] VT certificar

cf. ABBR (= *compare*) cf

CFC N ABBR (= *chlorofluorocarbon*) CFC m

chain [tʃeɪn] N corrente f; (*of islands*) grupo; (*of mountains*) cordilheira; (*of shops*) cadeia; (*of events*) série f ▶ VT (*also:* **~ up**) acorrentar

chair [tʃɛəʳ] N cadeira; (*armchair*) poltrona; (*of university*) cátedra; (*of meeting*) presidência, mesa ▶ VT (*meeting*) presidir; **chairlift** N teleférico; **chairman** *irreg* N presidente m; **chairperson** N presidente m/f; **chairwoman** *irreg* N presidente f

chalk [tʃɔ:k] N (*Geo*) greda; (*for writing*) giz m

challenge ['tʃælɪndʒ] N desafio ▶ VT desafiar; (*statement, right*) disputar, contestar; **challenging** ADJ desafiante; (*tone*) de desafio

chamber ['tʃeɪmbə'] N câmara; (*BRIT Jur: gen pl*) sala de audiências; **chambermaid** N arrumadeira (BR), empregada (PT); **chamber of commerce** N câmara de comércio

champagne [ʃæm'peɪn] N champanhe m or f

champion ['tʃæmpɪən] N campeão(-peã) m/f; (*of cause*) defensor(a) m/f; **championship** N campeonato

chance [tʃɑːns] N (*opportunity*) oportunidade, ocasião f; (*likelihood*) chance f; (*risk*) risco ▶ VT arriscar ▶ ADJ fortuito, casual; **to take a ~** arriscar-se; **by ~** por acaso; **to ~ it** arriscar-se

chancellor ['tʃɑːnsələ'] N chanceler m; **C~ of the Exchequer** (BRIT) Ministro da Economia (Fazenda e Planejamento)

chandelier [ʃændə'lɪə'] N lustre m

change [tʃeɪndʒ] VT (*alter*) mudar; (*wheel, bulb, money*) trocar; (*replace*) substituir; (*clothes, house*) mudar de, trocar de; (*nappy*) mudar, trocar; (*transform*): **to ~ sb into** transformar alguém em ▶ VI mudar(-se); (*change clothes*) trocar-se; (*trains*) fazer baldeação (BR), mudar (PT); (*be transformed*): **to ~ into** transformar-se em ▶ N mudança; (*exchange*) troca; (*difference*) diferença; (*of clothes*) muda; (*coins*) trocado; **to ~ gear** (*Aut*) trocar de marcha; **to ~ one's mind** mudar de ideia; **for a ~** para variar; **changeable** ADJ (*weather*) instável; (*mood*) inconstante

channel ['tʃænl] N canal m; (*of river*) leito; (*groove*) ranhura; (*fig: medium*) meio, via ▶ VT: **to ~ (into)** canalizar (para); **the (English) C~** o Canal da Mancha

chant [tʃɑːnt] N canto; (*Rel*) cântico ▶ VT cantar; (*word, slogan*) entoar

chaos ['keɪɔs] N caos m

chap [tʃæp] N (BRIT inf: man) sujeito (BR), tipo (PT)

chapel ['tʃæpəl] N capela

chapter ['tʃæptə'] N capítulo

character ['kærɪktə'] N caráter m; (*in novel, film*) personagem m/f; (*letter*) letra; **characteristic** [kærɪktə'rɪstɪk] ADJ característico

charcoal ['tʃɑːkəul] N carvão m de lenha; (*Art*) carvão m

charge [tʃɑːdʒ] N (*Jur*) encargo, acusação f; (*fee*) preço, custo; (*responsibility*) encargo ▶ VT (*battery*) carregar; (*Mil*) atacar; (*customer*) cobrar dinheiro de; (*Jur*): **to ~ sb (with)** acusar alguém (de) ▶ VI precipitar-se; **charges** NPL: **bank ~s** taxas fpl bancárias; **to reverse the ~s** (BRIT Tel) ligar a cobrar; **how much do you ~?** quanto você cobra?; **to ~ an expense (up) to sb's account** pôr a despesa na conta de alguém; **to take ~ of** encarregar-se de, tomar conta de; **to be in ~ of** estar a cargo de or encarregado de; **charge card** N cartão m de crédito (*emitido por uma loja*)

charity ['tʃærɪtɪ] N caridade f; (*organization*) obra de caridade; (*kindness*) compaixão f; (*money, gifts*) donativo

charm [tʃɑːm] N (*quality*) charme m; (*talisman*) amuleto; (*on bracelet*) berloque m ▶ VT encantar, deliciar; **charming** ADJ encantador(a)

chart [tʃɑːt] N (*graph*) gráfico; (*diagram*) diagrama m; (*map*) carta de navegação ▶ VT traçar; **charts** NPL (*hit parade*) paradas fpl (de sucesso)

charter ['tʃɑːtə'] VT fretar ▶ N (*document*) carta, alvará m; **chartered accountant** (BRIT) N perito-contador/perita-contadora m/f; **charter flight** N voo charter or fretado

chase [tʃeɪs] VT perseguir; (*also: ~ away*) enxotar ▶ N perseguição f, caça

chat [tʃæt] VI (*also: have a ~*) conversar, bater papo (BR), cavaquear (PT) ▶ N conversa, bate-papo m (BR), cavaqueira (PT); **chatroom** N sala f de bate-papo; **chat show** (BRIT) N programa m de entrevistas

chatter ['tʃætə'] VI (*person*) tagarelar; (*animal*) emitir sons; (*teeth*) tiritar ▶ N tagarelice f; emissão f de sons; (*of birds*) chilro

chauvinist ['ʃəuvɪnɪst] N (*also: male ~*) machista m; (*nationalist*) chauvinista m/f

cheap [tʃiːp] ADJ barato; (*poor quality*) barato, de pouca qualidade; (*behaviour*) vulgar; (*joke*) de mau gosto ▶ ADV barato; **cheaply** ADV barato, por baixo preço

cheat [tʃiːt] VI trapacear; (*at cards*) roubar (BR), fazer batota (PT); (*in exam*) colar (BR), cabular (PT) ▶ N fraude f; (*person*) trapaceiro(-a); **to ~ sb out of sth** defraudar alguém de algo

check [tʃɛk] VT (*examine*) controlar; (*facts*) verificar; (*halt*) conter, impedir; (*restrain*) parar, refrear ▶ N controle m, inspeção f; (*curb*) freio; (*US: bill*) conta; (*pattern: gen pl*) xadrez m; (*US*) = **cheque** ▶ ADJ (*pattern, cloth*) xadrez inv; **check in** VI (*in hotel*) registrar-se; (*in airport*)

apresentar-se ▸ VT (*luggage*) entregar;
check out VI pagar a conta e sair; **check
up** VI: **to ~ up on sth** verificar algo; **to ~
up on sb** investigar alguém; **checkers**
(*US*) N (jogo de) damas *fpl*; **check-in,
check-in desk** N check-in *m*; **checking
account** (*US*) N conta corrente;
checkout N caixa; **checkpoint** N (ponto
de) controle *m*; **checkroom** (*US*) N
depósito de bagagem; **checkup** N (*Med*)
check-up *m*

cheek [tʃiːk] N bochecha; (*impudence*)
folga, descaramento; **cheekbone** N
maçã *f* do rosto; **cheeky** ADJ insolente,
descarado

cheer [tʃɪəʳ] VT dar vivas a, aplaudir;
(*gladden*) alegrar, animar ▸ VI gritar com
entusiasmo ▸ N (*gen pl*) gritos *mpl* de
entusiasmo; **cheers** NPL (*of crowd*)
aplausos *mpl*; **~s!** saúde!; **cheer up** VI
animar-se, alegrar-se ▸ VT alegrar,
animar; **cheerful** ADJ alegre; **cheerio**
(*BRIT*) EXCL tchau (*BR*), adeus (*PT*);
cheerleader ['tʃɪəliːdəʳ] N animador(a)
de torcida *m/f*

cheese [tʃiːz] N queijo

chef [ʃɛf] N cozinheiro-chefe/
cozinheira-chefe *m/f*

chemical ['kɛmɪkəl] ADJ químico ▸ N
produto químico

chemist ['kɛmɪst] N (*BRIT: pharmacist*)
farmacêutico(-a); (*scientist*) químico(-a);
chemistry N química; **chemist's,
chemist's shop** (*BRIT*) N farmácia

cheque [tʃɛk] (*BRIT*) N cheque *m*;
chequebook N talão *m* (*BR*) or livro (*PT*)
de cheques; **cheque card** (*BRIT*) N cartão
m (de garantia) de cheques

cherry ['tʃɛrɪ] N cereja; (*also: ~ tree*)
cerejeira

chess [tʃɛs] N xadrez *m*

chest [tʃɛst] N (*Anat*) peito; (*box*) caixa,
cofre *m*

chestnut ['tʃɛsnʌt] N castanha

chest of drawers N cômoda

chew [tʃuː] VT mastigar; **chewing gum**
N chiclete *m* (*BR*), pastilha elástica (*PT*)

chic [ʃɪk] ADJ elegante

chick [tʃɪk] N pinto; (*inf: girl*) broto

chicken ['tʃɪkɪn] N galinha; (*food*)
galinha, frango; (*inf: coward*) covarde
m/f, galinha; **chicken out** (*inf*) VI
agalinhar-se; **chickenpox** N catapora
(*BR*), varicela (*PT*)

chief [tʃiːf] N (*of tribe*) cacique *m*,
morubixaba *m*; (*of organization*) chefe *m/f*
▸ ADJ principal; **chiefly** ADV
principalmente

child [tʃaɪld] (*pl* **children**) N criança;
(*offspring*) filho(-a); **childbirth** N parto;
childcare N serviço de cuidado infantil;
childhood N infância; **childish** ADJ
infantil; **child minder** (*BRIT*) N cuidadora
de crianças; **children** ['tʃɪldrən] NPL
of **child**

Chile ['tʃɪlɪ] N Chile *m*

chill [tʃɪl] N frio, friagem *f*; (*Med*)
resfriamento ▸ VT (*Culin*) semi-congelar;
(*person*) congelar

chilli ['tʃɪlɪ], (*US*) **chili** N pimentão *m*
picante

chilly ['tʃɪlɪ] ADJ frio; (*person*) friorento

chimpanzee [tʃɪmpæn'ziː] N
chimpanzé *m*

chin [tʃɪn] N queixo

China ['tʃaɪnə] N China

china ['tʃaɪnə] N porcelana; (*crockery*)
louça fina

Chinese [tʃaɪ'niːz] ADJ chinês(-esa) ▸ N
INV chinês(-esa) *m/f*; (*Ling*) chinês *m*

chip [tʃɪp] N (*gen pl*: *BRIT Culin*) batata
frita; (: *US: also*: **potato ~**) batatinha
frita; (*of wood*) lasca; (*of glass, stone*)
lasca, pedaço; (*Comput: also*: **micro~**)
chip *m* ▸ VT (*cup, plate*) lascar; **chip in**
(*inf*) VI interromper; (*contribute*)
compartilhar as despesas

chiropodist [kɪ'rɔpədɪst] (*BRIT*) N
pedicuro(-a)

chisel ['tʃɪzl] N (*for wood*) formão *m*; (*for
stone*) cinzel *m*

chives [tʃaɪvz] NPL cebolinha

chocolate ['tʃɔklɪt] N chocolate *m*

choice [tʃɔɪs] N (*selection*) seleção *f*;
(*option*) escolha; (*preference*) preferência
▸ ADJ seleto, escolhido

choir ['kwaɪəʳ] N coro

choke [tʃəuk] VI sufocar-se; (*on food*)
engasgar ▸ VT estrangular; (*block*)
obstruir ▸ N (*Aut*) afogador *m* (*BR*), ar *m*
(*PT*)

cholesterol [kə'lɛstərɔl] N colesterol *m*

choose [tʃuːz] (*pt* **chose**, *pp* **chosen**) VT
escolher; **to ~ to do** optar por fazer

chop [tʃɔp] VT (*wood*) cortar, talhar;
(*Culin: also*: **~ up**) cortar em pedaços;
(*meat*) picar ▸ N golpe *m*; (*Culin*)
costeleta; **chops** NPL (*inf: jaws*) beiços
mpl

chopsticks ['tʃɔpstɪks] NPL pauzinhos
mpl, palitos *mpl*

chord [kɔːd] N (*Mus*) acorde *m*

chore [tʃɔːʳ] N tarefa; (*routine task*)
trabalho de rotina

chorus ['kɔːrəs] N (*group*) coro; (*song*)
coral *m*; (*refrain*) estribilho

chose [tʃəuz] PT *of* **choose**; **chosen** PP
of **choose**

Christ [kraist] N Cristo

christen ['krisn] VT batizar; *(nickname)*
apelidar

Christian ['kristiən] ADJ, N cristão(-tã)
m/f; **Christianity** [kristi'æniti] N
cristianismo; **Christian name** N
prenome *m*, nome *m* de batismo

Christmas ['krisməs] N Natal *m;* **Happy
or Merry ~!** Feliz Natal!; **Christmas card**
N cartão *m* de Natal; **Christmas cracker**
N *ver nota*

> Um **Christmas cracker** é um
> cilindro de papelão que ao ser aberto
> faz estourar uma bombinha.
> Contém um presente surpresa e
> um chapéu de papel que cada
> convidado coloca na cabeça durante
> a ceia de Natal.

Christmas: Christmas Day N dia *m* de
Natal; **Christmas Eve** N véspera de
Natal; **Christmas tree** N árvore *f* de
Natal

chronic ['krɔnik] ADJ crônico; *(fig:
drunkenness)* inveterado

chubby ['tʃʌbi] ADJ roliço, gorducho

chuck [tʃʌk] VT jogar (BR), deitar (PT);
(BRIT: also: **~ up, ~ in**: *job)* largar; *(: person)*
acabar com; **chuck out** VT *(thing)* jogar
(BR) *or* deitar (PT) fora; *(person)* expulsar

chuckle ['tʃʌkl] VI rir

chuffed [tʃʌft] *(inf)* ADJ: **~ (about sth)**
encantado (com algo)

chum [tʃʌm] N camarada *m/f*

church [tʃəːtʃ] N igreja; **churchyard** N
adro, cemitério

churn [tʃəːn] N *(for butter)* batedeira;
(also: **milk ~**) lata, vasilha; **churn out** VT
produzir em série

chute [ʃuːt] N rampa; *(also:* **rubbish ~**)
despejador *m*

CIA (US) N ABBR (= *Central Intelligence
Agency*) CIA *f*

CID (BRIT) N ABBR = **Criminal
Investigation Department**

cider ['saidə^r] N sidra

cigar [si'gɑː^r] N charuto

cigarette [sigə'ret] N cigarro

cinema ['sinəmə] N cinema *m*

cinnamon ['sinəmən] N canela

circle ['səːkl] N círculo; *(in cinema)* balcão
m ▶ VI dar voltas ▶ VT *(surround)* rodear,
cercar; *(move round)* dar a volta de

circuit ['səːkit] N circuito; *(tour, lap)*
volta; *(track)* pista

circular ['səːkjulə^r] ADJ circular ▶ N
(carta) circular *f*

circulate ['səːkjuleit] VT, VI circular;
circulation [səːkju'leiʃən] N circulação *f;*
(of newspaper, book etc) tiragem *f*

circumstances ['səːkəmstənsiz] NPL
circunstâncias *fpl; (conditions)* condições
fpl; (financial condition) situação *f*
econômica

circus ['səːkəs] N circo

citizen ['sitizn] N *(of country)*
cidadão(-dã) *m/f; (of town)* habitante
m/f; **citizenship** N cidadania

city ['siti] N cidade *f;* **the C~** centro
financeiro de Londres

civic ['sivik] ADJ cívico, municipal

civil ['sivil] ADJ civil; *(polite)* delicado,
cortês; **civilian** [si'viliən] ADJ, N civil *m/f*

civilized ['sivilaizd] ADJ civilizado

civil servant N funcionário(-a)
público(-a)

Civil Service N administração *f* pública

civil war N guerra civil

claim [kleim] VT exigir, reclamar; *(rights
etc)* reivindicar; *(responsibility)* assumir;
(assert): **to ~ that/to be** afirmar que/ser
▶ VI *(for insurance)* reclamar ▶ N
reclamação *f; (assertion)* afirmação *f;*
(wage claim etc) reivindicação *f*

clam [klæm] N molusco

clamp [klæmp] N grampo ▶ VT prender;
clamp down on VT FUS reprimir

clan [klæn] N clã *m*

clap [klæp] VI bater palmas, aplaudir

clarinet [klæri'net] N clarinete *m*

clarity ['klæriti] N clareza

clash [klæʃ] N *(fight)* confronto;
(disagreement) desavença; *(of beliefs)*
divergência; *(of colours, styles)* choque *m;*
(of dates) coincidência ▶ VI *(gangs, beliefs)*
chocar-se; *(disagree)* entrar em conflito,
ter uma desavença; *(colours)* não
combinar; *(dates, events)* coincidir;
(weapons, cymbals etc) ressoar

clasp [klɑːsp] N fecho; *(embrace)* abraço
▶ VT prender; *(embrace)* abraçar

class [klɑːs] N classe *f; (lesson)* aula;
(type) tipo ▶ VT classificar

classic ['klæsik] ADJ clássico ▶ N clássico;
classical ADJ clássico

classmate ['klɑːsmeit] N colega *m/f* de
aula

classroom ['klɑːsrum] N sala de aula

clatter ['klætə^r] N ruído, barulho; *(of
hooves)* tropel *m* ▶ VI fazer barulho or
ruído

clause [klɔːz] N cláusula; *(Ling)* oração *f*

claw [klɔː] N *(of animal)* pata; *(of bird of
prey)* garra; *(of lobster)* pinça; **claw at** VT
FUS arranhar; *(tear)* rasgar

clay [kleɪ] N argila
clean [kli:n] ADJ limpo ▶ VT limpar; (hands, face etc) lavar; **clean out** VT limpar; **clean up** VT limpar, assear; **cleaner** N faxineiro(-a); (product) limpador m; **cleaner's** N (also: **dry cleaner's**) tinturaria; **cleaning** N limpeza; **clean technology** N tecnologia limpa

clear [klɪəʳ] ADJ claro; (footprint, photograph) nítido; (obvious) evidente; (glass, water) transparente; (road, way) limpo, livre; (conscience) tranquilo; (skin) macio ▶ VT (space) abrir; (room) esvaziar; (Jur: suspect) absolver; (fence, wall) saltar, transpor; (cheque) compensar ▶ VI (weather) abrir; (sky) clarear; (fog etc) dissipar-se ▶ ADV: **~ of** a salvo de; **to ~ the table** tirar a mesa; **clear up** VT limpar; (mystery) resolver, esclarecer; **clearance** N remoção f; (permission) permissão f; **clear-cut** ADJ bem definido, nítido; **clearing** N (in wood) clareira; **clearly** ADV distintamente; (obviously) claramente; (coherently) coerentemente; **clearway** (BRIT) N estrada onde não se pode estacionar

clench [klɛntʃ] VT apertar, cerrar; (teeth) trincar
clerk [klɑ:k, (US) klə:rk] N auxiliar m/f de escritório; (US: sales person) balconista m/f
clever [ˈklɛvəʳ] ADJ inteligente; (deft, crafty) hábil; (device, arrangement) engenhoso
click [klɪk] VT (tongue) estalar; (heels) bater; (Comput) clicar em ▶ VI (make sound) estalar; (Comput) clicar
client [ˈklaɪənt] N cliente m/f
cliff [klɪf] N penhasco
climate [ˈklaɪmɪt] N clima m; **climate change** N mudanças fpl climáticas
climax [ˈklaɪmæks] N clímax m, ponto culminante; (sexual) clímax
climb [klaɪm] VI subir; (plant) trepar; (plane) ganhar altitude; (prices etc) escalar ▶ VT (stairs) subir; (tree) trepar em; (hill) escalar ▶ N subida; (of prices etc) escalada; **climber** N alpinista m/f; (plant) trepadeira; **climbing** N alpinismo
clinch [klɪntʃ] VT (deal) fechar; (argument) decidir, resolver
cling [klɪŋ] (pt, pp **clung**) VI: **to ~ to** pegar-se a, aderir a; (support, idea) agarrar-se a; (clothes) ajustar-se a
Clingfilm® [ˈklɪŋfɪlm] N papel m filme
clinic [ˈklɪnɪk] N clínica

clip [klɪp] N (for hair) grampo (BR), gancho (PT); (also: **paper ~**) mola, clipe m; (TV, Cinema) clipe ▶ VT (cut) aparar; (papers) grampear
cloak [kləʊk] N capa, manto ▶ VT (fig) encobrir; **cloakroom** N vestiário; (BRIT: WC) sanitários mpl (BR), lavatórios mpl (PT)
clock [klɔk] N relógio; **clock in, clock on** (BRIT) VI assinar o ponto na entrada; **clock off, clock out** (BRIT) VI assinar o ponto na saída; **clockwise** ADV em sentido horário; **clockwork** N mecanismo de relógio ▶ ADJ de corda
clog [klɔg] N tamanco ▶ VT entupir ▶ VI (also: **~ up**) entupir-se
close [adj, adv kləʊs, vb, n kləʊz] ADJ próximo; (friend) íntimo; (examination) minucioso; (watch) atento; (contest) apertado; (weather) abafado ▶ ADV perto ▶ VT fechar; (end) encerrar ▶ VI fechar; (end) concluir-se, terminar-se ▶ N (end) fim m, conclusão f, terminação f; **~ by, ~ at hand** perto, pertinho; **to have a ~ shave** (fig) livrar-se por um triz; **~ to** perto de; **close down** VI fechar definitivamente; **closed** [kləʊzd] ADJ fechado
closely [ˈkləʊslɪ] ADV (watch) de perto; **we are ~ related** somos parentes próximos
closet [ˈklɔzɪt] N (cupboard) armário
close-up [kləʊs-] N close m, close-up m
closure [ˈkləʊʒəʳ] N fechamento
clot [klɔt] N (gen: blood clot) coágulo; (inf: idiot) imbecil m/f ▶ VI coagular-se
cloth [klɔθ] N (material) tecido, fazenda; (rag) pano
clothes [kləʊðz] NPL roupa
clothing [ˈkləʊðɪŋ] N = **clothes**
cloud [klaʊd] N nuvem f; **cloud computing** N computação f em nuvem; **cloudy** ADJ nublado; (liquid) turvo
clove [kləʊv] N cravo; **clove of garlic** N dente m de alho
clown [klaʊn] N palhaço ▶ VI (also: **~ about, ~ around**) fazer palhaçadas
club [klʌb] N (society) clube m; (weapon) cacete m; (also: **golf ~**) taco ▶ VT esbordoar ▶ VI: **to ~ together** cotizar-se; **clubs** NPL (Cards) paus mpl
clue [klu:] N indício, pista; (in crossword) definição f; **I haven't a ~** não faço ideia
clumsy [ˈklʌmzɪ] ADJ (person) desajeitado; (movement) deselegante, mal-feito; (attempt) inábil
clung [klʌŋ] PT, PP of **cling**
cluster [ˈklʌstəʳ] N grupo; (of flowers) ramo ▶ VI agrupar-se, apinhar-se

clutch [klʌtʃ] N (*grip, grasp*) garra; (*Aut*) embreagem *f* (BR), embraiagem *f* (PT) ▶ VT empunhar, pegar em

Co. ABBR = **county**; (= *company*) Cia.

c/o ABBR (= *care of*) a/c

coach [kəutʃ] N (*bus*) ônibus *m* (BR), autocarro (PT); (*horse-drawn*) carruagem *f*, coche *m*; (*of train*) vagão *m*; (*Sport*) treinador(a) *m/f*, instrutor(a) *m/f*; (*tutor*) professor(a) *m/f* particular ▶ VT (*Sport*) treinar; (*student*) preparar, ensinar; **coach station** [BRIT] N rodoviária; **coach trip** N passeio de ônibus (BR) or autocarro (PT)

coal [kəul] N carvão *m*

coalition [kəuə'lıʃən] N coalizão *f*

coarse [kɔːs] ADJ grosso, áspero; (*vulgar*) grosseiro, ordinário

coast [kəust] N costa, litoral *m* ▶ VI (*Aut*) ir em ponto morto; **coastal** ADJ costeiro; **coastguard** N (*service*) guarda costeira; (*person*) guarda-costeira *m/f*; **coastline** N litoral *m*

coat [kəut] N (*overcoat*) sobretudo; (*of animal*) pelo; (*of paint*) demão *f*, camada ▶ VT cobrir, revestir; **coat hanger** N cabide *m*; **coating** N camada

coax [kəuks] VT persuadir com meiguice

cobweb ['kɔbwɛb] N teia de aranha

cocaine [kə'keın] N cocaína

cock [kɔk] N (*rooster*) galo; (*male bird*) macho ▶ VT (*gun*) engatilhar; **cockerel** N frango, galo pequeno

cockney ['kɔknı] N londrino(-a) (*nativo dos bairros populares do leste de Londres*)

cockpit ['kɔkpıt] N (*in aircraft*) cabina

cockroach ['kɔkrəutʃ] N barata

cocktail ['kɔkteıl] N coquetel *m* (BR), cocktail *m* (PT)

cocoa ['kəukəu] N cacau *m*; (*drink*) chocolate *m*

coconut ['kəukənʌt] N coco

cod [kɔd] N INV bacalhau *m*

code [kəud] N cifra; (*Comput, dialling code, post code*) código ▶ VI escrever código; **code of practice** N deontologia

coffee ['kɔfı] N café *m*; **coffee bar** (BRIT) N café *m*, lanchonete *f*; **coffee bean** N grão *m* de café; **coffeepot** N cafeteira; **coffee table** N mesinha de centro

coffin ['kɔfın] N caixão *m*

cognitive ['kɔgnıtıv] ADJ cognitivo

coil [kɔıl] N rolo; (*Elec*) bobina; (*contraceptive*) DIU *m* ▶ VT enrolar

coin [kɔın] N moeda ▶ VT (*word*) cunhar, criar

coincide [kəuın'saıd] VI coincidir; **coincidence** [kəu'ınsıdəns] N coincidência

coke [kəuk] N (*coal*) coque *m*

colander ['kɔləndəʳ] N coador *m*, passador *m*

cold [kəuld] ADJ frio ▶ N frio; (*Med*) resfriado (BR), constipação *f* (PT); **it's ~** está frio; **to be** *or* **feel ~** (*person*) estar com frio; (*object*) estar frio; **to catch ~** pegar friagem; **to catch a ~** ficar resfriado (BR), apanhar uma constipação (PT); **in ~ blood** a sangue frio; **cold sore** N herpes *m* labial

coleslaw ['kəulslɔː] N salada de repolho cru

collapse [kə'læps] VI cair, tombar; (*building*) desabar; (*Med*) desmaiar ▶ N desabamento, desmoronamento; (*of government*) queda; (*Med*) colapso

collar ['kɔləʳ] N (*of shirt*) colarinho; (*of coat etc*) gola; (*for dog*) coleira; (*Tech*) aro, colar *m*; **collarbone** N clavícula

colleague ['kɔliːg] N colega *m/f*

collect [kə'lɛkt] VT (*as a hobby*) colecionar; (*gather*) recolher; (*wages, debts*) cobrar; (*donations, subscriptions*) colher; (*mail*) coletar; (BRIT: *call for*) (ir) buscar ▶ VI (*people*) reunir-se ▶ ADV: **to call ~** (US Tel) ligar a cobrar; **collection** N coleção *f*; (*of people*) grupo; (*of donations*) arrecadação *f*; (*of post, for charity*) coleta; (*of writings*) coletânea; **collector** N colecionador(a) *m/f*; (*of taxes etc*) cobrador(a) *m/f*

college ['kɔlıdʒ] N (*of university*) faculdade *f*; (*of technology, agriculture*) escola profissionalizante

> Além de "universidade", **college** também se refere a um centro de educação superior para jovens que terminaram a educação obrigatória, *secondary school*. Alguns oferecem cursos de especialização em matérias técnicas, artísticas ou comerciais, outros oferecem disciplinas universitárias.

collide [kə'laıd] VI: **to ~ (with)** colidir (com)

collision [kə'lıʒən] N colisão *f*

Colombia [kə'lɔmbıə] N Colômbia

colon ['kəulən] N (*sign*) dois pontos; (*Med*) cólon *m*

colonel ['kəːnl] N coronel *m*

colony ['kɔlənı] N colônia

colour ['kʌləʳ], (US) **color** N cor *f* ▶ VT colorir; (*with crayons*) colorir, pintar; (*dye*) tingir; (*fig: account*) falsear ▶ VI (*blush*) corar; **colours** NPL (*of party, club*) cores *fpl*; **in ~** (*photograph etc*) a cores; **colour in** VT (*drawing*) colorir; **colour-blind** ADJ

daltônico; **coloured** ADJ colorido;
colour film N filme m a cores; **colourful**
ADJ colorido; (*account*) vívido;
(*personality*) vivo, animado; **colouring** N
colorido; (*complexion*) tez f; (*in food*)
colorante m; **colour television** N
televisão f a cores

column ['kɔləm] N coluna; (*of smoke*)
faixa; (*of people*) fila

coma ['kəumə] N coma m

comb [kəum] N pente m; (*ornamental*)
crista ▶ VT pentear; (*area*) vasculhar

combat ['kɔmbæt] N combate m ▶ VT
combater

combination [kɔmbɪ'neɪʃən] N
combinação f; (*of safe*) segredo

combine [vt, vi kəm'baɪn, n 'kɔmbaɪn]
VT combinar; (*qualities*) reunir ▶ VI
combinar-se ▶ N (*Econ*) associação f

(KEYWORD)

come [kʌm] (*pt* **came**, *pp* **come**) VI
1 (*movement towards*) vir; **come with
me** vem comigo; **to come running** vir
correndo
2 (*arrive*) chegar; **she's come here to
work** ela veio aqui para trabalhar; **to
come home** chegar em casa
3 (*reach*): **to come to** chegar a; **the bill
came to £40** a conta deu £40; **her hair
came to her waist** o cabelo dela batia
na cintura
4 (*occur*): **an idea came to me** uma ideia
me ocorreu
5 (*be, become*) ficar; **to come loose/
undone** soltar-se/desfazer-se; **I've
come to like him** passei a gostar dele
come about VI suceder, acontecer
come across VT FUS (*person*) topar com;
(*thing*) encontrar
come away VI (*leave*) ir-se embora;
(*become detached*) desprender-se,
soltar-se
come back VI (*return*) voltar
come by VT FUS (*acquire*) conseguir
come down VI (*price*) baixar; (*tree*) cair;
(*building*) desmoronar-se
come forward VI apresentar-se
come from VT FUS (*subj: person*) ser de;
(: *thing*) originar-se de
come in VI entrar; (*on deal etc*) participar;
(*be involved*) estar envolvido
come in for VT FUS (*criticism etc*) receber
come into VT FUS (*money*) herdar;
(*fashion*) ser; (*be involved*) estar
envolvido em
come off VI (*button*) desprender-se,
soltar-se; (*attempt*) dar certo

come on VI (*pupil, work, project*) avançar;
(*lights, electricity*) ser ligado; **come on!**
vamos!, vai!
come out VI (*fact*) vir à tona; (*book*) ser
publicado; (*stain, sun*) sair
come round VI voltar a si
come to VI voltar a si
come up VI (*sun*) nascer; (*problem,
subject*) surgir; (*event*) acontecer
come up against VT FUS (*resistance,
difficulties*) enfrentar, esbarrar em
come upon VT FUS (*find*) encontrar,
achar
come up with VT FUS (*idea*) propor,
sugerir; (*money*) contribuir

comedian [kə'mi:dɪən] N cômico,
humorista m
comedy ['kɔmɪdɪ] N comédia
comfort ['kʌmfət] N (*well-being*)
bem-estar m; (*relief*) alívio ▶ VT consolar,
confortar; **comforts** NPL (*of home etc*)
conforto; **comfortable** ADJ confortável;
(*financially*) tranquilo; (*walk, climb etc*)
fácil
comic ['kɔmɪk] ADJ (*also*: **~al**) cômico ▶ N
(*person*) humorista m/f; (BRIT: *magazine*)
revista em quadrinhos (BR), revista de
banda desenhada (PT), gibi m (BR inf)
comma ['kɔmə] N vírgula
command [kə'mɑːnd] N ordem f,
mandado; (*control*) controle m; (Mil:
authority) comando; (*mastery*) domínio
▶ VT mandar; **commander** N (Mil)
comandante m/f
commemorate [kə'mɛmərɛɪt] VT (*with
monument*) comemorar; (*with celebration*)
celebrar
commence [kə'mɛns] VT, VI começar,
iniciar
commend [kə'mɛnd] VT elogiar, louvar;
(*recommend*) recomendar
comment ['kɔmɛnt] N comentário ▶ VI
comentar; **to ~ on sth** comentar algo;
"no ~" "sem comentário"; **commentary**
['kɔməntərɪ] N comentário;
commentator ['kɔmənteɪtəʳ] N
comentarista m/f
commerce ['kɔmə:s] N comércio
commercial [kə'mə:ʃəl] ADJ comercial
▶ N anúncio, comercial m
commission [kə'mɪʃən] N comissão f;
(*order for work of art etc*) empreitada,
encomenda ▶ VT (*work of art*)
encomendar; **out of ~** com defeito;
commissioner N comissário(-a)
commit [kə'mɪt] VT cometer; (*money,
resources*) alocar; (*to sb's care*) entregar;

to ~ o.s. (to do) comprometer-se (a fazer);
to ~ suicide suicidar-se; **commitment**
N compromisso; (*political etc*)
engajamento; (*undertaking*) promessa
committee [kə'mɪtɪ] N comitê *m*
commodity [kə'mɔdɪtɪ] N mercadoria
common ['kɔmən] ADJ comum; (*vulgar*)
ordinário, vulgar ▶ N *área verde aberta ao
público*; **Commons** NPL (BRIT Pol): **the
(House of) C~s** a Câmara dos Comuns;
to have sth in ~ (with sb) ter algo em
comum (con alguém); **commonly** ADV
geralmente; **commonplace** ADJ vulgar;
common sense N bom senso;
Commonwealth N: **the
Commonwealth** a Comunidade
Britânica
communal ['kɔmjuːnl] ADJ comun
commune [*n* 'kɔmjuːn, *vi* kə'mjuːn] N
(*group*) comuna ▶ VI: **to ~ with**
comunicar-se com
communicate [kə'mjuːnɪkeɪt] VT
comunicar ▶ VI: **to ~ (with)**
comunicar-se (com); **communication**
[kəmjuːnɪ'keɪʃən] N comunicação *f*;
(*letter, call*) mensagem *f*
communion [kə'mjuːnɪən] N (*also:
Holy C~) comunhão *f*
communism ['kɔmjunɪzəm] N
comunismo; **communist** ADJ, N
comunista *m/f*
community [kə'mjuːnɪtɪ] N
comunidade *f*; **community centre** N
centro social
commute [kə'mjuːt] VI viajar
diariamente ▶ VT comutar; **commuter**
N viajante *m/f* habitual
compact [*adj* kəm'pækt, *n* 'kɔmpækt]
ADJ compacto ▶ N (*also:* **powder ~**)
estojo; **compact disc** N disco laser;
compact disc player N som cd *m*
companion [kəm'pænɪən] N
companheiro(-a)
company ['kʌmpənɪ] N companhia;
(*Comm*) sociedade *f*, companhia; **to keep
sb ~** fazer companhia a alguém
comparative [kəm'pærətɪv] ADJ (*study*)
comparativo; (*peace, safety*) relativo;
comparatively ADJ relativamente
compare [kəm'pɛəʳ] VT comparar; **to ~
(to/with)** comparar (a/com) ▶ VI: **to ~
with** comparar-se com; **comparison**
[kəm'pærɪsn] N comparação *f*
compartment [kəm'pɑːtmənt] N
compartimento; (*of wallet*) divisão *f*
compass ['kʌmpəs] N bússola;
compasses NPL compasso
compassion [kəm'pæʃən] N compaixão *f*

compatible [kəm'pætɪbl] ADJ
compatível
compel [kəm'pɛl] VT obrigar
compensate ['kɔmpənseɪt] VT
indenizar ▶ VI: **to ~ for** compensar;
compensation [kɔmpən'seɪʃən] N
compensação *f*; (*damages*) indenização *f*
compete [kəm'piːt] VI (*take part*)
competir; (*vie*): **to ~ (with)** competir
(com), fazer competição (com)
competent ['kɔmpɪtənt] ADJ
competente
competition [kɔmpɪ'tɪʃən] N (*contest*)
concurso; (*Econ*) concorrência; (*rivalry*)
competição *f*
competitive [kəm'pɛtɪtɪv] ADJ
competitivo; (*person*) competidor(a)
competitor [kəm'pɛtɪtəʳ] N (*rival*)
competidor(a) *m/f*; (*participant, Econ*)
concorrente *m/f*
complain [kəm'pleɪn] VI queixar-se; **to
~ of** (*pain*) queixar-se de; **complaint** N
(*objection*) objeção *f*; (*criticism*) queixa;
(*Med*) achaque *m*, doença
complement ['kɔmplɪmənt] N
complemento; (*esp ship's crew*)
tripulação *f* ▶ VT complementar
complete [kəm'pliːt] ADJ completo;
(*finished*) acabado ▶ VT (*finish: building,
task*) acabar; (*set, group*) completar; (*a
form*) preencher; **completely** ADV
completamente; **completion** N
conclusão *f*, término; (*of contract etc*)
realização *f*
complex ['kɔmplɛks] ADJ complexo ▶ N
complexo; (*of buildings*) conjunto
complexion [kəm'plɛkʃən] N (*of face*)
cor *f*, tez *f*
complicate ['kɔmplɪkeɪt] VT complicar;
complicated ADJ complicado;
complication [kɔmplɪ'keɪʃən] N
problema *m*; (*Med*) complicação *f*
compliment [*n* 'kɔmplɪmənt, *vt*
'kɔmplɪmɛnt] N (*praise*) elogio ▶ VT
elogiar; **compliments** NPL
cumprimentos *mpl*; **to pay sb a ~**
elogiar alguém; **complimentary**
[kɔmplɪ'mɛntərɪ] ADJ lisonjeiro; (*free*)
gratuito
comply [kəm'plaɪ] VI: **to ~ with** cumprir
com
component [kəm'pəunənt] ADJ
componente ▶ N (*part*) peça
compose [kəm'pəuz] VT compor; **to be
~d of** compor-se de; **to ~ o.s.**
tranquilizar-se; **composer** N (*Mus*)
compositor(a) *m/f*; **composition**
[kɔmpə'zɪʃən] N composição *f*

compound ['kɔmpaund] N (Chem, Ling) composto; (enclosure) recinto ▸ ADJ composto

comprehensive [kɔmprɪ'hɛnsɪv] ADJ abrangente; (Insurance) total; **comprehensive school** (BRIT) N escola secundária de amplo programa

Criadas na década de 1960 pelo governo trabalhista da época, as **comprehensive schools** são estabelecimentos de ensino secundário polivalentes concebidos para acolher todos os alunos sem distinção e lhes oferecer oportunidades iguais, em oposição ao sistema seletivo das grammar schools. A maioria dos estudantes britânicos frequenta atualmente uma **comprehensive school**, mas as grammar schools não desapareceram de todo.

compress [vt kəm'prɛs, n 'kɔmprɛs] VT comprimir; (text, information etc) reduzir ▸ N (Med) compressa

comprise [kəm'praɪz] VT (also: **be ~d of**) compreender, constar de; (constitute) constituir

compromise ['kɔmprəmaɪz] N meio-termo ▸ VT comprometer ▸ VI chegar a um meio-termo

compulsive [kəm'pʌlsɪv] ADJ compulsivo

compulsory [kəm'pʌlsərɪ] ADJ obrigatório; (retirement) compulsório

computer [kəm'pju:tə*] N computador m; **computer game** N game m; **computerize** VT informatizar, computadorizar; **computer literate** ADJ capaz de lidar com um computador; **computing** N computação f; (science) informática

conceal [kən'si:l] VT ocultar; (information) omitir

conceited [kən'si:tɪd] ADJ vaidoso

conceive [kən'si:v] VT conceber ▸ VI conceber, engravidar

concentrate ['kɔnsəntreɪt] VI concentrar-se ▸ VT concentrar; **concentration** N concentração f

concept ['kɔnsɛpt] N conceito

concern [kən'sə:n] N (Comm) empresa; (anxiety) preocupação f ▸ VT preocupar; (involve) envolver; (relate to) dizer respeito a; **to be ~ed (about)** preocupar-se (com); **concerning** PREP sobre, a respeito de, acerca de

concert ['kɔnsət] N concerto

concession [kən'sɛʃən] N concessão f; **tax ~** redução no imposto

conclude [kən'klu:d] VT (finish) acabar, concluir; (treaty etc) firmar; (agreement) chegar a; (decide) decidir

conclusion [kən'klu:ʒən] N conclusão f

concrete ['kɔnkri:t] N concreto (BR), betão m (PT) ▸ ADJ concreto

concussion [kən'kʌʃən] N (Med) concussão f cerebral

condemn [kən'dɛm] VT denunciar; (prisoner, building) condenar

condensation [kɔndɛn'seɪʃən] N condensação f

condense [kən'dɛns] VI condensar-se ▸ VT condensar

condition [kən'dɪʃən] N condição f; (Med: illness) doença ▸ VT condicionar; **conditions** NPL (circumstances) circunstâncias fpl; **on ~ that** com a condição (de) que; **conditioner** N (for hair) condicionador m; (for fabrics) amaciante m

condom ['kɔndɔm] N preservativo, camisinha

condominium [kɔndə'mɪnɪəm] N (US) (building) edifício

condone [kən'dəun] VT admitir, aceitar

conduct [n 'kɔndʌkt, vt, vi kən'dʌkt] N conduta, comportamento ▸ VT (research etc) fazer; (heat, electricity) conduzir; (Mus) reger; **to ~ o.s.** comportar-se; **conducted tour** N viagem f organizada; **conductor** N (of orchestra) regente m/f; (on bus) cobrador(a) m/f; (US Rail) revisor(a) m/f; (Elec) condutor m

cone [kəun] N cone m; (Bot) pinha; (for ice-cream) casquinha

confectionery [kən'fɛkʃnərɪ] N (sweets) balas fpl; (sweetmeats) doces mpl

confer [kən'fə:*] VT: **to ~ on** outorgar a ▸ VI conferenciar

conference ['kɔnfərns] N congresso

confess [kən'fɛs] VT confessar ▸ VI (admit) admitir; **confession** N admissão f; (Rel) confissão f

confide [kən'faɪd] VI: **to ~ in** confiar em, fiar-se em

confidence ['kɔnfɪdns] N confiança; (faith) fé f; (secret) confidência; **in ~** em confidência; **confident** ADJ confiante, convicto; (positive) seguro; **confidential** [kɔnfɪ'dɛnʃəl] ADJ confidencial

confine [kən'faɪn] VT (shut up) encarcerar; (limit): **to ~ (to)** confinar (a); **confined** ADJ (space) reduzido

confirm [kən'fə:m] VT confirmar; **confirmation** [kɔnfə'meɪʃən] N confirmação f; (Rel) crisma

confiscate ['kɔnfɪskeɪt] VT confiscar

conflict [n 'kɒnflɪkt, vi kən'flɪkt] N (*disagreement*) divergência; (*of interests, loyalties*) conflito; (*fighting*) combate m ▶ vi estar em conflito; (*opinions*) divergir

conform [kən'fɔːm] vi conformar-se; **to ~ to** ajustar-se a, acomodar-se a

confront [kən'frʌnt] vt (*problems*) enfrentar; (*enemy, danger*) defrontar-se com; **confrontation** [kɒnfrən'teɪʃən] N confrontação f

confuse [kən'fjuːz] vt (*perplex*) desconcertar; (*mix up*) confundir, misturar; (*complicate*) complicar; **confused** ADJ confuso; **confusing** ADJ confuso; **confusion** [kən'fjuːʒən] N (*mix-up*) mal-entendido; (*perplexity*) perplexidade f; (*disorder*) confusão f

congestion [kən'dʒestʃən] N (*Med*) congestão f; (*traffic*) congestionamento

congratulate [kən'grætjuleɪt] vt parabenizar; **congratulations** [kəngrætju'leɪʃənz] NPL parabéns mpl

congress ['kɒŋgres] N congresso; (*us*): **C~** Congresso

O Congresso (**Congress**) é o Parlamento dos Estados Unidos. Consiste na *House of Representatives* e no Senado *Senate*. Os representantes e senadores são eleitos por sufrágio universal direto. O Congresso se reúne no *Capitol*, em Washington.

congressman (*us*) *irreg* N deputado

conjure ['kʌndʒəʳ] vi fazer truques; **conjure up** vt (*ghost, spirit*) fazer aparecer, invocar; (*memories*) evocar

connect [kə'nekt] vt (*Elec, Tel*) ligar; (*fig: associate*) associar; (*join*): **to ~ sth (to)** juntar *or* unir algo (a) ▶ vi: **to ~ with** (*train*) conectar com; **to be ~ed with** estar relacionado com; **I'm trying to ~ you** (*Tel*) estou tentando completar a ligação; **connecting flight** N conexão f; **connection** N ligação f; (*Comput, Elec, Rail*) conexão f; (*Tel*) ligação f

conquer ['kɒŋkəʳ] vt conquistar; (*enemy*) vencer; (*feelings*) superar; **conquest** ['kɒŋk] N conquista

conscience ['kɒnʃəns] N consciência; **conscientious** [kɒnʃi'enʃəs] ADJ consciencioso

conscious ['kɒnʃəs] ADJ: **~ (of)** consciente (de); (*deliberate*) intencional; **consciousness** N consciência; **to lose/regain consciousness** perder/recuperar os sentidos

consent [kən'sent] N consentimento ▶ vi: **to ~ to** consentir em

consequence ['kɒnsɪkwəns] N consequência; (*significance*): **of ~** de importância; **consequently** ADV por conseguinte

conservation [kɒnsə'veɪʃən] N conservação f; (*of the environment*) preservação f

conservative [kən'sə:vətɪv] ADJ conservador(a); (*cautious*) moderado; (*brit Pol*): **C~** conservador(a) ▶ N (*brit Pol*) conservador(a) m/f

conservatory [kən'sə:vətrɪ] N (*Mus*) conservatório; (*greenhouse*) estufa

consider [kən'sɪdəʳ] vt considerar; (*take into account*) levar em consideração; (*study*) estudar, examinar; **to ~ doing sth** pensar em fazer algo

considerable [kən'sɪdərəbl] ADJ considerável; (*sum*) importante

considerate [kən'sɪdərɪt] ADJ atencioso; **consideration** [kənsɪdə'reɪʃən] N consideração f; (*deliberation*) deliberação f; (*factor*) fator m

considering [kən'sɪdərɪŋ] PREP em vista de

consist [kən'sɪst] vi: **to ~ of** (*comprise*) consistir em

consistency [kən'sɪstənsɪ] N coerência; (*thickness*) consistência

consistent [kən'sɪstənt] ADJ (*person*) coerente, estável; (*argument, idea*) sólido

consolation [kɒnsə'leɪʃən] N conforto

console [*us*] vt kən'səul, *n* 'kɒnsəul] vt confortar ▶ N consolo

consonant ['kɒnsənənt] N consoante f

conspicuous [kən'spɪkjuəs] ADJ conspícuo

conspiracy [kən'spɪrəsɪ] N conspiração f, trama

constable ['kʌnstəbl] (*brit*) N policial m/f (*br*), polícia m/f (*pt*); **chief ~** chefe m/f de polícia

constant ['kɒnstənt] ADJ constante

constipated ['kɒnstɪpeɪtəd] ADJ com prisão de ventre

constipation [kɒnstɪ'peɪʃən] N prisão f de ventre

constituency [kən'stɪtjuənsɪ] N (*Pol*) distrito eleitoral; (*people*) eleitorado

constitution [kɒnstɪ'tjuːʃən] N constituição f; (*health*) compleição f

constraint [kən'streɪnt] N coação f, pressão f; (*restriction*) limitação f

construct [kən'strʌkt] vt construir; **construction** N construção f; (*structure*) estrutura

consul ['kɒnsl] N cônsul m/f; **consulate** ['kɒnsjulɪt] N consulado

consult [kən'sʌlt] vt consultar;
consultant N (Med) (médico(-a))
especialista m/f; (other specialist)
assessor(a) m/f, consultor(a) m/f;
consulting room (BRIT) N consultório

consume [kən'sju:m] vt (eat) comer;
(drink) beber; (fire etc, Comm) consumir;
consumer N consumidor(a) m/f

consumption [kən'sʌmpʃən] N
consumo

cont. ABBR = **continued**

contact ['kɔntækt] N contato ▶ vt
entrar or pôr-se em contato com;
contact lenses NPL lentes fpl de contato

contagious [kən'teɪdʒəs] ADJ
contagioso; (fig: laughter etc)
contagiante

contain [kən'teɪn] vt conter; **to ~ o.s.**
conter-se; **container** N recipiente m; (for
shipping etc) container m, cofre m de
carga

contaminate [kən'tæmɪneɪt] vt
contaminar

cont'd ABBR = **continued**

contemplate ['kɔntəmpleɪt] vt (idea)
considerar; (person, painting etc)
contemplar

contemporary [kən'tempərərɪ] ADJ
contemporâneo; (design etc) moderno
▶ N contemporâneo(-a)

contempt [kən'tempt] N desprezo;
contempt of court (Jur) desacato à
autoridade do tribunal

contend [kən'tend] vt (assert): **to ~ that**
afirmar que ▶ vi: **to ~ with** (struggle)
lutar com; (difficulty) enfrentar;
(compete): **to ~ for** competir por

content [adj, vt kən'tent, n 'kɔntent] ADJ
(happy) contente; (satisfied) satisfeito
▶ vt contentar, satisfazer ▶ N conteúdo;
(fat content, moisture content etc)
quantidade f; **contents** NPL (of packet,
book) conteúdo; **contented** ADJ
contente, satisfeito

contest [n 'kɔntest, vt kən'test] N
contenda; (competition) concurso ▶ vt
(legal case) defender; (Pol) ser candidato
a; (competition) disputar; (statement,
decision) contestar; **contestant**
[kən'testənt] N competidor(a) m/f; (in
fight) adversário(-a)

context ['kɔntekst] N contexto

continent ['kɔntɪnənt] N continente m;
the C~ (BRIT) o continente europeu;
continental [kɔntɪ'nentl] ADJ
continental; **continental quilt** (BRIT) N
edredom m (BR), edredão m (PT)

continual [kən'tɪnjuəl] ADJ contínuo

continue [kən'tɪnju:] vi prosseguir,
continuar ▶ vt continuar; (start again)
recomeçar, retomar; **continuous**
[kən'tɪnjuəs] ADJ contínuo

contour ['kɔntuər] N contorno; (also:
~ line) curva de nível

contraceptive [kɔntrə'septɪv] ADJ
anticoncepcional ▶ N anticoncepcional m

contract [n, cpd 'kɔntrækt, vt, vi
kən'trækt] N contrato ▶ CPD (work) de
empreitada ▶ vi (become smaller)
contrair-se, encolher-se; (Comm): **to ~ to
do sth** comprometer-se por contrato a
fazer algo ▶ vt contrair

contradict [kɔntrə'dɪkt] vt contradizer,
desmentir

contrary¹ ['kɔntrərɪ] ADJ contrário ▶ N
contrário; **on the ~** muito pelo
contrário; **unless you hear to the ~**
salvo aviso contrário

contrary² [kən'trɛərɪ] ADJ teimoso

contrast [n 'kɔntrɑ:st, vt kən'trɑ:st] N
contraste m ▶ vt comparar; **in ~ to** or
with em contraste com, ao contrário de

contribute [kən'trɪbju:t] vt contribuir
▶ vi dar; **to ~ to** (charity) contribuir para;
(newspaper) escrever para; (discussion)
participar de; **contribution**
[kɔntrɪ'bju:ʃən] N (donation) doação f;
(BRIT: for social security) contribuição f;
(to debate) intervenção f; (to journal)
colaboração f; **contributor** [kən'trɪbjutər]
N (to newspaper) colaborador(a) m/f

control [kən'trəul] vt controlar;
(machinery) regular; (temper) dominar
▶ N controle m; (of car) direção f (BR),
condução f (PT); (check) freio, controle;
controls NPL (of vehicle) comandos mpl;
(on radio, television etc) controle; **to be in
~ of** ter o controle de; (in charge of) ser
responsável por

controversial [kɔntrə'və:ʃl] ADJ
controvertido, polêmico

controversy ['kɔntrəvə:sɪ] N
controvérsia, polêmica

convenience [kən'vi:nɪəns] N (easiness)
facilidade f; (suitability) conveniência;
(advantage) vantagem f, conveniência; **at
your ~** quando lhe convier; **all modern
~s, all mod cons** (BRIT) com todos os
confortos

convenient [kən'vi:nɪənt] ADJ
conveniente

convent ['kɔnvənt] N convento

convention [kən'venʃən] N (custom)
costume m; (agreement) convenção f;
(meeting) assembleia; **conventional** ADJ
convencional

conversation [kɒnvə'seɪʃən] N conversação f, conversa

convert [vt kən'vɜːt, n 'kɒnvɜːt] VT converter ▶ N convertido(-a); **convertible** [kən'vɜːtəbl] N conversível m

convey [kən'veɪ] VT transportar, levar; (thanks) expressar; (information) passar; **conveyor belt** N correia transportadora

convict [vt kən'vɪkt, n 'kɒnvɪkt] VT condenar ▶ N presidiário(-a); **conviction** N condenação f; (belief) convicção f; (certainty) certeza

convince [kən'vɪns] VT (assure) assegurar; (persuade) convencer; **convincing** ADJ convincente

cook [kuk] VT cozinhar; (meal) preparar ▶ VI cozinhar ▶ N cozinheiro(-a); **cookbook** N livro de receitas; **cooker** N fogão m; **cookery** N culinária; **cookery book** (BRIT) N = **cookbook**; **cookie** (US) N bolacha, biscoito; (Comput) cookie m; **cooking** N cozinha

cool [kuːl] ADJ fresco; (calm) calmo; (unfriendly) frio ▶ VT resfriar ▶ VI esfriar

cop [kɒp] (inf) N policial m/f (BR), polícia m/f (PT), tira m (inf)

cope [kəup] VI: **to ~ with** poder com, arcar com; (problem) estar à altura de

copper ['kɒpəʳ] N (metal) cobre m; (BRIT inf: police officer) policial m/f (BR), polícia m/f (PT); **coppers** NPL (coins) moedas fpl de pouco valor

copy ['kɒpɪ] N cópia; duplicata; (of book etc) exemplar m ▶ VT copiar; (imitate) imitar; **copyright** N direitos mpl autorais, copirraite m

coral ['kɒrəl] N coral m

cord [kɔːd] N corda; (Elec) fio, cabo; (fabric) veludo cotelê

corduroy ['kɔːdərɔɪ] N veludo cotelê

core [kɔːʳ] N centro; (of fruit) caroço; (of problem) âmago ▶ VT descaroçar

cork [kɔːk] N rolha; (tree) cortiça; **corkscrew** N saca-rolhas m inv

corn [kɔːn] N (BRIT) trigo; (US: maize) milho; (on foot) calo; **~ on the cob** (Culin) espiga de milho

corned beef ['kɔːnd-] N carne f de boi enlatada

corner ['kɔːnəʳ] N (outside) esquina; (inside) canto; (in road) curva; (Football etc) córner m ▶ VT (trap) encurralar; (Comm) açambarcar, monopolizar ▶ VI fazer uma curva

cornflakes ['kɔːnfleɪks] NPL flocos mpl de milho

cornflour ['kɔːnflauəʳ] (BRIT) N farinha de milho, maisena®

cornstarch ['kɔːnstɑːtʃ] (US) N = **cornflour**

Cornwall ['kɔːnwəl] N Cornualha

coronary ['kɒrənərɪ] N: **~ (thrombosis)** trombose f (coronária)

coronation [kɒrə'neɪʃən] N coroação f

coroner ['kɒrənəʳ] N magistrado que investiga mortes suspeitas

corporal ['kɔːpərl] N cabo ▶ ADJ: **~ punishment** castigo corporal

corporate ['kɔːpərɪt] ADJ (finance) corporativo; (action) coletivo; (image) da empresa

corporation [kɔːpə'reɪʃən] N (of town) município, junta; (Comm) sociedade f

corps [kɔːʳ] (pl **corps** [kɔːz]) N (Mil) unidade f; (diplomatic) corpo; **the press ~** a imprensa

corpse [kɔːps] N cadáver m

correct [kə'rɛkt] ADJ exato; (proper) correto ▶ VT corrigir; **correction** N correção f

correspond [kɒrɪs'pɒnd] VI (write): **to ~ (with)** corresponder-se (com); (be equal to): **to ~ to** corresponder a; (be in accordance): **to ~ (with)** corresponder (a); **correspondence** N correspondência; **correspondent** N correspondente m/f

corridor ['kɒrɪdɔːʳ] N corredor m

corrode [kə'rəud] VT corroer ▶ VI corroer-se

corrupt [kə'rʌpt] ADJ corrupto; (Comput) corrupto, danificado ▶ VT corromper; **corruption** N corrupção f

Corsica ['kɔːsɪkə] N Córsega

cosmetic [kɒz'mɛtɪk] N cosmético ▶ ADJ (fig) simbólico, superficial

cost [kɒst] (pt, pp **cost**) N (price) preço ▶ VT custar; **costs** NPL (Comm) custos mpl; (Jur) custas fpl; **at all ~s** custe o que custar

co-star [kəu-] N coestrela m/f

Costa Rica ['kɔstə'riːkə] N Costa Rica

costly ['kɒstlɪ] ADJ caro

costume ['kɒstjuːm] N traje m; (BRIT: also: **swimming ~**: woman's) maiô m (BR), fato de banho (PT); (: man's) calção m (de banho) (BR), calções mpl de banho (PT)

cosy ['kəuzɪ], (US) **cozy** ADJ aconchegante; (life) confortável

cot [kɒt] N (BRIT) cama (de criança), berço; (US) cama de lona

cottage ['kɒtɪdʒ] N casa de campo; **cottage cheese** N queijo tipo cottage (BR), queijo creme (PT)

cotton ['kɒtn] N algodão m; (thread) fio, linha; **cotton on** (inf) VI: **to ~ on (to sth)**

sacar (algo); **cotton bud** (BRIT) N cotonete® m; **cotton candy** (US) N algodão m doce; **cotton wool** (BRIT) N algodão m (hidrófilo)

couch [kautʃ] N sofá m; (doctor's) cama; (psychiatrist's) divã m

cough [kɔf] VI tossir ▶ N tosse f

could [kud] PT, CONDITIONAL of **can²**

couldn't ['kudnt] = **could not**

council ['kaunsl] N conselho; **city** or **town ~** câmara municipal; **council estate** (BRIT) N conjunto habitacional; **council house** (BRIT) N casa popular; **councillor** N vereador(a) m/f

counsellor ['kaunsələ'], (US) **counselor** N conselheiro(-a); (US Jur) advogado(-a)

count [kaunt] VT contar; (include) incluir ▶ VI contar ▶ N (of votes etc) contagem f; (of pollen, alcohol) nível m; (nobleman) conde m; **count on** VT FUS contar com; **countdown** N contagem f regressiva

counter ['kauntə'] N (in shop) balcão m; (in post office etc) guichê m; (in games) ficha ▶ VT contrariar ▶ ADV: **~ to** ao contrário de

counterfeit ['kauntəfɪt] N falsificação f ▶ VT falsificar ▶ ADJ falso, falsificado

counterpart ['kauntəpa:t] N (opposite number) homólogo(-a); (equivalent) equivalente m/f; **counterterrorism** [kauntə'tɛrərɪzəm] N antiterrorismo

countess ['kauntɪs] N condessa

countless ['kauntlɪs] ADJ inumerável

country ['kʌntrɪ] N país m; (nation) nação f; (native land) terra; (as opposed to town) campo; (region) região f, terra; **countryside** N campo

county ['kauntɪ] N condado

coup [ku:] N golpe m de mestre; (also: **~ d'état**) golpe (de estado)

couple ['kʌpl] N (of things, people) par m; (married couple, courting couple) casal m; **a ~ of** um par de; (a few) alguns/algumas

coupon ['ku:pɔn] N cupom m (BR), cupão m (PT); (voucher) vale m

courage ['kʌrɪdʒ] N coragem f

courier ['kurɪə'] N correio; (for tourists) guia m/f, agente m/f de turismo

course [kɔ:s] N (direction) direção f; (process) desenvolvimento; (of river, Sch) curso; (of ship) rumo; (Golf) campo; (part of meal) prato; **of ~** naturalmente; (certainly) certamente; **of ~!** claro!, lógico!

court [kɔ:t] N (royal) corte f; (Jur) tribunal m; (Tennis etc) quadra ▶ VT (woman)

cortejar, namorar; **to take to ~** demandar, levar a julgamento

courtesy ['kə:təsɪ] N cortesia; **(by) ~ of** com permissão de

court-house (US) N palácio de justiça

courtroom ['kɔ:trum] N sala de tribunal

courtyard ['kɔ:tja:d] N pátio

cousin ['kʌzn] N primo(-a) m/f; **first ~** primo-irmão/prima-irmã m/f

cover ['kʌvə'] VT cobrir; (with lid) tampar; (chairs etc) revestir; (distance) percorrer; (include) abranger; (protect) abrigar; (issues) tratar ▶ N (lid) tampa; (for chair etc) capa; (for bed) cobertor m; (of book, magazine) capa; (shelter) abrigo; (Insurance) cobertura; **to take ~** abrigar-se; **under ~** (indoors) abrigado; **under separate ~** (Comm) em separado; **cover up** VI: **to ~ up for sb** cobrir alguém; **coverage** N cobertura; **cover charge** N couvert m

cover-up N encobrimento (dos fatos)

cow [kau] N vaca ▶ VT intimidar

coward ['kauəd] N covarde m/f; **cowardly** ADJ covarde

cowboy ['kaubɔɪ] N vaqueiro

cozy ['kəuzɪ] (US) ADJ = **cosy**

crab [kræb] N caranguejo

crack [kræk] N rachadura; (gap) brecha; (noise) estalo; (drug) crack m ▶ VT quebrar; (nut) partir, descascar; (wall) rachar; (whip etc) estalar; (joke) soltar; (mystery) resolver; (code) decifrar ▶ ADJ (expert) de primeira classe; **crack down on** VT FUS (crime) ser linha dura com; **crack up** VI (Psych) sofrer um colapso nervoso; **cracker** N (biscuit) biscoito; (Christmas cracker) busca pé surpresa m

crackle ['krækl] VI crepitar

cradle ['kreɪdl] N berço

craft [krɑːft] N (skill) arte f; (trade) ofício; (boat) barco; **craftsman** irreg N artífice m, artesão m; **craftsmanship** N acabamento

cram [kræm] VT (fill): **to ~ sth with** encher or abarrotar algo de; (put): **to ~ sth into** enfiar algo em ▶ VI (for exams) estudar na última hora

cramp [kræmp] N (Med) cãibra; **cramped** ADJ apertado, confinado

cranberry ['krænbərɪ] N oxicoco

crane [kreɪn] N (Tech) guindaste m; (bird) grou m

crash [kræʃ] N (noise) estrondo; (of car) batida; (of plane) desastre m de avião; (Comm) falência, quebra; (Stock Exchange) craque m ▶ VT (car) bater com; (plane) jogar ▶ VI (car) bater; (plane) cair; (two *cars*) colidir, bater; (*Comm*) falir, quebrar; **crash course** N curso intensivo

crate [kreɪt] N caixote *m*; (*for bottles*) engradado

crave [kreɪv] VT, VI: **to ~ for** ansiar por

crawl [krɔːl] VI arrastar-se; (*child*) engatinhar; (*insect*) andar; (*vehicle*) andar a passo de tartaruga ▶ N (*Swimming*) crawl *m*

crayfish ['kreɪfɪʃ] N INV (*freshwater*) camarão-d'água-doce *m*; (*saltwater*) lagostim *m*

crayon ['kreɪən] N lápis *m* de cera, crayon *m*

craze [kreɪz] N (*fashion*) moda

crazy ['kreɪzɪ] ADJ louco, maluco, doido

creak [kriːk] VI ranger

cream [kriːm] N (*of milk*) nata; (*artificial, cosmetic*) creme *m*; (*élite*): **the ~ of** a fina flor de ▶ ADJ (*colour*) creme *inv*; **cream cheese** N ricota (*BR*), queijo creme (*PT*); **creamy** ADJ (*colour*) creme *inv*; (*taste*) cremoso

crease [kriːs] N (*fold*) dobra, vinco; (*in trousers*) vinco; (*wrinkle*) ruga ▶ VT (*wrinkle*) amassar, amarrotar ▶ VI amassar-se, amarrotar-se

create [kriːˈeɪt] VT criar; (*produce*) produzir

creature ['kriːtʃəʳ] N (*animal*) animal *m*, bicho; (*living thing*) criatura

credit ['krɛdɪt] N crédito; (*merit*) mérito ▶ VT (*also*: **give ~ to**) acreditar; (*Comm*) creditar; **credits** NPL (*Cinema, TV*) crédito; **to ~ sb with sth** (*fig*) atribuir algo a alguém; **to be in ~** ter fundos; **credit card** N cartão *m* de crédito; **credit crunch** N contração *f* do crédito

creek [kriːk] N enseada; (*US*) riacho

creep [kriːp] (*pt, pp* **crept**) VI (*animal*) rastejar; (*person*) deslizar(-se)

cremate [krɪˈmeɪt] VT cremar; **crematorium** (*pl* **crematoria**) N crematório

crept [krɛpt] PT, PP of **creep**

crescent ['krɛsnt] N meia-lua; (*street*) rua semicircular

cress [krɛs] N agrião *m*

crest [krɛst] N (*of bird*) crista; (*of hill*) cimo, topo; (*of coat of arms*) timbre *m*

crew [kruː] N (*of ship etc*) tripulação *f*; (*Cinema*) equipe *f*

crib [krɪb] N manjedoura, presépio; (*US: cot*) berço ▶ VT (*inf*) colar

cricket ['krɪkɪt] N (*insect*) grilo; (*game*) críquete *m*, cricket *m*

crime [kraɪm] N (*no pl: illegal activities*) crime *m*; (*offence*) delito; (*fig*) pecado, maldade *f*; **criminal** ['krɪmɪnl] N

criminoso ▶ ADJ criminal; (*morally wrong*) imoral

crimson ['krɪmzn] ADJ carmesim *inv*

cringe [krɪndʒ] VI encolher-se

cripple ['krɪpl] VT aleijar

crisis ['kraɪsɪs] (*pl* **crises**) N crise *f*

crisp [krɪsp] ADJ fresco; (*bacon etc*) torrado; (*manner*) seco; **crisps** (*BRIT*) NPL batatinhas *fpl* fritas; **crispy** ADJ crocante

criterion [kraɪˈtɪərɪən] (*pl* **criteria**) N critério

critic ['krɪtɪk] N crítico(-a); **critical** ADJ crítico; (*illness*) grave; **to be critical of sth/sb** criticar algo/alguém; **criticism** ['krɪtɪsɪzm] N crítica; **criticize** ['krɪtɪsaɪz] VT criticar

Croatia [krəʊˈeɪʃə] N Croácia

crockery ['krɔkərɪ] N louça

crocodile ['krɔkədaɪl] N crocodilo

crocus ['krəʊkəs] N açafrão-da-primavera *m*

crook [kruk] N (*inf: criminal*) vigarista *m/f*; (*of shepherd*) cajado; **crooked** ['krukɪd] ADJ torto; (*dishonest*) desonesto

crop [krɔp] N (*produce*) colheita; (*amount produced*) safra; (*riding crop*) chicotinho ▶ VT cortar; **crop up** VI surgir

cross [krɔs] N cruz *f*; (*hybrid*) cruzamento ▶ VT cruzar; (*street etc*) atravessar; (*thwart*) contrariar ▶ ADJ zangado, mal-humorado; **cross out** VT riscar; **cross over** VI atravessar; **crossing** N (*sea passage*) travessia; (*also*: **pedestrian crossing**) faixa (para pedestres) (*BR*), passadeira (*PT*); **crossroads** N cruzamento; **crosswalk** (*US*) N faixa (para pedestres) (*BR*), passadeira (*PT*); **crossword** N palavras *fpl* cruzadas

crouch [krautʃ] VI agachar-se

crow [krəʊ] N (*bird*) corvo; (*of cock*) canto, cocoricó *m* ▶ VI (*cock*) cantar, cocoricar

crowd [kraud] N multidão *f* ▶ VT (*fill*) apinhar ▶ VI (*gather*) amontoar-se; (*cram*): **to ~ in** apinhar-se; **crowded** ADJ (*full*) lotado; (*densely populated*) superlotado

crown [kraun] N coroa; (*of head, hill*) topo ▶ VT coroar; (*fig*) rematar; **crown jewels** NPL joias *fpl* reais

crucial ['kruːʃl] ADJ (*decision*) vital; (*vote*) decisivo

crucifix ['kruːsɪfɪks] N crucifixo

crude [kruːd] ADJ (*materials*) bruto; (*fig: basic*) tosco; (: *vulgar*) grosseiro

cruel ['kruəl] ADJ cruel

cruise [kruːz] N cruzeiro ▶ VI (*ship*) fazer um cruzeiro; (*car*): **to ~ at ... km/h** ir a ... km por hora

crumb [krʌm] N (of bread) migalha; (of cake) farelo

crumble ['krʌmbl] VT esfarelar ▶ VI (building) desmoronar-se; (plaster, earth) esfacelar-se; (fig) desintegrar-se

crumpet ['krʌmpɪt] N bolo leve

crumple ['krʌmpl] VT (paper) amassar; (material) amarrotar

crunch [krʌntʃ] VT (food etc) mastigar; (underfoot) esmagar ▶ N (fig): **the ~** o momento decisivo; **crunchy** ADJ crocante

crush [krʌʃ] N (crowd) aglomeração f; (love): **to have a ~ on sb** ter um rabicho por alguém; (drink): **lemon ~** limonada ▶ VT (press) esmagar; (squeeze) espremer; (paper) amassar; (cloth) enrugar; (army, opposition) aniquilar; (hopes) destruir; (person) arrasar

crust [krʌst] N (of bread) casca; (of snow, earth) crosta

crutch [krʌtʃ] N muleta

cry [kraɪ] VI chorar; (shout: also: **~ out**) gritar ▶ N grito; (of bird) pio; (of animal) voz f; **cry off** VI desistir

crystal ['krɪstl] N cristal m

cub [kʌb] N filhote m; (also: **~ scout**) lobinho

Cuba ['kju:bə] N Cuba

cube [kju:b] N cubo ▶ VT (Math) elevar ao cubo; **cubic** ADJ cúbico

cubicle ['kju:bɪkl] N cubículo

cuckoo ['kuku:] N cuco

cucumber ['kju:kʌmbər] N pepino

cuddle ['kʌdl] VT abraçar ▶ VI abraçar-se

cue [kju:] N (Snooker) taco; (Theatre etc) deixa

cuff [kʌf] N (of shirt, coat etc) punho; (US: on trousers) bainha; (blow) bofetada; **off the ~** de improviso

cul-de-sac ['kʌldəsæk] N beco sem saída

cull [kʌl] VT (story, idea) escolher, selecionar ▶ N matança seletiva

culminate ['kʌlmɪneɪt] VI: **to ~ in** terminar em

culprit ['kʌlprɪt] N culpado(-a)

cult [kʌlt] N culto

cultivate ['kʌltɪveɪt] VT cultivar

cultural ['kʌltʃərəl] ADJ cultural

culture ['kʌltʃər] N cultura

cunning ['kʌnɪŋ] N astúcia ▶ ADJ astuto, malandro; (device, idea) engenhoso

cup [kʌp] N xícara (BR), chávena (PT); (prize, of bra) taça

cupboard ['kʌbəd] N armário

curator [kjuə'reɪtər] N diretor(a) m/f

curb [kə:b] VT refrear ▶ N freio; (US) = **kerb**

curdle ['kə:dl] VI coalhar

cure [kjuər] VT curar ▶ N tratamento, cura

curfew ['kə:fju:] N toque m de recolher

curious ['kjuərɪəs] ADJ curioso; (nosy) abelhudo; (unusual) estranho

curl [kə:l] N (of hair) cacho ▶ VT (loosely) frisar; (tightly) encrespar ▶ VI (hair) encaracolar; **curl up** VI encaracolar-se; **curler** N rolo, bobe m; **curly** ADJ cacheado, crespo

currant ['kʌrənt] N passa de corinto; (blackcurrant, redcurrant) groselha

currency ['kʌrənsɪ] N moeda; **to gain ~** (fig) consagrar-se

current ['kʌrənt] N corrente f ▶ ADJ corrente; (present) atual; **current account** (BRIT) N conta corrente; **current affairs** NPL atualidades fpl; **currently** ADV atualmente

curriculum [kə'rɪkjuləm] (**curriculums** or pl **curricula**) N programa m de estudos; **curriculum vitae** [-'vi:taɪ] N currículo

curry ['kʌrɪ] N caril m ▶ VT: **to ~ favour with** captar simpatia de

curse [kə:s] VI xingar (BR), praguejar (PT) ▶ VT (swear at) xingar (BR), praguejar a (PT); (bemoan) amaldiçoar ▶ N maldição f; (swearword) palavrão m (BR), baixo calão m (PT); (problem) castigo

cursor ['kə:sər] N (Comput) cursor m

curt [kə:t] ADJ seco, brusco

curtain ['kə:tn] N cortina; (Theatre) pano

curve [kə:v] N curva ▶ VI encurvar-se, torcer-se; (road) fazer (uma) curva

cushion ['kuʃən] N almofada ▶ VT amortecer

custard ['kʌstəd] N nata, creme m

custody ['kʌstədɪ] N custódia; **to take into ~** deter

custom ['kʌstəm] N (tradition) tradição f; (convention) costume m; (habit) hábito; (Comm) clientela; **customer** N cliente m/f; **customize** ['kʌstəmaɪz] VT personalizar

customs ['kʌstəmz] NPL alfândega; **customs officer** N inspetor(a) m/f da alfândega, aduaneiro(-a)

cut [kʌt] (pt, pp **cut**) VT cortar; (reduce) reduzir ▶ VI cortar ▶ N corte m; (in spending) redução f; (of garment) tacho; **cut down** VT (tree) derrubar; (reduce) reduzir; **cut off** VT (piece, Tel) cortar; (person, village) isolar; (supply) suspender; **cut out** VT (shape) recortar; (activity etc) suprimir; (remove) remover; **cut up** VT cortar em pedaços

cute [kju:t] ADJ bonitinho

cutlery ['kʌtlərɪ] N talheres mpl

cutlet ['kʌtlɪt] N costeleta

cut-price, (US) **cut-rate** ADJ a preço reduzido

cutting ADJ cortante ▶ N (BRIT: from newspaper) recorte m; (from plant) muda; **cutting-edge** ADJ (technology, research) de ponta

CV N ABBR = **curriculum vitae**

cyber attack ['saɪbərətæk] N ciberataque m

cyberbullying ['saɪbəbuliɪŋ] N ciberbullying m

cybercafé ['saɪbəkæfeɪ] N cibercafé m

cybercrime ['saɪbəkraɪm] N crime m virtual

cyberspace ['saɪbəspeɪs] N ciberespaço

cycle ['saɪkl] N ciclo; (bicycle) bicicleta ▶ VI andar de bicicleta

cycling ['saɪklɪŋ] N ciclismo

cyclist ['saɪklɪst] N ciclista m/f

cylinder ['sɪlɪndə ʳ] N cilindro; (of gas) bujão m

Cyprus ['saɪprəs] N Chipre f

cyst [sɪst] N cisto; **cystitis** N cistite f

czar [zɑːʳ] N czar m

Czech [tʃɛk] ADJ tcheco ▶ N tcheco(-a); (Ling) tcheco; **Czech Republic** N: **the Czech Republic** a República Tcheca

D¹ [diː] N (Mus) ré m

D² (US) ABBR (Pol) = **democrat, democratic**

dab [dæb] VT (eyes, wound) tocar (de leve); (paint, cream) aplicar de leve

dad [dæd] (inf) N papai m

daddy ['dædɪ] N = **dad**

daffodil ['dæfədɪl] N narciso-dos-prados m

daft [dɑːft] ADJ bobo, besta

dagger ['dægəʳ] N punhal m, adaga

daily ['deɪlɪ] ADJ diário ▶ N (paper) jornal m, diário ▶ ADV diariamente

dairy ['dɛərɪ] N leiteria

daisy ['deɪzɪ] N margarida

dam [dæm] N represa, barragem f ▶ VT represar

damage ['dæmɪdʒ] N (harm) prejuízo; (dents etc) avaria ▶ VT danificar; (harm) prejudicar; **damages** NPL (Jur) indenização f por perdas e danos

damn [dæm] VT condenar; (curse) maldizer ▶ N (inf): **I don't give a ~** não dou a mínima, estou me lixando ▶ ADJ (inf: also: **~ed**) danado, maldito; **~ (it)!** (que) droga!

damp [dæmp] ADJ úmido ▶ N umidade f ▶ VT (also: **~en**: cloth, rag) umedecer; (: enthusiasm etc) jogar água fria em

dance [dɑːns] N dança; (party etc) baile m ▶ VI dançar; **dancer** N dançarino(-a); (professional) bailarino(-a); **dancing** N dança

dandelion ['dændɪlaɪən] N dente-de-leão m

dandruff ['dændrəf] N caspa

Dane [deɪn] N dinamarquês(-esa) m/f

danger ['deɪndʒəʳ] N perigo; (risk) risco; **"~!"** (on sign) "perigo!"; **to be in ~ of** correr o risco de; **in ~** em perigo; **dangerous** ['deɪndʒərəs] ADJ perigoso

dangle ['dæŋgl] VT balançar ▶ VI pender
balançando

Danish ['deɪnɪʃ] ADJ dinamarquês(-esa)
▶ N (Ling) dinamarquês m

dare [dɛəʳ] VT: **to ~ sb to do sth** desafiar
alguém a fazer algo ▶ VI: **to ~ (to) do sth**
atrever-se a fazer algo, ousar fazer algo;
I ~ say (I suppose) acho provável que;
daring ADJ audacioso; (bold) ousado ▶ N
coragem f, destemor m

dark [dɑːk] ADJ escuro; (complexion)
moreno ▶ N escuro; **in the ~ about** (fig)
no escuro sobre; **after ~** depois de
escurecer; **darken** VT escurecer; (colour)
fazer mais escuro ▶ VI escurecer(-se);
darkness N escuridão f; **darkroom** N
câmara escura

darling ['dɑːlɪŋ] ADJ, N querido(-a)

dart [dɑːt] N dardo; (in sewing) alinhavo
▶ VI precipitar-se; **to ~ away/along**
ir-se/seguir precipitadamente; **darts** N
(game) jogo de dardos

dash [dæʃ] N (sign) hífen m; (: long)
travessão m; (small quantity) pontinha
▶ VT arremessar; (hopes) frustrar ▶ VI
precipitar-se, correr; **dash away** VI sair
apressado; **dash off** VI = **dash away**

dashboard ['dæʃbɔːd] N painel m de
instrumentos

data ['deɪtə] NPL dados mpl; **database** N
banco de dados; **data processing** N
processamento de dados

date [deɪt] N data; (with friend) encontro;
(fruit) tâmara ▶ VT datar; (person)
namorar; **to ~** até agora; **out of ~**
desatualizado; **up to ~** moderno; **dated**
['deɪtɪd] ADJ antiquado

daughter ['dɔːtəʳ] N filha; **daughter-in-
law** (pl **daughters-in-law**) N nora

daunting ['dɔːntɪŋ] ADJ desanimador(a)

dawn [dɔːn] N alvorada, amanhecer m;
(of period, situation) surgimento, início
▶ VI (day) amanhecer; (fig): **it ~ed on him
that ...** começou a perceber que ...

day [deɪ] N dia m; (working day) jornada,
dia útil; **the ~ before/after** a véspera/o
dia seguinte; **the ~ before yesterday**
anteontem; **the ~ after tomorrow**
depois de amanhã; **by ~** de dia;
day-care centre ['deɪkeə-] N (for elderly
etc) centro de convivência; (for children)
creche f; **daydream** VI devanear;
daylight N luz f (do dia); **day return**
(BRIT) N bilhete m de ida e volta no
mesmo dia; **daytime** N dia m;
day-to-day ADJ cotidiano

dazzle ['dæzl] VT (bewitch) deslumbrar;
(blind) ofuscar

dead [dɛd] ADJ morto; (numb) dormente;
(telephone) cortado; (Elec) sem corrente
▶ ADV completamente; (exactly)
absolutamente ▶ NPL: **the ~** os mortos;
to shoot sb ~ matar alguém a tiro;
~ tired morto de cansado; **to stop ~**
estacar; **dead end** N beco sem saída;
deadline N prazo final; **deadly** ADJ
mortal, fatal; (weapon) mortífero

deaf [dɛf] ADJ surdo; **deafen** VT
ensurdecer

deal [diːl] (pt, pp **dealt**) N (agreement)
acordo ▶ VT (cards, blows) dar; **a good** or
great ~ (of) bastante, muito; **deal in** VT
FUS (Comm) negociar em or com; **deal
with** VT FUS (people) tratar com;
(problem) ocupar-se de; (subject) tratar
de; **dealer** N negociante m/f; **dealings**
NPL transações fpl

dean [diːn] N (Rel) decano; (Sch: BRIT)
reitor(a) m/f; (: US) orientador(a) m/f de
estudos

dear [dɪəʳ] ADJ querido, caro; (expensive)
caro ▶ N: **my ~** meu querido/minha
querida ▶ EXCL: **~ me!** ai, meu Deus!;
D~ Sir/Madam (in letter) Prezado
Senhor/Prezada Senhora (BR), Exmo.
Senhor/Exma. Senhora (PT); **D~ Mr/
Mrs X** Prezado Sr. X/Prezada Sra. X;
dearly ADV (love) ternamente; (pay) caro

death [dɛθ] N morte f; (Admin) óbito;
death penalty N pena de morte; **death
row** (US) N corredor m da morte

debate [dɪ'beɪt] N debate m ▶ VT debater

debit ['dɛbɪt] N débito ▶ VT: **to ~ a sum
to sb** or **sb's account** lançar uma
quantia ao débito de alguém or à conta
de alguém; see also **direct debit**; **debit
card** N cartão m de débito

debt [dɛt] N dívida; (state)
endividamento; **to be in ~** ter dívidas,
estar endividado

decade ['dɛkeɪd] N década

decaffeinated [dɪ'kæfɪneɪtɪd] ADJ
descafeinado

decay [dɪ'keɪ] N ruína; (also: **tooth ~**)
cárie f ▶ VI (rot) apodrecer-se

deceased [dɪ'siːst] N: **the ~** o falecido/a
falecida

deceit [dɪ'siːt] N engano; (duplicity)
fraude f

deceive [dɪ'siːv] VT enganar

December [dɪ'sɛmbəʳ] N dezembro

decent ['diːsənt] ADJ (proper) decente;
(kind, honest) honesto, amável

deception [dɪ'sɛpʃən] N engano;
(deceitful act) fraude f; **deceptive** ADJ
enganador(a)

decide [dɪˈsaɪd] vt (*person*) convencer; (*question, argument*) resolver ▶ vi decidir; **to ~ on sth** decidir-se por algo

decimal [ˈdɛsɪməl] ADJ decimal ▶ N decimal *m*

decision [dɪˈsɪʒən] N (*choice*) escolha; (*act of choosing*) decisão *f*; (*decisiveness*) resolução *f*

decisive [dɪˈsaɪsɪv] ADJ (*action*) decisivo; (*person*) decidido

deck [dɛk] N (*Naut*) convés *m*; (*of bus*): **top ~** andar *m* de cima; (*of cards*) baralho; **record/cassette ~** toca-discos *m inv*/ toca-fitas *m inv*

declare [dɪˈklɛəʳ] vt (*intention*) revelar; (*result*) divulgar; (*income, at customs*) declarar

decline [dɪˈklaɪn] N declínio; (*lessening*) diminuição *f*, baixa ▶ vt recusar ▶ vi diminuir

decorate [ˈdɛkəreɪt] vt; **decoration** [dɛkəˈreɪʃən] N enfeite *m*; (*act*) decoração; (*medal*) condecoração *f*; **decorator** N (*painter*) pintor(a) *m/f*

decrease [*n* ˈdiːkriːs, *vt, vi* diːˈkriːs] N: **~ (in)** diminuição *f* (de) ▶ vt reduzir ▶ vi diminuir

decree [dɪˈkriː] N decreto

decrypt [diːˈkrɪpt] vt (*Comput, Tel*) desencriptar

dedicate [ˈdɛdɪkeɪt] vt dedicar; **dedication** [dɛdɪˈkeɪʃən] N dedicação *f*; (*in book*) dedicatória; (*on radio*) mensagem *f*

deduce [dɪˈdjuːs] vt deduzir

deduct [dɪˈdʌkt] vt deduzir; **deduction** N (*deducting*) redução *f*; (*amount*) subtração *f*; (*deducing*) dedução *f*

deed [diːd] N feito; (*Jur*) escritura, título

deep [diːp] ADJ profundo; (*voice*) baixo, grave; (*breath*) fundo; (*colour*) forte, carregado ▶ ADV: **the spectators stood 20 ~** havia 20 fileiras de espectadores; **to be 4 metres ~** ter 4 metros de profundidade; **deepen** vt aprofundar ▶ vi aumentar

deer [dɪəʳ] N INV veado, cervo

default [dɪˈfɔːlt] N (*Comput*) default *m*, padrão *m*; **by ~** (*win*) por desistência

defeat [dɪˈfiːt] N derrota; (*failure*) malogro ▶ vt derrotar, vencer

defect [*n* ˈdiːfɛkt, *vi* dɪˈfɛkt] N defeito ▶ vi: **to ~ to the enemy** desertar para se juntar ao inimigo; **defective** [dɪˈfɛktɪv] ADJ defeituoso

defence [dɪˈfɛns], (*US*) **defense** N defesa

defend [dɪˈfɛnd] vt defender; (*Jur*) contestar; **defendant** N acusado(-a); (*in civil case*) réu/ré *m/f*; **defender** N defensor(a) *m/f*; (*Sport*) defesa

defer [dɪˈfəʳ] vt (*postpone*) adiar

defiance [dɪˈfaɪəns] N desafio; rebeldia; **in ~ of** a despeito de

defiant [dɪˈfaɪənt] ADJ desafiador(a)

deficiency [dɪˈfɪʃənsɪ] N (*lack*) deficiência, falta; (*defect*) defeito

deficit [ˈdɛfɪsɪt] N déficit *m*

define [dɪˈfaɪn] vt definir

definite [ˈdɛfɪnɪt] ADJ (*fixed*) definitivo; (*clear, obvious*) claro, categórico; (*certain*) certo; **he was ~ about it** ele foi categórico; **definitely** ADV sem dúvida

deflate [diːˈfleɪt] vt esvaziar

deflect [dɪˈflɛkt] vt desviar

defraud [dɪˈfrɔːd] vt: **to ~ sb (of sth)** trapacear alguém (por causa de algo)

defriend [diːˈfrɛnd] vt (*on social network*) excluir (*em rede social*)

defrost [diːˈfrɔst] vt descongelar

defuse [diːˈfjuːz] vt tirar o estopim *or* a espoleta de; (*situation*) neutralizar

defy [dɪˈfaɪ] vt desafiar; (*resist*) opor-se a

degree [dɪˈgriː] N grau *m*; (*Sch*) diploma *m*, título; **~ in maths** formatura em matemática; **by ~s** (*gradually*) pouco a pouco; **to some ~, to a certain ~** até certo ponto

dehydrated [diːhaɪˈdreɪtɪd] ADJ desidratado; (*milk*) em pó

delay [dɪˈleɪ] vt (*decision etc*) retardar, atrasar; (*train, person*) atrasar ▶ vi hesitar ▶ N demora; (*postponement*) adiamento; **to be ~ed** estar atrasado; **without ~** sem demora *or* atraso

delegate [*n* ˈdɛlɪgɪt, *vt* ˈdɛlɪgeɪt] N delegado(-a) ▶ vt (*person*) autorizar; (*task*) delegar

delete [dɪˈliːt] vt eliminar, riscar; (*Comput*) deletar, excluir

deliberate [*adj* dɪˈlɪbərɪt, *vi* dɪˈlɪbəreɪt] ADJ (*intentional*) intencional; (*slow*) pausado, lento ▶ vi considerar; **deliberately** [dɪˈlɪbərɪtlɪ] ADV (*on purpose*) de propósito

delicacy [ˈdɛlɪkəsɪ] N delicadeza; (*of problem*) dificuldade *f*; (*choice food*) iguaria

delicate [ˈdɛlɪkɪt] ADJ delicado; (*health*) frágil

delicatessen [dɛlɪkəˈtɛsn] N delicatessen *m*

delicious [dɪˈlɪʃəs] ADJ delicioso; (*food*) saboroso

delight [dɪ'laɪt] N prazer m, deleite m; (*person*) encanto; (*experience*) delícia ▶ VT encantar, deleitar; **to take (a) ~ in** deleitar-se com; **delighted** ADJ: **delighted (at** *or* **with sth)** encantado (com algo); **delightful** ADJ encantador(a), delicioso

delinquent [dɪ'lɪŋkwənt] ADJ, N delinquente m/f

deliver [dɪ'lɪvər] VT (*distribute*) distribuir; (*hand over*) entregar; (*message*) comunicar; (*speech*) proferir; (*Med*) partejar; **delivery** N distribuição f; (*of speaker*) enunciação f; (*Med*) parto; **to take delivery of** receber

delusion [dɪ'luːʒən] N ilusão f

demand [dɪ'maːnd] VT exigir; (*rights*) reivindicar, reclamar ▶ N exigência; (*claim*) reivindicação f; (*Econ*) procura; **to be in ~** estar em demanda; **on ~** à vista; **demanding** ADJ (*boss*) exigente; (*work*) absorvente

demise [dɪ'maɪz] N falecimento

demo ['dɛməʊ] (*inf*) N ABBR (= *demonstration*) passeata

democracy [dɪ'mɔkrəsɪ] N democracia; **democrat** ['dɛməkræt] N democrata m/f; **democratic** [dɛmə'krætɪk] ADJ democrático

demolish [dɪ'mɔlɪʃ] VT demolir, derrubar; (*argument*) refutar, contestar

demonstrate ['dɛmənstreɪt] VT demonstrar ▶ VI: **to ~ (for/against)** manifestar-se (a favor de/contra); **demonstration** [dɛmən'streɪʃən] N (*Pol*) manifestação f; (: *march*) passeata; (*proof*) demonstração f; (*exhibition*) exibição f; **demonstrator** N manifestante m/f

demote [dɪ'məʊt] VT rebaixar de posto

den [dɛn] N (*of animal*) covil m; (*of thieves*) antro, esconderijo; (*room*) aposento privado, cantinho

denial [dɪ'naɪəl] N refutação f; (*refusal*) negativa

denim ['dɛnɪm] N brim m, zuarte m; **denims** NPL jeans m (BR), jeans mpl (PT)

Denmark ['dɛnmaːk] N Dinamarca

denomination [dɪnɔmɪ'neɪʃən] N valor m, denominação f; (*Rel*) confissão f, seita

denounce [dɪ'naʊns] VT denunciar

dense [dɛns] ADJ denso; (*inf*: *stupid*) estúpido, bronco

density ['dɛnsɪtɪ] N densidade f

dent [dɛnt] N amolgadura, depressão f ▶ VT amolgar, dentar

dental ['dɛntl] ADJ (*treatment*) dentário; (*hygiene*) dental; **dental floss** [-'flɔs] N fio dental

dentist ['dɛntɪst] N dentista m/f

dentures ['dɛntʃəz] NPL dentadura

deny [dɪ'naɪ] VT negar; (*refuse*) recusar

deodorant [diː'əʊdərənt] N desodorante m (BR), desodorizante m (PT)

depart [dɪ'paːt] VI ir-se, partir; (*train etc*) sair; **to ~ from** (*fig*: *differ from*) afastar-se de

department [dɪ'paːtmənt] N (*Sch*) departamento; (*Comm*) seção f; (*Pol*) repartição f; **department store** N magazine m (BR), grande armazém m (PT)

departure [dɪ'paːtʃər] N partida, ida; (*of train etc*) saída; (*of employee*) saída; **a new ~** uma nova orientação; **departure lounge** N sala de embarque

depend [dɪ'pɛnd] VI: **to ~ (up)on** depender de; (*rely on*) contar com; **it ~s** depende; **~ing on the result …** dependendo do resultado …; **dependant** N dependente m/f; **dependent** ADJ: **to be dependent (on)** depender (de), ser dependente (de) ▶ N = **dependant**

depict [dɪ'pɪkt] VT (*in picture*) retratar, representar; (*describe*) descrever

deport [dɪ'pɔːt] VT deportar

deposit [dɪ'pɔzɪt] N (*Comm*, *Geo*) depósito; (*Chem*) sedimento; (*of ore, oil*) jazida; (*down payment*) sinal m ▶ VT depositar; (*luggage*) guardar; **deposit account** N conta de depósito a prazo

depot ['dɛpəʊ] N (*storehouse*) depósito, armazém m; (*for vehicles*) garagem f, parque m; (*US*) estação f

depress [dɪ'prɛs] VT deprimir; (*press down*) apertar; **depressed** ADJ deprimido; (*area, market, trade*) em depressão; **depressing** ADJ deprimente; **depression** N depressão f; (*hollow*) achatamento

deprive [dɪ'praɪv] VT: **to ~ sb of** privar alguém de; **deprived** ADJ carente

depth [dɛpθ] N profundidade f; (*of feeling*) intensidade f; **in the ~s of despair** no auge do desespero; **to be out of one's ~** (BRIT: *swimmer*) estar sem pé; (*fig*) estar voando

deputy ['dɛpjutɪ] ADJ: **~ chairperson** vice-presidente(-a) m/f ▶ N (*assistant*) adjunto; (*Pol*: *MP*) deputado(-a)

derail [dɪ'reɪl] VT: **to be ~ed** descarrilhar

derelict ['dɛrɪlɪkt] ADJ abandonado

derive [dɪ'raɪv] VT: **to ~ (from)** obter *or* tirar (de) ▶ VI: **to ~ from** derivar-se de

descend [dɪ'sɛnd] VT, VI descer; **to ~ from** descer de; **to ~ to** descambar em; **descent** N descida; (origin) descendência

describe [dɪs'kraɪb] VT descrever; **description** [dɪs'krɪpʃən] N descrição f; (sort) classe f, espécie f

desert [n'dɛzət, vt, vi dɪ'zə:t] N deserto ▶ VT (place) desertar; (partner, family) abandonar ▶ VT (Mil) desertar

deserve [dɪ'zə:v] VT merecer

design [dɪ'zaɪn] N (sketch) desenho, esboço; (layout, shape) plano, projeto; (pattern) desenho, padrão m; (art) design m; (intention) propósito, intenção f ▶ VT (plan) projetar

designer [dɪ'zaɪnər] N (Art) artista m/f gráfico(-a); (Tech) desenhista m/f, projetista m/f; (fashion designer) estilista m/f

desire [dɪ'zaɪər] N anseio; (sexual) desejo ▶ VT querer; desejar, cobiçar

desk [dɛsk] N (in office) mesa, secretária; (for pupil) carteira f; (at airport) balcão m; (in hotel) recepção f; (BRIT: in shop, restaurant) caixa; **desktop** ['dɛsktɔp] N (Comput) área (BR) or ambiente m (PT) de trabalho

despair [dɪs'pɛər] N desesperança ▶ VI: **to ~ of** desesperar-se de

despatch [dɪs'pætʃ] N, VT = **dispatch**

desperate ['dɛspərɪt] ADJ desesperado; (situation) desesperador(a); **to be ~ for sth/to do** estar louco por algo/para fazer; **desperately** ADV desesperadamente; (very: unhappy) terrivelmente; (: ill) gravemente; **desperation** [dɛspə'reɪʃən] N despero, desesperança; **in (sheer) desperation** desesperado

despise [dɪs'paɪz] VT desprezar

despite [dɪs'paɪt] PREP apesar de, a despeito de

dessert [dɪ'zə:t] N sobremesa

destination [dɛstɪ'neɪʃən] N destino

destined ['dɛstɪnd] ADJ: **to be ~ to do sth** estar destinado a fazer algo; **~ for** com destino a

destiny ['dɛstɪnɪ] N destino

destroy [dɪs'trɔɪ] VT destruir; (animal) sacrificar; **destruction** N destruição f

detach [dɪ'tætʃ] VT separar; (unstick) desprender; **detached** ADJ (attitude) imparcial, objetivo; (house) independente, isolado

detail ['di:teɪl] N detalhe m; (trifle) bobagem f ▶ VT detalhar; **in ~** pormenorizado, em detalhe

detain [dɪ'teɪn] VT deter; (in captivity) prender; (in hospital) hospitalizar

detect [dɪ'tɛkt] VT perceber; (Med, Police) identificar; (Mil, Radar, Tech) detectar; **detection** N descoberta; **detective** N detetive m/f; **detective story** N romance m policial

detention [dɪ'tɛnʃən] N detenção f, prisão f; (Sch) castigo

deter [dɪ'tə:r] VT (discourage) desanimar; (dissuade) dissuadir

detergent [dɪ'tə:dʒənt] N detergente m

deteriorate [dɪ'tɪərɪəreɪt] VI deteriorar-se

determine [dɪ'tə:mɪn] VT descobrir; (limits etc) demarcar; **determined** ADJ (person) resoluto; **determined to do** decidido a fazer

detour ['di:tuər] N desvio

detract [dɪ'trækt] VI: **to ~ from** diminuir

detrimental [dɛtrɪ'mɛntl] ADJ: **~ (to)** prejudicial (a)

develop [dɪ'vɛləp] VT desenvolver; (Phot) revelar; (disease) contrair; (resources) explotar ▶ VI (advance) progredir; (evolve) evoluir; (appear) aparecer; **development** [dɪ'vɛləpmənt] N desenvolvimento; (advance) progresso; (of land) urbanização f

device [dɪ'vaɪs] N aparelho, dispositivo

devil ['dɛvl] N diabo

devious ['di:vɪəs] ADJ (person) malandro, esperto

devise [dɪ'vaɪz] VT (plan) criar; (machine) inventar

devote [dɪ'vəut] VT: **to ~ sth to** dedicar algo a; **devoted** [dɪ'vəutɪd] ADJ (friendship) leal; (partner) fiel; **to be devoted to** estar devotado a; **the book is devoted to politics** o livro trata de política; **devotion** N devoção f; (to duty) dedicação f

devour [dɪ'vauər] VT devorar

devout [dɪ'vaut] ADJ devoto

dew [dju:] N orvalho

diabetes [daɪə'bi:ti:z] N diabete f

diagnosis [daɪəg'nəusɪs] (pl **diagnoses**) N diagnóstico

diagonal [daɪ'ægənl] ADJ diagonal ▶ N diagonal f

diagram ['daɪəgræm] N diagrama m, esquema m

dial ['daɪəl] N disco ▶ VT (number) discar (BR), marcar (PT)

dial code (US) N = **dialling code**

dialect ['daɪəlɛkt] N dialeto

dialling code ['daɪəlɪŋ-] (BRIT) N código de discagem

dialling tone ['daɪəlɪŋ-] (BRIT) N sinal m de discagem (BR) or de marcar (PT)
dialogue ['daɪəlɔɡ], (US) **dialog** N diálogo; (conversation) conversa
diameter [daɪ'æmɪtəʳ] N diâmetro
diamond ['daɪəmənd] N diamante m; (shape) losango, rombo; **diamonds** NPL (Cards) ouros mpl
diarrhoea [daɪə'riːə], (US) **diarrhea** N diarreia
diary ['daɪərɪ] N (daily account) diário; (engagements book) agenda
dice [daɪs] N INV dado ▶ VT (Culin) cortar em cubos
dictate [dɪk'teɪt] VT ditar; **dictation** N ditado
dictator [dɪk'teɪtəʳ] N ditador(a) m/f
dictionary ['dɪkʃənrɪ] N dicionário
did [dɪd] PT of **do**
didn't ['dɪdnt] = **did not**
die [daɪ] N, VI morrer; (fig: fade) murchar; **to be dying for sth/to do sth** estar louco por algo/para fazer algo; **die away** VI (sound, light) extinguir-se lentamente; **die down** VI (fire) apagar-se; (wind) abrandar; (excitement) diminuir; **die out** VI desaparecer
diesel ['diːzl] N diesel m; (also: ~ **fuel**, ~ **oil**) óleo diesel
diet ['daɪət] N dieta; (restricted food) regime m ▶ VI (also: **be on a ~**) estar de dieta, fazer regime
differ ['dɪfəʳ] VI (be different): **to ~ from sth** ser diferente de algo, diferenciar-se de algo; (disagree): **to ~ (about)** discordar (sobre); **difference** N diferença; (disagreement) divergência; **different** ADJ diferente; **differentiate** [dɪfə'renʃɪeɪt] VI: **to differentiate (between)** distinguir (entre)
difficult ['dɪfɪkəlt] ADJ difícil; **difficulty** N dificuldade f
dig [dɪɡ] (pt, pp **dug**) VT cavar ▶ N (prod) pontada; (archaeological) escavação f; (remark) alfinetada; **to ~ one's nails into** cravar as unhas em; **dig into** VT FUS (savings) gastar; **dig up** VT (plant) arrancar; (information) trazer à tona
digest [vt daɪ'dʒest, n 'daɪdʒest] VT (food) digerir; (facts) assimilar ▶ N sumário; **digestion** [dɪ'dʒestʃən] N digestão f
digit ['dɪdʒɪt] N (Math) dígito; (finger) dedo; **digital** ADJ digital; **digital camera** N câmara digital; **digital TV** N televisão f digital
dignified ['dɪɡnɪfaɪd] ADJ digno
dignity ['dɪɡnɪtɪ] N dignidade f
dilemma [daɪ'lemə] N dilema m

dilute [daɪ'luːt] VT diluir
dim [dɪm] ADJ fraco; (outline) indistinto; (room) escuro; (inf: person) burro ▶ VT diminuir; (US Aut) baixar
dime [daɪm] (US) N (moeda de) dez centavos
dimension [dɪ'menʃən] N dimensão f; (measurement) medida; (also: ~**s**: scale, size) tamanho
diminish [dɪ'mɪnɪʃ] VI diminuir
din [dɪn] N zoeira
dine [daɪn] VI jantar; **diner** N comensal m/f; (US: eating place) lanchonete f
dinghy ['dɪŋɡɪ] N dingue m, bote m; **rubber ~** bote de borracha
dingy ['dɪndʒɪ] ADJ (room) sombrio, lúgubre; (clothes, curtains etc) sujo
dining car ['daɪnɪŋ-] (BRIT) N (Rail) vagão-restaurante m
dining room ['daɪnɪŋ-] N sala de jantar
dinkum ['dɪŋkəm] (AUST inf) ADJ (also: **fair ~**) de verdade
dinner ['dɪnəʳ] N (evening meal) jantar m; (lunch) almoço; (banquet) banquete m; **dinner jacket** N smoking m; **dinner party** N jantar m; **dinner time** N (midday) hora de almoçar; (evening) hora de jantar
dip [dɪp] N (slope) inclinação f; (in sea) mergulho; (Culin) pasta para servir com salgadinhos ▶ VT (in water) mergulhar; (ladle etc) meter; (BRIT Aut: lights) baixar ▶ VI descer subitamente
diploma [dɪ'pləumə] N diploma m
diplomat ['dɪpləmæt] N diplomata m/f
dipstick ['dɪpstɪk] N (Aut) vareta medidora
dire [daɪəʳ] ADJ terrível
direct [daɪ'rekt] ADJ direto; (route) reto; (manner) franco, sincero ▶ VT dirigir; (order): **to ~ sb to do sth** ordenar alguém para fazer algo ▶ ADV direto; **can you ~ me to ...?** pode me indicar o caminho a ...?; **direct debit** (BRIT) N (Banking) débito direto; **direction** N (way) indicação f; (TV, Radio, Cinema) direção f; **directions** NPL (instructions) instruções fpl; **directions for use** modo de usar; **directly** ADV diretamente; (at once) imediatamente; **director** N diretor(a) m/f
directory [dɪ'rektərɪ] N (Tel) lista (telefônica); (Comm) anuário comercial; (Comput) diretório; **directory enquiries**, (US) **directory assistance** N (serviço de) informações fpl
dirt [dəːt] N sujeira (BR), sujidade (PT); **dirty** ADJ sujo; (joke) indecente ▶ VT sujar

disability [dısə'bılıtı] N incapacidade f
disabled [dıs'eıbld] ADJ deficiente
disadvantage [dısəd'vɑ:ntıdʒ] N desvantagem f; (prejudice) inconveniente m
disagree [dısə'gri:] VI (differ) diferir; (be against, think otherwise): **to ~ (with)** não concordar (com), discordar (de); **disagreeable** ADJ desagradável; **disagreement** N desacordo; (quarrel) desavença
disappear [dısə'pıər] VI desaparecer, sumir; (custom etc) acabar; **disappearance** N desaparecimento, desaparição f
disappoint [dısə'pɔınt] VT decepcionar; **disappointed** ADJ decepcionado; **disappointment** N decepção f; (cause) desapontamento
disapproval [dısə'pru:vəl] N desaprovação f
disapprove [dısə'pru:v] VI: **to ~ of** desaprovar
disarmament N desarmamento
disaster [dı'zɑ:stər] N (accident) desastre m; (natural) catástrofe f
disbelief [dısbə'li:f] N incredulidade f
disc [dısk] N disco; (Comput) = **disk**
discard [dıs'kɑ:d] VT (old things) desfazer-se de; (fig) descartar
discharge [vt dıs'tʃɑ:dʒ, n 'dıstʃɑ:dʒ] VT (duties) cumprir, desempenhar; (patient) dar alta a; (employee) despedir; (soldier) dar baixa em, dispensar; (defendant) pôr em liberdade; (waste etc) descarregar, despejar ▶ N (Elec) descarga; (dismissal) despedida; (of duty) desempenho; (of debt) quitação f; (from hospital) alta; (from army) baixa; (Jur) absolvição f; (Med) secreção f
discipline ['dısıplın] N disciplina ▶ VT disciplinar; (punish) punir
disc jockey N (on radio) radialista m/f; (in discotheque) discotecário(-a)
disclose [dıs'kləuz] VT revelar
disco ['dıskəu] N ABBR = **discotheque**
discomfort [dıs'kʌmfət] N (unease) inquietação f; (physical) desconforto
disconnect [dıskə'nɛkt] VT desligar; (pipe, tap) desmembrar
discontent [dıskən'tɛnt] N descontentamento
discontinue [dıskən'tınju:] VT interromper; (payments) suspender; **"~d"** (Comm) "fora de linha"
discotheque ['dıskəutɛk] N discoteca
discount [n 'dıskaunt, vt dıs'kaunt] N desconto ▶ VT descontar; (idea) ignorar

discourage [dıs'kʌrıdʒ] VT (dishearten) desanimar; (advise against): **to ~ sth/sb from doing** desaconselhar algo/alguém a fazer
discover [dıs'kʌvər] VT descobrir; (missing person) encontrar; (mistake) achar; **discovery** N descoberta
discredit [dıs'krɛdıt] VT desacreditar; (claim) desmerecer
discreet [dı'skri:t] ADJ discreto; (careful) cauteloso
discrepancy [dı'skrɛpənsı] N diferença
discretion [dı'skrɛʃən] N discrição f; **at the ~ of** ao arbítrio de
discriminate [dı'skrımıneıt] VI: **to ~ between** fazer distinção entre; **to ~ against** discriminar contra; **discrimination** [dıskrımı'neıʃən] N (discernment) discernimento; (bias) discriminação f
discuss [dı'skʌs] VT discutir; (analyse) analisar; **discussion** N discussão f; (debate) debate m
disease [dı'zi:z] N doença
disembark [dısım'bɑ:k] VT, VI desembarcar
disgrace [dıs'greıs] N ignomínia; (shame) desonra ▶ VT (family) envergonhar; (name, country) desonrar; **disgraceful** ADJ vergonhoso; (behaviour) escandaloso
disgruntled [dıs'grʌntld] ADJ descontente
disguise [dıs'gaız] N disfarce m ▶ VT: **to ~ o.s. (as)** disfarçar-se (de); **in ~** disfarçado
disgust [dıs'gʌst] N repugnância ▶ VT repugnar a, dar nojo em; **disgusting** ADJ repugnante; (unacceptable) inaceitável
dish [dıʃ] N prato; (serving dish) travessa; **to do** or **wash the ~es** lavar os pratos or a louça; **dish out** VT repartir; **dish up** VT servir; **dishcloth** N pano de prato or de louça
dishonest [dıs'ɔnıst] ADJ (person) desonesto; (means) fraudulento
dishwasher ['dıʃwɔʃər] N máquina de lavar louça or pratos
disillusion [dısı'lu:ʒən] VT desiludir
disinfectant [dısın'fɛktənt] N desinfetante m
disintegrate [dıs'ıntıgreıt] VI desintegrar-se
disk [dısk] N (Comput) disco; (removable) disquete m; **disk drive** N unidade f de disco; **diskette** [dıs'kɛt] (US) N (Comput) disquete m

dislike [dɪs'laɪk] N desagrado ▶ VT
antipatizar com, não gostar de

dislocate ['dɪsləkeɪt] VT deslocar

disloyal [dɪs'lɔɪəl] ADJ desleal

dismal ['dɪzml] ADJ (depressing)
deprimente; (very bad) horrível

dismantle [dɪs'mæntl] VT desmontar,
desmantelar

dismay [dɪs'meɪ] N consternação f ▶ VT
consternar

dismiss [dɪs'mɪs] VT (worker) despedir;
(pupils) dispensar; (soldiers) dar baixa a;
(Jur, possibility) rejeitar; **dismissal** N
demissão f

disobedient [dɪsə'biːdɪənt] ADJ
desobediente

disobey [dɪsə'beɪ] VT desobedecer a;
(rules) transgredir

disorder [dɪs'ɔːdəʳ] N desordem f; (rioting)
distúrbios mpl, tumulto; (Med) distúrbio

disown [dɪs'əun] VT repudiar; (child)
rejeitar

dispatch [dɪs'pætʃ] VT (send: parcel etc)
expedir; (: messenger) enviar ▶ N (sending)
remessa; (Press) comunicado; (Mil) parte f

dispel [dɪs'pɛl] VT dissipar

dispense [dɪs'pɛns] VT (medicine)
preparar (e vender); **dispense with** VT
FUS prescindir de; **dispenser** N (device)
distribuidor m automático

disperse [dɪs'pəːs] VT espalhar; (crowd)
dispersar ▶ VI dispersar-se

display [dɪs'pleɪ] N (in shop) mostra;
(exhibition) exposição f; (Comput:
information) apresentação f visual;
(: device) display m; (of feeling)
manifestação f ▶ VT mostrar;
(ostentatiously) ostentar

displease [dɪs'pliːz] VT (offend) ofender;
(annoy) aborrecer

disposable [dɪs'pəuzəbl] ADJ
descartável; (income) disponível

disposal [dɪs'pəuzl] N (of rubbish)
destruição f; (of property etc) venda,
traspasse m; **at sb's ~** à disposição de
alguém; **disposition** [dɪspə'zɪʃən] N
disposição f; (temperament) índole f

dispute [dɪs'pjuːt] N (domestic) briga;
(also: **industrial ~**) conflito, disputa
▶ VT disputar; (question) questionar

disqualify [dɪs'kwɔlɪfaɪ] VT (Sport)
desclassificar; **to ~ sb for sth/from
doing sth** desqualificar alguém para
algo/de fazer algo

disregard [dɪsrɪ'gɑːd] VT ignorar

disrupt [dɪs'rʌpt] VT (plans) desfazer;
(conversation, proceedings) perturbar,
interromper

dissect [dɪ'sɛkt] VT dissecar

dissent [dɪ'sɛnt] N dissensão f

dissertation [dɪsə'teɪʃən] N (also: Sch)
dissertação f, tese f

dissolve [dɪ'zɔlv] VT dissolver ▶ VI
dissolver-se; **to ~ in(to) tears**
debulhar-se em lágrimas

distance ['dɪstəns] N distância; **in the ~**
ao longe

distant ['dɪstənt] ADJ distante; (manner)
afastado, reservado

distil [dɪs'tɪl], (US) **distill** VT destilar;
distillery N destilaria

distinct [dɪs'tɪŋkt] ADJ distinto; (clear)
claro; (unmistakable) nítido; **as ~ from**
em oposição a; **distinction** N diferença;
(honour) honra; (in exam) distinção f

distinguish [dɪs'tɪŋgwɪʃ] VT
(differentiate) diferenciar; (identify)
identificar; **to ~ o.s.** distinguir-se;
distinguished ADJ (eminent) eminente;
(in appearance) distinto

distort [dɪs'tɔːt] VT distorcer

distract [dɪs'trækt] VT distrair;
(attention) desviar; **distracted** ADJ
distraído; (anxious) aturdido;
distraction N distração f; (confusion)
aturdimento, perplexidade f;
(amusement) divertimento

distraught [dɪs'trɔːt] ADJ desesperado

distress [dɪs'trɛs] N angústia ▶ VT afligir;
distressing ADJ angustiante

distribute [dɪs'trɪbjuːt] VT distribuir;
(share out) repartir, dividir; **distribution**
[dɪstrɪ'bjuːʃən] N distribuição f; (of profits
etc) repartição f; **distributor** N (Aut)
distribuidor m; (Comm) distribuidor(a) m/f

district ['dɪstrɪkt] N (of country) região f;
(of town) zona; (Admin) distrito; **district
attorney** (US) N promotor(a) m/f
público(-a)

distrust [dɪs'trʌst] N desconfiança ▶ VT
desconfiar de

disturb [dɪs'təːb] VT (disorganize)
perturbar; (upset) incomodar; (interrupt)
atrapalhar; **disturbance** N (upheaval)
convulsão f; (political, violent) distúrbio;
(of mind) transtorno; **disturbed** ADJ
perturbado; (child) infeliz; **to be
emotionally disturbed** ter problemas
emocionais; **disturbing** ADJ
perturbador(a)

ditch [dɪtʃ] N fosso; (irrigation ditch) rego
▶ VT (inf: partner) abandonar; (: car, plan
etc) desfazer-se de

ditto ['dɪtəu] ADV idem

dive [daɪv] N (from board) salto; (underwater,
of submarine) mergulho ▶ VI mergulhar;

to ~ into (*bag, drawer etc*) enfiar a mão em; (*shop, car etc*) enfiar-se em; **diver** N mergulhador(a) *m/f*

diversion [daɪ'vəːʃən] N (*BRIT Aut*) desvio; (*distraction, Mil*) diversão *f*; (*of funds*) desvio

divert [daɪ'vəːt] VT desviar

divide [dɪ'vaɪd] VT (*Math*) dividir; (*separate*) separar; (*share out*) repartir ▶ VI dividir-se; (*road*) bifurcar-se; **divided highway** (US) N pista dupla

divine [dɪ'vaɪn] ADJ (*also fig*) divino

diving ['daɪvɪŋ] N salto; (*underwater*) mergulho; **diving board** N trampolim *m*

division [dɪ'vɪʒən] N divisão *f*; (*sharing out*) repartição *f*; (*disagreement*) discórdia; (*Football*) grupo

divorce [dɪ'vɔːs] N divórcio ▶ VT divorciar-se de; (*dissociate*) dissociar; **divorced** ADJ divorciado; **divorcee** N divorciado(-a)

DIY N ABBR = **do-it-yourself**

dizzy ['dɪzɪ] ADJ tonto

DJ N ABBR = **disc jockey**

do [duː] (*pt* **did**, *pp* **done**) AUX VB **1** (*in negative constructions*): **I don't understand** eu não compreendo **2** (*to form questions*): **didn't you know?** você não sabia?; **what do you think?** o que você acha? **3** (*for emphasis, in polite expressions*): **she does seem rather late** ela está muito atrasada; **do sit down/help yourself** sente-se/sirva-se; **do take care!** tome cuidado! **4** (*used to avoid repeating vb*): **she swims better than I do** ela nada melhor que eu; **do you agree? — yes, I do/no, I don't** você concorda? — sim, concordo/ não, não concordo; **she lives in Glasgow — so do I** ela mora em Glasgow — eu também; **who broke it? — I did** quem quebrou isso? — (fui) eu **5** (*in question tags*): **you like him, don't you?** você gosta dele, não é?; **he laughed, didn't he?** ele riu, não foi? ▶ VT **1** (*gen: carry out, perform etc*) fazer; **what are you doing tonight?** o que você vai fazer hoje à noite?; **to do the washing-up/cooking** lavar a louça/ cozinhar; **to do one's teeth/nails** escovar os dentes/fazer as unhas; **to do one's hair** (*comb*) pentear-se; (*style*) fazer um penteado; **we're doing Othello at school** (*studying*) nós estamos

estudando Otelo na escola; (*performing*) nós vamos encenar Otelo na escola **2** (*Aut etc*): **the car was doing 190** o carro andava a 190 por hora; **we've done 200 km already** já percorremos 200 km; **he can do 190 km/h in that car** ele consegue chegar a 190 km/h naquele carro ▶ VI **1** (*act, behave*) fazer; **do as I do** faça como eu faço **2** (*get on, fare*) ir; **how do you do?** como você está indo? **3** (*suit*) servir; **will it do?** serve? **4** (*be sufficient*) bastar; **will £10 do?** £10 dá?; **that'll do** é suficiente; **that'll do!** (*in annoyance*) basta!, chega!; **to make do (with)** contentar-se (com) ▶ N (*inf: party etc*) festa; **it was rather a do** foi uma festança

do away with VT FUS (*kill*) matar; (*law etc*) abolir; (*withdraw*) retirar

do up VT (*laces*) atar; (*zip*) fechar; (*dress, skirt*) abotoar; (*renovate, room, house*) arrumar, renovar

do with VT FUS (*be connected*) ter a ver com; (*need*): **I could do with a drink/ some help** eu bem que gostaria de tomar alguma coisa/eu bem que precisaria de uma ajuda; **what has it got to do with you?** o que é que isso tem a ver com você?

do without VI: **if you're late for tea then you'll do without** se você chegar atrasado ficará sem almoço ▶ VT FUS passar sem

dock [dɔk] N (*Naut*) doca; (*Jur*) banco (dos réus) ▶ VI (*Naut: enter dock*) atracar; (*Space*) unir-se no espaço; **docks** NPL docas *fpl*

doctor ['dɔktər] N médico(-a); (*PhD etc*) doutor(a) *m/f* ▶ VT (*drink etc*) falsificar

document ['dɔkjumənt] N documento; **documentary** [dɔkju'mɛntərɪ] ADJ documental ▶ N documentário

dodge [dɔdʒ] N (*trick*) trapaça ▶ VT esquivar-se de, evitar; (*tax*) sonegar; (*blow*) furtar-se a

does [dʌz] VB *see* **do**

doesn't ['dʌznt] = **does not**

dog [dɔg] N cachorro, cão *m* ▶ VT (*subj: person*) seguir; (: *bad luck*) perseguir; **doggy bag** ['dɔgɪ-] N quentinha

do-it-yourself N sistema *m* faça-você-mesmo

dole [dəul] (*BRIT*) N (*payment*) subsídio de desemprego; **on the ~** desempregado; **dole out** VT distribuir

doll [dɔl] N boneca; (*us inf: woman*) gatinha

dollar ['dɔləʳ] N dólar *m*

dolphin ['dɔlfɪn] N golfinho

dome [dəʊm] N (*Arch*) cúpula

domestic [də'mɛstɪk] ADJ doméstico; (*national*) nacional

dominate ['dɔmɪneɪt] VT dominar

domino ['dɔmɪnəʊ] (*pl* **dominoes**) N peça de dominó; **dominoes** N (*game*) dominó *m*

donate [də'neɪt] VT doar

done [dʌn] PP *of* **do**

donkey ['dɔŋkɪ] N burro

donor ['dəʊnəʳ] N doador(a) *m/f*; **donor card** N cartão *m* de doador

don't [dəʊnt] = **do not**

doodle ['du:dl] VI rabiscar

doom [du:m] N (*fate*) destino ▶ VT: **to be ~ed to failure** estar destinado *or* fadado ao fracasso

door [dɔːʳ] N porta; **doorbell** N campainha; **doorstep** N degrau *m* da porta, soleira; **doorway** N vão *m* da porta, entrada

dope [dəʊp] N (*inf: person*) imbecil *m/f*; (*: drugs*) maconha ▶ VT (*horse etc*) dopar

dormitory ['dɔːmɪtrɪ] N dormitório; (*us*) residência universitária

dose [dəʊs] N dose *f*

dot [dɔt] N ponto; (*speck*) pontinho ▶ VT: **~ted with** salpicado de; **on the ~** em ponto

dotcom [dɔt'kɔm] N empresa pontocom

double ['dʌbl] ADJ duplo ▶ ADV (*twice*): **to cost ~ (sth)** custar o dobro (de algo) ▶ N (*person*) duplo(-a) ▶ VT dobrar ▶ VI dobrar; **at the ~** (*BRIT*), **on the ~** em passo acelerado; **double bass** N contrabaixo; **double bed** N cama de casal; **double-click** VI (*Comput*) clicar duas vezes; **double-decker** [dʌbl'dɛkəʳ] N ônibus *m* (*BR*) *or* autocarro (*PT*) de dois andares; **double room** N quarto de casal

doubt [daut] N dúvida ▶ VT duvidar; (*suspect*) desconfiar de; **to ~ that ...** duvidar que ...; **doubtful** ADJ duvidoso; **doubtless** ADV sem dúvida

dough [dəʊ] N massa; **doughnut**, (*us*) **donut** N sonho (*BR*), bola de Berlim (*PT*)

dove [dʌv] N pomba

down [daun] N (*feathers*) penugem *f* ▶ ADV (*downwards*) para baixo; (*on the ground*) por terra ▶ PREP por, abaixo ▶ VT (*inf: drink*) tomar de um gole só; **~ with X!** abaixo X!; **down-and-out** N (*tramp*) vagabundo(-a); **downfall** N queda,

ruína; **downhill** ADV para baixo ▶ N (*Ski: also:* **downhill race**) descida; **to go downhill** descer, ir morro abaixo; (*fig: business*) degringolar

Downing Street ['daunɪŋ-] (*BRIT*) N *ver nota*

> **Downing Street** é a rua de Westminster (Londres) onde estão localizadas as residências oficiais do Primeiro-ministro (número 10) e do Ministro da Fazenda (número 11). O termo **Downing Street** é frequentemente utilizado para designar o governo britânico.

down: download ['daunləud] VT (*Comput*) baixar, fazer o download de; **downloadable** ADJ (*Comput*) baixável; **downright** ['daunraɪt] ADJ (*lie*) patente; (*refusal*) categórico

Down's syndrome [daunz-] N síndrome *f* de Down

down: downstairs ADV (*below*) lá em baixo; (*direction*) para baixo; **down-to-earth** ADJ prático, realista; **downtown** ADV no centro da cidade; **down under** ADV na Austrália (*or* Nova Zelândia); **downward** ['daunwəd] ADJ, ADV para baixo; **downwards** ADV = **downward**

doze [dəuz] VI dormitar; **doze off** VI cochilar

dozen ['dʌzn] N dúzia; **a ~ books** uma dúzia de livros; **~s of times** milhares de vezes

drab [dræb] ADJ sombrio

draft [drɑːft] N (*first copy*) rascunho; (*Pol: of bill*) projeto de lei; (*bank draft*) saque *m*, letra; (*us: call-up*) recrutamento ▶ VT (*plan*) esboçar; (*speech, letter*) rascunhar; *see also* **draught**

drag [dræg] VT arrastar; (*river*) dragar ▶ VI arrastar-se ▶ N (*inf*) chatice *f* (*BR*), maçada (*PT*); (*women's clothing*): **in ~** em travesti; **drag on** VI arrastar-se

dragon ['drægən] N dragão *m*

dragonfly ['drægənflaɪ] N libélula

drain [dreɪn] N bueiro; (*source of loss*) sorvedouro ▶ VT drenar; (*vegetables*) coar ▶ VI (*water*) escorrer, escoar-se; **drainage** N (*act*) drenagem *f*; (*system*) esgoto; **drainpipe** N cano de esgoto

drama ['drɑːmə] N (*art*) teatro; (*play, event*) drama *m*; **dramatic** [drə'mætɪk] ADJ dramático; (*theatrical*) teatral

drank [dræŋk] PT *of* **drink**

drape [dreɪp] VT ornar, cobrir

drastic ['dræstɪk] ADJ drástico

draught [drɑːft], (*us*) **draft** N (*of air*) corrente *f*; (*Naut*) calado; (*beer*) chope *m*;

on ~ (*beer*) de barril; **draughts** (BRIT) N (jogo de) damas *fpl*

draw [drɔ:] (*pt* **drew**, *pp* **drawn**) VT desenhar; (*cart*) puxar; (*curtain*) fechar; (*gun*) sacar; (*attract*) atrair; (*money*) tirar; (: *from bank*) sacar ▶ VI empatar ▶ N empate *m*; (*lottery*) sorteio; **to ~ near** aproximar-se; **draw out** VT (*money*) sacar; **draw up** VI (*stop*) parar(-se) ▶ VT (*chair etc*) puxar; (*document*) redigir; **drawback** N inconveniente *m*, desvantagem *f*; **drawer** [drɔ:ʳ] N gaveta; **drawing** N desenho; **drawing pin** (BRIT) N tachinha (BR), pionés *m* (PT); **drawing room** N sala de visitas

drawn [drɔ:n] PP *of* **draw**

dread [drɛd] N medo, pavor *m* ▶ VT temer, recear, ter medo de; **dreadful** ADJ terrível

dream [dri:m] (*pt*, *pp* **dreamed** *or* **dreamt**) N sonho ▶ VT, VI sonhar

dreary ['drɪərɪ] ADJ (*talk, time*) monótono; (*weather*) sombrio

drench [drɛntʃ] VT encharcar

dress [drɛs] N vestido; (*no pl: clothing*) traje *m* ▶ VT vestir; (*wound*) fazer curativo em ▶ VI vestir-se; **to get ~ed** vestir-se; **dress up** VI vestir-se com elegância; (*in fancy dress*) fantasiar-se; **dress circle** (BRIT) N balcão *m* nobre; **dresser** N (BRIT: *cupboard*) aparador *m*; (US: *chest of drawers*) cômoda de espelho; **dressing** N (*Med*) curativo; (*Culin*) molho; **dressing gown** (BRIT) N roupão *m*; (*woman's*) peignoir *m*; **dressing room** N (*Theatre*) camarim *m*; (*Sport*) vestiário; **dressing table** N penteadeira (BR), toucador *m* (PT); **dressmaker** N costureiro(-a)

drew [dru:] PT *of* **draw**

dribble ['drɪbl] VI (*baby*) babar ▶ VT (*ball*) driblar

dried [draɪd] ADJ seco; (*eggs, milk*) em pó

drier ['draɪəʳ] N = **dryer**

drift [drɪft] N (*of current etc*) força; (*of snow, sand etc*) monte *m*; (*meaning*) sentido ▶ VI (*boat*) derivar; (*sand, snow*) amontoar-se

drill [drɪl] N furadeira; (*bit, of dentist*) broca; (*for mining etc*) broca, furadeira; (*Mil*) exercícios *mpl* militares ▶ VT furar, brocar; (*Mil*) exercitar ▶ VI (*for oil*) perfurar

drink [drɪŋk] (*pt* **drank**, *pp* **drunk**) N bebida ▶ VT, VI beber; **a ~ of water** um copo d'água; **drinker** N bebedor(a) *m/f*; **drinking water** N água potável

drip [drɪp] N gotejar *m*; (*one drop*) gota, pingo; (*Med*) gota a gota *m* ▶ VI gotejar, pingar

drive [draɪv] (*pt* **drove**, *pp* **driven**) N passeio (de automóvel); (*journey*) trajeto, percurso; (*also:* **~way**) entrada; (*energy*) energia, vigor *m*; (*campaign*) campanha; (*Comput*) drive *m* ▶ VT (*car*) dirigir (BR), guiar (PT); (*push*) empurrar; (*Tech: motor*) acionar; (*nail*): **to ~ sth into** cravar algo em ▶ VI (*Aut: at controls*) dirigir (BR), guiar (PT); (: *travel*) ir de carro; **left-/ right-hand ~** direção à esquerda/ direita; **to ~ sb mad** deixar alguém louco

driver ['draɪvəʳ] N motorista *m/f*; (*Rail*) maquinista *m*; **driver's license** (US) N carteira de motorista (BR), carta de condução (PT)

driveway ['draɪvweɪ] N entrada

driving ['draɪvɪŋ] N direção *f* (BR), condução *f* (PT); **driving instructor** N instrutor(a) *m/f* de autoescola (BR) *or* de condução (PT); **driving licence** (BRIT) N carteira de motorista (BR), carta de condução (PT); **driving test** N exame *m* de motorista

drizzle ['drɪzl] N chuvisco

droop [dru:p] VI pender

drop [drɔp] N (*of water*) gota; (*lessening*) diminuição *f*; (*fall: distance*) declive *m* ▶ VT (*allow to fall*) deixar cair; (*voice, eyes, price*) baixar; (*set down from car*) deixar (saltar/descer); (*omit*) omitir ▶ VI cair; (*wind*) parar; **drops** NPL (*Med*) gotas *fpl*; **drop off** VI (*sleep*) cochilar ▶ VT (*passenger*) deixar; **drop out** VI (*withdraw*) retirar-se; **drop-out** N pessoa que abandona o trabalho, os estudos etc

drought [draut] N seca

drove [drəuv] PT *of* **drive**

drown [draun] VT afogar; (*also:* **~ out**: *sound*) encobrir ▶ VI afogar-se

drowsy ['drauzɪ] ADJ sonolento

drug [drʌg] N remédio, medicamento; (*narcotic*) droga ▶ VT drogar; **to be on ~s** (*an addict*) estar viciado em drogas; (*Med*) estar sob medicação; **drug addict** N toxicômano(-a); **druggist** (US) N farmacêutico(-a); **drugstore** (US) N drogaria

drum [drʌm] N tambor *m*; (*for oil, petrol*) tambor, barril *m*; **drums** NPL (*kit*) bateria; **drummer** N baterista *m/f*

drunk [drʌŋk] PP *of* **drink** ▶ ADJ bêbado ▶ N (*also:* **~ard**) bêbado(-a); **drunken** ADJ (*laughter*) de bêbado; (*party*) com muita bebida; (*person*) bêbado

dry [draɪ] ADJ seco; (*day*) sem chuva; (*humour*) irônico ▶ VT secar, enxugar; (*tears*) limpar ▶ VI secar; **dry up** VI secar

completamente; **dry-cleaner's** N
tinturaria; **dryer** N secador *m*; (*also:*
spin-dryer) secadora

DSS (BRIT) N ABBR (= *Department of Social Security*) ≈ INAMPS *m*

DTP N ABBR (= *desktop publishing*) DTP *m*

dual ['djuəl] ADJ dual, duplo; **dual carriageway** (BRIT) N pista dupla

dubious ['dju:bɪəs] ADJ duvidoso;
(*reputation, company*) suspeitoso

duck [dʌk] N pato ▸ VI abaixar-se
repentinamente

due [dju:] ADJ (*proper*) devido; (*expected*)
esperado ▸ N: **to give sb his** (*or* **her**) ~
ser justo com alguém ▸ ADV: ~ **north**
exatamente ao norte; **dues** NPL (*for club,
union*) quota; (*in harbour*) direitos *mpl*; **in
~ course** no devido tempo; (*eventually*)
no final; ~ **to** devido a

duet [dju:'ɛt] N dueto

dug [dʌg] PT, PP *of* **dig**

duke [dju:k] N duque *m*

dull [dʌl] ADJ (*light*) sombrio; (*intelligence,
wit*) lento; (*boring*) enfadonho; (*sound,
pain*) surdo; (*weather, day*) nublado,
carregado ▸ VT (*pain, grief*) aliviar; (*mind,
senses*) entorpecer

dumb [dʌm] ADJ (*stupid*) estúpido

dummy ['dʌmɪ] N (*tailor's model*)
manequim *m*; (*mock-up*) modelo; (BRIT:
for baby) chupeta ▸ ADJ falso

dump [dʌmp] N (*also:* **rubbish ~**)
depósito de lixo; (*inf: place*) chiqueiro
▸ VT (*put down*) depositar, descarregar;
(*get rid of*) desfazer-se de

dumpling ['dʌmplɪŋ] N bolinho cozido

dungarees [dʌŋgə'ri:z] NPL macacão *m*
(BR), fato macaco (PT)

dungeon ['dʌndʒən] N calabouço

duplex ['dju:plɛks] (US) N casa
geminada; (*also:* ~ **apartment**) duplex *m*

duplicate [*n* 'dju:plɪkət, *vt* 'dju:plɪkeɪt]
N (*of document*) duplicata; (*of key*) cópia
▸ VT duplicar; (*photocopy*) multigrafar;
(*repeat*) reproduzir

durable ['djuərəbl] ADJ durável; (*clothes,
metal*) resistente

during ['djuərɪŋ] PREP durante

dusk [dʌsk] N crepúsculo, anoitecer *m*

dust [dʌst] N pó *m*, poeira ▸ VT (*furniture*)
tirar o pó de; (*cake etc*): **to ~ with**
polvilhar com; **dustbin** N (BRIT) lata de
lixo; **duster** N pano de pó; **dustman**
(BRIT) *irreg* N lixeiro, gari *m* (BR *inf*); **dusty**
ADJ empoeirado

Dutch [dʌtʃ] ADJ holandês(-esa) ▸ N (*Ling*)
holandês *m* ▸ ADV: **let's go ~** (*inf*) cada
um paga o seu, vamos rachar; **the**

Dutch NPL (*people*) os holandeses;
Dutchman *irreg* N holandês *m*;
Dutchwoman *irreg* N holandesa

duty ['dju:tɪ] N dever *m*; (*tax*) taxa; **on ~**
de serviço; **off ~** de folga; **duty-free** ADJ
livre de impostos

duvet ['du:veɪ] (BRIT) N edredom *m* (BR),
edredão *m* (PT)

DVD N ABBR (= *digital versatile* or *video disc*)
DVD *m*; **DVD burner** N gravador *m* de
DVD; **DVD player** N DVD player *m*; **DVD
writer** N gravador *m* de DVD

dwarf [dwɔ:f] (*pl* **dwarves**) N (*pej*) anão/
anã *m/f* ▸ VT ananicar

dwindle ['dwɪndl] VI diminuir

dye [daɪ] N tintura, tinta ▸ VT tingir

dynamite ['daɪnəmaɪt] N dinamite *f*

dyslexia [dɪs'lɛksɪə] N dislexia

e

E [iː] N (*Mus*) mi *m*

each [iːtʃ] ADJ cada *inv* ▶ PRON cada um(a); **~ other** um ao outro; **they hate ~ other** (eles) se odeiam

eager ['iːgəʳ] ADJ ávido; **to be ~ to do sth** ansiar por fazer algo; **to be ~ for** ansiar por

eagle ['iːgl] N águia

ear [ɪəʳ] N (*external*) orelha; (*inner, fig*) ouvido; (*of corn*) espiga; **earache** N dor *f* de ouvidos; **eardrum** N tímpano

earl [əːl] N conde *m*

earlier ['əːlɪəʳ] ADJ mais adiantado; (*edition etc*) anterior ▶ ADV mais cedo

early ['əːlɪ] ADV cedo; (*before time*) com antecedência ▶ ADJ (*sooner than expected*) prematuro; (*reply*) pronto; (*Christians, settlers*) primeiro; (*man*) primitivo; (*life, work*) juvenil; **in the ~ or ~ in the spring/19th century** no princípio da primavera/do século dezenove

earmark ['ɪəmɑːk] VT: **to ~ sth for** reservar *or* destinar algo para

earn [əːn] VT ganhar; (*Comm: interest*) render; (*praise, reward*) merecer

earnest ['əːnɪst] ADJ (*wish*) intenso; (*manner*) sério; **in ~** a sério

earnings ['əːnɪŋz] NPL (*personal*) vencimentos *mpl*, salário, ordenado; (*of company*) lucro

earphones NPL fones *mpl* de ouvido

earring N brinco

earth [əːθ] N terra; (*BRIT Elec*) fio terra ▶ VT (*BRIT Elec*) ligar à terra; **earthquake** N terremoto (*BR*), terramoto (*PT*)

ease [iːz] N facilidade *f*; (*relaxed state*) sossego ▶ VT facilitar; (*pain, tension*) aliviar; (*help pass*): **to ~ sth in/out** meter/tirar algo com cuidado; **at ~!** (*Mil*) descansar!; **ease off** VI acalmar-se;

(*wind*) baixar; (*rain*) moderar-se; **ease up** VI = **ease off**

easily ['iːzɪlɪ] ADV facilmente, fácil (*inf*)

east [iːst] N leste *m* ▶ ADJ (*region*) leste; (*wind*) do leste ▶ ADV para o leste; **the E~** o Oriente; (*Pol*) o leste

Easter ['iːstəʳ] N Páscoa; **Easter egg** N ovo de Páscoa

eastern ['iːstən] ADJ do leste, oriental

easy ['iːzɪ] ADJ fácil; (*comfortable*) folgado, cômodo; (*relaxed*) natural, complacente; (*victim, prey*) desprotegido ▶ ADV: **to take it** *or* **things ~** (*not worry*) levar as coisas com calma; (*go slowly*) ir devagar; (*rest*) descansar; **easy-going** ADJ pacato, fácil

eat [iːt] (*pt* **ate**, *pp* **eaten**) VT, VI comer; **eat away** VT corroer; **eat away at** VT FUS corroer; **eat into** VT FUS = **eat away at**

eavesdrop ['iːvzdrɔp] VI: **to ~ (on)** escutar às escondidas

Ebola virus [iˈbəʊlə vaɪərəs] N ebola vírus *m* (*BR*), vírus *m* ébola (*PT*)

e-book ['iːbuk] N livro eletrônico

e-card ['iːkɑːd] N cartão *m* eletrônico

eccentric [ɪkˈsɛntrɪk] ADJ, N excêntrico(-a)

echo ['ɛkəʊ] (*pl* **echoes**) N eco ▶ VT ecoar, repetir ▶ VI ressoar, repetir

e-cigarette [iːsɪgəˈrɛt] N cigarro eletrônico

eclipse [ɪˈklɪps] N eclipse *m*

eco-friendly [iːkəʊˈfrɛndlɪ] ADJ ecológico

ecological [iːkəˈlɔdʒɪkəl] ADJ ecológico

ecology [ɪˈkɔlədʒɪ] N ecologia

e-commerce N ABBR (= *electronic commerce*) comércio eletrônico

economic [iːkəˈnɔmɪk] ADJ econômico; (*business etc*) rentável; **economical** ADJ econômico; **economics** N economia ▶ NPL aspectos *mpl* econômicos

economize [ɪˈkɔnəmaɪz] VI economizar, fazer economias

economy [ɪˈkɔnəmɪ] N economia; **economy class** N (*Aviat*) classe *f* econômica

ecstasy [ˈɛkstəsɪ] N êxtase *m*; **ecstatic** [ɛksˈtætɪk] ADJ extasiado

eczema [ˈɛksɪmə] N eczema *m*

edge [ɛdʒ] N (*of knife etc*) fio; (*of table, chair etc*) borda; (*of lake etc*) margem *f* ▶ VT (*trim*) embainhar; **on ~** (*fig*) = **edgy**; **to ~ away from** afastar-se pouco a pouco de; **edgy** ADJ nervoso, inquieto

edible [ˈɛdɪbl] ADJ comestível

Edinburgh [ˈɛdɪnbərə] N Edimburgo

edit ['ɛdɪt] vt (be editor of) dirigir; (cut) cortar, redigir; (Comput, TV) editar; (Cinema) montar; **edition** [ɪ'dɪʃən] N edição f; **editor** N redator(a) m/f; (of newspaper) diretor(a) m/f; **editorial** [ɛdɪ'tɔ:rɪəl] ADJ editorial

educate ['ɛdjukeɪt] vt educar

education [ɛdju'keɪʃən] N educação f; (schooling) ensino; (science) pedagogia; **educational** ADJ (policy, experience) educacional; (toy etc) educativo

eel [i:l] N enguia

eerie ['ɪərɪ] ADJ (strange) estranho; (mysterious) misterioso

effect [ɪ'fɛkt] N efeito ▶ vt (repairs) fazer; (savings) efetuar; **to take ~** (law) entrar em vigor; (drug) fazer efeito; **in ~** na realidade; **effective** [ɪ'fɛktɪv] ADJ eficaz; (actual) efetivo

efficiency [ɪ'fɪʃənsɪ] N eficiência

efficient [ɪ'fɪʃənt] ADJ eficiente; (machine) rentável

effort ['ɛfət] N esforço; **effortless** ADJ fácil

e.g. ADV ABBR (= exempli gratia) p. ex.

egg [ɛg] N ovo; **hard-boiled/soft-boiled ~** ovo duro/mole; **egg on** vt incitar; **eggcup** N oveiro; **eggplant** (esp US) N beringela; **eggshell** N casca de ovo

ego ['i:gəu] N ego

Egypt ['i:dʒɪpt] N Egito; **Egyptian** [ɪ'dʒɪpʃən] ADJ, N egípcio(-a)

eight [eɪt] NUM oito; **eighteen** ['eɪ'ti:n] NUM dezoito; **eighteenth** NUM décimo oitavo; **eighth** [eɪtθ] NUM oitavo; **eightieth** ['eɪtɪɪθ] NUM octogésimo; **eighty** ['eɪtɪ] NUM oitenta

Eire ['ɛərə] N (República da) Irlanda

either ['aɪðə'] ADJ (one or other) um ou outro; (each) cada; (both) ambos ▶ PRON: **~ (of them)** qualquer (dos dois) ▶ ADV: **no, I don't ~** eu também não ▶ CONJ: **~ yes or no** ou sim ou não

eject [ɪ'dʒɛkt] vt expulsar

elaborate [adj ɪ'læbərɪt, vt, vi ɪ'læbəreɪt] ADJ complicado ▶ vt (expand) expandir; (refine) aperfeiçoar ▶ vi: **to ~ on** acrescentar detalhes a

elastic [ɪ'læstɪk] ADJ elástico; (adaptable) flexível, adaptável ▶ N elástico; **elastic band** (BRIT) N elástico

elbow ['ɛlbəu] N cotovelo

elder ['ɛldə'] ADJ mais velho ▶ N (tree) sabugueiro; (person) o/a mais velho(-a); **elderly** ADJ idoso, de idade; **~ people** as pessoas de idade, os idosos

eldest ['ɛldɪst] ADJ mais velho ▶ N o/a mais velho(-a)

elect [ɪ'lɛkt] vt eleger ▶ ADJ: **the president ~** o presidente eleito; **to ~ to do** (choose) optar por fazer; **election** N (voting) votação f; (installation) eleição f; **electorate** N eleitorado

electric [ɪ'lɛktrɪk] ADJ elétrico; **electrical** ADJ elétrico; **electric fire** N aquecedor m elétrico

electrician [ɪlɛk'trɪʃən] N eletricista m/f

electricity [ɪlɛk'trɪsɪtɪ] N eletricidade f

electrify [ɪ'lɛktrɪfaɪ] vt (fence, Rail) eletrificar; (audience) eletrizar

electronic [ɪlɛk'trɔnɪk] ADJ eletrônico; **electronic mail** N correio eletrônico; **electronics** N eletrônica

elegant ['ɛlɪgənt] ADJ (person, building) elegante; (idea) refinado

element ['ɛlɪmənt] N elemento; **elementary** [ɛlɪ'mɛntərɪ] ADJ (gen) elementar; (primitive) rudimentar; (school, education) primário; **elementary school** (US) N ver nota

▌ Nos Estados Unidos e no Canadá, uma **elementary school** (também chamada de grade school ou grammar school nos Estados Unidos) é uma escola pública onde os alunos passam de seis a oito dos primeiros anos escolares.

elephant ['ɛlɪfənt] N elefante m

elevator ['ɛlɪveɪtə'] (US) N elevador m

eleven [ɪ'lɛvn] NUM onze; **eleventh** NUM décimo-primeiro

eligible ['ɛlɪdʒəbl] ADJ elegível, apto; **to be ~ for sth** (job etc) ter qualificações para algo

elm [ɛlm] N olmo

eloquent ['ɛləkwənt] ADJ eloquente

El Salvador [ɛl'sælvədɔ:'] N El Salvador

else [ɛls] ADV outro, mais; **something ~** outra coisa; **nobody ~ spoke** ninguém mais falou; **elsewhere** ADV (be) em outro lugar (BR), noutro sítio (PT); (go) para outro lugar (BR), a outro sítio (PT)

elusive [ɪ'lu:sɪv] ADJ esquivo; (quality) indescritível

email ['i:meɪl] N e-mail m, correio eletrônico ▶ vt (person) enviar um e-mail a; **email account** N conta de e-mail, conta de correio eletrônico; **email address** N e-mail m, endereço eletrônico

embark [ɪm'bɑ:k] vi embarcar ▶ vt embarcar; **to ~ on** (fig) empreender, começar

embarrass [ɪm'bærəs] vt (politician) embaraçar; (emotionally) constranger; **embarrassed** ADJ desconfortável; **embarrassing** ADJ embaraçoso,

constrangedor(a); **embarrassment** N
embaraço, constrangimento

embassy ['ɛmbəsɪ] N embaixada

embrace [ɪm'breɪs] VT abraçar, dar um
abraço em; (include) abarcar, abranger
▶ VI abraçar-se ▶ N abraço

embroider [ɪm'brɔɪdə'] VT bordar;
embroidery N bordado

emerald ['ɛmərəld] N esmeralda

emerge [ɪ'mə:dʒ] VI sair; (from sleep)
acordar; (fact, idea) emergir

emergency [ɪ'mə:dʒənsɪ] N
emergência; **in an ~** em caso de
urgência; **emergency exit** N saída de
emergência; **emergency landing** N
aterrissagem f forçada (BR), aterragem f
forçosa (PT)

emigrate ['ɛmɪgreɪt] VI emigrar

eminent ['ɛmɪnənt] ADJ eminente

emit [ɪ'mɪt] VT (smoke) soltar; (smell)
exalar; (sound) produzir

emoji [ɪ'məudʒɪ] N (Comput) emoji m

emoticon ['ɪ'məutɪkən] N (Comput)
emoticon m

emotion [ɪ'məuʃən] N emoção f;
emotional ADJ (needs, exhaustion)
emocional; (person) sentimental,
emotivo; (scene) comovente; (tone)
emocionante

emperor ['ɛmpərə'] N imperador m

emphasis ['ɛmfəsɪs] (pl **emphases**) N
ênfase f

emphasize ['ɛmfəsaɪz] VT (word, point)
enfatizar, acentuar; (feature) salientar

empire ['ɛmpaɪə'] N império

employ [ɪm'plɔɪ] VT empregar; (tool)
utilizar; **employee** N empregado(-a);
employer N empregador(a) m/f,
patrão(-troa) m/f; **employment** N (gen)
emprego; (work) trabalho

empress ['ɛmprɪs] N imperatriz f

emptiness ['ɛmptɪnɪs] N vazio, vácuo

empty ['ɛmptɪ] ADJ vazio; (place)
deserto; (house) desocupado; (threat)
vão/vã ▶ N, VT esvaziar; (place) evacuar
▶ VI esvaziar-se; (place) ficar deserto;
empty-handed ADJ de mãos vazias

emulsion [ɪ'mʌlʃən] N emulsão f; (also:
~ paint) tinta plástica

enable [ɪ'neɪbl] VT: **to ~ sb to do sth**
(allow) permitir que alguém faça algo;
(prepare) capacitar alguém para fazer
algo

enamel [ɪ'næməl] N esmalte m

enclose [ɪn'kləuz] VT (land) cercar; (with
letter etc) anexar, enviar junto (PT);
please find ~d segue junto

enclosure [ɪn'kləuʒə'] N cercado

encore [ɔŋ'kɔ:'] EXCL bis!, outra! ▶ N bis m

encounter [ɪn'kauntə'] N encontro ▶ VT
encontrar, topar com; (difficulty)
enfrentar

encourage [ɪn'kʌrɪdʒ] VT (activity)
encorajar; (growth) estimular; (person):
to ~ sb to do sth animar alguém a fazer
algo; **encouragement** N estímulo

encrypt [ɪn'krɪpt] VT (Comput, Tel)
criptografar

encyclopaedia, encyclopedia
[ɛnsaɪkləu'pi:dɪə] N enciclopédia

end [ɛnd] N fim m; (of table, line, rope etc)
ponta; (of street, town) final m ▶ VT
acabar, terminar; (also: **bring to an ~,
put an ~ to**) acabar com, pôr fim a ▶ VI
terminar, acabar; **in the ~** ao fim, por
fim, finalmente; **on ~** na ponta; **to
stand on ~** (hair) arrepiar-se; **for hours
on ~** por horas a fio; **end up** VI: **to ~ up
in** terminar em; (place) ir parar em

endanger [ɪn'deɪndʒə'] VT pôr em perigo

endearing [ɪn'dɪərɪŋ] ADJ simpático,
atrativo

endeavour [ɪn'dɛvə'], (US) **endeavor** N
esforço; (attempt) tentativa ▶ VI: **to ~ to
do** esforçar-se para fazer; (try) tentar
fazer

ending ['ɛndɪŋ] N fim m, conclusão f; (of
book) desenlace m; (Ling) terminação f

endless ['ɛndlɪs] ADJ interminável;
(possibilities) infinito

endorse [ɪn'dɔ:s] VT (cheque) endossar;
(approve) aprovar; **endorsement** N (BRIT:
on driving licence) descrição f das multas;
(approval) aval m

endure [ɪn'djuə'] VT (bear) aguentar,
suportar ▶ VI (last) durar

enemy ['ɛnəmɪ] ADJ, N inimigo(-a)

energy ['ɛnədʒɪ] N energia; **energy
drink** N energético, bebida energética

enforce [ɪn'fɔ:s] VT (Jur) fazer cumprir

engage [ɪn'geɪdʒ] VT (attention) chamar;
(interest) atrair; (lawyer) contratar;
(clutch) engrenar ▶ VI engrenar; **to ~ in**
dedicar-se a, ocupar-se com; **to ~ sb in
conversation** travar conversa com
alguém; **engaged** ADJ (BRIT: phone)
ocupado (BR), impedido (PT); (: toilet)
ocupado; (betrothed) noivo; **to get
engaged** ficar noivo; **engaged tone**
(BRIT) N (Tel) sinal m de ocupado (BR) or de
impedido (PT); **engagement** N
encontro; (booking) contrato; (to marry)
noivado; **engagement ring** N aliança de
noivado

engine ['ɛndʒɪn] N (Aut) motor m; (Rail)
locomotiva

engineer [ɛndʒɪ'nɪəʳ] N engenheiro(-a); (US Rail) maquinista m/f; (BRIT: for repairs) técnico(-a); **engineering** N engenharia

England ['ɪŋɡlənd] N Inglaterra

English ['ɪŋɡlɪʃ] ADJ inglês(-esa) ▶ N (Ling) inglês m; **the English** NPL (people) os ingleses; **English Channel** N: **the English Channel** o Canal da Mancha

engraving [ɪn'ɡreɪvɪŋ] N gravura

enhance [ɪn'hɑ:ns] VT (gen) ressaltar, salientar; (beauty) realçar; (position) melhorar; (add to) aumentar

enjoy [ɪn'dʒɔɪ] VT gostar de; (health, privilege) desfrutar de; **to ~ o.s.** divertir-se; **enjoyable** ADJ agradável; **enjoyment** N prazer m

enlarge [ɪn'lɑ:dʒ] VT aumentar; (Phot) ampliar ▶ VI: **to ~ on** (subject) desenvolver, estender-se sobre

enlist [ɪn'lɪst] VT alistar; (support) conseguir, aliciar ▶ VI alistar-se

enormous [ɪ'nɔ:məs] ADJ enorme

enough [ɪ'nʌf] ADJ: **~ time/books** tempo suficiente/livros suficientes ▶ PRON: **have you got ~?** você tem o suficiente? ▶ ADV: **big ~** suficientemente grande; **~!** basta!, chega!; **that's ~, thanks** chega, obrigado; **I've had ~ of him** estou farto dele; **which, funnily** or **oddly ~ ...** o que, por estranho que pareça ...

enquire [ɪn'kwaɪəʳ] VT, VI = **inquire**

enrage [ɪn'reɪdʒ] VT enfurecer, enraivecer

enrol [ɪn'rəul], (US) **enroll** VT inscrever; (Sch) matricular ▶ VI inscrever-se; matricular-se; **enrolment** N inscrição f; (Sch) matrícula

ensure [ɪn'ʃuəʳ] VT assegurar

entail [ɪn'teɪl] VT implicar

enter ['ɛntəʳ] VT entrar em; (club) ficar or fazer-se sócio de; (army) alistar-se em; (competition) inscrever-se em; (sb for a competition) inscrever; (write down) completar; (Comput) digitar ▶ VI entrar; **enter for** VT FUS inscrever-se em; **enter into** VT FUS estabelecer; (plans) fazer parte de; (debate, negotiations) entrar em; (agreement) chegar a, firmar

enterprise ['ɛntəpraɪz] N empresa; (undertaking) empreendimento; (initiative) iniciativa; **enterprising** ADJ empreendedor(a)

entertain [ɛntə'teɪn] VT divertir, entreter; (guest) receber (em casa); (idea, plan) estudar; **entertainer** N artista m/f; **entertaining** ADJ divertido;

entertainment N (amusement) entretenimento, diversão f; (show) espetáculo

enthusiasm [ɪn'θu:zɪæzəm] N entusiasmo

enthusiast [ɪn'θu:zɪæst] N entusiasta m/f; **enthusiastic** [ɪnθu:zɪ'æstɪk] ADJ entusiasmado; **to be enthusiastic about** entusiasmar-se por

entire [ɪn'taɪəʳ] ADJ inteiro; **entirely** ADV totalmente, completamente

entitle [ɪn'taɪtl] VT: **to ~ sb to sth** dar a alguém direito a algo; **entitled** [ɪn'taɪtld] ADJ (book etc) intitulado; **to be entitled to sth/to do sth** ter direito a algo/de fazer algo

entrance [n 'ɛntrəns, vt ɪn'trɑ:ns] N entrada; (arrival) chegada ▶ VT encantar, fascinar; **to gain ~ to** (university etc) ser admitido em; **entrance examination** N exame m de admissão; **entrance fee** N joia

entrant ['ɛntrənt] N participante m/f; (BRIT: in exam) candidato(-a)

entrepreneur [ɔntrəprə'nə:ʳ] N empresário(-a)

entrust [ɪn'trʌst] VT: **to ~ sth to sb** confiar algo a alguém

entry ['ɛntrɪ] N entrada; (in register) registro, assentamento; (in account) lançamento; (in dictionary) verbete m; **"no ~"** "entrada proibida"; (Aut) "contramão" (BR), "entrada proibida" (PT); **entry phone** (BRIT) N interfone m (em apartamento)

envelope ['ɛnvələup] N envelope m

envious ['ɛnvɪəs] ADJ invejoso; (look) de inveja

environment [ɪn'vaɪərnmənt] N meio ambiente m; **environmental** [ɪnvaɪərn'mentl] ADJ ambiental

envisage [ɪn'vɪzɪdʒ] VT prever

envoy ['ɛnvɔɪ] N enviado(-a)

envy ['ɛnvɪ] N inveja ▶ VT ter inveja de; **to ~ sb sth** invejar alguém por algo, cobiçar algo de alguém

epic ['ɛpɪk] N epopeia ▶ ADJ épico

epidemic [ɛpɪ'dɛmɪk] N epidemia

epilepsy ['ɛpɪlɛpsɪ] N epilepsia

episode ['ɛpɪsəud] N episódio

equal ['i:kwl] ADJ igual; (treatment) equitativo, equivalente ▶ N igual m/f ▶ VT ser igual a; **to be ~ to** (task) estar à altura de; **equality** [i:'kwɔlɪtɪ] N igualdade f; **equalize** VI igualar; (Sport) empatar; **equally** ADV igualmente; (share etc) por igual

equator [ɪ'kweɪtəʳ] N equador m

equip [ɪˈkwɪp] vt equipar; (*person*) prover, munir; **to be well ~ped** estar bem preparado *or* equipado; **equipment** N equipamento; (*machines etc*) equipamentos *mpl*, aparelhagem *f*

equivalent [ɪˈkwɪvəlnt] ADJ equivalente ▶ N equivalente *m*

era [ˈɪərə] N era, época

erase [ɪˈreɪz] vt apagar; **eraser** N borracha (de apagar)

e-reader [ˈiːˈriːdəʳ] N leitor *m* de livros digitais

erect [ɪˈrɛkt] ADJ (*posture*) ereto; (*tail, ears*) levantado ▶ vt erigir, levantar; (*assemble*) montar; **erection** N construção *f*; (*assembly*) montagem *f*; (*Physiol*) ereção *f*

erode [ɪˈrəud] vt (*Geo*) causar erosão em; (*confidence*) minar

erotic [ɪˈrɔtɪk] ADJ erótico

errand [ˈɛrnd] N recado, mensagem *f*

erratic [ɪˈrætɪk] ADJ imprevisível

error [ˈɛrəʳ] N erro

erupt [ɪˈrʌpt] vi entrar em erupção; (*fig*) explodir, estourar; **eruption** N erupção *f*; (*fig*) explosão *f*

escalate [ˈɛskəleɪt] vi intensificar-se

escalator [ˈɛskəleɪtəʳ] N escada rolante

escape [ɪˈskeɪp] N fuga; (*of gas*) escapatória ▶ vi escapar; (*flee*) fugir, evadir-se; (*leak*) vazar, escapar ▶ vt fugir de; (*elude*): **his name ~s me** o nome dele me foge a memória; **to ~ from** (*place*) escapar de; (*person*) escapulir de

escort [*n* ˈɛskɔːt, *vt* ɪˈskɔːt] N acompanhante *m/f*; (*Mil, Naut*) escolta ▶ vt acompanhar

especially [ɪˈspɛʃlɪ] ADV (*above all*) sobretudo; (*particularly*) em particular

espionage [ˈɛspɪənɑːʒ] N espionagem *f*

essay [ˈɛseɪ] N ensaio

essence [ˈɛsns] N essência

essential [ɪˈsɛnʃl] ADJ (*necessary*) indispensável; (*basic*) essencial ▶ N elemento essencial

establish [ɪˈstæblɪʃ] vt estabelecer; (*facts*) verificar; (*proof*) demonstrar; (*reputation*) firmar; **establishment** N estabelecimento; **the Establishment** a classe dirigente

estate [ɪˈsteɪt] N (*land*) fazenda (BR), propriedade *f* (PT); (*Jur*) herança; (*Pol*) estado; (BRIT: *also:* **housing ~**) conjunto habitacional; **estate agent** (BRIT) N corretor(a) *m/f* de imóveis (BR), agente *m/f* imobiliário(-a) (PT); **estate car** (BRIT) N perua (BR), canadiana (PT)

estimate [*n* ˈɛstɪmət, *vb* ˈɛstɪmeɪt] N (*assessment*) avaliação *f*; (*calculation*) cálculo; (*Comm*) orçamento ▶ vt estimar, avaliar, calcular

etc. ABBR (= *et cetera*) etc.

eternal [ɪˈtəːnl] ADJ eterno

eternity [ɪˈtəːnɪtɪ] N eternidade *f*

ethical [ˈɛθɪkl] ADJ ético

ethics [ˈɛθɪks] N ética ▶ NPL moral *f*

Ethiopia [iːθɪˈəupɪə] N Etiópia

ethnic [ˈɛθnɪk] ADJ étnico; (*culture*) folclórico

e-ticket [ˈiːtɪkɪt] N bilhete *m* eletrônico

etiquette [ˈɛtɪkɛt] N etiqueta

EU ABBR (= *European Union*) UE *f*

euro [ˈjuərəu] N (*currency*) euro *m*

Europe [ˈjuərəp] N Europa; **European** [juərəˈpiːən] ADJ, N europeu(-peia); **European Union** N: **the European Union** a União Europeia

evacuate [ɪˈvækjueɪt] vt evacuar

evade [ɪˈveɪd] vt (*person*) evitar; (*question, duties*) esquivar-se de; (*tax*) sonegar

evaporate [ɪˈvæpəreɪt] vi evaporar-se

eve [iːv] N: **on the ~ of** na véspera de

even [ˈiːvn] ADJ (*level*) plano; (*smooth*) liso; (*equal, Sport*) igual; (*number*) par ▶ ADV até, mesmo; **~ if** mesmo que; **~ though** mesmo que, embora; **~ more** ainda mais; **~ so** mesmo assim; **not ~** nem; **to get ~ with sb** ficar quite com alguém; **even out** vi nivelar-se

evening [ˈiːvnɪŋ] N (*early*) tarde *f*; (*late*) noite *f*; (*event*) noitada; **in the ~** à noite; **evening class** N aula noturna

event [ɪˈvɛnt] N acontecimento; (*Sport*) prova; **in the ~ of** no caso de; **eventful** ADJ cheio de acontecimentos; (*game etc*) cheio de emoção, agitado

eventual [ɪˈvɛntʃuəl] ADJ final; **eventually** ADV finalmente; (*in time*) por fim

ever [ˈɛvəʳ] ADV (*always*) sempre; (*at any time*) em qualquer momento; (*in question*): **why ~ not?** por que não, ora?; **the best ~** o melhor que já se viu; **have you ~ seen it?** você alguma vez já viu isto?; **better than ~** melhor que nunca; **~ since** adv desde então; *conj* depois que; **evergreen** N sempre-verde *f*

KEYWORD

every [ˈɛvrɪ] ADJ **1** (*each*) cada; **every one of them** cada um deles; **every shop in the town was closed** todas as lojas da cidade estavam fechadas

2 (all possible) todo(-a); **I have every confidence in her** tenho absoluta confiança nela; **we wish you every success** desejamos-lhe o maior sucesso; **he's every bit as clever as his brother** ele é tão inteligente quanto o irmão **3** (showing recurrence) todo(-a); **every other car had been broken into** cada dois carros foram arrombados; **she visits me every other/third day** ele me visita cada dois/três dias; **every now and then** de vez em quando

everybody ['ɛvrɪbɔdɪ] PRON todos, todo mundo (BR), toda a gente (PT)
everyday ['ɛvrɪdeɪ] ADJ (daily) diário; (usual) corrente; (common) comum
everyone ['ɛvrɪwʌn] PRON = **everybody**
everything ['ɛvrɪθɪŋ] PRON tudo
everywhere ['ɛvrɪwɛəʳ] ADV (be) em todo lugar (BR), em toda a parte (PT); (go) a todo lugar (BR), a toda a parte (PT); (wherever): **~ you go you meet ...** aonde quer que se vá, encontra-se ...
evict [ɪ'vɪkt] VT despejar
evidence ['ɛvɪdəns] N (proof) prova(s) f(pl); (of witness) testemunho, depoimento; (indication) sinal m; **to give ~** testemunhar, prestar depoimento
evident ['ɛvɪdənt] ADJ evidente; **evidently** ADV evidentemente; (apparently) aparentemente
evil ['iːvl] ADJ mau/má ▶ N mal m, maldade f
evoke [ɪ'vəuk] VT evocar
evolution [iːvə'luːʃən] N evolução f; (development) desenvolvimento
evolve [ɪ'vɔlv] VT desenvolver ▶ VI desenvolver-se
exact [ɪg'zækt] ADJ exato; (person) meticuloso ▶ VT: **to ~ sth (from)** exigir algo (de); **exactly** ADV exatamente; (indicating agreement) isso mesmo
exaggerate [ɪg'zædʒəreɪt] VT, VI exagerar; **exaggeration** [ɪgzædʒə'reɪʃən] N exagero
exam [ɪg'zæm] N ABBR = **examination**
examination [ɪgzæmɪ'neɪʃən] N exame m; (inquiry) investigação f
examine [ɪg'zæmɪn] VT examinar; (inspect) inspecionar; **examiner** N examinador(a) m/f
example [ɪg'zaːmpl] N exemplo; **for ~** por exemplo
excavate ['ɛkskəveɪt] VT escavar
exceed [ɪk'siːd] VT exceder; (number) ser superior a; (speed limit) ultrapassar; (limits) ir além de; (powers) exceder-se

em; (hopes) superar; **exceedingly** ADV extremamente
excellent ['ɛksələnt] ADJ excelente
except [ɪk'sɛpt] PREP (also: **~ for, ~ing**) exceto, a não ser ▶ VT: **to ~ sb from** excluir alguém de; **~ if/when** a menos que, a não ser que; **exception** N exceção f; **to take exception to** ressentir-se de
excerpt ['ɛksəːpt] N trecho
excess [ɪk'sɛs] N excesso; **excess baggage** N excesso de bagagem; **excessive** ADJ excessivo
exchange [ɪks'tʃeɪndʒ] N troca; (of teachers, students) intercâmbio; (also: **telephone ~**) estação f telefônica (BR), central f telefónica (PT) ▶ VT: **to ~ (for)** trocar (por); **exchange rate** N (taxa de) câmbio
excite [ɪk'saɪt] VT excitar; **to get ~d** entusiasmar-se; **excitement** N emoções fpl; (agitation) agitação f; **exciting** ADJ emocionante, empolgante
exclaim [ɪk'skleɪm] VI exclamar; **exclamation** [ɛksklə'meɪʃən] N exclamação f; **exclamation mark** N ponto de exclamação
exclude [ɪk'skluːd] VT excluir
exclusive [ɪk'skluːsɪv] ADJ exclusivo; **~ of tax** sem incluir os impostos
excruciating [ɪk'skruːʃɪeɪtɪŋ] ADJ doloroso, martirizante
excursion [ɪk'skəːʃən] N excursão f
excuse [n ɪk'skjuːs, vt ɪk'skjuːz] N desculpa ▶ VT desculpar, perdoar; **to ~ sb from doing sth** dispensar alguém de fazer algo; **~ me!** desculpe!; **if you will ~ me ...** com a sua licença ...
execute ['ɛksɪkjuːt] VT (plan) realizar; (order) cumprir; (person, movement) executar; **execution** N realização f; (killing) execução f
executive [ɪg'zɛkjutɪv] N (Comm, Pol) executivo(-a) ▶ ADJ executivo
exempt [ɪg'zɛmpt] ADJ: **~ from** isento de ▶ VT: **to ~ sb from** dispensar or isentar alguém de
exercise ['ɛksəsaɪz] N exercício ▶ VT exercer; (right) valer-se de; (dog) levar para passear ▶ VI (also: **to take ~**) fazer exercício; **exercise book** N caderno
exert [ɪg'zəːt] VT exercer; **to ~ o.s.** esforçar-se, empenhar-se; **exertion** N esforço
exhale [ɛks'heɪl] VT, VI expirar
exhaust [ɪg'zɔːst] N (Aut: also: **~ pipe**) escape m, exaustor m; (fumes) escapamento (de gás) ▶ VT esgotar; **exhaustion** N exaustão f

exhibit [ɪgˈzɪbɪt] N (Art) obra exposta; (Jur) objeto exposto ▶ VT (courage etc) manifestar, mostrar; (quality, emotion) demonstrar; (paintings) expor; **exhibition** [ɛksɪˈbɪʃən] N exposição f

exhilarating [ɪgˈzɪləreɪtɪŋ] ADJ estimulante, tônico

exile [ˈɛksaɪl] N exílio; (person) exilado(-a) ▶ VT desterrar, exilar

exist [ɪgˈzɪst] VI existir; (live) viver; **existence** N existência; (life) vida; **existing** ADJ atual

exit [ˈɛksɪt] N saída ▶ VI (Comput, Theatre) sair

exotic [ɪgˈzɔtɪk] ADJ exótico

expand [ɪkˈspænd] VT aumentar ▶ VI aumentar; (trade, gas etc) expandir-se; (metal) dilatar-se

expansion [ɪkˈspænʃən] N (of town) desenvolvimento; (of trade) expansão f; (of population) aumento

expect [ɪkˈspɛkt] VT esperar; (suppose) supor; (require) exigir ▶ VI: **to be ~ing** estar grávida; **expectation** [ɛkspɛkˈteɪʃən] N esperança; (belief) expectativa

expedition [ɛkspəˈdɪʃən] N expedição f

expel [ɪkˈspɛl] VT expelir; (from place, school) expulsar

expense [ɪkˈspɛns] N gasto, despesa; (expenditure) despesas fpl; **expenses** NPL (costs) despesas fpl; **at the ~ of** à custa de; **expense account** N relatório de despesas

expensive [ɪkˈspɛnsɪv] ADJ caro

experience [ɪkˈspɪərɪəns] N experiência ▶ VT (situation) enfrentar; (feeling) sentir; **experienced** ADJ experiente

experiment [ɪkˈspɛrɪmənt] N experimento, experiência ▶ VI: **to ~ (with/on)** fazer experiências (com/em)

expert [ˈɛkspəːt] ADJ hábil, perito ▶ N especialista m/f; **expertise** [ɛkspəːˈtiːz] N perícia

expire [ɪkˈspaɪər] VI expirar; (run out) vencer; **expiry** N expiração f, vencimento

explain [ɪkˈspleɪn] VT explicar; (clarify) esclarecer; **explain away** VT justificar

explicit [ɪkˈsplɪsɪt] ADJ explícito

explode [ɪkˈspləud] VI estourar, explodir

exploit [n ˈɛksplɔɪt, vt ɪkˈsplɔɪt] N façanha ▶ VT explorar; **exploitation** [ɛksplɔɪˈteɪʃən] N exploração f

explore [ɪkˈsplɔːr] VT explorar; (fig) examinar, pesquisar; **explorer** N explorador(a) m/f

explosion [ɪkˈspləuʒən] N explosão f

explosive [ɪkˈspləusɪv] ADJ explosivo ▶ N explosivo

export [vt ɛkˈspɔːt, n, cpd ˈɛkspɔːt] VT exportar ▶ N exportação f ▶ CPD de exportação; **exporter** N exportador(a) m/f

expose [ɪkˈspəuz] VT expor; (unmask) desmascarar; **exposed** ADJ (house etc) desabrigado

exposure [ɪkˈspəuʒər] N exposição f; (publicity) publicidade f; (Phot) revelação f; **to die from ~** (Med) morrer de frio

express [ɪkˈsprɛs] ADJ expresso, explícito; (BRIT: letter etc) urgente ▶ N rápido ▶ VT exprimir, expressar; (quantity) representar; **expression** N expressão f; **expressway** (US) N rodovia (BR), autoestrada (PT)

extend [ɪkˈstɛnd] VT (visit, street) prolongar; (building) aumentar; (offer) fazer; (hand) estender

extension [ɪkˈstɛnʃən] N (Elec) extensão f; (building) acréscimo, expansão f; (of rights) ampliação f; (Tel) ramal m (BR), extensão f (PT); (of deadline, campaign) prolongamento, prorrogação f

extensive [ɪkˈstɛnsɪv] ADJ extenso; (damage) considerável; (broad) vasto, amplo

extent [ɪkˈstɛnt] N (breadth) extensão f; (of damage etc) dimensão f; (scope) alcance m; **to some** or **to a certain ~** até certo ponto

exterior [ɛkˈstɪərɪər] ADJ externo ▶ N exterior m; (appearance) aspecto

external [ɛkˈstəːnl] ADJ externo

extinct [ɪkˈstɪŋkt] ADJ extinto

extinguish [ɪkˈstɪŋgwɪʃ] VT extinguir

extra [ˈɛkstrə] ADJ adicional ▶ ADV adicionalmente ▶ N (surcharge) extra m, suplemento; (Cinema, Theatre) figurante m/f

extract [vt ɪkˈstrækt, n ˈɛkstrækt] VT tirar, extrair; (tooth) arrancar; (mineral) extrair; (money) extorquir; (promise) conseguir, obter ▶ N extrato

extradite [ˈɛkstrədaɪt] VT (from country) extraditar; (to country) obter a extradição de

extraordinary [ɪkˈstrɔːdnrɪ] ADJ extraordinário; (odd) estranho

extravagance [ɪkˈstrævəgəns] N extravagância; (no pl: spending) esbanjamento

extravagant [ɪkˈstrævəgənt] ADJ (lavish) extravagante; (wasteful) gastador(a), esbanjador(a)

extreme [ɪk'striːm] ADJ extremo ▸ N extremo; **extremely** ADV muito, extremamente

extrovert ['ɛkstrəvəːt] N extrovertido(-a)

eye [aɪ] N olho; (of needle) buraco ▸ VT olhar, observar; **to keep an ~ on** vigiar, ficar de olho em; **eyebrow** N sobrancelha; **eyedrops** NPL gotas fpl para os olhos; **eyelash** N cílio; **eyelid** N pálpebra; **eyeliner** N delineador m; **eye shadow** N sombra de olhos; **eyesight** N vista, visão f

f

F [ɛf] N (Mus) fá m

fabric ['fæbrɪk] N tecido, pano

face [feɪs] N cara, rosto; (grimace) careta; (of clock) mostrador m; (side, surface) superfície f; (of building) frente f, fachada ▸ VT (facts, problem) enfrentar; (particular direction) dar para; **~ down** de bruços; (card) virado para baixo; **to lose ~** perder o prestígio; **to save ~** salvar as aparências; **to make** or **pull a ~** fazer careta; **in the ~ of** diante de, à vista de; **on the ~ of it** a julgar pelas aparências, à primeira vista; **face up to** VT FUS enfrentar; **face cloth** (BRIT) N pano de rosto; **face pack** (BRIT) N máscara facial

facilities [fə'sɪlɪtɪz] NPL facilidades fpl, instalações fpl; **credit ~** crediário

fact [fækt] N fato; **in ~** realmente, na verdade

factor ['fæktəʳ] N fator m

factory ['fæktərɪ] N fábrica

factual ['fæktjuəl] ADJ real, fatual

faculty ['fækəltɪ] N faculdade f; (US) corpo docente

fad [fæd] (inf) N mania, modismo

fade [feɪd] VI desbotar; (sound, hope) desvanecer-se; (light) apagar-se; (flower) murchar

fag [fæg] (inf) N cigarro

fail [feɪl] VT (candidate) reprovar; (exam) não passar em, ser reprovado em; (subj: leader) fracassar; (: courage) carecer; (: memory) falhar ▸ VI fracassar; (engine, brakes, voice) falhar; **to ~ to do sth** deixar de fazer algo; (be unable) não conseguir fazer algo; **without ~** sem falta; **failing** N defeito ▸ PREP na or à falta de; **failing that** senão; **failure** N fracasso; (mechanical etc) falha

faint [feɪnt] ADJ fraco; (*recollection*) vago; (*mark*) indistinto; (*smell, trace*) leve ▶ N desmaio ▶ VI desmaiar; **to feel ~** sentir tonteira

fair [fɛəʳ] ADJ justo; (*hair*) louro; (*complexion*) branco; (*weather*) bom; (*good enough*) razoável; (*sizeable*) considerável ▶ ADV: **to play ~** fazer jogo limpo ▶ N (*also*: **trade ~**) feira; (BRIT: *funfair*) parque m de diversões; **fairly** ADV (*justly*) com justiça; (*quite*) bastante; **fair trade** N comércio justo

fairy ['fɛərɪ] N fada

faith [feɪθ] N fé f; (*trust*) confiança; (*denomination*) seita; **faithful** ADJ fiel; (*account*) exato; **faithfully** ADV fielmente; **yours faithfully** (BRIT: *in letters*) atenciosamente

fake [feɪk] N (*painting etc*) falsificação f; (*person*) impostor(a) m/f ▶ ADJ falso ▶ VT fingir; (*painting etc*) falsificar

falcon ['fɔ:lkən] N falcão m

fall [fɔ:l] (*pt* **fell**, *pp* **fallen**) N queda; (US: *autumn*) outono ▶ VI cair; (*price*) baixar; **falls** NPL (*waterfall*) cascata, queda d'água; **to ~ flat** cair de cara no chão; (*plan*) falhar; (*joke*) não agradar; **fall back** VI retroceder; **fall back on** VT FUS recorrer a; **fall behind** VI ficar para trás; **fall down** VI (*person*) cair; (*building*) desabar; **fall for** VT FUS (*trick*) cair em; (*person*) enamorar-se de; **fall in** VI ruir; (*Mil*) alinhar-se; **fall off** VI cair; (*diminish*) declinar, diminuir; **fall out** VI cair; (*friends etc*) brigar; **fall through** VI (*plan, project*) furar

fallout ['fɔ:laut] N chuva radioativa

false [fɔ:ls] ADJ falso; **false teeth** (BRIT) NPL dentadura postiça

fame [feɪm] N fama

familiar [fə'mɪlɪəʳ] ADJ (*well-known*) conhecido; (*tone*) familiar, íntimo; **to be ~ with** (*subject*) estar familiarizado com

family ['fæmɪlɪ] N família

famine ['fæmɪn] N fome f

famous ['feɪməs] ADJ famoso, célebre

fan [fæn] N (*hand-held*) leque m; (*Elec*) ventilador m; (*person*) fã m/f ▶ VT abanar; (*fire, quarrel*) atiçar; **fan out** VI espalhar-se

fanatic [fə'nætɪk] N fanático(-a)

fan belt N correia do ventilador (BR) or da ventoinha (PT)

fan club N fã-clube m

fancy ['fænsɪ] N capricho; (*imagination*) imaginação f; (*fantasy*) fantasia ▶ ADJ ornamental; (*luxury*) luxuoso ▶ VT desejar, querer; (*imagine*) imaginar;

(*think*) acreditar, achar; **to take a ~ to** tomar gosto por; **he fancies her** (*inf*) ele está a fim dela; **fancy dress** N fantasia

fantastic [fæn'tæstɪk] ADJ fantástico

fantasy ['fæntəsɪ] N (*dream*) sonho; (*unreality*) fantasia; (*imagination*) imaginação f

far [fɑ:ʳ] ADJ (*distant*) distante ▶ ADV (*also*: **~ away, ~ off**) longe; **the ~ side/end** o lado de lá/a outra ponta; **~ better** muito melhor; **~ from** longe de; **by ~** de longe; **go as ~ as the farm** vá até a (BR) or à (PT) fazenda; **as ~ as I know** que eu saiba; **how ~?** até onde?; (*fig*) até que ponto?

farce [fɑ:s] N farsa

fare [fɛəʳ] N (*on trains, buses*) preço (da passagem); (*in taxi: cost*) tarifa; (*food*) comida; **half/full ~** meia/inteira passagem

Far East N: **the ~** o Extremo Oriente

farewell [fɛə'wɛl] EXCL adeus ▶ N despedida

farm [fɑ:m] N fazenda (BR), quinta (PT) ▶ VT cultivar; **farmer** N fazendeiro(-a), agricultor m; **farmhouse** *irreg* N casa da fazenda (BR) or da quinta (PT); **farming** N agricultura; (*tilling*) cultura; (*of animals*) criação f; **farmyard** N curral m

far-reaching [-'ri:tʃɪŋ] ADJ de grande alcance, abrangente

fart [fɑ:t] (!) VI soltar um peido (!), peidar (!)

farther ['fɑ:ðəʳ] ADV mais longe ▶ ADJ mais distante, mais afastado

farthest ['fɑ:ðɪst] SUPERL of **far**

fascinate ['fæsɪneɪt] VT fascinar

fashion ['fæʃən] N moda; (*fashion industry*) indústria da moda; (*manner*) maneira ▶ VT modelar, dar feitio a; **in ~** na moda; **fashionable** ADJ da moda, elegante; **fashion show** N desfile m de modas

fast [fɑ:st] ADJ rápido; (*dye, colour*) firme, permanente; (*clock*): **to be ~** estar adiantado ▶ ADV rápido, rapidamente, depressa; (*stuck, held*) firmemente ▶ N jejum m ▶ VI jejuar; **~ asleep** dormindo profundamente

fasten ['fɑ:sn] VT fixar, prender; (*coat*) fechar; (*belt*) apertar ▶ VI prender-se, fixar-se

fast food N fast food f

fat [fæt] ADJ gordo; (*book*) grosso; (*wallet*) recheado; (*profit*) grande ▶ N gordura; (*lard*) banha, gordura

fatal ['feɪtl] ADJ fatal; (*injury*) mortal

fate [feɪt] N destino; (*of person*) sorte f

father ['fɑːðəʳ] N pai m; **father-in-law** N sogro

fatigue [fə'tiːg] N fadiga, cansaço

fatty ['fætɪ] ADJ (food) gorduroso ▶ N (inf) gorducho(-a)

fault [fɔːlt] N (blame) culpa; (defect) defeito; (Geo) falha; (Tennis) falta, bola fora ▶ VT criticar; **to find ~ with** criticar, queixar-se de; **at ~** culpado; **faulty** ADJ defeituoso

favour ['feɪvəʳ], (US) **favor** N favor m ▶ VT favorecer; (assist) auxiliar; **to do sb a ~** fazer favor a alguém; **to find ~ with** cair nas boas graças de; **in ~ of** em favor de; **favourite** ['feɪvərɪt] ADJ predileto ▶ N favorito(-a)

fawn [fɔːn] N cervo novo, cervato ▶ ADJ (also: **~-coloured**) castanho-claro inv ▶ VI: **to ~ (up)on** bajular

fax [fæks] N fax m, fac-símile m ▶ VT enviar por fax or fac-símile

FBI (US) N ABBR (= Federal Bureau of Investigation) FBI m

fear [fɪəʳ] N medo ▶ VT ter medo de, temer; **for ~ of** com medo de; **fearful** ADJ medonho, temível; (cowardly) medroso; (awful) terrível

feasible ['fiːzəbl] ADJ viável

feast [fiːst] N banquete m; (Rel: also: **~ day**) festa ▶ VI banquetear-se

feat [fiːt] N façanha, feito

feather ['fɛðəʳ] N pena, pluma

feature ['fiːtʃəʳ] N característica; (article) reportagem f ▶ VT (subj: film) apresentar ▶ VI figurar; **features** NPL (of face) feições fpl; **feature film** N longa-metragem f

February ['fɛbruərɪ] N fevereiro

fed [fɛd] PT, PP of **feed**

federal ['fɛdərəl] ADJ federal

fed up ADJ: **to be ~** estar (de saco) cheio (BR), estar farto (PT)

fee [fiː] N taxa (BR), propina (PT); (of school) matrícula; (of doctor, lawyer) honorários mpl

feeble ['fiːbl] ADJ fraco; (attempt) ineficaz

feed [fiːd] (pt, pp **fed**) N (of baby) alimento infantil; (of animal) ração f; (on printer) mecanismo alimentador ▶ VT alimentar; (baby) amamentar; (animal) dar de comer a; (data, information): **to ~ into** introduzir em; **feed on** VT FUS alimentar-se de; **feedback** ['fiːdbæk] N reação f

feel [fiːl] (pt, pp **felt**) N sensação f; (sense of touch) tato; (impression) impressão f ▶ VT tocar, apalpar; (anger, cold etc) sentir; (think, believe) achar, acreditar; **to ~ hungry/cold** estar com fome/frio (BR),

ter fome/frio (PT); **to ~ lonely/better** sentir-se só/melhor; **I don't ~ well** não estou me sentindo bem; **it ~s soft** é macio; **to ~ like** querer; **to ~ about** or **around** tatear; **feeling** N sensação f; (emotion) sentimento; (impression) impressão f

feet [fiːt] NPL of **foot**

fell [fɛl] PT of **fall** ▶ VT (tree) lançar por terra, derrubar

fellow ['fɛləu] N camarada m/f; (inf: man) cara m (BR), tipo (PT); (of learned society) membro ▶ CPD: **~ students** colegas mpl/fpl de curso; **fellowship** N amizade f; (grant) bolsa de estudo; (society) associação f

felony ['fɛlənɪ] N crime m

felt [fɛlt] PT, PP of **feel** ▶ N feltro

female ['fiːmeɪl] N (pej: woman) mulher f; (Zool) fêmea ▶ ADJ fêmeo(-a); (sex, character) feminino; (vote etc) das mulheres; (child etc) do sexo feminino

feminine ['fɛmɪnɪn] ADJ feminino

feminist ['fɛmɪnɪst] N feminista m/f

fence [fɛns] N cerca ▶ VT (also: **~ in**) cercar ▶ VI esgrimir; **fencing** N (sport) esgrima

fend [fɛnd] VI: **to ~ for o.s.** defender-se, virar-se; **fend off** VT defender-se de

ferment [vi fə'mɛnt, n 'fəːmɛnt] VI fermentar ▶ N (fig) agitação f

fern [fəːn] N samambaia (BR), feto (PT)

ferocious [fə'rəuʃəs] ADJ feroz

ferret ['fɛrɪt] N furão m; **ferret out** VT (information) desenterrar, descobrir

ferry ['fɛrɪ] N (small) barco (de travessia); (large: also: **~boat**) balsa ▶ VT transportar

fertile ['fəːtaɪl] ADJ fértil; (Bio) fecundo; **fertilizer** ['fəːtɪlaɪzəʳ] N adubo, fertilizante m

festival ['fɛstɪvəl] N (Rel) festa; (Art, Mus) festival m

festive ['fɛstɪv] ADJ festivo; **the ~ season** (BRIT: Christmas) a época do Natal

fetch [fɛtʃ] VT ir buscar, trazer; (sell for) alcançar

fête [feɪt] N festa

feud [fjuːd] N disputa, rixa

fever ['fiːvəʳ] N febre f; **feverish** ADJ febril

few [fjuː] ADJ, PRON poucos(-as); **a ~ ...** alguns/algumas ...; **fewer** ['fjuːəʳ] ADJ menos; **fewest** ['fjuːɪst] ADJ o menor número de

fib [fɪb] N lorota

fickle ['fɪkl] ADJ inconstante; (weather) instável

fiction ['fɪkʃən] N ficção f; **fictional** ADJ de ficção

fiddle ['fɪdl] N (Mus) violino; (swindle) trapaça ▶ VT (BRIT: accounts) falsificar; **fiddle with** VT FUS brincar com

fidget ['fɪdʒɪt] VI estar irrequieto, mexer-se

field [fiːld] N campo; (fig) área, esfera, especialidade f

fierce [fɪəs] ADJ feroz; (wind, attack) violento; (heat) intenso

fifteen [fɪf'tiːn] NUM quinze

fifth [fɪfθ] NUM quinto

fifty ['fɪftɪ] NUM cinquenta; **fifty-fifty** ADV: **to share** or **go fifty-fifty with sb** dividir meio a meio com alguém, rachar com alguém ▶ ADJ: **to have a fifty-fifty chance** ter 50% de chance

fig [fɪg] N figo

fight [faɪt] (pt, pp fought) N briga; (Mil) combate m; (struggle: against illness etc) luta ▶ VT lutar contra; (cancer, alcoholism) combater; (election) competir ▶ VI brigar, bater-se

figure ['fɪgəʳ] N (Drawing, Math) figura, desenho; (number, cipher) número, cifra; (outline) forma; (person) personagem m ▶ VT (esp US) imaginar ▶ VI figurar; **figure out** VT compreender

file [faɪl] N (tool) lixa; (dossier) dossiê m, pasta; (folder) pasta; (Comput) arquivo; (row) fila, coluna ▶ VT (wood, nails) lixar; (papers) arquivar; (Jur: claim) apresentar, dar entrada em ▶ VI: **to ~ in/out** entrar/sair em fila; **file sharing** N (Comput) compartilhamento de arquivos

fill [fɪl] VT encher; (vacancy) preencher; (need) satisfazer ▶ N: **to eat one's ~** encher-se or fartar-se de comer; **fill in** VT (form) preencher; (hole) tapar; (time) encher; **fill up** VT encher ▶ VI (Aut) abastecer o carro

fillet ['fɪlɪt] N filete m, filé m; **fillet steak** N filé m

filling ['fɪlɪŋ] N (Culin) recheio; (for tooth) obturação f (BR), chumbo (PT); **filling station** N posto de gasolina

film [fɪlm] N filme m; (of liquid etc) camada fina, véu m ▶ VT rodar, filmar ▶ VI filmar; **film star** N astro/estrela do cinema

filter ['fɪltəʳ] N filtro ▶ VT filtrar

filth [fɪlθ] N sujeira (BR), sujidade f (PT); **filthy** ADJ sujo; (language) indecente, obsceno

fin [fɪn] N barbatana

final ['faɪnl] ADJ final, último; (definitive) definitivo ▶ N (Sport) final f; **finals** NPL (Sch) exames mpl finais; **finale** [fɪ'nɑːlɪ] N

final m; **finalize** VT concluir, completar; **finally** ADV finalmente, por fim

finance [faɪ'næns] N fundos mpl; (money management) finanças fpl ▶ VT financiar; **finances** NPL (personal finances) finanças; **financial** [faɪ'nænʃəl] ADJ financeiro

find [faɪnd] (pt, pp found) N encontrar, achar; (discover) descobrir ▶ N achado, descoberta; **to ~ sb guilty** (Jur) declarar alguém culpado; **find out** VT descobrir; (person) desmascarar ▶ VI: **to ~ out about** (by chance) saber de; **findings** NPL (Jur) veredito, decisão f; (of report) constatações fpl

fine [faɪn] ADJ fino; (excellent) excelente ▶ ADV muito bem ▶ N (Jur) multa ▶ VT (Jur) multar; **to be ~** (person) estar bem; (weather) estar bom; **fine arts** NPL belas artes fpl

finger ['fɪŋgəʳ] N dedo ▶ VT manusear; **fingernail** N unha; **fingerprint** N impressão f digital; **fingertip** N ponta do dedo

finish ['fɪnɪʃ] N fim m; (Sport) chegada; (on wood etc) acabamento ▶ VT, VI terminar, acabar; **to ~ doing sth** terminar de fazer algo; **to ~ third** chegar no terceiro lugar; **finish off** VT terminar; (kill) liquidar; **finish up** VT acabar ▶ VI ir parar

Finland ['fɪnlənd] N Finlândia

Finn [fɪn] N finlandês(-esa) m/f; **Finnish** ADJ finlandês(-esa) ▶ N (Ling) finlandês m

fir [fəːʳ] N abeto

fire ['faɪəʳ] N fogo; (accidental) incêndio; (gas fire, electric fire) aquecedor m ▶ VT (gun) disparar; (arrow) atirar; (interest) estimular; (dismiss) despedir ▶ VI disparar; **on ~** em chamas; **fire alarm** N alarme m de incêndio; **firearm** N arma de fogo; **fire brigade** N (corpo de) bombeiros mpl; **fire engine** N carro de bombeiro; **fire escape** N escada de incêndio; **fire exit** N saída de emergência; **fire extinguisher** N extintor m de incêndio; **firefighter** N bombeiro(-a); **fireman** irreg N bombeiro; **fireplace** N lareira; **fire station** N posto de bombeiros; **firewall** N (Comput) firewall m; **firewood** N lenha; **fireworks** NPL fogos mpl de artifício

firm [fəːm] ADJ firme ▶ N firma

first [fəːst] ADJ primeiro ▶ ADV (before others) primeiro; (when listing reasons etc) em primeiro lugar ▶ N (in race) primeiro(-a); (Aut) primeira; (BRIT Sch) menção f honrosa; **at ~** no início; **~ of all** antes de tudo, antes de mais nada;

first aid N primeiros socorros *mpl*;
first-aid kit N estojo de primeiros
socorros; **first-class** ADJ de primeira
classe; **first-hand** ADJ de primeira mão;
first lady (US) N primeira dama; **firstly**
ADV primeiramente, em primeiro lugar;
first name N primeiro nome *m*;
first-rate ADJ de primeira categoria

fish [fɪʃ] N INV peixe *m* ▶ VT, VI pescar; **to
go ~ing** ir pescar; **fisherman** *irreg* N
pescador *m*; **fishing boat** N barco de
pesca; **fishing line** N linha de pesca;
fishmonger ['fɪʃmʌŋɡəʳ] N peixeiro(-a);
fishmonger's (shop) peixaria; **fishy**
(*inf*) ADJ (*tale*) suspeito

fist [fɪst] N punho

fit [fɪt] ADJ em (boa) forma; (*suitable*)
adequado, apropriado ▶ VT (*subj: clothes*)
caber em; (*put in, attach*) colocar; (*equip*)
equipar ▶ VI (*clothes*) servir; (*parts*)
ajustar-se; (*in space, gap*) caber ▶ N (*Med*)
ataque *m*; **~ to** bom para; **~ for**
adequado para; **a ~ of anger/pride** um
acesso de raiva/orgulho; **by ~s and
starts** espasmodicamente; **fit in** VI
encaixar-se; (*person*) dar-se bem (com
todos); **fitness** N (*Med*) saúde *f*, boa
forma; **fitted kitchen** (BRIT) N cozinha
planejada; **fitting** ADJ apropriado ▶ N (*of
dress*) prova; **fittings** NPL (*in building*)
instalações *fpl*, acessórios *mpl*

five [faɪv] NUM cinco; **fiver** (*inf*) N (BRIT)
nota de cinco libras; (US) nota de cinco
dólares

fix [fɪks] VT (*secure*) fixar, colocar;
(*arrange*) arranjar; (*mend*) consertar;
(*meal, drink*) preparar ▶ N: **to be in a ~**
estar em apuros; **fix up** VT (*meeting*)
marcar; **to ~ sb up with sth** arranjar
algo para alguém; **fixed** ADJ (*prices, smile*)
fixo; **fixture** N (*furniture*) móvel *m* fixo;
(*Sport*) desafio, encontro

fizzy ['fɪzɪ] ADJ com gás, gasoso

flag [flæg] N bandeira; (*for signalling*)
bandeirola; (*flagstone*) laje *f* ▶ VI
acabar-se, descair; **flag down** VT: **to ~
sb down** fazer sinais a alguém para que
pare

flagpole ['flæɡpəul] N mastro de
bandeira

flair [flɛəʳ] N (*talent*) talento; (*style*)
habilidade *f*

flake [fleɪk] N (*of rust, paint*) lasca; (*of
snow, soap powder*) floco ▶ VI (*also: ~ off*)
lascar, descamar-se

flamboyant [flæm'bɔɪənt] ADJ (*dress*)
espalhafatoso; (*person*) extravagante

flame [fleɪm] N chama

flammable ['flæməbl] ADJ inflamável

flan [flæn] (BRIT) N torta

flannel ['flænl] N (BRIT: *also:* **face ~**)
pano de rosto; (*fabric*) flanela; **flannels**
NPL calça (BR) *or* calças *fpl* (PT) de flanela

flap [flæp] N (*of pocket, table*) aba; (*of
envelope*) dobra ▶ VT (*arms*) oscilar;
(*wings*) bater ▶ VI (*sail, flag*) ondular; (*inf:
also:* **be in a ~**) estar atarantado

flare [flɛəʳ] N fogacho, chama; (*Mil*)
foguete *m* sinalizador; (*in skirt etc*) folga;
flare up VI chamejar; (*fig: person*)
encolerizar-se; (: *violence*) irromper

flash [flæʃ] N (*of lightning*) clarão *m*; (*also:*
news ~) notícias *fpl* de última hora;
(*Phot*) flash *m* ▶ VT piscar; (*news, message*)
transmitir; (*look, smile*) brilhar ▶ VI
brilhar; (*light on ambulance, eyes etc*)
piscar; **in a ~** num instante; **to ~ by** *or*
past passar como um raio; **flash drive**
N (*Comput*) pen drive *m*; **flashlight** N
lanterna de bolso

flat [flæt] ADJ plano; (*battery*)
descarregado; (*tyre*) vazio; (*beer*) choco;
(*denial*) categórico; (*Mus*) abemolado;
(: *voice*) desafinado; (*rate*) único; (*fee*) fixo
▶ N (BRIT: *apartment*) apartamento;
(*Mus*) bemol *m*; (*Aut*) pneu *m* furado;
~ out (*work*) a toque de caixa; **flatscreen**
ADJ ['flætskri:n] de tela (BR) *or* ecrã (PT)
plana; **flatten** VT (*also:* **flatten out**)
aplanar; (*demolish*) arrasar

flatter ['flætəʳ] VT lisonjear; **flattering**
ADJ lisonjeiro; (*clothes etc*) favorecedor(a)

flaunt [flɔ:nt] VT ostentar, pavonear

flavour ['fleɪvəʳ], (US) **flavor** N sabor *m*
▶ VT condimentar, aromatizar;
strawberry-~ed com sabor de
morango

flaw [flɔ:] N defeito; (*in character*) falha;
flawless ADJ impecável

flea [fli:] N pulga

flee [fli:] (*pt, pp* **fled**) VT fugir de ▶ VI
fugir

fleece [fli:s] N tosão *m*; (*coat*) velo; (*wool*)
lã *f* ▶ VT (*inf*) espoliar

fleet [fli:t] N (*gen, of lorries etc*) frota; (*of
ships*) esquadra

fleeting ['fli:tɪŋ] ADJ fugaz

Flemish ['flɛmɪʃ] ADJ flamengo

flesh [flɛʃ] N carne *f*; (*of fruit*) polpa

flew [flu:] PT *of* **fly**

flex [flɛks] N fio ▶ VT (*muscles*) flexionar;
flexible ADJ flexível

flick [flɪk] N (*pancada leve*; (*with finger*)
peteleco, piparote *m*; (*with whip*)
chicotada ▶ VT dar um peteleo; (*switch*)
apertar; **flick through** VT FUS folhear

flicker ['flɪkə'] vɪ tremular; (*eyelids*) tremer

flight [flaɪt] N voo *m*; (*escape*) fuga; (*of steps*) lance *m*; **flight attendant** (*US*) N comissário(-a) de bordo

flimsy ['flɪmzɪ] ADJ (*thin*) delgado, franzino; (*weak*) débil; (*excuse*) fraco

flinch [flɪntʃ] vɪ encolher-se; **to ~ from sth/from doing sth** vacilar diante de algo/em fazer algo

fling [flɪŋ] (*pt, pp* **flung**) vT lançar

flint [flɪnt] N pederneira; (*in lighter*) pedra

flip-flops ['flɪpflɔps] (*esp BRIT*) NPL chinelo (de dedo)

flipper ['flɪpə'] N boia; (*of animal*) nadadeira; (*for swimmer*) pé de pato, nadadeira

flirt [flə:t] vɪ flertar ▶ N namorador(a) *m/f*, paquerador(a) *m/f*

float [fləut] N boia; (*in procession*) carro alegórico; (*sum of money*) caixa ▶ vɪ flutuar; (*swimmer*) boiar

flock [flɔk] N rebanho; (*of birds*) bando ▶ vɪ: **to ~ to** afluir a

flood [flʌd] N enchente *f*, inundação *f* ▶ vT inundar, alagar ▶ vɪ (*place*) alagar; (*people, goods*): **to ~ into** inundar; **flooding** N inundação *f*; **floodlight** *irreg* N refletor *m*, holofote *m*

floor [flɔ:'] N chão *m*; (*storey*) andar *m*; (*of sea*) fundo ▶ vT (*fig: confuse*) confundir, pasmar; **ground ~** (*BRIT*) or **first ~** (*US*) andar térreo (*BR*), rés-do-chão (*PT*); **first ~** (*BRIT*) or **second ~** (*US*) primeiro andar; **floorboard** N tábua de assoalho; **floor show** N show *m*

flop [flɔp] N fracasso ▶ vɪ fracassar; (*into chair etc*) cair pesadamente

floppy ['flɔpɪ] ADJ frouxo, mole ▶ N (*also:* **~ disk**) disquete *m*

florist ['flɔrɪst] N florista *m/f*; **florist's**, **florist's shop** N floricultura

flour ['flauə'] N farinha

flourish ['flʌrɪʃ] vɪ florescer ▶ vT brandir, menear ▶ N: **with a ~** con gestos floreados

flow [fləu] N fluxo; (*of river, Elec*) corrente *f*; (*of blood*) circulação *f* ▶ vɪ correr; (*traffic*) fluir; (*blood, Elec*) circular; (*clothes, hair*) ondular

flower ['flauə'] N flor *f* ▶ vɪ florescer, florir; **flower bed** N canteiro; **flowerpot** N vaso

flown [fləun] PP *of* **fly**

flu [flu:] N gripe *f*

fluctuate ['flʌktjueɪt] vɪ flutuar; (*temperature*) variar

fluent ['flu:ənt] ADJ fluente; **he speaks ~ French, he's ~ in French** ele fala francês fluentemente

fluff [flʌf] N felpa, penugem *f*; **fluffy** ADJ macio, fofo

fluid ['flu:ɪd] ADJ fluido ▶ N fluido

fluke [flu:k] (*inf*) N sorte *f*

flung [flʌŋ] PT, PP *of* **fling**

fluoride ['fluəraɪd] N fluoreto

flurry ['flʌrɪ] N (*of snow*) lufada; **~ of activity/excitement** muita atividade/animação

flush [flʌʃ] N (*on face*) rubor *m* ▶ vT lavar com água ▶ vɪ ruborizar-se ▶ ADJ: **~ with** rente com; **to ~ the toilet** dar descarga; **flush out** vT levantar

flute [flu:t] N flauta

flutter ['flʌtə'] N agitação *f*; (*of wings*) bater *m* ▶ vɪ esvoaçar

fly [flaɪ] (*pt* **flew**, *pp* **flown**) N mosca; (*on trousers: also:* **flies**) braguilha ▶ vT (*plane*) pilotar; (*passengers, cargo*) transportar (de avião); (*distances*) percorrer ▶ vɪ voar; (*passengers*) ir de avião; (*escape*) fugir; (*flag*) hastear-se; **fly away** vɪ voar; **fly off** vɪ = **fly away**; **flying** N aviação *f* ▶ ADJ: **flying visit** visita de médico; **with flying colours** brilhantemente; **flying saucer** N disco voador; **flyover** (*BRIT*) N viaduto

foal [fəul] N potro

foam [fəum] N espuma ▶ vɪ espumar; **foam rubber** N espuma de borracha

focus ['fəukəs] (*pl* **focuses**) N foco ▶ vT enfocar ▶ vɪ: **to ~ on** enfocar, focalizar; **in/out of ~** em foco/fora de foco

fog [fɔg] N nevoeiro; **foggy** ADJ nevoento

foil [fɔɪl] vT frustrar ▶ N folha metálica; (*also:* **kitchen ~**) folha or papel *m* de alumínio; (*complement*) contraste *m*, complemento; (*Fencing*) florete *m*

fold [fəuld] N dobra, vinco, prega; (*of skin*) ruga; (*Agr*) redil *m*, curral *m* ▶ vT dobrar; **to ~ one's arms** cruzar os braços; **fold up** vɪ dobrar; (*business*) abrir falência ▶ vT dobrar; **folder** N pasta; **folding** ADJ dobrável

folk [fəuk] NPL gente *f* ▶ CPD popular, folclórico; **folks** NPL (*family*) família, parentes *mpl*; **folklore** ['fəuklɔ:'] N folclore *m*

follow ['fɔləu] vT (*gen, on social media*) seguir ▶ vɪ seguir; (*result*) resultar; **I don't quite ~ you** não consigo acompanhar o seu raciocínio; **to ~ suit** fazer o mesmo; **follow up** vT (*letter*) responder a; (*offer*) levar adiante; (*case*) acompanhar; **follower** N (*gen, on social media*) seguidor(a) *m/f*; **following** ADJ seguinte ▶ N adeptos *mpl*

fond [fɔnd] ADJ carinhoso; (*hopes*) absurdo, descabido; **to be ~ of** gostar de

food [fuːd] N comida; **food miles** N distância entre o local de produção e consumo de alimentos; **food mixer** N batedeira; **food poisoning** N intoxicação *f* alimentar; **food processor** N multiprocessador *m* de cozinha

fool [fuːl] N tolo(-a); (*Culin*) puré *m* de frutas com creme ▶ VT enganar ▶ VI (*gen: fool around*) brincar; (*careless*) imprudente; **foolproof** ADJ infalível

foot [fut] (*pl* **feet**) N pé *m*; (*of animal*) pata; (*measure*) pé (304 *mm*; 12 *inches*) ▶ VT (*bill*) pagar; **on ~** a pé; **footage** N (*Cinema: length*) ≈ metragem *f*; (*: material*) sequências *fpl*; **football** N bola; (*game*: BRIT) futebol *m*; (*: US*) futebol norte-americano; **footballer** N, **football player** N jogador *m* de futebol; **footbridge** N passarela; **foothold** N apoio para o pé; **footing** N (*fig*) posição *f*; **to lose one's footing** escorregar; **footnote** N nota ao pé da página, nota de rodapé; **footpath** N caminho, atalho; **footprint** N pegada; **footstep** N passo; **footwear** N calçados *mpl*

(KEYWORD)

for [fɔːʳ] PREP **1** (*indicating destination, direction*) para; **he went for the paper** foi pegar o jornal; **is this for me?** é para mim?; **it's time for lunch** é hora de almoçar

2 (*indicating purpose*) para; **what's it for?** para quê serve?; **to pray for peace** orar pela paz

3 (*on behalf of, representing*) por; **he works for the government/a local firm** ele trabalha para o governo/uma firma local; **G for George** G de George

4 (*because of*) por; **for this reason** por esta razão; **for fear of being criticized** com medo de ser criticado

5 (*with regard to*) para; **it's cold for July** está frio para julho

6 (*in exchange for*) por; **it was sold for £5** foi vendido por £5

7 (*in favour of*) a favor de; **are you for or against us?** você está a favor de ou contra nós?; **I'm all for it** concordo plenamente, tem todo o meu apoio; **vote for X** vote em X

8 (*referring to distance*): **there are road works for 5 km** há obras na estrada por 5 quilômetros; **we walked for miles** andamos quilômetros

9 (*referring to time*): **she will be away for a month** ela ficará fora um mês; **I have known her for years** eu a conheço há anos; **can you do it for tomorrow?** você pode fazer isso para amanhã?

10 (*with infinite clause*): **it is not for me to decide** não cabe a mim decidir; **it would be best for you to leave** seria melhor que você fosse embora; **there is still time for you to do it** ainda há tempo para você fazer isso; **for this to be possible …** para que isso seja possível …

11 (*in spite of*) apesar de

▶ CONJ (*since, as: rather formal*) pois, porque

forbid [fə'bɪd] (*pt* **forbad(e)**, *pp* **forbidden**) VT proibir; **to ~ sb to do sth** proibir alguém de fazer algo

force [fɔːs] N força ▶ VT forçar; **the Forces** (BRIT) NPL as Forças Armadas; **in ~** em vigor; **forceful** ADJ enérgico, vigoroso

ford [fɔːd] N vau *m*

fore [fɔːʳ] N: **to come to the ~** salientar-se

forearm ['fɔːrɑːm] N antebraço

forecast ['fɔːkɑːst] (*irreg: like* **cast**) N previsão *f*; (*also: weather ~*) previsão do tempo ▶ VT prognosticar, prever

forefinger ['fɔːfɪŋgəʳ] N (dedo) indicador *m*

foreground ['fɔːgraund] N primeiro plano

forehead ['fɔrɪd] N testa

foreign ['fɔrɪn] ADJ estrangeiro; (*trade*) exterior; **foreigner** N estrangeiro(-a); **foreign exchange** N câmbio; **Foreign Office** (BRIT) N Ministério das Relações Exteriores

foreman ['fɔːmən] *irreg* N capataz *m*; (*in construction*) contramestre *m*; primeiro jurado

foremost ['fɔːməust] ADJ principal ▶ ADV: **first and ~** antes de mais nada

forensic [fə'rensɪk] ADJ forense; **~ medicine** medicina legal

foresee [fɔː'siː] (*irreg: like* **see**) VT prever; **foreseeable** ADJ previsível

forest ['fɔrɪst] N floresta

forestry ['fɔrɪstrɪ] N silvicultura

forever [fə'revəʳ] ADV para sempre

foreword ['fɔːwəːd] N prefácio

forfeit ['fɔːfɪt] VT perder (direito a)

forgave [fə'geɪv] PT *of* **forgive**

forge [fɔːdʒ] N ferraria ▶ VT falsificar; (*metal*) forjar; **forge ahead** VI avançar constantemente; **forger** N

falsificador(a) m/f; **forgery** N
falsificação f

forget [fə'gɛt] (pt **forgot**, pp **forgotten**)
VT, VI esquecer; **forgetful** ADJ
esquecido

forgive [fə'gɪv] (pt **forgave**, pp **forgiven**)
VT perdoar; **to ~ sb for sth** perdoar algo
a alguém, perdoar alguém de algo

forgot [fə'gɔt] PT of **forget**

forgotten [fə'gɔtn] PP of **forget**

fork [fɔːk] N (for eating) garfo; (for
gardening) forquilha; (of roads etc)
bifurcação f ▶ VI bifurcar-se; **fork out**
(inf) VT (pay) desembolsar, morrer em

forlorn [fə'lɔːn] ADJ desolado; (attempt)
desesperado; (hope) último

form [fɔːm] N forma; (type) tipo; (Sch)
série f; (questionnaire) formulário ▶ VT
formar; (organization) criar; **to ~ a queue**
(BRIT) fazer fila; **in top ~** em plena forma

formal ['fɔːməl] ADJ (offer, receipt) oficial;
(person etc) cerimonioso; (occasion,
education) formal; (dress) a rigor (BR), de
cerimônia (PT); (garden) simétrico

format ['fɔːmæt] N formato ▶ VT
(Comput) formatar

former ['fɔːmə'] ADJ anterior; (earlier)
antigo; **the ~ ... the latter ...** aquele ...
este ...; **formerly** ADV anteriormente

formidable ['fɔːmɪdəbl] ADJ terrível,
temível

formula ['fɔːmjulə] (pl **formulas** or
formulae) N fórmula

fort [fɔːt] N forte m

fortify ['fɔːtɪfaɪ] VT (city) fortificar;
(person) fortalecer

fortnight ['fɔːtnaɪt] (BRIT) N quinzena,
quinze dias mpl; **fortnightly** ADJ
quinzenal ▶ ADV quinzenalmente

fortunate ['fɔːtʃənɪt] ADJ (event) feliz;
(person): **to be ~** ter sorte; **it is ~ that ...**
é uma sorte que ...; **fortunately** ADV
felizmente

fortune ['fɔːtʃən] N sorte f; (wealth)
fortuna; **fortune-teller** N adivinho(-a)

forty ['fɔːtɪ] NUM quarenta

forward ['fɔːwəd] ADJ (movement) para a
frente; (position) avançado; (not shy)
imodesto, presunçoso ▶ N (Sport)
atacante m ▶ VT (letter) remeter; (goods,
parcel) expedir; (career) promover; (plans)
ativar; **to move ~** avançar; **~ planning**
planejamento para o futuro; **forwards**
ADV para a frente; **forward slash** N barra

foster ['fɔstə'] VT tutelar; (activity)
promover; **foster child** irreg N
tutelado(-a)

fought [fɔːt] PT, PP of **fight**

foul [faul] ADJ horrível; (language)
obsceno ▶ N (Sport) falta ▶ VT sujar; **foul
play** N (Jur) crime m

found [faund] PT, PP of **find** ▶ VT
(establish) fundar; **foundation**
[faun'deɪʃən] N (act) fundação f; (base)
base f; (also: **foundation cream**) creme
m base; **foundations** NPL (of building)
alicerces mpl

founder ['faundə'] N fundador(a) m/f
▶ VI naufragar

fountain ['fauntɪn] N chafariz m;
fountain pen N caneta-tinteiro f

four [fɔː'] NUM quatro; **on all ~s** de
quatro; **four-by-four** [fɔbaɪ'fɔ'] N 4X4 m
(quatro por quatro); **four-letter word** N
palavrão m; **fourteen** NUM catorze; see
also **five**; **fourth** NUM quarto

fowl [faul] N ave f (doméstica)

fox [fɔks] N raposa ▶ VT deixar perplexo

foyer ['fɔɪeɪ] N saguão m

fraction ['frækʃən] N fração f

fracture ['fræktʃə'] N fratura ▶ VT
fraturar

fragile ['frædʒaɪl] ADJ frágil

fragment ['frægmənt] N fragmento

frail [freɪl] ADJ (person) fraco; (structure)
frágil

frame [freɪm] N (of building) estrutura;
(body) corpo; (of picture, door) moldura;
(of spectacles: also: **~s**) armação f, aro ▶ VT
(picture) emoldurar; **framework** N
armação f

France [frɑːns] N França

frank [fræŋk] ADJ franco ▶ VT (letter)
franquear; **frankly** ADV francamente;
(candidly) abertamente

frantic ['fræntɪk] ADJ frenético; (person)
fora de si

fraud [frɔːd] N fraude f; (person)
impostor(a) m/f

fraught [frɔːt] ADJ tenso; **~ with** repleto
de

fray [freɪ] N combate m, luta ▶ VI
esfiapar-se; **tempers were ~ed**
estavam com os nervos em frangalhos

freak [friːk] N (person) anormal m/f;
(event) anomalia

freckle ['frɛkl] N sarda

free [friː] ADJ livre; (seat) desocupado;
(costing nothing) gratis, gratuito ▶ VT pôr
em liberdade; (jammed object) soltar;
~ (of charge) grátis, de graça; **freedom**
N liberdade f; **freelance** ADJ freelance;
freely ADV livremente; **free-range** N (egg)
caseiro; **freeway** (US) N via expressa;
free will N livre arbítrio; **of one's own
free will** por sua própria vontade

freeze [friːz] (*pt* **froze**, *pp* **frozen**) VI
gelar(-se), congelar-se ▶ VT congelar
▶ N geada; (*on arms, wages*)
congelamento; **freezer** N congelador *m*,
freezer *m* (BR); **freezing** ADJ: **freezing
(cold)** (*weather*) glacial; (*water*) gelado;
3 degrees below freezing 3 graus
abaixo de zero; **freezing point** N ponto
de congelamento

freight [freɪt] N (*goods*) carga; (*money
charged*) frete *m*; **freight train** (US) N
trem *m* de carga

French [frɛntʃ] ADJ francês(-esa) ▶ N
(*Ling*) francês *m*; **the French** NPL os
franceses; **French bean** (BRIT) N feijão *m*
comum; **French fried potatoes** NPL
batatas *fpl* fritas; **Frenchman** *irreg* N
francês *m*; **Frenchwoman** *irreg* N
francesa

frenzy ['frɛnzɪ] N frenesi *m*

frequent [*adj* 'friːkwənt, *vt* frɪ'kwɛnt]
ADJ frequente ▶ VT frequentar;
frequently ADV frequentemente, a
miúdo

fresh [frɛʃ] ADJ fresco; (*new*) novo;
(*cheeky*) atrevido; **freshen** VI (*wind, air*)
tornar-se mais forte; **freshen up** VI
(*person*) lavar-se, refrescar-se; **freshly**
ADV recentemente, há pouco

fret [frɛt] VI afligir-se

friction ['frɪkʃən] N fricção *f*; (*between
people*) atrito

Friday ['fraɪdɪ] N sexta-feira *f*

fridge [frɪdʒ] N geladeira (BR), frigorífico
(PT)

fried [fraɪd] ADJ frito; **~ egg** ovo
estrelado *or* frito

friend [frɛnd] N amigo(-a) ▶ VT (*on social
network*) adicionar como amigo;
friendly ADJ simpático ▶ N (*also:*
friendly match) amistoso; **friendship**
N amizade *f*

fries [fraɪz] (*esp* US) NPL = **French fried
potatoes**

fright [fraɪt] N terror *m*; (*scare*) pavor *m*;
to take ~ assustar-se; **frighten** VT
assustar; **frightened** ADJ: **to be
frightened of** ter medo de; **frightening**
ADJ assustador(a); **frightful** ADJ terrível,
horrível

frill [frɪl] N babado

fringe [frɪndʒ] N franja; (*on shawl etc*)
beira, orla; (*edge: of forest etc*) margem *f*

fritter ['frɪtə'] N bolinho frito; **fritter
away** VT desperdiçar

frivolous ['frɪvələs] ADJ frívolo; (*activity*)
fútil

fro [frəu] ADJ *see* **to**

frock [frɔk] N vestido

frog [frɔg] N rã *f*; **frogman** *irreg* N
homem-rã *m*

(KEYWORD)

from [frɔm] PREP **1** (*indicating starting
place*) de; **where do you come from?** de
onde você é?; **we flew from London to
Glasgow** fomos de avião de Londres
para Glasgow; **to escape from sth/sb**
escapar de algo/alguém
2 (*indicating origin etc*) de; **a letter/
telephone call from my sister** uma
carta/um telefonema da minha irmã;
tell him from me that ... diga a ele que
da minha parte ...; **to drink from the
bottle** beber na garrafa
3 (*indicating time*): **from one o'clock to** *or*
until *or* **till two** da uma hora até às duas;
from January (on) a partir de janeiro
4 (*indicating distance*) de; **we're still a
long way from home** ainda estamos
muito longe de casa
5 (*indicating price, number etc*) de; **prices
range from £10 to £50** os preços vão de
£10 a £50
6 (*indicating difference*) de; **he can't tell
red from green** ele não pode diferenciar
vermelho do verde
7 (*because of/on the basis of*): **from what
he says** pelo que ele diz; **to act from
conviction** agir por convicção; **weak
from hunger** fraco de fome

front [frʌnt] N frente *f*; (*of vehicle*) parte *f*
dianteira; (*of house*) fachada; (*also:*
sea ~) orla marítima ▶ ADJ da frente; **in ~
(of)** em frente (de); **front door** N porta
principal; **frontier** ['frʌntɪə'] N fronteira;
front page N primeira página

frost [frɔst] N geada; (*also:* **hoar~**) gelo;
frostbite N ulceração *f* produzida pelo
frio; **frosty** ADJ (*window*) coberto de
geada; (*welcome*) glacial

froth [frɔθ] N espuma

frown [fraun] VI franzir as sobrancelhas,
amarrar a cara

froze [frəuz] PT *of* **freeze**

frozen ['frəuzn] PP *of* **freeze**

fruit [fruːt] N INV fruta; (*fig*) fruto; **fruit
juice** N suco (BR) *or* sumo (PT) de frutas;
fruit machine (BRIT) N caça-níqueis *m*
inv (BR), máquina de jogo (PT); **fruit
salad** N salada de frutas

frustrate [frʌs'treɪt] VT frustrar

fry [fraɪ] (*pt, pp* **fried**) VT fritar; **frying
pan** N frigideira

fudge [fʌdʒ] N (*Culin*) ≈ doce *m* de leite

fuel [fjuəl] N (gen, for heating) combustível m; (for propelling) carburante m; **fuel tank** N depósito de combustível

fulfil [ful'fɪl], (US) **fulfill** VT (function) cumprir; (condition) satisfazer; (wish, desire) realizar

full [ful] ADJ cheio; (use, volume) máximo; (complete) completo; (information) detalhado; (price) integral; (skirt) folgado ▶ ADV: **~ well** perfeitamente; **I'm ~ (up)** estou satisfeito; **~ employment** pleno emprego; **a ~ two hours** duas horas completas; **at ~ speed** a toda a velocidade; **in ~** integralmente; **full stop** N ponto (final); **full-time** ADJ (work) de tempo completo or integral; **fully** ADV completamente; (at least) pelo menos

fumble ['fʌmbl] VI atrapalhar-se; **fumble with** VT FUS atrapalhar-se com

fume [fjuːm] VI fumegar; (be angry) estar com raiva; **fumes** NPL gases mpl

fun [fʌn] N divertimento; **to have ~** divertir-se; **for ~** de brincadeira; **to make ~ of** fazer troça de, zombar de

function ['fʌŋkʃən] N função f; (reception, dinner) recepção f ▶ VI funcionar

fund [fʌnd] N fundo; (source, store) fonte f; **funds** NPL (money) fundos mpl

fundamental [fʌndə'mentl] ADJ fundamental

funeral ['fjuːnərəl] N (burial) enterro

funfair ['fʌnfɛəʳ] (BRIT) N parque m de diversões

fungus ['fʌŋgəs] (pl **fungi**) N fungo; (mould) bolor m, mofo

funnel ['fʌnl] N funil m; (of ship) chaminé f

funny ['fʌnɪ] ADJ engraçado, divertido; (strange) esquisito, estranho

fur [fəːʳ] N pele f; (BRIT: in kettle etc) depósito, crosta

furious ['fjuərɪəs] ADJ furioso; (effort) incrível

furnish ['fəːnɪʃ] VT mobiliar (BR), mobilar (PT); (supply): **to ~ sb with sth** fornecer algo a alguém; **furnishings** NPL mobília

furniture ['fəːnɪtʃəʳ] N mobília, móveis mpl; **piece of ~** móvel m

furry ['fəːrɪ] ADJ peludo

further ['fəːðəʳ] ADJ novo, adicional ▶ ADV mais longe; (more) mais; (moreover) além disso ▶ VT promover; **further education** (BRIT) N educação f superior; **furthermore** ADV além disso

furthest ['fəːðɪst] SUPERL of **far**

fury ['fjuərɪ] N fúria

fuse [fjuːz] N fusível m; (for bomb etc) espoleta, mecha ▶ VT fundir; (fig) unir ▶ VI (metal) fundir-se; unir-se; **to ~ the lights** (BRIT Elec) queimar as luzes; **fuse box** N caixa de fusíveis

fuss [fʌs] N estardalhaço; (complaining) escândalo; **to make a ~** criar caso; **to make a ~ of sb** paparicar alguém; **fussy** ADJ (person) exigente; (dress, style) espalhafatoso

future ['fjuːtʃəʳ] ADJ futuro ▶ N futuro; **in (the) ~** no futuro

fuze [fjuːz] (US) = **fuse**

fuzzy ['fʌzɪ] ADJ (Phot) indistinto; (hair) frisado, encrespado

g

G [dʒi:] N (Mus) sol m

gadget ['gædʒɪt] N aparelho, engenhoca

Gaelic ['geɪlɪk] ADJ gaélico(-a) ▶ N (Ling) gaélico

gag [gæg] N (on mouth) mordaça; (joke) piada ▶ VT amordaçar

gain [geɪn] N ganho; (profit) lucro ▶ VT ganhar ▶ VI (watch) adiantar-se; (benefit): **to ~ from sth** tirar proveito de algo; **to ~ on sb** aproximar-se de alguém; **to ~ 3lbs (in weight)** engordar 3 libras

gal. ABBR = **gallon**

gale [geɪl] N ventania; **~ force 10** vento de força 10

gallery ['gælərɪ] N (in theatre etc) galeria; (also: **art ~**: public) museu m; (: private) galeria (de arte)

gallon ['gælən] N galão m (Brit = 4.5 litros, US = 3.8 litros)

gallop ['gæləp] N galope m ▶ VI galopar

gallstone ['gɔ:lstəun] N cálculo biliar

gamble ['gæmbl] N risco ▶ VT, VI jogar, arriscar; **gambler** N jogador(a) m/f; **gambling** N jogo

game [geɪm] N jogo; (match) partida; (Tennis) jogada; (strategy) plano, esquema m; (Hunting) caça ▶ ADJ (willing): **to be ~ for anything** topar qualquer parada; **big ~** caça grossa; **games console** [geɪmz-] N console m de videogames (BR), consola de videojogos (PT); **game show** N game show m; **gaming** ['geɪmɪŋ] N (with video games) jogos mpl de computador

gang [gæŋ] N bando, grupo; (of criminals) gangue f; (of workmen) turma ▶ VI: **to ~ up on sb** conspirar contra alguém

gangster ['gæŋstə'] N gângster m, bandido

gap [gæp] N brecha, fenda; (in trees, traffic) abertura; (in time) intervalo; (difference): **~ (between)** diferença (entre)

gape [geɪp] VI (person) estar or ficar boquiaberto; (hole) abrir-se

garage ['gærɑ:ʒ] N garagem f; (for car repairs) oficina (mecânica)

garbage ['gɑ:bɪdʒ] N (US) lixo; (inf: nonsense) disparates mpl; **garbage can** (US) N lata de lixo; **garbage collector** (US) N lixeiro(-a)

garden ['gɑ:dn] N jardim m; **gardens** NPL (public park) jardim público, parque m; **gardener** N jardineiro(-a); **gardening** N jardinagem f

garlic ['gɑ:lɪk] N alho

garment ['gɑ:mənt] N peça de roupa

garrison ['gærɪsn] N guarnição f

gas [gæs] N gás m; (US: gasoline) gasolina ▶ VT asfixiar com gás; **gas cooker** (BRIT) N fogão m a gás; **gas cylinder** N bujão m de gás; **gas fire** (BRIT) N aquecedor m a gás

gasket ['gæskɪt] N (Aut) junta, gaxeta

gasoline ['gæsəli:n] (US) N gasolina

gasp [gɑ:sp] N arfada ▶ VI arfar; **gasp out** VT dizer com voz entrecortada

gas station (US) N posto de gasolina

gastric ['gæstrɪk] ADJ gástrico; **gastric band** N (Med) banda gástrica

gate [geɪt] N portão m; **gate-crash** ['geɪtkræʃ] (BRIT) VT entrar de penetra em; **gated community** ['geɪtɪd-] N condomínio fechado; **gateway** N portão m, passagem f

gather ['gæðə'] VT colher; (assemble) reunir; (Sewing) franzir; (understand) compreender ▶ VI reunir-se; **to ~ speed** acelerar(-se); **gathering** N reunião f, assembleia

gauge [geɪdʒ] N (instrument) medidor m ▶ VT (fig: sb's capabilities, character) avaliar

gave [geɪv] PT of **give**

gay [geɪ] ADJ gay; (old-fashioned: cheerful) alegre; (colour) vistoso; (music) vivo

gaze [geɪz] N olhar m fixo ▶ VI: **to ~ at sth** fitar algo

GB ABBR = **Great Britain**

gear [gɪə'] N equipamento; (Tech) engrenagem f; (Aut) velocidade f, marcha (BR), mudança (PT) ▶ VT (fig: adapt): **to ~ sth to** preparar algo para; **top** (BRIT) or **high** (US)/**low ~** quinta/primeira (marcha); **in ~** engrenado

geese [gi:s] NPL of **goose**

gel [dʒɛl] N gel m

gem [dʒɛm] N joia, gema

Gemini ['dʒeminai] N Gêminis m, Gêmeos mpl

gender ['dʒendəʳ] N gênero

general ['dʒenərl] N general m ▶ ADJ geral; **in ~** em geral; **general anaesthetic** N anestesia geral; **generally** ADV geralmente; **general practitioner** N clínico(-a) geral

generate ['dʒenəreit] VT gerar; **generator** N gerador m

generous ['dʒenərəs] ADJ generoso; (measure etc) abundante

genetically [dʒɪ'netɪklɪ] ADV: **~ modified** (food etc) transgênico

Geneva [dʒɪ'niːvə] N Genebra

genitals ['dʒenɪtlz] NPL órgãos mpl genitais

genius ['dʒiːnɪəs] N gênio

genome ['dʒiːnəum] N genoma m

gentle ['dʒentl] ADJ (touch, breeze) leve, suave; (landscape) suave; (animal) manso

gentleman ['dʒentlmən] irreg N senhor m; (referring to social position) fidalgo; (well-bred man) cavalheiro

gently ['dʒentlɪ] ADV suavemente

gents [dʒents] N banheiro de homens (BR), casa de banho dos homens (PT)

genuine ['dʒenjuɪn] ADJ autêntico; (person) sincero

geography [dʒɪ'ɔgrəfɪ] N geografia

geology [dʒɪ'ɔlədʒɪ] N geologia

geometry [dʒɪ'ɔmətrɪ] N geometria

geranium [dʒɪ'reɪnjəm] N gerânio

geriatric [dʒerɪ'ætrɪk] ADJ geriátrico

germ [dʒəːm] N micróbio, bacilo

German ['dʒəːmən] ADJ alemão(-mã) ▶ N alemão(-mã) m/f; (Ling) alemão m; **German measles** N rubéola

Germany ['dʒəːmənɪ] N Alemanha

gesture ['dʒestʃəʳ] N gesto

(KEYWORD)

get [gɛt] (pt, pp **got**, (US) pp **gotten**) VI
1 (become, be) ficar, tornar-se; **to get old/ tired/cold** envelhecer/cansar-se/ resfriar-se; **to get annoyed/bored** aborrecer-se/amuar-se; **to get drunk** embebedar-se; **to get dirty** sujar-se; **to get killed/married** ser morto/casar-se; **when do I get paid?** quando eu recebo?, quando eu vou ser pago?; **it's getting late** está ficando tarde
2 (go): **to get to/from** ir para/de; **to get home** chegar em casa
3 (begin) começar a; **to get to know sb** começar a conhecer alguém; **let's get going** or **started** vamos lá!
▶ MODAL AUX VB: **you've got to do it** você tem que fazê-lo

▶ VT **1**: **to get sth done** (do) fazer algo; (have done) mandar fazer algo; **to get one's hair cut** cortar o cabelo; **to get the car going** or **to go** fazer o carro andar; **to get sb to do sth** convencer alguém a fazer algo; **to get sth/sb ready** preparar algo/arrumar alguém
2 (obtain) ter; (find) achar; (fetch) buscar; **to get sth for sb** arranjar algo para alguém; (fetch) ir buscar algo para alguém; **get me Mr Harris, please** (Tel) pode chamar o Sr Harris, por favor; **can I get you a drink?** você está servido?
3 (receive: present, letter) receber; (acquire: reputation, prize) ganhar
4 (catch) agarrar; (hit: target etc) pegar; **to get sb by the arm/throat** agarrar alguém pelo braço/pela garganta; **get him!** pega ele!
5 (take, move) levar; **to get sth to sb** levar algo para alguém; **I can't get it in/ out/through** não consigo enfiá-lo/ tirá-lo/passá-lo; **do you think we'll get it through the door?** você acha que conseguiremos passar isto na porta?
6 (plane, bus etc) pegar, tomar; **where do I get the train to Birmingham?** onde eu pego o trem para Birmingham?
7 (understand) entender; (hear) ouvir; **I've got it** entendi; **I don't get your meaning** não entendo o que você quer dizer
8 (have, possess): **to have got** ter

get about VI (news) espalhar-se

get along VI (agree) entender-se; (depart) ir embora; (manage) = **get by**

get around = **get round**

get at VT FUS (attack, criticize) atacar; (reach) alcançar; **what are you getting at?** o que você está querendo dizer?

get away VI (leave) partir; (escape) escapar

get away with VT FUS conseguir fazer impunemente

get back VI (return) regressar, voltar ▶ VT receber de volta, recobrar

get by VI (pass) passar; (manage) virar-se

get down VI descer ▶ VT FUS abaixar ▶ VT (object) abaixar, descer; (depress: person) deprimir

get down to VT FUS (work) pôr-se a (fazer)

get in VI entrar; (train) chegar; (arrive home) voltar para casa

get into VT FUS entrar em; (vehicle) subir em; (clothes) pôr, vestir, enfiar; **to get into bed/a rage** meter-se na cama/ ficar com raiva

get off VI (from train etc) saltar (BR), descer (PT); (depart) sair; (escape) escapar

▶ VT (remove: clothes, stain) tirar; (send off) mandar ▶ VT FUS (train, bus) saltar de (BR), sair de (PT)

get on VI (at exam etc): **how are you getting on?** como vai?; (agree): **to get on (with)** entender-se (com) ▶ VT FUS (train etc) subir em (BR), subir para (PT); (horse) montar em

get out VI (of place, vehicle) sair ▶ VT (take out) tirar

get out of VT FUS (duty etc) escapar de

get over VT FUS (illness) restabelecer-se de

get round VT FUS rodear; (fig: person) convencer

get through VI (Tel) completar a ligação

get through to VT FUS (Tel) comunicar-se com

get together VI (people) reunir-se ▶ VT reunir

get up VI levantar-se ▶ VT FUS levantar

get up to VT FUS (reach) chegar a; (BRIT: prank etc) fazer

getaway ['gɛtəweɪ] N fuga, escape m

ghastly ['gɑːstlɪ] ADJ horrível; (building) medonho; (appearance) horripilante; (pale) pálido

ghost [gəʊst] N fantasma m

giant ['dʒaɪənt] N gigante m ▶ ADJ gigantesco, gigante

gift [gɪft] N presente m, dádiva; (ability) dom m, talento; **gifted** ADJ bem-dotado; **gift shop**, (US) **gift store** N loja de presentes

gigabyte ['gɪgəbaɪt] N gigabyte m

gigantic [dʒaɪ'gæntɪk] ADJ gigantesco

giggle ['gɪgl] VI dar risadinha boba

gills [gɪlz] NPL (of fish) guelras fpl, brânquias fpl

gilt [gɪlt] ADJ dourado ▶ N dourado

gimmick ['gɪmɪk] N truque m or macete m (publicitário)

gin [dʒɪn] N gim m, genebra

ginger ['dʒɪndʒəʳ] N gengibre m

gipsy ['dʒɪpsɪ] N cigano

giraffe [dʒɪ'rɑːf] N girafa

girl [gəːl] N (small) menina (BR), rapariga (PT); (young woman) jovem f, moça; (daughter) filha; **girlfriend** N (of girl) amiga; (of boy) namorada

gist [dʒɪst] N essencial m

(KEYWORD)

give [gɪv] (pt **gave**, pp **given**) VT **1** (hand over) dar; **to give sb sth, give sth to sb** dar algo a alguém

2 (used with n to replace a vb): **to give a** cry/sigh/push etc dar um grito/suspiro/empurrão etc; **to give a speech/ a lecture** fazer um discurso/uma palestra

3 (tell, deliver: news, advice, message etc) dar; **to give the right/wrong answer** dar a resposta certa/errada

4 (supply, provide: opportunity, surprise, job etc) dar; (bestow: title, honour, right) conceder; **the sun gives warmth and light** o sol fornece calor e luz

5 (dedicate: time, one's life/attention) dedicar; **she gave it all her attention** ela dedicou toda sua atenção a isto

6 (organize): **to give a party/dinner** etc dar uma festa/jantar etc

▶ VI **1** (also: **give way**: break, collapse) dar folga; **his legs gave beneath him** suas pernas bambearam; **the roof/floor gave as I stepped on it** o telhado/chão desabou quando eu pisei nele

2 (stretch: fabric) dar de si

give away VT (money, opportunity) dar; (secret, information) revelar

give back VT devolver

give in VI (yield) ceder ▶ VT (essay etc) entregar

give off VT (heat, smoke) soltar

give out VT (distribute) distribuir; (make known) divulgar

give up VI (surrender) desistir, dar-se por vencido ▶ VT (job, boyfriend, habit) renunciar a; (idea, hope) abandonar; **to give up smoking** deixar de fumar; **to give o.s. up** entregar-se

give way VI (yield) ceder; (break, collapse: rope) arrebentar; (: ladder) quebrar; (BRIT Aut) dar a preferência (BR), dar prioridade (PT)

glacier ['glæsɪəʳ] N glaciar m, geleira

glad [glæd] ADJ contente

gladly ['glædlɪ] ADV com muito prazer

glamorous ['glæmərəs] ADJ encantador(a), glamuroso

glamour ['glæməʳ] N encanto, glamour m

glance [glɑːns] N relance m, vista de olhos ▶ VI: **to ~ at** olhar (de relance); **glance off** VT FUS (bullet) ricochetear de

gland [glænd] N glândula

glare [glɛəʳ] N (of anger) olhar m furioso; (of light) luminosidade f; (of publicity) foco ▶ VI brilhar; **to ~ at** olhar furioso para; **glaring** ADJ (mistake) notório

glass [glɑːs] N vidro, cristal m; (for drinking) copo; **glasses** NPL (spectacles) óculos mpl

glaze [gleɪz] VT (*door*) envidraçar; (*pottery*) vitrificar ▸ N verniz *m*

gleam [gli:m] VI brilhar

glide [glaɪd] VI deslizar; (*Aviat: birds*) planar; **glider** N (*Aviat*) planador *m*

glimmer ['glɪmə'] N luz *f* trêmula; (*of interest, hope*) lampejo

glimpse [glɪmps] N vista rápida, vislumbre *m* ▸ VT vislumbrar, ver de relance

glint [glɪnt] VI cintilar

glisten ['glɪsn] VI brilhar

glitter ['glɪtə'] VI reluzir, brilhar

global ['gləubl] ADJ mundial; **globalization** [gləubəlaɪ'zeɪʃən] N globalização *f*; **global warming** N aquecimento global

globe [gləub] N globo, esfera

gloom [glu:m] N escuridão *f*; (*sadness*) tristeza; **gloomy** ADJ escuro; (*sad*) triste

glorious ['glɔ:rɪəs] ADJ (*weather*) magnífico; (*future*) glorioso

glory ['glɔ:rɪ] N glória

gloss [glɔs] N (*shine*) brilho; (*also: ~ paint*) pintura brilhante, esmalte *m*; **gloss over** VT FUS encobrir

glossary ['glɔsərɪ] N glossário

glossy ['glɔsɪ] ADJ lustroso

glove [glʌv] N luva

glow [gləu] VI (*shine*) brilhar; (*fire*) arder

glucose ['glu:kəus] N glicose *f*

glue [glu:] N cola ▸ VT colar

GM ADJ ABBR (= *genetically modified*) geneticamente modificado; **GM crop** N plantação *f* geneticamente modificada; **GM foods** NPL alimentos *mpl* geneticamente modificados

gnaw [nɔ:] VT roer

(KEYWORD)

go [gəu] (*pt* **went**, *pp* **gone**, *pl* **goes**) VI **1** ir; (*travel, move*) viajar; **a car went by** um carro passou; **he has gone to Aberdeen** ele foi para Aberdeen

2 (*depart*) sair, ir embora

3 (*attend*) ir; **she went to university in Rio** ela fez universidade no Rio; **he goes to the local church** ele frequenta a igreja local

4 (*take part in an activity*) ir; **to go for a walk** ir passear

5 (*work*) funcionar; **the bell went just then** a campainha acabou de tocar

6 (*become*): **to go pale/mouldy** ficar pálido/mofado

7 (*be sold*): **to go for £10** ser vendido por £10

8 (*fit, suit*): **to go with** acompanhar, combinar com

9 (*be about to, intend to*): **he's going to do it** ele vai fazê-lo; **are you going to come?** você vem?

10 (*time*) passar

11 (*event, activity*) ser; **how did it go?** como foi?

12 (*be given*): **the job is to go to someone else** o emprego vai ser dado para outra pessoa

13 (*break*) romper-se; **the fuse went** o fusível queimou; **the leg of the chair went** a perna da cadeira quebrou

14 (*be placed*): **where does this cup go?** onde é que põe esta xícara?; **the milk goes in the fridge** pode guardar o leite na geladeira

▸ N **1** (*try*): **to have a go (at)** tentar

2 (*turn*) vez *f*

3 (*move*): **to be on the go** ter muito para fazer

go about VI (*also*: **go around**: *rumour*) espalhar-se ▸ VT FUS: **how do I go about this?** como é que eu faço isto?

go ahead VI (*make progress*) progredir; (*get going*) ir em frente

go along VI ir ▸ VT FUS ladear; **to go along with** concordar com

go away VI (*leave*) ir-se, ir embora

go back VI (*return*) voltar; (*go again*) ir de novo

go back on VT FUS (*promise*) faltar com

go by VI (*years, time*) passar ▸ VT FUS (*book, rule*) guiar-se por

go down VI (*descend*) descer, baixar; (*ship*) afundar; (*sun*) pôr-se ▸ VT FUS (*stairs, ladder*) descer

go for VT FUS (*fetch*) ir buscar; (*like*) gostar de; (*attack*) atacar

go in VI (*enter*) entrar

go in for VT FUS (*competition*) inscrever-se em; (*like*) gostar de

go into VT FUS (*enter*) entrar em; (*investigate*) investigar; (*embark on*) embarcar em

go off VI (*leave*) ir-se; (*food*) estragar, apodrecer; (*bomb, gun*) explodir; (*event*) realizar-se ▸ VT FUS (*person, place, food etc*) deixar de gostar de

go on VI (*continue*) seguir, continuar; (*happen*) acontecer, ocorrer

go out VI sair (*for entertainment*): **are you going out tonight?** você vai sair hoje à noite?; (*couple*): **they went out for 3 years** eles namoraram durante 3 anos; (*fire, light*) apagar-se

go over VI (*ship*) soçobrar ▸ VT FUS (*check*) revisar

go round VI (*news, rumour*) circular

go through VT FUS (*town etc*) atravessar; (*search through*) vasculhar; (*examine*) percorrer de cabo a rabo
go up VI (*ascend*) subir; (*price, level*) aumentar
go without VT FUS passar sem

go-ahead ADJ empreendedor(a) ▶ N luz f verde
goal [gəʊl] N meta, alvo; (*Sport*) gol m (BR), golo (PT); **goalkeeper** N goleiro(-a) (BR), guarda-redes m/f inv (PT)
goat [gəʊt] N cabra
gobble ['gɔbl] VT (*also:* **~ down, ~ up**) engolir rapidamente, devorar
god [gɔd] N deus m; **G~** Deus; **godchild** *irreg* N afilhado(-a); **goddess** N deusa; **godfather** N padrinho; **godmother** N madrinha
goggles ['gɔglz] NPL óculos mpl de proteção
going ['gəʊɪŋ] N (*conditions*) estado do terreno ▶ ADJ: **the ~ rate** tarifa corrente *or* em vigor
gold [gəʊld] N ouro ▶ ADJ de ouro; **golden** ADJ (*made of gold*) de ouro; (*gold in colour*) dourado; **goldfish** N INV peixe-dourado m; **gold-plated** ADJ plaquê inv
golf [gɔlf] N golfe m; **golf ball** N bola de golfe; (*on typewriter*) esfera; **golf club** N clube m de golfe; (*stick*) taco; **golf course** N campo de golfe; **golfer** N jogador(a) m/f de golfe, golfista m/f
gone [gɔn] PP of **go**
gong [gɔŋ] N gongo
good [gʊd] ADJ bom/boa; (*kind*) bom, bondoso; (*well-behaved*) educado ▶ N bem m; **goods** NPL (*Comm*) mercadorias fpl; **~!** bom!; **to be ~ at** ser bom em; **to be ~ for** servir para; **it's ~ for you** faz-lhe bem; **a ~ deal (of)** muito; **a ~ many** muitos; **to make ~** reparar; **it's no ~ complaining** não adianta se queixar; **for ~** para sempre, definitivamente; **~ morning/afternoon!** bom dia/boa tarde!; **~ evening!** boa noite!; **~ night!** boa noite!; **goodbye** EXCL até logo (BR), adeus (PT); **to say goodbye** despedir-se; **Good Friday** N Sexta-Feira Santa; **good-looking** ADJ bonito; **good-natured** ADJ (*person*) de bom gênio; (*pet*) de boa índole; **goodwill** N boa vontade f
Google® ['gu:gəl] VT, VI pesquisar no Google®
goose [gu:s] (*pl* **geese**) N ganso
gooseberry ['guzbəri] N groselha; **to play ~** (BRIT) ficar de vela

gorge [gɔːdʒ] N desfiladeiro ▶ VT: **to ~ o.s. (on)** empanturrar-se (de)
gorgeous ['gɔːdʒəs] ADJ magnífico, maravilhoso; (*person*) lindo
gorilla [gə'rɪlə] N gorila m
gosh [gɔʃ] (*inf*) EXCL puxa
gospel ['gɔspl] N evangelho
gossip ['gɔsɪp] N (*scandal*) fofocas fpl (BR), mexericos mpl (PT); (*chat*) conversa; (*scandalmonger*) fofoqueiro(-a) (BR), mexeriqueiro(-a) (PT) ▶ VI (*chat*) bater (um) papo (BR), cavaquear (PT)
got [gɔt] PT, PP of **get**
gotten ['gɔtn] (US) PP of **get**
govern ['gʌvən] VT governar; (*event*) controlar
government ['gʌvnmənt] N governo
governor ['gʌvənəʳ] N governador(a) m/f; (*of school, hospital, jail*) diretor(a) m/f
gown [gaʊn] N vestido; (*of teacher, judge*) toga
GP N ABBR (*Med*) = **general practitioner**
GPS N ABBR (= *global positioning system*) GPS m
grab [græb] VT agarrar ▶ VI: **to ~ at** tentar agarrar
grace [greɪs] N (*Rel*) graça; (*gracefulness*) elegância, fineza ▶ VT (*honour*) honrar; (*adorn*) adornar; **5 days' ~** um prazo de 5 dias; **graceful** ADJ elegante, gracioso; **gracious** ['greɪʃəs] ADJ gracioso, afável
grade [greɪd] N (*quality*) classe f, qualidade f; (*degree*) grau m; (US: *Sch*) série f, classe ▶ VT classificar; **grade crossing** (US) N passagem f de nível; **grade school** (US) N escola primária
gradient ['greɪdɪənt] N declive m
gradual ['grædjuəl] ADJ gradual, gradativo; **gradually** ADV gradualmente, gradativamente, pouco a pouco
graduate [n 'grædjuɪt, vi 'grædjueɪt] N graduado, licenciado; (US) diplomado do colégio ▶ VI formar-se, licenciar-se; **graduation** [grædju'eɪʃən] N formatura
graffiti [grə'fi:ti] N, NPL pichações fpl
graft [grɑːft] N (*Agr, Med*) enxerto; (BRIT *inf*) trabalho pesado; (*bribery*) suborno ▶ VT enxertar
grain [greɪn] N grão m; (*no pl: cereals*) cereais mpl; (*in wood*) veio, fibra
gram [græm] N grama m
grammar ['græməʳ] N gramática; **grammar school** N (BRIT) ≈ liceo
gramme [græm] N = **gram**
gran [græn] (BRIT *inf*) N vó f
grand [grænd] ADJ grandioso; (*inf*: *wonderful*) ótimo; **granddad** N vovô m;

granddaughter N neta; **grandfather** N
avô *m*; **grandma** ['grænmɑ:] N avó *f*,
vovó *f*; **grandmother** N avó *f*; **grandpa**
['grænpɑ:] N = **granddad**;
grandparents NPL avós *mpl*; **grand
piano** N piano de cauda; **grandson** N
neto

granite ['grænɪt] N granito

granny ['grænɪ] (*inf*) N avó *f*, vovó *f*

grant [grɑ:nt] VT (*concede*) conceder; (*a
request etc*) anuir a; (*admit*) admitir ▶ N
(*Sch*) bolsa; (*Admin*) subvenção *f*,
subsídio; **to take sth for ~ed** dar algo
por certo

grape [greɪp] N uva

grapefruit ['greɪpfru:t] N toranja,
grapefruit *m* (BR)

graph [grɑ:f] N gráfico; **graphic**
['græfɪk] ADJ gráfico; **graphics** N (*art*)
artes *fpl* gráficas ▶ NPL (*drawings*)
desenhos *mpl*

grasp [grɑ:sp] VT agarrar, segurar;
(*understand*) compreender, entender ▶ N
mão *f*; (*understanding*) compreensão *f*

grass [grɑ:s] N grama (BR), relva (PT);
grasshopper N gafanhoto

grate [greɪt] N (*fireplace*) lareira ▶ VI
ranger ▶ VT (*Culin*) ralar

grateful ['greɪtful] ADJ agradecido, grato

grater ['greɪtə'] N ralador *m*

gratitude ['grætɪtju:d] N
agradecimento

grave [greɪv] N cova, sepultura ▶ ADJ
sério; (*mistake*) grave

gravestone ['greɪvstəun] N lápide *f*

graveyard ['greɪvjɑ:d] N cemitério

gravity ['grævɪtɪ] N (*Phys*) gravidade *f*;
(*seriousness*) seriedade *f*, gravidade *f*

gravy ['greɪvɪ] N molho (de carne)

gray [greɪ] (US) ADJ = **grey**

graze [greɪz] VI pastar ▶ VT (*touch lightly*)
roçar; (*scrape*) raspar ▶ N (*Med*)
esfoladura, arranhadura

grease [gri:s] N (*fat*) gordura; (*lubricant*)
graxa, lubrificante *m* ▶ VT (*dish*) untar;
(*brakes etc*) lubrificar, engraxar; **greasy**
ADJ gordurento, gorduroso; (*skin, hair*)
oleoso

great [greɪt] ADJ grande; (*inf*) genial;
(*pain, heat*) forte; (*important*)
importante; **Great Britain** N
Grã-Bretanha

> A Grã-Bretanha, **Great Britain** ou
> **Britain** em inglês, designa a maior das
> ilhas britânicas e, portanto, engloba a
> Escócia e o País de Gales. Junto com a
> Irlanda, a ilha de Man e as ilhas
> Anglo-normandas, a Grã-Bretanha

> forma as ilhas Britânicas, ou *British
> Isles*. Reino Unido, em inglês *United
> Kingdom* ou *UK*, é o nome oficial da
> entidade política que compreende a
> Grã-Bretanha e a Irlanda do Norte.

great: great-grandfather N bisavô *m*;
great-grandmother N bisavó *f*; **greatly**
ADV imensamente, muito

Greece [gri:s] N Grécia

greed [gri:d] N (*also:* **~iness**) avidez *f*,
cobiça; **greedy** ADJ avarento; (*for food*)
guloso

Greek [gri:k] ADJ grego ▶ N grego(-a);
(*Ling*) grego

green [gri:n] ADJ verde; (*inexperienced*)
inexperiente, ingênuo ▶ N verde *m*;
(*stretch of grass*) gramado (BR), relvado
(PT); (*on golf course*) green *m*; **greens** NPL
(*vegetables*) verduras *fpl*; **greenhouse** N
estufa; **greenhouse effect** N: **the
greenhouse effect** o efeito estufa;
greenhouse gas N gás *m* de efeito estufa

Greenland ['gri:nlənd] N Groenlândia

green tax N imposto ecológico

greet [gri:t] VT acolher; (*news*) receber;
greeting N acolhimento; **greeting
card, greetings card** N cartão *m*
comemorativo

grew [gru:] PT *of* **grow**

grey [greɪ], (US) **gray** ADJ cinzento;
(*dismal*) sombrio; **grey-haired** ADJ
grisalho; **greyhound** N galgo; **grey
vote** N voto dos idosos

grid [grɪd] N grade *f*; (*Elec*) rede *f*; **gridlock**
N (*traffic jam*) paralisia do trânsito

grief [gri:f] N dor *f*, pesar *m*

grievance ['gri:vəns] N motivo de
queixa, agravo

grieve [gri:v] VI sofrer ▶ VT dar pena a,
afligir; **to ~ for** chorar por

grill [grɪl] N (*on cooker*) grelha; (*also:*
mixed ~) prato de grelhados ▶ VT (BRIT)
grelhar; (*question*) interrogar
cerradamente

grille [grɪl] N grade *f*; (*Aut*) grelha

grim [grɪm] ADJ desagradável;
(*unattractive*) feio; (*stern*) severo

grime [graɪm] N sujeira (BR), sujidade *f* (PT)

grin [grɪn] N sorriso largo ▶ VI: **to ~ (at)**
dar um sorriso largo (para)

grind [graɪnd] (*pt, pp* **ground**) VT triturar;
(*coffee, pepper etc*) moer; (*make sharp*)
afiar; (US: *meat*) picar ▶ N (*work*) trabalho
(repetitivo e maçante)

grip [grɪp] N (*of hands*) aperto; (*handle*)
punho; (*of tyre, shoe*) aderência; (*holdall*)
valise *f* ▶ VT agarrar; (*attention*) prender;
to come *or* **get to ~s with** arcar com

gripping ['grɪpɪŋ] ADJ absorvente, emocionante

grit [grɪt] N areia, grão m de areia; (*courage*) coragem f ▶ VT (*road*) pôr areia em; **to ~ one's teeth** cerrar os dentes

groan [grəun] N gemido ▶ VI gemer

grocer ['grəusə'] N dono(-a) de mercearia; **grocer's, grocer's shop** N mercearia; **grocery** N mercearia; **groceries** NPL comestíveis *mpl*

groin [grɔɪn] N virilha

groom [gru:m] N cavalariço; (*also:* **bride~**) noivo ▶ VT (*horse*) tratar; (*fig*): **to ~ sb for sth** preparar alguém para algo; **well-~ed** bem-posto

groove [gru:v] N ranhura, entalhe *m*

grope [grəup] VI: **to ~ for** procurar às cegas

gross [grəus] ADJ (*flagrant*) grave; (*vulgar*) vulgar; (: *building*) de mau-gosto; (*Comm*) bruto

ground [graund] PT, PP of **grind** ▶ N terra, chão m; (*Sport*) campo; (*land*) terreno; (*reason: gen pl*) motivo, razão f; (*us: also:* **~ wire**) (ligação f à) terra, fio-terra m ▶ VT (*plane*) manter em terra; (*us Elec*) ligar à terra; **grounds** NPL (*of coffee etc*) borra; (*gardens etc*) jardins *mpl*, parque m; **on the ~** no chão; **to the ~** por terra; **groundsheet** (*BRIT*) N capa impermeável; **groundwork** N base f, preparação f

group [gru:p] N grupo; (*also:* **pop ~**) conjunto ▶ VT (*also:* **~ together**) agrupar ▶ VI (*also:* **~ together**) agrupar-se

grouse [graus] N INV (*bird*) tetraz m, galo-silvestre m ▶ VI (*complain*) queixar-se, resmungar

grovel ['grɔvl] VI: **to ~ (before)** abaixar-se (diante de)

grow [grəu] (*pt* **grew**, *pp* **grown**) VI crescer; (*increase*) aumentar; (*develop*): **to ~ (out of/from)** originar-se (de) ▶ VT plantar, cultivar; (*beard*) deixar crescer; **to ~ rich/weak** enriquecer(-se)/ enfraquecer(-se); **grow up** VI crescer, fazer-se homem/mulher

growl [graul] VI rosnar

grown [grəun] PP of **grow**

grown-up N adulto(-a), pessoa mais velha

growth [grəuθ] N crescimento; (*increase*) aumento; (*Med*) abcesso, tumor *m*

grub [grʌb] N larva, lagarta; (*inf: food*) comida, rango (*BR*)

grubby ['grʌbɪ] ADJ encardido

grudge [grʌdʒ] N motivo de rancor ▶ VT: **to ~ sb sth** dar algo a alguém de má vontade, invejar algo a alguém; **to**

bear sb a ~ for sth guardar rancor de alguém por algo

gruelling ['gruəlɪŋ], (*us*) **grueling** ADJ duro, árduo

gruesome ['gru:səm] ADJ horrível

grumble ['grʌmbl] VI resmungar, bufar

grumpy ['grʌmpɪ] ADJ rabugento

grunt [grʌnt] VI grunhir

guarantee [gærən'ti:] N garantia ▶ VT garantir

guard [ga:d] N guarda; (*one person*) guarda m; (*BRIT Rail*) guarda-freio; (*on machine*) dispositivo de segurança; (*also:* **fire~**) guarda-fogo ▶ VT (*protect*): **to ~ (against)** proteger (contra); (*prisoner*) vigiar; **to be on one's ~** estar prevenido; **guard against** VT FUS prevenir-se contra; **guardian** N protetor(a) *m/f*; (*of minor*) tutor(a) *m/f*

Guatemala [gwɑtə'mɑ:lə] N Guatemala

guerrilla [gə'rɪlə] N guerrilheiro(-a)

guess [gɛs] VT, VI (*estimate*) avaliar, conjeturar; (*correct answer*) adivinhar; (*us*) achar, supor ▶ N suposição f, conjetura; **to take** *or* **have a ~** adivinhar, chutar (*inf*)

guest [gɛst] N convidado(-a); (*in hotel*) hóspede *m/f*

guidance ['gaɪdəns] N conselhos *mpl*

guide [gaɪd] N (*person*) guia *m/f*; (*book, fig*) guia m; (*BRIT: also:* **girl ~**) escoteira ▶ VT guiar; **guidebook** N guia m; **guide dog** N cão m de guia; **guided tour** N visita guiada; **guidelines** NPL (*advice*) orientação f

guilt [gɪlt] N culpa; **guilty** ADJ culpado

guinea pig ['gɪnɪpɪg] N porquinho-da-Índia m, cobaia; (*fig*) cobaia

guitar [gɪ'tɑ:'] N violão m

gulf [gʌlf] N golfo; (*abyss: also fig*) abismo

gull [gʌl] N gaivota

gulp [gʌlp] VI engolir em seco ▶ VT (*also:* **~ down**) engolir

gum [gʌm] N (*Anat*) gengiva; (*glue*) goma; (*also:* **~ drop**) bala de goma; (*also:* **chewing-~**) chiclete *m* (*BR*), pastilha elástica (*PT*) ▶ VT colar

gun [gʌn] N (*gen*) arma (de fogo); (*revolver*) revólver m; (*small*) pistola; (*rifle*) espingarda; (*cannon*) canhão m; **gunfire** N tiroteio; **gunman** *irreg* N pistoleiro; **gunpoint** N: **at gunpoint** sob a ameaça de uma arma; **gunpowder** N pólvora; **gunshot** N tiro (de arma de fogo)

gust [gʌst] N (*of wind*) rajada

gut [gʌt] N intestino, tripa; **guts** NPL (*Anat*) entranhas *fpl*; (*inf: courage*) coragem f, raça (*inf*)

gutter [ˈgʌtəʳ] N (of roof) calha; (in street) sarjeta

guy [gaɪ] N (also: **~rope**) corda; (inf: man) cara m (BR), tipo (PT); **Guy Fawkes' Night** N ver nota

A **Guy Fawkes' Night**, também chamada de *bonfire night*, é a ocasião em que se comemora o fracasso da conspiração (a *Gunpowder Plot*) contra James I e o Parlamento, em 5 de novembro de 1605. Um dos conspiradores, Guy Fawkes, foi surpreendido no porão do Parlamento quando estava prestes a atear fogo a explosivos. Todo ano, no dia 5 de novembro, as crianças preparam antecipadamente um boneco de Guy Fawkes e pedem às pessoas que passam na rua *a penny for the Guy* (uma moedinha para o Guy), com o qual compram fogos de artifício.

gym [dʒɪm] N (also: **gymnasium**) ginásio; (also: **gymnastics**) ginástica

gymnast [ˈdʒɪmnæst] N ginasta m/f

gymnastics [dʒɪmˈnæstɪks] N ginástica

gynaecologist [gaɪnɪˈkɔlədʒɪst], (US) **gynecologist** N ginecologista m/f

gypsy [ˈdʒɪpsɪ] N = **gipsy**

h

haberdashery [ˈhæbəˈdæʃərɪ] (BRIT) N armarinho

habit [ˈhæbɪt] N hábito, costume m; (addiction) vício; (Rel) hábito

hack [hæk] VT (cut) cortar; (chop) talhar ▶ N (pej: writer) escrevinhador(a) m/f; **hacker** N (Comput) hacker m

had [hæd] PT, PP of **have**

haddock [ˈhædək] (**haddocks** or pl **haddock**) N hadoque m (BR), eglefim m (PT)

hadn't [ˈhædnt] = **had not**

haemorrhage [ˈhɛmərɪdʒ], (US) **hemorrhage** N hemorragia

haemorrhoids [ˈhɛmərɔɪdz], (US) **hemorrhoids** NPL hemorróidas fpl

haggle [ˈhægl] VI pechinchar, regatear

hail [heɪl] N granizo; (of objects) chuva; (of criticism) torrente f ▶ VT (greet) cumprimentar, saudar; (call) chamar ▶ VI chover granizo; **hailstone** N pedra de granizo

hair [hɛəʳ] N (of human) cabelo; (of animal, on legs) pelo; **to do one's ~** pentear-se; **hairbrush** N escova de cabelo; **haircut** N corte m de cabelo; **hairdo** N penteado; **hairdresser** N cabeleireiro(-a); **hairdresser's** N cabeleireiro; **hair dryer** N secador m de cabelo; **hair gel** N gel m para o cabelo; **hair spray** N laquê m (BR), laca (PT); **hairstyle** N penteado; **hairy** ADJ cabeludo, peludo; (inf: situation) perigoso

hake [heɪk] (pl **hakes** or **hake**) N abrótea

half [hɑːf] (pl **halves**) N metade f ▶ ADJ meio ▶ ADV meio, pela metade; **~ a pound** meia libra; **two and a ~** dois e meio; **~ a dozen** meia-dúzia; **to cut sth in ~** cortar algo ao meio; **half-hearted** ADJ irresoluto, indiferente; **half-hour** N meia hora; **half-price** ADJ, ADV pela metade do preço; **half term** (BRIT) N (Sch) *dias de folga no meio do semestre*; **half-time** N meio tempo; **halfway** ADV a meio caminho; (in time) no meio

hall [hɔ:l] N (for concerts) sala; (entrance way) hall m, entrada

hallmark ['hɔ:lmɑ:k] N (also fig) marca

hall of residence (BRIT) (pl **halls of residence**) N residência universitária

Hallowe'en ['hæləu'i:n] N Dia m das Bruxas (31 de outubro)

Segundo a tradição, **Hallowe'en** é a noite dos fantasmas e dos bruxos. Na Escócia e nos Estados Unidos, sobretudo (bem menos na Inglaterra), as crianças, para festejar o **Hallowe'en**, se fantasiam e batem de porta em porta pedindo prendas (chocolates, maçãs etc).

hallway ['hɔ:lweɪ] N hall m, entrada

halo ['heɪləu] N (of saint etc) auréola

halt [hɔ:lt] N parada (BR), paragem f (PT) ▶ VI parar ▶ VT deter; (process) interromper

halve [hɑ:v] VT (divide) dividir ao meio; (reduce by half) reduzir à metade

halves [hɑ:vz] NPL of half

ham [hæm] N presunto, fiambre m (PT)

hamburger ['hæmbə:gəʳ] N hambúrguer m

hammer ['hæməʳ] N martelo ▶ VT martelar ▶ VI (on door) bater insistentemente

hammock ['hæmək] N rede f

hamper ['hæmpəʳ] VT dificultar, atrapalhar ▶ N cesto

hamster ['hæmstəʳ] N hamster m

hand [hænd] N mão f; (of clock) ponteiro; (writing) letra; (of cards) cartas fpl; (worker) trabalhador m ▶ VT dar, passar; **to give** or **lend sb a ~** dar uma mãozinha a alguém, dar uma ajuda a alguém; **at ~** à mão, disponível; **in ~** livre; (situation) sob controle; **to be on ~** (person) estar disponível; (emergency services) estar num estado de prontidão; **on the one ~ ...**, **on the other ~ ...** por um lado ..., por outro (lado) ...; **hand in** VT entregar; **hand out** VT distribuir; **hand over** VT entregar; (powers etc) transmitir; **handbag** N bolsa; **handbook** N manual m; **handbrake** N freio (BR) or travão m (PT) de mão; **handcuffs** NPL algemas fpl; **handful** N punhado; (of people) grupo

handicap ['hændɪkæp] N (disadvantage) desvantagem f; (Sport) handicap m ▶ VT prejudicar

handkerchief ['hæŋkətʃɪf] N lenço

handle ['hændl] N (of door etc) maçaneta; (of cup etc) asa; (of knife etc) cabo; (for winding) manivela ▶ VT manusear; (deal with) tratar de; (treat: people) lidar com; **"~ with care"** "cuidado — frágil"; **to fly off the ~** perder as estribeiras; **handlebar** N, **handlebars** ['hɑ:ndlbɑ:z] NPL guidom m (BR), guidão m (PT)

handmade ['hændmeɪd] ADJ feito a mão

handout ['hændaut] N (money, food) doação f; (leaflet) folheto; (at lecture) apostila

hands-free kit ['hændzfri:-] N viva-voz m

handsome ['hænsəm] ADJ bonito; (building) elegante; (profit) considerável

handwriting ['hændraɪtɪŋ] N letra, caligrafia

handy ['hændɪ] ADJ (close at hand) à mão; (useful) útil; (skilful) habilidoso, hábil

hang [hæŋ] (pt, pp **hung**) VT pendurar; (criminal: pt, pp **hanged**) enforcar ▶ VI estar pendurado; (hair, drapery) cair ▶ N (inf): **to get the ~ of (doing) sth** pegar o jeito de (fazer) algo; **hang about** VI vadiar, vagabundear; **hang around** VI = **hang about**; **hang on** VI (wait) esperar; **hang up** VT (coat) pendurar ▶ VI (Tel) desligar; **to ~ up on sb** bater o telefone na cara de alguém

hanger ['hæŋəʳ] N cabide m

hang-gliding N voo livre

hangover ['hæŋəuvəʳ] N ressaca

happen ['hæpən] VI acontecer; **as it ~s ...** acontece que ...

happily ['hæpɪlɪ] ADV (luckily) felizmente; (cheerfully) alegremente

happiness ['hæpɪnɪs] N felicidade f

happy ['hæpɪ] ADJ feliz; (cheerful) contente; **to be ~ (with)** estar contente (com); **to be ~ to do** (willing) estar disposto a fazer; **~ birthday!** feliz aniversário

harass ['hærəs] VT importunar; **harassment** N perseguição f

harbour ['hɑ:bəʳ], (US) **harbor** N porto ▶ VT (hope etc) abrigar; (hide) esconder

hard [hɑ:d] ADJ duro; (difficult) difícil; (work) árduo; (person) severo, cruel; (facts) verdadeiro ▶ ADV (work) muito, diligentemente; (think, try) seriamente; **to look ~ at** olhar firme or fixamente para; **no ~ feelings!** sem ressentimentos!; **to be ~ of hearing** ser surdo; **to be ~ done by** ser tratado injustamente; **hardback** N livro de capa dura; **hard disk** N (Comput) disco rígido;

hard drive N (*Comput*) disco rígido;
harden VT endurecer; (*steel*) temperar;
(*fig*) tornar insensível ▶ VI endurecer-se
hardly ['hɑːdlɪ] ADV (*scarcely*) apenas; (*no
sooner*) mal; **~ ever** quase nunca
hardship ['hɑːdʃɪp] N privação f
hardware ['hɑːdwɛəʳ] N ferragens fpl;
(*Comput*) hardware m
hard-working ADJ trabalhador(a);
(*student*) aplicado
hardy ['hɑːdɪ] ADJ forte; (*plant*) resistente
hare [hɛəʳ] N lebre f
harm [hɑːm] N mal m; (*damage*) dano
▶ VT (*person*) fazer mal a, prejudicar;
(*thing*) danificar; **out of ~'s way** a salvo;
harmful ADJ prejudicial, nocivo;
harmless ADJ inofensivo
harmony ['hɑːmənɪ] N harmonia
harness ['hɑːnɪs] N (*for horse*) arreios mpl;
(*for child*) correia; (*safety harness*) correia
de segurança ▶ VT (*horse*) arrear, pôr
arreios em; (*resources*) aproveitar
harp [hɑːp] N harpa ▶ VI: **to ~ on about**
bater sempre na mesma tecla sobre
harsh [hɑːʃ] ADJ (*life*) duro
harvest ['hɑːvɪst] N colheita ▶ VT colher
has [hæz] VB *see* **have**
hash [hæʃ] N (*symbol*) sustenido;
hashtag ['hæʃtæg] N (*on Twitter*)
hashtag f
hasn't ['hæznt] = **has not**
hassle ['hæsl] (*inf*) N complicação f
haste [heɪst] N pressa; **hasten** ['heɪsn]
VT acelerar ▶ VI: **to hasten to do sth**
apressar-se em fazer algo; **hastily** ADV
depressa; **hasty** ADJ apressado; (*rash*)
precipitado
hat [hæt] N chapéu m
hatch [hætʃ] N (*Naut: also: ~way*)
escotilha; (*also: service ~*) comunicação
f entre a cozinha e a sala de jantar ▶ VI
sair do ovo, chocar
hate [heɪt] VT odiar, detestar ▶ N ódio;
hatred ['heɪtrɪd] N ódio
haul [hɔːl] VT puxar ▶ N (*of fish*) redada;
(*of stolen goods etc*) pilhagem f, presa
haunt [hɔːnt] VT (*subj: ghost*) assombrar;
(: *problem, memory*) perseguir ▶ N reduto;
(*haunted house*) casa mal-assombrada

(KEYWORD)

have [hæv] (*pt, pp* **had**) AUX VB **1** (*gen*) ter;
to have arrived/gone/eaten/slept
ter chegado/ido/comido/dormido; **he
has been kind/promoted** ele foi
bondoso/promovido; **having finished
or when he had finished, he left**
quando ele terminou, foi embora

2 (*in tag questions*): **you've done it,
haven't you?** você fez isto, não foi?;
he hasn't done it, has he? ele não fez
isto, fez?
3 (*in short questions and answers*): **you've
made a mistake — no I haven't/so
I have** você fez um erro — não, eu não
fiz/sim, eu fiz; **I've been there before,
have you?** eu já estive lá, e você?
▶ MODAL AUX VB (*be obliged*): **to have
(got) to do sth** ter que fazer algo;
**I haven't got *or* I don't have to wear
glasses** eu não preciso usar óculos
▶ VT **1** (*possess*) ter; **he has (got) blue
eyes/dark hair** ele tem olhos azuis/
cabelo escuro
2 (*referring to meals etc*): **to have
breakfast** tomar café (BR), tomar o
pequeno almoço (PT); **to have lunch/
dinner** almoçar/jantar; **to have a
drink/a cigarette** tomar um drinque/
fumar um cigarro
3 (*receive, obtain etc*): **may I have your
address?** pode me dar seu endereço?;
you can have it for 5 pounds você pode
levá-lo por 5 libras; **to have a baby** dar à
luz (BR), ter um nenê *or* bebê (PT)
4 (*maintain, allow*): **he will have it that
he is right** ele vai insistir que ele está
certo; **I won't have it/this nonsense!**
não vou aguentar isso/este absurdo!;
we can't have that não podemos
permitir isto
5: **to have sth done** mandar fazer algo;
to have one's hair cut ir cortar o
cabelo; **to have sb do sth** mandar
alguém fazer algo
6 (*experience, suffer*): **to have a cold/flu**
estar resfriado (BR) *or* constipado (PT)/
com gripe; **she had her bag stolen/her
arm broken** ela teve sua bolsa roubada/
ela quebrou o braço; **to have an
operation** fazer uma operação
7 (+ *n: take, hold etc*): **to have a swim/
walk/bath/rest** ir nadar/passear/
tomar um banho/descansar; **let's have
a look** vamos dar uma olhada; **to have
a party** fazer uma festa
8 (*inf: dupe*): **he's been had** ele comprou
gato por lebre
have out VT: **to have it out with sb**
(*settle a problem*) explicar-se com alguém

haven ['heɪvn] N porto; (*fig*) abrigo,
refúgio
haven't ['hævnt] = **have not**
havoc ['hævək] N destruição f; **to play ~
with** (*fig*) estragar

hawk [hɔ:k] N falcão m
hay [heɪ] N feno; **hay fever** N febre f do feno; **haystack** N palheiro
hazard [ˈhæzəd] N perigo, risco ▶ VT aventurar, arriscar; **hazard warning lights** NPL (Aut) pisca-alerta m
haze [heɪz] N névoa
hazelnut [ˈheɪzlnʌt] N avelã f
hazy [ˈheɪzɪ] ADJ nublado; (idea) confuso
he [hi:] PRON ele; **he who ...** quem ..., aquele que ...
head [hɛd] N cabeça; (of table) cabeceira; (of queue) frente f; (of organization) chefe m/f; (of school) diretor(a) m/f ▶ VT (list) encabeçar; (group) liderar; **~s or tails** cara ou coroa; **~ first** de cabeça; **~ over heels** de pernas para o ar; **~ over heels in love** apaixonadíssimo; **to ~ the ball** cabecear a bola; **head for** VT FUS dirigir-se a; (disaster) estar procurando; **headache** N dor f de cabeça; **heading** N título, cabeçalho; **headlamp** (BRIT) N = **headlight**; **headlight** N farol m; **headline** N manchete f; **head office** N matriz f; **headphones** NPL fones mpl de ouvido; **headquarters** NPL sede f; (Mil) quartel m general; **headroom** N (in car) espaço (para a cabeça); (under bridge) vão m livre; **headscarf** irreg N lenço de cabeça
heal [hi:l] VT curar ▶ VI cicatrizar
health [hɛlθ] N saúde f; **good ~!** saúde!; **health care** N assistência médica; **healthy** ADJ (person) saudável; (air, walk) sadio; (economy) próspero, forte
heap [hi:p] N pilha, montão m ▶ VT (plate) encher; **~s (of)** (inf) um monte (de)
hear [hɪəʳ] (pt, pp **heard**) VT ouvir; (listen to) escutar; (news) saber; **to ~ about** ouvir falar de; **to ~ from sb** ter notícias de alguém; **hearing** N (sense) audição f; (Jur) audiência; **hearing aid** N aparelho para a surdez
hearse [hə:s] N carro fúnebre
heart [ha:t] N coração m; (of problem, city) centro; **hearts** NPL (Cards) copas fpl; **to lose/take ~** perder o ânimo/criar coragem; **at ~** no fundo; **by ~** (learn, know) de cor; **heart attack** N ataque m de coração; **heartbeat** N batida do coração; **heartbroken** ADJ: **to be heartbroken** estar inconsolável; **heartburn** N azia
hearty [ˈha:tɪ] ADJ (person) energético; (laugh) animado; (appetite) bom/boa; (welcome) sincero; (dislike) absoluto
heat [hi:t] N calor m; (excitement) ardor m; (Sport: also: **qualifying ~**) (prova) eliminatória ▶ VT esquentar; (room, house) aquecer; **heat up** VI aquecer-se, esquentar ▶ VT esquentar; **heated** ADJ aquecido; (fig) acalorado; **heater** N aquecedor m
heather [ˈhɛðəʳ] N urze f
heating [ˈhi:tɪŋ] N aquecimento, calefação f
heaven [ˈhɛvn] N céu m, paraíso; **heavenly** ADJ celestial; (Rel) divino
heavily [ˈhɛvɪlɪ] ADV pesadamente; (drink, smoke) excessivamente; (sleep, depend) profundamente
heavy [ˈhɛvɪ] ADJ pesado; (work) duro; (responsibility) grande; (rain, meal) forte; (drinker, smoker) inveterado; (weather) carregado
Hebrew [ˈhi:bru:] ADJ hebreu/hebreia ▶ N (Ling) hebraico
Hebrides [ˈhɛbrɪdi:z] NPL: **the ~** as (ilhas) Hébridas
hectic [ˈhɛktɪk] ADJ agitado
he'd [hi:d] = **he would**; = **he had**
hedge [hɛdʒ] N cerca viva, sebe f ▶ VI dar evasivas ▶ VT: **to ~ one's bets** (fig) resguardar-se
hedgehog [ˈhɛdʒhɔg] N ouriço
heed [hi:d] VT (also: **take ~ of**) prestar atenção a
heel [hi:l] N (of shoe) salto; (of foot) calcanhar m ▶ VT (shoe) pôr salto em
hefty [ˈhɛftɪ] ADJ (person) robusto; (parcel) pesado; (profit) alto
height [haɪt] N (of person) estatura; (of building, tree) altura; (of plane) altitude f; (high ground) monte m; (fig: of power) auge m; (: of luxury) máximo; (: of stupidity) cúmulo; **heighten** VT elevar; (fig) aumentar
heir [ɛəʳ] N herdeiro; **heiress** N herdeira
held [hɛld] PT, PP of **hold**
helicopter [ˈhɛlɪkɔptəʳ] N helicóptero
hell [hɛl] N inferno; **~!** (inf) droga!
he'll [hi:l] = **he will**; = **he shall**
hello [həˈləu] EXCL oi! (BR), olá! (PT); (surprise) ora essa!
helmet [ˈhɛlmɪt] N capacete m
help [hɛlp] N ajuda; (charwoman) faxineira ▶ VT ajudar; **~!** socorro!; **~ yourself** sirva-se; **he can't ~ it** não tem culpa; **help desk** N atendimento telefônico; **helper** N ajudante m/f; **helpful** ADJ prestativo; (advice) útil; **helping** N porção f; **helpless** ADJ (incapable) incapaz; (defenceless) indefeso; **helpline** N disque-ajuda m (BR), linha de apoio (PT)
hem [hɛm] N bainha ▶ VT embainhar; **hem in** VT cercar, encurralar

hemorrhage ['hɛmərɪdʒ] (US) N =
  haemorrhage
hemorrhoids ['hɛmərɔɪdz] (US) NPL =
  haemorrhoids
hen [hɛn] N galinha; (female bird) fêmea
hence [hɛns] ADV daí, portanto; **2 years ~**
  daqui a 2 anos
her [həːʳ] PRON (direct) a; (indirect) lhe;
  (stressed, after prep) ela ▶ ADJ seu/sua,
  dela; see also **me, my**
herb [həːb] N erva
herd [həːd] N rebanho
here [hɪəʳ] ADV aqui; (at this point) nesse
  ponto; **~!** (present) presente!; **~ is/are**
  aqui está/estão; **~ he/she is!** aqui está
  ele/ela!
heritage ['hɛrɪtɪdʒ] N patrimônio
hernia ['həːnɪə] N hérnia
hero ['hɪərəu] (pl **heroes**) N herói m; (of
  book, film) protagonista m
heroin ['hɛrəuɪn] N heroína
heroine ['hɛrəuɪn] N heroína; (of book,
  film) protagonista
heron ['hɛrən] N garça
herring ['hɛrɪŋ] (pl **herrings** or **herring**)
  N arenque m
hers [həːz] PRON (o) seu/(a) sua, (o/a)
  dela; see also **mine¹**
herself [həːˈsɛlf] PRON (reflexive) se;
  (emphatic) ela mesma; (after prep) si
  (mesma); see also **oneself**
he's [hiːz] = **he is**; = **he has**
hesitant ['hɛzɪtənt] ADJ hesitante,
  indeciso
hesitate ['hɛzɪteɪt] VI hesitar;
  hesitation [hɛzɪˈteɪʃən] N hesitação f,
  indecisão f
heterosexual ['hɛtərəuˈsɛksjuəl] ADJ
  heterossexual
heyday ['heɪdeɪ] N: **the ~ of** o auge or
  apogeu de
hi [haɪ] EXCL oi!
hibernate ['haɪbəneɪt] VI hibernar
hiccup ['hɪkʌp] VI soluçar ▶ NPL: **~s**
  soluço; **to have (the) ~s** estar com
  soluço
hide [haɪd] (pt **hid**, pp **hidden**) N (skin)
  pele f ▶ VT esconder, ocultar; (view)
  obscurecer ▶ VI: **to ~ (from sb)**
  esconder-se or ocultar-se (de alguém)
hideous ['hɪdɪəs] ADJ horrível
hiding ['haɪdɪŋ] N (beating) surra; **to be
  in ~** (concealed) estar escondido
hi-fi ['haɪfaɪ] N alta-fidelidade f; (system)
  som m ▶ ADJ de alta-fidelidade
high [haɪ] ADJ alto; (number) grande;
  (price) alto, elevado; (wind) forte; (voice)
  agudo; (opinion) ótimo; (principles) nobre

▶ ADV alto, a grande altura; **it is 20 m ~**
  tem 20 m de altura; **~ in the air** nas
  alturas; **highchair** N cadeira alta (para
  criança); **higher education** N ensino
  superior; **high jump** N (Sport) salto em
  altura; **highlands** NPL: **the Highlands**
  (in Scotland) a Alta Escócia; **highlight** N
  (fig) ponto alto; (in hair) mecha ▶ VT
  realçar, ressaltar; **highly** ADV: **highly
  paid** muito bem pago; **to speak highly
  of** falar elogiosamente or; **high-rise** ADJ
  alto; **high school** N (BRIT) escola
  secundária; (US) científico

  Uma **high school** é um
  estabelecimento de ensino
  secundário. Nos Estados Unidos,
  existem a Junior High School, que
  equivale aproximadamente aos dois
  últimos anos do primeiro grau, e a
  Senior High School, que corresponde ao
  segundo grau. Na Grã-Bretanha, esse
  termo às vezes é utilizado para as
  escolas secundárias.

high street (BRIT) N rua principal
highway (US) N estrada; (main road)
  rodovia
hijab [hɪˈdʒæb] N lenço islâmico
hijack ['haɪdʒæk] VT sequestrar;
  hijacker N sequestrador(a) m/f (de
  avião)
hike [haɪk] VI caminhar ▶ N caminhada,
  excursão f a pé; **hiker** N caminhante m/f,
  andarilho(-a)
hilarious [hɪˈlɛərɪəs] ADJ hilariante
hill [hɪl] N colina; (high) montanha;
  (slope) ladeira, rampa; **hillside** N
  vertente f; **hilly** ADJ montanhoso
him [hɪm] PRON (direct) o; (indirect) lhe;
  (stressed, after prep) ele; see also **me**;
  himself PRON (reflexive) se; (emphatic) ele
  mesmo; (after prep) si (mesmo); see also
  oneself
hinder ['hɪndəʳ] VT retardar
hindsight ['haɪndsaɪt] N: **with (the
  benefit of) ~** em retrospecto
Hindu ['hɪnduː] ADJ hindu
hinge [hɪndʒ] N dobradiça ▶ VI (fig): **to ~
  on** depender de
hint [hɪnt] N (suggestion) indireta; (advice)
  dica; (sign) sinal m ▶ VT: **to ~ that**
  insinuar que ▶ VI: **to ~ at** fazer alusão a
hip [hɪp] N quadril m
hippopotamus [hɪpəˈpɔtəməs] (pl
  hippopotamuses or **hippopotami**) N
  hipopótamo
hipster ['hɪpstə] N (inf) hipster mf
hire ['haɪəʳ] VT (BRIT: car, equipment)
  alugar; (worker) contratar ▶ N aluguel m;

for ~ aluga-se; (*taxi*) livre; **hire purchase**
(BRIT) N compra a prazo
his [hɪz] PRON (o) seu/(a) sua, (o/a) dele
▶ ADJ seu/sua, dele; *see also* **my, mine¹**
hiss [hɪs] vi (*snake, fat*) assoviar; (*gas*)
silvar; (*boo*) vaiar
historic [hɪ'stɔrɪk], **historical**
[hɪ'stɔrɪkl] ADJ histórico
history ['hɪstərɪ] N história
hit [hɪt] (*pt, pp* **hit**) vt bater em; (*target*)
acertar, alcançar; (*car*) bater em, colidir
com; (*fig: affect*) atingir ▶ N golpe m;
(*success*) sucesso; (*internet visit*) visita; **to
~ it off with sb** dar-se bem com alguém
hitch [hɪtʃ] vt (*fasten*) atar, amarrar;
(*also:* **~ up**) levantar ▶ N (*difficulty*)
dificuldade f; **to ~ a lift** pegar carona
(BR), arranjar uma boleia (PT)
hitch-hike vi pegar carona (BR), andar à
boleia (PT); **hitch-hiker** N carona m/f
(BR), viajante m/f à boleia (PT)
hi-tech ADJ tecnologicamente avançado
▶ N alta tecnologia
HIV ABBR: **~-negative/-positive** HIV
negativo/positivo
hive [haɪv] N colmeia; **hive off** (*inf*) vt
transferir
hoard [hɔːd] N provisão f; (*of money*)
tesouro ▶ vt acumular
hoarse [hɔːs] ADJ rouco
hoax [həuks] N trote m
hob [hɔb] N *parte de cima do fogão*
hobble ['hɔbl] vi coxear
hobby ['hɔbɪ] N hobby m, passatempo
predileto
hobo ['həubəu] (*us*) N vagabundo
hockey ['hɔkɪ] N hóquei m
hog [hɔg] N porco ▶ vt (*fig*) monopolizar;
to go the whole ~ ir até o fim
hoist [hɔɪst] vt içar
hold [həuld] (*pt, pp* **held**) vt segurar;
(*contain*) conter; (*have*) ter; (*meeting*)
realizar; (*detain*) deter; (*consider*): **to ~ sb
responsible (for sth)** responsabilizar
alguém (por algo) ▶ vi (*withstand
pressure*) resistir; (*be valid*) ser válido ▶ N
(*fig*) influência, domínio; (*of ship*) porão
m; (*of plane*) compartimento para cargo;
~ the line! (*Tel*) não desligue!; **to ~ one's
own** (*fig*) virar-se, sair-se bem; **to catch
or get (a) ~ of** agarrar, pegar; **hold back**
vt reter; (*secret*) manter, guardar; **hold
down** vt (*person*) segurar; (*job*) manter;
hold off vt (*enemy*) afastar, repelir; **hold
on** vi agarrar-se; (*wait*) esperar; **~ on!**
espera aí!; (*Tel*) não desligue!; **hold on to**
vt FUS agarrar-se a; (*keep*) guardar, ficar
com; **hold out** vt estender ▶ vi (*resist*)

resistir; **hold up** vt (*raise*) levantar;
(*support*) apoiar; (*delay*) atrasar; (*rob*)
assaltar; **holdall** (BRIT) N bolsa de
viagem; **holder** N (*of ticket*) portador(a)
m/f; (*of record*) detentor(a) m/f; (*of office,
title etc*) titular m/f; **hold-up** N (*robbery*)
assalto; (*delay*) demora; (BRIT: *in traffic*)
engarrafamento
hole [həul] N buraco; (*small, in sock etc*)
furo ▶ vt esburacar
holiday ['hɔlədɪ] N (BRIT: *vacation*) férias
fpl; (*day off*) dia m de folga; (*public holiday*)
feriado; **to be on ~** estar de férias;
holiday camp (BRIT) N colônia de férias;
holiday-maker (BRIT) N pessoa (que
está) de férias; **holiday resort** N local m
de férias
Holland ['hɔlənd] N Holanda
hollow ['hɔləu] ADJ oco, vazio; (*cheeks*)
côncavo; (*eyes*) fundo; (*sound*) surdo;
(*laugh, claim*) falso ▶ N (*in ground*)
cavidade f, depressão f ▶ vt: **to ~ out**
escavar
holly ['hɔlɪ] N azevinho
holy ['həulɪ] ADJ sagrado; (*person*) santo;
bento
home [həum] N casa, lar m; (*country*)
pátria; (*institution*) asilo ▶ CPD caseiro,
doméstico; (*Econ, Pol*) nacional, interno;
(*Sport: team*) de casa; (: *game*) no próprio
campo ▶ ADV (*direction*) para casa; (*right
in: nail etc*) até o fundo; **at ~** em casa;
make yourself at ~ fique à vontade;
home address N endereço residencial;
homeland N terra (natal); **homeless** ADJ
sem casa, desabrigado; **homely** ADJ
(*simple*) simples inv; **home-made** ADJ
caseiro; **Home Office** (BRIT) N Ministério
do Interior; **home page** N (*Comput*)
página inicial; **Home Secretary** (BRIT) N
Ministro(a) do Interior; **homesick** ADJ:
to be homesick estar com saudades (do
lar); **home town** N cidade f natal;
homework N dever m de casa
homoeopathic [həumɪə'pæθɪk], (*us*)
homeopathic ADJ homeopático
homosexual [hɔməu'sɛksjuəl] ADJ, N
homossexual m/f
Honduras [hɔn'djuərəs] N Honduras m
(*no article*)
honest ['ɔnɪst] ADJ (*truthful*) franco;
(*trustworthy*) honesto; (*sincere*) sincero;
honestly ADV honestamente; **honesty**
N honestidade f, sinceridade f
honey ['hʌnɪ] N mel m; **honeymoon** N
lua-de-mel f; (*trip*) viagem f de lua-de-mel
honorary ['ɔnərərɪ] ADJ (*unpaid*) não
remunerado; (*duty, title*) honorário

honour ['ɔnəʳ], (US) **honor** VT honrar ▶ N honra; **honourable** ADJ honrado

hood [hud] N capuz m; (of cooker) tampa; (BRIT Aut) capota; (US Aut) capô m

hoof [hu:f] (pl hooves) N casco, pata

hook [huk] N gancho; (on dress) colchete m; (for fishing) anzol m ▶ VT prender com gancho (or colchete); (fish) fisgar

hooligan ['hu:lɪgən] N desordeiro(-a), bagunceiro(-a)

hoop [hu:p] N arco

hooray [hu:'reɪ] EXCL = **hurrah**

hoot [hu:t] VI (Aut) buzinar; (siren) tocar; (owl) piar

hooves [hu:vz] NPL of **hoof**

hop [hɔp] VI saltar, pular; (on one foot) pular num pé só

hope [həup] VI esperar ▶ N esperança; **I ~ so/not** espero que sim/não; **hopeful** ADJ (person) otimista, esperançoso; (situation) promissor(a); **hopefully** ADV esperançosamente; **hopefully, they'll come back** é de esperar or esperamos que voltem; **hopeless** ADJ desesperado, irremediável; (useless) inútil

horizon [hə'raɪzn] N horizonte m; **horizontal** [hɔrɪ'zɔntl] ADJ horizontal

horn [hɔ:n] N corno, chifre m; (material) chifre; (Mus) trompa; (Aut) buzina

horoscope ['hɔrəskəup] N horóscopo

horrendous [hə'rɛndəs] ADJ horrendo

horrible ['hɔrɪbl] ADJ horrível; (terrifying) terrível

horrid ['hɔrɪd] ADJ horrível

horror ['hɔrəʳ] N horror m; **horror film** N filme m de terror

horse [hɔ:s] N cavalo; **horseback: on horseback** ADJ, ADV a cavalo; **horse chestnut** N castanha-da-índia; **horsepower** N cavalo-vapor m; **horse-racing** N corridas fpl de cavalo, turfe m

hose [həuz] N (also: **~pipe**) mangueira

hospital ['hɔspɪtl] N hospital m

hospitality [hɔspɪ'tælɪtɪ] N hospitalidade f

host [həust] N anfitrião m; (TV, Radio) apresentador(a) m/f; (Rel) hóstia; (large number): **a ~ of** uma multidão de

hostage ['hɔstɪdʒ] N refém m/f

hostel ['hɔstl] N albergue m, abrigo; (also: **youth ~**) albergue da juventude

hostess ['həustɪs] N anfitriã f; (BRIT: air hostess) aeromoça (BR), hospedeira de bordo (PT); (TV, Radio) apresentadora

hostile ['hɔstaɪl] ADJ hostil

hostility [hɔ'stɪlɪtɪ] N hostilidade f

hot [hɔt] ADJ quente; (as opposed to only warm) muito quente; (spicy) picante; (fierce) ardente; **to be ~** (person) estar com calor; (thing, weather) estar quente; **hot dog** N cachorro-quente m

hotel [həu'tɛl] N hotel m

hotspot ['hɔtspɔt] N (Comput: also: **wireless ~**) hotspot m (local público com acesso à Internet sem fio)

hound [haund] VT acossar, perseguir ▶ N cão m de caça, sabujo

hour ['auəʳ] N hora; **hourly** ADJ de hora em hora; (rate) por hora

house [n haus, vt hauz] N (gen, firm) casa; (Pol) câmara; (Theatre) assistência, lotação f ▶ VT (person) alojar; (collection) abrigar; **on the ~** (fig) por conta da casa; **household** N família; (house) casa; **housekeeper** N governanta; **housekeeping** N (work) trabalhos mpl domésticos; (money) economia doméstica; **housewife** irreg N dona de casa; **housework** N trabalhos mpl domésticos; **housing** N (provision) alojamento; (houses) residências fpl; **housing development** N conjunto residencial; **housing estate** (BRIT) N = **housing development**

hover ['hɔvəʳ] VI pairar; **hovercraft** N aerobarco

[KEYWORD]

how [hau] ADV **1** (in what way) como; **how was the film?** que tal o filme?; **how are you?** como vai? **2** (to what degree) quanto; **how much milk/many people?** quanto de leite/ quantas pessoas?; **how long have you been here?** há quanto tempo você está aqui?; **how old are you?** quantos anos você tem?; **how tall is he?** qual é a altura dele?; **how lovely/awful!** que ótimo/terrível!

however [hau'ɛvəʳ] ADV de qualquer modo; (+adj) por mais ... que; (in questions) como ▶ CONJ no entanto, contudo

howl [haul] VI uivar

H.P. (BRIT) N ABBR = **hire purchase**

h.p. ABBR (Aut: = horsepower) CV

HQ N ABBR (= headquarters) QG m

HTML N ABBR (= Hypertext Mark-up Language) HTML f

huddle ['hʌdl] VI: **to ~ together** aconchegar-se

huff [hʌf] N: **in a ~** com raiva

hug [hʌg] VT abraçar; (thing) agarrar, prender

huge [hju:dʒ] ADJ enorme, imenso
hull [hʌl] N (of ship) casco
hum [hʌm] VT cantarolar ▶ VI cantarolar;
(insect, machine etc) zumbir
human ['hju:mən] ADJ humano ▶ N
(also: **~ being**) ser m humano
humane [hju:'meɪn] ADJ humano
humanitarian [hju:mænɪ'tɛərɪən] ADJ
humanitário
humanity [hju:'mænɪtɪ] N
humanidade f
human rights NPL direitos mpl humanos
humble ['hʌmbl] ADJ humilde ▶ VT
humilhar
humid ['hju:mɪd] ADJ úmido
humiliate [hju:'mɪlɪeɪt] VT humilhar
humorous ['hju:mərəs] ADJ
humorístico; (person) engraçado
humour ['hju:mə'], (US) **humor** N
humorismo, senso de humor; (mood)
humor m ▶ VT fazer a vontade de
hump [hʌmp] N (in ground) elevação f;
(camel's) corcova, giba; (deformity)
corcunda
hunch [hʌntʃ] N (premonition)
pressentimento, palpite m
hundred ['hʌndrəd] NUM cem; (before
lower numbers) cento; **~s of people**
centenas de pessoas; **hundredth** NUM
centésimo
hung [hʌŋ] PT, PP of **hang**
Hungary ['hʌŋgərɪ] N Hungria
hunger ['hʌŋgə'] N fome f ▶ VI: **to ~ for**
(desire) desejar ardentemente
hungry ['hʌŋgrɪ] ADJ faminto,
esfomeado; (keen): **~ for** (fig) ávido de,
ansioso por; **to be ~** estar com fome
hunt [hʌnt] VT buscar, perseguir; (Sport)
caçar ▶ VI caçar ▶ N caça, caçada;
hunter N caçador(a) m/f; **hunting** N
caça
hurdle ['hə:dl] N (Sport) barreira; (fig)
obstáculo
hurl [hə:l] VT arremessar, lançar; (abuse)
gritar
hurrah [hu'rɑ:] EXCL oba!, viva!
hurray [hu'reɪ] EXCL = **hurrah**
hurricane ['hʌrɪkən] N furacão m
hurry ['hʌrɪ] N pressa ▶ VI (also: **~ up**)
apressar-se ▶ VT (also: **~ up**: person)
apressar; (: work) acelerar; **to be in a ~**
estar com pressa
hurt [hə:t] (pt, pp **hurt**) VT machucar;
(injure) ferir; (fig) magoar ▶ VI doer
husband ['hʌzbənd] N marido, esposo
hush [hʌʃ] N silêncio, quietude f ▶ VT
silenciar, fazer calar; **~!** silêncio!, psiu!;
hush up VT abafar, encobrir

husky ['hʌskɪ] ADJ rouco ▶ N cão m
esquimó
hut [hʌt] N cabana, choupana; (shed)
alpendre m
hyacinth ['haɪəsɪnθ] N jacinto
hybrid ['haɪbrɪd] ADJ, N (gen, Aut) híbrido
hydrofoil ['haɪdrəfɔɪl] N hidrofoil m,
aliscafo
hydrogen ['haɪdrədʒən] N hidrogênio
hygiene ['haɪdʒi:n] N higiene f
hymn [hɪm] N hino
hype [haɪp] (inf) N tititi m, falatório
hyperlink ['haɪpəlɪŋk] N hiperlink m
hypermarket ['haɪpəmɑ:kɪt] (BRIT) N
hipermercado
hyphen ['haɪfn] N hífen m
hypnotize ['hɪpnətaɪz] VT hipnotizar
hypocrite ['hɪpəkrɪt] N hipócrita m/f;
hypocritical ADJ hipócrita
hysterical [hɪ'stɛrɪkl] ADJ histérico;
(funny) hilariante; **hysterics** NPL
(nervous) crise f histérica; (laughter)
ataque m de riso; **to be in** or **have
hysterics** ter uma crise histérica

I

I [aɪ] PRON eu ▶ ABBR (= *island, isle*) I
ice [aɪs] N gelo; (*ice cream*) sorvete *m* ▶ VT (*cake*) cobrir com glacê ▶ VI (*also*: **~ over, ~ up**) gelar; **iceberg** N iceberg *m*; **ice cream** N sorvete *m* (*BR*), gelado (*PT*); **ice cube** N pedra de gelo; **ice hockey** N hóquei *m* sobre o gelo
Iceland ['aɪslənd] N Islândia
ice lolly (*BRIT*) N picolé *m*
ice rink N pista de gelo, rinque *m*
icing ['aɪsɪŋ] N (*Culin*) glacê *m*; **icing sugar** (*BRIT*) N açúcar *m* glacê
icon ['aɪkɔn] N (*gen, Comput*) ícone *m*
ICT N ABBR (= *Information and Communication(s) Technology*) TIC *f*
icy ['aɪsɪ] ADJ gelado
I'd [aɪd] = **I would**; = **I had**
idea [aɪ'dɪə] N ideia
ideal [aɪ'dɪəl] N ideal *m* ▶ ADJ ideal
identical [aɪ'dɛntɪkl] ADJ idêntico
identification [aɪdɛntɪfɪ'keɪʃən] N identificação *f*; **means of ~** documentos pessoais
identify [aɪ'dɛntɪfaɪ] VT identificar
identity [aɪ'dɛntɪtɪ] N identidade *f*; **identity card** N carteira de identidade; **identity theft** N roubo de identidade
idiom ['ɪdɪəm] N expressão *f* idiomática; (*style of speaking*) idioma *m*, linguagem *f*
idiot ['ɪdɪət] N idiota *m/f*
idle ['aɪdl] ADJ ocioso; (*lazy*) preguiçoso; (*unemployed*) desempregado; (*pointless*) inútil, vão/vã ▶ VI (*machine*) funcionar com a transmissão desligada; **idle away** VT: **to ~ away the time** perder *or* desperdiçar tempo
idol ['aɪdl] N ídolo
i.e. ABBR (= *id est*) i.e., isto é

if [ɪf] CONJ **1** (*conditional use*) se; **if necessary** se necessário; **if I were you** se eu fôsse você
2 (*whenever*) quando
3 (*although*): **(even) if** mesmo que
4 (*whether*) se
5: **if so/not** sendo assim/do contrário; **if only** se pelo menos; *see also* **as**

ignition [ɪg'nɪʃən] N (*Aut*) ignição *f*; **to switch on/off the ~** ligar/desligar o motor
ignorant ['ɪgnərənt] ADJ ignorante; **to be ~ of** ignorar
ignore [ɪg'nɔː'] VT (*person*) não fazer caso de; (*fact*) não levar em consideração, ignorar
ill [ɪl] ADJ doente; (*harmful: effects*) nocivo ▶ N mal *m* ▶ ADV: **to speak/think ~ of sb** falar/pensar mal de alguém; **to take** *or* **be taken ~** ficar doente
I'll [aɪl] = **I will**; = **I shall**
illegal [ɪ'liːgl] ADJ ilegal
illegible [ɪ'lɛdʒɪbl] ADJ ilegível
illegitimate [ɪlɪ'dʒɪtɪmət] ADJ ilegítimo
illiterate [ɪ'lɪtərət] ADJ analfabeto
illness ['ɪlnɪs] N doença
illuminate [ɪ'luːmɪneɪt] VT iluminar, clarear
illusion [ɪ'luːʒən] N ilusão *f*
illustrate ['ɪləstreɪt] VT ilustrar; (*point*) exemplificar; **illustration** [ɪlə'streɪʃən] N ilustração *f*; (*example*) exemplo; (*explanation*) esclarecimento
I'm [aɪm] = **I am**
image ['ɪmɪdʒ] N imagem *f*
imaginary [ɪ'mædʒɪnərɪ] ADJ imaginário
imagination [ɪmædʒɪ'neɪʃən] N imaginação *f*; (*inventiveness*) inventividade *f*
imagine [ɪ'mædʒɪn] VT imaginar
imbalance [ɪm'bæləns] N desigualdade *f*
imitate ['ɪmɪteɪt] VT imitar; **imitation** [ɪmɪ'teɪʃən] N imitação *f*; (*copy*) cópia; (*mimicry*) mímica
immaculate [ɪ'mækjulət] ADJ impecável; (*Rel*) imaculado
immature [ɪmə'tjuə'] ADJ imaturo; (*fruit*) verde
immediate [ɪ'miːdɪət] ADJ imediato; (*pressing*) urgente, premente; (*neighbourhood, family*) próximo; **immediately** ADV imediatamente; **immediately next to** bem junto a
immense [ɪ'mɛns] ADJ imenso; (*importance*) enorme

immerse [ɪ'məːs] VT submergir; **to be ~d in** (fig) estar absorto em

immigrant ['ɪmɪɡrənt] N imigrante m/f

immigration [ɪmɪ'ɡreɪʃən] N imigração f

imminent ['ɪmɪnənt] ADJ iminente

immoral [ɪ'mɔrl] ADJ imoral

immortal [ɪ'mɔːtl] ADJ imortal

immune [ɪ'mjuːn] ADJ: **~ to** imune a, imunizado contra; **immune system** N sistema m imunológico

impact ['ɪmpækt] N impacto (BR), impacte m (PT)

impair [ɪm'pɛəʳ] VT prejudicar

impartial [ɪm'pɑːʃl] ADJ imparcial

impatience [ɪm'peɪʃəns] N impaciência

impatient [ɪm'peɪʃənt] ADJ impaciente; **to get** or **grow ~** impacientar-se

impeccable [ɪm'pɛkəbl] ADJ impecável

impending [ɪm'pɛndɪŋ] ADJ iminente, próximo

imperative [ɪm'pɛrətɪv] ADJ (tone) imperioso, obrigatório; (necessary) indispensável ▶ N (Ling) imperativo

imperfect [ɪm'pəːfɪkt] ADJ imperfeito; (goods etc) defeituoso ▶ N (Ling: also: **~ tense**) imperfeito

imperial [ɪm'pɪərɪəl] ADJ imperial

impersonal [ɪm'pəːsənl] ADJ impessoal

impersonate [ɪm'pəːsəneɪt] VT fazer-se passar por, personificar; (Theatre) imitar

implement [n 'ɪmplɪmənt, vt 'ɪmplɪment] N instrumento, ferramenta; (for cooking) utensílio ▶ VT efetivar

implicit [ɪm'plɪsɪt] ADJ implícito; (complete) absoluto

imply [ɪm'plaɪ] VT (mean) significar; (hint) dar a entender que

impolite [ɪmpə'laɪt] ADJ indelicado, mal-educado

import [vt ɪm'pɔːt, n, cpd 'ɪmpɔːt] VT importar ▶ N importação f; (article) mercadoria importada

importance [ɪm'pɔːtəns] N importância

important [ɪm'pɔːtənt] ADJ importante; **it's not ~** não tem importância, não importa

impose [ɪm'pəuz] VT impor ▶ VI: **to ~ on sb** abusar de alguém; **imposing** ADJ imponente

impossible [ɪm'pɔsɪbl] ADJ impossível; (situation) inviável; (person) insuportável

impotent ['ɪmpətənt] ADJ impotente

impoverished [ɪm'pɔvərɪʃt] ADJ empobrecido; (land) esgotado

impractical [ɪm'præktɪkl] ADJ pouco prático

impress [ɪm'prɛs] VT impressionar; (mark) imprimir; **to ~ sth on sb** inculcar algo em alguém

impression [ɪm'prɛʃən] N impressão f; **to be under the ~ that** estar com a impressão de que

impressive [ɪm'prɛsɪv] ADJ impressionante

imprison [ɪm'prɪzn] VT encarcerar

improbable [ɪm'prɔbəbl] ADJ improvável; (story) inverossímil (BR), inverosímil (PT)

improper [ɪm'prɔpəʳ] ADJ (unsuitable) impróprio; (dishonest) desonesto

improve [ɪm'pruːv] VT melhorar ▶ VI melhorar; (pupils) progredir; **improvement** N melhora; progresso

improvise ['ɪmprəvaɪz] VT, VI improvisar

impulse ['ɪmpʌls] N impulso, ímpeto; (Elec) impulso; **to act on ~** agir sem pensar or num impulso

(KEYWORD)

in [ɪn] PREP **1** (indicating place, position) em; **in the house/garden** na casa/no jardim; **I have the money in my hand** estou com o dinheiro na mão; **in here/there** aqui dentro/lá dentro
2 (with place names: of town, country, region) em; **in London** em Londres; **in England/Japan/Canada/the United States** na Inglaterra/no Japão/no Canadá/nos Estados Unidos; **in Rio** no Rio
3 (indicating time: during) em; **in spring/autumn** na primavera/no outono; **in 1988** em 1988; **in May** em maio; **I'll see you in July** até julho; **in the morning** de manhã; **at 4 o'clock in the afternoon** às 4 da tarde
4 (indicating time: in the space of) em; **I did it in 3 hours/days** fiz isto em 3 horas/dias; **in 2 weeks, in 2 weeks' time** daqui a 2 semanas
5 (indicating manner etc): **in a loud/soft voice** em voz alta/numa voz suave; **written in pencil/ink** escrito a lápis/à caneta; **in English/Portuguese** em inglês/português; **the boy in the blue shirt** o menino de camisa azul
6 (indicating circumstances): **in the sun** ao or sob o sol; **in the rain** na chuva; **a rise in prices** um aumento nos preços
7 (indicating mood, state): **in tears** aos prantos; **in anger/despair** com raiva/desesperado; **in good condition** em boas condições

8 (*with ratios, numbers*): **1 in 10** 1 em 10, 1 em cada 10; **20 pence in the pound** vinte pênis numa libra; **they lined up in twos** eles se alinharam dois a dois **9** (*referring to people, works*) em **10** (*indicating profession etc*): **to be in teaching/publishing** ser professor/trabalhar numa editora **11** (*after superl*): **the best pupil in the class** o melhor aluno da classe; **the biggest/smallest in Europe** o maior/menor na Europa **12** (*with present participle*): **in saying this** ao dizer isto ▶ ADV: **to be in** (*person: at home*) estar em casa; (*: at work*) estar no trabalho; (*fashion*) estar na moda; (*ship, plane, train*): **it's in** chegou; **is he in?** ele está?; **to ask sb in** convidar alguém para entrar; **to run/limp etc in** entrar correndo/mancando *etc* ▶ N: **the ins and outs** (*of proposal, situation etc*) os cantos e recantos, os pormenores

in. ABBR = **inch**
inability [ɪnə'bɪlɪtɪ] N: ~ **(to do)** incapacidade *f* (de fazer)
inaccurate [ɪn'ækjurət] ADJ inexato, impreciso
inadequate [ɪn'ædɪkwət] ADJ insuficiente; (*person*) impróprio
inadvertently [ɪnəd'vəːtntlɪ] ADV inadvertidamente, sem querer
inappropriate [ɪnə'prəupriət] ADJ inadequado; (*word, expression*) impróprio
inbox ['ɪnbɒks] N (*Comput*) caixa de entrada; (*US: for papers*) cesta para correspondência de entrada
incapable [ɪn'keɪpəbl] ADJ incapaz
incense [*n* 'ɪnsɛns, *vt* ɪn'sɛns] N incenso ▶ VT (*anger*) exasperar, enraivecer
incentive [ɪn'sɛntɪv] N incentivo
inch [ɪntʃ] N polegada (= 25 *mm*; 12 *in a foot*); **to be within an ~ of** estar a um passo de; **he didn't give an ~** ele não cedeu nem um milímetro; **inch forward** VI avançar palmo a palmo
incident ['ɪnsɪdnt] N incidente *m*, evento
inclination [ɪnklɪ'neɪʃən] N (*tendency*) tendência; (*disposition*) inclinação *f*
incline [*n* 'ɪnklaɪn, *vt, vi* ɪn'klaɪn] N inclinação *f*, ladeira ▶ VT curvar, inclinar ▶ VI inclinar-se; **to be ~d to** tender a, ser propenso a
include [ɪn'kluːd] VT incluir
including [ɪn'kluːdɪŋ] PREP inclusive

inclusive [ɪn'kluːsɪv] ADJ incluído, incluso; ~ **of** incluindo
income ['ɪnkʌm] N (*earnings*) renda, rendimentos *mpl*; (*unearned*) renda; **income tax** N imposto de renda (BR), imposto complementar (PT)
incoming ['ɪnkʌmɪŋ] ADJ (*flight, passenger*) de chegada; (*mail*) de entrada; (*government, tenant*) novo
incompetent [ɪn'kɒmpɪtənt] ADJ incompetente
incomplete [ɪnkəm'pliːt] ADJ incompleto; (*unfinished*) por terminar
inconsistent [ɪnkən'sɪstnt] ADJ inconsistente; ~ **with** incompatível com
inconvenience [ɪnkən'viːnjəns] N (*quality*) inconveniência; (*problem*) inconveniente *m* ▶ VT incomodar
inconvenient [ɪnkən'viːnjənt] ADJ inconveniente, incômodo; (*time, place*) inoportuno
incorporate [ɪn'kɔːpəreɪt] VT incorporar; (*contain*) compreender
incorrect [ɪnkə'rɛkt] ADJ incorreto
increase [*n* 'ɪnkriːs, *vi, vt* ɪn'kriːs] N aumento ▶ VI, VT aumentar
incredible [ɪn'krɛdɪbl] ADJ inacreditável; (*enormous*) incrível
incur [ɪn'kəː'] VT incorrer em; (*expenses*) contrair
indecent [ɪn'diːsnt] ADJ indecente
indeed [ɪn'diːd] ADV de fato; (*certainly*) certamente; (*furthermore*) aliás; **yes ~!** claro que sim!
indefinitely [ɪn'dɛfɪnɪtlɪ] ADV indefinidamente
independence [ɪndɪ'pɛndns] N independência; **Independence Day** N *ver nota*

O dia da Independência **Independence Day** é a festa nacional dos Estados Unidos. Todo dia 4 de julho os americanos comemoram a adoção, em 1776, da declaração de Independência escrita por Thomas Jefferson que proclamava a separação das 13 colônias americanas da Grã-Bretanha.

independent [ɪndɪ'pɛndnt] ADJ independente; (*inquiry*) imparcial
index ['ɪndɛks] N (*pl* **indexes**) (*in book*) índice *m*; (*in library etc*) catálogo; (*pl* **indices**) (*ratio, sign*) índice *m*, expoente *m*
India ['ɪndɪə] N Índia; **Indian** ADJ, N (*from India*) indiano(-a); (*American, Brazilian*) índio(-a)

indicate ['ɪndɪkeɪt] vt (show) sugerir; (point to) indicar; **indication** [ɪndɪ'keɪʃən] n indício, sinal m; **indicative** [ɪn'dɪkətɪv] ADJ indicativo ▶ n (Ling) indicativo; **to be indicative of sth** ser sintomático de algo; **indicator** n indicador m; (Aut) pisca-pisca m

indices ['ɪndɪsi:z] NPL of **index**

indifferent [ɪn'dɪfrənt] ADJ indiferente; (quality) medíocre

indigenous [ɪn'dɪdʒɪnəs] ADJ indígena, nativo

indigestion [ɪndɪ'dʒɛstʃən] n indigestão f

indignant [ɪn'dɪgnənt] ADJ: **to be ~ about sth/with sb** estar indignado com algo/alguém, indignar-se de algo/alguém

indirect [ɪndɪ'rɛkt] ADJ indireto

individual [ɪndɪ'vɪdjuəl] n indivíduo ▶ ADJ individual; (personal) pessoal; (characteristic) particular

Indonesia [ɪndə'ni:zɪə] n Indonésia

indoor ['ɪndɔ:ʳ] ADJ (inner) interno, interior; (inside) dentro de casa; (swimming pool) coberto; (games, sport) de salão; **indoors** ADV em lugar fechado

induce [ɪn'dju:s] vt (Med) induzir; (bring about) causar, produzir

indulge [ɪn'dʌldʒ] vt (desire) satisfazer; (whim) condescender com; (person) comprazer; (child) fazer a vontade de ▶ vi: **to ~ in** entregar-se a, satisfazer-se com; **indulgent** ADJ indulgente

industrial [ɪn'dʌstrɪəl] ADJ industrial

industry ['ɪndəstrɪ] n indústria; (diligence) aplicação f, diligência

inefficient [ɪnɪ'fɪʃənt] ADJ ineficiente

inequality [ɪnɪ'kwɒlɪtɪ] n desigualdade f

inevitable [ɪn'ɛvɪtəbl] ADJ inevitável; **inevitably** ADV inevitavelmente

inexpensive [ɪnɪk'spɛnsɪv] ADJ barato, econômico

inexperienced [ɪnɪk'spɪərɪənst] ADJ inexperiente

infamous ['ɪnfəməs] ADJ infame, abominável

infant ['ɪnfənt] n (baby) bebê m; (young child) criança

infant school (BRIT) n pré-escola

infect [ɪn'fɛkt] vt (person) contagiar; (food) contaminar; **infection** n infecção f; **infectious** ADJ contagioso; (fig) infeccioso

infer [ɪn'fə:ʳ] vt deduzir, inferir

inferior [ɪn'fɪərɪəʳ] ADJ inferior; (goods) de qualidade inferior ▶ n inferior m/f; (in rank) subalterno(-a)

infertile [ɪn'fə:taɪl] ADJ infértil; (person, animal) estéril

infinite ['ɪnfɪnɪt] ADJ infinito

infirmary [ɪn'fə:mərɪ] n enfermaria, hospital m

inflamed [ɪn'fleɪmd] ADJ inflamado

inflammation [ɪnflə'meɪʃən] n inflamação f

inflatable [ɪn'fleɪtəbl] ADJ inflável

inflate [ɪn'fleɪt] vt (tyre, balloon) inflar, encher; (price) inflar; **inflation** n (Econ) inflação f

inflict [ɪn'flɪkt] vt: **to ~ sth on sb** infligir algo em alguém

influence ['ɪnfluəns] n influência ▶ vt influir em, influenciar; **under the ~ of alcohol** sob o efeito do álcool; **influential** [ɪnflu'ɛnʃl] ADJ influente

influenza [ɪnflu'ɛnzə] n gripe f

inform [ɪn'fɔ:m] vt: **to ~ sb of sth** informar alguém de algo ▶ vi: **to ~ on sb** delatar alguém

informal [ɪn'fɔ:ml] ADJ informal; (visit, discussion) extraoficial

information [ɪnfə'meɪʃən] n informação f, informações fpl; (knowledge) conhecimento; **a piece of ~** uma informação

informative [ɪn'fɔ:mətɪv] ADJ informativo

infuriating [ɪn'fjuərɪeɪtɪŋ] ADJ de dar raiva, enfurecedor(a)

ingenious [ɪn'dʒi:njəs] ADJ engenhoso

ingredient [ɪn'gri:dɪənt] n ingrediente m; (of situation) fator m

inhabit [ɪn'hæbɪt] vt habitar; **inhabitant** n habitante m/f

inhale [ɪn'heɪl] vt inalar ▶ vi (in smoking) tragar; **inhaler** [ɪn'heɪləʳ] n inalador m

inherent [ɪn'hɪərənt] ADJ: **~ in or to** inerente a

inherit [ɪn'hɛrɪt] vt herdar; **inheritance** n herança

inhibit [ɪn'hɪbɪt] vt inibir; **inhibition** [ɪnhɪ'bɪʃən] n inibição f

initial [ɪ'nɪʃl] ADJ inicial ▶ n inicial f ▶ vt marcar com iniciais; **initials** NPL (of name) iniciais fpl; **initially** ADV inicialmente, no início

initiate [ɪ'nɪʃɪeɪt] vt (start) iniciar, começar; (person) iniciar; **to ~ sb into a secret** revelar um segredo a alguém; **to ~ proceedings against sb** (Jur) abrir um processo contra alguém

initiative [ɪ'nɪʃətɪv] n iniciativa

inject [ɪn'dʒɛkt] vt (liquid, fig: money) injetar; (person) dar uma injeção em; **injection** n injeção f

injure ['ɪndʒəʳ] vт ferir; (*reputation etc*) prejudicar; (*offend*) ofender; **injured** ADJ ferido; (*feelings*) ofendido, magoado; **injury** N ferida

injustice [ɪn'dʒʌstɪs] N injustiça

ink [ɪŋk] N tinta

inland [*adj* 'ɪnlənd, *adv* ɪn'lænd] ADJ interior, interno ▶ ADV para o interior; **Inland Revenue** (BRIT) N ≈ fisco, ≈ receita federal (BR)

inmate ['ɪnmeɪt] N (*in prison*) presidiário(-a); (*in asylum*) internado(-a)

inn [ɪn] N hospedaria, taberna

inner ['ɪnəʳ] ADJ (*place*) interno; (*feeling*) interior; **inner city** N aglomeração f urbana, metrópole f

innocent ['ɪnəsnt] ADJ inocente

in-patient N paciente m/f interno(-a)

input ['ɪnput] N entrada; (*resources*) investimento

inquest ['ɪnkwɛst] N inquérito judicial

inquire [ɪn'kwaɪəʳ] vı pedir informação ▶ vт perguntar; **inquire into** vт FUS investigar, indagar; **inquiry** N pergunta; (*Jur*) investigação f, inquérito

ins. ABBR = **inches**

insane [ɪn'seɪn] ADJ louco, doido; (*Med*) demente, insano; **insanity** [ɪn'sænɪtɪ] N loucura; (*Med*) insanidade f, demência

inscrutable [ɪn'skruːtəbl] ADJ inescrutável, impenetrável

insect ['ɪnsɛkt] N inseto

insecure [ɪnsɪ'kjuəʳ] ADJ inseguro

insensitive [ɪn'sɛnsɪtɪv] ADJ insensível

insert [ɪn'səːt] vт (*between things*) intercalar; (*into sth*) introduzir, inserir

inside ['ɪn'saɪd] N interior m ▶ ADJ interior, interno ▶ ADV (*be*) dentro; (*go*) para dentro ▶ PREP dentro de; (*of time*): **~ 10 minutes** em menos de 10 minutos; **insides** NPL (*inf*) entranhas fpl; **inside out** ADV ás avessas; (*know*) muito bem; **to turn sth inside out** virar algo pelo avesso

insight ['ɪnsaɪt] N insight m

insignificant [ɪnsɪg'nɪfɪknt] ADJ insignificante

insincere [ɪnsɪn'sɪəʳ] ADJ insincero

insist [ɪn'sɪst] vı insistir; **to ~ on doing** insistir em fazer; **to ~ that** insistir que; (*claim*) cismar que; **insistent** ADJ insistente, pertinaz; (*continual*) persistente

insomnia [ɪn'sɔmnɪə] N insônia

inspect [ɪn'spɛkt] vт inspecionar; (*building*) vistoriar; (BRIT: *tickets*) fiscalizar; (*troops*) passar revista em;

inspection N inspeção f; (*of building*) vistoria; (BRIT: *of tickets*) fiscalização f; **inspector** N inspetor(a) m/f; (BRIT: *on buses, trains*) fiscal m

inspire [ɪn'spaɪəʳ] vт inspirar

install [ɪn'stɔːl] vт instalar; (*official*) nomear; **installation** [ɪnstə'leɪʃən] N instalação f

installment [ɪn'stɔːlmənt] (US) N = **instalment**

instalment [ɪn'stɔːlmənt] N (*of money*) prestação f; (*of story*) fascículo; (*of TV serial etc*) capítulo; **in ~s** (*pay*) a prestações; (*receive*) em várias vezes

instance ['ɪnstəns] N exemplo; **for ~** por exemplo; **in the first ~** em primeiro lugar

instant ['ɪnstənt] N instante m, momento ▶ ADJ imediato; (*coffee*) instantâneo; **instantly** ADV imediatamente; **instant message** N mensagem f instantânea; **instant messaging** N sistema m de mensagens instantâneas

instead [ɪn'stɛd] ADV em vez disso; **~ of** em vez de, em lugar de

instinct ['ɪnstɪŋkt] N instinto

institute ['ɪnstɪtjuːt] N instituto; (*professional body*) associação f ▶ vт (*inquiry*) começar, iniciar; (*proceedings*) instituir, estabelecer

institution [ɪnstɪ'tjuːʃən] N instituição f; (*organization*) instituto; (*Med: home*) asilo; (*asylum*) manicômio; (*custom*) costume m

instruct [ɪn'strʌkt] vт: **to ~ sb in sth** instruir alguém em or sobre algo; **to ~ sb to do sth** dar instruções a alguém para fazer algo; **instruction** N (*teaching*) instrução f; **instructions** N ordens fpl; **instructions (for use)** modo de usar; **instructor** N instrutor(a) m/f

instrument ['ɪnstrumənt] N instrumento

insufficient [ɪnsə'fɪʃənt] ADJ insuficiente

insulate ['ɪnsjuleɪt] vт isolar; (*protect*) segregar; **insulation** [ɪnsju'leɪʃən] N isolamento

insulin ['ɪnsjulɪn] N insulina

insult [n 'ɪnsʌlt, vt ɪn'sʌlt] N ofensa ▶ vт insultar, ofender

insurance [ɪn'ʃuərəns] N seguro; **fire/life ~** seguro contra incêndio/de vida

insure [ɪn'ʃuəʳ] vт segurar

intact [ɪn'tækt] ADJ intacto, íntegro; (*unharmed*) ileso, são e salvo

intake ['ɪnteɪk] N (*of food*) quantidade *f* ingerida; (*BRIT Sch*) **an ~ of 200 a year** 200 matriculados por ano

integral ['ɪntɪɡrəl] ADJ (*part*) integrante, essencial

integrate ['ɪntɪɡreɪt] VT integrar ▶ VI integrar-se

intellect ['ɪntəlɛkt] N intelecto; **intellectual** [ɪntə'lɛktjuəl] ADJ, N intelectual *m/f*

intelligence [ɪn'tɛlɪdʒəns] N inteligência; (*Mil etc*) informações *fpl*

intelligent [ɪn'tɛlɪdʒənt] ADJ inteligente

intend [ɪn'tɛnd] VT (*gift etc*): **to ~ sth for** destinar algo a; **to ~ to do sth** tencionar *or* pretender fazer algo; (*plan*) planejar fazer algo

intense [ɪn'tɛns] ADJ intenso; (*person*) muito emotivo

intensive [ɪn'tɛnsɪv] ADJ intensivo; **intensive care unit** N unidade *f* de tratamento intensivo

intent [ɪn'tɛnt] N intenção *f* ▶ ADJ: **to be ~ on doing sth** estar resolvido a fazer algo; **to all ~s and purposes** para todos os efeitos

intention [ɪn'tɛnʃən] N intenção *f*, propósito; **intentional** ADJ intencional, proposital

interact [ɪntər'ækt] VI interagir; **interactive** [ɪntər'æktɪv] ADJ interativo

interchange ['ɪntətʃeɪndʒ] N intercâmbio; (*exchange*) troca, permuta; (*on motorway*) trevo

intercourse ['ɪntəkɔːs] N: **sexual ~** relações *fpl* sexuais

interest ['ɪntrɪst] N interesse *m*; (*Comm: sum of money*) juros *mpl*; (*: in company*) participação *f* ▶ VT interessar; **to be ~ed in** interessar-se por, estar interessado em; **interesting** ADJ interessante

interface ['ɪntəfeɪs] N (*Comput*) interface *f*

interfere [ɪntə'fɪə'] VI: **to ~ in** interferir *or* intrometer-se em; **to ~ with** (*objects*) mexer em; (*hinder*) impedir; (*plans*) interferir em

interference [ɪntə'fɪərəns] N intromissão *f*; (*Radio, TV*) interferência

interior [ɪn'tɪərɪə'] N interior *m* ▶ ADJ interno; (*ministry*) do interior

intermediate [ɪntə'miːdɪət] ADJ intermediário

intermission [ɪntə'mɪʃən] N intervalo

intern [*vt* ɪn'təːn, *n* 'ɪntəːn] VT internar ▶ N (*US: in hospital*) médico interno/ médica interna; (*on work placement*) estagiário(-a)

internal [ɪn'təːnl] ADJ interno

international [ɪntə'næʃənl] ADJ internacional ▶ N (*BRIT Sport: game*) jogo internacional

Internet ['ɪntənɛt] N: **the ~** a Internet; **Internet café** N cibercafé *m*; **Internet Service Provider** N provedor de acesso à Internet; **Internet user** N internauta *m/f*

interpret [ɪn'təːprɪt] VT interpretar; (*translate*) traduzir ▶ VI interpretar; **interpreter** N intérprete *m/f*

interrogate [ɪn'tɛrəugeɪt] VT interrogar; **interrogation** [ɪntɛrə'geɪʃən] N interrogatório

interrupt [ɪntə'rʌpt] VT, VI interromper; **interruption** N interrupção *f*

interval ['ɪntəvl] N intervalo

intervene [ɪntə'viːn] VI intervir; (*event*) ocorrer; (*time*) decorrer

interview ['ɪntəvjuː] N entrevista ▶ VT entrevistar; **interviewer** N entrevistador(a) *m/f*

intimate [*adj* 'ɪntɪmət, *vt* 'ɪntɪmeɪt] ADJ íntimo; (*knowledge*) profundo ▶ VT insinuar, sugerir

(KEYWORD)

into ['ɪntu] PREP

1 (*indicating motion or direction*) em; **come into the house/garden** venha para dentro/o jardim; **research into cancer** pesquisa sobre o câncer; **he worked late into the night** ele trabalhou até altas horas

2 (*indicating change of condition, result*): **she burst into tears** ela desatou a chorar; **he was shocked into silence** ele ficou mudo de choque; **into 3 pieces/French** em 3 pedaços/para o francês

intolerant [ɪn'tɔlərənt] ADJ: **~ (of)** intolerante (com *or* para com)

intranet ['ɪntrənɛt] N intranet *f*

intricate ['ɪntrɪkət] ADJ complexo, complicado

intrigue [ɪn'triːg] N intriga ▶ VT intrigar; **intriguing** ADJ intrigante

introduce [ɪntrə'djuːs] VT introduzir; **to ~ sb (to sb)** apresentar alguém (a alguém); **to ~ sb to** (*pastime, technique*) iniciar alguém em; **introduction** N introdução *f*; (*of person*) apresentação *f*; **introductory** ADJ introdutório

intrude [ɪn'truːd] VI: **to ~ (on or into)** intrometer-se (em); **intruder** N intruso(-a)

inundate ['ɪnʌndeɪt] VT: **to ~ with** inundar de

invade [ɪn'veɪd] VT invadir

invalid [n 'ɪnvəlɪd, adj ɪn'vælɪd] N inválido(-a) ▶ ADJ inválido, nulo

invaluable [ɪn'væljuəbl] ADJ valioso, inestimável

invariably [ɪn'vɛərɪəblɪ] ADV invariavelmente

invent [ɪn'vɛnt] VT inventar; **invention** N invenção f; (inventiveness) engenho; (lie) ficção f, mentira; **inventor** N inventor(a) m/f

inventory ['ɪnvəntrɪ] N inventário, relação f

invest [ɪn'vɛst] VT investir ▶ VI: **to ~ in** investir em; (acquire) comprar

investigate [ɪn'vɛstɪgeɪt] VT investigar; **investigation** [ɪnvɛstɪ'geɪʃən] N investigação f

investment [ɪn'vɛstmənt] N investimento

invisible [ɪn'vɪzɪbl] ADJ invisível

invitation [ɪnvɪ'teɪʃən] N convite m

invite [ɪn'vaɪt] VT convidar; (opinions etc) solicitar; **inviting** ADJ convidativo

invoice ['ɪnvɔɪs] N fatura ▶ VT faturar

involve [ɪn'vɔlv] VT (entail) implicar; (require) exigir; **to ~ sb (in)** envolver alguém (em); **involved** ADJ (complex) complexo; **to be/get involved in sth** estar/ficar envolvido em algo; **involvement** N envolvimento

inward ['ɪnwəd] ADJ (movement) interior, interno; (thought, feeling) íntimo ▶ ADV para dentro; **inwards** ADV para dentro

iPod® ['aɪpɒd] N iPod® m

IQ N ABBR (= intelligence quotient) QI m

IRA N ABBR (= Irish Republican Army) IRA m

Iran [ɪ'rɑːn] N Irã m (BR), Irão m (PT)

Iraq [ɪ'rɑːk] N Iraque m

Ireland ['aɪələnd] N Irlanda

iris ['aɪrɪs] (pl **irises**) N íris f

Irish ['aɪrɪʃ] ADJ irlandês(-esa); **the Irish** NPL os irlandeses; **Irishman** irreg N irlandês m; **Irish Sea** N: **the Irish Sea** o mar da Irlanda; **Irishwoman** irreg N irlandesa

iron ['aɪən] N ferro; (for clothes) ferro de passar roupa ▶ ADJ de ferro ▶ VT (clothes) passar; **iron out** VT (problem) resolver

ironic [aɪ'rɒnɪk], **ironical** [aɪ'rɒnɪkl] ADJ irônico

ironing ['aɪənɪŋ] N (activity) passar roupa; (clothes) roupa passada; **ironing board** N tábua de passar roupa

irony ['aɪrənɪ] N ironia

irrational [ɪ'ræʃənl] ADJ irracional

irregular [ɪ'rɛgjuləʳ] ADJ irregular; (surface) desigual

irrelevant [ɪ'rɛləvənt] ADJ irrelevante

irresistible [ɪrɪ'zɪstɪbl] ADJ irresistível

irresponsible [ɪrɪ'spɒnsɪbl] ADJ irresponsável

irrigation [ɪrɪ'geɪʃən] N irrigação f

irritate ['ɪrɪteɪt] VT irritar; **irritating** ADJ irritante; **irritation** [ɪrɪ'teɪʃən] N irritação f

is [ɪz] VB see **be**

Islam ['ɪzlɑːm] N islamismo

island ['aɪlənd] N ilha; **islander** N ilhéu/ilhoa m/f

isle [aɪl] N ilhota, ilha

isn't ['ɪznt] = **is not**

ISP N ABBR (= Internet Service Provider) ISP m

Israel ['ɪzreɪl] N Israel; **Israeli** [ɪz'reɪlɪ] ADJ, N israelense m/f

issue ['ɪsjuː] N questão f, tema m; (of book) edição f; (of stamps) emissão f ▶ VT (rations, equipment) distribuir; (orders) dar; **at ~** em debate; **to take ~ with sb (over sth)** discordar de alguém (sobre algo); **to make an ~ of sth** criar caso com algo

KEYWORD

it [ɪt] PRON **1** (specific: subject) ele/ela; (: direct object) o/a; (: indirect object) lhe; **it's on the table** está em cima da mesa; **I can't find it** não consigo achá-lo; **give it to me** dê-mo; **about/from it** sobre/de isto; **did you go to it?** (party, concert etc) você foi?

2 (impers) isto, isso; (after prep) ele, ela; **it's raining** está chovendo (BR) or a chover (PT); **it's six o'clock/the 10th of August** são seis horas/hoje é (dia) 10 de agosto; **who is it? — it's me** quem é? — sou eu

Italian [ɪ'tæljən] ADJ italiano ▶ N italiano(-a); (Ling) italiano

italics [ɪ'tælɪks] NPL itálico

Italy ['ɪtəlɪ] N Itália

itch [ɪtʃ] N comichão f, coceira ▶ VI (person) estar com or sentir comichão or coceira; (part of body) comichar, coçar; **I'm ~ing to do something** estou louco para fazer algo; **itchy** ADJ que coça; **to be itchy** (person) estar com or sentir comichão or coceira; (part of body) comichar, coçar

it'd ['ɪtd] = **it would**; = **it had**

item ['aɪtəm] N item m; (on agenda) assunto; (in programme) número; (also: **news ~**) notícia

itinerary [aɪ'tɪnərərɪ] N itinerário

it'll ['ɪtl] = **it will;** = **it shall**

its [ɪts] ADJ seu/sua, dele/dela ▶ PRON o seu/a sua, o dele/a dela

it's [ɪts] = **it is;** = **it has**

itself [ɪt'sɛlf] PRON (*reflexive*) si mesmo(-a); (*emphatic*) ele mesmo/ela mesma

ITV (BRIT) N ABBR (= *Independent Television*) canal de televisão comercial

I've [aɪv] = **I have**

ivory ['aɪvərɪ] N marfim *m*

ivy ['aɪvɪ] N hera

jab [dʒæb] VT cutucar ▶ N cotovelada, murro; (*Med: inf*) injeção *f*; **to ~ sth into sth** cravar algo em algo

jack [dʒæk] N (*Aut*) macaco; (*Cards*) valete *m*; **jack up** VT (*Aut*) levantar com macaco

jacket ['dʒækɪt] N jaqueta, casaco curto; (*of boiler etc*) forro; (*of book*) sobrecapa

jackpot ['dʒækpɔt] N bolada, sorte *f* grande

jagged ['dʒægɪd] ADJ dentado, denteado

jail [dʒeɪl] N prisão *f*, cadeia ▶ VT encarcerar

jam [dʒæm] N geleia; (*also*: **traffic ~**) engarrafamento; (*inf*) apuro ▶ VT obstruir, atravancar; (*mechanism*) emperrar; (*Radio*) bloquear, interferir ▶ VI (*mechanism, drawer etc*) emperrar; **to ~ sth into sth** forçar algo dentro de algo

Jamaica [dʒə'meɪkə] N Jamaica

janitor ['dʒænɪtə'] N zelador *m*

January ['dʒænjuərɪ] N janeiro

Japan [dʒə'pæn] N Japão *m*; **Japanese** [dʒæpə'niːz] ADJ japonês(-esa) ▶ N INV japonês(-esa) *m/f*; (*Ling*) japonês *m*

jar [dʒɑːʳ] N jarro ▶ VI (*sound*) ranger, chiar; (*colours*) destoar

jargon ['dʒɑːgən] N jargão *m*

javelin ['dʒævlɪn] N dardo de arremesso

jaw [dʒɔː] N mandíbula, maxilar *m*

jazz [dʒæz] N jazz *m*; **jazz up** VT animar, avivar

jealous ['dʒɛləs] ADJ ciumento; **jealousy** N ciúmes *mpl*

jeans [dʒiːnz] NPL jeans *m* (BR), jeans *mpl* (PT)

jelly ['dʒɛlɪ] N (*jam*) geleia; **jellyfish** ['dʒɛlɪfɪʃ] N INV água-viva

jerk [dʒəːk] N solavanco, sacudida; (wrench) puxão m; (inf: idiot) babaca m ▶ VT sacudir ▶ VI dar um solavanco

jersey ['dʒəːzɪ] N suéter m (BR), camisola (PT); (fabric) jérsei m, malha

Jesus ['dʒiːzəs] N Jesus m (Cristo)

jet [dʒet] N (of gas, liquid) jato; (Aviat) (avião m a) jato; (stone) azeviche m; **jet lag** N cansaço devido à diferença de fuso horário

jetty ['dʒetɪ] N quebra-mar m, cais m

Jew [dʒuː] N judeu(-dia) m/f

jewel ['dʒuːəl] N joia; **jeweller**, (US) **jeweler** N joalheiro(-a); **jewellery**, (US) **jewelry** N joias fpl, pedrarias fpl

Jewish ['dʒuːɪʃ] ADJ judeu/judia

jigsaw ['dʒɪgsɔː] N (also: ~ puzzle) quebra-cabeça m

jihad [dʒɪ'hæd] N jihad f

job [dʒɔb] N trabalho; (task) tarefa; (duty) dever m; (post) emprego; **it's not my ~** não faz parte das minhas funções; **it's a good ~ that ...** ainda bem que ...; **just the ~!** justo o que queria!; **jobless** ADJ desempregado

jockey ['dʒɔkɪ] N jóquei m ▶ VI: **to ~ for position** manobrar para conseguir uma posição

jog [dʒɔg] VT empurrar, sacudir ▶ VI fazer jogging or cooper; **jog along** VI ir levando; **jogging** N jogging m

john [dʒɔn] (US inf) N trono m (inf) (no banheiro)

join [dʒɔɪn] VT (things) juntar, unir; (queue) entrar em; (become member of) associar-se a; (meet) encontrar-se com; (accompany) juntar-se a ▶ VI (roads, rivers) confluir ▶ N junção f; **join in** VI participar ▶ VT FUS participar em; **join up** VI unir-se; (Mil) alistar-se

joint [dʒɔɪnt] N (Tech) junta, união f; (wood) encaixe m; (Anat) articulação f; (BRIT Culin) quarto; (inf: place) espelunca; (: marijuana cigarette) baseado ▶ ADJ comum; (combined) conjunto; (committee) misto

joke [dʒəuk] N piada; (also: **practical ~**) brincadeira, peça ▶ VI brincar; **to play a ~ on** pregar uma peça em; **joker** N (Cards) curingão m

jolly ['dʒɔlɪ] ADJ (merry) alegre; (enjoyable) divertido ▶ ADV (BRIT inf) muito, extremamente

jolt [dʒəult] N (shake) sacudida, solavanco; (shock) susto ▶ VT sacudir; (emotionally) abalar

Jordan ['dʒɔːdən] N Jordânia; (river) Jordão m

journal ['dʒəːnl] N jornal m; (magazine) revista; (diary) diário; **journalism** N jornalismo; **journalist** N jornalista m/f

journey ['dʒəːnɪ] N viagem f; (distance covered) trajeto

joy [dʒɔɪ] N alegria

judge [dʒʌdʒ] N juiz/juíza m/f; (in competition) árbitro; (fig: expert) especialista m/f, conhecedor(a) m/f ▶ VT julgar; (competition) arbitrar; (estimate) avaliar; (consider) considerar

judo ['dʒuːdəu] N judô m

jug [dʒʌg] N jarro

juggle ['dʒʌgl] VI fazer malabarismos; **juggler** N malabarista m/f

juice [dʒuːs] N suco (BR), sumo (PT); **juicy** ADJ suculento

July [dʒuː'laɪ] N julho

jumble ['dʒʌmbl] N confusão f, mixórdia ▶ VT (also: ~ up: mix up) misturar; **jumble sale** (BRIT) N bazar m

As **jumble sales** têm lugar dentro de igrejas, salões de festa e escolas, onde são vendidos diversos tipos de mercadorias, em geral baratas e sobretudo de segunda mão, a fim de coletar dinheiro para uma obra de caridade, uma escola ou uma igreja.

jump [dʒʌmp] VI saltar, pular; (start) sobressaltar-se; (increase) disparar ▶ VT pular, saltar ▶ N pulo, salto; (increase) alta; (fence) obstáculo; **to ~ the queue** (BRIT) furar a fila (BR), pôr-se à frente (PT)

jumper ['dʒʌmpəʳ] N (BRIT: pullover) suéter m (BR), camisola (PT); (US: pinafore dress) avental m; **jumper cables** (US) NPL = **jump leads**

jump leads, (US) **jumper cables** NPL cabos mpl para ligar a bateria

Jun. ABBR = **junior**

junction ['dʒʌŋkʃən] (BRIT) N (of roads) cruzamento; (Rail) entroncamento

June [dʒuːn] N junho

jungle ['dʒʌŋgl] N selva, mato

junior ['dʒuːnɪəʳ] ADJ (in age) mais novo or moço; (position) subalterno ▶ N jovem m/f

junk [dʒʌŋk] N (cheap goods) tranqueira, velharias fpl; (rubbish) lixo; **junk food** N comida pronta de baixo valor nutritivo; **junk mail** N correspondência não-solicitada

jury ['dʒuərɪ] N júri m

just [dʒʌst] ADJ justo ▶ ADV (exactly) justamente, exatamente; (only) apenas, somente; **he's ~ done it/left** ele acabou (BR) or acaba (PT) de fazê-lo/ir; **~ right** perfeito; **~ two o'clock** duas (horas) em ponto; **she's ~ as clever as you** ela é tão inteligente como você; **~ as well that ...** ainda bem que ...; **~ as he was leaving** no momento em que ele saía; **~ before/enough** justo antes/o suficiente; **~ here** bem aqui; **he ~ missed** falhou por pouco; **~ listen** escute aqui!

justice ['dʒʌstɪs] N justiça; (US: judge) juiz/juíza m/f; **to do ~ to** (fig) apreciar devidamente

justify ['dʒʌstɪfaɪ] VT justificar

jut [dʒʌt] VI (also: **~ out**) sobressair

juvenile ['dʒuːvənaɪl] ADJ juvenil; (court) de menores; (books) para adolescentes ▶ N menor m/f de idade

K

K ABBR (= kilobyte) K ▶ N ABBR (= one thousand) mil

kangaroo [kæŋgəˈruː] N canguru m

karate [kəˈrɑːtɪ] N karatê m

kebab [kəˈbæb] N churrasquinho, espetinho

keen [kiːn] ADJ (interest, desire) grande, vivo; (eye, intelligence) penetrante; (competition) acirrado, intenso; (edge) afiado; (eager) entusiasmado; **to be ~ to do** or **on doing sth** sentir muita vontade de fazer algo; **to be ~ on sth/sb** gostar de algo/alguém

keep [kiːp] (pt, pp **kept**) VT ficar com; (house etc) cuidar; (detain) deter; (shop etc) tomar conta de; (preserve) conservar; (family etc) manter; (promise) cumprir; (chickens, bees etc) criar; (prevent): **to ~ sb from doing sth** impedir alguém de fazer algo ▶ VI (food) conservar-se; (remain) ficar ▶ N (of castle) torre f de menagem; (food etc): **to earn one's ~** ganhar a vida; (inf): **for ~s** para sempre; **to ~ doing sth** continuar fazendo algo; **to ~ sb happy** manter alguém satisfeito; **to ~ a place tidy** manter um lugar limpo; **keep on** VI: **to ~ on doing** continuar fazendo; **keep out** VT impedir de entrar; **"~ out"** "entrada proibida"; **keep up** VT manter ▶ VI não atrasar-se, acompanhar; **to ~ up with** (pace) acompanhar; (level) manter-se ao nível de; **keeper** N guarda m, guardião(-diã) m/f

kennel ['kɛnl] N casa de cachorro; **kennels** N (establishment) canil m

kept [kɛpt] PT, PP of **keep**

kerb [kəːb] (BRIT) N meio-fio (BR), borda do passeio (PT)

kettle ['kɛtl] N chaleira

key [kiː] N chave f; (Mus) clave f; (of piano, typewriter) tecla ▶ CPD (issue etc) chave ▶ VT (also: **~ in**) digitar; **keyboard** N teclado; **keyhole** N buraco da fechadura; **keyring** N chaveiro

khaki ['kɑːkɪ] ADJ cáqui

kick [kɪk] VT dar um pontapé em; (ball) chutar; (inf: habit) conseguir superar ▶ VI (horse) dar coices ▶ N (from person) pontapé m; (from animal) coice m, patada; (to ball) chute m; (inf: thrill): **he does it for ~s** faz isso para curtir; **kick off** VI (Sport) dar o chute inicial

kid [kɪd] N (inf: child) criança; (animal) cabrito; (leather) pelica ▶ VI (inf) brincar

kidnap ['kɪdnæp] VT sequestrar

kidney ['kɪdnɪ] N rim m

kill [kɪl] VT matar; (murder) assassinar ▶ N ato de matar; **killer** N assassino(-a); **killing** N assassinato; **to make a killing** (inf) faturar uma boa nota

kiln [kɪln] N forno

kilo ['kiːləʊ] N quilo; **kilobyte** N kilobyte m; **kilogram, kilogramme** N quilograma m; **kilometre**, (US) **kilometer** N quilômetro; **kilowatt** N quilowatt m

kilt [kɪlt] N saiote m escocês

kin [kɪn] N see **next-of-kin**

kind [kaɪnd] ADJ (friendly) gentil; (generous) generoso; (good) bom/boa, bondoso, amável ▶ N espécie f, classe f; (species) gênero; **in ~** (Comm) em espécie

kindergarten ['kɪndəgɑːtn] N jardim m de infância

kindly ['kaɪndlɪ] ADJ (good) bom/boa, bondoso; (gentle) gentil, carinhoso ▶ ADV bondosamente, amavelmente; **will you ~ ...** você pode fazer o favor de ...

kindness ['kaɪndnɪs] N bondade f, gentileza

king [kɪŋ] N rei m; **kingdom** N reino; **kingfisher** N martim-pescador m

kiosk ['kiːɔsk] N banca (BR), quiosque m (PT); (BRIT: also: **telephone ~**) cabine f

kipper ['kɪpər] N tipo de arenque defumado

kiss [kɪs] N beijo ▶ VT beijar; **to ~ (each other)** beijar-se; **kiss of life** (BRIT) N respiração f boca-a-boca

kit [kɪt] N (for sport etc) kit m; (equipment) equipamento; (set of tools etc) caixa de ferramentas; (for assembly) kit m para montar

kitchen ['kɪtʃɪn] N cozinha

kite [kaɪt] N (toy) papagaio, pipa

kitten ['kɪtn] N gatinho

kitty ['kɪtɪ] N fundo comum, vaquinha

km ABBR (= kilometre) km

knack [næk] N: **there's a ~ (to it)** tem um jeito

knee [niː] N joelho; **kneecap** N rótula

kneel [niːl] (pt, pp **knelt**) VI (also: **~ down**) ajoelhar-se

knew [njuː] PT of **know**

knickers ['nɪkəz] (BRIT) NPL calcinha (BR), cuecas fpl (PT)

knife [naɪf] (pl **knives**) N faca ▶ VT esfaquear

knight [naɪt] N cavaleiro; (Chess) cavalo

knit [nɪt] VT tricotar; (brows) franzir ▶ VI tricotar (BR), fazer malha (PT); (bones) consolidar-se; **knitting** N ato de tricotar, tricô (BR), malha (PT); **knitting needle** N agulha de tricô (BR) or de malha (PT); **knitwear** N roupa de malha

knives [naɪvz] NPL of **knife**

knob [nɔb] N (of door) maçaneta; (of stick) castão m; (on radio, TV etc) botão m

knock [nɔk] VT bater em; (bump into) colidir com; (inf) criticar, malhar ▶ N pancada, golpe m; (on door) batida ▶ VI: **to ~ at** or **on the door** bater à porta; **knock down** VT derrubar; (pedestrian) atropelar; **knock off** VI (inf: finish) terminar ▶ VT (inf: steal) abafar; (from price): **to ~ off £10** dar um desconto de £10; **knock out** VT pôr nocaute, nocautear; (defeat) eliminar; **knock over** VT derrubar; (pedestrian) atropelar

knot [nɔt] N nó m ▶ VT dar nó em

know [nəʊ] (pt **knew**, pp **known**) VT saber; (person, author, place) conhecer ▶ VI: **to ~ about** or **of sth** saber de algo; **to ~ how to swim** saber nadar; **know-how** N know-how m, experiência; **knowingly** ADV (purposely) de propósito; (spitefully) maliciosamente

knowledge ['nɔlɪdʒ] N conhecimento; (range of learning) saber m, conhecimentos mpl; **knowledgeable** ADJ entendido, versado

known [nəʊn] PP of **know**

knuckle ['nʌkl] N nó m

Koran [kɔ'rɑːn] N: **the ~** o Alcorão

Korea [kə'rɪə] N Coreia

kosher ['kəʊʃər] ADJ kosher inv

Kosovo ['kɒsəvəʊ] N Kosovo m

L ABBR (BRIT Aut: = learner) (condutor(a) m/f) aprendiz m/f

lab [læb] N ABBR = **laboratory**

label ['leɪbl] N etiqueta, rótulo ▶ VT etiquetar, rotular

labor ['leɪbə'] (US) = **labour**

laboratory [lə'bɔrətərɪ] N laboratório

labour ['leɪbə'], (US) **labor** N trabalho; (work force) mão-de-obra f; (Med): **to be in ~** estar em trabalho de parto ▶ VI: **to ~ (at)** trabalhar (em) ▶ VT insistir em; **the L~ Party** (BRIT) o Partido Trabalhista; **labourer** N operário; **farm labourer** trabalhador m rural, peão m

lace [leɪs] N renda; (of shoe etc) cadarço ▶ VT (shoe) amarrar

lack [læk] N falta ▶ VT (money, confidence) faltar; (intelligence) carecer de; **through** or **for ~ of** por falta de; **to be ~ing** faltar; **to be ~ing in** carecer de

lacquer ['lækə'] N laca; (hair) fixador m

lad [læd] N menino, rapaz m, moço

ladder ['lædə'] N escada f de mão; (BRIT: in tights) defeito (em forma de escada)

ladle ['leɪdl] N concha (de sopa)

lady ['leɪdɪ] N senhora; (distinguished, noble) dama; (in address): **ladies and gentlemen, ...** senhoras e senhores, ...; **young ~** senhorita; **"ladies' (toilets)"** "senhoras"; **ladybird**, (US) **ladybug** N joaninha

lag [læg] N atraso, retardamento ▶ VI (also: **~ behind**) ficar para trás ▶ VT (pipes) revestir com isolante térmico

lager ['lɑːgə'] N cerveja leve e clara

lagoon [lə'guːn] N lagoa

laid [leɪd] PT, PP of **lay**

lain [leɪn] PP of **lie**

lake [leɪk] N lago

lamb [læm] N cordeiro

lame [leɪm] ADJ coxo, manco; (excuse, argument) pouco convincente, fraco

lament [lə'ment] N lamento, queixa ▶ VT lamentar-se de

lamp [læmp] N lâmpada; **lamppost** (BRIT) N poste m; **lampshade** N abajur m, quebra-luz m

land [lænd] N terra; (country) país m; (piece of land) terreno; (estate) terras fpl, propriedades fpl ▶ VI (from ship) desembarcar; (Aviat) pousar, aterrissar (BR), aterrar (PT); (fig: arrive unexpectedly) cair, terminar ▶ VT desembarcar; **to ~ sb with sth** (inf) sobrecarregar alguém com algo; **land up** VI: **to ~ up in/at** ir parar em; **landfill site** ['lændfɪl-] N aterro sanitário; **landing** N (Aviat) pouso, aterrissagem f (BR), aterragem f (PT); (of staircase) patamar m; **landlady** N senhoria; (of pub) dona, proprietária; **landline** N telefone m fixo; **landlord** N senhorio, locador m; (of pub etc) dono, proprietário; **landmark** N lugar m conhecido; (fig) marco; **landowner** N latifundiário(-a)

landscape ['lændskeɪp] N paisagem f

landslide ['lændslaɪd] N (Geo) desmoronamento, desabamento; (fig: Pol) vitória esmagadora

lane [leɪn] N caminho, estrada estreita; (Aut) pista; (in race) raia

language ['læŋgwɪdʒ] N língua; (way one speaks, Comput, style) linguagem f; **bad ~** palavrões mpl; **language laboratory** N laboratório de línguas; **language school** N escola de línguas

lantern ['læntn] N lanterna

lap [læp] N (of track) volta; (of person) colo ▶ VT (also: **~ up**) lamber ▶ VI (waves) marulhar; **lap up** VT (fig) receber com sofreguidão

lapel [lə'pɛl] N lapela

lapse [læps] N lapso; (bad behaviour) deslize m ▶ VI (law) prescrever; **to ~ into bad habits** adquirir maus hábitos

laptop ['læptɔp], **laptop computer** N laptop m

lard [lɑːd] N banha de porco

larder ['lɑːdə'] N despensa

large [lɑːdʒ] ADJ grande; **at ~** (free) em liberdade; (generally) em geral; **largely** ADV em grande parte; (introducing reason) principalmente; **large-scale** ADJ (map) em grande escala; (fig) importante, de grande alcance

lark [lɑːk] N (bird) cotovia; (joke) brincadeira, peça; **lark about** VI divertir-se, brincar

laryngitis [lærɪn'dʒaɪtɪs] N laringite f
laser ['leɪzəʳ] N laser m; **laser printer** N impressora a laser
lash [læʃ] N (blow) chicotada; (also: **eye~**) pestana, cílio ▶ VT chicotear, açoitar; (subj: rain, wind) castigar; (tie) atar; **lash out** VI: **to ~ out (at sb)** atacar (alguém) violentamente; **to ~ out at** or **against sb** (criticize) atacar alguém verbalmente
lass [læs] (BRIT) N moça
last [lɑːst] ADJ último; (final) derradeiro ▶ ADV em último lugar ▶ VI durar; (continue) continuar; **~ week** na semana passada; **~ night** ontem à noite; **at ~** finalmente; **~ but one** penúltimo; **lastly** ADV por fim, por último; (finally) finalmente; **last-minute** ADJ de última hora
latch [lætʃ] N trinco, fecho, tranca
late [leɪt] ADJ (not on time) atrasado; (far on in day etc) tardio; (former) antigo, ex-, anterior; (dead) falecido ▶ ADV tarde; (behind time, schedule) atrasado; **of ~** recentemente; **in ~ May** no final de maio; **latecomer** N retardatário(-a); **lately** ADV ultimamente; **later** ADJ (date etc) posterior; (version etc) mais recente ▶ ADV mais tarde, depois; **later on** mais tarde; **latest** ADJ último; **at the latest** no mais tardar
lather ['lɑːðəʳ] N espuma (de sabão) ▶ VT ensaboar
Latin ['lætɪn] N (Ling) latim m ▶ ADJ latino; **Latin America** N América Latina; **Latin American** ADJ, N latino-americano(-a)
latitude ['lætɪtjuːd] N latitude f
latter ['lætəʳ] ADJ último; (of two) segundo ▶ N: **the ~** o último, este
laugh [lɑːf] N riso, risada ▶ VI rir, dar risada (or gargalhada); **(to do sth) for a ~** (fazer algo) só de curtição; **laugh at** VT FUS rir de; **laugh off** VT disfarçar sorrindo; **laughter** N riso, risada
launch [lɔːntʃ] N (boat) lancha, (Comm, of rocket etc) lançamento ▶ VT lançar; **launch into** VT FUS lançar-se a
laundry ['lɔːndrɪ] N lavanderia; (clothes) roupa para lavar
lava ['lɑːvə] N lava
lavatory ['lævətərɪ] N privada (BR), casa de banho (PT)
lavender ['lævəndəʳ] N lavanda
lavish ['lævɪʃ] ADJ (amount) generoso; (person): **~ with** pródigo em, generoso com ▶ VT: **to ~ sth on sb** encher or cobrir alguém de algo

law [lɔː] N lei f; (rule) regra; (Sch) direito; **lawful** ADJ legal, lícito
lawn [lɔːn] N gramado (BR), relvado (PT); **lawnmower** N cortador m de grama (BR) or de relva (PT)
lawsuit ['lɔːsuːt] N ação f judicial, processo
lawyer ['lɔːjəʳ] N advogado(-a); (for sales, wills etc) notário(-a), tabelião(-liã) m/f
lax [læks] ADJ (discipline) relaxado; (person) negligente
laxative ['læksətɪv] N laxante m
lay [leɪ] (pt, pp **laid**) PT of **lie** ▶ ADJ leigo ▶ VT colocar; (eggs, table) pôr; **lay aside** VT pôr de lado; **lay by** VT = **lay aside**; **lay down** VT depositar; (rules etc) impor, estabelecer; **to ~ down the law** (pej) impor regras; **to ~ down one's life** sacrificar voluntariamenta a vida; **lay off** VT (workers) demitir; **lay on** VT (meal, entertainment) prover; **lay out** VT (spread out) dispor em ordem; **lay-by** (BRIT) N acostamento
layer ['leɪəʳ] N camada
layman ['leɪmən] irreg N leigo
layout ['leɪaut] N (of garden, building) desenho; (of piece of writing) leiaute m
lazy ['leɪzɪ] ADJ preguiçoso; (movement) lento
lb. ABBR (weight) = **pound**
lead[1] [liːd] (pt, pp **led**) N (front position) dianteira; (Sport) liderança; (fig) vantagem f; (clue) pista; (Elec) fio; (for dog) correia; (in play, film) papel m principal ▶ VT levar; (be leader of) chefiar; (start, guide: activity) encabeçar ▶ VI encabeçar; **to be in the ~** (Sport: in race) estar na frente; (: in match) estar ganhando; **to ~ the way** assumir a direção; **lead away** VT levar; **lead back** VT levar de volta; **lead on** VT (tease) provocar; **lead to** VT FUS levar a, conduzir a; **lead up to** VT FUS conduzir a
lead[2] [lɛd] N chumbo; (in pencil) grafite f
leader ['liːdəʳ] N líder m/f; **leadership** N liderança; (quality) poder m de liderança
lead-free [lɛd-] ADJ sem chumbo
leading ['liːdɪŋ] ADJ principal; (role) de destaque; (first, front) primeiro, dianteiro
lead singer [liːd-] N cantor(a) m/f
leaf [liːf] (pl **leaves**) N folha ▶ VI: **to ~ through** (book) folhear; **to turn over a new ~** mudar de vida, partir para outra (inf)
leaflet ['liːflɪt] N folheto
league [liːg] N liga; **to be in ~ with** estar de comum acordo com

leak [li:k] N (of liquid, gas) escape m, vazamento; (hole) buraco, rombo; (in roof) goteira; (fig: of information) vazamento ▶ vi (ship) fazer água; (shoe) deixar entrar água; (roof) gotejar; (pipe, container, liquid) vazar; (gas) escapar ▶ vT (news) vazar

lean [li:n] (pt, pp **leaned** or **leant**) ADJ magro ▶ vT: **to ~ sth on** encostar or apoiar algo em ▶ vi inclinar-se; **to ~ against** encostar-se or apoiar-se contra; **to ~ on** encostar-se or apoiar-se em; **lean back** vi inclinar-se para trás; **lean forward** vi inclinar-se para frente; **lean out** vi: **to ~ out (of)** inclinar-se para fora (de); **lean over** vi debruçar-se ▶ vT FUS debruçar-se sobre

leap [li:p] (pt, pp **leaped** or **leapt**) N salto, pulo ▶ vi saltar; **leap year** N ano bissexto

learn [lə:n] (pt, pp **learned** or **learnt**) vT aprender; (by heart) decorar ▶ vi aprender; **to ~ about sth** (hear, read) saber de algo; **learner** N principiante m/f; (BRIT: also: **learner driver**) aprendiz m/f de motorista

lease [li:s] N arrendamento ▶ vT arrendar

leash [li:ʃ] N correia

least [li:st] ADJ: **the ~** (+ n) o/a menor; (smallest amount of) a menor quantidade de ▶ ADV: **the ~** (+ adj) o/a menos; **at ~** pelo menos; **not in the ~** de maneira nenhuma

leather [ˈlɛðəʳ] N couro

leave [li:v] (pt, pp **left**) vT deixar; (go away from) abandonar ▶ vi ir-se, sair; (train) sair ▶ N licença; **to ~ sth to sb** deixar algo para alguém; **to be left** sobrar; **leave behind** vT deixar para trás; (forget) esquecer; **leave out** vT omitir

leaves [li:vz] NPL of **leaf**

Lebanon [ˈlɛbənən] N Líbano

lecture [ˈlɛktʃəʳ] N conferência, palestra; (Sch) aula ▶ vi dar aulas, lecionar ▶ vT (scold) passar um sermão em; **lecturer** N (BRIT: at university) professor(a) m/f

led [lɛd] PT, PP of **lead¹**

ledge [lɛdʒ] N (of window) peitoril m; (of mountain) saliência, proeminência

leek [li:k] N alho-poró m

left [lɛft] PT, PP of **leave** ▶ ADJ esquerdo ▶ N esquerda ▶ ADV à esquerda; **on the ~** à esquerda; **to the ~** para a esquerda; **the L~** (Pol) a Esquerda; **left-handed** ADJ canhoto; **left-luggage**, (BRIT) **left-luggage office** N depósito de bagagem

left-wing ADJ (Pol) de esquerda, esquerdista

leg [lɛg] N perna; (of animal) pata; (Culin: of meat) perna; (of journey) etapa; **1st/2nd ~** (Sport) primeiro/segundo turno

legacy [ˈlɛgəsɪ] N legado; (fig) herança

legal [ˈli:gl] ADJ legal

legend [ˈlɛdʒənd] N lenda; (person) mito

leggings [ˈlɛgɪŋz] NPL legging f

legislation [lɛdʒɪsˈleɪʃən] N legislação f

legitimate [lɪˈdʒɪtɪmət] ADJ legítimo

leisure [ˈlɛʒəʳ] N lazer m; **at ~** desocupado, livre

lemon [ˈlɛmən] N limão(-galego) m; **lemonade** [lɛməˈneɪd] N limonada; **lemon tea** N chá m de limão

lend [lɛnd] (pt, pp **lent**) vT: **to ~ sth to sb** emprestar algo a alguém

length [lɛŋθ] N comprimento, extensão f; (amount of time) duração f; **at ~** (at last) finalmente, afinal; (lengthily) por extenso; **lengthen** vT encompridar, alongar ▶ vi encompridar-se; **lengthways** ADV longitudinalmente, ao comprido; **lengthy** ADJ comprido, longo; (meeting) prolongado

lens [lɛnz] N (of spectacles) lente f; (of camera) objetiva

Lent [lɛnt] N Quaresma

lent [lɛnt] PT, PP of **lend**

lentil [ˈlɛntl] N lentilha

Leo [ˈli:əu] N Leão m

leotard [ˈli:ətɑ:d] N collant m

lesbian [ˈlɛzbɪən] N lésbica

less [lɛs] ADJ, PRON, ADV menos ▶ PREP: **~ tax/10% discount** menos imposto/10% de desconto; **~ than ever** menos do que nunca; **~ and ~** cada vez menos; **the ~ he works ...** quanto menos trabalha ...

lessen [ˈlɛsn] vi diminuir, minguar ▶ vT diminuir, reduzir

lesser [ˈlɛsəʳ] ADJ menor; **to a ~ extent** or **degree** nem tanto

lesson [ˈlɛsn] N aula; (example, warning) lição f; **to teach sb a ~** (fig) dar uma lição em alguém

let [lɛt] (pt, pp **let**) vT (allow) deixar; (BRIT: lease) alugar; **to ~ sb know sth** avisar alguém de algo; **~'s go!** vamos!; **"to ~"** "aluga-se"; **let down** vT (tyre) esvaziar; (disappoint) desapontar; **let go** vT, vi soltar; **let in** vT deixar entrar; (visitor etc) fazer entrar; **let off** vT (culprit) perdoar; (firework etc) soltar; **let on** vi revelar; **let out** vT deixar sair; (scream) soltar; **let up** vi cessar, afrouxar

lethal ['liːθl] ADJ letal
letter ['lɛtəʳ] N (of alphabet) letra; (correspondence) carta; **letterbox** (BRIT) N caixa do correio
lettuce ['lɛtɪs] N alface f
leukaemia [luː'kiːmɪə], (US) **leukemia** N leucemia
level ['lɛvl] ADJ (flat) plano ▶ ADV no mesmo nível ▶ N nível m; (height) altura ▶ VT aplanar; **"A" ~s** npl (BRIT) ≈ vestibular m; **"O" ~s** npl (BRIT) provas prestadas no final do ensino fundamental; **to be ~ with** estar no mesmo nível que; **on the ~** em nível; (fig: honest) sincero; **level off** vi (prices etc) estabilizar-se; **level out** vi, vt = **level off**; **level crossing** (BRIT) N passagem f de nível
lever ['liːvəʳ] N alavanca; (fig) estratagema m; **leverage** N força de uma alavanca; (fig: influence) influência
liability [laɪə'bɪlətɪ] N responsabilidade f; (handicap) desvantagem f; **liabilities** NPL (Comm) exigibilidades fpl, obrigações fpl
liable ['laɪəbl] ADJ (subject): **~ to** sujeito a; (responsible): **~ for** responsável por; (likely): **~ to do** capaz de fazer
liaise [liː'eɪz] vi: **to ~ (with)** cooperar (com)
liar ['laɪəʳ] N mentiroso(-a)
libel ['laɪbl] N difamação f ▶ VT caluniar, difamar
liberal ['lɪbərl] ADJ liberal; (generous) generoso
liberation N liberação f, libertação f
liberty ['lɪbətɪ] N liberdade f; (criminal): **to be at ~** estar livre; **to be at ~ to do** ser livre de fazer
Libra ['liːbrə] N Libra, Balança
librarian [laɪ'brɛərɪən] N bibliotecário(-a)
library ['laɪbrərɪ] N biblioteca
Libya ['lɪbɪə] N Líbia
licence ['laɪsns], (US) **license** N (gen, Comm) licença; (Aut) carta de motorista (BR), carta de condução (PT)
license ['laɪsns] N (US) = **licence** ▶ VT autorizar, dar licença a; **licensed** ADJ (car) autorizado oficialmente; (for alcohol) autorizado para vender bebidas alcoólicas; **license plate** (US) N (Aut) placa (de identificação) (do carro)
lick [lɪk] VT lamber; (inf: defeat) arrasar, surrar; **to ~ one's lips** (also fig) lamber os beiços
lid [lɪd] N tampa; (eyelid) pálpebra
lie [laɪ] vi (pt **lay**, pp **lain**) (act) deitar-se; (state) estar deitado; (object: be situated)

estar, encontrar-se; (fig: problem, cause) residir; (in race, league) ocupar; (pt, pt **lied**) (tell lies) mentir ▶ N mentira; **to ~ low** (fig) esconder-se; **lie about** vi (things) estar espalhado; (people) vadiar; **lie around** vi = **lie about**; **lie-in** (BRIT) N: **to have a lie-in** dormir até tarde
lieutenant [lɛf'tɛnənt], (US) luː'tɛnənt] N (Mil) tenente m
life [laɪf] (pl **lives**) N vida; **to come to ~** animar-se; **lifeboat** N barco salva-vidas; **lifeguard** N salva-vidas m/f; **life jacket** N colete m salva-vidas; **lifelike** ADJ natural; (realistic) realista; **life preserver** (US) N = **life jacket**; **life sentence** N pena de prisão perpétua; **lifetime** N vida
lift [lɪft] VT levantar ▶ vi (fog) dispersar-se, dissipar-se ▶ N (BRIT: elevator) elevador m; **to give sb a ~** (BRIT) dar uma carona para alguém (BR), dar uma boleia a alguém (PT); **lift-off** N decolagem f
light [laɪt] (pt, pp **lit**) N luz f; (Aut: headlight) farol m; (: rear light) luz traseira; (for cigarette etc): **have you got a ~?** tem fogo? ▶ VT acender; (room) iluminar ▶ ADJ (colour, room) claro; (not heavy, also fig) leve; (rain, traffic) fraco; (movement, action) delicado; **lights** NPL (Aut) sinal m de trânsito; **to come to ~** vir à tona; **in the ~ of** à luz de; **light up** vi iluminar-se ▶ VT iluminar; **light bulb** N lâmpada; **lighten** VT tornar mais leve; **lighter** N (also: **cigarette lighter**) isqueiro, acendedor m; **light-hearted** ADJ alegre, despreocupado; **lighthouse** N farol m; **lighting** N iluminação f; **lightly** ADV ligeiramente; **to get off lightly** conseguir se safar, livrar a cara (inf)
lightning ['laɪtnɪŋ] N relâmpago, raio
lightweight ['laɪtweɪt] ADJ (suit) leve; (Boxing) peso-leve
like [laɪk] VT gostar de ▶ PREP como; (such as) tal qual ▶ ADJ parecido, semelhante ▶ N: **the ~** coisas fpl parecidas; **his ~s and dislikes** seus gostos e aversões; **I would ~, I'd ~** (eu) gostaria de; **to be or look ~ sb/sth** parecer-se com alguém/algo, parecer alguém/algo; **do it ~ this** faça isso assim; **it is nothing ~ ...** não se parece nada com ...; **likeable** ADJ simpático, agradável
likelihood ['laɪklɪhud] N probabilidade f
likely ['laɪklɪ] ADJ provável; **he's ~ to leave** é provável que ele se vá; **not ~!** (inf) nem morto!

likewise ['laɪkwaɪz] ADV igualmente; **to do ~** fazer o mesmo

liking ['laɪkɪŋ] N afeição f, simpatia; **to be to sb's ~** ser ao gosto de alguém

lilac ['laɪlək] N lilás m

lily ['lɪlɪ] N lírio, açucena

limb [lɪm] N membro

limbo ['lɪmbəu] N: **to be in ~** (fig) viver na expectativa

lime [laɪm] N (tree) limeira; (fruit) limão m; (also: ~ **juice**) suco (BR) or sumo (PT) de limão; (Geo) cal f

limelight ['laɪmlaɪt] N: **to be in the ~** ser o centro das atenções

limestone ['laɪmstəun] N pedra calcária

limit ['lɪmɪt] N limite m ▶ VT limitar; **limited** ADJ limitado; **to be limited to** limitar-se a

limp [lɪmp] N: **to have a ~** mancar, ser coxo ▶ VI mancar ▶ ADJ frouxo

line [laɪn] N linha; (rope) corda; (wire) fio; (row) fila, fileira; (on face) ruga ▶ VT (road, room) encarreirar; (container, clothing): **to ~ sth (with)** forrar algo (de); **to ~ the streets** ladear as ruas; **in ~ with** de acordo com; **line up** VI enfileirar-se ▶ VT enfileirar; (set up, have ready) preparar, arranjar

linen ['lɪnɪn] N artigos de cama e mesa; (cloth) linho

liner ['laɪnəʳ] N navio de linha regular; (also: **bin ~**) saco para lata de lixo

linger ['lɪŋgəʳ] VI demorar-se, retardar-se; (smell, tradition) persistir

lining ['laɪnɪŋ] N forro; (Anat) parede f

link [lɪŋk] N (of a chain) elo; (connection) conexão f ▶ VT vincular, unir; (associate): **to ~ with** or **to** unir a; **links** NPL (Golf) campo de golfe; **link up** VT acoplar ▶ VI unir-se

lion ['laɪən] N leão m; **lioness** N leoa

lip [lɪp] N lábio; **lipread** irreg VI ler os lábios; **lip salve** N pomada para os lábios; **lipstick** N batom m

liqueur [lɪ'kjuəʳ] N licor m

liquid ['lɪkwɪd] ADJ líquido ▶ N líquido

liquor ['lɪkəʳ] N licor m, bebida alcoólica; **liquor store** (US) N loja que vende bebidas alcoólicas

Lisbon ['lɪzbən] N Lisboa

lisp [lɪsp] N ceceio ▶ VI cecear, falar com a língua presa

list [lɪst] N lista ▶ VT (write down) fazer uma lista or relação de; (enumerate) enumerar

listen ['lɪsn] VI escutar, ouvir; **to ~ to** escutar; **listener** N ouvinte m/f

lit [lɪt] PT, PP of **light**

liter ['liːtəʳ] (US) N = **litre**

literacy ['lɪtərəsɪ] N capacidade f de ler e escrever, alfabetização f

literal ['lɪtərl] ADJ literal

literary ['lɪtərərɪ] ADJ literário

literate ['lɪtərət] ADJ alfabetizado, instruído; (educated) culto, letrado

literature ['lɪtərɪtʃəʳ] N literatura; (brochures etc) folhetos mpl

litre ['liːtəʳ], (US) **liter** N litro

litter ['lɪtəʳ] N (rubbish) lixo; (young animals) ninhada; **litter bin** (BRIT) N lata de lixo

little ['lɪtl] ADJ (small) pequeno; (not much) pouco ▶ ADV pouco; **a ~** um pouco (de); **~ house** casinha; **for a ~ while** por um instante; **as ~ as possible** o menos possível; **~ by ~** pouco a pouco

live [vi, vt lɪv, adj laɪv] VI viver; (reside) morar ▶ ADJ vivo; (wire) eletrizado; (broadcast) ao vivo; (shell) carregado; **~ ammunition** munição de guerra; **live down** VT redimir; **live on** VT FUS viver de, alimentar-se de; **to ~ on £50 a week** viver com £50 por semana; **live together** VI viver juntos; **live up to** VT FUS (fulfil) cumprir

livelihood ['laɪvlɪhud] N meio de vida, subsistência

lively ['laɪvlɪ] ADJ vivo

liven up ['laɪvn-] VT animar ▶ VI animar-se

liver ['lɪvəʳ] N fígado

lives [laɪvz] NPL of **life**

livestream ['laivstriːm] N (Comput) transmissão f ao vivo pela Internet ▶ VT transmitir ao vivo pela Internet

living ['lɪvɪŋ] ADJ vivo ▶ N: **to earn** or **make a ~** ganhar a vida; **living room** N sala de estar; **living will** N testamento em vida

lizard ['lɪzəd] N lagarto

load [ləud] N carga; (weight) peso ▶ VT (gen, Comput) carregar; **a ~ of, ~s of** (fig) um monte de, uma porção de; **loaded** ADJ (question, word) intencionado; (inf: rich) cheio da nota; (vehicle): **to be loaded with** estar carregado de

loaf [ləuf] (pl **loaves**) N pão-de-forma m

loan [ləun] N empréstimo ▶ VT emprestar; **on ~** emprestado

loathe [ləuð] VT detestar, odiar

loaves [ləuvz] NPL of **loaf**

lobby ['lɔbɪ] N vestíbulo, saguão m; (Pol: pressure group) grupo de pressão, lobby m ▶ VT pressionar

lobster ['lɔbstəʳ] N lagostim m; (large) lagosta

local ['ləukl] ADJ local ▶ N (*pub*) bar m
(local); **the locals** NPL (*local inhabitants*)
os moradores locais; **local anaesthetic**
N anestesia local

locate [ləu'keɪt] VT (*find*) localizar, situar;
(*situate*): **to be ~d in** estar localizado em

location [ləu'keɪʃən] N local m, posição f;
on ~ (*Cinema*) em externas

loch [lɔx] N lago

lock [lɔk] N (*of door, box*) fechadura; (*of
canal*) eclusa; (*of hair*) anel m, mecha ▶ VT
(*with key*) trancar ▶ VI (*door etc*) fechar-se
à chave; (*wheels*) travar-se; **lock in** VT
trancar dentro; **lock out** VT trancar do
lado de fora; **lock up** VT (*criminal*)
prender; (*house*) trancar ▶ VI fechar tudo

locker ['lɔkə'] N compartimento com
chave; **locker-room** (*US*) N (*Sport*)
vestiário

locksmith ['lɔksmɪθ] N serralheiro(-a)

lodge [lɔdʒ] N casa do guarda, guarita;
(*hunting lodge*) pavilhão m de caça ▶ VI
(*person*): **to ~ (with)** alojar-se (na casa
de) ▶ VT (*complaint*) apresentar; **lodger** N
inquilino(-a), hóspede m/f

loft [lɔft] N sótão m

log [lɔg] N (*of wood*) tora; (*book*) =
logbook ▶ VT registrar; **logbook** N
(*Naut*) diário de bordo; (*Aviat*) diário de
voo; (*of car*) documentação f (do carro)

logic ['lɔdʒɪk] N lógica; **logical** ADJ lógico

login ['lɔgɪn] N (*Comput*) login m

LOL (*inf*) ABBR (= *laugh out loud*) rs, LOL

lollipop ['lɔlɪpɔp] N pirulito (*BR*),
chupa-chupa m (*PT*); **lollipop lady** (*BRIT*)
N mulher que ajuda as crianças a
atravessarem a rua; **lollipop man** (*BRIT*)
N homem que ajuda as crianças a atravessarem
a rua

> Lollipop men/ladies são as pessoas
> que ajudam as crianças a atravessar a
> rua nas proximidades das escolas na
> hora da entrada e da saída. São
> facilmente localizados graças a suas
> longas capas brancas e à placa
> redonda com a qual pedem aos
> motoristas que parem. São chamados
> assim por causa da forma circular
> da placa, que lembra um pirulito
> (*lollipop*).

lolly ['lɔlɪ] (*inf*) N (*ice*) picolé m; (*lollipop*)
pirulito

London ['lʌndən] N Londres; **Londoner**
N londrino(-a)

lone [ləun] ADJ (*person*) solitário; (*thing*)
único

loneliness ['ləunlɪnɪs] N solidão f,
isolamento

lonely ['ləunlɪ] ADJ (*person*) só; (*place,
childhood*) solitário, isolado

long [lɔŋ] ADJ longo; (*road, hair, table*)
comprido ▶ ADV muito tempo ▶ VI: **to ~
for sth** ansiar or suspirar por algo; **how
~ is the street?** qual é a extensão da
rua?; **how ~ is the lesson?** quanto dura
a lição?; **all night ~** a noite inteira; **he
no ~er comes** ele não vem mais; **~
before/after** muito antes/depois; **before ~** (+ *future*) dentro de pouco;
(+ *past*) pouco tempo depois; **at ~ last**
por fim, no final; **so** or **as ~ as** contanto
que; **long-distance** ADJ (*travel*) de longa
distância; (*call*) interurbano; **longing** N
desejo, anseio

longitude ['lɔŋgɪtjuːd] N longitude f;

long: long jump N salto em distância;
long-sighted ADJ presbita; **long-
standing** ADJ de muito tempo; **long-
term** ADJ a longo prazo

loo [luː] (*BRIT inf*) N banheiro (*BR*), casa de
banho (*PT*)

look [luk] VI olhar; (*seem*) parecer;
(*building etc*): **to ~ south/(out) onto the
sea** dar para o sul/o mar ▶ N olhar m;
(*glance*) olhada, vista de olhos;
(*appearance*) aparência, aspecto; **looks**
NPL (*good looks*) físico, aparência;
~ (here)! (*annoyance*) escuta aqui!; **~!**
(*surprise*) olha!; **look after** VT FUS cuidar
de; (*deal with*) lidar com; **look at** VT FUS
olhar (para); (*read quickly*) ler
rapidamente; (*consider*) considerar; **look
back** VI: **to ~ back on** (*remember*)
recordar, rever; **look down on** VT FUS
(*fig*) desdenhar, desprezar; **look for** VT
FUS procurar; **look forward to** VT FUS
aguardar com prazer, ansiar por; (*in
letter*): **we ~ forward to hearing from
you** no aguardo de suas notícias; **look
into** VT FUS investigar; **look on** VI
assistir; **look out** VI (*beware*): **to ~ out
(for)** tomar cuidado (com); **look out for**
VT FUS (*await*) esperar; **look round** VI
virar a cabeça, voltar-se; **look through**
VT FUS (*papers, book*) examinar; **look to**
VT FUS (*rely on*) contar com; **look up** VI
levantar os olhos; (*improve*) melhorar
▶ VT (*word*) procurar

loop [luːp] N laço ▶ VT: **to ~ sth round
sth** prender algo em torno de algo

loose [luːs] ADJ solto; (*not tight*) frouxo
▶ N: **to be on the ~** estar solto; **loosely**
ADV frouxamente, folgadamente;
loosen VT (*free*) soltar; (*slacken*) afrouxar

loot [luːt] N saque m, despojo ▶ VT
saquear, pilhar

lord [lɔ:d] N senhor m; **L~ Smith** Lord Smith; **the L~** (Rel) o Senhor; **good L~!** Deus meu!; **the (House of) L~s** (BRIT) a Câmara dos Lordes

lorry ['lɔrɪ] (BRIT) N caminhão m (BR), camião m (PT); **lorry driver** (BRIT) N caminhoneiro (BR), camionista m/f (PT)

lose [lu:z] (pt, pp **lost**) VT, VI perder; **to ~ (time)** (clock) atrasar-se; **loser** N perdedor(a) m/f; (inf: failure) derrotado(-a), fracassado(-a)

loss [lɔs] N perda; (Comm): **to make a ~** sair com prejuízo; **heavy ~es** (Mil) grandes perdas; **to be at a ~** estar perplexo

lost [lɔst] PT, PP of **lose** ▶ ADJ perdido; **~ and found** (US) (seção f de) perdidos e achados mpl; **lost property** (BRIT) N (objetos mpl) perdidos e achados mpl

lot [lɔt] N (set of things) porção f; (at auctions) lote m; **the ~** tudo, todos(-as); **a ~** muito, bastante; **a ~ of, ~s of** muito(s); **I read a ~** leio bastante; **to draw ~s** tirar à sorte

lotion ['ləuʃən] N loção f

lottery ['lɔtərɪ] N loteria

loud [laud] ADJ (voice) alto; (shout) forte; (noise) barulhento; (support, condemnation) veemente; (gaudy) berrante ▶ ADV alto; **out ~** em voz alta; **loudly** ADV ruidosamente; (aloud) em voz alta; **loudspeaker** N alto-falante m

lounge [laundʒ] N sala de estar f; (of airport) salão m; (BRIT: also: **~ bar**) bar m social ▶ VI recostar-se, espreguiçar-se; **lounge about, lounge around** VI ficar à-toa

lousy ['lauzɪ] (inf) ADJ ruim, péssimo; (ill): **to feel ~** sentir-se mal

love [lʌv] N amor m ▶ VT amar; (like a lot) adorar; **to ~ to do** adorar fazer; **~ (from) Anne** (on letter) um abraço or um beijo, Anne; **I ~ you** eu te amo; **I ~ coffee** adoro o café; **"15 ~"** (Tennis) "15 a zero"; **to be in ~ with** estar apaixonado por; **to fall in ~ with** apaixonar-se por; **to make ~** fazer amor; **love affair** N aventura (amorosa), caso (de amor); **love life** N vida sentimental

lovely ['lʌvlɪ] ADJ (delightful) encantador(a), delicioso; (beautiful) lindo, belo; (holiday, surprise) muito agradável, maravilhoso

lover ['lʌvəʳ] N amante m/f

loving ['lʌvɪŋ] ADJ carinhoso, afetuoso; (actions) dedicado

low [ləu] ADJ baixo; (depressed) deprimido; (ill) doente ▶ ADV baixo ▶ N (Meteorology) área de baixa pressão; **to be ~ on** (supplies) ter pouco; **to reach a new** or **an all-time ~** cair para o seu nível mais baixo; **low-alcohol** ADJ de baixo teor alcoólico; **low-calorie** ADJ de baixo teor calórico; **low-carb** (inf) ADJ (diet, meal) com baixo carboidrato; **lower** ADJ mais baixo; (less important) inferior ▶ VT abaixar; (reduce) reduzir, diminuir; **low-fat** ADJ magro

loyal ['lɔɪəl] ADJ leal; **loyalty** N lealdade f

loyalty card (BRIT) N cartão m de fidelidade

L-plates ['ɛlpleɪts] (BRIT) NPL placas fpl de aprendiz de motorista

> As **L-plates** são placas quadradas com um "L" vermelho que são colocadas na parte de trás do carro para mostrar que a pessoa ao volante ainda não tem carteira de motorista. Até a obtenção da carteira, o motorista aprendiz possui uma permissão provisória e não tem direito de dirigir sem um motorista qualificado ao lado. Os motoristas aprendizes não podem dirigir em estradas mesmo que estejam acompanhados.

Ltd (BRIT) ABBR (= limited (liability) company) SA

luck [lʌk] N sorte f; **bad ~** azar m; **good ~!** boa sorte!; **bad** or **hard** or **tough ~!** que azar!; **luckily** ADV por sorte, felizmente; **lucky** ADJ (person) sortudo; (situation) afortunado; (object) de sorte

ludicrous ['lu:dɪkrəs] ADJ ridículo

luggage ['lʌgɪdʒ] N bagagem f; **luggage rack** N porta-bagagem m, bagageiro

lukewarm ['lu:kwɔ:m] ADJ morno, tépido; (fig) indiferente

lull [lʌl] N pausa, interrupção f ▶ VT: **to ~ sb to sleep** acalentar alguém; **to be ~ed into a false sense of security** ser acalmado com uma falsa sensação de segurança

lullaby ['lʌləbaɪ] N canção f de ninar

lumber ['lʌmbəʳ] N (junk) trastes mpl velhos; (wood) madeira serrada, tábua ▶ VT: **to ~ sb with sth/sb** empurrar algo/alguém para cima de alguém

luminous ['lu:mɪnəs] ADJ luminoso

lump [lʌmp] N torrão m; (fragment) pedaço; (on body) galo, caroço; (also: **sugar ~**) cubo de açúcar ▶ VT: **to ~ together** amontoar; **lump sum** N montante m único; **lumpy** ADJ encaroçado

lunatic ['lu:nətɪk] ADJ louco(-a)

lunch [lʌntʃ] N almoço; **lunch break,
lunch hour** N hora do almoço
lung [lʌŋ] N pulmão m
lure [luəʳ] N isca ▶ VT atrair, seduzir
lurk [lə:k] VI (hide) esconder-se; (wait)
estar à espreita
lush [lʌʃ] ADJ exuberante
lust [lʌst] N luxúria; (greed) cobiça; **lust
after** VT FUS cobiçar; **lust for** VT FUS =
lust after
Luxembourg ['lʌksəmbə:g] N
Luxemburgo
luxurious [lʌg'zjuərɪəs] ADJ luxuoso
luxury ['lʌkʃərɪ] N luxo ▶ CPD de luxo
lying ['laɪɪŋ] N mentira(s) f(pl) ▶ ADJ
mentiroso, falso
lyrics ['lɪrɪks] NPL (of song) letra

M.A. ABBR (Sch) = **Master of Arts**
mac [mæk] (BRIT) N capa impermeável
macaroni [mækə'rəunɪ] N macarrão m
machine [mə'ʃi:n] N máquina ▶ VT (dress
etc) costurar à máquina; (Tech) usinar;
machine gun N metralhadora;
machinery N maquinaria; (fig) máquina
mackerel ['mækrl] N INV cavala
mackintosh ['mækɪntɔʃ] (BRIT) N capa
impermeável
mad [mæd] ADJ louco; (foolish) tolo;
(angry) furioso, brabo; (keen): **to be ~
about** ser louco por
madam ['mædəm] N senhora, madame f
made [meɪd] PT, PP of **make**;
made-to-measure (BRIT) ADJ feito sob
medida; **made-up** ['meɪdʌp] ADJ (story)
inventado
madly ['mædlɪ] ADV loucamente; **~ in
love** louco de amor
madman ['mædmən] irreg N louco
madness ['mædnɪs] N loucura;
(foolishness) tolice f
magazine [mægə'zi:n] N (Press) revista;
(Radio, TV) programa m de atualidades
maggot ['mægət] N larva de inseto
magic ['mædʒɪk] N magia, mágica ▶ ADJ
mágico; **magical** ADJ mágico; **magician**
[mə'dʒɪʃən] N mago(-a); (entertainer)
mágico(-a)
magistrate ['mædʒɪstreɪt] N
magistrado(-a), juiz/juíza m/f
magnet ['mægnɪt] N ímã m; **magnetic**
[mæg'nɛtɪk] ADJ magnético
magnificent [mæg'nɪfɪsnt] ADJ
magnífico
magnify ['mægnɪfaɪ] VT aumentar;
magnifying glass N lupa, lente f de
aumento
magpie ['mægpaɪ] N pega

mahogany [mə'hɔgənı] N mogno, acaju m

maid [meɪd] N empregada; **old ~** (pej) solteirona

maiden name ['meɪdn-] N nome m de solteira

mail [meɪl] N correio; (letters) cartas fpl ▶ VT pôr no correio; **mailbox** N (US) caixa do correio; **mailing list** N lista de clientes, mailing list m

main [meɪn] ADJ principal ▶ N (pipe) cano or esgoto principal; **the mains** NPL (Elec, gas, water) a rede; **in the ~** na maior parte; **mainland** N: **the mainland** o continente; **mainly** ADV principalmente; **main road** N estrada principal; **mainstream** N corrente f principal

maintain [meɪn'teɪn] VT manter; (keep up) conservar (em bom estado); (affirm) sustentar, afirmar; **maintenance** ['meɪntənəns] N manutenção f; (alimony) alimentos mpl, pensão f alimentícia

maize [meɪz] N milho

majesty ['mædʒɪstɪ] N majestade f

major ['meɪdʒəʳ] N (Mil) major m ▶ ADJ (main) principal; (considerable) importante; (Mus) maior

Majorca [mə'jɔːkə] N Maiorca

majority [mə'dʒɔrɪtɪ] N maioria

make [meɪk] (pt, pp made) VT fazer; (manufacture) fabricar, produzir; (cause to be): **to ~ sb sad** entristecer alguém, fazer alguém ficar triste; (force): **to ~ sb do sth** fazer com que alguém faça algo; (equal): **2 and 2 ~ 4** dois e dois são quatro ▶ N marca; **to ~ a profit/loss** ter um lucro/uma perda; **to ~ it** (arrive) chegar; (succeed) ter sucesso; **what time do you ~ it?** que horas você tem?; **to ~ do with** contentar-se com; **make for** VT FUS (place) dirigir-se a; **make out** VT (decipher) decifrar; (understand) compreender; (see) divisar, avistar; **make up** VT (constitute) constituir; (invent) inventar; (parcel) embrulhar ▶ VI reconciliar-se; (with cosmetics) maquilar-se (BR), maquilhar-se (PT); **make up for** VT FUS compensar; **maker** N (of film, programme) criador m; (manufacturer) fabricante m/f; **makeshift** ADJ provisório; **make-up** N maquilagem f (BR), maquilhagem f (PT)

malaria [mə'lɛərɪə] N malária

Malaysia [mə'leɪzɪə] N Malaísia (BR), Malásia (PT)

male [meɪl] N macho ▶ ADJ masculino; (child etc) do sexo masculino

malignant [mə'lɪgnənt] ADJ (Med) maligno

mall [mɔːl] N (also: **shopping ~**) shopping m

mallet ['mælɪt] N maço, marreta

malt [mɔːlt] N malte m

Malta ['mɔːltə] N Malta

malware ['mælwɛəʳ] N (Comput) software m malicioso

mammal ['mæml] N mamífero

mammoth ['mæməθ] N mamute m ▶ ADJ gigantesco, imenso

man [mæn] (pl men) N homem m ▶ VT (Naut) tripular; (Mil) guarnecer; (machine) operar; **an old ~** um velho; **~ and wife** marido e mulher

manage ['mænɪdʒ] VI arranjar-se, virar-se ▶ VT (be in charge of) dirigir, administrar; (business) gerenciar; (ship, person) controlar; **manageable** ADJ manejável; (task etc) viável; **management** N administração f, direção f, gerência; **manager** N gerente m/f; (Sport) técnico(-a); **manageress** N gerente f; **managerial** [mænə'dʒɪəːrɪəl] ADJ administrativo, gerencial; **managing director** N diretor(a) m/f, diretor-gerente/diretora-gerente m/f

mandarin ['mændərɪn] N (also: **~ orange**) tangerina; (person) mandarim m

mandatory ['mændətərɪ] ADJ obrigatório

mane [meɪn] N (of horse) crina; (of lion) juba

maneuver [mə'nuːvəʳ] (US) = **manoeuvre**

mango ['mæŋgəu] (pl mangoes) N manga

manhole ['mænhəul] N poço de inspeção

manhood ['mænhud] N (age) idade f adulta; (masculinity) virilidade f

mania ['meɪnɪə] N mania; **maniac** ['meɪnɪæk] N maníaco(-a); (fig) louco(-a)

manic ['mænɪk] ADJ maníaco

manicure ['mænɪkjuəʳ] N manicure f (BR), manicura (PT)

manifest ['mænɪfɛst] VT manifestar, mostrar ▶ ADJ manifesto, evidente

manipulate [mə'nɪpjuleɪt] VT manipular

mankind [mæn'kaɪnd] N humanidade f, raça humana

man-made ADJ sintético, artificial

manner ['mænəʳ] N modo, maneira; (behaviour) conduta, comportamento; **manners** NPL (conduct) boas maneiras fpl, educação f; **bad ~s** falta de educação; **all ~ of** todo tipo de; **all ~ of things** todos os tipos de coisa

manoeuvre [məˈnuːvəʳ], (US) **maneuver** VT manobrar; (manipulate) manipular ▶ VI manobrar ▶ N manobra

manpower [ˈmænpauəʳ] N potencial m humano, mão-de-obra f

mansion [ˈmænʃən] N mansão f, palacete m

manslaughter [ˈmænslɔːtəʳ] N homicídio involuntário

mantelpiece [ˈmæntlpiːs] N consolo da lareira

manual [ˈmænjuəl] ADJ manual ▶ N manual m

manufacture [mænjuˈfæktʃəʳ] VT manufaturar, fabricar ▶ N fabricação f; **manufacturer** N fabricante m/f

manure [məˈnjuəʳ] N estrume m, adubo

manuscript [ˈmænjuskrɪpt] N manuscrito

many [ˈmɛnɪ] ADJ, PRON muitos(-as); **a great ~** muitíssimos; **~ a time** muitas vezes

map [mæp] N mapa m; **map out** VT traçar

maple [ˈmeɪpl] N bordo

mar [mɑːʳ] VT estragar

marathon [ˈmærəθən] N maratona

marble [ˈmɑːbl] N mármore m; (toy) bola de gude

March [mɑːtʃ] N março

march [mɑːtʃ] VI marchar; (demonstrators) desfilar ▶ N marcha, passeata

mare [mɛəʳ] N égua

margarine [mɑːdʒəˈriːn] N margarina

margin [ˈmɑːdʒɪn] N margem f; **marginal** ADJ marginal; **marginal seat** (Pol) cadeira ganha por pequena maioria

marigold [ˈmærɪɡəuld] N malmequer m

marijuana [mærɪˈwɑːnə] N maconha

marine [məˈriːn] ADJ marinho; (engineer) naval ▶ N fuzileiro naval

marital [ˈmærɪtl] ADJ matrimonial, marital; **~ status** estado civil

marjoram [ˈmɑːdʒərəm] N manjerona

mark [mɑːk] N marca, sinal m; (imprint) impressão f; (stain) mancha; (BRIT Sch) nota; (currency) marco ▶ VT marcar; (stain) manchar; (indicate) indicar; (commemorate) comemorar; (BRIT Sch) dar nota em; (: correct) corrigir; **to ~ time** marcar passo; **marker** N (sign) marcador m, marca; (bookmark) marcador

market [ˈmɑːkɪt] N mercado ▶ VT (Comm) comercializar; **marketing** N marketing m; **marketplace** N mercado;

market research N pesquisa de mercado

marmalade [ˈmɑːməleɪd] N geleia de laranja

maroon [məˈruːn] VT: **to be ~ed** ficar abandonado (numa ilha) ▶ ADJ vinho inv

marquee [mɑːˈkiː] N toldo, tenda

marriage [ˈmærɪdʒ] N casamento

married [ˈmærɪd] ADJ casado; (life, love) conjugal

marrow [ˈmærəu] N medula; (vegetable) abóbora

marry [ˈmærɪ] VT casar(-se) com; (subj: father, priest etc) casar, unir ▶ VI (also: **get married**) casar(-se)

Mars [mɑːz] N Marte m

marsh [mɑːʃ] N pântano; (salt marsh) marisma

marshal [ˈmɑːʃl] N (Mil: also: **field ~**) marechal m; (at sports meeting etc) oficial m ▶ VT (thoughts, support) organizar; (soldiers) formar

martyr [ˈmɑːtəʳ] N mártir m/f

marvel [ˈmɑːvl] N maravilha ▶ VI: **to ~ (at)** maravilhar-se (de or com); **marvellous**, (US) **marvelous** ADJ maravilhoso

Marxist [ˈmɑːksɪst] ADJ, N marxista m/f

mascara [mæsˈkɑːrə] N rímel m

masculine [ˈmæskjulɪn] ADJ masculino

mash [mæʃ] VT (Culin) fazer um purê de; (crush) amassar

mask [mɑːsk] N máscara ▶ VT (face) encobrir; (feelings) esconder, ocultar

mason [ˈmeɪsn] N (also: **stone ~**) pedreiro(-a); (also: **free~**) maçom m; **masonry** N alvenaria

mass [mæs] N quantidade f; (people) multidão f; (Phys) massa; (Rel) missa; (great quantity) montão m ▶ CPD de massa ▶ VI reunir-se; (Mil) concentrar-se; **the masses** NPL (ordinary people) as massas; **~es of** (inf) montes de

massacre [ˈmæsəkəʳ] N massacre m, carnificina

massage [ˈmæsɑːʒ] N massagem f

massive [ˈmæsɪv] ADJ (large) enorme; (support) massivo

mass media NPL meios mpl de comunicação de massa, mídia

mast [mɑːst] N (Naut) mastro; (Radio etc) antena

master [ˈmɑːstəʳ] N mestre m; (fig: of situation) dono; (in secondary school) professor m; (title for boys): **M~ X** o menino X ▶ VT controlar; (learn) conhecer a fundo; **mastermind** N (fig) cabeça ▶ VT dirigir, planejar; **masterpiece** N obra-prima

mat [mæt] N esteira; (*also:* **door~**) capacho; (*also:* **table ~**) descanso

match [mætʃ] N fósforo; (*game*) jogo, partida; (*equal*) igual m/f ▶ vт (*also:* **~ up**) casar, emparelhar; (*go well with*) combinar com; (*equal*) igualar; (*correspond to*) corresponder a ▶ vi combinar; **to be a good ~** (*couple*) formar um bom casal; **matchbox** N caixa de fósforos; **matching** ADJ que combina (com)

mate [meit] N (*inf*) colega m/f; (*assistant*) ajudante m/f; (*animal*) macho/fêmea; (*in merchant navy*) imediato ▶ vi acasalar-se

material [mə'tɪərɪəl] N (*substance*) matéria; (*equipment*) material m; (*cloth*) pano, tecido; (*data*) dados mpl ▶ ADJ material; **materials** NPL (*equipment*) material

maternal [mə'tə:nl] ADJ maternal

maternity [mə'tə:nɪtɪ] N maternidade f

mathematical [mæθə'mætɪkl] ADJ matemático

mathematics [mæθə'mætɪks] N matemática

maths [mæθs], (*US*) **math** N matemática

matron ['meitrən] N (*in hospital*) enfermeira-chefe f; (*in school*) inspetora

matter ['mætə'] N questão f, assunto; (*Phys*) matéria; (*substance*) substância; (*reading matter etc*) material m; (*Med: pus*) pus m ▶ vi importar; **matters** NPL (*affairs*) questões fpl; **it doesn't ~** não importa; (*I don't mind*) tanto faz; **what's the ~?** o que (é que) há?, qual é o problema?; **no ~ what** aconteça o que acontecer; **as a ~ of course** por rotina; **as a ~ of fact** na realidade, de fato

mattress ['mætrɪs] N colchão m

mature [mə'tjuə'] ADJ maduro; (*cheese, wine*) amadurecido ▶ vi amadurecer

maul [mɔ:l] vт machucar, maltratar

mauve [məuv] ADJ cor de malva inv

maximum ['mæksɪməm] (*pl* **maxima** or **maximums**) ADJ máximo ▶ N máximo

May [mei] N maio

may [mei] (*conditional* **might**) AUX VB (*indicating possibility*): **he ~ come** pode ser que ele venha, é capaz de vir; (*be allowed to*): **~ I smoke?** posso fumar?; (*wishes*): **~ God bless you!** que Deus lhe abençoe

maybe ['meibi:] ADV talvez; **~ not** talvez não

mayhem ['meihɛm] N caos m

mayonnaise [meiə'neiz] N maionese f

mayor [mɛə'] N prefeito (*BR*), presidente m do município (*PT*); **mayoress** N prefeita (*BR*), presidenta do município (*PT*)

maze [meiz] N labirinto

(KEYWORD)

me [mi:] PRON **1** (*direct*) me; **he heard me** ele me ouviu; **it's me** sou eu
2 (*indirect*) me; **he gave me the money** ele me deu o dinheiro; **give it to me** dá isso para mim
3 (*stressed, after prep*) mim; **with me** comigo; **without me** sem mim

meadow ['mɛdəu] N prado, campina

meagre ['mi:gə'], (*US*) **meager** ADJ escasso

meal [mi:l] N refeição f; (*flour*) farinha; **mealtime** N hora da refeição

mean [mi:n] (*pt, pp* **meant**) ADJ (*with money*) sovina, avarento, pão-duro inv (*BR*); (*unkind*) mesquinho; (*shabby*) malcuidado, dilapidado; (*average*) médio ▶ vт (*signify*) significar, querer dizer; (*refer to*): **I thought you ~t her** eu pensei que você estivesse se referindo a ela; (*intend*): **to ~ to do sth** pretender or tencionar fazer algo ▶ N meio, meio termo; **means** NPL (*way, money*) meio; **by ~s of** por meio de, mediante; **by all ~s!** claro que sim!, pois não; **do you ~ it?** você está falando sério?

meaning ['mi:nɪŋ] N sentido, significado; **meaningful** ADJ significativo; (*relationship*) sério; **meaningless** ADJ sem sentido

meant [mɛnt] PT, PP *of* **mean**

meantime ['mi:ntaim] ADV (*also:* **in the ~**) entretanto, enquanto isso

meanwhile ['mi:nwail] ADV = **meantime**

measles ['mi:zlz] N sarampo

measure ['mɛʒə'] vт, vi medir ▶ N medida; (*also:* **tape ~**) fita métrica

measurement ['mɛʒəmənt] N medida; **measurements** NPL (*size*) medidas fpl

meat [mi:t] N carne f; **cold ~s** (*BRIT*) frios; **meatball** N almôndega

Mecca ['mɛkə] N Meca; (*fig*): **a ~ (for)** a meca (de)

mechanic [mɪ'kænɪk] N mecânico; **mechanical** ADJ mecânico

mechanism ['mɛkənɪzəm] N mecanismo

medal ['mɛdl] N medalha

meddle ['mɛdl] vi: **to ~ in** meter-se em, intrometer-se em; **to ~ with sth** mexer em algo

media ['miːdɪə] NPL meios mpl de comunicação, mídia

mediaeval [medɪ'iːvl] ADJ = **medieval**

mediate ['miːdɪeɪt] VI mediar

medical ['medɪkl] ADJ médico ▶ N (examination) exame m médico

medication [medɪ'keɪʃən] N medicação f

medicine ['medsɪn] N medicina; (drug) remédio, medicamento

medieval [medɪ'iːvl] ADJ medieval

mediocre [miːdɪ'əʊkəʳ] ADJ medíocre

meditate ['medɪteɪt] VI meditar

Mediterranean [medɪtə'reɪnɪən] ADJ mediterrâneo; **the ~ (Sea)** o (mar) Mediterrâneo

medium ['miːdɪəm] (pl **media** or **mediums**) ADJ médio ▶ N (means) meio; (pl **mediums**: person) médium m/f

meek [miːk] ADJ manso, dócil

meet [miːt] (pt, pp **met**) VT encontrar; (accidentally) topar com, dar de cara com; (by arrangement) encontrar-se com, ir ao encontro de; (for the first time) conhecer; (go and fetch) ir buscar; (opponent, problem) enfrentar; (obligations) cumprir; (need) satisfazer ▶ VI encontrar-se; (for talks) reunir-se; (join) unir-se; (get to know) conhecer-se; **meet with** VT FUS reunir-se com; (difficulty) encontrar; **meeting** N encontro; (session: of club, Comm) reunião f; (assembly) assembleia; (Sport) corrida

megabyte ['megəbaɪt] N (Comput) megabyte m

megaphone ['megəfəʊn] N megafone m

megapixel ['megəpɪksl] N megapixel m

melancholy ['melənkəlɪ] N melancolia ▶ ADJ melancólico

melody ['melədɪ] N melodia

melon ['melən] N melão m

melt [melt] VI (metal) fundir-se; (snow) derreter ▶ VT derreter; **melt down** VT fundir

member ['membəʳ] N membro(-a); (of club) sócio(-a); (Anat) membro; **M~ of Parliament** (BRIT) deputado(-a); **membership** N (state) adesão f; (members) número de sócios; **membership card** N carteira de sócio

meme [miːm] N (Comput) meme m

memento [mə'mentəu] N lembrança

memo ['meməu] N memorando, nota

memorandum [memə'rændəm] (pl **memoranda**) N memorando

memorial [mɪ'mɔːrɪəl] N monumento comemorativo ▶ ADJ comemorativo; **Memorial Day** (US) N ver nota

> **Memorial Day** é um feriado nos Estados Unidos, a última segunda-feira de maio na maior parte dos estados, em memória aos soldados americanos mortos em combate.

memorize ['meməraɪz] VT decorar, aprender de cor

memory ['memərɪ] N memória; (recollection) lembrança; **memory stick** N (Comput: flash pen) pen drive m; (card) cartão m de memória

men [men] NPL of **man**

menace ['menəs] N ameaça; (nuisance) droga ▶ VT ameaçar

mend [mend] VT consertar, reparar; (darn) remendar ▶ N: **to be on the ~** estar melhorando

meningitis [menɪn'dʒaɪtɪs] N meningite f

menopause ['menəupɔːz] N menopausa

menstruation [menstru'eɪʃən] N menstruação f

mental ['mentl] ADJ mental; **mentality** [men'tælɪtɪ] N mentalidade f

mention ['menʃən] N menção f ▶ VT (speak of) falar de; **don't ~ it!** não tem de quê!, de nada!

menu ['menjuː] N (set menu, Comput) menu m; (printed) cardápio (BR), ementa (PT)

MEP N ABBR (= Member of the European Parliament) deputado(-a)

mercenary ['məːsɪnərɪ] ADJ mercenário ▶ N mercenário

merchandise ['məːtʃəndaɪz] N mercadorias fpl

merchant ['məːtʃənt] N comerciante m/f

merciless ['məːsɪlɪs] ADJ desumano, inclemente

mercury ['məːkjurɪ] N mercúrio

mercy ['məːsɪ] N piedade f; (Rel) misericórdia; **at the ~ of** à mercê de

mere [mɪəʳ] ADJ mero, simples inv; **merely** ADV simplesmente, somente, apenas

merge [məːdʒ] VT unir ▶ VI unir-se; (Comm) fundir-se; **merger** N fusão f

meringue [mə'ræŋ] N suspiro, merengue m

merit ['merɪt] N mérito; (advantage) vantagem f ▶ VT merecer

mermaid ['məːmeɪd] N sereia

merry ['merɪ] ADJ alegre; **M~ Christmas!** Feliz Natal!; **merry-go-round** N carrossel m

mesh [meʃ] N malha

mess [mɛs] N confusão f; (in room)
bagunça; (Mil) rancho; **to be in a ~** ser
uma bagunça, estar numa bagunça;
mess about (inf) VI perder tempo;
(pass the time) vadiar; **mess about
with** (inf) VT FUS mexer com; **mess
around** (inf) VI = **mess about**; **mess up**
VT (spoil) estragar; (dirty) sujar

message ['mɛsɪdʒ] N recado, mensagem
f ▸ VT enviar uma mensagem para;
message board N (on internet) fórum m
de discussão

messenger ['mɛsɪndʒəʳ] N
mensageiro(-a)

messy ['mɛsɪ] ADJ (dirty) sujo; (untidy)
desarrumado

met [mɛt] PT, PP of **meet**

metal ['mɛtl] N metal m

meteorology [miːtɪə'rɔlədʒɪ] N
meteorologia

meter ['miːtəʳ] N (instrument) medidor m;
(also: **parking ~**) parcômetro; (US: unit) =
metre

method ['mɛθəd] N método;
methodical [mɪ'θɔdɪkl] ADJ
metódico

metre ['miːtəʳ], (US) **meter** N metro

metric ['mɛtrɪk] ADJ métrico

metropolitan [mɛtrə'pɔlɪtən] ADJ
metropolitano

Mexico ['mɛksɪkəu] N México

mice [maɪs] NPL of **mouse**

micro... ['maɪkrəu] PREFIX micro;
microblog ['maɪkrəublɔg] N
microblog(ue) m; **microchip** N
microchip m; **microphone** N microfone
m; **microscope** N microscópio;
microwave N (also: **microwave oven**)
micro-ondas m inv

mid [mɪd] ADJ: **in ~ May** em meados de
maio; **in ~ afternoon** no meio da tarde;
in ~ air em pleno ar; **midday** N
meio-dia m

middle ['mɪdl] N meio; (waist) cintura
▸ ADJ meio; (quantity, size) médio,
mediano; **middle-aged** ADJ de
meia-idade; **Middle Ages** NPL: **the
Middle Ages** a Idade Média; **Middle
East** N: **the Middle East** o Oriente
Médio; **middle name** N segundo
nome m

midge [mɪdʒ] N mosquito

midget ['mɪdʒɪt] N anão(-anã) m/f

midnight ['mɪdnaɪt] N meia-noite f

midst [mɪdst] N: **in the ~ of** no meio de,
entre

midsummer [mɪd'sʌməʳ] N: **a ~ day**
um dia em pleno verão

midway [mɪd'weɪ] ADJ, ADV: **~ (between)**
no meio do caminho (entre)

midweek [mɪd'wiːk] ADV no meio da
semana

midwife ['mɪdwaɪf] (pl **midwives**) N
parteira

might [maɪt] VB see **may** ▸ N poder m;
força; **mighty** ADJ poderoso, forte

migraine ['miːgreɪn] N enxaqueca

migrant ['maɪgrənt] ADJ migratório;
(worker) emigrante

migrate [maɪ'greɪt] VI emigrar; (birds)
arribar

mike [maɪk] N ABBR = **microphone**

mild [maɪld] ADJ (character) pacífico;
(climate) temperado; (taste) suave;
(illness) leve, benigno; (interest) pequeno

mile [maɪl] N milha (1609 m); **mileage** N
número de milhas; (Aut)
≈ quilometragem f; **milestone**
['maɪlstəun] N marco miliário

military ['mɪlɪtərɪ] ADJ militar

milk [mɪlk] N leite m ▸ VT (cow) ordenhar;
(fig) explorar, chupar; **milk chocolate** N
chocolate m de leite; **milkman** irreg N
leiteiro; **milky** ADJ leitoso

mill [mɪl] N (windmill etc) moinho; (coffee
mill) moedor m de café; (factory) moinho,
engenho ▸ VT moer ▸ VI (also: **~ about**)
aglomerar-se, remoinhar

millimetre, (US) **millimeter**
['mɪlɪmiːtəʳ] N milímetro

million ['mɪljən] N milhão m; **a ~ times**
um milhão de vezes; **millionaire** N
milionário(-a); **millionth** NUM
milionésimo

mime [maɪm] N mimo; (actor)
mímico(-a), comediante m/f ▸ VT imitar
▸ VI fazer mímica

mimic ['mɪmɪk] N mímico(-a),
imitador(a) m/f ▸ VT imitar, parodiar

min. ABBR (= minute, minimum) min

mince [mɪns] VT moer ▸ VI (in walking)
andar com afetação ▸ N (BRIT Culin)
carne f moída; **mincemeat** N recheio de
sebo e frutas picadas; (US: meat) carne f
moída; **mince pie** N pastel com recheio de
sebo e frutas picadas

mind [maɪnd] N mente f; (intellect)
intelecto; (opinion): **to my ~** a meu ver;
(sanity): **to be out of one's ~** estar fora
de si ▸ VT (attend to, look after) tomar
conta de, cuidar de; (be careful of) ter
cuidado com; (object to): **I don't ~ the
noise** o barulho me não incomoda; **it is
on my ~** não me sai da cabeça; **to keep**
or **bear sth in ~** levar algo em
consideração, não esquecer-se de algo;

to make up one's ~ decidir-se; **I don't ~** (*it doesn't worry me*) eu nem ligo; (*it's all the same to me*) para mim tanto faz; **~ you, ...** se bem que ...; **never ~!** não faz mal; (*don't worry*) não se preocupe!; **"~ the step"** "cuidado com o degrau"; **mindless** ADJ (*violence, crime*) insensato; (*job*) monótono

mine¹ [maın] PRON o meu/a minha; **a friend of ~** um amigo meu

mine² [maın] N mina ▶ VT (*coal*) extrair, explorar; (*ship, beach*) minar

miner ['maınə'] N mineiro

mineral ['mınərəl] ADJ mineral ▶ N mineral m; **minerals** NPL (*BRIT: soft drinks*) refrigerantes mpl; **mineral water** N água mineral

mingle ['mıŋgl] VI: **to ~ with** misturar-se com

miniature ['mınətʃə'] ADJ em miniatura ▶ N miniatura

minibus ['mınıbʌs] N micro-ônibus m

minimal ['mınıml] ADJ mínimo

minimum ['mınıməm] (*pl* **minima**) ADJ mínimo ▶ N mínimo

mining ['maınıŋ] N exploração f de minas

miniskirt ['mınıskə:t] N minissaia

minister ['mınıstə'] N (*BRIT Pol*) ministro(-a); (*Rel*) pastor m ▶ VI: **to ~ to sb** prestar assistência a alguém; **to ~ to sb's needs** atender às necessidades de alguém

ministry ['mınıstrı] N (*BRIT Pol*) ministério; (*Rel*): **to go into the ~** ingressar no sacerdócio

minor ['maınə'] ADJ menor; (*unimportant*) de pouca importância; (*Mus*) menor ▶ N (*Jur*) menor m/f de idade

minority [maɪ'nɔrıtı] N minoria

mint [mınt] N (*plant*) hortelã f; (*sweet*) bala de hortelã ▶ VT (*coins*) cunhar; **the (Royal) M~** (*BRIT*) **or the (US) M~** (*US*) ≈ a Casa da Moeda; **in ~ condition** em perfeito estado

minus ['maınəs] N (*also*: **~ sign**) sinal m de subtração ▶ PREP menos

minute¹ [maı'nju:t] ADJ miúdo, diminuto; (*search*) minucioso

minute² ['mınıt] N minuto; **minutes** NPL (*of meeting*) atas fpl; **at the last ~** no último momento

miracle ['mırəkl] N milagre m

mirage ['mıra:ʒ] N miragem f

mirror ['mırə'] N espelho; (*in car*) retrovisor m

misbehave [mısbı'heıv] VI comportar-se mal

miscarriage ['mıskærıdʒ] N (*Med*) aborto (espontâneo); (*failure*): **~ of justice** erro judicial

miscellaneous [mısı'leınıəs] ADJ (*items, expenses*) diverso; (*selection*) variado

mischief ['mıstʃıf] N (*naughtiness*) travessura; (*fun*) diabrura; (*maliciousness*) malícia; **mischievous** ['mıstʃıvəs] ADJ (*naughty*) travesso; (*playful*) traquino

misconception [mıskən'sepʃən] N concepção f errada, conceito errado

misconduct [mıs'kɔndʌkt] N comportamento impróprio; **professional ~** má conduta profissional

miser ['maızə'] N avaro(-a), sovina m/f

miserable ['mızərəbl] ADJ triste; (*wretched*) miserável; (*weather, person*) deprimente; (*contemptible: offer*) desprezível; (: *failure*) humilhante

misery ['mızərı] N (*unhappiness*) tristeza; (*wretchedness*) miséria

misfortune [mıs'fɔ:tʃən] N desgraça, infortúnio

misguided [mıs'gaıdıd] ADJ enganado

mishap ['mıshæp] N desgraça, contratempo

misinterpret [mısın'tə:prıt] VT interpretar mal

misjudge [mıs'dʒʌdʒ] VT fazer um juízo errado de, julgar mal

mislay [mıs'leı] *irreg* VT extraviar, perder

mislead [mıs'li:d] *irreg* VT induzir em erro, enganar; **misleading** ADJ enganoso, errôneo

misplace [mıs'pleıs] VT extraviar, perder

misprint ['mısprınt] N erro tipográfico

Miss [mıs] N Senhorita (*BR*), a menina (*PT*)

miss [mıs] VT (*train, class, opportunity*) perder; (*fail to hit*) errar, não acertar em; (*fail to see*): **you can't ~ it** é impossível não ver; (*regret the absence of*): **I ~ him** sinto a falta dele ▶ VI falhar ▶ N (*shot*) tiro perdido *or* errado; **miss out** (*BRIT*) VT omitir

missile ['mısaıl] N míssil m; (*object thrown*) projétil m

missing ['mısıŋ] ADJ (*pupil*) ausente; (*thing*) perdido; (*removed*) que está faltando; (*Mil*) desaparecido; **to be ~** estar desaparecido; **to go ~** desaparecer

mission ['mıʃən] N missão f; (*official representatives*) delegação f

mist [mıst] N (*light*) neblina; (*heavy*) névoa; (*at sea*) bruma ▶ VI (*eyes: also*: **~ over**) enevoar-se; (*BRIT: also*: **~ over**, **~ up**: *windows*) embaçar

mistake [mɪs'teɪk] *irreg* N erro, engano
▶ VT entender *or* interpretar mal; **by ~**
por engano; **to make a ~** fazer um erro;
to ~ A for B confundir A com B; **mistaken**
PP *of* **mistake** ▶ ADJ errado; **to be**
mistaken enganar-se, equivocar-se

mister ['mɪstəʳ] (*inf*) N senhor *m*; *see* **Mr**

mistletoe ['mɪsltəu] N visco

mistook [mɪs'tuk] PT *of* **mistake**

mistress ['mɪstrɪs] N (*lover*) amante *f*;
(*of house*) dona (da casa); (BRIT: *in school*)
professora, mestra; (*of situation*) dona;
see **Mrs**

mistrust [mɪs'trʌst] VT desconfiar de

misty ['mɪstɪ] ADJ (*day*) nublado; (*glasses*
etc) embaçado

misunderstand [mɪsʌndə'stænd] *irreg*
VT, VI entender *or* interpretar mal;
misunderstanding N mal-entendido;
(*disagreement*) desentendimento

misuse [*n* mɪs'juːs, *vt* mɪs'juːz] N uso
impróprio; (*of power*) abuso; (*of funds*)
desvio ▶ VT abusar de; desviar

mix [mɪks] VT misturar; (*combine*)
combinar ▶ VI (*people*) entrosar-se ▶ N
mistura; (*combining*) combinação *f*;
mix up VT (*confuse: things*) misturar;
(*: people*) confundir; **mixed** ADJ misto;
mixed-up ADJ confuso; **mixer** N (*for food*)
batedeira; (*person*) pessoa sociável;
mixture N mistura; (*Med*) preparado;
mix-up N trapalhada, confusão *f*

mm ABBR (= *millimetre*) mm

moan [məun] N gemido ▶ VI gemer; (*inf*:
complain): **to ~ (about)** queixar-se (de),
bufar (sobre) (*inf*)

moat [məut] N fosso

mob [mɔb] N multidão *f* ▶ VT cercar

mobile ['məubaɪl] ADJ móvel ▶ N móvel
m; **mobile phone** N telefone *m* celular
(BR), telemóvel *m* (PT)

mock [mɔk] VT ridicularizar; (*laugh at*)
zombar de, gozar de ▶ ADJ falso, fingido;
(*exam, battle*) simulado; **mockery** N
zombaria; **to make a mockery of sth**
ridicularizar algo

mode [məud] N modo; (*of transport*)
meio

model ['mɔdl] N modelo; (*Arch*)
maqueta; (*person: for fashion, Art*) modelo
m/f ▶ ADJ exemplar ▶ VT modelar; **to ~**
o.s. on mirar-se em ▶ VI servir de
modelo; (*in fashion*) trabalhar como
modelo

modem ['məudɛm] N modem *m*

moderate [*adj*, *n* 'mɔdərət, *vi*, *vt*
'mɔdəreɪt] ADJ, N moderado(-a) ▶ VI
moderar-se, acalmar-se ▶ VT moderar

modern ['mɔdən] ADJ moderno;
modernize VT modernizar, atualizar

modest ['mɔdɪst] ADJ modesto;
modesty N modéstia

modify ['mɔdɪfaɪ] VT modificar

moist [mɔɪst] ADJ úmido (BR), húmido
(PT), molhado; **moisture** N umidade *f*
(BR), humidade *f* (PT); **moisturizer** N
creme *m* hidratante

mojo ['məudʒəu] N (*inf*) encanto

mole [məul] N (*animal*) toupeira; (*spot*)
sinal *m*, lunar *m*; (*fig*) espião(-piã) *m/f*

molest [məu'lɛst] VT molestar; (*attack*
sexually) atacar sexualmente

molten ['məultən] ADJ fundido; (*lava*)
liquefeito

mom [mɔm] (US) N = **mum**

moment ['məumənt] N momento; **at**
the ~ neste momento; **momentary** ADJ
momentâneo; **momentous**
[məu'mɛntəs] ADJ importantíssimo

momentum [məu'mɛntəm] N
momento; (*fig*) ímpeto; **to gather ~**
ganhar ímpeto

mommy ['mɔmɪ] (US) N = **mummy**

Monaco ['mɔnəkəu] N Mônaco (*no*
article)

monarch ['mɔnək] N monarca *m/f*;
monarchy N monarquia

monastery ['mɔnəstərɪ] N mosteiro,
convento

Monday ['mʌndɪ] N segunda-feira

monetary ['mʌnɪtərɪ] ADJ monetário

money ['mʌnɪ] N dinheiro; (*currency*)
moeda; **to make ~** ganhar dinheiro;
money order N vale *m* (postal)

mongrel ['mʌngrəl] N (*dog*) vira-lata *m*

monitor ['mɔnɪtəʳ] N (*Comput*) monitor
m ▶ VT (*heartbeat, pulse*) controlar;
(*broadcasts, progress*) monitorar

monk [mʌŋk] N monge *m*

monkey ['mʌŋkɪ] N macaco

monopoly [mə'nɔpəlɪ] N monopólio

monotonous [mə'nɔtənəs] ADJ
monótono

monsoon [mɔn'suːn] N monção *f*

monster ['mɔnstəʳ] N monstro

month [mʌnθ] N mês *m*; **monthly** ADJ
mensal ▶ ADV mensalmente

monument ['mɔnjumənt] N
monumento

mood [muːd] N humor *m*; (*of crowd*)
atmosfera; **to be in a good/bad ~** estar
de bom/mau humor; **moody** ADJ
(*variable*) caprichoso, de veneta; (*sullen*)
rabugento

moon [muːn] N lua; **moonlight** N luar *m*
▶ VI ter dois empregos, ter um bico

moor [muə^r] N charneca ▶ VT (ship) amarrar ▶ VI fundear, atracar

moose [mu:s] N INV alce m

mop [mɔp] N esfregão m; (for dishes) esponja com cabeça; (of hair) grenha ▶ VT esfregar; **mop up** VT limpar

mope [məup] VI estar or andar deprimido or desanimado

moped ['məupɛd] N moto f pequena (BR), motorizada (PT)

moral ['mɔrl] ADJ moral ▶ N moral f; **morals** NPL (principles) moralidade f, costumes mpl

morale [mɔ'rɑ:l] N moral f, estado de espírito

morality [mə'rælɪtɪ] N moralidade f; (correctness) retidão f, probidade f

(KEYWORD)

more [mɔ:^r] ADJ 1 (greater in number etc) mais; **more people/work/letters than we expected** mais pessoas/trabalho/ cartas do que esperávamos 2 (additional) mais; **do you want (some) more tea?** você quer mais chá?; **I have no** or **I don't have any more money** não tenho mais dinheiro ▶ PRON 1 (greater amount) mais; **more than 10** mais de 10; **it cost more than we expected** custou mais do que esperávamos 2 (further or additional amount) mais; **is there any more?** tem ainda mais?; **there's no more** não tem mais ▶ ADV mais; **more dangerous/difficult etc than** mais perigoso/difícil etc do que; **more easily/economically/quickly (than)** mais fácil/econômico/ rápido (do que); **more and more** cada vez mais; **more or less** mais ou menos; **more than ever** mais do que nunca

moreover [mɔ:'rəuvə^r] ADV além do mais, além disso

morning ['mɔ:nɪŋ] N manhã f; (early morning) madrugada ▶ CPD da manhã; **in the ~** de manhã; **7 o'clock in the ~** (as) 7 da manhã; **morning sickness** N náusea matinal

Morocco [mə'rɔkəu] N Marrocos m

moron ['mɔ:rɔn] (inf: offensive) N débil mental m/f, idiota m/f

Morse [mɔ:s] N (also: **~ code**) código Morse

mortar ['mɔ:tə^r] N (cannon) morteiro; (Constr) argamassa; (dish) pilão m, almofariz m

mortgage ['mɔ:gɪdʒ] N hipoteca ▶ VT hipotecar

mortuary ['mɔ:tjuərɪ] N necrotério

mosaic [məu'zeɪɪk] N mosaico

Moscow ['mɔskəu] N Moscou (BR), Moscovo (PT)

Moslem ['mɔzləm] ADJ, N = **Muslim**

mosque [mɔsk] N mesquita

mosquito [mɔs'ki:təu] (pl **mosquitoes**) N mosquito

moss [mɔs] N musgo

(KEYWORD)

most [məust] ADJ 1 (almost all: people, things etc) a maior parte de, a maioria de; **most people** a maioria das pessoas 2 (largest, greatest: interest) máximo; (money): **who has (the) most money?** quem é que tem mais dinheiro?; **he derived the most pleasure from her visit** ele teve o maior prazer em recebê-la ▶ PRON (greatest quantity, number) a maior parte, a maioria; **most of it/them** a maioria dele/deles; **most of the money** a maior parte do dinheiro; **do the most you can** faça o máximo que você puder; **I saw the most** vi mais; **to make the most of sth** aproveitar algo ao máximo; **at the (very) most** quando muito, no máximo ▶ ADV (+ vb, adj, adv) o mais; **the most intelligent/expensive** etc o mais inteligente/caro etc; (very: polite, interesting etc) muito; **a most interesting book** um livro interessantíssimo

mostly ['məustlɪ] ADV principalmente, na maior parte

MOT (BRIT) N ABBR = **Ministry of Transport**; **the ~ (test)** vistoria anual dos veículos automotores

motel [məu'tɛl] N motel m

moth [mɔθ] N mariposa; (clothes moth) traça

mother ['mʌðə^r] N mãe f ▶ ADJ materno ▶ VT (care for) cuidar de (como uma mãe); **motherhood** N maternidade f; **mother-in-law** N sogra; **mother-of-pearl** N madrepérola; **mother-to-be** N futura mamãe f; **mother tongue** N língua materna

motion ['məuʃən] N movimento; (gesture) gesto, sinal m; (at meeting) moção f ▶ VT, VI: **to ~ (to) sb to do sth** fazer sinal a alguém para que faça algo; **motionless** ADJ imóvel; **motion picture** N filme m (cinematográfico)

motive ['məʊtɪv] N motivo

motor ['məʊtəʳ] N motor m; (BRIT inf: vehicle) carro, automóvel m ▶ CPD (industry) de automóvel; **motorbike** N moto(cicleta) f, motoca (inf); **motorboat** N barco a motor; **motorcar** (BRIT) N carro, automóvel m; **motorcycle** N motocicleta; **motorist** N motorista m/f; **motor racing** (BRIT) N corrida de carros, automobilismo; **motorway** (BRIT) N rodovia (BR), autoestrada (PT)

motto ['mɔtəʊ] (pl **mottoes**) N lema m

mound [maʊnd] N (of earth) monte m; (of blankets, leaves etc) pilha, montanha

mount [maʊnt] N monte m ▶ VT (horse etc) montar em, subir a; (stairs) subir; (exhibition) montar; (picture) emoldurar ▶ VI (increase) aumentar; **mount up** VI aumentar

mountain ['maʊntɪn] N montanha ▶ CPD de montanha; **mountain bike** N mountain bike f; **mountaineer** [maʊntɪ'nɪəʳ] N alpinista m/f, montanhista m/f; **mountaineering** N alpinismo; **mountainous** ADJ montanhoso

mourn [mɔːn] VT chorar, lamentar ▶ VI: **to ~ for** chorar or lamentar a morte de; **mourning** N luto; **(to be) in mourning** (estar) de luto

mouse [maʊs] (pl **mice**) N camundongo (BR), rato (PT); (Comput) mouse m; **mouse mat, mouse pad** N (Comput) mouse pad m

mousse [muːs] N musse f; (for hair) mousse f

moustache [məs'tɑːʃ], (US) **mustache** N bigode m

mouth [maʊθ] N boca; (of cave, hole) entrada; (of river) desembocadura; **mouthful** N bocado; **mouth organ** N gaita; **mouthwash** N colutório

move [muːv] N movimento; (in game) lance m, jogada; (: turn to play) turno, vez f; (of house, job) mudança ▶ VT (change position of) mudar; (in game) jogar; (emotionally) comover; (Pol: resolution etc) propor ▶ VI mexer-se, mover-se; (traffic) circular; (also: ~ house) mudar-se; (develop: situation) desenvolver; **to ~ sb to do sth** convencer alguém a fazer algo; **to get a ~ on** apressar-se; **move about** VI (fidget) mexer-se; (travel) deslocar-se; **move along** VI avançar; **move away** VI = **move about**; **move away** VI afastar-se; **move back** VI voltar; **move forward** VI avançar; **move in** VI

(to a house) instalar-se (numa casa); **move on** VI ir andando; **move out** VI sair (de uma casa); **move over** VI afastar-se; **move up** VI ser promovido

movement ['muːvmənt] N movimento; (gesture) gesto; (of goods) transporte m; (in attitude, policy) mudança

movie ['muːvɪ] N filme m; **to go to the ~s** ir ao cinema

moving ['muːvɪŋ] ADJ (emotional) comovente; (that moves) móvel

mow [məʊ] (pt **mowed**, pp **mowed** or **mown**) VT (grass) cortar; (corn) ceifar; **mow down** VT (massacre) chacinar; **mower** N ceifeira; (also: **lawnmower**) cortador m de grama (BR) or de relva (PT)

Mozambique [məʊzəm'biːk] N Moçambique m (no article)

MP N ABBR = **Member of Parliament**

MP3 N MP3 m; **MP4** N MP4 m; **MP4 file** arquivo MP4

mph ABBR = **miles per hour**

Mr ['mɪstəʳ], (US) **Mr.** N: **Mr Smith** (o) Sr. Smith

Mrs ['mɪsɪz], (US) **Mrs.** N: **~ Smith** (a) Sra. Smith

Ms [mɪz], (US) **Ms.** N (= Miss or Mrs): **Ms X** (a) Sa X

> **Ms** é um título utilizado em lugar de Mrs (senhora) ou de Miss (senhorita) para evitar a distinção tradicional entre mulheres casadas e solteiras. É aceito, portanto, como o equivalente de Mr (senhor) para os homens. Muitas vezes reprovado por ter surgido como manifestação de um feminismo exacerbado, é uma forma de tratamento muito comum hoje em dia.

MSc N ABBR = **Master of Science**

(KEYWORD)

much [mʌtʃ] ADJ muito; **how much money/time do you need?** quanto dinheiro/tempo você precisa?; **he's done so much work for the charity** ele trabalhou muito para a obra de caridade; **as much as** tanto como ▶ PRON muito; **much has been gained from our discussions** nossas discussões foram muito proveitosas; **how much does it cost? — too much** quanto custa isso? — caro demais ▶ ADV **1** (greatly, a great deal) muito; **thank you very much** muito obrigado(-a); **we are very much looking forward to your visit** estamos aguardando a sua visita com muito ansiedade; **he is very much the gentleman/politician** ele é muito cavalheiro/político; **as much as** tanto como; **as much as you** tanto quanto você

2 (by far) de longe; **I'm much better now** estou bem melhor agora

3 (almost) quase; **how are you feeling? — much the same** como você está (se sentindo)? — do mesmo jeito

muck [mʌk] N (dirt) sujeira (BR), sujidade f (PT); **muck about** (inf) VI fazer besteiras; **muck around** VI = **muck about; muck up** (inf) VT estragar

mud [mʌd] N lama

muddle ['mʌdl] N confusão f, bagunça; (mix-up) trapalhada ▶ VT (also: ~ **up**: person, story) confundir; (: things) misturar; **muddle through** VI virar-se

muddy ['mʌdɪ] ADJ (road) lamacento

mudguard ['mʌdgɑːd] N para-lama m

muesli ['mjuːzlɪ] N muesli m

muffin ['mʌfɪn] N bolinho redondo e chato

mug [mʌg] N (cup) caneca; (for beer) caneco, canecão; (inf: face) careta; (: fool) bobo(-a) ▶ VT (assault) assaltar; **mugging** N assalto

muggy ['mʌgɪ] ADJ abafado

mule [mjuːl] N mula

multimedia [mʌltɪ'miːdɪə] ADJ multimídia

multiple ['mʌltɪpl] ADJ múltiplo ▶ N múltiplo; **multiple sclerosis** [-sklɪ'rəʊsɪs] N esclerose f múltipla

multiply ['mʌltɪplaɪ] VT multiplicar ▶ VI multiplicar-se

multistorey ['mʌltɪ'stɔːrɪ] (BRIT) ADJ de vários andares

mum [mʌm] N (BRIT inf) mamãe f ▶ ADJ: **to keep ~** ficar calado

mumble ['mʌmbl] VT, VI resmungar, murmurar

mummy ['mʌmɪ] N (BRIT: mother) mamãe f; (embalmed) múmia

mumps [mʌmps] N caxumba

municipal [mjuː'nɪsɪpl] ADJ municipal

murder ['məːdər] N assassinato ▶ VT assassinar; **murderer** N assassino

murky ['məːkɪ] ADJ escuro; (water) turvo

murmur ['məːmər] N murmúrio ▶ VT, VI murmurar

muscle ['mʌsl] N músculo; (fig: strength) força (muscular); **muscle in** VI imiscuir-se, impor-se; **muscular** ['mʌskjulər] ADJ muscular; (person) musculoso

museum [mjuː'zɪəm] N museu m

mushroom ['mʌʃrum] N cogumelo ▶ VI crescer da noite para o dia, pipocar

music ['mjuːzɪk] N música; **musical** ADJ musical; (harmonious) melodioso ▶ N musical m; **musician** [mjuː'zɪʃən] N músico(-a)

Muslim ['mʌzlɪm] ADJ, N muçulmano(-a)

mussel ['mʌsl] N mexilhão m

must [mʌst] AUX VB (obligation): **I ~ do it** tenho que or devo fazer isso; (probability): **he ~ be there by now** ele já deve estar lá; (suggestion, invitation): **you ~ come and see me soon** você tem que vir me ver em breve; (indicating sth unwelcome): **why ~ he behave so badly?** por que ele tem que se comportar tão mal? ▶ N necessidade f; **it's a ~** é imprescindível

mustache ['mʌstæʃ] (US) N = **moustache**

mustard ['mʌstəd] N mostarda

mustn't ['mʌsnt] = **must not**

mutiny ['mjuːtɪnɪ] N motim m, rebelião f

mutter ['mʌtər] VT, VI resmungar, murmurar

mutton ['mʌtn] N carne f de carneiro

mutual ['mjuːtʃuəl] ADJ mútuo; (shared) comum

muzzle ['mʌzl] N (of animal) focinho; (guard: for dog) focinheira; (of gun) boca ▶ VT pôr focinheira em

my [maɪ] ADJ meu/minha; **this is my house/car/brother** esta é a minha casa/meu carro/meu irmão; **I've washed my hair/cut my finger** lavei meu cabelo/cortei meu dedo

myself [maɪ'sɛlf] PRON (reflexive) me; (emphatic) eu mesmo; (after prep) mim mesmo; see also **oneself**

mysterious [mɪs'tɪərɪəs] ADJ misterioso

mystery ['mɪstərɪ] N mistério

mystify ['mɪstɪfaɪ] VT mistificar

myth [mɪθ] N mito; **mythology** [mɪ'θɒlədʒɪ] N mitologia

n

nag [næg] VT ralhar, apoquentar
nail [neɪl] N (*human*) unha; (*metal*) prego
▶ VT pregar; **to ~ sb down to a date/
price** conseguir que alguém se defina
sobre a data/o preço; **nailbrush** N
escova de unhas; **nailfile** N lixa de
unhas; **nail polish** N esmalte *m* (BR) or
verniz *m* (PT) de unhas; **nail polish
remover** N removedor *m* de esmalte (BR)
or verniz (PT); **nail scissors** NPL
tesourinha de unhas; **nail varnish** (BRIT)
N = **nail polish**
naïve [naɪˈiːv] ADJ ingênuo
naked [ˈneɪkɪd] ADJ nu(a)
name [neɪm] N nome *m*; (*surname*)
sobrenome *m*; (*reputation*) reputação *f*,
fama ▶ VT (*child*) pôr nome em; (*criminal*)
apontar; (*price*) fixar; (*date*) marcar;
what's your ~? qual é o seu nome?,
como (você) se chama?; **by ~** de nome;
in the ~ of em nome de; **namely** ADV a
saber, isto é
nanny [ˈnænɪ] N babá *f*
nap [næp] N (*sleep*) soneca ▶ VI: **to be
caught ~ping** ser pego de surpresa
napkin [ˈnæpkɪn] N (*also*: **table ~**)
guardanapo
nappy [ˈnæpɪ] (BRIT) N fralda
narrative [ˈnærətɪv] N narrativa
narrow [ˈnærəʊ] ADJ estreito; (*fig:
majority*) pequeno; (: *ideas*) tacanho ▶ VI
(*road*) estreitar-se; (*difference*) diminuir;
to have a ~ escape escapar por um triz;
to ~ sth down to restringir or reduzir
algo a; **narrowly** ADV (*miss*) por pouco;
narrow-minded ADJ de visão limitada,
bitolado
nasty [ˈnɑːstɪ] ADJ (*unpleasant: remark*)
desagradável; (: *person*) mau, ruim;
(*malicious*) maldoso; (*rude*) grosseiro,

obsceno; (*taste, smell*) repugnante,
asqueroso; (*wound, disease etc*) grave,
sério
nation [ˈneɪʃən] N nação *f*
national [ˈnæʃənl] ADJ, N nacional *m/f*;
national anthem N hino nacional;
National Health Service (BRIT) N serviço
nacional de saúde; **nationality**
[næʃəˈnælɪtɪ] N nacionalidade *f*;
nationalize VT nacionalizar; **national
park** N parque *m* nacional; **National
Trust** (BRIT) N *ver nota*

> O **National Trust** é uma instituição
> independente, sem fins lucrativos,
> cuja missão é proteger e valorizar os
> monumentos e a paisagem da
> Grã-Bretanha devido a seu interesse
> histórico ou beleza natural.

nationwide [ˈneɪʃənwaɪd] ADJ de
âmbito or a nível nacional ▶ ADV em todo
o país
native [ˈneɪtɪv] N natural *m/f*, nativo(-a);
(*in colonies*) indígena *m/f*, nativo(-a) ▶ ADJ
(*indigenous*) indígena; (*of one's birth*)
natal; (*language*) materno; (*innate*) inato,
natural; **a ~ speaker of Portuguese**
uma pessoa de língua (materna)
portuguesa
NATO [ˈneɪtəʊ] N ABBR (= *North Atlantic
Treaty Organization*) OTAN *f*
natural [ˈnætʃrəl] ADJ natural; **naturally**
ADV naturalmente; (*of course*) claro,
evidentemente
nature [ˈneɪtʃəʳ] N natureza; (*character*)
caráter *m*, índole *f*
naughty [ˈnɔːtɪ] ADJ travesso, levado
nausea [ˈnɔːsɪə] N náusea
naval [ˈneɪvl] ADJ naval
nave [neɪv] N nave *f*
navel [ˈneɪvl] N umbigo
navigate [ˈnævɪɡeɪt] VI navegar; (*Aut*)
ler o mapa; **navigation** [nævɪˈɡeɪʃən] N
(*action*) navegação *f*; (*science*) náutica
navy [ˈneɪvɪ] N marinha (de guerra)
Nazi [ˈnɑːtsɪ] N nazista *m/f* (BR),
nazi *m/f* (PT)
NB ABBR (= *nota bene*) NB
near [nɪəʳ] ADJ (*place*) vizinho; (*time*)
próximo; (*relation*) íntimo ▶ ADV perto
▶ PREP (*also*: **~ to**: *space*) perto de; (: *time*)
perto de, quase ▶ VT aproximar-se de;
nearby [nɪəˈbaɪ] ADJ próximo, vizinho
▶ ADV à mão, perto; **nearly** ADV quase;
I nearly fell quase que caí; **near-
sighted** ADJ míope
neat [niːt] ADJ (*place*) arrumado, em
ordem; (*person*) asseado, arrumado;
(*work*) caprichado; (*plan*) engenhoso,

bem bolado; (*spirits*) puro; **neatly** ADV
caprichosamente, com capricho;
(*skilfully*) habilmente
necessarily ['nɛsɪsərɪlɪ] ADV
necessariamente
necessary ['nɛsɪsrɪ] ADJ necessário
necessity [nɪ'sɛsɪtɪ] N (*thing needed*)
necessidade f, requisito; (*compelling
circumstances*) necessidade; **necessities**
NPL (*essentials*) artigos mpl de primeira
necessidade
neck [nɛk] N (*Anat*) pescoço; (*of garment*)
gola; (*of bottle*) gargalo ▶ VI (*inf*) ficar de
agarramento; **~ and ~** emparelhados
necklace ['nɛklɪs] N colar m
necktie ['nɛktaɪ] (*esp US*) N gravata
need [niːd] N (*lack*) falta, carência;
(*necessity*) necessidade f; (*thing needed*)
requisito, necessidade ▶ VT precisar de;
I ~ to do it preciso fazê-lo
needle ['niːdl] N agulha ▶ VT (*inf*)
provocar, alfinetar
needless ['niːdlɪs] ADJ inútil,
desnecessário; **~ to say ...**
desnecessário dizer que ...
needlework ['niːdlwəːk] N costura
needn't ['niːdnt] = **need not**
needy ['niːdɪ] ADJ necessitado, carente
negative ['nɛɡətɪv] ADJ negativo ▶ N
(*Phot*) negativo; (*Ling*) negativa
neglect [nɪ'ɡlɛkt] VT (*one's duty*)
negligenciar, não cumprir com; (*child*)
descuidar, esquecer-se de ▶ N (*of child*)
descuido, desatenção f; (*of house etc*)
abandono; (*of duty*) negligência
negotiate [nɪ'ɡəusɪeɪt] VI negociar ▶ VT
(*treaty, transaction*) negociar; (*obstacle*)
contornar; (*bend in road*) fazer;
negotiation [nɪɡəusɪ'eɪʃən] N
negociação f
neighbour ['neɪbər], (*US*) **neighbor** N
vizinho(-a); **neighbourhood** N (*place*)
vizinhança, bairro; (*people*) vizinhos mpl;
neighbouring ADJ vizinho
neither ['naɪðər] CONJ: **I didn't move
and ~ did he** não me movi nem ele ▶ ADJ,
PRON nenhum (dos dois), nem um nem
outro ▶ ADV: **~ good nor bad** nem bom
nem mau; **~ story is true** nenhuma das
estórias é verdade
neon ['niːɔn] N neônio, néon m
nephew ['nɛvjuː] N sobrinho
nerve [nəːv] N (*Anat*) nervo; (*courage*)
coragem f; (*impudence*) descaramento,
atrevimento; **to have a fit of ~s** ter uma
crise nervosa
nervous ['nəːvəs] ADJ (*Anat*) nervoso;
(*anxious*) apreensivo; (*timid*) tímido,

acanhado; **nervous breakdown** N
esgotamento nervoso
nest [nɛst] VI aninhar-se ▶ N (*of bird*)
ninho; (*of wasp*) vespeiro
net [nɛt] N rede f; (*fabric*) filó m ▶ ADJ
(*Comm*) líquido ▶ VT pegar na rede;
(*money: subj: person*) faturar; (: *deal, sale*)
render; **the Net** (*Internet*) a Rede;
netball N espécie de basquetebol
Netherlands ['nɛðələndz] NPL: **the ~**
os Países Baixos
nett [nɛt] ADJ = **net**
nettle ['nɛtl] N urtiga
network ['nɛtwəːk] N rede f; **there's no
~ coverage here** (*Tel*) aqui não tem
cobertura
neurotic [njuə'rɔtɪk] ADJ, N
neurótico(-a)
neuter ['njuːtər] ADJ neutro ▶ VT (*cat etc*)
castrar, capar
neutral ['njuːtrəl] ADJ neutro ▶ N (*Aut*)
ponto morto
never ['nɛvər] ADV nunca; *see also* **mind**;
never-ending ADJ sem fim, interminável;
nevertheless ADV todavia, contudo
new [njuː] ADJ novo; **New Age** N
esoterismo; **newborn** ADJ recém-
nascido; **newcomer** N recém-
chegado(-a), novato(-a); **newly** ADV
recém, novamente
news [njuːz] N notícias fpl; (*Radio, TV*)
noticiário; **a piece of ~** uma notícia;
newsagent (*BRIT*) N jornaleiro(-a);
newscaster N locutor(a) m/f;
newsletter N boletim m informativo;
newspaper N jornal m; **newsreader** N =
newscaster
newt [njuːt] N tritão m
New Year N ano novo; **New Year's Day**
N dia m de ano novo; **New Year's Eve** N
véspera de ano novo
New Zealand [-'ziːlənd] N Nova
Zelândia; **New Zealander** N
neozelandês(-esa) m/f
next [nɛkst] ADJ (*in space*) próximo,
vizinho; (*in time*) seguinte, próximo
▶ ADV depois; depois, logo; **~ time** na
próxima vez; **~ year** o ano que vem; **~ to**
ao lado de; **~ to nothing** quase nada;
next door ADV na casa do lado ▶ ADJ
vizinho; **next-of-kin** N parentes mpl
mais próximos
NHS (*BRIT*) N ABBR = **National Health
Service**
nibble ['nɪbl] VT mordiscar, beliscar
Nicaragua [nɪkə'ræɡjuə] N Nicarágua
nice [naɪs] ADJ (*likeable*) simpático; (*kind*)
amável, atencioso; (*pleasant*) agradável;

(*attractive*) bonito; **nicely** ADV
agradavelmente, bem

nick [nɪk] N (*wound*) corte m; (*cut,
indentation*) entalhe m, incisão f ▶ VT (*inf:
steal*) furtar; **in the ~ of time** na hora H,
em cima da hora

nickel ['nɪkl] N níquel m; (*US*) moeda de 5
centavos

nickname ['nɪkneɪm] N apelido (BR),
alcunha (PT) ▶ VT apelidar de (BR),
alcunhar de (PT)

niece [niːs] N sobrinha

Nigeria [naɪ'dʒɪərɪə] N Nigéria

night [naɪt] N noite f; **at** or **by ~** à or de
noite; **the ~ before last** anteontem à
noite; **nightclub** N boate f; **nightlife**
['naɪtlaɪf] N vida noturna; **nightly**
['naɪtlɪ] ADJ noturno, de noite ▶ ADV
todas as noites, cada noite; **nightmare**
['naɪtmɛəʳ] N pesadelo; **night-time** N
noite f

nil [nɪl] N nada; (BRIT *Sport*) zero

nine [naɪn] NUM nove; **nineteen**
[naɪn'tiːn] NUM dezenove (BR),
dezanove (PT); **nineteenth** [naɪn'tiːnθ]
NUM décimo nono; **ninetieth** ['naɪntɪɪθ]
NUM nonagésimo; **ninety** ['naɪntɪ] NUM
noventa; **ninth** [naɪnθ] NUM nono

nip [nɪp] VT (*pinch*) beliscar; (*bite*) morder

nipple ['nɪpl] N (*Anat*) bico do seio, mamilo

nitrogen ['naɪtrədʒən] N nitrogênio

KEYWORD

no [nəu] (*pl* **noes**) ADV (*opposite of "yes"*)
não; **are you coming? — no (I'm not)**
você vem? — não (não vou)
▶ ADJ (*not any*) nenhum(a), não ...
algum(a); **I have no more money/
time/books** não tenho mais dinheiro/
tempo/livros; **"no entry"** "entrada
proibida"; **"no smoking"** "é proibido
fumar"
▶ N não m, negativa

nobility [nəu'bɪlɪtɪ] N nobreza

noble ['nəubl] ADJ (*person*) nobre; (*title*)
de nobreza

nobody ['nəubədɪ] PRON ninguém

no-brainer [nəu'breɪnəʳ] (*inf*) N: **it's a ~**
isso é meio óbvio

nod [nɔd] VI (*greeting*) cumprimentar com
a cabeça; (*in agreement*) acenar (que sim)
com a cabeça; (*doze*) cochilar, dormitar
▶ VT: **to ~ one's head** inclinar a cabeça
▶ N inclinação f da cabeça; **nod off** VI
cochilar

noise [nɔɪz] N barulho; **noisy** ADJ
barulhento

nominate ['nɔmɪneɪt] VT (*propose*)
propor; (*appoint*) nomear; **nominee**
[nɔmɪ'niː] N pessoa nomeada,
candidato(-a)

none [nʌn] PRON (*person*) ninguém;
(*thing*) nenhum(a), nada; **~ of you**
nenhum de vocês; **I've ~ left** não tenho
mais

nonetheless [nʌnðə'lɛs] ADV no
entanto, apesar disso, contudo

non-fiction [nɔn-] N literatura de
não-ficção

nonsense ['nɔnsəns] N disparate m,
besteira, absurdo; **~!** bobagem!, que nada!

non-smoker N não-fumante m/f

non-stick ADJ tefal®, não-aderente

noodles ['nuːdlz] NPL talharim m

noon [nuːn] N meio-dia m

no-one PRON = **nobody**

nor [nɔːʳ] CONJ = **neither** ▶ ADV *see*
neither

norm [nɔːm] N (*convention*) norma;
(*requirement*) regra

normal ['nɔːml] ADJ normal

north [nɔːθ] N norte m ▶ ADJ do norte,
setentrional ▶ ADV ao or para o norte;
North America N América do Norte;
north-east N nordeste m; **northern**
['nɔːðən] ADJ do norte, setentrional;
Northern Ireland N Irlanda do Norte;
North Pole N: **the North Pole** o Pólo
Norte; **North Sea** N: **the North Sea** o
Mar do Norte; **north-west** N noroeste m

Norway ['nɔːweɪ] N Noruega;
Norwegian [nɔː'wiːdʒən] ADJ
norueguês(-esa) ▶ N norueguês(-esa)
m/f; (*Ling*) norueguês m

nose [nəuz] N (*Anat*) nariz m; (*Zool*)
focinho; (*sense of smell: of person*) olfato;
(*: of animal*) faro; **nose about** VI
bisbilhotar; **nose around** VI = **nose
about**; **nosebleed** N hemorragia nasal;
nosey (*inf*) ADJ = **nosy**

nostalgia [nɔs'tældʒɪə] N nostalgia

nostril ['nɔstrɪl] N narina

nosy ['nəuzɪ] (*inf*) ADJ intrometido,
abelhudo

not [nɔt] ADV não; **he is ~** or **isn't here**
ele não está aqui; **it's too late, isn't it?**
é muito tarde, não?; **he asked me ~ to
do it** ele me pediu para não fazer isto;
~ yet/now ainda/agora não; *see also* **all,
only**

notably ['nəutəblɪ] ADV (*particularly*)
particularmente; (*markedly*)
notavelmente

notch [nɔtʃ] N (*in wood*) entalhe m; (*in
blade*) corte m

note [nəut] N (*Mus, banknote*) nota;
(*letter*) nota, bilhete *m*; (*record*) nota,
anotação *f*; (*tone*) tom *m* ▶ VT (*observe*)
observar, reparar em; (*also*: **~ down**)
anotar, tomar nota de; **notebook** N
caderno; **notepad** N bloco de anotações;
notepaper N papel *m* de carta
nothing ['nʌθɪŋ] N nada; (*zero*) zero; **he**
does ~ ele não faz nada; **~ new/much**
nada de novo/de mais; **for ~** de graça,
grátis; (*in vain*) à toa, por nada
notice ['nəutɪs] N (*sign*) aviso, anúncio;
(*warning*) aviso; (*of leaving or losing job*)
aviso prévio ▶ VT reparar em, notar; **at**
short ~ de repente, em cima da hora;
until further ~ até nova ordem; **to**
hand in *or* **give one's ~** demitir, pedir a
demissão; **to take ~ of** prestar atenção
a, fazer caso de; **to bring sth to sb's ~**
levar algo ao conhecimento de alguém;
noticeable ADJ evidente, visível; **notice**
board (*BRIT*) N quadro de avisos
notify ['nəutɪfaɪ] VT: **to ~ sb of sth**
avisar alguém de algo
notion ['nəuʃən] N noção *f*, ideia
nought [nɔːt] N zero
noun [naun] N substantivo
nourish ['nʌrɪʃ] VT nutrir, alimentar; (*fig*)
fomentar, alentar; **nourishment** N
alimento, nutrimento
novel ['nɔvl] N romance *m* ▶ ADJ novo,
recente; **novelist** N romancista *m/f*;
novelty N novidade *f*
November [nəu'vɛmbəʳ] N novembro
now [nau] ADV agora; (*these days*)
atualmente, hoje em dia ▶ CONJ:
~ (that) agora que; **right ~** agora
mesmo; **by ~** já; **just ~** agora; **~ and**
then, ~ and again de vez em quando;
from ~ on de agora em diante;
nowadays ADV hoje em dia
nowhere ['nəuwɛəʳ] ADV (*go*) a lugar
nenhum; (*be*) em nenhum lugar
nozzle ['nɔzl] N bocal *m*
nuclear ['njuːklɪəʳ] ADJ nuclear
nucleus ['njuːklɪəs] (*pl* **nuclei**) N núcleo
nude [njuːd] ADJ nu(a) ▶ N (*Art*) nu *m*; **in**
the ~ nu, pelado
nudge [nʌdʒ] VT acotovelar, cutucar (*BR*)
nudist ['njuːdɪst] N nudista *m/f*
nuisance ['njuːsns] N amolação *f*,
aborrecimento; (*person*) chato; **what**
a ~! que saco! (*BR*), que chatice! (*PT*)
numb [nʌm] ADJ dormente; **~ with cold**
duro de frio; **~ with fear** paralisado de
medo
number ['nʌmbəʳ] N número; (*numeral*)
algarismo ▶ VT (*pages etc*) numerar;

(*amount to*) montar a; **a ~ of** vários,
muitos; **to be ~ed among** figurar entre;
they were ten in ~ eram em número de
dez; **number plate** (*BRIT*) N placa (do
carro)
numerous ['njuːmərəs] ADJ numeroso
nun [nʌn] N freira
nurse [nəːs] N enfermeiro(-a); (*also*:
~maid) ama-seca, babá *f* ▶ VT (*patient*)
cuidar de, tratar de
nursery ['nəːsərɪ] N (*institution*) creche *f*;
(*room*) quarto das crianças; (*for plants*)
viveiro; **nursery rhyme** N poesia
infantil; **nursery school** N escola
maternal
nursing ['nəːsɪŋ] N (*profession*)
enfermagem *f*; (*care*) cuidado,
assistência; **nursing home** N sanatório,
clínica de repouso
nut [nʌt] N (*Tech*) porca; (*Bot*) noz *f*
nutmeg ['nʌtmeg] N noz-moscada
nutritious [njuː'trɪʃəs] ADJ nutritivo
nuts [nʌts] (*inf*) ADJ: **he's ~** ele é doido
nylon ['naɪlɔn] N náilon *m* (*BR*), nylon *m*
(*PT*) ▶ ADJ de náilon *or* nylon

O

oak [əuk] N carvalho ▶ ADJ de carvalho

OAP (BRIT) N ABBR = **old-age pensioner**

oar [ɔːʳ] N remo

oasis [əu'eɪsɪs] (pl **oases**) N oásis m inv

oath [əuθ] N juramento; (swear word) palavrão m

oatmeal ['əutmiːl] N farinha or mingau m de aveia

oats [əuts] N aveia

obedient [ə'biːdɪənt] ADJ obediente

obey [ə'beɪ] VT obedecer a; (instructions, regulations) cumprir

obituary [ə'bɪtjuərɪ] N necrológio

object [n 'ɔbdʒɪkt, vi əb'dʒɛkt] N objeto; (purpose) objetivo ▶ VI: **to ~ to** (attitude) desaprovar, objetar a; (proposal) opor-se a; **I ~!** protesto!; **he ~ed that …** ele objetou que …; **expense is no ~** o preço não é problema; **objection** [əb'dʒɛkʃən] N objeção f; **I have no objection to …** não tenho nada contra …; **objective** N objetivo

obligation [ɔblɪ'geɪʃən] N obrigação f; **without ~** sem compromisso

obligatory [ə'blɪgətərɪ] ADJ obrigatório

oblige [ə'blaɪdʒ] VT (do a favour for) obsequiar, fazer um favor a; (force) obrigar, forçar; **to be ~d to sb for doing sth** ficar agradecido por alguém fazer algo

oblong ['ɔblɔŋ] ADJ oblongo, retangular ▶ N retângulo

obnoxious [əb'nɔkʃəs] ADJ odioso, detestável; (smell) enjoativo

oboe ['əubəu] N oboé m

obscene [əb'siːn] ADJ obsceno

obscure [əb'skjuəʳ] ADJ obscuro, desconhecido; (difficult to understand) pouco claro ▶ VT ocultar, escurecer; (hide: sun etc) esconder

observant [əb'zəːvnt] ADJ observador(a)

observation [ɔbzə'veɪʃən] N observação f; (Med) exame m

observatory [əb'zəːvətrɪ] N observatório

observe [əb'zəːv] VT observar; (rule) cumprir; **observer** N observador(a) m/f

obsess [əb'sɛs] VT obsedar, obcecar

obsolete ['ɔbsəliːt] ADJ obsoleto

obstacle ['ɔbstəkl] N obstáculo; (hindrance) estorvo, impedimento

obstinate ['ɔbstɪnɪt] ADJ obstinado

obstruct [əb'strʌkt] VT obstruir; (hinder) estorvar

obtain [əb'teɪn] VT obter; (achieve) conseguir

obvious ['ɔbvɪəs] ADJ óbvio; **obviously** ADV evidentemente; **obviously not!** (é) claro que não!

occasion [ə'keɪʒən] N ocasião f; (event) acontecimento; **occasional** ADJ de vez em quando; **occasionally** ADV de vez em quando

occupation [ɔkju'peɪʃən] N ocupação f; (job) profissão f

occupy ['ɔkjupaɪ] VT ocupar; (house) morar em; **to ~ o.s. in doing** ocupar-se de fazer

occur [ə'kəːʳ] VI ocorrer; (phenomenon) acontecer; **to ~ to sb** ocorrer a alguém; **occurrence** N ocorrência, acontecimento; (existence) existência

ocean ['əuʃən] N oceano

o'clock [ə'klɔk] ADV: **it is 5 ~** são cinco horas

October [ɔk'təubəʳ] N outubro

octopus ['ɔktəpəs] N polvo

odd [ɔd] ADJ (strange) estranho, esquisito; (number) ímpar; (sock etc) desemparelhado; **60-~** 60 e tantos; **at ~ times** às vezes, de vez em quando; **to be the ~ one out** ficar sobrando, ser a exceção; **oddly** ADV curiosamente; see also **enough**; **odds** NPL (in betting) pontos mpl de vantagem; **it makes no odds** dá no mesmo; **at odds** brigados(-as), de mal

odour ['əudəʳ], (US) **odor** N odor m, cheiro; (unpleasant) fedor m

of [ɔv, əv] PREP **1** (gen) de; **a friend of ours** um amigo nosso; **a boy of 10** um menino de 10 anos; **that was very kind of you** foi muito gentil da sua parte **2** (expressing quantity, amount, dates etc) de; **how much of this do you need?** de quanto você precisa?; **3 of them** 3 deles;

3 of us went 3 de nós foram; **the 5th of July** dia 5 de julho
3 (*from, out of*) de; **made of wood** feito de madeira

(KEYWORD)

off [ɔf] ADV **1** (*distance, time*): **it's a long way off** fica bem longe; **the game is 3 days off** o jogo é daqui a 3 dias
2 (*departure*): **I'm off** estou de partida; **to go off to Paris/Italy** ir para Paris/a Itália; **I must be off** devo ir-me
3 (*removal*): **to take off one's hat/coat/ clothes** tirar o chapéu/o casaco/a roupa; **the button came off** o botão caiu; **10% off** (*Comm*) 10% de abatimento or desconto
4 (*not at work*): **to have a day off** tirar um dia de folga; (: *sick*): **to be off sick** estar ausente por motivo de saúde
▶ ADJ **1** (*not turned on: machine, water, gas*) desligado; (: *light*) apagado; (: *tap*) fechado
2 (*cancelled*) cancelado
3 (*not fresh: food*) passado; (: *milk*) talhado, anulado
4: **on the off chance** (*just in case*) ao acaso; **today I had an off day** (*not as good as usual*) hoje não foi o meu dia
▶ PREP **1** (*indicating motion, removal, etc*) de; **the button came off my coat** o botão do meu casaco caiu
2 (*distant from*) de; **5 km off (the road)** a 5 km (da estrada); **off the coast** em frente à costa
3: **to be off meat** (*no longer eat it*) não comer mais carne; (*no longer like it*) enjoar de carne

offence [ə'fɛns], (*US*) **offense** N (*crime*) delito; **to take ~ at** ofender-se com, melindrar-se com

offend [ə'fɛnd] VT ofender; **offender** N delinquente *m/f*

offensive [ə'fɛnsɪv] ADJ (*weapon, remark*) ofensivo; (*smell etc*) repugnante ▶ N (*Mil*) ofensiva

offer ['ɔfər] N oferta; (*proposal*) proposta ▶ VT oferecer; (*opportunity*) proporcionar; **"on ~"** (*Comm*) "em oferta"

office ['ɔfɪs] N (*place*) escritório; (*room*) gabinete *m*; (*position*) cargo, função *f*; **to take ~** tomar posse; **doctor's ~** (*US*) consultório; **office block**, (*US*) **office building** N conjunto de escritórios

officer ['ɔfɪsər] N (*Mil etc*) oficial *m/f*; (*of organization*) diretor(a) *m/f*; (*also*: **police ~**) agente *m/f* policial or de polícia

office worker N empregado(-a) or funcionário(-a) de escritório

official [ə'fɪʃl] ADJ oficial ▶ N oficial *m/f*; (*civil servant*) funcionário(-a) público(-a)

off-licence (*BRIT*) N *loja de bebidas alcoólicas*

Uma loja **off-licence** vende bebidas alcoólicas (para viagem) nos horários em que os pubs estão fechados. Nesses estabelecimentos também se pode comprar bebidas não-alcoólicas, cigarros, batatas fritas, balas, chocolates etc.

offline ADJ, ADV (*Comput*) off-line

off-peak ADJ (*heating etc*) de período de pouco consumo; (*ticket, train*) de período de pouco movimento

off-putting (*BRIT*) ADJ desconcertante

off-season ADJ, ADV fora de estação or temporada

offset ['ɔfsɛt] *irreg* VT compensar, contrabalançar

offshore [ɔf'ɔːr] ADJ (*breeze*) de terra; (*fishing*) costeiro; **~ oilfield** campo petrolífero ao largo

offside ['ɔf'saɪd] ADJ (*Sport*) impedido; (*Aut*) do lado do motorista

offspring ['ɔfsprɪŋ] N descendência, prole *f*

often ['ɔfn] ADV muitas vezes, frequentemente; **how ~ do you go?** com que frequência você vai?

oil [ɔɪl] N (*Culin*) azeite *m*; (*petroleum*) petróleo; (*for heating*) óleo ▶ VT (*machine*) lubrificar; **oil painting** N pintura a óleo; **oil rig** N torre *f* de perfuração; **oil slick** N mancha de óleo; **oil tanker** N (*ship*) petroleiro; (*truck*) carro-tanque *m* de petróleo; **oil well** N poço petrolífero; **oily** ADJ oleoso; (*food*) gorduroso

ointment ['ɔɪntmənt] N pomada

O.K. ['əu'keɪ] EXCL está bem, está bom, tá (bem or bom) (*inf*) ▶ ADJ bom; (*correct*) certo ▶ VT aprovar

old [əuld] ADJ velho; (*former*) antigo, anterior; **how ~ are you?** quantos anos você tem?; **he's 10 years ~** ele tem 10 anos; **~er brother** irmão mais velho; **old age** N velhice *f*; **old-age pensioner** (*BRIT*) N aposentado(-a) (*BR*), reformado(-a) (*PT*); **old-fashioned** ADJ fora de moda; (*person*) antiquado; (*values*) obsoleto, retrógrado

olive ['ɔlɪv] N (*fruit*) azeitona; (*tree*) oliveira ▶ ADJ (*also*: **~-green**) verde-oliva *inv*; **olive oil** N azeite *m* de oliva

Olympic® [əu'lɪmpɪk] ADJ olímpico

omelette, (*US*) **omelet** ['ɔmlɪt] N omelete *f*

omen ['əumən] N presságio, agouro

OMG (*inf*) ABBR (= *Oh my God!*) OMG

ominous ['ɔmɪnəs] ADJ preocupante
omit [əu'mɪt] VT omitir

(KEYWORD)

on [ɔn] PREP **1** (*indicating position*) sobre, em (cima de); **on the wall** na parede; **on the left** à esquerda
2 (*indicating means, method, condition etc*): **on foot** a pé; **on the train/plane** no trem/avião; **on the telephone/radio** no telefone/rádio; **on television** na televisão; **to be on drugs** (*addicted*) ser viciado em drogas; (*Med*) estar sob medicação; **to be on holiday/business** estar de férias/a negócio
3 (*referring to time*): **on Friday** na sexta-feira; **a week on Friday** sem ser esta sexta-feira, a outra; **on arrival** ao chegar; **on seeing this** ao ver isto
4 (*about, concerning*) sobre
▶ ADV **1** (*referring to dress*): **to have one's coat on** estar de casaco; **what's she got on?** o que ela está usando?; **she put her boots on** ela calçou as botas; **he put his gloves/hat on** ele colocou as luvas/o chapéu
2: **screw the lid on tightly** atarraxar bem a tampa
3 (*further, continuously*): **to walk/drive on** continuar andando/dirigindo; **to go on** continuar (em frente); **to read on** continuar a ler
▶ ADJ **1** (*functioning, in operation: machine*) em funcionamento; (: *light*) aceso; (: *radio*) ligado; (: *tap*) aberto; (: *brakes: of car etc*): **to be on** estar freado; (*meeting*): **is the meeting still on?** (*in progress*) a reunião ainda está sendo realizada?; (*not cancelled*) ainda vai haver reunião?; **there's a good film on at the cinema** tem um bom filme passando no cinema
2: **that's not on!** (*inf: of behaviour*) isso não se faz!

once [wʌns] ADV uma vez; (*formerly*) outrora ▶ CONJ depois que; **~ he had left/it was done** depois que ele saiu/foi feito; **at ~** imediatamente; (*simultaneously*) de uma vez, ao mesmo tempo; **~ more** mais uma vez; **~ and for all** uma vez por todas; **~ upon a time** era uma vez

oncoming ['ɔnkʌmɪŋ] ADJ (*traffic*) que vem de frente

(KEYWORD)

one [wʌn] NUM um(a); **one hundred and fifty** cento e cinquenta; **one by**

one um por um
▶ ADJ **1** (*sole*) único; **the one book which ...** o único livro que ...
2 (*same*) mesmo; **they came in the one car** eles vieram no mesmo carro
▶ PRON **1** um(a); **this one** este/esta; **that one** esse/essa, aquele/aquela; **I've already got one/ a red one** eu já tenho um/um vermelho
2: **one another** um ao outro; **do you two ever see one another?** vocês dois se veem de vez em quando?
3 (*impers*): **one never knows** nunca se sabe; **to cut one's finger** cortar o dedo; **one needs to eat** é preciso comer

oneself [wʌn'sɛlf] PRON (*reflexive*) se; (*after prep, emphatic*) si (mesmo(-a)); **by ~** sozinho(-a); **to hurt ~** ferir-se; **to keep sth for ~** guardar algo para si mesmo; **to talk to ~** falar consigo mesmo
one-sided ADJ parcial
one-way ADJ (*street, traffic*) de mão única (BR), de sentido único (PT)
ongoing ['ɔngəuɪŋ] ADJ (*project*) em andamento; (*situation*) existente
onion ['ʌnjən] N cebola
online [ɔn'laɪn] ADJ, ADV (*Comput*) on-line, online; **online banking** N netbanking m
onlooker ['ɔnlukəʳ] N espectador(a) m/f
only ['əunlɪ] ADV somente, apenas ▶ ADJ único, só ▶ CONJ só que, porém; **an ~ child** um filho único; **not ~ ... but also ...** não só ... mas também ...
onset ['ɔnsɛt] N começo
onto ['ɔntu] PREP = **on to**
onward ['ɔnwəd], **onwards** ['ɔnwədz] ADV (*move*) para diante, para a frente; **from this time ~(s)** de (ag)ora em diante
ooze [u:z] VI ressumar, filtrar-se
opaque [əu'peɪk] ADJ opaco, fosco
open ['əupn] ADJ aberto; (*car*) descoberto; (*road*) livre; (*fig: frank*) aberto, franco; (*meeting*) aberto, sem restrições ▶ VT abrir ▶ VI abrir(-se); (*book etc*) começar; **in the ~ (air)** ao ar livre; **open on to** VT FUS (*subj: room, door*) dar para; **open up** VT abrir; (*blocked road*) desobstruir ▶ VI (*Comm*) abrir; **opening** ADJ de abertura ▶ N abertura; (*start*) início; (*opportunity*) oportunidade f; **openly** ADV abertamente; **open-minded** ADJ aberto, imparcial; **open-necked** ADJ aberto no colo; **open-plan** ADJ sem paredes divisórias; **Open University** (BRIT) N *ver nota*

Fundada em 1969, a **Open University** oferece um tipo de ensino que compreende cursos (alguns blocos da programação da TV e do rádio são reservados para esse fim), deveres que são enviados pelo aluno ao diretor ou diretora de estudos e uma estada obrigatória em uma universidade de verão. É preciso cumprir um certo número de unidades ao longo de um período determinado e obter a média em um certo número delas para receber o diploma almejado.

opera ['ɔpərə] N ópera

operate ['ɔpəreɪt] VT fazer funcionar, pôr em funcionamento ▶ VI funcionar; (Med): **to ~ on sb** operar alguém

operation [ɔpə'reɪʃən] N operação f; (of machine) funcionamento; **to be in ~** (system) estar em vigor

operator ['ɔpəreɪtə^r] N (of machine) operador(a) m/f; manipulador(a) m/f; (Tel) telefonista m/f

opinion [ə'pɪnɪən] N opinião f; **in my ~** na minha opinião, a meu ver

opponent [ə'pəunənt] N oponente m/f; (Mil, Sport) adversário(-a)

opportunity [ɔpə'tjuːnɪtɪ] N oportunidade f; **to take the ~ of doing** aproveitar a oportunidade para fazer

oppose [ə'pəuz] VT opor-se a; **to be ~d to sth** opor-se a algo, estar contra algo; **as ~d to** em oposição a

opposite ['ɔpəzɪt] ADJ oposto; (house etc) em frente ▶ ADV (lá) em frente ▶ PREP em frente de, defronte de ▶ N oposto, contrário

opposition [ɔpə'zɪʃən] N oposição f

opt [ɔpt] VI: **to ~ for** optar por; **to ~ to do** optar por fazer; **opt out** VI: **to ~ out of doing sth** optar por não fazer algo

optician [ɔp'tɪʃən] N oculista m/f

optimist ['ɔptɪmɪst] N otimista m/f; **optimistic** [ɔptɪ'mɪstɪk] ADJ otimista

option ['ɔpʃən] N opção f; **optional** ADJ opcional, facultativo

or [ɔː^r] CONJ ou; (with negative): **he hasn't seen or heard anything** ele não viu nem ouviu nada; **or else** senão

oral ['ɔːrəl] ADJ oral ▶ N prova f oral

orange ['ɔrɪndʒ] N (fruit) laranja ▶ ADJ cor de laranja inv, alaranjado

orbit ['ɔːbɪt] N órbita ▶ VT orbitar

orchard ['ɔːtʃəd] N pomar m

orchestra ['ɔːkɪstrə] N orquestra; (us: seating) plateia

orchid ['ɔːkɪd] N orquídea

ordeal [ɔː'diːl] N experiência penosa, provação f

order ['ɔːdə^r] N ordem f; (Comm) encomenda ▶ VT (also: **put in ~**) pôr em ordem, arrumar; (in restaurant) pedir; (Comm) encomendar; (command) mandar, ordenar; **in (working) ~** em bom estado; **in ~ to do/that** para fazer/que (+ sub); **good ~** bom estado; **on ~** (Comm) encomendado; **out of ~** com defeito, enguiçado; **order form** N impresso para encomendas; **orderly** N (Mil) ordenança m; (Med) servente m/f ▶ ADJ (room) arrumado, ordenado; (person) metódico

ordinary ['ɔːdnrɪ] ADJ comum, usual; (pej) ordinário, medíocre; **out of the ~** fora do comum, extraordinário

ore [ɔː^r] N minério

organ ['ɔːgən] N órgão m; **organic** [ɔː'gænɪk] ADJ orgânico

organization [ɔːgənaɪ'zeɪʃən] N organização f

organize ['ɔːgənaɪz] VT organizar

orgasm ['ɔːgæzəm] N orgasmo

origin ['ɔrɪdʒɪn] N origem f

original [ə'rɪdʒɪnl] ADJ original ▶ N original m

originate [ə'rɪdʒɪneɪt] VI: **to ~ from** originar-se de, surgir de; **to ~ in** ter origem em

Orkney ['ɔːknɪ] N (also: **the ~ Islands, the ~s**) as ilhas Órcadas

ornament ['ɔːnəmənt] N ornamento; (on dress) enfeite m; **ornamental** [ɔːnə'mentl] ADJ decorativo, ornamental

ornate [ɔː'neɪt] ADJ enfeitado, requintado

orphan ['ɔːfn] N órfão/órfã m/f

orthopaedic [ɔːθə'piːdɪk], (us) **orthopedic** ADJ ortopédico

ostrich ['ɔstrɪtʃ] N avestruz m/f

other ['ʌðə^r] ADJ outro ▶ PRON: **the ~ (one)** o outro/a outra ▶ ADV (usually in negatives): **~ than** (apart from) além de; (anything but) exceto; **~s** (other people) outros; **otherwise** ADV (in a different way) de outra maneira; (apart from that) além disso ▶ CONJ (if not) senão

otter ['ɔtə^r] N lontra

ouch [autʃ] EXCL ai!

ought [ɔːt] (pt ought) AUX VB: **I ~ to do it** eu deveria fazê-lo; **he ~ to win** (probability) ele deve ganhar

ounce [auns] N onça (= 28.35g)

our ['auə^r] ADJ nosso; see also **my**; **ours** PRON (o) nosso/(a) nossa etc; see also

mine¹; **ourselves** [auə'sɛlvz] PRON PL
(*reflexive, after prep*) nós; (*emphatic*) nós
mesmos(-as); *see also* **oneself**
oust [aust] VT expulsar

(KEYWORD)

out [aut] ADV **1** (*not in*) fora; **(to stand)**
out in the rain/snow (estar em pé) na
chuva/neve; **out loud** em voz alta
2 (*not at home, absent*) fora (de casa);
Mr Green is out at the moment Sr.
Green não está no momento; **to have a**
day/night out passar o dia fora/sair à
noite
3 (*indicating distance*): **the boat was 10**
km out o barco estava a 10 km da costa
4 (*Sport*): **the ball is/has gone out** a
bola caiu fora; **out!** (*Tennis etc*) fora!
▶ ADJ **1: to be out** (*unconscious*) estar
inconsciente; (*out of game*) estar fora; (*out*
of fashion) estar fora de moda
2 (*have appeared: news, secret*) do
conhecimento público; **the flowers are**
out as flores desabrocharam
3 (*extinguished: light, fire*) apagado;
before the week was out (*finished*)
antes da semana acabar
4: **to be out to do sth** (*intend*) pretender
fazer algo; **to be out in one's**
calculations (*wrong*) enganar-se nos
cálculos
▶ **out of** PREP **1** (*outside, beyond*) fora de;
to go out of the house sair da casa; **to**
look out of the window olhar pela
janela
2 (*cause, motive*) por
3 (*origin*): **to drink sth out of a cup**
beber algo na xícara
4 (*from among*): **1 out of every 3 smokers**
1 entre 3 fumantes
5 (*without*) sem; **to be out of milk/**
sugar/petrol *etc* não ter leite/açúcar/
gasolina *etc*

outback ['autbæk] N (*in Australia*): **the ~**
o interior; **outbox** ['autbɔks] N (*Comput*)
caixa de saída; (*us: for papers*) cesta de
saída
outbreak ['autbreik] N (*of war*)
deflagração *f*; (*of disease*) surto; (*of*
violence etc) explosão *f*
outburst ['autbə:st] N explosão *f*
outcast ['autkɑ:st] N pária *m/f*
outcome ['autkʌm] N resultado
outcry ['autkrai] N clamor *m* (de
protesto)
outdated [aut'deitid] ADJ antiquado,
fora de moda

outdoor [aut'dɔ:ʳ] ADJ ao ar livre;
(*clothes*) de sair; **outdoors** ADV ao ar livre
outer ['autəʳ] ADJ exterior, externo;
outer space N espaço (exterior)
outfit ['autfit] N roupa, traje *m*
outgoing ['autgəuiŋ] ADJ de saída;
(*character*) extrovertido, sociável;
outgoings (*BRIT*) NPL despesas *fpl*
outing ['autiŋ] N excursão *f*
outlaw ['autlɔ:] N fora-da-lei *m/f* ▶ VT
(*person*) declarar fora da lei; (*practice*)
declarar ilegal
outlay ['autlei] N despesas *fpl*
outlet ['autlet] N saída, escape *m*; (*of*
pipe) desague *m*, escoadouro; (*us Elec*)
tomada; (*also*: **retail ~**) posto de venda
outline ['autlain] N (*shape*) contorno,
perfil *m*; (*of plan*) traçado; (*sketch*)
esboço, linhas *fpl* gerais ▶ VT (*theory, plan*)
traçar, delinear
outlook ['autluk] N (*attitude*) ponto de
vista; (*fig: prospects*) perspectiva; (: *for*
weather) previsão *f*
outnumber [aut'nʌmbəʳ] VT exceder
em número
out-of-date ADJ (*passport, ticket*) sem
validade; (*clothes*) fora de moda
out-of-the-way ADJ remoto, afastado
outpatient ['autpeiʃənt] N paciente *m/f*
externo(-a) *or* de ambulatório
outpost ['autpəust] N posto avançado
output ['autput] N (volume *m* de)
produção *f*; (*Comput*) saída ▶ VT (*Comput*)
dar saída em
outrage ['autreidʒ] N escândalo;
(*atrocity*) atrocidade *f* ▶ VT ultrajar;
outrageous [aut'reidʒəs] ADJ ultrajante,
escandaloso
outright [*adv* aut'rait, *adj* 'autrait] ADV
(*kill, win*) completamente; (*ask, refuse*)
abertamente ▶ ADJ completo; franco
outset ['autset] N início, princípio
outside [aut'said] N exterior *m* ▶ ADJ
exterior, externo ▶ ADV (lá) fora ▶ PREP
fora de; (*beyond*) além (dos limites) de;
at the ~ (*fig*) no máximo; **outsider** N
(*stranger*) estranho(-a), forasteiro(-a)
outsize ['autsaiz] ADJ (*clothes*) de
tamanho extra-grande *or* especial
outskirts ['autskə:ts] NPL arredores *mpl*,
subúrbios *mpl*
outspoken [aut'spəukən] ADJ franco,
sem rodeios
outstanding [aut'stændiŋ] ADJ
excepcional; (*work, debt*) pendente
outward ['autwəd] ADJ externo;
(*journey*) de ida; **outwards** (*esp BRIT*) ADV
para fora

outweigh [aut'weɪ] VT ter mais valor do que

oval ['əuvl] ADJ ovalado ▶ N oval m; **Oval Office** N ver nota

> O Salão Oval (**Oval Office**) é o escritório particular do presidente dos Estados Unidos na Casa Branca, assim chamado devido a sua forma oval. Por extensão, o termo se refere à presidência em si.

ovary ['əuvərɪ] N ovário

oven ['ʌvn] N forno

(KEYWORD)

over ['əuvəʳ] ADV **1** (across: walk, jump, fly etc) por cima; **to cross over to the other side of the road** atravessar para o outro lado da rua; **over here** por aqui, cá; **over there** por ali, lá; **to ask sb over** (to one's home) convidar alguém
2: **to fall over** cair; **to knock over** derrubar; **to turn over** virar; **to bend over** curvar-se, debruçar-se
3 (finished): **to be over** estar acabado
4 (excessively: clever, rich, fat etc) muito, demais; **she's not over intelligent** ela não é superdotada
5 (remaining: money, food etc): **there are 3 over** tem 3 sobrando/sobraram 3
6: **all over** (everywhere) por todos os lados; **over and over (again)** repetidamente
▶ PREP **1** (on top of) sobre; (above) acima de
2 (on the other side of) no outro lado de; **he jumped over the wall** ele pulou o muro
3 (more than) mais de; **over and above** além de
4 (during) durante

overall [n, adj 'əuvərɔ:l, adv əuvər'ɔ:l] ADJ (length) total; (study) global ▶ ADV (view) globalmente; (measure, paint) totalmente; **overalls** NPL macacão m (BR), (fato) macaco (PT)

overboard ['əuvəbɔ:d] ADV (Naut) ao mar

overcast ['əuvəkɑ:st] ADJ nublado, fechado

overcharge [əuvə'tʃɑ:dʒ] VT: **to ~ sb** cobrar em excesso a alguém

overcoat ['əuvəkəut] N sobretudo

overcome [əuvə'kʌm] irreg VT vencer, dominar; (difficulty) superar

overcrowded [əuvə'kraudɪd] ADJ superlotado

overdo [əuvə'du:] irreg VT exagerar; (overcook) cozinhar demais; **to ~ it** (work too hard) exceder-se

overdose ['əuvədəus] N overdose f, dose f excessiva

overdraft ['əuvədrɑ:ft] N saldo negativo

overdrawn [əuvə'drɔ:n] ADJ (account) sem fundos, a descoberto

overdue [əuvə'dju:] ADJ atrasado; (change) tardio

overestimate [əuvər'ɛstɪmeɪt] VT sobrestimar

overflow [vi əuvə'fləu, n 'əuvəfləu] VI transbordar ▶ N (also: **~ pipe**) tubo de descarga, ladrão m

overgrown [əuvə'grəun] ADJ (garden) coberto de vegetação

overhaul [vt əuvə'hɔ:l, n 'əuvəhɔ:l] VT revisar ▶ N revisão f

overhead [adv əuvə'hɛd, adj, n 'əuvəhɛd] ADV por cima, em cima; (in the sky) no céu ▶ ADJ (lighting) superior; (railway) suspenso ▶ N (US) = **overheads**; **overheads** NPL (expenses) despesas fpl gerais

overhear [əuvə'hɪəʳ] irreg VT ouvir por acaso

overheat [əuvə'hi:t] VI (engine) aquecer demais

overland ['əuvəlænd] ADJ, ADV por terra

overlap [əuvə'læp] VI (edges) sobrepor-se em parte; (fig) coincidir

overload [əuvə'ləud] VT sobrecarregar

overlook [əuvə'luk] VT (have view on) dar para; (miss) omitir; (forgive) fazer vista grossa a

overnight [adv əuvə'naɪt, adj 'əuvənaɪt] ADV durante a noite; (fig) da noite para o dia ▶ ADJ de uma (or de) noite; **to stay ~** passar a noite, pernoitar

overpass ['əuvəpɑ:s] (esp US) N viaduto

overpower [əuvə'pauəʳ] VT dominar, subjugar; (fig) assolar

overrule [əuvə'ru:l] VT (decision) anular; (claim) indeferir

overrun [əuvə'rʌn] irreg VT (country etc) invadir; (time limit) ultrapassar, exceder

overseas [əuvə'si:z] ADV (abroad) no estrangeiro, no exterior ▶ ADJ (trade) exterior; (visitor) estrangeiro

overshadow [əuvə'ʃædəu] VT ofuscar

oversight ['əuvəsaɪt] N descuido

oversleep [əuvə'sli:p] irreg VI dormir além da hora

overt [əu'və:t] ADJ aberto, indissimulado

overtake [əuvə'teɪk] irreg VT ultrapassar

overthrow [əuvə'θrəu] irreg VT (government) derrubar

overtime ['əuvətaɪm] N horas fpl extras

overturn [əuvə'tə:n] VT virar; (system) derrubar; (decision) anular ▶ VI capotar

overweight [əuvə'weɪt] ADJ acima do peso

overwhelm [əuvə'wɛlm] VT esmagar, assolar; **overwhelming** ADJ (victory, defeat) esmagador(a); (heat) sufocante; (desire) irresistível

owe [əu] VT: **to ~ sb sth, to ~ sth to sb** dever algo a alguém; **owing to** PREP devido a, por causa de

owl [aul] N coruja

own [əun] ADJ próprio ▶ VT possuir, ter; **a room of my ~** meu próprio quarto; **to get one's ~ back** ir à forra; **on one's ~** sozinho; **own up** VI: **to ~ up to sth** confessar algo; **owner** N dono(-a), proprietário(-a); **ownership** N posse f

ox [ɔks] (pl **oxen**) N boi m

oxygen ['ɔksɪdʒən] N oxigênio

oyster ['ɔɪstə] N ostra

oz. ABBR = **ounce**

ozone ['əuzəun] N ozônio

p [piː] ABBR (= page) p; (BRIT) = **penny, pence**

p.a. ABBR (= per annum) por ano

pace [peɪs] N passo; (speed) velocidade f ▶ VI: **to ~ up and down** andar de um lado para o outro; **to keep ~ with** acompanhar o passo de; **pacemaker** N (Med) marcapasso m

Pacific [pə'sɪfɪk] N: **the ~ (Ocean)** o (Oceano) Pacífico

pack [pæk] N pacote m, embrulho; (of hounds) matilha; (of thieves etc) bando, quadrilha; (of cards) baralho; (backpack) mochila ▶ VT encher; (in suitcase etc) arrumar (na mala); (cram): **to ~ into** entupir de, entulhar com ▶ VI: **to ~ (one's bags)** fazer as malas; **~ it in!** para com isso!; **pack off** VT (person) despedir

package ['pækɪdʒ] N pacote m; (bulky) embrulho, fardo; (also: **~ deal**) pacote; **package tour** (BRIT) N excursão f organizada

packed lunch [pækt-] (BRIT) N merenda

packet ['pækɪt] N pacote m; (of cigarettes) maço; (of washing powder etc) caixa

packing ['pækɪŋ] N embalagem f; (act) empacotamento

pad [pæd] N (of paper) bloco; (to prevent friction) acolchoado; (inf: home) casa ▶ VT acolchoar, enchumaçar

paddle ['pædl] N remo curto; (US: for table tennis) raquete f ▶ VT remar ▶ VI patinhar; **paddling pool** (BRIT) N lago de recreação

paddock ['pædək] N cercado; (at race course) paddock m

padlock ['pædlɔk] N cadeado

paedophile, (US) **pedophile** ['piːdəufaɪl] N pedófilo(-a)

page [peɪdʒ] N página; (also: **~ boy**)
mensageiro ▶ VT mandar chamar
pager ['peɪdʒəʳ] N bip m
paid [peɪd] PT, PP of **pay** ▶ ADJ (work)
remunerado; (holiday) pago; (official)
assalariado; **to put ~ to** (BRIT) acabar
com
pain [peɪn] N dor f; **to be in ~** sofrer or
sentir dor; **to take ~s to do sth** dar-se
ao trabalho de fazer algo; **painful** ADJ
doloroso; (laborious) penoso;
(unpleasant) desagradável; **painkiller** N
analgésico; **painstaking** ['peɪnzteɪkɪŋ]
ADJ (work) esmerado; (person)
meticuloso
paint [peɪnt] N pintura ▶ VT pintar;
paintbrush N (artist's) pincel m;
(decorator's) broxa; **painter** N pintor(a)
m/f; **painting** N pintura; (picture) tela,
quadro
pair [pɛəʳ] N par m; **a ~ of scissors** uma
tesoura; **a ~ of trousers** uma calça (BR),
umas calças (PT)
pajamas [pɪ'dʒɑːməz] (US) NPL pijama m
Pakistan [pɑːkɪ'stɑːn] N Paquistão m;
Pakistani ADJ, N paquistanês(-esa) m/f
pal [pæl] (inf) N camarada m/f, colega m/f
palace ['pæləs] N palácio
pale [peɪl] ADJ pálido; (colour) claro;
(light) fraco ▶ VI empalidecer ▶ N: **to be
beyond the ~** passar dos limites
Palestine ['pælɪstaɪn] N Palestina;
Palestinian [pælɪs'tɪnɪən] ADJ, N
palestino(-a)
palm [pɑːm] N (hand, leaf) palma; (also: **~
tree**) palmeira ▶ VT: **to ~ sth off on sb**
(inf) impingir algo a alguém
pamper ['pæmpəʳ] VT paparicar, mimar
pamphlet ['pæmflət] N panfleto
pan [pæn] N (also: **sauce~**) panela (BR),
caçarola (PT); (also: **frying ~**) frigideira
Panama ['pænəmɑː] N Panamá m
pancake ['pænkeɪk] N panqueca
panda ['pændə] N panda m/f
pandemic [pæn'dɛmɪk] N pandemia
pane [peɪn] N vidraça, vidro
panel ['pænl] N (of wood, Radio, TV)
painel m
panic ['pænɪk] N pânico ▶ VI entrar em
pânico
pansy ['pænzɪ] N (Bot) amor-perfeito;
(inf, pej) bicha (BR), maricas m (PT)
pant [pænt] VI arquejar, ofegar
panther ['pænθəʳ] N pantera
panties ['pæntɪz] NPL calcinha (BR),
cuecas fpl (PT)
pantomime ['pæntəmaɪm] (BRIT) N
pantomima

Uma **pantomime**, também chamada
simplesmente de panto, é um gênero
de comédia em que o personagem
principal em geral é um rapaz e na qual
há sempre uma dame, isto é, uma
mulher idosa representada por um
homem, e um vilão. Na maior parte
das vezes, a história é baseada em um
conto de fadas, como "A gata
borralheira" ou "O gato de botas",
e a plateia é encorajada a participar
prevenindo os heróis dos perigos que
estão por vir. Esse tipo de espetáculo,
voltado sobretudo para as crianças,
visa também ao público adulto por
meio de diversas brincadeiras que
fazem alusão aos fatos atuais.

pants [pænts] NPL (BRIT: underwear:
woman's) calcinha (BR), cuecas fpl (PT);
(: man's) cueca (BR), cuecas (PT); (US:
trousers) calça (BR), calças fpl (PT)
paper ['peɪpəʳ] N papel m; (also: **news~**)
jornal m; (also: **wall~**) papel de parede;
(study, article) artigo, dissertação f;
(exam) exame m, prova ▶ ADJ de papel
▶ VT (room) revestir (com papel de
parede); **papers** NPL (also: **identity ~s**)
documentos mpl; **paperback** N livro de
capa mole; **paper bag** N saco de papel;
paper clip N clipe m; **paperwork** N
trabalho burocrático; (pej) papelada
par [pɑːʳ] N paridade f, igualdade f; (Golf)
média f; **on a ~ with** em pé de igualdade
com
parachute ['pærəʃuːt] N para-quedas m
inv
parade [pə'reɪd] N desfile m ▶ VT (show
off) exibir ▶ VI (Mil) passar revista
paradise ['pærədaɪs] N paraíso
paraffin ['pærəfɪn] (BRIT) N: **~ (oil)**
querosene m
paragraph ['pærəgrɑːf] N parágrafo
Paraguay ['pærəgwaɪ] N Paraguai m
parallel ['pærəlɛl] ADJ (lines etc) paralelo;
(fig) correspondente ▶ N paralela;
correspondência
paralysis [pə'rælɪsɪs] (pl **paralyses**) N
paralisia
paranoid ['pærənɔɪd] ADJ paranoico
parcel ['pɑːsl] N pacote m ▶ VT (also: **~ up**)
embrulhar, empacotar
pardon ['pɑːdn] N (Jur) indulto ▶ VT
perdoar; **~ me!, I beg your ~** (apologizing)
desculpe(-me); **(I beg your) ~?** (BRIT),
~ me? (US) (not hearing) como?, como disse?
parent ['pɛərənt] N (father) pai m;
(mother) mãe f; **parents** NPL (mother and
father) pais mpl

Paris ['pærɪs] N Paris
parish ['pærɪʃ] N paróquia, freguesia
park [pɑ:k] N parque m ▶ VT, VI
estacionar; **park and ride** N esquema de
transporte feito parcialmente com carro, que
em seguida é estacionado para o uso de
transporte público
parking ['pɑ:kɪŋ] N estacionamento;
"no ~" "estacionamento proibido";
parking lot (US) N (parque m de)
estacionamento; **parking meter** N
parquímetro; **parking ticket** N multa
por estacionamento proibido
parliament ['pɑ:ləmənt] (BRIT) N
parlamento
parole [pə'rəul] N: **on ~** em liberdade
condicional, sob promessa
parrot ['pærət] N papagaio
parsley ['pɑ:slɪ] N salsa
parsnip ['pɑ:snɪp] N cherivia, pastinaga
parson ['pɑ:sn] N padre m, clérigo; (in
Church of England) pastor m
part [pɑ:t] N parte f; (of machine) peça;
(Theatre etc) papel m; (of serial) capítulo;
(US: in hair) risca, repartido ▶ ADV =
partly ▶ VT dividir; (hair) repartir ▶ VI
(people) separar-se; (crowd) dispersar-se;
to take ~ in participar de, tomar parte
em; **to take sb's ~** defender alguém; **for
my ~** pela minha parte; **for the most ~**
na maior parte; **to take sth in good ~**
não se ofender com algo; **part with** VT
FUS ceder, entregar; (money) pagar
partial ['pɑ:ʃl] ADJ parcial; **to be ~ to**
gostar de, ser apreciador(a) de
participate [pɑ:'tɪsɪpeɪt] VI: **to ~ in**
participar de
particle ['pɑ:tɪkl] N partícula; (of dust)
grão m
particular [pə'tɪkjulə'] ADJ (special)
especial; (specific) específico; (fussy)
exigente, minucioso; **in ~** em particular;
particularly ADV em particular,
especialmente; **particulars** NPL
detalhes mpl; (personal details) dados mpl
pessoais
parting ['pɑ:tɪŋ] N (act) separação f;
(farewell) despedida; (BRIT: in hair) risca,
repartido ▶ ADJ de despedida; **~ shot** (fig)
flecha de parto
partition [pɑ:'tɪʃən] N (Pol) divisão f;
(wall) tabique m, divisória
partly ['pɑ:tlɪ] ADV em parte
partner ['pɑ:tnə'] N (Comm) sócio(-a);
(Sport) parceiro(-a); (at dance) par m;
(spouse) cônjuge m/f; **partnership** N
associação f, parceria; (Comm)
sociedade f

partridge ['pɑ:trɪdʒ] N perdiz f
part-time ADJ, ADV de meio expediente
party ['pɑ:tɪ] N (Pol) partido; (celebration)
festa; (group) grupo; (Jur) parte f
interessada, litigante m/f ▶ CPD (Pol) do
partido, partidário
pass [pɑ:s] VT passar; (exam) passar em;
(place) passar por; (overtake, surpass)
ultrapassar; (approve) aprovar ▶ VI
passar; (Sch) ser aprovado, passar ▶ N
(permit) passe m; (membership card)
carteira; (in mountains) desfiladeiro;
(Sport) passe m; (Sch): **to get a ~ in** ser
aprovado em; **to make a ~ at sb** tomar
liberdade com alguém; **pass away** VI
falecer; **pass by** VI passar ▶ VT passar por
cima de; **pass for** VT FUS passar por;
pass on (news, illness) transmitir;
(object) passar para; **pass out** VI
desmaiar; **pass up** VT deixar passar;
passable ADJ (road) transitável; (work)
aceitável
passage ['pæsɪdʒ] N (also: **~way**: indoors)
corredor m; (: outdoors) passagem f;
(Anat) via; (act of passing) trânsito; (in
book) trecho; (by boat) travessia;
(Mechanics, Med) conduto
passenger ['pæsɪndʒə'] N passageiro(-a)
passer-by ['pɑ:sə'-] (pl **passers-by**) N
transeunte m/f
passion ['pæʃən] N paixão f; **passionate**
ADJ apaixonado; **passion fruit** N
maracujá m
passive ['pæsɪv] ADJ passivo
passport ['pɑ:spɔ:t] N passaporte m
password ['pɑ:swə:d] N senha
past [pɑ:st] PREP (drive, walk etc: in front
of) por; (: beyond) mais além de; (later
than) depois de ▶ ADJ passado; (president
etc) ex-, anterior ▶ N passado; **he's ~
forty** ele tem mais de quarenta anos;
ten/quarter ~ four quatro e dez/
quinze; **for the ~ few/3 days** nos
últimos/3 dias
pasta ['pæstə] N massa
paste [peɪst] N pasta; (glue) grude m, cola
▶ VT grudar; **tomato ~** massa de tomate
pasteurized ['pæstəraɪzd] ADJ
pasteurizado
pastime ['pɑ:staɪm] N passatempo
pastry ['peɪstrɪ] N massa; (cake) bolo
pasture ['pɑ:stʃə'] N pasto
pasty [n 'pæstɪ, adj 'peɪstɪ] N empadão m
de carne ▶ ADJ (complexion) pálido
pat [pæt] VT dar palmadinhas em; (dog
etc) fazer festa em
patch [pætʃ] N retalho; (eye patch)
tapa-olho m; (area) área pequena; (mend)

remendo ▶ VT remendar; **(to go through) a bad ~** (passar por) um mau pedaço; **patch up** VT consertar provisoriamente; (*quarrel*) resolver; **patchy** ADJ (*colour*) desigual; (*information*) incompleto

pâté ['pæteɪ] N patê *m*

patent ['peɪtnt] N patente *f* ▶ VT patentear ▶ ADJ patente, evidente

paternal [pə'tɜːnl] ADJ paternal; (*relation*) paterno

path [pɑːθ] N caminho; (*trail, track*) trilha, senda; (*trajectory*) trajetória

pathetic [pə'θɛtɪk] ADJ (*pitiful*) patético, digno de pena; (*very bad*) péssimo

pathway ['pɑːθweɪ] N caminho, trilha

patience ['peɪʃns] N paciência

patient ['peɪʃnt] ADJ, N paciente *m/f*

patio ['pætɪəʊ] N pátio

patrol [pə'trəʊl] N patrulha ▶ VT patrulhar; **patrol car** N carro de patrulha

patron ['peɪtrən] N (*customer*) cliente *m/f*, freguês(-esa) *m/f*; (*of charity*) benfeitor(a) *m/f*; **~ of the arts** mecenas *m*

pattern ['pætən] N (*Sewing*) molde *m*; (*design*) desenho

pause [pɔːz] N pausa ▶ VI fazer uma pausa

pave [peɪv] VT pavimentar; **to ~ the way for** preparar o terreno para

pavement ['peɪvmənt] N (*BRIT*) calçada (*BR*), passeio (*PT*)

pavilion [pə'vɪlɪən] N (*Sport*) barraca

paving ['peɪvɪŋ] N pavimento, calçamento

paw [pɔː] N pata; (*of cat*) garra

pawn [pɔːn] N (*Chess*) peão *m*; (*fig*) títere *m* ▶ VT empenhar; **pawnbroker** N agiota *m/f*

pay [peɪ] (*pt, pp* **paid**) N salário; (*of manual worker*) paga ▶ VT pagar; (*debt*) liquidar, saldar; (*visit*) fazer ▶ VI valer a pena, render; **to ~ attention (to)** prestar atenção (a); **to ~ one's respects to sb** fazer uma visita de cortesia a alguém; **pay back** VT (*money*) devolver; (*person*) pagar; **pay for** VT FUS pagar a; (*fig*) recompensar; **pay in** VT depositar; **pay off** VT (*debts*) saldar, liquidar; (*creditor*) pagar, reembolsar ▶ VI (*plan, patience*) valer a pena; **pay up** VT pagar; **payable** ADJ pagável; (*cheque*): **payable to** nominal em favor de; **payment** N pagamento; **monthly payment** pagamento mensal; **pay packet** (*BRIT*) N envelope *m* de pagamento; **pay-per-click** N (*Comput*) sistema *m* pague por clique; **pay phone** N telefone *m* público;

payroll N folha de pagamento; **pay television** N televisão *f* por assinatura; **paywall** N (*Comput*) paywall *m* (*PT f*), muro de cobrança BR

PC N ABBR (= *personal computer*) PC *m*

PDA N ABBR (= *personal digital assistant*) PDA *m* (*assistente digital pessoal*)

pea [piː] N ervilha

peace [piːs] N paz *f*; (*calm*) tranquilidade *f*, quietude *f*; **peaceful** ADJ (*person*) tranquilo, pacífico; (*place, time*) tranquilo, sossegado

peach [piːtʃ] N pêssego

peacock ['piːkɔk] N pavão *m*

peak [piːk] N (*of mountain: top*) cume *m*; (*of cap*) pala, viseira; (*fig*) apogeu *m*

peanut ['piːnʌt] N amendoim *m*; **peanut butter** N manteiga de amendoim

pear [pɛəʳ] N pera

pearl [pɜːl] N pérola

peasant ['pɛznt] N camponês(-esa) *m/f*

peat [piːt] N turfa

pebble ['pɛbl] N seixo, calhau *m*

peck [pɛk] VT (*also: ~ at*) bicar, dar bicadas em ▶ N bicada; (*kiss*) beijoca; **peckish** (*BRIT inf*) ADJ: **I feel peckish** estou a fim de comer alguma coisa

peculiar [pɪ'kjuːlɪəʳ] ADJ (*strange*) estranho, esquisito; **~ to** (*belonging to*) próprio de

pedal ['pɛdl] N pedal *m* ▶ VI pedalar

pedestrian [pɪ'dɛstrɪən] N pedestre *m/f* (*BR*), peão *m* (*PT*) ▶ ADJ (*fig*) prosaico; **pedestrian crossing** (*BRIT*) N passagem *f* para pedestres (*BR*), passadeira (*PT*)

pedigree ['pɛdɪgriː] N raça; (*fig*) genealogia ▶ CPD (*animal*) de raça

pedophile ['piːdəʊfaɪl] (*US*) N = **paedophile**

pee [piː] (*inf*) VI fazer xixi, mijar

peek [piːk] VI: **to ~ at** espiar, espreitar

peel [piːl] N casca ▶ VT descascar ▶ VI (*paint, skin*) descascar; (*wallpaper*) desprender-se

peep [piːp] N (*BRIT: look*) espiadela; (*sound*) pio ▶ VI espreitar; **peep out** (*BRIT*) VI mostrar-se, surgir

peer [pɪəʳ] VI: **to ~ at** perscrutar, fitar ▶ N (*noble*) par *m/f*; (*equal*) igual *m/f*; (*contemporary*) contemporâneo(-a)

peg [pɛg] N (*for coat etc*) cabide *m*; (*BRIT: also*: **clothes ~**) pregador *m*

pelican ['pɛlɪkən] N pelicano

pelt [pɛlt] VT: **to ~ sb with sth** atirar algo em alguém ▶ VI (*rain: also*: **~ down**) chover a cântaros; (*inf: run*) correr ▶ N pele *f* (não curtida)

pelvis ['pɛlvɪs] N pelvis *f*, bacia

pen [pɛn] N caneta; (for sheep etc) redil m, cercado

penalty ['pɛnltɪ] N pena, penalidade f; (fine) multa; (Sport) punição f

pence [pɛns] (BRIT) NPL of **penny**

pencil ['pɛnsl] N lápis m; **pencil case** N lapiseira, porta-lápis m inv; **pencil sharpener** N apontador m (de lápis) (BR), apara-lápis m inv (PT)

pendant ['pɛndnt] N pingente m

pending ['pɛndɪŋ] PREP até ▶ ADJ pendente

penetrate ['pɛnɪtreɪt] VT penetrar

penfriend ['pɛnfrɛnd] (BRIT) N amigo(-a) por correspondência

penguin ['pɛŋgwɪn] N pinguim m

peninsula [pə'nɪnsjulə] N península

penis ['piːnɪs] N pênis m

penitentiary [pɛnɪ'tɛnʃərɪ] (US) N penitenciária, presídio

penknife ['pɛnnaɪf] irreg N canivete m

penniless ['pɛnɪlɪs] ADJ sem dinheiro, sem um tostão

penny ['pɛnɪ] (pl **pennies**, BRIT **pence**) N pêni m; (US) cêntimo

penpal ['pɛnpæl] N amigo(-a) por correspondência

pension ['pɛnʃən] N pensão f; (old-age pension) aposentadoria; **pensioner** (BRIT) N aposentado(-a) (BR), reformado(-a) (PT)

Pentagon ['pɛntəgən] N: **the ~** o Pentágono

O Pentágono (**Pentagon**) é o nome dado aos escritórios do Ministério da Defesa americano, localizados em Arlington, no estado da Virgínia, por causa da forma pentagonal do edifício onde se encontram. Por extensão, o termo é utilizado também para se referir ao ministério.

penthouse ['pɛnthaus] N cobertura

people ['piːpl] NPL gente f, pessoas fpl; (inhabitants) habitantes mpl/fpl; (citizens) povo; (Pol): **the ~** o povo ▶ N (nation, race) povo; **several ~ came** vieram várias pessoas; **~ say that ...** dizem que ...

pepper ['pɛpəʳ] N pimenta; (vegetable) pimentão m ▶ VT apimentar; (fig): **to ~ with** salpicar de; **peppermint** N (sweet) bala de hortelã

per [pəːʳ] PREP por

perceive [pə'siːv] VT perceber; (notice) notar; (realize) compreender

per cent N por cento

percentage [pə'sɛntɪdʒ] N porcentagem f, percentagem f

perch [pəːtʃ] (pl **perches**) N (for bird) poleiro; (fish) perca ▶ VI: **to ~ (on)** (bird) empoleirar-se (em); (person) encarapitar-se (em)

perfect [adj, n 'pəːfɪkt, vt pə'fɛkt] ADJ perfeito; (utter) completo ▶ N (also: **~ tense**) perfeito ▶ VT aperfeiçoar; **perfectly** ADV perfeitamente

perform [pə'fɔːm] VT (carry out) realizar, fazer; (piece of music) interpretar ▶ VI (well, badly) interpretar; **performance** N desempenho; (of play, by artist) atuação f; (of car) performance f; **performer** N (actor) artista m/f, ator/atriz m/f; (Mus) intérprete m/f

perfume ['pəːfjuːm] N perfume m

perhaps [pə'hæps] ADV talvez

perimeter [pə'rɪmɪtəʳ] N perímetro

period ['pɪərɪəd] N período; (Sch) aula; (US: full stop) ponto final; (Med) menstruação f, regra ▶ ADJ (costume, furniture) da época

perish ['pɛrɪʃ] VI perecer; (decay) deteriorar-se

perjury ['pəːdʒərɪ] N (Jur) perjúrio, falso testemunho

perk [pəːk] (inf) N mordomia, regalia; **perk up** VI (cheer up) animar-se

perm [pəːm] N permanente f

permanent ['pəːmənənt] ADJ permanente

permission [pə'mɪʃən] N permissão f; (authorization) autorização f

permit [n 'pəːmɪt, vt pə'mɪt] N licença; (to enter) passe m ▶ VT permitir; (authorize) autorizar

perplex [pə'plɛks] VT deixar perplexo

persecute [pə'sɪkjuːt] VT perseguir

persevere [pəːsɪ'vɪəʳ] VI perseverar

Persian ['pəːʃən] ADJ persa ▶ N (Ling) persa m; **the (~) Gulf** o golfo Pérsico

persist [pə'sɪst] VI: **to ~ (in doing sth)** persistir (em fazer algo); **persistent** [pə'sɪstənt] ADJ persistente; (determined) teimoso

person ['pəːsn] N pessoa; **in ~** em pessoa; **personal** ADJ pessoal; (private) particular; (visit) em pessoa, pessoal; **personal assistant** N secretário(-a) particular; **personal computer** N computador m pessoal; **personality** [pəːsə'nælɪtɪ] N personalidade f; **personal organizer** N agenda

personnel [pəːsə'nɛl] N pessoal m

perspective [pə'spɛktɪv] N perspectiva

perspiration [pəːspɪ'reɪʃən] N transpiração f

persuade [pə'sweɪd] VT: **to ~ sb to do sth** persuadir alguém a fazer algo

Peru [pə'ruː] N Peru m

pervert [n 'pɜːvɜːt, vt pə'vɜːt] N pervertido(-a) ▶ VT perverter, corromper; (*truth*) distorcer

pessimist ['pɛsɪmɪst] N pessimista m/f; **pessimistic** [pɛsɪ'mɪstɪk] ADJ pessimista

pest [pɛst] N (*animal*) praga; (*fig*) peste f

pester ['pɛstəʳ] VT incomodar

pet [pɛt] N animal m de estimação ▶ CPD predileto ▶ VT acariciar ▶ VI (*inf*) acariciar-se; **teacher's ~** (*favourite*) preferido(-a) do professor

petal ['pɛtl] N pétala

petite [pə'tiːt] ADJ delicado, mignon

petition [pə'tɪʃən] N petição f; (*list of signatures*) abaixo-assinado

petrified ['pɛtrɪfaɪd] ADJ (*fig*) petrificado, paralisado

petrol ['pɛtrəl] (BRIT) N gasolina; **two/ four-star ~** gasolina comum/premium

petroleum [pə'trəʊlɪəm] N petróleo

petrol: petrol pump (BRIT) N bomba de gasolina; **petrol station** (BRIT) N posto (BR) or bomba (PT) de gasolina; **petrol tank** (BRIT) N tanque m de gasolina

petticoat ['pɛtɪkəʊt] N anágua

petty ['pɛtɪ] ADJ (*mean*) mesquinho; (*unimportant*) insignificante

pew [pjuː] N banco (de igreja)

pewter ['pjuːtəʳ] N peltre m

phantom ['fæntəm] N fantasma m

pharmacy ['fɑːməsɪ] N farmácia

phase [feɪz] N fase f ▶ VT: **to ~ in/out** introduzir/retirar por etapas

PhD N ABBR = **Doctor of Philosophy** ≈ doutorado

pheasant ['fɛznt] N faisão m

phenomenon [fə'nɔmɪnən] (*pl* **phenomena**) N fenômeno

philosophical [fɪlə'sɔfɪkl] ADJ filosófico; (*fig*) calmo, sereno

philosophy [fɪ'lɔsəfɪ] N filosofia

phishing ['fɪʃɪŋ] N phishing m; **~ attack** golpe m de phishing

phobia ['fəʊbjə] N fobia

phone [fəʊn] N telefone m ▶ VT telefonar para, ligar para; **to be on the ~** ter telefone; (*be calling*) estar no telefone; **phone back** VT, VI ligar de volta; **phone up** VT telefonar para ▶ VI telefonar; **phone book** N lista telefônica; **phone box** (BRIT) N cabine f telefônica; **phone call** N telefonema m, ligação f; **phone card** N cartão m telefônico; **phone number** N número de telefone

phonetics [fə'nɛtɪks] N fonética

phoney ['fəʊnɪ] ADJ falso; (*person*) fingido

photo ['fəʊtəʊ] N foto f

photo... ['fəʊtəʊ] PREFIX foto...; **photobomb** VT estragar a fotografia de (*aparecendo na foto sem ser solicitado*); **photocopier** N fotocopiadora f; **photocopy** N fotocópia, xerox® m ▶ VT fotocopiar, xerocar

photograph ['fəʊtəgrɑːf] N fotografia ▶ VT fotografar; **photographer** [fə'tɔgrəfəʳ] N fotógrafo(-a); **photography** [fə'tɔgrəfɪ] N fotografia

phrase [freɪz] N frase f ▶ VT expressar; **phrase book** N livro de expressões idiomáticas (para turistas)

physical ['fɪzɪkl] ADJ físico

physician [fɪ'zɪʃən] N médico(-a)

physics ['fɪzɪks] N física

physiotherapy [fɪzɪəʊ'θɛrəpɪ] N fisioterapia

physique [fɪ'ziːk] N físico

pianist ['piːənɪst] N pianista m/f

piano [pɪ'ænəʊ] N piano

pick [pɪk] N (*also*: **~axe**) picareta ▶ VT (*select*) escolher, selecionar; (*gather*) colher; (*remove*) tirar; (*lock*) forçar; **take your ~** escolha o que quiser; **the ~ of** o melhor de; **to ~ one's nose** colocar o dedo no nariz; **to ~ one's teeth** palitar os dentes; **to ~ a quarrel** or **a fight with sb** comprar uma briga com alguém; **pick at** VT FUS (*food*) beliscar; **pick on** VT FUS (*person: criticize*) criticar; (: *treat badly*) azucrinar, aporrinhar; **pick out** VT escolher; (*distinguish*) distinguir; **pick up** VI (*improve*) melhorar ▶ VT (*from floor, Aut*) apanhar; (*Police*) prender; (*collect*) buscar; (*for sexual encounter*) paquerar; (*learn*) aprender; (*Radio, TV, Tel*) pegar; **to ~ up speed** acelerar; **to ~ o.s. up** levantar-se

pickle ['pɪkl] N (*also*: **~s**: *as condiment*) picles mpl; (*fig: mess*) apuro ▶ VT (*in vinegar*) conservar em vinagre; (*in salt*) conservar em sal e água

pickpocket ['pɪkpɔkɪt] N batedor(a) m/f de carteira (BR), carteirista m/f (PT)

picnic ['pɪknɪk] N piquenique m

picture ['pɪktʃəʳ] N quadro; (*painting*) pintura; (*drawing*) desenho; (*etching*) água-forte f; (*photograph*) foto(grafia) f; (*TV*) imagem f; (*film*) filme m; (*fig: description*) descrição f; (: *situation*) conjuntura ▶ VT imaginar-se; **the pictures** NPL (BRIT *inf*) o cinema; **picture messaging** N serviço de mensagens multimídia

pie [paɪ] N (*vegetable*) pastelão m; (*fruit*) torta; (*meat*) empadão m

piece [piːs] N (*portion*) fatia; (*item*): **a ~ of clothing/furniture/advice** uma roupa/um móvel/um conselho ▶ VT: **to ~ together** juntar; **to take to ~s** desmontar

pie chart N gráfico de setores

pier [pɪəʳ] N cais m; (*jetty*) embarcadouro, molhe m

pierce [pɪəs] VT furar, perfurar

pig [pɪg] N porco; (*fig*) porcalhão(-lhona) m/f; (*pej: unkind person*) grosseiro(-a); (: *greedy person*) ganancioso(-a)

pigeon [ˈpɪdʒən] N pombo

piggy bank [ˈpɪgɪ-] N cofre em forma de porquinho

pigsty [ˈpɪgstaɪ] N chiqueiro

pigtail [ˈpɪgteɪl] N rabo-de-cavalo, trança

pike [paɪk] (*pl* **pike** *or* **pikes**) N (*fish*) lúcio

pilchard [ˈpɪltʃəd] N sardinha

pile [paɪl] N (*heap*) monte m; (*of carpet*) pelo; (*of cloth*) lado felpudo ▶ VT (*also: ~ up*) empilhar ▶ VI (*also: ~ up: objects*) empilhar-se; (: *problems, work*) acumular-se; **pile into** VT FUS (*car*) apinhar-se

piles [paɪlz] NPL hemorróidas fpl

pile-up N (*Aut*) engavetamento

pilgrim [ˈpɪlgrɪm] N peregrino(-a)

pill [pɪl] N pílula; **the ~** a pílula

pillar [ˈpɪləʳ] N pilar m; **pillar box** (*BRIT*) N caixa coletora (do correio) (*BR*), marco do correio (*PT*)

pillow [ˈpɪləu] N travesseiro (*BR*), almofada (*PT*); **pillowcase** N fronha

pilot [ˈpaɪlət] N piloto(-a) ▶ CPD (*scheme etc*) piloto *inv* ▶ VT pilotar; **pilot light** N piloto

pimple [ˈpɪmpl] N espinha

PIN N ABBR (= *personal identification number*) senha

pin [pɪn] N alfinete m ▶ VT alfinetar; **~s and needles** comichão f, sensação f de formigamento; **to ~ sth on sb** (*fig*) culpar alguém de algo; **pin down** VT (*fig*): **to ~ sb down** conseguir que alguém se defina *or* tome atitude

pinafore [ˈpɪnəfɔːʳ] N (*also: ~ dress*) avental m

pinch [pɪntʃ] N (*of salt etc*) pitada ▶ VT beliscar; (*inf: steal*) afanar; **at a ~** em último caso

pine [paɪn] N pinho ▶ VI: **to ~ for** ansiar por; **pine away** VI consumir-se, definhar

pineapple [ˈpaɪnæpl] N abacaxi m (*BR*), ananás m (*PT*)

pink [pɪŋk] ADJ cor de rosa *inv* ▶ N (*colour*) cor f de rosa; (*Bot*) cravo, cravina

pinpoint [ˈpɪnpɔɪnt] VT (*discover*) descobrir; (*explain*) identificar; (*locate*) localizar com precisão

pint [paɪnt] N quartilho (*Brit* = 568cc, *US* = 473cc)

pioneer [paɪəˈnɪəʳ] N pioneiro(-a)

pious [ˈpaɪəs] ADJ pio, devoto

pip [pɪp] N (*seed*) caroço, semente f; **the pips** NPL (*BRIT: time signal on radio*) ≈ o toque de seis segundos

pipe [paɪp] N cano; (*for smoking*) cachimbo ▶ VT canalizar, encanar; **pipes** NPL (*also: bag~s*) gaita de foles; **pipe down** (*inf*) VI calar o bico, meter a viola no saco; **pipeline** N (*for oil*) oleoduto; (*for gas*) gaseoduto

pirate [ˈpaɪərət] N pirata m ▶ VT piratear

Pisces [ˈpaɪsiːz] N Pisces m, Peixes mpl

piss [pɪs] (!) VI mijar; **pissed** (!) ADJ (*drunk*) bêbado, de porre

pistol [ˈpɪstl] N pistola

piston [ˈpɪstən] N pistão m, êmbolo

pit [pɪt] N cova, fossa; (*quarry, hole in surface of sth*) buraco; (*also:* **coal ~**) mina de carvão ▶ VT: **to ~ one's wits against sb** competir em conhecimento *or* inteligência contra alguém; **pits** NPL (*Aut*) box m

pitch [pɪtʃ] N (*Mus*) tom m; (*fig: degree*) intensidade f; (*BRIT Sport*) campo; (*tar*) piche m, breu m ▶ VT (*throw*) arremessar, lançar; (*tent*) armar ▶ VI (*fall forwards*) cair (para frente); **pitch-black** ADJ escuro como o breu

pitfall [ˈpɪtfɔːl] N perigo (imprevisto), armadilha

pitiful [ˈpɪtɪful] ADJ comovente, tocante

pity [ˈpɪtɪ] N compaixão f, piedade f ▶ VT ter pena de, compadecer-se de

pixel [ˈpɪksl] N pixel m

pizza [ˈpiːtsə] N pizza

placard [ˈplækɑːd] N placar m; (*in march etc*) cartaz m

place [pleɪs] N lugar m; (*rank, position*) posição f; (*post*) posto; (*role*) papel m; (*home*): **at/to his ~** na/para a casa dele ▶ VT pôr, colocar; (*identify*) identificar, situar; **to take ~** realizar-se; (*occur*) ocorrer; **out of ~** (*not suitable*) fora de lugar, deslocado; **in the first ~** em primeiro lugar; **to change ~s with sb** trocar de lugar com alguém; **to be ~d** (*in race, exam*) classificar-se

plague [pleɪg] N (*Med*) peste f; (*fig*) praga ▶ VT atormentar, importunar

plaice [pleɪs] N INV solha

plain [pleɪn] ADJ (*unpatterned*) liso; (*clear*) claro, evidente; (*simple*) simples *inv*, despretensioso; (*not handsome*) sem atrativos ▶ ADV claramente, com franqueza ▶ N planície f, campina; **plain chocolate** N chocolate m amargo; **plainly** ADV claramente, obviamente; (*hear, see*) facilmente; (*state*) francamente

plaintiff ['pleɪntɪf] N querelante m/f, queixoso(-a)

plait [plæt] N trança, dobra

plan [plæn] N plano; (*scheme*) projeto; (*schedule*) programa m ▶ VT planejar (BR), planear (PT) ▶ VI fazer planos; **to ~ to do** pretender fazer

plane [pleɪn] N (*Aviat*) avião m; (*also: ~ tree*) plátano; (*fig: level*) nível m; (*tool*) plaina; (*Math*) plano

planet ['plænɪt] N planeta m

plank [plæŋk] N tábua

planning ['plænɪŋ] N planejamento (BR), planeamento (PT); **family ~** planejamento or planeamento familiar

plant [plɑ:nt] N planta; (*machinery*) maquinaria; (*factory*) usina, fábrica ▶ VT plantar; (*field*) semear; (*bomb*) colocar, pôr

plaster ['plɑ:stə'] N (*for walls*) reboco; (*also: ~ of Paris*) gesso; (BRIT: *also:* **sticking ~**) esparadrapo, band-aid m ▶ VT rebocar; (*cover*): **to ~ with** encher or cobrir de

plastic ['plæstɪk] N plástico ▶ ADJ de plástico; **plastic bag** N sacola de plástico; **plastic surgery** N cirurgia plástica

plate [pleɪt] N prato; (*on door, Phot, dental*) chapa; (*in book*) gravura; **gold/silver ~** placa de ouro/prata

plateau ['plætəu] (*pl* **plateaus** *or* **plateaux**) N planalto

platform ['plætfɔ:m] N (*Rail*) plataforma (BR), cais m (PT); (*at meeting*) tribuna; (*raised structure: for landing etc*) plataforma; (BRIT: *of bus*) plataforma; (*Pol*) programa m partidário

platinum ['plætɪnəm] N platina

plausible ['plɔ:zɪbl] ADJ plausível; (*person*) convincente

play [pleɪ] N (*Theatre*) obra, peça ▶ VT jogar; (*team, opponent*) jogar contra; (*instrument, music, record*) tocar ▶ VI (*music*) tocar; (*frolic*) brincar; **to ~ safe** não se arriscar, não correr riscos; **play down** VT minimizar; **play up** VI (*person*) dar trabalho; (*TV, car*) estar com defeito; **player** N jogador(a) m/f;

(*Theatre*) ator/atriz m/f; (*Mus*) músico(-a); **playful** ADJ brincalhão(-lhona); **playground** N (*in park*) playground m; (*in school*) pátio de recreio; **playgroup** N espécie de jardim de infância; **playing card** N carta de baralho; **playing field** N campo de esportes (BR) or jogos (PT); **playtime** N (*Sch*) recreio; **playwright** N dramaturgo(-a)

plea [pli:] N (*request*) apelo, petição f; (*Jur*) defesa

plead [pli:d] VT (*Jur*) defender, advogar; (*give as excuse*) alegar ▶ VI (*Jur*) declarar-se; (*beg*): **to ~ with sb** suplicar or rogar a alguém

pleasant ['plɛznt] ADJ agradável; (*person*) simpático

please [pli:z] EXCL por favor ▶ VT agradar a, dar prazer a ▶ VI agradar, dar prazer; (*think fit*): **do as you ~** faça o que or como quiser; **~ yourself!** (*inf*) como você quiser!, você que sabe!; **pleased** ADJ: **pleased (with)** satisfeito (com); **pleased to meet you** prazer (em conhecê-lo)

pleasure ['plɛʒə'] N prazer m; **"it's a ~"** "não tem de quê"

pleat [pli:t] N prega

pledge [plɛdʒ] N (*promise*) promessa ▶ VT prometer; **to ~ support for sb** empenhar-se a apoiar alguém

plentiful ['plɛntɪful] ADJ abundante

plenty ['plɛntɪ] N: **~ of** (*food, money*) bastante; (*jobs, people*) muitos(-as)

pliers ['plaɪəz] NPL alicate m

plod [plɔd] VI caminhar pesadamente; (*fig*) trabalhar laboriosamente

plonk [plɔŋk] (*inf*) N (BRIT: *wine*) zurrapa ▶ VT: **to ~ sth down** deixar cair algo (pesadamente)

plot [plɔt] N (*scheme*) conspiração f, complô m; (*of story, play*) enredo, trama; (*of land*) lote m ▶ VT (*conspire*) tramar, planejar (BR), planear (PT); (*Aviat, Naut, Math*) plotar ▶ VI conspirar; **a vegetable ~** (BRIT) uma horta

plough [plau], (US) **plow** N arado ▶ VT arar; **to ~ money into** investir dinheiro em; **plough through** VT FUS abrir caminho por; **ploughman's lunch** (BRIT) N lanche de pão, queijo e picles

ploy [plɔɪ] N estratagema m

pls ABBR (= *please*) por favor

pluck [plʌk] VT (*fruit*) colher; (*musical instrument*) dedilhar; (*bird*) depenar ▶ N coragem f, puxão m; **to ~ one's eyebrows** fazer as sobrancelhas; **to ~ up courage** criar coragem

plug [plʌg] N (Elec) tomada (BR), ficha (PT); (in sink) tampa; (Aut: also: **spark(ing) ~**) vela (de ignição) ▶ VT (hole) tapar; (inf: advertise) fazer propaganda de; **plug in** VT (Elec) ligar; **plug-in** N (Comput) plug-in m

plum [plʌm] N (fruit) ameixa ▶ CPD (inf): **a ~ job** um emprego joia

plumber ['plʌmə'] N bombeiro(-a) (BR), encanador(a) m/f (BR), canalizador(a) m/f (PT)

plumbing ['plʌmɪŋ] N (trade) ofício de encanador; (piping) encanamento

plummet ['plʌmɪt] VI: **to ~ (down)** (bird, aircraft) cair rapidamente; (price) baixar rapidamente

plump [plʌmp] ADJ roliço, rechonchudo ▶ VI: **to ~ for** (inf: choose) escolher, optar por; **plump up** VT (cushion) afofar

plunge [plʌndʒ] N (dive) salto; (fig) queda ▶ VT (hand, knife) enfiar, meter ▶ VI (fall, fig) cair; (dive) mergulhar; **to take the ~** topar a parada

plural ['pluərl] ADJ plural ▶ N plural m

plus [plʌs] N (also: **~ sign**) sinal m de adição ▶ PREP mais; **ten/twenty ~** dez/vinte e tantos; **plus-one** ['plʌs'wʌn] (inf) N acompanhante m/f

ply [plaɪ] N (of wool) fio ▶ VT (a trade) exercer ▶ VI (ship) ir e vir; **to ~ sb with drink/questions** bombardear alguém com bebidas/perguntas; **plywood** N madeira compensada

p.m. ADV ABBR (= post meridiem) da tarde, da noite

PMT N ABBR (= premenstrual tension) TPM f, tensão f pré-menstrual

pneumatic drill [nju:mætɪk drɪl] N perfuratriz f

poach [pəutʃ] VT (cook: fish) escaldar; (: eggs) fazer pochê (BR), escalfar (PT); (steal) furtar ▶ VI caçar (or pescar) em propriedade alheia

pocket ['pɔkɪt] N bolso; (fig: small area) pedaço ▶ VT meter no bolso; (steal) embolsar; **to be out of ~** (BRIT) ter prejuízo; **pocketbook** (US) N carteira; **pocket money** N dinheiro para despesas miúdas; (for child) mesada

pod [pɔd] N vagem f

podcast ['pɔdkɑːst] N podcast m; **podcasting** N podcasting m

podiatrist [pɔ'diːətrɪst] (US) N pedicuro(-a)

poem ['pəuɪm] N poema m

poet ['pəuɪt] N poeta/poetisa m/f; **poetic** [pəu'ɛtɪk] ADJ poético; **poetry** ['pəuɪtrɪ] N poesia

point [pɔɪnt] N ponto; (of needle, knife etc) ponta; (purpose) finalidade f; (significant part) ponto principal; (position, place) lugar m, posição f; (moment) momento; (stage) estágio; (Elec: also: **power ~**) tomada; (also: **decimal ~**): **2 ~ 3 (2.3)** dois vírgula três ▶ VT mostrar; (gun etc): **to ~ sth at sb** apontar algo para alguém ▶ VI apontar; **points** NPL (Aut) platinado, contato; (Rail) agulhas fpl; **to ~ at** apontar para; **to be on the ~ of doing sth** estar prestes a or a ponto de fazer algo; **to make a ~ of** fazer questão de, insistir em; **to get the ~** perceber; **to miss the ~** compreender mal; **to come to the ~** ir ao assunto; **there's no ~ (in doing)** não há razão (para fazer); **~ of view** ponto de vista; **point out** VT (in debate etc) ressaltar; **point to** VT FUS (fig) indicar; **point-blank** ADV categoricamente; (also: **at point-blank range**) à queima-roupa; **pointed** ADJ (stick etc) pontudo; (remark) mordaz; **pointer** N (on chart) indicador m; (on machine) ponteiro; (fig) dica; **pointless** ADJ (useless) inútil; (senseless) sem sentido

poison ['pɔɪzn] N veneno ▶ VT envenenar; **poisonous** ADJ venenoso; (fumes etc) tóxico

poke [pəuk] VT cutucar; (put): **to ~ sth in(to)** enfiar or meter algo em; **poke about** VI escarafunchar, espionar

poker ['pəukə'] N atiçador m (de brasas); (Cards) pôquer m

Poland ['pəulənd] N Polônia

polar ['pəulə'] ADJ polar; **polar bear** N urso polar

Pole [pəul] N polonês(-esa) m/f

pole [pəul] N vara; (Geo) polo; (telegraph pole) poste m; (flagpole) mastro; **pole bean** (US) N feijão-trepador m; **pole vault** N salto com vara

police [pə'liːs] N polícia ▶ VT policiar; **police car** N rádio-patrulha f; **policeman** irreg N policial m (BR), polícia m (PT); **police officer** N policial m/f (BR), polícia m/f (PT); **police station** N delegacia (de polícia) (BR), esquadra (PT); **policewoman** irreg N policial f (feminina) (BR), mulher f polícia (PT)

policy ['pɔlɪsɪ] N política; (also: **insurance ~**) apólice f

polio ['pəulɪəu] N polio(mielite) f

Polish ['pəulɪʃ] ADJ polonês(-esa) ▶ N (Ling) polonês m

polish ['pɔlɪʃ] N (for shoes) graxa; (for floor) cera (para encerar); (shine) brilho; (fig) refinamento, requinte m ▶ VT (shoes) engraxar; (*make shiny*) lustrar, dar brilho a; **polish off** VT (*work*) dar os arremates a; (*food*) raspar

polite [pəˈlaɪt] ADJ educado; **politeness** N gentileza, cortesia

political [pəˈlɪtɪkl] ADJ político

politician [pɔlɪˈtɪʃən] N político(-a)

politics [ˈpɔlɪtɪks] N, NPL política

poll [pəul] N (*votes*) votação f; (*also*: **opinion ~**) pesquisa, sondagem f ▶ VT (*votes*) receber, obter

pollen [ˈpɔlən] N pólen m

pollute [pəˈluːt] VT poluir; **pollution** N poluição f

polyester [pɔlɪˈɛstəʳ] N poliéster m

polystyrene [pɔlɪˈstaɪriːn] N isopor® m

polythene [ˈpɔliθiːn] N politeno

pomegranate [ˈpɔmɪɡrænɪt] N romã f

pond [pɔnd] N (*natural*) lago pequeno; (*artificial*) tanque m

ponder [ˈpɔndəʳ] VT, VI ponderar, meditar (sobre)

pony [ˈpəunɪ] N pônei m; **ponytail** N rabo-de-cavalo; **pony trekking** (BRIT) N excursão f em pônei

poodle [ˈpuːdl] N cão-d'água m

pool [puːl] N (*puddle*) poça, charco; (*pond*) lago; (*also*: **swimming ~**) piscina; (*fig: of light*) feixe m; (: *of liquid*) poça; (*Sport*) sinuca ▶ VT juntar; **pools** NPL (*football pools*) loteria esportiva (BR), totobola (PT); **typing** (BRIT) or **secretary** (US) **~** seção f de datilografia

poor [puəʳ] ADJ pobre; (*bad*) inferior, mau ▶ NPL: **the ~** os pobres; **~ in** (*resources etc*) deficiente em; **poorly** ADJ adoentado, indisposto ▶ ADV mal

pop [pɔp] N (*sound*) estalo, estouro; (*Mus*) pop m; (US inf: *father*) papai m; (*inf: fizzy drink*) bebida gasosa ▶ VT: **to ~ sth into/ onto** etc (*put*) pôr algo em/sobre etc ▶ VI estourar; (*cork*) saltar; **pop in** VI dar um pulo; **pop out** VI dar uma saída; **pop up** VI surgir, aparecer inesperadamente; **popcorn** N pipoca

pope [pəup] N papa m

poplar [ˈpɔpləʳ] N álamo, choupo

poppy [ˈpɔpɪ] N papoula

popular [ˈpɔpjuləʳ] ADJ popular; (*person*) querido

population [pɔpjuˈleɪʃən] N população f

porcelain [ˈpɔːslɪn] N porcelana

porch [pɔːtʃ] N pórtico; (US: *verandah*) varanda

pore [pɔːʳ] N poro ▶ VI: **to ~ over** examinar minuciosamente

pork [pɔːk] N carne f de porco

pornography [pɔːˈnɔɡrəfɪ] N pornografia

porridge [ˈpɔrɪdʒ] N mingau m (de aveia)

port [pɔːt] N (*harbour*) porto; (*Naut: left side*) bombordo; (*wine*) vinho do Porto; **~ of call** porto de escala

portable [ˈpɔːtəbl] ADJ portátil

porter [ˈpɔːtəʳ] N (*for luggage*) carregador m; (*doorkeeper*) porteiro

portfolio [pɔːtˈfəuliəu] N (*case*) pasta; (*Pol*) pasta ministerial; (*Finance*) carteira de ações ou títulos; (*of artist*) pasta, portfólio

portion [ˈpɔːʃən] N porção f, quinhão m; (*of food*) ração f

portrait [ˈpɔːtreɪt] N retrato

portray [pɔːˈtreɪ] VT retratar; (*act*) interpretar

Portugal [ˈpɔːtjugl] N Portugal m (*no article*)

Portuguese [pɔːtjuˈɡiːz] ADJ português(-esa) ▶ N INV português(-esa) m/f; (*Ling*) português m

pose [pəuz] N postura, pose f ▶ VI (*pretend*): **to ~ as** fazer-se passar por ▶ VT (*question*) fazer; (*problem*) causar; **to ~ for** (*painting*) posar para

posh [pɔʃ] (*inf*) ADJ fino, chique; (*upper-class*) de classe alta

position [pəˈzɪʃən] N posição f; (*job*) cargo; (*situation*) situação f ▶ VT colocar, situar

positive [ˈpɔzɪtɪv] ADJ positivo; (*certain*) certo; (*definite*) definitivo

possess [pəˈzɛs] VT possuir; **possession** N posse f, possessão f; **possessions** NPL (*belongings*) pertences mpl; **to take possession of sth** tomar posse de algo

possibility [pɔsɪˈbɪlɪtɪ] N possibilidade f; (*of sth happening*) probabilidade f

possible [ˈpɔsɪbl] ADJ possível; **possibly** ADV pode ser, talvez; (*surprise*): **what could they possibly want with me?** o que eles podem querer comigo?; (*emphasizing effort*): **they did everything they possibly could** eles fizeram tudo o que podiam; **I cannot possibly go** não posso ir de jeito nenhum

post [pəust] N (BRIT: *mail*) correio; (*job*) cargo, posto; (*pole*) poste m; (*on internet*) post m; (*Mil*) nomeação f ▶ VT (BRIT: *send by post*) pôr no correio; (*on internet*) postar; (BRIT: *appoint*): **to ~ to** destinar a; **postage** N porte m, franquia; **postal order** N vale m postal; **postbox** (BRIT) N caixa de correio; **postcard** N cartão m postal; **postcode** (BRIT) N código postal, ≈ CEP m (BR)

poster [ˈpəustəʳ] N cartaz m; (*as decoration*) pôster m

postman ['pəustmən] *irreg* N carteiro

postmark ['pəustmɑːk] N carimbo do correio

post office N (*building*) agência do correio, correio; (*organization*) ≈ Empresa Nacional dos Correios e Telégrafos (BR), ≈ Correios, Telégrafos e Telefones (PT)

postpone [pəs'pəun] VT adiar

posture ['pɒstʃəʳ] N postura; (*fig*) atitude *f*

pot [pɒt] N (*for cooking*) panela; (*for flowers*) vaso; (*container*) pote *m*; (*teapot*) bule *m*; (*inf: marijuana*) maconha ▶ VT (*plant*) plantar em vaso; **to go to ~** (*inf*) arruinar-se, degringolar

potato [pə'teɪtəu] (*pl* **potatoes**) N batata; **potato peeler** N descascador *m* de batatas

potent ['pəutnt] ADJ poderoso; (*drink*) forte; (*man*) potente

potential [pə'tɛnʃl] ADJ potencial ▶ N potencial *m*

pothole ['pɒthəul] N (*in road*) buraco; (BRIT: *underground*) caldeirão *m*, cova

potter ['pɒtəʳ] N (*artistic*) ceramista *m/f*; (*artisan*) oleiro(-a) ▶ VI (BRIT): **to ~ around, ~ about** ocupar-se com pequenos trabalhos; **pottery** N cerâmica; (*factory*) olaria

potty ['pɒti] ADJ (*inf: mad*) maluco, doido ▶ N penico

pouch [pautʃ] N (*Zool*) bolsa; (*for tobacco*) tabaqueira

poultry ['pəultri] N aves *fpl* domésticas; (*meat*) carne *f* de aves domésticas

pounce [pauns] VI: **to ~ on** lançar-se sobre; (*person*) agarrar em; (*fig: mistake etc*) apontar

pound [paund] N libra (*weight = 453g, 16 ounces; money = 100 pence*) ▶ VT (*beat*) socar, esmurrar; (*crush*) triturar ▶ VI (*heart*) bater

pour [pɔːʳ] VT despejar; (*drink*) servir ▶ VI correr, jorrar; **pour away** VT esvaziar, decantar; **pour in** VI (*people*) entrar numa enxurrada; (*information*) chegar numa enxurrada; **pour off** VT esvaziar, decantar; **pour out** VI (*people*) sair aos borbotões ▶ VT (*drink*) servir; (*fig*) extravasar; **pouring** ['pɔːrɪŋ] ADJ: **pouring rain** chuva torrencial

pout [paut] VI fazer beicinho or biquinho

poverty ['pɒvəti] N pobreza, miséria

powder ['paudəʳ] N pó *m*; (*face powder*) pó-de-arroz *m* ▶ VT (*face*) empoar, passar pó em; **powdered milk** N leite *m* em pó

power ['pauəʳ] N poder *m*; (*of explosion, engine*) força, potência; (*ability, Pol*) poder; (*electricity*) força; **to be in ~** estar no poder; **power cut** (BRIT) N corte *m* de energia, blecaute *m* (BR); **powerful** ADJ poderoso; (*engine*) potente; (*body*) vigoroso; (*blow*) violento; (*argument*) convincente; (*emotion*) intenso; **powerless** ADJ impotente; **power point** (BRIT) N tomada; **power station** N central *f* elétrica

PR N ABBR = **public relations**

practical ['præktɪkl] ADJ prático; **practical joke** N brincadeira, peça

practice ['præktɪs] N (*habit, Rel*) costume *m*, hábito; (*exercise*) prática; (*of profession*) exercício; (*training*) treinamento; (*Med*) consultório; (*Jur*) escritório ▶ VT, VI (US) = **practise**; **in ~** na prática; **out of ~** destreinado

practise ['præktɪs], (US) **practice** VT praticar; (*profession*) exercer; (*sport*) treinar ▶ VI (*doctor*) ter consultório; (*lawyer*) ter escritório; (*train*) treinar, praticar

practitioner [præk'tɪʃənəʳ] N (*Med*) médico(-a)

prairie ['prɛəri] N campina, pradaria

praise [preɪz] N louvor *m*; (*admiration*) elogio ▶ VT elogiar, louvar

pram [præm] (BRIT) N carrinho de bebê

prank [præŋk] N travessura, peça

prawn [prɔːn] N pitu *m*; (*small*) camarão *m*

pray [preɪ] VI: **to ~ for/that** rezar por/para que; **prayer** [prɛəʳ] N (*activity*) reza; (*words*) oração *f*, prece *f*

preach [priːtʃ] VT pregar ▶ VI pregar; (*pej*) catequizar

precede [prɪ'siːd] VT preceder

precedent ['prɛsɪdənt] N precedente *m*

preceding [prɪ'siːdɪŋ] ADJ anterior

precinct ['priːsɪŋkt] N (US: *district*) distrito policial; **precincts** NPL (*of large building*) arredores *mpl*; **pedestrian ~** (BRIT) zona para pedestres (BR) *or* peões (PT); **shopping ~** (BRIT) zona comercial

precious ['prɛʃəs] ADJ precioso

precise [prɪ'saɪs] ADJ exato, preciso; (*plans*) detalhado

predecessor ['priːdɪsɛsəʳ] N predecessor(a) *m/f*, antepassado(-a)

predicament [prɪ'dɪkəmənt] N situação *f* difícil, apuro

predict [prɪ'dɪkt] VT prever, predizer, prognosticar; **predictable** ADJ previsível

predominantly [prɪ'dɔmɪnəntlɪ] ADV predominantemente; na maioria

preface ['prɛfəs] N prefácio

prefect ['priːfɛkt] N (BRIT *Sch*) monitor(a) *m/f*, tutor(a) *m/f*; (*in Brazil*) prefeito(-a)

prefer [prɪ'fəːʳ] vt preferir; **preferably** ['prɛfrəblɪ] adv de preferência

prefix ['priːfɪks] n prefixo

pregnancy ['prɛgnənsɪ] n gravidez f; (animal) prenhez f

pregnant ['prɛgnənt] adj grávida; (animal) prenha

prehistoric [priːhɪs'tɔrɪk] adj pré-histórico

prejudice ['prɛdʒudɪs] n preconceito; **prejudiced** adj (person) preconceituoso

premature ['prɛmətʃuəʳ] adj prematuro

première ['prɛmɪɛəʳ] n estreia

premium ['priːmɪəm] n prêmio; **to be at a ~** ser caro

premonition [prɛmə'nɪʃən] n presságio, pressentimento

preoccupied [priː'ɔkjupaɪd] adj (worried) preocupado

prepaid [priː'peɪd] adj com porte pago

preparation [prɛpə'reɪʃən] n preparação f; **preparations** npl (arrangements) preparativos mpl

prepare [prɪ'pɛəʳ] vt preparar ▶ vi: **to ~ for** preparar-se or aprontar-se para; **~d to** disposto a; **~d for** pronto para

preposition [prɛpə'zɪʃən] n preposição f

prerequisite [priː'rɛkwɪzɪt] n pré-requisito, condição f prévia

prescribe [prɪ'skraɪb] vt prescrever; (Med) receitar

prescription [prɪ'skrɪpʃən] n receita

presence ['prɛzns] n presença; (spirit) espectro

present [adj, n 'prɛznt, vt prɪ'zɛnt] adj presente; (current) atual ▶ n presente m; (actuality): **the ~** o presente ▶ vt (give) entregar algo a alguém; (describe) descrever; **at ~** no momento, agora; **to give sb a ~** presentear alguém; **presentation** [prɛzn'teɪʃən] n apresentação f; (ceremony) entrega; (of plan etc) exposição f; **present-day** adj atual, de hoje; **presenter** n apresentador(a) m/f; **presently** adv (soon after) logo depois; (soon) logo, em breve; (now) atualmente

preservative [prɪ'zəːvətɪv] n conservante m

preserve [prɪ'zəːv] vt (situation) conservar, manter; (building, manuscript) preservar; (food) pôr em conserva ▶ n (often pl: jam) geleia; (: fruit) compota, conserva

president ['prɛzɪdənt] n presidente(-a) m/f; **presidential** [prɛzɪ'dɛnʃl] adj presidencial

press [prɛs] n (printer's) imprensa, prelo; (newspapers) imprensa; (of switch) pressão f ▶ vt apertar; (clothes: iron) passar; (put pressure on: person) pressionar; (insist): **to ~ sth on sb** insistir para que alguém aceite algo ▶ vi (squeeze) apertar; (pressurize): **to ~ for** pressionar por; **we are ~ed for time/ money** estamos com pouco tempo/dinheiro; **press on** vi continuar; **pressing** adj urgente; **press stud** (brit) n botão m de pressão; **press-up** (brit) n flexão f

pressure ['prɛʃəʳ] n pressão f; **to put ~ on sb (to do sth)** pressionar alguém (a fazer algo); **pressure cooker** n panela de pressão

prestige [prɛs'tiːʒ] n prestígio

presume [prɪ'zjuːm] vt supor

pretence [prɪ'tɛns], (us) **pretense** n pretensão f; **under false ~s** por meios fraudulentos

pretend [prɪ'tɛnd] vt, vi fingir

pretense [prɪ'tɛns] (us) n = **pretence**

pretty ['prɪtɪ] adj bonito ▶ adv (quite) bastante

prevail [prɪ'veɪl] vi triunfar; (be current) imperar

prevalent ['prɛvələnt] adj (common) predominante

prevent [prɪ'vɛnt] vt impedir

preview ['priːvjuː] n pré-estreia

previous ['priːvɪəs] adj (earlier) anterior; **previously** adv (before) previamente; (in the past) anteriormente

prey [preɪ] n presa ▶ vi: **to ~ on** (feed on) alimentar-se de; **it was ~ing on his mind** preocupava-o, atormentava-o

price [praɪs] n preço ▶ vt fixar o preço de; **priceless** adj inestimável; (inf: amusing) impagável

prick [prɪk] n picada ▶ vt picar; (make hole in) furar; **to ~ up one's ears** aguçar os ouvidos

pride [praɪd] n orgulho; (pej) soberba ▶ vt: **to ~ o.s. on** orgulhar-se de

priest [priːst] n (Christian) padre m; (non-Christian) sacerdote m

primarily ['praɪmərɪlɪ] adv principalmente

primary ['praɪmərɪ] adj primário; (first in importance) principal ▶ n (us: election) eleição f primária; **primary school** (brit) n escola primária

> As **primary schools** da Grã-Bretanha acolhem crianças de 5 a 11 anos. Assinalam o início do ciclo escolar obrigatório e são compostas de duas partes: a pré-escola (infant school) e o primário (junior school).

prime [praɪm] ADJ primeiro, principal; (*excellent*) de primeira ▶ VT (*wood*) imprimir; (*fig*) preparar ▶ N: **in the ~ of life** na primavera da vida; **~ example** exemplo típico; **prime minister** N primeiro-ministro/primeira-ministra

primitive ['prɪmɪtɪv] ADJ primitivo; (*crude*) rudimentar

primrose ['prɪmrəuz] N prímula, primavera

prince [prɪns] N príncipe *m*

princess [prɪn'sɛs] N princesa

principal ['prɪnsɪpl] ADJ principal ▶ N (*of school, college*) diretor(a) *m/f*

principle ['prɪnsɪpl] N princípio; **in ~** em princípio; **on ~** por princípio

print [prɪnt] N (*letters*) letra de forma; (*fabric*) estampado; (*Art*) estampa, gravura; (*Phot*) cópia; (*footprint*) pegada; (*fingerprint*) impressão *f* digital ▶ VT imprimir; (*write in capitals*) escrever em letra de imprensa; **out of ~** esgotado; **printer** N (*person*) impressor(a) *m/f*; (*firm*) gráfica; (*machine*) impressora; **printout** N (*Comput*) cópia impressa

prior ['praɪər] ADJ anterior, prévio; (*more important*) prioritário; **~ to doing** antes de fazer

priority [praɪ'ɔrɪtɪ] N prioridade *f*

prison ['prɪzn] N prisão *f* ▶ CPD carcerário; **prisoner** N (*in prison*) preso(-a), presidiário(-a); (*under arrest*) detido(-a)

privacy ['prɪvəsɪ] N isolamento, solidão *f*

private ['praɪvɪt] ADJ privado; (*personal*) particular; (*confidential*) confidencial, reservado; (*personal: belongings*) pessoal; (*: thoughts, plans*) secreto, íntimo; (*place*) isolado; (*quiet: person*) reservado; (*intimate*) íntimo ▶ N soldado raso; **"~"** (*on envelope*) "confidencial"; (*on door*) "privativo"; **in ~** em particular; **privatize** VT privatizar

privilege ['prɪvɪlɪdʒ] N privilégio

prize [praɪz] N prêmio ▶ ADJ de primeira classe ▶ VT valorizar; **prizewinner** N premiado(-a)

pro [prəu] N (*Sport*) profissional *m/f* ▶ PREP a favor de; **the ~s and cons** os prós e os contras

probability [prɔbə'bɪlɪtɪ] N probabilidade *f*

probable ['prɔbəbl] ADJ provável; (*plausible*) verossímil

probation [prə'beɪʃən] N: **on ~** (*employee*) em estágio probatório; (*Jur*) em liberdade condicional

probe [prəub] N (*Med, Space*) sonda; (*enquiry*) pesquisa ▶ VT investigar, esquadrinhar

problem ['prɔbləm] N problema *m*

procedure [prə'si:dʒər] N procedimento; (*method*) método, processo

proceed [prə'si:d] VI (*do afterwards*): **to ~ to do sth** passar a fazer algo; (*continue*): **to ~ (with)** continuar *or* prosseguir (com); (*activity, event*) continuar; (*go*) ir em direção a, dirigir-se a; **proceedings** NPL evento, acontecimento; **proceeds** ['prəusi:dz] NPL produto, proventos *mpl*

process ['prəusɛs] N processo ▶ VT processar; **procession** [prə'sɛʃən] N desfile *m*, procissão *f*; **funeral procession** cortejo fúnebre

proclaim [prə'kleɪm] VT anunciar

prod [prɔd] VT empurrar; (*with finger, stick*) cutucar ▶ N empurrão *m*; cotovelada; espetada

produce [n 'prɔdju:s, vt prə'dju:s] N (*Agr*) produtos *mpl* agrícolas ▶ VT produzir; (*cause*) provocar; (*evidence, argument*) apresentar, mostrar; (*show*) apresentar, exibir; (*Theatre*) pôr em cena *or* em cartaz; **producer** N (*Theatre*) diretor(a) *m/f*; (*Agr, Cinema, of record*) produtor(a) *m/f*; (*country*) produtor *m*

product ['prɔdʌkt] N produto

production [prə'dʌkʃən] N produção *f*; (*of electricity*) geração *f*; (*Theatre*) encenação *f*

profession [prə'fɛʃən] N profissão *f*; (*people*) classe *f*; **professional** N profissional *m/f* ▶ ADJ profissional; (*work*) de profissional

professor [prə'fɛsər] N (*BRIT*) catedrático(-a); (*US, CANADA*) professor(a) *m/f*

profile ['prəufaɪl] N perfil *m*

profit ['prɔfɪt] N (*Comm*) lucro ▶ VI: **to ~ by** *or* **from** (*benefit*) aproveitar-se de, tirar proveito de; **profitable** ADJ (*Econ*) lucrativo, rendoso

profound [prə'faund] ADJ profundo

programme ['prəugræm], (*US or* COMPUT) **program** N programa *m* ▶ VT programar; **programming**, **programing** N programação *f*

progress [n 'prəugrɛs, vi prə'grɛs] N progresso ▶ VI progredir, avançar; **in ~** em andamento; **progressive** [prə'grɛsɪv] ADJ progressivo; (*person*) progressista

prohibit [prə'hɪbɪt] VT proibir

project [n 'prɔdʒɛkt, vt, vi prə'dʒɛkt] N projeto; (*Sch: research*) pesquisa ▶ VT

projetar; (*figure*) estimar ▶vɪ (*stick out*)
ressaltar, sobressair

projection [prəˈdʒɛkʃən] N projeção f;
(*overhang*) saliência

projector [prəˈdʒɛktəʳ] N projetor m

prolong [prəˈlɒŋ] ᴠᴛ prolongar

prom [prɒm] N ABBR = **promenade,
promenade concert**; (ᴜs: *ball*) baile m
de estudantes

promenade [prɒməˈnɑːd] N (*by sea*)
passeio (à orla marítima); **promenade
concert** (ʙʀɪᴛ) N concerto (de música
clássica)

> Na Grã-Bretanha, um **promenade
> concert** (ou **prom**) é um concerto de
> música clássica, assim chamado
> porque originalmente o público não
> ficava sentado, mas de pé ou
> caminhando. Hoje em dia, uma parte
> do público permanece de pé, mas há
> também lugares sentados (mais
> caros). Os **Proms** mais conhecidos
> são os londrinos. A última sessão (*the
> Last Night of the Proms*) é um
> acontecimento carregado de emoção,
> quando são executadas árias
> tradicionais e patrióticas. Nos Estados
> Unidos e no Canadá, o **prom**, ou
> **promenade**, é um baile organizado
> pelas escolas secundárias.

prominent [ˈprɒmɪnənt] ADJ (*standing
out*) proeminente; (*important*) eminente,
notório

promise [ˈprɒmɪs] N promessa; (*hope*)
esperança ▶ᴠᴛ, ᴠɪ prometer; **promising**
ADJ promissor(a), prometedor(a)

promote [prəˈməʊt] ᴠᴛ promover;
(*product*) promover, fazer propaganda de;
promotion N promoção f

prompt [prɒmpt] ADJ pronto, rápido
▶ADV (*exactly*) em ponto, pontualmente
▶N (Comput) sinal m de orientação,
prompt m ▶ᴠᴛ (*urge*) incitar, impelir;
(*cause*) provocar, ocasionar; **to ~ sb to
do sth** induzir alguém a fazer algo;
promptly ADV imediatamente; (*exactly*)
pontualmente

prone [prəʊn] ADJ (*lying*) de bruços; **~ to**
propenso a, predisposto a

pronoun [ˈprəʊnaʊn] N pronome m

pronounce [prəˈnaʊns] ᴠᴛ pronunciar;
(*verdict, opinion*) declarar

pronunciation [prənʌnsɪˈeɪʃən] N
pronúncia

proof [pruːf] N prova ▶ADJ: **~ against** à
prova de

prop [prɒp] N suporte m, escora; (*fig*)
amparo, apoio ▶ᴠᴛ (*also*: **~ up**) apoiar,

escorar; (*lean*): **to ~ sth against** apoiar
algo contra

propaganda [prɒpəˈgændə] N
propaganda

proper [ˈprɒpəʳ] ADJ (*correct*) correto;
(*socially acceptable*) respeitável, digno;
(*authentic*) genuíno, autêntico; (*referring
to place*): **the village ~** a cidadezinha
propriamente dita; **properly** ADV (*eat,
study*) bem; (*behave*) decentemente

property [ˈprɒpətɪ] N propriedade f;
(*goods*) posses fpl, bens mpl; (*buildings*)
imóveis mpl

prophet [ˈprɒfɪt] N profeta m/f

proportion [prəˈpɔːʃən] N proporção f;
proportional ADJ proporcional

proposal [prəˈpəʊzl] N proposta; (*of
marriage*) pedido

propose [prəˈpəʊz] ᴠᴛ propor; (*toast*)
erguer ▶ᴠɪ propor casamento; **to ~ to
do** propor-se fazer

proposition [prɒpəˈzɪʃən] N proposta,
proposição f; (*offer*) oferta

proprietor [prəˈpraɪətəʳ] N
proprietário(-a), dono(-a)

prose [prəʊz] N prosa

prosecute [ˈprɒsɪkjuːt] ᴠᴛ processar;
prosecution [prɒsɪˈkjuːʃən] N acusação
f; (*accusing side*) autor m da demanda

prospect [n ˈprɒspɛkt, vt, vi prəˈspɛkt] N
(*chance*) probabilidade f; (*outlook,
potential*) perspectiva ▶ᴠɪ: **to ~ (for)**
prospectar (por); **prospects** NPL (*for
work etc*) perspectivas fpl

prospectus [prəˈspɛktəs] N prospecto,
programa m

prostitute [ˈprɒstɪtjuːt] N prostituta;
male ~ prostituto

protect [prəˈtɛkt] ᴠᴛ proteger;
protection N proteção f; **protective** ADJ
protetor(a)

protein [ˈprəʊtiːn] N proteína

protest [n ˈprəʊtɛst, vi, vt prəˈtɛst] N
protesto ▶ᴠɪ protestar ▶ᴠᴛ insistir

Protestant [ˈprɒtɪstənt] ADJ, N
protestante m/f

protester [prəˈtɛstəʳ] N manifestante m/f

proud [praʊd] ADJ orgulhoso; (*pej*)
vaidoso, soberbo

prove [pruːv] ᴠᴛ comprovar ▶ᴠɪ: **to ~
(to be) correct** *etc* vir a ser correto *etc*;
to ~ o.s. mostrar seu valor

proverb [ˈprɒvəːb] N provérbio

provide [prəˈvaɪd] ᴠᴛ fornecer,
proporcionar; **to ~ sb with sth** fornecer
alguém de algo, fornecer algo a alguém;
provide for ᴠᴛ FUS (*person*) prover à
subsistência de

providing [prə'vaɪdɪŋ] CONJ: **~ (that)** contanto que (+ sub)

province ['prɒvɪns] N província; (fig) esfera; **provincial** [prə'vɪnʃəl] ADJ provincial; (pej) provinciano

provision [prə'vɪʒən] N (supplying) abastecimento; (in contract) cláusula, condição f; **provisions** NPL (food) mantimentos mpl; **provisional** ADJ provisório, interino; (agreement, licence) provisório

provocative [prə'vɒkətɪv] ADJ provocante; (sexually) excitante

provoke [prə'vəuk] VT provocar; (cause) causar

prowl [praul] VI (also: **~ about**, **~ around**) rondar, andar à espreita ▶ N: **on the ~** de ronda, rondando

proxy ['prɒksɪ] N: **by ~** por procuração

prudent ['pru:dənt] ADJ prudente

prune [pru:n] N ameixa seca ▶ VT podar

pry [praɪ] VI: **to ~ (into)** intrometer-se (em)

PS N ABBR (= postscript) PS m

pseudonym ['sju:dənɪm] N pseudônimo

psychiatrist [saɪ'kaɪətrɪst] N psiquiatra m/f

psychic ['saɪkɪk] ADJ psíquico; (also: **~al**: person) sensível a forças psíquicas

psychologist [saɪ'kɒlədʒɪst] N psicólogo(-a)

psychology [saɪ'kɒlədʒɪ] N psicologia

PTO ABBR (= please turn over) v.v., vire

pub [pʌb] N ABBR (= public house) pub m, bar m, botequim m

> Um **pub** geralmente consiste em duas salas: uma (the lounge) é bastante confortável, com poltronas e bancos estofados, enquanto a outra ("the public bar") é simplesmente um bar onde a consumação é em geral mais barata. O ("the public bar") é muitas vezes também um salão de jogos, dos quais os mais comuns são os dardos, dominó e bilhar. Atualmente muitos pubs servem refeições, sobretudo na hora do almoço, e essa é a única hora em que a entrada de crianças é permitida, desde que estejam acompanhadas por adultos. Em geral os pubs funcionam das 11 às 23 horas, mas isso pode variar de acordo com sua permissão de funcionamento; alguns pubs fecham à tarde.

public ['pʌblɪk] ADJ público ▶ N público; **in ~** em público; **to make ~** tornar público; **public convenience** (BRIT) N

banheiro público; **public holiday** N feriado; **public house** (BRIT) N pub m, bar m, taberna

publicity [pʌb'lɪsɪtɪ] N publicidade f

publicize ['pʌblɪsaɪz] VT divulgar

public: public relations N relações fpl públicas; **public school** (BRIT) escola particular; (US) escola pública; **public transport**, (US) **public transportation** N transporte m coletivo

publish ['pʌblɪʃ] VT publicar; **publisher** N editor(a) m/f; (company) editora; **publishing** N a indústria editorial

pudding ['pudɪŋ] N (BRIT: dessert) sobremesa; (cake) pudim m, doce m; **black** (BRIT) or **blood** (US) **~** morcela

puddle ['pʌdl] N poça

puff [pʌf] N sopro; (of cigarette) baforada; (of air, smoke) lufada ▶ VT: **to ~ one's pipe** tirar baforadas do cachimbo ▶ VI (pant) arquejar; **puff out** VT (cheeks) encher; **puff pastry**, (US) **puff paste** N massa folhada

pull [pul] N (tug): **to give sth a ~** dar um puxão em algo ▶ VT puxar; (trigger) apertar; (curtain, blind) fechar ▶ VI puxar, dar um puxão; **to ~ to pieces** picar em pedacinhos; **to ~ one's punches** não usar toda a força; **to ~ one's weight** fazer a sua parte; **to ~ o.s. together** recompor-se; **to ~ sb's leg** (fig) brincar com alguém, sacanear alguém (inf); **pull apart** VT (break) romper; **pull down** VT (building) demolir, derrubar; **pull in** VI (Aut: at the kerb) encostar; (Rail) chegar (na plataforma); **pull off** VT tirar; (fig: deal etc) acertar; **pull out** VI (Aut: from kerb) sair; (Rail) partir ▶ VT tirar, arrancar; **pull over** VI (Aut) encostar; **pull through** VI (Med) sobreviver; **pull up** VI (stop) deter-se, parar ▶ VT levantar; (uproot) desarraigar, arrancar

pulley ['pulɪ] N roldana

pullover ['puləuvəʳ] N pulôver m

pulp [pʌlp] N (of fruit) polpa

pulse [pʌls] N (Anat) pulso; (of music, engine) cadência; (Bot) legume m

pump [pʌmp] N bomba; (shoe) sapatilha (de dança) ▶ VT bombear; **pump up** VT encher

pumpkin ['pʌmpkɪn] N abóbora

pun [pʌn] N jogo de palavras, trocadilho

punch [pʌntʃ] N (blow) soco, murro; (tool) punção m; (drink) ponche m ▶ VT (hit): **to ~ sb/sth** esmurrar or socar alguém/algo

punctual ['pʌŋktjuəl] ADJ pontual

punish ['pʌnɪʃ] vt punir, castigar; **punishment** N castigo, punição f

punk [pʌŋk] N (also: ~ **rocker**) punk m/f; (also: ~ **rock**) punk m; (us inf: hoodlum) pinta-brava m

pupil ['pjuːpl] N aluno(-a); (of eye) pupila

puppet ['pʌpɪt] N marionete f, títere m; (fig) fantoche m

puppy ['pʌpɪ] N cachorrinho (BR), cachorro (PT)

purchase ['pəːtʃɪs] N compra ▶ vt comprar

pure [pjuər] ADJ puro

purple ['pəːpl] ADJ roxo, purpúreo

purpose ['pəːpəs] N propósito, objetivo; **on** ~ de propósito

purse [pəːs] N (BRIT) carteira; (US) bolsa ▶ vt enrugar, franzir

pursue [pəˈsjuː] vt perseguir; (fig: activity) exercer; (: interest, plan) dedicar-se a; (: result) lutar por

pursuit [pəˈsjuːt] N perseguição f; (fig) busca

push [puʃ] N empurrão m; (of button) aperto ▶ vt empurrar; (button) apertar; (promote) promover ▶ vi empurrar; (press) apertar; (fig): **to** ~ **for** reivindicar; **push aside** vt afastar com a mão; **push off** (inf) vi dar o fora; **push on** vi prosseguir; **push through** vi abrir caminho ▶ vt (measure) forçar a aceitação de; **push up** vt forçar a alta de; **pushchair** (BRIT) N carrinho; **pusher** N (also: **drug pusher**) traficante m/f; **push-up** (US) N flexão f

put [put] (pt, pp **put**) vt pôr, colocar; (put into) meter; (person: in institution etc) internar; (say) dizer, expressar; (case) expor; (question) fazer; (estimate) avaliar, calcular; (write, type etc) colocar; **put about** vt (rumour) espalhar; **put across** vt (ideas) comunicar; **put away** vt guardar; **put back** vt (replace) repor; (postpone) adiar; (delay) atrasar; **put by** vt (money etc) poupar, pôr de lado; **put down** vt pôr em; (animal) sacrificar; (in writing) anotar, inscrever; (revolt etc) sufocar; (attribute): **to** ~ **sth down to** atribuir algo a; **put forward** vt apresentar, propor; **put in** vt (application, complaint) apresentar; (time, effort) investir, gastar; **put off** vt adiar, protelar; (discourage) desanimar; **put on** vt (clothes, make-up, dinner) pôr; (light) acender; (play) encenar; (weight) ganhar; (brake) aplicar; (record, video, kettle) ligar; (accent, manner) assumir; **put out** vt (take out) colocar fora; (fire, cigarette,

light) apagar; (one's hand) estender; (inf: person): **to be** ~ **out** estar aborrecido; **put through** vt (call) transferir; (plan) aprovar; **put up** vt (raise) levantar, erguer; (hang) prender; (build) construir, edificar; (tent) armar; (increase) aumentar; (accommodate) hospedar; **put up with** vt FUS suportar, aguentar

puzzle ['pʌzl] N charada; (jigsaw) quebra-cabeça m; (also: **crossword** ~) palavras cruzadas fpl; (mystery) mistério ▶ vt desconcertar, confundir ▶ vi: **to** ~ **over sth** tentar entender algo; **puzzling** ADJ intrigante, confuso

pyjamas [pɪˈdʒɑːməz], (US) **pajamas** NPL pijama m or f

pylon ['paɪlən] N pilono, poste m, torre f

pyramid ['pɪrəmɪd] N pirâmide f

Pyrenees [pɪrəˈniːz] NPL: **the** ~ os Pirineus

q

quack [kwæk] N grasnido; (*pej: doctor*) curandeiro(-a), charlatão(-tã) m/f

quaint [kweɪnt] ADJ (*ideas*) curioso, esquisito; (*village etc*) pitoresco

quake [kweɪk] VI (*with fear*) tremer ▶ N ABBR = **earthquake**

qualification [kwɔlɪfɪ'keɪʃən] N (*skill, quality*) qualificação f; (*reservation*) restrição f, ressalva; (*modification*) modificação f; (*often pl: degree, training*) título, qualificação

qualified ['kwɔlɪfaɪd] ADJ (*trained*) habilitado, qualificado; (*professionally*) diplomado; (*fit*): ~ **to** apto para, capaz de; (*limited*) limitado

qualify ['kwɔlɪfaɪ] VT (*modify*) modificar ▶ VI: **to ~ (for)** reunir os requisitos (para)

quality ['kwɔlɪtɪ] N qualidade f; **quality (news)papers** (BRIT) NPL *ver nota*

> Os **quality (news)papers** (ou **quality press**) englobam os jornais "sérios", diários ou semanais, em oposição aos jornais populares (**tabloid press**). Esses jornais visam a um público que procura informações detalhadas sobre uma grande variedade de assuntos e que está disposto a dedicar um bom tempo à leitura. Geralmente os *quality newspapers* são publicados em formato grande.

quantify ['kwɔntɪfaɪ] VT quantificar

quantity ['kwɔntɪtɪ] N quantidade f

quarantine ['kwɔrntiːn] N quarentena

quarrel ['kwɔrl] N (*argument*) discussão f ▶ VI: **to ~ (with)** brigar (com)

quarry ['kwɔrɪ] N (*for stone*) pedreira; (*animal*) presa, caça

quart [kwɔːt] N quarto de galão (1.136 l)

quarter ['kwɔːtəʳ] N quarto, quarta parte f; (*of year*) trimestre m; (*district*) bairro; (*US: 25 cents*) (moeda de) 25 centavos mpl de dólar ▶ VT dividir em quatro; (*Mil: lodge*) aquartelar; **quarters** NPL (*Mil*) quartel m; (*living quarters*) alojamento; **a ~ of an hour** um quarto de hora; **quarter final** N quarta de final; **quarterly** ADJ trimestral ▶ ADV trimestralmente

quay [kiː] N (*also:* **~side**) cais m

queasy ['kwiːzɪ] ADJ (*sickly*) enjoado

queen [kwiːn] N rainha; (*also:* **~ bee**) abelha-mestra, rainha; (*Cards etc*) dama

queer [kwɪəʳ] ADJ (*odd*) esquisito, estranho ▶ N (*inf: homosexual*) bicha m (BR), maricas m inv (PT)

quench [kwɛntʃ] VT: **to ~ one's thirst** matar a sede

query ['kwɪərɪ] N pergunta ▶ VT questionar

quest [kwɛst] N busca

question ['kwɛstʃən] N pergunta; (*doubt*) dúvida; (*issue, in test*) questão f ▶ VT (*doubt*) duvidar; (*interrogate*) interrogar, inquirir; **beyond ~** sem dúvida; **out of the ~** fora de cogitação, impossível; **questionable** ADJ discutível; (*doubtful*) duvidoso; **question mark** N ponto de interrogação; **questionnaire** [kwɛstʃə'nɛəʳ] N questionário

queue [kjuː] (BRIT) N fila (BR), bicha (PT) ▶ VI (*also:* **~ up**) fazer fila (BR) or bicha (PT)

quick [kwɪk] ADJ rápido; (*agile*) ágil; (*mind*) sagaz, despachado ▶ N: **to cut sb to the ~** ferir alguém; **be ~!** ande depressa!, vai rápido!; **quickly** ADV rapidamente, depressa

quid [kwɪd] (BRIT inf) N INV libra

quiet ['kwaɪət] ADJ (*voice, music*) baixo; (*peaceful: place*) tranquilo; (*calm: person*) calmo; (*not noisy: place*) silencioso; (*not talkative: person*) calado; (*silent*) silencioso; (*ceremony*) discreto ▶ N (*peacefulness*) sossego; (*silence*) quietude f ▶ VT, VI (US) = **quieten**; **quieten, quieten down** VI (*grow calm*) acalmar-se; (*grow silent*) calar-se ▶ VT tranquilizar; fazer calar; **quietly** ADV silenciosamente; (*talk*) baixo

quilt [kwɪlt] N acolchoado, colcha; (BRIT: *also* **continental ~**) edredom m (BR), edredão m (PT)

quit [kwɪt] (*pt, pp* **quit** or **quitted**) VT (*smoking etc*) deixar; (*job*) deixar; (*premises*) desocupar ▶ VI desistir; (*resign*) pedir demissão

quite [kwaɪt] ADV (*rather*) bastante; (*entirely*) completamente, totalmente; **that's not ~ big enough** não é suficientemente grande; **~ a few of them** um bom número deles; **~ (so)!** exatamente!, isso mesmo!

quiver ['kwɪvəʳ] vɪ estremecer

quiz [kwɪz] N concurso (de cultura geral) ▶ vᴛ interrogar

quota ['kwəutə] N cota, quota

quotation [kwəu'teɪʃən] N citação f; (*estimate*) orçamento; **quotation marks** NPL aspas fpl

quote [kwəut] N citação f; (*estimate*) orçamento ▶ vᴛ citar; (*price*) propor; (*figure, example*) citar, dar; **quotes** NPL aspas fpl

rabbi ['ræbaɪ] N rabino

rabbit ['ræbɪt] N coelho

rabies ['reɪbiːz] N raiva

RAC (*BRIT*) N ABBR (= *Royal Automobile Club*) ≈ TCB m (*BR*), ≈ ACP m (*PT*)

race [reɪs] N corrida; (*species*) raça ▶ vᴛ (*horse*) fazer correr ▶ vɪ (*compete*) competir; (*run*) correr; (*pulse*) bater rapidamente; **race car** (*US*) N = **racing car**; **racecourse** N hipódromo; **racehorse** N cavalo de corridas; **racetrack** N pista de corridas; (*for cars*) autódromo

racing ['reɪsɪŋ] N corrida; **racing car** (*BRIT*) N carro de corrida; **racing driver** (*BRIT*) N piloto(-a) de corrida

racism ['reɪsɪzəm] N racismo; **racist** ADJ, N racista m/f

rack [ræk] N (*also:* **luggage ~**) bagageiro; (*shelf*) estante f; (*also:* **roof ~**) xalmas fpl, porta-bagagem m; (*also:* **dish ~**) secador m de prato ▶ vᴛ: **~ed by** (*pain, anxiety*) tomado por; **to ~ one's brains** quebrar a cabeça

racket ['rækɪt] N (*for tennis*) raquete f (*BR*), raqueta (*PT*); (*noise*) barulheira, zoeira; (*swindle*) negócio ilegal, fraude f

racquet ['rækɪt] N raquete f (*BR*), raqueta (*PT*)

radiation [reɪdɪ'eɪʃən] N radiação f

radiator ['reɪdɪeɪtəʳ] N radiador m

radical ['rædɪkl] ADJ radical

radio ['reɪdɪəu] N rádio ▶ vᴛ: **to ~ sb** comunicar-se por rádio com alguém

radio... [reɪdɪəu] PREFIX radio...; **radioactive** ['reɪdɪəu'æktɪv] ADJ radioativo; **radio station** N emissora, estação f de rádio

radish ['rædɪʃ] N rabanete m

raffle ['ræfl] N rifa

raft [rɑːft] N balsa

rag [ræg] N trapo; (*torn cloth*) farrapo; (*pej: newspaper*) jornaleco; (*University*) atividades estudantis beneficentes; **rags** NPL (*torn clothes*) trapos mpl, farrapos mpl

rage [reɪdʒ] N (*fury*) raiva, furor m ▶ VI (*person*) estar furioso; (*debate*) continuar calorosamente; **it's all the ~** é a última moda

ragged ['rægɪd] ADJ (*edge*) irregular, desigual; (*clothes*) puído, gasto; (*appearance*) esfarrapado, andrajoso

raid [reɪd] N (*Mil*) incursão f; (*criminal*) assalto; (*attack*) ataque m; (*by police*) batida ▶ VT invadir, atacar; assaltar; atacar; fazer uma batida em

rail [reɪl] N (*on stair*) corrimão m; (*on bridge, balcony*) parapeito, anteparo; (*of ship*) amurada; **rails** NPL (*for train*) trilhos mpl; **by ~** de trem (BR), por caminho de ferro (PT); **railing** N, **railings** NPL grade f; **railroad** (US) N = **railway**; **railway** N estrada (BR) or caminho (PT) de ferro; **railway line** (BRIT) N linha de trem (BR) or de comboio (PT); **railway station** (BRIT) N estação f ferroviária (BR) or de caminho de ferro (PT)

rain [reɪn] N chuva ▶ VI chover; **it's ~ing** está chovendo (BR), está a chover (PT); **rainbow** (BR) N arco-íris m inv; **raincoat** N impermeável m, capa de chuva; **raindrop** N gota de chuva; **rainfall** N chuva; (*measurement*) pluviosidade f; **rainforest** N floresta tropical; **rainy** ADJ chuvoso; **a rainy day** um dia de chuva

raise [reɪz] N aumento ▶ VT levantar; (*salary, production*) aumentar; (*morale, standards*) melhorar; (*doubts*) suscitar, despertar; (*cattle, family*) criar; (*crop*) cultivar, plantar; (*army*) recrutar, alistar; (*funds*) angariar; (*loan*) levantar, obter; **to ~ one's voice** levantar a voz

raisin ['reɪzn] N passa, uva seca

rake [reɪk] N ancinho ▶ VT (*garden*) revolver or limpar com o ancinho; (*with machine gun*) varrer

rally ['rælɪ] N (*Pol etc*) comício; (*Aut*) rally m, rali m; (*Tennis*) rebatida ▶ VT reunir ▶ VI reorganizar-se; (*sick person, stock exchange*) recuperar-se; **rally round** VT FUS dar apoio a

RAM [ræm] N ABBR (*Comput: = random access memory*) RAM f

ram [ræm] N carneiro ▶ VT (*push*) cravar; (*crash into*) colidir com

ramble ['ræmbl] N caminhada, excursão f a pé ▶ VI caminhar; (*talk: also: ~ on*) divagar; **rambler** N caminhante m/f;

(*Bot*) roseira trepadeira; **rambling** ADJ (*speech*) desconexo, incoerente; (*house*) cheio de recantos; (*plant*) rastejante

ramp [ræmp] N (*incline*) rampa; **on/off ~** (US Aut) entrada (para a rodovia)/saída da rodovia

rampage [ræm'peɪdʒ] N: **to be on the ~** alvoroçar-se

ran [ræn] PT of **run**

ranch [rɑːntʃ] N rancho, fazenda, estância

random ['rændəm] ADJ ao acaso, casual, fortuito; (*Comput, Math*) aleatório ▶ N: **at ~** a esmo, aleatoriamente

rang [ræŋ] PT of **ring**

range [reɪndʒ] N (*of mountains*) cadeia, cordilheira; (*of missile*) alcance m; (*of voice*) extensão f; (*series*) série f; (*of products*) gama, sortimento; (*Mil: also:* **shooting ~**) estande m; (*also:* **kitchen ~**) fogão m ▶ VT (*place*) colocar; (*arrange*) arrumar, ordenar ▶ VI: **to ~ over** (*extend*) estender-se por; **to ~ from ... to ...** variar de ... a ..., oscilar entre ... e ...

rank [ræŋk] N (*row*) fila, fileira; (*Mil*) posto; (*status*) categoria, posição f; (*BRIT: also:* **taxi ~**) ponto de táxi ▶ VI: **to ~ among** figurar entre ▶ ADJ fétido, malcheiroso; **the ~ and file** (*fig*) a gente comum

ransom ['rænsəm] N resgate m; **to hold sb to ~** (*fig*) encostar alguém contra a parede

rant [rænt] VI arengar

rap [ræp] N, VT bater de leve; (*also:* **~ music**) rap m

rape [reɪp] N estupro; (*Bot*) colza ▶ VT violentar, estuprar

rapid ['ræpɪd] ADJ rápido

rapids ['ræpɪdz] NPL (*Geo*) cachoeira

rapist ['reɪpɪst] N estuprador m

rapport [ræ'pɔːʳ] N harmonia, afinidade f

rare [rɛəʳ] ADJ raro; (*Culin: steak*) mal passado

rascal ['rɑːskl] N maroto, malandro

rash [ræʃ] ADJ impetuoso, precipitado ▶ N (*Med*) exantema m, erupção f cutânea; (*of events*) série f, torrente f

rasher ['ræʃəʳ] N fatia fina

raspberry ['rɑːzbərɪ] N framboesa

rat [ræt] N rato (BR), ratazana (PT)

rate [reɪt] N (*ratio*) razão f; (*price*) preço, taxa; (*: of hotel*) diária; (*of interest, change*) taxa; (*speed*) velocidade f ▶ VT (*value*) taxar; (*estimate*) avaliar; **rates** NPL (BRIT) imposto predial e territorial; (*fees*) pagamento; **to ~ sb/sth as** considerar alguém/algo como

rather ['rɑːðəʳ] ADV (*somewhat*) um tanto, meio; (*to some extent*) até certo ponto; (*more accurately*): **or ~** ou melhor; **it's ~ expensive** (*quite*) é meio caro; (*too*) é caro demais; **there's ~ a lot** há bastante *or* muito; **I would** *or* **I'd ~ go** preferiria *or* preferia ir; **or ~** ou melhor

ratio ['reɪʃɪəu] N razão f, proporção f

ration ['ræʃən] N ração f ▸ VT racionar; **rations** NPL (*Mil*) mantimentos *mpl*, víveres *mpl*

rational ['ræʃənl] ADJ lógico; (*person*) sensato, razoável

rat race N: **the ~** a competição acirrada na vida moderna

rattle ['rætl] N (*of door*) batida; (*of train etc*) chocalhada; (*of coins*) chocalhar *m*; (*object: for baby*) chocalho ▸ VI (*small objects*) tamborilar; (*vehicle*): **to ~ along** mover-se ruidosamente ▸ VT sacudir, fazer bater; (*unnerve*) perturbar

rave [reɪv] VI (*in anger*) encolerizar-se; (*Med*) delirar; (*with enthusiasm*): **to ~ about** vibrar com

raven ['reɪvən] N corvo

ravine [rə'viːn] N ravina, barranco

raw [rɔː] ADJ (*uncooked*) cru(a); (*not processed*) bruto; (*sore*) vivo; (*inexperienced*) inexperiente, novato; (*weather*) muito frio

ray [reɪ] N raio; **~ of hope** fio de esperança

razor ['reɪzəʳ] N (*open*) navalha; (*safety razor*) aparelho de barbear; (*electric*) aparelho de barbear elétrico; **razor blade** N gilete *m* (BR), lâmina de barbear (PT)

Rd ABBR = **road**

re [riː] PREP referente a

reach [riːtʃ] N alcance *m*; (*of river etc*) extensão f ▸ VT alcançar; (*arrive at: place*) chegar em; (: *agreement, conclusion*) chegar a; (*by telephone*) conseguir falar com ▸ VI (*stretch out*) esticar-se; **within ~** ao alcance (da mão); **out of** *or* **beyond ~** fora de alcance; **reach out** VT (*hand*) esticar ▸ VI: **to ~ out for sth** estender *or* esticar a mão para pegar (em) algo

react [riːˈækt] VI reagir; **reaction** N reação f; **reactions** NPL (*reflexes*) reflexos *mpl*

reactor [riːˈæktəʳ] N (*also*: **nuclear ~**) reator *m* nuclear

read [riːd] (*pt, pp* **read** [rɛd]) VI ler ▸ VT ler; (*understand*) compreender; (*study*) estudar; **read out** VT ler em voz alta; **reader** N leitor(a) *m/f*; (*book*) livro de leituras; (BRIT: *at university*) professor(a) *m/f* adjunto(-a)

readily ['rɛdɪlɪ] ADV (*willingly*) de boa vontade; (*easily*) facilmente; (*quickly*) sem demora, prontamente

reading ['riːdɪŋ] N leitura; (*on instrument*) indicação f, registro (BR), registo (PT)

ready ['rɛdɪ] ADJ pronto, preparado; (*willing*) disposto; (*available*) disponível ▸ N: **at the ~** (*Mil*) pronto para atirar; **to get ~** VI preparar-se; VT preparar; **ready-made** ADJ (*já*) feito; (*clothes*) pronto

real [rɪəl] ADJ real; (*genuine*) verdadeiro, autêntico; **in ~ terms** em termos reais; **real estate** N bens *mpl* imobiliários *or* de raiz; **realistic** [rɪəˈlɪstɪk] ADJ realista

reality [riːˈælɪtɪ] N realidade f; **reality TV** N reality TV f

realization [rɪəlaɪˈzeɪʃən] N (*fulfilment*) realização f; (*understanding*) compreensão f; (*Comm*) conversão f em dinheiro, realização

realize ['rɪəlaɪz] VT (*understand*) perceber; (*fulfil, Comm*) realizar

really ['rɪəlɪ] ADV (*for emphasis*) realmente; (*actually*): **what ~ happened?** o que aconteceu na verdade?; **~?** (*interest*) é mesmo?; (*surprise*) verdade!; **~!** (*annoyance*) realmente!

realm [rɛlm] N reino; (*fig*) esfera, domínio

realtor ['rɪəltəʳ] (US) N corretor(a) *m/f* de imóveis (BR), agente *m/f* imobiliário(-a) (PT)

reappear [riːəˈpɪəʳ] VI reaparecer

rear [rɪəʳ] ADJ traseiro, de trás ▸ N traseira ▸ VT criar ▸ VI (*also*: **~ up**) empinar-se

reason ['riːzn] N (*cause*) razão f; (*ability to think*) raciocínio; (*sense*) bom-senso ▸ VI: **to ~ with sb** argumentar com alguém, persuadir alguém; **it stands to ~ that** é razoável *or* lógico que; **reasonable** ADJ (*fair*) razoável; (*sensible*) sensato; **reasonably** ADV razoavelmente; (*sensibly*) sensatamente; **reasoning** N raciocínio

reassurance [riːəˈʃuərəns] N garantia

reassure [riːəˈʃuəʳ] VT tranquilizar; **to ~ sb of** reafirmar a confiança de alguém acerca de

rebate ['riːbeɪt] N devolução f

rebel [n 'rɛbl, vi rɪ'bɛl] N rebelde *m/f* ▸ VI rebelar-se; **rebellious** [rɪ'bɛljəs] ADJ insurreto; (*behaviour*) rebelde

recall [rɪ'kɔːl] VT (*remember*) recordar, lembrar; (*parliament*) reunir de volta; (*ambassador etc*) chamar de volta ▸ N (*memory*) recordação f, lembrança; (*of ambassador etc*) chamada (de volta)

receipt [rɪ'siːt] N recibo; (*act of receiving*) recebimento (BR), receção f (PT); **receipts** NPL (*Comm*) receitas fpl

receive [rɪ'siːv] VT receber; (*guest*) acolher; (*wound, criticism*) sofrer; **receiver** N (*Tel*) fone m (BR), auscultador m (PT); (*Radio, TV*) receptor m; (*of stolen goods*) receptador(a) m/f; (*Comm*) curador(a) m/f síndico(-a) de massa falida

recent ['riːsnt] ADJ recente; **recently** ADV recentemente; (*in recent times*) ultimamente

reception [rɪ'sɛpʃən] N recepção f; (*welcome*) acolhida; **reception desk** N (mesa de) recepção f; **receptionist** N recepcionista m/f

recession [rɪ'sɛʃən] N recessão f

recipe ['rɛsɪpɪ] N receita

recipient [rɪ'sɪpɪənt] N recipiente m/f, recebedor(a) m/f; (*of letter*) destinatário(-a)

recite [rɪ'saɪt] VT recitar

reckless ['rɛkləs] ADJ (*driver*) imprudente; (*speed*) imprudente, excessivo; (*spending*) irresponsável

reckon ['rɛkən] VT (*calculate*) calcular, contar; (*think*) **I ~ that ...** acho que ...; **reckon on** VT FUS contar com

reclaim [rɪ'kleɪm] VT (*demand back*) reivindicar; (*waste materials*) reaproveitar

recline [rɪ'klaɪn] VI reclinar-se

recognition [rɛkəg'nɪʃən] N reconhecimento

recognize ['rɛkəgnaɪz] VT reconhecer

recommend [rɛkə'mɛnd] VT recomendar

reconcile ['rɛkənsaɪl] VT reconciliar; (*two facts*) conciliar, harmonizar; **to ~ o.s. to sth** resignar-se a or conformar-se com algo

reconsider [riːkən'sɪdər] VT reconsiderar

reconstruct [riːkən'strʌkt] VT reconstruir; (*event*) reconstituir

record [n, adj 'rɛkɔːd, vt rɪ'kɔːd] N (*Mus*) disco; (*of meeting etc*) ata, minuta; (*Comput, of attendance*) registro (BR), registo (PT); (*written*) história; (*also:* **criminal ~**) antecedentes mpl; (*Sport*) recorde m ▶ VT (*write down*) anotar; (*temperature, speed*) registrar (BR), registar (PT); (*Mus: song etc*) gravar ▶ ADJ: **in ~ time** num tempo recorde; **off the ~** adj confidencial; adv confidencialmente; **recorder** N (*Mus*) flauta; **recording** N (*Mus*) gravação f;

record player N toca-discos m inv (BR), gira-discos m inv (PT)

recover [rɪ'kʌvər] VT recuperar ▶ VI (*from illness*) recuperar-se; (*from shock*) refazer-se; **recovery** N recuperação f; (*Med*) recuperação, melhora

recreation [rɛkrɪ'eɪʃən] N recreio; **recreational drug** N droga recreacional

recruit [rɪ'kruːt] N recruta m/f; (*in company*) novato(-a) ▶ VT recrutar

rectangle ['rɛktæŋgl] N retângulo

rector ['rɛktər] N (*Rel*) pároco

recur [rɪ'kəːr] VI repetir-se, ocorrer outra vez; (*symptoms*) reaparecer

recyclable [riː'saɪkləbl] ADJ reciclável; **recycle** VT reciclar; **recycling** N reciclagem f

red [rɛd] N vermelho; (*Pol: pej*) vermelho(-a) ▶ ADJ vermelho; (*hair*) ruivo; (*wine*) tinto; **to be in the ~** não ter fundos; **Red Cross** N Cruz f Vermelha

redeem [rɪ'diːm] VT (*Rel*) redimir; (*sth in pawn*) tirar do prego; (*loan, fig: situation*) salvar

red: red-haired ADJ ruivo; **redhead** ['rɛdhɛd] N ruivo(-a); **red-hot** ADJ incandescente; **red-light district** N zona (de meretrício)

reduce [rɪ'djuːs] VT reduzir; (*lower*) rebaixar; **"~ speed now"** (*Aut*) "diminua a velocidade"; **to ~ sb to** (*silence, begging*) levar alguém a; (*tears*) reduzir alguém a; **reduction** [rɪ'dʌkʃən] N redução f; (*of price*) abatimento

redundancy [rɪ'dʌndənsɪ] N (BRIT: *dismissal*) demissão f; (*unemployment*) desemprego

redundant [rɪ'dʌndnt] ADJ (BRIT: *worker*) desempregado; (*detail, object*) redundante, supérfluo; **to be made ~** ficar desempregado or sem trabalho

reed [riːd] N (*Bot*) junco; (*Mus: of clarinet etc*) palheta

reef [riːf] N (*at sea*) recife m

reel [riːl] N carretel m, bobina; (*of film*) rolo, filme m; (*on fishing-rod*) carretilha; (*dance*) dança típica da Escócia ▶ VI (*sway*) cambalear, oscilar; **reel in** VT puxar enrolando a linha

ref [rɛf] (*inf*) N ABBR = **referee**

refectory [rɪ'fɛktərɪ] N refeitório

refer [rɪ'fəːr] VT (*matter, problem*): **to ~ sth to** submeter algo à apreciação de; (*person, patient*): **to ~ sb to** encaminhar alguém a ▶ VI: **to ~ to** referir-se or aludir a; (*consult*) recorrer a

referee [rɛfə'riː] N árbitro(-a); (BRIT: *for job application*) referência ▶ VT apitar

reference ['rɛfrəns] N referência; (*mention*) menção *f*; **with ~ to** com relação a; (*Comm: in letter*) com referência a; **"please quote this ~"** (*Comm*) "queira citar esta referência"

refill [*vt* riːˈfɪl, *n* ˈriːfɪl] VT reencher; (*lighter etc*) reabastecer ▶ N (*for pen*) carga nova

refine [rɪˈfaɪn] VT refinar; **refined** ADJ refinado, culto

reflect [rɪˈflɛkt] VT refletir ▶ VI (*think*) refletir, meditar; **it ~s badly/well on him** isso repercute mal/bem para ele; **reflection** N reflexo; (*thought, act*) reflexão *f*; (*criticism*) **reflection on** crítica de; **on reflection** pensando bem

reflex [ˈriːflɛks] ADJ, N reflexo

reform [rɪˈfɔːm] N reforma ▶ VT reformar

refrain [rɪˈfreɪn] VI: **to ~ from doing** abster-se de fazer ▶ N estribilho, refrão *m*

refresh [rɪˈfrɛʃ] VT refrescar; **refreshing** ADJ refrescante; (*sleep*) repousante

refreshment [rɪˈfrɛʃmənt] N (*eating*): **for some ~** para comer alguma coisa; **refreshments** NPL comes e bebes *mpl*

refrigerator [rɪˈfrɪdʒəreɪtəʳ] N refrigerador *m*, geladeira (BR), frigorífico (PT)

refuel [riːˈfjuəl] VI reabastecer

refuge [ˈrɛfjuːdʒ] N refúgio; **to take ~ in** refugiar-se em

refugee [rɛfjuˈdʒiː] N refugiado(-a)

refund [*n* ˈriːfʌnd, *vt* rɪˈfʌnd] N reembolso ▶ VT devolver, reembolsar

refurbish [riːˈfəːbɪʃ] VT renovar

refusal [rɪˈfjuːzəl] N recusa, negativa; **first ~** primeira opção

refuse¹ [rɪˈfjuːz] VT recusar; (*order*) recusar-se a ▶ VI recusar-se, negar-se; (*horse*) recusar-se a pular a cerca

refuse² [ˈrɛfjuːs] N refugo, lixo

regain [rɪˈgeɪn] VT recuperar, recobrar

regard [rɪˈgɑːd] N (*gaze*) olhar *m* firme; (*attention*) atenção *f*; (*esteem*) estima, consideração *f* ▶ VT (*consider*) considerar; **to give one's ~s to** dar lembranças a; **"with kindest ~s"** "cordialmente"; **as ~s, with ~ to** com relação a, com respeito a, quanto a; **regarding** PREP com relação a; **regardless** ADV apesar de tudo; **regardless of** apesar de

regiment [ˈrɛdʒɪmənt] N regimento

region [ˈriːdʒən] N região *f*; **in the ~ of** (*fig*) por volta de, ao redor de; **regional** ADJ regional

register [ˈrɛdʒɪstəʳ] N registro (BR), registo (PT); (*Sch*) chamada ▶ VT registrar (BR), registar (PT); (*subj: instrument*) marcar, indicar ▶ VI (*at hotel*) registrar-se (BR), registar-se (PT); (*for work*) candidatar-se; (*as student*) inscrever-se; (*make impression*) causar impressão; **registered** ADJ (*letter, parcel*) registrado (BR), registado (PT)

registrar [ˈrɛdʒɪstrɑːʳ] N oficial *m/f* de registro (BR) or registo (PT), escrivão(-vã) *m/f*; (*in college*) funcionário(-a) administrativo(-a) sênior; (*in hospital*) médico(-a) sênior

registration [rɛdʒɪsˈtreɪʃən] N (*act*) registro (BR), registo (PT); (*Aut: also*: **~ number**) número da placa

regret [rɪˈgrɛt] N desgosto, pesar *m* ▶ VT lamentar; (*repent of*) arrepender-se de

regular [ˈrɛgjuləʳ] ADJ regular; (*frequent*) frequente; (*usual*) habitual; (*soldier*) de linha ▶ N habitual *m/f*; **regularly** ADV regularmente; (*shaped*) simetricamente; (*often*) frequentemente

regulate [ˈrɛgjuleɪt] VT (*speed*) regular; (*spending*) controlar; (*Tech*) regular, ajustar; **regulation** [rɛgjuˈleɪʃən] N (*rule*) regra, regulamento; (*adjustment*) ajuste *m*

rehearsal [rɪˈhəːsəl] N ensaio

rehearse [rɪˈhəːs] VT ensaiar

reign [reɪn] N reinado; (*fig*) domínio ▶ VI reinar; imperar

reimburse [riːɪmˈbəːs] VT reembolsar

rein [reɪn] N (*for horse*) rédea

reindeer [ˈreɪndɪəʳ] N INV rena

reinforce [riːɪnˈfɔːs] VT reforçar

reinstate [riːɪnˈsteɪt] VT (*worker*) readmitir; (*tax, law*) reintroduzir

reject [*n* ˈriːdʒɛkt, *vt* rɪˈdʒɛkt] N (*Comm*) artigo defeituoso ▶ VT rejeitar; (*offer of help*) recusar; (*goods*) refugar; **rejection** N rejeição *f*; (*of offer of help*) recusa

rejoice [rɪˈdʒɔɪs] VI: **to ~ at** or **over** regozijar-se or alegrar-se de

relate [rɪˈleɪt] VT (*tell*) contar, relatar; (*connect*): **to ~ sth to** relacionar algo com ▶ VI: **to ~ to** relacionar-se com; **~d to** ligado a, relacionado a

relation [rɪˈleɪʃən] N (*person*) parente *m/f*; (*link*) relação *f*; **relations** NPL (*dealings*) relações *fpl*; (*relatives*) parentes *mpl*; **relationship** N relacionamento; (*between two things*) relação *f*; (*also*: **family relationship**) parentesco

relative [ˈrɛlətɪv] N parente *m/f* ▶ ADJ relativo; **relatively** ADV relativamente

relax [rɪˈlæks] VI (*unwind*) descontrair-se; (*muscle*) relaxar-se ▶ VT (*grip*) afrouxar; (*control*) relaxar; (*mind, person*) descansar; **relaxation** [riːlækˈseɪʃən] N (*rest*) descanso; (*of muscle, control*) relaxamento; (*of grip*) afrouxamento; (*recreation*) lazer *m*; **relaxed** ADJ relaxado; (*tranquil*) descontraído

relay ['riːleɪ] N (*race*) (corrida de) revezamento ▶ VT (*message*) retransmitir

release [rɪ'liːs] N (*from prison*) libertação *f*; (*from obligation*) liberação *f*; (*of gas*) escape *m*; (*of water*) despejo; (*of film, book etc*) lançamento ▶ VT (*prisoner*) pôr em liberdade; (*book, film*) lançar; (*report, news*) publicar; (*gas etc*) soltar; (*free: from wreckage etc*) soltar; (*Tech: catch, spring etc*) desengatar, desapertar

relegate ['relɪgeɪt] VT relegar; (*Sport*): **to be ~d** ser rebaixado

relent [rɪ'lɛnt] VI (*yield*) ceder; **relentless** ADJ (*unceasing*) contínuo; (*determined*) implacável

relevant ['rɛləvənt] ADJ pertinente; **~ to** relacionado com

reliable [rɪ'laɪəbl] ADJ (*person, firm*) de confiança, confiável, sério; (*method, machine*) seguro; (*news*) fidedigno

relic ['rɛlɪk] N (*Rel*) relíquia; (*of the past*) vestígio

relief [rɪ'liːf] N alívio; (*help, supplies*) ajuda, socorro; (*Art, Geo*) relevo

relieve [rɪ'liːv] VT (*pain, fear*) aliviar; (*bring help to*) ajudar, socorrer; (*take over from: gen*) substituir, revezar; (: *guard*) render; **to ~ sb of sth** (*load*) tirar algo de alguém; (*duties*) destituir alguém de algo; **to ~ o.s.** fazer as necessidades

religion [rɪ'lɪdʒən] N religião *f*; **religious** ADJ religioso

relish ['rɛlɪʃ] N (*Culin*) condimento, tempero; (*enjoyment*) entusiasmo ▶ VT (*food etc*) saborear; (*thought*) ver com satisfação

reluctant [rɪ'lʌktənt] ADJ relutante; **reluctantly** ADV relutantemente, de má vontade

rely on [rɪ'laɪ-] VT FUS confiar em, contar com; (*be dependent on*) depender de

remain [rɪ'meɪn] VI (*survive*) sobreviver; (*stay*) ficar, permanecer; (*be left*) sobrar; (*continue*) continuar; **remainder** N resto, restante *m*; **remaining** ADJ restante; **remains** NPL (*of body*) restos *mpl*; (*of meal*) sobras *fpl*; (*of building*) ruínas *fpl*

remand [rɪ'mɑːnd] N: **on ~** sob prisão preventiva ▶ VT: **to be ~ed in custody** continuar sob prisão preventiva, manter sob custódia

remark [rɪ'mɑːk] N observação *f*, comentário ▶ VT comentar; **remarkable** ADJ (*outstanding*) extraordinário

remarry [riː'mærɪ] VI casar-se de novo

remedy ['rɛmədɪ] N: **~ (for)** remédio (contra or a) ▶ VT remediar

remember [rɪ'mɛmbə^r] VT lembrar-se de, lembrar; (*bear in mind*) ter em mente; (*send greetings*): **~ me to her** dê lembranças a ela

remembrance [rɪ'mɛmbrəns] N (*memory*) memória; (*souvenir*) lembrança, recordação *f*; **Remembrance Sunday** N ver nota

> **Remembrance Sunday** ou **Remembrance Day** é o domingo mais próximo do dia 11 de novembro, dia em que a Primeira Guerra Mundial terminou oficialmente e no qual se homenageia as vítimas das duas guerras mundiais. Nessa ocasião são observados dois minutos de silêncio às 11 horas, horário da assinatura do armistício com a Alemanha em 1918. Nos dias anteriores, papoulas de papel são vendidas por associações de caridade e a renda é revertida aos ex-combatentes e suas famílias.

remind [rɪ'maɪnd] VT: **to ~ sb to do sth** lembrar a alguém que tem de fazer algo; **to ~ sb of sth** lembrar algo a alguém, lembrar alguém de algo; **reminder** N lembrança; (*letter*) carta de advertência

remnant ['rɛmnənt] N resto; (*of cloth*) retalho; **remnants** NPL (*Comm*) retalhos *mpl*

remorse [rɪ'mɔːs] N remorso

remote [rɪ'məut] ADJ remoto; (*person*) reservado, afastado; **remote control** N controle *m* remoto; **remotely** ADV remotamente; (*slightly*) levemente

removal [rɪ'muːvəl] N (*taking away*) remoção *f*; (BRIT: *from house*) mudança; (*from office: sacking*) afastamento; (*Med*) extração *f*; **removal van** (BRIT) N caminhão *m* (BR) or camião *m* (PT) de mudanças

remove [rɪ'muːv] VT tirar, retirar; (*clothing*) tirar; (*stain*) remover; (*employee*) afastar, demitir; (*name from list, obstacle*) eliminar, remover; (*doubt, abuse*) afastar; (*Med*) extrair, extirpar

render ['rɛndə^r] VT (*thanks*) trazer; (*service*) prestar; (*make*) fazer, tornar

rendezvous ['rɔndɪvuː] N encontro; (*place*) ponto de encontro

renew [rɪ'njuː] VT retomar, recomeçar; (*loan etc*) prorrogar; (*negotiations, acquaintance*) reatar

renovate ['rɛnəveɪt] VT renovar; (*house, room*) reformar

rent [rɛnt] N aluguel m (BR), aluguer m (PT) ▶ VT (also: **~ out**) alugar; **rental** N (for television, car) aluguel m (BR), aluguer m (PT)

rep [rɛp] N ABBR (Comm) = **representative**

repair [rɪ'pɛəʳ] N reparação f, conserto ▶ VT consertar; **in good/bad ~** em bom/mau estado; **repair kit** N caixa de ferramentas

repay [ri:'peɪ] irreg VT (money) reembolsar, restituir; (person) pagar de volta; (debt) saldar, liquidar; (sb's efforts) corresponder, retribuir; (favour) retribuir; **repayment** N reembolso; (of debt) pagamento

repeat [rɪ'pi:t] N (Radio, TV) repetição f ▶ VT repetir; (Comm: order) renovar ▶ VI repetir-se

repetitive [rɪ'pɛtɪtɪv] ADJ repetitivo

replace [rɪ'pleɪs] VT (put back) repor, devolver; (take the place of) substituir; **replacement** N (substitution) substituição f; (substitute) substituto(-a)

replay ['ri:pleɪ] N (of match) partida decisiva; (TV: also: **action ~**) replay m

replica ['rɛplɪkə] N réplica, cópia, reprodução f

reply [rɪ'plaɪ] N resposta ▶ VI responder

report [rɪ'pɔ:t] N relatório; (Press etc) reportagem f; (BRIT: also: **school ~**) boletim m escolar; (of gun) estampido, detonação f ▶ VT informar sobre; (Press etc) fazer uma reportagem sobre; (bring to notice) comunicar, anunciar ▶ VI (make a report): **to ~ (on)** apresentar um relatório (sobre); (present o.s.): **to ~ (to sb)** apresentar-se (a alguém); (be responsible to): **to ~ to sb** obedecer as ordens de alguém; **report card** (US, SCOTLAND) N boletim m escolar; **reportedly** ADV: **she is reportedly living in Spain** dizem que ela mora na Espanha; **reporter** N repórter m/f

represent [rɛprɪ'zɛnt] VT representar; (constitute) constituir; (Comm) ser representante de; **representation** [rɛprɪzɛn'teɪʃən] N representação f; (picture, statue) representação, retrato; (petition) petição f; **representations** NPL (protest) reclamação f, protesto; **representative** [rɛprɪ'zɛntətɪv] N representante m/f; (US Pol) deputado(-a) ▶ ADJ: **representative (of)** representativo (de)

repress [rɪ'prɛs] VT reprimir; **repression** N repressão f

reproduce [ri:prə'dju:s] VT reproduzir ▶ VI reproduzir-se

reptile ['rɛptaɪl] N réptil m

republic [rɪ'pʌblɪk] N república; **republican** ADJ, N republicano(-a); (US Pol): **Republican** membro(-a) do Partido Republicano

reputable ['rɛpjutəbl] ADJ (make etc) bem conceituado, de confiança; (person) honrado, respeitável

reputation [rɛpju'teɪʃən] N reputação f

request [rɪ'kwɛst] N pedido; (formal) petição f ▶ VT: **to ~ sth of or from sb** pedir algo a alguém; (formally) solicitar algo a alguém; **request stop** (BRIT) N (for bus) parada não obrigatória

require [rɪ'kwaɪəʳ] VT (need: subj: person) precisar de, necessitar; (: thing, situation) requerer, exigir; (want) pedir; (order): **to ~ sb to do sth/sth of sb** exigir que alguém faça algo/algo de alguém; **requirement** N (need) necessidade f; (want) pedido

rescue ['rɛskju:] N salvamento, resgate m ▶ VT: **to ~ (from)** resgatar (de); (save, fig) salvar (de)

research [rɪ'sə:tʃ] N pesquisa ▶ VT pesquisar

resemblance [rɪ'zɛmbləns] N semelhança

resemble [rɪ'zɛmbl] VT parecer-se com

resent [rɪ'zɛnt] VT (attitude) ressentir-se de; (person) estar ressentido com; **resentful** ADJ ressentido

reservation [rɛzə'veɪʃən] N reserva

reserve [rɪ'zə:v] N reserva; (Sport) suplente m/f, reserva m/f (BR) ▶ VT reservar; **reserves** NPL (Mil) (tropas fpl da) reserva; (Comm) reserva; **in ~** de reserva; **reserved** ADJ reservado

residence ['rɛzɪdəns] N residência; (formal: home) domicílio; **residence permit** (BRIT) N autorização f de residência

resident ['rɛzɪdənt] N (of country, town) habitante m/f; (in hotel) hóspede m/f ▶ ADJ (population) permanente; (doctor) interno, residente; **residential** [rɛzɪ'dɛnʃəl] ADJ residencial

residue ['rɛzɪdju:] N resto

resign [rɪ'zaɪn] VT renunciar a, demitir-se de ▶ VI: **to ~ (from)** demitir-se (de); **to ~ o.s. to** resignar-se a; **resignation** [rɛzɪg'neɪʃən] N demissão f; (state of mind) resignação f

resist [rɪ'zɪst] VT resistir a

resolution [rɛzə'lu:ʃən] N resolução f; (of problem) solução f

resolve [rɪˈzɔlv] N resolução f ▶ VT resolver ▶ VI: **to ~ to do** resolver-se a fazer

resort [rɪˈzɔːt] N local m turístico, estação f de veraneio; (*recourse*) recurso ▶ VI: **to ~ to** recorrer a; **in the last ~** em último caso, em última instância

resource [rɪˈsɔːs] N (*raw material*) recurso natural; **resources** NPL (*coal, money, energy*) recursos mpl; **resourceful** ADJ engenhoso, habilidoso

respect [rɪsˈpɛkt] N respeito ▶ VT respeitar; **respects** NPL (*greetings*) cumprimentos mpl; **respectable** ADJ respeitável; (*large*) considerável; (*result, player*) razoável; **respectful** ADJ respeitoso

respond [rɪsˈpɔnd] VI (*answer*) responder; (*react*) reagir; **response** N resposta; (*reaction*) reação f

responsibility [rɪspɔnsɪˈbɪlɪtɪ] N responsabilidade f; (*duty*) dever m

responsible [rɪsˈpɔnsɪbl] ADJ sério, responsável; (*job*) de responsabilidade; (*liable*): **~ (for)** responsável (por)

responsive [rɪsˈpɔnsɪv] ADJ receptivo

rest [rɛst] N descanso, repouso; (*pause*) pausa, intervalo; (*support*) apoio; (*remainder*) resto; (*Mus*) pausa ▶ VI descansar; (*stop*) parar; (*be supported*): **to ~ on** apoiar-se em ▶ VT descansar; (*lean*): **to ~ sth on/against** apoiar algo em or sobre/contra; **the ~ of them** os outros; **it ~s with him to do it** cabe a ele fazê-lo

restaurant [ˈrɛstərɔn] N restaurante m; **restaurant car** (BRIT) N vagão-restaurante m

restless [ˈrɛstlɪs] ADJ desassossegado, irrequieto

restore [rɪsˈtɔːr] VT (*building, order*) restaurar; (*sth stolen*) restituir; (*peace, health*) restabelecer

restrain [rɪsˈtreɪn] VT (*feeling*) reprimir; (*growth, inflation*) refrear; (*person*): **to ~ (from doing)** impedir (de fazer); **restraint** N (*restriction*) restrição f; (*moderation*) moderação f, comedimento; (*of style*) sobriedade f

restrict [rɪsˈtrɪkt] VT restringir, limitar; (*people, animals*) confinar; (*activities*) limitar; **restriction** N restrição f, limitação f

rest room (US) N banheiro (BR), lavabo (PT)

result [rɪˈzʌlt] N resultado ▶ VI: **to ~ in** resultar em; **as a ~ of** como resultado or consequência de

resume [rɪˈzjuːm] VT (*work, journey*) retomar, recomeçar ▶ VI recomeçar

résumé [ˈreɪzjuːmeɪ] N (*summary*) resumo; (*US: curriculum vitae*) curriculum vitae m, currículo

resuscitate [rɪˈsʌsɪteɪt] VT (*Med*) ressuscitar, reanimar

retail [ˈriːteɪl] ADJ a varejo (BR), a retalho (PT) ▶ ADV a varejo (BR), a retalho (PT); **retailer** N varejista m/f (BR), retalhista m/f (PT)

retain [rɪˈteɪn] VT (*keep*) reter, conservar

retire [rɪˈtaɪər] VI aposentar-se; (*withdraw*) retirar-se; (*go to bed*) deitar-se; **retired** ADJ aposentado (BR), reformado (PT); **retirement** N aposentadoria (BR), reforma (PT)

retort [rɪˈtɔːt] VI replicar, retrucar

retreat [rɪˈtriːt] N (*place*) retiro; (*act*) retirada ▶ VI retirar-se

retrieve [rɪˈtriːv] VT (*sth lost*) reaver, recuperar; (*situation, honour*) salvar; (*error, loss*) reparar

retrospect [ˈrɛtrəspɛkt] N: **in ~** retrospectivamente, em retrospecto; **retrospective** [rɛtrəˈspɛktɪv] ADJ retrospectivo; (*law*) retroativo

return [rɪˈtəːn] N regresso, volta; (*of sth stolen etc*) devolução f; (*Finance: from land, shares*) rendimento ▶ CPD (*journey*) de volta; (BRIT: *ticket*) de ida e volta; (*match*) de revanche ▶ VI voltar, regressar; (*symptoms etc*) voltar; (*regain*): **to ~ to** (*consciousness*) recobrar; (*power*) retornar a ▶ VT devolver; (*favour, love etc*) retribuir; (*verdict*) proferir, anunciar; (*Pol: candidate*) eleger; **returns** NPL (*Comm*) receita; **in ~ (for)** em troca (de); **many happy ~s (of the day)!** parabéns!; **by ~ (of post)** por volta do correio

retweet [riːˈtwiːt] N (*on Twitter*) retweet m

reunion [riːˈjuːnɪən] N (*family*) reunião f; (*two people, class*) reencontro

reunite [riːjuːˈnaɪt] VT reunir; (*reconcile*) reconciliar

revamp [ˈriːˈvæmp] VT dar um jeito em

reveal [rɪˈviːl] VT revelar; (*make visible*) mostrar; **revealing** ADJ revelador(a)

revel [ˈrɛvl] VI: **to ~ in sth/in doing sth** deleitar-se com algo/em fazer algo

revenge [rɪˈvɛndʒ] N vingança, desforra; **to take ~ on** vingar-se de

revenue [ˈrɛvənjuː] N receita, renda

reversal [rɪˈvəːsl] N (*of order*) reversão f; (*of direction*) mudança em sentido contrário; (*of decision*) revogação f; (*of roles*) inversão f

reverse [rɪ'vəːs] N (*opposite*) contrário; (*back: of cloth*) avesso; (: *of coin*) reverso; (: *of paper*) dorso; (*Aut: also:* **~ gear**) marcha à ré (BR), marcha atrás (PT); (*setback*) revés m, derrota ▶ ADJ (*order*) inverso, oposto; (*direction*) contrário; (*process*) inverso ▶ VT inverter; (*position*) mudar; (*process, decision*) revogar; (*car*) dar ré com ▶ VI (BRIT Aut) dar (marcha à) ré (BR), fazer marcha atrás (PT); **reverse-charge call** (BRIT) N (*Tel*) ligação f a cobrar

revert [rɪ'vəːt] VI: **to ~ to** voltar a; (*Jur*) reverter a

review [rɪ'vjuː] N (*magazine, Mil*) revista; (*of book, film*) crítica, resenha; (*examination*) recapitulação f, exame m ▶ VT rever, examinar; (*Mil*) passar em revista; (*book, film*) fazer a crítica or resenha de

revise [rɪ'vaɪz] VT (*manuscript*) corrigir; (*opinion, procedure*) alterar; (*price*) revisar; **revision** [rɪ'vɪʒən] N correção f; (*for exam*) revisão f

revival [rɪ'vaɪvəl] N (*recovery*) restabelecimento; (*of interest*) renascença, renascimento; (*Theatre*) reestreia; (*of faith*) despertar m

revive [rɪ'vaɪv] VT (*person*) reanimar, ressuscitar; (*economy*) recuperar; (*custom*) restabelecer, restaurar; (*hope, courage*) despertar; (*play*) reapresentar ▶ VI (*person: from faint*) voltar a si, recuperar os sentidos; (: *from ill-health*) recuperar-se; (*activity, economy*) reativar-se; (*hope, interest*) renascer

revolt [rɪ'vəult] N revolta, rebelião f, insurreição f ▶ VI revoltar-se ▶ VT causar aversão a, repugnar; **revolting** ADJ revoltante, repulsivo

revolution [revə'luːʃən] N revolução f; (*of wheel, earth*) rotação f

revolve [rɪ'vɔlv] VI girar

revolver [rɪ'vɔlvə'] N revólver m

reward [rɪ'wɔːd] N recompensa ▶ VT: **to ~ (for)** recompensar or premiar (por); **rewarding** ADJ (*fig*) gratificante, compensador(a)

rewind [riː'waɪnd] *irreg* VT (*tape*) voltar para trás

rewritable [rɪ'raɪtəbl] ADJ regravável

rheumatism ['ruːmətɪzəm] N reumatismo

rhinoceros [raɪ'nɔsərəs] N rinoceronte m

rhubarb ['ruːbɑːb] N ruibarbo

rhyme [raɪm] N rima; (*verse*) verso(s) m(pl) rimado(s), poesia

rhythm ['rɪðm] N ritmo

rib [rɪb] N (*Anat*) costela ▶ VT (*mock*) zombar de, encarnar em

ribbon ['rɪbən] N fita; **in ~s** (*torn*) em tirinhas, esfarrapado

rice [raɪs] N arroz m; **rice pudding** N arroz m doce

rich [rɪtʃ] ADJ rico; (*clothes*) valioso; (*soil*) fértil; (*food*) suculento, forte; (*colour*) intenso; (*voice*) suave, cheio ▶ NPL: **the ~** os ricos; **riches** NPL (*wealth*) riquezas fpl

rid [rɪd] (*pt, pp* **rid**) VT: **to ~ sb of sth** livrar alguém de algo; **to get ~ of** livrar-se de; (*sth no longer required*) desfazer-se de

riddle ['rɪdl] N (*conundrum*) adivinhação f; (*mystery*) enigma m, charada ▶ VT: **to be ~d with** estar cheio de

ride [raɪd] (*pt* **rode**, *pp* **ridden**) N (*gen*) passeio; (*on horse*) passeio a cavalo; (*distance covered*) percurso, trajeto ▶ VI (*as sport*) montar; (*go somewhere: on horse, bicycle*) ir (a cavalo, de bicicleta); (*journey: on bicycle, motorcycle, bus*) viajar ▶ VT (*a horse*) montar a; (*bicycle, motorcycle*) andar de; (*distance*) percorrer; **to ~ at anchor** (*Naut*) estar ancorado; **to take sb for a ~** (*fig*) enganar alguém; **rider** N (*on horse: male*) cavaleiro; (: *female*) amazona; (*on bicycle*) ciclista m/f; (*on motorcycle*) motociclista m/f

ridge [rɪdʒ] N (*of hill*) cume m, topo; (*of roof*) cumeeira; (*wrinkle*) ruga

ridicule ['rɪdɪkjuːl] N escárnio, zombaria, mofa ▶ VT ridicularizar, zombar de; **ridiculous** ADJ ridículo

riding ['raɪdɪŋ] N equitação f

rife [raɪf] ADJ: **to be ~** ser comum; **to be ~ with** estar repleto de, abundar em

rifle ['raɪfl] N rifle m, fuzil m ▶ VT saquear; **rifle through** VT FUS vascular

rift [rɪft] N fenda, fratura; (*in clouds*) brecha; (*fig: between friends*) desentendimento; (: *in party*) rompimento, divergência

rig [rɪg] N (*also:* **oil ~**) torre f de perfuração ▶ VT adulterar or falsificar os resultados de; **rig out** (BRIT) VT: **to ~ out as/in** ataviar or vestir como/com; **rig up** VT instalar, montar, improvisar

right [raɪt] ADJ certo, correto; (*suitable*) adequado, conveniente; (: *decision*) certo; (*just*) justo; (*morally good*) bom; (*not left*) direito ▶ N direito; (*not left*) direita ▶ ADV bem, corretamente; (*fairly*) adequadamente, justamente; (*not on the left*) à direita; (*exactly*): **~ now** agora mesmo ▶ VT colocar em pé; (*correct*)

corrigir, indireitar ▶ EXCL boml; **to be ~**
(*person*) ter razão; (*answer, clock*) estar
certo; **by ~s** por direito; **on the ~** à
direita; **to be in the ~** ter razão; **~ away**
imediatamente, logo, já; **~ in the
middle** bem no meio; **rightful** ADJ (*heir*)
legítimo; (*place*) justo, legítimo;
right-handed ADJ destro; **rightly** ADV
(*with reason*) com razão; **right of way** N
prioridade f de passagem; (*Aut*)
preferência; **right-wing** ADJ de direita

rigid ['rɪdʒɪd] ADJ rígido; (*principle*)
inflexível

rim [rɪm] N borda, beira; (*of spectacles,
wheel*) aro

rind [raɪnd] N (*of bacon*) pele f; (*of lemon
etc*) casca; (*of cheese*) crosta, casca

ring [rɪŋ] (*pt* **rang**, *pp* **rung**) N (*of metal*)
aro; (*on finger*) anel m; (*of people, objects*)
círculo, grupo; (*for boxing*) ringue m; (*of
circus*) pista, picadeiro; (*bullring*)
picadeiro, arena; (*of light, smoke*) círculo;
(*sound: of small bell*) toque m; (: *of large
bell*) badalada, repique m ▶ VI (*on
telephone*) telefonar; (*bell*) tocar; (*also: ~
out*) soar; (*ears*) zumbir ▶ VT (*BRIT Tel*)
telefonar a, ligar para; (*bell etc*) badalar;
(*doorbell*) tocar; **to give sb a ~** (*BRIT Tel*)
dar uma ligada or ligar para alguém; **ring
back** (*BRIT*) VI (*Tel*) telefonar or ligar de
volta ▶ VT telefonar or ligar de volta para;
ring off (*BRIT*) VI (*Tel*) desligar; **ring up**
(*BRIT*) VT (*Tel*) telefonar a, ligar para;
ring-fence VT (*money, tax*) restringir (o
uso de alguma verba); **ringing tone**
(*BRIT*) N (*Tel*) sinal m de chamada;
ringleader N cabeça m/f, cérebro; **ring
road** (*BRIT*) N estrada periférica or
perimetral; **ringtone** N (*on cellphone*)
toque m

rink [rɪŋk] N (*also:* **ice ~**) pista de
patinação, rinque m

rinse [rɪns] N enxaguada ▶ VT enxaguar;
(*also: ~ out: mouth*) bochechar

riot ['raɪət] N distúrbio, motim m,
desordem f; (*of colour*) festival m,
profusão f ▶ VI provocar distúrbios,
amotinar-se; **to run ~** desenfrear-se

rip [rɪp] N rasgão m ▶ VT rasgar ▶ VI
rasgar-se

ripe [raɪp] ADJ maduro

ripple ['rɪpl] N ondulação f, encrespação
f; (*of laughter etc*) onda ▶ VI encrespar-se

rise [raɪz] (*pt* **rose**, *pp* **risen**) N elevação f,
ladeira; (*hill*) colina, rampa; (*increase:
BRIT: in wages*) aumento; (: *in prices,
temperature*) subida; (*to power etc*)
ascensão f ▶ VI levantar-se, erguer-se;

(*prices, waters*) subir; (*sun*) nascer; (*from
bed etc*) levantar(-se); (*sound, voice*)
aumentar, erguer-se; (*also: ~ up:
building*) erguer-se; (: *rebel*) sublevar-se;
(*in rank*) ascender, subir; **to give ~ to**
ocasionar, dar origem a; **to ~ to the
occasion** mostrar-se à altura da
situação; **rising** ADJ (*increasing: prices*)
em alta; (: *number*) crescente, cada vez
maior; (*tide*) montante; (*sun, moon*)
nascente

risk [rɪsk] N risco, perigo; (*Insurance*) risco
▶ VT pôr em risco; (*chance*) arriscar,
aventurar; **to take** or **run the ~ of doing**
correr o risco de fazer; **at ~** em perigo;
at one's own ~ por sua própria conta e
risco; **risky** ADJ perigoso

rite [raɪt] N rito; **last ~s** últimos
sacramentos

ritual ['rɪtjuəl] ADJ ritual ▶ N ritual m; (*of
initiation*) rito

rival ['raɪvl] ADJ, N rival m/f; (*in business*)
concorrente m/f ▶ VT competir com;
rivalry N rivalidade f

river ['rɪvəʳ] N rio ▶ CPD (*port, traffic*)
fluvial; **up/down ~** rio acima/abaixo;
riverbank N margem f (do rio)

road [rəud] N via; (*motorway etc*) estrada
(de rodagem); (*in town*) rua ▶ CPD
rodoviário; **road accident** N acidente m
de trânsito; **roadblock** N barricada;
road map N mapa m rodoviário; **road
rage** N conduta agressiva dos motoristas no
trânsito; **roadside** N beira da estrada;
road sign N placa de sinalização;
roadworks ['rəudwə:ks] NPL obras fpl de
estrada

roam [rəum] VI vagar, perambular, errar

roar [rɔːʳ] N (*of animal*) rugido, urro; (*of
crowd*) bramido; (*of vehicle, storm*)
estrondo; (*of laughter*) barulho ▶ VI
(*animal, engine*) rugir; (*person, crowd*)
bradar; **to ~ with laughter** dar
gargalhadas

roast [rəust] N carne f assada, assado
▶ VT assar; (*coffee*) torrar; **roast beef** N
rosbife m

rob [rɔb] VT roubar; (*bank*) assaltar; **to ~
sb of sth** roubar algo de alguém; (*fig:
deprive*) despojar alguém de algo; **robber**
N ladrão/ladra m/f; **robbery** N roubo

robe [rəub] N toga, beca; (*also:* **bath ~**)
roupão m (de banho)

robin ['rɔbɪn] N pisco-de-peito-ruivo
(BR), pintarroxo (PT)

robot ['rəubɔt] N robô m

robust [rəu'bʌst] ADJ robusto, forte;
(*appetite*) sadio; (*economy*) forte

rock [rɔk] N rocha; (*boulder*) penhasco, rochedo; (*US: small stone*) cascalho; (*BRIT: sweet*) pirulito ▶ VT (*swing gently: cradle*) balançar, oscilar; (: *child*) embalar, acalentar; (*shake*) sacudir ▶ VI (*object*) balançar-se; (*person*) embalar-se; **on the ~s** (*drink*) com gelo; (*marriage etc*) arruinado, em dificuldades; **rock and roll** N rock-and-roll m

rocket ['rɔkɪt] N foguete m

rocky ['rɔkɪ] ADJ rochoso; bambo, instável; (*marriage etc*) instável

rod [rɔd] N vara, varinha; (*also*: **fishing ~**) vara de pescar

rode [rəud] PT of **ride**

rodent ['rəudnt] N roedor m

rogue [rəug] N velhaco, maroto

role [rəul] N papel m; **role model** N modelo

roll [rəul] N rolo; (*of banknotes*) maço; (*also*: **bread ~**) pãozinho; (*register*) rol m, lista; (*of drums etc*) rufar m ▶ VT rolar; (*also*: **~ up**: *string*) enrolar; (: *sleeves*) arregaçar; (*cigarette*) enrolar; (*eyes*) virar; (*also*: **~ out**: *pastry*) esticar; (*lawn, road etc*) aplanar ▶ VI rolar; (*drum*) rufar; (*vehicle*: *also*: **~ along**) rodar; (*ship*) balançar, jogar; **roll about** VI ficar rolando; **roll around** VI = **roll about**; **roll by** VI (*time*) passar; **roll in** VI (*mail, cash*) chegar em grande quantidade; **roll over** VI dar uma volta; **roll up** VI (*inf*) pintar, chegar, aparecer ▶ VT (*carpet etc*) enrolar; **roller** N (*in machine*) rolo, cilindro; (*wheel*) roda, roldana; (*for lawn, road*) rolo compressor; (*for hair*) rolo; **roller coaster** N montanha-russa; **roller skates** NPL patins mpl de roda

rolling pin N rolo de pastel

ROM [rɔm] N ABBR (*Comput*: = *read-only memory*) ROM f

Roman ['rəumən] ADJ, N romano(-a); **Roman Catholic** ADJ, N católico(-a) (romano(-a))

romance [rə'mæns] N aventura amorosa, romance m; (*book etc*) história de amor; (*charm*) romantismo

Romania [ruː'meɪnɪə] N Romênia; **Romanian** ADJ romeno ▶ N romeno(-a); (*Ling*) romeno

romantic [rə'mæntɪk] ADJ romântico

Rome [rəum] N Roma

roof [ruːf] N (*of house*) telhado; (*of car*) capota, teto ▶ VT telhar, cobrir com telhas; **the ~ of the mouth** o céu da boca; **roof rack** N (*Aut*) bagageiro

rook [ruk] N (*bird*) gralha; (*Chess*) torre f

room [ruːm] N (*in house*) quarto, aposento; (*also*: **bed~**) quarto, dormitório; (*in school etc*) sala; (*space*) espaço, lugar m; (*scope for improvement etc*) espaço; **rooms** NPL (*lodging*) alojamento; **"~s to let"** (*BRIT*), **"~s for rent"** (*US*) "alugam-se quartos or apartamentos"; **roommate** N companheiro(-a) de quarto; **room service** N serviço de quarto; **roomy** ADJ espaçoso; (*garment*) folgado

rooster ['ruːstə] N galo

root [ruːt] N raiz f; (*fig*) origem f ▶ VI enraizar, arraigar; **roots** NPL (*family origins*) raízes fpl; **root about** VI (*fig*): **to ~ about in** (*drawer*) vasculhar; (*house*) esquadrinhar; **root for** VT FUS torcer por; **root out** VT extirpar

rope [rəup] N corda; (*Naut*) cabo ▶ VT (*tie*) amarrar; (*climbers*: *also*: **~ together**) amarrar or atar com uma corda; (*area*: *also*: **~ off**) isolar; **to know the ~s** (*fig*) estar por dentro (do assunto); **rope in** VT (*fig*): **to ~ sb** persuadir alguém a tomar parte

rose [rəuz] PT of **rise** ▶ N rosa; (*also*: **~bush**) roseira; (*on watering can*) crivo

rosé ['rəuzeɪ] N rosado, rosé m

rosemary ['rəuzmərɪ] N alecrim m

rosy ['rəuzɪ] ADJ rosado, rosáceo; (*cheeks*) rosado; (*situation*) cor-de-rosa inv; **a ~ future** um futuro promissor

rot [rɔt] N (*decay*) putrefação f, podridão f; (*fig: pej*) besteira ▶ VT, VI apodrecer

rota ['rəutə] N lista de tarefas, escala de serviço

rotate [rəu'teɪt] VT fazer girar, dar voltas em ▶ VI girar, dar voltas

rotten ['rɔtn] ADJ podre; (*wood*) carcomido; (*fig*) corrupto; (*inf: bad*) péssimo; **to feel ~** (*ill*) sentir-se podre

rough [rʌf] ADJ (*skin, surface*) áspero; (*terrain*) acidentado; (*road*) desigual; (*voice*) áspero, rouco; (*weather*) tempestuoso; (*treatment*) brutal, mau/má; (*sea*) agitado; (*district*) violento; (*plan*) preliminar; (*work, cloth*) grosseiro; (*guess*) aproximado ▶ N (*Golf*): **in the ~** na grama crescida; **to sleep ~** (*BRIT*) dormir na rua; **roughly** ADV bruscamente; (*make*) toscamente; (*approximately*) aproximadamente

roulette [ruː'lɛt] N roleta

round [raund] ADJ redondo ▶ N (*BRIT: of toast*) rodela; (*of police officer*) ronda; (*of milkman*) trajeto; (*of doctor*) visitas fpl; (*game: of cards, golf, in competition*) partida; (*of ammunition*) cartucho; (*Boxing*) rounde m, assalto; (*of talks*) ciclo

▶ VT virar, dobrar ▶ PREP (*surrounding*): **~ his neck/the table** em volta de seu pescoço/ao redor da mesa; (*in a circular movement*): **to go ~ the world** dar a volta ao mundo; (*in various directions*): **to move ~ a house** mover-se por uma casa; (*approximately*): **~ about** aproximadamente ▶ ADV: **all ~** por todos os lados; **the long way ~** o caminho mais comprido; **all the year ~** durante todo o ano; **it's just ~ the corner** (*fig*) está pertinho; **~ the clock** ininterrupto; **to go ~ the back** passar por detrás; **to go ~ a house** visitar uma casa; **enough to go ~** suficiente para todos; **a ~ of applause** uma salva de palmas; **a ~ of drinks** uma rodada de bebidas; **~ of sandwiches** sanduíche m (BR), sandes f *inv* (PT); **round off** VT terminar, completar; **round up** VT (*cattle*) encurralar; (*people*) reunir; (*price, figure*) arredondar; **roundabout** N (BRIT: *Aut*) rotatória; (: *at fair*) carrossel m ▶ ADJ indireto; **round trip** N viagem f de ida e volta

rouse [rauz] VT (*wake up*) despertar, acordar; (*stir up*) suscitar

route [ruːt] N caminho, rota; (*of bus*) trajeto; (*of shipping*) rumo, rota; (*of procession*) rota; **router** ['ruːtə] N (*Cómput*) roteador m (BR), router m (PT)

routine [ruː'tiːn] ADJ (*work*) rotineiro; (*procedure*) de rotina ▶ N rotina; (*Theatre*) número

row¹ [rəu] N (*line*) fila, fileira; (*in theatre, boat*) fileira; (*Knitting*) carreira, fileira ▶ VI, VT remar; **in a ~** (*fig*) a fio, seguido

row² [rau] N barulho, balbúrdia; (*dispute*) discussão f, briga; (*scolding*) repreensão f ▶ VI brigar; **to have a ~** ter uma briga

rowboat ['rəubəut] (US) N barco a remo

rowing ['rəuɪŋ] N remo; **rowing boat** (BRIT) N barco a remo

royal ['rɔɪəl] ADJ real

Royal Academy (BRIT) N *ver nota*

A **Royal Academy**, ou **Royal Academy of Arts**, fundada em 1768 por George III para desenvolver a pintura, a escultura e a arquitetura, situa-se em Burlington House, Piccadilly. A cada verão há uma exposição de obras de artistas contemporâneos. A **Royal Academy** também oferece cursos de pintura, escultura e arquitetura.

royalty N família real, realeza; (*payment: to author*) direitos *mpl* autorais

rpm ABBR (= *revolutions per minute*) rpm

rub [rʌb] VT (*part of body*) esfregar; (*object*) friccionar ▶ N: **to give sth a ~** dar uma esfregada em algo; **to ~ sb up** (BRIT) or **~ sb** (US) **the wrong way** irritar alguém; **rub off** VI sair esfregando; **rub off on** VT FUS transmitir-se para, influir sobre; **rub out** VT apagar

rubber ['rʌbə] N borracha; (BRIT: *eraser*) borracha; **rubber band** N elástico, tira elástica

rubbish ['rʌbɪʃ] N (*waste*) refugo; (*from household, in street*) lixo; (*junk*) coisas *fpl* sem valor; (*fig: pej: nonsense*) disparates *mpl*, asneiras *fpl*; **rubbish bin** (BRIT) N lata de lixo; **rubbish dump** N (*in town*) depósito (de lixo)

rubble ['rʌbl] N (*debris*) entulho; (*Constr*) escombros *mpl*

ruby ['ruːbɪ] N rubi m

rucksack ['rʌksæk] N mochila

rudder ['rʌdə'] N leme m; (*of plane*) leme de direção

rude [ruːd] ADJ (*person*) grosso, mal-educado; (*word, manners*) grosseiro; (*shocking*) obsceno, chocante

rug [rʌg] N tapete m; (BRIT: *for knees*) manta (de viagem)

rugby ['rʌgbɪ] N (*also*: **~ football**) rúgbi m (BR), râguebi m (PT)

rugged ['rʌgɪd] ADJ (*landscape*) acidentado, irregular; (*features*) marcado; (*character*) severo, austero

ruin ['ruːɪn] N ruína; (*of plans*) destruição f; (*downfall*) queda; (*bankruptcy*) bancarrota ▶ VT destruir; (*future, person*) arruinar; (*spoil*) estragar; **ruins** NPL (*of building*) ruínas *fpl*

rule [ruːl] N (*norm*) regra; (*regulation*) regulamento; (*government*) governo, domínio; (*ruler*) régua ▶ VT governar ▶ VI governar; (*monarch*) reger; (*Jur*): **to ~ in favour of/against** decidir oficialmente a favor de/contra; **as a ~** por via de regra, geralmente; **rule out** VT excluir; **ruler** N (*sovereign*) soberano(-a); (*for measuring*) régua; **ruling** ADJ (*party*) dominante; (*class*) dirigente ▶ N (*Jur*) parecer m, decisão f

rum [rʌm] N rum m

rumble ['rʌmbl] N ruído surdo, barulho; (*of thunder*) estrondo, ribombo ▶ VI ribombar, ressoar; (*stomach*) roncar; (*pipe*) fazer barulho; (*thunder*) ribombar

rumour ['ruːmə'], (US) **rumor** N rumor m, boato ▶ VT: **it is ~ed that ...** corre o boato de que ...

rump steak [rʌmp-] N alcatra

run [rʌn] (pt **ran**, pp **run**) N corrida; (in car) passeio (de carro); (distance travelled) trajeto, percurso; (journey) viagem f; (series) série f; (Theatre) temporada; (Ski) pista; (in stockings) fio puxado ▶ VT (race) correr; (operate: business) dirigir; (: competition, course) organizar; (: hotel, house) administrar; (water) deixar correr; (bath) encher; (Press: feature) publicar; (Comput) rodar; (hand, finger) passar ▶ VI correr; (work: machine) funcionar; (bus, train: operate) circular; (: travel) ir; (continue: play) continuar em cartaz; (: contract) ser válido; (river, bath) fluir, correr; (colours, washing) desbotar; (in election) candidatar-se; (nose) escorrer; **there was a ~ on** houve muita procura de; **in the long ~** no final das contas, mais cedo ou mais tarde; **on the ~** em fuga, foragido; **run about** VI correr por todos os lados; **run across** VT FUS encontrar por acaso, topar com, dar com; **run around** VI = **run about**; **run away** VI fugir; **run down** VT (Aut) atropelar; (production) reduzir; (criticize) criticar; **to be ~ down** estar enfraquecido or exausto; **run in** (BRIT) VT (car) rodar; **run into** VT FUS (meet: person) dar com, topar com; (: trouble) esbarrar em; (collide with) bater em; **run off** VI fugir; **run out** VI (person) sair correndo; (liquid) escorrer, esgotar-se; (lease, passport) caducar, vencer; (money) acabar; **run out of** VT FUS ficar sem; **run over** VT (Aut) atropelar ▶ VT FUS (revise) recapitular; **run through** VT FUS (instructions) recapitular; **run up** VT (debt) acumular ▶ VI: **to ~ up against** esbarrar em; **runaway** ADJ (horse) desembestado; (truck) desgovernado; (person) fugitivo

rung [rʌŋ] PP of **ring** ▶ N (of ladder) degrau m

runner ['rʌnəʳ] N (in race) corredor(a) m/f; (: horse) corredor m; (on sledge) patim m, lâmina; (for drawer) corrediça; **runner bean** (BRIT) N (Bot) vagem f (BR), feijão m verde (PT); **runner-up** N segundo(-a) colocado(-a)

running ['rʌnɪŋ] N (sport, race) corrida; (of business) direção f ▶ ADJ (water) corrente; (commentary) contínuo, seguido; **6 days ~** 6 dias seguidos or consecutivos; **to be in/out of the ~ for sth** disputar algo/estar fora da disputa por algo

runny ['rʌnɪ] ADJ aguado; (egg) mole; **to have a ~ nose** estar com coriza, estar com o nariz escorrendo

run-up N: **~ to sth** (election etc) período que antecede algo; **during** or **in the ~ to** nas vésperas de

runway ['rʌnweɪ] N (Aviat) pista (de decolagem or de pouso)

rupture ['rʌptʃəʳ] N (Med) hérnia

rural ['ruərl] ADJ rural

rush [rʌʃ] N (hurry) pressa; (Comm) grande procura or demanda; (Bot) junco; (current) torrente f; (of emotion) ímpeto ▶ VT apressar ▶ VI apressar-se, precipitar-se; **rush hour** N rush m (BR), hora de ponta (PT)

Russia ['rʌʃə] N Rússia; **Russian** ADJ russo ▶ N russo(-a); (Ling) russo

rust [rʌst] N ferrugem f ▶ VI enferrujar

rusty ['rʌstɪ] ADJ enferrujado

ruthless ['ruːθlɪs] ADJ implacável, sem piedade

rye [raɪ] N centeio

S

Sabbath ['sæbəθ] N (*Christian*) domingo; (*Jewish*) sábado

sabotage ['sæbətɑːʒ] N sabotagem f ▶ VT sabotar

saccharin, saccharine ['sækərɪn] N sacarina

sachet ['sæʃeɪ] N sachê m

sack [sæk] N (*bag*) saco, saca ▶ VT (*dismiss*) despedir; (*plunder*) saquear; **to get the ~** ser demitido

sacred ['seɪkrɪd] ADJ sagrado

sacrifice ['sækrɪfaɪs] N sacrifício ▶ VT sacrificar

sad [sæd] ADJ triste; (*deplorable*) deplorável, triste

saddle ['sædl] N sela; (*of cycle*) selim m ▶ VT selar; **to ~ sb with sth** (*inf: task, bill*) pôr algo nas costas de alguém; (: *responsibility*) sobrecarregar alguém com algo

sadistic [sə'dɪstɪk] ADJ sádico

sadly ['sædlɪ] ADV tristemente; (*regrettably*) infelizmente; (*mistaken, neglected*) gravemente; **~ lacking (in)** muito carente (de)

sadness ['sædnɪs] N tristeza

safe [seɪf] ADJ seguro; (*out of danger*) fora de perigo; (*unharmed*) ileso, incólume ▶ N cofre m, caixa-forte f; **~ from** protegido de; **~ and sound** são e salvo; **(just) to be on the ~ side** por via das dúvidas; **safely** ADV com segurança, a salvo; (*without mishap*) sem perigo

safety ['seɪftɪ] N segurança; **safety belt** N cinto de segurança; **safety pin** N alfinete m de segurança

sag [sæg] VI (*breasts*) cair; (*roof*) afundar; (*hem*) desmanchar

sage [seɪdʒ] N salva; (*man*) sábio

Sagittarius [sædʒɪ'tɛərɪəs] N Sagitário

Sahara [sə'hɑːrə] N: **the ~ (Desert)** o Saara

said [sɛd] PT, PP *of* **say**

sail [seɪl] N (*on boat*) vela; (*trip*): **to go for a ~** dar um passeio de barco a vela ▶ VT (*boat*) governar ▶ VI (*travel: ship*) navegar, velejar; (: *passenger*) ir de barco; (*Sport*) velejar; (*set off*) zarpar; **they ~ed into Rio de Janeiro** entraram no porto do Rio de Janeiro; **sail through** VT FUS (*fig*) fazer com facilidade; **sailboat** (*US*) N barco a vela; **sailing** N (*Sport*) navegação f a vela, vela; **to go sailing** ir velejar

sailor ['seɪlər] N marinheiro, marujo

saint [seɪnt] N santo(-a)

sake [seɪk] N: **for the ~ of** por (causa de), em consideração a; **for sb's/sth's ~** pelo bem de alguém/algo

salad ['sæləd] N salada; **salad cream** (*BRIT*) N maionese f; **salad dressing** N tempero *or* molho da salada

salami [sə'lɑːmɪ] N salame m

salary ['sælərɪ] N salário

sale [seɪl] N venda; (*at reduced prices*) liquidação f, saldo; (*auction*) leilão m; **sales** NPL (*total amount sold*) vendas fpl; **"for ~"** "vende-se"; **on ~** à venda; **on ~ or return** em consignação; **sales assistant**, (*US*) **sales clerk** N vendedor(a) m/f

salmon ['sæmən] N INV salmão m

salon ['sælɔn] N (*hairdressing salon*) salão m (de cabeleireiro); (*beauty salon*) salão (de beleza)

saloon [sə'luːn] N (*US*) bar m, botequim m; (*BRIT Aut*) sedã m; (*ship's lounge*) salão m

salt [sɔːlt] N sal m ▶ VT salgar; **saltwater** ADJ de água salgada; **salty** ADJ salgado

salute [sə'luːt] N (*greeting*) saudação f; (*of guns*) salva; (*Mil*) continência ▶ VT saudar; (*Mil*) fazer continência a

salvage ['sælvɪdʒ] N (*saving*) salvamento, recuperação f; (*things saved*) salvados mpl ▶ VT salvar

same [seɪm] ADJ mesmo ▶ PRON: **the ~** o mesmo/a mesma; **the ~ book as** o mesmo livro que; **all *or* just the ~** apesar de tudo, mesmo assim; **the ~ to you!** igualmente!

sample ['sɑːmpl] N amostra ▶ VT (*food, wine*) provar, experimentar

sanction ['sæŋkʃən] N sanção f ▶ VT sancionar

sanctuary ['sæŋktjʊərɪ] N (*holy place*) santuário; (*refuge*) refúgio, asilo; (*for animals*) reserva

sand [sænd] N areia; (*beach: also*: **~s**) praia ▶ VT (*also*: **~ down**) lixar
sandal ['sændl] N sandália
sand: sandbox ['sændbɒks] (*US*) N (*for children*) caixa de areia; **sand castle** N castelo de areia; **sandpaper** ['sændpeɪpəʳ] N lixa; **sandpit** ['sændpɪt (*BRIT*)] N (*for children*) caixa de areia; **sandstone** ['sændstəun] N arenito, grés *m*
sandwich ['sændwɪtʃ] N sanduíche *m* (*BR*), sandes *f inv* (*PT*) ▶ VT: **~ed between** encaixado entre
sandy ['sændɪ] ADJ arenoso; (*colour*) vermelho amarelado
sane [seɪn] ADJ são/sã do juízo; (*sensible*) ajuizado, sensato
sang [sæŋ] PT *of* **sing**
sanity ['sænɪtɪ] N sanidade *f*, equilíbrio mental; (*common sense*) juízo, sensatez *f*
sank [sæŋk] PT *of* **sink**
Santa Claus [sæntə'klɔ:z] N Papai Noel *m*
sap [sæp] N (*of plants*) seiva ▶ VT (*strength*) esgotar, minar
sapphire ['sæfaɪəʳ] N safira
sarcasm ['sɑ:kæzm] N sarcasmo
sardine [sɑː'diːn] N sardinha
Sardinia [sɑː'dɪnɪə] N Sardenha
sat [sæt] PT, PP *of* **sit**
satchel ['sætʃl] N sacola
satellite ['sætəlaɪt] N satélite *m*; **satellite dish** N antena parabólica; **satellite television** N televisão *f* via satélite
satin ['sætɪn] N cetim *m* ▶ ADJ acetinado
satire ['sætaɪəʳ] N sátira
satisfaction [sætɪs'fækʃən] N satisfação *f*; (*refund, apology etc*) compensação *f*; **satisfactory** ADJ satisfatório
satisfy ['sætɪsfaɪ] VT satisfazer; (*convince*) convencer, persuadir
Saturday ['sætədɪ] N sábado
sauce [sɔːs] N molho; (*sweet*) calda; **saucepan** N panela (*BR*), caçarola (*PT*)
saucer ['sɔːsəʳ] N pires *m inv*
Saudi ['saudɪ] ADJ, N (*also*: **~ Arabia**) Arábia Saudita; (*also*: **~ Arabian**) saudita *m/f*
sauna ['sɔːnə] N sauna
sausage ['sɒsɪdʒ] N salsicha, linguiça; (*cold meat*) frios *mpl*; **sausage roll** N folheado de salsicha
savage ['sævɪdʒ] ADJ (*cruel, fierce*) cruel, feroz; (*primitive*) selvagem ▶ N selvagem *m/f*

save [seɪv] VT (*rescue, Comput*) salvar; (*money*) poupar, economizar; (*time*) ganhar; (*Sport*) impedir; (*avoid: trouble*) evitar; (*keep: seat*) guardar ▶ VI (*also*: **~ up**) poupar ▶ N (*Sport*) salvamento ▶ PREP salvo, exceto
saw [sɔː] (*pt* **sawed**, *pp* **sawed** *or* **sawn**) PT *of* **see** ▶ N (*tool*) serra ▶ VT serrar; **sawdust** N serragem *f*, pó *m* de serra
saxophone ['sæksəfəun] N saxofone *m*
say [seɪ] (*pt, pp* **said**) N: **to have one's ~** exprimir sua opinião, vender seu peixe (*inf*) ▶ VT dizer, falar; **to have a** *or* **some ~ in sth** opinar sobre algo, ter que ver com algo; **could you ~ that again?** poderia repetir?; **that is to ~** ou seja; **saying** N ditado, provérbio
scab [skæb] N casca, crosta (*de ferida*); (*pej*) fura-greve *m/f inv*
scald [skɔːld] N escaldadura ▶ VT escaldar, queimar
scale [skeɪl] N escala; (*of fish*) escama; (*of salaries, fees etc*) tabela ▶ VT (*mountain*) escalar; **scales** NPL (*for weighing*) balança; **~ of charges** tarifa, lista de preços; **scale down** VT reduzir
scallop ['skɔləp] N (*Zool*) vieira, venera; (*Sewing*) barra, arremate *m*
scalp [skælp] N couro cabeludo ▶ VT escalpar
scam [skæm] (*inf*) N maracutaia, falcatrua
scampi ['skæmpɪ] NPL camarões *mpl* fritos
scan [skæn] VT (*examine*) esquadrinhar, perscrutar; (*glance at quickly*) passar uma vista de olhos por; (*TV, Radar*) explorar ▶ N (*Med*) exame *m*
scandal ['skændl] N escândalo; (*gossip*) fofocas *fpl*; (*fig: disgrace*) vergonha
Scandinavian [skændɪ'neɪvɪən] ADJ, N escandinavo(-a)
scanner ['skænəʳ] N (*Med, Comput*) scanner *m*
scapegoat ['skeɪpgəut] N bode *m* expiatório
scar [skɑː] N cicatriz *f* ▶ VT marcar (com uma cicatriz)
scarce [skɛəs] ADJ escasso, raro; **to make o.s. ~** (*inf*) dar o fora, cair fora; **scarcely** ADV mal, quase não; (*barely*) apenas
scare [skɛəʳ] N susto; (*panic*) pânico ▶ VT assustar; **to ~ sb stiff** deixar alguém morrendo de medo; **bomb ~** alarme de bomba; **scare away** espantar; **scare off** VT = **scare away**; **scarecrow** N espantalho; **scared** ADJ:

to be scared estar assustado or com medo

scarf [skɑːf] (pl **scarfs** or **scarves**) N cachecol m; (square) lenço (de cabeça)

scarlet ['skɑːlɪt] ADJ escarlate

scary ['skɛərɪ] (inf) ADJ assustador(a)

scatter ['skætə'] VT espalhar; (put to flight) dispersar ▶ VI espalhar-se

scene [siːn] N (Theatre, fig) cena; (of crime, accident) cenário; (sight) vista, panorama m; (fuss) escândalo; **scenery** ['siːnərɪ] N (Theatre) cenário; (landscape) paisagem f; **scenic** ADJ pitoresco

scent [sɛnt] N perfume m; (smell) aroma; (track, fig) pista, rastro

schedule [(BRIT) 'ʃɛdjuːl, (US) 'skɛdjuːl] N (of trains) horário; (of events) programa m; (list) lista ▶ VT (timetable) planejar; (visit) marcar (a hora de); **on ~** na hora, sem atraso; **to be ahead of/behind ~** estar adiantado/atrasado

scheme [skiːm] N (plan, plot) maquinação f; (pension scheme etc) projeto; (arrangement) arranjo ▶ VI conspirar

scholar ['skɔlə'] N aluno(-a), estudante m/f; (learned person) sábio(-a), erudito(-a); **scholarship** N erudição f; (grant) bolsa de estudos

school [skuːl] N escola; (secondary school) colégio; (US: university) universidade f ▶ CPD escolar; **schoolboy** N aluno; **schoolchildren** NPL alunos mpl; **schoolgirl** N aluna; **schoolteacher** N professor(a) m/f

science ['saɪəns] N ciência; **science fiction** N ficção f científica; **scientific** [saɪən'tɪfɪk] ADJ científico; **scientist** N cientista m/f

scissors ['sɪzəz] NPL tesoura; **a pair of ~** uma tesoura

scold [skəuld] VT ralhar

scone [skɔn] N bolinho de trigo

scoop [skuːp] N colherona; (for flour etc) pá f; (Press) furo (jornalístico); **scoop out** VT escavar; **scoop up** VT recolher

scooter ['skuːtə'] N (also: **motor ~**) lambreta; (toy) patinete m

scope [skəup] N liberdade f de ação; (of plan, undertaking) âmbito; (of person) competência; (opportunity) oportunidade f

score [skɔː'] N (points etc) escore m, contagem f; (Mus) partitura; (twenty) vintena ▶ VT (goal, point) fazer; (mark) marcar, entalhar; (success) alcançar ▶ VI (in game) marcar; (Football) marcar or fazer um gol; (keep score) marcar o

escore; **on that ~** a esse respeito, por esse motivo; **~s of** (fig) um monte de; **to ~ 6 out of 10** tirar nota 6 num total de 10; **score out** VT riscar; **scoreboard** N marcador m, placar m

scorn [skɔːn] N desprezo ▶ VT desprezar, rejeitar

Scorpio ['skɔːpɪəu] N Escorpião m

Scot [skɔt] N escocês(-esa) m/f

Scotch [skɔtʃ] N uísque m (BR) or whisky m (PT) escocês

Scotland ['skɔtlənd] N Escócia; **Scots** ADJ escocês(-esa); **Scotsman** irreg N escocês m; **Scotswoman** irreg N escocesa; **Scottish** ADJ escocês(-esa)

scout [skaut] N (Mil) explorador m, batedor m; (also: **boy ~**) escoteiro; **girl ~** (US) escoteira; **scout around** VI explorar

scowl [skaul] VI franzir a testa; **to ~ at sb** olhar de cara feia para alguém

scramble ['skræmbl] N (climb) escalada (difícil); (struggle) luta ▶ VI: **to ~ out/ through** conseguir sair com dificuldade; **to ~ for** lutar por; **scrambled eggs** NPL ovos mpl mexidos

scrap [skræp] N (of paper) pedacinho; (of material) fragmento; (fig: of truth) mínimo; (fight) rixa, luta; (also: **~ iron**) ferro velho, sucata ▶ VT sucatar, jogar no ferro velho; (fig) descartar, abolir ▶ VI brigar; **scraps** NPL (leftovers) sobras fpl, restos mpl; **scrapbook** N álbum m de recortes

scrape [skreɪp] N (fig): **to get into a ~** meter-se numa enrascada ▶ VT raspar; (also: **~ against**: hand, car) arranhar, roçar ▶ VI: **to ~ through** (in exam) passar raspando; **scrape together** VT (money) juntar com dificuldade

scrap paper N papel m de rascunho

scratch [skrætʃ] N arranhão m; (from claw) arranhadura ▶ CPD: **~ team** time m improvisado, escrete m ▶ VT (rub) coçar; (with claw, nail) arranhar, unhar; (damage) arranhar ▶ VI coçar(-se); **to start from ~** partir do zero; **to be up to ~** estar à altura (das circunstâncias)

scream [skriːm] N grito ▶ VI gritar

screen [skriːn] N (Cinema, TV, Comput) tela (BR); ecrã m (PT); (movable) biombo; (fig) cortina ▶ VT (conceal) esconder, tapar; (from the wind etc) proteger; (film) projetar; (candidates etc, Med) examinar; **screenplay** N roteiro; **screensaver** ['skriːnseɪvə'] N protetor m de tela; **screenshot** N (Comput) captura de tela

screw [skruː] N parafuso ▶ VT aparafusar; (also: **~ in**) apertar, atarraxar; **screw up** vt (*paper etc*) amassar; **to ~ up one's eyes** franzir os olhos; **screwdriver** N chave *f* de fenda *or* de parafuso

scribble ['skrɪbl] N garrancho ▶ vt escrevinhar ▶ vi rabiscar

script [skrɪpt] N (*Cinema etc*) roteiro, script *m*; (*writing*) escrita, caligrafia

scroll [skrəʊl] N rolo de pergaminho

scrub [skrʌb] N mato, cerrado ▶ vt esfregar; (*inf*) cancelar, eliminar

scruffy ['skrʌfɪ] ADJ desmazelado

scrutiny ['skru:tɪnɪ] N escrutínio, exame *m* cuidadoso

sculptor ['skʌlptər] N escultor(a) *m/f*

sculpture ['skʌlptʃər] N escultura

scum [skʌm] N (*on liquid*) espuma; (*pej: people*) ralé *f*, gentinha

scurry ['skʌrɪ] vi sair correndo; **scurry off** vi sair correndo, dar no pé

sea [si:] N mar *m* ▶ cpd do mar, marino; **on the ~** (*boat*) no mar; (*town*) junto ao mar; **to go by ~** viajar por mar; **out to** *or* **at ~** em alto mar; **to be all at ~** (*fig*) estar confuso *or* desorientado; **seafood** N mariscos *mpl*; **seagull** N gaivota

seal [si:l] N (*animal*) foca; (*stamp*) selo ▶ vt fechar; **seal off** vt fechar

sea level N nível *m* do mar

seam [si:m] N costura; (*where edges meet*) junta; (*of coal*) veio, filão *m*

search [sə:tʃ] N busca, procura; (*Comput*) busca; (*inspection*) exame *m*, investigação *f* ▶ vt (*look in*) procurar em; (*examine*) examinar; (*person, place*) revistar ▶ vi: **to ~ for** procurar; **in ~ of** à procura de; **search through** vt fus dar busca em; **search engine** N (*on Internet*) site *m* de busca; **search party** N equipe *f* de salvamento

sea: seashore N praia, beira-mar *f*, litoral *m*; **seasick** ADJ: **to be** *or* **get seasick** enjoar; **seaside** N praia; **seaside resort** N balneário

season ['si:zn] N (*of year*) estação *f*; (*sporting etc*) temporada; (*of films etc*) série *f* ▶ vt (*food*) temperar; **to be in/out of ~** (*fruit*) estar na época/fora de época; **season ticket** N bilhete *m* de temporada

seat [si:t] N (*in bus, train: place*) assento; (*chair*) cadeira; (*Pol*) lugar *m*, cadeira; (*buttocks*) traseiro, nádegas *fpl*; (*of trousers*) fundilhos *mpl* ▶ vt sentar; (*have room for*) ter capacidade para; **to be ~ed** estar sentado; **seat belt** N cinto de segurança

sea water N água do mar

seaweed ['si:wi:d] N alga marinha

sec. ABBR (= *second*) seg.

secluded [sɪ'klu:dɪd] ADJ (*place*) afastado; (*life*) solitário

second¹ [sɪ'kɔnd] (BRIT) vt (*employee*) transferir temporariamente

second² ['sɛkənd] ADJ segundo ▶ ADV (*in race etc*) em segundo lugar ▶ N segundo; (*Aut: also:* **~ gear**) segunda; (*Comm*) artigo defeituoso; (*BRIT Sch: degree*) *uma qualificação boa mas sem distinção* ▶ vt (*motion*) apoiar, secundar; **secondary** ADJ secundário; **secondary school** N escola secundária, colégio

▎Na Grã-Bretanha, uma **secondary
▎school** é um estabelecimento de
▎ensino para alunos de 11 a 18 anos,
▎alguns dos quais interrompem os
▎estudos aos 16 anos.

second: second-class ADV em segunda classe; **secondhand** ADJ de (BR) *or* em (PT) segunda mão, usado; **second hand** N (*on clock*) ponteiro de segundos; **secondly** ADV em segundo lugar; **second-rate** ADJ de segunda categoria; **second thoughts** N PL, (US) **second thought**: **to have second thoughts (about doing sth)** pensar duas vezes (antes de fazer algo); **on second thoughts** pensando bem

secrecy ['si:krəsɪ] N sigilo

secret ['si:krɪt] ADJ secreto ▶ N segredo

secretary ['sɛkrətərɪ] N secretário(-a); (BRIT Pol): **S~ of State** Ministro(-a) de Estado

secretive ['si:krətɪv] ADJ sigiloso, reservado

section ['sɛkʃən] N seção *f*; (*part*) parte *f*, porção *f*; (*of document*) parágrafo, artigo; (*of opinion*) setor *m*; **cross-~** corte *m* transversal

sector ['sɛktər] N setor *m*

secular ['sɛkjulər] ADJ (*priest*) secular; (*music, society*) leigo

secure [sɪ'kjuər] ADJ (*safe*) seguro; (*firmly fixed*) firme, rígido ▶ vt (*fix*) prender; (*get*) conseguir, obter; **security** N segurança; (*for loan*) fiança, garantia; **security guard** N segurança *m/f*

sedate [sɪ'deɪt] ADJ calmo ▶ vt sedar, tratar com calmantes; **sedative** N calmante *m*, sedativo

seduce [sɪ'dju:s] vt seduzir; **seductive** ADJ sedutor(a)

see [si:] (*pt* **saw**, *pp* **seen**) vt ver; (*understand*) entender; (*accompany*): **to ~ sb to the door** acompanhar *or* levar alguém até a porta ▶ vi ver; (*find out*) achar ▶ N sé *f*, sede *f*; **to ~ that** (*ensure*) assegurar que; **~ you soon/later/ tomorrow!** até logo/mais tarde/ amanhã!; **see about** VT FUS tratar de; **see off** VT despedir-se de; **see through** VT FUS enxergar através de ▶ VT levar a cabo; **see to** VT FUS providenciar

seed [si:d] N semente f; (*sperm*) esperma m; (*fig: gen pl*) germe m; (*Tennis*) pré-selecionado(-a); **to go to ~** produzir sementes; (*fig*) deteriorar-se

seeing ['si:ɪŋ] CONJ: **~ (that)** visto (que), considerando (que)

seek [si:k] (*pt, pp* sought) VT procurar; (*post*) solicitar

seem [si:m] VI parecer; **there ~s to be ...** parece que há ...

seen [si:n] PP *of* see

seesaw ['si:sɔ:] N gangorra, balanço

segment ['sɛgmənt] N segmento m; (*of orange*) gomo

seize [si:z] VT agarrar, pegar; (*power, hostage*) apoderar-se de, confiscar; (*territory*) tomar posse de; (*opportunity*) aproveitar; **seize on** VT FUS valer-se de; **seize up** VI (*Tech*) gripar; **seize upon** VT FUS = seize on; **seizure** N (*Med*) ataque m, acesso; (*Jur, of power*) confisco, embargo

seldom ['sɛldəm] ADV raramente

select [sɪ'lɛkt] ADJ seleto, fino ▶ VT escolher, selecionar; (*Sport*) selecionar, escalar; **selection** N seleção f, escolha; (*Comm*) sortimento

self [sɛlf] (*pl* selves) PRON *see* herself, himself, itself, myself, oneself, ourselves, themselves, yourself ▶ N: **the ~** o eu; **self-assured** ADJ seguro de si; **self-catering** (BRIT) ADJ (*flat*) com cozinha; (*holiday*) em casa alugada; **self-centred**, (US) **self-centered** ADJ egocêntrico; **self-confidence** N autoconfiança, confiança em si; **self-conscious** ADJ inibido, constrangido; **self-control** N autocontrole m, autodomínio; **self-defence**, (US) **self-defense** N legítima defesa, autodefesa; **in self-defence** em legítima defesa; **self-employed** ADJ autônomo; **self-harm** N autoimolação f; **selfie** N ['sɛlfɪ] selfie f; **selfie stick** N pau m de selfie (BR), selfie stick m (PT); **self-interest** N egoísmo; **selfish** ADJ egoísta; **self-pity** N pena de si mesmo; **self-respect** N amor m próprio; **self-service** ADJ de autosserviço

sell [sɛl] (*pt, pp* sold) VT vender; (*fig*): **to ~ sb an idea** convencer alguém de uma

ideia ▶ VI vender-se; **to ~ at** *or* **for £10** vender a *or* por £10; **sell off** VT liquidar; **sell out** VI vender todo o estoque ▶ VT: **the tickets are all sold out** todos os ingressos já foram vendidos; **sell-by date** N vencimento; **seller** N vendedor(a) m/f

selves [sɛlvz] PL *of* self

semi... ['sɛmɪ] PREFIX semi..., meio...; **semicircle** N semicírculo; **semidetached**, **semidetached house** (BRIT) N (*casa*) geminada

seminar ['sɛmɪnɑ:ʳ] N seminário

senate ['sɛnɪt] N senado; **senator** N senador(a) m/f

send [sɛnd] (*pt, pp* sent) VT mandar, enviar; (*dispatch*) expedir, remeter; (*transmit*) transmitir; **send away** VT (*letter, goods*) expedir, mandar; (*unwelcome visitor*) mandar embora; **send away for** VT FUS encomendar, pedir pelo correio; **send back** VT devolver, mandar de volta; **send for** VT FUS mandar buscar; (*by post*) pedir pelo correio, encomendar; **send off** VT (*goods*) despachar, expedir; (BRIT *Sport: player*) expulsar; **send on** VT (BRIT: *letter*) remeter; (*luggage etc: in advance*) mandar com antecedência; **send out** VT (*invitation*) distribuir; (*signal*) emitir; **send up** VT (*person, price*) fazer subir; (BRIT: *parody*) parodiar; **sender** N remetente m/f; **send-off** N: **a good send-off** uma boa despedida

senior ['si:nɪəʳ] ADJ (*older*) mais velho *or* idoso; (*on staff*) mais antigo; (*of higher rank*) superior; **senior citizen** N idoso(-a)

sensation [sɛn'seɪʃən] N sensação f; **sensational** ADJ sensacional; (*headlines, result*) sensacionalista

sense [sɛns] N sentido; (*feeling*) sensação f; (*good sense*) bom senso ▶ VT sentir, perceber; **it makes ~** faz sentido; **senseless** ADJ insensato, estúpido; (*unconscious*) sem sentidos, inconsciente; **sensible** ADJ sensato, de bom senso; (*reasonable: price*) razoável; (: *advice, decision*) sensato

sensitive ['sɛnsɪtɪv] ADJ sensível; (*fig: touchy*) suscetível

sensual ['sɛnsjuəl] ADJ sensual

sensuous ['sɛnsjuəs] ADJ sensual

sent [sɛnt] PT, PP *of* send

sentence ['sɛntəns] N (*Ling*) frase f, oração f; (*Jur*) sentença ▶ VT: **to ~ sb to death/to 5 years** condenar alguém à morte/a 5 anos de prisão

sentiment ['sɛntɪmənt] N sentimento; (*opinion: also pl*) opinião f; **sentimental** [sɛntɪ'mɛntl] ADJ sentimental

separate [*adj* 'sɛprɪt, *vt*, *vi* 'sɛpəreɪt] ADJ separado; (*distinct*) diferente ▶ VT separar; (*part*) dividir ▶ VI separar-se; **separately** ADV separadamente

September [sɛp'tɛmbəʳ] N setembro

septic ['sɛptɪk] ADJ sético; (*wound*) infeccionado

sequel ['si:kwl] N consequência, resultado; (*of film, story*) continuação f

sequence ['si:kwəns] N série f, sequência; (*Cinema*) série

sequin ['si:kwɪn] N lantejoula, paetê m

sergeant ['sɑ:dʒənt] N sargento

serial ['sɪərɪəl] N seriado; **serial killer** N assassino(-a) em série, serial killer m/f; **serial number** N número de série

series ['sɪəri:z] N INV série f

serious ['sɪərɪəs] ADJ sério; (*matter*) importante; (*illness*) grave; **seriously** ADV a sério, com seriedade; (*hurt*) gravemente

sermon ['sə:mən] N sermão m

servant ['sə:vənt] N empregado(-a); (*fig*) servidor(a) m/f

serve [sə:v] VT servir; (*customer*) atender; (*subj: train*) passar por; (*apprenticeship*) fazer; (*prison term*) cumprir ▶ VI (*at table*) servir-se; (*Tennis*) sacar; (*be useful*): **to ~ as/for/to do** servir como/para/para fazer ▶ N (*Tennis*) saque m; **it ~s him right** é bem feito para ele; **serve out** VT (*food*) servir; **serve up** VT = **serve out**; **server** ['sə:vəʳ] N (*Comput*) servidor m

service ['sə:vɪs] N serviço; (*Rel*) culto; (*Aut*) revisão f; (*Tennis*) saque m; (*also*: **dinner ~**) aparelho de jantar ▶ VT (*car, washing machine*) fazer a revisão de, revisar; **the Services** NPL (*army, navy etc*) as Forças Armadas; **to be of ~ to sb** ser útil a alguém; **service area** N (*on motorway*) posto de gasolina com bar, restaurante etc; **service charge** (BRIT) N serviço; **serviceman** irreg N militar m; **service station** N posto de gasolina (BR), estação f de serviço (PT)

serviette [sə:vɪ'ɛt] (BRIT) N guardanapo

session ['sɛʃən] N sessão f; **to be in ~** estar reunido em sessão

set [sɛt] (*pt, pp* **set**) N (*collection of things*) jogo; (*radio set, TV set*) aparelho; (*of utensils*) bateria de cozinha; (*of cutlery*) talher m; (*of books*) coleção f; (*of group of people*) grupo; (*Tennis*) set m; (*Theatre, Cinema*) cenário; (*Hairdressing*) penteado;

(*Math*) conjunto ▶ ADJ fixo; (*ready*) pronto ▶ VT pôr, colocar; (*table*) pôr; (*price*) fixar; (*rules etc*) estabelecer, decidir; (*record*) estabelecer; (*time*) marcar; (*adjust*) ajustar; (*task, exam*) passar ▶ VI (*sun*) pôr-se; (*jam, jelly, concrete*) endurecer, solidificar-se; **to be ~ on doing sth** estar decidido a fazer algo; **to ~ to music** musicar, pôr música em; **to ~ on fire** botar fogo em, incendiar; **to ~ free** libertar; **to ~ sth going** pôr algo em movimento; **set about** VT FUS começar com; **set aside** VT deixar de lado; **set back** VT (*cost*): **it ~ me back £50** custou £50; (*in time*): **to ~ sb back (by)** atrasar alguém (em); **set off** VI partir, ir indo ▶ VT (*bomb*) fazer explodir; (*alarm*) disparar; (*chain of events*) iniciar; (*show up well*) ressaltar; **set out** VI partir ▶ VT (*arrange*) colocar, dispor; (*state*) expor, explicar; **to ~ out to do sth** pretender fazer algo; **set up** VT fundar, estabelecer; **setback** N revés m, contratempo; **set menu** N refeição f a preço fixo

settee [sɛ'ti:] N sofá m

setting ['sɛtɪŋ] N (*background*) cenário; (*position*) posição f; (*of sun*) pôr (do sol) m; (*of jewel*) engaste m

settle ['sɛtl] VT (*argument, matter*) resolver, esclarecer; (*accounts*) ajustar, liquidar; (*Med: calm*) acalmar, tranquilizar ▶ VI (*dust etc*) assentar; (*calm down: children*) acalmar-se; (*also*: **~ down**) instalar-se, estabilizar-se; **to ~ for sth** concordar em aceitar algo; **to ~ on sth** optar por algo; **settle in** VI instalar-se; **settle up** VI: **to ~ up with sb** ajustar as contas com alguém; **settlement** N (*payment*) liquidação f; (*agreement*) acordo, convênio; (*village etc*) povoado, povoação f

setup ['sɛtʌp] N (*organization*) organização f; (*situation*) situação f

seven ['sɛvn] NUM sete; **seventeen** ['sɛvn'ti:n] NUM dezessete; **seventeenth** [sɛvn'ti:nθ] NUM décimo sétimo; **seventh** ['sɛvnθ] NUM sétimo; **seventieth** ['sɛvntɪɪθ] NUM septuagésimo; **seventy** ['sɛvntɪ] NUM setenta

sever ['sɛvəʳ] VT cortar; (*relations*) romper

several ['sɛvərl] ADJ, PRON vários(-as); **~ of us** vários de nós

severe [sɪ'vɪəʳ] ADJ severo; (*serious*) grave; (*hard*) duro; (*pain*) intenso; (*dress*) austero

sew [səu] (*pt* **sewed**, *pp* **sewn**) VT coser, costurar; **sew up** VT coser, costurar

sewage ['su:ɪdʒ] N detritos mpl
sewer ['su:əʳ] N (cano do) esgoto, bueiro
sewing ['səuɪŋ] N costura; **sewing machine** N máquina de costura
sewn [səun] PP of **sew**
sex [sɛks] N sexo; **sexist** ADJ sexista
sexual ['sɛksjuəl] ADJ sexual; **sexuality** [sɛksju'ælɪtɪ] N sexualidade f
sexy ['sɛksɪ] ADJ sexy
shabby ['ʃæbɪ] ADJ (person) esfarrapado, maltrapilho; (clothes) usado, surrado; (behaviour) indigno
shack [ʃæk] N choupana, barraca
shade [ʃeɪd] N sombra; (for lamp) quebra-luz m; (of colour) tom m, tonalidade f; (small quantity): **a ~ (more/too big)** um pouquinho (mais/grande) ▶ VT dar sombra a; (eyes) sombrear; **in the ~** à sombra
shadow ['ʃædəu] N sombra ▶ VT (follow) seguir de perto (sem ser visto)
shady ['ʃeɪdɪ] ADJ à sombra; (fig: dishonest: person) suspeito, duvidoso; (: deal) desonesto
shaft [ʃɑ:ft] N (of arrow, spear) haste f; (Aut, Tech) eixo, manivela; (of mine, of lift) poço; (of light) raio
shake [ʃeɪk] (pt **shook**, pp **shaken**) VT sacudir; (building, confidence) abalar; (surprise) surpreender ▶ VI tremer; **to ~ hands with sb** apertar a mão de alguém; **to ~ one's head** (in refusal etc) dizer não com a cabeça; (in dismay) sacudir a cabeça; **shake off** VT sacudir; (fig) livrar-se de; **shake up** VT sacudir; (fig) reorganizar; **shaky** ADJ (hand, voice) trêmulo; (table) instável; (building) abalado
shall [ʃæl] AUX VB: **I ~ go** irei; **~ I open the door?** posso abrir a porta?; **I'll get some, ~ I?** eu vou pegar algum, está bem?
shallow ['ʃæləu] ADJ raso; (breathing) fraco; (fig) superficial
sham [ʃæm] N fraude f, fingimento ▶ VT fingir, simular
shambles ['ʃæmblz] N confusão f
shame [ʃeɪm] N vergonha ▶ VT envergonhar; **it is a ~ (that/to do)** é (uma) pena (que/fazer); **what a ~!** que pena!; **shameful** ADJ vergonhoso; **shameless** ADJ sem vergonha, descarado
shampoo [ʃæm'pu:] N xampu m (BR), champô m (PT) ▶ VT lavar o cabelo (com xampu or champô)
shandy ['ʃændɪ] N mistura de cerveja com refresco gaseificado

shan't [ʃɑ:nt] = **shall not**
shape [ʃeɪp] N forma ▶ VT (form) moldar; (sb's ideas) formar; (sb's life) definir, determinar; **to take ~** tomar forma; **shape up** VI (events) desenrolar-se; (person) tomar jeito
share [ʃɛəʳ] N parte f; (contribution) cota; (Comm) ação f ▶ VT dividir; (have in common) compartilhar; **share out** VI distribuir; **shareholder** N acionista m/f
shark [ʃɑ:k] N tubarão m
sharp [ʃɑ:p] ADJ (razor, knife) afiado; (point, features) pontiagudo; (outline) definido, bem marcado; (pain, curve) agudo; (taste) acre; (Mus) desafinado; (contrast) marcado; (quick-witted) perspicaz; (dishonest) desonesto ▶ N (Mus) sustenido ▶ ADV: **at 2 o'clock ~** às 2 (horas) em ponto; **sharpen** VT afiar; (pencil) apontar, fazer a ponta de; (fig) açúcar; **sharpener** N (also: **pencil sharpener**) apontador m (BR), apara-lápis m inv (PT); **sharply** ADV (abruptly) bruscamente; (clearly) claramente; (harshly) severamente
shatter ['ʃætəʳ] VT despedaçar, estilhaçar; (fig: ruin) destruir, acabar com; (: upset) arrasar ▶ VI despedaçar-se, estilhaçar-se
shave [ʃeɪv] VT barbear, fazer a barba de ▶ VI fazer a barba, barbear-se ▶ N: **to have a ~** fazer a barba; **shaver** N barbeador m; **electric shaver** barbeador elétrico; **shaving cream** N creme m de barbear; **shaving foam** N espuma de barbear
shawl [ʃɔ:l] N xale m
she [ʃi:] PRON ela ▶ PREFIX: **~-elephant** etc elefante etc fêmea
sheath [ʃi:θ] N bainha; (contraceptive) camisa-de-vênus f, camisinha
shed [ʃɛd] (pt, pp **shed**) N alpendre m, galpão m ▶ VT (skin) mudar; (load, leaves, fur) perder; (tears, blood) derramar; (workers) despedir
she'd [ʃi:d] = **she had**; = **she would**
sheep [ʃi:p] N INV ovelha; **sheepdog** N cão m pastor; **sheepskin** N pele f de carneiro, pelego
sheer [ʃɪəʳ] ADJ (utter) puro, completo; (steep) íngreme, empinado; (almost transparent) fino, translúcido ▶ ADV a pique
sheet [ʃi:t] N (on bed) lençol m; (of paper) folha; (of glass, metal) lâmina, chapa; (of ice) camada
sheik, sheikh [ʃeɪk] N xeque m

shelf [ʃelf] (pl **shelves**) N prateleira

shell [ʃel] N (on beach) concha; (of egg, nut etc) casca; (explosive) obus m; (of building) armação f, esqueleto ▶ VT (peas) descascar; (Mil) bombardear

she'll [ʃiːl] = **she will**; = **she shall**

shellfish [ʃelfɪʃ] N INV crustáceo; (as food) frutos mpl do mar, mariscos mpl

shelter [ʃeltəʳ] N (building) abrigo; (protection) refúgio ▶ VT (protect) proteger; (give lodging to) abrigar ▶ VI abrigar-se, refugiar-se

shepherd [ʃepəd] N pastor m ▶ VT guiar, conduzir; **shepherd's pie** (BRIT) N empadão m de carne e batata

sheriff [ʃerɪf] (US) N xerife m

sherry [ʃerɪ] N (vinho de) Xerez m

she's [ʃiːz] = **she is**; = **she has**

Shetland [ʃetlənd] N (also: **the ~s, the ~ Isles**) as ilhas Shetland

shield [ʃiːld] N escudo; (Sport) escudo, brasão m; (protection) proteção f ▶ VT: **to ~ (from)** proteger (contra)

shift [ʃɪft] N mudança; (of work) turno; (of workers) turma ▶ VT transferir; (remove) tirar ▶ VI mudar

shin [ʃɪn] N canela (da perna)

shine [ʃaɪn] (pt, pp **shone**) N brilho, lustre m ▶ VI brilhar ▶ VT (shoes: pt, pp **shined**) lustrar; **to ~ a torch on sth** apontar uma lanterna para algo

shingles [ʃɪŋglz] N (Med) herpes-zoster m

shiny [ʃaɪnɪ] ADJ brilhante, lustroso

ship [ʃɪp] N barco ▶ VT (goods) embarcar; (send) transportar or mandar (por via marítima); **shipment** N carregamento; **shipping** N (ships) navios mpl; (cargo) transporte m de mercadorias (por via marítima); (traffic) navegação f; **shipwreck** N (event) malogro; (ship) naufrágio ▶ VT: **to be shipwrecked** naufragar; **shipyard** N estaleiro

shirt [ʃəːt] N (man's) camisa; (woman's) blusa; **in ~ sleeves** em manga de camisa

shit [ʃɪt] (!) EXCL merda (!)

shiver [ʃɪvəʳ] N tremor m, arrepio ▶ VI tremer, estremecer, tiritar

shock [ʃɔk] N (impact) choque m; (Elec) descarga; (emotional) comoção f, abalo; (start) susto, sobressalto; (Med) trauma m ▶ VT dar um susto em, chocar; (offend) escandalizar; **shocking** ADJ chocante, lamentável; (outrageous) revoltante, chocante

shoe [ʃuː] (pt, pp **shod**) N sapato; (for horse) ferradura ▶ VT (horse) ferrar; **shoelace** N cadarço, cordão m (de

sapato); **shoe polish** N graxa de sapato; **shoeshop** N sapataria

shone [ʃɔn] PT, PP of **shine**

shook [ʃuk] PT of **shake**

shoot [ʃuːt] (pt, pp **shot**) N (on branch, seedling) broto ▶ VT disparar; (kill) matar à bala, balear; (wound) ferir à bala, balear; (execute) fuzilar; (film) filmar, rodar ▶ VI: **to ~ (at)** atirar (em); (Football) chutar; **shoot down** VT (plane) derrubar, abater; **shoot in** VI entrar correndo; **shoot out** VI sair correndo; **shoot up** VI (fig) subir vertiginosamente

shop [ʃɔp] N loja; (workshop) oficina ▶ VI (also: **go ~ping**) ir fazer compras; **shop assistant** (BRIT) N vendedor(a) m/f; **shopkeeper** N lojista m/f; **shoplifting** N furto (em lojas); **shopping** N (goods) compras fpl; **shopping bag** N bolsa (de compras); **shopping cart** (US) N carrinho de compras; **shopping centre**, (US) **shopping center** N shopping (center) m; **shopping mall** N shopping m; **shopping trolley** (BRIT) N carrinho de compras; **shop window** N vitrine f (BR), montra (PT)

shore [ʃɔːʳ] N (of sea) costa, praia; (of lake) margem f ▶ VT: **to ~ (up)** reforçar, escorar; **on ~** em terra

short [ʃɔːt] ADJ curto; (in time) breve, de curta duração; (person) baixo; (curt) seco, brusco; (insufficient) insuficiente, em falta; **to be ~ of sth** estar em falta de algo; **in ~** em resumo; **~ of doing ...** a não ser fazer ...; **everything ~ of ...** tudo o não ser ...; **it is ~ for** é a abreviatura de; **to cut ~** (speech, visit) encurtar; **to fall ~ of** não ser à altura de; **to run ~ of sth** ficar sem algo; **to stop ~** parar de repente; **to stop ~ of** chegar quase a; **shortage** N escassez f, falta; **shortbread** N biscoito amanteigado; **shortcoming** N defeito, imperfeição f, falha; **shortcrust pastry**, (BRIT) **short pastry** N massa amanteigada; **shortcut** N atalho; **shorten** VT encurtar; (visit) abreviar; **shorthand** (BRIT) N estenografia; **shortly** ADV em breve, dentro em pouco; **shorts** NPL: **(a pair of) shorts** um calção (BR), um short (BR), uns calções (PT); **short-sighted** (BRIT) ADJ míope; (fig) imprevidente; **short story** N conto; **short-tempered** ADJ irritadiço; **short-term** ADJ a curto prazo

shot [ʃɔt] PT, PP of **shoot** ▶ N (of gun) tiro; (pellets) chumbo; (try, Football) tentativa;

(*injection*) injeção f; (*Phot*) fotografia;
to be a good/bad ~ (*person*) ter boa/
má pontaria; **like a ~** como um
relâmpago, de repente; **shotgun** N
espingarda

should [ʃud] AUX VB: **I ~ go now** devo ir
embora agora; **he ~ be there now** ele já
deve ter chegado; **I ~ go if I were you** se
eu fosse você eu iria; **I ~ like to** eu
gostaria de

shoulder [ˈʃəuldəʳ] N ombro ▶ VT (*fig*)
arcar com; **shoulder blade** N
omoplata m

shouldn't [ˈʃudnt] = **should not**

shout [ʃaut] N grito ▶ VT gritar ▶ VI (*also:*
~ out) gritar, berrar; **shout down** VT
fazer calar com gritos

shove [ʃʌv] VT empurrar; (*inf: put*) **to ~
sth in** botar algo em; **shove off** VI (*inf*)
dar o fora

shovel [ˈʃʌvl] N pá f; (*mechanical*)
escavadeira ▶ VT cavar com pá

show [ʃəu] (*pt* showed, *pp* shown) N (*of
emotion*) demonstração f; (*semblance*)
aparência; (*exhibition*) exibição f;
(*Theatre*) espetáculo, representação f;
(*Cinema*) sessão f ▶ VT mostrar; (*courage
etc*) demonstrar, dar prova de; (*exhibit*)
exibir, expor; (*depict*) ilustrar; (*film*) exibir
▶ VI mostrar-se; (*appear*) aparecer; **to be
on ~** estar em exposição; **show in** VT
mandar entrar; **show off** VI (*pej*)
mostrar-se, exibir-se ▶ VT (*display*) exibir,
mostrar; **show out** VT levar até a porta;
show up VI (*stand out*) destacar-se; (*inf:
turn up*) aparecer, pintar ▶ VT descobrir;
show business N o mundo do
espetáculo

shower [ˈʃauəʳ] N (*rain*) pancada de
chuva; (*of stones etc*) chuva, enxurrada;
(*also:* **~ bath**) chuveiro ▶ VI tomar banho
(de chuveiro) ▶ VT: **to ~ sb with** (*gifts etc*)
cumular alguém de; **to have** *or* **take a ~**
tomar banho (de chuveiro)

showing [ˈʃəuɪŋ] N (*of film*) projeção f,
exibição f

show jumping [-ˈdʒʌmpɪŋ] N hipismo

shown [ʃəun] PP *of* **show**

show-off (*inf*) N (*person*) exibicionista
m/f, faroleiro(-a)

showpiece [ˈʃəupiːs] N (*of exhibition etc*)
obra mais importante

showroom [ˈʃəurum] N sala de
exposição

shrank [ʃræŋk] PT *of* **shrink**

shred [ʃrɛd] N (*gen pl*) tira, pedaço ▶ VT
rasgar em tiras, retalhar; (*Culin*)
desfiar, picar

shrewd [ʃruːd] ADJ perspicaz

shriek [ʃriːk] N grito ▶ VI gritar, berrar

shrimp [ʃrɪmp] N camarão m

shrine [ʃraɪn] N santuário

shrink [ʃrɪŋk] (*pt* shrank, *pp* shrunk) VI
encolher; (*be reduced*) reduzir-se; (*also:*
~ away) encolher-se ▶ VT (*cloth*) fazer
encolher ▶ N (*inf, pej*) psicanalista m/f;
to ~ from doing sth não se atrever a
fazer algo

shrivel [ˈʃrɪvl] VT (*also:* **~ up**: *dry*) secar;
(: *crease*) enrugar ▶ VI secar-se;
enrugar-se, murchar

Shrove Tuesday [ʃrəuv-] N terça-feira
gorda

shrub [ʃrʌb] N arbusto

shrug [ʃrʌg] N encolhimento dos ombros
▶ VT, VI: **to ~ (one's shoulders)**
encolher os ombros, dar de ombros (BR);
shrug off VT negar a importância de

shrunk [ʃrʌŋk] PP *of* **shrink**

shudder [ˈʃʌdəʳ] N estremecimento,
tremor m ▶ VI estremecer, tremer de
medo

shuffle [ˈʃʌfl] VT (*cards*) embaralhar ▶ VI:
to ~ (one's feet) arrastar os pés

shun [ʃʌn] VT evitar, afastar-se de

shut [ʃʌt] (*pt, pp* shut) VT fechar ▶ VI
fechar(-se); **shut down** VT, VI fechar;
shut off VT cortar, interromper; **shut up**
VI (*inf: keep quiet*) calar-se, calar a boca
▶ VT (*close*) fechar; (*silence*) calar;
shutter N veneziana; (*Phot*)
obturador m

shuttle [ˈʃʌtl] N (*plane: also:* **~ service**)
ponte f aérea; (*space shuttle*) ônibus m
espacial

shuttlecock [ˈʃʌtlkɔk] N peteca

shy [ʃaɪ] ADJ tímido; (*reserved*) reservado

sick [sɪk] ADJ (*ill*) doente; (*nauseated*)
enjoado; (*humour*) negro; (*vomiting*): **to
be ~** vomitar; **to feel ~** estar enjoado;
to be ~ of (*fig*) estar cheio *or* farto de;
sickening ADJ (*fig*) repugnante; **sick
leave** N licença por doença; **sickly** ADJ
doentio; (*causing nausea*) nauseante;
sickness N doença, indisposição f;
(*vomiting*) náusea, enjoo

side [saɪd] N lado; (*of body*) flanco; (*of
lake*) margem f; (*aspect*) aspecto; (*team*)
time m (BR), equipa (PT); (*of hill*)
declive m ▶ CPD (*door, entrance*) lateral
▶ VI: **to ~ with sb** tomar o partido de
alguém; **by the ~ of** ao lado de;
~ by ~ lado a lado, juntos; **from ~ to ~**
para lá e para cá; **to take ~s with**
pôr-se ao lado de; **sideboard** N
aparador m; **sideboards** NPL (BRIT)

= **sideburns**; **sideburns** N PL suíças f pl, costeletas f pl; **side effect** N efeito colateral; **sidelight** N (Aut) luz f lateral; **side order** N acompanhamento; **sidetrack** VT (fig) desviar (do seu propósito); **sidewalk** (US) N calçada; **sideways** ADV de lado

siege [siːdʒ] N sítio, assédio

sieve [sɪv] N peneira ▶ VT peneirar

sift [sɪft] VT peneirar; (fig) esquadrinhar, analisar minuciosamente

sigh [saɪ] N suspiro ▶ VI suspirar

sight [saɪt] N (faculty) vista, visão f; (spectacle) espetáculo; (on gun) mira ▶ VT avistar; **in ~** à vista; **on ~** (shoot) no local; **out of ~** longe dos olhos; **sightseeing** N turismo; **to go sightseeing** fazer turismo, passear

sign [saɪn] N (with hand) sinal m, aceno; (indication) indício; (notice) letreiro, tabuleta; (written, of zodiac) signo ▶ VT assinar; **to ~ sth over to sb** assinar a transferência de algo para alguém; **sign on** VI (Mil) alistar-se; (BRIT: as unemployed) cadastrar-se para receber auxílio-desemprego; (for course) inscrever-se ▶ VT (Mil) alistar; (employee) efetivar; **sign up** VI (Mil) alistar-se; (for course) inscrever-se ▶ VT recrutar

signal ['sɪgnl] N sinal m, aviso; (Tel) rede f ▶ VI (also: Aut) sinalizar, dar sinal ▶ VT (person) fazer sinais para; (message) transmitir

signature ['sɪgnətʃər] N assinatura

significance [sɪg'nɪfɪkəns] N importância; **significant** ADJ significativo; (important) importante

sign language N mímica, linguagem f através de sinais

silence ['saɪləns] N silêncio ▶ VT silenciar, impor silêncio a

silent ['saɪlənt] ADJ silencioso; (not speaking) calado; (film) mudo; **to keep** or **remain ~** manter-se em silêncio

silhouette [sɪluːˈet] N silhueta

silicon chip ['sɪlɪkən tʃɪp] N placa or chip m de silício

silk [sɪlk] N seda ▶ ADJ de seda

silly ['sɪlɪ] ADJ (person) bobo, idiota, imbecil; (idea) absurdo, ridículo

silver ['sɪlvər] N prata; (money) moedas f pl; (also: ~ware) prataria ▶ ADJ de prata; **silver-plated** ADJ prateado, banhado a prata

SIM card ['sɪm-] N (Tel) cartão m SIM, chip m

similar ['sɪmɪlər] ADJ: **~ to** parecido com, semelhante a

simmer ['sɪmər] VI cozer em fogo lento, ferver lentamente

simple ['sɪmpl] ADJ simples inv; (foolish) ingênuo; **simply** ADV de maneira simples; (merely) simplesmente

simultaneous [sɪməl'teɪnɪəs] ADJ simultâneo

sin [sɪn] N pecado ▶ VI pecar

since [sɪns] ADV desde então, depois ▶ PREP desde ▶ CONJ (time) desde que; (because) porque, visto que, já que; **~ then** desde então; **(ever) ~ I arrived** desde que eu cheguei

sincere [sɪn'sɪər] ADJ sincero; **sincerely** ADV: **yours sincerely** (BRIT), **sincerely yours** (US) (at end of letter) atenciosamente

sing [sɪŋ] (pt **sang**, pp **sung**) VT, VI cantar

Singapore [sɪŋɡə'pɔːr] N Cingapura (no article)

singer ['sɪŋər] N cantor(a) m/f

singing ['sɪŋɪŋ] N canto; (songs) canções f pl

single ['sɪŋgl] ADJ único, só; (unmarried) solteiro; (not double) simples inv ▶ N (BRIT: also: **~ ticket**) passagem f de ida; (record) compacto; **single out** VT (choose) escolher; (distinguish) distinguir; **single file** N: **in single file** em fila indiana; **single-handed** ADV sem ajuda, sozinho; **single-minded** ADJ determinado; **single room** N quarto individual

singular ['sɪŋgjulər] ADJ (odd) esquisito; (outstanding) extraordinário, excepcional; (Ling) singular ▶ N (Ling) singular m

sinister ['sɪnɪstər] ADJ sinistro

sink [sɪŋk] (pt **sank**, pp **sunk**) N pia ▶ VT (ship) afundar; (foundations) escavar ▶ VI afundar-se; (heart) partir; (spirits) ficar deprimido; (also: **~ back**, **~ down**) cair or mergulhar gradativamente; **to ~ sth into** enterrar algo em; **sink in** VI (fig) penetrar

sinus ['saɪnəs] N (Anat) seio (paranasal)

sip [sɪp] N gole m ▶ VT sorver, bebericar

sir [səːr] N senhor m; **S~ John Smith** John Smith; **yes, ~** sim, senhor

siren ['saɪərən] N sirena

sirloin ['səːlɔɪn] N lombo de vaca

sister ['sɪstər] N irmã f; (BRIT: nurse) enfermeira-chefe f; (nun) freira; **sister-in-law** N cunhada

sit [sɪt] (pt, pp **sat**) VI sentar-se; (be sitting) estar sentado; (assembly) reunir-se; (for painter) posar ▶ VT (exam) prestar; **sit**

down vi sentar-se; **sit in on** vt fus assistir a; **sit up** vi (after lying) levantar-se; (straight) endireitar-se; (not go to bed) aguardar acordado, velar

sitcom ['sɪtkɔm] N ABBR (= situation comedy) comédia de costumes

site [saɪt] N local m, sítio; (also: **building ~**) lote m (de terreno) ▶ vt situar, localizar

sitting ['sɪtɪŋ] N (in canteen) turno; **sitting room** N sala de estar

situation [sɪtjuˈeɪʃən] N situação f; (job) posição f; (location) local m; **"~s vacant/ wanted"** (BRIT) "empregos oferecem-se/ procuram-se"

six [sɪks] NUM seis; **sixteen** NUM dezesseis; **sixteenth** [sɪksˈtiːnθ] NUM décimo sexto; **sixth** NUM sexto; **sixtieth** ['sɪkstiːθ] NUM sexagésimo; **sixty** NUM sessenta

size [saɪz] N tamanho; (extent) extensão f; (of clothing) tamanho, medida; (of shoes) número; **size up** vt avaliar, formar uma opinião sobre; **sizeable** ADJ considerável, importante

sizzle ['sɪzl] vi chiar

skate [skeɪt] N patim m; (fish: pl inv) arraia ▶ vi patinar; **skateboard** N skate m, patim-tábua m; **skating** N patinação f; **skating rink** N rinque m de patinação

skeleton ['skɛlɪtn] N esqueleto; (Tech) armação f; (outline) esquema m, esboço

sketch [skɛtʃ] N (drawing) desenho; (outline) esboço, croqui m; (Theatre) quadro, esquete m ▶ vt desenhar, esboçar; (ideas: also: **~ out**) esboçar

skewer ['skjuːə'] N espetinho

ski [skiː] N esqui m ▶ vi esquiar; **ski boot** N bota de esquiar

skid [skɪd] N derrapagem f ▶ vi deslizar; (Aut) derrapar

skier ['skiːə'] N esquiador(a) m/f

skiing ['skiːɪŋ] N esqui m

skilful ['skɪlful], (US) **skillful** ADJ habilidoso, jeitoso

ski lift N ski lift m

skill [skɪl] N habilidade f, perícia; (for work) técnica; **skilled** ADJ hábil, perito; (worker) especializado, qualificado

skim [skɪm] vt (milk) desnatar; (glide over) roçar ▶ vi: **to ~ through** (book) folhear; **skimmed milk** N leite m desnatado

skin [skɪn] N pele f; (of fruit, vegetable) casca ▶ vt (fruit etc) descascar; (animal) tirar a pele de; **skinny** ADJ magro, descarnado

skip [skɪp] N salto, pulo; (BRIT: container) balde m ▶ vi saltar; (with rope) pular corda ▶ vt (pass over) omitir, saltar; (miss) deixar de

skipper ['skɪpə'] N capitão m

skipping rope ['skɪpɪŋ-] (BRIT) N corda (de pular)

skirt [skəːt] N saia ▶ vt orlar, circundar; **skirting board** (BRIT) N rodapé m

skull [skʌl] N caveira; (Anat) crânio

skunk [skʌŋk] N gambá m

sky [skaɪ] N céu m; **skyscraper** N arranha-céu m

slab [slæb] N (stone) bloco; (flat) laje f; (of cake) fatia grossa

slack [slæk] ADJ (loose) frouxo; (slow) lerdo; (careless) descuidado, desmazelado; **slacks** NPL (trousers) calça (BR), calças fpl (PT)

slain [sleɪn] PP of slay

slam [slæm] vt (door) bater or fechar (com violência); (throw) atirar violentamente; (criticize) malhar, criticar ▶ vi fechar-se (com violência)

slander ['slɑːndə'] N calúnia, difamação f

slang [slæŋ] N gíria; (jargon) jargão m

slant [slɑːnt] N declive m, inclinação f; (fig) ponto de vista

slap [slæp] N tapa m or f ▶ vt dar um(a) tapa em; (paint etc): **to ~ sth on sth** passar algo em algo descuidadamente ▶ ADV diretamente, exatamente

slash [slæʃ] vt cortar, talhar; (fig: prices) cortar

slate [sleɪt] N ardósia ▶ vt (fig: criticize) criticar duramente, arrasar

slaughter ['slɔːtə'] N (of animals) matança; (of people) carnificina ▶ vt abater; matar, massacrar; **slaughterhouse** N matadouro

slave [sleɪv] N escravo(-a) ▶ vi (also: **~ away**) trabalhar como escravo; **slavery** N escravidão f

slay [sleɪ] (pt slew, pp slain) vt (literary) matar

sleazy ['sliːzɪ] ADJ sórdido

sledge [slɛdʒ] N trenó m

sleek [sliːk] ADJ (hair, fur) macio, lustroso; (car, boat) aerodinâmico

sleep [sliːp] (pt, pp slept) N sono ▶ vi dormir; **to go to ~** dormir, adormecer; **sleep around** vi ser promíscuo sexualmente; **sleep in** vi (oversleep) dormir demais; **sleeper** N (Rail: train) vagão-leitos m (BR), carruagem-camas (PT); **sleeping bag** N saco de dormir; **sleeping car** N vagão-leitos m (BR),

carruagem-camas f (PT); **sleeping pill** N
pílula para dormir; **sleepy** ADJ
sonolento; (fig) morto

sleet [sli:t] N chuva com neve or granizo

sleeve [sli:v] N manga; (of record) capa

sleigh [sleɪ] N trenó m

slender ['slɛndə'] ADJ esbelto, delgado;
(means) escasso, insuficiente

slept [slɛpt] PT, PP of **sleep**

slew [slu:] PT of **slay**

slice [slaɪs] N (of meat, bread) fatia; (of
lemon) rodela; (utensil) pá f or espátula de
bolo ▶ VT cortar em fatias

slick [slɪk] ADJ (skilful) jeitoso, ágil,
engenhoso; (clever) esperto, astuto ▶ N
(also: **oil ~**) mancha de óleo

slide [slaɪd] (pt, pp **slid**) N deslizamento,
escorregão m; (in playground)
escorregador m; (Phot) slide m; (BRIT:
also: **hair ~**) passador m ▶ VT deslizar ▶ VI
escorregar; **slide show** N apresentação f
de slides; **sliding** ADJ (door) corrediço

slight [slaɪt] ADJ (slim) fraco, franzino;
(frail) delicado; (error, pain, increase)
pequeno; (trivial) insignificante ▶ N
desfeita, desconsideração f; **not in the
~est** em absoluto, de maneira alguma;
slightly ADV ligeiramente, um pouco

slim [slɪm] ADJ esbelto, delgado; (chance)
pequeno ▶ VI emagrecer

slimming N emagrecimento

sling [slɪŋ] (pt, pp **slung**) N (Med) tipoia;
(for baby) bebêbag m; (weapon) estilingue
m, funda ▶ VT atirar, arremessar, lançar

slip [slɪp] N (fall) escorregão m; (mistake)
erro, lapso; (underskirt) combinação f; (of
paper) tira ▶ VT deslizar ▶ VI (slide)
deslizar; (lose balance) escorregar;
(decline) decair; (move smoothly): **to ~
into/out of** entrar furtivamente em/
sair furtivamente de; **to ~ sth on/off**
enfiar/tirar algo; **to give sb the ~**
esgueirar-se de alguém; **a ~ of the
tongue** um lapso da língua; **slip away**
VI escapulir; **slip in** VT meter ▶ VI (errors)
surgir; **slip out** VI (go out) sair (um
momento); **slip up** VI cometer um erro

slipper ['slɪpə'] N chinelo

slippery ['slɪpərɪ] ADJ escorregadio

slip-up N equívoco, mancada

slit [slɪt] (pt, pp **slit**) N fenda; (cut) corte m
▶ VT (cut) rachar, cortar; (open) abrir

slog [slɔg] (BRIT) VI mourejar ▶ N: **it was
a ~** deu um trabalho louco

slogan ['sləugən] N lema m, slogan m

slope [sləup] N ladeira; (side of mountain)
encosta, vertente f; (ski slope) pista;
(slant) inclinação f, declive m ▶ VI: **to ~
down** estar em declive; **to ~ up**
inclinar-se; **sloping** ADJ inclinado, em
declive; (handwriting) torto

sloppy ['slɔpɪ] ADJ (work) descuidado;
(appearance) relaxado

slot [slɔt] N (in machine) fenda ▶ VT: **to ~
into** encaixar em

slow [sləu] ADJ lento; (not clever) bronco,
de raciocínio lento; (watch): **to be ~**
atrasar ▶ ADV lentamente, devagar ▶ VT,
VI ir (mais) devagar; **"~"** (road sign)
"devagar"; **slowly** ADV lentamente,
devagar; **slow motion** N: **in slow
motion** em câmara lenta

slug [slʌg] N lesma f; **sluggish** ADJ
vagaroso; (business) lento

slum [slʌm] N (area) favela; (house)
cortiço, barraco

slump [slʌmp] N (economic) depressão f;
(Comm) baixa, queda ▶ VI (person) cair;
(prices) baixar repentinamente

slung [slʌŋ] PT, PP of **sling**

slur [slə:'] N calúnia ▶ VT pronunciar
indistintamente

slush [slʌʃ] N neve f meio derretida

sly [slaɪ] ADJ (person) astuto; (smile,
remark) malicioso, velhaco

smack [smæk] N palmada ▶ VT bater;
(child) dar uma palmada em; (on face) dar
um tabefe em ▶ VI: **to ~ of** cheirar a,
saber a

small [smɔ:l] ADJ pequeno; **small
change** N trocado

smart [smɑ:t] ADJ elegante; (clever, Tel)
inteligente; (quick) vivo, esperto ▶ VI
sofrer; **SMART Board®** N quadro
interativo; **smart phone** N
smartphone m

smash [smæʃ] N (also: **~-up**) colisão f,
choque m; (smash hit) sucesso de
bilheteira ▶ VT (break) escangalhar,
despedaçar; (car etc) bater com; (Sport:
record) quebrar ▶ VI despedaçar-se;
(against wall etc) espatifar-se; **smashing**
(inf) ADJ excelente

smear [smɪə'] N mancha, nódoa; (Med)
esfregaço ▶ VT untar; (to make dirty)
lambuzar

smell [smɛl] (pt, pp **smelt** or **smelled**) N
cheiro; (sense) olfato ▶ VT cheirar ▶ VI
(food etc) cheirar; (pej) cheirar mal; **to ~
of** cheirar a; **smelly** (pej) ADJ fedorento,
malcheiroso

smile [smaɪl] N sorriso ▶ VI sorrir

smirk [smə:k] (pej) N sorriso falso or
afetado

smog [smɔg] N nevoeiro com fumaça
(BR) or fumo (PT)

smoke [sməuk] N fumaça (BR), fumo (PT)
▶ vı fumar; (chimney) fumegar ▶ vT
(cigarettes) fumar; **smoked** ADJ (bacon)
defumado; (glass) fumée; **smoker** N
(person) fumante m/f; (Rail) vagão m para
fumantes; **smoking** N: **"no smoking"**
(sign) "proibido fumar"; **he's given up
smoking** ele deixou de fumar; **smoky**
ADJ enfumaçado; (taste) defumado

smooth [smu:ð] ADJ liso, macio; (sauce)
cremoso; (sea) tranquilo, calmo; (flavour,
movement) suave ▶ vT (also: ~ out) alisar;
(: difficulties) aplainar

smother ['smʌðəʳ] vT (fire) abafar;
(person) sufocar; (emotions) reprimir

SMS N ABBR (= short message service) SMS
m

smudge [smʌdʒ] N mancha ▶ vT
manchar, sujar

smug [smʌg] (pej) ADJ convencido

smuggle ['smʌgl] vT contrabandear;
smuggling N contrabando

snack [snæk] N lanche m (BR), merenda
(PT); **snack bar** N lanchonete f (BR),
snackbar m (PT)

snag [snæg] N dificuldade f, obstáculo

snail [sneıl] N caracol m

snake [sneık] N cobra

snap [snæp] N (sound) estalo;
(photograph) foto f ▶ ADJ repentino ▶ vT
quebrar; (fingers, whip) estalar ▶ vı
quebrar; (fig: person) retrucar
asperamente; **to ~ shut** fechar com um
estalo; **snap at** vT FUS (subj: dog) tentar
morder; **snap off** vT (break) partir; **snap
up** vT arrebatar, comprar rapidamente;
snapshot N foto f (instantânea)

snarl [snɑ:l] vı grunhir

snatch [snætʃ] N (small piece) trecho ▶ vT
agarrar; (fig: look) roubar

sneak [sni:k] vı: **to ~ in/out** entrar/sair
furtivamente ▶ N (inf) dedo-duro; **to ~
up on sb** chegar de mansinho perto de
alguém; **sneakers** NPL tênis m (BR),
sapatos mpl de treino (PT)

sneer [snıəʳ] vı rir-se com desdém;
(mock): **to ~ at** zombar de, desprezar

sneeze [sni:z] N espirro ▶ vı espirrar

sniff [snıf] N fungada; (of dog) farejada;
(of person) fungadela ▶ vı fungar ▶ vT
fungar, farejar; (glue, drug) cheirar

snigger ['snıgəʳ] vı rir-se com
dissimulação

snip [snıp] N tesourada; (BRIT inf)
pechincha ▶ vT cortar com tesoura

sniper ['snaıpəʳ] N franco-
atirador(a) m/f

snob [snɔb] N esnobe m/f

snooker ['snu:kəʳ] N sinuca

snoop [snu:p] vı: **to ~ about**
bisbilhotar

snooze [snu:z] N soneca ▶ vı tirar uma
soneca, dormitar

snore [snɔ:ʳ] vı roncar ▶ N ronco

snorkel ['snɔ:kl] N tubo snorkel

snort [snɔ:t] N bufo, bufido ▶ vı bufar

snow [snəu] N neve f ▶ vı nevar;
snowball N bola de neve ▶ vı (fig)
aumentar (como bola de neve);
snowboarding ['snəubɔ:dıŋ] N
snowboard m; **snowdrift** N monte m de
neve (formado pelo vento); **snowman**
irreg N boneco de neve; **snowplough**,
(US) **snowplow** N máquina limpa-neve,
removedor m de neve; **snowstorm** N
nevasca, tempestade f de neve

snub [snʌb] vT desdenhar, menosprezar
▶ N repulsa

snug [snʌg] ADJ (sheltered) abrigado,
protegido; (fitted) justo, cômodo

(KEYWORD)

so [səu] ADV 1 (thus, likewise) assim, deste
modo; **so saying he walked away**
falou isto e foi embora; **if so** se for assim,
se assim é; **I didn't do it — you did so**
não fiz isso — você fez!; **so do I, so am I**
etc eu também; **so it is!** é verdade!;
I hope/think so espero/acho que sim;
so far até aqui

2 (in comparisons etc: to such a degree) tão;
so big/quickly (that) tão grande/
rápido (que)

3: **so much** (adj, adv) tanto; **I've got so
much work** tenho tanto trabalho; **so
many** tantos(-as); **there are so
many people to see** tem tanta gente
para ver

4 (phrases): **10 or so** uns 10; **so long!** (inf:
goodbye) tchau!

▶ CONJ 1 (expressing purpose): **so as to do**
para fazer; **we hurried so as not to be
late** nós nos apressamos para não
chegarmos atrasados; **so (that)** para
que, a fim de que

2 (result) de modo que; **he didn't arrive
so I left** como ele não chegou, eu fui
embora; **so I was right after all** então
eu estava certo no final das contas

soak [səuk] vT embeber, ensopar; (put in
water) pôr de molho ▶ vı estar de molho,
impregnar-se; **soak in** vı infiltrar; **soak
up** vT absorver

soap [səup] N sabão m; **soap opera** N
novela; **soap powder** N sabão m em pó

soar [sɔːʳ] VI (*on wings*) elevar-se em voo; (*rocket, temperature*) subir; (*building etc*) levantar-se; (*price, production*) disparar

sob [sɔb] N soluço ▶ VI soluçar

sober ['səubəʳ] ADJ (*serious*) sério; (*not drunk*) sóbrio; (*colour, style*) discreto; **sober up** VI ficar sóbrio

so-called [-kɔːld] ADJ chamado

soccer ['sɔkəʳ] N futebol m

social ['səuʃl] ADJ social ▶ N reunião f social; **socialism** N socialismo; **socialist** ADJ, N socialista m/f; **socialize** VI: **to socialize (with)** socializar (com); **social media** NPL mídias fpl sociais (BR), meios mpl de comunicação social (PT); **social networking** [-'nɛtwəːkɪŋ] N redes fpl sociais; **social networking site** N rede f social; **social security** (BRIT) N previdência social; **social work** N assistência social, serviço social; **social worker** N assistente m/f social

society [sə'saɪətɪ] N sociedade f; (*club*) associação f; (*also:* **high ~**) alta sociedade

sociology [səusɪ'ɔlədʒɪ] N sociologia

sock [sɔk] N meia (BR), peúga (PT)

socket ['sɔkɪt] N bocal m, encaixe m; (BRIT Elec) tomada

soda ['səudə] N (Chem) soda; (*also:* **~ water**) água com gás; (US: *also:* **~ pop**) soda

sofa ['səufə] N sofá m

soft [sɔft] ADJ mole; (*voice, music, light*) suave; (*kind*) meigo, bondoso; **soft drink** N refrigerante m; **soften** VT amolecer, amaciar; (*effect*) abrandar; (*expression*) suavizar ▶ VI amolecer-se; (*voice, expression*) suavizar-se; **softly** ADV suavemente; (*gently*) delicadamente; **software** N software m

soggy ['sɔgɪ] ADJ ensopado, encharcado

soil [sɔɪl] N terra, solo; (*territory*) território ▶ VT sujar, manchar

solar ['səuləʳ] ADJ solar; **solar panel** N painel m solar; **solar power** N energia solar

sold [səuld] PT, PP of **sell** ▶ ADJ: **~ out** (*Comm*) esgotado

soldier ['səuldʒəʳ] N soldado; (*army man*) militar m

sole [səul] N (*of foot, shoe*) sola; (*fish: pl inv*) solha, linguado ▶ ADJ único

solicitor [sə'lɪsɪtəʳ] (BRIT) N (*for wills etc*) tabelião(-lioa) m/f; (*in court*) ≈ advogado(-a)

solid ['sɔlɪd] ADJ sólido; (*gold etc*) maciço; (*person*) sério ▶ N sólido; **solids** NPL (*food*) comida sólida

solitary ['sɔlɪtərɪ] ADJ solitário, só; (*walk*) só; (*isolated*) isolado, retirado; (*single*) único

solo ['səuləu] N, ADV solo; **soloist** N solista m/f

solution [sə'luːʃən] N solução f

solve [sɔlv] VT resolver, solucionar

solvent ['sɔlvənt] ADJ (Comm) solvente ▶ N (Chem) solvente m

KEYWORD

some [sʌm] ADJ **1** (*a certain number or amount*): **some tea/water/biscuits** um pouco de chá/água/uns biscoitos; **some children came** algumas crianças vieram **2** (*certain: in contrasts*) algum(a); **some people say that ...** algumas pessoas dizem que ... **3** (*unspecified*) um pouco de; **some woman was asking for you** uma mulher estava perguntando por você; **some day** um dia ▶ PRON **1** (*a certain number*) alguns/ algumas; **I've got some** (*books etc*) tenho alguns; **some went for a taxi and some walked** alguns foram pegar um táxi e outros foram andando **2** (*a certain amount*) um pouco; **I've got some** (*milk, money etc*) tenho um pouco ▶ ADV: **some 10 people** umas 10 pessoas

somebody ['sʌmbədɪ] PRON = **someone**

somehow ['sʌmhau] ADV de alguma maneira; (*for some reason*) por uma razão ou outra

someone ['sʌmwʌn] PRON alguém

someplace ['sʌmpleɪs] (US) ADV = **somewhere**

something ['sʌmθɪŋ] PRON alguma coisa, algo (BR)

sometime ['sʌmtaɪm] ADV (*in future*) algum dia, em outra oportunidade; (*in past*): **~ last month** durante o mês passado

sometimes ['sʌmtaɪmz] ADV às vezes, de vez em quando

somewhat ['sʌmwɔt] ADV um tanto

somewhere ['sʌmwɛəʳ] ADV (*be*) em algum lugar; (*go*) para algum lugar; **~ else** (*be*) em outro lugar; (*go*) para outro lugar

son [sʌn] N filho

song [sɔŋ] N canção f; (*of bird*) canto

son-in-law ['sʌnɪnlɔː] N genro

soon [suːn] ADV logo, brevemente; (*a short time after*) logo após; (*early*) cedo; **~ afterwards** pouco depois; *see also* **as**; **sooner** ADV antes, mais cedo;

(*preference*): **I would sooner do that**
preferia fazer isso; **sooner or later** mais
cedo ou mais tarde

soothe [suːð] VT acalmar, sossegar;
(*pain*) aliviar, suavizar

soprano [səˈprɑːnəu] N soprano *m/f*

sore [sɔːʳ] ADJ dolorido ▸ N chaga, ferida

sorrow [ˈsɔrəu] N tristeza, mágoa, dor *f*;
sorrows NPL (*causes of grief*) tristezas *fpl*

sorry [ˈsɔrɪ] ADJ (*regretful*) arrependido;
(*condition, excuse*) lamentável; **~!**
desculpe!, perdão!, sinto muito!; **to feel
~ for sb** sentir pena de alguém

sort [sɔːt] N tipo ▸ VT (*also*: **~ out**: *papers*)
classificar; (: *problems*) solucionar,
resolver

SOS N ABBR (= *save our souls*) S.O.S. *m*

so-so ADV mais ou menos, regular

sought [sɔːt] PT, PP of **seek**

soul [səul] N alma; (*person*) criatura

sound [saund] ADJ (*healthy*) saudável,
sadio; (*safe, not damaged*) sólido,
completo; (*secure*) seguro; (*reliable*)
confiável; (*sensible*) sensato ▸ ADV:
~ asleep dormindo profundamente ▸ N
(*noise*) som *m*, ruído, barulho; (*volume: on
TV etc*) volume *m*; (*Geo*) estreito, braço
(de mar) ▸ VT (*alarm*) soar ▸ VI soar,
tocar; (*fig: seem*) parecer; **to ~ like**
parecer; **sound out** VI sondar;
soundtrack N trilha sonora

soup [suːp] N sopa; **in the ~** (*fig*) numa
encrenca

sour [ˈsauəʳ] ADJ azedo, ácido; (*milk*)
talhado; (*fig*) mal-humorado,
rabugento; **it's ~ grapes!** (*fig*) é
despeito!

source [sɔːs] N fonte *f*

south [sauθ] N sul *m* ▸ ADJ do sul,
meridional ▸ ADV ao ou para o sul; **South
Africa** N África do Sul; **South African**
ADJ, N sul-africano(-a); **South America**
N América do Sul; **South American** ADJ,
N sul-americano(-a); **south-east** N
sudeste *m*; **southern** [ˈsʌðən] ADJ (*to the
south*) para o sul, em direção do sul; (*from
the south*) do sul, sulista; **the southern
hemisphere** o Hemisfério Sul; **South
Pole** N Pólo Sul; **southward,
southwards** ADV para o sul; **south-west**
N sudoeste *m*

souvenir [suːvəˈnɪəʳ] N lembrança

sovereign [ˈsɔvrɪn] N soberano(-a)

sow¹ [sau] N porca

sow² [səu] (*pt* **sowed**, *pp* **sown**) VT
semear; (*fig: spread*) disseminar, espalhar

soya [ˈsɔɪə], (*US*) **soy** [sɔɪ] N soja; **soya
bean**, (*US*) **soybean** N semente *f* de soja;

soya sauce, (*US*) **soy sauce** N molho
de soja

spa [spɑː] N (*town*) estância hidro-
mineral; (*US: also*: **health ~**) estância
balnear

space [speɪs] N (*gen*) espaço; (*room*) lugar
m ▸ CPD espacial ▸ VT (*also*: **~ out**)
espaçar; **spacecraft** N nave *f* espacial;
spaceship N = **spacecraft**; **spacious**
[ˈspeɪʃəs] ADJ espaçoso

spade [speɪd] N pá *f*; **spades** NPL (*Cards*)
espadas *fpl*

Spain [speɪn] N Espanha

spam [ˈspæm] N (*junk email*) spam *m*

span [spæn] N (*also*: **wing~**)
envergadura; (*of arch*) vão *m*; (*in time*)
lapso, espaço ▸ VT estender-se sobre,
atravessar; (*fig*) abarcar

Spaniard [ˈspænjəd] N espanhol(a) *m/f*

Spanish [ˈspænɪʃ] ADJ espanhol(a) ▸ N
(*Ling*) espanhol *m*, castelhano; **the
Spanish** NPL os espanhóis

spanner [ˈspænəʳ] (*BRIT*) N chave *f*
inglesa

spare [spεəʳ] ADJ vago, desocupado;
(*surplus*) de sobra, a mais ▸ N = **spare
part** ▸ VT dispensar, passar sem; (*make
available*) dispor de; (*refrain from hurting*)
perdoar, poupar; **to ~** de sobra; **spare
part** N peça sobressalente; **spare time**
N tempo livre; **spare wheel** N estepe *m*

spark [spɑːk] N chispa, faísca; (*fig*)
centelha

sparkle [ˈspɑːkl] N cintilação *f*, brilho ▸ VI
(*shine*) brilhar, faiscar; **sparkling** ADJ
(*mineral water*) gasoso; (*wine*)
espumante; (*conversation*) animado;
(*performance*) brilhante

sparrow [ˈspærəu] N pardal *m*

sparse [spɑːs] ADJ escasso; (*hair*) ralo

spasm [ˈspæzəm] N (*Med*) espasmo

spat [spæt] PT, PP of **spit**

speak [spiːk] (*pt* **spoke**, *pp* **spoken**) VT
(*language*) falar; (*truth*) dizer ▸ VI falar;
(*make a speech*) discursar; **~ up!** fale alto!;
speaker N (*in public*) orador(a) *m/f*; (*also*:
loudspeaker) alto-falante *m*; (*Pol*): **the
Speaker** o Presidente da Câmara

spear [spɪəʳ] N lança ▸ VT lancear,
arpoar

special [ˈspεʃl] ADJ especial; (*edition etc*)
extra; (*delivery*) rápido; **specialist** N
especialista *m/f*; **speciality** [spεʃɪˈælɪtɪ]
N especialidade *f*; **specialize** VI: **to
specialize (in)** especializar-se (em);
specially ADV especialmente; **specialty**
[ˈspεʃəltɪ] (*esp US*) N = **speciality**

species [ˈspiːʃiːz] N INV espécie *f*

specific [spəˈsɪfɪk] ADJ específico

specimen [ˈspɛsɪmən] N espécime m, amostra; (for testing, Med) espécime

speck [spɛk] N mancha, pinta

spectacle [ˈspɛktəkl] N espetáculo; **spectacles** NPL (glasses) óculos mpl; **spectacular** [spɛkˈtækjuləʳ] ADJ espetacular ▶ N (Cinema etc) superprodução f

spectator [spɛkˈteɪtəʳ] N espectador(a) m/f

spectrum [ˈspɛktrəm] (pl **spectra**) N espectro

sped [spɛd] PT, PP of **speed**

speech [spiːtʃ] N (faculty, Theatre) fala; (formal talk) discurso; **speechless** ADJ estupefato, emudecido

speed [spiːd] (pt, pp **sped**) N velocidade f; (rate) rapidez f; (haste) pressa; (promptness) prontidão f; **at full** or **top ~** a toda a velocidade; **speed up** (pt, pp **speeded up**) VT, VI acelerar; **speedboat** N lancha; **speed camera** N radar m de velocidade; **speeding** N (Aut) excesso de velocidade; **speed limit** N limite m de velocidade, velocidade f máxima; **speedometer** [spɪˈdɒmɪtəʳ] N velocímetro; **speedy** ADJ veloz, rápido; (prompt) pronto, imediato

spell [spɛl] (pt, pp **spelled** or **spelt**) N (also: **magic ~**) encanto, feitiço; (period of time) período, temporada ▶ VT (also: **~ out**) soletrar; (fig) pressagiar, ser sinal de; **to cast a ~ on sb** enfeitiçar alguém; **he can't ~** não sabe escrever bem, comete erros de ortografia; **spellchecker** [ˈspɛltʃɛkəʳ] N (Comput) corretor m ortográfico

spend [spɛnd] (pt, pp **spent**) VT (money) gastar; (time) passar

sperm [spəːm] N esperma

sphere [sfɪəʳ] N esfera

spice [spaɪs] N especiaria ▶ VT condimentar

spicy [ˈspaɪsɪ] ADJ condimentado

spider [ˈspaɪdəʳ] N aranha

spike [spaɪk] N (point) ponta, espigão m; (Bot) espiga

spill [spɪl] (pt, pp **spilt** or **spilled**) VT entornar, derramar ▶ VI derramar-se; **spill over** VI transbordar

spin [spɪn] (pt, pp **spun**) N (Aviat) parafuso; (trip in car) volta or passeio de carro; (ball): **to put ~ on** fazer rolar ▶ VT (wool etc) fiar, tecer ▶ VI girar, rodar; (make thread) tecer; **spin out** VT prolongar; (money) fazer render

spinach [ˈspɪnɪtʃ] N espinafre m

spinal cord [ˈspaɪnl kɔːd] N espinha dorsal

spin doctor (inf) N marqueteiro(-a)

spin-dryer (BRIT) N secadora

spine [spaɪn] N espinha dorsal; (thorn) espinho

spiral [ˈspaɪərl] N espiral f ▶ VI (prices) disparar

spire [ˈspaɪəʳ] N flecha, agulha

spirit [ˈspɪrɪt] N (soul) alma; (ghost) fantasma m; (courage) coragem f, ânimo; (frame of mind) estado de espírito; (sense) sentido; **spirits** NPL (drink) álcool m; **in good ~s** alegre, de bom humor; **spiritual** ADJ espiritual ▶ N (also: **Negro spiritual**) canto religioso dos negros

spit [spɪt] (pt, pp **spat**) N (for roasting) espeto; (saliva) saliva ▶ VI cuspir; (sound) escarrar; (rain) chuviscar

spite [spaɪt] N rancor m, ressentimento ▶ VT contrariar; **in ~ of** apesar de, a despeito de; **spiteful** ADJ maldoso, malévolo

splash [splæʃ] N (sound) borrifo, respingo; (of colour) mancha ▶ VT: **to ~ (with)** salpicar (de) ▶ VI (also: **~ about**) borrifar, respingar

splendid [ˈsplɛndɪd] ADJ esplêndido; (impressive) impressionante

splinter [ˈsplɪntəʳ] N (of wood, glass) lasca; (in finger) farpa ▶ VI lascar-se, estilhaçar-se, despedaçar-se

split [splɪt] (pt, pp **split**) N fenda, brecha; (fig: division) rompimento; (: difference) diferença; (Pol) divisão f ▶ VT partir, fender; (party, work) dividir; (profits) repartir ▶ VI (divide) dividir-se, repartir-se; **split up** VI (couple) separar-se, acabar; (meeting) terminar

spoil [spɔɪl] (pt, pp **spoilt** or **spoiled**) VT (damage) danificar; (mar) estragar, arruinar; (child) mimar

spoke [spəuk] PT of **speak** ▶ N raio

spoken [ˈspəukn] PP of **speak**

spokesman [ˈspəuksmən] irreg N porta-voz m

spokeswoman [ˈspəukswumən] irreg N porta-voz f

sponge [spʌndʒ] N esponja; (cake) pão de ló m ▶ VT lavar com esponja ▶ VI: **to ~ on sb** viver às custas de alguém; **sponge bag** (BRIT) N bolsa de toalete

sponsor [ˈspɒnsəʳ] N patrocinador(a) m/f ▶ VT patrocinar; apadrinhar; fiar; (applicant, proposal) apoiar, defender; **sponsorship** N patrocínio

spontaneous [spɒnˈteɪnɪəs] ADJ espontâneo

spooky ['spuːkɪ] (inf) ADJ arrepiante
spoon [spuːn] N colher f; **spoonful** N colherada
sport [spɔːt] N esporte m (BR), desporto (PT); (person) bom perdedor/boa perdedora m/f ▶ VT (wear) exibir; **sport jacket** (US) N = **sports jacket**; **sports car** N carro esporte (BR), carro de sport (PT); **sports drink** N isotônico; **sports jacket** (BRIT) N casaco esportivo (BR) or desportivo (PT); **sportsman** irreg N esportista m (BR), desportista m (PT); **sportswear** N roupa esportiva (BR) or desportiva (PT) or esporte; **sportswoman** irreg N esportista (BR), desportista (PT); **sporty** ADJ esportivo (BR), desportivo (PT)
spot [spɔt] N (mark) marca; (place) lugar m, local m; (dot: on pattern) mancha, ponto; (on skin) espinha; (Radio, TV) hora; (small amount): **a ~ of** um pouquinho de ▶ VT notar; **on the ~** na hora; (there) ali mesmo; (in difficulty) em apuros; **spotless** ADJ sem mancha, imaculado; **spotlight** N holofote m, refletor m
spouse [spauz] N cônjuge m/f
sprain [spreɪn] N distensão f, torcedura ▶ VT torcer
sprang [spræŋ] PT of **spring**
sprawl [sprɔːl] VI esparramar-se
spray [spreɪ] N borrifo; (container) spray m, atomizador m; (garden spray) vaporizador m; (of flowers) ramalhete m ▶ VT pulverizar; (crops) borrifar, regar
spread [spred] (pt, pp **spread**) N extensão f; (distribution) expansão f, difusão f; (Culin) pasta; (inf: food) banquete m ▶ VT espalhar; (butter) untar, passar; (wings, sails) abrir, desdobrar; (workload, wealth) distribuir; (scatter) disseminar ▶ VI (news, stain) espalhar-se; (disease) alastrar-se; **spread out** VI dispersar-se; **spreadsheet** N (Comput) planilha
spree [spriː] N: **to go on a ~** cair na farra
spring [sprɪŋ] (pt **sprang**, pp **sprung**) N salto, pulo; (coiled metal) mola; (season) primavera; (of water) fonte f; **spring up** VI aparecer de repente
sprinkle ['sprɪŋkl] VT (liquid) salpicar; (salt, sugar) borrifar; **to ~ water on, ~ with water** salpicar de água
sprint [sprɪnt] N corrida de pequena distância ▶ VI correr a toda velocidade
sprung [sprʌŋ] PP of **spring**
spun [spʌn] PT, PP of **spin**

spur [spəːʳ] N espora; (fig) estímulo ▶ VT (also: ~ **on**) incitar, estimular; **on the ~ of the moment** de improviso, de repente
spurt [spəːt] N (of energy) acesso; (of blood etc) jorro ▶ VI jorrar
spy [spaɪ] N espião/espiã m/f ▶ VI: **to ~ on** espiar, espionar ▶ VT enxergar, avistar; **spyware** ['spaɪwɛəʳ] N (Comput) spyware m, software m espião
sq. ABBR (Math etc) = **square**
squabble ['skwɔbl] VI brigar, discutir
squad [skwɔd] N (Mil, Police) pelotão m, esquadra; (Football) seleção f
squadron ['skwɔdrən] N (Mil) esquadrão m; (Aviat) esquadrilha; (Naut) esquadra
squander ['skwɔndəʳ] VT esbanjar, dissipar; (chances) desperdiçar
square [skwɛəʳ] N quadrado; (in town) praça; (inf: person) quadrado(-a), careta m/f ▶ ADJ quadrado; (inf: ideas, tastes) careta, antiquado ▶ VT (arrange) ajustar, acertar; (Math) elevar ao quadrado; (reconcile) conciliar; **all ~** igual, quite; **a ~ meal** uma refeição substancial; **2 metres ~** um quadrado de dois metros de lado; **2 ~ metres** 2 metros quadrados
squash [skwɔʃ] N (BRIT: drink): **lemon/orange ~** limonada/laranjada concentrada; (Sport) squash m; (US: vegetable) abóbora ▶ VT esmagar
squat [skwɔt] ADJ atarracado ▶ VI (also: ~ **down**) agachar-se, acocorar-se; **squatter** N posseiro(-a)
squeak [skwiːk] VI (door) ranger; (mouse) guinchar
squeal [skwiːl] VI guinchar, gritar agudamente
squeeze [skwiːz] N (gen, of hand) aperto; (Econ) arrocho ▶ VT comprimir, socar; (hand, arm) apertar; **squeeze out** VT espremer; (fig) extorquir
squid [skwɪd] N (pl **squids** or **squid**) N lula
squint [skwɪnt] VI olhar or ser vesgo ▶ N (Med) estrabismo
squirm [skwəːm] VI retorcer-se
squirrel ['skwɪrəl] N esquilo
squirt [skwəːt] VI, VT jorrar, esguichar
Sr ABBR = **senior**
St ABBR (= saint) S.; = **street**
stab [stæb] N (with knife etc) punhalada; (of pain) pontada; (inf: try): **to have a ~ at (doing) sth** tentar (fazer) algo ▶ VT apunhalar
stable ['steɪbl] ADJ estável ▶ N estábulo, cavalariça
stack [stæk] N montão m, pilha ▶ VT amontoar, empilhar

stadium ['steɪdɪəm] (pl **stadia** or **stadiums**) N estádio

staff [stɑːf] N (work force) pessoal m, quadro; (BRIT Sch: also: **teaching ~**) corpo docente ▶ VT prover de pessoal

stag [stæg] N veado, cervo

stage [steɪdʒ] N palco, cena; (point) etapa, fase f; (platform) plataforma, estrado; (profession): **the ~** o palco, o teatro ▶ VT pôr em cena, representar; (demonstration) montar, organizar; **in ~s** por etapas

stagger ['stægə'] VI cambalear ▶ VT (amaze) surpreender, chocar; (hours, holidays) escalonar; **staggering** ADJ (amazing) surpreendente, chocante

stain [steɪn] N mancha; (colouring) tinta, tintura ▶ VT manchar; (wood) tingir

stair [stɛə'] N (step) degrau m; **stairs** NPL (flight of steps) escada; **staircase** N escadaria, escada; **stairway** N = **staircase**

stake [steɪk] N estaca, poste m; (Comm: interest) interesse m, participação f; (Betting: gen pl) aposta ▶ VT apostar; (claim) reivindicar; **to be at ~** estar em jogo

stale [steɪl] ADJ (bread) dormido; (food) estragado; (air) viciado; (smell) mofado; (beer) velho

stalk [stɔːk] N talo, haste f ▶ VT caçar de tocaia; **to ~ in/out** entrar/sair silenciosamente; **to ~ off** andar com arrogância

stall [stɔːl] N (BRIT: in market) barraca; (in stable) baia ▶ VT (Aut) fazer morrer; (fig: delay) impedir, atrasar ▶ VI morrer; esquivar-se, ganhar tempo; **stalls** NPL (BRIT: in cinema, theatre) plateia

stamina ['stæmɪnə] N resistência

stammer ['stæmə'] N gagueira ▶ VI gaguejar, balbuciar

stamp [stæmp] N selo; (rubber stamp) carimbo, timbre m; (mark, also fig) marca, impressão f ▶ VI (also: **~ one's foot**) bater com o pé ▶ VT (letter) selar; (mark) marcar; (with rubber stamp) carimbar

stampede [stæm'piːd] N debandada, estouro (da boiada)

stance [stæns] N postura, posição f

stand [stænd] (pt, pp **stood**) N posição f, postura; (for taxis) ponto; (also: **hall ~**) pedestal m; (also: **music ~**) estante f; (Sport) tribuna, palanque m; (stall) barraca ▶ VI (be) estar, encontrar-se; (be on foot) estar em pé; (rise) levantar-se; (remain: decision, offer) estar de pé; (in election) candidatar-se ▶ VT (place) pôr, colocar; (tolerate, withstand) aguentar, suportar; (cost) pagar; **to make a ~** resistir; (fig) ater-se a um princípio; **to ~ for parliament** (BRIT) apresentar-se como candidato ao parlamento; **stand by** VI estar a postos ▶ VT FUS (opinion) aferrar-se a; (person) ficar ao lado de; **stand down** VI retirar-se; **stand for** VT FUS (signify) significar; (represent) representar; (tolerate) tolerar, permitir; **stand in for** VT FUS substituir; **stand out** VI (be prominent) destacar-se; **stand up** VI levantar-se; **stand up for** VT FUS defender; **stand up to** VT FUS enfrentar

standard ['stændəd] N padrão m, critério; (flag) estandarte m; (level) nível m ▶ ADJ padronizado, regular, normal; **standards** NPL (morals) valores mpl morais; **standard of living** N padrão m de vida (BR), nível m de vida (PT)

stand-by ADJ de reserva ▶ N: **to be on ~** estar de sobreaviso or de prontidão; **stand-by ticket** N bilhete m de stand-by

standing ['stændɪŋ] ADJ (on foot) em pé; (permanent) permanente ▶ N posição f, reputação f; **of many years' ~** de muitos anos

standpoint ['stændpɔɪnt] N ponto de vista

standstill ['stændstɪl] N: **at a ~** paralisado, parado; **to come to a ~** (car) parar; (factory, traffic) ficar paralisado

stank [stæŋk] PT of **stink**

staple ['steɪpl] N (for papers) grampo ▶ ADJ (food etc) básico ▶ VT grampear

star [stɑː'] N estrela; (celebrity) astro/estrela ▶ VI: **to ~ in** ser a estrela em, estrelar ▶ VT (Cinema) ser estrelado por; **the stars** NPL (horoscope) o horóscopo

starboard ['stɑːbəd] N estibordo

starch [stɑːtʃ] N (in food) amido, fécula; (for clothes) goma

stardom ['stɑːdəm] N estrelato

stare [stɛə'] N olhar m fixo ▶ VI: **to ~ at** olhar fixamente, fitar

stark [stɑːk] ADJ severo, áspero ▶ ADV: **~ naked** completamente nu, em pelo

start [stɑːt] N princípio, começo; (departure) partida; (sudden movement) sobressalto, susto; (advantage) vantagem f ▶ VT começar, iniciar; (cause) causar; (found) fundar; (engine) ligar ▶ VI começar, iniciar; (with fright) sobressaltar-se, assustar-se; (train etc) sair; **start off** VI começar, principiar; (leave) sair, pôr-se a caminho; **start up** VI começar; (car) pegar, pôr-se em marcha ▶ VT começar; (car) ligar; **starter** N (Aut) arranque m; (Sport: official) juiz/juíza m/f da partida; **starting point** N ponto de partida

startle ['stɑːtl] VT assustar, aterrar; **startling** ADJ surpreendente

starvation [stɑːˈveɪʃən] N fome f

starve ['stɑːv] VI passar fome; (to death) morrer de fome ▶ VT fazer passar fome; (fig): **to ~ (of)** privar (de)

state [steɪt] N estado ▶ VT afirmar, declarar; **the States** NPL (Geo) os Estados Unidos; **to be in a ~** estar agitado; **statement** N declaração f; **statesman** irreg N estadista m

static ['stætɪk] N (Radio, TV) interferência ▶ ADJ estático

station ['steɪʃən] N estação f; (Police) delegacia; (Radio) emissora ▶ VT colocar

stationary ['steɪʃnərɪ] ADJ estacionário

station wagon (US) N perua (BR), canadiana (PT)

statistic [stəˈtɪstɪk] N estatística; **statistics** [stəˈtɪstɪks] N (science) estatística

statue ['stætjuː] N estátua

status ['steɪtəs] N posição f; (official classification) categoria; (importance) status m

staunch [stɔːntʃ] ADJ fiel

stay [steɪ] N estadia, estada ▶ VI ficar; (as guest) hospedar-se; (spend some time) demorar-se; **to ~ put** não se mexer; **to ~ the night** pernoitar; **stay behind** VI ficar atrás; **stay in** VI ficar em casa; **stay on** VI ficar; **stay out** VI ficar fora de casa; **stay up** VI (at night) velar, ficar acordado

steadily ['stedɪlɪ] ADV (firmly) firmemente; (unceasingly) sem parar, constantemente; (walk) regularmente

steady ['stedɪ] ADJ (job, boyfriend) constante; (speed) fixo; (regular) regular; (person, character) sensato; (calm) calmo, sereno ▶ VT (stabilize) estabilizar; (nerves) acalmar

steak [steɪk] N filé m; (beef) bife m

steal [stiːl] (pt **stole**, pp **stolen**) VT roubar ▶ VI mover-se furtivamente

steam [stiːm] N vapor m ▶ VT (Culin) cozinhar no vapor ▶ VI fumegar; **steamy** ADJ vaporoso; (room) cheio de vapor, úmido (BR), húmido (PT); (heat, atmosphere) vaporoso

steel [stiːl] N aço ▶ ADJ de aço

steep [stiːp] ADJ íngreme; (increase) acentuado; (price) exorbitante ▶ VT (food) colocar de molho; (cloth) ensopar, encharcar

steeple ['stiːpl] N campanário, torre f

steer [stɪər] VT (person) guiar; (vehicle) dirigir ▶ VI conduzir; **steering** N (Aut) direção f; **steering wheel** N volante m

stem [stem] N (of plant) caule m, haste f; (of glass) pé m ▶ VT deter, reter; (blood) estancar; **stem from** VT FUS originar-se de

step [step] N passo; (stair) degrau m ▶ VI: **to ~ forward** dar um passo a frente/ atrás; **steps** NPL (BRIT) = **stepladder**; **to be in ~ (with)** (fig) manter a paridade (com); **to be out of ~ (with)** (fig) estar em disparidade (com); **step down** VI (fig) renunciar; **step on** VT FUS pisar; **step up** VT aumentar; **stepbrother** N meio-irmão m; **stepdaughter** N enteada; **stepfather** N padrasto; **stepladder** (BRIT) N escada portátil or de abrir; **stepmother** N madrasta; **stepsister** N meia-irmã f; **stepson** N enteado

stereo ['sterɪəu] N estéreo; (record player) (aparelho de) som m ▶ ADJ (also: **~phonic**) estereofônico

sterile ['steraɪl] ADJ esterelizado; (barren) estéril; **sterilize** ['sterɪlaɪz] VT esterilizar

sterling ['stɜːlɪŋ] ADJ esterlino; (silver) de lei ▶ N (currency) libra esterlina; **one pound ~** uma libra esterlina

stern [stɜːn] ADJ severo, austero ▶ N (Naut) popa, ré f

stew [stjuː] N guisado, ensopado ▶ VT guisar, ensopar; (fruit) cozinhar

steward ['stjuːəd] N (Aviat) comissário de bordo; **stewardess** N aeromoça (BR), hospedeira de bordo (PT)

stick [stɪk] (pt, pp **stuck**) N pau m; (as weapon) cacete m; (walking stick) bengala, cajado ▶ VT (glue) colar; (inf: put) meter; (: tolerate) aguentar, suportar; (thrust): **to ~ sth into** cravar or enfiar algo em ▶ VI (become attached) colar-se; (be unmoveable) emperrar; (in mind etc) gravar-se; **stick out** VI estar saliente, projetar-se; **stick up** VI estar saliente, projetar-se; **stick up for** VT FUS defender; **sticker** N adesivo; **sticking plaster** N esparadrapo

sticky ['stɪkɪ] ADJ pegajoso; (label) adesivo; (fig) delicado

stiff [stɪf] ADJ (strong) forte; (hard) duro; (difficult) difícil; (moving with difficulty: person) teso; (: door, zip) empenado; (formal) formal ▶ ADV (bored, worried) extremamente

stigma ['stɪgmə] N estigma m

stiletto [stɪˈletəu] (BRIT) N (also: **~ heel**) salto alto e fino

still [stɪl] ADJ parado ▶ ADV (*up to this time*) ainda; (*even, yet*) ainda; (*nonetheless*) entretanto, contudo

stimulate ['stɪmjuleɪt] VT estimular

stimulus ['stɪmjuləs] (*pl* **stimuli**) N estímulo, incentivo

sting [stɪŋ] (*pt, pp* **stung**) N (*wound*) picada; (*pain*) ardência; (*of insect*) ferrão *m* ▶ VT aguilhar ▶ VI (*insect, animal*) picar; (*eyes, ointment*) queimar

stink [stɪŋk] (*pt* **stank**, *pp* **stunk**) N fedor *m*, catinga ▶ VI feder, cheirar mal

stir [stəːʳ] N (*fig*) comoção *f*, rebuliço ▶ VT mexer; (*fig*) comover ▶ VI mover-se, remexer-se; **stir up** VT excitar; (*trouble*) provocar

stitch [stɪtʃ] N (*Sewing, Knitting, Med*) ponto; (*pain*) pontada ▶ VT costurar; (*Med*) dar pontos em, suturar

stock [stɔk] N suprimento; (*Comm: reserves*) estoque *m*, provisão *f*; (: *selection*) sortimento; (*Agr*) gado; (*Culin*) caldo; (*lineage*) estirpe *f*, linhagem *f*; (*Finance*) valores *mpl*, títulos *mpl* ▶ ADJ (*reply etc*) de sempre, costumeiro ▶ VT ter em estoque, estocar; **in ~** em estoque; **out of ~** esgotado; **to take ~ of** (*fig*) fazer um balanço de; **~s and shares** valores e títulos mobiliários; **stock up** VI: **to ~ up (with)** abastecer-se (de); **stockbroker** N corretor(a) *m/f* de valores; **stock cube** (BRIT) N cubo de caldo; **stock exchange** N Bolsa de Valores

stocking ['stɔkɪŋ] N meia

stock market (BRIT) N Bolsa, mercado de valores

stole [stəul] PT *of* **steal** ▶ N estola

stolen ['stəuln] PP *of* **steal**

stomach ['stʌmək] N (*Anat*) estômago; (*belly*) barriga, ventre *m* ▶ VT suportar, tolerar

stone [stəun] N pedra; (*pebble*) pedrinha; (*in fruit*) caroço; (*Med*) cálculo, pedra; (BRIT: *weight*) = 6.348kg; 14 *pounds* ▶ ADJ de pedra ▶ VT apedrejar; (*fruit*) tirar o(s) caroço(s) de

stood [stud] PT, PP *of* **stand**

stool [stuːl] N tamborete *m*, banco

stoop [stuːp] VI (*also*: **have a ~**) ser corcunda; (*also*: **~ down**) debruçar-se, curvar-se

stop [stɔp] N parada, interrupção *f*; (*for bus etc*) parada (BR), ponto (BR), paragem *f* (PT); (*also*: **full ~**) ponto ▶ VT parar, deter; (*break off*) interromper; (*pay, cheque*) sustar, suspender; (*also*: **put a ~ to**) impedir ▶ VI parar, deter-se;

(*watch, noise*) parar; (*end*) acabar; **to ~ doing sth** deixar de fazer algo; **stop dead** VI parar de repente; **stop off** VI dar uma parada; **stop up** VT tapar; **stopover** N parada rápida; (*Aviat*) escala

storage ['stɔːrɪdʒ] N armazenagem *f*

store [stɔːʳ] N (*stock*) suprimento; (*depot*) armazém *m*; (*reserve*) estoque *m*; (BRIT: *large shop*) loja de departamentos; (US: *shop*) loja ▶ VT armazenar; **stores** NPL (*provisions*) víveres *mpl*, provisões *fpl*; **who knows what is in ~ for us?** quem sabe o que nos espera?; **store up** VT acumular

storey ['stɔːrɪ], (US) **story** N andar *m*

storm [stɔːm] N tempestade *f*; (*fig*) tumulto ▶ VI (*fig*) enfurecer-se ▶ VT tomar de assalto, assaltar; **stormy** ADJ tempestuoso

story ['stɔːrɪ] N história, estória; (*lie*) mentira; (US) = **storey**

stout [staut] ADJ sólido, forte; (*fat*) gordo, corpulento; (*resolute*) decidido, resoluto ▶ N cerveja preta

stove [stəuv] N (*for cooking*) fogão *m*; (*for heating*) estufa, fogareiro

straight [streɪt] ADJ reto; (*back*) esticado; (*hair*) liso; (*honest*) honesto; (*simple*) simples *inv* ▶ ADV reto; (*drink*) puro; **to put** *or* **get sth ~** esclarecer algo; **~ away, ~ off** (*at once*) imediatamente; **straighten** VT arrumar; **to straighten things out** arrumar as coisas; **straighten out** VT endireitar; (*fig*) esclarecer; **straightforward** ADJ (*simple*) simples *inv*, direto; (*honest*) honesto, franco

strain [streɪn] N tensão *f*; (*Tech*) esforço; (*Med: back strain*) distensão *f*; (: *tension*) luxação *f*; (*breed*) raça, estirpe *f* ▶ VT forçar, torcer, distender; (*stretch*) puxar, estirar; (*Culin*) coar; **strains** NPL (*Mus*) acordes *mpl*; **strained** ADJ distendido; (*laugh*) forçado; (*relations*) tenso; **strainer** N coador *m*; (*sieve*) peneira

strait [streɪt] N estreito; **straits** NPL: **to be in dire ~s** estar em apuros

strand [strænd] N (*of thread, hair*) fio; (*of rope*) tira; **stranded** ADJ preso

strange [streɪndʒ] ADJ (*not known*) desconhecido; (*odd*) estranho, esquisito; **strangely** ADV estranhamente; **stranger** N desconhecido(-a); (*from another area*) forasteiro(-a)

strangle ['stræŋgl] VT estrangular; (*fig*) sufocar

strap [stræp] N correia; (*of slip, dress*) alça

strategic [strə'ti:dʒɪk] ADJ estratégico

strategy ['strætɪdʒɪ] N estratégia

straw [strɔ:] N palha; (*drinking straw*) canudo; **that's the last ~!** essa foi a última gota!

strawberry ['strɔ:bərɪ] N morango

stray [streɪ] ADJ (*animal*) extraviado; (*bullet*) perdido; (*scattered*) espalhado ▶ VI perder-se

streak [stri:k] N listra, traço; (*in hair*) mecha ▶ VT listrar ▶ VI: **to ~ past** passar como um raio

stream [stri:m] N riacho, córrego; (*of people, vehicles*) fluxo; (*of smoke*) rastro; (*of questions etc*) torrente f ▶ VT (*Sch*) classificar; (*Comput*) fazer stream de ▶ VI correr, fluir; **to ~ in/out** entrar/sair em massa

street [stri:t] N rua; **streetcar** (*US*) N bonde m (BR), eléctrico (PT); **street plan** N mapa m

strength [strɛŋθ] N força; (*of girder, knot etc*) firmeza, resistência; (*fig*) poder m; **strengthen** VT fortificar; (*fig*) fortalecer

strenuous ['strɛnjuəs] ADJ enérgico; (*determined*) tenaz

stress [strɛs] N pressão f; (*mental strain*) tensão f, stress m; (*emphasis*) ênfase f; (*Tech*) tensão ▶ VT realçar, dar ênfase a; (*syllable*) acentuar; **stressed** ADJ (*tense*) estressado; (*syllable*) tônico

stretch [strɛtʃ] N (*of sand etc*) trecho, extensão f ▶ VI espreguiçar-se; (*extend*): **to ~ to** or **as far as** estender-se até ▶ VT estirar, esticar; (*fig: subj: job, task*) exigir o máximo de; **stretch out** VI esticar-se ▶ VT (*arm etc*) esticar; (*spread*) estirar

stretcher ['strɛtʃər] N maca, padiola

strict [strɪkt] ADJ (*person*) severo, rigoroso; (*meaning*) exato, estrito

stride [straɪd] (*pt* **strode**, *pp* **stridden**) N passo largo ▶ VI andar a passos largos

strike [straɪk] (*pt, pp* **struck**) N greve f; (*of oil etc*) descoberta; (*attack*) ataque m ▶ VT bater em; (*oil etc*) descobrir; (*deal*) fechar, acertar; (*fig*): **the thought** or **it ~s me that ...** me ocorre que ...; ▶ VI estar em greve; (*attack: soldiers, illness*) atacar; (: *disaster*) assolar; (*clock*) bater; **on ~** em greve; **to ~ a match** acender um fósforo; **strike down** VT derrubar; **strike up** VT (*Mus*) começar a tocar; (*conversation, friendship*) travar; **striker** N grevista m/f; (*Sport*) atacante m/f; **striking** ADJ impressionante

string [strɪŋ] (*pt, pp* **strung**) N (*cord*) barbante m (BR), cordel m (PT); (*of beads*) cordão m; (*of onions*) réstia; (*Mus*) corda

▶ VT: **to ~ out** esticar; **the strings** NPL (*Mus*) os instrumentos de corda; **to ~ together** (*words*) unir; (*ideas*) concatenar; **to get a job by pulling ~s** (*fig*) usar pistolão

strip [strɪp] N tira; (*of land*) faixa; (*of metal*) lâmina, tira ▶ VT despir ▶ VI despir-se

stripe [straɪp] N listra; (*Mil*) galão m; **striped** ADJ listrado, com listras

strive [straɪv] (*pt* **strove**, *pp* **striven**) VI: **to ~ for sth/to do sth** esforçar-se por or batalhar para algo/para fazer algo

strode [strəud] PT of **stride**

stroke [strəuk] N (*blow*) golpe m; (*Med*) derrame m cerebral; (*of paintbrush*) pincelada; (*Swimming: style*) nado ▶ VT acariciar, afagar; **at a ~** de repente, de golpe

stroll [strəul] N volta, passeio ▶ VI passear, dar uma volta; **stroller** (*US*) N carrinho (de criança)

strong [strɔŋ] ADJ forte; (*imagination*) fértil; (*personality*) forte, dominante; (*nerves*) de aço; **they are 50 ~** são em 50 pessoas; **stronghold** N fortaleza; (*fig*) baluarte m; **strongly** ADV firmemente; (*push, defend*) vigorosamente; (*believe*) profundamente

strove [strəuv] PT of **strive**

struck [strʌk] PT, PP of **strike**

structure ['strʌktʃər] N estrutura; (*building*) construção f

struggle ['strʌgl] N luta, contenda ▶ VI (*fight*) lutar; (*try hard*) batalhar

strung [strʌŋ] PT, PP of **string**

stub [stʌb] N (*of ticket etc*) canhoto; (*of cigarette*) toco, ponta; **to ~ one's toe** dar uma topada; **stub out** VT apagar

stubble ['stʌbl] N restolho; (*on chin*) barba por fazer

stubborn ['stʌbən] ADJ teimoso, cabeçudo, obstinado

stuck [stʌk] PT, PP of **stick** ▶ ADJ (*jammed*) emperrado

stud [stʌd] N (*shirt stud*) botão m; (*earring*) tarraxa, rosca; (*of boot*) cravo; (*also*: **~ farm**) fazenda de cavalos; (*also*: **~ horse**) garanhão m ▶ VT (*fig*): **~ded with** salpicado de

student ['stju:dənt] N estudante m/f ▶ ADJ estudantil; **student driver** (*US*) N aprendiz m/f

studio ['stju:dɪəu] N estúdio; (*sculptor's*) ateliê m

study ['stʌdɪ] N estudo; (*room*) sala de leitura or estudo ▶ VT estudar; (*examine*) examinar, investigar ▶ VI estudar;

studies NPL (*subjects*) estudos *mpl*, matérias *fpl*

stuff [stʌf] N (*substance*) troço; (*things*) troços *mpl*, coisas *fpl* ▶ VT (*Culin*) rechear; (*animals*) empalhar; (*inf: push*) enfiar; **~ed toy** brinquedo de pelúcia; **stuffing** N recheio; **stuffy** ADJ (*room*) abafado, mal ventilado; (*person*) rabujento, melindroso

stumble ['stʌmbl] VI tropeçar; **to ~ across** or **on** (*fig*) topar com

stump [stʌmp] N (*of tree*) toco; (*of limb*) coto ▶ VT: **to be ~ed** ficar perplexo

stun [stʌn] VT (*subj: blow*) aturdir; (: *news*) pasmar

stung [stʌŋ] PT, PP *of* **sting**

stunk [stʌŋk] PP *of* **stink**

stunning ['stʌnɪŋ] ADJ (*news*) atordoante; (*appearance*) maravilhoso

stunt [stʌnt] N façanha sensacional; (*publicity stunt*) truque *m* publicitário

stupid ['stjuːpɪd] ADJ estúpido, idiota

sturdy ['stɜːdɪ] ADJ (*person*) robusto, firme; (*thing*) sólido

stutter ['stʌtəʳ] N gagueira, gaguez *f* ▶ VI gaguejar

style [staɪl] N estilo; (*elegance*) elegância; **stylish** ADJ elegante, chique

subconscious [sʌb'kɔnʃəs] ADJ do subconsciente

subject [*n* 'sʌbdʒɪkt, *vt* səb'dʒɛkt] N (*of king*) súdito(-a); (*theme*) assunto; (*Sch*) matéria; (*Ling*) sujeito ▶ VT: **to ~ sb to sth** submeter alguém a algo; **to be ~ to** estar sujeito a; **subjective** [səb'dʒɛktɪv] ADJ subjetivo; **subject matter** N assunto; (*content*) conteúdo

submarine ['sʌbməriːn] N submarino

submission [səb'mɪʃən] N submissão *f*; (*to committee*) petição *f*; (*of plan*) apresentação *f*, exposição *f*

submit [səb'mɪt] VT submeter ▶ VI submeter-se

subordinate [sə'bɔːdɪnət] ADJ, N subordinado(-a)

subscribe [səb'skraɪb] VI subscrever; **to ~ to** (*opinion*) concordar com; (*fund*) contribuir para; (*newspaper*) assinar; **subscription** [səb'skrɪpʃən] N assinatura

subsequent ['sʌbsɪkwənt] ADJ subsequente, posterior; **subsequently** ADV posteriormente, depois

subside [səb'saɪd] VI (*feeling, wind*) acalmar-se; (*flood*) baixar

subsidiary [səb'sɪdɪərɪ] ADJ secundário ▶ N (*also:* **~ company**) subsidiária

subsidize ['sʌbsɪdaɪz] VT subsidiar

subsidy ['sʌbsɪdɪ] N subsídio

substance ['sʌbstəns] N substância

substantial [səb'stænʃl] ADJ (*solid*) sólido; (*reward, meal*) substancial

substitute ['sʌbstɪtjuːt] N substituto(-a); (*person*) suplente *m/f* ▶ VT: **to ~ A for B** substituir B por A

subtitled ['sʌbtaɪtld] ADJ (*film*) legendado

subtle ['sʌtl] ADJ sutil

subtract [səb'trækt] VT subtrair, deduzir

suburb ['sʌbəːb] N subúrbio; **suburban** [sə'bəːbən] ADJ suburbano; (*train etc*) de subúrbio

subway ['sʌbweɪ] N (*BRIT*) passagem *f* subterrânea; (*US*) metrô *m* (*BR*), metro(-politano) (*PT*)

succeed [sək'siːd] VI (*person*) ser bem sucedido, ter êxito; (*plan*) sair bem ▶ VT suceder a; **to ~ in doing** conseguir fazer

success [sək'sɛs] N êxito, (*hit, person*) sucesso; **successful** ADJ (*venture*) bem sucedido; (*writer*) de sucesso, bem sucedido; **to be successful (in doing)** conseguir (fazer); **successfully** ADV com sucesso, com êxito

succession [sək'sɛʃən] N sucessão *f*, série *f*; (*to throne*) sucessão

such [sʌtʃ] ADJ tal, semelhante; (*of that kind: singular*): **~ a book** um livro parecido, tal livro; (: *plural*): **~ books** tais livros; (*so much*): **~ courage** tanta coragem ▶ ADV tão; **~ a long trip** uma viagem tão longa; **~ a lot of** tanto; **~ as** tal como; **as ~** como tal; **such-and-such** ADJ tal e qual

suck [sʌk] VT chupar; (*breast*) mamar

sudden ['sʌdn] ADJ (*rapid*) repentino, súbito; (*unexpected*) imprevisto; **all of a ~** inesperadamente; **suddenly** ADV inesperadamente

sudoku [su'dəuku:] N sudoku *m*

sue [suː] VT processar

suede [sweɪd] N camurça

suffer ['sʌfəʳ] VT sofrer; (*bear*) aguentar, suportar ▶ VI sofrer, padecer; **to ~ from** sofrer de, estar com; **suffering** N sofrimento

sufficient [sə'fɪʃənt] ADJ suficiente, bastante

suffocate ['sʌfəkeɪt] VI sufocar(-se), asfixiar(-se)

sugar ['ʃugəʳ] N açúcar *m* ▶ VT pôr açúcar em, açucarar

suggest [sə'dʒɛst] VT sugerir; (*indicate*) indicar; **suggestion** N sugestão *f*; (*indication*) indicação *f*

suicide ['suɪsaɪd] N suicídio; (*person*) suicida *m/f*; *see also* **commit**; **suicide attack** N ataque *m* suicida, atentado suicida; **suicide bomber** N homem-bomba *m*, mulher-bomba *f*; **suicide bombing** N ataque *m* suicida

suit [su:t] N (*man's*) terno (BR), fato (PT); (*woman's*) conjunto; (*Jur*) processo; (*Cards*) naipe *m* ▸ VT convir a; (*clothes*) ficar bem a; (*adapt*): **to ~ sth to** adaptar *or* acomodar algo a; **they are well ~ed** fazem um bom par; **suitable** ADJ conveniente; (*appropriate*) apropriado

suitcase ['su:tkeɪs] N mala

suite [swi:t] N (*of rooms*) conjunto de salas; (*Mus*) suite *f*; **a three-piece ~** um conjunto estofado (sofá e duas poltronas)

sulfur ['sʌlfə^r] (US) = **sulphur**

sulk [sʌlk] VI ficar emburrado, fazer beicinho *or* biquinho (*inf*)

sulphur ['sʌlfə^r], (US) **sulfur** N enxofre *m*

sultana [sʌl'tɑ:nə] N passa branca

sum [sʌm] N soma; (*calculation*) cálculo; **sum up** VT, VI resumir

summarize ['sʌməraɪz] VT resumir

summary ['sʌmərɪ] N resumo

summer ['sʌmə^r] N verão *m* ▸ ADJ de verão; **in (the) ~** no verão; **summertime** N (*season*) verão *m*

summit ['sʌmɪt] N topo, cume *m*; (*also*: **~ conference**) (conferência de) cúpula

summon ['sʌmən] VT (*person*) mandar chamar; (*meeting*) convocar; (*Jur: witness*) convocar; **summon up** VT concentrar

sun [sʌn] N sol *m*; **sunbathe** VI tomar sol; **sunblock** N bloqueador *m* solar; **sunburn** N queimadura do sol

Sunday ['sʌndɪ] N domingo

sunflower ['sʌnflauə^r] N girassol *m*

sung [sʌŋ] PP *of* **sing**

sunglasses ['sʌnglɑ:sɪz] NPL óculos *mpl* de sol

sunk [sʌŋk] PP *of* **sink**

sun: sunlight N (luz *f* do) sol *m*; **sunny** ADJ cheio de sol; (*day*) ensolarado, de sol; **sunrise** N nascer *m* do sol; **sun roof** N (*Aut*) teto solar; **sunscreen** N protetor *m* solar; **sunset** N pôr *m* do sol; **sunshade** N para-sol *m*; **sunshine** N (luz *f* do) sol *m*; **sunstroke** N insolação *f*; **suntan** N bronzeado; **suntan lotion** N loção *f* de bronzear

super ['su:pə^r] (*inf*) ADJ bacana (BR), muito giro (PT)

superb [su:'pə:b] ADJ excelente

superfood ['su:pəfu:d] N superalimento

superintendent [su:pərɪn'tɛndənt] N superintendente *m/f*; (*Police*) chefe *m/f* de polícia

superior [su'pɪərɪə^r] ADJ superior; (*smug*) desdenhoso ▸ N superior *m*

supermarket ['su:pəmɑ:kɪt] N supermercado

supernatural [su:pə'nætʃərəl] ADJ sobrenatural ▸ N: **the ~** o sobrenatural

superpower ['su:pəpauə^r] N (*Pol*) superpotência

superstitious [su:pə'stɪʃəs] ADJ supersticioso

supervise ['su:pəvaɪz] VT supervisar, supervisionar; **supervision** [su:pə'vɪʒən] N supervisão *f*; **supervisor** N supervisor(a) *m/f*; (*academic*) orientador(a) *m/f*

supper ['sʌpə^r] N jantar *m*; (*late evening*) ceia

supple ['sʌpl] ADJ flexível

supplement [*n* 'sʌplɪmənt, *vt* sʌplɪ'mɛnt] N suplemento ▸ VT suprir, completar

supplier [sə'plaɪə^r] N abastecedor(a) *m/f*, fornecedor(a) *m/f*

supply [sə'plaɪ] VT (*provide*): **to ~ sth (to sb)** fornecer algo (a alguém); (*equip*): **to ~ (with)** suprir (de) ▸ N fornecimento, provisão *f*; (*stock*) estoque *m*; (*supplying*) abastecimento

support [sə'pɔ:t] N (*moral, financial etc*) apoio; (*Tech*) suporte *m* ▸ VT apoiar; (*financially*) manter; (*Tech: hold up*) sustentar; (*theory etc*) defender; **supporter** N (*Pol etc*) partidário(-a); (*Sport*) torcedor(a) *m/f*

suppose [sə'pəuz] VT supor; (*imagine*) imaginar; (*duty*): **to be ~d to do sth** dever fazer algo; **supposedly** [sə'pəuzɪdlɪ] ADV supostamente, pretensamente; **supposing** CONJ caso, supondo-se que

suppress [sə'prɛs] VT (*information*) suprimir; (*feelings, revolt*) reprimir; (*yawn*) conter

supreme [su'pri:m] ADJ supremo

surcharge ['sə:tʃɑ:dʒ] N sobretaxa

sure [ʃuə^r] ADJ seguro; (*definite*) certo; (*aim*) certeiro; **to make ~ of sth/that** assegurar-se de algo/que; **~!** (*of course*) claro que sim!; **~ enough** efetivamente; **surely** ADV (*certainly*: US: *also*: **sure**) certamente

surf [sə:f] N (*waves*) ondas *fpl*, arrebentação *f*

surface ['sə:fɪs] N superfície *f* ▸ VT (*road*) revestir ▸ VI vir à superfície *or* à tona; (*fig: news, feeling*) vir à tona

surfboard ['sɜːfbɔːd] N prancha de surfe

surfer ['sɜːfəʳ] N surfista m/f; (on the Internet) internauta m/f

surfing ['sɜːfɪŋ] N surfe m

surge [sɜːdʒ] N onda ▶ vɪ (sea) encapelar-se; (people, vehicles) precipitar-se; (feeling) aumentar repentinamente

surgeon ['sɜːdʒən] N cirurgião(-giã) m/f

surgery ['sɜːdʒərɪ] N cirurgia; (BRIT: room) consultório; (also: ~ **hours**) horas fpl de consulta

surname ['sɜːneɪm] N sobrenome m (BR), apelido (PT)

surplus ['sɜːpləs] N excedente m; (Comm) superávit m ▶ ADJ excedente, de sobra

surprise [sə'praɪz] N surpresa ▶ vT surpreender; **surprising** ADJ surpreendente

surrender [sə'rɛndəʳ] N rendição f, entrega ▶ vɪ render-se, entregar-se

surround [sə'raund] vT circundar, rodear; (Mil etc) cercar; **surrounding** ADJ circundante, adjacente; **surroundings** NPL arredores mpl, cercanias fpl

surveillance [sɜː'veɪləns] N vigilância

survey [n 'sɜːveɪ, vt sɜː'veɪ] N inspeção f; (of habits etc) pesquisa; (of house) inspeção f; (of land) levantamento ▶ vT observar, contemplar; (land) fazer um levantamento de; **surveyor** N (of land) agrimensor(a) m/f; (of building) inspetor(a) m/f

survival [sə'vaɪvl] N sobrevivência; (relic) remanescente m

survive [sə'vaɪv] vɪ sobreviver; (custom etc) perdurar ▶ vT sobreviver a; **survivor** N sobrevivente m/f

suspect [adj, n 'sʌspɛkt, vt səs'pɛkt] ADJ, N suspeito(-a) ▶ vT suspeitar, desconfiar

suspend [səs'pɛnd] vT suspender; **suspenders** NPL (BRIT) ligas fpl; (US) suspensórios mpl

suspense [səs'pɛns] N incerteza, ansiedade f; (in film etc) suspense m; **to keep sb in ~** manter alguém em suspense or na expectativa

suspension [səs'pɛnʃən] N suspensão f; (of driving licence) cassação f

suspicion [səs'pɪʃən] N suspeita; **suspicious** ADJ (suspecting) suspeitoso; (causing suspicion) suspeito

sustain [səs'teɪn] vT sustentar; (suffer) sofrer; **sustainable** ADJ sustentável

SUV N ABBR (= sports utility vehicle) SUV m

swallow ['swɔləu] N (bird) andorinha ▶ vT engolir, tragar; (fig: story) engolir; **swallow up** vT (savings etc) consumir

swam [swæm] PT of **swim**

swamp [swɔmp] N pântano, brejo ▶ vT atolar, inundar; (fig) assoberbar

swan [swɔn] N cisne m

swap [swɔp] N troca, permuta ▶ vT: **to ~ (for)** trocar (por); (replace (with)) substituir (por)

swarm [swɔːm] N (of bees) enxame m; (of people) multidão f ▶ vɪ enxamear; aglomerar-se; (place): **to be ~ing with** estar apinhado de

sway [sweɪ] vɪ balançar-se, oscilar ▶ vT (influence) influenciar

swear [sweəʳ] (pt **swore**, pp **sworn**) vɪ (curse) xingar ▶ vT (promise) jurar; **swearword** N palavrão m

sweat [swɛt] N suor m ▶ vɪ suar

sweater N suéter m or f (BR), camisola (PT)

sweaty ADJ suado

Swede [swiːd] N sueco(-a)

swede [swiːd] N tipo de nabo

Sweden ['swiːdən] N Suécia; **Swedish** ADJ sueco ▶ N (Ling) sueco

sweep [swiːp] (pt, pp **swept**) N (act) varredura; (also: **chimney ~**) limpador m de chaminés ▶ vT varrer; (with arm) empurrar; (subj: current) arrastar; (: fashion, craze) espalhar-se por ▶ vɪ varrer; **sweep away** vT varrer; **sweep past** vɪ passar rapidamente; **sweep up** vɪ varrer

sweet [swiːt] N (candy) bala (BR), rebuçado (PT); (BRIT: pudding) sobremesa ▶ ADJ doce; (fig: air) fresco; (: water, smell) doce; (: sound) suave; (: baby, kitten) bonitinho; (kind) meigo; **sweetheart** N namorado(-a)

swell [swɛl] (pt **swelled**, pp **swollen** or **swelled**) N (of sea) vaga, onda ▶ ADJ (US inf: excellent) bacana ▶ vɪ (increase) aumentar; (get stronger) intensificar-se; (also: ~ **up**) inchar(-se); **swelling** N (Med) inchação f

swept [swɛpt] PT, PP of **sweep**

swerve [swɜːv] vɪ desviar-se

swift [swɪft] N (bird) andorinhão m ▶ ADJ rápido

swim [swɪm] (pt **swam**, pp **swum**) N: **to go for a ~** ir nadar ▶ vɪ nadar; (head, room) rodar ▶ vT atravessar a nado; (distance) percorrer (a nado); **swimmer** N nadador(a) m/f; **swimming** N natação f; **swimming costume** (BRIT) N (woman's) maiô m (BR), fato de banho (PT); (man's) calção m de banho (BR), calções mpl de banho (PT);

swimming pool N piscina; **swimming trunks** NPL sunga (BR), calções mpl de banho (PT); **swimsuit** N maiô m (BR), fato de banho (PT)

swine flu ['swaɪn-] N gripe f suína

swing [swɪŋ] (pt, pp **swung**) N (in playground) balanço; (movement) balanceio, oscilação f; (change: in opinion) mudança; virada; (rhythm) ritmo ▶ VT balançar; (also: ~ **round**) girar, rodar ▶ VI oscilar; (on swing) balançar; (also: ~ **round**) voltar-se bruscamente; **to be in full ~** estar a todo vapor

swipe [swaɪp] VT (hit) bater em; (card, Comput) passar

swirl [swəːl] VI redemoinhar

Swiss [swɪs] ADJ, N INV suíço(-a)

switch [swɪtʃ] N (for light, radio etc) interruptor m; (change) mudança ▶ VT (change) trocar; **switch off** VT apagar; (engine) desligar; **switch on** VT acender; ligar; **switchboard** N (Tel) mesa telefônica

Switzerland ['swɪtsələnd] N Suíça

swollen ['swəulən] PP of **swell**

swoop [swuːp] N (by police etc) batida ▶ VI (also: ~ **down**) precipitar-se, cair

swop [swɔp] N, VT = **swap**

sword [sɔːd] N espada

swore [swɔːʳ] PT of **swear**

sworn [swɔːn] PP of **swear** ▶ ADJ (statement) sob juramento; (enemy) declarado

swum [swʌm] PP of **swim**

swung [swʌŋ] PT, PP of **swing**

syllable ['sɪləbl] N sílaba

syllabus ['sɪləbəs] N programa m de estudos

symbol ['sɪmbl] N símbolo

sympathetic [sɪmpə'θɛtɪk] ADJ (understanding) compreensivo; (likeable) agradável; (supportive): ~ **to(wards)** solidário com

sympathize ['sɪmpəθaɪz] VI: **to ~ with** (person) compadecer-se de; (sb's feelings) compreender; (cause) simpatizar com

sympathy ['sɪmpəθɪ] N compaixão f; **sympathies** NPL (tendencies) simpatia; **in ~ with** em acordo com; (strike) em solidariedade com; **with our deepest ~** com nossos mais profundos pêsames

symphony ['sɪmfənɪ] N sinfonia

symptom ['sɪmptəm] N sintoma m; (sign) indício

syndicate ['sɪndɪkɪt] N sindicato; (of newspapers) cadeia

synthetic [sɪn'θɛtɪk] ADJ sintético

Syria ['sɪrɪə] N Síria

syringe [sɪ'rɪndʒ] N seringa

syrup ['sɪrəp] N xarope m; (also: **golden ~**) melaço

system ['sɪstəm] N sistema m; (method) método; (Anat) organismo; **systematic** [sɪstə'mætɪk] ADJ sistemático

t

tab [tæb] N lingueta, aba; (*label*) etiqueta; **to keep ~s on** (*fig*) vigiar

table ['teɪbl] N mesa ▶ VT (*motion etc*) apresentar; **to lay** *or* **set the ~** pôr a mesa; **~ of contents** índice *m*, sumário; **tablecloth** N toalha de mesa; **tablespoon** N colher *f* de sopa; (*also:* **tablespoonful**: *as measurement*) colherada

tablet ['tæblɪt] N (*Med*) comprimido; (*also:* **~ computer**) tablet *m*; (*of stone*) lápide *f*

table tennis N pingue-pongue *m*, tênis *m* de mesa

tabloid ['tæblɔɪd] N tabloide *m*; **tabloid press** N *ver nota*

> O termo **tabloid press** refere-se aos jornais populares de formato meio jornal que apresentam muitas fotografias e adotam um estilo bastante conciso. O público-alvo desses jornais é composto por leitores que se interessam pelos fatos do dia que contenham um certo toque de escândalo; veja **quality (news)papers**.

tack [tæk] N (*nail*) tachinha, percevejo ▶ VT prender com tachinha; (*stitch*) alinhavar ▶ VI virar de bordo

tackle ['tækl] N (*gear*) equipamento; (*also:* **fishing ~**) apetrechos *mpl*; (*for lifting*) guincho; (*Football*) ato de tirar a bola de adversário ▶ VT (*difficulty*) atacar; (*challenge: person*) desafiar; (*grapple with*) atracar-se com; (*Football*) tirar a bola de

tacky ['tækɪ] ADJ pegajoso, grudento; (*inf: tasteless*) cafona

tact [tækt] N tato, diplomacia; **tactful** ADJ diplomático

tactics ['tæktɪks] N, NPL tática

tactless ['tæktlɪs] ADJ sem diplomacia

tag [tæg] N (*label*) etiqueta; **tag along** VI seguir

tail [teɪl] N rabo; (*of bird, comet, plane*) cauda; (*of shirt, coat*) aba ▶ VT (*follow*) seguir bem de perto; *see also* **head**; **tail away** VI diminuir gradualmente; **tail off** VI diminuir gradualmente

tailor ['teɪlər] N alfaiate *m*

take [teɪk] (*pt* **took**, *pp* **taken**) VT tomar; (*photo, holiday*) tirar; (*grab*) pegar (em); (*prize*) ganhar; (*effort, courage*) requerer, exigir; (*tolerate*) aguentar; (*accompany, bring, carry: person*) acompanhar, trazer; (: *thing*) trazer, carregar; (*exam*) fazer; (*passengers etc*): **it ~s 50 people** cabem 50 pessoas; **to ~ sth from** (*drawer etc*) tirar algo de; (*person*) pegar algo de; **I ~ it that ...** suponho que ...; **take after** VT FUS parecer-se com; **take apart** VT desmontar; **take away** VT (*extract*) tirar; (*carry off*) levar; (*subtract*) subtrair; **take back** VT (*return*) devolver; (*one's words*) retirar; **take down** VT (*building*) demolir; (*dismantle*) desmontar; (*letter etc*) tomar por escrito; **take in** VT (*deceive*) enganar; (*understand*) compreender; (*include*) abranger; (*lodger*) receber; **take off** VI (*Aviat*) decolar; (*go away*) ir-se ▶ VT (*remove*) tirar; **take on** VT (*work*) empreender; (*employee*) empregar; (*opponent*) desafiar; **take out** VT tirar; (*extract*) extrair; (*invite*) acompanhar; **take over** VT (*business*) assumir; (*country*) tomar posse de ▶ VI: **to ~ over from sb** suceder a alguém; **take to** VT FUS (*person*) simpatizar com; (*activity*) afeiçoar-se a; **to ~ to doing sth** criar o hábito de fazer algo; **take up** VT (*dress*) encurtar; (*time, space*) ocupar; (*hobby etc*) dedicar-se a; (*offer, challenge*) aceitar; **to ~ sb up on a suggestion/ offer** aceitar a oferta/sugestão de alguém sobre algo; **takeaway** (BRIT) ADJ (*food*) para levar; **takeoff** N (*Aviat*) decolagem *f*; **takeover** N (*Comm*) aquisição *f* de controle; **takings** NPL (*Comm*) receita, renda

talc [tælk] N (*also:* **talcum powder**) talco

tale [teɪl] N (*story*) conto; (*account*) narrativa; **to tell ~s** (*fig: lie*) dizer mentiras

talent ['tælənt] N talento; **talented** ADJ talentoso

talk [tɔːk] N conversa, fala; (*gossip*) mexerico, fofocas *fpl*; (*conversation*) conversa, conversação *f* ▶ VI falar; **talks** NPL (*Pol etc*) negociações *fpl*; **to ~ about**

falar sobre; **to ~ sb into doing sth** convencer alguém a fazer algo; **to ~ sb out of doing sth** dissuadir alguém de fazer algo; **to ~ shop** falar sobre negócios/questões profissionais; **talk over** VT discutir

tall [tɔ:l] ADJ alto; **to be 6 feet ~** medir 6 pés, ter 6 pés de altura

tame [teɪm] ADJ domesticado; (fig: story, style) sem graça, insípido

tamper ['tæmpə'] VI: **to ~ with** mexer em

tampon ['tæmpɔn] N tampão m

tan [tæn] N (also: **sun~**) bronzeado ▶ VI bronzear-se ▶ ADJ (colour) bronzeado, marrom claro

tangerine [tændʒə'ri:n] N tangerina, mexerica

tangle ['tæŋgl] N emaranhado; **to get in(to) a ~** meter-se num rolo

tank [tæŋk] N depósito, tanque m; (for fish) aquário; (Mil) tanque m

tanker ['tæŋkə'] N (ship) navio-tanque m; (truck) caminhão-tanque m

tantrum ['tæntrəm] N chilique m, acesso (de raiva)

tap [tæp] N (on sink etc) torneira; (gentle blow) palmadinha; (gas tap) chave f ▶ VT dar palmadinha em, bater de leve; (resources) utilizar, explorar; (telephone) grampear; **on ~** disponível

tape [teɪp] N fita; (also: **magnetic ~**) fita magnética; (sticky tape) fita adesiva ▶ VT (record) gravar (em fita); (stick with tape) colar; **tape measure** N fita métrica, trena

tar [tɑ:'] N alcatrão m

target ['tɑ:gɪt] N alvo

tariff ['tærɪf] N tarifa

tarmac ['tɑ:mæk] N (BRIT: on road) macadame m; (Aviat) pista

tarpaulin [tɑ:'pɔ:lɪn] N lona alcatroada

tart [tɑ:t] N (Culin) torta; (BRIT inf, pej: woman) piranha ▶ ADJ (flavour) ácido, azedo; **tart up** (inf) VT arrumar, dar um jeito em; **to ~ o.s. up** arrumar-se; (pej) empetecar-se

tartan ['tɑ:tn] N pano escocês axadrezado, tartan m ▶ ADJ axadrezado

tartar ['tɑ:tə'] N (on teeth) tártaro

taste [teɪst] N gosto; (also: **after~**) gosto residual; (sample, fig) amostra, ideia ▶ VT provar; (test) experimentar ▶ VI: **to ~ of** or **like** ter gosto or sabor de; **you can ~ the garlic (in it)** sente-se o gosto de alho; **in good/bad ~** de bom/mau gosto; **tasteful** ADJ de bom gosto; **tasteless** ADJ insípido, insosso; (remark)

de mau gosto; **tasty** ADJ saboroso, delicioso

tatters ['tætəz] NPL: **in ~** (clothes) em farrapos; (papers etc) em pedaços

tattoo [tə'tu:] N tatuagem f; (spectacle) espetáculo militar ▶ VT tatuar

taught [tɔ:t] PT, PP of **teach**

taunt [tɔ:nt] N zombaria, escárnio ▶ VT zombar de, mofar de

Taurus ['tɔ:rəs] N Touro

taut [tɔ:t] ADJ esticado

tax [tæks] N imposto ▶ VT tributar; (fig: test) sobrecarregar; (: patience) esgotar; **tax-free** ADJ isento de impostos

taxi ['tæksɪ] N táxi m ▶ VI (Aviat) taxiar; **taxi driver** N motorista m/f de táxi; **taxi rank** (BRIT) N ponto de táxi; **taxi stand** N ponto de táxi

tax: tax payer N contribuinte m/f; **tax return** N declaração f de rendimentos

TB ABBR of **tuberculosis**

tea [ti:] N chá m; (BRIT: meal) refeição f à noite; **high ~** (BRIT) ajantarado; **tea bag** N saquinho (BR) or carteira (PT) de chá; **tea break** N (BRIT) pausa (para o chá)

teach [ti:tʃ] (pt, pp **taught**) VT: **to ~ sb sth, ~ sth to sb** ensinar algo a alguém; (in school) lecionar ▶ VI ensinar; (be a teacher) lecionar; **teacher** N professor(a) m/f; **teaching** N ensino; (as profession) magistério

teacup ['ti:kʌp] N xícara (BR) or chávena (PT) de chá

team [ti:m] N (Sport) time m (BR), equipa (PT); (group) equipe f (BR), equipa (PT); (of animals) parelha

teapot ['ti:pɔt] N bule m de chá

tear¹ [tɪə'] N lágrima; **in ~s** chorando, em lágrimas

tear² [tɛə'] (pt **tore**, pp **torn**) N rasgão m ▶ VT rasgar ▶ VI rasgar-se; **tear along** VI (rush) precipitar-se; **tear up** VT rasgar

tearful ['tɪəful] ADJ choroso

tear gas N gás m lacrimogênio

tearoom ['ti:ru:m] N salão m de chá

tease [ti:z] VT implicar com

teaspoon ['ti:spu:n] N colher f de chá; (also: **~ful**: as measurement) (conteúdo de) colher de chá

teatime ['ti:taɪm] N hora do chá

tea towel (BRIT) N pano de prato

technical ['tɛknɪkl] ADJ técnico

technician [tɛk'nɪʃn] N técnico(-a)

technique [tɛk'ni:k] N técnica

technology [tɛk'nɔlədʒɪ] N tecnologia

teddy ['tɛdɪ], **teddy bear** N ursinho de pelúcia

tedious ['ti:dɪəs] ADJ maçante, chato

teenage ['ti:neɪdʒ] ADJ (*fashions etc*) de or para adolescentes; **teenager** N adolescente *m/f*, jovem *m/f*

teens [ti:nz] NPL: **to be in one's ~** estar entre os 13 e 19 anos, estar na adolescência

teeth [ti:θ] NPL *of* **tooth**

teetotal ['ti:'təutl] ADJ abstêmio

teleconferencing ['telɪkɔnfərənsɪŋ] N teleconferência *f*

telegram ['telɪɡræm] N telegrama *m*

telephone ['telɪfəun] N telefone *m* ▶ VT (*person*) telefonar para; (*message*) telefonar; **to be on the ~** (*BRIT*), **to have a ~** (*subscriber*) ter telefone; **to be on the ~** (*be speaking*) estar falando no telefone; **telephone booth**, (*BRIT*) **telephone box** N cabine *f* telefônica; **telephone call** N telefonema *m*; **telephone directory** N lista telefônica, catálogo (*BR*); **telephone number** N (número de) telefone *m*

telesales ['teliseilz] NPL televendas *fpl*

telescope ['teliskəup] N telescópio

television ['telɪvɪʒən] N televisão *f*; **on ~** na televisão

tell [tel] (*pt, pp* **told**) VT dizer; (*relate: story*) contar; (*distinguish*): **to ~ sth from** distinguir algo de ▶ VI (*have effect*) ter efeito; (*talk*): **to ~ (of)** falar (de or em); **to ~ sb to do sth** dizer para alguém fazer algo; **tell off** VT repreender

telly ['teli] (*BRIT inf*) N ABBR = **television**

temp [temp] (*BRIT inf*) N temporário(-a) ▶ VI trabalhar como temporário(-a)

temper ['tempər] N (*nature*) temperamento; (*mood*) humor *m*; (*fit of anger*) cólera ▶ VT (*moderate*) moderar; **to be in a ~** estar de mau humor; **to lose one's ~** perder a paciência or a calma, ficar zangado

temperament ['temprəmənt] N temperamento; **temperamental** [temprə'mentl] ADJ temperamental

temperature ['temprətʃər] N temperatura; **to have** or **run a ~** ter febre

temple ['templ] N (*building*) templo; (*Anat*) têmpora

temporary ['tempərəri] ADJ temporário, (*passing*) transitório

tempt [tempt] VT tentar; **tempting** ['temptɪŋ] ADJ tentador(a)

ten [ten] NUM dez; *see also* **five**

tenant ['tenənt] N inquilino(-a), locatário(-a)

tend [tend] VT (*sick etc*) cuidar de ▶ VI: **to ~ to do sth** tender a fazer algo

tendency ['tendənsi] N tendência

tender ['tendər] ADJ terno; (*age*) tenro; (*sore*) sensível, dolorido; (*meat*) macio ▶ N (*Comm: offer*) oferta, proposta; (*money*): **legal ~** moeda corrente or legal ▶ VT oferecer; **to ~ one's resignation** pedir demissão

tennis ['tenɪs] N tênis *m*; **tennis ball** N bola de tênis; **tennis court** N quadra de tênis; **tennis player** N jogador(a) *m/f* de tênis; **tennis racket** N raquete *f* de tênis

tenor ['tenər] N (*Mus*) tenor *m*

tense [tens] ADJ tenso; (*muscle*) rígido, teso ▶ N (*Ling*) tempo

tension ['tenʃən] N tensão *f*

tent [tent] N tenda, barraca

tentative ['tentətɪv] ADJ provisório, tentativo; (*person*) hesitante, indeciso

tenth [tenθ] NUM décimo

tent peg N estaca

tent pole N pau *m*

tepid ['tepɪd] ADJ tépido, morno

term [tə:m] N (*word, expression*) termo, expressão *f*; (*period*) período; (*Sch*) trimestre *m* ▶ VT denominar; **terms** NPL (*conditions*) condições *fpl*; (*Comm*) cláusulas *fpl*, termos *mpl*; **in the short/ long ~** a curto/longo prazo; **to be on good ~s with sb** dar-se bem com alguém; **to come to ~s with** aceitar

terminal ['tə:mɪnl] ADJ incurável ▶ N (*Elec*) borne *m*; (*BRIT: also*: **air ~**) terminal *m*; (*for oil, ore etc, also*: *Comput*) terminal *m*; (*BRIT: also*: **coach ~**) estação *f* rodoviária

terminate ['tə:mɪneɪt] VT terminar; **to ~ a pregnancy** fazer um aborto

terminus ['tə:mɪnəs] (*pl* **termini**) N terminal *m*

terrace ['terəs] N terraço; (*BRIT: row of houses*) lance *m* de casas; **the terraces** NPL (*BRIT Sport*) a arquibancada (*BR*), a geral (*PT*); **terraced** ADJ (*house*) ladeado por outras casas; (*garden*) em dois níveis

terrain [te'reɪn] N terreno

terrible ['terɪbl] ADJ terrível, horroroso; (*conditions*) precário; (*inf: awful*) terrível; **terribly** ADV terrivelmente; (*very badly*) pessimamente

terrific [tə'rɪfɪk] ADJ terrível, magnífico; (*wonderful*) maravilhoso, sensacional

terrify ['terɪfaɪ] VT apavorar

territory ['terɪtəri] N território

terror ['terər] N terror *m*; **terrorist** N terrorista *m/f*

test [test] N (*trial, check*) prova, ensaio; (*of courage etc, Chem*) prova; (*Med*) exame *m*;

(*exam*) teste *m*, prova; (*also*: **driving ~**) exame de motorista ▸ vт testar, pôr à prova

testicle ['tɛstɪkl] N testículo

testify ['tɛstɪfaɪ] vɪ (*Jur*) depor, testemunhar; **to ~ to sth** atestar algo; testemunhar algo

testimony ['tɛstɪmənɪ] N (*Jur*) testemunho, depoimento; **to be (a) ~ to** ser uma prova de

test match N (*Cricket, Rugby*) jogo internacional

test tube N proveta, tubo de ensaio

tetanus ['tɛtənəs] N tétano

text [tɛkst] N texto; (*also*: **~ message**) mensagem *f* de texto, torpedo (*inf*) ▸ vт mandar uma mensagem de texto *or* (*inf*) um torpedo para; **textbook** N livro didático; (*Sch*) livro escolar; **text message** N mensagem *f* de texto, torpedo (*inf*)

texture ['tɛkstʃəʳ] N textura

Thailand ['taɪlænd] N Tailândia

Thames [tɛmz] N: **the ~** o Tâmisa (BR), o Tamisa (PT)

than [ðæn, ðən] CONJ (*in comparisons*) do que; **more ~ 10** mais de 10; **I have more/less ~ you** tenho mais/menos do que você; **she has more apples ~ pears** ela tem mais maçãs do que peras; **she is older ~ you think** ela é mais velha do que você pensa

thank [θæŋk] vт agradecer; **~ you (very much)** muito obrigado(-a); **thanks** NPL agradecimentos *mpl* ▸ EXCL obrigado(-a)!

Thanksgiving ['θæŋksgɪvɪŋ], **Thanksgiving Day** N Dia *m* de Ação de Graças

O feriado de Ação de graças (**Thanksgiving Day**) nos Estados Unidos, quarta quinta-feira do mês de novembro, é o dia em que se comemora a boa colheita feita pelos peregrinos originários da Grã-Bretanha em 1621; tradicionalmente, é um dia em que se agradece a Deus e se organiza um grande banquete. Uma festa semelhante é celebrada no Canadá na segunda segunda-feira de outubro.

that [ðæt, ðət] (*pl* **those**) ADJ (*demonstrative*) esse/essa; (*more remote*) aquele/aquela; **that man/woman/ book** aquele homem/aquela mulher/ aquele livro; **that one** esse/essa
▸ PRON **1** (*demonstrative*) esse/essa,

aquele/aquela; (*neuter*) isso, aquilo; **who's/what's that?** quem é?/o que é isso?; **is that you?** é você?; **I prefer this to that** eu prefiro isto a aquilo; **that's what he said** foi isso o que ele disse; **that is (to say)** isto é, quer dizer

2 (*relative, direct: thing, person*) que; (: *person*) quem; (*relative, indirect: thing, person*) o/a qual *sg*, os/as quais *pl*; (: *person*) quem; **the book (that) I read** o livro que eu li; **the box (that) I put it in** a caixa na qual eu o coloquei; **the man (that) I spoke to** o homem com quem *or* o qual falei

3 (*relative, of time*): **on the day that he came** no dia em que ele veio
▸ CONJ que; **she suggested that I phone you** ela sugeriu que eu telefonasse para você
▸ ADV (*demonstrative*): **I can't work that much** não posso trabalhar tanto; **I didn't realize it was that bad** não pensei que fôsse tão ruim; **that high** dessa altura, até essa altura

thatched [θætʃt] ADJ (*roof*) de sapê; **~ cottage** chalé *m* com telhado de sapê *or* de colmo

thaw [θɔ:] N degelo ▸ vɪ (*ice*) derreter-se; (*food*) descongelar-se ▸ vт (*food*) descongelar

the [ði:, ðə] DEF ART **1** (*gen: singular*) o/a; (: *plural*) os/as; **the books/children are in the library** os livros/as crianças estão na biblioteca; **she put it on the table** ela colocou-o na mesa; **he took it from the drawer** ele tirou isto da gaveta; **to play the piano/violin** tocar piano/ violino; **I'm going to the cinema** vou ao cinema
2 (+ *adj to form n*): **the rich and the poor** os ricos e os pobres; **to attempt the impossible** tentar o impossível
3 (*in titles*): **Richard the Second** Ricardo II; **Peter the Great** Pedro o Grande
4 (*in comparisons*): **the more he works, the more he earns** quanto mais ele trabalha, mais ele ganha

theatre ['θɪətəʳ], (*US*) **theater** N teatro; (*Med: also*: **operating ~**) sala de operação

theft [θɛft] N roubo

their [ðɛəʳ] ADJ seu/sua, deles/delas; **theirs** PRON (o) seu/(a) sua

them [ðɛm, ðəm] PRON (*direct*) os/as; (*indirect*) lhes; (*stressed, after prep*) a eles/a elas

theme [θi:m] N tema *m*; **theme park** N *parque de diversões em torno de um único tema*

themselves [ðəmˈsɛlvz] PRON (*subject*) eles mesmos/elas mesmas; se; (*after prep*) si (*mesmos/as*)

then [ðɛn] ADV (*at that time*) então; (*next*) em seguida; (*later*) logo, depois; (*and also*) além disso ▶ CONJ (*therefore*) então, nesse caso, portanto ▶ ADJ: **the ~ president** o então presidente; **by ~** (*past*) até então; (*future*) até lá; **from ~ on** a partir de então

theology [θɪˈɔlədʒɪ] N teologia

theory [ˈθɪərɪ] N teoria; **in ~** em teoria, teoricamente

therapy [ˈθɛrəpɪ] N terapia

(KEYWORD)

there [ðɛəʳ] ADV 1: **there is, there are** há, tem; **there are 3 of them** são três; **there is no-one here/no bread left** não tem ninguém aqui/não tem mais pão; **there has been an accident** houve um acidente

2 (*referring to place*) aí, ali, lá; **put it in/on/up/down there** põe isto lá dentro/cima/em cima/embaixo; **I want that book there** quero aquele livro lá; **there he is!** lá está ele!

3: **there, there!** (*esp to child*) calma!

thereabouts [ˈðɛərəbauts] ADV por aí; (*amount*) aproximadamente

thereafter [ðɛərˈɑːftəʳ] ADV depois disso

thereby [ˈðɛəbaɪ] ADV assim, deste modo

therefore [ˈðɛəfɔː] ADV portanto

there's [ðɛəz] = **there is**; = **there has**

thermal [ˈθəːml] ADJ térmico

thermometer [θəˈmɔmɪtəʳ] N termômetro

thermostat [ˈθəːməustæt] N termostato

these [ðiːz] PL ADJ, PRON estes/estas

thesis [ˈθiːsɪs] (*pl* **theses**) N tese *f*

they [ðeɪ] PRON PL eles/elas; **~ say that ...** (*it is said that*) diz-se que ..., dizem que ...; **they'd** = **they had**; = **they would**; **they'll** = **they shall**; = **they will**; **they've** = **they have**

thick [θɪk] ADJ espesso; (*mud, fog, forest*) denso; (*sauce*) grosso; (*stupid*) burro ▶ N: **in the ~ of the battle** em plena batalha; **it's 20 cm ~** tem 20 cm de espessura; **thicken** VI (*fog*) adensar-se; (*plot etc*)

complicar-se ▶ VT engrossar; **thickness** N espessura, grossura

thief [θiːf] (*pl* **thieves**) N ladrão/ladra *m/f*

thigh [θaɪ] N coxa

thin [θɪn] ADJ magro; (*slice, line, book*) fino; (*light*) leve; (*hair*) ralo; (*crowd*) pequeno; (*soup, sauce*) aguado ▶ VT (*also*: **~ down**) diluir

thing [θɪŋ] N coisa; (*object*) negócio; (*matter*) assunto, negócio; (*mania*) mania; **things** NPL (*belongings*) pertences *mpl*; **to have a ~ about sb/sth** ser vidrado em alguém/algo; **the best ~ would be to ...** o melhor seria ...; **how are ~s?** como vai?, tudo bem?; **she's got a ~ about ...** ela detesta ...; **poor ~!** coitadinho(-a)!

think [θɪŋk] (*pt, pp* **thought**) VI pensar; (*believe*) achar ▶ VT pensar, achar; (*imagine*) imaginar; **what did you ~ of them?** o que você achou deles?; **to ~ about sth/sb** pensar em algo/alguém; **I'll ~ about it** vou pensar sobre isso; **to ~ of doing sth** pensar em fazer algo; **I ~ so/not** acho que sim/não; **to ~ well of sb** fazer bom juízo de alguém; **think over** VT refletir sobre, meditar sobre; **think up** VT inventar, bolar

third [θəːd] ADJ terceiro ▶ N terceiro(-a); (*fraction*) terço; (*Aut*) terceira; (*Sch: degree*) terceira categoria; **thirdly** ADV em terceiro lugar; **third party insurance** N seguro contra terceiros; **Third World** N: **the Third World** o Terceiro Mundo

thirst [θəːst] N sede *f*; **thirsty** ADJ (*person*) sedento, com sede; (*work*) que dá sede; **to be thirsty** estar com sede

thirteen [ˈθəːˈtiːn] NUM treze

thirty [ˈθəːtɪ] NUM trinta

(KEYWORD)

this [ðɪs] (*pl* **these**) ADJ (*demonstrative*) este/esta; **this man/woman/book** este homem/esta mulher/este livro; **these people/children/records** estas pessoas/crianças/estes discos; **this one** este aqui

▶ PRON (*demonstrative*) este/esta; (*neuter*) isto; **who/what is this?** quem é esse?/o que é isso?; **this is where I live** é aqui que eu moro; **this is Mr Brown** este é o Sr. Brown; (*on phone*) aqui é o Sr. Brown

▶ ADV (*demonstrative*): **this high** desta altura; **this long** deste comprimento; **we can't stop now we've gone this far** não podemos parar agora que fomos tão longe

thistle ['θɪsl] N cardo
thorn [θɔːn] N espinho
thorough ['θʌrə] ADJ (*search*) minucioso; (*knowledge, research, person*) metódico, profundo; **thoroughly** ADV minuciosamente; (*search*) profundamente; (*wash*) completamente; (*very*) muito
those [ðəuz] PRON PL, ADJ esses/essas
though [ðəu] CONJ embora, se bem que ▸ ADV no entanto
thought [θɔːt] PT, PP *of* **think** ▸ N pensamento; (*idea*) ideia; (*opinion*) opinião f; (*reflection*) reflexão f; **thoughtful** ADJ pensativo, (*serious*) sério; (*considerate*) atencioso; **thoughtless** ADJ desatencioso; (*words, person*) inconsequente
thousand ['θauzənd] NUM mil; **two ~** dois mil; **~s (of)** milhares mpl (de); **thousandth** ADJ milésimo
thrash [θræʃ] VT surrar, malhar; (*defeat*) derrotar; **thrash about** VI debater-se; **thrash out** VT discutir exaustivamente
thread [θred] N fio, linha; (*of screw*) rosca ▸ VT (*needle*) enfiar
threat [θret] N ameaça; **threaten** VI ameaçar ▸ VT: **to threaten sb with sth/to do** ameaçar alguém com algo/de fazer
three [θriː] NUM três; **three-dimensional** ADJ tridimensional, em três dimensões; **three-piece suit** N terno (3 peças) (BR), fato de 3 peças (PT)
threshold ['θreʃhəuld] N limiar m
threw [θruː] PT *of* **throw**
thrill [θrɪl] N emoção f; (*shudder*) estremecimento ▸ VT emocionar, vibrar; **to be ~ed** (*with gift etc*) estar emocionado; **thriller** N romance m or filme m de suspense; **thrilling** ADJ emocionante
throat [θrəut] N garganta; **to have a sore ~** estar com dor de garganta
throb [θrɔb] N (*of heart*) batida; (*of engine*) vibração f; (*of pain*) latejo ▸ VI (*heart*) bater, palpitar; (*pain*) dar pontadas; (*engine*) vibrar
throne [θrəun] N trono
through [θruː] PREP por, através de; (*time*) durante; (*by means of*) por meio de, por intermédio de; (*owing to*) devido a ▸ ADJ (*ticket, train*) direto ▸ ADV através; **to put sb ~ to sb** (*Tel*) ligar alguém com alguém; **to be ~** (*Tel*) estar na linha; (*have finished*) acabar; "**no ~ road**" "rua sem saída"; **I'm halfway ~ the book** estou na metade do livro; **throughout**

PREP (*place*) por todo(-a); (*time*) durante todo(-a) ▸ ADV por or em todas as partes
throw [θrəu] (*pt* **threw**, *pp* **thrown**) N arremesso, tiro; (*Sport*) lançamento ▸ VT jogar, atirar; (*Sport*) lançar; (*rider*) derrubar; (*fig*) desconcertar; **to ~ a party** dar uma festa; **throw away** VT (*dispose of*) jogar fora; (*waste*) desperdiçar; **throw off** VT desfazer-se de; (*habit, cold*) livrar-se; **throw out** VT expulsar; (*rubbish*) jogar fora; (*idea*) rejeitar; **throw up** VI vomitar, botar para fora
thru [θruː] (*US*) PREP, ADJ, ADV = **through**
thrush [θrʌʃ] N (*Zool*) tordo
thrust [θrʌst] (*pt*, *pp* **thrust**) N impulso; (*Tech*) empuxo ▸ VT empurrar
thud [θʌd] N baque m, som m surdo
thug [θʌg] N facínora m/f
thumb [θʌm] N (*Anat*) polegar m; **to ~ a lift** pegar carona (BR), arranjar uma boleia (PT); **thumb through** VT FUS folhear; **thumbtack** (*US*) N percevejo, tachinha
thump [θʌmp] N murro, pancada; (*sound*) baque m ▸ VT dar um murro em ▸ VI bater
thunder ['θʌndə'] N trovão m ▸ VI trovejar; (*train etc*) **to ~ past** passar como um raio; **thunderstorm** N tempestade f com trovoada, temporal m
Thursday ['θəːzdɪ] N quinta-feira
thyme [taɪm] N tomilho
tick [tɪk] N (*of clock*) tique-taque m; (*mark*) tique m, marca; (*Zool*) carrapato; (*BRIT inf*): **in a ~** num instante ▸ VI fazer tique-taque ▸ VT marcar, ticar; **tick off** VT assinalar, ticar; (*person*) dar uma bronca em; **tick over** (*BRIT*) VI (*engine*) funcionar em marcha lenta; (*fig*) ir indo
ticket ['tɪkɪt] N (*for bus, plane*) passagem f; (*for theatre, raffle*) bilhete m; (*for cinema*) entrada; (*in shop: on goods*) etiqueta; (*for library*) cartão m; (*also*: **parking ~**: *fine*) multa; **to get a (parking) ~** (*Aut*) ganhar uma multa (por estacionamento ilegal); **ticket barrier** (*BRIT*) N (*Rail*) catraca de embarque/desembarque; **ticket collector** N revisor(a) m/f; **ticket office** N bilheteria (BR), bilheteira (PT)
tickle ['tɪkl] VT fazer cócegas em ▸ VI fazer cócegas; **ticklish** ADJ coceguento; (*problem*) delicado
tide [taɪd] N maré f; (*fig*) curso; **high/low ~** maré alta/baixa; **the ~ of public opinion** a corrente da opinião pública; **tide over** VT ajudar num período difícil

tidy ['taɪdɪ] ADJ (*room*) arrumado; (*dress, work*) limpo; (*person*) bem arrumado ▶ VT (*also:* **~ up**) pôr em ordem, arrumar

tie [taɪ] N (*string etc*) fita, corda; (*BRIT: also:* **neck~**) gravata; (*fig: link*) vínculo, laço; (*Sport: draw*) empate m ▶ VT amarrar ▶ VI (*Sport*) empatar; **to ~ in a bow** dar um laço em; **to ~ a knot in sth** dar um nó em algo; **tie down** VT amarrar; (*fig: restrict*) limitar, restringir; (*: to date, price etc*) obrigar; **tie up** VT embrulhar; (*dog*) prender; (*boat, prisoner etc*) amarrar; (*arrangements*) concluir; **to be ~d up** estar ocupado

tier [tɪəʳ] N fileira; (*of cake*) camada

tiger ['taɪgəʳ] N tigre m

tight [taɪt] ADJ (*rope*) esticado, firme; (*money*) escasso; (*clothes, shoes*) justo; (*bend*) fechado; rigoroso; (*inf: drunk*) bêbado ▶ ADV (*squeeze*) bem forte; (*shut*) hermeticamente; **tighten** VT (*rope*) esticar; (*screw, grip*) apertar; (*security*) aumentar ▶ VI esticar-se; apertar-se; **tightly** ADV firmemente

tile [taɪl] N (*on roof*) telha; (*on floor*) ladrilho; (*on wall*) azulejo, ladrilho

till [tɪl] N caixa (registradora) ▶ VT (*land*) cultivar ▶ PREP, CONJ = **until**

tilt [tɪlt] VT inclinar ▶ VI inclinar-se

timber ['tɪmbəʳ] N (*material*) madeira; (*trees*) mata, floresta

time [taɪm] N tempo; (*epoch: often pl*) época; (*by clock*) hora; (*moment*) momento; (*occasion*) vez f; (*Mus*) compasso ▶ VT calcular or medir o tempo de; (*visit etc*) escolher o momento para; **a long ~** muito tempo; **4 at a ~** quatro de uma vez; **for the ~ being** por enquanto; **from ~ to ~** de vez em quando; **at ~s** às vezes; **in ~** (*soon enough*) a tempo; (*after some time*) com o tempo; (*Mus*) no compasso; **in a week's ~** dentro de uma semana; **in no ~** num abrir e fechar de olhos; **any ~** a qualquer hora; **on ~** na hora; **5 ~s 5 is 25** 5 vezes 5 são 25; **what ~ is it?** que horas são?; **to have a good ~** divertir-se; **timely** ADJ oportuno; **timetable** N horário; **time zone** N fuso horário

timid ['tɪmɪd] ADJ tímido

timing ['taɪmɪŋ] N escolha do momento; (*Sport*) cronometragem f; **the ~ of his resignation** o momento que escolheu para se demitir

tin [tɪn] N estanho; (*also:* **~ plate**) folha-de-flandres f; (*BRIT: can*) lata

tingle ['tɪŋgl] VI formigar

tinned [tɪnd] (*BRIT*) ADJ (*food*) em lata, em conserva

tin opener (*BRIT*) N abridor m de latas (*BR*), abre-latas m inv (*PT*)

tinsel ['tɪnsl] N ouropel m

tint [tɪnt] N matiz m; (*for hair*) tintura, tinta; **tinted** ADJ (*hair*) pintado; (*spectacles, glass*) fumê inv

tiny ['taɪnɪ] ADJ pequenininho, minúsculo

tip [tɪp] N ponta; (*gratuity*) gorjeta; (*BRIT: for rubbish*) depósito; (*advice*) dica ▶ VT dar uma gorjeta a; (*tilt*) inclinar; (*overturn: also:* **~ over**) virar, emborcar; (*empty: also:* **~ out**) esvaziar, entornar

tiptoe ['tɪptəu] N: **on ~** na ponta dos pés

tire ['taɪəʳ] N (*US*) = **tyre** ▶ VT cansar ▶ VI cansar-se; (*become bored*) chatear-se; **tired** ADJ cansado; **to be tired of sth** estar farto or cheio de algo; **tiring** ADJ cansativo

tissue ['tɪʃuː] N tecido; (*paper handkerchief*) lenço de papel; **tissue paper** N papel m de seda

tit [tɪt] N (*bird*) passarinho; **to give ~ for tat** pagar na mesma moeda

title ['taɪtl] N título

TM N ABBR = **trademark**

(KEYWORD)

to [tuː, tə] PREP **1** (*direction*) a, para; (*towards*) para; **to go to France/ London/school/the station** ir à França/a Londres/ao colégio/à estação; **to go to Lígia's/the doctor's** ir à casa da Lígia/ao médico; **the road to Edinburgh** a estrada para Edinburgo; **to the left/right** à esquerda/direita **2** (*as far as*) até; **to count to 10** contar até 10; **from 40 to 50 people** de 40 a 50 pessoas **3** (*with expressions of time*): **a quarter to 5** quinze para as 5 (*BR*), 5 menos um quarto (*PT*) **4** (*for, or*) de, para; **the key to the front door** a chave da porta da frente; **a letter to his wife** uma carta para a sua mulher **5** (*expressing indirect object*): **to give sth to sb** dar algo a alguém; **to talk to sb** falar com alguém; **I sold it to a friend** vendi isto para um amigo; **to cause damage to sth** causar danos em algo **6** (*in relation to*) para; **3 goals to 2** 3 a 2; **8 apples to the kilo** 8 maçãs por quilo **7** (*purpose, result*) para; **to come to sb's aid** prestar ajuda a alguém; **to sentence sb to death** condenar alguém à morte; **to my surprise** para minha surpresa

▶WITH VB **1** (*simple infin*): **to go/eat** ir/comer

2 (*following another vb*): **to want/try to do** querer/tentar fazer; **to start to do** começar a fazer

3 (*with vb omitted*): **I don't want to** eu não quero; **you ought to** você deve

4 (*purpose, result*) para

5 (*equivalent to relative clause*) para, a; **I have things to do** eu tenho coisas para fazer; **the main thing is to try** o principal é tentar

6 (*after adj etc*) para; **ready to go** pronto para ir; **too old/young to ...** muito velho/jovem para ...

▶ADV: **pull/push the door to** puxar/empurrar a porta

toad [təud] N sapo

toadstool ['təudstu:l] N chapéu-de-cobra m, cogumelo venenoso

toast [təust] N (*Culin*) torradas fpl; (*drink, speech*) brinde m ▶ VT torrar; (*drink to*) brindar; **toaster** N torradeira

tobacco [tə'bækəu] N tabaco, fumo (BR)

today [tə'deɪ] ADV, N hoje m

toddler ['tɔdlə'] N criança que começa a andar

toe [təu] N dedo do pé; (*of shoe*) bico ▶ VT: **to ~ the line** (*fig*) conformar-se, cumprir as obrigações

toffee ['tɔfɪ] N puxa-puxa m (BR), caramelo (PT)

together [tə'gɛðə'] ADV juntos; (*at same time*) ao mesmo tempo; **~ with** junto com

toilet ['tɔɪlət] N privada, vaso sanitário, (BRIT: *lavatory*) banheiro (BR), casa de banho (PT) ▶ CPD de toalete; **toilet paper** N papel m higiênico; **toiletries** NPL artigos mpl de toalete; **toilet roll** N rolo de papel higiênico

token ['təukən] N (*sign*) sinal m, símbolo, prova; (*souvenir*) lembrança; (*substitute coin*) ficha ▶ CPD simbólico; **book/record ~** (BRIT) vale para comprar livros/discos

told [təuld] PT, PP *of* **tell**

tolerant ['tɔlərənt] ADJ: **~ of** tolerante com

tolerate ['tɔləreɪt] VT suportar; (*Med, Tech*) tolerar

toll [təul] N (*of casualties*) número de baixas; (*tax, charge*) pedágio (BR), portagem f (PT) ▶ VI dobrar, tanger

tomato [tə'mɑ:təu] (*pl* **tomatoes**) N tomate m

tomb [tu:m] N tumba

tombstone ['tu:mstəun] N lápide f

tomorrow [tə'mɔrəu] ADV, N amanhã m; **the day after ~** depois de amanhã; **~ morning** amanhã de manhã

ton [tʌn] N tonelada; **~s of** (*inf*) um monte de

tone [təun] N tom m ▶ VI harmonizar; **tone down** VT (*colour, criticism*) suavizar; (*sound*) baixar; (*Mus*) entoar; **tone up** VT (*muscles*) tonificar

tongs [tɔŋz] NPL (*for coal*) tenaz f; (*for hair*) ferros mpl de frisar cabelo

tongue [tʌŋ] N língua; **~ in cheek** ironicamente

tonic ['tɔnɪk] N (*Med*) tônico; (*also:* **~ water**) (água) tônica

tonight [tə'naɪt] ADV, N esta noite, hoje à noite

tonsil ['tɔnsəl] N amígdala; **tonsillitis** [tɔnsɪ'laɪtɪs] N amigdalite f

too [tu:] ADV (*excessively*) demais; muito; (*also*) também; **~ much** (*adv*) demais; (*adj*) demasiado; **~ many** demasiados(-as)

took [tuk] PT *of* **take**

tool [tu:l] N ferramenta

tooth [tu:θ] (*pl* **teeth**) N (*Anat, Tech*) dente m; (*molar*) molar m; **toothache** N dor f de dente; **to have toothache** estar com dor de dente; **toothbrush** N escova de dentes; **toothpaste** N pasta de dentes, creme m dental; **toothpick** N palito

top [tɔp] N (*of mountain*) cume m, cimo; (*of tree*) topo; (*of head*) cocuruto; (*of cupboard, table*) superfície f, topo; (*of box, jar, bottle*) tampa; (*of ladder, page*) topo; (*toy*) pião m; (*blouse etc*) top m, blusa ▶ ADJ (*highest: shelf, step*) mais alto; (: *marks*) máximo; (*in rank*) principal, superior ▶ VT exceder; (*be first in*) estar à cabeça de; **on ~ of** sobre, em cima de; (*in addition to*) além de; **from ~ to toe** (BRIT) da cabeça aos pés; **from ~ to bottom** de cima abaixo; **top up**, (US) **top off** VT completar; (*mobile phone*) recarregar; **top floor** N último andar m

topic ['tɔpɪk] N tópico, assunto; **topical** ADJ atual

topless ['tɔplɪs] ADJ (*bather etc*) topless inv, sem a parte superior do biquíni

topple ['tɔpl] VT derrubar ▶ VI cair para frente

top-up card N cartão de recarga (para celular)

torch [tɔ:tʃ] N (BRIT) lanterna

tore [tɔ:'] PT *of* **tear²**

torment [*n* 'tɔːmɛnt, *vt* tɔː'mɛnt] N tormento, suplício ▸ VT atormentar; (*fig: annoy*) chatear, aborrecer

torn [tɔːn] PP *of* **tear²**

tornado [tɔː'neɪdəu] (*pl* **tornadoes**) N tornado

torrent ['tɔrənt] N torrente *f*

tortoise ['tɔːtəs] N tartaruga

torture ['tɔːtʃə'] N tortura ▸ VT torturar; (*fig*) atormentar

Tory ['tɔːrɪ] (*BRIT*) ADJ, N (*Pol*) conservador(a) *m/f*

toss [tɔs] VT atirar, arremessar; (*head*) lançar para trás ▸ VI: **to ~ and turn in bed** virar de um lado para o outro na cama; **to ~ a coin** tirar cara ou coroa; **to ~ up for sth** (*BRIT*) jogar cara ou coroa por algo

total ['təutl] ADJ total ▸ N total *m*, soma ▸ VT (*add up*) somar; (*amount to*) montar a

touch [tʌtʃ] N (*sense*) toque *m*; (*contact*) contato ▸ VT tocar (em); (*tamper with*) mexer com; (*make contact with*) fazer contato com; (*emotionally*) comover; **a ~ of** (*fig*) um traço de; **to get in ~ with sb** entrar em contato com alguém; **to lose ~** perder o contato; **touch on** VT FUS (*topic*) tocar em, fazer menção de; **touch up** VT (*paint*) retocar; **touchdown** N aterrissagem *f* (*BR*), aterragem *f* (*PT*); (*on sea*) amerissagem *f* (*BR*), amaragem *f* (*PT*); (*US Football*) touchdown *m* (*colocação da bola no chão atrás da linha de gol*); **touching** ADJ comovedor(a); **touchless** ADJ (*Comput*) sem contato, touchless; **touch screen** N (*Comput*) touch screen *m*, ecrã táctil (*PT*)

tough [tʌf] ADJ duro; (*difficult*) difícil; (*resistant*) resistente; (*person: physically*) forte; (*: mentally*) tenaz; (*firm*) firme, inflexível

tour ['tuə'] N viagem *f*, excursão *f*; (*also:* **package ~**) excursão organizada; (*of town, museum*) visita; (*by artist*) turnê *f* ▸ VT (*country, city*) excursionar por; (*factory*) visitar

tourism ['tuərɪzm] N turismo

tourist ['tuərɪst] N turista *m/f* ▸ CPD turístico; **tourist office** N (*in country*) escritório de turismo; (*in embassy etc*) departamento de turismo

tournament ['tuənəmənt] N torneio

tow [təu] VT rebocar; **"on ~"** (*BRIT*), **"in ~"** (*US*) (*Aut*) "rebocado"

toward [tə'wɔːd], **towards** [tə'wɔːdz] PREP em direção a; (*of attitude*) para com; (*of purpose*) para; **~(s) noon/the end of the year** perto do meio-dia/do fim do ano

towel ['tauəl] N toalha; **towelling** N (*fabric*) tecido para toalhas

tower ['tauə'] N torre *f*; **tower block** (*BRIT*) N prédio alto, espigão *m*, cortiço (*BR*)

town [taun] N cidade *f*; **to go to ~** ir à cidade; (*fig*) fazer com entusiasmo, mandar brasa (*BR*); **town centre** N centro (da cidade); **town hall** N prefeitura (*BR*), concelho (*PT*)

toy [tɔɪ] N brinquedo; **toy with** VT FUS brincar com; (*idea*) contemplar

trace [treɪs] N (*sign*) sinal *m*; (*small amount*) traço ▸ VT (*draw*) traçar, esboçar; (*follow*) seguir a pista de; (*locate*) encontrar

track [træk] N (*mark*) pegada, vestígio; (*path: gen*) caminho, vereda; (*: of bullet etc*) trajetória; (*: of suspect, animal*) pista, rasto; (*Rail*) trilhos (*BR*), carris *mpl* (*PT*); (*on tape*) trilha; (*Sport*) pista; (*on record*) faixa ▸ VT seguir a pista de; **to keep ~ of** não perder de vista; (*fig*) manter-se informado sobre; **track down** VT (*prey*) seguir a pista de; (*sth lost*) procurar e encontrar

tractor ['træktə'] N trator *m*

trade [treɪd] N comércio; (*skill, job*) ofício ▸ VI negociar, comerciar ▸ VT: **to ~ sth (for sth)** trocar algo (por algo); **trade in** VT dar como parte do pagamento; **trademark** N marca registrada; **trader** N comerciante *m/f*; **tradesman** *irreg* N lojista *m*; **trade union** N sindicato

tradition [trə'dɪʃən] N tradição *f*; **traditional** ADJ tradicional

traffic ['træfɪk] N trânsito; (*air traffic etc*) tráfego; (*illegal*) tráfico ▸ VI: **to ~ in** (*pej: liquor, drugs*) traficar com, fazer tráfico com; **traffic circle** (*US*) N rotatória; **traffic jam** N engarrafamento, congestionamento; **traffic lights** NPL sinal *m* luminoso; **traffic warden** N guarda *m/f* de trânsito

tragedy ['trædʒədɪ] N tragédia

tragic ['trædʒɪk] ADJ trágico

trail [treɪl] N (*tracks*) rasto, pista; (*path*) caminho, trilha; (*of smoke, dust*) rasto ▸ VT (*drag*) arrastar; (*follow*) seguir a pista de ▸ VI arrastar-se; (*hang loosely*) pender; (*in game, contest*) ficar para trás; **trail behind** VI atrasar-se; **trailer** N (*Aut*) reboque *m*; (*US: caravan*) trailer *m* (*BR*), rulote *f* (*PT*); (*Cinema*) trailer

train [treɪn] N trem *m* (*BR*), comboio (*PT*); (*of dress*) cauda ▸ VT formar; (*teach skills to*) instruir; (Sport) treinar; (dog) adestrar, amestrar; (point: gun etc): **to ~ on** apontar para ▶ vi (learn a skill) instruir-se; (Sport) treinar; (be educated) ser treinado; **to lose one's ~ of thought** perder o fio; **trainee** [treɪ'niː] N estagiário(-a); **trainer** N (Sport) treinador(a) m/f; (of animals) adestrador(a) m/f; **trainers** NPL (shoes) tênis m; **training** N instrução f; (Sport, for occupation) treinamento; (professional) formação

trait [treɪt] N traço

traitor ['treɪtə'] N traidor(a) m/f

tram [træm] (BRIT) N (also: **~car**) bonde m (BR), eléctrico (PT)

tramp [træmp] N (person) vagabundo(-a); (inf, pej: woman) piranha ▶ vi caminhar pesadamente

trample ['træmpl] VT: **to ~ (underfoot)** calcar aos pés

trampoline ['træmpəliːn] N trampolim m

tranquil ['træŋkwɪl] ADJ tranquilo; **tranquillizer** N (Med) tranquilizante m

transfer [n 'trænsfə', vt træns'fə:'] N transferência; (picture, design) decalcomania ▶ vt transferir; **to ~ the charges** (BRIT Tel) ligar a cobrar

transform [træns'fɔ:m] VT transformar

transfusion [træns'fjuːʒən] N (also: **blood ~**) transfusão f (de sangue)

transit ['trænzɪt] N: **in ~** em trânsito, de passagem

translate [trænz'leɪt] VT traduzir; **translation** N tradução f; **translator** N tradutor(a) m/f

transmission [trænz'mɪʃən] N transmissão f

transmit [trænz'mɪt] VT transmitir

transparent [træns'pærnt] ADJ transparente

transplant [vt træns'plɑːnt, n 'trænsplɑːnt] VT transplantar ▶ N (Med) transplante m

transport [n 'trænspɔːt, vt træns'pɔːt] N transporte m ▶ vt transportar; (carry) acarretar; **transportation** [trænspɔː'teɪʃən] N transporte m

trap [træp] N (snare) armadilha, cilada; (trick) cilada; (carriage) aranha, charrete f ▶ vt (animal, person) pegar numa armadilha; (immobilize) bloquear; **to be ~ped** (in bad marriage, fire) estar preso(-a)

trash [træʃ] N (US: rubbish) lixo; **trash can** (US) N lata de lixo

trauma ['trɔːmə] N trauma m

travel ['trævl] N viagem f ▶ vi viajar; (sound) propagar-se; (news) levar; (wine):

this wine ~s well este vinho não sofre alteração ao ser transportado ▶ vt percorrer; **travels** NPL (journeys) viagens fpl; **travel agent** N agente m/f de viagens; **traveller**, (US) **traveler** N viajante m/f; (Comm) caixeiro(-a) viajante; **traveller's cheque**, (US) **traveler's check** N cheque m de viagem; **travelling**, (US) **traveling** N as viagens, viajar m ▶ ADJ (circus, exhibition) itinerante; (salesman) viajante ▶ CPD de viagem; **travel sickness** N enjoo

tray [treɪ] N bandeja; (on desk) cesta

treacherous ['trɛtʃərəs] ADJ traiçoeiro; (ground, tide) perigoso

treacle ['triːkl] N melado

tread [trɛd] (pt **trod**, pp **trodden**) N (step) passo, pisada; (sound) passada; (of stair) piso; (of tyre) banda de rodagem ▶ vi pisar; **tread on** VT FUS pisar (em)

treasure ['trɛʒə'] N tesouro; (person) joia ▶ vt (value) apreciar, estimar; **treasures** NPL (art treasures etc) preciosidades fpl

treasurer ['trɛʒərə'] N tesoureiro(-a)

treasury ['trɛʒərɪ] N tesouraria

treat [triːt] N regalo, deleite m ▶ vt tratar; **to ~ sb to sth** convidar alguém para algo

treatment ['triːtmənt] N tratamento

treaty ['triːtɪ] N tratado, acordo

treble ['trɛbl] ADJ tríplice ▶ vt triplicar ▶ vi triplicar(-se)

tree [triː] N árvore f

trek [trɛk] N (long journey) jornada; (walk) caminhada

tremble ['trɛmbl] vi tremer

tremendous [trɪ'mɛndəs] ADJ tremendo; (enormous) enorme; (excellent) sensacional, fantástico

trench [trɛntʃ] N trincheira

trend [trɛnd] N (tendency) tendência; (of events) curso; (fashion) modismo, tendência; (on social network: also: **~ing topic**) trending topic m ▶ vi (on social network) ser compartilhado no Twitter até virar trending topic; **trendy** ADJ (idea) de acordo com a tendência atual; (clothes) da última moda

trespass ['trɛspəs] vi: **to ~ on** invadir; **"no ~ing"** "entrada proibida"

trial ['traɪəl] N (Jur) processo; (test: of machine etc) prova, teste m; **trials** NPL (unpleasant experiences) dissabores mpl; **by ~ and error** por tentativas; **to be on ~** ser julgado; **trial period** N período de experiência

triangle ['traɪæŋgl] N (Math, Mus) triângulo

tribe [traɪb] N tribo f
tribunal [traɪ'bjuːnl] N tribunal m
tribute ['trɪbjuːt] N homenagem f; **to pay ~ to** prestar homenagem a, homenagear
trick [trɪk] N truque m; (joke) peça, brincadeira; (skill, knack) habilidade f; (Cards) vaza ▶ VT enganar; **to play a ~ on sb** pregar uma peça em alguém; **that should do the ~** (inf) isso deveria dar resultado
trickle ['trɪkl] N (of water etc) fio (de água) ▶ VI gotejar, pingar
tricky ['trɪkɪ] ADJ difícil, complicado
trifle ['traɪfl] N bobagem f, besteira; (Culin) tipo de bolo com fruta e creme ▶ ADV: **a ~ long** um pouquinho longo
trigger ['trɪgər] N (of gun) gatilho; **trigger off** VT desencadear
trim [trɪm] ADJ (figure) elegante; (house) arrumado; (garden) bem cuidado ▶ N (haircut etc) habilidade f, knack) (on car) estofamento ▶ VT aparar, cortar; (decorate): **to ~ (with)** enfeitar (com); (Naut: sail) ajustar
trip [trɪp] N viagem f; (outing) excursão f; (stumble) tropeção m ▶ VI tropeçar; (go lightly) andar com passos ligeiros; **on a ~** de viagem; **trip up** VI tropeçar ▶ VT passar uma rasteira em
triple ['trɪpl] ADJ triplo, tríplice; **triplets** NPL trigêmeos(-as) mpl/fpl
tripod ['traɪpɔd] N tripé m
triumph ['traɪʌmf] N (satisfaction) satisfação f; (great achievement) triunfo ▶ VI: **to ~ (over)** triunfar (sobre)
trivial ['trɪvɪəl] ADJ insignificante; (commonplace) trivial
trod [trɔd] PT of **tread**; **trodden** PP of **tread**
troll [trɔl, trəʊl] (inf: Comput) N troll m ▶ VI trollar
trolley ['trɔlɪ] N carrinho; (table on wheels) mesa volante
trombone [trɔm'bəʊn] N trombone m
troop [truːp] N bando, grupo ▶ VI: **to ~ in/out** entrar/sair em bando; **troops** NPL (Mil) tropas fpl; **~ing the colour** (BRIT) saudação da bandeira
trophy ['trəʊfɪ] N troféu m
tropic ['trɔpɪk] N trópico; **tropical** ADJ tropical
trot [trɔt] N trote m; (fast pace) passo rápido ▶ VI trotar; (person) andar rapidamente; **on the ~** (fig: inf) a fio
trouble ['trʌbl] N problema(s) m(pl), dificuldade(s) f(pl); (worry) preocupação f; (bother, effort) incômodo, trabalho; (Pol)

distúrbios mpl; (Med): **stomach ~** etc problemas mpl gástricos etc ▶ VT perturbar; (worry) preocupar, incomodar ▶ VI: **to ~ to do sth** incomodar-se or preocupar-se de fazer algo; **troubles** NPL (Pol etc) distúrbios mpl; **to be in ~** estar num aperto; (ship, climber etc) estar em dificuldade; **what's the ~?** qual é o problema?; **troubled** ADJ preocupado; (epoch, life) agitado; **troublemaker** N criador(a)-de-casos m/f; (child) encrenqueiro(-a); **troublesome** ADJ importuno; (child, cough) incômodo
trough [trɔf] N (also: **drinking ~**) bebedouro, cocho; (also: **feeding ~**) gamela; (depression) depressão f
trousers ['traʊzəz] NPL calça (BR), calças fpl (PT)
trout [traʊt] N INV truta
truant ['truːənt] (BRIT) N: **to play ~** matar aula (BR), fazer gazeta (PT)
truce [truːs] N trégua, armistício
truck [trʌk] N caminhão m (BR), camião m (PT); (Rail) vagão m; **truck driver** N caminhoneiro(-a) (BR), camionista m/f (PT)
true [truː] ADJ verdadeiro; (accurate) exato; (genuine) autêntico; (faithful) fiel, leal; **to come ~** realizar-se, tornar-se realidade
truly ['truːlɪ] ADV realmente; (truthfully) verdadeiramente; (faithfully) fielmente; **yours ~** (in letter) atenciosamente
trumpet ['trʌmpɪt] N trombeta
trunk [trʌŋk] N tronco; (of elephant) tromba; (case) baú m; (US Aut) mala (BR), porta-bagagens m (PT); **trunks** NPL (also: **swimming ~s**) sunga (BR), calções mpl de banho (PT)
trust [trʌst] N confiança; (responsibility) responsabilidade f; (Jur) fideicomisso ▶ VT (rely on) confiar em; (entrust): **to ~ sth to sb** confiar algo a alguém; (hope): **to ~ (that)** esperar que; **to take sth on ~** aceitar algo sem verificação prévia; **trusted** ADJ de confiança; **trustworthy** ADJ digno de confiança
truth [truːθ] N verdade f; **truthful** ADJ (person) sincero, honesto
try [traɪ] N tentativa; (Rugby) ensaio ▶ VT (Jur) julgar; (test: sth new) provar, pôr à prova; (strain) cansar ▶ VI tentar; **to have a ~** fazer uma tentativa; **to ~ to do sth** tentar fazer algo; **try on** VT (clothes) experimentar, provar; **trying** ADJ exasperante
T-shirt N camiseta (BR), T-shirt f (PT)
tub [tʌb] N tina; (bath) banheira

tube [tjuːb] N tubo; (*pipe*) cano; (BRIT: *underground*) metrô *m* (BR), metro(-politano) (PT); (*for tyre*) câmara-de-ar *f*

tuberculosis [tjubəːkjuˈləusɪs] N tuberculose *f*

tuck [tʌk] VT (*put*) enfiar, meter; **tuck away** VT esconder; **to be ~ed away** estar escondido; **tuck in** VT enfiar para dentro; (*child*) aconchegar ▶ VI (*eat*) comer com apetite; **tuck up** VT (*child*) aconchegar

Tuesday [ˈtjuːzdɪ] N terça-feira

tug [tʌg] N (*ship*) rebocador *m* ▶ VT puxar

tuition [tjuːˈɪʃən] N ensino; (*private tuition*) aulas *fpl* particulares; (US: *fees*) taxas *fpl* escolares

tulip [ˈtjuːlɪp] N tulipa

tumble [ˈtʌmbl] N (*fall*) queda ▶ VI cair, tombar; **to ~ to sth** (*inf*) sacar algo

tumbler [ˈtʌmbləʳ] N copo

tummy [ˈtʌmɪ] (*inf*) N (*belly*) barriga; (*stomach*) estômago

tumour [ˈtjuːməʳ], (US) **tumor** N tumor *m*

tuna [ˈtjuːnə] N INV (*also*: **~ fish**) atum *m*

tune [tjuːn] N melodia ▶ VT (*Mus*) afinar; (*Radio, TV*) sintonizar; (*Aut*) regular; **to be in/out of ~** (*instrument*) estar afinado/desafinado; (*singer*) cantar afinado/desafinar; **to be in/out of ~ with** (*fig*) harmonizar-se com/destoar de; **tune in** VI (*Radio, TV*): **to ~ in (to)** sintonizar (com); **tune up** VI (*musician*) afinar (seu instrumento)

tunic [ˈtjuːnɪk] N túnica

Tunisia [tjuːˈnɪzɪə] N Tunísia

tunnel [ˈtʌnl] N túnel *m*; (*in mine*) galeria ▶ VI abrir um túnel (*or* uma galeria)

turbulence [ˈtəːbjuləns] N (*Aviat*) turbulência

turf [təːf] N torrão *m* ▶ VT relvar, gramar; **turf out** (*inf*) VT (*person*) pôr no olho da rua

Turk [təːk] N turco(-a)

Turkey [ˈtəːkɪ] N Turquia

turkey [ˈtəːkɪ] N peru(a) *m/f*

Turkish [ˈtəːkɪʃ] ADJ turco(-a) ▶ N (*Ling*) turco

turmoil [ˈtəːmɔɪl] N tumulto, distúrbio, agitação *f*; **in ~** agitado, tumultuado

turn [təːn] N volta, turno; (*in road*) curva; (*of mind, events*) propensão *f*, tendência; (*Theatre*) número; (*Med*) choque *m* ▶ VT dar volta a, fazer girar; (*collar*) virar; (*change*): **to ~ sth into** converter algo em ▶ VI virar; (*person: look back*) voltar-se; (*reverse direction*) mudar de direção; (*milk*) azedar; (*become*) tornar-se, virar; **to ~ nasty** engrossar; **to ~ forty** fazer quarenta anos; **a good ~** um favor; **it gave me quite a ~** me deu um susto enorme; **"no left ~"** (*Aut*) "proibido virar à esquerda"; **it's your ~** é a sua vez; **in ~** por sua vez; **to take ~s (at)** revezar (em); **turn away** VI virar a cabeça ▶ VT (*business, applicants*) recusar; **turn back** VI voltar atrás ▶ VT voltar para trás; (*clock*) atrasar; **turn down** VT (*refuse*) recusar; (*reduce*) baixar; (*fold*) dobrar, virar para baixo; **turn in** VI (*inf: go to bed*) ir dormir ▶ VT (*fold*) dobrar para dentro; **turn off** VI (*from road*) virar, sair do caminho ▶ VT (*light, radio etc*) apagar; (*engine*) desligar; **turn on** VT (*light*) acender; (*engine, radio*) ligar; (*tap*) abrir; **turn out** VT (*light, gas*) apagar; (*produce*) produzir ▶ VI (*troops*) ser mobilizado; **to ~ out to be ...** revelar-se (ser) ..., resultar (ser) ..., vir a ser ...; **turn over** VI (*person*) virar-se ▶ VT (*object*) virar; **turn round** VI voltar-se, virar-se; **turn up** VI (*person*) aparecer, pintar; (*lost object*) aparecer ▶ VT (*collar*) levantar; (*volume, radio etc*) aumentar; **turning** N (*in road*) via lateral

turnip [ˈtəːnɪp] N nabo

turnout [ˈtəːnaut] N assistência; (*in election*) comparecimento às urnas

turnover [ˈtəːnəuvəʳ] N (*Comm: amount of money*) volume *m* de negócios; (: *of goods*) movimento; (*of staff*) rotatividade *f*

turn-up (BRIT) N (*on trousers*) volta, dobra

turquoise [ˈtəːkwɔɪz] N (*stone*) turquesa ▶ ADJ azul-turquesa *inv*

turtle [ˈtəːtl] N tartaruga, cágado

tusk [tʌsk] N defesa (de elefante)

tutor [ˈtjuːtəʳ] N professor(a) *m/f*; (*private tutor*) professor(a) *m/f* particular; **tutorial** [tjuːˈtɔːrɪəl] N (*Sch*) seminário

tuxedo [tʌkˈsiːdəu] (US) N smoking *m*

TV N ABBR (= *television*) TV *f*

tweed [twiːd] N tweed *m*, pano grosso de lã

tweet [twiːt] (*on Twitter*) N tweet *m* ▶ VT, VI tuitar

tweezers [ˈtwiːzəz] NPL pinça (pequena)

twelfth [twɛlfθ] NUM décimo segundo

twelve [twɛlv] NUM doze; **at ~ (o'clock)** (*midday*) ao meio-dia; (*midnight*) à meia-noite

twentieth [ˈtwɛntɪɪθ] NUM vigésimo

twenty [ˈtwɛntɪ] NUM vinte

twice [twaɪs] ADV duas vezes; **~ as much** duas vezes mais

twig [twɪg] N graveto, varinha ▶ vɪ (*inf*) sacar

twilight ['twaɪlaɪt] N crepúsculo, meia-luz *f*

twin [twɪn] ADJ gêmeo(-a); (*beds*) separado ▶ N gêmeo(-a) ▶ vᴛ irmanar; **twin-bedded room** N quarto com duas camas

twinkle ['twɪŋkl] vɪ cintilar; (*eyes*) pestanejar

twist [twɪst] N torção *f*; (*in road, coil*) curva; (*in wire, flex*) virada; (*in story*) mudança imprevista ▶ vᴛ torcer, retorcer; (*ankle*) torcer; (*weave*) entrelaçar; (*roll around*) enrolar; (*fig*) deturpar ▶ vɪ serpentear

twit [twɪt] (*inf*) N idiota *m/f*, bobo(-a)

twitch [twɪtʃ] N puxão *m*; (*nervous*) tique *m* nervoso ▶ vɪ contrair-se

two [tuː] NUM dois; **to put ~ and ~ together** (*fig*) tirar conclusões; **two-way** ADJ: **two-way traffic** trânsito em mão dupla

type [taɪp] N (*category*) tipo, espécie *f*; (*model*) modelo; (*Typ*) tipo, letra ▶ vᴛ (*letter etc*) datilografar, bater (à máquina); **typewriter** N máquina de escrever

typhoid ['taɪfɔɪd] N febre *f* tifoide

typical ['tɪpɪkl] ADJ típico

typing ['taɪpɪŋ] N datilografia

typist ['taɪpɪst] N datilógrafo(-a) *m/f*

tyre ['taɪəʳ], (*US*) **tire** N pneu *m*

UFO ['juːfəu] N ABBR (= *unidentified flying object*) óvni *m*

Uganda [juːˈɡændə] N Uganda (*no article*)

ugly ['ʌɡlɪ] ADJ feio; (*dangerous*) perigoso

UK N ABBR = **United Kingdom**

ulcer ['ʌlsəʳ] N úlcera; **mouth ~** afta

ultimate ['ʌltɪmət] ADJ último, final; (*authority*) máximo; **ultimately** ADV (*in the end*) no final, por último; (*fundamentally*) no fundo

ultrasound ['ʌltrəsaund] N (*Med*) ultrassom *m*

umbrella [ʌmˈbrɛlə] N guarda-chuva *m*; (*for sun*) guarda-sol *m*, barraca (da praia)

umpire ['ʌmpaɪəʳ] N árbitro ▶ vᴛ arbitrar

UN N ABBR (= *United Nations*) ONU *f*

unable [ʌnˈeɪbl] ADJ: **to be ~ to do sth** não poder fazer algo

unanimous [juːˈnænɪməs] ADJ unânime

unarmed [ʌnˈɑːmd] ADJ (*without a weapon*) desarmado; (*defenceless*) indefeso

unattended [ʌnəˈtɛndɪd] ADJ (*car, luggage*) abandonado

unattractive [ʌnəˈtræktɪv] ADJ sem atrativos; (*building, appearance, idea*) pouco atraente

unavoidable [ʌnəˈvɔɪdəbl] ADJ inevitável

unaware [ʌnəˈwɛəʳ] ADJ: **to be ~ of** ignorar, não perceber

unawares [ʌnəˈwɛəz] ADV improvisadamente, de surpresa

unbearable [ʌnˈbɛərəbl] ADJ insuportável

unbeatable [ʌnˈbiːtəbl] ADJ (*team*) invencível; (*price*) sem igual

unbelievable [ʌnbɪˈliːvəbl] ADJ inacreditável; (*amazing*) incrível

unborn [ʌn'bɔːn] ADJ por nascer

unbutton [ʌn'bʌtn] VT desabotoar

uncalled-for [ʌn'kɔːld-] ADJ desnecessário, gratuito

uncanny [ʌn'kænɪ] ADJ estranho; (knack) excepcional

uncertain [ʌn'sɜːtn] ADJ incerto; (character) indeciso; (unsure) **~ about** inseguro sobre; **in no ~ terms** em termos precisos; **uncertainty** N incerteza; (also pl: doubts) dúvidas fpl

uncle ['ʌŋkl] N tio

uncomfortable [ʌn'kʌmfətəbl] ADJ incômodo; (uneasy) pouco à vontade; (situation) desagradável

uncommon [ʌn'kɔmən] ADJ raro, incomum, excepcional

unconditional [ʌnkən'dɪʃənl] ADJ incondicional

unconscious [ʌn'kɔnʃəs] ADJ sem sentidos, desacordado; (unaware) **~ of** inconsciente de ▶ N: **the ~** o inconsciente

uncontrollable [ʌnkən'trəuləbl] ADJ (temper) ingovernável; (child, animal, laughter) incontrolável

unconventional [ʌnkən'vɛnʃənl] ADJ inconvencional

uncover [ʌn'kʌvər] VT descobrir; (take lid off) destapar, destampar

undecided [ʌndɪ'saɪdɪd] ADJ indeciso; (question) não respondido, pendente

under ['ʌndər] PREP embaixo de (BR), debaixo de (PT); (fig) sob; (less than) menos de; (according to) segundo, de acordo com ▶ ADV embaixo; (movement) por baixo; **~ there** ali embaixo; **~ repair** em conserto; **undercover** ADJ secreto, clandestino; **underdog** N o mais fraco; **underdone** ADJ (Culin) mal passado; **underestimate** VT subestimar; **undergo** irreg VT sofrer; (test) passar por; (operation, treatment) ser submetido a; **undergraduate** N universitário(-a); **underground** N (BRIT) metrô m (BR), metro(-politano) (PT); (Pol) organização f clandestina ▶ ADJ subterrâneo; (fig) clandestino ▶ ADV (work) embaixo da terra; (fig) na clandestinidade; **undergrowth** N vegetação f rasteira; **underline** VT sublinhar; **undermine** VT minar, solapar; **underneath** ADV embaixo, debaixo, por baixo ▶ PREP embaixo de (BR), debaixo de (PT); **underpaid** ADJ mal pago; **underpants** (BRIT) NPL cueca (BR), cuecas fpl (PT); **underpass** (BRIT) N passagem f inferior; **underprivileged** ADJ menos favorecido

understand [ʌndə'stænd] irreg VT entender, compreender ▶ VI: **to ~ that** acreditar que; **understandable** ADJ compreensível; **understanding** ADJ compreensivo ▶ N compreensão f; (knowledge) entendimento; (agreement) acordo

understatement [ʌndə'steɪtmənt] N (quality) subestimação f; (euphemism) eufemismo; **it's an ~ to say that ...** é uma subestimação dizer que ...

understood [ʌndə'stud] PT, PP of **understand** ▶ ADJ entendido; (implied) subentendido, implícito

undertake [ʌndə'teɪk] (irreg: like **take**) VT incumbir-se de, encarregar-se de; **to ~ to do sth** comprometer-se a fazer algo

undertaking ['ʌndəteɪkɪŋ] N empreendimento; (promise) promessa

underwater [ʌndə'wɔːtər] ADV sob a água ▶ ADJ subaquático

underwear ['ʌndəwɛər] N roupa de baixo

underworld ['ʌndəwɜːld] N (of crime) submundo

undo [ʌn'duː] (irreg: like **do**) VT (unfasten) desatar; (spoil) desmanchar

undress [ʌn'drɛs] VI despir-se, tirar a roupa

unearth [ʌn'ɜːθ] VT desenterrar; (fig) revelar

uneasy [ʌn'iːzɪ] ADJ (person) preocupado; (feeling) incômodo; (peace, truce) desconfortável

uneducated [ʌn'ɛdjukeɪtɪd] ADJ inculto, sem instrução, não escolarizado

unemployed [ʌnɪm'plɔɪd] ADJ desempregado ▶ NPL: **the ~** os desempregados

unemployment [ʌnɪm'plɔɪmənt] N desemprego

uneven [ʌn'iːvn] ADJ desigual; (road etc) irregular, acidentado

unexpected [ʌnɪk'spɛktɪd] ADJ inesperado; **unexpectedly** [ʌnɪk'spɛktɪdlɪ] ADV inesperadamente

unfair [ʌn'fɛər] ADJ: **~ (to)** injusto (com); **it's ~ that ...** não é justo que ...

unfaithful [ʌn'feɪθful] ADJ infiel

unfamiliar [ʌnfə'mɪlɪər] ADJ pouco familiar, desconhecido; **to be ~ with sth** não estar familiarizado com algo

unfashionable [ʌn'fæʃnəbl] ADJ fora da moda

unfasten [ʌn'fɑːsn] VT desatar; (open) abrir

unfavourable [ʌn'feɪvərəbl], (US) **unfavorable** ADJ desfavorável

unfinished [ʌn'fɪnɪʃt] ADJ incompleto, inacabado

unfit [ʌn'fɪt] ADJ sem preparo físico; (*incompetent*) incompetente, incapaz; **~ for work** inapto para trabalhar

unfold [ʌn'fəuld] VT desdobrar ▶ VI (*story, situation*) desdobrar-se

unfortunate [ʌn'fɔːtʃənət] ADJ infeliz; (*event, remark*) inoportuno

unfriend [ʌn'frɛnd] VT excluir (em rede social)

unfriendly [ʌn'frɛndlɪ] ADJ antipático

unhappiness [ʌn'hæpɪnɪs] N infelicidade f

unhappy [ʌn'hæpɪ] ADJ triste; (*unfortunate*) desventurado; (*childhood*) infeliz; (*dissatisfied*): **~ with** descontente com, insatisfeito com

unhealthy [ʌn'hɛlθɪ] ADJ insalubre; (*person*) doentio; (*fig*) anormal

unheard-of [ʌn'həːd-] ADJ insólito

unhurt [ʌn'həːt] ADJ ileso

uniform ['juːnɪfɔːm] N uniforme m ▶ ADJ uniforme

uninhabited [ʌnɪn'hæbɪtɪd] ADJ inabitado

uninstall ['ʌnɪnstɔːl] VT (*Comput*) desinstalar

unintentional [ʌnɪn'tɛnʃənəl] ADJ involuntário, não intencional

union ['juːnjən] N união f; (*also*: **trade ~**) sindicato (de trabalhadores) ▶ CPD sindical; **Union Jack** N bandeira britânica

unique [juː'niːk] ADJ único, sem igual

unit ['juːnɪt] N unidade f; (*of furniture etc*) segão f; (*team, squad*) equipe f; **kitchen ~** armário de cozinha

unite [juː'naɪt] VT unir ▶ VI unir-se; **united** ADJ unido; (*effort*) conjunto; **United Kingdom** N Reino Unido; **United Nations, United Nations Organization** N (Organização f das) Nações fpl Unidas; **United States, United States of America** N Estados Unidos mpl (da América)

universal [juːnɪ'vəːsl] ADJ universal

universe ['juːnɪvəːs] N universo

university [juːnɪ'vəːsɪtɪ] N universidade f

unjust [ʌn'dʒʌst] ADJ injusto

unkind [ʌn'kaɪnd] ADJ maldoso; (*comment etc*) cruel

unknown [ʌn'nəun] ADJ desconhecido

unlawful [ʌn'lɔːful] ADJ ilegal

unleaded [ʌn'lɛdɪd] ADJ (*petrol, fuel*) sem chumbo

unleash [ʌn'liːʃ] VT (*fig*) desencadear

unless [ʌn'lɛs] CONJ a menos que, a não ser que; **~ he comes** a menos que ele venha

unlike [ʌn'laɪk] ADJ diferente ▶ PREP diferentemente de, ao contrário de

unlikely [ʌn'laɪklɪ] ADJ (*not likely*) improvável; (*unexpected*) inesperado

unlisted [ʌn'lɪstɪd] ADJ (*us Tel*): **an ~ number** um número que não consta na lista telefônica

unload [ʌn'ləud] VT descarregar

unlock [ʌn'lɔk] VT destrancar

unlucky [ʌn'lʌkɪ] ADJ infeliz; (*object, number*) de mau agouro; **to be ~** ser azarado, ter azar

unmarried [ʌn'mærɪd] ADJ solteiro

unmistakable, unmistakeable [ʌnmɪs'teɪkəbl] ADJ inconfundível

unnatural [ʌn'nætʃrəl] ADJ antinatural, artificial; (*manner*) afetado; (*habit*) depravado

unnecessary [ʌn'nɛsəsərɪ] ADJ desnecessário, inútil

UNO ['juːnəu] N ABBR (= *United Nations Organization*) ONU f

unofficial [ʌnə'fɪʃl] ADJ não-oficial, informal; (*strike*) desautorizado

unpack [ʌn'pæk] VI desembrulhar ▶ VT desfazer

unpleasant [ʌn'plɛznt] ADJ desagradável; (*person, manner*) antipático

unplug [ʌn'plʌg] VT desligar

unpopular [ʌn'pɔpjuləʳ] ADJ impopular

unprecedented [ʌn'prɛsɪdəntɪd] ADJ sem precedentes

unpredictable [ʌnprɪ'dɪktəbl] ADJ imprevisível

unravel [ʌn'rævl] VT desemaranhar; (*mystery*) desvendar

unreal [ʌn'rɪəl] ADJ irreal, ilusório; (*extraordinary*) extraordinário

unrealistic [ʌnrɪə'lɪstɪk] ADJ pouco realista

unreasonable [ʌn'riːznəbl] ADJ insensato; (*demand*) absurdo

unrelated [ʌnrɪ'leɪtɪd] ADJ sem relação; (*family*) sem parentesco

unreliable [ʌnrɪ'laɪəbl] ADJ (*person*) indigno de confiança; (*machine*) incerto, perigoso

unrest [ʌn'rɛst] N inquietação f, desassossego; (*Pol*) distúrbios mpl

unroll [ʌn'rəul] VT desenrolar

unruly [ʌn'ruːlɪ] ADJ indisciplinado; (*hair*) desalinhado

unsafe [ʌn'seɪf] ADJ perigoso

unsatisfactory [ʌnsætɪsˈfæktərɪ] ADJ insatisfatório

unscrew [ʌnˈskruː] VT desparafusar

unsettled [ʌnˈsɛtld] ADJ (*weather*) instável; (*person*) inquieto

unsightly [ʌnˈsaɪtlɪ] ADJ feio, disforme

unskilled [ʌnˈskɪld] ADJ não-especializado

unstable [ʌnˈsteɪbl] ADJ em falso; (*government, mentally*) instável

unsteady [ʌnˈstɛdɪ] ADJ (*hand, person*) trêmulo; (*ladder*) instável

unsuccessful [ʌnsəkˈsɛsful] ADJ (*attempt*) frustrado, vão/vã; (*writer, proposal*) sem êxito; **to be ~** (*in attempting sth*) ser mal sucedido, não conseguir; (*application*) ser recusado

unsuitable [ʌnˈsuːtəbl] ADJ inadequado; (*time, moment*) inconveniente

unsure [ʌnˈʃuəʳ] ADJ inseguro, incerto; **to be ~ of o.s.** não ser seguro de si

untidy [ʌnˈtaɪdɪ] ADJ (*room*) desarrumado, desleixado; (*appearance*) desmazelado, desalinhado

untie [ʌnˈtaɪ] VT desatar, desfazer; (*dog, prisoner*) soltar

until [ənˈtɪl] PREP até ▶ CONJ até que; **~ he comes** até que ele venha; **~ now** até agora; **~ then** até então

unused¹ [ʌnˈjuːzd] ADJ novo, sem uso

unused² [ʌnˈjuːst] ADJ: **to be ~ to sth/to doing sth** não estar acostumado com algo/a fazer algo

unusual [ʌnˈjuːʒuəl] ADJ (*strange*) estranho; (*rare*) incomum; (*exceptional*) extraordinário

unveil [ʌnˈveɪl] VT desvelar, descobrir

unwanted [ʌnˈwɔntɪd] ADJ não desejado, indesejável

unwell [ʌnˈwɛl] ADJ: **to be ~** estar doente; **to feel ~** estar indisposto

unwilling [ʌnˈwɪlɪŋ] ADJ: **to be ~ to do sth** relutar em fazer algo, não querer fazer algo

unwind [ʌnˈwaɪnd] (*irreg*) VT desenrolar ▶ VI (*relax*) relaxar-se

unwise [ʌnˈwaɪz] ADJ imprudente

unwrap [ʌnˈræp] VT desembrulhar

(KEYWORD)

up [ʌp] PREP: **to go/be up sth** subir algo/estar em cima de algo; **we climbed/walked up the hill** nós subimos/andamos até em cima da colina; **they live further up the street** eles moram mais adiante nesta rua

▶ ADV **1** (*upwards, higher*) em cima, para cima; **up in the sky/the mountains** lá no céu/nas montanhas; **up there** lá em cima; **up above** em cima

2: **to be up** (*out of bed*) estar de pé; (*prices, level*) estar elevado; (*building, tent*) estar erguido

3: **up to** (*as far as*) até; **up to now** até agora

4: **to be up to** (*depending on*): **it is up to you** você é quem sabe, você decide

5: **to be up to** (*equal to*) estar à altura de; **he's not up to it** (*job, task etc*) ele não é capaz de fazê-lo; **his work is not up to the required standard** seu trabalho não atende aos padrões exigidos

6: **to be up to** (*inf: be doing*) estar fazendo (BR) or a fazer (PT); **what is he up to?** o que ele está querendo?, o que ele está tramando?

▶ N: **ups and downs** altos *mpl* e baixos

upbringing [ˈʌpbrɪŋɪŋ] N educação f, criação f

update [ʌpˈdeɪt] VT atualizar, pôr em dia

upgrade [ʌpˈgreɪd] VT (*person*) promover; (*job*) melhorar; (*house*) reformar

upheaval [ʌpˈhiːvl] N transtorno; (*unrest*) convulsão f

uphill [ʌpˈhɪl] ADJ ladeira acima; (*fig: task*) trabalhoso, árduo ▶ ADV: **to go ~** ir morro acima

upload [ˈʌpləʊd] VT (*Comput*) fazer upload, transferir

upon [əˈpɔn] PREP sobre

upper [ˈʌpəʳ] ADJ superior, de cima ▶ N (*of shoe*) gáspea, parte f superior; **upper-class** ADJ de classe alta

upright [ˈʌpraɪt] ADJ vertical; (*straight*) reto; (*fig*) honesto

uprising [ˈʌpraɪzɪŋ] N revolta, rebelião f, sublevação f

uproar [ˈʌprɔːʳ] N tumulto, algazarra

upset [*n* ˈʌpsɛt, *vt, adj* ʌpˈsɛt] (*irreg: like* **set**) N (*to plan etc*) revés *m*, reviravolta; (*stomach upset*) indisposição f ▶ VT (*glass etc*) virar; (*plan*) perturbar; (*person: annoy*) aborrecer ▶ ADJ aflito; (*stomach*) indisposto

upside down [ˈʌpsaɪd-] ADV de cabeça para baixo; **to turn a place ~** (*fig*) deixar um lugar de cabeça para baixo

upstairs [ʌpˈstɛəz] ADV (*be*) em cima; (*go*) lá em cima ▶ ADJ (*room*) de cima ▶ N andar *m* de cima

up-to-date ADJ (*person*) moderno, atualizado; (*information*) atualizado

upward [ˈʌpwəd] ADJ ascendente, para cima ▶ ADV para cima

upwards [ˈʌpwədz] ADV = **upward**

urban ['ə:bən] ADJ urbano, da cidade
urge [ə:dʒ] N desejo ▶ VT: **to ~ sb to do sth** incitar alguém a fazer algo
urgent ['ə:dʒənt] ADJ urgente; (*tone, plea*) insistente
urinal [ju'raɪnl] (BRIT) N (*vessel*) urinol m; (*building*) mictório
urine ['juərɪn] N urina
URL ABBR (= *uniform resource locator*) URL m
Uruguay ['juərəgwaɪ] N Uruguai m
US N ABBR (= *United States*) EUA mpl
us [ʌs] PRON nos, (*after prep*) nós; *see also* **me**
USA N ABBR (= *United States of America*) EUA mpl
USB ABBR (*Comput*) (= *universal serial bus*) USB m; **USB stick** N (*Comput*) pen drive m
use [n ju:s, vt ju:z] N uso, emprego; (*usefulness*) utilidade f ▶ VT usar, utilizar; (*phrase*) empregar; **in ~** em uso; **out of ~** fora de uso; **to be of ~** ser útil; **it's no ~** (*pointless*) é inútil; (*not useful*) não serve; **to be ~d to** estar acostumado a; **she ~d to do it** ela costumava fazê-lo; **use up** VT esgotar, consumir; (*money*) gastar; **used** [ju:zd] ADJ usado; **useful** ['ju:sful] ADJ útil; **useless** ['ju:slɪs] ADJ inútil; (*person*) incapaz; **user** ['ju:zəʳ] N usuário(-a) (BR), utente m/f (PT); **user-friendly** ADJ de fácil utilização; **username** N (*Comput*) nome m de usuário (BR) or utilizador (PT)
USP N ABBR (= *unique selling proposition*) proposta única de valor
usual ['ju:ʒuəl] ADJ usual, habitual; **as ~** como de hábito, como sempre; **usually** ['ju:ʒuəlɪ] ADV normalmente
utensil [ju:'tɛnsl] N utensílio
utmost ['ʌtməust] ADJ maior ▶ N: **to do one's ~** fazer todo o possível
utter ['ʌtəʳ] ADJ total ▶ VT (*sounds*) emitir; (*words*) proferir, pronunciar; **utterly** ADV completamente, totalmente
U-turn N retorno

vacancy ['veɪkənsɪ] N (BRIT: *job*) vaga; (*room*) quarto livre
vacant ['veɪkənt] ADJ desocupado, livre; (*expression*) distraído
vacate [və'keɪt] VT (*house*) desocupar; (*job*) deixar
vacation [və'keɪʃən] (*esp* US) N férias fpl
vacuum ['vækjum] N vácuo m; **vacuum cleaner** N aspirador m de pó
vagina [və'dʒaɪnə] N vagina
vague [veɪg] ADJ vago; (*blurred: memory*) fraco
vain [veɪn] ADJ vaidoso; (*useless*) vão/vã, inútil; **in ~** em vão
valentine ['væləntaɪn] N (*also: ~ card*) cartão m do Dia dos Namorados; (*person*) namorado
valid ['vælɪd] ADJ válido
valley ['vælɪ] N vale m
valuable ['væljuəbl] ADJ (*jewel*) de valor; (*time*) valioso; (*help*) precioso; **valuables** NPL objetos mpl de valor
value ['vælju:] N valor m; (*importance*) importância ▶ VT (*fix price of*) avaliar; (*appreciate*) valorizar, estimar; **values** NPL (*principles*) valores mpl
valve [vælv] N válvula
van [væn] N (*Aut*) camionete f (BR), camioneta (PT)
vandal ['vændl] N vândalo(-a); **vandalize** VT destruir, depredar
vanilla [və'nɪlə] N baunilha
vanish ['vænɪʃ] VI desaparecer, sumir
vanity ['vænɪtɪ] N vaidade f
vape [veɪp] VI fumar cigarro eletrônico
vapour ['veɪpəʳ], (US) **vapor** N vapor m
variety [və'raɪətɪ] N variedade f, diversidade f; (*type, quantity*) variedade
various ['vɛərɪəs] ADJ vários(-as), diversos(-as); (*several*) vários(-as)

varnish ['vɑːnɪʃ] N verniz m; (*nail varnish*) esmalte m ▶ VT envernizar; (*nails*) pintar (com esmalte)

vary ['vɛərɪ] VT mudar ▶ VI variar; (*become different*): **to ~ with** or **according to** variar de acordo com

vase [vɑːz] N vaso

vast [vɑːst] ADJ enorme

VAT [væt] (BRIT) N ABBR (= *value added tax*) ≈ ICM m (BR), IVA m (PT)

vault [vɔːlt] N (*of roof*) abóbada; (*tomb*) sepulcro; (*in bank*) caixa-forte f ▶ VT (*also*: **~ over**) saltar (por cima de)

veal [viːl] N carne f de vitela

vegan ['viːgən] N vegetalista m/f

vegetable ['vɛdʒtəbl] N (*Bot*) vegetal m; (*edible plant*) legume m, hortaliça ▶ ADJ vegetal

vegetarian [vɛdʒɪ'tɛərɪən] ADJ, N vegetariano(-a)

vehicle ['viːɪkl] N veículo

veil [veɪl] N véu m ▶ VT velar

vein [veɪn] N veia; (*of ore etc*) filão m; (*on leaf*) nervura

velvet ['vɛlvɪt] N veludo ▶ ADJ aveludado

vending machine ['vɛndɪŋ-] N vendedor m automático

Venezuela [vɛnɛ'zweɪlə] N Venezuela

vengeance ['vɛndʒəns] N vingança; **with a ~** (*fig*) para valer

venison ['vɛnɪsn] N carne f de veado

venom ['vɛnəm] N veneno; (*bitterness*) malevolência

vent [vɛnt] N (*opening, in jacket*) abertura; (*also*: **air ~**) respiradouro ▶ VT (*fig: feelings*) desabafar, descarregar

venture ['vɛntʃəʳ] N empreendimento ▶ VT (*opinion*) arriscar ▶ VI arriscar-se; **business ~** empreendimento comercial

venue ['vɛnjuː] N local m

verb [vəːb] N verbo

verdict ['vəːdɪkt] N veredicto, decisão f; (*fig*) opinião f, parecer m

verge [vəːdʒ] N beira, margem f; (*on road*) acostamento (BR), berma (PT); (*BRIT Aut*) "acostamento mole"; **to be on the ~ of doing sth** estar a ponto or à beira de fazer algo; **verge on** VT FUS beirar em

versatile ['vəːsətaɪl] ADJ (*person*) versátil; (*machine, tool etc*) polivalente

verse [vəːs] N verso, poesia; (*stanza*) estrofe f; (*in bible*) versículo

version ['vəːʃən] N versão f

versus ['vəːsəs] PREP contra, versus

vertical ['vəːtɪkl] ADJ vertical

very ['vɛrɪ] ADV muito ▶ ADJ: **the ~ book which** o mesmo livro que; **the ~ last** o último (de todos), bem o último; **at the ~ least** no mínimo; **~ much** muitíssimo

vessel ['vɛsl] N (*Naut*) navio, barco; (*container*) vaso, vasilha

vest [vɛst] N (BRIT) camiseta (BR), camisola interior (PT); (US: *waistcoat*) colete m

vet [vɛt] N ABBR (= *veterinary surgeon*) veterinário(-a) ▶ VT examinar

veteran ['vɛtərən] N (*also*: **war ~**) veterano de guerra

veto ['viːtəu] (*pl* **vetoes**) N veto ▶ VT vetar

via ['vaɪə] PREP por, via

vibrate [vaɪ'breɪt] VI vibrar

vicar ['vɪkəʳ] N vigário

vice [vaɪs] N (*evil*) vício; (*Tech*) torno mecânico

vice- [vaɪs] PREFIX vice-

vice versa ['vaɪsɪ'vəːsə] ADV vice-versa

vicinity [vɪ'sɪnɪtɪ] N proximidade f; **in the ~ of** nas proximidades de

vicious ['vɪʃəs] ADJ violento; (*cruel*) cruel

victim ['vɪktɪm] N vítima f

victor ['vɪktəʳ] N vencedor(a) m/f

Victorian [vɪk'tɔːrɪən] ADJ vitoriano

victory ['vɪktərɪ] N vitória

video ['vɪdɪəu] N (*video film*) vídeo; (*also*: **~ cassette**) videocassete m; (*also*: **~ cassette recorder**) videocassete m; **video camera** N filmadora; **videophone** N videofone m

Vienna [vɪ'ɛnə] N Viena

Vietnam ['vjɛt'næm] N Vietnã m (BR), Vietname m (PT); **Vietnamese** [vjɛtnə'miːz] ADJ vietnamita ▶ N INV vietnamita m/f; (*Ling*) vietnamita m

view [vjuː] N vista; (*outlook*) perspectiva; (*opinion*) opinião f, parecer m ▶ VT olhar; **in full ~ (of)** à plena vista (de); **in my ~** na minha opinião; **in ~ of the weather/ the fact that** em vista do tempo/do fato de que; **viewer** N telespectador(a) m/f; **viewpoint** N ponto de vista; (*place*) lugar m

vigorous ['vɪgərəs] ADJ vigoroso; (*plant*) vigoso

vile [vaɪl] ADJ vil, infame; (*smell*) repugnante, repulsivo; (*temper*) violento

villa ['vɪlə] N (*country house*) casa de campo; (*suburban house*) vila, quinta

village ['vɪlɪdʒ] N aldeia, povoado; **villager** N aldeão/aldeã m/f

villain ['vɪlən] N (*scoundrel*) patife m; (BRIT: *in novel etc*) vilão m; (*criminal*) marginal m/f

vine [vaɪn] N planta trepadeira

vinegar ['vɪnɪgəʳ] N vinagre m

vineyard ['vɪnjɑːd] N vinha, vinhedo
vintage ['vɪntɪdʒ] N vindima; (year) safra, colheita ▶ CPD (comedy) de época; (performance) clássico; **the 1970 ~** a safra de 1970
viola [vɪ'əʊlə] N viola
violate ['vaɪəleɪt] VT violar
violence ['vaɪələns] N violência; (strength) força
violent ['vaɪələnt] ADJ violento; (intense) intenso
violet ['vaɪələt] ADJ violeta ▶ N violeta
violin [vaɪə'lɪn] N violino
VIP N ABBR (= very important person) VIP m/f
viral ['vaɪərəl] ADJ (Med) viral; **to go ~** (Comput) propagar-se rapidamente
virgin ['vəːdʒɪn] N virgem m/f ▶ ADJ virgem
Virgo ['vəːgəʊ] N Virgem f
virtually ['vəːtjʊəlɪ] ADV praticamente
virtual reality ['vəːtjʊəl-] N (Comput) realidade f virtual
virtue ['vəːtjuː] N virtude f; (advantage) vantagem f; **by ~ of** em virtude de
virus ['vaɪərəs] N vírus m
visa ['viːzə] N visto
visible ['vɪzəbl] ADJ visível
vision ['vɪʒən] N (sight) vista, visão f; (foresight, in dream) visão f
visit ['vɪzɪt] N visita ▶ VT (person: us: also: ~ with) visitar, fazer uma visita a; (place) ir a, ir conhecer; **visiting hours** NPL horário de visita; **visitor** N visitante m/f; (to a house) visita; (tourist) turista m/f
visual ['vɪzjʊəl] ADJ visual; **visualize** VT visualizar
vital ['vaɪtl] ADJ essencial, indispensável; (important) de importância vital; (crucial) crucial; (person) vivo; (of life) vital
vitamin ['vɪtəmɪn] N vitamina
vivid ['vɪvɪd] ADJ (account) vívido; (light) claro, brilhante; (imagination, colour) vivo
V-neck N (also: ~ **jumper, ~ pullover**) suéter f com decote em V
vocabulary [vəʊ'kæbjʊlərɪ] N vocabulário
vocal ['vəʊkl] ADJ vocal; (noisy) clamoroso; (articulate) claro, eloquente
vodka ['vɔdkə] N vodca
vogue [vəʊg] N voga, moda; **to be in ~** estar na moda
voice [vɔɪs] N voz f ▶ VT expressar; **voice mail** N (system) correio m de voz; (device) caixa f postal
void [vɔɪd] N vazio; (hole) oco ▶ ADJ nulo; (empty): **~ of** destituído de
volatile ['vɔlətaɪl] ADJ volátil; (situation, person) imprevisível

volcano [vɔl'keɪnəʊ] (pl **volcanoes**) N vulcão m
volt [vəʊlt] N volt m
volume ['vɔljuːm] N volume m; (of tank) capacidade f
voluntarily ['vɔləntrɪlɪ] ADV livremente, voluntariamente
voluntary ['vɔləntərɪ] ADJ voluntário; (unpaid) (a título) gratuito
volunteer [vɔlən'tɪər] N voluntário(-a) ▶ VT oferecer voluntariamente ▶ VI (Mil) alistar-se voluntariamente; **to ~ to do** oferecer-se voluntariamente para fazer
vomit ['vɔmɪt] N vômito ▶ VT, VI vomitar
vote [vəʊt] N voto; (votes cast) votação f; (right to vote) direito de votar ▶ VT: **to be ~d chairperson** etc ser eleito presidente etc; (propose): **to ~ that** propor que; (in election) votar ▶ VI votar; **voter** N votante m/f, eleitor(a) m/f
voucher ['vaʊtʃər] N (with petrol etc) vale m; (gift voucher) vale m para presente
vow [vaʊ] N voto ▶ VT: **to ~ to do/that** prometer solenemente fazer/que
vowel ['vaʊəl] N vogal f
voyage ['vɔɪɪdʒ] N viagem f
vulgar ['vʌlgər] ADJ grosseiro, ordinário; (in bad taste) vulgar, baixo
vulture ['vʌltʃər] N abutre m, urubu m

W

wade [weɪd] VI: **to ~ through** andar em; (*fig: a book*) ler com dificuldade

wafer ['weɪfəʳ] N (*biscuit*) bolacha

waffle ['wɔfl] N (*Culin*) waffle *m*; (*empty talk*) lengalenga ▶ VI encher linguiça

wag [wæg] VT (*tail*) sacudir; (*finger*) menear ▶ VI abanar

wage [weɪdʒ] N (*also: ~s*) salário, ordenado ▶ VT: **to ~ war** empreender *or* fazer guerra

waggon, wagon ['wægən] N (*horse-drawn*) carroça; (*BRIT Rail*) vagão *m*

wail [weɪl] N lamento, gemido ▶ VI lamentar-se, gemer; (*siren*) tocar

waist [weɪst] N cintura; **waistcoat** N colete *m*

wait [weɪt] N espera ▶ VI esperar; **I can't ~ to** (*fig*) estou morrendo de vontade de; **to ~ for sb/sth** esperar por alguém/ algo; **wait behind** VI ficar para trás; **wait on** VT FUS servir; **waiter** N garçom *m* (*BR*), empregado (*PT*); **waiting list** N lista de espera; **waiting room** N sala de espera; **waitress** N garçonete *f* (*BR*), empregada (*PT*)

waive [weɪv] VT abrir mão de

wake [weɪk] (*pt* **woke**, *pp* **woken**) VT (*also: ~ up*) acordar ▶ VI acordar ▶ N (*for dead person*) velório; (*Naut*) esteira

Wales [weɪlz] N País *m* de Gales

walk [wɔːk] N passeio; (*hike*) excursão *f* a pé, caminhada; (*gait*) passo, modo de andar; (*in park etc*) alameda, passeio ▶ VI andar; (*for pleasure, exercise*) passear ▶ VT (*distance*) percorrer a pé, andar; (*dog*) levar para passear; **it's 10 minutes' ~ from here** daqui são 10 minutos a pé; **people from all ~s of life** pessoas de todos os níveis; **walk out** VI sair; (*audience*) retirar-se; (*strike*) entrar em

greve; **walk out on** VT FUS abandonar; **walkie-talkie** ['wɔːkɪ'tɔːkɪ] N transmissor-receptor *m* portátil, walkie-talkie *m*; **walking** N o andar; **walking shoes** NPL sapatos *mpl* de caminhada; **walking stick** N bengala; **walkway** N passeio, passadiço

wall [wɔːl] N parede *f*; (*exterior*) muro; (*city wall etc*) muralha

wallet ['wɔlɪt] N carteira

wallpaper ['wɔːlpeɪpəʳ] N papel *m* de parede ▶ VT colocar papel de parede em

walnut ['wɔːlnʌt] N noz *f*; (*tree, wood*) nogueira

walrus ['wɔːlrəs] (*pl* **walrus** *or* **walruses**) N morsa

waltz [wɔːlts] N valsa ▶ VI valsar

wand [wɔnd] N (*also:* **magic ~**) varinha de condão

wander ['wɔndəʳ] VI (*person*) vagar, perambular; (*thoughts*) divagar ▶ VT perambular

want [wɔnt] VT querer; (*demand*) exigir; (*need*) precisar de, necessitar; **wanted** ADJ (*criminal etc*) procurado (pela polícia); **"cook wanted"** (*in advertisement*) "precisa-se cozinheiro"

war [wɔːʳ] N guerra; **to make ~ (on)** fazer guerra (contra)

ward [wɔːd] N (*in hospital*) ala; (*Pol*) distrito eleitoral; (*Jur: child*) tutelado(-a), pupilo(-a); **ward off** VT desviar, aparar; (*attack*) repelir

warden ['wɔːdn] N (*BRIT: of institution*) diretor(a) *m/f*; (*of park, game reserve*) administrador(a) *m/f*; (*BRIT: also:* **traffic ~**) guarda *m/f*

wardrobe ['wɔːdrəub] N guarda-roupa *m*

warehouse ['wɛəhaus] N armazém *m*, depósito

warfare ['wɔːfɛəʳ] N guerra, combate *m*

warhead ['wɔːhɛd] N ogiva

warm [wɔːm] ADJ quente; (*thanks, welcome*) caloroso; **it's ~** está quente; **I'm ~** estou com calor; **warm up** VI esquentar ▶ VT esquentar; **warmly** ADV calorosamente; **warmth** N calor *m*; (*friendliness*) calor humano

warn [wɔːn] VT prevenir, avisar; **to ~ sb that/of/(not) to do** prevenir alguém de que/de/para (não) fazer

warning ['wɔːnɪŋ] N advertência; (*in writing*) aviso; (*signal*) sinal *m*

warrant ['wɔrnt] N (*voucher*) comprovante *m*; (*Jur: to arrest*) mandado de prisão; (: *to search*) mandado de busca; **warranty** N garantia

warrior ['wɔrɪər] N guerreiro(-a)

Warsaw ['wɔːsɔː] N Varsóvia

warship ['wɔːʃɪp] N navio de guerra

wart [wɔːt] N verruga

wartime ['wɔːtaɪm] N: **in ~** em tempo de guerra

wary ['wɛərɪ] ADJ cauteloso, precavido

was [wɔz] PT *of* **be**

wash [wɔʃ] VT lavar ▶ VI lavar-se; (*sea etc*): **to ~ over/against sth** bater/chocar-se contra algo ▶ N (*clothes etc*) lavagem f; (*of ship*) esteira; **to have a ~** lavar-se; **wash away** VT (*stain*) tirar ao lavar; (*subj: river etc*) levar, arrastar; **wash off** VT tirar lavando ▶ VI sair ao lavar; **wash up** VI (*BRIT*) lavar a louça; (*US*) lavar-se; **washbasin** N pia (*BR*), lavatório (*PT*); **washing** (*BRIT*) N (*dirty*) roupa suja; (*clean*) roupa lavada; **washing machine** N máquina de lavar roupa, lavadora; **washing powder** (*BRIT*) N sabão m em pó; **washing-up** N: **to do the washing-up** lavar a louça; **washing-up liquid** N detergente m; **washroom** (*US*) N banheiro (*BR*), casa de banho (*PT*)

wasn't ['wɔznt] = **was not**

wasp [wɔsp] N vespa

waste [weɪst] N desperdício, esbanjamento; (*of time*) perda; (*also:* **household ~**) detritos mpl domésticos; (*rubbish*) lixo ▶ ADJ (*material*) de refugo; (*left over*) de sobra; (*land*) baldio ▶ VT (*squander*) esbanjar, desperdiçar; (*time, opportunity*) perder; **wastes** NPL ermos mpl; **to lay ~** devastar; **waste away** VI definhar

watch [wɔtʃ] N (*clock*) relógio; (*also:* **wrist~**) relógio de pulso; (*act of watching*) vigia; (*guard: Mil*) sentinela; (*Naut: spell of duty*) quarto ▶ VT (*look at*) observar, olhar; (*programme, match*) assistir a; (*television*) ver; (*spy on, guard*) vigiar; (*be careful of*) tomar cuidado com ▶ VI ver, olhar; (*keep guard*) montar guarda; **watch out** VI ter cuidado; **watchdog** N cão m de guarda; (*fig*) vigia m/f

water ['wɔːtər] N água ▶ VT (*plant*) regar ▶ VI (*eyes*) lacrimejar; (*mouth*) salivar; **in British ~s** nas águas territoriais britânicas; **water down** VT (*milk*) aguar; (*fig*) diluir; **watercolour**, (*US*) **watercolor** N aquarela; **waterfall** N cascata, cachoeira; **watering can** N regador m; **watermelon** N melancia; **waterproof** ADJ impermeável; **water-skiing** N esqui m aquático;

watt [wɔt] N watt m

wave [weɪv] N onda; (*of hand*) aceno, sinal m; (*in hair*) onda, ondulação f ▶ VI acenar com a mão; (*flag, grass, branches*) tremular ▶ VT (*hand*) acenar; (*handkerchief*) acenar com; (*weapon*) brandir; **wavelength** N comprimento de onda; **to be on the same wavelength as** ter os mesmos gostos e atitudes que

waver ['weɪvər] VI vacilar; (*voice, eyes, love*) hesitar

wavy ['weɪvɪ] ADJ (*hair*) ondulado; (*line*) ondulante

wax [wæks] N cera ▶ VT encerar; (*car*) polir ▶ VI (*moon*) crescer

way [weɪ] N caminho; (*distance*) percurso; (*direction*) direção f, sentido; (*manner*) maneira, modo; (*habit*) costume m; **which ~? — this ~** por onde? — por aqui; **on the ~ (to)** a caminho (de); **to be on one's ~** estar a caminho; **to be in the ~** atrapalhar; **to go out of one's ~ to do sth** dar-se ao trabalho de fazer algo; **to lose one's ~** perder-se; **to be under ~** estar em andamento; **in a ~** de certo modo, até certo ponto; **in some ~s** a certos respeitos; **by the ~** a propósito; **"~ in"** (*BRIT*) "entrada"; **"~ out"** (*BRIT*) "saída"; **the ~ back** o caminho de volta; **"give ~"** (*BRIT Aut*) "dê a preferência"; **no ~!** (*inf*) de jeito nenhum!

WC ['dʌblju'siː] N ABBR (= *water closet*) privada

we [wiː] PRON PL nós

weak [wiːk] ADJ fraco, débil; (*morally, currency*) fraco; (*excuse*) pouco convincente; (*tea*) aguado, ralo; **weaken** VI enfraquecer(-se); (*give way*) ceder; (*influence, power*) diminuir ▶ VT enfraquecer; **weakness** N fraqueza; (*fault*) ponto fraco; **to have a weakness for** ter uma queda por

wealth [wɛlθ] N riqueza; (*of details*) abundância; **wealthy** ADJ rico, abastado; (*country*) rico

weapon ['wɛpən] N arma; **~s of mass destruction** armas de destruição em massa

wear [wɛər] (*pt* **wore**, *pp* **worn**) N (*use*) uso; (*deterioration through use*) desgaste m; (*clothing*): **baby/sports ~** roupa infantil/de esporte ▶ VT (*clothes*) usar; (*shoes*) usar, calçar; (*put on*) vestir; (*damage: through use*) desgastar ▶ VI (*last*) durar; (*rub through etc*) gastar-se; **town/evening ~** traje m de passeio/

de gala; **wearable** ['wɛərəbəl] ADJ
(Comput) vestível; **wear away** VT gastar
▸ VI desgastar-se; **wear down** VT gastar;
(strength) esgotar; **wear off** VI (pain etc)
passar; **wear out** VT desgastar; (person,
strength) esgotar

weary ['wɪərɪ] ADJ cansado; (dispirited)
deprimido ▸ VI: **to ~ of** cansar-se de

weasel ['wiːzl] N (Zool) doninha

weather ['wɛðəʳ] N tempo ▸ VT (storm,
crisis) resistir a; **under the ~** (fig: ill)
doente; **weather forecast** N previsão f
do tempo

weave [wiːv] (pt, pp **wove** or **woven**) VT
tecer

web [wɛb] N (of spider) teia; (on foot)
membrana; (network) rede f; **the (World
Wide) W~** a (WorldWide) Web; **web
address** N endereço web; **webcam**
['wɛbkæm] N webcam f; **webinar**
['wɛbɪnɑːʳ] N seminário online, webinar
m; **weblog** N weblog m; **webmail** N
(serviço m de) webmail m; **web page** N
página (da) web; **website** N site m,
website m

wed [wɛd] (pt, pp **wedded**) VT casar ▸ VI
casar-se

we'd [wiːd] = **we had**; = **we would**

wedding ['wɛdɪŋ] N casamento, núpcias
fpl; **wedding dress** N vestido de noiva;
wedding ring N anel m or aliança de
casamento

wedge [wɛdʒ] N (of wood etc) cunha,
calço; (of cake) fatia ▸ VT (pack tightly)
apinhar; (door) pôr calço em

Wednesday ['wɛdnzdɪ] N quarta-feira

wee [wiː] (SCOTLAND) ADJ pequeno,
pequenino

weed [wiːd] N erva daninha ▸ VT capinar;
weedkiller N herbicida m

week [wiːk] N semana; **a ~ today** daqui
a uma semana; **a ~ on Tuesday** sem ser
essa terça-feira, a outra; **every other ~**
uma semana sim, uma semana não;
weekday N dia m de semana; (Comm) dia
útil; **weekend** N fim m de semana;
weekly ADV semanalmente ▸ ADJ
semanal ▸ N semanário

weep [wiːp] (pt, pp **wept**) VI (person)
chorar

weigh [weɪ] VT, VI pesar; **to ~ anchor**
levantar ferro; **weigh down** VT
sobrecarregar; (fig: with worry) deprimir,
acabrunhar; **weigh up** VT ponderar,
avaliar

weight [weɪt] N peso; **to lose/put on ~**
emagrecer/engordar

weird [wɪəd] ADJ esquisito, estranho

welcome ['wɛlkəm] ADJ bem-vindo ▸ N
acolhimento, recepção f ▸ VT dar as
boas-vindas a; (be glad of) saudar;
you're ~ (after thanks) de nada

weld [wɛld] N solda ▸ VT soldar, unir

welfare ['wɛlfɛəʳ] N bem-estar m; (social
aid) assistência social; **welfare state** N
país auto-financiador da sua assistência
social

well [wɛl] N poço ▸ ADV bem ▸ ADJ: **to
be ~** estar bem (de saúde) ▸ EXCL bem!,
então!; **as ~** também; **as ~ as** assim
como; **~ done!** muito bem!; **get ~ soon!**
melhoras!; **to do ~** ir or sair-se bem;
(business) ir bem; **well up** VI brotar

we'll [wiːl] = **we will**; = **we shall**

well: well-behaved [-bɪˈheɪvd] ADJ bem
comportado; **well-built** ADJ robusto;
(house) bem construído; **well-dressed**
[-drɛst] ADJ bem vestido

wellingtons ['wɛlɪŋtənz] N (also:
wellington boots) botas de borracha até
os joelhos

well-known ADJ conhecido

well-off ADJ próspero, rico

Welsh [wɛlʃ] ADJ galês/galesa ▸ N (Ling)
galês m; **the Welsh** NPL (people) os
galeses; **Welshman** irreg N galês m;
Welshwoman irreg N galesa

went [wɛnt] PT of **go**

wept [wɛpt] PT, PP of **weep**

were [wəːʳ] PT of **be**

we're [wɪəʳ] = **we are**

weren't [wəːnt] = **were not**

west [wɛst] N oeste m ▸ ADJ ocidental, do
oeste ▸ ADV para o oeste or ao oeste; **the
W~** (Pol) o Oeste, o Ocidente; **western**
ADJ ocidental ▸ N (Cinema) western m,
bangue-bangue (BR inf); **West Indian**
ADJ, N antilhano(-a); **West Indies** NPL
Antilhas fpl

wet [wɛt] ADJ molhado; (damp) úmido;
(wet through) encharcado; (rainy)
chuvoso ▸ N (BRIT Pol) político de
tendência moderada; **to get ~**
molhar-se; **"~ paint"** "tinta fresca";
wetsuit N roupa de mergulho

we've [wiːv] = **we have**

whale [weɪl] N (Zool) baleia

wharf [wɔːf] (pl **wharves**) N cais m inv

(KEYWORD)

what [wɒt] ADJ **1** (in direct/indirect
questions) que, qual; **what size is it?** que
tamanho é este?; **what colour/shape is
it?** qual é a cor/o formato?; **he asked me
what books I needed** ele me perguntou
de quais os livros eu precisava

2 (*in exclamations*) quê!, como!; **what a mess!** que bagunça!
▶ PRON **1** (*interrogative*) que, o que; **what are you doing?** o que é que você está fazendo?; **what is it called?** como se chama?; **what about me?** e eu?; **what about doing ...?** que tal fazer ...?
2 (*relative*) o que; **I saw what you did/ was on the table** eu vi o que você fez/ estava na mesa; **he asked me what she had said** ele me perguntou o que ela tinha dito
▶ EXCL (*disbelieving*): **what, no coffee?** ué, não tem café?

whatever [wɔt'ɛvəʳ] ADJ: **~ book you choose** qualquer livro que você escolha
▶ PRON: **do ~ is necessary/you want** faça tudo o que for preciso/o que você quiser; **~ happens** aconteça o que acontecer; **no reason ~** or **whatsoever** nenhuma razão seja qual for or em absoluto; **nothing ~** nada em absoluto
whatsoever [wɔtsəu'ɛvəʳ] ADJ = **whatever**
wheat [wi:t] N trigo
wheel [wi:l] N roda; (*also*: **steering ~**) volante m; (*Naut*) roda do leme ▶ VT (*pram etc*) empurrar ▶ VI (*birds*) dar voltas; (*also*: **~ round**) girar, dar voltas, virar-se; **wheelbarrow** N carrinho de mão; **wheelchair** N cadeira de rodas; **wheel clamp** N (*Aut*) grampo com que se imobiliza carros estacionados ilegalmente
wheeze [wi:z] VI respirar ruidosamente

when [wɛn] ADV quando
▶ CONJ **1** (*at, during, after the time that*) quando; **when you've read it, tell me what you think** depois que você tiver lido isto, diga-me o que acha; **that was when I needed you** foi quando eu precisei de você
2 (*on, at which*) quando, em que; **on the day when I met him** no dia em que o conheci; **one day when it was raining** um dia quando estava chovendo
3 (*whereas*) ao passo que; **you said I was wrong when in fact I was right** você disse que eu estava errado quando, na verdade, eu estava certo

whenever [wɛn'ɛvəʳ] CONJ quando, quando quer que; (*every time that*) sempre que ▶ ADV quando você quiser
where [wɛəʳ] ADV onde ▶ CONJ onde, aonde; **this is ~ ...** aqui é onde ...;

whereabouts ['wɛərəbauts] ADV (por) onde ▶ N: **nobody knows his whereabouts** ninguém sabe o seu paradeiro; **whereas** [wɛər'æz] CONJ uma vez que, ao passo que; **whereby** ADV (*formal*) pelo qual (or pela qual etc); **wherever** [wɛər'ɛvəʳ] CONJ onde quer que ▶ ADV (*interrogative*) onde?
whether ['wɛðəʳ] CONJ se; **I don't know ~ to accept or not** não sei se aceito ou não; **~ you go or not** quer você vá quer não; **it's doubtful ~ ...** não é certo que ...

which [wɪtʃ] ADJ **1** (*interrogative*) que, qual; **which picture do you want?** que quadro você quer?; **which books are yours?** quais são os seus livros?; **which one?** qual?
2: **in which case** em cujo caso; **by which time** momento em que
▶ PRON **1** (*interrogative*) qual; **which (of these) are yours?** quais (destes) são seus?
2 (*relative*) que, o que, o qual etc; **the apple which you ate** a maçã que você comeu; **the chair on which you are sitting** a cadeira na qual você está sentado; **he said he knew, which is true** ele disse que sabia, o que é verdade; **after which** depois do que

whichever [wɪtʃ'ɛvəʳ] ADJ: **take ~ book you prefer** pegue o livro que preferir; **~ book you take** qualquer livro que você pegue
while [waɪl] N tempo, momento ▶ CONJ enquanto, ao mesmo tempo que; (*as long as*) contanto que; (*although*) embora; **for a ~** durante algum tempo; **while away** VT (*time*) encher
whim [wɪm] N capricho, veneta
whine [waɪn] N (*of pain*) gemido; (*of engine, siren*) zunido ▶ VI gemer; zunir; (*fig*) lamuriar-se
whip [wɪp] N açoite m; (*for riding*) chicote m; (*Pol*) líder m/f da bancada ▶ VT chicotear; (*snatch*) apanhar de repente; (*cream, eggs*) bater; (*move quickly*): **to ~ sth out/off/away** etc arrancar algo; **whipped cream** [wɪpt-] N creme m chantilly
whirl [wəːl] VT fazer girar ▶ VI (*dancers*) rodopiar; (*leaves, water etc*) redemoinhar
whisk [wɪsk] N (*Culin*) batedeira ▶ VT bater; **to ~ sb away** or **off** levar alguém rapidamente

whiskers ['wɪskəz] NPL (of animal)
bigodes mpl; (of man) suíças fpl
whisky ['wɪskɪ], (US, IRELAND) **whiskey**
N uísque m (BR), whisky m (PT)
whisper ['wɪspə'] N sussurro, murmúrio
▶ VT, VI sussurrar
whistle ['wɪsl] N (sound) assobio; (object)
apito ▶ VT, VI assobiar
white [waɪt] ADJ branco; (pale) pálido ▶ N
branco; (of egg) clara; **whiteboard** N
quadro branco; **interactive
whiteboard** quadro interativo; **white
coffee** N café m com leite; **White House**
N ver nota

> A Casa Branca (**White House**) é um
> grande edifício branco situado em
> Washington D.C. onde reside o
> presidente dos Estados Unidos. Por
> extensão, o termo se refere também
> ao poder executivo americano.

whitewash ['waɪtwɔʃ] N (paint) cal f ▶ VT
caiar; (fig) encobrir
whiting ['waɪtɪŋ] N INV pescada-
marlonga
Whitsun ['wɪtsn] N Pentecostes m
whizz [wɪz] VI: **to ~ past** or **by** passar a
toda velocidade

who [hu:] PRON **1** (interrogative) quem?;
who is it? quem é?
2 (relative) que, o qual etc, quem; **my
cousin, who lives in New York** meu
primo/que mora em Nova Iorque; **the
man/woman who spoke to me** o
homem/a mulher que falou comigo

whole [həul] ADJ (complete) todo, inteiro;
(not broken) intacto ▶ N (all): **the ~ of the
time** o tempo todo; (entire unit)
conjunto; **on the ~, as a ~** como um
todo, no conjunto; **wholemeal** (BRIT)
ADJ integral; **wholesale** N venda por
atacado ▶ ADJ por atacado; (destruction)
em grande escala ▶ ADV por atacado;
wholewheat ADJ = **wholemeal**;
wholly ['həulɪ] ADV totalmente,
completamente

whom [hu:m] PRON **1** (interrogative)
quem?; **to whom did you give it?** para
quem você deu isto?
2 (relative) que, quem; **the man whom I
saw/to whom I spoke** o homem que eu
vi/com quem eu falei

whore [hɔ:'] (inf, pej) N puta

whose [hu:z] ADJ **1** (possessive,
interrogative): **whose book is this?,
whose is this book?** de quem é este
livro?; **I don't know whose it is** eu não
sei de quem é isto
2 (possessive, relative): **the man whose
son you rescued** o homem cujo filho
você salvou; **the woman whose car
was stolen** a mulher de quem o carro foi
roubado
▶ PRON de quem

why [waɪ] ADV por que (BR), porque (PT);
(at end of sentence) por quê (BR), porquê (PT)
▶ CONJ por que; **that's not why I'm
here** não é por isso que estou aqui; **the
reason why** a razão por que
▶ EXCL (expressing surprise, shock,
annoyance) ora essa!; (explaining) bem!;
why, it's you! ora, é você!

wicked ['wɪkɪd] ADJ perverso; (smile)
malicioso
wicket ['wɪkɪt] N (Cricket) arco
wide [waɪd] ADJ largo; (area, publicity,
knowledge) amplo ▶ ADV: **to open ~** abrir
totalmente; **to shoot ~** atirar longe do
alvo; **widely** ADV extremamente;
(travelled, spaced) muito; (believed, known)
ampliamente; **widen** VT alargar; (one's
experience) aumentar ▶ VI alargar-se;
wide open ADJ (eyes) arregalado; (door)
escancarado; **widespread** ADJ (belief etc)
difundido, comum
widget ['wɪdʒɪt] N (Comput) widget m
widow ['wɪdəu] N viúva; **widower** N
viúvo
width [wɪdθ] N largura
wield [wi:ld] VT (sword) brandir,
empunhar; (power) exercer
wife [waɪf] (pl **wives**) N mulher f, esposa
Wi-Fi ['waɪfaɪ] N Wi-Fi m
wig [wɪg] N peruca
wild [waɪld] ADJ (animal) selvagem;
(plant) silvestre; (rough) violento, furioso;
(idea) disparatado, extravagante;
(person) insensato; **wilderness**
['wɪldənɪs] N ermo; **wildlife** N animais
mpl (e plantas fpl) selvagens; **wildly** ADV
(behave) freneticamente; (hit, guess)
irrefletidamente; (happy) extremamente

will [wɪl] (pt, pp **willed**) AUX VB **1** (forming
future tense): **I will finish it tomorrow**

vou acabar isto amanhã; **I will have finished it by tomorrow** até amanhã eu terei terminado isto; **will you do it? — yes I will/no I won't** você vai fazer isto? — sim, vou/não eu não vou
2 (*in conjectures, predictions*): **he will come** ele virá; **he will** *or* **he'll be there by now** nesta altura ele está lá; **that will be the postman** deve ser o carteiro; **this medicine will/won't help you** este remédio vai/não vai fazer efeito em você
3 (*in commands, requests, offers*): **will you be quiet!** fique quieto, por favor!; **will you come?** você vem?; **will you help me?** você pode me ajudar?; **will you have a cup of tea?** você vai querer uma xícara de chá *or* um chá?; **I won't put up with it** eu não vou tolerar isto
▶ VT: **to will sb to do sth** desejar que alguém faça algo; **he willed himself to go on** reuniu grande força de vontade para continuar
▶ N (*volition*) vontade *f*; (*testament*) testamento

willing ['wɪlɪŋ] ADJ disposto, pronto; (*enthusiastic*) entusiasmado; **willingly** ADV de bom grado, de boa vontade
willow ['wɪləu] N salgueiro
willpower ['wɪlpauə'] N força de vontade
wilt [wɪlt] VI (*flower*) murchar; (*plant*) morrer
win [wɪn] (*pt, pp* **won**) N vitória ▶ VT ganhar, vencer; (*obtain*) conseguir, obter; (*support*) alcançar ▶ VI ganhar; **win over** VT conquistar; **win round** (*BRIT*) VT = **win over**
wince [wɪns] VI encolher-se, estremecer
wind¹ [wɪnd] N vento; (*Med*) gases *mpl*, flatulência; (*breath*) fôlego ▶ VT deixar sem fôlego
wind² [waɪnd] (*pt, pp* **wound**) VT enrolar, bobinar; (*wrap*) envolver; (*clock, toy*) dar corda a ▶ VI (*road, river*) serpentear; **wind up** VT (*clock*) dar corda em; (*debate*) rematar, concluir
windfall ['wɪndfɔːl] N golpe *m* de sorte
wind farm N parque *m* eólico
winding ['waɪndɪŋ] ADJ (*road*) sinuoso, tortuoso; (*staircase*) de caracol, em espiral
windmill ['wɪndmɪl] N moinho de vento
window ['wɪndəu] N janela; (*in shop etc*) vitrine *f* (*BR*), montra (*PT*); **window box** N jardineira (no peitoril da janela); **window cleaner** N limpador(a) *m/f* de janelas; **window-shopping** N: **to go window-shopping** ir ver vitrines
windscreen ['wɪndskriːn] (*BRIT*) N para-brisa *m*; **windscreen wiper** (*BRIT*) N limpador *m* de para-brisa
windshield ['wɪndʃiːld] (*US*) N = **windscreen**
wind turbine ['wɪndtəːbaɪn] N turbina eólica
windy ['wɪndɪ] ADJ com muito vento, batido pelo vento; **it's ~** está ventando (*BR*), faz vento (*PT*)
wine [waɪn] N vinho; **wine bar** N bar *m* para degustação de vinhos; **wine glass** N cálice *m* (de vinho); **wine list** N lista de vinhos
wing [wɪŋ] N asa; (*of building*) ala; (*Aut*) aleta, para-lamas *m inv*; **wings** NPL (*Theatre*) bastidores *mpl*
wink [wɪŋk] N piscadela ▶ VI piscar o olho; (*light etc*) piscar
winner ['wɪnə'] N vencedor(a) *m/f*
winning ['wɪnɪŋ] ADJ (*team*) vencedor(a); (*goal*) decisivo; (*smile*) sedutor(a)
winter ['wɪntə'] N inverno; **winter sports** NPL esportes *mpl* (*BR*) *or* desportos *mpl* (*PT*) de inverno
wipe [waɪp] N: **to give sth a ~** limpar algo com um pano ▶ VT limpar; (*rub*) èsfregar; (*erase: tape*) apagar; **wipe off** VT remover esfregando; **wipe out** VT (*debt*) liquidar; (*memory*) apagar; (*destroy*) exterminar; **wipe up** VT limpar
wire ['waɪə'] N arame *m*; (*Elec*) fio (elétrico); (*telegram*) telegrama *m* ▶ VT (*house*) instalar a rede elétrica em; (*also: ~ up*) conectar; (*telegram*) telegrafar para
wireless ['waɪəlɪs] ADJ sem fio (*BR*), sem fios (*PT*)
wiring ['waɪərɪŋ] N instalação *f* elétrica
wisdom ['wɪzdəm] N prudência; (*of action, remark*) bom-senso, sabedoria; **wisdom tooth** *irreg* N dente *m* do siso
wise [waɪz] ADJ prudente; (*action, remark*) sensato
wish [wɪʃ] N desejo ▶ VT (*want*) querer; **best ~es** (*on birthday etc*) parabéns *mpl*, felicidades *fpl*; **with best ~es** (*in letter*) cumprimentos; **to ~ sb goodbye** despedir-se de alguém; **he ~ed me well** me desejou boa sorte; **to ~ to do/sb to do sth** querer fazer/que alguém faça algo; **to ~ for** desejar
wistful ['wɪstful] ADJ melancólico
wit [wɪt] N (*wittiness*) presença de espírito, engenho; (*intelligence: also: ~s*) entendimento; (*person*) espirituoso(-a)
witch [wɪtʃ] N bruxa

with [wɪð, wɪθ] PREP **1** (accompanying, in the company of) com; **I was with him** eu estava com ele; **to stay overnight with friends** dormir na casa de amigos; **we'll take the children with us** vamos levar as crianças conosco; **I'll be with you in a minute** vou vê-lo num minuto; **I'm with you** (I understand) compreendo; **to be with it** (inf) estar por dentro; (: aware) estar a par da situação; (: up-to-date) estar atualizado com
2 (descriptive) com, de; **a room with a view** um quarto com vista; **the man with the grey hat/blue eyes** o homem do chapéu cinza/de olhos azuis
3 (indicating manner, means, cause) com, de; **with tears in her eyes** com os olhos cheios de lágrimas; **to fill sth with water** encher algo de água

withdraw [wɪð'drɔ:] irreg VT tirar, remover; (offer) retirar ▶ VI retirar-se; **to ~ money (from the bank)** retirar dinheiro (do banco); **withdrawal** N retirada; **withdrawal symptoms** NPL síndrome f de abstinência; **withdrawn** ADJ (person) reservado, introvertido
wither ['wɪðəʳ] VI murchar
withhold [wɪð'həuld] (irreg: like hold) VT (money) reter; (permission) negar; (information) esconder
within [wɪð'ɪn] PREP dentro de ▶ ADV dentro; **~ reach** ao alcance da mão; **~ sight** à vista; **~ the week** antes do fim da semana; **~ a mile of** a uma milha de
without [wɪð'aut] PREP sem; **~ anybody knowing** sem ninguém saber; **to go** or **do ~ sth** passar sem algo
withstand [wɪð'stænd] (irreg: like stand) VT resistir a
witness ['wɪtnɪs] N testemunha ▶ VT testemunhar, presenciar; (document) legalizar; **to bear ~ to sth** (fig) testemunhar algo
witty ['wɪtɪ] ADJ espirituoso
wives [waɪvz] NPL of **wife**
wizard ['wɪzəd] N feiticeiro, mago
wk ABBR = **week**
wobble ['wɔbl] VI oscilar; (chair) balançar
woe [wəu] N dor f, mágoa
woke [wəuk] PT of **wake**; **woken** PP of **wake**
wolf [wulf] (pl **wolves**) N lobo
woman ['wumən] (pl **women**) N mulher f; **~ doctor** médica

womb [wu:m] N (Anat) matriz f, útero
women ['wɪmɪn] NPL of **woman**
won [wʌn] PT, PP of **win**
wonder ['wʌndəʳ] N maravilha, prodígio; (feeling) espanto ▶ VI: **to ~ whether/ why** perguntar-se a si mesmo se/por quê; **to ~ at** admirar-se de; **to ~ about** pensar sobre or em; **it's no ~ that** não é de admirar que; **wonderful** ADJ maravilhoso; (miraculous) impressionante
won't [wəunt] = **will not**
wood [wud] N (timber) madeira; (forest) floresta, bosque m; **wooden** ADJ de madeira; (fig) inexpressivo; **woodwind** N (Mus) instrumentos mpl de sopro de madeira; **woodwork** N carpintaria
wool [wul] N lã f; **to pull the ~ over sb's eyes** (fig) enganar alguém, vender a alguém gato por lebre; **woollen** ADJ de lã; **woolly**, (US) **wooly** ADJ de lã; (fig) confuso
word [wə:d] N palavra; (news) notícia ▶ VT redigir; **in other ~s** em outras palavras, ou seja; **to break/keep one's ~** faltar à palavra/cumprir a promessa; **to have ~s with sb** discutir com alguém; **wording** N fraseado; **word processing** N processamento de textos; **word processor** N processador m de textos
wore [wɔ:ʳ] PT of **wear**
work [wə:k] N trabalho; (job) emprego, trabalho; (Art, Literature) obra ▶ VI trabalhar; (mechanism) funcionar; (medicine etc) surtir efeito, ser eficaz ▶ VT (clay) moldar; (wood etc) talhar; (mine etc) explorar; (machine) fazer trabalhar, manejar; (effect, miracle) causar; **to ~ loose** (part) soltar-se; (knot) afrouxar-se; **work on** VT FUS trabalhar em, dedicar-se a; (principle) basear-se em; **work out** VI dar certo, surtir efeito ▶ VT (problem) resolver; (plan) elaborar, formular; **it ~s out at £100** dá £100; **worker** N trabalhador(a) m/f, operário(-a); **working class** N proletariado, classe f operária ▶ ADJ: **working-class** do proletariado, da classe operária; **workman** irreg N operário, trabalhador m; **worksheet** N (with exercises) folha de exercícios; **workshop** N oficina; (practical session) aula prática
world [wə:ld] N mundo ▶ CPD mundial; **to think the ~ of sb** (fig) ter alguém em alto conceito

worm [wə:m] N (also: **earth~**) minhoca, lombriga

worn [wɔ:n] PP of **wear** ▶ ADJ gasto; **worn-out** ADJ (object) gasto; (person) esgotado, exausto

worry ['wʌrɪ] N preocupação f ▶ VT preocupar, inquietar ▶ VI preocupar-se, afligir-se

worse [wə:s] ADJ, ADV pior ▶ N o pior; **a change for the ~** uma mudança para pior, uma piora; **worsen** VT, VI piorar; **worse off** ADJ com menos dinheiro; (fig): **you'll be worse off this way** assim você ficará pior que nunca

worship ['wə:ʃɪp] N adoração f ▶ VT adorar, venerar; (person, thing) adorar; **Your W~** (BRIT: to mayor) vossa Excelência; (: to judge) senhor Juiz

worst [wə:st] ADJ (o/a) pior ▶ ADV pior ▶ N o pior; **at ~** na pior das hipóteses

worth [wə:θ] N valor m, mérito ▶ ADJ: **to be ~** valer; **it's ~ it** vale a pena; **to be ~ one's while (to do)** valer a pena (fazer); **worthless** ADJ (person) imprestável; (thing) inútil; **worthwhile** ADJ (activity) que vale a pena; (cause) de mérito, louvável

worthy ['wə:ðɪ] ADJ (person) merecedor(a), respeitável; (motive) justo; **~ of** digno de

(KEYWORD)

would [wʊd] AUX VB **1** (conditional tense): **if you asked him, he would do it** se você pedisse, ele faria isto; **if you had asked him, he would have done it** se você tivesse pedido, ele teria feito isto **2** (in offers, invitations, requests): **would you like a biscuit?** você quer um biscoito?; **would you ask him to come in?** pode pedir a ele para entrar?; **would you close the door, please?** quer fechar a porta por favor? **3** (in indirect speech): **I said I would do it** eu disse que eu faria isto **4** (emphatic): **youWOULD say that, wouldn't you?** é lógico que você vai dizer isso **5** (insistence): **she wouldn't behave** não houve jeito dela se comportar **6** (conjecture): **it would have been midnight** devia ser meia-noite; **it would seem so** parece que sim **7** (indicating habit): **he would go on Mondays** costumava ir nas segundas-feiras

wouldn't ['wʊdnt] = **would not**

wound¹ [waʊnd] PT, PP of **wind²**

wound² [wu:nd] N ferida ▶ VT ferir

wove [wəʊv] PT of **weave**; **woven** PP of **weave**

wrap [ræp] N (stole) xale m; (cape) capa ▶ VT (cover) envolver; (also: **~ up**) embrulhar; **wrapper** N invólucro; (BRIT: of book) capa; **wrapping paper** N papel m de embrulho; (fancy) papel de presente

wreath [ri:θ] N coroa

wreck [rɛk] N (of vehicle) destroços mpl; (ship) restos mpl do naufrágio; (pej: person) caco ▶ VT destruir, danificar; (fig) arruinar, arrasar; **wreckage** N (of car, plane) destroços mpl; (of ship) restos mpl; (of building) escombros mpl

wren [rɛn] N (Zool) carriça

wrench [rɛntʃ] N (Tech) chave f inglesa; (tug) puxão m; (fig) separação f penosa ▶ VT torcer com força; **to ~ sth from sb** arrancar algo de alguém

wrestle ['rɛsl] VI: **to ~ (with sb)** lutar (com or contra alguém); **wrestler** N lutador m; **wrestling** N luta (livre)

wretched ['rɛtʃɪd] ADJ desventurado, infeliz; (inf) maldito

wriggle ['rɪgl] VI (also: **~ about**) retorcer-se, contorcer-se

wring [rɪŋ] (pt, pp **wrung**) VT (clothes, neck) torcer; (hands) apertar; (fig): **to ~ sth out of sb** arrancar algo de alguém

wrinkle ['rɪŋkl] N (on skin) ruga; (on paper) prega ▶ VT franzir ▶ VI enrugar-se

wrist [rɪst] N pulso

write [raɪt] (pt **wrote**, pp **written**) VT escrever; (cheque, prescription) passar ▶ VI escrever; **to ~ to sb** escrever para alguém; **write down** VT (note) anotar; (put on paper) pôr no papel; **write off** VT cancelar; **write out** VT escrever por extenso; (cheque etc) passar; **write up** VT redigir; **write-off** N perda total; **writer** N escritor(a) m/f

writing ['raɪtɪŋ] N escrita; (handwriting) caligrafia, letra; (of author) obra; **in ~** por escrito

wrong [rɒŋ] ADJ (bad) errado, mau; (unfair) injusto; (incorrect) errado, equivocado; (inappropriate) impróprio ▶ ADV mal, errado ▶ N injustiça ▶ VT ser injusto com; **you are ~ to do it** você se engana ao fazê-lo; **you are ~ about that, you've got it ~** você está enganado sobre isso; **to be in the ~** não ter razão; **what's ~?** o que é que há?; **to go ~** (person) desencaminhar-se; (plan) dar errado; (machine) sofrer uma avaria; **wrongly** ADV errado

wrote [rəut] PT *of* **write**
wrung [rʌŋ] PT, PP *of* **wring**
WWW N ABBR = **World Wide Web; the ~**
  a WWW

Xmas [ˈɛksməs] N ABBR = **Christmas**
X-ray [ɛksˈreɪ] N radiografia ▶ VT
  radiografar, tirar uma chapa de

y

yacht [jɔt] N iate *m*; **yachting** N iatismo
yard [jɑːd] N pátio, quintal *m*; (*measure*)
jarda (914 *mm*; 3 *feet*)
yarn [jɑːn] N fio; (*tale*) história
inverossímil
yawn [jɔːn] N bocejo ▶ vɪ bocejar
yeah [jɛə] (*inf*) ADV é
year [jɪəʳ] N ano; **to be 8 ~s old** ter 8
anos; **an eight-~-old child** uma criança
de oito anos (de idade); **yearly** ADJ anual
▶ ADV anualmente
yearn [jəːn] vɪ: **to ~ to do/for sth** ansiar
fazer/por algo
yeast [jiːst] N levedura, fermento
yell [jɛl] N grito, berro ▶ vɪ gritar, berrar
yellow ['jɛləu] ADJ amarelo; **Yellow
Pages**® NPL (*Tel*) Páginas Amarelas *fpl*
yes [jɛs] ADV, N sim *m*
yesterday ['jɛstədɪ] ADV, N ontem *m*
yet [jɛt] ADV ainda ▶ CONJ porém, no
entanto; **the best ~** o melhor até agora;
as ~ até agora, ainda
yew [juː] N teixo
yield [jiːld] N (*Agr*) colheita; (*Comm*)
rendimento ▶ vᴛ produzir; (*profit*)
render; (*surrender*) ceder ▶ vɪ render-se,
ceder; (*us Aut*) ceder
yoghurt, yogurt ['jɔugət] N iogurte *m*
yolk [jəuk] N gema (do ovo)

you [juː] PRON **1** (*subj: singular*) tu, você;
(: *plural*) vós, vocês; **you French enjoy
your food** vocês franceses gostam de
comer; **you and I will go** nós iremos
2 (*direct object: singular*) te, o/a; (: *plural*)
vos, os/as; (*indirect object: singular*) te,
lhe; (: *plural*) vos, lhes; **I know you** eu
lhe conheço; **I gave it to you** dei isto
para você
3 (*stressed*) você; **I told YOU to do it** eu
disse para você fazer isto
4 (*after prep, in comparisons: singular*) ti,
você; (: *plural*) vós, vocês; (*polite form:
singular*) o senhor/a senhora; (: *plural*) os
senhores/as senhoras; **it's for you** é
para você; **with you** contigo, com você;
convosco, com vocês; com o senhor *etc*
5 (*impers: one*): **you never know** nunca
se sabe; **apples do you good** as maçãs
fazem bem à saúde

you'd [juːd] = **you had**; = **you would**
you'll [juːl] = **you will**; = **you shall**
young [jʌŋ] ADJ jovem ▶ NPL (*of animal*)
filhotes *mpl*, crias *fpl*; (*people*): **the ~** a
juventude, os jovens; **younger** ADJ mais
novo
your [jɔːʳ] ADJ teu/tua, seu/sua; (*plural*)
vosso, seu/sua; (*formal*) do senhor/da
senhora; *see also* **my**
you're [juəʳ] = **you are**
yours [jɔːz] PRON teu/tua, seu/sua;
(*plural*) vosso, seu/sua; (*formal*) do
senhor/da senhora; **~ sincerely** or
faithfully atenciosamente; *see also*
mine¹
yourself [jɔːˈsɛlf] PRON (*emphatic*) tu
mesmo, você mesmo; (*object, reflexive*)
te, se; (*after prep*) ti mesmo, si mesmo;
(*formal*) o senhor mesmo/a senhora
mesma; **yourselves** PRON vós mesmos,
vocês mesmos; (*object, reflexive*) vos, se;
(*after prep*) vós mesmos, vôces mesmos;
(*formal*) os senhores mesmos/as
senhoras mesmas; *see also* **oneself**
youth [juːθ] N mocidade *f*, juventude *f*;
(*young man*) jovem *m*; **youth club** N
associação *f* de juventude; **youthful** ADJ
juvenil; **youth hostel** N albergue *m* da
juventude
you've [juːv] = **you have**

Z

zebra ['zi:brə] N zebra; **zebra crossing**
(BRIT) N faixa (para pedestres) (BR),
passadeira (PT)

zero ['zɪərəu] N zero
zest [zɛst] N vivacidade *f*, entusiasmo;
(*of lemon etc*) zesto
zigzag ['zɪgzæg] N ziguezague *m* ▸ VI
ziguezaguear
Zika virus ['dzika vaɪərəs] N vírus *m*
Zika
zinc [zɪŋk] N zinco
zip [zɪp] N (*also:* ~ **fastener**) fecho ecler
(BR) *or* éclair (PT) ▸ VT (*also:* ~ **up**)
fechar o fecho ecler de, subir o fecho
ecler de; **zip code** (US) N código postal;
zip file N arquivo zipado; **zipper** (US)
N = **zip**
zit [zɪt] (*inf*) N espinha
zodiac ['zəudɪæk] N zodíaco
zone [zəun] N zona
zoo [zu:] N (jardim *m*) zoológico
zoom [zu:m] VI: **to** ~ **past** passar
zunindo; **zoom lens** N zoom *m*, zum *m*
zucchini [zu:'ki:nɪ] (US) NPL abobrinha

Gramática inglesa

1 Substantivos e sintagma nominal

1.1 Substantivos contáveis/incontáveis (countable/uncountable)

Algumas coisas são consideradas elementos individuais, ou seja, podem ser contadas uma a uma. Os substantivos que se referem a elas são chamados contáveis e, portanto, dispõem tanto de uma forma singular como de plural, expresso normalmente pela terminação **-s**. Note que poderão ocorrer mudanças ortográficas decorrentes do acréscimo dos sufixos:

… one **table**, … two **cats**, … three hundred **pounds**

⚠ Alguns substantivos de uso frequente têm plurais irregulares, que não são formados com o sufixo **-s**:

child → children	foot → feet
man → men	mouse → mice
tooth → teeth	woman → women

Por outro lado, considera-se que existam coisas que não podem ser contadas uma a uma; para se referir a elas, são usados os substantivos incontáveis:

The donkey needed food and water.
O burro precisava de comida e água.

All prices include travel to London.
Todos os preços incluem transporte até Londres.

Estes geralmente fazem referência a:

substâncias: coal, food, ice, iron, rice, steel, water
qualidades humanas: courage, cruelty, honesty, patience
sentimentos: anger, happiness, joy, pride, relief, respect
atividades: aid, help, sleep, travel, work
ideias abstratas: beauty, death, freedom, fun, life, luck

Cuidado: note que, às vezes, no inglês usa-se um substantivo incontável para algo que em português é contável; nesse caso, os elementos são considerados um conjunto em vez de um a um. Por exemplo, *furniture* significa "mobiliário, móveis", mas, para dizer "um móvel", é preciso usar a expressão *a piece of furniture*. O uso dos substantivos incontáveis deve levar em conta as seguintes regras:

1.2 Os substantivos incontáveis têm uma única forma, não dispondo, portanto, de plural:

advice, baggage, equipment, furniture, homework, information, knowledge, luggage, machinery, money, news, traffic

I needed help with my homework.
Eu precisava de ajuda com meu dever de casa.

We want to spend more money on roads.
Queremos gastar mais dinheiro nas estradas.

1.3 Substantivos coletivos

Os substantivos coletivos (pois se referem a um grupo de pessoas ou de coisas) podem ser acompanhados do verbo no plural ou no singular, já que é possível considerar o grupo tanto como uma unidade quanto como vários indivíduos juntos:

army, audience, committee, company, crew, data, enemy, family, flock, gang, government, group, herd, media, navy, press, public, staff, team

Our family is very worried.
Nossa família está muito preocupada.

My family are all football fans.
Toda minha família torce no futebol.

2 Pronomes

Usa-se um pronome pessoal:

• para voltar a se referir a algo ou alguém que já tenha sido mencionado
• para se referir diretamente a coisas ou pessoas que estão presentes ou são implicadas em determinada situação

He rang Mary and invited her to dinner.
Ele ligou para Maria e a convidou para jantar.

2.1 Estes pronomes podem ter duas formas distintas, dependendo de sua função em relação ao verbo: como sujeito ou objeto.

As formas de objeto são usadas, como objeto de um verbo, logo após uma preposição ou após o verbo principal.

Formas de sujeito:

I, you, he, she, it, we, you, they

Formas de objeto:

me, you, him, her, it, us, you, them

We were all sitting in a cafe with him.
Estávamos todos sentados em um café com ele.

Did you buy it?
Você o comprou?

2.2 Pronomes possessivos

Para dizer a quem algo pertence, usam-se os pronomes possessivos:

mine, yours, his, hers, ours, theirs

Is that coffee yours or mine?
Esse café é seu ou meu?

It was his fault, not ours.
A culpa foi dele, não nossa.

3 Determinantes

À frente do substantivo ou de qualquer adjetivo (isto é, no princípio do sintagma nominal), usa-se com frequência um determinante.

Há vários tipos: alguns fazem referência a algo concreto ou já mencionado enquanto outros se referem a algo mais geral ou não mencionado antes.

Muitos deles também podem ser usados como pronomes.

Os determinantes são:

- **the; this, these, that, those; a/an; some, any, no**
- os quantificadores **much, many, little, few, all, most, a little, a few, the whole, every, each, both, half, either, other, another, more, less, fewer**
- os adjetivos possessivos **my, your, his, her, its, our, their**
- os determinantes interrogativos **what, which, whose**
- os numerais **one, two, three, four …**

   I met the two Swedish girls in London.
   Conheci as duas garotas suecas em Londres.

   I don't like this picture.
   Não gosto deste quadro.

3.1

Geralmente usa-se *the* nos mesmos casos que o artigo definido em português:

   The girls were not at home.
   As meninas não estavam em casa.

   I don't like using the phone.
   Não gosto de usar o telefone.

3.2 Exceções

Quando se fala de um tipo de coisa, animal ou pessoa de maneira geral, é usado em inglês somente o substantivo no plural:

   Many adults don't listen to children.
   Muitos adultos não escutam as crianças.

   Dogs are mammals.
   Os cães são mamíferos.

3.3 This, that, these, those

This significa "este, esta, isto". *These* é a forma de plural ("estes, estas"). *That* significa "esse, essa, isso" ou "aquele, aquela, aquilo", de acordo com o contexto. *Those* é a forma de plural:

   This book is a present from my mother.
   Este livro é um presente da minha mãe.

   When did you buy that hat?
   Quando você comprou esse chapéu?

Esses determinantes também são usados como pronomes:

   That looks interesting.
   (Isso) parece interessante.
   These are mine.
   (Estes) são meus.

4

3.4 **A/an** são usados nos mesmos casos que seus equivalentes em português:

> **I got a postcard from Susan.**
> *Recebi um cartão postal de Susan.*

Usa-se **an** quando a palavra seguinte começa com um som vocálico:

> **an apple**
> **an honest man** ['ɔnist]
> **an hour** ['aur]

⚠ Se o som não é vocálico, mas semivocálico, usa-se **a**:

> **a university** [juni'vəːsiti]
> **a European** [jʊərə'pi(ː)ən]

4 Adjetivos

4.1 Em inglês, os adjetivos são colocados, como regra geral, antes do substantivo, e não depois, como no português:

> **She bought a loaf of white bread.**
> *Ela comprou um pão branco.*

4.2 Alguns adjetivos são usados exclusivamente antes do substantivo.
Por exemplo, diz-se **an atomic bomb**, mas não **The bomb was atomic**.
Entre eles:

> **atomic, countless, digital, existing, indoor, introductory, maximum, neighbouring, occasional, outdoor, eastern, northern, southern, western**

> **He sent countless letters to the newspapers.**
> *Ele enviou inúmeras cartas aos jornais.*

Outros são usados somente após um verbo de ligação. Por exemplo, pode-se dizer **She was glad**, mas não **a glad woman**:

> **afraid, alive, alone, asleep, aware, content, due, glad, ill, ready, sorry, sure, unable, well**

> **I wanted to be alone.**
> *Queria estar sozinho.*

5 Verbos e sintagma verbal

5.1 Em inglês, são usadas bem menos flexões que em português para se referir à pessoa ou ao tempo verbal, indicados respectivamente pelo uso obrigatório dos pronomes e dos verbos auxiliares ou modais:

> **We wanted to know what happened.**
> *Queríamos saber o que aconteceu.*

> **Did she phone you?**
> *Ela ligou para você?*

> **I might not go.**
> *Talvez eu não vá.*

5.2 Os verbos aos quais se pode acrescentar a terminação **-ed**, que são a maioria, chamam-se verbos regulares. Há certos verbos que têm uma ou duas formas diferentes em vez desta terminação; são os chamados verbos irregulares.

Os verbos regulares têm quatro formas:

a) a forma base, que é aquela mencionada, por exemplo, em um dicionário, e que é usada para quase todas as pessoas no presente, com os verbos modais e na construção **to**...

b) a forma com **-s**, que é usada somente no presente quando o sujeito está na terceira pessoa do singular.

c) a forma de gerúndio **-ing**

d) a forma de particípio **-ed**

Observe que as eventuais mudanças ortográficas produzidas com o acréscimo de terminação não fazem com que os verbos sejam irregulares:

ask → asks → asking → asked

try → tries → trying → tried

reach → reaches → reaching → reached

dance → dances → dancing → danced

dip → dips → dipping → dipped

5.3 Os verbos irregulares podem ter três, quatro ou cinco formas diferentes, pois podem ter uma forma diferente para o passado e às vezes outra para o particípio. Todas essas formas aparecem na parte inglês-português do dicionário depois da forma base:

cost → costs → costing → cost → cost

think → thinks → thinking → thought → thought

5.4 O verbo principal pode ser precedido de:

• verbos auxiliares e modais

I had met him in Zermatt.
Eu o havia conhecido em Zermatt.

You can go now.
Agora você pode ir.

She would have been delighted to see you.
Ela teria ficado encantada em vê-la.

5.5 Os verbos auxiliares: **be**, **have**, **do**

Em inglês, há três verbos auxiliares: **be**, **have** e **do**.

	be	have	do
presente	am/is/are	have/has	do/does
-ing	being	having	doing
passado	was/were	had	did
particípio	been	had	done

Como verbo auxiliar, **be** pode ser acompanhado de:

- um verbo com a forma **-ing** para formar os tempos contínuos:

  He is living in Germany.
  Ele está morando na Alemanha.

- um particípio para formar a voz passiva:

  These cars are made in Japan.
  Estes carros são fabricados no Japão.

Have é usado como verbo auxiliar com um particípio para formar os tempos perfeitos:

  I have changed my mind.
  Mudei de ideia.

Do é empregado como auxiliar para:

- a forma negativa ou interrogativa dos verbos no presente simples e no passado simples

  Do you like her new haircut?
  Você gostou do novo corte de cabelo dela?

  She didn't buy the house.
  Ela não comprou a casa.

5.6 Tempos contínuos

Os tempos contínuos são os seguintes:

- presente contínuo = presente do verbo **be** + **-ing**

  They're (= They are) having a meeting.
  Eles estão tendo uma reunião.

- futuro contínuo = **will** + **be** + **-ing**:

  She'll (= She will) be leaving tomorrow.
  Ela vai ir embora amanhã.

- passado contínuo = passado de **be** + **-ing**:

  The train was going very fast.
  O trem ia muito rápido.

- presente perfeito contínuo = presente de **have** + **been** + **-ing**:

  I've (= I have) been living here since last year.
  Estou morando aqui desde o ano passado.

- passado perfeito contínuo = passado de **have** + **been** + **-ing**:

  I'd (= I had) been walking for hours when I saw the road.
  Eu já estava andando por horas quando vi a estrada.

5.7 Tempos simples

Os tempos simples são assim chamados porque são os únicos usados sem um verbo auxiliar na forma afirmativa. O verbo é colocado logo depois do sujeito:

  I live in San Francisco.
  Moro em São Francisco.

  George comes every Monday.
  George vem todas as segundas-feiras.

Os tempos simples são os seguintes:

- **presente simples** = a forma base do verbo (+ **-s** para *He/She/It*):

    I live just outside London.
    Eu moro logo saindo de Londres.

    He likes Australia.
    Ele gosta da Austrália.

- **passado simples** (ou pretérito perfeito simples) = a forma base + **-ed** para os verbos regulares:

    I liked her a lot.
    Eu gostava muito dela.

- e o passado simples, no caso dos verbos irregulares:

    I bought six CDs.
    Comprei seis CDs.

5.8 Tempos de presente:

O presente perfeito (ou pretérito perfeito composto) é formado com o presente de **have** + **-ed**:

I've (= I have) lost my passport.
Perdi meu passaporte.

O presente simples é usado para:

- falar do presente em geral ou de uma ação habitual ou que acontece com regularidade:

    George lives in Birmingham.
    George vive em Birmingham.

    Do you eat meat?
    Você come carne?

- afirmar uma verdade universal:

    Water boils at 100 degrees centigrade.
    A água ferve a 100 graus centígrados.

5.9 Os tempos do passado são:

- o passado simples, o passado contínuo, o passado perfeito e o passado perfeito contínuo.

O passado perfeito (ou mais-que-perfeito) é formado com o passado de **have** + particípio passado:

He had lived in the same village all his life.
Ele tinha morado a vida toda no mesmo vilarejo.

I had forgotten my book.
Eu tinha esquecido meu livro.

O passado simples é usado para:

- referir-se a um evento que ocorreu no passado:

    I woke up early and got out of bed.
    Acordei cedo e me levantei da cama.

- falar de uma situação que durou certo período no passado:

> **She lived just outside Los Angeles.**
> *Ela vivia (ou viveu) nos arredores de Los Angeles.*

- referir-se a algo que costumava ocorrer no passado:

> **We usually spent the winter at Aunt Meg's house.**
> *Costumávamos passar (ou passávamos) o inverno na casa de tia Meg.*

5.10 O uso dos tempos com for, since, ago

Com ***ago***, o verbo da frase principal fica sempre no passado simples:

> **We moved into this house five years ago.**
> *Nós nos mudamos para esta casa há cinco anos.*

Com ***for***, o verbo da oração principal pode ficar:

- no passado, se a ação ocorre inteiramente no passado:

> **We lived in China for two years.**
> *Vivemos na China por dois anos.*

- no presente perfeito, e geralmente na forma contínua, para indicar que a ação começou no passado e se prolonga no presente:

> **We have been living here for five years.**
> *Estamos morando aqui há cinco anos.*

- no passado perfeito ou no passado perfeito contínuo, quando se fala de duas ações que ocorreram no passado:

> **We had been working** ou **We had worked there for nine months when the company closed.**
> *Vínhamos trabalhando ali havia nove meses quando a empresa fechou.*

- no futuro:

> **I'll be staying with you for a month.**
> *Ficarei na sua casa por um mês.*

Com ***since***, o verbo da oração principal pode estar:

- no presente perfeito, e geralmente na forma contínua, para indicar que a ação começou no passado e se prolonga no presente:

> **We have been living here since 2015.**
> *Estamos morando aqui desde 2015.*

> **I've been in politics since I was at university.**
> *Dedico-me à política desde que estava na universidade.*

5.11 Os verbos modais são:

> **will, shall, would, can, could, may, might, must, should, ought to**

Têm uma única forma e, à exceção de ***ought***, são usados com o infinitivo sem ***to***.

5.12 Nunca se podem usar dois modais juntos nem podem ser precedidos de um verbo auxiliar. Por exemplo, não se pode dizer He will can come. Em vez disso, deve-se dizer **He will be able to come**, usando uma expressão com significado idêntico ao do modal.

5.13 *Will* é um verbo modal que na maioria das vezes é usado para falar do futuro:

> **The weather will be warm and sunny tomorrow.**
> *Amanhã o tempo estará quente e ensolarado.*

> **Don't be late. I'll be waiting for you.**
> *Não se atrase. Estarei esperando você.*

5.14 Também se usa *will* para solicitar algo ou fazer um convite:

> **Will you do me a favour?**
> *Você quer me fazer um favor?*

> **Will you come to my party on Saturday?**
> *Você vem à minha festa no sábado?*

5.15 Usa-se *shall* somente com *I* e *we*, principalmente na forma interrogativa para fazer uma sugestão a outra pessoa:

> **Shall we go to the theatre?**
> *Vamos ao teatro?*

> **Shall I shut the door?**
> *Fecho a porta?/Quer que eu feche a porta?*

5.16 No inglês falado, usa-se *would* com *you* para fazer um convite a alguém ou pedir de maneira educada que faça algo:

> **Would you tell her Adrian phoned?**
> *Você poderia dizer-lhe que Adrian ligou?*

> **Would you like a drink?**
> *Gostaria de beber um drinque?*

5.17 can, could, be able to

Can é usado para dizer que algo pode ser ou acontecer:

> **Cooking can be a real pleasure.**
> *Cozinhar pode ser um verdadeiro prazer.*

Usa-se *could* para dizer que algo poderia ter sido ou acontecido:

> **You could have gone to Chicago.**
> *Você poderia ter ido a Chicago.*

Can e *could* são usados para falar da capacidade de fazer algo:

Também são usados para dizer que alguém sabe ou sabia fazer algo, pois aprendeu e pode fazer:

> **He can't dance.**
> *Ele não sabe dançar.*

5.18 Para expressar estes significados com formas verbais que não permitem o uso de *can*, são usadas formas da expressão equivalente *be able to*:

> **Nobody else will be able to read it.**
> *Ninguém mais conseguirá lê-lo.*

5.19 *Can* e *could* são usados no inglês falado para pedir algo de uma maneira educada ou para alguém se oferecer para fazer algo:

> **Can I help you with the dishes?**
> *Posso ajudar com os pratos?*

> **Could you do me a favour?**
> *Você poderia me fazer um favor?*

5.20 *Can*, *could*, *may* ou *be allowed to* são usados para pedir permissão.

A construção com *may* é a mais formal:

> **Can I ask a question?**
> *Posso fazer uma pergunta?*

> **Could I just interrupt a minute?**
> *Poderia interromper um minuto?*

> **May I have a cigarette?**
> *Você poderia me dar um cigarro?*

Somente *can* e *may* são usados para dar permissão:

> **You may leave as soon as you have finished.**
> *Você pode sair assim que tiver terminado.*

5.21 *May* e *might* são usados para dizer que existe a possibilidade de que algo aconteça ou tenha acontecido:

> **He might come.**
> *Pode ser que ele venha.*

> **You may have noticed this advertisement.**
> *Pode ser que você tenha notado este anúncio.*

5.22 *Should* e *ought to* são sinônimos e têm os mesmos significados que "deveria" em português:

> **We should send her a postcard.**
> *Deveríamos enviar-lhe um postal.*

> **We ought to have stayed in tonight.**
> *Deveríamos ter ficado em casa esta noite.*

> **You ought not to see him again.**
> *Você não deveria voltar a vê-lo.*

5.23 Imperativos

A forma afirmativa do imperativo é a mesma que a forma base de um verbo, não sendo precedida de um pronome:

> **Come to my place.**
> *Venha me visitar lá em casa.*

5.24 Nos phrasal verbs, combina-se um verbo com um advérbio ou uma preposição. O significado do verbo às vezes pode mudar radicalmente:

> **Turn right at the next corner.**
> *Vire à direita na próxima esquina.*

She turned off the radio.
Ela desligou o rádio.

She broke her arm in the accident.
Ela quebrou o braço no acidente.

They broke out of prison on Thursday night.
Eles escaparam da prisão na noite de quinta-feira.

5.25 As diferentes composições verbais desse tipo se distribuem em quatro grupos.

Os do primeiro grupo não têm objeto:

break out, catch on, check up, come in, get by, give in, go away, grow up, stand down, start up, stay up, stop off, watch out, wear off

War broke out in September.
A guerra estourou em setembro.

You'll have to stay up late tonight.
Você terá que ficar acordado até tarde da noite.

Os do segundo grupo tomam o objeto depois da composição verbal. Embora pareça ser um grupo nominal com uma preposição, esta é considerada parte do verbo porque lhe confere um significado distinto:

fall for, bargain for, deal with, look after, part with, pick on, set about, take after

She looked after her mother while she was ill.
Ela cuidou da mãe enquanto estava doente.

Peter takes after his father but John is more like me.
Peter é parecido com o pai, mas o John é mais como eu.

Os do terceiro grupo recebem o objeto logo depois do verbo:

bring around, keep up, knock out

The boxer knocked his opponent out.
O boxeador nocauteou o oponente.

Alguns verbos pertencem ao segundo e ao terceiro grupo, ou seja, o objeto pode ir depois da composição verbal ou logo depois do verbo:

fold up, hand over, knock over, point out, pull down, put away, put up, rub out, sort out, take up, tear up, throw away, try out

It took ages to clean up the mess. / It took ages to clean the mess up.
Levou uma eternidade para arrumar a bagunça.

No entanto, se o objeto é um pronome, é colocado sempre logo depois do verbo.

There was such a mess. It took ages to clean it up.
Estava uma bagunça. Levou uma eternidade para arrumar tudo.

5.26 Quando se deseja chamar a atenção para a pessoa ou coisa afetada pela ação, mais que na pessoa ou coisa que pratica a ação, usam-se as formas verbais na voz passiva. Somente os verbos que geralmente recebem objeto admitem tais construções:

Mr. Smith locks the gate at six o'clock every night.
O Sr. Smith fecha o portão às seis horas todas as tardes.

The gate is locked at six o'clock every night.
O portão é trancado às seis horas todas as tardes.

The storm destroyed dozens of trees.
A tempestade destruiu dezenas de árvores.

Dozens of trees were destroyed.
Dezenas de árvores foram destruídas.

5.27 *There is/there are* são usados com uma forma verbal no singular (*is...*, *has...*, *appears...*, *seems...*) se o grupo nominal que segue o verbo (ou o primeiro substantivo, caso haja mais de um) está no singular ou é incontável:

There is one point we must add here.
Há um ponto que devemos acrescentar aqui.

There was a sofa and two chairs.
Havia um sofá e duas cadeiras.

Usa-se uma forma verbal no plural se o grupo nominal está no plural e antes de frases como *a number (of)*, *a lot (of)* e *a few (of)*:

There were two men in the room.
Havia dois homens na sala.

There were a lot of shoppers in the streets.
Havia muitos compradores nas ruas.

5.28 A forma verbal de gerúndio com *-ing* pode ser usada para formar um adjetivo a partir de um verbo e é colocada logo antes do substantivo:

Britain is an aging society.
A Grã-Bretanha tem uma sociedade em processo de envelhecimento.

Rising prices are making food very expensive.
O aumento de preço está encarecendo muito a comida.

5.29 A forma verbal de gerúndio com *-ing* é usada depois do verbo principal para falar de uma ação quando o sujeito é o mesmo do verbo principal. Também pode ser usada na forma passiva. Outros verbos são seguidos de uma forma de infinitivo *to...*, e alguns como *bother*, *try* ou *prefer* admitem as duas construções:

I don't mind telling you.
Não me importo de lhe dizer.

I've just finished reading that book.
Acabei de terminar esse livro.

5.30 A forma verbal de infinitivo *to...* é usada depois de alguns verbos para se referir a uma ação quando o sujeito for igual ao do verbo principal. Geralmente equivale ao infinitivo em português:

She had agreed to let us use her car.
Ela tinha concordado em nos deixar usar seu carro.

I have decided not to go out for the evening.
Decidi não sair esta noite.

13

A forma verbal de infinitivo *to...* é usada depois de alguns verbos e seu objeto ou seu grupo nominal com preposição. O equivalente em português é uma forma de subjuntivo precedida de "que":

I asked her to explain.
Pedi a ela que desse uma explicação.

I waited for him to speak.
Esperei que ele falasse.

Cuidado: o verbo *want* é usado com o infinitivo *to...*

I want you to help me.
Quero que me ajude.

5.31 A forma verbal do particípio pode ser usada da mesma maneira que um adjetivo:

The bird had a broken wing.
O pássaro tinha uma asa quebrada.

6 Perguntas

6.1 Para as perguntas cuja resposta é simplesmente sim ou não, o verbo auxiliar da forma verbal é colocado no começo, seguido do sujeito e o restante das palavras segue sua ordem habitual.

Is he coming? — Yes, he is./No, he isn't.
Ele está vindo? – Sim, está. / Não, não está.

Have you finished yet? — Yes, I have./No, I haven't.
Você já terminou? – Sim, já. / Não, ainda não.

Observe que os tempos simples levam *do* como verbo auxiliar em perguntas deste tipo:

Do you like wine? — Yes, I do/No, I don't.
Gosta de vinho? – Sim, gosto./Não, não gosto.

Do you have any questions? — Yes, we do./No, we don't.
Tem alguma pergunta? – Sim, temos./Não, não temos.

6.2 No inglês falado, é muito comum perguntar algo com uma frase seguido de uma *question tag* (pergunta curta) ao final para pedir confirmação do que acaba de ser dito. Essa pequena pergunta repete a forma verbal da oração, mas usando unicamente o verbo auxiliar correspondente seguido do sujeito. A *question tag* leva a negação *not* depois do verbo auxiliar se na frase anterior não há nenhuma negação:

It is quite warm, isn't it?
Está bem quente, né?

6.3 As partículas interrogativas em inglês são:

what, which, when, where, who, whom, whose, why, how,
how much, how many, how long

Observe que *whom* é usado somente no inglês culto.

As partículas interrogativas são sempre a primeira palavra nas perguntas em que são usadas.

Com essas partículas, a ordem do verbo auxiliar com o sujeito fica invertida, como em qualquer pergunta:

How many are there?
Quantos há?

Which do you like best?
De qual você gosta mais?

When are you going to Liverpool?
Quando você vai para Liverpool?

Why did you do it?
Por que você fez isso?

Where did you get that from?
De onde você conseguiu isso?

Whose idea was it?
De quem foi a ideia?

A única exceção se dá quando se está perguntando pelo sujeito do verbo. Nesse caso, segue-se a ordem habitual da oração. Observe que nesse caso são usadas formas verbais simples, e não a forma com verbo auxiliar *do*:

Who could have done it?
Quem poderia ter feito isso?

What happened?
O que aconteceu?

Which is the best restaurant?
Qual é o melhor restaurante?

6.4 Se houver uma preposição, esta é colocada no final. No entanto, com *whom*, ela é sempre posta antes do pronome:

What's this for?
Para que isso?

What's the book about?
Sobre o que é o livro?

With whom were you talking?
Com quem você estava falando?

6.5 Não tendo somente o significado de "como", *how* também pode acompanhar adjetivos e advérbios, ou *many* e *much*:

How old are your children?
Que idade têm seus filhos?

How long have you lived here?
Você mora aqui há quanto tempo?

How many were there?
Quantos havia?

7 Negações

A negação das formas verbais é composta da palavra *not* (contraída ou não) após o primeiro verbo. É preciso tomar cuidado com as formas verbais simples que necessitam de um auxiliar na forma negativa:

They do not need to talk.
Eles não precisam falar.

I was not smiling.
Eu não estava sorrindo.

I haven't been playing football.
Eu não tenho jogado futebol.

Estas são algumas das contrações mais frequentes:

isn't	haven't	doesn't	mightn't	won't
aren't	hasn't	didn't	mustn't	wouldn't
wasn't	hadn't	—	oughtn't	—
weren't	—	can't	shan't	daren't
—	don't	couldn't	shouldn't	needn't

Em inglês, não se repetem duas negações como é costume em português, portanto não se usa *not* com os seguintes termos: *no one*, *nobody*, *nothing*, *nowhere*, *none*, *never*, *neither* (*... nor...*). Caso a partícula *not* seja usada, ou se houver outra negação, os seguintes correspondentes são empregados:

anyone, anybody, anything, anywhere, any, ever, either

There is nothing you can do./There isn't anything you can do.
Não há nada que você possa fazer.

Portuguese Grammar

1 Verbs

1.1 Simple tenses: formation

In Portuguese, the following are simple tenses: present; preterite; imperfect; future; conditional; imperative; present subjunctive; imperfect subjunctive; future subjunctive. These simple tenses are formed by adding endings to a verb stem. The endings show the number and person of the subject of the verb:

Eu cant*o*.	*I sing.*
Nós cant*amos*.	*We sing.*

Third-person endings for você and vocês: even though **você** and **vocês** mean *you* (singular and plural), they are used with third-person verb endings.

Você cant*a*.	*You sing.*
Ele cant*a*.	*He sings.*

Traditional second-person endings: these are for subjects **tu** and **vós**, which also mean *you* (singular and plural).

Tu cant*as*.	*You sing.*
Vós cant*ais*.	*You sing. (plural)*

Singular endings for **tu** will be shown separately in the verb tables, identified as: **2nd person**. Plural endings for **vós** will also appear, but in brackets, as they are no longer in current use.

Regular verbs

There are three regular verb patterns (known as conjugations), each identifiable by the ending of the infinitive:

First conjugation verbs end in **-ar**, e.g. **cantar** *to sing*.
Second conjugation verbs end in **-er**, e.g. **comer** *to eat*.
Third conjugation verbs end in **-ir**, e.g. **partir** *to leave, depart*.

1.2 Simple tenses: first conjugation

For all tenses other than the future, the conditional and the future subjunctive, the stem is formed removing **ar** from the infinitive. To this stem we add the appropriate endings for each person, as shown in the table below. The stem of the future, the conditional and the future subjunctive is the same as the infinitive.

Example

person	(1) present	(2) preterite	(3) imperfect
eu	cant-o	cant-ei	cant-ava
tu	cant-as	cant-aste	cant-avas
você, ele/ela	cant-a	cant-ou	cant-ava
nós	cant-amos	cant-amos(°)	cant-ávamos
vocês, eles/elas	cant-am	cant-aram	cant-avam

(°) alternative spelling, mainly in Portugal: **cantámos**

1.3 Simple tenses: second conjugation

For all tenses other than the future, the conditional and the future subjunctive, the stem is formed removing **er** from the infinitive. To this stem, we add the appropriate endings for each person, as shown in the table below. The stem of the future, the conditional and the future subjunctive is the same as the infinitive.

Example

person	(1) present	(2) preterite	(3) imperfect
eu	com-o	com-i	com-ia
tu	com-es	com-este	com-ias
você, ele/ela	com-e	com-eu	com-ia
nós	com-emos	com-emos	com-íamos
vocês, eles/elas	com-em	com-eram	com-iam

1.4 Simple tenses: third conjugation

For all tenses other than the future, the conditional and the future subjunctive, the stem is formed removing **ir** from the infinitive. To this stem, we add the appropriate endings for each person, as shown in the table below. The stem of the future, the conditional and the future subjunctive is the same as the infinitive.

Example

person	(1) present	(2) preterite	(3) imperfect
eu	part-o	part-i	part-ia
tu	part-es	part-iste	part-ias
você, ele/ela	part-e	part-iu	part-ia
nós	part-imos	part-imos	part-íamos
vocês, eles/elas	part-em	part-iram	part-iam

1.5 Compound tenses: formation

In Portuguese, the following are compound tenses: present perfect; pluperfect; future perfect; conditional perfect; present perfect subjunctive; pluperfect subjunctive; future perfect subjunctive.

Compound tenses consist of the past participle of the verb preceded by an auxiliary verb and are formed the same way for both regular and irregular verbs.

The auxiliary verb is normally **ter**.

The past participle may be regular or irregular but remains invariable, i.e. it does not change to agree with the subject in gender or number. For past participle formation, see page 5.

> **Elas tinham cantado.**   *They (fem.) had sung.*

Present Perfect
(Present of the auxiliary verb plus past participle)
> **Tem chovido muito.**   *It has been raining a lot.*

Pluperfect
(Imperfect of the auxiliary verb plus past participle)
> **Tinha chovido muito.**   *It had been raining a lot.*

Colloquial future
Future
(Present of *ir*, used as an auxiliary verb, plus the infinitive of the main verb)
> **Eu vou cantar.**   *I am going to sing.*

When the main verb is *ir* itself, a simple tense is used:

> **Eu vou lá.**   *I am going there.*
> **Eu ia lá.**   *I was going there.*

Present Continuous

(Present of **estar** plus preposition **a** plus the infinitive of the main verb (Eur))

(Present of **estar** plus the present participle of the main verb (Br))

> **Eu estou a ler um livro.** (Eur)
> **Eu estou lendo um livro.** (Br)   *I am reading a book.*

Past Continuous

(Imperfect of **estar** plus preposition **a** plus the infinitive of the main verb (Eur))

(Imperfect of **estar** plus the present participle of the main verb (Br))

> **Eu estava a ler um livro.** (Eur)
> **Eu estava lendo um livro.** (Br)   *I was reading a book.*

1.6 Reflexive verbs

A reflexive verb is one that is accompanied by a reflexive pronoun to show that the subject both *performs* and *receives* the action (e.g. *I hurt myself*).

reflexive pronouns			
	singular		**plural**	
1st person	**me**	*myself*	**nos**	*ourselves*
2nd person	**se** (general) **te** (familiar)	*yourself*	**se** (both general and familiar)	*yourselves*
3rd person	**se**	*him/her/itself*	**se**	*themselves*

> **Elas não se magoaram.**   *They didn't hurt themselves.*
> **Eles beijam-se.** (Eur), **Eles se beijam.** (Br)   *They kiss (each other).*

Other common reflexive verbs in Portuguese:

> **deitar-se**, *to go to bed* • **despedir-se**, *to say goodbye* • **divertir-se**, *to have a nice time* • **esquecer-se**, *to forget* • **lembrar-se**, *to remember* • **levantar-se**, *to get up* • **pentear-se**, *to comb one's hair* • **sentar-se**, *to sit down* • **vestir-se**, *to get dressed*

1.7 The passive

In the passive, the subject *receives* the action (e.g. *I was called*) as opposed to *performing* it (e.g. *I called*). The Portuguese passive is formed in very much the same way as the English one, i.e. using a form of the verb **ser** meaning *to be*, and a past participle. In the passive in Portuguese, the past participle agrees in gender and number with the subject:

> **O carro foi vendido.**   *The car has been sold.*
> **Elas foram recompensadas.**   *They (fem.) were rewarded.*

1.8 Impersonal verbs

In English, **it** is often used as an impersonal subject. In Portuguese, however, the subject pronoun is omitted in such cases:

> **Vale a pena.**   *It is worthwhile.*

Below are some frequently used impersonal verbs in Portuguese:

• Verbs for the weather and other natural phenomena:

> **Choveu ontem.**   *It rained yesterday.*
> **Anoiteceu cedo.**   *It got dark early.*

- **haver**

for talking about existence or events:

Há lojas perto daqui?	*Are there any shops nearby?*
Haverá um desfile de Carnaval.	*There will be a Carnival parade.*

- **estar**

for weather:

Está frio hoje.	*It's cold today.*

- **ser**

for weather and seasons:

É verão.	*It is summer.*

for telling the time:

É uma hora.	*It's one o'clock.*

for distance:

São cinco quilómetros (Eur) /	
quilômetros (Br) **daqui até lá.**	*It's five km away.*

for days of the week and dates:

Ontem foi quarta-feira.	*Yesterday was Wednesday.*

in impersonal expressions:

É fácil.	*It's easy.*
É importante.	*It's important.*

1.9 Present and past participles

Formation of present participle

To form the present participle of the first, second and third conjugation, replace the final **-r** of the infinitive with **-ndo**:

cantar *to sing*	→	**cantando** *singing*
comer *to eat*	→	**comendo** *eating*
partir *to leave*	→	**partindo** *leaving*

Formation of past participle

To form the past participle of the first conjugation, replace the infinitive ending **-ar** with **-ado**:

cantar *to sing*	→	**cantado** *sung*

To form the past participle of the second and third conjugations, replace the infinitive endings **-er** and **-ir -ido**:

comer *to eat*	→	**comido** *eaten*
partir *to leave*	→	**partido** *left*

Some past participles are irregular, even when the verb is otherwise regular:

abrir *to open*	→	**aberto** *open(ed)*
escrever *to write*	→	**escrito** *written*

The Portuguese **past participle** is used in the following ways:

- As part of a perfect tense:

Ela tinha acendido a luz.	*She had switched on the light.*

21

- In the passive voice:

> **O exército foi derrotado pelo inimigo.**
> *The army was defeated by the enemy.*

- As an adjective:

> **Estas contas estão pagas.**   *These bills are paid.*

1.10 Ser and estar

Portuguese has two verbs that both correspond to *to be*: **ser** and **estar**. They are not interchangeable, however. Their different meanings and uses are explained below.

Ser

Ser is used for things that are considered inherent to the subject. This includes nationality; profession; possession; location of non-movable things; geographical location; numbers; time; and impersonal general statements:

Ela é de São Paulo.	*She is from São Paulo.*
Elas são irmãs.	*They are sisters.*
Ele é professor.	*He is a teacher.*
Portugal é na Europa.	*Portugal is in Europe.*

Estar

Estar is used for things that are considered non-inherent to the subject and, as such, often transitory. This includes personal location; location of movable things; temporary conditions; certain expressions of feeling; and time span:

Eles estão em casa.	*They are at home.*
O livro está em cima da mesa.	*The book is on the table.*
Hoje estou muito cansada.	*Today I am very tired.*
Estávamos de férias.	*We were on holiday.*

1.11 Modal auxiliary verbs

In Portuguese, some modal auxiliary verbs are followed by a verb in the infinitive and others by a verb in the gerund (also known as the present participle). How they are used and what they mean is explained below:

- Modals followed directly by a verb in the infinitive

dever *must; should; be predictable*

> **Devemos telefonar para ele ainda hoje.**
> *We must phone him by the end of today.*
> **Você devia ser professor.**   *You should be a teacher.*

poder *to be able to, can; may* (permission); *may* (probability)

> **Eu posso ir lá amanhã.**   *I can go there tomorrow.*

- Modals linked to a following infinitive by a connector (often a preposition)

acabar de *to have just ...*

> **Acabamos de chegar.**   *We have just arrived.*

acabar por *to end up ...*

> **Eles acabaram por ficar em casa.**   *They ended up staying at home.*

• Modals followed by a present participle (or gerund)

acabar *to end up ... -ing*

> **Eles acabaram rindo.** *They ended up laughing.*

começar *to start ...-ing*

> **Ele já começou a fazer o trabalho.** *He has already started doing the job.*

continuar *to go on ...-ing*

> **Vocês continuam trabalhando juntos?**
> **Vocês continuam a trabalhar juntos?** (Eur) *Are you still working together?*

2 Nouns

2.1 Gender of nouns

In Portuguese, all nouns are either masculine or feminine. This grammatical gender applies not only to people and animals but also to inanimate objects and abstract concepts:

homem	*man*	(masculine)
vaca	*cow*	(feminine)
carro	*car*	(masculine)
felicidade	*happiness*	(feminine)

There are some guidelines that can help you work out whether a noun is masculine or feminine.

Generally, males and females are masculine and feminine respectively:

homem (masculine) / **mulher** (feminine)	*man / woman*
cavalo (masculine) / **égua** (feminine)	*horse / mare*
gato (masculine) / **gata** (feminine)	*cat / she-cat*

Usually masculine: nouns ending in the vowels **-o** and **-u**, the consonants **-l**, **-r**, and **-z**, and the letters **-ume**:

> **gato, livro, peru, hotel, mar, rapaz, legume**

Usually feminine: nouns ending in the vowel **-a** and the letters **-gem**, **-dade**, **-tude** and **-ão** (when the ending corresponds to **-ion** in the English translation):

> **gata, escola, garagem, identidade, juventude, atenção**

However, since there are exceptions, it is always advisable to learn a noun with its definite article, i.e., the word for *the*, which indicates its gender. Please see **The definite article**, on page 9.

Some nouns have only one gender, often feminine, which applies to both male and female. The following nouns are always feminine even when they refer to a male:

> **pessoa, criança**

A masculine plural can cover both genders:

irmão	brother	**irmãos**	*brothers or siblings*
senhor	gentleman	**senhores**	*gentlemen or ladies and gentlemen*

2.2 Formation of feminines

As in English, males and females are sometimes differentiated by the use of two different words in Portuguese, e.g.:

homem / mulher	*man / woman*
pai / mãe	*father / mother*

However, the male-female distinction is often shown by a change of ending.

Words ending in **-o** (but not **-ão**) in the masculine change to **-a** in the feminine:

menino / menina	*boy / girl*
filho / filha	*son / daughter*

Some words ending in **-ão** drop the final **-o**:

irmão / irmã	*brother / sister*
cidadão / cidadã	(male) *citizen* / (female) *citizen*

A few words ending in **-ão** change to **-oa**:

patrão / patroa	(male) *boss* / (female) *boss*
leão / leoa	*lion / lioness*

Words ending in **-or** generally add **a**:

senhor / senhora	*gentleman / lady*
professor / professora	(male) *teacher* / (female) *teacher*

Words ending in **-ês** normally add **a** and lose their written accent:

português / portuguesa	*Portuguese man / Portuguese woman*
freguês / freguesa	(male) *customer* / (female) *customer*

Words ending in **-ista** do not change:

dentista	(male) *dentist* / (female) *dentist*
motorista	(male) *driver* / (female) *driver*

Most words ending in **-a** or **-e** do not change:

estudante	(male) *student* / (female) *student*
habitante	(male) *inhabitant* / (female) *inhabitant*
colega	(male) *colleague* / (female) *colleague*

2.3 Formation of plurals

As a general rule, simply add an **-s** to nouns ending in a single vowel:

menino	*boy*	**meninos**	*boys*
chave	*key*	**chaves**	*keys*

There are some specific endings which require a different plural form in Portuguese.

Words ending in **-m** change to **-ns**:

homem	*man*	**homens**	*men*
nuvem	*cloud*	**nuvens**	*clouds*

Words ending in the consonants **-r**, **-z** and **-n** add **-es**:

mulher	*woman*	**mulheres**	*women*
rapaz	*boy, young man*	**rapazes**	*boys, young men*

Words ending in **-ês** add **es** and lose their accent:

freguês	*customer*	**fregueses**	*customers*
mês	*month*	**meses**	*months*

Words ending in **-al** change to **-ais**:

animal	*animal*	**animais**	*animals*

Words ending in stressed **-el** change to **-éis** and those ending in unstressed **-el** change to **-eis**:

hotel	*hotel*	**hotéis**	*hotels*
nível	*level*	**níveis**	*levels*

Some words ending in **-ão** add **-s** while others change to **-ões** or **-ães**.

irmão	*brother*	**irmãos**	*brothers/siblings*
avião	*aeroplane*	**aviões**	*aeroplanes*
capitão	*captain*	**capitães**	*captains*

Words ending in **-s** have the same form for both singular and plural:

pires	*saucer*	**pires**	*saucers*

3 Articles

3.1 The definite article

The Portuguese definite article agrees in gender (i.e. masc. or fem.) and number (i.e. sing. or plur.) with the noun to which it relates. As such, it has the following forms:

o	masculine singular	**os**	masculine plural
a	feminine singular	**as**	feminine plural
o homem	*the man*	**os homens**	*the men*
a chave	*the key*	**as chaves**	*the keys*

(Please note that Portuguese **a** translates English *the*, not *a/an*.)

For nouns that mean different things depending on their gender, it is the article that helps identify the sense in question:

o capital	*capital* (money)	**a capital**	*capital* (city)

Basically the role of the definite article is much the same in Portuguese as it is in English, but its use is broader in Portuguese, e.g.:

• with nouns when making generalizations

O ouro é um metal precioso.	*Gold is a precious metal.*

• with parts of the body, belongings, close relations and friends

Vou lavar o cabelo.	*I am going to wash my hair.*
Ela saiu com os amigos.	*She went out with her friends.*

with possessives, although its use here is optional:

Este é o meu livro.	*This is my book.*

• with a title followed by a name

O doutor Oliveira não está.	*Doctor Oliveira is not in.*

• with names of people – in Portugal and some parts of Brazil

Comprei um presente para a Lúcia.	*I have bought a present for Lúcia.*

3.2 The indefinite article

The Portuguese indefinite article agrees with the noun to which it relates. As such it has a masculine (**um**) and a feminine (**uma**) form:

um homem	*a man*
uma chave	*a key*

The Portuguese indefinite article also has plural forms. These often correspond to *some* and *a few* in English:

uns homens	*some / a few men*
umas chaves	*some / a few keys*

4 Adjectives

Most adjectives agree in gender and number with the noun they modify.

Descriptive adjectives generally follow their nouns:

> **O lápis preto está em cima da mesa.**
> *The black pencil is on the table.*

Some adjectives have different meanings depending on whether they go before or after the noun:

Ele é um homem grande.	*He is a big man.*
Ele é um grande homem.	*He is a great man.*

4.1 Formation of feminines

Words ending in **-o** (but not **-ão**) change to **-a**:

alto / alta, vermelho / vermelha, brasileiro / brasileira

Some words ending in **-ão** drop the final **-o**:

são / sã, cristão / cristã, alemão / alemã

4.2 Formation of plurals

Most words ending in a single vowel add **-s**:

brasileiro, brasileiros	*Brazilian*

Words ending in **-m** change to **-ns**:

jovem, jovens	*young*

Words ending in **-r** or **-z** add **-es**:

feliz, felizes	*happy*

Words ending in **-ês** add **-es** (and lose their accent):

português, portugueses	*Portuguese*

Words ending in **-al** change to **-ais**:

internacional, internacionais	*international*

Words ending in **-el** generally change to **-eis**:

possível, possíveis	*possible*

4.3 Demonstrative adjectives

Demonstrative adjectives agree with the noun in both gender (i.e. masc. or fem.) and number (i.e. sing. or plur.):

	masculine	feminine	
singular	este, esse, aquele	esta, essa, aquela	*this; that*
plural	estes, esses, aqueles	estas, essas, aquelas	*these; those*

    Este casaco é meu.   *This coat is mine.*
    Aquelas malas são deles.   *Those suitcases are theirs.*

The difference between **este**, **esse**, **aquele** is shown below:

* **este** (and its feminine and plural) indicate something or someone close to the speaker, i.e. to the 1st person.

* **esse** (and its feminine and plural) indicate something or someone close to the listener, i.e. to the 2nd person.

* **aquele** (and its feminine and plural) indicate something or someone at a distance from both the 1st and 2nd persons.

4.4 Interrogative adjectives

Que...? can translate both English *What...?* and *Which...?*. It is used when seeking identification or a definition:

    Que rua é esta?   *What street is this?*

Qual...? translates English *Which...?*. It implies the notion of choice or selection. It agrees in number with its noun and has the form **Quais...?** for the plural:

    Qual livro você vai escolher?   *Which book are you going to choose?*

Quanto...?, Quanta...?, Quantos...?, Quantas...? translates English *How much...?* and *How many...?*. It agrees in gender and number with the noun it relates to:

    Quanto tempo vai demorar?   *How long is it going to take?*
    Quantos livros você leu?   *How many books have you read?*

4.5 Possessive adjectives

Possessor	Possessives		
	Masculine, singular and plural	Feminine, singular and plural	
1st person sing. (*I*)	o(s) meus(s)	a(s) minha(s)	*my*
2nd person sing. (*you*)	o(s) seu(s) (relating to você / o senhor / a senhora) o(s) [noun] de ... o(s) teu(s)	a(s) sua(s) (relating to você, o senhor, a senhora) a(s) [noun] de ... a(s) tua(s)	*your*
3rd person sing. (*he / she / it*)	o(s) seu(s) o(s) [noun] dele / dela	a(s) sua(s) a(s) [noun] dele / dela	*his / her / its*
1st person plur. (*we*)	o(s) nosso(s)	a(s) nossa(s)	*our*
2nd person plur. (*you*)	o(s) seu(s) (relating to vocês etc) o(s) vosso(s) o(s) [noun] de ...	a(s) sua(s) (relating to vocês etc) a(s) vossa(s) a(s) [noun] de ...	*your*
3rd person plur. (*they*)	o(s) seu(s) o(s) [noun] deles / delas	a(s) sua(s) a(s) [noun] deles / delas	*their*

5 Pronouns

5.1 Personal pronouns

Subject pronouns

	singular		plural	
1st person	eu	*I*	nós	*we*
2nd person	você tu	*you*	vocês	*you*
3rd person (masc.) (fem.)	ele ela	*he; it* *she; it*	eles elas	*they* *they*

A masculine plural can refer to both genders:

Eles gostam de viajar. (Cecilia e Eduardo)
They like travelling. (Cecília and Eduardo)

você, tu

In today's Portuguese, **você** is a second-person singular subject marker, although it is followed by a verb in the third person. The other subject marker, **tu**, is the traditional second-person singular subject pronoun. Both **você** and **tu** share the same plural, **vocês**.

There is variation in the use of **você** and **tu**. In European Portuguese **tu** is very much alive and well. In many parts of Brazil, preference is given to **você** at a national level, but some Brazilian speakers use the subject pronoun **tu**, often conjugated with the verb ending for **você**. The use of **tu** in some parts of Brazil has nothing to do with familiarity with the person being spoken to, as in other languages such as French and Spanish.

Cecília, você gosta de viajar?   *Cecília, do you like travelling?*
Cecília, tu gostas de viajar? (Eur)   *Cecília, do you like travelling?*

Where the verb ending indicates the subject clearly, the subject marker can be dropped:

(Eu) telefonei ontem.   *I phoned yesterday.*
(Nós) vamos para à praia amanhã.   *We are going to the beach tomorrow.*

Direct object pronouns

	singular		plural	
1st person	me	*me*	nos	*us*
2nd person	o/a você te	*you*	os/as, vos (Eur) (Wr Br) vocês	*you*
3rd person (masc.) (fem.)	o ele (Coll Br) a ela (Coll Br)	*him; it* *her; it*	os eles (Coll Br) as elas (Coll Br)	*them* *them*

Eu não te vi.   *I didn't see you.*
Eles não nos viram.   *They didn't see us.*

The preposition **com** (*with*) combines with personal pronouns in the following ways:

comigo	*with me*
contigo	*with you*
connosco (Eur), **conosco** (Br)	*with us*
consigo (Eur) (Wr Br) = **com você**	*with you*
convosco (Eur) (Wr Br) = **com vocês**	*with you*

5.2 Tu, você and o senhor / a senhora

In today's English, there is an all-embracing pronoun used for addressing people: *you*. The closest Portuguese translation is **você**:

Você está de férias? *Are you on holiday?* (addressing one person)

In Portuguese, a more formal form of address is achieved by replacing **você** with the nouns **o senhor** (literally, *the gentleman*) and **a senhora** (*the lady*), when wishing to show more respect:

O senhor está de férias? *Are you on holiday?*
A senhora está de férias? *Are you on holiday?*

In Portugal, including Madeira and the Azores, as well as in Portuguese-speaking regions of Africa and Asia, **tu** is the main choice for this purpose, along with its related object pronouns, **te** and **ti**:

Tu estás de férias? *Are you on holiday?*
Eu não te vi na praia. (Eur) *I didn't see you on the beach.*

In Brazil, both **você** and **tu** can be heard in conjunction with the object pronouns **te** and **ti**:

Você está de férias? *Are you on holiday?*
Eu não te vi na praia. (Br) *I didn't see you on the beach.*

When talking to more than one person, **você** is pluralized to **vocês**.

Vocês estão de férias? *Are you on holiday?*

The verb endings used for both the more formal **o senhor / a senhora** and less formal **você** are third-person forms:

O senhor está de férias? *Are you on holiday?*
Você está de férias? *Are you on holiday?*

In Portugal, and the other geographical locations listed above, the subject pronoun **tu** has retained its traditional second-person singular verb endings. Because they are distinctive as a second-person marker, **tu** can be omitted without loss of meaning:

Tu estás de férias? (Eur) or **Estás de férias?** *Are you on holiday?*

5.3 Relative pronouns

Que (*that, which, who, whom*) is the most frequently used relative pronoun in Portuguese. It is invariable and can be used both as subject and direct object:

A minha amiga é a pessoa que você vê ali.
My friend is the person (whom or who or that) *you can see over there.*

Tenho o livro que você pediu. *I have the book* (which or that) *you asked for.*

(Please note that, unlike English, Portuguese never omits the relative pronoun.)

5.4 Interrogative pronouns

Quem...? translates English *Who...?* and *Whom...?*, both singular and plural:

Quem veio aqui ontem?   *Who came here yesterday?*

Que...? and **Qual...?** are equivalent to *What?* and *Which?* in English.

Que...? is used when the questioner is expecting an answer that identifies or defines. **Qual...?** (plural **Quais...?**) is used when the possible answers are more restricted and there is an implicit idea of choice:

Qual você prefere?   *Which do you prefer?*
                      (choosing one out of two or more options)

O que is also translated into English as *What...?*

O que você está fazendo?   *What are you doing?*

Quanto...?, **Quanta...?**, **Quantos...?**, **Quantas...?** corresponds to *How much?*, *How many?* in English and agrees in gender and number with the noun:

Quanto custa?   *How much does it cost?*
Quantas são?   *How many are there?*

5.5 Possessive pronouns

Possessor	Possessives		
	Masculine, singular and plural	Feminine, singular and plural	
1st person sing. (*I*)	o(s) meu(s)	a(s) minha(s)	*mine*
2nd person sing. (*you*)	o(s) seu(s) (relating to você, o senhor, a senhora) o(s) de ... o(s) teu(s)	a(s) sua(s) (relating to você, o senhor, a senhora) a(s) de ... a(s) tua(s)	*yours*
3rd person sing. (*he / she / it*)	o(s) seu(s) o(s) dele / dela	a(s) sua(s) a(s) dele / dela	*his / hers / its*
1st person plur. (*we*)	o(s) nosso(s)	a(s) nossa(s)	*ours*
2nd person plur. (*you*)	o(s) seu(s) (relating to vocês etc) o(s) vosso(s) o(s) de ...	a(s) sua(s) (relating to vocês etc) a(s) vossa(s) a(s) de ...	*yours*
3rd person plur. (*they*)	o(s) seu(s) o(s) deles / delas	a(s) sua(s) a(s) deles / delas	*theirs*

5.6 Demonstrative pronouns

Demonstrative pronouns have forms that agree in gender (i.e. masc. or fem.) and number (i.e. sing. or plur.) with the noun they replace:

	masculine	feminine	
singular	este, esse, aquele	esta, essa, aquela	*this; that (one)*
plural	estes, esses, aqueles	estas, essas, aquelas	*these; those (ones)*

There are also invariable neuter forms, for something or someone yet to be identified:

isto, isso, aquilo   *this; that (one)*
Este é o meu casaco.   *This is my coat.*
Esse é o teu guarda-chuva.   *That is your umbrella.*
Aquelas são as malas deles.   *Those are their suitcases.*

The difference between **isto**, **isso** and **aquilo** is shown below:

- **isto** (and the feminine and plural forms) is used to indicate something close to the speaker, i.e. to the 1st person.

- **isso** (and the feminine and plural forms) is used to indicate something close to the listener, i.e. to the 2nd person.

- **aquilo** (and the feminine and plural forms) is used to indicate something at a distance away from both the 1st and 2nd persons.

6 Negatives

Unlike in English, a Portuguese sentence can be made negative just by placing the word **não**, *not*, before the verb. No auxiliary verb is required:

Aquele carro não é novo.	*That car is not new.*
Eu não trabalho aqui.	*I don't work here.*

If there is an object pronoun, this will come between **não** and the verb:

Ela não me telefonou.	*She hasn't phoned me.*

In addition to translating *not*, **não** also translates *no* as opposed to *yes*:

Sim!	*Yes!*
Não!	*No!*

Other important negatives are:

- adverbs **nunca** and **nunca mais**

Eu nunca fui lá.	*I have never been there.*
Ele nunca mais trabalhou aqui.	*He has never worked here again.*

- indefinite pronouns **nada**, **ninguém**, **nenhum** (**nenhuma**, **nenhuns**, **nenhumas**)

Nada a declarar.	*Nothing to declare.*
Ninguém vem aqui.	*No one comes here.*
Nenhum deles chegou atrasado.	*None of them arrived late.*

7 Questions

Questions for yes/no replies

When asking a question in Portuguese, the normal word order is generally followed and the question is indicated only by the rising intonation of the voice at the end of the sentence:

Você vai para a praia?	*Are you going to the beach?*
Eles já chegaram?	*Have they arrived yet?*
Você fala português?	*Do you speak Portuguese?*

You can reply with **Sim**, *Yes*, or **Não**, *No*. However, particularly in affirmative replies, native speakers tend to repeat elements from the question while changing the verb ending as required:

O jantar foi bom?	*Was dinner good?*
Não, não foi.	*No, it wasn't.*
Você fala português.	*Do you speak Portuguese?*
Falo.	*Yes, I do.*

8   Use of numbers and time

8.1   Numbers

In Portuguese, no number or indefinite article precedes the words for 100 or 1,000:

cem carros	*one/a hundred cars*
mil carros	*one/a thousand cars*

In Portuguese, the word for 100 (**cem**) changes form before lower numbers:

cento e dez carros	*one hundred and ten cars*

Unlike in English, there is a preposition **de** after the word for million(s):

um milhão de carros	*one million cars*

Note that hundreds, tens and units are linked together using **e** (*and*) but a comma is used for thousands and millions when followed by more than two lower numbers:

cento e vinte e dois	*one hundred and twenty-two*
mil, cento e vinte e três	*one thousand, one hundred and twenty-three*

In Portuguese, commas and dots are used in the opposite way to English, since commas are used to show decimal places while the role of dots is to separate out larger numbers (thousands, millions, etc):

zero vírgula cinco	**0,5**	*zero point five*	*0.5*
mil	**1.000**	*one thousand*	*1,000*

There are masculine and feminine forms for cardinals 1 and 2, the multiples of 100 (which are expressed in the plural), and the ordinals:

um carro e uma bicicleta	*one car and one bicycle*
dois carros e duas bicicletas	*two cars and two bicycles*
duzentos carros	*two hundred cars*
duzentas bicicletas	*two hundred bicycles*
o primeiro carro	*the first car*
a segunda bicicleta	*the second bicycle*

8.2   Time

While English always uses the singular form of the verb to talk about time, in Portuguese a plural form is used if the plural noun **horas** is expressed or understood:

Que horas são?	*What time is it?*
São seis horas.	*It is six o'clock.*
É uma hora.	*It is one o'clock.*

Time past and to the hour is expressed differently from the way it is in English. Minutes are used on both sides of the Atlantic, but, in Portugal, **quarto** (*quarter*) is also widely used:

É uma e dez.	*It is one ten (ten past one).*
São dez para as duas.	*It is ten to two.*
São seis e trinta. or **São seis e meia.**	*It is six thirty. / It is half past six.*
É uma e quinze. (Br) or **É uma e um quarto.** (Eur)	
It is one fifteen. / It is a quarter past one.	

Português – Inglês

Portuguese – English

a

a [a] ART DEF the; *ver tb* **o**
▶ PRON (*ela*) her; (*você*) you; (*coisa*) it; *ver tb* **o**
▶ PREP (*a + o(s) = ao(s); a + a(s) = à(s); a + aquele/a(s) = àquele/a(s)*)
1 (*direção*) to; **à direita/esquerda** to *ou* on the right/left
2 (*distância*): **está a 15 km daqui** it's 15 km from here
3 (*posição*): **ao lado de** beside, at the side of
4 (*tempo*) at; **a que horas?** at what time?; **às 5 horas** at 5 o'clock; **à noite** at night; **aos 15 anos** at 15 years of age
5 (*maneira*): **à francesa** in the French way; **a cavalo/pé** on horseback/foot
6 (*meio, instrumento*): **à força** by force; **a mão** by hand; **a lápis** in pencil; **fogão a gás** gas stove
7 (*razão*): **a R$10 o quilo** at R$10 a kilo; **a mais de 100 km/h** at over 100 km/h
8 (*depois de certos verbos*): **começou a nevar** it started snowing *ou* to snow; **passar a fazer** to become
9 (*+ infin*): **ao vê-lo, reconheci-o imediatamente** when I saw him, I recognized him immediately; **ele ficou muito nervoso ao falar com o professor** he became very nervous while he was talking to the teacher
10 (*PT: + infin, gerúndio*): **a correr** running; **estou a trabalhar** I'm working

à [a] = **a + a**; *ver a*
(a) ABR (= *assinado*) signed
aba ['aba] F (*de chapéu*) brim; (*de casaco*) tail; (*de montanha*) foot
abacate [aba'katʃi] M avocado (pear)
abacaxi [aba'kaʃi] (BR) M pineapple
abafado, -a [aba'fadu, a] ADJ (*ar*) stuffy; (*tempo*) humid, close; (*ocupado*) (extremely) busy; (*angustiado*) anxious
abaixar [abaj'ʃar] VT to lower; (*luz, som*) to turn down; **abaixar-se** VR to stoop
abaixo [a'bajʃu] ADV down ▶ PREP: **~ de** below; **~ o governo!** down with the government!; **morro ~** downhill; **rio ~** downstream; **mais ~** further down; **~ e acima** up and down; **~ assinado** undersigned; **abaixo-assinado** [-asi'nadu] (*pl* **-s**) M petition
abalado, -a [aba'ladu, a] ADJ unstable, unsteady; (*fig*) shaken
abalar [aba'lar] VT to shake; (*fig: comover*) to affect ▶ VI to shake; **abalar-se** VR to be moved
abalo [a'balu] M (*comoção*) shock; (*ação*) shaking; **~ sísmico** earth tremor
abanar [aba'nar] VT to shake; (*rabo*) to wag; (*com leque*) to fan
abandonar [abãdo'nar] VT to leave; (*ideia*) to reject; (*esperança*) to give up; (*descuidar*) to neglect
abarrotado, -a [abaho'tadu, a] ADJ (*gaveta*) crammed full; (*lugar*) packed
abastecer [abaste'ser] VT to supply; (*motor*) to fuel; (*Auto*) to fill up; (*Aer*) to refuel; **abastecer-se** VR: **~-se de** to stock up with
abastecimento [abastesi'mẽtu] M supply; (*comestíveis*) provisions *pl*; (*ato*) supplying; **abastecimentos** MPL (*suprimentos*) supplies
abater [aba'ter] VT (*gado*) to slaughter; (*preço*) to reduce; (*desalentar*) to upset; **abatido, -a** [aba'tʃidu, a] ADJ depressed, downcast; **abatimento** [abatʃi'mẽtu] M (*fraqueza*) weakness; (*de preço*) reduction; (*prostração*) depression; **fazer um abatimento em** to give a discount on
abdômen [ab'domẽ] M abdomen
á-bê-cê [abe'se] M alphabet
abecedário [abese'darju] M alphabet, ABC
abelha [a'beʎa] F bee
abelhudo, -a [abe'ʎudu, a] ADJ nosy
abençoar [abẽ'swar] VT to bless
aberto, -a [a'bɛrtu, a] PP *de* **abrir** ▶ ADJ open; (*céu*) clear; (*sinal*) green; (*torneira*) on
abestalhado, -a [abesta'ʎadu, a] ADJ stupid
abismado, -a [abiz'madu, a] ADJ astonished
ABL ABR F = **Academia Brasileira de Letras**
abnegado, -a [abne'gadu, a] ADJ self-sacrificing

abnegar [abne'gar] vt to renounce

abóbada [a'bɔbada] F vault; (*telhado*) arched roof

abobalhado, -a [aboba'ʎadu, a] ADJ (*criança*) simple

abóbora [a'bɔbora] F pumpkin

abobrinha [abo'briɲa] F courgette (BRIT), zucchini (US)

abolir [abo'lir] vt to abolish

aborrecer [abohe'ser] vt (*chatear*) to annoy; (*maçar*) to bore; **aborrecer-se** vR to get upset; to get bored; **aborrecido, -a** [abohe'sidu, a] ADJ boring; (*chateado*) annoyed; **aborrecimento** [abohesi'mētu] M boredom; (*chateação*) annoyance

abortar [abor'tar] vi (Med) to have a miscarriage; (: *de propósito*) to have an abortion; **aborto** [a'bortu] M miscarriage; (*forçado*) abortion; **fazer/ter um aborto** to have an abortion/a miscarriage

abotoadura [abotwa'dura] F cufflink

abotoar [abo'twar] vt to button up ▶ vi (Bot) to bud

abraçar [abra'sar] vt to hug; (*causa*) to embrace; **abraçar-se** vR to embrace; **ele abraçou-se a mim** he embraced me; **abraço** [a'brasu] M embrace, hug; **com um abraço** (*em carta*) with best wishes

abre-garrafas ['abri-] (PT) M INV bottle opener

abre-latas ['abri-] (PT) M INV tin (BRIT) ou can opener

abreviar [abre'vjar] vt to abbreviate; (*texto*) to abridge; **abreviatura** [abrevja'tura] F abbreviation

abridor [abri'dor] (BR) M: **~ (de lata)** tin (BRIT) ou can opener; **~ de garrafa** bottle opener

abrigar [abri'gar] vt to shelter; (*proteger*) to protect; **abrigar-se** vR to take shelter

abrigo [a'brigu] M shelter, cover; **~ antiaéreo** air-raid shelter; **~ antinuclear** fall-out shelter

abril [a'briw] M April

> On 25 April (**25 de abril**) 1974 in Portugal, the MAF (Armed Forces Movement) instigated the bloodless revolution that was to topple the 48-year-old dictatorship presided over until 1968 by António de Oliveira Salazar. The red carnation has come to symbolize the coup, as it is said that the Armed Forces took to the streets with carnations in the barrels of their rifles. 25 April is now a public holiday in Portugal.

abrir [a'brir] vt to open; (*fechadura*) to unlock; (*vestuário*) to unfasten; (*torneira*) to turn on; (*buraco, exceção*) to make ▶ vi to open; (*sinal*) to go green; **abrir-se** vR: **~-se com alguém** to confide in sb

abrupto, -a [a'bruptu, a] ADJ abrupt; (*repentino*) sudden

absolutamente [absoluta'mētʃi] ADV absolutely; (*em resposta*) absolutely not, not at all

absoluto, -a [abso'lutu, a] ADJ absolute; **em ~** absolutely not, not at all

absorto, -a [ab'sortu, a] PP *de* **absorver** ▶ ADJ absorbed, engrossed

absorvente [absor'vētʃi] ADJ (*papel etc*) absorbent; (*livro etc*) absorbing

absorver [absor'ver] vt to absorb; **absorver-se** vR: **~-se em** to concentrate on

abstêmio, -a [abs'temju, a] ADJ abstemious; (*álcool*) teetotal ▶ M/F abstainer; teetotaller (BRIT), teetotaler (US)

abster-se [ab'stersi] (*irreg: como* **ter**) vR: **~ de** to abstain ou refrain from

abstinência [abstʃi'nēsja] F abstinence; (*jejum*) fasting

abstrato, -a [abs'tratu, a] ADJ abstract

absurdo, -a [abi'surdu, a] ADJ absurd ▶ M nonsense

abundante [abū'dātʃi] ADJ abundant; **abundar** [abū'dar] vi to abound

abusar [abu'zar] vi to go too far; **~ de** to abuse

abuso [a'buzu] M abuse; (Jur) indecent assault

a.C. ABR (= *antes de Cristo*) B.C.

a/c ABR (= *aos cuidados de*) Attn:

acabado, -a [aka'badu, a] ADJ finished; (*esgotado*) worn out

acabamento [akaba'mētu] M finish

acabar [aka'bar] vt to finish, complete; (*consumir*) to use up; (*rematar*) to finish off ▶ vi to finish, end; **acabar-se** vR to be over; (*prazo*) to expire; (*esgotar-se*) to run out; **~ com** to put an end to; **~ de chegar** to have just arrived; **~ por fazer** to end up (by) doing; **acabou-se!** it's all over!; (*basta!*) that's enough!

academia [akade'mia] F academy; **Academia Brasileira de Letras** *see note*

> Founded in 1896 in Rio de Janeiro, on the initiative of the author Machado de Assis, the **Academia Brasileira de Letras**, or ABL, aims to preserve and develop the Portuguese language and Brazilian literature. Machado de Assis was its president until 1908. It is made

up of forty life members known as the *imortais*. The Academia's activities include publication of reference books, promotion of literary prizes, and running a library, museum and archive.

acadêmico, -a [aka'demiku, a] ADJ, M/F academic

açafrão [asa'frãw] M saffron

acalmar [akaw'mar] VT to calm ▶ VI (*vento etc*) to abate; **acalmar-se** VR to calm down

acampamento [akãpa'mẽtu] M camping; (*Mil*) camp, encampment

acampar [akã'par] VI to camp

acanhado, -a [aka'ɲadu, a] ADJ shy

acanhamento [akaɲa'mẽtu] M shyness

acanhar-se [aka'ɲarsi] VR to be shy

ação [a'sãw] (*pl* **-ões**) F action; (*ato*) act, deed; (*Mil*) battle; (*enredo*) plot; (*Jur*) lawsuit; (*Com*) share; **~ ordinária/preferencial** (*Com*) ordinary/preference share

acarajé [akara'ʒɛ] M (*Culin*) beans fried in palm oil

acarretar [akahe'tar] VT to result in, bring about

acaso [a'kazu] M chance; **ao ~** at random; **por ~** by chance

acatar [aka'tar] VT to respect; (*lei*) to obey

aceitação [asejta'sãw] F acceptance; (*aprovação*) approval

aceitar [asej'tar] VT to accept; (*aprovar*) to approve; **aceitável** [asej'tavew] (*pl* **-eis**) ADJ acceptable; **aceito, -a** [a'sejtu, a] PP *de* **aceitar**

acelerador [aselera'dor] M accelerator

acelerar [asele'rar] VT, VI to accelerate; **~ o passo** to go faster

acenar [ase'nar] VI (*com a mão*) to wave; (*com a cabeça*) to nod

acender [asẽ'der] VT (*cigarro, fogo*) to light; (*luz*) to switch on; (*fig*) to excite, inflame

acento [a'sẽtu] M accent; (*de intensidade*) stress; **acentuar** [asẽ'twar] VT to accent; (*salientar*) to stress, emphasize

acepção [asep'sãw] (*pl* **-ões**) F (*de uma palavra*) sense

acerca [a'serka] ADV: **~ de** about, concerning

acertado, -a [aser'tadu, a] ADJ right, correct; (*sensato*) sensible

acertar [aser'tar] VT (*ajustar*) to put right; (*relógio*) to set; (*alvo*) to hit; (*acordo*) to reach; (*pergunta*) to get right

▶ VI to get it right, be right; **~ o caminho** to find the right way; **~ com** to hit upon

aceso, -a [a'sezu, a] PP *de* **acender** ▶ ADJ (*luz, gás, TV*) on; (*fogo*) alight; (*excitado*) excited; (*furioso*) furious

acessar [ase'sar] VT (*Comput*) to access

acessível [ase'sivew] (*pl* **-eis**) ADJ accessible; (*pessoa*) approachable; (*preço*) reasonable, affordable

acesso [a'sɛsu] M access; (*Med*) fit, attack

acessório, -a [ase'sɔrju, a] ADJ (*máquina, equipamento*) backup ▶ M accessory

achado [a'ʃadu] M find, discovery; (*pechincha*) bargain; (*sorte*) godsend

achar [a'ʃar] VT (*descobrir*) to find; (*pensar*) to think; **achar-se** VR to think (that) one is; (*encontrar-se*) to be; **~ de fazer** (*resolver*) to decide to do; **o que é que você acha disso?** what do you think of it?; **acho que sim** I think so

achatar [aʃa'tar] VT to squash, flatten

acidentado, -a [aside'tadu, a] ADJ (*terreno*) rough; (*estrada*) bumpy; (*viagem*) eventful; (*vida*) difficult ▶ M/F injured person

acidental [aside'taw] (*pl* **-ais**) ADJ accidental

acidente [asi'detʃi] M accident; **por ~** by accident; **~ de trânsito** road accident

acidez [asi'dez] F acidity

ácido, -a ['asidu, a] ADJ acid; (*azedo*) sour ▶ M acid

acima [a'sima] ADV above; (*para cima*) up ▶ PREP: **~ de** above; (*além de*) beyond; **mais ~** higher up; **rio ~** up river; **passar rua ~** to go up the street; **~ de 1000** more than 1000

acionar [asjo'nar] VT to set in motion; (*máquina*) to operate; (*Jur*) to sue

acionista [asjo'nista] M/F shareholder

acirrado, -a [asi'hadu, a] ADJ (*luta, competição*) tough

acirrar [asi'har] VT to incite, stir up

aclamar [akla'mar] VT to acclaim; (*aplaudir*) to applaud

aço ['asu] M steel

acocorar-se [akoko'rarsi] VR to squat, crouch

acode [a'kɔdʒi] VB *ver* **acudir**

ações [a'sõjs] FPL *de* **ação**

acolá [ako'la] ADV over there

acolchoado [akow'ʃwadu] M quilt

acolhedor, a [akoʎe'dor(a)] ADJ welcoming; (*hospitaleiro*) hospitable

acolher [ako'ʎer] VT to welcome; (*abrigar*) to shelter; (*aceitar*) to accept;

acolher-se VR to shelter; **acolhida**
[akoˈʎida] F (recepção) reception,
welcome; (refúgio) refuge; **acolhimento**
[akoʎiˈmẽtu] M = **acolhida**
acomodação [akomodaˈsãw] (pl -ões) F
accommodation; (arranjo) arrangement;
(adaptação) adaptation
acomodar [akomoˈdar] VT to
accommodate; (arrumar) to arrange;
(adaptar) to adapt
acompanhamento [akõpaɲaˈmẽtu] M
attendance; (cortejo) procession; (Mús)
accompaniment; (Culin) side dish
acompanhante [akõpaˈɲãtʃi] M/F
companion; (Mús) accompanist; (de
idoso, doente) carer (BRIT), caregiver (US)
acompanhar [akõpaˈɲar] VT to
accompany
aconchegante [akõʃeˈɡãtʃi] ADJ cosy
(BRIT), cozy (US)
aconselhar [akõseˈʎar] VT to advise;
aconselhar-se VR: **~-se com** to consult
acontecer [akõteˈser] VI to happen;
acontecimento [akõtesiˈmẽtu] M event
acordar [akorˈdar] VT to wake (up);
(concordar) to agree (on) ▶ VI to wake up
acorde [aˈkɔrdʒi] M chord
acordo [aˈkordu] M agreement; **"de ~!"**
"agreed!"; **de ~ com** (pessoa) in
agreement with; (conforme) in
accordance with; **estar de ~** to agree
Açores [aˈsoris] MPL: **os ~** the Azores;
açoriano, -a [asoˈrjanu, a] ADJ, M/F
Azorean
acossar [akoˈsar] VT (perseguir) to
pursue; (atormentar) to harass
acostamento [akostaˈmẽtu] M hard
shoulder (BRIT), berm (US)
acostumado, -a [akostuˈmadu, a] ADJ
usual, customary; **estar ~ a algo** to be
used to sth
acostumar [akostuˈmar] VT to
accustom; **acostumar-se** VR: **~-se a** to
get used to
açougue [aˈsoɡi] M butcher's (shop);
açougueiro [asoˈɡejru] M butcher
acovardar-se [akovarˈdarsi] VR
(desanimar) to lose courage; (amedrontar-
se) to flinch, cower
acreditado, -a [akredʒiˈtadu, a] ADJ
accredited
acreditar [akredʒiˈtar] VT to believe;
(Com) to credit; (afiançar) to guarantee
▶ VI: **~ em** to believe in
acrescentar [akresẽˈtar] VT to add
açúcar [aˈsukar] M sugar; **açucareiro**
[asukaˈrejru] M sugar bowl
açude [aˈsudʒi] M dam

acudir [akuˈdʒir] VT (ir em socorro) to
help, assist ▶ VI (responder) to reply,
respond; **~ a** to come to the aid of
acumular [akumuˈlar] VT to
accumulate; (reunir) to collect; (funções)
to combine
acusação [akuzaˈsãw] (pl -ões) F
accusation, charge; (Jur) prosecution
acusar [akuˈzar] VT to accuse; (revelar) to
reveal; (culpar) to blame; **~ o
recebimento de** to acknowledge
receipt of
acústico, -a [aˈkustʃiku, a] ADJ acoustic
adaptar [adapˈtar] VT to adapt;
(acomodar) to fit; **adaptar-se** VR: **~-se a**
to adapt to
adega [aˈdɛɡa] F cellar
ademais [adʒiˈmajs] ADV besides,
moreover
adentro [aˈdẽtru] ADV inside, in; **mata ~**
into the woods
adequado, -a [adeˈkwadu, a] ADJ
appropriate
adereço [adeˈresu] M adornment;
adereços MPL (Teatro) stage props
aderente [adeˈrẽtʃi] ADJ adhesive, sticky
▶ M/F supporter
aderir [adeˈrir] VI to adhere
adesão [adeˈzãw] F adhesion;
(patrocínio) support
adesivo, -a [adeˈzivu, a] ADJ adhesive,
sticky ▶ M adhesive tape; (Med) sticking
plaster
adestrar [adesˈtrar] VT to train; (cavalo)
to break in
adeus [aˈdews] EXCL goodbye!
adiantado, -a [adʒjãˈtadu, a] ADJ
advanced; (relógio) fast; **chegar ~** to
arrive ahead of time; **pagar ~** to pay in
advance
adiantamento [adʒjãtaˈmẽtu] M
progress; (dinheiro) advance (payment)
adiantar [adʒjãˈtar] VT (dinheiro, salário)
to advance; (relógio) to put forward; **não
adianta reclamar/insistir** there's no
point ou it's no use complaining/insisting
adiante [aˈdʒjãtʃi] ADV (na frente) in front;
(para a frente) forward; **mais ~** further
on; (no futuro) later on
adiar [aˈdʒjar] VT to postpone, put off;
(sessão) to adjourn
adição [adʒiˈsãw] (pl -ões) F addition;
(Mat) sum; **adicionar** [adʒisjoˈnar] VT to
add
adido, -a [aˈdʒidu, a] M/F attaché
adiro [aˈdiru] VB ver **aderir**
adivinhar [adʒiviˈɲar] VT to guess;
(ler a sorte) to foretell ▶ VI to guess;

~ o pensamento de alguém to read sb's mind; **adivinho, -a** [adʒi'viɲu, a] M/F fortune-teller

adjetivo [adʒe'tʃivu] M adjective

adjudicar [adʒudʒi'kar] VT to award, grant

administração [adʒiministra'sãw] (*pl -ões*) F administration; (*direção*) management; (*comissão*) board

administrador, a [adʒiministra'dor(a)] M/F administrator; (*diretor*) director; (*gerente*) manager

administrar [adʒiminis'trar] VT to administer, manage; (*governar*) to govern

admiração [adʒimira'sãw] F wonder; (*estima*) admiration; **ponto de ~** (*PT*) exclamation mark

admirado, -a [adʒimi'radu, a] ADJ astonished, surprised

admirar [adʒimi'rar] VT to admire; **admirar-se** VR: **~-se de** to be astonished *ou* surprised at; **admirável** [adʒimi'ravew] (*pl -eis*) ADJ amazing

admissão [adʒimi'sãw] (*pl -ões*) F admission; (*consentimento para entrar*) admittance; (*de escola*) intake

admitir [adʒimi'tʃir] VT to admit; (*permitir*) to allow; (*funcionário*) to take on

adoção [ado'sãw] F adoption

adoçar [ado'sar] VT to sweeten

adoecer [adoe'ser] VI to fall ill ▶ VT to make ill; **~ de** *ou* **com** to fall ill with

adoidado, -a [adoj'dadu, a] ADJ crazy

adolescente [adole'sẽtʃi] ADJ, M/F adolescent

adorar [ado'rar] VT to adore; (*venerar*) to worship

adormecer [adorme'ser] VI to fall asleep; (*entorpecer-se*) to go numb; **adormecido, -a** [adorme'sidu, a] ADJ sleeping ▶ M/F sleeper

adorno [a'dornu] M adornment

adotar [ado'tar] VT to adopt; **adotivo, -a** [ado'tʃivu, a] ADJ (*filho*) adopted

adquirir [adʒiki'rir] VT to acquire

Adriático, -a [a'drjatʃiku, a] ADJ: **o (mar) ~** the Adriatic (Sea)

adro ['adru] M (church) forecourt; (*em volta da igreja*) churchyard

adulação [adula'sãw] F flattery

adulterar [aduwte'rar] VT to adulterate; (*contas*) to falsify ▶ VI to commit adultery

adultério [aduw'terju] M adultery

adulto, -a [a'duwtu, a] ADJ, M/F adult

advento [ad'vẽtu] M advent; **o A~** Advent

advérbio [adʒ'vɛrbju] M adverb

adverso, -a [adʒi'vɛrsu, a] ADJ adverse; (*oposto*): **~ a** opposed to

advertência [adʒiver'tẽsja] F warning

advertir [adʒiver'tʃir] VT to warn; (*repreender*) to reprimand; (*chamar a atenção a*) to draw attention to

advogado, -a [adʒivo'gadu, a] M/F lawyer

advogar [adʒivo'gar] VT to advocate; (*Jur*) to plead ▶ VI to practise (*BRIT*) *ou* practice (*US*) law

aéreo, -a [a'ɛrju, a] ADJ air *atr*

aerobarco [aero'barku] M jetfoil

aeromoço, -a [aero'mosu, a] (*BR*) M/F flight attendant

aeronáutica [aero'nawtʃika] F air force; (*ciência*) aeronautics *sg*

aeronave [aero'navi] F aircraft

aeroporto [aero'portu] M airport

aerossol [aero'sɔw] (*pl -óis*) M aerosol

afã [a'fã] M (*entusiasmo*) enthusiasm; (*diligência*) diligence; (*ânsia*) eagerness; (*esforço*) effort

afagar [afa'gar] VT to caress; (*cabelo*) to stroke

afastado, -a [afas'tadu, a] ADJ (*distante*) remote; (*isolado*) secluded; **manter-se ~** to keep to o.s.

afastamento [afasta'mẽtu] M removal; (*distância*) distance; (*de pessoal*) lay-off

afastar [afas'tar] VT to remove; (*separar*) to separate; (*ideia*) to put out of one's mind; (*pessoal*) to lay off; **afastar-se** VR to move away

afável [a'favew] (*pl -eis*) ADJ friendly

afazeres [afa'zeris] MPL business *sg*; (*dever*) duties, tasks; **~ domésticos** household chores

afeição [afej'sãw] F affection, fondness; (*dedicação*) devotion; **afeiçoado, -a** [afej'swadu, a] ADJ: **afeiçoado a** (*amoroso*) fond of; (*devotado*) devoted to; **afeiçoar-se** [afej'swarsi] VR: **afeiçoar-se a** to take a liking to

afeito, -a [a'fejtu, a] ADJ: **~ a** accustomed to, used to

aferrado, -a [afe'hadu, a] ADJ obstinate, stubborn

afetar [afe'tar] VT to affect; (*fingir*) to feign

afetivo, -a [afe'tʃivu, a] ADJ affectionate; (*problema*) emotional

afeto [a'fetu] M affection; **afetuoso, -a** [afe'twozu, ɔza] ADJ affectionate

afiado, -a [a'fjadu, a] ADJ sharp; (*pessoa*) well-trained

afiar [a'fjar] VT to sharpen

aficionado, -a [afisjo'nadu, a] M/F enthusiast

afilhado, -a [afi'ʎadu, a] M/F godson/goddaughter

afim [a'fĩ] (*pl* **-ns**) ADJ (*semelhante*) similar; (*consanguíneo*) related ▶ M/F relative, relation

afinado, -a [afi'nadu, a] ADJ in tune

afinal [afi'naw] ADV at last, finally; **~ (de contas)** after all

afinar [afi'nar] VT (*Mús*) to tune

afinco [a'fĩku] M tenacity, persistence

afins [a'fĩs] PL *de* **afim**

afirmação [afirma'sãw] (*pl* **-ões**) F affirmation; (*declaração*) statement

afirmar [afir'mar] VT, VI to affirm, assert; (*declarar*) to declare

afirmativo, -a [afirma'tʃivu, a] ADJ affirmative

afixar [afik'sar] VT (*cartazes*) to stick, post

aflição [afli'sãw] F affliction; (*ansiedade*) anxiety; (*angústia*) anguish

afligir [afli'ʒir] VT to distress; (*atormentar*) to torment; (*inquietar*) to worry; **afligir-se** VR: **~-se com** to worry about; **aflito, -a** [a'flitu, a] PP *de* **afligir** ▶ ADJ distressed, anxious

afluência [a'flwẽsja] F affluence; (*corrente copiosa*) flow; (*de pessoas*) stream; **afluente** [a'flwẽtʃi] ADJ copious; (*rico*) affluent ▶ M tributary

afobação [afoba'sãw] F fluster; (*ansiedade*) panic

afobado, -a [afo'badu, a] ADJ flustered; (*ansioso*) panicky, nervous

afobar [afo'bar] VT to fluster; (*deixar ansioso*) to make nervous *ou* panicky ▶ VI to get flustered; to panic, get nervous; **afobar-se** VR to get flustered

afogar [afo'gar] VT to drown ▶ VI (*Auto*) to flood; **afogar-se** VR to drown

afoito, -a [a'fojtu, a] ADJ bold, daring

afortunado, -a [afortu'nadu, a] ADJ fortunate, lucky

África ['afrika] F: **a ~** Africa; **a ~ do Sul** South Africa; **africano, -a** [afri'kanu, a] ADJ, M/F African

afro-brasileiro, -a [afru-] (*pl* **-s**) ADJ Afro-Brazilian

afronta [a'frõta] F insult, affront; **afrontar** [afrõ'tar] VT to insult; (*ofender*) to offend

afrouxar [afro'ʃar] VT (*desapertar*) to slacken; (*soltar*) to loosen ▶ VI to come loose

afta ['afta] F (mouth) ulcer

afugentar [afuʒẽ'tar] VT to drive away, put to flight

afundar [afũ'dar] VT to sink; (*cavidade*) to deepen; **afundar-se** VR to sink

agachar-se [aga'ʃarsi] VR (*acaçapar-se*) to crouch, squat; (*curvar-se*) to stoop

agarrar [aga'har] VT to seize, grasp; **agarrar-se** VR: **~-se a** to cling to, hold on to

agasalhar [agaza'ʎar] VT to dress warmly, wrap up; **agasalhar-se** VR to wrap o.s. up

agasalho [aga'zaʎu] M (*casaco*) coat; (*suéter*) sweater

ágeis ['aʒejs] PL *de* **ágil**

agência [a'ʒẽsja] F agency; (*escritório*) office; **~ de correio** (BR) post office; **~ de viagens** travel agency

agenda [a'ʒẽda] F diary; **~ eletrônica** personal organizer

agente [a'ʒẽtʃi] M/F agent; (*de polícia*) police officer

ágil ['aʒiw] (*pl* **-eis**) ADJ agile

agir [a'ʒir] VI to act

agitação [aʒita'sãw] (*pl* **-ões**) F agitation; (*perturbação*) disturbance; (*inquietação*) restlessness

agitado, -a [aʒi'tadu, a] ADJ agitated, disturbed; (*inquieto*) restless

agitar [aʒi'tar] VT to agitate, disturb; (*sacudir*) to shake; (*cauda*) to wag; (*mexer*) to stir; **agitar-se** VR to get upset; (*mar*) to get rough

aglomeração [aglomera'sãw] (*pl* **-ões**) F gathering; (*multidão*) crowd

aglomerar [aglome'rar] VT to heap up, pile up; **aglomerar-se** VR (*multidão*) to crowd together

agonia [ago'nia] F agony, anguish; (*ânsia da morte*) death throes *pl*; **agonizante** [agoni'zãtʃi] ADJ dying ▶ M/F dying person; **agonizar** [agoni'zar] VI to be dying; (*afligir-se*) to agonize

agora [a'gɔra] ADV now; **~ mesmo** right now; (*há pouco*) a moment ago; **até ~** so far, up to now; **por ~** for now

agosto [a'gostu] M August

agouro [a'goru] M omen

agraciar [agra'sjar] VT to decorate

agradar [agra'dar] VT to please; (*fazer agrados a*) to be nice to ▶ VI to be pleasing; (*satisfazer*) to go down well

agradável [agra'davew] (*pl* **-eis**) ADJ pleasant

agradecer [agrade'ser] VT: **~ algo a alguém, ~ a alguém por algo** to thank sb for sth; **agradecido, -a** [agrade'sidu, a] ADJ grateful; **mal**

agradecido ungrateful; **agradecimento** [agradesi'mẽtu] M gratitude; **agradecimentos** (*gratidão*) thanks

agrado [a'gradu] M: **fazer um ~ a alguém** (*afagar*) to be affectionate with sb; (*ser agradável*) to be nice to sb

agrário, -a [a'grarju, a] ADJ agrarian; **reforma agrária** land reform

agravante [agra'vãtʃi] ADJ aggravating ▶ F aggravating circumstance

agravar [agra'var] VT to aggravate, make worse; **agravar-se** VR (*piorar*) to get worse

agredir [agre'dʒir] VT to attack; (*insultar*) to insult

agregar [agre'gar] VT (*juntar*) to collect; (*acrescentar*) to add

agressão [agre'sãw] (*pl* -**ões**) F aggression; (*ataque*) attack; (*assalto*) assault

agressivo, -a [agre'sivu, a] ADJ aggressive

agressões [agre'sõjs] FPL *de* **agressão**

agreste [a'grɛstʃi] ADJ rural, rustic; (*terreno*) wild

agrião [a'grjãw] M watercress

agrícola [a'grikola] ADJ agricultural

agricultor [agrikuw'tor] M farmer

agricultura [agrikuw'tura] F agriculture, farming

agrido [a'gridu] VB *ver* **agredir**

agridoce [agri'dosi] ADJ bittersweet

agronegócio [agrone'gɔsju] M agribusiness

agronomia [agrono'mia] F agronomy

agropecuária [agrope'kwarja] F farming, agriculture

agrupar [agru'par] VT to group; **agrupar-se** VR to group together

agrura [a'grura] F bitterness

água ['agwa] F water; **águas** FPL (*mar*) waters; (*chuvas*) rain *sg*; (*maré*) tides; **~ abaixo/acima** downstream/ upstream; **dar ~ na boca** (*comida*) to be mouthwatering; **estar na ~** (*bêbado*) to be drunk; **fazer ~** (*Náut*) to leak; **~ benta** holy water; **~ corrente** running water; **~ de coco** coconut water; **~ doce** fresh water; **~ dura/leve** hard/soft water; **~ mineral** mineral water; **~ oxigenada** peroxide; **~ salgada** salt water; **~ sanitária** household bleach

água-de-colônia (*pl* **águas-de-colônia**) F eau-de-cologne

aguado, -a [a'gwadu, a] ADJ watery

aguardar [agwar'dar] VT to wait for; (*contar com*) to expect ▶ VI to wait

aguardente [agwar'dẽtʃi] M spirit (BRIT), liquor (US)

aguçado, -a [agu'sadu, a] ADJ pointed; (*espírito, sentidos*) acute

agudo, -a [a'gudu, a] ADJ sharp; shrill; (*intenso*) acute

aguentar [agwẽ'tar] VT (*muro etc*) to hold up; (*dor, injustiças*) to stand, put up with; (*peso*) to withstand ▶ VI to last; **aguentar-se** VR to remain, hold on; **~ fazer algo** to manage to do sth; **não ~ de** not to be able to stand

águia ['agja] F eagle; (*fig*) genius

agulha [a'guʎa] F (*de coser, tricô*) needle; (*Náut*) compass; (*Ferro*) points *pl* (BRIT), switch (US); **trabalho de ~** needlework

ai [aj] EXCL (*suspiro*) oh!; (*de dor*) ouch! ▶ M (*suspiro*) sigh; (*gemido*) groan; **ai de mim** poor me!

aí [a'i] ADV there; (*então*) then; **por aí** (*em lugar indeterminado*) somewhere over there, thereabouts; **espera aí** wait!, hang on a minute!; **está aí!** (*col*) right!; **e aí?** and then what?

AIDS ['ajdʒs] F AIDS

ainda [a'ĩda] ADV still; (*mesmo*) even; **~ agora** just now; **~ assim** even so, nevertheless; **~ bem** just as well; **~ por cima** on top of all that, in addition; **~ não** not yet; **~ que** even if; **maior ~** even bigger

aipo ['ajpu] M celery

ajeitar [aʒej'tar] VT (*adaptar*) to fit, adjust; (*arranjar*) to arrange; **ajeitar-se** VR to adapt

ajo ['aʒu] VB *ver* **agir**

ajoelhar [aʒweʎar] VI to kneel (down); **ajoelhar-se** VR to kneel down

ajuda [a'ʒuda] F help; (*subsídio*) grant, subsidy; **dar ~ a alguém** to lend *ou* give sb a hand; **~ de custo** allowance; **ajudante** [aʒu'dãtʃi] M/F assistant, helper; (*Mil*) adjutant

ajudar [aʒu'dar] VT to help

ajuizado, -a [aʒwi'zadu, a] ADJ (*sensato*) sensible; (*sábio*) wise; (*prudente*) discreet

ajuntamento [aʒũta'mẽtu] M gathering

ajustagem [aʒus'taʒẽ] (BR) (*pl* -**ns**) F (*Tec*) adjustment

ajustamento [aʒusta'mẽtu] M adjustment; (*de contas*) settlement

ajustar [aʒus'tar] VT to adjust; (*conta, disputa*) to settle; (*acomodar*) to fit; (*roupa*) to take in; (*preço*) to agree on; **ajustar-se** VR: **~-se a** to conform to; (*adaptar-se*) to adapt to

ajuste [a'ʒustʃi] M (acordo) agreement; (de contas) settlement; (adaptação) adjustment

ala ['ala] F (fileira) row; (passagem) aisle; (de edifício, exército, ave) wing

alagar [ala'gar] VT, VI to flood

alameda [ala'meda] F (avenida) avenue; (arvoredo) grove

alarde [a'lardʒi] M ostentation; (jactância) boasting; **fazer ~ de** to boast about; **alardear** [alar'dʒjar] VT to show off; (gabar-se de) to boast of ▶ VI to boast; **alardear-se** VR to boast

alargar [alar'gar] VT to extend; (fazer mais largo) to widen, broaden; (afrouxar) to loosen, slacken

alarma [a'larma] F alarm; (susto) panic; (tumulto) tumult; (vozearia) outcry; **dar o sinal de ~** to raise the alarm; **~ de roubo** burglar alarm; **alarmante** [alar'mãtʃi] ADJ alarming; **alarmar** [alar'mar] VT to alarm; **alarmar-se** VR to be alarmed

alarme [a'larmi] M = **alarma**

alastrar [alas'trar] VT to scatter; (disseminar) to spread; **alastrar-se** VR (epidemia, rumor) to spread

alavanca [ala'vãka] F lever; (pé de cabra) crowbar; **~ de mudanças** gear lever

albergue [aw'bɛrgi] M (estalagem) inn; (refúgio) hospice, shelter; **~ noturno** hotel; **~ para jovens** youth hostel

álbum ['awbũ] (pl **-ns**) M album; **~ de recortes** scrapbook

alça ['awsa] F strap; (asa) handle; (de fusil) sight

alcachofra [awka'ʃofra] F artichoke

alcançar [awkã'sar] VT to reach; (estender) to hand, pass; (obter) to obtain, get; (atingir) to attain; (compreender) to understand; (desfalcar): **~ uma firma em $1 milhão** to embezzle $1 million from a firm

alcance [aw'kãsi] M reach; (competência) power; (compreensão) understanding; (de tiro, visão) range; **ao ~ de** within reach ou range of; **ao ~ da voz** within earshot; **de grande ~** far-reaching; **fora do ~ da mão** out of reach; **fora do ~ de alguém** beyond sb's grasp

alcaparra [awka'paha] F caper

alcatrão [awka'trãw] M tar

álcool ['awkɔw] M alcohol; **alcoólatra** [aw'kɔlatra] M/F alcoholic; **alcoólico, -a** [aw'kɔliku, a] ADJ, M/F alcoholic

Alcorão [awko'rãw] M Koran

alcova [aw'kova] F bedroom

alcunha [aw'kuɲa] F nickname

aldeão, -deã [aw'dʒjãw, jã] (pl **-ões/-s**) M/F villager

aldeia [aw'deja] F village

aldeões [aw'dʒjõjs] MPL de **aldeão**

alecrim [ale'krĩ] M rosemary

alegar [ale'gar] VT to allege; (Jur) to plead

alegoria [alego'ria] F allegory

alegórico, -a [ale'gɔriku, a] ADJ allegorical; **carro ~** float

alegrar [ale'grar] VT to cheer (up), gladden; (ambiente) to brighten up; (animar) to liven (up); **alegrar-se** VR to cheer up

alegre [a'lɛgri] ADJ cheerful; (contente) happy, glad; (cores) bright; (embriagado) merry, tight; **alegria** [ale'gria] F joy, happiness

aleijado, -a [alej'ʒadu, a] ADJ lame, crippled ▶ M/F lame person

aleijar [alej'ʒar] VT to maim

além [a'lẽj] ADV (lá ao longe) over there; (mais adiante) further on ▶ M: **o ~** the hereafter ▶ PREP: **~ de** beyond; (no outro lado de) on the other side of; (para mais de) over; (ademais de) apart from, besides; **~ disso** moreover; **mais ~** further

alemã [ale'mã] F de **alemão**

alemães [ale'mãjs] MPL de **alemão**

Alemanha [ale'mãɲa] F: **a ~** Germany

alemão, -mã [ale'mãw, 'mã] (pl **-ães/-s**) ADJ, M/F German ▶ M (Ling) German

alento [a'lẽtu] M (fôlego) breath; (ânimo) courage; **dar ~** to encourage; **tomar ~** to draw breath

alergia [aler'ʒia] F: **~ (a)** allergy (to); (fig) aversion (to); **alérgico, -a** [a'lɛrʒiku, a] ADJ: **alérgico (a)** allergic (to)

alerta [a'lɛrta] ADJ alert ▶ ADV on the alert ▶ M alert

alfabetizar [awfabetʃi'zar] VT to teach to read and write; **alfabetizar-se** VR to learn to read and write

alfabeto [awfa'bɛtu] M alphabet

alface [aw'fasi] F lettuce

alfaiate [awfa'jatʃi] M tailor

alfândega [aw'fãdʒiga] F customs pl, customs house; **alfandegário, -a** [awfãde'garju, a] M/F customs officer

alfazema [awfa'zema] F lavender

alfinete [awfi'netʃi] M pin; **~ de segurança** safety pin

alga ['awga] F seaweed

Algarve [aw'garvi] M: **o ~** the Algarve

algazarra [awga'zaha] F uproar, racket

álgebra ['awʒebra] F algebra

algemas [aw'ʒɛmas] FPL handcuffs

algo ['awgu] ADV somewhat, rather ▶ PRON something; (*qualquer coisa*) anything

algodão [awgo'dãw] M cotton; **~ (hidrófilo)** cotton wool (*BRIT*), absorbent cotton (*US*)

alguém [aw'gēj] PRON someone, somebody; (*em frases interrogativas ou negativas*) anyone, anybody

algum, a [aw'gũ, 'guma] ADJ some; (*em frases interrogativas ou negativas*) any ▶ PRON one; (*no plural*) some; (*negativa*): **de modo ~** in no way; **coisa ~a** nothing; **~ dia** one day; **~ tempo** for a while; **~a coisa** something; **~a vez** sometime

alheio, -a [a'ʎeju, a] ADJ (*de outra pessoa*) someone else's; (*de outras pessoas*) other people's; (*estranho*) alien; (*estrangeiro*) foreign; (*impróprio*) irrelevant

alho ['aʎu] M garlic

ali [a'li] ADV there; **até ~** up to there; **por ~** around there; (*direção*) that way; **~ por** (*tempo*) round about; **de ~ por diante** from then on; **~ dentro** in there

aliado, -a [a'ljadu, a] ADJ allied ▶ M/F ally

aliança [a'ljãsa] F alliance; (*anel*) wedding ring

aliar [a'ljar] VT to ally; **aliar-se** VR to form an alliance

aliás [a'ljajs] ADV (*a propósito*) as a matter of fact; (*ou seja*) rather, that is; (*contudo*) nevertheless; (*diga-se de passagem*) incidentally

álibi ['alibi] M alibi

alicate [ali'katʃi] M pliers *pl*; **~ de unhas** nail clippers *pl*

alienação [aljena'sãw] F alienation; (*de bens*) transfer (of property); **~ mental** insanity

alienado, -a [alje'nadu, a] ADJ alienated; (*demente*) insane; (*bens*) transferred ▶ M/F lunatic

alienar [alje'nar] VT (*bens*) to transfer; (*afastar*) to alienate

alimentação [alimẽta'sãw] F (*alimentos*) food; (*ação*) feeding; (*nutrição*) nourishment; (*Elet*) supply

alimentar [alimẽ'tar] VT to feed; (*fig*) to nurture ▶ ADJ (*produto*) food *atr*; (*hábitos*) eating *atr*; **alimentar-se** VR: **~-se de** to feed on

alimento [ali'mẽtu] M food; (*nutrição*) nourishment

alisar [ali'zar] VT to smooth; (*cabelo*) to straighten; (*acariciar*) to stroke

aliviar [ali'vjar] VT to relieve

alívio [a'livju] M relief

alma ['awma] F soul; (*entusiasmo*) enthusiasm; (*caráter*) character

almejar [awme'ʒar] VT to long for, yearn for

almirante [awmi'rãtʃi] M admiral

almoçar [awmo'sar] VI to have lunch ▶ VT: **~ peixe** to have fish for lunch

almoço [aw'mosu] M lunch; **pequeno ~** (*PT*) breakfast

almofada [awmo'fada] F cushion; (*PT: travesseiro*) pillow

almoxarifado [awmoʃari'fadu] M storeroom

alô [a'lo] (*BR*) EXCL (*Tel*) hello!

alocar [alo'kar] VT to allocate

alojamento [aloʒa'mẽtu] M accommodation (*BRIT*), accommodations *pl* (*US*); (*habitação*) housing

alojar [alo'ʒar] VT to lodge; (*Mil*) to billet; **alojar-se** VR to stay

alongar [alõ'gar] VT to lengthen; (*prazo*) to extend; (*prolongar*) to prolong; (*braço*) to stretch out; **alongar-se** VR (*sobre um assunto*) to dwell

aloprado, -a [alo'pradu, a] (*col*) ADJ nutty

alpendre [aw'pẽdri] M (*telheiro*) shed; (*pórtico*) porch

Alpes ['awpis] MPL: **os ~** the Alps

alpinismo [awpi'nizmu] M mountaineering, climbing; **alpinista** [awpi'nista] M/F mountaineer, climber

alta ['awta] F (*de preços*) rise; (*de hospital*) discharge

altar [aw'tar] M altar

alterado, -a [awte'radu, a] ADJ bad-tempered, irritated

alterar [awte'rar] VT to alter; (*falsificar*) to falsify; **alterar-se** VR (*mudar-se*) to change; (*enfurecer-se*) to lose one's temper

alternar [awter'nar] VT, VI to alternate; **alternar-se** VR to alternate; (*por turnos*) to take turns

alternativa [awterna'tʃiva] F alternative

alternativo, -a [awterna'tʃivu, a] ADJ alternative; (*Elet*) alternating

alteza [aw'teza] F highness

altitude [awtʃi'tudʒi] F altitude

alto, -a ['awtu, a] ADJ high; (*pessoa*) tall; (*som*) loud; (*Geo*) upper ▶ ADV (*falar*) loudly, loud; (*voar*) high ▶ EXCL halt! ▶ M top, summit; **do ~** from above; **por ~** superficially; **alta fidelidade** high fidelity, hi-fi; **alta noite** dead of night

alto-falante (*pl* **-s**) M loudspeaker

altura [aw'tura] F height; (*momento*) point, juncture; (*altitude*) altitude; (*de um som*) pitch; **em que ~ da Rio Branco fica a livraria?** whereabouts in Rio Branco is the bookshop?; **nesta ~** at this juncture; **estar à ~ de** (*ser capaz de*) to be up to; **ter 1.80 metros de ~** to be 1.80 metres (BRIT) ou meters (US) tall

alucinado, -a [alusi'nadu, a] ADJ crazy

alugar [alu'gar] VT (*tomar de aluguel*) to rent, hire; (*dar de aluguel*) to let, rent out; **alugar-se** VR to let; **aluguel** [alu'gew] (*pl* **-éis**) (BR) M rent; (*ação*) renting; **aluguel de carro** car hire (BRIT) ou rental (US); **aluguer** [alu'gɛr] (PT) M = **aluguel**

alumínio [alu'minju] M aluminium (BRIT), aluminum (US)

aluno, -a [a'lunu, a] M/F pupil, student

alvejar [awve'ʒar] VT (*tomar como alvo*) to aim at; (*branquear*) bleach

alvenaria [awvena'ria] F masonry; **de ~** brick atr, brick-built

alvéolo [aw'vɛolu] M cavity

alvo, -a ['awvu, a] ADJ white ▶ M target

alvorada [awvo'rada] F dawn

alvorecer [awvore'ser] VI to dawn

alvoroço [awvo'rosu] M commotion; (*entusiasmo*) enthusiasm

amabilidade [amabili'dadʒi] F kindness; (*simpatia*) friendliness

amaciante [ama'sjãtʃi] M: **~ (de roupa)** fabric conditioner

amaciar [ama'sjar] VT (*tornar macio*) to soften; (*carro*) to run in

amado, -a [a'madu, a] M/F beloved, sweetheart

amador, a [ama'dor(a)] ADJ, M/F amateur

amadurecer [amadure'ser] VT, VI (*frutos*) to ripen; (*fig*) to mature

âmago ['amagu] M (*centro*) heart, core; (*medula*) pith; (*essência*) essence

amalgamar [amawga'mar] VT to amalgamate; (*combinar*) to fuse (BRIT), fuze (US), blend

amalucado, -a [amalu'kadu, a] ADJ crazy, whacky

amamentar [amamē'tar] VT, VI to breast-feed

amanhã [ama'ɲã] ADV, M tomorrow

amanhecer [amaɲe'ser] VI (*alvorecer*) to dawn; (*encontrar-se pela manhã*): **amanhecemos em Paris** we were in Paris at daybreak ▶ M dawn; **ao ~** at daybreak

amansar [amã'sar] VT (*animais*) to tame; (*cavalos*) to break in; (*aplacar*) to placate

amante [a'mãtʃi] M/F lover

amar [a'mar] VT to love; **eu te amo** I love you

amarelo, -a [ama'rɛlu, a] ADJ yellow ▶ M yellow

amargar [amar'gar] VT to make bitter; (*fig*) to embitter

amargo, -a [a'margu, a] ADJ bitter; **amargura** [amar'gura] F bitterness

amarrar [ama'har] VT to tie (up); (*Náut*) to moor; **~ a cara** to frown, scowl

amarrotar [amaho'tar] VT to crease

amassar [ama'sar] VT (*pão*) to knead; (*misturar*) to mix; (*papel*) to screw up; (*roupa*) to crease; (*carro*) to dent

amável [a'mavew] (*pl* **-eis**) ADJ kind

Amazonas [ama'zɔnas] M: **o ~** the Amazon

Amazônia [ama'zonja] F: **a ~** the Amazon region

> **Amazônia** is the region formed by the basin of the river Amazon (the river with the largest volume of water in the world) and its tributaries. With a total area of almost 7 million square kilometres, it stretches from the Atlantic to the Andes. Most of **Amazônia** is in Brazilian territory, although it also extends into Peru, Colombia, Venezuela and Bolivia. It contains the richest biodiversity and largest area of tropical rainforest in the world.

ambição [ambi'sãw] (*pl* **-ões**) F ambition; **ambicionar** [ābisjo'nar] VT to aspire to; **ambicioso, -a** [ābi'sjozu, ɔza] ADJ ambitious

ambidestro, -a [ābi'destru, a] ADJ ambidextrous

ambientar [ābjē'tar] VT (*filme etc*) to set; (*adaptar*) **~ alguém a algo** to get sb used to sth; **ambientar-se** VR to fit in

ambiente [ā'bjētʃi] M atmosphere; (*meio, Comput*) environment; **meio ~** environment; **temperatura ~** room temperature

ambíguo, -a [ā'bigwu, a] ADJ ambiguous

âmbito ['abitu] M extent; (*campo de ação*) scope, range

ambos, ambas ['abus, as] ADJ PL both

ambulância [ābu'lãsja] F ambulance

ambulante [ābu'lãtʃi] ADJ walking; (*errante*) wandering; (*biblioteca*) mobile

ambulatório [ābula'tɔrju] M outpatient department

ameaça [ame'asa] F threat; **~ de bomba** bomb scare; **ameaçar** [amea'sar] VT to threaten

amedrontar [amedrõ'tar] vt to scare, intimidate; **amedrontar-se** vr to be frightened

ameixa [a'mejʃa] f plum; (passa) prune

amém [a'mēj] excl amen!

amêndoa [a'mēdwa] f almond; **amendoeira** [amē'dwejra] f almond tree

amendoim [amēdo'ĩ] (pl -ns) m peanut

amenidade [ameni'dadʒi] f wellbeing; **amenidades** fpl (assuntos superficiais) small talk sg

amenizar [ameni'zar] vt (abrandar) to soften; (tornar agradável) to make pleasant; (facilitar) to ease

ameno, -a [a'mɛnu, a] adj pleasant; (clima) mild

América [a'mɛrika] f: **a ~** America; **a ~ do Norte/do Sul** North/South America; **a ~ Central/Latina** Central/Latin America; **americano, -a** [ameri'kanu, a] adj, m/f American

amestrar [ames'trar] vt to train

amianto [a'mjãtu] m asbestos

amido [a'midu] m starch

amigável [ami'gavew] (pl -eis) adj amicable

amígdala [a'migdala] f tonsil; **amigdalite** [amigda'litʃi] f tonsillitis

amigo, -a [a'migu, a] adj friendly ▶ m/f friend; **ser ~ de** to be friends with

amistoso, -a [amis'tozu, ɔza] adj friendly, cordial ▶ m (jogo) friendly

amiúde [a'mjudʒi] adv often, frequently

amizade [ami'zadʒi] f (relação) friendship; (simpatia) friendliness

amnistia [amnis'tia] (PT) f = **anistia**

amolação [amola'sãw] (pl -ões) f bother, annoyance

amolar [amo'lar] vt to sharpen; (aborrecer) to annoy, bother ▶ vi to be annoying

amolecer [amole'ser] vt to soften ▶ vi to soften; (abrandar-se) to relent

amônia [a'monja] f ammonia

amoníaco [amo'niaku] m ammonia

amontoar [amõ'twar] vt to pile up, accumulate; **~ riquezas** to amass a fortune

amor [a'mor] m love; **por ~ de** for the sake of; **fazer ~** to make love

amora [a'mɔra] f (amora-preta) blackberry; **~ silvestre** blackberry

amordaçar [amorda'sar] vt to gag

amoroso, -a [amo'rozu, ɔza] adj loving, affectionate

amor-perfeito (pl **amores-perfeitos**) m pansy

amortização [amortʃiza'sãw] f payment in instalments (BRIT) ou installments (US)

amortizar [amortʃi'zar] vt to pay in instalments (BRIT) ou installments (US)

amostra [a'mɔstra] f sample

amparar [ãpa'rar] vt to support; (ajudar) to assist; **amparar-se** vr: **~-se em/contra** to lean on/against

amparo [ã'paru] m support; (auxílio) help, assistance

ampliação [amplja'sãw] (pl -ões) f enlargement; (extensão) extension

ampliar [ã'pljar] vt to enlarge; (conhecimento) to broaden

amplificador [ãplifika'dor] m amplifier

amplificar [ãplifi'kar] vt to amplify

amplitude [ãpli'tudʒi] f (espaço) spaciousness; (fig: extensão) extent

amplo, -a ['ãplu, a] adj (sala) spacious; (conhecimento, sentido) broad; (possibilidade) ample

amputar [ãpu'tar] vt to amputate

Amsterdã [amister'dã] (BR) n Amsterdam

Amsterdão [amister'dãw] (PT) n = **Amsterdã**

amuado, -a [a'mwadu, a] adj sulky

aná [a'na] f de **anão**

anais [a'najs] mpl annals

analfabeto, -a [anawfa'bɛtu, a] adj, m/f illiterate

analgésico, -a [anaw'ʒeziku, a] adj analgesic ▶ m painkiller

analisar [anali'zar] vt to analyse; **análise** [a'nalizi] f analysis; **analista** [ana'lista] m/f analyst

ananás [ana'nas] (pl **ananases**) m (BR) variety of pineapple; (PT) pineapple

anão, anã [a'nãw, a'nã] (pl -ões/-s) m/f dwarf (pej)

anarquia [anar'kia] f anarchy; **anarquista** [anar'kista] m/f anarchist

anatomia [anato'mia] f anatomy

anca ['ãka] f (de pessoa) hip; (de animal) rump

ancião, anciã [ã'sjãw, ã'sjã] (pl -ões/-s) adj old ▶ m/f old man/woman; (de uma tribo) elder

anciões [ã'sjõjs] mpl de **ancião**

âncora ['ãkora] f anchor; **ancorar** [ãko'rar] vt, vi to anchor

andaime [ã'dajmi] m (Arq) scaffolding

andamento [ãda'mẽtu] m (progresso) progress; (rumo) course; (Mús) tempo; **em ~** in progress

andar [ã'dar] vi to walk; (máquina) to work; (progredir) to progress; (estar): **ela**

anda triste she's been sad lately ▶ M gait; (*pavimento*) floor, storey (BRIT), story (US); **anda!** hurry up!; **~ a cavalo** to ride; **~ de trem/avião/bicicleta** to travel by train/to fly/to ride a bike

Andes [ˈãdʒis] MPL: **os ~** the Andes

andorinha [ãdoˈriɲa] F (*pássaro*) swallow

anedota [aneˈdɔta] F anecdote

anel [aˈnɛw] (*pl* **-éis**) M ring; (*elo*) link; (*de cabelo*) curl; **~ de casamento** wedding ring

anestesia [anesteˈzia] F anaesthesia (BRIT), anesthesia (US); (*anestésico*) anaesthetic (BRIT), anesthetic (US)

anexar [anekˈsar] VT to annex; (*juntar*) to attach; (*documento*) to enclose; **anexo, -a** [aˈneksu, a] ADJ attached ▶ M annexe; (*em carta*) enclosure; (*em e-mail*) attachment; **segue em anexo** please find enclosed

anfitrião, -triã [ãfiˈtrjãw, ˈtrjã] (*pl* **-ões/-s**) M/F host/hostess

angina [ãˈʒina] F: **~ do peito** angina (pectoris)

Angola [ãˈgɔla] F Angola

angu [ãˈgu] M corn-meal purée

ângulo [ˈãgulu] M angle; (*canto*) corner

angústia [ãˈgustʃja] F anguish, distress

animado, -a [aniˈmadu, a] ADJ lively; (*alegre*) cheerful; **~ com** enthusiastic about

animador, a [animaˈdor(a)] ADJ encouraging ▶ M/F (BR TV) presenter; (*de festa*) entertainer; **~(a) de torcida** cheerleader

animal [aniˈmaw] (*pl* **-ais**) ADJ, M animal; **~ de estimação** pet (animal)

animar [aniˈmar] VT to liven up; (*encorajar*) to encourage; **animar-se** VR to cheer up; (*festa etc*) to liven up; **~-se a** to bring o.s. to

ânimo [ˈanimu] M (*coragem*) courage; **~!** cheer up!; **perder o ~** to lose heart; **recobrar o ~** to pluck up courage; (*alegrar-se*) to cheer up

aninhar [aniˈɲar] VT to nestle; **aninhar-se** VR to nestle

anis [aˈnis] M aniseed

anistia [anisˈtʃia] F amnesty

aniversário [aniverˈsarju] M anniversary; (*de nascimento*) birthday; (: *festa*) birthday party

anjo [ˈãʒu] M angel; **~ da guarda** guardian angel

ano [ˈanu] M year; **Feliz A~ Novo!** Happy New Year!; **o ~ que vem** next year; **por ~** per annum; **fazer ~s** to have a birthday;

ter dez ~s to be ten (years old); **dia de ~s** (PT) birthday; **~ letivo** academic year; (*da escola*) school year

anões [aˈnõjs] MPL *de* **anão**

anoitecer [anojteˈser] VI to grow dark ▶ M nightfall

anomalia [anomaˈlia] F anomaly

anônimo, -a [aˈnonimu, a] ADJ anonymous

anoraque [anoˈraki] M anorak

anormal [anorˈmaw] (*pl* **-ais**) ADJ abnormal; (*excepcional*) disabled; **anormalidade** [anormaliˈdadʒi] F abnormality

anotação [anotaˈsãw] (*pl* **-ões**) F annotation; (*nota*) note

anotar [anoˈtar] VT (*tomar nota*) to note down; (*esclarecer*) to annotate

anseio [ãˈseju] VB *ver* **ansiar**

ânsia [ˈãsja] F anxiety; (*desejo*): **~ (de)** longing (for); **ter ~s (de vômito)** to feel sick

ansiar [ãˈsjar] VI: **~ por** (*desejar*) to yearn for; **~ por fazer** to long to do

ansiedade [ãsjeˈdadʒi] F anxiety; (*desejo*) eagerness

ansioso, -a [ãˈsjozu, ɔza] ADJ anxious; (*desejoso*) eager

antártico, -a [ãˈtartʃiku, a] ADJ antarctic ▶ M: **o A~** the Antarctic

ante [ˈãtʃi] PREP (*na presença de*) before; (*em vista de*) in view of, faced with

antecedência [ãteseˈdẽsja] F: **com ~** in advance; **3 dias de ~** three days' notice

antecedente [ãteseˈdẽtʃi] ADJ preceding ▶ M antecedent; **antecedentes** MPL (*registro*) record *sg*; (*passado*) background *sg*

anteceder [ãteseˈder] VT to precede

antecipação [ãtesipaˈsãw] F anticipation; **com um mês de ~** a month in advance; **~ de pagamento** advance (payment)

antecipadamente [ãtesipadaˈmẽtʃi] ADV in advance, beforehand

antecipado, -a [ãtesiˈpadu, a] ADJ (*pagamento*) (in) advance

antecipar [ãtesiˈpar] VT to anticipate, forestall; (*adiantar*) to bring forward

antemão [anteˈmãw] ADV: **de ~** beforehand

antena [ãˈtena] F (*Bio*) antenna, feeler; (*Rádio*, *TV*) aerial

anteontem [ãtʃiˈõtẽ] ADV the day before yesterday

antepassado [ãtʃipaˈsadu] M ancestor

anterior [ãteˈrjor] ADJ previous; (*antigo*) former; (*de posição*) front

antes ['ãtʃis] ADV before; (*antigamente*) formerly; (*ao contrário*) rather ▶ PREP: **~ de** before; **o quanto ~** as soon as possible; **~ de partir** before leaving; **~ de tudo** above all; **~ que** before

anti- [ãtʃi] PREFIXO anti-

antiácido, -a [ã'tʃjasidu, a] ADJ, M antacid

antibiótico, -a [ãtʃi'bjɔtʃiku, a] ADJ, M antibiotic

anticaspa [ãtʃi'kaspa] ADJ INV anti-dandruff

anticlímax [ãtʃi'klimaks] M anticlimax

anticoncepcional [ãtʃikõsepsjo'naw] (*pl* **-ais**) ADJ, M contraceptive

antidepressivo, -a [ãtʃidepre'sivu, a] ADJ, M anti-depressant

antigamente [ãtʃiga'mẽtʃi] ADV formerly; (*no passado*) in the past

antiglobalização [ãtʃiglobaliza'sãw] F antiglobalization

antigo, -a [ã'tʃigu, a] ADJ old; (*histórico*) ancient; (*de estilo*) antique; (*chefe etc*) former

antiguidade [ãtʃigwi'dadʒi] F antiquity, ancient times *pl*; (*de emprego*) seniority; **antiguidades** FPL (*monumentos*) ancient monuments; (*artigos*) antiques

anti-horário, -a ADJ anticlockwise

antilhano, -a [ãtʃi'ʎanu, a] ADJ, M/F West Indian

Antilhas [ã'tʃiʎas] FPL: **as ~** the West Indies

antipatia [ãtʃipa'tʃia] F dislike; **antipático, -a** [ãtʃi'patʃiku, a] ADJ unpleasant, unfriendly

antipatizar [ãtʃipatʃi'zar] VI: **~ com alguém** to dislike sb

antiquado, -a [ãtʃi'kwadu, a] ADJ antiquated; (*fora de moda*) out of date, old-fashioned

antiquário, -a [ãtʃi'kwarju, a] M/F antique dealer ▶ M (*loja*) antique shop

antissemita ADJ anti-Semitic

antisséptico, -a ADJ, M antiseptic

antissocial (*pl* **-ais**) ADJ antisocial

antivírus [ãtʃi'virus] M INV (*Comput*) antivirus

antologia [ãtolo'ʒia] F anthology

anual [a'nwaw] (*pl* **-ais**) ADJ annual, yearly

anulação [anula'sãw] (*pl* **-ões**) F cancellation; (*de contrato, casamento*) annulment

anunciante [anũ'sjãtʃi] M (*Com*) advertiser

anunciar [anũ'sjar] VT to announce; (*Com*) to advertise

anúncio [a'nũsju] M announcement; (*Com*) advertisement; (*cartaz*) notice; **~s classificados** small ou classified ads

ânus ['anus] M INV anus

anzol [ã'zɔw] (*pl* **-óis**) M fish-hook

ao [aw] = **a + o**; *ver* **a**

aonde [a'õdʒi] ADV where; **~ quer que** wherever

aos [aws] = **a + os**; *ver* **a**

Ap. ABR = **apartamento**

apagado, -a [apa'gadu, a] ADJ (*fogo*) out; (*luz elétrica*) off

apagão [apa'gãw] (*pl* **-ões**) M power cut (*BRIT*), power outage (*US*)

apagar [apa'gar] VT to put out; (*luz elétrica*) to switch off; (*vela*) to blow out; (*com borracha*) to rub out, erase; **apagar-se** VR to go out

apaixonado, -a [apajʃo'nadu, a] ADJ (*discurso*) impassioned; (*pessoa*): **ele está ~ por ela** he is in love with her; **ele é ~ por tênis** he's mad about tennis

apaixonar-se [apajʃo'narsi] VR: **~ por** to fall in love with

apalpar [apaw'par] VT to touch, feel; (*Med*) to examine

apanhado [apa'ɲadu] M (*de flores*) bunch; (*resumo*) summary

apanhar [apa'ɲar] VT to catch; (*algo à mão, do chão*) to pick up; (*ir buscar, surra, táxi*) to get; (*flores, frutas*) to pick; (*agarrar*) to grab ▶ VI to get a beating; **~ sol/chuva** to sunbathe/get soaked

aparador [apara'dor] M sideboard

apara-lápis [apara'lapis] (*PT*) M INV pencil sharpener

aparar [apa'rar] VT (*cabelo*) to trim; (*lápis*) to sharpen; (*algo arremessado*) to catch

aparato [apa'ratu] M pomp; (*coleção*) array

aparecer [apare'ser] VI to appear; (*apresentar-se*) to turn up; (*ser publicado*) to be published; **~ em casa de alguém** to call on sb; **aparecimento** [aparesi'mẽtu] M appearance; (*publicação*) publication

aparelho [apa'reʎu] M apparatus; (*equipamento*) equipment; (*Pesca*) tackle; (*máquina*) machine; (*BR: fone*) telephone; **~ de barbear** electric shaver; **~ de chá** tea set; **~ de rádio/TV** radio/TV set; **~ doméstico** domestic appliance

aparência [apa'rẽsja] F appearance; **na ~** apparently; **sob a ~ de** under the guise of; **ter ~ de** to look like, seem

aparentar [aparẽ'tar] VT (*fingir*) to feign; (*parecer*) to give the appearance of

aparente [apa'rẽtʃi] ADJ apparent
aparição [apari'sãw] (pl -ões) F (visão) apparition; (fantasma) ghost
apartamento [aparta'mẽtu] M apartment, flat (BRIT)
apartar [apar'tar] VT to separate; **apartar-se** VR to separate
apatia [apa'tʃia] F apathy
apático, -a [a'patʃiku, a] ADJ apathetic
apavorado, -a [apavo'radu, a] ADJ terrified
apavorante [apavo'rãtʃi] ADJ terrifying
apavorar [apavo'rar] VT to terrify ▶ VI to be terrifying; **apavorar-se** VR to be terrified
apear-se [a'pjarsi] VR: ~ **de** (cavalo) to dismount from
apegado, -a [ape'gadu, a] ADJ: **ser** ~ **a** (gostar de) to be attached to
apegar-se [ape'garsi] VR: ~ **a** (afeiçoar-se) to become attached to
apego [a'pegu] M (afeição) attachment
apelar [ape'lar] VI to appeal; ~ **da sentença** (Jur) to appeal against the sentence; ~ **para** to appeal to; ~ **para a ignorância/violência** to resort to abuse/violence
apelido [ape'lidu] M (PT: nome de família) surname; (BR: alcunha) nickname
apelo [a'pelu] M appeal
apenas [a'pɛnas] ADV only
apendicite [apẽdʒi'sitʃi] F appendicitis
aperfeiçoar [aperfej'swar] VT to perfect; (melhorar) to improve
apertado, -a [aper'tadu, a] ADJ tight; (estreito) narrow; (sem dinheiro) hard-up; (vida) hard
apertar [aper'tar] VT (agarrar) to hold tight; (roupa) to take in; (esponja) to squeeze; (botão) to press; (despesas) to limit; (vigilância) to step up; (coração) to break; (fig: pessoa) to put pressure on ▶ VI (sapatos) to pinch; (chuva, frio) to get worse; (estrada) to narrow; ~ **em** (insistir) to insist on; ~ **a mão de alguém** to shake hands with sb
aperto [a'pertu] M (pressão) pressure; (situação difícil) spot of bother, jam; **um** ~ **de mãos** a handshake
apesar [ape'zar] PREP: ~ **de** in spite of, despite; ~ **disso** nevertheless; ~ **de que** even though
apetecer [apete'ser] VI (comida) to be appetizing
apetite [ape'tʃitʃi] M appetite; **bom** ~! enjoy your meal!
apetrechos [ape'treʃus] MPL gear sg; (Pesca) tackle sg

apinhado, -a [api'ɲadu, a] ADJ crowded
apitar [api'tar] VI to whistle; **apito** [a'pitu] M whistle
aplacar [apla'kar] VT to placate ▶ VI to calm down; **aplacar-se** VR to calm down
aplaudir [aplaw'dʒir] VT to applaud
aplauso [a'plawzu] M applause; (apoio) support; (elogio) praise; (aprovação) approval
aplicação [aplika'sãw] (pl -ões) F application; (esforço) effort; (da lei) enforcement; (de dinheiro) investment; (PT Comput) application, app (col)
aplicado, -a [apli'kadu, a] ADJ hard-working
aplicar [apli'kar] VT to apply; (lei) to enforce; (dinheiro) to invest; **aplicar-se** VR: ~**se a** to devote o.s. to
aplicativo [aplika'tʃivu] M (BR Comput) application, app (col)
apoderar-se [apode'rarsi] VR: ~ **de** to seize, take possession of
apodrecer [apodre'ser] VT to rot; (dente) to decay ▶ VI to rot; to decay
apogeu [apo'ʒew] M (fig) height, peak
apoiar [apo'jar] VT to support; (basear) to base; (moção) to second; **apoiar-se** VR: ~**se em** to rest on
apoio [a'poju] M support; (financeiro) backing
apólice [a'polisi] F (certificado) policy, certificate; (ação) share, bond; ~ **de seguro** insurance policy
apontamento [apõta'mẽtu] M (nota) note
apontar [apõ'tar] VT (fusil) to aim; (erro) to point out; (com o dedo) to point at ou to; (razão) to put forward ▶ VI to begin to appear; (brotar) to sprout; (com o dedo) to point; ~ **para** to point to; (com arma) to aim at
após [a'pojs] PREP after
aposentado, -a [apozẽ'tadu, a] ADJ retired ▶ M/F retired person, pensioner; **ser** ~ to be retired; **aposentadoria** [apozẽtado'ria] F retirement; (dinheiro) pension
aposentar [apozẽ'tar] VT to retire; **aposentar-se** VR to retire
aposento [apo'zẽtu] M room
apossar-se [apo'sarsi] VR: ~ **de** to take possession of, seize
apostar [apos'tar] VT to bet ▶ VI: ~ **em** to bet on
apóstrofo [a'postrofu] M apostrophe
apreciar [apre'sjar] VT to appreciate; (gostar de) to enjoy

apreço [a'presu] M esteem, regard; (*consideração*) consideration; **em ~** in question

apreender [apriẽ'der] VT to apprehend; (*tomar*) to seize; (*entender*) to grasp

apreensão [apriẽ'sãw] (*pl* -ões) F (*percepção*) perception; (*tomada*) seizure; (*receio*) apprehension

apreensivo, -a [apriẽ'sivu, a] ADJ apprehensive

apreensões [apriẽ'sõjs] FPL *de* **apreensão**

apregoar [apre'gwar] VT to proclaim, announce; (*mercadorias*) to cry

aprender [aprẽ'der] VT, VI to learn; **~ a ler** to learn to read; **~ de cor** to learn by heart

aprendizagem [aprẽdʒi'zaʒẽ] F (*num ofício*) apprenticeship; (*numa profissão*) training; (*escolar*) learning

apresentação [aprezẽta'sãw] (*pl* -ões) F presentation; (*de peça, filme*) performance; (*de pessoas*) introduction; (*porte pessoal*) appearance

apresentador, a [aprezẽta'dor(a)] M/F presenter

apresentar [aprezẽ'tar] VT to present; (*pessoas*) to introduce; **apresentar-se** VR to introduce o.s.; (*problema*) to present itself; (*à polícia etc*) to report; **quero ~-lhe ...** may I introduce you to ...

apressado, -a [apre'sadu, a] ADJ hurried, hasty; **estar ~** to be in a hurry

apressar [apre'sar] VT to hurry; **apressar-se** VR to hurry (up)

aprisionar [aprizjo'nar] VT (*cativar*) to capture; (*encarcerar*) to imprison

aprontar [aprõ'tar] VT to get ready, prepare; **aprontar-se** VR to get ready

apropriado, -a [apro'prjadu, a] ADJ appropriate, suitable

aprovado, -a [apro'vadu, a] ADJ approved; **ser ~ num exame** to pass an exam

aprovar [apro'var] VT to approve of; (*exame*) to pass ▶ VI to make the grade

aproveitador, a [aprovejta'dor(a)] M/F opportunist

aproveitamento [aprovejta'mẽtu] M use, utilization; (*nos estudos*) progress

aproveitar [aprovej'tar] VT to take advantage of; (*utilizar*) to use; (*oportunidade*) to take ▶ VI to make the most of it; (*PT*) to be of use; **aproveite!** enjoy yourself!

aproximação [aprosima'sãw] (*pl* -ões) F approximation; (*chegada*) approach; (*proximidade*) nearness

aproximar [aprosi'mar] VT to bring near; (*aliar*) to bring together; **aproximar-se** VR: **~-se de** (*acercar-se*) to approach

aptidão [aptʃi'dãw] F aptitude; (*jeito*) knack; **~ física** physical fitness

apto, -a ['aptu, a] ADJ apt; (*capaz*) capable

apto. ABR = **apartamento**

apunhalar [apuɲa'lar] VT to stab

apurado, -a [apu'radu, a] ADJ refined

apurar [apu'rar] VT to perfect; (*averiguar*) to investigate; (*dinheiro*) to raise, get; (*votos*) to count; **apurar-se** VR to dress up

aquarela [akwa'rɛla] F watercolour (BRIT), watercolor (US)

aquário [a'kwarju] M aquarium; **A~** (*Astrologia*) Aquarius

aquático, -a [a'kwatʃiku, a] ADJ aquatic, water *atr*

aquecer [ake'ser] VT to heat ▶ VI to heat up; **aquecer-se** VR to heat up; **aquecido, -a** [ake'sidu, a] ADJ heated; **aquecimento** [akesi'mẽtu] M heating; **aquecimento central** central heating; **aquecimento global** global warming

aquele, -ela [a'keli, ɛla] ADJ (*sg*) that; (*pl*) those ▶ PRON (*sg*) that one; (*pl*) those (ones)

àquele, -ela [a'keli, ɛla] = **a + aquele, -ela**

aquém [a'kẽj] ADV on this side; **~ de** on this side of

aqui [a'ki] ADV here; **eis ~** here is/are; **~ mesmo** right here; **até ~** up to here; **por ~** hereabouts; (*nesta direção*) this way

aquilo [a'kilu] PRON that; **~ que** what

àquilo [a'kilu] = **a + aquilo**

aquisição [akizi'sãw] (*pl* -ões) F acquisition

ar [ar] M air; (*aspecto*) look; (*brisa*) breeze; (*PT Auto*) choke; **ares** MPL (*atitude*) airs; (*clima*) climate *sg*; **ao ar livre** in the open air; **no ar** (*TV, Rádio*) on air; (*fig: planos*) up in the air; **dar-se ares** to put on airs

árabe ['arabi] ADJ, M/F Arab ▶ M (*Ling*) Arabic

Arábia [a'rabja] F: **a ~ Saudita** Saudi Arabia

arame [a'rami] M wire

aranha [a'raɲa] F spider

arara [a'rara] F macaw

arbitragem [arbi'traʒẽ] F arbitration

arbitrar [arbi'trar] VT to arbitrate; (*Esporte*) to referee

arbitrário, -a [arbi'trarju, a] ADJ arbitrary

arbítrio [ar'bitrju] M decision; **ao ~ de**
at the discretion of

árbitro ['arbitru] M (juiz) arbiter; (Jur)
arbitrator; (Futebol) referee; (Tênis)
umpire

arbusto [ar'bustu] M shrub, bush

arca ['arka] F chest, trunk; **~ de Noé**
Noah's Ark

arcar [ar'kar] VT: **~ com**
(responsabilidades) to shoulder; (despesas)
to handle; (consequencias) to take

arcebispo [arse'bispu] M archbishop

arco ['arku] M (Arq) arch; (Mil, Mús) bow;
(Elet, Mat) arc

arco-íris (pl **arcos-íris**) M rainbow

ar-condicionado (pl **ares-**
condicionados) M (aparelho) air
conditioner; (sistema) air conditioning

arder [ar'der] VI to burn; (pele, olhos) to
sting; **~ de raiva** to seethe (with rage)

ardiloso, -a [ardʒi'lozu, ɔza] ADJ
cunning

ardor [ar'dor] M ardour (BRIT), ardor (US);
ardoroso, -a [ardo'rozu, ɔza] ADJ ardent

árduo, -a ['ardwu, a] ADJ arduous;
(difícil) hard, difficult

área ['arja] F area; (Esporte) penalty area;
(fig) field; **~ (de serviço)** balcony (for
hanging washing etc)

areia [a'reja] F sand; **~ movediça**
quicksand

arejar [are'ʒar] VT to air ▶ VI to get some
air; (descansar) to have a breather;
arejar-se VR to get some air; to have a
break

arena [a'rɛna] F arena; (de circo) ring

Argélia [ar'ʒɛlja] F: **a ~** Algeria

Argentina [arʒẽ'tʃina] F: **a ~** Argentina

argila [ar'ʒila] F clay

argola [ar'gɔla] F ring; **argolas** FPL
(brincos) hooped earrings; **~ (de porta)**
door-knocker

argumentação [argumẽta'sãw] F line
of argument

argumentar [argumẽ'tar] VT, VI to
argue

argumento [argu'mẽtu] M argument;
(de obra) theme

aridez [ari'dez] F dryness; (esterilidade)
barrenness; (falta de interesse) dullness

árido, -a ['aridu, a] ADJ arid, dry; (estéril)
barren; (maçante) dull

Áries ['aris] F Aries

aritmética [aritʃ'mɛtʃika] F arithmetic

arma ['arma] F weapon; **armas** FPL
(nucleares etc) arms; (brasão) coat sg of
arms; **passar pelas ~s** to shoot,
execute; **~ convencional/nuclear**

conventional/nuclear weapon; **~s de**
destruição em massa weapons of
mass destruction; **~ de fogo** firearm

armação [arma'sãw] (pl **-ões**) F
(armadura) frame; (Pesca) tackle; (Náut)
rigging; (de óculos) frames pl

armado, -a [ar'madu, a] ADJ armed

armar [ar'mar] VT to arm; (montar) to
assemble; (barraca) to pitch; (um
aparelho) to set up; (armadilha) to set;
(Náut) to fit out; **armar-se** to arm
o.s.; **~ uma briga com** to pick a quarrel
with

armarinho [arma'riɲu] M haberdashery
(BRIT), notions pl (US)

armário [ar'marju] M cupboard; (de
roupa) wardrobe

armazém [arma'zẽj] (pl **-ns**) M (depósito)
warehouse; (loja) grocery store;
armazenar [armaze'nar] VT to store;
(provisões) to stock

aro ['aru] M (argola) ring; (de óculos, roda)
rim; (de porta) frame

aroma [a'rɔma] M aroma; **aromático,**
-a [aro'matʃiku, a] ADJ (comida)
aromatic; (perfume) fragrant

arpão [ar'pãw] (pl **-ões**) M harpoon

arqueiro, -a [ar'kejru, a] M/F archer;
(goleiro) goalkeeper

arqueologia [arkjolo'ʒia] F archaeology
(BRIT), archeology (US); **arqueólogo, -a**
[ar'kjɔlogu, a] M/F archaeologist (BRIT),
archeologist (US)

arquiteto, -a [arki'tɛtu, a] M/F
architect; **arquitetónico, -a**
[arkite'toniku, a] ADJ architectural;
arquitetura [arkite'tura] F architecture

arquivar [arki'var] VT to file; (projeto) to
shelve

arquivo [ar'kivu] M (ger, Comput) file;
(lugar) archive; (de empresa) files pl;
(móvel) filing cabinet; **~ zipado** (Comput)
zip file

arraial [aha'jaw] (pl **-ais**) M (PT: festa) fair

arrancada [ahã'kada] F (puxão) jerk; **dar**
uma ~ (em carro) to pull away (suddenly)

arrancar [ahã'kar] VT to pull out; (botão
etc) to pull off; (arrebatar) to snatch
(away); (fig: confissão) to extract ▶ VI to
start (off); **arrancar-se** VR to leave;
(fugir) to run off

arranha-céu [a'haɲa-] (pl **-s**) M
skyscraper

arranhão [aha'ɲãw] (pl **-ões**) M scratch

arranhar [aha'ɲar] VT to scratch

arranjar [ahã'ʒar] VT to arrange;
(emprego etc) to get, find; (doença) to get,
catch; (questão) to settle; **arranjar-se**

to manage; (*conseguir emprego*) to get a job; **~-se sem** to do without

arranjo [aˈʁãʒu] M arrangement

arrasar [ahaˈzar] VT to devastate; (*demolir*) to demolish; (*estragar*) to ruin; **arrasar-se** VR to be devastated; (*destruir-se*) to destroy o.s.; (*arruinar-se*) to lose everything

arrastão [ahasˈtãw] (*pl* **-ões**) M tug; (*rede*) dragnet

arrastar [ahasˈtar] VT to drag; (*atrair*) to draw ▶ VI to trail; **arrastar-se** VR to crawl; (*tempo*) to drag; (*processo*) to drag on

arrebatado, -a [ahebaˈtadu, a] ADJ rash, impetuous

arrebatar [ahebaˈtar] VT to snatch (away); (*levar*) to carry off; (*enlevar*) to entrance; (*enfurecer*) to enrage; **arrebatar-se** VR to be entranced

arrebentado, -a [ahebēˈtadu, a] ADJ broken; (*estafado*) worn out

arrebentar [ahebēˈtar] VT to break; (*porta*) to break down; (*corda*) to snap ▶ VI to break; to snap; (*guerra*) to break out

arrebitado, -a [ahebiˈtadu, a] ADJ turned-up; (*nariz*) snub

arrecadar [ahekaˈdar] VT (*impostos etc*) to collect

arredondado, -a [ahedõˈdadu, a] ADJ round, rounded

arredondar [ahedõˈdar] VT to round (off); (*conta*) to round up

arredores [aheˈdɔris] MPL suburbs; (*cercanias*) outskirts

arrefecer [ahefeˈser] VT to cool; (*febre*) to lower; (*desanimar*) to discourage ▶ VI to cool (off); to get discouraged

arregaçar [ahegaˈsar] VT to roll up

arregalado, -a [ahegaˈladu, a] ADJ (*olhos*) wide

arregalar [ahegaˈlar] VT: **~ os olhos** to stare in amazement

arrematar [ahemaˈtar] VT (*dizer concluindo*) to conclude; (*comprar*) to buy by auction; (*vender*) to sell by auction; (*Costura*) to finish off

arremessar [ahemeˈsar] VT to throw, hurl; **arremesso** [aheˈmesu] M throw

arremeter [ahemeˈter] VI to lunge; **~ contra** (*acometer*) to attack, assail

arrendar [ahẽˈdar] VT to lease

arrepender-se [ahepēˈdersi] VR to repent; (*mudar de opinião*) to change one's mind; **~ de** to regret, be sorry for; **arrependido, -a** [ahepēˈdʒidu, a] ADJ (*pessoa*) sorry; **arrependimento**

[ahepēdʒiˈmētu] M regret; (*Rel, de crime*) repentance

arrepiar [aheˈpjar] VT (*amedrontar*) to horrify; (*cabelo*) to cause to stand on end; **arrepiar-se** VR to shiver; (*cabelo*) to stand on end; **(ser) de ~ os cabelos** (to be) hair-raising

arrepio [aheˈpiu] M shiver; (*de frio*) chill; **isso me dá ~s** it gives me the creeps

arriar [aˈhjar] VT to lower; (*depor*) to lay down ▶ VI to drop; (*vergar*) to sag; (*desistir*) to give up; (*fig*) to collapse

arriscado, -a [ahisˈkadu, a] ADJ risky; (*audacioso*) daring

arriscar [ahisˈkar] VT to risk; (*pôr em perigo*) to endanger, jeopardize; **arriscar-se** VR to take a risk; **~-se a fazer** to risk doing

arrogante [ahoˈgãtʃi] ADJ arrogant

arrojado, -a [ahoˈʒadu, a] ADJ (*design*) bold; (*temerário*) rash; (*ousado*) daring

arrolar [ahoˈlar] VT to list

arrombar [ahõˈbar] VT (*porta*) to break down; (*cofre*) to crack

arrotar [ahoˈtar] VI to belch ▶ VT (*alardear*) to boast of

arroz [aˈhoz] M rice; **~ doce** rice pudding

arruinar [ahwiˈnar] VT to ruin; (*destruir*) to destroy; **arruinar-se** VR to be ruined; (*perder a saúde*) to ruin one's health

arrumação [ahumaˈsãw] F arrangement; (*de um quarto etc*) tidying up; (*de malas*) packing

arrumadeira [ahumaˈdejra] F cleaning lady; (*num hotel*) chambermaid

arrumar [ahuˈmar] VT to put in order, arrange; (*quarto etc*) to tidy up; (*malas*) to pack; (*emprego*) to get; (*vestir*) to dress up; (*desculpa*) to make up, find; (*vida*) to sort out; **arrumar-se** VR (*aprontar-se*) to get dressed, get ready; (*na vida*) to sort o.s. out; (*virar-se*) to manage

arte [ˈartʃi] F art; (*habilidade*) skill; (*ofício*) trade, craft

artefato [artʃiˈfatu], (*PT*) **artefacto** M (manufactured) article

artéria [arˈtɛrja] F (*Anat*) artery

artesão, -sã [arteˈzãw, zã] (*pl* **-s/-s**) M/F artisan, craftsman/woman

ártico, -a [ˈartʃiku, a] ADJ Arctic ▶ M: **o Á~** the Arctic

artificial [artʃifiˈsjaw] (*pl* **-ais**) ADJ artificial

artifício [artʃiˈfisju] M stratagem, trick

artigo [arˈtʃigu] M article; (*Com*) item; **artigos** MPL (*produtos*) goods

artista [arˈtʃista] M/F artist; **artístico, -a** [arˈtʃistʃiku, a] ADJ artistic

artrite [ar'tritʃi] F (*Med*) arthritis
árvore ['arvori] F tree; (*Tec*) shaft; **~ de Natal** Christmas tree
as [as] ART DEF *ver* **a**
ás [ajs] M ace
às [as] = **a** + **as**; *ver* **a**
asa ['aza] F wing; (*de xícara etc*) handle
ascendência [asẽ'dẽsja] F (*antepassados*) ancestry; (*domínio*) ascendancy, sway; **ascendente** [asẽ'dẽtʃi] ADJ rising, upward
ascender [asẽ'der] VI to rise, ascend
ascensão [asẽ'sãw] (*pl* **-ões**) F ascent; (*Rel*): **dia da A~** Ascension Day
asco ['asku] M loathing, revulsion; **dar ~ a** to revolt, disgust
asfalto [as'fawtu] M asphalt
asfixia [asfik'sia] F asphyxia, suffocation
Ásia ['azja] F: **a ~** Asia
asiático, -a [a'zjatʃiku, a] ADJ, M/F Asian
asilo [a'zilu] M (*refúgio*) refuge; (*estabelecimento*) home; **~ político** political asylum
asma ['azma] F asthma
asneira [az'nejra] F (*tolice*) stupidity; (*ato, dito*) stupid thing
asno ['aznu] M donkey; (*fig*) ass
aspas ['aspas] FPL inverted commas
aspecto [as'pɛktu] M aspect; (*aparência*) look, appearance; (*característica*) feature; (*ponto de vista*) point of view
aspereza [aspe'reza] F roughness; (*severidade*) harshness; (*rudeza*) rudeness
áspero, -a ['asperu, a] ADJ rough; (*severo*) harsh; (*rude*) rude
aspiração [aspira'sãw] (*pl* **-ões**) F aspiration; (*inalação*) inhalation
aspirador [aspira'dor] M: **~ (de pó)** vacuum cleaner; **passar o ~ (em)** to vacuum
aspirante [aspi'rãtʃi] ADJ aspiring ▶ M/F candidate
aspirar [aspi'rar] VT to breathe in; (*bombear*) to suck up ▶ VI to breathe; (*soprar*) to blow; (*desejar*): **~ a algo** to aspire to sth
aspirina [aspi'rina] F aspirin
asqueroso, -a [aske'rozu, ɔza] ADJ disgusting, revolting
assado, -a [a'sadu, a] ADJ roasted; (*Culin*) roast ▶ M roast; **carne assada** roast beef
assaltante [asaw'tãtʃi] M/F assailant; (*de banco*) robber; (*de casa*) burglar; (*na rua*) mugger
assaltar [asaw'tar] VT to attack; (*casa*) to break into; (*banco*) to rob; (*pessoa na rua*) to mug; **assalto** [a'sawtu] M attack, raid; (*a um banco etc*) robbery; (*a uma casa*) burglary, break-in; (*a uma pessoa na rua*) mugging; (*Boxe*) round
assar [a'sar] VT to roast; (*na grelha*) to grill
assassinar [asasi'nar] VT to murder, kill; (*Pol*) to assassinate; **assassinato** [asasi'natu] M murder, killing; (*Pol*) assassination; **assassino, -a** [asa'sinu, a] M/F murderer; (*Pol*) assassin; **assassino em série** serial killer
assaz [a'saz] ADV (*suficientemente*) sufficiently; (*muito*) rather
assediar [ase'dʒjar] VT (*sitiar*) to besiege; (*importunar*) to pester; **assédio** [a'sɛdʒu] M siege; (*insistência*) insistence
assegurar [asegu'rar] VT to secure; (*garantir*) to ensure; (*afirmar*) to assure; **assegurar-se** VR: **~-se de** to make sure of
asseio [a'seju] M cleanliness
assembleia [asẽ'bleja] F assembly; (*reunião*) meeting; **~ geral (ordinária)** annual general meeting
assentar [asẽ'tar] VT (*fazer sentar*) to seat; (*colocar*) to place; (*estabelecer*) to establish; (*decidir*) to decide upon ▶ VI (*pó etc*) to settle; **assentar-se** VR to sit down; **~ em** *ou* **a** (*roupa*) to suit
assentir [asẽ'tʃir] VI: **~ (em)** to consent *ou* agree (to)
assento [a'sẽtu] M seat; (*base*) base
assíduo, -a [a'sidwu, a] ADJ (*aluno*) who attends regularly; (*diligente*) assiduous; (*constante*) constant; **ser ~ num lugar** to be a regular visitor to a place
assim [a'sĩ] ADV (*deste modo*) like this, in this way, thus; (*portanto*) therefore; (*igualmente*) likewise; **~ ~** so-so; **~ mesmo** in any case; **e ~ por diante** and so on; **~ como** as well as; **como ~?** how do you mean?; **~ que** (*logo que*) as soon as
assimilar [asimi'lar] VT to assimilate; (*apreender*) to take in; (*assemelhar*) to compare
assinante [asi'nãtʃi] M/F (*de jornal etc*) subscriber
assinar [asi'nar] VT to sign
assinatura [asina'tura] F (*nome*) signature; (*de jornal etc*) subscription; (*Teatro*) season ticket
assinto [a'sĩtu] VB *ver* **assentir**
assistência [asis'tẽsja] F (*presença*) presence; (*público*) audience; (*auxílio*) aid; **~ médica** medical aid; **~ social** social work

assistente [asis'tẽtʃi] ADJ assistant ▶ M/F spectator, onlooker; (*ajudante*) assistant; **~ social** social worker

assistir [asis'tʃir] VT, VI: **~ (a)** (*Med*) to attend (to); **~ a** to assist; (*TV, filme, jogo*) to watch; (*reunião*) to attend

assoar [aso'ar] VT: **~ o nariz** to blow one's nose; **assoar-se** VR (*PT*) to blow one's nose

assobiar [aso'bjar] VI to whistle

assobio [aso'biu] M whistle

associação [asosja'sãw] (*pl* **-ões**) F association; (*organização*) society; (*parceria*) partnership

associado, -a [aso'sjadu, a] ADJ associate ▶ M/F associate, member; (*Com*) associate; (*sócio*) partner

associar [aso'sjar] VT to associate; **associar-se** VR: **~-se a** to associate with

assombração [asõbra'sãw] (*pl* **-ões**) F ghost

assombro [a'sõbru] M amazement, astonishment; (*maravilha*) marvel; **assombroso, -a** [asõ'brozu, ɔza] ADJ astonishing, amazing

assoviar [aso'vjar] VT = **assobiar**

assovio [aso'viu] M = **assobio**

assumir [asu'mir] VT to assume, take on; (*reconhecer*) to accept

assunto [a'sũtu] M subject, matter; (*enredo*) plot

assustador, a [asusta'dor(a)] ADJ (*alarmante*) startling; (*amedrontador*) frightening

assustar [asus'tar] VT to frighten, startle; **assustar-se** VR to be frightened

asteca [as'tɛka] ADJ, M/F Aztec

astral [as'traw] (*pl* **-ais**) M mood; **bom ~** good vibe; **alto ~** upbeat mood; **baixo ~** gloom; **estar de baixo ~** to be feeling glum

astrologia [astrolo'ʒia] F astrology

astronauta [astro'nawta] M/F astronaut

astronave [astro'navi] F spaceship

astronomia [astrono'mia] F astronomy

astúcia [as'tusja] F cunning

ata ['ata] F (*de reunião*) minutes pl

atacado, -a [ata'kadu, a] ADJ (*col: pessoa*) in a bad mood ▶ M: **por ~** wholesale

atacante [ata'kãtʃi] ADJ attacking ▶ M/F attacker, assailant ▶ M (*Futebol*) forward

atacar [ata'kar] VT to attack; (*problema etc*) to tackle

atado, -a [a'tadu, a] ADJ (*desajeitado*) clumsy, awkward; (*perplexo*) puzzled

atalho [a'taʎu] M (*caminho*) short cut

ataque [a'taki] M attack; **~ aéreo** air raid; **~ suicida** suicide attack

atar [a'tar] VT to tie (up), fasten; **não ~ nem desatar** (*pessoa*) to waver; (*negócio*) to be in the air

atarefado, -a [atare'fadu, a] ADJ busy

atarracado, -a [ataha'kadu, a] ADJ stocky

até [a'tɛ] PREP (*PT*: **+ a**: *lugar*) up to, as far as; (*tempo etc*) until, till ▶ ADV (*tb*: **~ mesmo**) even; **~ certo ponto** to a certain extent; **~ em cima** to the top; **~ já** see you soon; **~ logo** bye!; **~ onde** as far as; **~ que** until; **~ que enfim!** at last!

atear [ate'ar] VT (*fogo*) to kindle; (*fig*) to incite, inflame; **atear-se** VR to blaze; (*paixões*) to flare up

ateia [a'teja] F *de* **ateu**

atemorizar [atemori'zar] VT to frighten; (*intimidar*) to intimidate

Atenas [a'tenas] N Athens

atenção [atẽ'sãw] (*pl* **-ões**) F attention; (*cortesia*) courtesy; (*bondade*) kindness; **~!** be careful!; **chamar a ~** to attract attention; **atencioso, -a** [atẽ'sjozu, ɔza] ADJ considerate

atender [atẽ'der] VT: **~ (a)** to attend to; (*receber*) to receive; (*deferir*) to grant; (*telefone etc*) to answer; (*paciente*) to see ▶ VI to answer; (*dar atenção*) to pay attention; **atendimento** [atẽdʒi'mẽtu] M service; (*recepção*) reception; **horário de atendimento** opening hours; (*em consultório*) surgery (*BRIT*) *ou* office (*US*) hours

atentado [atẽ'tadu] M attack; (*crime*) crime; (*contra a vida de alguém*) attempt on sb's life; **~ suicida** suicide attack

atento, -a [a'tẽtu, a] ADJ attentive; **estar ~ a** to be aware *ou* mindful of

atenuante [ate'nwãtʃi] ADJ extenuating ▶ M extenuating circumstance

atenuar [ate'nwar] VT to reduce, lessen

aterragem [ate'haʒẽj] (*PT*) (*pl* **-ns**) F (*Aer*) landing

aterrar [ate'har] VI (*PT Aer*) to land

aterrissagem [atehi'saʒẽ] (*BR*) (*pl* **-ns**) F (*Aer*) landing

aterrissar [atehi'sar] (*BR*) VI (*Aer*) to land

aterro [a'tehu] M: **~ sanitário** landfill (site)

aterrorizante [atehori'zãtʃi] ADJ terrifying

aterrorizar [atehori'zar] VT to terrorize

atestado, -a [ates'tadu, a] ADJ certified ▶ M certificate; (*prova*) proof; (*Jur*) testimony

ateu, ateia [a'tew, a'tɛja] ADJ, M/F atheist

atinar [atʃi'nar] VT (*acertar*) to guess correctly ▶ VI: **~ com** (*solução*) to find; **~ em** to notice; **~ a fazer algo** to succeed in doing sth

atingir [atʃi'ʒir] VT to reach; (*acertar*) to hit; (*afetar*) to affect; (*objetivo*) to achieve; (*compreender*) to grasp

atirador, a [atʃira'dor(a)] M/F marksman/woman; **~ de tocaia** sniper

atirar [atʃi'rar] VT to throw, fling ▶ VI (*arma*) to shoot; **atirar-se** VR: **~-se a** to hurl o.s. at

atitude [atʃi'tudʒi] F attitude; (*postura*) posture

atividade [atʃivi'dadʒi] F activity

ativo, -a [a'tʃivu, a] ADJ active ▶ M (*Com*) assets *pl*

atlântico, -a [at'lãtʃiku, a] ADJ Atlantic ▶ M: **o (Oceano) A~** the Atlantic (Ocean)

atlas ['atlas] M INV atlas

atleta [at'lɛta] M/F athlete; **atlético, -a** [at'lɛtʃiku, a] ADJ athletic; **atletismo** [atle'tʃizmu] M athletics *sg*

atmosfera [atmos'fera] F atmosphere

ato [a'tu] M act, action; (*cerimônia*) ceremony; (*Teatro*) act; **em ~ contínuo** straight after; **no ~** on the spot; **no mesmo ~** at the same time

atômico, -a [a'tomiku, a] ADJ atomic

átomo ['atomu] M atom

atônito, -a [a'tonitu, a] ADJ astonished, amazed

ator [a'tor] M actor

atordoado, -a [ator'dwadu, a] ADJ dazed

atordoar [ator'dwar] VT to daze, stun

atormentar [atormẽ'tar] VT to torment

atração [atra'sãw] (*pl* -ões) F attraction

atracar [atra'kar] VT, VI (*Náut*) to moor; **atracar-se** VR to grapple

atrações [atra'sõjs] FPL *de* **atração**

atraente [atra'ẽtʃi] ADJ attractive

atrair [atra'ir] VT to attract; (*fascinar*) to fascinate

atrapalhar [atrapa'ʎar] VT to confuse; (*perturbar*) to disturb; (*dificultar*) to hinder ▶ VI to be a nuisance

atrás [a'trajs] ADV behind; (*no fundo*) at the back ▶ PREP: **~ de** behind; (*no tempo*) after; **dois meses ~** two months ago

atrasado, -a [atra'zadu, a] ADJ late; (*país etc*) backward; (*relógio etc*) slow; (*pagamento*) overdue; **atrasados** [atra'zadus] MPL (*Com*) arrears

atrasar [atra'zar] VT to delay; (*progresso, desenvolvimento*) to hold back; (*relógio*) to put back; (*pagamento*) to be late with ▶ VI (*relógio etc*) to be slow; (*avião, pessoa*) to be late; **atrasar-se** VR to be late; (*num trabalho*) to fall behind; (*num pagamento*) to get into arrears

atraso [a'trazu] M delay; (*de país etc*) backwardness; **atrasos** MPL (*Com*) arrears; **com 20 minutos de ~** 20 minutes late

atrativo, -a [atra'tʃivu, a] ADJ attractive ▶ M attraction; (*incentivo*) incentive; **atrativos** MPL (*encantos*) charms

através [atra'vɛs] ADV across; **~ de** across; (*pelo centro de*) through

atravessar [atrave'sar] VT to cross; (*pôr ao través*) to put ou lay across; (*traspassar*) to pass through

atrever-se [atre'versi] VR: **~ a** to dare to; **atrevido, -a** [atre'vidu, a] ADJ cheeky; (*corajoso*) bold; **atrevimento** [atrevi'mẽtu] M (*ousadia*) boldness; (*insolência*) cheek

atribuir [atri'bwir] VT: **~ algo a** to attribute sth to; (*prêmios, regalias*) to confer sth on

atributo [atri'butu] M attribute

átrio ['atrju] M hall; (*pátio*) courtyard

atrito [a'tritu] M (*fricção*) friction; (*desentendimento*) disagreement

atriz [a'triz] F actress

atropelamento [atropela'mẽtu] M (*de pedestre*) accident involving a pedestrian

atropelar [atrope'lar] VT to knock down, run over; (*empurrar*) to jostle

atuação [atwa'sãw] (*pl* -ões) F acting; (*de ator etc*) performance

atual [a'twaw] (*pl* -ais) ADJ current; (*pessoa, carro*) modern; **atualidade** [atwali'dadʒi] F present (time); **atualidades** FPL (*notícias*) news *sg*; **atualizar** [atwali'zar] VT to update; **atualmente** [atwaw'mẽtʃi] ADV at present, currently; (*hoje em dia*) nowadays

atuante [a'twãtʃi] ADJ active

atuar [a'twar] VI to act; **~ para** to contribute to; **~ sobre** to influence

atum [a'tũ] (*pl* -ns) M tuna (fish)

aturdido, -a [atur'dʒidu, a] ADJ stunned; (*com barulho*) deafened; (*com confusão, movimento*) bewildered

audácia [aw'dasja] F boldness; (*insolência*) insolence; **audacioso, -a** [awda'sjozu, ɔza] ADJ daring; (*insolente*) insolent

audição [awdʒi'sãw] (*pl* -ões) F audition

audiência [aw'dʒjẽsja] F audience; (*de tribunal*) session, hearing

auditar [awdʒi'tar] vt to audit

auditor, a [awdʒi'tor(a)] M/F auditor; (*juiz*) judge; (*ouvinte*) listener

auditoria [awdʒito'ria] F: **fazer a ~ de** to audit

auditório [awdʒi'tɔrju] M audience; (*recinto*) auditorium

auge ['awʒi] M height, peak

aula ['awla] F (*PT: sala*) classroom; (*lição*) lesson, class; **dar ~** to teach

aumentar [awmē'tar] vt to increase; (*salários, preços*) to raise; (*sala, casa*) to expand, extend; (*suj: lente*) to magnify; (*acrescentar*) to add ▶ vi to increase; (*preço, salário*) to rise, go up

aumento [aw'mētu] M increase; (*de preços*) rise; (*ampliação*) enlargement; (*crescimento*) growth

ausência [aw'zẽsja] F absence

ausentar-se [awzẽ'tarsi] vr (*ir-se*) to go away; (*afastar-se*) to stay away

ausente [aw'zẽtʃi] ADJ absent

austral [aws'traw] (*pl* -**ais**) ADJ southern

Austrália [aws'tralja] F: **a ~** Australia; **australiano, -a** [awstra'ljanu, a] ADJ, M/F Australian

Áustria ['awstrja] F: **a ~** Austria; **austríaco, -a** [aws'triaku, a] ADJ, M/F Austrian

autêntico, -a [aw'tẽtʃiku, a] ADJ authentic; (*pessoa*) genuine; (*verdadeiro*) true, real

auto ['awtu] M car; **autos** MPL (*Jur: processo*) legal proceedings; (*documentos*) legal papers

autobiografia [awtobjogra'fia] F autobiography

autobronzeador [awtobrõzja'dor] ADJ self-tanning

autocarro [awto'kahu] (*PT*) M bus

autodefesa [awtode'feza] F self-defence (*BRIT*), self-defense (*US*)

autódromo [aw'tɔdromu] M race track

autoestrada [awtois'trada] F motorway (*BRIT*), expressway (*US*)

autografar [awtogra'far] vt to autograph

autógrafo [aw'tɔgrafu] M autograph

automático, -a [awto'matʃiku, a] ADJ automatic

automobilismo [awtomobi'lizmu] M motoring; (*Esporte*) motor car racing

automóvel [awto'mɔvew] (*pl* -**eis**) M motor car (*BRIT*), automobile (*US*)

autonomia [awtono'mia] F autonomy

autor, a [aw'tor(a)] M/F author; (*de um crime*) perpetrator; (*Jur*) plaintiff

autoral [awto'raw] (*pl* -**ais**) ADJ: **direitos autorais** copyright *sg*

autoridade [awtori'dadʒi] F authority

autorização [awtoriza'sãw] (*pl* -**ões**) F permission, authorization; **dar ~ a alguém para** to authorize sb to

autorizar [awtori'zar] vt to authorize

autosserviço [awtoser'visu] M self-service

auxiliar [awsi'ljar] ADJ auxiliary ▶ M/F assistant ▶ vt to help; **auxílio** [aw'silju] M help, assistance

Av. ABR (= *avenida*) Ave.

aval [a'vaw] (*pl* -**ais**) M guarantee

avalancha [ava'lãʃa] F avalanche

avaliar [ava'ljar] vt to value; to assess

avançado, -a [avã'sadu, a] ADJ advanced; (*ideias, pessoa*) progressive

avançar [avã'sar] vt to move forward ▶ vi to advance; **avanço** [a'vãsu] M advancement; (*progresso*) progress

avaria [ava'ria] F (*Tec*) breakdown; **avariado, -a** [ava'rjadu, a] ADJ (*máquina*) out of order; (*carro*) broken down; **avariar** [ava'rjar] vt to damage ▶ vi to suffer damage; (*Tec*) to break down

avatar [ava'tar] M (*Comput*) avatar

ave ['avi] F bird

aveia [a'veja] F oats *pl*

avelã [ave'lã] F hazelnut

avenida [ave'nida] F avenue

avental [avẽ'taw] (*pl* -**ais**) M apron; (*vestido*) pinafore dress (*BRIT*), jumper (*US*)

averiguar [averi'gwar] vt to investigate; (*verificar*) to verify

avermelhado, -a [averme'ʎadu, a] ADJ reddish

avesso, -a [a'vesu, a] ADJ (*lado*) opposite, reverse ▶ M wrong side, reverse; **ao ~** inside out; **às avessas** (*inverso*) upside down; (*oposto*) the wrong way round

avestruz [aves'truz] M ostrich

aviação [avja'sãw] F aviation, flying

aviador, a [avja'dor(a)] M/F aviator, airman/woman

avião [a'vjãw] (*pl* -**ões**) M aeroplane; **~ a jato** jet

ávido, -a ['avidu, a] ADJ greedy; (*desejoso*) eager

aviões [a'vjõjs] MPL *de* **avião**

avisar [avi'zar] vt to warn; (*informar*) to tell, let know; **aviso** [a'vizu] M (*comunicação*) notice

avistar [avis'tar] vt to catch sight of

avô, avó [a'vo, a'vɔ] M/F grandfather/ mother; **avós** MPL grandparents

avulso, -a [a'vuwsu, a] ADJ separate, detached

axila [ak'sila] F armpit

azar [a'zar] M bad luck; **~!** too bad!, bad luck!; **estar com ~, ter ~** to be unlucky; **azarento, -a** [aza'rẽtu, a] ADJ unlucky

azedar [aze'dar] VT to turn sour ▶ VI to turn sour; (*leite*) to go off; **azedo, -a** [a'zedu, a] ADJ sour; (*leite*) off; (*fig*) grumpy

azeite [a'zejtʃi] M oil; (*de oliva*) olive oil

azeitona [azej'tɔna] F olive

azia [a'zia] F heartburn

azougue [a'zogi] M (*Quím*) mercury

azul [a'zuw] (*pl* **-uis**) ADJ blue

azulejo [azu'leʒu] M (glazed) tile

azul-marinho ADJ INV navy blue

azul-turquesa ADJ INV turquoise

baba ['baba] F dribble

babá [ba'ba] F nanny

babado [ba'badu] M frill; (*col*) piece of gossip

babador [baba'dor] M bib

babar [ba'bar] VI to dribble; **babar-se** VR to dribble

baby-sitter ['bejbisiter] (*pl* **-s**) M/F baby-sitter

bacalhau [baka'ʎaw] M (dried) cod

bacana [ba'kana] (*col*) ADJ great

bacharel [baʃa'rɛw] (*pl* **-éis**) M graduate

bacia [ba'sia] F basin; (*Anat*) pelvis

backup [ba'kapi] (*pl* **-s**) M (*Comput*) back-up; **fazer um ~ de** to back up

bactéria [bak'tɛrja] F germ, bacterium; **bactérias** MPL bacteria *pl*

badalar [bada'lar] VT, VI to ring

baderna [ba'dɛrna] F commotion

bafo ['bafu] M (bad) breath

bagaço [ba'gasu] M (*de frutos*) pulp; (*PT: cachaça*) brandy; **estar/ficar um ~** (*fig: pessoa*) to be/get run down

bagageiro [baga'ʒejru] M (*Auto*) roof rack; (*PT*) porter

bagagem [ba'gaʒẽ] F luggage; (*fig*) baggage; **recebimento de ~** (*Aer*) baggage reclaim

bagulho [ba'guʎu] M (*objeto*) piece of junk

bagunça [ba'gũsa] F mess, shambles *sg*; **bagunçado, -a** [bagũ'sadu, a] ADJ messy; **bagunçar** [bagũ'sar] VT to mess up; **bagunceiro, -a** [bagũ'sejru, a] ADJ messy

baía [ba'ia] F bay

bailado [baj'ladu] M dance; (*balé*) ballet

bailarino, -a [bajla'rinu, a] M/F ballet dancer

baile ['bajli] M dance; (*formal*) ball; **~ à fantasia** fancy-dress ball

bainha [ba'iɲa] F (de arma) sheath; (de costura) hem

bairro ['bajʁu] M district

baixa ['bajʃa] F decrease; (de preço) reduction, fall; drop; (em combate) casualty; (do serviço) discharge

baixar [baj'ʃar] VT to lower; (ordem) to issue; (lei) to pass; (Comput) to download ▶ VI to go (ou come) down; (temperatura, preço) to drop, fall

baixinho [baj'ʃiɲu] ADV (falar) softly, quietly; (em segredo) secretly

baixo, -a ['bajʃu, a] ADJ low; (pessoa) short, small; (rio) shallow; (linguagem) common; (olhos) lowered; (atitude) mean; (metal) base ▶ ADV low; (em posição baixa) low down; (falar) softly ▶ M (Mús) bass; **em ~** below; (em casa) downstairs; **em voz baixa** in a quiet voice; **para ~** down, downwards; (em casa) downstairs; **por ~ de** under, underneath

bala ['bala] F bullet; (BR: doce) sweet

balança [ba'lãsa] F scales pl; **B~** (Astrologia) Libra; **~ comercial** balance of trade; **~ de pagamentos** balance of payments

balançar [balã'sar] VT to swing; (pesar) to weigh (up) ▶ VI to swing; (carro, avião) to shake; (em cadeira) to rock; **balançar-se** VR to swing; **balanço** [ba'lãsu] M (movimento) swinging; (brinquedo) swing; (de carro, avião) shaking; (Com: registro) balance (sheet); (: verificação) audit; **fazer um balanço de** (fig) to take stock of

balão [ba'lãw] (pl -ões) M balloon

balbúrdia [baw'burdʒja] F uproar, bedlam

balcão [baw'kãw] (pl -ões) M balcony; (de loja) counter; (Teatro) circle; **balconista** [bawko'nista] M/F shop assistant

balde ['bawdʒi] M bucket, pail

balé [ba'lɛ] M ballet

baleia [ba'leja] F whale

baliza [ba'liza] F (estaca) post; (boia) buoy; (luminosa) beacon; (Esporte) goal

balneário [baw'njarju] M bathing resort

balões [ba'lõjs] MPL de **balão**

baloiço [ba'lojsu] (PT) M (de criança) swing; (ação) swinging

balsa ['bawsa] F raft; (barca) ferry

bamba ['bãba] ADJ, M/F expert

bambo, -a ['bãbu, a] ADJ slack, loose

banana [ba'nana] F banana; **bananeira** [bana'nejra] F banana tree

banca ['bãka] F bench; (escritório) office; (em jogo) bank; **~ (de jornais)** newsstand; **bancada** [bã'kada] F (banco, Pol) bench; (de cozinha) worktop

bancar [bã'kar] VT to finance ▶ VI (fingir): **~ que** to pretend that; **bancário, -a** [bã'karju, a] ADJ bank atr ▶ M/F bank employee

bancarrota [bãka'ʁota] F bankruptcy; **ir à ~** to go bankrupt

banco ['bãku] M (assento) bench; (Com) bank; **~ de areia** sandbank; **~ de dados** (Comput) database

banda ['bãda] F band; (lado) side; (cinto) sash; **de ~** sideways; **pôr de ~** to put aside; **~ desenhada** (PT) cartoon; **~ larga** (Tel) broadband

bandeira [bã'dejra] F flag; (estandarte, fig) banner; **bandeirinha** [bãdej'riɲa] M (Esporte) linesman

bandeja [bã'deʒa] F tray

bandido [bã'dʒidu] M bandit

bando ['bãdu] M band; (grupo) group; (de malfeitores) gang; (de ovelhas) flock; (de gado) herd; (de livros etc) pile

banha ['baɲa] F fat; (de porco) lard

banhar [ba'ɲar] VT to wet; (mergulhar) to dip; (lavar) to wash; **banhar-se** VR to bathe

banheira [ba'ɲejra] F bath

banheiro [ba'ɲejru] M bathroom

banho ['baɲu] M bath; (mergulho) dip; **tomar ~** to have a bath; (de chuveiro) to have a shower; **~ de chuveiro** shower; **~ de sol** sunbathing

banir [ba'nir] VT to banish

banqueiro, -a [bã'kejru, a] M/F banker

banquete [bã'ketʃi] M banquet

bar [bar] M bar

baralho [ba'raʎu] M pack of cards

barata [ba'rata] F cockroach

barateiro, -a [bara'tejru, a] ADJ cheap

barato, -a [ba'ratu, a] ADJ cheap ▶ ADV cheaply

barba ['barba] F beard; **fazer a ~** to shave

bárbaro, -a ['barbaru, a] ADJ barbaric; (dor, calor) terrible; (maravilhoso) great

barbeador [barbja'dor] M razor; (tb: ~ elétrico) shaver

barbear [bar'bjar] VT to shave; **barbear-se** VR to shave; **barbearia** [barbja'ria] F barber's (shop)

barbeiro [bar'bejru] M barber; (loja) barber's

barca ['barka] F barge; (de travessia) ferry

barco ['barku] M boat; **~ a motor** motorboat; **~ a remo** rowing boat; **~ a vela** sailing boat

barganha [bar'gaɲa] F bargain; **barganhar** [barga'ɲar] VT, VI to negotiate

barman [bar'mã] (pl **-men**) M barman

barra ['baha] F bar; (faixa) strip; (traço) stroke; (alavanca) lever; (em endereço web) forward slash

barraca [ba'haka] F (tenda) tent; (de feira) stall; (de madeira) hut; (de praia) sunshade; **barracão** [baha'kãw] (pl **-ões**) M shed; **barraco** [ba'haku] M shack, shanty; (col: confusão) scene

barragem [ba'haʒẽ] (pl **-ns**) F dam; (impedimento) barrier

barrar [ba'har] VT to bar

barreira [ba'hejra] F barrier; (cerca) fence; (Esporte) hurdle

barricada [bahi'kada] F barricade

barriga [ba'higa] F belly; **estar de ~** to be pregnant; **~ da perna** calf; **barrigudo, -a** [bahi'gudu, a] ADJ paunchy, pot-bellied

barril [ba'hiw] (pl **-is**) M barrel, cask

barro ['bahu] M clay; (lama) mud

barulhento, -a [baru'ʎẽtu, a] ADJ noisy

barulho [ba'ruʎu] M (ruído) noise; (tumulto) din

base ['bazi] F base; (fig) basis; **sem ~** groundless; **com ~ em** based on; **na ~ de** by means of

basear [ba'zjar] VT to base; **basear-se** VR: **~se em** to be based on

básico, -a ['baziku, a] ADJ basic

basquete [bas'kɛtʃi] M = **basquetebol**

basquetebol [baskete'bɔw] M basketball

basta ['basta] M: **dar um ~ em** to call a halt to

bastante [bas'tãtʃi] ADJ (suficiente) enough; (muito) quite a lot (of) ▶ ADV enough; a lot

bastão [bas'tãw] (pl **-ões**) M stick

bastar [bas'tar] VI to be enough, be sufficient; **bastar-se** VR to be self-sufficient; **basta!** (that's) enough!; **~ para** to be enough to

bastardo, -a [bas'tardu, a] ADJ, M/F bastard

bastões [bas'tõjs] MPL de **bastão**

bata ['bata] F (de mulher) smock; (de médico) overall

batalha [ba'taʎa] F battle; **batalhador, a** [bataʎa'dor(a)] ADJ struggling ▶ M/F fighter; **batalhão** [bata'ʎãw] (pl **-ões**) M battalion; **batalhar** [bata'ʎar] VI to battle, fight; (esforçar-se) to make an effort, try hard ▶ VT (emprego) to go after

batata [ba'tata] F potato; **~ doce** sweet potato; **~ frita** chips pl (BRIT), French fries pl; (de pacote) crisps pl (BRIT), (potato) chips pl (US)

bate-boca ['batʃi-] (pl **-s**) M row, quarrel

batedeira [bate'dejra] F beater; (de manteiga) churn; **~ elétrica** mixer

batente [ba'tẽtʃi] M doorpost

bate-papo ['batʃi-] (pl **-s**) (BR) M chat

bater [ba'ter] VT to beat; to strike; (pé) to stamp; (foto) to take; (porta) to slam; (asas) to flap; (recorde) to break; (roupa) to wear all the time ▶ VI to slam; (sino) to ring; (janela) to bang; (coração) to beat; (sol) to beat down; **bater-se** VR: **~se para fazer/por** to fight to do/for; **~ (à porta)** to knock (at the door); **~ à maquina** to type; **~ em** to hit; **~ com o carro** to crash one's car; **~ com a cabeça** to bang one's head; **~ com o pé (em)** to kick

bateria [bate'ria] F battery; (Mús) drums pl; **~ de cozinha** kitchen utensils pl; **baterista** [bate'rista] M/F drummer

batida [ba'tʃida] F beat; (da porta) slam; (à porta) knock; (da polícia) raid; (Auto) crash; (bebida) cocktail of cachaça, fruit and sugar

batido, -a [ba'tʃidu, a] ADJ beaten; (roupa) worn ▶ M: **~ de leite** (PT) milk shake

batina [ba'tʃina] F (Rel) cassock

batismo [ba'tʃizmu] M baptism, christening

batizar [batʃi'zar] VT to baptize, christen

batom [ba'tõ] (pl **-ns**) M lipstick

batucada [batu'kada] F dance percussion group

batucar [batu'kar] VT, VI to drum

baú [ba'u] M trunk

baunilha [baw'niʎa] F vanilla

bazar [ba'zar] M bazaar; (loja) shop

bêbado, -a ['bebadu, a] ADJ, M/F drunk

bebê [be'be] M baby

bebedeira [bebe'dejra] F drunkenness; **tomar uma ~** to get drunk

bêbedo, -a ['bebedu, a] ADJ, M/F = **bêbado**

bebedouro [bebe'douru] M drinking fountain

beber [be'ber] VT to drink; (absorver) to soak up ▶ VI to drink; **bebida** [be'bida] F drink

beça ['bɛsa] (col) F: **à ~** (com vb) a lot; (com n) a lot of

beco ['beku] M alley, lane; **~ sem saída** cul-de-sac

bege ['bɛʒi] ADJ INV beige

beija-flor [bejʒaˈflɔr] (pl -**es**) M
hummingbird

beijar [bejˈʒar] VT to kiss; **beijar-se** VR to
kiss (one another); **beijo** [ˈbejʒu] M kiss;
dar beijos em alguém to kiss sb

beira [ˈbejra] F edge; (de rio) bank; (orla)
border; **à ~ de** on the edge of; (ao lado de)
beside, by; (fig) on the verge of; **~ do
telhado** eaves pl; **beira-mar** F seaside

belas-artes FPL fine arts

beldade [bewˈdadʒi] F beauty

beleza [beˈleza] F beauty; **que ~!** how
lovely!

belga [ˈbɛwga] ADJ, M/F Belgian

Bélgica [ˈbɛwʒika] F: **a ~** Belgium

beliche [beˈliʃi] M bunk

beliscão [belisˈkãw] (pl -**ões**) M pinch;
beliscar [belisˈkar] VT to pinch, nip;
(comida) to nibble

Belize [beˈlizi] M Belize

belo, -a [ˈbɛlu, a] ADJ beautiful

(PALAVRA-CHAVE)

bem [bẽj] ADV **1** (de maneira satisfatória,
correta etc) well; **trabalha/come bem**
she works/eats well; **respondeu bem**
he answered correctly; **me sinto/não
me sinto bem** I feel fine/I don't feel very
well; **tudo bem? — tudo bem** how's it
going? — fine
2 (valor intensivo) very; **um quarto bem
quente** a nice warm room; **bem se vê
que ...** it's clear that ...
3 (bastante) quite, fairly; **a casa é bem
grande** the house is quite big
4 (exatamente): **bem ali** right there; **não
é bem assim** it's not quite like that
5 (estar bem): **estou muito bem aqui** I
feel very happy here; **está bem! vou
fazê-lo** oh all right, I'll do it!
6 (de bom grado): **eu bem que iria mas ...**
I'd gladly go but ...
7 (cheirar) good, nice
▶ M **1** (bem-estar) good; **estou dizendo
isso para o seu bem** I'm telling you for
your own good; **o bem e o mal** good
and evil
2 (posses): **bens** goods, property sg; **bens
de consumo** consumer goods; **bens de
família** family possessions; **bens
móveis/imóveis** moveable property
sg/real estate sg
▶ EXCL **1** (aprovação): **bem!** OK!; **muito
bem!** well done!
2 (desaprovação): **bem feito!** it serves you
right!
▶ ADJ INV (tom depreciativo): **gente bem**
posh people

▶ CONJ **1**: **nem bem** as soon as, no
sooner than; **nem bem ela chegou
começou a dar ordens** as soon as she
arrived she started to give orders, no
sooner had she arrived than she started
to give orders
2: **se bem que** though; **gostaria de ir
se bem que não tenho dinheiro** I'd like
to go even though I've got no money
3: **bem como** as well as; **o livro bem
como a peça foram escritos por ele**
the book as well as the play was written
by him

bem-conceituado, -a [-kõsejˈtwadu,
a] ADJ highly regarded

bem-disposto, -a [-dʒisˈpostu, ˈpɔsta]
ADJ well, in good form

bem-me-quer (pl -**es**) M daisy

bem-vindo, -a [-vĩdo] ADJ welcome

bênção [ˈbẽsãw] (pl -**s**) F blessing

beneficência [benefiˈsẽsja] F kindness;
(caridade) charity

beneficiar [benefiˈsjar] VT to benefit;
(melhorar) to improve; **beneficiar-se** VR
to benefit

benefício [beneˈfisju] M benefit, profit;
(favor) favour (BRIT), favor (US); **em ~ de**
in aid of; **benéfico, -a** [beˈnɛfiku, a] ADJ
beneficial; (generoso) generous

bengala [bẽˈgala] F walking stick

benigno, -a [beˈnignu, a] ADJ kind;
(agradável) pleasant; (Med) benign

bens [bẽjs] MPL de **bem**

bento, -a [ˈbẽtu, a] PP de **benzer** ▶ ADJ
blessed; (água) holy

benzer [bẽˈzer] VT to bless; **benzer-se** VR
to cross o.s.

berço [ˈbersu] M cradle; (cama) cot;
(origem) birthplace

Berlim [berˈlĩ] N Berlin

berma [ˈbɛrma] (PT) F hard shoulder
(BRIT), berm (US)

berrar [beˈhar] VI to bellow; (criança) to
bawl; **berreiro** [beˈhejru] M: **abrir o
berreiro** to burst out crying; **berro**
[ˈbɛhu] M yell

besta [ˈbesta] ADJ stupid; (convencido) full
of oneself; **~ de carga** beast of burden;
besteira [besˈtejra] F foolishness; **dizer
besteiras** to talk nonsense; **fazer uma
besteira** to do something silly; **bestial**
[besˈtʃjaw] (pl -**ais**) ADJ bestial;
(repugnante) repulsive

best-seller [bɛstˈsɛler] (pl -**s**) M best
seller

betão [beˈtãw] (PT) M concrete

beterraba [beteˈhaba] F beetroot

bexiga [be'ʃiga] F bladder

bezerro, -a [be'zehu, a] M/F calf

BI (PT) ABR M *see note*

> All Portuguese citizens are required to carry an identity card which was formerly known as the **BI** or *bilhete de identidade*. This has now been replaced by a smart-card version known as the **cartão de cidadão**. As well as providing a photograph and giving standard details such as the owner's name, date of birth, height and names of parents, it includes on the same card electoral, medical and tax-payer identification details. Like the BI, this card can be used instead of a passport for travel within the European Union.

Bíblia ['biblja] F Bible

bibliografia [bibljogra'fia] F bibliography

biblioteca [bibljo'tɛka] F library; (*estante*) bookcase; **bibliotecário, -a** [bibljote'karju, a] M/F librarian

bica ['bika] F tap; (PT) black coffee, expresso

bicha ['biʃa] F (*lombriga*) worm; (PT: *fila*) queue

bicho ['biʃu] M animal; (*inseto*) insect, bug

bicicleta [bisi'klɛta] F bicycle; (*col*) bike; **andar de ~** to cycle

bico ['biku] M (*de ave*) beak; (*ponta*) point; (*de chaleira*) spout; (*boca*) mouth; (*de pena*) nib; (*do peito*) nipple; (*de gás*) jet; (*col: emprego*) casual job; (*chupeta*) dummy; **calar o ~** to shut up

bidê [bi'de] M bidet

bife ['bifi] M (beef) steak; **~ a cavalo** steak with fried eggs; **~ à milanesa** beef escalope; **~ de panela** beef stew

bifurcação [bifurka'sãw] (*pl* **-ões**) F fork

bifurcar-se [bifur'karsi] VR to fork, divide

bigode [bi'gɔdʒi] M moustache

bijuteria [biʒute'ria] F (*costume*) jewellery (BRIT) *ou* jewelry (US)

bilhão [bi'ʎãw] (*pl* **-ões**) M billion

bilhar [bi'ʎar] M (*jogo*) billiards *sg*

bilhete [bi'ʎetʃi] M ticket; (*cartinha*) note; **~ eletrônico** e-ticket; **~ de ida** single (BRIT) *ou* one-way ticket; **~ de ida e volta** return (BRIT) *ou* round-trip (US) ticket; **bilheteira** [biʎe'tejra] (PT) F ticket office; (*Teatro*) box office; **bilheteiro, -a** [biʎe'tejru, a] M/F ticket seller; **bilheteria** [biʎete'ria] F ticket office

bilhões [bi'ʎõjs] MPL *de* **bilhão**

bilíngue [bi'lĩgwi] ADJ bilingual

binóculo [bi'nɔkulu] M binoculars *pl*; (*para teatro*) opera glasses *pl*

biocombustível [bjokõbus'tʃivew] (*pl* **-eis**) M biofuel

biodiesel [bjo'dʒizew] M biodiesel

biodiversidade [bjodʒiversi'dadʒi] F biodiversity

biografia [bjogra'fia] F biography

biologia [bjolo'ʒia] F biology

biombo ['bjõbu] M screen

bioterrorismo [bjoteho'rizmu] M bioterrorism

bip [bip] N pager

biquíni [bi'kini] M bikini

birita [bi'rita] (*col*) F drink

biruta [bi'ruta] ADJ crazy ▶ F windsock

bis [bis] EXCL encore!

bisavô, -vó [biza'vo, vɔ] M/F great-grandfather/great-grandmother; **bisavós** [biza'vɔs] MPL great-grandparents

biscate [bis'katʃi] M odd job

biscoito [bis'kojtu] M biscuit (BRIT), cookie (US)

bispo ['bispu] M bishop

bissexto, -a [bi'sestu, a] ADJ: **ano ~** leap year

bit ['bitʃi] M (*Comput*) bit

bizarro, -a [bi'zahu, a] ADJ bizarre

blasfemar [blasfe'mar] VT to curse ▶ VI to blaspheme; **blasfêmia** [blas'femja] F blasphemy

blazer ['blejzer] (*pl* **-s**) M blazer

blecaute [ble'kawtʃi] M power cut

blindado, -a [blĩ'dadu, a] ADJ armoured (BRIT), armored (US)

blitz [blits] F police road block

bloco ['blɔku] M block; (*Pol*) bloc; (*de escrever*) writing pad; **~ de carnaval** carnival troupe

blog ['blɔgi] M blog; **blogar** [blo'gar] VI to blog; **blogosfera** [blɔgos'fɛra] F blogosphere; **blogue** ['blɔgi] M blog; **blogueiro, -a** [blo'gejru, a] M/F blogger

bloqueador [blokja'dor] M: **~ solar** sunblock

bloquear [blo'kjar] VT to blockade; (*obstruir*) to block; **bloqueio** [blo'keju] M (*Mil*) blockade; (*obstrução*) blockage

blusa ['bluza] F (*de mulher*) blouse; (*de homem*) shirt; **~ de lã** jumper; **blusão** [blu'zãw] (*pl* **-ões**) M jacket

boa ['boa] ADJ F *de* **bom** ▶ F boa constrictor

boate ['bwatʃi] F nightclub

boato ['bwatu] M rumour (BRIT), rumor (US)

bobagem [bo'baʒẽ] (*pl* **-ns**) F silliness, nonsense; (*dito, ato*) silly thing

bobo, -a ['bobu, a] ADJ silly, daft ▶ M/F fool ▶ M (*de corte*) jester; **fazer-se de ~** to act the fool

bobó [bo'bɔ] M beans, palm oil and manioc

boca ['boka] F mouth; (*entrada*) entrance; (*de fogão*) ring; **de ~ aberta** amazed; **bater ~** to argue

bocadinho [boka'dʒiɲu] M: **um ~** (*pouco tempo*) a little while; (*pouquinho*) a little bit

bocado [bo'kadu] M mouthful, bite; (*pedaço*) piece, bit; **um ~ de tempo** quite some time

boçal [bo'saw] (*pl* **-ais**) ADJ ignorant; (*grosseiro*) uncouth

bocejar [bose'ʒar] VI to yawn; **bocejo** [bo'seʒu] M yawn

bochecha [bo'ʃeʃa] F cheek; **bochecho** [bo'ʃeʃu] M mouthwash

boda ['boda] F wedding; **bodas** FPL (*aniversário de casamento*) wedding anniversary *sg*

bode ['bɔdʒi] M goat; **~ expiatório** scapegoat

bofetada [bofe'tada] F slap

bofetão [bofe'tãw] (*pl* **-ões**) M punch

boi [boj] M ox

boia ['bɔja] F buoy; (*col*) grub; (*de braço*) armband, water wing

boiar [bo'jar] VT, VI to float

boi-bumbá [-bũ'ba] N *see note*

The **boi-bumbá**, or *bumba-meu-boi*, is a traditional folk dance from north-eastern Brazil, which brings together human, animal and mythological characters in a theatrical performance. The ox, which the dance is named after, is played by a dancer wearing an iron frame covered in pieces of colourful fabric. Eventually the beast is "killed" and its meat is symbolically shared out before it comes back to life in the finale.

boicotar [bojko'tar] VT to boycott; **boicote** [boj'kɔtʃi] M boycott

bola ['bɔla] F ball; **dar ~ para** (*flertar*) to flirt with; **ela não dá a menor ~ (para isso)** she couldn't care less (about it); **não ser certo da ~** (*col*) not to be right in the head

bolacha [bo'laʃa] F biscuit (BRIT), cookie (US); (*col: bofetada*) wallop; (*para chope*) beer mat

boleia [bo'leja] F (*de caminhão*) cab; (PT: *carona*) lift; **dar uma ~ a alguém** (PT) to give sb a lift

boletim [bole'tʃĩ] (*pl* **-ns**) M report; (*publicação*) newsletter; **~ meteorológico** weather forecast

bolha ['boʎa] F (*na pele*) blister; (*de ar, sabão*) bubble

boliche [bo'liʃi] M bowling, skittles *sg*

bolinho [bo'liɲu] M: **~ de carne** meat ball; **~ de arroz/bacalhau** rice/dry cod cake

Bolívia [bo'livja] F: **a ~** Bolivia

bolo ['bolu] M cake; (*monte: de gente*) bunch; (: *de papéis*) bundle; **dar o ~ em alguém** to stand sb up; **vai dar ~** (*col*) there's going to be trouble

bolor [bo'lor] M mould (BRIT), mold (US); (*nas plantas*) mildew; (*bafio*) mustiness

bolota [bo'lɔta] F acorn

bolsa ['bowsa] F bag; (*Com: tb:* **~ de valores**) stock exchange; **~ (de estudos)** scholarship

bolso ['bowsu] M pocket; **de ~** pocket *atr*

(PALAVRA-CHAVE)

bom, boa [bõ, 'boa] (*pl* **bons/boas**) ADJ
1 (*ótimo*) good; **é um livro bom** *ou* **um bom livro** it's a good book; **a comida está boa** the food is delicious; **o tempo está bom** the weather's fine; **ele foi muito bom comigo** he was very nice *ou* kind to me
2 (*apropriado*): **ser bom para** to be good for; **acho bom você não ir** I think it's better if you don't go
3 (*irônico*): **um bom quarto de hora** a good quarter of an hour; **que bom motorista você é!** a fine *ou* some driver you are!; **seria bom que ...!** a fine thing it would be if ...!; **essa é boa!** what a cheek!
4 (*saudação*): **bom dia!** good morning!; **boa tarde!** good afternoon!; **boa noite!** good evening!; (*ao deitar-se*) good night!; **tudo bom?** how's it going?
5 (*outras frases*): **está bom?** OK?
▶ EXCL: **bom!** all right!; **bom, ...** right, ...

---

bomba ['bõba] F bomb; (*Tec*) pump; (*fig*) bombshell; **~ atômica/relógio/de fumaça** atomic/time/smoke bomb; **~ de gasolina** petrol (BRIT) *ou* gas (US) pump; **~ de incêndio** fire extinguisher

bombardear [bõbar'dʒjar] VT to bomb; (*fig*) to bombard; **bombardeio** [bõbar'deju] M bombing, bombardment; **bombardeio suicida** suicide bombing

bombeiro [bõ'bejru] M firefighter; (BR: *encanador*) plumber; **o corpo de ~s** fire brigade

bombom [bõ'bõ] (pl **-ns**) M chocolate

bondade [bõ'dadʒi] F goodness, kindness; **tenha a ~ de vir** would you please come

bonde ['bõdʒi] (BR) M tram

bondoso, -a [bõ'dozu, ɔza] ADJ kind, good

boné [bo'nɛ] M cap

boneca [bo'nɛka] F doll

boneco [bo'nɛku] M dummy

bonito, -a [bo'nitu, a] ADJ pretty; (gesto, dia) nice ▶ M (peixe) tuna (fish), tunny

bônus ['bonus] M INV bonus

boquiaberto, -a [bokja'bɛrtu, a] ADJ dumbfounded, astonished

borboleta [borbo'leta] F butterfly; (BR: roleta) turnstile

borbotão [borbo'tãw] (pl **-ões**) M gush, spurt; **sair aos borbotões** to gush out

borbulhar [borbu'ʎar] VI to bubble

borda ['borda] F edge; (do rio) bank; **à ~ de** on the edge of

bordado [bor'dadu] M embroidery

bordar [bor'dar] VT to embroider

bordo ['bordu] M (de navio) side; **a ~** on board

borra ['boha] F dregs pl

borracha [bo'haʃa] F rubber; **borracheiro** [boha'ʃejru] M tyre (BRIT) ou tire (US) specialist

borrão [bo'hãw] (pl **-ões**) M (rascunho) rough draft; (mancha) blot

borrifar [bohi'far] VT to sprinkle; **borrifo** [bo'hifu] M spray

borrões [bo'hõjs] MPL de **borrão**

bosque ['boski] M wood, forest

bossa ['bɔsa] F charm; (inchaço) swelling; **Bossa nova** (Mús) see note

> Bossa nova is a type of music invented by young, middle-class inhabitants of Rio de Janeiro at the end of the 1950s. It has an obvious jazz influence, an unusual, rhythmic beat and lyrics praising beauty and love. **Bossa nova** became known around the world through the work of the conductor and composer Antônio Carlos Jobim, whose compositions, working with the poet Vinícius de Morais, include the famous song "The Girl from Ipanema".

bota ['bɔta] F boot; **~s de borracha** wellingtons

botânica [bo'tanika] F botany

botão [bo'tãw] (pl **-ões**) M button; (flor) bud

botar [bo'tar] VT to put; (roupa, sapatos) to put on; (mesa) to set; (defeito) to find; (ovos) to lay

bote ['bɔtʃi] M boat; (com arma) thrust; (salto) spring

botequim [botʃi'kĩ] (pl **-ns**) M bar

botija [bo'tʃiʒa] F (earthenware) jug

botões [bo'tõjs] MPL de **botão**

boxe ['bɔksi] M boxing

brabo, -a ['brabu, a] ADJ fierce; (zangado) angry; (ruim) bad; (calor) unbearable

braçada [bra'sada] F armful; (Natação) stroke

bracelete [brase'letʃi] M bracelet

braço ['brasu] M arm; **de ~s cruzados** with arms folded; (fig) without lifting a finger; **de ~ dado** arm-in-arm

bradar [bra'dar] VT, VI to shout, yell; **brado** ['bradu] M shout, yell

braguilha [bra'giʎa] F flies pl

branco, -a ['brãku, a] ADJ white ▶ M/F white man/woman ▶ M (espaço) blank; **em ~** blank; **noite em ~** sleepless night; **brancura** [brã'kura] F whiteness

brando, -a ['brãdu, a] ADJ gentle; (mole) soft

brasão [bra'zãw] (pl **-ões**) M coat of arms

braseiro [bra'zejru] M brazier

Brasil [bra'ziw] M: **o ~** Brazil; **brasileiro, -a** [brazi'lejru, a] ADJ, M/F Brazilian

Brasília [bra'zilja] N Brasília

brasões [bra'zõjs] MPL de **brasão**

bravata [bra'vata] F bravado, boasting

bravio, -a [bra'viu, a] ADJ (selvagem) wild; (feroz) ferocious

bravo, -a ['bravu, a] ADJ brave; (furioso) angry; (mar) rough ▶ M brave man; **~!** bravo!; **bravura** [bra'vura] F courage, bravery

brecar [bre'kar] VT (carro) to stop; (reprimir) to curb ▶ VI to brake

breu [brew] M tar, pitch

breve ['brɛvi] ADJ short; (conciso, rápido) brief ▶ ADV soon; **em ~** soon, shortly; **até ~** see you soon

bridge ['bridʒi] M bridge

briga ['briga] F fight; (verbal) quarrel

brigada [bri'gada] F brigade

brigão, -gona [bri'gãw, ɔna] (pl **-ões/-s**) ADJ quarrelsome ▶ M/F troublemaker

brigar [bri'gar] VI to fight; (altercar) to quarrel

brigões [bri'gõjs] MPL de **brigão**

brigona [bri'gona] F de **brigão**

brilhante [bri'ʎãtʃi] ADJ brilliant ▶ M diamond

brilhar [bri'ʎar] VI to shine

brincadeira [brĩka'dejra] F fun; (gracejo) joke; (de criança) game; **deixe de ~s!** stop fooling!; **de ~** for fun

brincalhão, -lhona [brīka'ʎãw, ɔna] (*pl* -ões/-s) ADJ playful ▸ M/F joker, teaser

brincar [brī'kar] VI to play; (*gracejar*) to joke; **estou brincando** I'm only kidding; **~ de soldados** to play (at) soldiers; **~ com alguém** to tease sb

brinco ['brĩku] M (*joia*) earring

brindar [brĩ'dar] VT to drink to; (*presentear*) to give a present to; **brinde** ['brĩdʒi] M toast; (*presente*) free gift

brinquedo [brĩ'kedu] M toy

brio ['briu] M self-respect, dignity

brisa ['briza] F breeze

britânico, -a [bri'taniku, a] ADJ British ▸ M/F Briton

broche ['brɔʃi] M brooch

brochura [bro'ʃura] F (*livro*) paperback; (*folheto*) brochure, pamphlet

brócolis ['brɔkolis] MPL broccoli *sg*

bronca ['brõka] (*col*) F telling off; **dar uma ~ em** to tell off; **levar uma ~** to get told off

bronco, -a ['brõku, a] ADJ (*rude*) coarse; (*burro*) thick

bronquite [brõ'kitʃi] F bronchitis

bronze ['brõzi] M bronze; **bronzear** [brõ'zjar] VT to tan; **bronzear-se** VR to get a tan

broto ['brotu] M bud; (*fig*) youngster

broxa ['brɔʃa] F (large) paint brush

bruços ['brusus] MPL: **de ~** face down

bruma ['bruma] F mist, haze

brusco, -a ['brusku, a] ADJ brusque; (*súbito*) sudden

brutal [bru'taw] (*pl* -ais) ADJ brutal

bruto, -a ['brutu, a] ADJ brutish; (*grosseiro*) coarse; (*móvel*) heavy; (*petróleo*) crude; (*peso, Com*) gross ▸ M brute; **em ~** raw, unworked

bruxa ['bruʃa] F witch; **bruxaria** [bruʃa'ria] F witchcraft

Bruxelas [bru'ʃelas] N Brussels

bruxo ['bruʃu] M wizard

budismo [bu'dʒizmu] M Buddhism

bufar [bu'far] VI to puff, pant; (*com raiva*) to snort; (*reclamar*) to moan, grumble

bufê [bu'fe] M sideboard; (*comida*) buffet

buffer ['bafer] (*pl* -s) M (*Comput*) buffer

bula ['bula] F (*Med*) directions *pl* for use

bule ['buli] M (*de chá*) teapot; (*de café*) coffeepot

Bulgária [buw'garja] F: **a ~** Bulgaria; **búlgaro, -a** ['buwgaru, a] ADJ, M/F Bulgarian ▸ M (*Ling*) Bulgarian

bulimia [buli'mia] F bulimia

bunda ['bũda] (*col*) F bottom, backside

buquê [bu'ke] M bouquet

buraco [bu'raku] M hole; (*de agulha*) eye;

ser um ~ to be tough; **~ da fechadura** keyhole

burguês, -guesa [bur'ges, 'geza] ADJ middle-class, bourgeois; **burguesia** [burge'zia] F middle class, bourgeoisie

burocracia [burokra'sia] F bureaucracy

burro, -a ['buhu, a] ADJ stupid ▸ M/F (*Zool*) donkey; (*pessoa*) fool, idiot; **pra ~** (*col*) a lot; (*com adj*) really; **~ de carga** (*fig*) hard worker

busca ['buska] F search; **em ~ de** in search of; **dar ~ a** to search for

buscador [buska'dor] M search engine

buscar [bus'kar] VT to fetch; (*procurar*) to look *ou* search for; **ir ~** to fetch, go for; **mandar ~** to send for

bússola ['busola] F compass

busto ['bustu] M bust

buzina [bu'zina] F horn; **buzinar** [buzi'nar] VI to sound one's horn, toot the horn ▸ VT to hoot

búzio ['buzju] M conch

c/ ABR = **com**

cá [ka] ADV here; **de cá** on this side; **para cá** here, over here; **para lá e para cá** back and forth; **de lá para cá** since then

caatinga [ka'tʃĩga] (BR) F scrub(-land)

cabana [ka'bana] F hut

cabeça [ka'besa] F head; (inteligência) brain; (de uma lista) top ▶ M/F leader; **de ~** off the top of one's head; (calcular) in one's head; **de ~ para baixo** upside down; **por ~** per person, per head; **cabeçada** [kabe'sada] F (pancada com cabeça) butt; (Futebol) header; (asneira) blunder; **cabeçalho** [kabe'saʎu] M (de livro) title page; (de página, capítulo) heading

cabeceira [kabe'sejra] F (de cama) head

cabeçudo, -a [kabe'sudu, a] ADJ with a big head; (teimoso) headstrong

cabeleira [kabe'lejra] F head of hair; (postiça) wig; **cabeleireiro, -a** [kabelej'rejru, a] M/F hairdresser

cabelo [ka'belu] M hair; **cortar/fazer o ~** to have one's hair cut/done; **cabeludo, -a** [kabe'ludu, a] ADJ hairy

caber [ka'ber] VI: **~ (em)** to fit; (ser compatível) to be appropriate (in); **~ a** (em partilha) to fall to; **cabe a alguém fazer** it is up to sb to do; **não cabe aqui fazer comentários** this is not the time or place to comment

cabide [ka'bidʒi] M (coat) hanger; (móvel) hat stand; (fixo à parede) coat rack

cabine [ka'bini] F cabin; (em loja) fitting room; **~ do piloto** (Aer) cockpit; **~ telefônica** telephone box (BRIT) ou booth

cabo ['kabu] M (extremidade) end; (de faca, vassoura etc) handle; (corda) rope; (elétrico etc) cable; (Geo) cape; (Mil) corporal; **ao ~ de** at the end of; **de ~ a rabo** from beginning to end; **levar a ~** to carry out; **dar ~ de** to do away with

caboclo, -a [ka'boklu, a] (BR) M/F mestizo

cabra ['kabra] F goat

cabreiro, -a [ka'brejru, a] (col) ADJ suspicious

cabrito [ka'britu] M kid

caça ['kasa] F hunting; (busca) hunt; (animal) quarry, game ▶ M (Aer) fighter (plane); **caçador, a** [kasa'dor(a)] M/F hunter

cação [ka'sãw] (pl -ões) M shark

caçar [ka'sar] VT to hunt; (com espingarda) to shoot; (procurar) to seek ▶ VI to hunt, go hunting

caçarola [kasa'rɔla] F (sauce)pan

cacau [ka'kaw] M cocoa; (Bot) cacao

cacetada [kase'tada] F blow (with a stick)

cachaça [ka'ʃasa] F (white) rum

cachaceiro, -a [kaʃa'sejru, a] ADJ drunk ▶ M/F drunkard

cachê [ka'ʃe] M fee

cachecol [kaʃe'kɔw] (pl -óis) M scarf

cachimbo [ka'ʃĩbu] M pipe

cacho ['kaʃu] M bunch; (de cabelo) curl; (longo) ringlet

cachoeira [kaʃ'wejra] F waterfall

cachorra [ka'ʃoʁa] F bitch, (female) puppy

cachorrinho, -a [kaʃo'hiɲu, a] M/F puppy

cachorro [ka'ʃoʁu] M dog, puppy; **cachorro-quente** (pl **cachorros-quentes**) M hot dog

cacique [ka'siki] M (Indian) chief; (mandachuva) local boss

caco ['kaku] M bit, fragment; (pessoa velha) old relic

caçoar [ka'swar] VT, VI to mock

cacoete [ka'kwetʃi] M twitch, tic

cacto ['kaktu] M cactus

cada ['kada] ADJ INV each; (todo) every; **~ um** each one; **~ semana** each week; **a ~ 3 horas** every 3 hours; **~ vez mais** more and more

cadastrar [kadas'trar] VT to register; **cadastrar-se** VR to register

cadastro [ka'dastru] M register; (ato) registration; (de criminosos) criminal record

cadáver [ka'daver] M corpse, (dead) body

cadê [ka'de] (col) ADV: **~ ...?** where's/where are ...?, what's happened to ...?

cadeado [ka'dʒjadu] M padlock

cadeia [ka'deja] F chain; (*prisão*) prison; (*rede*) network

cadeira [ka'dejra] F chair; (*disciplina*) subject; (*Teatro*) stall; (*função*) post; **cadeiras** FPL (*Anat*) hips; **~ de balanço** rocking chair; **~ de rodas** wheelchair; **cadeirante** M/F (*BR*) wheelchair user

cadela [ka'dɛla] F (*cão*) bitch

caderneta [kader'neta] F notebook; **~ de poupança** savings account

caderno [ka'dɛrnu] M exercise book; (*de notas*) notebook; (*de jornal*) section

caducar [kadu'kar] VI to lapse, expire; **caduco, -a** [ka'duku, a] ADJ invalid, expired; (*senil*) senile; (*Bot*) deciduous

cães [kãjs] MPL *de* **cão**

cafajeste [kafa'ʒɛstʃi] (*col*) ADJ roguish; (*vulgar*) vulgar, coarse ▶ M/F rogue; rough customer

café [ka'fɛ] M coffee; (*estabelecimento*) café; **~ com leite** white coffee (*BRIT*), coffee with cream (*US*); **~ preto** black coffee; **~ da manhã** (*BR*) breakfast

cafeteira [kafe'tejra] F coffeepot; (*máquina*) percolator; **cafezal** [kafe'zaw] (*pl* **-ais**) M coffee plantation; **cafezinho** [kafe'ziɲu] M *small black coffee*

cagada [ka'gada] (!) F shit (!)

cágado [ˈkagadu] M turtle

cagar [ka'gar] (!) VI to (have a) shit (!)

caguetar [kagwe'tar] VT to inform on; **caguete** [ka'gwetʃi] M informer

caiba [ˈkajba] VB *ver* **caber**

cãibra [ˈkãjbra] F (*Med*) cramp

caída [ka'ida] F = **queda**

caído, -a [ka'idu, a] ADJ dejected; (*derrubado*) fallen; (*pendente*) droopy; **~ por** (*apaixonado*) in love with

câimbra [ˈkãjbra] F = **cãibra**

caipirinha [kajpi'riɲa] F *cocktail of cachaça, lemon and sugar*

cair [ka'ir] VI to fall; **~ bem/mal** (*roupa*) to fit well/badly; (*col: pessoa*) to look good/bad; **~ em si** to come to one's senses; **ao ~ da noite** at nightfall; **essa comida me caiu mal** that food did not agree with me

Cairo [ˈkajru] M: **o ~** Cairo

cais [kajs] M (*Náut*) quay; (*PT Ferro*) platform

caixa [ˈkajʃa] F box; (*cofre*) safe; (*de uma loja*) cash desk ▶ M/F (*pessoa*) cashier; **~ automática** *ou* **eletrônico** cash machine; **pequena ~** petty cash; **~ de correio** letter box; **~ de mudanças** (*BR*) *ou* **de velocidades** gear box; **~ econômica** savings bank; **~ postal** P.O. box; **~ registradora** cash register; **caixa-forte** (*pl* **caixas-fortes**) F vault

caixão [kaj'ʃãw] (*pl* **-ões**) M (*ataúde*) coffin; (*caixa grande*) large box

caixeiro-viajante, caixeira-viajante (*pl* **caixeiros-viajantes/caixeiras-viajantes**) M/F commercial traveller (*BRIT*) *ou* traveler (*US*)

caixilho [kaj'ʃiʎu] M (*moldura*) frame

caixões [kaj'ʃõjs] MPL *de* **caixão**

caixote [kaj'ʃɔtʃi] M packing case; **~ do lixo** (*PT*) dustbin (*BRIT*), garbage can (*US*)

caju [ka'ʒu] M cashew fruit

cal [kaw] F lime; (*na água*) chalk; (*para caiar*) whitewash

calabouço [kala'bosu] M dungeon

calado, -a [ka'ladu, a] ADJ quiet

calafrio [kala'friu] M shiver; **ter ~s** to shiver

calamidade [kalami'dadʒi] F calamity, disaster

calão [ka'lãw] M: **(baixo) ~** slang

calar [ka'lar] VT (*não dizer*) to keep quiet about; (*impor silêncio a*) to silence ▶ VI to go quiet; (*manter-se calado*) to keep quiet; **calar-se** VR to go quiet; to keep quiet; **cala a boca!** shut up!

calça [ˈkawsa] F (*tb*: **~s**) trousers *pl* (*BRIT*), pants *pl* (*US*)

calçada [kaw'sada] F (*PT: rua*) roadway; (*BR: passeio*) pavement (*BRIT*), sidewalk (*US*)

calçadão [kawsa'dãw] (*pl* **-ões**) M pedestrian precinct (*BRIT*), pedestrian zone (*US*)

calçado, -a [kaw'sadu, a] ADJ (*rua*) paved ▶ M shoe; **calçados** MPL (*para os pés*) footwear *sg*

calçadões [kawsa'dõjs] MPL *de* **calçadão**

calçamento [kawsa'mẽtu] M paving

calcanhar [kawka'ɲar] M (*Anat*) heel

calção [kaw'sãw] (*pl* **-ões**) M shorts *pl*; **~ de banho** swimming trunks *pl*

calcar [kaw'kar] VT to tread on; (*espezinhar*) to trample (on)

calçar [kaw'sar] VT (*sapatos, luvas*) to put on; (*pavimentar*) to pave; **calçar-se** VR to put on one's shoes; **ela calça (número) 28** she takes size 28 (in shoes)

calcário, -a [kaw'karju, a] ADJ (*água*) hard ▶ M limestone

calcinha [kaw'siɲa] F panties *pl*

calço [ˈkawsu] M wedge

calções [kaw'sõjs] MPL *de* **calção**

calculador [kawkula'dor] M = **calculadora**

calculadora [kawkula'dora] F calculator

calcular [kawku'lar] VT to calculate; (*imaginar*) to imagine; **~ que** to reckon that

cálculo ['kawkulu] M calculation; (*Mat*) calculus; (*Med*) stone

calda ['kawda] F (*de doce*) syrup; **caldas** FPL (*águas termais*) hot springs

caldeirada [kawdej'rada] (*PT*) F (*guisado*) fish stew

caldo ['kawdu] M broth; (*de fruta*) juice; **~ de carne/galinha** beef/chicken stock; **~ verde** potato and cabbage broth

calendário [kalẽ'darju] M calendar

calhar [ka'ʎar] VI: **calhou viajarmos no mesmo avião** we happened to travel on the same plane; **calhou que** it so happened that; **~ a** (*cair bem*) to suit; **se ~** (*PT*) perhaps, maybe

calibre [ka'libri] M (*de cano*) calibre (*BRIT*), caliber (*US*)

cálice ['kalisi] M wine glass; (*Rel*) chalice

calista [ka'lista] M/F chiropodist (*BRIT*), podiatrist (*US*)

calma ['kawma] F calm

calmante [kaw'mãtʃi] ADJ soothing ▶ M (*Med*) tranquillizer

calmo, -a ['kawmu, a] ADJ calm

calo ['kalu] M callus; (*no pé*) corn

calor [ka'lor] M heat; (*fig*) warmth; **está ou faz ~** it is hot; **estar com ~** to be hot

calorento, -a [kalo'rẽtu, a] ADJ (*pessoa*) sensitive to heat; (*lugar*) hot

caloria [kalo'ria] F calorie

caloroso, -a [kalo'rozu, ɔza] ADJ warm; (*entusiástico*) enthusiastic

calouro, -a [ka'loru, a] M/F (*Educ*) fresher (*BRIT*), freshman (*US*)

calúnia [ka'lunja] F slander

calvo, -a ['kawvu, a] ADJ bald

cama ['kama] F bed; **~ de casal** double bed; **~ de solteiro** single bed; **de ~** (*doente*) ill (in bed)

camada [ka'mada] F layer; (*de tinta*) coat

câmara ['kamara] F chamber; (*PT Foto*) camera; **~ de ar** inner tube; **~ municipal** (*BR*) town council; (*PT*) town hall

camarão [kama'rãw] (*pl* **-ões**) M shrimp; (*graúdo*) prawn

camarões [kama'rõjs] MPL *de* **camarão**

camarote [kama'rɔtʃi] M (*Náut*) cabin; (*Teatro*) box

cambaleante [kãba'ljãtʃi] ADJ unsteady (on one's feet)

cambalhota [kãba'ʎɔta] F somersault

câmbio ['kãbju] M (*dinheiro etc*) exchange; (*preço de câmbio*) rate of exchange; **~ livre** free trade; **~ oficial/ paralelo** official/black market

cambista [kã'bista] M money changer

Camboja [kã'bɔja] M: **o ~** Cambodia

camelo [ka'melu] M camel

câmera ['kamera] (*BR*) F camera; **em ~ lenta** in slow motion; **~ de segurança** security camera, CCTV camera; **~ digital** digital camera

camião [ka'mjãw] (*pl* **-ões**) (*PT*) M lorry (*BRIT*), truck (*US*)

caminhada [kami'nada] F walk

caminhão [kami'nãw] (*pl* **-ões**) (*BR*) M lorry (*BRIT*), truck (*US*)

caminhar [kami'nar] VI to walk; (*processo*) to get under way; (*negócios*) to progress

caminho [ka'minu] M way; (*vereda*) road, path; **~ de ferro** (*PT*) railway (*BRIT*), railroad (*US*); **a ~** on the way, en route; **cortar ~** to take a short cut; **pôr-se a ~** to set off

caminhões [kami'nõjs] MPL *de* **caminhão**

caminhoneiro, -a [kamino'nejru, a] M/F lorry driver (*BRIT*), truck driver (*US*)

camiões [ka'mjõjs] MPL *de* **camião**

camioneta [kamjo'neta] (*PT*) F (*para passageiros*) coach; (*comercial*) van

camionista [kamjo'nista] (*PT*) M/F lorry driver (*BRIT*), truck driver (*US*)

camisa [ka'miza] F shirt; **~ de dormir** nightshirt; **~ de força** straitjacket; **~ esporte/polo/social** sports/polo/ dress shirt

camiseta [kami'zeta] (*BR*) F T-shirt; (*interior*) vest

camisinha [kami'zina] (*col*) F condom

camisola [kami'zɔla] F (*BR*) nightdress; (*PT: pulôver*) sweater; **~ interior** (*PT*) vest

campainha [kampa'ina] F bell

campanário [kãpa'narju] M church tower, steeple

campeão, -peã [kã'pjãw, 'pjã] (*pl* **-ões/-s**) M/F champion; **campeonato** [kãpjo'natu] M championship

campestre [kã'pɛstri] ADJ rural, rustic

camping ['kãpĩ] (*BR*) (*pl* **-s**) M camping; (*lugar*) campsite

campismo [kã'pizmu] M camping; **parque de ~** campsite

campista [kã'pista] M/F camper

campo ['kãpu] M field; (*fora da cidade*) countryside; (*Esporte*) ground; (*acampamento*) camp; (*Tênis*) court

camponês, -esa [kãpo'nes, eza] M/F countryman/woman; (*agricultor*) farmer

campus ['kãpus] M INV campus

camuflagem [kamu'flaʒẽ] F camouflage

camundongo [kamũ'dõgu] (*BR*) M mouse

camurça [ka'mursa] F suede

cana ['kana] F cane; (*col: cadeia*) nick; (*de açúcar*) sugar cane

Canadá [kana'da] M: **o ~** Canada;
canadense [kana'dẽsi] ADJ, M/F
Canadian

canal [ka'naw] (*pl* **-ais**) M channel; (*de
navegação*) canal; (*Anat*) duct

canalização [kanaliza'sãw] F plumbing

canalizador, a [kanaliza'dor(a)] (*PT*)
M/F plumber

canário [ka'narju] M canary

canastra [ka'nastra] F (big) basket

canção [kã'sãw] (*pl* **-ões**) F song; **~ de
ninar** lullaby

cancela [kã'sɛla] F gate

cancelamento [kãsela'mẽtu] M
cancellation

cancelar [kãse'lar] VT to cancel; (*riscar*)
to cross out

câncer ['kãser] M cancer; **C~** (*Astrologia*)
Cancer

canções [kã'sõjs] FPL *de* **canção**

cancro ['kãkru] (*PT*) M cancer

candelabro [kãde'labru] M candlestick;
(*lustre*) chandelier

candidato, -a [kãdʒi'datu, a] M/F
candidate; (*a cargo*) applicant

cândido, -a ['kãdʒidu, a] ADJ naive;
(*inocente*) innocent

candomblé [kãdõ'blɛ] M *see note*

> **Candomblé** is Brazil's most influential
> Afro-Brazilian religion. Practised
> mainly in Bahia, it mixes catholicism
> with Yoruba traditions. According to
> **candomblé**, believers become
> possessed by spirits and thus become
> an instrument of communication
> between divine and mortal forces.
> **Candomblé** ceremonies are great
> spectacles of African rhythm and
> dance held in *terreiros*.

caneca [ka'nɛka] F mug

canela [ka'nɛla] F cinnamon; (*Anat*) shin

caneta [ka'neta] F pen; **~ esferográfica**
ballpoint pen; **~ pilot** felt-tip pen

cangaceiro [kãga'sejru] (*BR*) M bandit

canguru [kãgu'ru] M kangaroo

canhão [ka'ɲãw] (*pl* **-ões**) M cannon;
(*Geo*) canyon

canhoto, -a [ka'ɲotu, a] ADJ left-handed
▶ M/F left-handed person ▶ M (*de cheque*)
stub

canibal [kani'baw] (*pl* **-ais**) M/F cannibal

canil [ka'niw] (*pl* **-is**) M kennel

canja ['kãʒa] F chicken broth; (*col*) cinch,
pushover

canjica [kã'ʒika] F maize porridge

cano ['kanu] M pipe; (*tubo*) tube; (*de
arma de fogo*) barrel; (*de bota*) top; **~ de
esgoto** sewer

canoa [ka'noa] F canoe

cansaço [kã'sasu] M tiredness

cansado, -a [kã'sadu, a] ADJ tired

cansar [kã'sar] VT to tire; (*entediar*) to
bore ▶ VI to get tired; **cansar-se** VR to
get tired; **cansativo, -a** [kãsa'tʃivu, a]
ADJ tiring; (*tedioso*) tedious

cantar [kã'tar] VT, VI to sing ▶ M song

canteiro [kã'tejru] M stonemason; (*de
flores*) flower bed

cantiga [kã'tʃiga] F ballad; **~ de ninar**
lullaby

cantil [kã'tʃiw] (*pl* **-is**) M canteen

cantina [kã'tʃina] F canteen

cantis [kã'tʃis] MPL *de* **cantil**

canto ['kãtu] M corner; (*lugar*) place;
(*canção*) song

cantor, a [kã'tor(a)] M/F singer

cão [kãw] (*pl* **cães**) M dog

caolho, -a [ka'oʎu, a] ADJ cross-eyed

caos ['kaos] M chaos

capa ['kapa] F cape; (*cobertura*) cover;
livro de ~ dura/mole hardback/
paperback (book)

capacete [kapa'setʃi] M helmet

capacidade [kapasi'dadʒi] F capacity;
(*aptidão*) ability, competence

capaz [ka'paz] ADJ able, capable; **ser ~
de** to be able to (*ou* capable of); **sou ~ de
...** (*talvez*) I might ...; **é ~ de chover hoje**
it might rain today

capela [ka'pɛla] F chapel

capim [ka'pĩ] M grass

capitães [kapi'tãjs] MPL *de* **capitão**

capital [kapi'taw] (*pl* **-ais**) ADJ, M capital
▶ F (*cidade*) capital; **~ (em) ações** (*Com*)
share capital

capitalismo [kapita'lizmu] M
capitalism; **capitalista** [kapita'lista]
M/F capitalist

capitalizar [kapitali'zar] VT to
capitalize on; (*Com*) to capitalize

capitão [kapi'tãw] (*pl* **-ães**) M captain

capítulo [ka'pitulu] M chapter

capô [ka'po] M (*Auto*) bonnet (*BRIT*),
hood (*US*)

capoeira [ka'pwejra] F (*PT*) hencoop

> **Capoeira** is a fusion of martial arts
> and dance which originated among
> African slaves in colonial Brazil. It is
> danced in a circle to the sound of the
> *berimbau*, a percussion instrument of
> African origin. Opposed by the
> Brazilian authorities until the
> beginning of the twentieth century,
> today **capoeira** is regarded as a
> national sport.

capota [ka'pɔta] F (*Auto*) hood, top

capotar [kapo'tar] vi to overturn

capricho [ka'priʃu] м whim, caprice; (*teimosia*) obstinacy; (*apuro*) care; **caprichoso, -a** [kapri'ʃozu, ɔza] ADJ capricious; (*com apuro*) meticulous

Capricórnio [kapri'kɔrnju] м Capricorn

cápsula [kapsula] ꜰ capsule

captar [kap'tar] vt (*atrair*) to win; (*Rádio*) to pick up

captura [kap'tura] ꜰ capture; **~ de tela** (*Comput*) screenshot; **capturar** [kaptu'rar] vt to capture

capuz [ka'puz] м hood

cáqui ['kaki] ADJ khaki

cara ['kara] ꜰ face; (*aspecto*) appearance ▶ м (*col*) guy; **~ ou coroa?** heads or tails?; **de ~** straightaway; **dar de ~ com** to bump into; **ser a ~ de** (*col*) to be the spitting image of; **ter ~ de** to look (like)

caracol [kara'kɔw] (*pl* -óis) м snail; (*de cabelo*) curl; **escada em ~** spiral staircase

caracteres [karak'tɛris] MPL *de* **caráter**

característica [karakte'ristʃika] ꜰ characteristic, feature

característico, -a [karakte'ristʃiku, a] ADJ characteristic

cara de pau ꜰ cheek ▶ ADJ INV brazen

caramelo [kara'mɛlu] м caramel; (*bala*) toffee

caranguejo [karã'geʒu] м crab

caratê [kara'te] м karate

caráter [ka'rater] (*pl* **caracteres**) м character

caravana [kara'vana] ꜰ caravan

carboidrato [karboi'dratu] м carbohydrate

cardápio [kar'dapju] (BR) м menu

cardeal [kar'dʒjaw] (*pl* -ais) ADJ, м cardinal

cardigã [kardʒi'gã] м cardigan

careca [ka'rɛka] ADJ bald

carecer [kare'ser] vi: **~ de** to lack; (*precisar*) to need

carência [ka'rẽsja] ꜰ lack; (*necessidade*) need; (*privação*) deprivation; **carente** [ka'rẽtʃi] ADJ wanting; (*pessoa*) needy, deprived

carga ['karga] ꜰ load; (*de navio, avião*) cargo; (*ato de carregar*) loading; (*Elet*) charge; (*fig: peso*) burden; (*Mil*) attack, charge

cargo ['kargu] м responsibility; (*função*) post; **a ~ de** in charge of; **ter a ~** to be in charge of; **tomar a ~** to take charge of

Caribe [ka'ribi] м: **o ~** the Caribbean (Sea)

caridade [kari'dadʒi] ꜰ charity; **obra de ~** charity

cárie ['kari] ꜰ tooth decay

carimbar [karĩ'bar] vt to stamp; (*no correio*) to postmark

carimbo [ka'rĩbu] м stamp; (*postal*) postmark

carinho [ka'riɲu] м affection, fondness; (*carícia*) caress; **fazer ~** to caress; **com ~** affectionately; (*com cuidado*) with care; **carinhoso, -a** [kari'ɲozu, ɔza] ADJ affectionate

carioca [ka'rjɔka] ADJ of Rio de Janeiro ▶ м/ꜰ native of Rio de Janeiro ▶ м (*café*) type of weak coffee

carnal [kar'naw] (*pl* -ais) ADJ carnal; **primo ~** first cousin

carnaval [karna'vaw] (*pl* -ais) м carnival

> In Brazil, **Carnaval** is the popular festival held each year in the four days before Lent. It is celebrated in very different ways in different parts of the country. In Rio de Janeiro, for example, the big attraction is the parades of the *escolas de samba*, in Salvador the *trios elétricos*, in Recife the *frevo* and, in Olinda, the giant figures, such as the *Homen da meia-noite* and *Mulher do meio-dia*. In Portugal, **Carnaval** is celebrated on Shrove Tuesday, with street parties and processions taking place throughout the country.

carne ['karni] ꜰ flesh; (*Culin*) meat; **em ~ e osso** in the flesh

carnê [kar'ne] м (*para compras*) payment book

carneiro [kar'nejru] м sheep; (*macho*) ram; **perna/costeleta de ~** leg of lamb/ lamb chop

carnificina [karnifi'sina] ꜰ slaughter

caro, -a ['karu, a] ADJ dear; **cobrar/ pagar ~** to charge a lot/pay dearly

carochinha [karo'ʃiɲa] ꜰ: **conto da ~** fairy tale

caroço [ka'rosu] м (*de frutos*) stone; (*endurecimento*) lump

carona [ka'rɔna] ꜰ lift; **viajar de ~** to hitchhike; **pegar uma ~** to get a lift

carpete [kar'petʃi] м (*fitted*) carpet

carpinteiro [karpĩ'tejru] м carpenter

carrapato [kaha'patu] м (*inseto*) tick

carrasco [ka'hasku] м executioner; (*fig*) tyrant

carregado, -a [kahe'gadu, a] ADJ loaded; (*semblante*) sullen; (*céu*) dark; (*ambiente*) tense

carregador [kahega'dor] м porter

carregamento [kahega'mẽtu] м (*ação*) loading; (*carga*) load, cargo

carregar [kahe'gar] VT to load; (*levar*) to carry; (*bateria*) to charge; (PT: *apertar*) to press; (*levar para longe*) to take away ▶ VI: **~ em** to overdo; (*pôr enfase*) to bring out

carreira [ka'hejra] F run, running; (*profissão*) career; (*Turfe*) race; (*Náut*) slipway; (*fileira*) row; **às ~s** in a hurry

carretel [kahe'tɛw] (*pl* **-éis**) M spool, reel

carrinho [ka'hiɲu] M trolley; (*brinquedo*) toy car; **~ (de criança)** pram; **~ de mão** wheelbarrow; **~ de compras** shopping trolley (BRIT), shopping cart (US)

carro ['kaho] M car; (*de bois*) cart; (*de mão*) barrow; (*de máquina de escrever*) carriage; **~ de corrida** racing car; **~ de passeio** saloon car; **~ de praça** cab; **~ de bombeiro** fire engine; **~ esporte** sports car

carroça [ka'hɔsa] F cart, wagon

carroçeria [kahose'ria] F (*Auto*) bodywork

carro-chefe (*pl* **carros-chefe(s)**) M (*de desfile*) main float; (*fig*) flagship, centrepiece (BRIT), centerpiece (US)

carrossel [kaho'sɛw] (*pl* **-éis**) M merry-go-round

carruagem [ka'hwaʒẽ] (*pl* **-ns**) F carriage, coach

carta ['karta] F letter; (*de jogar*) card; (*mapa*) chart; **~ aérea** airmail letter; **~ registrada** registered letter; **~ de condução** (PT) driving licence (BRIT), driver's license (US); **dar as ~s** to deal

cartão [kar'tãw] (*pl* **-ões**) M card; (PT: *material*) cardboard; **~ de cidadão** (PT) identity card (*see also note at* **BI**); **~ de crédito** credit card; **~ de débito** debit card; **~ de memória** memory card; **~ de recarga** (*para celular*) top-up card; **~ telefónico** phone card; **cartão-postal** (*pl* **cartões-postais**) M postcard; (*lugar turístico*) sight

cartaz [kar'taz] M poster, bill (US); **(estar) em ~** (*Teatro, Cinema*) (to be) showing

carteira [kar'tejra] F desk; (*para dinheiro*) wallet; (*de ações*) portfolio; **~ de identidade** (BR) identity card; **~ de motorista** driving licence (BRIT), driver's license (US)

carteiro [kar'tejru] M postman (BRIT), mailman (US)

cartões [kar'tõjs] MPL *de* **cartão**

cartola [kar'tɔla] F top hat

cartolina [karto'lina] F card

cartório [kar'tɔrju] M registry office

cartucho [kar'tuʃu] M cartridge; (*saco de papel*) packet

cartum [kar'tũ] (*pl* **-ns**) M cartoon

carvalho [kar'vaʎu] M oak

carvão [kar'vãw] (*pl* **-ões**) M coal; (*de madeira*) charcoal

casa ['kaza] F house; (*lar*) home; (*Com*) firm; (*Mat: decimal*) place; **em/para ~** (at) home/home; **~ de saúde** hospital; **~ da moeda** mint; **~ de banho** (PT) bathroom; **~ e comida** board and lodging; **~ de câmbio** bureau de change; **~ de cômodos** tenement; **~ de repouso** old people's home (BRIT), retirement home (US); **~ popular** ≈ council house

casacão [kaza'kãw] (*pl* **-ões**) M overcoat

casaco [ka'zaku] M coat; (*paletó*) jacket

casacões [kaza'kõjs] MPL *de* **casacão**

casado, -a [ka'zadu, a] ADJ married

casal [ka'zaw] (*pl* **-ais**) M couple

casamento [kaza'mẽtu] M marriage; (*boda*) wedding

casar [ka'zar] VT to marry; (*combinar*) to match (up); **casar-se** VR to get married; (*harmonizar-se*) to combine well

casarão [kaza'rãw] (*pl* **-ões**) M mansion

casca ['kaska] F (*de árvore*) bark; (*de banana*) skin; (*de ferida*) scab; (*de laranja*) peel; (*de nozes, ovos*) shell; (*de milho etc*) husk; (*de pão*) crust

cascata [kas'kata] F waterfall

casco ['kasku] M skull; (*de animal*) hoof; (*de navio*) hull; (*para bebidas*) empty bottle; (*de tartaruga*) shell

caseiro, -a [ka'zejru, a] ADJ home-made; (*pessoa, vida*) domestic ▶ M/F housekeeper

caso ['kazu] M case; (*tb:* **~ amoroso**) affair; (*estória*) story ▶ CONJ in case, if; **no ~ de** in case (of); **em todo ~** in any case; **neste ~** in that case; **~ necessário** if necessary; **criar ~** to cause trouble; **não fazer ~ de** to ignore; **~ de emergência** emergency

caspa ['kaspa] F dandruff

casquinha [kas'kiɲa] F (*de sorvete*) cone; (*pele*) skin

cassar [ka'sar] VT (*direitos, licença*) to cancel, withhold; (*políticos*) to ban

cassete [ka'sɛtʃi] M cassette

cassino [ka'sinu] M casino

castanha [kas'taɲa] F chestnut; **~ de caju** cashew nut; **castanha-do-pará** [-pa'ra] (*pl* **castanhas-do-pará**) F Brazil nut

castanheiro [kasta'ɲejru] M chestnut tree

castanho, -a [kas'taɲu, a] ADJ brown

castelo [kas'tɛlu] M castle

castiçal [kaʃtʃiˈsaw] (*pl* **-ais**) M
candlestick

castiço, -a [kasˈtʃisu, a] ADJ pure

castidade [kaʃtʃiˈdadʒi] F chastity

castigar [kaʃtʃiˈgar] VT to punish;
castigo [kasˈtʃigu] M punishment; (*fig:
mortificação*) pain

casto, -a [ˈkastu, a] ADJ chaste

casual [kaˈzwaw] (*pl* **-ais**) ADJ chance *atr*,
accidental; (*fortuito*) fortuitous;
casualidade [kazwaliˈdadʒi] F chance;
(*acidente*) accident

cata [ˈkata] F: **à ~ de** in search of

catalizador, a [katalizaˈdor(a)] ADJ
catalytic ▶ M catalyst

catalogar [kataloˈgar] VT to catalogue
(*BRIT*), catalog (*US*)

catálogo [kaˈtalogu] M catalogue (*BRIT*),
catalog (*US*); **~ (telefônico)** telephone
directory

catapora [kataˈpora] (*BR*) F chickenpox

catar [kaˈtar] VT to pick (up); (*procurar*) to
look for, search for; (*recolher*) to collect,
gather

catarata [kataˈrata] F waterfall; (*Med*)
cataract

catarro [kaˈtahu] M catarrh

catástrofe [kaˈtastrofi] F catastrophe

cata-vento M weathercock

catedral [kateˈdraw] (*pl* **-ais**) F cathedral

categoria [kategoˈria] F category;
(*social*) rank; (*qualidade*) quality; **de alta ~**
first-rate

cativar [katʃiˈvar] VT to enslave;
(*fascinar*) to captivate; (*atrair*) to charm

cativeiro [katʃiˈvejru] M captivity;
(*escravidão*) slavery; (*cadeia*) prison

católico, -a [kaˈtɔliku, a] ADJ, M/F
Catholic

catorze [kaˈtorzi] NUM fourteen

catraca [kaˈtraka] F turnstile; **~ de
embarque/desembarque** (*em estação*)
ticket barrier

caução [kawˈsãw] (*pl* **-ões**) F security,
guarantee; (*Jur*) bail; **sob ~** on bail

caule [ˈkauli] M stalk, stem

causa [ˈkawza] F cause; (*motivo*) motive,
reason; (*Jur*) lawsuit, case; **por ~ de**
because of; **causador, a** [kawzaˈdor(a)]
ADJ which caused ▶ M cause; **causar**
[kawˈzar] VT to cause, bring about

cautela [kawˈtɛla] F caution; (*senha*)
ticket; **~ (de penhor)** pawn ticket;
cauteloso, -a [kawteˈlozu, ɔza] ADJ
cautious, wary

cavado, -a [kaˈvadu, a] ADJ (*olhos*)
sunken; (*roupa*) low-cut

cavala [kaˈvala] F mackerel

cavaleiro [kavaˈlejru] M rider,
horseman; (*medieval*) knight

cavalheiro, -a [kavaˈʎejru, a] ADJ
courteous, gallant ▶ M gentleman

cavalo [kaˈvalu] M horse; (*Xadrez*)
knight; **a ~** on horseback; **50
~s(-vapor), 50 ~s de força** 50
horsepower; **~ de corrida** racehorse

cavaquinho [kavaˈkiɲu] M small guitar

cavar [kaˈvar] VT to dig; (*esforçar-se para
obter*) to try to get ▶ VI to dig; (*fig*) to
delve; (*animal*) to burrow

cave [ˈkavi] (*PT*) F wine cellar

caveira [kaˈvejra] F skull

cavidade [kaviˈdadʒi] F cavity

caxumba [kaˈʃũba] F mumps *sg*

CD ABR M CD

cê [se] (*col*) PRON = **você**

cear [sjar] VT to have for supper ▶ VI to
dine

cebola [seˈbola] F onion; **cebolinha**
[seboˈliɲa] F spring onion

ceder [seˈder] VT to give up; (*dar*) to hand
over; (*emprestar*) to lend ▶ VI to give in,
yield; (*porta etc*) to give (way)

cedilha [seˈdʒiʎa] F cedilla

cedo [ˈsedu] ADV early; (*em breve*) soon

cedro [ˈsɛdru] M cedar

cédula [ˈsɛdula] F banknote; (*eleitoral*)
ballot paper; **~ de identidade** (*BR*)
identity card

CEE ABR F (= *Comunidade Econômica
Europeia*) EEC

cegar [seˈgar] VT to blind; (*ofuscar*) to
dazzle ▶ VI to be dazzling

cego, -a [ˈsɛgu, a] ADJ blind; (*total*)
complete, total; (*tesoura*) blunt ▶ M/F
blind man/woman; **às cegas** blindly

ceia [ˈseja] F supper

cela [ˈsɛla] F cell

celebração [selebraˈsãw] (*pl* **-ões**) F
celebration

celebrar [seleˈbrar] VT to celebrate;
(*exaltar*) to praise; (*acordo*) to seal

celebridade [selebriˈdadʒi] F celebrity

celeiro [seˈlejru] M granary; (*depósito*)
barn

celeste [seˈlɛstʃi] ADJ celestial, heavenly

celibatário, -a [selibaˈtarju, a] ADJ
unmarried, single ▶ M/F bachelor/
spinster

celofane [seloˈfani] M cellophane;
papel ~ cling film

célula [ˈsɛlula] F (*Bio, Elet*) cell; **celular**
[seluˈlar] ADJ cellular ▶ N: (*telefone*)
celular mobile (phone) (*BRIT*),
cellphone (*US*); **celular com câmera**
camera phone

cem [sẽ] NUM hundred

cemitério [semi'tɛrju] M cemetery, graveyard

cena ['sɛna] F scene; (*palco*) stage

cenário [se'narju] M scenery; (*Cinema*) scenario; (*de um acontecimento*) setting

cenoura [se'nora] F carrot

censo ['sẽsu] M census

censor, a [sẽ'sor(a)] M/F censor

censura [sẽ'sura] F censorship; (*reprovação*) censure, criticism; **censurar** [sẽsu'rar] VT to censure; (*filme, livro etc*) to censor

centavo [sẽ'tavu] M cent; **estar sem um ~** to be penniless

centeio [sẽ'teju] M rye

centelha [sẽ'teʎa] F spark

centena [sẽ'tɛna] F hundred; **às ~s** in hundreds

centenário, -a [sẽte'narju, a] ADJ centenary ▶ M centenary

centígrado [sẽ'tʃigradu] M centigrade

centímetro [sẽ'tʃimetru] M centimetre (*BRIT*), centimeter (*US*)

cento ['sẽtu] M: **~ e um** one hundred and one; **por ~** per cent

centopeia [sẽto'peja] F centipede

central [sẽ'traw] (*pl* **-ais**) ADJ central ▶ F (*de polícia etc*) head office; **~ elétrica** (electric) power station; **~ telefônica** telephone exchange; **centralizar** [sẽtrali'zar] VT to centralize

centrar [sẽ'trar] VT to centre (*BRIT*), center (*US*)

centro ['sẽtru] M centre (*BRIT*), center (*US*); (*de uma cidade*) town centre; **centroavante** [sẽtroa'vãtʃi] M (*Futebol*) centre forward

CEP ['sɛpi] (*BR*) ABR M (= *Código de Endereçamento Postal*) postcode (*BRIT*), zip code (*US*)

cera ['sera] F wax

cerâmica [se'ramika] F pottery

cerca ['serka] F fence ▶ PREP: **~ de** (*aproximadamente*) around, about; **~ viva** hedge

cercado, -a [ser'kadu, a] ADJ surrounded ▶ M enclosure; (*para animais*) pen; (*para crianças*) playpen

cercanias [serka'nias] FPL outskirts; (*vizinhança*) neighbourhood *sg* (*BRIT*), neighborhood *sg* (*US*)

cerco ['serku] M siege; **pôr ~ a** to besiege

cereal [se'rjaw] (*pl* **-ais**) M cereal

cérebro ['sɛrebru] M brain; .(*fig*) brains *pl*

cereja [se'reʒa] F cherry

cerimônia [seri'monja] F ceremony

cerração [seha'sãw] F fog

cerrado, -a [se'hadu, a] ADJ shut, closed; (*denso*) thick ▶ M scrub(land)

certeza [ser'teza] F certainty; **com ~** certainly, surely; (*provavelmente*) probably; **ter ~ de** to be certain ou sure of; **ter ~ de que** to be sure that

certidão [sertʃi'dãw] (*pl* **-ões**) F certificate

certificado [sertʃifi'kadu] M certificate

certificar [sertʃifi'kar] VT to certify; (*assegurar*) to assure; **certificar-se** VR: **~-se de** to make sure of

certo, -a ['sertu, a] ADJ certain, sure; (*exato, direito*) right; (*um, algum*) a certain ▶ ADV correctly, right; **ao ~** for certain; **está ~** okay, all right

cerveja [ser'veʒa] F beer; **cervejaria** [serveʒa'ria] F (*fábrica*) brewery; (*bar*) bar, public house

cervical [servi'kaw] (*pl* **-ais**) ADJ cervical

cessação [sesa'sãw] F halting, ceasing

cessão [se'sãw] (*pl* **-ões**) F surrender

cessar [se'sar] VI to cease, stop; **sem ~** continually; **cessar-fogo** M INV cease-fire

cessões [se'sõjs] FPL *de* **cessão**

cesta ['sesta] F basket; **~ básica** food parcel

cesto ['sestu] M basket; (*com tampa*) hamper

cético, -a ['sɛtʃiku, a] M/F sceptic (*BRIT*), skeptic (*US*)

cetim [se'tʃĩ] M satin

céu [sɛw] M sky; (*Rel*) heaven; (*da boca*) roof

cevada [se'vada] F barley

CFTV ABR M (= *circuito fechado de TV*) CCTV

chá [ʃa] M tea

chácara ['ʃakara] F farm; (*casa de campo*) country house

chacina [ʃa'sina] F slaughter; **chacinar** [ʃasi'nar] VT (*matar*) to slaughter

chacota [ʃa'kɔta] F mockery

chafariz [ʃafa'riz] M fountain

chalé [ʃa'lɛ] M chalet

chaleira [ʃa'lejra] F kettle; (*bajulador*) crawler, toady

chama ['ʃama] F flame

chamada [ʃa'mada] F call; (*Mil*) roll call; (*Educ*) register; (*no jornal*) headline; **dar uma ~ em alguém** to tell sb off

chamar [ʃa'mar] VT to call; (*convidar*) to invite; (*atenção*) to attract ▶ VI to call; (*telefone*) to ring; **chamar-se** VR to be called; **chamo-me João** my name is John; **~ alguém de idiota/Dudu** to call sb an idiot/Dudu; **mandar ~** to summon, send for

chamariz [ʃamaˈriz] M decoy

chamativo, -a [ʃamaˈtʃivu, a] ADJ showy, flashy

chaminé [ʃamiˈnɛ] F chimney; (de navio) funnel

champanha [ʃãˈpaɲa] M ou F champagne

champanhe [ʃãˈpaɲi] M ou F = **champanha**

champu [ʃãˈpu] (PT) M shampoo

chance [ˈʃãsi] F chance

chantagear [ʃãtaˈʒjar] VT to blackmail

chantagem [ʃãˈtaʒẽ] F blackmail

chão [ʃãw] (pl **chãos**) M ground; (terra) soil; (piso) floor

chapa [ˈʃapa] F (placa) plate; (eleitoral) list; ~ **de matrícula** (PT Auto) number (BRIT) ou license (US) plate; **oi, meu ~!** hi, mate!

chapéu [ʃaˈpɛw] M hat

charco [ˈʃarku] M marsh, bog

charme [ˈʃarmi] M charm; **fazer ~** to be nice, use one's charm; **charmoso, -a** [ʃarˈmozu, ɔza] ADJ charming

charrete [ʃaˈhɛtʃi] F cart

charuto [ʃaˈrutu] M cigar

chassi [ʃaˈsi] M (Auto, Elet) chassis

chata [ˈʃata] F barge; ver tb **chato**

chateação [ʃatʃjaˈsãw] (pl **-ões**) F bother, hassle; (maçada) bore

chatear [ʃaˈtʃjar] VT to bother, upset; (importunar) to pester; (entediar) to bore; (irritar) to annoy ► VI to be upsetting; to be boring; to be annoying; **chatear-se** VR to get upset; to get bored; to get annoyed

chatice [ʃaˈtʃisi] F nuisance

chato, -a [ˈʃatu, a] ADJ flat; (tedioso) boring; (irritante) annoying; (que fica mal) rude ► M/F bore; (quem irrita) pain

chauvinista [ʃawviˈnista] ADJ chauvinistic ► M/F chauvinist

chavão [ʃaˈvãw] (pl **-ões**) M cliché

chave [ˈʃavi] F key; (Elet) switch; ~ **de porcas** spanner; ~ **inglesa** (monkey) wrench; ~ **de fenda** screwdriver

chávena [ˈʃavena] (PT) F cup

checar [ʃeˈkar] VT to check

check-up [tʃeˈkapi] (pl **-s**) M check-up

chefe [ˈʃefi] M/F head, chief; (patrão) boss; ~ **de estação** stationmaster; **chefia** [ʃeˈfia] F leadership; (direção) management; (repartição) headquarters sg; **chefiar** [ʃeˈfjar] VT to lead

chegada [ʃeˈgada] F arrival

chegado, -a [ʃeˈgadu, a] ADJ near; (íntimo) close

chegar [ʃeˈgar] VT to bring near ► VI to arrive; (ser suficiente) to be enough; **chegar-se a** VR to approach; **chega!** that's enough!; ~ **a** (atingir) to reach; (conseguir) to manage to

cheio, -a [ˈʃeju, a] ADJ full; (repleto) full up; (col: farto) fed up

cheirar [ʃejˈrar] VT, VI to smell; ~ **a** to smell of; **cheiro** [ˈʃejru] M smell; **ter cheiro de** to smell of; **cheiroso, -a** [ʃejˈrozu, ɔza] ADJ: **ser** ou **estar cheiroso** to smell nice

cheque [ˈʃɛki] M cheque (BRIT), check (US); ~ **de viagem** traveller's cheque (BRIT), traveler's check (US)

chiar [ʃjar] VI to squeak; (porta) to creak; (vapor) to hiss; (col: reclamar) to grumble

chiclete [ʃiˈklɛtʃi] M chewing gum

chicória [ʃiˈkɔrja] F chicory

chicote [ʃiˈkɔtʃi] M whip

chifre [ˈʃifri] M horn

Chile [ˈʃili] M: **o ~** Chile

chimarrão [ʃimaˈhãw] (pl **-ões**) M mate tea without sugar taken from a pipe-like cup

chimpanzé [ʃĩpãˈzɛ] M chimpanzee

China [ˈʃina] F: **a ~** China

chinelo [ʃiˈnɛlu] M slipper; ~ **(de dedo)** flip-flop

chinês, -esa [ʃiˈnes, eza] ADJ, M/F Chinese ► M (Ling) Chinese

chip [ˈʃipi] M (Comput) chip

Chipre [ˈʃipri] F Cyprus

chique [ˈʃiki] ADJ stylish, chic

chocalho [ʃoˈkaʎu] M (Mús, brinquedo) rattle; (para animais) bell

chocante [ʃoˈkãtʃi] ADJ shocking; (col) amazing

chocar [ʃoˈkar] VT to hatch, incubate; (ofender) to shock, offend ► VI to shock; **chocar-se** VR to crash, collide; to be shocked

chocho, -a [ˈʃoʃu, a] ADJ hollow, empty; (fraco) weak; (sem graça) dull

chocolate [ʃokoˈlatʃi] M chocolate

chofer [ʃoˈfer] M driver

chope [ˈʃopi] M draught beer

choque¹ [ˈʃɔki] M shock; (colisão) collision; (impacto) impact; (conflito) clash

choque² [ˈʃɔki] VB ver **chocar**

choramingar [ʃoramĩˈgar] VI to whine, whimper

chorão, -rona [ʃoˈrãw, rɔna] (pl **-ões/-s**) ADJ tearful ► M/F crybaby ► M (Bot) weeping willow

chorar [ʃoˈrar] VT, VI to weep, cry

chorinho [ʃoˈriɲu] M type of Brazilian music

choro [ˈʃoru] M crying; (Mús) type of Brazilian music

choupana [ʃoˈpana] F shack, hut

chouriço [ʃoˈɾisu] M (BR) black pudding; (PT) spicy sausage

chover [ʃoˈver] VI to rain; **~ a cântaros** to rain cats and dogs

chulé [ʃuˈlɛ] M foot odour (BRIT) ou odor (US)

chulo, -a [ˈʃulu, a] ADJ vulgar

chumbo [ˈʃũbu] M lead; (de caça) gunshot; (PT: de dente) filling; **sem ~** (gasolina) unleaded

chupar [ʃuˈpar] VT to suck

chupeta [ʃuˈpeta] F dummy (BRIT), pacifier (US)

churrasco [ʃuˈhasku] M barbecue; **churrasqueira** [ʃuhasˈkejra] F barbecue

churrasquinho [ʃuhasˈkiɲu] M kebab

chutar [ʃuˈtar] VT to kick; (col: adivinhar) to guess at; (: dar o fora em) to dump ▶ VI to kick; to guess; (col: mentir) to lie

chute [ˈʃutʃi] M kick; (col: mentira) lie; **dar o ~ em alguém** (col) to give sb the boot

chuteira [ʃuˈtejra] F football boot

chuva [ˈʃuva] F rain; **chuveiro** [ʃuˈvejru] M shower

chuviscar [ʃuvisˈkar] VI to drizzle; **chuvisco** [ʃuˈvisku] M drizzle

chuvoso, -a [ʃuˈvozu, ɔza] ADJ rainy

Cia. ABR (= companhia) Co

ciberbullying [siberˈbuliiŋ] M cyberbullying

cibercafé [siberkaˈfɛ] M cybercafé

ciberespaço [siberisˈpasu] M cyberspace

cicatriz [sikaˈtriz] F scar; **cicatrizar** [sikatriˈzar] VI to heal; (rosto) to scar

cicerone [siseˈrɔni] M tourist guide

ciclismo [siˈklizmu] M cycling

ciclista [siˈklista] M/F cyclist

ciclo [ˈsiklu] M cycle

ciclovia [sikloˈvia] F cycle path

cidadã [sidaˈdã] F de **cidadão**

cidadania [sidadaˈnia] F citizenship

cidadão, cidadã [sidaˈdãw] (pl **-s/-s**) M/F citizen

cidade [siˈdadʒi] F town; (grande) city

ciência [ˈsjẽsja] F science

ciente [ˈsjẽtʃi] ADJ aware

científico, -a [sjẽˈtʃifiku, a] ADJ scientific

cientista [sjẽˈtʃista] M/F scientist

cifra [ˈsifra] F cipher; (algarismo) number, figure; (total) sum

cigano, -a [siˈganu, a] ADJ, M/F gypsy

cigarra [siˈgaha] F cicada; (Elet) buzzer

cigarrilha [sigaˈhiʎa] F cheroot

cigarro [siˈgahu] M cigarette; **~ eletrônico** e-cigarette

cilada [siˈlada] F ambush; (armadilha) trap; (embuste) trick

cilindro [siˈlĩdru] M cylinder; (rolo) roller

cima [ˈsima] F: **de ~ para baixo** from top to bottom; **para ~** up; **em ~ de** on, on top of; **por ~ de** over; **de ~** from above; **lá em ~** up there; (em casa) upstairs; **ainda por ~** on top of that

cimento [siˈmẽtu] M cement; (fig) foundation

cimo [ˈsimu] M top, summit

cinco [ˈsĩku] NUM five

cineasta [sineˈasta] M/F film maker

cinema [siˈnɛma] F cinema

Cingapura [sĩgaˈpura] F Singapore

cinquenta [sĩˈkwẽta] NUM fifty

cinta [ˈsĩta] F sash; (de mulher) girdle

cinto [ˈsĩtu] M belt; **~ de segurança** safety belt; (Auto) seat belt

cintura [sĩˈtura] F waist; (linha) waistline

cinza [ˈsĩza] ADJ INV grey (BRIT), gray (US) ▶ F ash, ashes pl

cinzeiro [sĩˈzejru] M ashtray

cinzento, -a [sĩˈzẽtu, a] ADJ grey (BRIT), gray (US)

cio [siu] M: **no ~** on heat, in season

cipreste [siˈprɛstʃi] M cypress (tree)

cipriota [siˈprjɔta] ADJ, M/F Cypriot

circo [ˈsirku] M circus

circuito [sirˈkwitu] M circuit

circulação [sirkulaˈsãw] F circulation

circular [sirkuˈlar] ADJ circular ▶ F (carta) circular ▶ VI to circulate; (girar, andar) to go round ▶ VT to circulate; (estar em volta de) to surround; (percorrer em roda) to go round

círculo [ˈsirkulu] M circle

circundar [sirkũˈdar] VT to surround

circunferência [sirkũfeˈrẽsja] F circumference

circunflexo, -a [sirkũˈflɛksu, a] ADJ circumflex ▶ M circumflex (accent)

circunstância [sirkũsˈtãsja] F circumstance; **~s atenuantes** mitigating circumstances

cirurgia [sirurˈʒia] F surgery; **~ plástica/estética** plastic/cosmetic surgery

cirurgião, -giã [sirurˈʒjãw, ˈʒjã] (pl **-ões/-s**) M/F surgeon

cisco [ˈsisku] M speck

cismado, -a [sizˈmadu, a] ADJ with fixed ideas

cismar [sizˈmar] VI (pensar): **~ em** to brood over; (antipatizar): **~ com** to take a dislike to ▶ VT: **~ que** to be convinced that; **~ de** ou **em fazer** (meter na cabeça) to get into one's head to do; (*insistir*) to insist on doing

cisne ['siʒni] M swan

cisterna [sis'tɛrna] F cistern, tank

citação [sita'sãw] (*pl* **-ões**) F quotation; (*Jur*) summons *sg*

citar [si'tar] VT to quote; (*Jur*) to summon

ciúme ['sjumi] M jealousy; **ter ~s de** to be jealous of; **ciumento, -a** [sju'mẽtu, a] ADJ jealous

cívico, -a ['siviku, a] ADJ civic

civil [si'viw] (*pl* **-is**) ADJ civil ▶ M/F civilian; **civilidade** [sivili'dadʒi] F politeness

civilização [siviliza'sãw] (*pl* **-ões**) F civilization

civis [si'vis] PL *de* **civil**

clamar [kla'mar] VT to clamour (BRIT) *ou* clamor (US) for ▶ VI to cry out, clamo(u)r

clamor [kla'mor] M outcry, uproar

clandestino, -a [klãdes'tʃinu, a] ADJ clandestine; (*ilegal*) underground

clara ['klara] F egg white

clarão [kla'rãw] (*pl* **-ões**) M (*cintilação*) flash; (*claridade*) gleam

clarear [kla'rjar] VI (*dia*) to dawn; (*tempo*) to clear up, brighten up ▶ VT to clarify

claridade [klari'dadʒi] F brightness

clarim [kla'rĩ] (*pl* **-ns**) M bugle

clarinete [klari'netʃi] M clarinet

clarins [kla'rĩs] MPL *de* **clarim**

claro, -a ['klaru, a] ADJ clear; (*luminoso*) bright; (*cor*) light; (*evidente*) clear, evident ▶ M (*na escrita*) space; (*clareira*) clearing ▶ ADV clearly; **~!** of course!; **~ que sim!/não!** of course!/of course not!; **às claras** openly

classe ['klasi] F class; **~ econômica/ executiva** economy/business class

clássico, -a ['klasiku, a] ADJ classical; (*fig*) classic; (*habitual*) usual ▶ M classic

classificação [klasifika'sãw] (*pl* **-ões**) F classification; (*Esporte*) place, placing

classificado, -a [klasifi'kadu, a] ADJ (*em exame*) successful; (*anúncio*) classified; (*Esporte*) placed ▶ M classified ad

classificar [klasifi'kar] VT to classify; **classificar-se** VR: **~-se de algo** to call o.s. sth, describe o.s. as sth

cláusula ['klawzula] F clause

clausura [klaw'zura] F enclosure

clavícula [kla'vikula] F collar bone

clemência [kle'mẽsja] F mercy

clero ['klɛru] M clergy

clicar [kli'kar] VI (*Comput*) to click; **~ duas vezes em** to double-click on

cliente ['kljẽtʃi] M client; customer; (*de médico*) patient; **clientela** [kljẽ'tɛla] F clientele; (*de loja*) customers *pl*

clima ['klima] M climate

clímax ['klimaks] M INV climax

clipe ['klipi] M clip; (*para papéis*) paper clip

clique ['kliki] M (*Comput*) click

cloro ['klɔru] M chlorine

close ['klɔzi] M close-up

clube ['klubi] M club

coadjuvante [koadʒu'vãtʃi] ADJ supporting ▶ M/F (*num crime*) accomplice; (*Teatro, Cinema*) co-star

coador [koa'dor] M strainer; (*de café*) filter bag; (*para legumes*) colander

coalhada [koa'ʎada] F curd

coalizão [koali'zãw] (*pl* **-ões**) F coalition

coar [ko'ar] VT (*líquido*) to strain

coberta [ko'bɛrta] F cover, covering; (*Náut*) deck

cobertor [kober'tor] M blanket

cobertura [kober'tura] F covering; (*telhado*) roof; (*apartamento*) penthouse; (*TV, Rádio, Jornalismo*) coverage; (*Seguros*) cover; (*Tel*) network coverage; **aqui não tem ~** there's no network coverage here

cobiça [ko'bisa] F greed

cobra ['kɔbra] F snake

cobrador, a [kobra'dor(a)] M/F collector; (*em transporte*) conductor; **~ de ônibus** bus conductor

cobrança [ko'brãsa] F collection; (*ato de cobrar*) charging

cobrar [ko'brar] VT to collect; (*preço*) to charge

cobre ['kɔbri] M copper; **cobres** MPL (*dinheiro*) money *sg*

cobrir [ko'brir] VT to cover

cocada [ko'kada] F coconut sweet

cocaína [koka'ina] F cocaine

coçar [ko'sar] VT to scratch ▶ VI to itch; **coçar-se** VR to scratch o.s.

cócegas ['kɔsegas] FPL: **fazer ~ em** to tickle; **tenho ~ nos pés** I have tickly feet; **sentir ~** to be ticklish

coceira [ko'sejra] F itch; (*qualidade*) itchiness

cochichar [koʃi'ʃar] VI to whisper; **cochicho** [ko'ʃiʃu] M whispering

cochilar [koʃi'lar] VI to snooze, doze; **cochilo** [ko'ʃilu] M nap

coco ['koku] M coconut

cócoras ['kɔkoras] FPL: **de ~** squatting; **ficar de ~** to squat (down)

código ['kɔdʒigu] M code; **~ de barras** bar code

coelho [ko'eʎu] M rabbit

coerente [koe'rẽtʃi] ADJ coherent; (*consequente*) consistent

cofre ['kɔfri] M safe; (caixa) strongbox;
os ~s públicos public funds

cogitar [koʒi'tar] VT, VI to contemplate

cognitivo, -a [kogni'tʃivu, a] ADJ
cognitive

cogumelo [kogu'mɛlu] M mushroom;
~ venenoso toadstool

coice ['kojsi] M kick; (de arma) recoil; dar
~s em to kick

coincidência [koĩsi'dẽsja] F
coincidence

coincidir [koĩsi'dʒir] VI to coincide;
(concordar) to agree

coisa ['kojza] F thing; (assunto) matter;
~ de about

coitado, -a [koj'tadu, a] ADJ poor,
wretched

cola ['kɔla] F glue

colaborador, a [kolabora'dor(a)] M/F
collaborator; (em jornal) contributor

colaborar [kolabo'rar] VI to collaborate;
(ajudar) to help; (escrever artigos etc) to
contribute

colante [ko'lãtʃi] ADJ (roupa) skin-tight

colapso [ko'lapsu] M collapse;
~ cardíaco heart failure

colar [ko'lar] VT to stick, glue; (BR: copiar)
to crib ▶ VI to stick; to cheat ▶ M
necklace

colarinho [kola'riɲu] M collar

colarinho-branco (pl colarinhos-
brancos) M white-collar worker

colcha ['kowʃa] F bedspread

colchão [kow'ʃãw] (pl -ões) M mattress

colchete [kow'ʃetʃi] M clasp, fastening;
(parêntese) square bracket; ~ de gancho
hook and eye; ~ de pressão press stud,
popper

colchões [kow'ʃõjs] MPL de colchão

coleção [kole'sãw] (pl coleções) F
collection; **colecionador, a**
[kolesjona'dor(a)] M/F collector;
colecionar [kolesjo'nar] VT to collect

colega [ko'lɛga] M/F colleague; (de
escola) classmate

colegial [kole'ʒjaw] (pl -ais) M/F
schoolboy/girl

colégio [ko'lɛʒu] M school

coleira [ko'lejra] F collar

cólera ['kɔlera] F anger ▶ M ou F (Med)
cholera

colesterol [koleste'rɔw] M cholesterol

colete [ko'letʃi] M waistcoat (BRIT), vest
(US); ~ salva-vidas life jacket (BRIT), life
preserver (US)

coletivo, -a [kole'tʃivu, a] ADJ collective;
(transportes) public ▶ M bus

colheita [ko'ʎejta] F harvest

colher [ko'ʎer] VT to gather, pick; (dados)
to gather ▶ F spoon; ~ de chá/sopa
teaspoon/tablespoon

colidir [koli'dʒir] VI: ~ com to collide
with, crash into

coligação [koliga'sãw] (pl -ões) F
coalition

colina [ko'lina] F hill

colisão [koli'zãw] (pl -ões) F collision

collant [ko'lã] (pl -s) M tights pl (BRIT),
pantihose (US); (blusa) leotard

colmeia [kow'meja] F beehive

colo ['kɔlu] M neck; (regaço) lap

colocar [kolo'kar] VT to put, place;
(empregar) to find a job for, place; (Com)
to market; (pneus, tapetes) to fit;
(questão, ideia) to put forward

Colômbia [ko'lõbja] F: a ~ Colombia

colônia [ko'lonja] F colony; (perfume)
cologne; **colonial** [kolo'njaw] (pl -ais)
ADJ colonial

colonizador, a [koloniza'dor(a)] M/F
colonist, settler

coloquial [kolo'kjaw] (pl -ais) ADJ
colloquial

colóquio [ko'lɔkju] M conversation;
(congresso) conference

colorido, -a [kolo'ridu, a] ADJ colourful
(BRIT), colorful (US) ▶ M colouring (BRIT),
coloring (US)

colorir [kolo'rir] VT to colour (BRIT), color
(US)

coluna [ko'luna] F column; (pilar) pillar;
~ dorsal ou vertebral spine; **colunável**
[kolu'navew] (pl -eis) ADJ famous ▶ M/F
celebrity; **colunista** [kolu'nista] M/F
columnist

com [kõ] PREP with; estar ~ fome to be
hungry; ~ cuidado carefully; estar ~
dinheiro/câncer to have some money
on one/have cancer

coma ['kɔma] F coma

comandante [komã'dãtʃi] M
commander; (Mil) commandant; (Náut)
captain

comandar [komã'dar] VT to command

comando [ko'mãdu] M command

combate [kõ'batʃi] M combat;
combater [kõba'ter] VT to fight; (opor-
se a) to oppose ▶ VI to fight; **combater-se**
VR to fight

combinação [kõbina'sãw] (pl -ões) F
combination; (Quím) compound;
(acordo) arrangement; (plano) scheme;
(roupa) slip

combinar [kõbi'nar] VT to combine;
(jantar etc) to arrange; (fuga etc) to plan
▶ VI (roupas etc) to go together;

combinar-se vr to combine; (*pessoas*) to get on well together; **~ com** (*harmonizar-se*) to go with; **~ de fazer** to arrange to do; **combinado!** agreed!

comboio [kõ'boju] M (PT) train; (*de navios, carros*) convoy

combustível [kõbus'tʃivew] M fuel

começar [kome'saɾ] vt, vi to begin, start; **~ a fazer** to begin *ou* start to do

começo [ko'mesu] M beginning, start

comédia [ko'mɛdʒja] F comedy

comemorar [komemo'raɾ] vt to commemorate, celebrate

comentar [komẽ'taɾ] vt to comment on; (*maliciosamente*) to make comments about

comentário [komẽ'taɾju] M comment, remark; (*análise*) commentary

comer [ko'meɾ] vt to eat; (*Damas, Xadrez*) to take, capture ▶ vi to eat; **dar de ~ a** to feed

comercial [komeɾ'sjaw] (*pl* **-ais**) ADJ commercial; (*relativo ao negócio*) business *atr* ▶ M commercial

comercializar [komeɾsjali'zaɾ] vt to market

comerciante [komeɾ'sjãtʃi] M/F trader

comércio [ko'mɛɾsju] M commerce; (*tráfico*) trade; (*negócio*) business; (*lojas*) shops *pl*; **~ eletrônico** e-commerce; **~ justo** fair trade

comes ['kɔmis] MPL: **~ e bebes** food and drink

comestíveis [komes'tʃiveis] MPL foodstuffs, food *sg*

comestível [komes'tʃivew] (*pl* **-eis**) ADJ edible

cometer [kome'teɾ] vt to commit

comício [ko'misju] M (*Pol*) rally, meeting; (*assembleia*) assembly

cômico, -a ['komiku, a] ADJ comic(al) ▶ M comedian; (*de teatro*) actor

comida [ko'mida] F (*alimento*) food; (*refeição*) meal; **~ pronta** ready meal (BRIT), TV dinner (US)

comigo [ko'migu] PRON with me

comilão, -lona [komi'lãw, lona] (*pl* **-ões/-s**) ADJ greedy ▶ M/F glutton

comiserar [komize'raɾ] vt to move to pity; **comiserar-se** vr: **~-se (de)** to sympathize (with)

comissão [komi'sãw] (*pl* **-ões**) F commission; (*comitê*) committee

comissário [komi'saɾju] M commissioner; (*Com*) agent; **~ de bordo** (*Aer*) steward; (*Náut*) purser

comissões [komi'sõjs] FPL *de* **comissão**

comitê [komi'te] M committee

como ['komu] ADV **1** (*modo*) as; **ela fez como eu pedi** she did as I asked; **como se** as if; **como quiser** as you wish; **seja como for** be that as it may

2 (*assim como*) like; **ela tem olhos azuis como o pai** she has blue eyes like her father's; **ela trabalha numa loja, como a mãe** she works in a shop, as does her mother

3 (*de que maneira*) how; **como?** pardon?; **como!** what!; **como assim?** what do you mean?; **como não!** of course!

▶ CONJ (*porque*) as, since; **como estava tarde ele dormiu aqui** since it was late he slept here

comoção [komo'sãw] (*pl* **-ões**) F distress; (*revolta*) commotion

cômoda ['komoda] F chest of drawers (BRIT), bureau (US)

comodidade [komodʒi'dadʒi] F comfort; (*conveniência*) convenience

comodismo [komo'dʒizmu] M complacency

cômodo, -a ['komodu, a] ADJ comfortable; (*conveniente*) convenient ▶ M room

comovente [komo'vẽtʃi] ADJ moving, touching

comover [komo'veɾ] vt to move ▶ vi to be moving; **comover-se** vr to be moved

compacto, -a [kõ'paktu, a] ADJ compact; (*espesso*) thick; (*sólido*) solid ▶ M (*disco*) single

compadecer-se [kõpade'seɾsi] vr: **~ de** to pity

compadre [kõ'padɾi] M (*col: companheiro*) buddy, pal

compaixão [kõpaj'ʃãw] M compassion; (*misericórdia*) mercy

companheiro, -a [kõpa'ɲejɾu, a] M/F companion; (*colega*) friend; (*col*) buddy, mate

companhia [kõpa'ɲia] F company

comparação [kõpara'sãw] (*pl* **-ões**) F comparison

comparar [kõpa'raɾ] vt to compare; **~ com** to compare with; **~ a** to liken to

comparecer [kõpare'seɾ] vi to appear, make an appearance; **~ a uma reunião** to attend a meeting

comparsa [kõ'parsa] M/F (*Teatro*) extra; (*cúmplice*) accomplice

compartilhar [kõpartʃi'ʎaɾ] vt to share ▶ vi: **~ de** to share in, participate in

compartimento [kõpartʃi'mẽtu] M compartment; (*aposento*) room

compasso [kõ'pasu] M (*instrumento*) pair of compasses; (*Mús*) time; (*ritmo*) beat

compatível [kõpa'tʃivew] (*pl* **-eis**) ADJ compatible

compensar [kõpẽ'sar] VT to make up for, compensate for; (*equilibrar*) to offset; (*cheque*) to clear

competência [kõpe'tẽsja] F competence, ability; (*responsabilidade*) responsibility; **competente** [kõpe'tẽtʃi] ADJ competent; (*apropriado*) appropriate; (*responsável*) responsible

competição [kõpetʃi'sãw] (*pl* **-ões**) F competition

competidor, a [kõpetʃi'dor(a)] M/F competitor

competir [kõpe'tʃir] VI to compete; **~ a alguém** to be sb's responsibility; (*caber*) to be up to sb

competitivo, -a [kõpetʃi'tʃivu, a] ADJ competitive

compito [kõ'pitu] VB *ver* **competir**

complementar [kõplemẽ'tar] ADJ complementary ▶ VT to supplement

complemento [kõple'mẽtu] M complement

completamente [kõpleta'mẽtʃi] ADV completely, quite

completar [kõple'tar] VT to complete; to fill up; **~ dez anos** to be ten

completo, -a [kõ'plɛtu, a] ADJ complete; (*cheio*) full (up); **por ~** completely

complexo, -a [kõ'plɛksu, a] ADJ complex ▶ M complex

complicação [kõplika'sãw] (*pl* **-ões**) F complication

complicado, -a [kõpli'kadu, a] ADJ complicated

complicar [kõpli'kar] VT to complicate

complô [kõ'plo] M plot, conspiracy

componente [kõpo'nẽtʃi] ADJ, M component

compor [kõ'por] (*irreg: como* **pôr**) VT to compose; (*discurso, livro*) to write; (*arranjar*) to arrange ▶ VI to compose; **compor-se** VR (*controlar-se*) to compose o.s.; **~-se de** to consist of

comportamento [kõporta'mẽtu] M behaviour (BRIT), behavior (US)

comportar [kõpor'tar] VT to put up with; **comportar-se** VR (*portar-se*) to behave; **~-se mal** to misbehave, behave badly

composição [kõpozi'sãw] (*pl* **-ões**) F composition; (*Tip*) typesetting

compositor, a [kõpozi'tor(a)] M/F composer; (*Tip*) typesetter

compota [kõ'pɔta] F fruit in syrup

compra ['kõpra] F purchase; **fazer ~s** to go shopping; **comprador, a** [kõpra'dor(a)] M/F buyer, purchaser

comprar [kõ'prar] VT to buy

compreender [kõprjen'der] VT to understand; (*constar de*) to comprise, consist of, be composed of; (*abranger*) to cover

compreensão [kõprjẽ'sãw] F understanding, comprehension; **compreensivo, -a** [kõprjẽ'sivu, a] ADJ understanding

compressa [kõ'prɛsa] F compress

comprido, -a [kõ'pridu, a] ADJ long; (*alto*) tall; **ao ~** lengthways

comprimento [kõpri'mẽtu] M length

comprimido, -a [kõpri'midu, a] ADJ compressed ▶ M pill; tablet

comprimir [kõpri'mir] VT to compress

comprometer [kõprome'ter] VT to compromise; (*envolver*) to involve; (*arriscar*) to jeopardize; (*empenhar*) to pledge; **comprometer-se** VR: **~-se a** to undertake to, promise to

compromisso [kõpro'misu] M promise; (*obrigação*) commitment; (*hora marcada*) appointment; (*acordo*) agreement

comprovante [kõpro'vãtʃi] M receipt; **~ de residência** proof of address

comprovar [kõpro'var] VT to prove; (*confirmar*) to confirm

compulsivo, -a [kõpuw'sivu, a] ADJ compulsive

compulsório, -a [kõpuw'sɔrju, a] ADJ compulsory

computação [kõputa'sãw] F computer science, computing; **~ em nuvem** cloud computing

computador [kõputa'dor] M computer

computar [kõpu'tar] VT (*calcular*) to calculate; (*contar*) to count

comum [ko'mũ] (*pl* **-ns**) ADJ ordinary, common; (*habitual*) usual; **em ~** in common

comungar [komũ'gar] VI to take communion

comunhão [komu'ɲãw] (*pl* **-ões**) F communion

comunicação [komunika'sãw] (*pl* **-ões**) F communication; (*mensagem*) message; (*acesso*) access

comunicado [komuni'kadu] M notice

comunicar [komuni'kar] VT, VI to communicate; **comunicar-se** VR to communicate; **~-se com** (*entrar em contato*) to get in touch with

comunidade [komuni'dadʒi] F
community; **C~ (Econômica) Europeia**
European (Economic) Community

comunismo [komu'nizmu] M
communism; **comunista** [komu'nista]
ADJ, M/F communist

comuns [ko'mũs] PL *de* **comum**

conceber [kõse'ber] VT, VI to conceive

conceder [kõse'der] VT to allow;
(*outorgar*) to grant; (*dar*) to give ▶ VI:
~ em to agree to

conceito [kõ'sejtu] M concept, idea;
(*fama*) reputation; (*opinião*) opinion;
conceituado, -a [kõsej'twadu, a] ADJ
well thought of, highly regarded

concentração [kõsẽtra'sãw] (*pl* **-ões**) F
concentration

concepção [kõsep'sãw] (*pl* **-ões**) F
(*geração*) conception; (*noção*) idea,
concept; (*opinião*) opinion

concerto [kõ'sertu] M concert

concessão [kõse'sãw] (*pl* **-ões**) F
concession; (*permissão*) permission

concha ['kõʃa] F shell; (*para líquidos*) ladle

conchavo [kõ'ʃavu] M conspiracy

conciliar [kõsi'ljar] VT to reconcile

concluir [kõ'klwir] VT, VI to conclude

conclusão [kõklu'zãw] (*pl* **-ões**) F end;
(*dedução*) conclusion

conclusões [kõklu'zõjs] FPL *de*
conclusão

concordância [kõkor'dãsja] F
agreement

concordar [kõkor'dar] VI, VT to agree

concorrência [kõko'hẽsja] F
competition; (*a um cargo*) application

concorrente [kõko'hẽtʃi] M/F
contestant; (*candidato*) candidate

concorrer [kõko'her] VI to compete; **~ a**
to apply for

concretizar [kõkretʃi'zar] VT to make
real; **concretizar-se** VR (*sonho*) to come
true; (*ambições*) to be realized

concreto, -a [kõ'krɛtu, a] ADJ concrete
▶ M concrete

concurso [kõ'kursu] M contest; (*exame*)
competition

conde ['kõdʒi] M count

condenar [kõde'nar] VT to condemn;
(*Jur: sentenciar*) to sentence; (: *declarar
culpado*) to convict

condensar [kõdẽ'sar] VT to condense;
condensar-se VR to condense

condessa [kõ'desa] F countess

condimento [kõdʒi'mẽtu] M seasoning

condomínio [kõdo'minju] M
condominium; **~ fechado** gated
community

condução [kõdu'sãw] F driving;
(*transporte*) transport; (*ônibus*) bus

condutor, a [kõdu'tor(a)] M/F (*de
veículo*) driver ▶ M (*Elet*) conductor

conduzir [kõdu'zir] VT (*levar*) to lead;
(*Fís*) to conduct; **conduzir-se** VR to
behave; **~ a** to lead to

cone ['kɔni] M cone

conectar [konek'tar] VT to connect

conexão [konek'sãw] (*pl* **-ões**) F
connection; (*voo*) connecting flight

confecção [kõfek'sãw] (*pl* **-ões**) F
making; (*de um boletim*) production;
(*roupa*) ready-to-wear clothes *pl*; (*negócio*)
business selling ready-to-wear clothes

confeccionar [kõfeksjo'nar] VT to
make; (*fabricar*) to manufacture

confecções [kõfek'sõjs] FPL *de*
confecção

confeitaria [kõfejta'ria] F patisserie

conferência [kõfe'rẽsja] F conference;
(*discurso*) lecture

conferir [kõfe'rir] VT to check;
(*comparar*) to compare; (*outorgar*) to
grant ▶ VI to tally

confessar [kõfe'sar] VT, VI to confess;
confessar-se VR to confess

confiança [kõ'fjãsa] F confidence; (*fé*)
trust; **de ~** reliable; **ter ~ em alguém** to
trust sb

confiar [kõ'fjar] VT to entrust; (*segredo*)
to confide ▶ VI: **~ em** to trust; (*ter fé*) to
have faith in

confiável [kõ'fjavew] (*pl* **-eis**) ADJ reliable

confidência [kõfi'dẽsja] F secret; **em ~**
in confidence; **confidencial**
[kõfidẽ'sjaw] (*pl* **-ais**) ADJ confidential

confirmação [kõfirma'sãw] (*pl* **-ões**) F
confirmation

confirmar [kõfir'mar] VT to confirm

confiro [kõ'firu] VB *ver* **conferir**

confissão [kõfi'sãw] (*pl* **-ões**) F
confession

conformar [kõfor'mar] VT to form
▶ VI: **~ com** to conform to; **conformar-se**
VR: **~-se com** to resign o.s. to;
(*acomodar-se*) to conform to

conforme [kõ'fɔrmi] PREP according to;
(*dependendo de*) depending on ▶ CONJ
(*logo que*) as soon as; (*como*) as, according
to what; (*à medida que*) as; **você vai?** — **~**
are you going? — it depends

conformidade [kõformi'dadʒi] F
agreement; **em ~ com** in accordance with

confortar [kõfor'tar] VT to comfort,
console

confortável [kõfor'tavew] (*pl* **-eis**)
ADJ comfortable

conforto [kõ'fortu] M comfort
confrontar [kõfrõ'tar] VT to confront; (*comparar*) to compare
confronto [kõ'frõtu] M confrontation; (*comparação*) comparison
confusão [kõfu'zãw] (*pl* **-ões**) F confusion; (*tumulto*) uproar; (*problemas*) trouble
confuso, -a [kõ'fuzu, a] ADJ confused; (*problema*) confusing
confusões [kõfu'zõjs] FPL *de* **confusão**
congelador [kõʒela'dor] M freezer, deep freeze
congelamento [kõʒela'mẽtu] M freezing; (*Econ*) freeze
congelar [kõʒe'lar] VT to freeze; **congelar-se** VR to freeze
congestão [kõʒes'tãw] F congestion; **congestionado, -a** [kõʒestʃjo'nadu, a] ADJ congested; (*olhos*) bloodshot; (*rosto*) flushed; **congestionamento** [kõʒestʃjona'mẽtu] M congestion; **um congestionamento (de tráfego)** a traffic jam
congestionar [kõʒestʃjo'nar] VT to congest; **congestionar-se** VR (*rosto*) to go red
congressista [kõgre'sista] M/F congressman/woman
congresso [kõ'grɛsu] M congress, conference
conhaque [ko'ɲaki] M cognac, brandy
conhecedor, a [koɲese'dor(a)] ADJ knowing ▶ M/F connoisseur, expert
conhecer [koɲe'ser] VT to know; (*travar conhecimento com*) to meet; (*descobrir*) to discover; **conhecer-se** VR to meet; (*ter conhecimento*) to know each other
conhecido, -a [koɲe'sidu, a] ADJ known; (*célebre*) well-known ▶ M/F acquaintance
conhecimento [koɲesi'mẽtu] M knowledge; (*ideia*) idea; (*conhecido*) acquaintance; (*Com*) bill of lading; **conhecimentos** MPL (*informações*) knowledge *sg*; **levar ao ~ de alguém** to bring to sb's notice
conjugado [kõʒu'gadu] M studio
cônjuge ['kõʒuʒi] M spouse
conjunção [kõʒũ'sãw] (*pl* **-ões**) F union; (*Ling*) conjunction
conjuntivo [kõʒũ'tʃivu] (PT) M (*Ling*) subjunctive
conosco [ko'nosku] PRON with us
conquista [kõ'kista] F conquest; **conquistador, a** [kõkista'dor(a)] ADJ conquering ▶ M conqueror; **conquistar** [kõkis'tar] VT to conquer; (*alcançar*) to achieve; (*ganhar*) to win

consciência [kõ'sjẽsja] F conscience; (*percepção*) awareness; (*senso de responsabilidade*) conscientiousness
consciente [kõ'sjẽtʃi] ADJ conscious
conseguinte [kõse'gĩtʃi] ADJ: **por ~** consequently
conseguir [kõse'gir] VT to get, obtain; **~ fazer** to manage to do, succeed in doing
conselho [kõ'seʎu] M piece of advice; (*corporação*) council; **conselhos** MPL (*advertência*) advice *sg*; **~ de guerra** court martial; **C~ de ministros** (*Pol*) Cabinet
consentimento [kõsẽtʃi'mẽtu] M consent
consentir [kõsẽ'tʃir] VT to allow, permit; (*aprovar*) to agree to ▶ VI: **~ em** to agree to
consequência [kõse'kwẽsja] F consequence; **por ~** consequently
consertar [kõser'tar] VT to mend, repair; (*remediar*) to put right; **conserto** [kõ'sertu] M repair
conserva [kõ'serva] F pickle; **em ~** pickled
conservação [kõserva'sãw] F conservation; (*de vida, alimentos*) preservation
conservador, a [kõserva'dor(a)] ADJ conservative ▶ M/F (*Pol*) conservative
conservante [kõser'vãtʃi] M preservative
conservar [kõser'var] VT to preserve, maintain; (*reter, manter*) to keep, retain; **conservar-se** VR to keep
conservatório [kõserva'tɔrju] M conservatory
consideração [kõsidera'sãw] (*pl* **-ões**) F consideration; (*estima*) respect, esteem; **levar em ~** to take into account
considerar [kõside'rar] VT to consider; (*prezar*) to respect ▶ VI to consider
considerável [kõside'ravew] (*pl* **-eis**) ADJ considerable
consigo¹ [kõ'sigu] PRON (*m*) with him; (*f*) with her; (*pl*) with them; (*com você*) with you
consigo² VB *ver* **conseguir**
consinto [kõ'sĩtu] VB *ver* **consentir**
consistente [kõsis'tẽtʃi] ADJ solid; (*espesso*) thick
consistir [kõsis'tʃir] VI: **~ em** to be made up of, consist of
consoante [kõso'ãtʃi] F consonant ▶ PREP according to ▶ CONJ: **~ prometera** as he had promised

consolação [kõsola'sãw] (pl -ões) F
consolation

consolar [kõso'lar] VT to console

console [kõ'sɔli], **consola** [kõ'sɔla] F
(Comput) console

consolidar [kõsoli'dar] VT to
consolidate; (fratura) to knit ▸ VI to
become solid; to knit together

consolo [kõ'solu] M consolation

consome [kõ'somi] VB ver **consumir**

consórcio [kõ'sɔrsju] M (união)
partnership; (Com) consortium

conspiração [kõspira'sãw] (pl -ões) F
plot, conspiracy

conspirar [kõspi'rar] VT, VI to plot

constante [kõs'tãtʃi] ADJ constant

constar [kõs'tar] VI to be in; **ao que me
consta** as far as I know

constatar [kõsta'tar] VT to establish;
(notar) to notice; (evidenciar) to show up

consternado, -a [kõster'nadu, a] ADJ
depressed; (desolado) distressed

constipação [kõstʃipa'sãw] (pl -ões) F
(PT) cold

constipado, -a [kõstʃi'padu, a] (PT) ADJ:
estar - to have a cold

constituição [kõstʃitwi'sãw] (pl -ões) F
constitution

constituinte [kõstʃi'twĩtʃi] M/F
(deputado) member ▸ F: **a C-** the
Constituent Assembly

constituir [kõstʃi'twir] VT to constitute;
(formar) to form; (estabelecer) to
establish; (nomear) to appoint

constrangimento [kõstrãʒi'mẽtu] M
constraint; (acanhamento)
embarrassment

construção [kõstru'sãw] (pl -ões) F
building, construction

construir [kõs'trwir] VT to build,
construct

construtivo, -a [kõstru'tʃivu, a] ADJ
constructive

construtor, a [kõstru'tor(a)] M/F builder

cônsul ['kõsuw] (pl cônsules) M consul;
consulado [kõsu'ladu] M consulate

consulta [kõ'suwta] F consultation;
livro de - reference book; **horário de -**
surgery hours pl (BRIT), office hours pl
(US); **consultar** [kõsuw'tar] VT to
consult; **consultor, a** [kõsuw'tor(a)]
M/F consultant

consultório [kõsuw'tɔrju] M surgery

consumidor, a [kõsumi'dor(a)] ADJ
consumer atr ▸ M/F consumer

consumir [kõsu'mir] VT to consume;
(gastar) to use up; **consumir-se** VR to
waste away

consumo [kõ'sumu] M consumption;
artigos de - consumer goods

conta ['kõta] F count; (em restaurante)
bill; (fatura) invoice; (bancária) account;
(de colar) bead; **contas** FPL (Com)
accounts; **levar** ou **ter em -** to take into
account; **tomar - de** to take care of;
(dominar) to take hold of; **afinal de -s**
after all; **dar-se - de** to realize; (notar) to
notice; **- corrente** current account;
- de e-mail ou **de correio eletrônico**
email account

contabilista [kõtabi'lista] (PT) M/F
accountant

contabilizar [kõtabili'zar] VT to write
up, book

contacto [kõ'tatu] (PT) M = **contato**

contador, a [kõta'dor(a)] M/F (Com)
accountant ▸ M (Tec: medidor) meter

contagiante [kõta'ʒjãtʃi] ADJ (alegria)
contagious

contagiar [kõta'ʒjar] VT to infect

contágio [kõ'taʒju] M infection

contagioso, -a [kõta'ʒjozu, ɔza] ADJ
(doença) contagious

contaminar [kõtami'nar] VT to
contaminate

contanto que [kõ'tãtu ki] CONJ
provided that

conta-quilómetros (PT) M INV
speedometer

contar [kõ'tar] VT to count; (narrar) to
tell; (pretender) to intend ▸ VI to count;
- com to count on; (esperar) to expect;
- em fazer to count on doing, expect
to do

contatar [kõta'tar] VT to contact;
contato [kõ'tatu] M contact; **entrar em
contato com** to get in touch with,
contact

contemplar [kõtẽ'plar] VT to
contemplate; (olhar) to gaze at

contemplativo, -a [kõtẽpla'tʃivu, a]
ADJ (pessoa) thoughtful

contemporâneo, -a [kõtẽpo'ranju, a]
ADJ, M/F contemporary

contentamento [kõtẽta'mẽtu] M
(felicidade) happiness; (satisfação)
contentment

contente [kõ'tẽtʃi] ADJ happy; (satisfeito)
pleased, satisfied

contento [kõ'tẽtu] M: **a -**
satisfactorily

conter [kõ'ter] (irreg: como **ter**) VT to
contain, hold; (refrear) to restrain, hold
back; (gastos) to curb

contestação [kõtesta'sãw] (pl -ões) F
challenge; (negação) denial

contestar [kõtes'tar] vt to dispute, contest; (*impugnar*) to challenge
conteúdo [kõte'udu] m contents pl; (*de um texto*) content
contexto [kõ'testu] m context
contigo [kõ'tʃigu] PRON with you
contíguo, -a [kõ'tʃigwu, a] ADJ: ~ **a** next to
continental [kõtʃinẽ'taw] (*pl* -**ais**) ADJ continental
continente [kõtʃi'nẽtʃi] m continent
continuação [kõtʃinwa'sãw] F continuation
continuar [kõtʃi'nwar] vt, vi to continue; ~ **falando** ou **a falar** to go on talking; **ela continua doente** she is still sick
continuidade [kõtʃinwi'dadʒi] F continuity
conto ['kõtu] m story, tale; (PT: *dinheiro*) 1000 escudos
contorcer [kõtor'ser] vt to twist; **contorcer-se** VR to writhe
contornar [kõtor'nar] vt (*rodear*) to go round; (*ladear*) to skirt; (*fig: problema*) to get round
contorno [kõ'tornu] m outline; (*da terra*) contour; (*do rosto*) profile
contra ['kõtra] PREP against ▶ m: **os prós e os ~s** the pros and cons; **dar o ~ (a)** to be opposed (to)
contra-ataque m counterattack
contrabandear [kõtrabã'dʒjar] vt to smuggle; **contrabandista** [kõtrabã'dʒista] m/f smuggler; **contrabando** [kõtra'bãdu] m smuggling; (*artigos*) contraband
contraceptivo, -a [kõtrasep'tʃivu, a] ADJ contraceptive ▶ m contraceptive
contracheque [kõtra'ʃeki] m pay slip (BRIT), check stub (US)
contradição [kõtradʒi'sãw] (*pl* -**ões**) F contradiction
contraditório, -a [kõtradʒi'tɔrju, a] ADJ contradictory
contradizer [kõtradʒi'zer] (*irreg: como* **dizer**) vt to contradict
contragosto [kõtra'gostu] m: **a ~** against one's will, unwillingly
contrair [kõtra'ir] vt to contract; (*hábito*) to form
contramão [kõtra'mãw] ADJ one-way ▶ F: **na ~** the wrong way down a one-way street
contraproducente [kõtraprodu'sẽtʃi] ADJ counterproductive
contrário, -a [kõ'trarju, a] ADJ (*oposto*) opposite; (*pessoa*) opposed;

(*desfavorável*) unfavourable (BRIT), unfavorable (US), adverse ▶ m opposite; **do ~** otherwise; **pelo** ou **ao ~** on the contrary; **ao ~** the other way round
contrassenso [kõtra'sẽsu] m nonsense
contrastar [kõtras'tar] vt to contrast; **contraste** [kõ'trastʃi] m contrast
contratação [kõtrata'sãw] F (*de pessoal*) employment
contratar [kõtra'tar] vt (*serviços*) to contract; (*pessoal*) to employ, take on
contratempo [kõtra'tẽpu] m setback; (*aborrecimento*) upset; (*dificuldade*) difficulty
contrato [kõ'tratu] m contract; (*acordo*) agreement
contribuição [kõtribwi'sãw] (*pl* -**ões**) F contribution; (*imposto*) tax
contribuinte [kõtri'bwĩtʃi] m/f contributor; (*que paga impostos*) taxpayer
contribuir [kõtri'bwir] vt to contribute ▶ vi to contribute; (*pagar impostos*) to pay taxes
controlar [kõtro'lar] vt to control
controle [kõ'trɔli] m control; ~ **remoto** remote control; ~ **de crédito** (Com) credit control; ~ **de qualidade** (Com) quality control
controvérsia [kõtro'vɛrsja] F controversy; (*discussão*) debate; **controverso, -a** [kõtro'vɛrsu, a] ADJ controversial
contudo [kõ'tudu] CONJ nevertheless, however
contumaz [kõtu'majz] ADJ obstinate, stubborn
contusão [kõtu'zãw] (*pl* -**ões**) F bruise
convenção [kõvẽ'sãw] (*pl* -**ões**) F convention; (*acordo*) agreement
convencer [kõvẽ'ser] vt to convince; (*persuadir*) to persuade; **convencer-se** VR: ~-**se de** to be convinced about; **convencido, -a** [kõvẽ'sidu, a] ADJ convinced; (*col: imodesto*) conceited, smug
convencional [kõvẽsjo'naw] (*pl* -**ais**) ADJ conventional
convenções [kõvẽ'sõjs] FPL *de* **convenção**
conveniência [kõve'njẽsja] F convenience
conveniente [kõve'njẽtʃi] ADJ convenient, suitable; (*vantajoso*) advantageous
convênio [kõ'venju] m (*reunião*) convention; (*acordo*) agreement
convento [kõ'vẽtu] m convent
conversa [kõ'vɛrsa] F conversation; ~ **fiada** idle talk; (*promessa falsa*) hot air

conversão [kõver'sãw] (*pl* -ões) F conversion

conversar [kõver'sar] VI to talk; to chat

conversões [kõver'sõjs] FPL *de* **conversão**

converter [kõver'ter] VT to convert

convés [kõ'vɛs] (*pl* -eses) M (*Náut*) deck

convexo, -a [kõ'vɛksu, a] ADJ convex

convicção [kõvik'sãw] (*pl* -ões) F conviction

convidado, -a [kõvi'dadu, a] M/F guest

convidar [kõvi'dar] VT to invite

convincente [kõvĩ'sẽtʃi] ADJ convincing

convir [kõ'vir] (*irreg: como* **vir**) VI to suit, be convenient; (*ficar bem*) to be appropriate; (*concordar*) to agree; **convém fazer isso o mais rápido possível** we must do this as soon as possible

convite [kõ'vitʃi] M invitation

convivência [kõvi'vẽsja] F living together; (*familiaridade*) familiarity, intimacy

conviver [kõvi'ver] VI: **~ com** (*viver em comum*) to live with; (*ter familiaridade*) to get on with; **convívio** [kõ'vivju] M living together; (*familiaridade*) familiarity

convocar [kõvo'kar] VT to summon, call upon; (*reunião, eleições*) to call; (*para o serviço militar*) to call up

convosco [kõ'vosku] ADV with you

convulsão [kõvuw'sãw] (*pl* -ões) F convulsion

cookie ['kuki] M (*Comput*) cookie

cooper ['kuper] M jogging; **fazer ~** to go jogging *ou* running

cooperação [koopera'sãw] F cooperation

cooperar [koope'rar] VI to cooperate

coordenada [koorde'nada] F coordinate

copa ['kɔpa] F (*de árvore*) top; (*torneio*) cup; **copas** FPL (*Cartas*) hearts

cópia ['kɔpja] F copy; **tirar ~ de** to copy; **copiadora** [kopja'dora] F duplicating machine

copiar [ko'pjar] VT to copy

copo ['kɔpu] M glass

coque ['kɔki] M (*penteado*) bun

coqueiro [ko'kejru] M (*Bot*) coconut palm

coquetel [koke'tɛw] (*pl* -éis) M cocktail; (*festa*) cocktail party

cor¹ [kɔr] M: **de ~** by heart

cor² [kor] F colour (BRIT), color (US); **de ~** colo(u)red

coração [kora'sãw] (*pl* -ões) M heart; **de bom ~** kind-hearted; **de todo o ~** wholeheartedly

corado, -a [ko'radu, a] ADJ ruddy

coragem [ko'raʒẽ] F courage; (*atrevimento*) nerve

corais [ko'rajs] MPL *de* **coral**

corajoso, -a [kora'ʒozu, ɔza] ADJ courageous

coral [ko'raw] (*pl* -ais) M (*Mús*) choir; (*Zool*) coral

corar [ko'rar] VT (*roupa*) to bleach (in the sun) ▶ VI to blush; (*tornar-se branco*) to bleach

corda ['kɔrda] F rope, line; (*Mús*) string; (*varal*) clothes line; (*de relógio*) spring; **dar ~ em** to wind up; **~s vocais** vocal chords

cordão [kor'dãw] (*pl* -ões) M string, twine; (*joia*) chain; (*no carnaval*) group; (*Elet*) lead; (*fileira*) row

cordeiro [kor'dejru] M lamb

cordel [kor'dɛw] (*pl* -éis) M string; **literatura de ~** pamphlet literature

cor-de-rosa [kor-] ADJ INV pink

cordões [kor'dõjs] MPL *de* **cordão**

coreano, -a [ko'rjanu, a] ADJ Korean ▶ M/F Korean ▶ M (*Ling*) Korean

Coreia [ko'reja] F: **a ~** Korea

coreto [ko'retu] M bandstand

córner ['kɔrner] M (*Futebol*) corner

coro ['koru] M chorus; (*conjunto de cantores*) choir

coroa [ko'roa] F crown; (*de flores*) garland ▶ M/F (BR col) old timer

coroar [koro'ar] VT to crown; (*premiar*) to reward

coronel [koro'nɛw] (*pl* -éis) M colonel; (*político*) local political boss

corpo ['kɔrpu] M body; (*aparência física*) figure; (: *de homem*) build; (*de vestido*) bodice; (*Mil*) corps *sg*; **de ~ e alma** (*fig*) wholeheartedly; **~ diplomático** diplomatic corps *sg*

corpulento, -a [korpu'lẽtu, a] ADJ stout

correção [kohe'sãw] (*pl* -ões) F correction; (*exatidão*) correctness; **casa de ~** reformatory

corre-corre [kɔhi'kɔhi] (*pl* -s) M (*pressa*) scramble; (*de muitas pessoas*) stampede

corredor, a [kohe'dor(a)] M/F runner ▶ M corridor; (*em avião etc*) aisle; (*cavalo*) racehorse

correia [ko'heja] F strap; (*de máquina*) belt; (*para cachorro*) leash

correio [ko'heju] M mail, post; (*local*) post office; (*carteiro*) postman (BRIT), mailman (US); **~ aéreo** air mail; **pôr no ~** to post; **~ eletrônico** email; **~ de voz** voice mail

corrente [ko'hẽtʃi] ADJ (atual) current; (águas) running; (comum) usual, common ▶ F current; (cadeia, joia) chain; ~ **de ar** draught (BRIT), draft (US); **correnteza** [kohẽ'teza] F (de ar) draught (BRIT), draft (US); (de rio) current

correr [ko'her] VT to run; (viajar por) to travel across ▶ VI to run; (em carro) to drive fast, speed; (o tempo) to elapse; (boato) to go round; (atuar com rapidez) to rush; **correria** [kohe'ria] F rush

correspondência [kohespõ'dẽsja] F correspondence; **correspondente** [kohespõ'dẽtʃi] ADJ corresponding ▶ M correspondent

corresponder [kohespõ'der] VI: ~ **a** to correspond to; (ser igual) to match (up to); **corresponder-se** VR: ~-**se com** to correspond with

correto, -a [ko'hetu, a] ADJ correct; (conduta) right; (pessoa) straight, honest

corretor, a [kohe'tor(a)] M/F broker; ~ **de fundos** ou **de bolsa** stockbroker; ~ **de imóveis** estate agent (BRIT), realtor (US); ~ **ortográfico** spellchecker

corrida [ko'hida] F running; (certame) race; (de taxi) fare; ~ **de cavalos** horse race

corrido, -a [ko'hidu, a] ADJ quick; (expulso) driven out ▶ ADV quickly

corrigir [kohi'ʒir] VT to correct

corriqueiro, -a [kohi'kejru, a] ADJ common; (problema) trivial

corromper [kohõ'per] VT to corrupt; (subornar) to bribe; **corromper-se** VR to be corrupted

corrosão [koho'zãw] F corrosion; (fig) erosion

corrosivo, -a [koho'zivu, a] ADJ corrosive

corrupção [kohup'sãw] F corruption

corrupto, -a [ko'huptu, a] ADJ corrupt

Córsega ['kɔrsega] F: **a** ~ Corsica

cortada [kor'tada] F: **dar uma** ~ **em alguém** (fig) to cut sb short

cortante [kor'tãtʃi] ADJ cutting

cortar [kor'tar] VT to cut; (eliminar) to cut out; (água, telefone etc) to cut off; (efeito) to stop ▶ VI to cut; (encurtar caminho) to take a short cut; ~ **o cabelo** (no cabeleireiro) to have one's hair cut; ~ **a palavra de alguém** to interrupt sb

corte¹ ['kɔrtʃi] M cut; (de luz) power cut; **sem** ~ (tesoura etc) blunt; ~ **de cabelo** haircut

corte² ['kɔrtʃi] F court; **cortes** FPL (PT) parliament sg

cortejo [kor'teʒu] M procession

cortesia [korte'zia] F politeness; (de empresa) free offer

cortiça [kor'tʃisa] F cork

cortiço [kor'tʃisu] M slum tenement

cortina [kor'tʃina] F curtain

coruja [ko'ruʒa] F owl

corvo ['korvu] M crow

coser [ko'zer] VT, VI to sew

cosmético, -a [koz'mεtʃiku, a] ADJ, M cosmetic

cospe ['kɔspi] VB ver **cuspir**

costa ['kɔsta] F coast; **costas** FPL (dorso) back sg; **dar as** ~**s a** to turn one's back on

Costa Rica F: **a** ~ Costa Rica

costela [kos'tεla] F rib

costeleta [koste'leta] F chop, cutlet; **costeletas** FPL (suíças) side-whiskers

costumar [kostu'mar] VT (habituar) to accustom ▶ VI: **ele costuma chegar às 6.00** he usually arrives at 6.00; **costumava dizer ...** he used to say ...

costume [kos'tumi] M custom, habit; (traje) costume; **costumes** MPL (comportamento) behaviour sg (BRIT), behavior sg (US); (conduta) conduct sg; (de um povo) customs; **de** ~ usual; **como de** ~ as usual

costura [kos'tura] F sewing; (sutura) seam; **costurar** [kostu'rar] VT, VI to sew; **costureira** [kostu'rejra] F dressmaker

cota ['kɔta] F quota, share

cotação [kota'sãw] (pl -**ões**) F (de preços) list, quotation; (Bolsa) price; (consideração) esteem; ~ **bancária** bank rate

cotado, -a [ko'tadu, a] ADJ (Com: ação) quoted; (bem-conceituado) well thought of; (num concurso) fancied

cotar [ko'tar] VT (ações) to quote; ~ **algo em** to value sth at

cotejar [kote'ʒar] VT to compare

cotidiano, -a [kotʃi'dʒjanu, a] ADJ daily, everyday ▶ M: **o** ~ daily life

cotonete® [koto'nεtʃi] M cotton bud (BRIT)

cotovelada [kotove'lada] F shove; (cutucada) nudge

cotovelo [koto'velu] M (Anat) elbow; (curva) bend; **falar pelos** ~**s** to talk non-stop

coube ['kobi] VB ver **caber**

couro ['koru] M leather; (de um animal) hide

couve ['kovi] F spring greens pl; **couve-flor** (pl **couves-flor(es)**) F cauliflower

couvert [ku'vεr] M cover charge

cova ['kɔva] F pit; (*caverna*) cavern; (*sepultura*) grave

covarde [ko'vardʒi] ADJ cowardly ▶ M/F coward; **covardia** [kovar'dʒia] F cowardice

covil [ko'viw] (*pl* **-is**) M den, lair

covis [ko'vis] MPL *de* **covil**

coxa ['kɔʃa] F thigh

coxear [ko'ʃjar] VI to limp

coxia [ko'ʃia] F aisle, gangway

coxo, -a ['koʃu, a] ADJ lame

cozer [ko'zer] VT, VI to cook

cozido [ko'zidu] M stew

cozinha [ko'ziɲa] F kitchen; (*arte*) cookery; (*móvel*) fitted kitchen

cozinhar [kozi'ɲar] VT, VI to cook

cozinheiro, -a [kozi'ɲejru, a] M/F cook

CP ABR = **Caminhos de Ferro Portugueses**

CPF (BR) ABR M (= *Cadastro de Pessoa Física*) identification number

CPLP ABR F *see note*

> The **CPLP** o the *Comunidade de Países de Língua Portuguesa* was set up in 1996 to establish economic and diplomatic links between all countries where the official language is Portuguese. The members are Brazil, Portugal, Angola, Mozambique, Guinea-Bissau, Cape Verde and São Tomé e Príncipe. Portuguese is spoken by around 170 million people around the world today.

crachá [kra'ʃa] M badge

crânio ['kranju] M skull

craque ['kraki] M/F ace, expert

crasso, -a ['krasu, a] ADJ crass

cratera [kra'tera] F crater

cravar [kra'var] VT (*prego etc*) to drive (in); (*com os olhos*) to stare at; **cravar-se** VR to penetrate

cravo ['kravu] M carnation; (*Mús*) harpsichord; (*especiaria*) clove; (*na pele*) blackhead; (*prego*) nail

creche ['krɛʃi] F crèche, day-care centre

credenciais [krede'sjajs] FPL credentials

creditar [kredʒi'tar] VT to guarantee; (*Com*) to credit; **~ algo a alguém** to credit sb with sth; (*garantir*) to assure sb of sth

crédito ['krɛdʒitu] M credit; **digno de ~** reliable

creme ['krɛmi] ADJ INV cream ▶ M cream; (*Culin: doce*) custard; **~ dental** toothpaste; **cremoso, -a** [kre'mozu, ɔza] ADJ creamy

crença ['krẽsa] F belief

crente ['krẽtʃi] M/F believer

crepúsculo [kre'puskulu] M dusk, twilight

crer [krer] VT, VI to believe; **crer-se** VR to believe o.s. to be; **~ em** to believe in; **creio que sim** I think so

crescer [kre'ser] VI to grow; **crescimento** [kresi'mẽtu] M growth

crespo, -a ['krespu, a] ADJ (*cabelo*) curly

cretinice [kretʃi'nisi] F stupidity; (*ato, dito*) stupid thing

cretino [kre'tʃinu] M cretin, imbecile

cria ['kria] F (*animal: sg*) baby animal; (: *pl*) young *pl*

criação [krja'sãw] (*pl* **-ões**) F creation; (*de animais*) raising, breeding; (*educação*) upbringing; (*animais domésticos*) livestock *pl*; **filho de ~** adopted child

criado, -a ['krjadu, a] M/F servant

criador, a [krja'dor(a)] M/F creator; **~ de gado** cattle breeder

criança ['krjãsa] ADJ childish ▶ F child; **criançada** [krjã'sada] F: **a criançada** the kids

criar [krjar] VT to create; (*crianças*) to bring up; (*animais*) to raise; (*amamentar*) to suckle, nurse; (*planta*) to grow; **criar-se** VR: **~-se (com)** to grow up (with); **~ caso** to make trouble

criatura [kria'tura] F creature; (*indivíduo*) individual

crime ['krimi] M crime; **criminal** [krimi'naw] (*pl* **-ais**) ADJ criminal; **criminalidade** [kriminali'dadʒi] F crime; **criminoso, -a** [krimi'nozu, ɔza] ADJ, M/F criminal

crina ['krina] F mane

crioulo, -a ['krjolu, a] ADJ creole ▶ M/F creole

criptografar [kriptogra'far] VT *Comput* to encrypt

crise ['krizi] F crisis; (*escassez*) shortage; (*Med*) attack, fit

crista ['krista] F (*de serra, onda*) crest; (*de galo*) cock's comb

cristal [kris'taw] (*pl* **-ais**) M crystal; (*vidro*) glass; **cristais** MPL (*copos*) glassware *sg*; **cristalino, -a** [krista'linu, a] ADJ crystal-clear

cristão, -tã [kris'tãw, 'tã] (*pl* **-s/-s**) ADJ, M/F Christian

cristianismo [kristʃja'nizmu] M Christianity

Cristo ['kristu] M Christ

critério [kri'terju] M criterion; (*juízo*) discretion, judgement; **criterioso, -a** [krite'rjozu, ɔza] ADJ thoughtful, careful

crítica ['kritʃika] F criticism; *ver tb* **crítico**

criticar [kritʃi'kar] VT to criticize; (*um livro*) to review

crítico, -a ['kritʃiku, a] ADJ critical ▶ M/F critic

crivar [kri'var] VT (*com balas etc*) to riddle

crivo ['krivu] M sieve

crocante [kro'kãtʃi] ADJ (*pão, alface*) crispy; (*nozes, chocolate*) crunchy

crônica ['kronika] F chronicle; (*coluna de jornal*) newspaper column; (*texto jornalístico*) feature; (*conto*) short story

crônico, -a ['kroniku, a] ADJ chronic

cronológico, -a [krono'lɔʒiku, a] ADJ chronological

croquete [kro'kɛtʃi] M croquette

cru, a [kru, 'krua] ADJ raw; (*não refinado*) crude

crucial [kru'sjaw] (*pl* -**ais**) ADJ crucial

crucificar [krusifi'kar] VT to crucify

crucifixo [krusi'fiksu] M crucifix

cruel [kru'ɛw] (*pl* -**éis**) ADJ cruel; **crueldade** [kruew'dadʒi] F cruelty

cruz [kruz] F cross; **C~ Vermelha** Red Cross

cruzado, -a [kru'zadu, a] ADJ crossed ▶ M (*moeda*) cruzado

cruzamento [kruza'mẽtu] M crossroads

cruzar [kru'zar] VT to cross ▶ VI (*Náut*) to cruise; (*pessoas*) to pass each other by; **~ com** to meet

cruzeiro [kru'zejru] M (*cruz*) (monumental) cross; (*moeda*) cruzeiro; (*viagem de navio*) cruise

cu [ku] (!) M arse (!); **vai tomar no cu** fuck off (!)

Cuba ['kuba] F Cuba

cubro ['kubru] VB *ver* **cobrir**

cuca ['kuka] (*col*) F head; **fundir a ~** (*quebrar a cabeça*) to rack one's brain; (*baratinar*) to boggle the mind; (*perturbar*) to drive crazy

cuco ['kuku] M cuckoo

cueca ['kwɛka] F (BR) underpants *pl*; **cuecas** FPL (PT) underpants *pl*; (*para mulheres*) panties *pl*

cuíca ['kwika] F *kind of musical instrument*

cuidado [kwi'dadu] M care; **aos ~s de** in the care of; **ter ~** to be careful; **~!** watch out!, be careful!; **tomar ~ (de)** to be careful (of); **cuidadoso, -a** [kwida'dozu, ɔza] ADJ careful

cuidar [kwi'dar] VI: **~ de** to take care of, look after; **cuidar-se** VR to look after o.s.

cujo, -a ['kuʒu, a] PRON (*de quem*) whose; (*de que*) of which

culinária [kuli'narja] F cookery

culpa ['kuwpa] F fault; (*Jur*) guilt; **ter ~ de** to be to blame for; **por ~ de** because

of; **culpado, -a** [kuw'padu, a] ADJ guilty ▶ M/F culprit; **culpar** [kuw'par] VT to blame; (*acusar*) to accuse; **culpar-se** VR to take the blame; **culpável** [kuw'pavew] (*pl* -**eis**) ADJ guilty

cultivar [kuwtʃi'var] VT to cultivate; (*plantas*) to grow; **cultivo** [kuw'tʃivu] M cultivation

culto, -a ['kuwtu, a] ADJ cultured ▶ M (*homenagem*) worship; (*religião*) cult

cultura [kuw'tura] F culture; (*da terra*) cultivation; **cultural** [kuwtu'raw] (*pl* **culturais**) ADJ cultural

cume ['kumi] M top, summit; (*fig*) climax

cúmplice ['kũplisi] M/F accomplice

cumprimentar [kũprimẽ'tar] VT to greet; (*dar parabéns*) to congratulate

cumprimento [kũpri'mẽtu] M fulfilment; (*saudação*) greeting; (*elogio*) compliment; **cumprimentos** MPL (*saudações*) best wishes; **~ de uma lei/ ordem** compliance with a law/an order

cumprir [kũ'prir] VT (*desempenhar*) to carry out; (*promessa*) to keep; (*lei*) to obey; (*pena*) to serve ▶ VI to be necessary; **~ a palavra** to keep one's word; **fazer ~** to enforce

cúmulo ['kumulu] M height; **é o ~!** that's the limit!

cunha ['kuɲa] F wedge

cunhado, -a [ku'ɲadu, a] M/F brother-in-law/sister-in-law

cunho ['kuɲu] M (*marca*) hallmark; (*caráter*) nature

cupim [ku'pĩ] (*pl* -**ns**) M termite

cupins [ku'pĩs] MPL *de* **cupim**

cúpula ['kupula] F dome; (*de abajur*) shade; (*de partido etc*) leadership; (**reunião de**) **~** summit (meeting)

cura ['kura] F cure; (*tratamento*) treatment; (*de carnes etc*) curing, preservation ▶ M priest

curar [ku'rar] VT (*doença*) to cure; (*ferida*) to treat; **curar-se** VR to get well

curativo [kura'tʃivu] M dressing

curiosidade [kurjozi'dadʒi] F curiosity; (*objeto raro*) curio

curioso, -a [ku'rjozu, ɔza] ADJ curious ▶ M/F snooper, inquisitive person; **curiosos** MPL (*espectadores*) onlookers

curral [ku'haw] (*pl* -**ais**) M pen, enclosure

currículo [ku'hikulu] M (*curriculum*) curriculum vitae

cursar [kur'sar] VT (*aulas, escola*) to attend; (*cursos*) to follow; **ele está cursando História** he's studying *ou* doing history

curso ['kursu] M course; (direção)
direction; **em ~** (ano etc) current;
(processo) in progress

cursor [kur'sor] M (Comput) cursor

curtição [kurtʃi'sãw] F fun

curtir [kur'tʃir] VT (couro) to tan; (tornar
rijo) to toughen up; (padecer) to suffer,
endure; (col) to enjoy

curto, -a ['kurtu, a] ADJ short ▶ M (Elet)
short (circuit); **curto-circuito** (pl
curtos-circuitos) M short circuit

curva ['kurva] F curve; (de estrada, rio)
bend; **~ fechada** hairpin bend

curvo, -a ['kurvu, a] ADJ curved; (estrada)
winding

cuscuz [kus'kuz] M couscous

cuspe ['kuspi] M spit, spittle

cuspir [kus'pir] VT, VI to spit

custa ['kusta] F: **à ~ de** at the expense
of; **custas** FPL (Jur) costs

custar [kus'tar] VI to cost; **~ a fazer** to
have trouble doing; (demorar) to take a
long time to do

custo ['kustu] M cost; **a ~** with difficulty;
a todo ~ at all costs

cutelo [ku'telu] M cleaver

cutícula [ku'tʃikula] F cuticle

cutucar [kutu'kar] VT (com o dedo) to
prod, poke; (com o cotovelo) to nudge

d

D ABR = **Dona**; (= direito) r; (= deve) d

d/ ABR = **dia**

da [da] = **de + a**

dá [da] VB ver **dar**

dactilografar [datilogra'far] (PT)
= **datilografar** etc

dado, -a ['dadu, a] ADJ given; (sociável)
sociable ▶ M (em jogo) die; (fato) fact;
dados MPL dice; (fatos, Comput) data sg;
~ que supposing that; (uma vez que)
given that

daí [da'ji] ADV (= **de + aí**) (desse lugar) from
there; (desse momento) from then; **~ a
um mês** a month later

dali [da'li] ADV = **de + ali**

daltônico, -a [daw'toniku, a] ADJ
colour-blind (BRIT), color-blind (US)

dama ['dama] F lady; (Xadrez, Cartas)
queen; **damas** FPL (jogo) draughts (BRIT),
checkers (US); **~ de honra** bridesmaid

damasco [da'masku] M apricot

danado, -a [da'nadu, a] ADJ damned;
(zangado) furious; (menino) mischievous

dança ['dãsa] F dance; **dançar** [dã'sar] VI
to dance

danificar [danifi'kar] VT to damage

dano ['danu] M (tb: **~s**) damage; harm;
(a uma pessoa) injury

dantes ['dãtʃis] ADV before, formerly

daquele, -a [da'kele, 'kɛla] = **de +
aquele**

daqui [da'ki] ADV (= **de + aqui**) (deste
lugar) from here; **~ a pouco** soon, in a
little while; **~ a uma semana** a week
from now; **~ em diante** from now on

daquilo [da'kilu] = **de + aquilo**

(PALAVRA-CHAVE)

dar [dar] VT **1** (ger) to give; (festa) to hold;
(problemas) to cause; **dar algo a alguém**

to give sb sth, give sth to sb; **dar de beber a alguém** to give sb a drink; **dar aula de francês** to teach French
2 (*produzir: fruta etc*) to produce
3 (*notícias no jornal*) to publish
4 (*cartas*) to deal
5 (+ *n, perífrase de vb*): **me dá medo/pena** it frightens/upsets me
▶ VI **1**: **dar com** (*coisa*) to find; (*pessoa*) to meet
2: **dar em** (*bater*) to hit; (*resultar*) to lead to; (*lugar*) to come to
3: **dá no mesmo** it's all the same
4: **dar de si** (*sapatos etc*) to stretch, give
5: **dar para** (*impess: ser possível*) to be able to; **dá para trocar dinheiro aqui?** can I change money here?; **vai dar para eu ir amanhã** I'll be able to go tomorrow; **dá para você vir amanhã? — não, amanhã não vai dar** can you come tomorrow? — no, I can't
6 (*ser suficiente*): **dar para/para fazer** to be enough for/to do; **dá para todo mundo?** is there enough for everyone?
dar-se VR **1** (*sair-se*): **dar-se bem/mal** to do well/badly
2: **dar-se (com alguém)** to be acquainted (with sb); **dar-se bem (com alguém)** to get on well (with sb)
3: **dar-se por vencido** to give up

das [das] = **de + as**
data ['data] F date; (*época*) time; **datar** [da'tar] VT to date ▶ VI: **datar de** to date from
datilografar [datʃilogra'far] VT to type; **datilografia** [datʃilogra'fia] F typing; **datilógrafo, -a** [datʃi'lɔgrafu, a] M/F typist (BRIT), stenographer (US)
d.C. ABR (= *depois de Cristo*) A.D.
DDD ABR F (= *discagem direta a distância*) direct long-distance dialling ▶ ABR M (*código*) dialling code (BRIT), area code (US)
DDI ABR F (= *discagem direta internacional*) IDD ▶ ABR M (*código de país*) country code

(PALAVRA-CHAVE)

de [dʒi] (*de + o(s)/a(s)* = *do(s)/da(s)*; + *ele(s)/a(s)* = *dele(s)/a(s)*; + *esse(s)/a(s)* = *desse(s)/a(s)*; + *isso* = *disso*; + *este(s)/a(s)* = *deste(s)/a(s)*; + *isto* = *disto*; + *aquele(s)/a(s)* = *daquele(s)/a(s)*; + *aquilo* = *daquilo*) PREP **1** (*posse*) of; **a casa de João/da irmã** João's/my sister's house; **é dele** it's his; **um romance de** a novel by
2 (*origem, distância, com números*) from; **sou de São Paulo** I'm from São Paulo; **de 8 a 20** from 8 to 20; **sair do cinema** to leave the cinema; **de dois em dois** two by two, two at a time
3 (*valor descritivo*): **um copo de vinho** a glass of wine; **um homem de cabelo comprido** a man with long hair; **o infeliz do homem** (*col*) the poor man; **um bilhete de avião** an air ticket; **uma criança de três anos** a three-year-old (child); **uma máquina de costurar** a sewing machine; **aulas de inglês** English lessons; **feito de madeira** made of wood; **vestido de branco** dressed in white
4 (*modo*): **de trem/avião** by train/plane; **de lado** sideways
5 (*hora, tempo*): **às 8 da manhã** at 8 o'clock in the morning; **de dia/noite** by day/night; **de hoje a oito dias** a week from now; **de dois em dois dias** every other day
6 (*comparações*): **mais/menos de cem pessoas** more/less than a hundred people; **é o mais caro da loja** it's the most expensive in the shop; **ela é mais bonita do que sua irmã** she's prettier than her sister; **gastei mais do que pretendia** I spent more than I intended
7 (*causa*): **estou morto de calor** I'm boiling hot; **ela morreu de câncer** she died of cancer
8 (*adj + de + infin*): **fácil de entender** easy to understand

dê [de] VB *ver* **dar**
debaixo [de'bajʃu] ADV below, underneath ▶ PREP: **~ de** under, beneath
debate [de'batʃi] M discussion, debate; (*disputa*) argument; **debater** [deba'ter] VT to debate; (*discutir*) to discuss; **debater-se** VR to struggle
débil ['debiw] (*pl* **-eis**) ADJ weak, feeble ▶ M: **~ mental** person with learning difficulties; **debilidade** [debili'dadʒi] F weakness; **debilidade mental** learning difficulties; **debilitar** [debili'tar] VT to weaken; **debilitar-se** VR to become weak, weaken; **debiloide** [debi'lɔjdʒi] (*col*) ADJ idiotic ▶ M/F idiot
debitar [debi'tar] VT: **~ $40 à** *ou* **na conta de alguém** to debit $40 to sb's account; **débito** ['dɛbitu] M debit
debochado, -a [debo'ʃadu, a] ADJ (*pessoa*) sardonic; (*jeito, tom*) mocking
década ['dɛkada] F decade
decadência [deka'dẽsja] F decadence

decair [deka'ir] vɪ to decline
decente [de'sẽtʃi] ADJ decent;
(*apropriado*) proper; (*honrado*)
honourable (BRIT), honorable (US);
(*trabalho*) neat; **decentemente**
[desẽtʃi'mẽtʃi] ADV decently;
(*apropriadamente*) properly;
(*honradamente*) honourably (BRIT),
honorably (US)
decepção [desep'sãw] (*pl* **-ões**) F
disappointment; **decepcionar**
[desepsjo'nar] vᴛ to disappoint;
(*desiludir*) to disillusion; **decepcionar-se**
vʀ to be disappointed; to be disillusioned
decidir [desi'dʒir] vᴛ to decide;
(*solucionar*) to resolve; **decidir-se** vʀ:
~-se a to make up one's mind to; **~-se
por** to decide on, go for
decifrar [desi'frar] vᴛ to decipher;
(*futuro*) to foretell; (*compreender*) to
understand
decimal [desi'maw] (*pl* **-ais**) ADJ, M
decimal
décimo, -a ['dɛsimu, a] ADJ tenth ▶ M
tenth; *ver tb* **quinto**
decisão [desi'zãw] (*pl* **-ões**) F decision;
decisivo, -a [desi'zivu, a] ADJ (*fator*)
decisive; (*jogo*) deciding
declaração [deklara'sãw] (*pl* **-ões**) F
declaration; (*depoimento*) statement
declarado, -a [dekla'radu, a] ADJ
(*intenção*) declared; (*opinião*) professed;
(*inimigo*) sworn; (*alcoólatra*) self-
confessed; (*cristão etc*) avowed
declarar [dekla'rar] vᴛ to declare;
(*confessar*) to confess
declinar [dekli'nar] vᴛ to decline ▶ vɪ
(*sol*) to go down; (*terreno*) to slope down;
declínio [de'klinju] M decline
declive [de'klivi] M slope, incline
decolagem [deko'laʒẽ] (*pl* **-ns**) F (*Aer*)
take-off
decolar [deko'lar] vɪ (*Aer*) to take off
decompor [dekõ'por] (*irreg: como* **pôr**) vᴛ
to analyse; (*apodrecer*) to rot;
decompor-se vʀ to rot, decompose
decomposição [dekõpozi'sãw] (*pl* **-ões**)
F decomposition; (*análise*) dissection
decorar [deko'rar] vᴛ to decorate;
(*aprender*) to learn by heart; **decorativo,
-a** [dekora'tʃivu, a] ADJ decorative
decoro [de'koru] M decency; (*dignidade*)
decorum
decorrente [deko'hẽtʃi] ADJ: **~ de**
resulting from
decorrer [deko'her] vɪ (*tempo*) to pass;
(*acontecer*) to take place, happen ▶ M: **no
~ de** in the course of; **~ de** to result from

decrescer [dekre'ser] vɪ to decrease,
diminish
decretar [dekre'tar] vᴛ to decree, order;
decreto [de'krɛtu] M decree, order;
decreto-lei (*pl* **decretos-leis**) M act,
law
dedetizar [dedetʃi'zar] vᴛ to spray with
insecticide
dedicação [dedʒika'sãw] F dedication;
(*devotamento*) devotion
dedicar [dedʒi'kar] vᴛ to dedicate;
(*tempo, atenção*) to devote; **dedicar-se**
vʀ: **~-se a** to devote o.s. to; **dedicatória**
[dedʒika'torja] F (*de obra*) dedication
dedo ['dedu] M finger; (*do pé*) toe;
~ anular ring finger; **~ indicador** index
finger; **~ mínimo** *ou* **mindinho** little
finger
dedução [dedu'sãw] (*pl* **-ões**) F
deduction
deduzir [dedu'zir] vᴛ (*concluir*): **~ (de)** to
deduce (from), infer (from); (*quantia*) to
deduct
defasagem [defa'zaʒẽ] (*pl* **-ns**) F
discrepancy
defeito [de'fejtu] M defect, flaw; **pôr ~s
em** to find fault with; **com ~** broken, out
of order; **para ninguém botar ~** (*col*)
perfect; **defeituoso, -a** [defej'twozu,
ɔza] ADJ defective, faulty
defender [defẽ'der] vᴛ to defend;
defender-se vʀ to stand up for o.s.;
(*numa língua*) to get by
defensiva [defẽ'siva] F: **estar** *ou* **ficar
na ~** to be on the defensive
defensor, a [defẽ'sor(a)] M/F defender;
(*Jur*) defending counsel
defesa [de'feza] F defence (BRIT), defense
(US); (*Jur*) counsel for the defence ▶ M
(*Futebol*) back
deficiente [defi'sjẽtʃi] ADJ (*imperfeito*)
defective; (*carente*): **~ (em)** deficient (in)
déficit ['dɛfisitʃi] (*pl* **-s**) M deficit
definição [defini'sãw] (*pl* **-ões**) F
definition
definir [defi'nir] vᴛ to define; **definir-se**
vʀ to make a decision; (*explicar-se*) to
make one's position clear; **~-se a favor
de/contra algo** to come out in favo(u)r
of/against sth
definitivamente [definitʃiva'mẽtʃi]
ADV definitively; (*permanentemente*) for
good; (*sem dúvida*) definitely
definitivo, -a [defini'tʃivu, a] ADJ final,
definitive; (*permanente*) permanent;
(*resposta, data*) definite
defronte [de'frõtʃi] ADV opposite ▶ PREP:
~ de opposite

defumar [defu'mar] VT (*presunto*) to smoke; (*perfumar*) to perfume

defunto, -a [de'fũta, a] ADJ dead ▸ M/F dead person

degelar [deʒe'lar] VT to thaw; (*geladeira*) to defrost ▸ VI to thaw out; to defrost

degradar [degra'dar] VT to degrade, debase; **degradar-se** VR to demean o.s.

degrau [de'graw] M step; (*de escada de mão*) rung

degustação [degusta'sãw] (*pl* -**ões**) F tasting, sampling; (*saborear*) savouring (BRIT), savoring (US)

degustar [degus'tar] VT (*provar*) to taste; (*saborear*) to savour (BRIT), savor (US)

dei [dej] VB *ver* **dar**

deitada [dej'tada] (*col*) F: **dar uma ~** to have a lie-down

deitado, -a [dej'tadu, a] ADJ (*estendido*) lying down; (*na cama*) in bed

deitar [dej'tar] VT to lay down; (*na cama*) to put to bed; (*colocar*) to put, place; (*lançar*) to cast; (PT: *líquido*) to pour; **deitar-se** VR to lie down; to go to bed; **~ sangue** (PT) to bleed; **~ abaixo** to knock down, flatten; **~ a fazer algo** to start doing sth; **~ uma carta** (PT) to post a letter; **~ fora** (PT) to throw away *ou* out; **~ e rolar** (*col*) to do as one likes

deixa ['dejʃa] F clue, hint; (*Teatro*) cue; (*chance*) chance

deixar [dej'ʃar] VT to leave; (*abandonar*) to abandon; (*permitir*) to let, allow ▸ VI: **~ de** (*parar*) to stop; (*não fazer*) to fail to; **não posso ~ de ir** I must go; **~ cair** to drop; **~ alguém louco** to drive sb crazy *ou* mad; **~ alguém cansado/nervoso** *etc* to make sb tired/nervous *etc*; **deixa disso!** (*col*) come off it!; **deixa para lá!** (*col*) forget it!

dela ['dɛla] = **de + ela**

delatar [dela'tar] VT (*pessoa*) to inform on; (*abusos*) to reveal; (*à polícia*) to report; **delator, a** [dela'tor(a)] M/F informer

dele ['deli] = **de + ele**

delegacia [delega'sia] F office; **~ de polícia** police station

delegado, -a [dele'gadu, a] M/F delegate, representative; **~ de polícia** police chief

delegar [dele'gar] VT to delegate

deleitar [delej'tar] VT to delight; **deleitar-se** VR: **~-se com** to delight in

delgado, -a [dew'gadu, a] ADJ thin; (*esbelto*) slim; (*fino*) fine

deliberação [delibera'sãw] (*pl* -**ões**) F deliberation; (*decisão*) decision

deliberar [delibe'rar] VT to decide, resolve ▸ VI to deliberate

delicadeza [delika'deza] F delicacy; (*cortesia*) kindness

delicado, -a [deli'kadu, a] ADJ delicate; (*frágil*) fragile; (*cortês*) polite; (*sensível*) sensitive

delícia [de'lisja] F delight; (*prazer*) pleasure; **que ~!** how lovely!; **deliciar** [deli'sjar] VT to delight; **deliciar-se** VR: **deliciar-se com algo** to take delight in sth

delicioso, -a [deli'sjozu, ɔza] ADJ lovely; (*comida, bebida*) delicious

delinear [deli'njar] VT to outline

delinquente [delĩ'kwẽtʃi] ADJ, M/F delinquent, criminal

delirar [deli'rar] VI (*com febre*) to be delirious; (*de ódio, prazer*) to go mad, go wild

delírio [de'lirju] M (*Med*) delirium; (*êxtase*) ecstasy; (*excitação*) excitement

delito [de'litu] M (*crime*) crime; (*falta*) offence (BRIT), offense (US)

demais [dʒi'majs] ADV (*em demasia*) too much; (*muitíssimo*) a lot, very much ▸ PRON: **os/as ~** the rest (of them); **já é ~!** this is too much!; **é bom ~** it's really good; **foi ~** (*col: bacana*) it was great

demanda [de'mãda] F lawsuit; (*disputa*) claim; (*requisição*) request; (*Econ*) demand; **em ~ de** in search of; **demandar** [demã'dar] VT (*Jur*) to sue; (*exigir, reclamar*) to demand

demasia [dema'zia] F excess, surplus; (*imoderação*) lack of moderation; **em ~** (*dinheiro, comida etc*) too much; (*cartas, problemas etc*) too many

demasiadamente [demazjada'mẽtʃi] ADV too much; (*com adj*) too

demasiado, -a [dema'zjadu, a] ADJ too much; (*pl*) too many ▸ ADV too much; (*com adj*) too

demitir [demi'tʃir] VT to dismiss; (*col*) to sack, fire; **demitir-se** VR to resign

democracia [demokra'sia] F democracy

democrático, -a [demo'kratʃiku, a] ADJ democratic

demolir [demo'lir] VT to demolish, knock down; (*fig*) to destroy

demonstração [demõstra'sãw] (*pl* -**ões**) F demonstration; (*de amizade*) show, display; (*prova*) proof

demonstrar [demõs'trar] VT to demonstrate; (*provar*) to prove; (*amizade etc*) to show

demora [de'mɔra] F delay; (*parada*) stop; **sem ~** at once, without delay; **qual é**

a ~ disso? how long will this take?;
demorado, -a [demo'radu, a] ADJ slow;
demorar [demo'rar] VT to delay, slow
down ▶ VI (*permanecer*) to stay; (*tardar a
vir*) to be late; (*conserto*) to take (a long)
time; **demorar-se** VR to stay for a long
time, linger; **demorar a chegar** to be a
long time coming; **vai demorar muito?**
will it take long?; **não vou demorar** I
won't be long
dendê [dë'dё] M (*Culin: óleo*) palm oil;
(*Bot*) oil palm
dengoso, -a [dё'gozu, ɔza] ADJ coy;
(*criança: choraminguento*): **ser ~** to be a
crybaby
dengue ['dёgi] F (*Med*) dengue
denominar [denomi'nar] VT: **~ algo/
alguém ...** to call sth/sb ...;
denominar-se VR to be called; (*a si
mesmo*) to call o.s.
denotar [deno'tar] VT (*indicar*) to show,
indicate; (*significar*) to signify
densidade [dёsi'dadʒi] F density
denso, -a [dёsu, a] ADJ dense; (*espesso*)
thick; (*compacto*) compact
dentada [dё'tada] F bite
dentadura [dёta'dura] F teeth pl, set of
teeth; (*artificial*) dentures pl
dente ['dёtʃi] M tooth; (*de animal*) fang;
(*de elefante*) tusk; (*de alho*) clove; **falar
entre os ~s** to mutter, mumble; **~ de
leite/do siso** milk/wisdom tooth; **~s
postiços** false teeth
dentista [dё'tʃista] M/F dentist
dentre ['dётri] PREP (from) among
dentro ['dёtru] ADV inside ▶ PREP:
~ de inside; (*tempo*) within; **de ~ para
fora** inside out; **dar uma ~** (*col*) to
get it right; **aí ~** in there; **por ~** on the
inside; **estar por ~** (*col: fig*) to be in the
know
denúncia [de'nūsja] F denunciation;
(*acusação*) accusation; (*de roubo*) report;
denunciar [denū'sjar] VT (*acusar*) to
denounce; (*delatar*) to inform on;
(*revelar*) to reveal
deparar [depa'rar] VT to reveal; (*fazer
aparecer*) to present ▶ VI: **~ com** to come
across, meet; **deparar-se** VR: **~-se com**
to come across, meet
departamento [departa'mёtu] M
department
dependência [depё'dёsja] F
dependence; (*edificação*) annexe (BRIT),
annex (US); (*colonial*) dependency;
(*cômodo*) room
dependente [depё'dёtʃi] M/F
dependant

depender [depё'der] VI: **~ de** to
depend on
depilar [depi'lar] VT to wax; **depilatório**
[depila'tɔrju] M hair-remover
deplorável [deplo'ravew] (*pl* **-eis**) ADJ
deplorable; (*lamentável*) regrettable
depoimento [depoj'mёtu] M
testimony, evidence; (*na polícia*)
statement
depois [de'pojs] ADV afterwards ▶ PREP:
~ de after; **~ de comer** after eating;
~ que after
depor [de'por] (*irreg: como* **pôr**) VT (*pôr*) to
place; (*indicar*) to indicate; (*rei*) to
depose; (*governo*) to overthrow ▶ VI (*Jur*)
to testify, give evidence; (*na polícia*) to
give a statement
depositar [depozi'tar] VT to deposit;
(*voto*) to cast; (*colocar*) to place
depósito [de'pozitu] M deposit;
(*armazém*) warehouse, depot; (*de lixo*)
dump; (*reservatório*) tank; **~ de
bagagens** left-luggage office (BRIT),
checkroom (US)
depreciação [depresja'sãw] F
depreciation
depredar [depre'dar] VT to wreck
depressa [dʒi'prɛsa] ADV fast, quickly;
vamos ~ let's get a move on!
depressão [depre'sãw] (*pl* **-ões**) F
depression
deprimente [depri'mёtʃi] ADJ
depressing
deprimido, -a [depri'midu, a] ADJ
depressed
deprimir [depri'mir] VT to depress;
deprimir-se VR to get depressed
deputado, -a [depu'tadu, a] M/F deputy;
(*agente*) agent; (*Pol*) ≈ Member of
Parliament (BRIT), ≈ Representative (US)
der [der] VB *ver* **dar**
deriva [de'riva] F drift; **ir à ~** to drift;
ficar à ~ to be adrift
derivar [deri'var] VT to divert; (*Ling*) to
derive ▶ VI to drift; **derivar-se** VR to be
derived; (*ir à deriva*) to drift; (*provir*):
~(-se) (de) to derive *ou* be derived
(from)
derradeiro, -a [deha'dejru, a] ADJ last,
final
derramamento [dehama'mёtu] M
spilling; (*de sangue, lágrimas*) shedding
derramar [deha'mar] VT to spill;
(*entornar*) to pour; (*sangue, lágrimas*) to
shed; **derramar-se** VR to pour out
derrame [de'hami] M haemorrhage
(BRIT), hemorrhage (US)
derrapar [deha'par] VI to skid

derreter [dehe'ter] VT to melt;
derreter-se VR to melt; (*coisa congelada*) to thaw; (*enternecer-se*) to be touched

derrota [de'hɔta] F defeat, rout; (*Náut*) route; **derrotar** [deho'tar] VT (*vencer*) to defeat; (*em jogo*) to beat

derrubar [dehu'bar] VT to knock down; (*governo*) to bring down; (*suj: doença*) to lay low; (*col: prejudicar*) to put down

desabafar [dʒizaba'far] VT (*sentimentos*) to give vent to ▸ VI: **~ (com)** to unburden o.s. (to); **desabafar-se** VR: **~-se (com)** to unburden o.s. (to); **desabafo** [dʒiza'bafu] M confession

desabamento [dʒizaba'mẽtu] M collapse

desabar [dʒiza'bar] VI (*edifício, ponte*) to collapse; (*chuva*) to pour down; (*tempestade*) to break

desabitado, -a [dʒizabi'tadu, a] ADJ uninhabited

desabotoar [dʒizabo'twar] VT to unbutton

desabrigado, -a [dʒizabri'gadu, a] ADJ (*sem casa*) homeless; (*exposto*) exposed

desabrochar [dʒizabro'ʃar] VI (*flores, fig*) to blossom

desacatar [dʒizaka'tar] VT (*desrespeitar*) to have *ou* show no respect for; (*afrontar*) to defy; (*desprezar*) to scorn; **desacato** [dʒiza'katu] M disrespect; (*desprezo*) disregard

desaconselhar [dʒizakõse'ʎar] VT: **~ algo (a alguém)** to advise (sb) against sth

desacordado, -a [dʒizakor'dadu, a] ADJ unconscious

desacordo [dʒiza'kordu] M disagreement; (*desarmonia*) discord

desacostumado, -a [dʒizakostumadu, a] ADJ: **~ (a)** unaccustomed (to)

desacreditar [dʒizakredʒi'tar] VT to discredit; **desacreditar-se** VR to lose one's reputation

desafiador, a [dʒizafja'dor(a)] ADJ challenging; (*pessoa*) defiant ▸ M/F challenger

desafiar [dʒiza'fjar] VT to challenge; (*afrontar*) to defy

desafinado, -a [dʒizafi'nadu, a] ADJ out of tune

desafio [dʒiza'fiu] M challenge; (*PT Esporte*) match, game

desaforado, -a [dʒizafo'radu, a] ADJ rude, insolent

desaforo [dʒiza'foru] M insolence, abuse

desafortunado, -a [dʒizafortu'nadu, a] ADJ unfortunate, unlucky

desagradar [dʒizagra'dar] VT to displease ▸ VI: **~ a alguém** to displease sb; **desagradável** [dʒizagra'davew] (*pl* **-eis**) ADJ unpleasant; **desagrado** [dʒiza'gradu] M displeasure

desaguar [dʒiza'gwar] VT to drain ▸ VI: **~ (em)** to flow *ou* empty (into)

desajeitado, -a [dʒizaʒej'tadu, a] ADJ clumsy, awkward

desalentado, -a [dʒizalẽ'tadu, a] ADJ disheartened

desalentar [dʒizalẽ'tar] VT to discourage; (*deprimir*) to depress; **desalento** [dʒiza'lẽtu] M discouragement

desalmado, -a [dʒizaw'madu, a] ADJ cruel, inhuman

desalojar [dʒizalo'ʒar] VT (*expulsar*) to oust; **desalojar-se** VR to move out

desamarrar [dʒizama'har] VT to untie ▸ VI (*Náut*) to cast off

desamor [dʒiza'mor] M dislike

desamparado, -a [dʒizãpa'radu, a] ADJ abandoned; (*sem apoio*) helpless

desanimação [dʒizanima'sãw] F dejection

desanimado, -a [dʒizani'madu, a] ADJ (*pessoa*) fed up, dispirited; (*festa*) dull; **ser ~** (*pessoa*) to be apathetic

desanuviar [dʒizanu'vjar] VT (*céu*) to clear; **desanuviar-se** VR to clear; (*fig*) to stop; **~ alguém** to put sb's mind at rest

desaparafusar [dʒizaparafu'zar] VT to unscrew

desaparecer [dʒizapare'ser] VI to disappear, vanish; **desaparecido, -a** [dʒizapare'sidu, a] ADJ lost, missing ▸ M/F missing person; **desaparecimento** [dʒizaparesi'mẽtu] M disappearance; (*falecimento*) death

desapego [dʒiza'pegu] M indifference, detachment

desapercebido, -a [dʒizaperse'bidu, a] ADJ unnoticed

desapertar [dʒizaper'tar] VT to loosen; (*livrar*) to free

desapontamento [dʒizapõta'mẽtu] M disappointment

desapontar [dʒizapõ'tar] VT to disappoint

desapropriar [dʒizapro'prjar] VT (*bens*) to expropriate; (*pessoa*) to dispossess

desaprovar [dʒizapro'var] VT to disapprove of; (*censurar*) to object to

desarmamento [dʒizarma'mẽtu] M
disarmament

desarmar [dʒizar'mar] VT to disarm;
(*desmontar*) to dismantle; (*bomba*) to
defuse

desarmonia [dʒizarmo'nia] F discord

desarranjo [dʒiza'haʒu] M disorder;
(*enguiço*) breakdown; (*diarreia*) diarrhoea
(*BRIT*), diarrhea (*US*)

desarrumado, -a [dʒizahu'madu, a]
ADJ untidy, messy

desarrumar [dʒizahu'mar] VT to mess
up; (*mala*) to unpack

desassossego [dʒizaso'segu] M
(*inquietação*) disquiet; (*perturbação*)
restlessness

desastrado, -a [dʒizas'tradu, a] ADJ
clumsy

desastre [dʒi'zastri] M disaster;
(*acidente*) accident; (*de avião*) crash

desatar [dʒiza'tar] VT (*nó*) to undo, untie
▶ VI: **~ a fazer** to begin to do; **~ a chorar**
to burst into tears; **~ a rir** to burst out
laughing

desatento, -a [dʒiza'tẽtu, a] ADJ
inattentive

desatinado, -a [dʒizatʃi'nadu, a] ADJ
crazy, wild ▶ M/F lunatic

desatino [dʒiza'tʃinu] M madness; (*ato*)
folly

desativar [dʒizatʃi'var] VT (*firma, usina*)
to shut down; (*veículos*) to withdraw
from service; (*bomba*) to deactivate,
defuse

desatualizado, -a [dʒizatwali'zadu, a]
ADJ out of date; (*pessoa*) out of touch

desavença [dʒiza'vẽsa] F (*briga*) quarrel;
(*discórdia*) disagreement; **em ~** at
loggerheads

desavergonhado, -a
[dʒizavergo'ɲadu, a] ADJ shameless

desavisado, -a [dʒizavi'zadu, a] ADJ
careless

desbastar [dʒizbas'tar] VT (*cabelo,
plantas*) to thin (out); (*vegetação*) to
trim

desbocado, -a [dʒizbo'kadu, a] ADJ
foul-mouthed

desbotar [dʒizbo'tar] VT to discolour
(*BRIT*), discolor (*US*) ▶ VI to fade

desbragadamente
[dʒizbragada'mẽtʃi] ADV (*beber*) to
excess; (*mentir*) blatantly

desbravar [dʒizbra'var] VT (*terras
desconhecidas*) to explore

descabelar [dʒiskabe'lar] VT: **~ alguém**
to mess up sb's hair; **descabelar-se** VR to
get one's hair messed up

descabido, -a [dʒiska'bidu, a] ADJ
improper; (*inoportuno*) inappropriate

descafeinado [dʒiskafej'nadu] ADJ
decaffeinated ▶ N decaf

descalçar [dʒiskaw'sar] VT (*sapatos*) to
take off; **descalçar-se** VR to take off
one's shoes

descalço, -a [dʒis'kawsu, a] ADJ
barefoot

descansado, -a [dʒiskã'sadu, a] ADJ
calm, quiet; (*vagaroso*) slow; **fique ~**
don't worry; **pode ficar ~ que ...** you
can rest assured that ...

descansar [dʒiskã'sar] VT to rest;
(*apoiar*) to lean ▶ VI to rest; to lean;
descanso [dʒis'kãsu] M rest; (*folga*)
break; (*para prato*) mat

descarregamento [dʒiskahega'mẽtu]
M (*de carga*) unloading; (*Elet*) discharge

descarregar [dʒiskahe'gar] VT (*carga*) to
unload; (*Elet*) to discharge; (*aliviar*) to
relieve; (*raiva*) to vent, give vent to;
(*arma*) to fire ▶ VI to unload; (*bateria*) to
run out; **~ a raiva em alguém** to take it
out on sb

descartar [dʒiskar'tar] VT to discard;
descartar-se VR: **~-se de** to get rid of;
descartável [dʒiskar'tavew] (*pl* -**eis**) ADJ
disposable

descascar [dʒiskas'kar] VT (*fruta*) to
peel; (*ervilhas*) to shell ▶ VI (*depois do sol*)
to peel; (*cobra*) to shed its skin

descaso [dʒis'kazu] M disregard

descendência [desẽ'dẽsja] F
descendants *pl*, offspring *pl*

descendente [desẽ'dẽtʃi] ADJ
descending, going down ▶ M/F
descendant

descer [de'ser] VT (*escada*) to go (*ou*
come) down; (*bagagem*) to take down
▶ VI (*saltar*) to get off; (*baixar*) to go (*ou*
come) down; **descida** [de'sida] F
descent; (*declive*) slope; (*abaixamento*)
fall, drop

desclassificar [dʒisklasifi'kar] VT to
disqualify; (*desacreditar*) to discredit

descoberta [dʒisko'berta] F discovery;
(*invenção*) invention

descoberto, -a [dʒisko'bertu, a] PP *de*
descobrir ▶ ADJ bare, naked; (*exposto*)
exposed ▶ M overdraft; **a ~** openly;
conta a ~ overdrawn account; **pôr** *ou*
sacar a ~ (*conta*) to overdraw

descobridor, a [dʒiskobri'dor(a)] M/F
discoverer; (*explorador*) explorer

descobrimento [dʒiskobri'mẽtu] M
discovery; **Descobrimentos** MPL
see note

Mainly due to the seafaring expertise of Henry the Navigator, Portugal enjoyed a period of unrivalled overseas expansion during the 15th century. He organized and financed several voyages to Africa, which eventually led to the rounding of the Cape of Good Hope in 1488 by Bartolomeu Dias. In 1497, Vasco da Gama became the first European to travel by sea to India, where he established a lucrative spice trade, and a few years later, in 1500, Pedro Álvares Cabral reached Brazil, which he claimed for Portugal. Brazil remained under Portuguese rule until 1822.

descobrir [dʒiskoˈbrir] vt to discover; (tirar a cobertura de) to uncover; (panela) to take the lid off; (averiguar) to find out; (enigma) to solve

descolar [dʒiskoˈlar] vt to unstick ▶ vi: **a criança não descola da mãe** the child won't leave its mother's side

descolorante [dʒiskoloˈrãtʃi] m bleach

descolorir [dʒiskoloˈrir] vt to discolour (BRIT), discolor (US); (cabelo) to bleach ▶ vi to fade

descompostura [dʒiskõposˈtura] f (repreensão) dressing-down; (insulto) abuse; **passar uma ~ em alguém** to give sb a dressing-down; to hurl abuse at sb

desconcentrar [dʒiskõsẽˈtrar] vt to distract; **desconcentrar-se** vr to lose one's concentration

desconfiado, -a [dʒiskõˈfjadu, a] ADJ suspicious, distrustful ▶ m/f suspicious person

desconfiança [dʒiskõˈfjãsa] f suspicion, distrust

desconfiar [dʒiskõˈfjar] vi to be suspicious; **~ de alguém** (não ter confiança em) to distrust sb; (suspeitar) to suspect sb; **~ que ...** to have the feeling that ...

desconfortável [dʒiskõforˈtavew] (pl **-eis**) ADJ uncomfortable

desconforto [dʒiskõˈfortu] m discomfort

desconhecer [dʒiskoɲeˈser] vt (ignorar) not to know; (não reconhecer) not to recognize; (um benefício) not to acknowledge; (não admitir) not to accept; **desconhecido, -a** [dʒiskoɲeˈsidu, a] ADJ unknown ▶ m/f stranger; **desconhecimento** [dʒiskoɲesiˈmẽtu] m ignorance

desconsolado, -a [dʒiskõˈsoladu, a] ADJ miserable, disconsolate

descontar [dʒiskõˈtar] vt to deduct; (não levar em conta) to discount; (não fazer caso de) to make light of

descontentamento [dʒiskõtẽtaˈmẽtu] m discontent; (desprazer) displeasure

desconto [dʒisˈkõtu] m discount; **com ~** at a discount; **dar um ~ (para)** (fig) to make allowances (for)

descontraído, -a [dʒiskõtraˈidu, a] ADJ casual, relaxed

descontrair [dʒiskõtraˈir] vt to relax; **descontrair-se** vr to relax

descontrolar-se [dʒiskõtroˈlarsi] vr (situação) to get out of control; (pessoa) to lose one's self-control

desconversar [dʒiskõverˈsar] vi to change the subject

descortesia [dʒiskorteˈzia] f rudeness, impoliteness

descoser [dʒiskoˈzer] vt (descosturar) to unstitch; (rasgar) to rip apart; **descoser-se** vr to come apart at the seams

descrença [dʒisˈkrẽsa] f disbelief, incredulity

descrente [dʒisˈkrẽtʃi] ADJ sceptical (BRIT), skeptical (US) ▶ m/f sceptic (BRIT), skeptic (US)

descrever [dʒiskreˈver] vt to describe

descrição [dʒiskriˈsãw] (pl **-ões**) f description

descriptografar [dʒiskriptograˈfar] vt Comput to decrypt

descritivo, -a [dʒiskriˈtʃivu, a] ADJ descriptive

descrito, -a [dʒisˈkritu, a] pp de **descrever**

descubro [dʒisˈkubru] vb ver **descobrir**

descuidar [dʒiskwiˈdar] vt to neglect ▶ vi: **~ de** to neglect, disregard; **descuido** [dʒisˈkwidu] m carelessness; (negligência) neglect; (erro) oversight, slip; **por descuido** inadvertently

desculpa [dʒisˈkuwpa] f excuse; (perdão) pardon; **pedir ~s a alguém por** ou **de algo** to apologize to sb for sth; **desculpar** [dʒiskuwˈpar] vt to excuse; (perdoar) to pardon, forgive; **desculpar-se** vr to apologize; **desculpar algo a alguém** to forgive sb for sth; **desculpe!** (I'm) sorry, I beg your pardon; **desculpável** [dʒiskuwˈpavew] (pl **-eis**) ADJ forgivable

PALAVRA-CHAVE

desde ['dezdʒi] PREP **1** (*lugar*): **desde ... até ...** from ... to ...; **andamos desde a praia até o restaurante** we walked from the beach to the restaurant **2** (*tempo, + adv, n*): **desde então** from then on, ever since; **desde já** (*de agora*) from now on; (*imediatamente*) at once, right now; **desde o casamento** since the wedding **3** (*tempo, + vb*) since; for; **conhecemo-nos desde 1978/há 20 anos** we've known each other since 1978/for 20 years; **não o vejo desde 1983** I haven't seen him since 1983 **4** (*variedade*): **desde os mais baratos até os mais luxuosos** from the cheapest to the most luxurious ▶ CONJ: **desde que** since; **desde que comecei a trabalhar não o vi mais** I haven't seen him since I started work; **não saiu de casa desde que chegou** he hasn't been out since he arrived

desdizer [dʒizdʒi'zer] (*irreg: como* **dizer**) VT to contradict; **desdizer-se** VR to go back on one's word

desdobrar [dʒizdo'brar] VT (*abrir*) to unfold; (*esforços*) to increase, redouble; (*tropas*) to deploy; (*bandeira*) to unfurl; (*dividir em grupos*) to split up; **desdobrar-se** VR to unfold; (*empenhar-se*) to work hard, make a big effort

desejar [dese'ʒar] VT to want, desire

desejo [de'zeʒu] M wish, desire; **desejoso, -a** [deze'ʒozu, ɔza] ADJ: **desejoso de algo** wishing for sth; **desejoso de fazer** keen to do

desembaraçar [dʒizẽbara'sar] VT (*livrar*) to free; (*cabelo*) to untangle; **desembaraçar-se** VR (*desinibir-se*) to lose one's inhibitions; **~-se de** to get rid of

desembaraço [dʒizẽba'rasu] M liveliness; (*facilidade*) ease; (*confiança*) self-assurance

desembarcar [dʒizẽbar'kar] VT (*carga*) to unload; (*passageiros*) to let off ▶ VI to disembark; **desembarque** [dʒizẽ'barki] M landing, disembarkation; **"desembarque"** (*no aeroporto*) "arrivals"

desembolsar [dʒizẽbow'sar] VT to spend

desembrulhar [dʒizẽbru'ʎar] VT to unwrap

desempacotar [dʒizẽpako'tar] VT to unpack

desempatar [dʒizẽpa'tar] VT to decide ▶ VI to decide the match (*ou race etc*); **desempate** [dʒizẽ'patʃi] M: **partida de desempate** (*jogo*) play-off, decider

desempenhar [dʒizẽpe'ɲar] VT (*cumprir*) to carry out, fulfil (BRIT), fulfill (US); (*papel*) to play; **desempenho** [dʒizẽ'peɲu] M performance; (*de obrigações etc*) fulfilment (BRIT), fulfillment (US)

desempregado, -a [dʒizẽpre'gadu, a] ADJ unemployed ▶ M/F unemployed person

desempregar-se [dʒizẽpre'garsi] VR to lose one's job

desemprego [dʒizẽ'pregu] M unemployment

desencadear [dʒizẽka'dʒjar] VT to unleash; (*despertar*) to provoke, trigger off ▶ VI (*chuva*) to pour; **desencadear-se** VR to break loose; (*tempestade*) to break

desencaixar [dʒizẽkaj'ʃar] VT to put out of joint; (*deslocar*) to dislodge; **desencaixar-se** VR to become dislodged

desencaixotar [dʒizẽkajʃo'tar] VT to unpack

desencarregar-se [dʒizẽkahe'garsi] VR (*de obrigação*) to discharge o.s.

desencontrar [dʒizẽkõ'trar] VT to keep apart; **desencontrar-se** VR (*não se encontrar*) to miss each other; (*perder-se um do outro*) to lose each other; **~-se de** to miss; to get separated from

desencorajar [dʒizẽkora'ʒar] VT to discourage

desencostar [dʒizẽkos'tar] VT to move away; **desencostar-se** VR: **~-se de** to move away from

desencriptar [dʒizẽkrip'tar] VT (*Comput, Tel*) to decrypt

desenfreado, -a [dʒizẽ'frjadu, a] ADJ wild

desenganado, -a [dʒizẽga'nadu, a] ADJ incurable; (*desiludido*) disillusioned

desenganar [dʒizẽga'nar] VT: **~ alguém** to disillusion sb; (*de falsas crenças*) to open sb's eyes; (*doente*) to give up hope of curing; **desenganar-se** VR to become disillusioned; (*sair de erro*) to realize the truth; **desengano** [dʒizẽ'ganu] M disillusionment; (*desapontamento*) disappointment

desengonçado, -a [dʒizẽgõ'sadu, a] ADJ (*malseguro*) rickety; (*pessoa*) ungainly

desenhar [deze'ɲar] VT to draw; (*Tec*) to design; **desenhar-se** VR (*destacar-se*) to stand out; (*figurar-se*) to take shape; **desenhista** [deze'ɲista] M/F (*Tec*) designer

desenho [de'zɐɲu] M drawing; (*modelo*) design; (*esboço*) sketch; (*plano*) plan; **~ animado** cartoon

desenlace [dʒizẽ'lasi] M outcome

desenrolar [dʒizẽho'lar] VT to unroll; (*narrativa*) to develop; **desenrolar-se** VR to unfold

desentender [dʒizẽtẽ'der] VT to misunderstand; **desentender-se** VR: **~-se com** to have a disagreement with; **desentendido, -a** [dʒizẽtẽ'dʒidu, a] ADJ: **fazer-se de desentendido** to pretend not to understand; **desentendimento** [dʒizẽtẽdʒi'mẽtu] M misunderstanding

desenterrar [dʒizẽte'har] VT (*cadáver*) to exhume; (*tesouro*) to dig up; (*descobrir*) to bring to light

desentupir [dʒizẽtu'pir] VT to unblock

desenvoltura [dʒizẽvow'tura] F self-confidence

desenvolver [dʒizẽvow'ver] VT to develop; **desenvolver-se** VR to develop; **desenvolvimento** [dʒizẽvowvi'mẽtu] M development; (*crescimento*) growth; **país em desenvolvimento** developing country

deserção [dezer'sãw] F desertion

desertar [deser'tar] VT to desert, abandon ▶ VI to desert; **deserto, -a** [de'zɛrtu, a] ADJ deserted ▶ M desert; **desertor, a** [dezer'tor(a)] M/F deserter

desesperado, -a [dʒizespe'radu, a] ADJ desperate; (*furioso*) furious

desesperador, a [dʒizespera'dor(a)] ADJ desperate; (*enfurecedor*) maddening

desesperança [dʒizespe'rãsa] F despair

desesperar [dʒizespe'rar] VT to drive to despair; (*enfurecer*) to infuriate; **desesperar-se** VR to despair; (*enfurecer-se*) to become infuriated; **desespero** [dʒizes'peru] M despair, desperation; (*raiva*) fury

desestimular [dʒizestʃimu'lar] VT to discourage

desfalcar [dʒisfaw'kar] VT (*dinheiro*) to embezzle; (*reduzir*) **~ (de)** to reduce (by); **o jogo está desfalcado** the game is incomplete

desfalecer [dʒisfale'ser] VT (*enfraquecer*) to weaken ▶ VI (*enfraquecer*) to weaken; (*desmaiar*) to faint

desfalque [dʒis'fawki] M (*de dinheiro*) embezzlement; (*diminuição*) reduction

desfavorável [dʒisfavo'ravew] (*pl* -**eis**) ADJ unfavourable (BRIT), unfavorable (US)

desfazer [dʒisfa'zer] (*irreg: como* **fazer**) VT (*costura*) to undo; (*dúvidas*) to dispel; (*agravo*) to redress; (*grupo*) to break up; (*contrato*) to dissolve; (*noivado*) to break off ▶ VI: **~ de alguém** to belittle sb; **desfazer-se** VR to vanish; (*tecido*) to come to pieces; (*grupo*) to break up; (*vaso*) to break; **~-se de** (*livrar-se*) to get rid of; **~-se em lágrimas/gentilezas** to burst into tears/go out of one's way to please

desfecho [dʒis'feʃu] M ending, outcome

desfeito, -a [dʒis'fejtu, a] ADJ undone; (*cama*) unmade; (*contrato*) broken

desfilar [dʒisfi'lar] VI to parade; **desfile** [dʒis'fili] M parade, procession

desforra [dʒis'fɔha] F revenge; (*reparação*) redress; **tirar ~** to get even

desfrutar [dʒisfru'tar] VT to enjoy ▶ VI: **~ de** to enjoy

desgarrado, -a [dʒizga'hadu, a] ADJ stray; (*navio*) off course

desgastante [dʒizgas'tãtʃi] ADJ (*fig*) stressful

desgrudar [dʒizgru'dar] VT to unstick ▶ VI: **~ de** to tear o.s. away from; **~ algo de algo** to take sth off sth

desidratar [dʒizidra'tar] VT to dehydrate

design [dʒi'zãjn] M design

designar [dezig'nar] VT to designate; (*nomear*) to name, appoint; (*dia, data*) to fix

desigual [dezi'gwaw] (*pl* -**ais**) ADJ unequal; (*terreno*) uneven; **desigualdade** [dʒizigwaw'dadʒi] F inequality

desiludir [dʒizilu'dʒir] VT to disillusion; (*causar decepção a*) to disappoint; **desiludir-se** VR to lose one's illusions

desimpedido, -a [dʒizĩpe'dʒidu, a] ADJ free

desinfetante [dʒizĩfe'tãtʃi] ADJ, M disinfectant

desinfetar [dʒizĩfe'tar] VT to disinfect

desinstalar [dʒizĩsta'lar] VT (*Comput*) to uninstall

desintegração [dʒizĩtegra'sãw] F disintegration, break-up

desintegrar [dʒizĩte'grar] VT to separate; **desintegrar-se** VR to disintegrate, fall to pieces

desistir [dezis'tʃir] VI to give up; **~ de fumar** to stop smoking; **ele ia, mas no final desistiu** he was going, but in the end he gave up the idea *ou* he decided not to

desjejum [dʒizʒe'ʒũ] M breakfast

deslavado, -a [dʒizla'vadu, a] ADJ (*pessoa, atitude*) shameless; (*mentira*) blatant

desleal [dʒizle'aw] (*pl* **-ais**) ADJ disloyal

desleixo [dʒiz'lejʃu] M sloppiness

desligado, -a [dʒizli'gadu, a] ADJ (*eletricidade*) off; (*pessoa*) absent-minded; **estar ~** to be miles away

desligar [dʒizli'gar] VT (*Tec*) to disconnect; (*luz, TV, motor*) to switch off; (*telefone*) to hang up; **desligar-se** VR: **~-se de algo** (*afastar-se*) to leave sth; (*problemas etc*) to turn one's back on sth; **não desligue** (*Tel*) hold the line

deslizar [dʒizli'zar] VI to slide; (*por acidente*) to slip; (*passar de leve*) to glide; **deslize** [dʒiz'lizi] M lapse; (*escorregadela*) slip

deslocado, -a [dʒizlo'kadu, a] ADJ (*membro*) dislocated; (*desambientado*) out of place

deslumbramento [dʒizlũbra'mẽtu] M dazzle; (*fascinação*) fascination

deslumbrante [dʒizlũ'brãtʃi] ADJ dazzling; (*casa, festa*) amazing

deslumbrar [dʒizlũ'brar] VT to dazzle; (*maravilhar*) to amaze; (*fascinar*) to fascinate ▶ VI to be dazzling; to be amazing; **deslumbrar-se** VR: **~-se com** to be fascinated by

desmaiado, -a [dʒizma'jadu, a] ADJ unconscious; (*cor*) pale

desmaiar [dʒizma'jar] VI to faint; **desmaio** [dʒiz'maju] M faint

desmanchar [dʒizman'ʃar] VT (*costura*) to undo; (*contrato*) to break; (*noivado*) to break off; (*penteado*) to mess up; **desmanchar-se** VR (*costura*) to come undone

desmarcar [dʒizmar'kar] VT (*compromisso*) to cancel

desmascarar [dʒizmaska'rar] VT to unmask

desmazelado, -a [dʒizmaze'ladu, a] ADJ slovenly, untidy

desmedido, -a [dʒizme'dʒidu, a] ADJ excessive

desmentido [dʒizmẽ'tʃidu] M (*negação*) denial; (*contradição*) contradiction

desmentir [dʒizmẽ'tʃir] VT (*contradizer*) to contradict; (*negar*) to deny

desmiolado, -a [dʒizmjo'ladu, a] ADJ brainless; (*esquecido*) forgetful

desmoronamento [dʒizmorona'mẽtu] M collapse

desmoronar [dʒizmoro'nar] VT to knock down ▶ VI to collapse

desnatado, -a [dʒizna'tadu, a] ADJ (*leite*) skimmed

desnaturado, -a [dʒiznatu'radu, a] ADJ inhumane ▶ M/F monster

desnecessário, -a [dʒiznese'sarju, a] ADJ unnecessary

desnutrição [dʒiznutri'sãw] F malnutrition

desobedecer [dʒizobede'ser] VT to disobey; **desobediência** [dʒizobe'dʒjẽsja] F disobedience; **desobediente** [dʒizobe'dʒjẽtʃi] ADJ disobedient

desobstruir [dʒizobis'trwir] VT to unblock

desocupado, -a [dʒizoku'padu, a] ADJ (*casa*) empty, vacant; (*disponível*) free; (*sem trabalho*) unemployed

desocupar [dʒizoku'par] VT (*casa*) to vacate; (*liberar*) to free

desodorante [dʒizodo'rãtʃi], (*PT*) **desodorizante** [dʒizodori'zãtʃi] M deodorant

desolação [dezola'sãw] F (*consternação*) grief; (*de um lugar*) desolation; **desolado, -a** [dezo'ladu, a] ADJ distressed; (*lugar*) desolate

desonesto, -a [dezo'nɛstu, a] ADJ dishonest

desordem [dʒi'zordẽ] F disorder, confusion; **em ~** (*casa*) untidy

desorganizar [dʒizorgani'zar] VT to disorganize; (*dissolver*) to break up; **desorganizar-se** VR to become disorganized; to break up

desorientação [dʒizorjẽta'sãw] F bewilderment, confusion

desorientar [dʒizorjẽ'tar] VT (*desnortear*) to throw off course; (*perturbar*) to confuse; (*desvairar*) to unhinge; **desorientar-se** VR to lose one's way; to get confused; to go mad

desovar [dʒizo'var] VT to lay; (*peixe*) to spawn

despachado, -a [dʒispa'ʃadu, a] ADJ (*pessoa*) efficient

despachar [dʒispa'ʃar] VT to dispatch, send off; (*atender, resolver*) to deal with; (*despedir*) to sack; **despachar-se** VR to hurry (up); **despacho** [dʒis'paʃu] M dispatch; (*de negócios*) handling; (*nota em requerimento*) ruling; (*reunião*) consultation; (*macumba*) witchcraft

despeço [dʒis'pɛsu] VB *ver* **despedir**

despedaçar [dʒispeda'sar] VT (*quebrar*) to smash; (*rasgar*) to tear apart; **despedaçar-se** VR to smash; to tear

despedida [dʒiʃpe'dʒida] F farewell; (de trabalhador) dismissal

despedir [dʒiʃpe'dʒir] VT (de emprego) to dismiss, sack; **despedir-se** VR: **~-se (de)** to say goodbye (to)

despeitado, -a [dʒiʃpej'tadu, a] ADJ spiteful; (ressentido) resentful

despeito [dʒiʃ'pejtu] M spite; **a ~ de** in spite of, despite

despejar [dʒiʃpe'ʒar] VT (água) to pour; (esvaziar) to empty; (inquilino) to evict; **despejo** [dʒiʃ'peʒu] M eviction; **quarto de despejo** junk room

despencar [dʒiʃpẽ'kar] VI to fall down, tumble down

despentear [dʒiʃpẽ'tʃjar] VT (cabelo: sem querer) to mess up; (: de propósito) to let down; **despentear-se** VR to mess one's hair up; to let one's hair down

despercebido, -a [dʒiʃperse'bidu, a] ADJ unnoticed

desperdiçar [dʒiʃperdʒi'sar] VT to waste; (dinheiro) to squander; **desperdício** [dʒiʃper'dʒisju] M waste

despertador [dʒiʃperta'dor] M (tb: **relógio ~**) alarm clock

despertar [dʒiʃper'tar] VT to wake; (suspeitas, interesse) to arouse; (reminiscências) to revive; (apetite) to whet ▶ VI to wake up ▶ M awakening; **desperto, -a** [dʒiʃ'pɛrtu, a] ADJ awake

despesa [dʒiʃ'peza] F expense; **despesas** FPL (de uma empresa) expenses, costs; **~s gerais** (Com) overheads

despido, -a [dʒiʃ'pidu, a] ADJ naked, bare; (livre) free

despir [dʒiʃ'pir] VT (roupa) to take off; (pessoa) to undress; (despojar) to strip; **despir-se** VR to undress

despojar [dʒiʃpo'ʒar] VT (casas) to loot, sack; (pessoas) to rob

despontar [dʒiʃpõ'tar] VI to emerge; (sol) to come out; (: ao amanhecer) to come up; **ao ~ do dia** at daybreak

desporto [dʒiʃ'portu] M sport

desprender [dʒiʃprẽ'der] VT to loosen; (desatar) to unfasten; (emitir) to emit; **desprender-se** VR (botão) to come off; (cheiro) to be given off

desprezar [dʒiʃpre'zar] VT to despise, disdain; (não dar importância a) to disregard, ignore; **desprezível** [dʒiʃpre'zivew] (pl -**eis**) ADJ despicable; **desprezo** [dʒiʃ'prezu] M scorn, contempt; **dar ao desprezo** to ignore

desproporcional [dʒiʃproporsjo'naw] ADJ disproportionate

despropósito [dʒiʃpro'pozitu] M nonsense

desprovido, -a [dʒiʃpro'vidu, a] ADJ deprived; **~ de** without

desqualificar [dʒiʃkwalifi'kar] VT (Esporte etc) to disqualify; (tornar indigno) to disgrace, lower

desregrado, -a [dʒiʒhe'gradu, a] ADJ disorderly, unruly; (devasso) immoderate

desrespeito [dʒiʒhe'spejtu] M disrespect

desse¹, -a ['desi, a] = **de + esse**, **~ a**

desse² VB ver **dar**

destacar [dʒiʃta'kar] VT (Mil) to detail; (separar) to detach; (enfatizar) to emphasize ▶ VI to stand out; **destacar-se** VR to stand out; (pessoa) to be outstanding

destampar [dʒiʃtã'par] VT to take the lid off

destapar [dʒiʃta'par] VT to uncover

destaque [dʒiʃ'taki] M distinction; (pessoa, coisa) highlight

deste, -a ['destʃi, a] = **de + este**, **~ a**

destemido, -a [deste'midu, a] ADJ fearless, intrepid

destilar [destʃi'lar] VT to distil (BRIT), distill (US)

destinação [destʃina'sãw] (pl -**ões**) F destination

destinar [des'tʃinar] VT to destine; (dinheiro): **~ (para)** to set aside (for); **destinar-se** VR: **~-se a** to be intended for; (carta) to be addressed to

destinatário, -a [destʃina'tarju, a] M/F addressee

destino [des'tʃinu] M destiny, fate; (lugar) destination; **com ~ a** bound for

destituir [destʃi'twir] VT to dismiss; **~ de** (privar de) to deprive of

destrancar [dʒiʃtrã'kar] VT to unlock

destratar [dʒiʃtra'tar] VT to abuse, insult

destreza [des'treza] F skill; (agilidade) dexterity

destro, -a ['dɛstru, a] ADJ skilful (BRIT), skillful (US); (ágil) agile; (não canhoto) right-handed

destrocar [dʒiʃtro'kar] VT to give back, return

destroçar [dʒiʃtro'sar] VT to destroy; (quebrar) to smash, break; **destroços** [dʒiʃ'trɔsus] MPL wreckage sg

destruição [dʒiʃtrwi'sãw] F destruction

destruir [dʒiʃ'trwir] VT to destroy

desvairado, -a [dʒiʒvaj'radu, a] ADJ (louco) crazy, demented; (desorientado) bewildered

desvalorizar [dʒiʒvalori'zar] VT to devalue

desvantagem [dʒizvã'taʒẽ] (pl **-ns**) F
disadvantage

desvão [dʒiz'vãw] (pl **-s**) M loft

desventura [dʒizvẽ'tura] F misfortune;
(*infelicidade*) unhappiness

desvio [dʒiz'viu] M diversion, detour;
(*curva*) bend; (*fig*) deviation; (*de dinheiro*)
embezzlement

detalhadamente [detaʎada'mẽtʃi]
ADV in detail

detalhado, -a [deta'ʎadu, a] ADJ
detailed

detalhe [de'taʎi] M detail

detectar [detek'tar] VT to detect

detector [detek'tor] M detector

detenção [detẽ'sãw] (pl **-ões**) F
detention

deter [de'ter] (*irreg*: *como* **ter**) VT to stop;
(*prender*) to arrest, detain; (*reter*) to keep;
(*conter: riso*) to contain; **deter-se** VR
to stop; (*ficar*) to stay; (*conter-se*) to
restrain o.s.

detergente [deter'ʒẽtʃi] M detergent

deteriorar [deterjo'rar] VT to spoil,
damage; **deteriorar-se** VR to
deteriorate; (*relações*) to worsen

determinação [determina'sãw] F
determination; (*decisão*) decision;
(*ordem*) order

determinado, -a [determi'nadu, a] ADJ
determined; (*certo*) certain, given

determinar [determi'nar] VT to
determine; (*decretar*) to order; (*resolver*)
to decide (on); (*causar*) to cause

detestar [detes'tar] VT to hate;
detestável [detes'tavew] (pl **-eis**) ADJ
horrible, hateful

detetive [dete'tʃivi] M/F detective

detido, -a [de'tʃidu, a] ADJ (*preso*) under
arrest; (*minucioso*) thorough ▶ M/F
person under arrest, prisoner

detonação [detona'sãw] (pl **-ões**) F
explosion

detonar [deto'nar] VI, VT to detonate

detrás [de'trajs] ADV behind ▶ PREP: **~ de**
behind

detrimento [detri'mẽtu] M: **em ~ de** to
the detriment of

detrito [de'tritu] M debris *sg*; (*de comida*)
remains *pl*; (*resíduo*) dregs *pl*

deturpação [deturpa'sãw] F
corruption; (*de palavras*) distortion

deturpar [detur'par] VT to corrupt;
(*desfigurar*) to disfigure; (*palavras*) to
twist

deu [dew] VB *ver* **dar**

deus, a [dews, 'dewza] M/F god/
goddess; **D~ me livre!** God forbid!;

graças a D~ thank goodness; **meu D~!**
good Lord!

devagar [dʒiva'gar] ADV slowly

devaneio [deva'neju] M daydream

devassa [de'vasa] F investigation, inquiry

devassidão [devasi'dãw] F debauchery

devasso, -a [de'vasu, a] ADJ dissolute

deve ['dɛvi] M debit

dever [de'ver] M duty ▶ VT to owe ▶ VI
(*suposição*): **deve (de) estar doente** he
must be ill; (*obrigação*): **devo partir às
oito** I must go at eight; **você devia ir ao
médico** you should go to the doctor;
que devo fazer? what shall I do?

devido, -a [de'vidu, a] ADJ (*maneira*)
proper; (*respeito*) due; **~ a** due to, owing
to; **no ~ tempo** in due course

devoção [devo'sãw] F devotion

devolução [devolu'sãw] F devolution;
(*restituição*) return; (*reembolso*) refund;
~ de impostos tax rebate

devolver [devow'ver] VT to give back,
return; (*Com*) to refund

devorar [devo'rar] VT to devour;
(*destruir*) to destroy

devotar [devo'tar] VT to devote

dez [dɛz] NUM ten

dezanove [deza'nɔvə] (PT) NUM
= **dezenove**

dezasseis [deza'sejs] (PT) NUM
= **dezesseis**

dezassete [deza'setə] (PT) NUM
= **dezessete**

dezembro [de'zẽbru] M December

dezena [de'zena] F: **uma ~** ten

dezenove [deze'nɔvi] NUM nineteen

dezesseis [deze'sejs] NUM sixteen

dezessete [dezi'setʃi] NUM seventeen

dezoito [dʒi'zojtu] NUM eighteen

dia ['dʒia] M day; (*claridade*) daylight;
~ a ~ day by day; **~ santo** holy day; **~ útil**
weekday; **estar** *ou* **andar em ~ (com)**
to be up to date (with); **de ~** in the
daytime, by day; **mais ~ menos ~**
sooner or later; **~ sim, ~ não** every other
day; **no ~ seguinte** the next day; **bom ~**
good morning; **um ~ desses** one of
these days; **~s a fio** days on end;
~ cheio/morto busy/quiet *ou* slow day;
todo santo ~ (*col*) every single day, day
after day; **recebo por ~** I'm paid by the
day; **um bebê de ~s** a newborn baby;
ele está com os ~s contados his days
are numbered; **dia a dia** M daily life,
everyday life

diabete, diabetes [dʒia'bɛtʃi(s)] F
diabetes *sg*; **diabético, -a** [dʒia'bɛtʃiku,
a] ADJ, M/F diabetic

diabo ['dʒjabu] M devil; **que ~!** (col)
damn it!

diabrura [dʒja'brura] F prank;
diabruras FPL (travessura) mischief sg

diagnóstico [dʒjag'nɔstʃiku] M
diagnosis

diagonal [dʒjago'naw] (pl -ais) ADJ, F
diagonal

diagrama [dʒja'grama] M diagram

dialeto [dʒja'lɛtu] M dialect

dialogar [dʒjalo'gar] VI: **~ (com
alguém)** to talk (to sb); (Pol) to have ou
hold talks (with sb)

diálogo ['dʒjalogu] M dialogue;
(conversa) talk, conversation

diamante [dʒja'mãtʃi] M diamond

diâmetro ['dʒjametru] M diameter

diante ['dʒjãtʃi] PREP: **~ de** before; (na
frente de) in front of; (problemas etc) in the
face of; **e assim por ~** and so on; **para ~**
forward

dianteira [dʒjã'tejra] F front, vanguard;
tomar a ~ to get ahead

dianteiro, -a [dʒjã'tejru, a] ADJ front

diapositivo [dʒjapozi'tʃivu] M (Foto)
slide

diária ['dʒjarja] F (de hotel) daily rate

diário, -a ['dʒjarju, a] ADJ daily ▶ M diary;
(jornal) (daily) newspaper; **~ de bordo**
(Aer) logbook

diarreia [dʒja'ʀeja] F diarrhoea (BRIT),
diarrhea (US)

dica ['dʒika] (col) F hint

dicionário [dʒisjo'narju] M dictionary

dieta ['dʒjeta] F diet; **fazer ~** to go on
a diet

diferença [dʒife'ʀẽsa] F difference; **ela
tem uma ~ comigo** she's got something
against me

diferenciar [dʒiferẽ'sjar] VT to
differentiate

diferente [dʒife'ʀẽtʃi] ADJ different;
estar ~ com alguém to be at odds
with sb

difícil [dʒi'fisiw] (pl -eis) ADJ difficult;
(improvável) unlikely; **o ~ é ...** the difficult
thing is ...; **acho ~ ela aceitar nossa
proposta** I think it's unlikely she will
accept our proposal; **dificilmente**
[dʒifisiw'mẽtʃi] ADV with difficulty;
(mal) hardly; (raramente) hardly ever

dificuldade [dʒifikuw'dadʒi] F
difficulty; **em ~s** in trouble

dificultar [dʒifikuw'tar] VT to make
difficult; (complicar) to complicate

difundir [dʒifũ'dʒir] VT to diffuse;
to spread

digerir [dʒiʒe'rir] VT, VI to digest

digestão [dʒiʒes'tãw] F digestion

digital [dʒiʒi'taw] (pl -ais) ADJ:
impressão ~ fingerprint

digitar [dʒiʒi'tar] VT (Comput: dados) to
key (in)

dígito ['dʒiʒitu] M digit

dignidade [dʒiɡni'dadʒi] F dignity

digno, -a ['dʒiɡnu, a] ADJ (merecedor)
worthy; (nobre) dignified

digo ['dʒiɡu] VB ver **dizer**

dilatar [dʒila'tar] VT to dilate, expand;
(prolongar) to prolong; (retardar) to delay

dilema [dʒi'lema] M dilemma

diluir [dʒi'lwir] VT to dilute

dilúvio [dʒi'luvju] M flood

dimensão [dʒimẽ'sãw] (pl -ões) F
dimension; **dimensões** FPL (medidas)
measurements

diminuição [dʒiminwi'sãw] F reduction

diminuir [dʒimi'nwir] VT to reduce;
(som) to turn down; (interesse) to lessen
▶ VI to lessen, diminish; (preço) to go
down; (dor) to wear off; (barulho) to die
down

diminutivo, -a [dʒiminu'tʃivu, a] ADJ
diminutive ▶ M (Ling) diminutive

Dinamarca [dʒina'marka] F Denmark;
dinamarquês, -quesa [dʒinamar'kes,
'keza] ADJ Danish ▶ M/F Dane ▶ M (Ling)
Danish

dinâmico, -a [dʒi'namiku, a] ADJ
dynamic

dínamo ['dʒinamu] M dynamo

dinheirão [dʒiɲej'rãw] M: **um ~** loads pl
of money

dinheiro [dʒi'ɲejru] M money; **~ à vista**
cash for paying in cash; **~ em caixa**
money in the till; **~ em espécie** cash

dinossauro [dʒino'sawru] M dinosaur

diploma [dʒip'lɔma] M diploma

diplomacia [dʒiploma'sia] F diplomacy;
(fig) tact

diplomata [dʒiplo'mata] M/F diplomat;
diplomático, -a [dʒiplo'matʃiku, a] ADJ
diplomatic

dique ['dʒiki] M dam; (Geo) dyke

direção [dʒire'sãw] (pl -ões) F direction;
(endereço) address; (Auto) steering;
(administração) management; (comando)
leadership; (diretoria) board of directors;
em ~ a towards

direi [dʒi'rej] VB ver **dizer**

direita [dʒi'rejta] F (mão) right hand;
(lado) right-hand side; (Pol) right wing;
à ~ on the right

direito, -a [dʒi'rejtu, a] ADJ (lado)
right-hand; (mão) right; (honesto)
honest; (devido) proper; (justo) right, just

▶ M right; (*Jur*) law ▶ ADV straight; (*bem*) right; (*de maneira certa*) properly; **direitos** MPL (*humanos*) rights; (*alfandegários*) duty *sg*

direto, -a [dʒi'rɛtu, a] ADJ direct ▶ ADV straight; **transmissão direta** (*TV*) live broadcast

diretor, a [dʒire'tor(a)] ADJ directing, guiding ▶ M/F director; (*de jornal*) editor; (*de escola*) head teacher; **diretoria** [dʒireto'ria] F (*Com*) management

dirigente [dʒiri'ʒẽtʃi] M/F (*de país, partido*) leader; (*diretor*) director; (*gerente*) manager

dirigir [dʒiri'ʒir] VT to direct; (*Com*) to manage; (*veículo*) to drive ▶ VI to drive; **dirigir-se** VR: **~-se a** (*falar com*) to speak to; (*ir, recorrer*) to go to; (*esforços*) to be directed towards

discagem [dʒis'kaʒẽ] F (*Tel*) dialling

discar [dʒis'kar] VT to dial

disciplina [dʒisi'plina] F discipline; **disciplinar** [dʒisipli'nar] VT to discipline

discípulo, -a [dʒi'sipulu, a] M/F disciple; (*aluno*) pupil

disco ['dʒisku] M disc; (*Comput*) disk; (*Mús*) record; (*de telefone*) dial; **~ rígido** (*Comput*) hard drive, hard disk; **~ do sistema** system disk; **~ voador** flying saucer

discordar [dʒiskor'dar] VI: **~ de alguém em algo** to disagree with sb on sth

discórdia [dʒis'kɔrdʒia] F discord, strife

discoteca [dʒisko'tɛka] F discotheque, disco (*col*)

discrepância [dʒiskre'pãsja] F discrepancy; (*desacordo*) disagreement; **discrepante** [dʒiskre'pãtʃi] ADJ conflicting

discreto, -a [dʒis'krɛtu, a] ADJ discreet; (*modesto*) modest; (*prudente*) shrewd; (*roupa*) plain; **discrição** [dʒiskri'sãw] F discretion

discriminação [dʒiskrimina'sãw] F discrimination

discriminar [dʒiskrimi'nar] VT to distinguish ▶ VI: **~ entre** to discriminate between

discurso [dʒis'kursu] M speech

discussão [dʒisku'sãw] F (*pl* -ões) F discussion; (*contenda*) argument

discutir [dʒisku'tʃir] VT to discuss ▶ VI: **~ (sobre algo)** to talk (about sth); (*contender*) to argue (about sth)

disenteria [dʒizẽte'ria] F dysentery

disfarçar [dʒisfar'sar] VT to disguise ▶ VI to pretend; **disfarçar-se** VR: **~-se em** ou

de algo to disguise o.s. as sth; **disfarce** [dʒis'farsi] M disguise; (*máscara*) mask

dislexia [dʒizlek'sia] F dyslexia

disparar [dʒispa'rar] VT to shoot, fire ▶ VI to fire; (*arma*) to go off; (*correr*) to shoot off, bolt

disparatado, -a [dʒispara'tadu, a] ADJ silly, absurd

disparate [dʒispa'ratʃi] M nonsense, rubbish

disparidade [dʒispari'dadʒi] F disparity

dispensar [dʒispẽ'sar] VT to excuse; (*prescindir de*) to do without; (*conferir*) to grant; **dispensável** [dʒispẽ'savew] (*pl* -**eis**) ADJ expendable

dispersar [dʒisper'sar] VT, VI to disperse; **disperso, -a** [dʒis'pɛrsu, a] ADJ scattered

displicência [dʒispli'sẽsja] (BR) F negligence, carelessness; **displicente** [dʒispli'sẽtʃi] ADJ careless

dispo ['dʒispu] VB *ver* **despir**

disponível [dʒispo'nivew] (*pl* -**eis**) ADJ available

dispor [dʒis'por] (*irreg: como* **pôr**) VT to arrange ▶ VI: **~ de** to have the use of; (*ter*) to have, own; (*pessoas*) to have at one's disposal; **dispor-se** VR: **~-se a** (*estar pronto a*) to be prepared to, be willing to; (*decidir*) to decide to; **~ sobre** to talk about; **disponha!** feel free!

disposição [dʒispozi'sãw] (*pl* -**ões**) F arrangement; (*humor*) disposition; (*inclinação*) inclination; **à sua ~** at your disposal

dispositivo [dʒispozi'tʃivu] M gadget, device; (*determinação de lei*) provision

disputa [dʒis'puta] F dispute, argument; (*competição*) contest; **disputar** [dʒispu'tar] VT to dispute; (*concorrer a*) to compete for; (*lutar por*) to fight over ▶ VI to quarrel, argue; to compete; **disputar uma corrida** to run a race

disquete [dʒis'ketʃi] M (*Comput*) diskette

disse ['dʒisi] VB *ver* **dizer**

disseminar [dʒisemi'nar] VT to disseminate; (*espalhar*) to spread

dissertar [dʒiser'tar] VI to speak

dissidência [dʒisi'dẽsja] F (*cisão*) difference of opinion

disso ['dʒisu] = **de** + **isso**

dissolução [dʒisolu'sãw] F (*libertinagem*) debauchery; (*de casamento*) dissolution

dissolver [dʒisow'ver] VT to dissolve; (*dispersar*) to disperse; (*motim*) to break up

dissuadir [dʒiswa'dʒir] VT to dissuade; **~ alguém de fazer algo** to talk sb out of doing sth, dissuade sb from doing sth

distância [dʒis'tãsja] F distance; **a 3 quilômetros de ~** 3 kilometres (BRIT) ou kilometers (US) away

distanciar [dʒistã'sjar] VT to distance, set apart; (*colocar por intervalos*) to space out; **distanciar-se** VR to move away; (*fig*) to distance o.s.

distante [dʒis'tãtʃi] ADJ distant

distender [dʒistẽ'der] VT to expand; (*estirar*) to stretch; (*dilatar*) to distend; (*músculo*) to pull; **distender-se** VR to expand; to distend

distinção [dʒistʃi'sãw] (*pl* **-ões**) F distinction; **fazer ~** to make a distinction

distinguir [dʒistʃi'gir] VT to distinguish; (*avistar, ouvir*) to make out; **distinguir-se** VR to stand out

distinto, -a [dʒis'tʃĩtu, a] ADJ different; (*eminente*) distinguished; (*claro*) distinct; (*refinado*) refined

disto ['dʒistu] = **de + isto**

distorcer [dʒistor'ser] VT to distort

distração [dʒistra'sãw] (*pl* **-ões**) F (*alheamento*) absent-mindedness; (*divertimento*) pastime; (*descuido*) oversight

distraído, -a [dʒistra'idu, a] ADJ absent-minded; (*não atento*) inattentive

distrair [dʒistra'ir] VT to distract; (*divertir*) to amuse

distribuição [dʒistribwi'sãw] F distribution; (*de cartas*) delivery

distribuidor, a [dʒistribwi'dor(a)] M/F distributor ▶ M (*Auto*) distributor ▶ F (*Com*) distribution company, distributor

distribuir [dʒistri'bwir] VT to distribute; (*repartir*) to share out; (*cartas*) to deliver

distrito [dʒis'tritu] M district; (*delegacia*) police station; **~ eleitoral** constituency; **~ federal** federal area

distúrbio [dʒis'turbju] M disturbance

ditado [dʒi'tadu] M dictation; (*provérbio*) saying

ditador [dʒita'dor] M dictator; **ditadura** [dʒita'dura] F dictatorship

ditar [dʒi'tar] VT to dictate; (*impor*) to impose

dito, -a ['dʒitu, a] PP *de* **dizer**; **~ e feito** no sooner said than done

diurno, -a ['dʒjurnu, a] ADJ daytime *atr*

divã [dʒi'vã] M couch, divan

divergir [dʒiver'ʒir] VI to diverge; (*discordar*): **~ (de alguém)** to disagree (with sb)

diversão [dʒiver'sãw] (*pl* **-ões**) F amusement; (*passatempo*) pastime

diverso, -a [dʒi'versu, a] ADJ different; (*pl*) various

diversões [dʒiver'sõjs] FPL *de* **diversão**

diversos [dʒi'versus] MPL sundries

divertido, -a [dʒiver'tʃidu, a] ADJ amusing, funny

divertimento [dʒivertʃi'mẽtu] M amusement, entertainment

divertir [dʒiver'tʃir] VT to amuse, entertain; **divertir-se** VR to enjoy o.s., have a good time

dívida ['dʒivida] F debt; **contrair ~s** to run into debt; **~ externa** foreign debt

dividir [dʒivi'dʒir] VT to divide; (*despesas, lucro, comida etc*) to share; (*separar*) to separate ▶ VI (*Mat*) to divide; **dividir-se** VR to divide, split up

divino, -a [dʒi'vinu, a] ADJ divine ▶ M Holy Ghost

divirjo [dʒi'virʒu] VB *ver* **divergir**

divisa [dʒi'viza] F emblem; (*frase*) slogan; (*fronteira*) border; (*Mil*) stripe; **divisas** FPL (*câmbio*) foreign exchange *sg*

divisão [dʒivi'zãw] (*pl* **-ões**) F division; (*discórdia*) split; (*partilha*) sharing

divisões [dʒivi'zõjs] FPL *de* **divisão**

divisória [dʒivi'zɔrja] F partition

divorciado, -a [dʒivor'sjadu, a] ADJ divorced ▶ M/F divorcé(e)

divorciar [dʒivor'sjar] VT to divorce; **divorciar-se** VR to get divorced; **divórcio** [dʒi'vɔrsju] M divorce

divulgar [dʒivuw'gar] VT (*notícias*) to spread; (*segredo*) to divulge; (*produto*) to market; (*livro*) to publish; **divulgar-se** VR to leak out

dizer [dʒi'zer] VT to say ▶ M saying; **dizer-se** VR to claim to be; **diz-se** *ou* **dizem que ...** it is said that ...; **~ algo a alguém** to tell sb sth; (*falar*) to say sth to sb; **~ a alguém que ...** to tell sb that ...; **o que você diz da minha sugestão?** what do you think of my suggestion?; **querer ~** to mean; **quer ~** that is to say; **digo** (*ou seja*) I mean; **não diga!** you don't say!; **por assim ~** so to speak; **até ~ chega** as much as possible

do [du] = **de + o**

doação [doa'sãw] (*pl* **-ões**) F donation

doador, a [doa'dor(a)] M/F donor

doar [do'ar] VT to donate, give

dobra ['dɔbra] F fold; (*prega*) pleat; (*de calças*) turn-up

dobradiça [dobra'dʒisa] F hinge

dobradinha [dobra'dʒiɲa] F (*Culin*) tripe stew

dobrar [do'brar] VT to double; (*papel*) to fold; (*joelho*) to bend; (*esquina*) to turn, go round; (*fazer ceder*): **~ alguém** to talk sb round ▶ vi to double; (*sino*) to toll; (*vergar*) to bend; **dobrar-se** vʀ to double (up)

dobro ['dobru] m double

doce ['dosi] ADJ sweet; (*terno*) gentle ▶ m sweet

dóceis ['dosejs] ADJ PL *de* **dócil**

dócil ['dɔsiw] (*pl* **-eis**) ADJ docile

documentação [dokumẽta'sãw] f documentation; (*documentos*) papers pl

documentário, -a [dokumẽ'tarju, a] ADJ, m documentary

documento [doku'mẽtu] m document

doçura [do'sura] f sweetness; (*brandura*) gentleness

doença [do'ẽsa] f illness

doente [do'ẽtʃi] ADJ ill, sick ▶ m/f sick person; (*cliente*) patient

doentio, -a [doẽ'tʃiu, a] ADJ (*pessoa*) sickly; (*clima*) unhealthy; (*curiosidade*) morbid

doer [do'er] vi to hurt, ache; **~ a alguém** (*pesar*) to grieve sb

doido, -a ['dojdu, a] ADJ mad, crazy ▶ m/f madman/woman

doído, -a [do'idu, a] ADJ painful; (*moralmente*) hurt; (*que causa dor*) painful

dois, duas [dojs, 'duas] NUM two; **conversa a ~** tête-à-tête

dólar ['dɔlar] m dollar; **~ oficial** dollar at the official rate; **~ turismo** dollar at the special tourist rate; **doleiro, -a** [do'lejru, a] m/f (*black market*) dollar dealer

dolorido, -a [dolo'ridu, a] ADJ painful, sore

dom [dõ] m gift; (*aptidão*) knack

domar [do'mar] vt to tame

doméstica [do'mɛstʃika] f maid

domesticar [domestʃi'kar] vt to domesticate; (*povo*) to tame

doméstico, -a [do'mɛstʃiku, a] ADJ domestic; (*vida*) home atr

domicílio [domi'silju] m home, residence; **"entregamos a ~"** "we deliver"

dominador, a [domina'dor(a)] ADJ (*pessoa*) domineering; (*olhar*) imposing ▶ m/f ruler

dominar [domi'nar] vt to dominate; (*reprimir*) to overcome ▶ vi to dominate; **dominar-se** vʀ to control o.s.

domingo [do'mĩgu] m Sunday

domínio [do'minju] m power; (*dominação*) control; (*território*) domain; (*esfera*) sphere; **~ próprio** self-control

dona ['dɔna] f owner; (*col: mulher*) lady; **~ de casa** housewife; **D~ Lígia** Lígia; **D~ Luísa Souza** Mrs Luísa Souza

donde ['dõdə] (PT) ADV from where; (*daí*) thus

dono ['donu] m owner

dopar [do'par] vt (*cavalo*) to dope

dor [dor] f ache; (*aguda*) pain; (*fig*) grief, sorrow; **~ de cabeça** headache; **~ de dentes** toothache; **~ de estômago** stomachache

dormente [dor'mẽtʃi] ADJ numb ▶ m (*Ferro*) sleeper

dormir [dor'mir] vi to sleep; **~ fora** to spend the night away

dormitório [dormi'tɔrju] m bedroom; (*coletivo*) dormitory

dorso ['dorsu] m back

dos [dus] = **de** + **os**

dosagem [do'zaʒẽ] f dosage

dose ['dɔzi] f dose

dossiê [do'sje] m dossier, file

dotado, -a [do'tadu, a] ADJ gifted; **~ de** endowed with

dotar [do'tar] vt to endow

dou [do] vʙ *ver* **dar**

dourado, -a [do'radu, a] ADJ golden; (*com camada de ouro*) gilt ▶ m gilt

doutor, a [do'tor(a)] m/f doctor; **D~** (*forma de tratamento*) Sir; **D~ Eduardo Souza** Mr Eduardo Souza

doutrina [do'trina] f doctrine

doze ['dozi] NUM twelve

Dr. ABR (= *Doutor*) Dr

Dra. ABR (= *Doutora*) Dr

dragão [dra'gãw] (*pl* **-ões**) m dragon

dragões [dra'gõjs] MPL *de* **dragão**

drama ['drama] m drama; **dramático, -a** [dra'matʃiku, a] ADJ dramatic; **dramatizar** [dramatʃi'zar] vt, vi to dramatize

drástico, -a ['drastʃiku, a] ADJ drastic

dreno ['drɛnu] m drain

driblar [dri'blar] vt (*Futebol*) to dribble

drinque ['drĩki] m drink

droga ['drɔga] f drug; (*fig*) rubbish; **drogado, -a** [dro'gadu, a] m/f drug addict; **drogar** [dro'gar] vt to drug; **drogar-se** vʀ to take drugs

drogaria [droga'ria] f chemist's shop (BRIT), drugstore (US)

duas ['duas] f *de* **dois**

ducha ['duʃa] f shower

dueto ['dwetu] m duet

duna ['duna] f dune

dupla ['dupla] f pair; (*Esporte*): **~ masculina/feminina/mista** men's/ women's/mixed doubles

duplicar [dupli'kar] vt to duplicate ▶ vi to double; **duplicata** [dupli'kata] f duplicate; (*título*) trade note, bill

duplo, -a ['duplu, a] ADJ, M double
duque ['duki] M duke
duração [dura'sãw] F duration; **de pouca ~** short-lived
durante [du'rãtʃi] PREP during; **~ uma hora** for an hour
durar [du'rar] VI to last
durável [du'ravew] (pl **-eis**) ADJ lasting
durex® [du'rɛks] ADJ: **fita ~** adhesive tape, Sellotape® (BRIT), Scotch tape® (US)
durmo ['durmu] VB ver **dormir**
duro, -a ['duru, a] ADJ hard; (severo) harsh; (resistente, fig) tough; **estar ~** (col) to be broke
dúvida ['duvida] F doubt; **sem ~** undoubtedly, without a doubt; **duvidar** [duvi'dar] VT to doubt ▶ VI to have one's doubts; **duvidar de alguém/algo** to doubt sb/sth; **duvidar que ...** to doubt that ...; **duvido!** I doubt it!; **duvidoso, -a** [duvi'dozu, ɔza] ADJ doubtful; (suspeito) dubious
duzentos, -as [du'zẽtus, as] NUM two hundred
dúzia ['duzja] F dozen; **meia ~** half a dozen
DVD ABR M (= disco digital versátil) DVD
dz. ABR = **dúzia**

e [i] CONJ and; **e a bagagem?** what about the luggage?
é [ɛ] VB ver **ser**
Ebola vírus [ebola virus] (BR) M Ebola virus
eclipse [e'klipsi] M eclipse
eco ['ɛku] M echo; **ter ~** to catch on; **ecoar** [e'kwar] VT to echo ▶ VI (ressoar) to echo
ecologia [ekolo'ʒia] F ecology
ecológico, -a [eko'lɔʒiku, a] ADJ ecological, eco-friendly
economia [ekono'mia] F economy; (ciência) economics sg; **economias** FPL (poupanças) savings; **fazer ~ (de)** to economize (with)
econômico, -a [eko'nomiku, a] ADJ economical; (pessoa) thrifty; (Com) economic
economizar [ekonomi'zar] VT (gastar com economia) to economize on; (poupar) to save (up) ▶ VI to economize; to save up
ecoturismo [eko'turizmu] M ecotourism
ecrã, écran ['ɛkrã] (PT) M screen; **~ tactil** touch screen
edição [edʒi'sãw] (pl **-ões**) F publication; (conjunto de exemplares) edition; (TV, Cinema) editing
edifício [edʒi'fisju] M building; **~ garagem** multistorey car park (BRIT), multistory parking lot (US)
Edimburgo [edʒi'burgu] N Edinburgh
editar [edʒi'tar] VT to publish; (Comput etc) to edit
editor, a [edʒi'tor(a)] ADJ publishing atr ▶ M/F publisher; (redator) editor ▶ F publishing company; **casa ~a** publishing house

editoração [edʒitora'sãw] F:
~ **eletrônica** desktop publishing;
editorial [edʒitor'jaw] (pl -**ais**) ADJ
publishing atr ▶ M editorial
edredão [ədrɐ'dãw] (pl -**ões**) (PT) M
= **edredom**
edredom [edre'dõ] (pl -**ns**) M
eiderdown
educação [eduka'sãw] F education;
(criação) upbringing; (de animais)
training; (maneiras) good manners pl;
educacional [edukasjo'naw] (pl -**ais**)
ADJ education atr
educar [edu'kar] VT to educate; (criar) to
bring up; (animal) to train
efeito [e'fejtu] M effect; **fazer** ~ to work;
levar a ~ to put into effect; **com** ~
indeed
efeminado, -a [efemi'nadu, a] ADJ
effeminate
efervescente [eferve'sẽtʃi] ADJ fizzy
efetivamente [efetʃiva'mẽtʃi] ADV
effectively; (realmente) really, in fact
efetivo, -a [efe'tʃivu, a] ADJ effective;
(real) actual, real; (cargo, funcionário)
permanent
efetuar [efe'twar] VT to carry out; (soma)
to do, perform
eficaz [efi'kaz] ADJ (pessoa) efficient;
(tratamento) effective
eficiência [efi'sjẽsja] F efficiency;
eficiente [efi'sjẽtʃi] ADJ efficient
egípcio, -a [e'ʒipsju, a] ADJ, M/F
Egyptian
Egito [e'ʒitu] M: **o** ~ Egypt
egoísmo [ego'izmu] M selfishness,
egoism; **egoísta** [ego'ista] ADJ selfish,
egoistic ▶ M/F egoist
égua ['ɛgwa] F mare
ei [ej] EXCL hey!
ei-lo = **eis** + **o**
eis [ejs] ADV (sg) here is; (pl) here are; ~ **aí**
there is; there are
ejacular [eʒaku'lar] VT (sêmen) to
ejaculate; (líquido) to spurt ▶ VI to
ejaculate
ela ['ɛla] PRON (pessoa) she; (coisa) it;
(com prep) her; it; **elas** FPL they;
(com prep) them; ~**s por** ~**s** (col) tit for
tat
elaboração [elabora'sãw] (pl -**ões**) F (de
uma teoria) working out; (preparo)
preparation
elaborar [elabo'rar] VT to prepare;
(fazer) to make
elástico, -a [e'lastʃiku, a] ADJ elastic;
(flexível) flexible; (colchão) springy ▶ M
elastic band

ele ['eli] PRON he; (coisa) it; (com prep)
him; it; **eles** MPL they; (com prep) them
elefante, -a [ele'fãtʃi, ta] M/F elephant
elegante [ele'gãtʃi] ADJ elegant; (da
moda) fashionable
eleger [ele'ʒer] VT to elect; (escolher) to
choose
eleição [elej'sãw] (pl -**ões**) F election;
(escolha) choice
eleito, -a [e'lejtu, a] PP de **eleger** ▶ ADJ
elected; (escolhido) chosen
eleitor, a [elej'tor(a)] M/F voter
elejo [e'leʒu] VB ver **eleger**
elementar [elemẽ'tar] ADJ elementary;
(fundamental) basic, fundamental
elemento [ele'mẽtu] M element; (parte)
component; (recurso) means;
(informação) grounds pl; **elementos** MPL
(rudimentos) rudiments
elenco [e'lẽku] M list; (de atores) cast
eletricidade [eletrisi'dadʒi] F electricity
eletricista [eletri'sista] M/F electrician
elétrico, -a [e'lɛtriku, a] ADJ electric;
(fig: agitado) worked up ▶ M tram (BRIT),
streetcar (US)
eletrificar [eletrifi'kar] VT to electrify
eletrizar [eletri'zar] VT to electrify; (fig)
to thrill
eletro... [eletru] PREFIXO electro...;
eletrocutar [eletroku'tar] VT to
electrocute; **eletrodo** [ele'trodu], (PT)
elétrodo [e'letrodu] M electrode;
eletrodomésticos [eletrodo'mɛstʃikus]
(BR) MPL (electrical) household
appliances
eletrônica [ele'tronika] F electronics sg
eletrônico, -a [ele'troniku, a] ADJ
electronic
elevação [eleva'sãw] (pl -**ões**) F (Arq)
elevation; (aumento) rise; (ato) raising;
(altura) height; (promoção) promotion;
(ponto elevado) bump
elevador [eleva'dor] M lift (BRIT),
elevator (US)
elevar [ele'var] VT to lift up; (voz, preço) to
raise; (exaltar) to exalt; (promover) to
promote; **elevar-se** VR to rise
eliminar [elimi'nar] VT to remove;
(suprimir) to delete; (possibilidade) to rule
out; (Med, banir) to expel; (Esporte) to
eliminate; **eliminatória** [elimina'tɔrja]
F (Esporte) heat, preliminary round;
(exame) test
elite [e'litʃi] F elite
elogiar [elo'ʒjar] VT to praise; **elogio**
[elo'ʒiu] M praise; (cumprimento)
compliment
El Salvador [ew-] N El Salvador

em [ẽ] (em + o(s)/a(s) = no(s)/na(s); +
ele(s)/a(s) = nele(s)/a(s); + esse(s)/a(s)
= nesse(s)/a(s); + isso = nisso; + este(s)/a(s)
= neste(s)/a(s); + isto = nisto; + aquele(s)/
a(s) = naquele(s)/a(s); + aquilo = naquilo)
PREP **1** (posição) in; (: sobre) on; **está na
gaveta/no bolso** it's in the drawer/
pocket; **está na mesa/no chão** it's on
the table/floor
2 (lugar) in; (: casa, escritório etc) at;
(: andar, meio de transporte) on; **no Brasil/
em São Paulo** in Brazil/São Paulo; **em
casa/no dentista** at home/the dentist;
no avião on the plane; **no quinto
andar** on the fifth floor
3 (ação) into; **ela entrou na sala de aula**
she went into the classroom; **colocar
algo na bolsa** to put sth into one's bag
4 (tempo) in; on; **em 1962/3 semanas** in
1962/3 weeks; **no inverno** in the winter;
em janeiro, no mês de janeiro in
January; **nessa ocasião/altura** on that
occasion/at that time; **em breve** soon
5 (diferença): **reduzir/aumentar em
20%** to reduce/increase by 20%
6 (modo): **escrito em inglês** written in
English
7 (após vb que indica gastar etc) on; **a
metade do seu salário vai em comida**
he spends half his salary on food
8 (tema, ocupação): **especialista no
assunto** expert on the subject; **ele
trabalha na construção civil** he works
in the building industry

emagrecer [imagre'ser] VT to make thin
▶ VI to grow thin; (mediante regime) to
slim; **emagrecimento** [imagresi'mẽtu]
M (mediante regime) slimming
e-mail [i'mew] M email; **mandar um ~
para alguém** to email sb; **mandar algo
por ~** to email sth
emaranhado, -a [imara'ɲadu, a] ADJ
tangled ▶ M tangle
embaixada [ẽbaj'ʃada] F embassy
embaixador, a [ẽbajʃa'dor(a)] M/F
ambassador
embaixatriz [ẽbajʃa'triz] F ambassador;
(mulher de embaixador) ambassador's wife
embaixo [ẽ'bajʃu] ADV below,
underneath ▶ PREP: **~ de** under,
underneath; **(lá) ~** (em andar inferior)
downstairs
embalagem [ẽba'laʒẽ] F packing; (de
produto: caixa etc) packaging
embalar [ẽba'lar] VT to pack; (balançar)
to rock

embaraçar [ẽbara'sar] VT to hinder;
(complicar) to complicate; (encabular) to
embarrass; (confundir) to confuse;
(obstruir) to block; **embaraçar-se** VR to
become embarrassed
embaraço [ẽba'rasu] M hindrance;
(cábula) embarrassment; **embaraçoso,
-a** [ẽbara'sozu, ɔza] ADJ embarrassing
embarcação [ẽbarka'sãw] (pl -ões) F
vessel
embarcar [ẽbar'kar] VT to embark, put
on board; (mercadorias) to ship, stow ▶ VI
to go on board, embark
embarque [ẽ'barkɪ] M (de pessoas)
boarding, embarkation; (de mercadorias)
shipment
embebedar [ẽbebe'dar] VT to make
drunk ▶ VI: **o vinho embebeda** wine
makes you drunk; **embebedar-se** VR to
get drunk
emblema [ẽ'blɛma] M emblem; (na
roupa) badge
êmbolo [ẽbolu] M piston
embolsar [ẽbow'sar] VT to pocket;
(herança etc) to come into
embora [ẽ'bɔra] CONJ though, although
▶ EXCL even so; **ir(-se) ~** to go away
emboscada [ẽbos'kada] F ambush
embriagar [ẽbrja'gar] VT to make
drunk, intoxicate; **embriagar-se** VR to
get drunk; **embriaguez** [ẽbrja'gez] F
drunkenness; (fig) rapture
embrião [e'brjãw] (pl -ões) M embryo
embromar [ẽbro'mar] VT (adiar) to put
off; (enganar) to cheat ▶ VI (prometer e não
cumprir) to make empty promises, be all
talk (and no action); (protelar) to stall;
(falar em rodeios) to beat about the bush
embrulhar [ẽbru'ʎar] VT (pacote) to
wrap; (enrolar) to roll up; (confundir) to
muddle up; (enganar) to cheat;
(estômago) to upset; **embrulhar-se** VR to
get into a muddle
embrulho [ẽ'bruʎu] M package, parcel;
(confusão) mix-up
emburrar [ẽbu'har] VI to sulk
embutido, -a [ẽbu'tʃidu, a] ADJ (armário)
built-in, fitted
emenda [e'mẽda] F correction; (Jur)
amendment; (de uma pessoa)
improvement; (ligação) join;
(sambladura) joint; (Costura) seam
emendar [emẽ'dar] VT to correct;
(reparar) to mend; (injustiças) to make
amends for; (Jur) to amend; (ajuntar) to
put together; **emendar-se** VR to mend
one's ways
ementa [e'mẽta] (PT) F menu

emergência [imer'ʒẽsja] F emergence; (*crise*) emergency

emigrado, -a [emi'gradu, a] ADJ emigrant

emigrante [emi'grãtʃi] M/F emigrant

emigrar [emi'grar] VI to emigrate; (*aves*) to migrate

eminência [emi'nẽsja] F eminence; (*altura*) height; **eminente** [emi'nẽtʃi] ADJ eminent, distinguished; (*Geo*) high

emissão [emi'sãw] (*pl* **-ões**) F emission; (*Rádio*) broadcast; (*de moeda, ações*) issue; **emissões de carbono** carbon emissions

emissor, a [emi'sor(a)] ADJ (*de moeda-papel*) issuing ▸ M (*Rádio*) transmitter ▸ F (*estação*) broadcasting station; (*empresa*) broadcasting company

emitir [emi'tʃir] VT (*som*) to give out; (*cheiro*) to give off; (*moeda, ações*) to issue; (*Rádio*) to broadcast; (*opinião*) to express ▸ VI (*emitir moeda*) to print money

emoção [emo'sãw] (*pl* **-ões**) F emotion; (*excitação*) excitement; **emocional** [imosjo'naw] (*pl* **-ais**) ADJ emotional; **emocionante** [imosjo'nãtʃi] ADJ moving; (*excitante*) exciting; **emocionar** [imosjo'nar] VT to move; (*perturbar*) to upset; (*excitar*) to excite, thrill ▸ VI to be exciting; (*comover*) to be moving; **emocionar-se** VR to get emotional

emoji [e'modʒi] M emoji

emotivo, -a [emo'tʃivu, a] ADJ emotional

empacotar [ẽpako'tar] VT to pack, wrap up

empada [ẽ'pada] F pie

empadão [ẽpa'dãw] (*pl* **-ões**) M pie

empalidecer [ẽpalide'ser] VI to turn pale

empanturrar [ẽpãtu'har] VT: **~ alguém de algo** to stuff sb full of sth

empatar [ẽpa'tar] VT to hinder; (*dinheiro*) to tie up; (*no jogo*) to draw; (*tempo*) to take up ▸ VI (*no jogo*): **~ (com)** to draw (with); **empate** [ẽ'patʃi] M draw; (*numa corrida etc*) tie; (*Xadrez*) stalemate; (*em negociações*) deadlock

empecilho [ẽpe'siʎu] M obstacle; (*col*) snag

empenhar [ẽpe'ɲar] VT (*objeto*) to pawn; (*palavra*) to pledge; (*empregar*) to exert; (*compelir*) to oblige; **empenhar-se** VR: **~-se em fazer** to strive to do, do one's utmost to do; **empenho** [ẽ'peɲu] M pawning; (*palavra*) pledge; (*insistência*): **empenho (em)** commitment (to)

empilhar [ẽpi'ʎar] VT to pile up

empinado, -a [ẽpi'nadu, a] ADJ upright; (*cavalo*) rearing; (*colina*) steep

empinar [ẽpi'nar] VT to raise, uplift

empobrecer [ẽpobre'ser] VT to impoverish ▸ VI to become poor; **empobrecimento** [ẽpobresi'mẽtu] M impoverishment

empolgação [ẽpowga'sãw] F excitement; (*entusiasmo*) enthusiasm

empolgante [ẽpow'gãtʃi] ADJ exciting

empolgar [ẽpow'gar] VT to stimulate, fill with enthusiasm; (*prender a atenção de*): **~ alguém** to keep sb riveted

empossar [ẽpo'sar] VT to appoint

empreendedor, a [ẽprjẽde'dor(a)] ADJ enterprising ▸ M/F entrepreneur

empreender [ẽprjẽ'der] VT to undertake; **empreendimento** [ẽprjẽdʒi'mẽtu] M undertaking

empregada [ẽpre'gada] F (*BR*: *doméstica*) maid; (*PT*: *de restaurante*) waitress; *ver tb* **empregado**

empregado, -a [ẽpre'gadu, a] M/F employee; (*em escritório*) clerk ▸ M (*PT*: *de restaurante*) waiter

empregador, a [ẽprega'dor(a)] M/F employer

empregar [ẽpre'gar] VT (*pessoa*) to employ; (*coisa*) to use; **empregar-se** VR to get a job

emprego [ẽ'pregu] M job; (*uso*) use

empreiteiro [ẽprej'tejru] M contractor

empresa [ẽ'preza] F undertaking; (*Com*) enterprise, firm; **~ pontocom** dotcom; **empresário, -a** [ẽpre'zarju, a] M/F businessman/woman; (*de cantor, boxeador etc*) manager

emprestado, -a [ẽpres'tadu, a] ADJ on loan; **pedir ~** to borrow; **tomar algo ~** to borrow sth

emprestar [ẽpres'tar] VT to lend; **empréstimo** [ẽ'prestʃimu] M loan

empunhar [ẽpu'ɲar] VT to grasp, seize

empurrão [ẽpu'hãw] (*pl* **-ões**) M push, shove; **aos empurrões** jostling

empurrar [ẽpu'har] VT to push

empurrões [ẽpu'hõjs] MPL *de* **empurrão**

emudecer [emude'ser] VT to silence ▸ VI to fall silent, go quiet

enamorado, -a [enamo'radu, a] ADJ enchanted; (*apaixonado*) in love

encabulado, -a [ẽkabu'ladu, a] ADJ shy

encadernação [ẽkaderna'sãw] (*pl* **-ões**) F (*de livro*) binding

encadernado, -a [ẽkader'nadu, a] ADJ bound; (*de capa dura*) hardback

encadernar [ẽkader'nar] VT to bind

encaixar [ẽkajˈʃar] vt (colocar) to fit in; (inserir) to insert ▶ vi to fit; **encaixe** [ẽˈkajʃi] м (ato) fitting; (ranhura) groove; (buraco) socket

encalço [ẽˈkawsu] м pursuit; **ir no ~ de** to pursue

encaminhar [ẽkamiˈɲar] vt to direct; (no bom caminho) to put on the right path; (processo) to set in motion; **encaminhar-se** vr: **~-se para/a** to set out for/to

encanar [ẽkaˈnar] vt to channel

encantado, -a [ẽkãˈtadu, a] adj delighted; (castelo etc) enchanted; (fascinado): **~ (por alguém/algo)** smitten (with sb/sth)

encantamento [ẽkãtaˈmẽtu] м (magia) spell; (fascinação) charm

encanto [ẽˈkãtu] м delight; (fascinação) charm

encarar [ẽkaˈrar] vt to face; (olhar) to look at; (considerar) to consider

encargo [ẽˈkargu] м responsibility; (ocupação) job, assignment; (oneroso) burden

encarnação [ẽkarnaˈsãw] (pl **-ões**) f incarnation

encarnado, -a [ẽkarˈnadu, a] adj red, scarlet

encarnar [ẽkarˈnar] vt to embody, personify; (Teatro) to play

encarregado, -a [ẽkaheˈgadu, a] adj: **~ de** in charge of ▶ м/ғ person in charge ▶ м (de operários) foreman

encarregar [ẽkaheˈgar] vt: **~ alguém de algo** to put sb in charge of sth; **encarregar-se** vr: **~-se de fazer** to undertake to do

encenação [ẽsenaˈsãw] (pl **-ões**) f (de peça) staging, putting on; (produção) production; (fingimento) play-acting; (atitude fingida) put-on

encerar [ẽseˈrar] vt to wax

encerramento [ẽsehaˈmẽtu] м close, end

encerrar [ẽseˈhar] vt to shut in, lock up; (conter) to contain; (concluir) to close

encharcar [ẽʃarˈkar] vt to flood; (ensopar) to soak, drench; **encharcar-se** vr to get soaked ou drenched

enchente [ẽˈʃẽtʃi] f flood

encher [ẽˈʃer] vt to fill (up); (balão) to blow up; (tempo) to fill, take up ▶ vi (col) to be annoying; **encher-se** vr to fill up; **~-se (de)** (col) to get fed up (with); **enchimento** [ẽʃiˈmẽtu] м filling

enciclopédia [ẽsikloˈpɛdʒja] f encyclopedia, encyclopaedia (brit)

encoberto, -a [ẽkoˈbɛrtu, a] pp de **encobrir** ▶ adj concealed; (tempo) overcast

encobrir [ẽkoˈbrir] vt to conceal, hide

encolher [ẽkoˈʎer] vt (pernas) to draw up; (os ombros) to shrug; (roupa) to shrink ▶ vi to shrink; **encolher-se** vr (de frio) to huddle

encomenda [ẽkoˈmẽda] f order; **feito de ~** made to order, custom-made; **encomendar** [ẽkomẽˈdar] vt: **encomendar algo a alguém** to order sth from sb

encontrar [ẽkõˈtrar] vt to find; (inesperadamente) to come across, meet; (dar com) to bump into ▶ vi: **~ com** to bump into; **encontrar-se** vr (achar-se) to be; (ter encontro): **~-se (com alguém)** to meet (sb)

encontro [ẽˈkõtru] м (de pessoas) meeting; (Mil) encounter; **~ marcado** appointment; **ir/vir ao ~ de** to go/come and meet; (aspirações) to meet, fulfil (brit), fulfill (us)

encorajar [ẽkoraˈʒar] vt to encourage

encosta [ẽˈkɔsta] f slope

encostar [ẽkosˈtar] vt (cabeça) to put down; (carro) to park; (pôr de lado) to put to one side; (pôr junto) to put side by side; (porta) to leave ajar ▶ vi to pull in; **encostar-se** vr: **~-se em** to lean against; (deitar-se) to lie down on; **~ em** to lean against; **~ a mão em** (bater) to hit

encosto [ẽˈkostu] м (arrimo) support; (de cadeira) back

encrencar [ẽkrẽˈkar] (col) vt (situação) to complicate; (pessoa) to get into trouble ▶ vi to get complicated; (carro) to break down; **encrencar-se** vr to get complicated; to get into trouble

encriptar [ẽkripˈtar] vt (Comput, Tel) to encrypt

encruzilhada [ẽkruziˈʎada] f crossroads sg

encurtar [ẽkurˈtar] vt to shorten

endereçar [ẽdereˈsar] vt (carta) to address; (encaminhar) to direct

endereço [ẽdeˈresu] м address; **~ de e-mail** email address; **~ web** web address

endiabrado, -a [ẽdʒjaˈbradu, a] adj devilish; (travesso) mischievous

endinheirado, -a [ẽdʒiɲejˈradu, a] adj rich, wealthy

endireitar [ẽdʒirejˈtar] vt (objeto) to straighten; (retificar) to put right; **endireitar-se** vr to straighten up

endividar [ēdʒivi'dar] vt to put into
debt; **endividar-se** vr to run into debt
endossar [ēdo'sar] vt to endorse
endurecer [ēdure'ser] vt, vi to harden
energético, -a [ener'ʒɛtʃiku, a] ADJ
energy atr ► m energy source; (tb:
bebida energética) energy drink
energia [enɛr'ʒia] F energy, drive; (Tec)
power, energy; **~ solar** solar power;
enérgico, -a [e'nɛrʒiku, a] ADJ energetic,
vigorous
enervante [ener'vātʃi] ADJ annoying
enevoado, -a [ene'vwadu, a] ADJ misty,
hazy
enfado [ē'fadu] m annoyance
ênfase ['ēfazi] F emphasis, stress
enfastiado, -a [ēfas'tʃjadu, a] ADJ
bored
enfático, -a [ē'fatʃiku, a] ADJ emphatic
enfatizar [ēfatʃi'zar] vt to emphasize
enfeitar [ēfej'tar] vt to decorate;
enfeitar-se vr to dress up; **enfeite**
[ē'fejtʃi] m decoration
enfermeiro, -a [ēfer'mejru, a] m/F
nurse
enfermidade [ēfermi'dadʒi] F illness
enfermo, -a [ē'fermu, a] ADJ ill, sick
► m/F sick person, patient
enferrujar [ēfehu'ʒar] vt to rust,
corrode ► vi to go rusty
enfiar [ē'fjar] vt (meter) to put; (agulha)
to thread; (vestir) to slip on; **enfiar-se**
vr: **~-se em** to slip into
enfim [ē'fĩ] ADV finally, at last; (em suma)
in short; **até que ~!** at last!
enfoque [ē'fɔki] m approach
enforcar [ēfor'kar] vt to hang;
(trabalho, aulas) to skip; **enforcar-se** vr
to hang o.s.
enfraquecer [ēfrake'ser] vt to weaken
► vi to grow weak
enfrentar [ēfrē'tar] vt to face;
(confrontar) to confront; (problemas) to
face up to
enfurecer [ēfure'ser] vt to infuriate;
enfurecer-se vr to get furious
enganado, -a [ēga'nadu, a] ADJ
mistaken; (traído) deceived
enganar [ēga'nar] vt to deceive;
(desonrar) to seduce; (cônjuge) to be
unfaithful to; (fome) to stave off;
enganar-se vr to be wrong, be
mistaken; (iludir-se) to deceive o.s.
engano [ē'gānu] m mistake; (ilusão)
deception; (logro) trick; **é ~** (Tel) I've (ou
you've) got the wrong number
engarrafamento [ēgahafa'mētu] m
bottling; (de trânsito) traffic jam

engarrafar [ēgaha'far] vt to bottle;
(trânsito) to block
engasgar [ēgaz'gar] vt to choke ► vi to
choke; (máquina) to splutter;
engasgar-se vr to choke
engatinhar [ēgatʃi'ɲar] vi to crawl
engenharia [ēʒeɲa'ria] F engineering;
engenheiro, -a [ēʒe'ɲejru, a] m/F
engineer
engenhoso, -a [ēʒe'ɲozu, ɔza] ADJ
clever, ingenious
engessar [ēʒe'sar] vt (perna) to put in
plaster; (parede) to plaster
englobar [ēglo'bar] vt to include
engodo [ē'godu] m bait
engolir [ēgo'lir] vt to swallow
engordar [ēgor'dar] vt to fatten ► vi to
put on weight
engraçado, -a [ēgra'sadu, a] ADJ funny,
amusing
engradado [ēgra'dadu] m crate
engraxador [ēgraʃa'dor] (PT) m shoe
shiner
engraxar [ēgra'far] vt to polish
engrenagem [ēgre'naʒē] (pl -ns) F
(Auto) gear
engrenar [ēgre'nar] vt to put into gear;
(fig: conversa) to strike up ► vi: **~ com
alguém** to get on with sb
engrossar [ēgro'sar] vt (sopa) to
thicken; (aumentar) to swell; (voz) to
raise ► vi to thicken; to swell; to rise;
(col: pessoa, conversa) to turn nasty
enguia [ē'gia] F eel
enguiçar [ēgi'sar] vi (máquina) to break
down ► vt to cause to break down;
enguiço [ē'gisu] m snag; (desarranjo)
breakdown
enigma [e'nigima] m enigma; (mistério)
mystery
enjeitado, -a [ēʒej'tadu, a] m/F
foundling, waif
enjoado, -a [ē'ʒwadu, a] ADJ sick;
(enfastiado) bored; (enfadonho) boring;
(mal-humorado) in a bad mood
enjoar [ē'ʒwar] vt to make sick;
(enfastiar) to bore ► vi (pessoa) to be sick;
(remédio, comida) to cause nausea;
enjoar-se vr: **~-se de** to get sick of
enjoo [ē'ʒou] m sickness; (em carro) travel
sickness; (em navio) seasickness;
(aborrecimento) boredom
enlatado, -a [ēla'tadu, a] ADJ tinned
(BRIT), canned ► m (pej: filme) foreign
import; **enlatados** mpl (comida) tinned
(BRIT) ou canned foods
enlouquecer [ēloke'ser] vt to drive mad
► vi to go mad

enlutado, -a [ēlu'tadu, a] ADJ in
mourning
enorme [e'nɔrmi] ADJ enormous, huge;
enormidade [enormi'dadʒi] F
enormity; **uma enormidade (de)** (col) a
hell of a lot (of)
enquanto [ē'kwātu] CONJ while;
(considerado como) as; **~ isso** meanwhile;
por ~ for the time being; **~ ele não vem**
until he comes; **~ que** whereas
enquete [ē'kɛtʃi] F survey
enraivecer [ēhajve'ser] VT to enrage
enredo [ē'hedu] M (de uma obra) plot;
(intriga) intrigue
enriquecer [ēhike'ser] VT to make rich;
(fig) to enrich ▶ VI to get rich;
enriquecer-se VR to get rich
enrolar [ēho'lar] VT to roll up; (agasalhar)
to wrap up; (col: enganar) to con ▶ VI (col)
to waffle; **enrolar-se** VR to roll up; to
wrap up; (col: confundir-se) to get mixed
ou muddled up
enroscar [ēhos'kar] VT (torcer) to twist,
wind (round); **enroscar-se** VR to coil up
enrugar [ēhu'gar] VT (pele) to wrinkle;
(testa) to furrow; (tecido) to crease ▶ VI
(pele, mãos) to go wrinkly; (pessoa) to get
wrinkles
ensaiar [ēsa'jar] VT to test, try out;
(treinar) to practise (BRIT), practice (US);
(Teatro) to rehearse
ensaio [ē'saju] M test; (tentativa)
attempt; (treino) practice; (Teatro)
rehearsal; (literário) essay
enseada [ē'sjada] F inlet, cove; (baía)
bay
ensejo [ē'seʒu] M chance, opportunity
ensinamento [ēsina'mētu] M teaching;
(exemplo) lesson
ensinar [ēsi'nar] VT, VI to teach
ensino [ē'sinu] M teaching, tuition;
(educação) education; **~ fundamental**
primary education; **~ médio** secondary
education
ensopado, -a [ēso'padu, a] ADJ soaked
▶ M stew
ensurdecer [ēsurde'ser] VT to deafen
▶ VI to go deaf
entalar [ēta'lar] VT to wedge, jam;
(encher): **ela me entalou de comida** she
stuffed me full of food
entalhar [ēta'ʎar] VT to carve; **entalhe**
[ē'taʎi] M groove, notch
entanto [ē'tātu] ADV: **no ~** yet,
however
então [ē'tãw] ADV then; **até ~** up to that
time; **desde ~** ever since; **e ~?** well
then?; **para ~** so that; **pois ~** in that

case; **~, você vai ou não?** so, are you
going or not?
entardecer [ētarde'ser] VI to get late
▶ M sunset
ente ['ētʃi] M being
enteado, -a [ē'tʃjadu, a] M/F stepson/
stepdaughter
entediar [ēte'dʒjar] VT to bore;
entediar-se VR to get bored
entender [ētē'der] VT to understand;
(pensar) to think; (ouvir) to hear;
entender-se VR to understand one
another; **dar a ~** to imply; **no meu ~** in
my opinion; **~ de música** to know about
music; **~ de fazer** to decide to do; **~-se**
por to be meant by; **~-se com alguém**
to get along with sb; (dialogar) to sort
things out with sb
entendimento [ētēdʒi'mētu] M
understanding
enterrar [ēte'har] VT to bury; (faca) to
plunge; (lever à ruina) to ruin; (assunto) to
close
enterro [ē'tehu] M burial; (funeral)
funeral
entidade [ētʃi'dadʒi] F (ser) being;
(corporação) body; (coisa que existe) entity
entornar [ētor'nar] VT to spill; (fig: copo)
to drink ▶ VI to drink a lot
entorpecente [ētorpe'sētʃi] M narcotic
entorpecimento [ētorpesi'mētu] M
numbness; (torpor) lethargy
entorse [ē'tɔrsi] F sprain
entortar [ētor'tar] VT (curvar) to bend;
(empenar) to warp; **~ os olhos** to squint
entrada [ē'trada] F (ato) entry; (lugar)
entrance; (Tec) inlet; (de casa) doorway;
(começo) beginning; (bilhete) ticket;
(Culin) starter, entrée; (Comput) input;
(pagamento inicial) down payment;
(corredor de casa) hall; **entradas** FPL (no
cabelo) receding hairline; **~ gratuita**
admission free; **"~ proibida"** "no entry",
"no admittance"; **meia ~** half-price ticket
entra e sai ['ētraj'saj] M comings and
goings pl
entranhado, -a [ētra'ɲadu, a] ADJ
deep-rooted
entranhas [ē'traɲas] FPL bowels,
entrails; (sentimentos) feelings; (centro)
heart sg
entrar [ē'trar] VI to go (ou come) in,
enter; **~ com** (Comput: dados etc) to enter;
eu entrei com £100 I put in £100; **~ de**
férias/licença to start one's holiday
(BRIT) ou vacation (US)/leave; **~ em** to go
(ou come) into, enter; (assunto) to get
onto; (comida, bebida) to start in on

entrave [ẽ'travi] M (*fig*) impediment

entre ['ẽtri] PREP (*dois*) between; (*mais de dois*) among(st); **~ si** amongst themselves

entreaberto, -a [ẽtrja'bɛrtu, a] ADJ half-open; (*porta*) ajar

entrega [ẽ'trɛga] F (*de mercadorias*) delivery; (*a alguém*) handing over; (*rendição*) surrender; **~ rápida** special delivery

entregar [ẽtre'gar] VT to hand over; (*mercadorias*) to deliver; (*confiar*) to entrust; (*devolver*) to return; **entregar-se** VR (*render-se*) to give o.s. up; (*dedicar-se*) to devote o.s.

entregue [ẽ'trɛgi] PP *de* **entregar**

entrelinha [ẽtre'liɲa] F line space; **ler nas ~s** to read between the lines

entreolhar-se [ẽtrio'ʎarsi] VR to exchange glances

entretanto [ẽtri'tãtu] CONJ however

entretenimento [ẽtriteni'mẽtu] M entertainment; (*distração*) pastime

entreter [ẽtri'ter] (*irreg: como* **ter**) VT to entertain, amuse; (*ocupar*) to occupy; (*manter*) to keep up; (*esperanças*) to cherish; **entreter-se** VR to amuse o.s.; to occupy o.s.

entrevista [ẽtre'vista] F interview; **~ coletiva (à imprensa)** press conference; **entrevistar** [ẽtrevis'tar] VT to interview; **entrevistar-se** VR to have an interview

entristecer [ẽtriste'ser] VT to sadden, grieve ▶ VI to feel sad; **entristecer-se** VR to feel sad

entroncamento [ẽtrõka'mẽtu] M junction

entrudo [ẽ'trudu] (PT) M carnival; (*Rel*) Shrovetide

entulhar [ẽtu'ʎar] VT to cram full; (*suj: multidão*) to pack

entupido, -a [ẽtu'pidu, a] ADJ blocked; **estar ~** (*col: congestionado*) to have a blocked-up nose; (*de comida*) to be fit to burst, be full up

entupimento [ẽtupi'mẽtu] M blockage

entupir [ẽtu'pir] VT to block, clog; **entupir-se** VR to become blocked; (*de comida*) to stuff o.s.

entusiasmar [ẽtuzjaz'mar] VT to fill with enthusiasm; (*animar*) to excite; **entusiasmar-se** VR to get excited

entusiasmo [ẽtu'zjazmu] M enthusiasm; (*júbilo*) excitement

entusiasta [ẽtu'zjasta] ADJ enthusiastic ▶ M/F enthusiast

enumerar [enume'rar] VT to enumerate; (*com números*) to number

envelhecer [ẽveʎe'ser] VT to age ▶ VI to grow old, age

envelope [ẽve'lɔpi] M envelope

envenenamento [ẽvenena'mẽtu] M poisoning; **~ do sangue** blood poisoning

envenenar [ẽvene'nar] VT to poison; (*fig*) to corrupt; (: *declaração, palavras*) to distort, twist; (*tornar amargo*) to sour ▶ VI to be poisonous; **envenenar-se** VR to poison o.s.

envergonhado, -a [ẽvergo'ɲadu, a] ADJ ashamed; (*tímido*) shy

envergonhar [ẽvergo'ɲar] VT to shame; (*degradar*) to disgrace; **envergonhar-se** VR to be ashamed

enviado, -a [ẽ'vjadu, a] M/F envoy, messenger

enviar [ẽ'vjar] VT to send

envio [ẽ'viu] M sending; (*expedição*) dispatch; (*remessa*) remittance; (*de mercadorias*) consignment

enviuvar [ẽvju'var] VI to be widowed

envolver [ẽvow'ver] VT to wrap (up); (*cobrir*) to cover; (*comprometer, acarretar*) to involve; (*nos braços*) to embrace; **envolver-se** VR (*intrometer-se*) to become involved; (*cobrir-se*) to wrap o.s. up; **envolvimento** [ẽvowvi'mẽtu] M involvement

enxada [ẽ'ʃada] F hoe

enxaguar [ẽʃa'gwar] VT to rinse

enxame [ẽ'ʃami] M swarm

enxaqueca [ẽʃa'keka] F migraine

enxergar [ẽʃer'gar] VT (*avistar*) to catch sight of; (*divisar*) to make out; (*notar*) to observe, see

enxofre [ẽ'ʃofri] M sulphur (BRIT), sulfur (US)

enxotar [ẽʃo'tar] VT to drive out

enxoval [ẽʃo'vaw] (*pl* **-ais**) M (*de noiva*) trousseau; (*de recém-nascido*) layette

enxugar [ẽʃu'gar] VT to dry; (*fig: texto*) to tidy up

enxurrada [ẽʃu'hada] F (*de água*) torrent; (*fig*) spate

enxuto, -a [ẽ'ʃutu, a] ADJ dry; (*corpo*) shapely; (*bonito*) good-looking

épico, -a ['ɛpiku, a] ADJ epic ▶ M epic poet

epidemia [epide'mia] F epidemic

epilepsia [epile'psia] F epilepsy

episódio [epi'zɔdʒu] M episode

época ['ɛpoka] F time, period; (*da história*) age, epoch; **naquela ~** at that time; **fazer ~** to be epoch-making

equação [ekwa'sãw] (*pl* **-ões**) F equation

Equador [ekwa'dor] M: **o ~** Ecuador

equador [ekwa'dor] M equator

equilibrar [ekili'brar] VT to balance;
equilibrar-se VR to balance; **equilíbrio**
[eki'librju] M balance

equipa [e'kipa] (PT) F team

equipamento [ekipa'mẽtu] M
equipment, kit

equipar [eki'par] VT (*navio*) to fit out;
(*prover*) to equip

equipe [e'kipi] (BR) F team

equitação [ekita'sãw] F (*ato*) riding;
(*arte*) horsemanship

equivalente [ekiva'lẽtʃi] ADJ, M
equivalent

equivaler [ekiva'ler] VI: **~ a** to be the
same as, equal

equivocado, -a [ekivo'kadu, a] ADJ
mistaken, wrong

equivocar-se [ekivo'karsi] VR to make a
mistake, be wrong

era¹ ['ɛra] F era, age

era² VB *ver* **ser**

erário [e'rarju] M exchequer

ereto, -a [e'rɛtu, a] ADJ upright, erect

erguer [er'ger] VT to raise, lift; (*edificar*)
to build, erect; **erguer-se** VR to rise;
(*pessoa*) to stand up

eriçar [eri'sar] VT: **~ o cabelo de alguém**
to make sb's hair stand on end; **eriçar-se**
VR to bristle; (*cabelos*) to stand on end

erigir [eri'ʒir] VT to erect

erosão [ero'zãw] F erosion

erótico, -a [e'rɔtʃiku, a] ADJ erotic

errado, -a [e'hadu, a] ADJ wrong; **dar ~**
to go wrong

errar [e'har] VT (*alvo*) to miss; (*conta*) to
get wrong ▶ VI to wander, roam;
(*enganar-se*) to be wrong, make a
mistake; **~ o caminho** to lose one's way

erro ['ehu] M mistake; **salvo ~** unless I
am mistaken; **~ de imprensa** misprint

errôneo, -a [e'honju, a] ADJ wrong,
mistaken; (*falso*) false, untrue

erva ['ɛrva] F herb; **~ daninha** weed; (*col:
dinheiro*) dosh; (: *maconha*) dope

erva-mate (*pl* **ervas-mate(s)**) F maté

ervilha [er'viʎa] F pea

esbanjar [izbã'ʒar] VT to squander,
waste

esbarrar [izba'har] VI: **~ em** to bump
into; (*obstáculo, problema*) to come up
against

esbelto, -a [iz'bɛwtu, a] ADJ slim,
slender

esboçar [izbo'sar] VT to sketch;
(*delinear*) to outline; (*plano*) to draw up;

esboço [iz'bosu] M sketch; (*primeira
versão*) draft; (*fig: resumo*) outline

esbofetear [izbofe'tʃjar] VT to slap, hit

esburacar [izbura'kar] VT to make holes
(*ou* a hole) in

esc (PT) ABR = **escudo**

escabroso, -a [iska'brozu, ɔza] ADJ
(*difícil*) tough; (*indecoroso*) indecent

escada [is'kada] F (*dentro da casa*)
staircase, stairs *pl*; (*fora da casa*) steps *pl*;
(*de mão*) ladder; **~ de incêndio** fire
escape; **~ rolante** escalator; **escadaria**
[iskada'ria] F staircase

escala [is'kala] F scale; (*Náut*) port of
call; (*parada*) stop; **fazer ~ em** to call at;
sem ~ non-stop

escalada [iska'lada] F (*de guerra*)
escalation

escalão [iska'lãw] (*pl* **-ões**) M step; (*Mil*)
echelon

escalar [iska'lar] VT (*montanha*) to climb;
(*muro*) to scale; (*designar*) to select

escaldar [iskaw'dar] VT to scald;
escaldar-se VR to scald o.s.

escalões [ɛska'lõjs] MPL *de* **escalão**

escama [is'kama] F (*de peixe*) scale; (*de
pele*) flake

escancarado, -a [iskãka'radu, a] ADJ
wide open

escandalizar [iskãdali'zar] VT to shock;
escandalizar-se VR to be shocked;
(*ofender-se*) to be offended

escândalo [is'kãdalu] M scandal;
(*indignação*) outrage; **fazer** *ou* **dar um ~**
to make a scene; **escandaloso, -a**
[iskãda'lozu, ɔza] ADJ shocking,
scandalous

Escandinávia [iskãdʒi'navja] F: **a ~**
Scandinavia; **escandinavo, -a**
[iskãdʒi'navu, a] ADJ, M/F Scandinavian

escangalhar [iskãga'ʎar] VT to break,
smash (up); **escangalhar-se** VR: **~-se de
rir** to split one's sides laughing

escapar [iska'par] VI: **~ a** *ou* **de** to
escape from; (*fugir*) to run away from;
escapar-se VR to run away, flee; **deixar
~** (*uma oportunidade*) to miss; (*palavras*) to
blurt out; **~ de boa** (*col*) to have a close
shave

escapatória [iskapa'tɔrja] F way out;
(*desculpa*) excuse

escape [is'kapi] M (*de gás*) leak; (*Auto*)
exhaust

escapulir [iskapu'lir] VI: **~ (de)** to get
away (from); (*suj: coisa*) to slip (from)

escarrar [iska'har] VT to spit, cough up
▶ VI to spit

escarro [is'kahu] M phlegm, spit

escassear [iska'sjar] vт to skimp on ▶ vi
to become scarce

escassez [iska'sez] ғ (*falta*) shortage

escavar [iska'var] vт to excavate

esclarecer [isklare'ser] vт (*situação*) to
explain; (*mistério*) to clear up, explain;
esclarecer-se vʀ: **~-se (sobre algo)** to
find out (about sth); **esclarecimento**
[isklaresi'mẽtu] м explanation;
(*informação*) information

escoadouro [iskoa'doru] м drain;
(*cano*) drainpipe

escocês, -esa [isko'ses, seza] ᴀᴅᴊ
Scottish, Scots ▶ м/ғ Scot, Scotsman/
woman

Escócia [is'kɔsja] ғ Scotland

escola [is'kɔla] ғ school; **~ de línguas**
language school; **~ naval** naval college;
~ primária/secundária primary (BRIT)
ou elementary (US) /secondary (BRIT) *ou*
high (US) school; **~ particular/pública**
private/state (BRIT) *ou* public (US) school;
~ superior college

> **Escolas de samba** are musical and
> recreational associations made up,
> among others, of samba dancers,
> percussionists and carnival dancers.
> Although they exist throughout Brazil,
> the most famous schools are in Rio de
> Janeiro. The schools in Rio rehearse all
> year long for the **carnaval**, when they
> parade along the *Sambódromo*, a
> purpose-built avenue flanked by
> stands for spectators, and compete for
> the samba school championship.
> Characterised by their extravagance,
> the biggest schools have up to 4,000
> members and are one of Brazil's major
> tourist attractions.

escolar [isko'lar] ᴀᴅᴊ school *atr* ▶ м/ғ
schoolboy/girl

escolha [is'koʎa] ғ choice

escolher [isko'ʎer] vт to choose, select

escolho [is'koʎu] м (*recife*) reef; (*rocha*)
rock

escolta [is'kɔwta] ғ escort; **escoltar**
[iskow'tar] vт to escort

escombros [is'kõbrus] мᴘʟ ruins,
debris *sg*

esconde-esconde [iskõdʒis'kõdʒi] м
hide-and-seek

esconder [iskõ'der] vт to hide, conceal;
esconder-se vʀ to hide

escondidas [iskõ'dʒidas] ғᴘʟ: **às ~**
secretly

escopo [is'kɔpu] м aim, purpose

escorar [isko'rar] vт to prop (up);
(*amparar*) to support; (*esperar de espreita*)

to lie in wait for ▶ vi to lie in wait;
escorar-se vʀ: **~-se em** (*fundamentar-se*)
to go by; (*amparar-se*) to live off

escore [is'kɔri] м score

escoriação [iskorja'sãw] (*pl* **-ões**) ғ
abrasion, scratch

escorpião [iskorpi'ãw] (*pl* **-ões**) м
scorpion; **E~** (*Astrologia*) Scorpio

escorrega [isko'hega] ғ slide;
escorregadela [iskohega'dɛla] ғ slip;
escorregadio, -a [iskohega'dʒiu, a] ᴀᴅᴊ
slippery; **escorregão** [iskohe'gãw] (*pl*
-ões) м slip; (*fig*) slip(-up); **escorregar**
[iskohe'gar] vi to slip; (*errar*) to slip up ·

escorrer [isko'her] vт to drain (off);
(*verter*) to pour out ▶ vi (*pingar*) to drip;
(*correr em fio*) to trickle

escoteiro [isko'tejru] м scout

escova [is'kova] ғ brush; (*penteado*)
blow-dry; **~ de dentes** toothbrush;
~ progressiva keratin straightening;
escovar [isko'var] vт to brush

escravatura [iskrava'tura] ғ (*tráfico*)
slave trade; (*escravidão*) slavery

escravidão [iskravi'dãw] ғ slavery

escravizar [iskravi'zar] vт to enslave;
(*cativar*) to captivate

escravo, -a [is'kravu, a] ᴀᴅᴊ captive
▶ м/ғ slave

escrever [iskre'ver] vт, vi to write;
escrever-se vʀ to write to each other;
~ à máquina to type

escrita [es'krita] ғ writing; (*pessoal*)
handwriting

escrito, -a [es'kritu, a] ᴘᴘ *de* **escrever**
▶ ᴀᴅᴊ written ▶ м piece of writing; **~ à
mão** handwritten; **dar por ~** to put in
writing

escritor, a [iskri'tor(a)] м/ғ writer;
(*autor*) author

escritório [iskri'tɔrju] м office; (*em
casa*) study

escritura [iskri'tura] ғ (*Jur*) deed; (*na
compra de imóveis*) ≈ exchange of
contracts; **as Sagradas E~s** the
Scriptures

escrivã [iskri'vã] ғ *de* **escrivão**

escrivaninha [iskriva'niɲa] ғ writing
desk

escrivão, -vã [iskri'vãw, vã] (*pl* **-ões/-s**)
м/ғ registrar, recorder

escrupuloso, -a [iskrupu'lozu, ɔza] ᴀᴅᴊ
scrupulous; (*cuidadoso*) careful

escudo [is'kudu] м shield; (*moeda*)
escudo

esculhambado, -a [iskuʎã'badu, a] (*!*)
ᴀᴅᴊ shabby, slovenly; (*estragado*)
knackered

esculhambar [iskuʎa'bar] (!) VT to mess up, fuck up (!); **~ alguém** (criticar) to give sb stick; (descompor) to give sb a bollocking (!)

esculpir [iskuw'pir] VT to carve, sculpt; (gravar) to engrave

escultor, a [iskuw'tor(a)] M/F sculptor

escultura [iskuw'tura] F sculpture

escuras [is'kuras] FPL: **às ~** in the dark

escurecer [iskure'ser] VT to darken ▶ VI to get dark; **ao ~** at dusk

escuridão [iskuri'dãw] F (trevas) darkness

escuro, -a [is'kuru, a] ADJ dark; (dia) overcast; (pessoa) swarthy ▶ M dark

escuso, -a [is'kuzu, a] ADJ shady

escuta [is'kuta] F listening; **à ~** listening out; **ficar na ~** to stand by

escutar [isku'tar] VT to listen to; (sem prestar atenção) to hear ▶ VI to listen; to hear

esfacelar [isfase'lar] VT to destroy

esfaquear [isfaki'ar] VT to stab

esfarrapado, -a [isfaha'padu, a] ADJ (roupa) ragged, tattered; (desculpa) lame

esfera [is'fɛra] F sphere; (globo) globe

esfolar [isfo'lar] VT to skin; (arranhar) to graze; (cobrar demais a) to overcharge, fleece

esfomeado, -a [isfo'mjadu, a] ADJ famished, starving

esforçado, -a [isfor'sadu, a] ADJ committed, dedicated

esforçar-se [isfor'sarsi] VR: **~ para** to try hard to, strive to

esforço [is'forsu] M effort

esfregar [isfre'gar] VT to rub; (com água) to scrub

esfriar [is'frjar] VT to cool, chill ▶ VI to get cold; (fig) to cool off

esganar [izga'nar] VT to strangle, choke

esgotado, -a [izgo'tadu, a] ADJ exhausted; (consumido) used up; (livros) out of print; **os ingressos estão ~s** the tickets are sold out

esgotamento [izgota'mẽtu] M exhaustion

esgotar [izgo'tar] VT to drain, empty; (recursos) to use up; (pessoa, assunto) to exhaust; **esgotar-se** VR to become exhausted; (mercadorias, edição) to be sold out; (recursos) to run out

esgoto [iz'gotu] M drain; (público) sewer

esgrima [iz'grima] F (Esporte) fencing

esgueirar-se [izgej'rarsi] VR to slip away, sneak off

esguelha [iz'geʎa] F slant; **olhar alguém de ~** to look at sb out of the corner of one's eye

esguio, -a [ez'giu, a] ADJ slender

esmagador, a [izmaga'dor(a)] ADJ crushing; (provas) irrefutable; (maioria) overwhelming

esmalte [iz'mawtʃi] M enamel; (de unhas) nail polish

esmeralda [izme'rawda] F emerald

esmerar-se [izme'rarsi] VR: **~ em** to take great care to

esmigalhar [izmiga'ʎar] VT to crumble; (despedaçar) to shatter; (esmagar) to crush; **esmigalhar-se** VR to crumble; (vaso) to smash, shatter

esmo ['ezmu] M: **a ~** at random; **falar a ~** to prattle

esmola [iz'mɔla] F alms pl; **pedir ~s** to beg

esmurrar [izmu'har] VT to punch

esoterismo [ezote'rizmu] M New Age

espacial [ispa'sjaw] (pl **-ais**) ADJ space atr; **nave ~** spaceship

espaço [is'pasu] M space; (tempo) period; **~ para 3 pessoas** room for 3 people; **a ~s** from time to time; **espaçoso, -a** [ispa'sozu, ɔza] ADJ spacious, roomy

espada [is'pada] F sword; **espadas** FPL (Cartas) spades

espadarte [ispa'dartʃi] M swordfish

espairecer [ispajre'ser] VT to amuse, entertain ▶ VI to relax; **espairecer-se** VR to relax

espaldar [ispaw'dar] M (chair) back

espalhafato [ispaʎa'fatu] M din, commotion

espalhar [ispa'ʎar] VT to scatter; (boato, medo) to spread; (luz) to shed; **espalhar-se** VR to spread; (refestelar-se) to lounge

espanador [ispana'dor] M duster

espancar [ispã'kar] VT to beat up

Espanha [is'paɲa] F: **a ~** Spain; **espanhol, a** [ispa'ɲɔw, ɔla] (pl **-óis/-s**) ADJ Spanish ▶ M/F Spaniard ▶ M (Ling) Spanish; **os espanhóis** MPL the Spanish

espantado, -a [ispã'tadu, a] ADJ astonished

espantalho [ispã'taʎu] M scarecrow

espantar [ispã'tar] VT to frighten; (admirar) to amaze, astonish; (afugentar) to frighten away ▶ VI to be amazing; **espantar-se** VR to be amazed; (assustar-se) to be frightened

espanto [is'pãtu] M fright, fear; (admiração) amazement; **espantoso, -a** [ispã'tozu, ɔza] ADJ amazing

esparadrapo [ispara'drapu] M (sticking) plaster (BRIT), Band-Aid® (US)

esparramar [ispaha'mar] VT to splash; (espalhar) to scatter

esparso, -a [is'parsu, a] ADJ scattered; (solto) loose

espasmo [is'pazmu] M spasm, convulsion

espatifar [ispatʃi'far] VT to smash; **espatifar-se** VR to smash; (avião) to crash

especial [ispe'sjaw] (pl **-ais**) ADJ special; **em ~** especially; **especialidade** [ispesjali'dadʒi] F speciality (BRIT), specialty (US); (ramo de atividades) specialization; **especialista** [ispesja'lista] M/F specialist; (perito) expert; **especializar-se** [ispesjali'zarsi] VR: **especializar-se (em)** to specialize (in)

espécie [is'pɛsi] F (Bio) species; (tipo) sort, kind; **causar ~** to be surprising; **pagar em ~** to pay in cash

especificar [ispesifi'kar] VT to specify; **específico, -a** [ispe'sifiku, a] ADJ specific

espécime [is'pɛsimi] M specimen

espécimen [is'pɛsimẽ] (pl **-s**) M = **espécime**

espectador, a [ispekta'dor(a)] M/F onlooker; (TV) viewer; (Esporte) spectator; (Teatro) member of the audience; **espectadores** MPL audience sg

especular [ispeku'lar] VI: **~ (sobre)** to speculate (on)

espelho [is'peʎu] M mirror; (fig) model; **~ retrovisor** (Auto) rear-view mirror

espera [is'pɛra] F (demora) wait; (expectativa) expectation; **à ~ de** waiting for; **à minha ~** waiting for me

esperança [ispe'rãsa] F hope; (expectativa) expectation; **dar ~s a alguém** to get sb's hopes up; **esperançoso, -a** [isperã'sozu, ɔza] ADJ hopeful

esperar [ispe'rar] VT to wait for; (desejar) to hope for; (contar com, bebê) to expect ▶ VI to wait; to hope; to expect

esperma [is'perma] M sperm

espertalhão, -lhona [isperta'ʎãw, ʎɔna] (pl **-ões/-s**) ADJ crafty, shrewd

esperteza [isper'teza] F cleverness; (astúcia) cunning

esperto, -a [is'pɛrtu, a] ADJ clever; (espertalhão) crafty

espetacular [ispetaku'lar] ADJ spectacular

espetáculo [ispe'takulu] M (Teatro) show; (vista) sight; (cena ridícula) spectacle; **dar ~** to make a spectacle of o.s.

espetar [ispe'tar] VT (carne) to put on a spit; (cravar) to stick; **espetar-se** VR to prick o.s.; **~ algo em algo** to pin sth to sth

espeto [is'petu] M spit; (pau) pointed stick; **ser um ~** (ser difícil) to be awkward

espevitado, -a [ispevi'tadu, a] ADJ (fig: vivo) lively

espiã [is'pjã] F de **espião**

espiada [is'pjada] F: **dar uma ~** to have a look

espião, -piã [is'pjãw, 'pjã] (pl **-ões/-s**) M/F spy

espiar [is'pjar] VT to spy on; (uma ocasião) to watch out for; (olhar) to watch ▶ VI to spy; (olhar) to peer

espiga [is'piga] F (de milho) ear

espinafre [ispi'nafri] M spinach

espingarda [ispĩ'garda] F shotgun, rifle

espinha [is'piɲa] F (de peixe) bone; (na pele) spot, zit (col); (coluna vertebral) spine

espinho [is'piɲu] M thorn; (de animal) spine; (fig: dificuldade) snag; **espinhoso, -a** [ispi'ɲozu, ɔza] ADJ (planta) prickly, thorny; (fig: difícil) difficult; (: problema) thorny

espiões [is'pjõjs] MPL de **espião**

espionar [ispjo'nar] VT to spy on ▶ VI to spy, snoop

espírito [is'piritu] M spirit; (pensamento) mind; **~ esportivo** sense of humo(u)r; **E~ Santo** Holy Spirit

espiritual [ispiri'twaw] (pl **-ais**) ADJ spiritual

espirituoso, -a [ispiri'twozu, ɔza] ADJ witty

espirrar [ispi'har] VI to sneeze; (jorrar) to spurt out ▶ VT (água) to spurt; **espirro** [is'pihu] M sneeze

esplêndido, -a [is'plẽdʒidu, a] ADJ splendid

esplendor [isplẽ'dor] M splendour (BRIT), splendor (US)

esponja [is'põʒa] F sponge

espontâneo, -a [ispõ'tanju, a] ADJ spontaneous; (pessoa) straightforward

esporádico, -a [ispo'radʒiku, a] ADJ sporadic

esporte [is'portʃi] (BR) M sport; **esportista** [ispor'tʃista] ADJ sporting ▶ M/F sportsman/woman; **esportivo, -a** [ispor'tʃivu, a] ADJ sporting

esposa [is'poza] F wife

esposo [is'pozu] M husband

espreguiçadeira [ispregisa'dejra] F deck chair; (*com lugar para as pernas*) lounger

espreguiçar-se [ispregi'sarsi] VR to stretch

espreita [is'prejta] F: **ficar à ~** to keep watch

espreitar [isprej'tar] VT to spy on; (*observar*) to observe, watch

espremer [ispre'mer] VT (*fruta*) to squeeze; (*roupa molhada*) to wring out; (*pessoas*) to squash; **espremer-se** VR (*multidão*) to be squashed together; (*uma pessoa*) to squash up

espuma [is'puma] F foam; (*de cerveja*) froth, head; (*de sabão*) lather; (*de ondas*) surf; **~ de borracha** foam rubber; **espumante** [ispu'mãtʃi] ADJ frothy, foamy; (*vinho*) sparkling

esq. ABR (= *esquerdo*) l.; = **esquina**

esquadra [is'kwadra] F (*Náut*) fleet; (*PT: da polícia*) police station

esquadrão [iskwa'drãw] (*pl* -**ões**) M squadron

esquadrilha [iskwa'driʎa] F squadron

esquadrões [iskwa'drõjs] MPL *de* **esquadrão**

esquartejar [iskwarte'ʒar] VT to quarter

esquecer [iske'ser] VT, VI to forget; **esquecer-se** VR: **~-se de** to forget; **esquecido, -a** [iske'sidu, a] ADJ forgotten; (*pessoa*) forgetful

esqueleto [iske'letu] M skeleton; (*arcabouço*) framework

esquema [is'kema] M outline; (*plano*) scheme; (*diagrama*) diagram, plan

esquentar [iskẽ'tar] VT to heat (up), warm (up); (*fig: irritar*) to annoy ▶ VI to warm up; (*casaco*) to be warm; **esquentar-se** VR to get annoyed

esquerda [is'kerda] F (*tb Pol*) left; **à ~** on the left

esquerdista [isker'dʒista] ADJ left-wing ▶ M/F left-winger

esquerdo, -a [is'kerdu, a] ADJ left

esqui [is'ki] M (*patim*) ski; (*esporte*) skiing; **~ aquático** water skiing; **fazer ~** to go skiing; **esquiar** [is'kjar] VI to ski

esquilo [is'kilu] M squirrel

esquina [is'kina] F corner

esquisito, -a [iski'zitu, a] ADJ strange, odd

esquivar-se [iski'varsi] VR: **~ de** to escape from, get away from; (*deveres*) to get out of

esquivo, -a [is'kivu, a] ADJ aloof, standoffish

essa ['ɛsa] PRON: **~ é/foi boa** that is/was a good one!; **~ não, sem ~** come off it!; **vamos nessa** let's go!; **ainda mais ~!** that's all I need!; **corta ~!** cut it out!; **por ~s e outras** for these and other reasons; **~ de fazer ...** this business of doing ...

esse ['esi] ADJ (*sg*) that; (*pl*) those; (BR: *este: sg*) this; (: *pl*) these ▶ PRON (*sg*) that one; (*pl*) those (ones); (BR: *este: sg*) this one; (: *pl*) these (ones)

essência [e'sẽsja] F essence; **essencial** [esẽ'sjaw] (*pl* -**ais**) ADJ essential; (*principal*) main ▶ M: **o essencial** the main thing

esta ['ɛsta] F **de este²**

estabelecer [istabele'ser] VT to establish; (*fundar*) to set up

estabelecimento [istabelesi'mẽtu] M establishment; (*casa comercial*) business

estábulo [is'tabulu] M cow-shed

estaca [is'taka] F post, stake; (*de barraca*) peg

estação [ista'sãw] (*pl* -**ões**) F station; (*do ano*) season; **~ de águas** spa; **~ balneária** seaside resort; **~ emissora** broadcasting station

estacionamento [istasjona'mẽtu] M (*ato*) parking; (*lugar*) car park (BRIT), parking lot (US)

estacionar [istasjo'nar] VT to park ▶ VI to park; (*não mover*) to remain stationary

estacionário, -a [istasjo'narju, a] ADJ (*veículo*) stationary; (*Com*) slack

estações [ista'sõjs] FPL *de* **estação**

estada [is'tada] F stay

estadia [ista'dʒia] F = **estada**

estádio [is'tadʒu] M stadium

estadista [ista'dʒista] M/F statesman/ woman

estado [i'stadu] M state; **E~s Unidos (da América)** United States (of America); **~ civil** marital status; **~ de espírito** state of mind; **~ maior** staff; **estadual** [ista'dwaw] (*pl* -**ais**) ADJ state *atr*

estafa [is'tafa] F fatigue; (*esgotamento*) nervous exhaustion

estagiário, -a [ista'ʒjarju, a] M/F (*empregado*) trainee; (*estudante*) intern; (*professor*) student teacher; (*médico*) junior doctor

estágio [is'taʒu] M (*aprendizado: de empregado*) traineeship; (: *de estudante*) internship; (*fase*) stage

estagnado, -a [istag'nadu, a] ADJ stagnant

estalar [ista'lar] VT to break; (*os dedos*) to snap ▶ VI to split, crack; (*crepitar*) to crackle

estalido [ista'lidu] M pop

estalo [is'talu] M (do chicote) crack; (dos dedos) snap; (dos lábios) smack; (de foguete) bang; **~ de trovão** thunderclap; **de ~** suddenly

estampa [is'tãpa] F (figura impressa) print; (ilustração) picture

estampado, -a [istã'padu, a] ADJ printed ▶ M (tecido) print; (num tecido) pattern

estampar [istã'par] VT to print; (marcar) to stamp

estancar [istã'kar] VT to staunch; (fazer cessar) to stop; **estancar-se** VR to stop

estância [is'tãsja] F ranch, farm

estandarte [istã'dartʃi] M standard, banner

estanho [is'taɲu] M (metal) tin

estante [is'tãtʃi] F bookcase; (suporte) stand

(PALAVRA-CHAVE)

estar [is'tar] VI **1** (lugar) to be; (em casa) to be in; (no telefone): **a Lúcia está? — não, ela não está** is Lúcia there? — no, she's not in

2 (estado) to be; **estar doente** to be ill; **estar bem** (de saúde) to be well; (financeiramente) to be well off; **estar calor/frio** to be hot/cold; **estar com fome/sede/medo** to be hungry/thirsty/afraid

3 (ação contínua): **estar fazendo** (BR) ou **a fazer** (PT) to be doing

4 (+ pp, como adj): **estar sentado/cansado** to be sitting down/tired

5 (+ pp, uso passivo): **está condenado à morte** he's been condemned to death; **o livro está emprestado** the book's been borrowed

6: **estar de férias/licença** to be on holiday (BRIT) ou vacation (US)/leave; **ela estava de chapéu** she had a hat on, she was wearing a hat

7: **estar para fazer** to be about to do; **ele está para chegar a qualquer momento** he'll be here any minute; **não estar para conversas** not to be in the mood for talking

8: **estar por fazer** to be still to be done

9: **estar sem dinheiro** to have no money; **estar sem dormir** not to have slept; **estou sem dormir há três dias** I haven't slept for three days; **está sem terminar** it isn't finished yet

10 (frases): **tá (bem)** (col) OK; **estar bem com** to be on good terms with

estardalhaço [istarda'ʎasu] M fuss; (ostentação) ostentation

estas ['estas] FPL de **este²**

estatal [ista'taw] (pl **-ais**) ADJ nationalized, state-owned ▶ F state-owned company

estático, -a [is'tatʃiku, a] ADJ static

estatística [ista'tʃistʃika] F statistic; (ciência) statistics sg

estatizar [istatʃi'zar] VT to nationalize

estátua [is'tatwa] F statue

estatura [ista'tura] F stature

estável [is'tavew] (pl **-eis**) ADJ stable

este¹ ['estʃi] M east ▶ ADJ INV (região) eastern; (vento, direção) easterly

este², esta ['estʃi, 'esta] ADJ (sg) this; (pl) these ▶ PRON this one; (pl) these; (a quem/que se referiu por último) the latter; **esta noite** (noite passada) last night; (noite de hoje) tonight

esteira [is'tejra] F mat; (de navio) wake; (rumo) path

esteja [is'teʒa] VB ver **estar**

estelionato [isteljo'natu] M fraud

estender [istẽ'der] VT to extend; (mapa) to spread out; (pernas) to stretch; (massa) to roll out; (conversa) to draw out; (corda) to pull tight; (roupa molhada) to hang out; **estender-se** VR to lie down; (fila, terreno) to stretch, extend; **~-se sobre algo** to dwell on sth, expand on sth; **~ a mão** to hold out one's hand

estéreis [is'terejs] ADJ PL de **estéril**

estereo... [isterju] PREFIXO stereo...; **estereofônico, -a** [isterjo'foniku, a] ADJ stereo(phonic); **estereótipo** [iste'rjɔtʃipu] M stereotype

estéril [is'teriw] (pl **-eis**) ADJ sterile; (terra) infertile; (fig) futile; **esterilizar** [isterili'zar] VT to sterilize

esteve [is'tevi] VB ver **estar**

esticar [istʃi'kar] VT to stretch; **esticar-se** VR to stretch out

estigma [is'tʃigima] M mark, scar; (fig) stigma

estilhaçar [istʃiʎa'sar] VT to splinter; (despedaçar) to shatter; **estilhaçar-se** VR to shatter; **estilhaço** [istʃi'ʎasu] M fragment; (de pedra) chip; (de madeira, metal) splinter

estilo [is'tʃilu] M style; (Tec) stylus; **~ de vida** way of life

estima [is'tʃima] F esteem; (afeto) affection

estimação [istʃima'sãw] F: **... de ~** favourite (BRIT) ..., favorite (US) ...

estimado, -a [istʃi'madu, a] ADJ respected; (em cartas): **E~ Senhor** Dear Sir

estimar [istʃi'mar] vт to appreciate; (*avaliar*) to value; (*ter estima a*) to have a high regard for; (*calcular aproximadamente*) to estimate

estimativa [istʃima'tʃiva] ꜰ estimate

estimulante [istʃimu'lãtʃi] ᴀᴅᴊ stimulating ▶ ᴍ stimulant

estimular [istʃimu'lar] vт to stimulate; (*incentivar*) to encourage; **estímulo** [is'tʃimulu] ᴍ stimulus; (*ânimo*) encouragement

estipular [istʃipu'lar] vт to stipulate

estirar [istʃi'rar] vт to stretch (out); **estirar-se** vʀ to stretch

estive [is'tʃivi] vʙ *ver* **estar**

estocada [isto'kada] ꜰ stab, thrust

estocar [isto'kar] vт to stock

estofo [is'tofu] ᴍ (*tecido*) material; (*para acolchoar*) padding, stuffing

estojo [is'toʒu] ᴍ case; **~ de ferramentas** tool kit; **~ de unhas** manicure set

estômago [is'tomagu] ᴍ stomach; **ter ~ para (fazer) algo** to be up to (doing) sth

estontear [istõ'tʃjar] vт to stun, daze

estoque [is'tɔki] ᴍ (Com) stock

estourado, -a [isto'radu, a] ᴀᴅᴊ (*temperamental*) explosive; (col: *cansado*) knackered, worn out

estourar [isto'rar] vɪ to explode; (*pneu*) to burst; (*escândalo*) to blow up; (*guerra*) to break out; (ʙʀ: *chegar*) to turn up, arrive; **~ (com alguém)** (*zangar-se*) to blow up (at sb)

estouro [is'toru] ᴍ explosion; **dar o ~** (fig: *zangar-se*) to blow up, blow one's top

estrábico, -a [is'trabiku, a] ᴀᴅᴊ cross-eyed

estraçalhar [istrasa'ʎar] vт (*livro, objeto*) to pull to pieces; (*pessoa*) to tear to pieces

estrada [is'trada] ꜰ road; **~ de ferro** (ʙʀ) railway (ʙʀɪᴛ), railroad (ᴜs); **~ principal** main road (ʙʀɪᴛ), state highway (ᴜs)

estrado [is'tradu] ᴍ (*tablado*) platform; (*de cama*) base

estragado, -a [istra'gadu, a] ᴀᴅᴊ ruined; (*fruta*) rotten; (*muito mimado*) spoiled, spoilt (ʙʀɪᴛ)

estraga-prazeres [istraga-] ᴍ/ꜰ ɪɴᴠ spoilsport

estragar [istra'gar] vт to spoil; (*arruinar*) to ruin, wreck; (*desperdiçar*) to waste; (*saúde*) to damage; (*mimar*) to spoil; **estrago** [is'tragu] ᴍ destruction; (*desperdício*) waste; (*dano*) damage; **os estragos da guerra** the ravages of war

estrangeiro, -a [istrã'ʒejru, a] ᴀᴅᴊ foreign ▶ ᴍ/ꜰ foreigner; **no ~** abroad

estrangular [istrãgu'lar] vт to strangle

estranhar [istra'ɲar] vт to be surprised at; (*achar estranho*) **~ algo** to find sth strange; **estranhei o clima** the climate did not agree with me; **não é de se ~** it's not surprising

estranho, -a [is'traɲu, a] ᴀᴅᴊ strange, odd; (*influências*) outside ▶ ᴍ/ꜰ (*desconhecido*) stranger; (*de fora*) outsider

estratégia [istra'tɛʒa] ꜰ strategy

estrear [is'trjar] vт (*vestido*) to wear for the first time; (*peça de teatro*) to perform for the first time; (*veículo*) to use for the first time; (*filme*) to show for the first time, première; (*iniciar*) **~ uma carreira** to embark on *ou* begin a career ▶ vɪ (*ator, jogador*) to make one's first appearance; (*filme, peça*) to open

estrebaria [istreba'ria] ꜰ stable

estreia [is'treja] ꜰ (*de artista*) debut; (*de uma peça*) first night; (*de um filme*) première, opening

estreitar [istrej'tar] vт to narrow; (*roupa*) to take in; (*abraçar*) to hug; (*laços de amizade*) to strengthen ▶ vɪ (*estrada*) to narrow

estreito, -a [is'trejtu, a] ᴀᴅᴊ narrow; (*saia*) straight; (*vínculo, relação*) close; (*medida*) strict ▶ ᴍ strait

estrela [is'trela] ꜰ star; **~ cadente** falling star; **estrelado, -a** [istre'ladu, a] ᴀᴅᴊ (*céu*) starry; (*ovo*) fried

estremecer [istreme'ser] vт to shake; (*amizade*) to strain; (*fazer tremer*): **~ alguém** to make sb shudder ▶ vɪ to shake; (*tremer*) to tremble; (*horrorizar-se*) to shudder; (*amizade*) to be strained

estremecimento [istremesi'mẽtu] ᴍ shaking, trembling; (*tremor*) tremor; (*numa amizade*) tension

estresse [is'tresi] ᴍ stress

estribeira [istri'bejra] ꜰ: **perder as ~s** (col) to fly off the handle, lose one's temper

estridente [istri'dẽtʃi] ᴀᴅᴊ shrill, piercing

estrofe [is'trɔfi] ꜰ stanza

estrondo [is'trõdu] ᴍ (*de trovão*) rumble; (*de armas*) din

estrutura [istru'tura] ꜰ structure; (*armação*) framework; (*de edifício*) fabric

estudante [istu'dãtʃi] ᴍ/ꜰ student; **estudantil** [istudã'tʃiw] (*pl* -**is**) ᴀᴅᴊ student *atr*

estudar [istu'dar] vт, vɪ to study

estúdio [is'tudʒu] ᴍ studio

estudo [is'tudu] M study

estufa [is'tufa] F (fogão) stove; (de plantas) greenhouse; (de fogão) plate warmer; **efeito ~** greenhouse effect

estufado [istu'fadu] (PT) M stew

estupefato, -a [istupe'fatu, a], (PT) **estupefacto** ADJ dumbfounded

estupendo, -a [istu'pēdu, a] ADJ wonderful; (col) terrific

estupidez [istupi'deʒ] F stupidity; (ato, dito) stupid thing; (grosseria) rudeness

estúpido, -a [is'tupidu, a] ADJ stupid; (grosseiro) rude, churlish ▶ M/F idiot; (grosseiro) oaf

estuprar [istu'prar] VT to rape; **estupro** [is'trupu] M rape

esvaziar [izva'zjar] VT to empty; **esvaziar-se** VR to empty

etapa [e'tapa] F stage

etc. ABR (= et cetera) etc

eternidade [eterni'dadʒi] F eternity

ética ['etʃika] F ethics pl

ético, -a ['etʃiku, a] ADJ ethical

Etiópia [e'tʃjɔpja] F: **a ~** Ethiopia

etiqueta [etʃi'keta] F etiquette; (rótulo, em roupa) label; (que se amarra) tag

étnico, -a ['etʃniku, a] ADJ ethnic

etos ['etus] M INV ethos

eu [ew] PRON I ▶ M self; **sou eu** it's me

EUA ABR MPL (= Estados Unidos da América) USA

eucaristia [ewkaris'tʃia] F Holy Communion

euro ['ewru] M (moeda) euro

Europa [ew'rɔpa] F: **a ~** Europe; **europeu, -peia** [ewro'peu, 'pɛja] ADJ, M/F European

evacuar [eva'kwar] VT to evacuate; (sair de) to leave; (Med) to discharge ▶ VI to defecate

evadir [eva'dʒir] VT to evade; **evadir-se** VR to escape

evangelho [evā'ʒeʎu] M gospel

evaporar [evapo'rar] VT, VI to evaporate; **evaporar-se** VR to evaporate; (desaparecer) to vanish

evasão [eva'zāw] (pl -ões) F escape, flight; (fig) evasion

evasiva [eva'ziva] F excuse

evasivo, -a [eva'zivu, a] ADJ evasive

evasões [eva'zõjs] FPL de **evasão**

evento [e'vētu] M event; (eventualidade) eventuality

eventual [evē'tuaw] (pl -ais) ADJ fortuitous, accidental; **eventualidade** [evētwali'dadʒi] F eventuality

evidência [evi'dēsja] F evidence, proof; **evidenciar** [evidē'sjar] VT to prove; (mostrar) to show; **evidenciar-se** VR to be evident, be obvious

evidente [evi'dētʃi] ADJ obvious, evident

evitar [evi'tar] VT to avoid; **~ de fazer algo** to avoid doing sth

evocar [evo'kar] VT to evoke; (espíritos) to invoke

evolução [evolu'sāw] (pl -ões) F development; (Mil) manoeuvre (BRIT), maneuver (US); (movimento) movement; (Bio) evolution

evoluir [evo'lwir] VI to evolve; **~ para** to evolve into

Ex.a ABR = **excelência**

exagerar [ezaʒe'rar] VT to exaggerate ▶ VI to exaggerate; (agir com exagero) to overdo it; **exagero** [eza'ʒeru] M exaggeration

exalar [eza'lar] VT (odor) to give off

exaltado, -a [ezaw'tadu, a] ADJ fanatical; (apaixonado) overexcited

exaltar [ezaw'tar] VT (elevar: pessoa, virtude) to exalt; (louvar) to praise; (excitar) to excite; (irritar) to annoy; **exaltar-se** VR (irritar-se) to get worked up; (arrebatar-se) to get carried away

exame [e'zami] M (Educ) examination, exam; (Med etc) examination; **fazer um ~** (Educ) to take an exam; (Med) to have an examination

examinar [ezami'nar] VT to examine

exatidão [ezatʃi'dāw] F accuracy; (perfeição) correctness

exato, -a [e'zatu, a] ADJ right, correct; (preciso) exact; **~!** exactly!

exaustão [ezaw'stāw] F exhaustion; **exausto, -a** [e'zawstu, a] ADJ exhausted

exaustor [ezaw'stor] M extractor fan

exceção [ese'sāw] (pl -ões) F exception; **com ~ de** with the exception of; **abrir ~** to make an exception

excecional (PT) ADJ = **excepcional**

excedente [ese'dētʃi] ADJ excess; (Com) surplus ▶ M (Com) surplus

exceder [ese'der] VT to exceed; (superar) to surpass; **exceder-se** VR (cometer excessos) to go too far; (cansar-se) to overdo things

excelência [ese'lēsja] F excellence; **por ~** par excellence; **Vossa E~** Your Excellency; **excelente** [ese'lētʃi] ADJ excellent

excêntrico, -a [e'sētriku, a] ADJ, M/F eccentric

excepcional [esepsjo'naw] (pl -ais) ADJ exceptional; (especial) special; (Med) disabled

excesso [e'sɛsu] M excess; (Com) surplus

exceto [e'sɛtu] PREP except (for), apart from

excitação [esita'sãw] F excitement

excitado, -a [esi'tadu, a] ADJ excited; (*estimulado*) aroused

excitante [esi'tãtʃi] ADJ exciting

exclamação [isklama'sãw] (*pl* -**ões**) F exclamation

exclamar [iskla'mar] VI to exclaim

excluir [is'klwir] VT to exclude, leave out; (*eliminar*) to rule out; (*ser incompatível com*) to preclude; **exclusão** [isklu'zãw] F exclusion; **exclusivo, -a** [isklu'zivu, a] ADJ exclusive

excursão [iskur'sãw] (*pl* -**ões**) F outing; excursion; **~ a pé** hike; **excursionista** [iskursjo'nista] M/F tourist; (*para o dia*) day-tripper; (*a pé*) hiker

execução [ezeku'sãw] (*pl* -**ões**) F execution; (*de música*) performance

executar [ezeku'tar] VT to execute; (*Mús*) to perform; (*plano*) to carry out; (*papel teatral*) to play

executivo, -a [ezeku'tʃivu, a] ADJ, M/F executive

exemplar [ezẽ'plar] ADJ exemplary ▶ M model, example; (*Bio*) specimen; (*livro*) copy; (*peça*) piece

exemplo [e'zẽplu] M example; **por ~** for example

exercer [ezer'ser] VT to exercise; (*influência, pressão*) to exert; (*função*) to perform; (*profissão*) to practise (BRIT), practice (US); (*obrigações*) to carry out

exercício [ezer'sisju] M exercise; (*de medicina*) practice; (*Mil*) drill; (*Com*) financial year

exercitar [ezersi'tar] VT (*profissão*) to practise (BRIT), practice (US); (*direitos, músculos*) to exercise; (*adestrar*) to train

exército [e'zɛrsitu] M army

exibição [ezibi'sãw] (*pl* -**ões**) F show, display; (*de filme*) showing

exibir [ezi'bir] VT to show, display; (*alardear*) to show off; (*filme*) to show, screen; **exibir-se** VR to show off; (*indecentemente*) to expose o.s.

exigência [ezi'ʒẽsja] F demand; (*o necessário*) requirement; **exigente** [ezi'ʒẽtʃi] ADJ demanding

exigir [ezi'ʒir] VT to demand

exíguo, -a [e'zigwu, a] ADJ (*diminuto*) small; (*escasso*) scanty

exilado, -a [ezi'ladu, a] M/F exile

exilar [ezi'lar] VT to exile; **exilar-se** VR to go into exile; **exílio** [e'zilju] M exile; (*forçado*) deportation

existência [ezis'tẽsja] F existence; (*vida*) life

existir [ezis'tʃir] VI to exist; **existe/ existem ...** (*há*) there is/are ...

êxito ['ezitu] M result; (*sucesso*) success; (*música, filme etc*) hit; **ter ~ (em)** to succeed (in), be successful (in)

Exmo, -a (*pl* -**s**/-**s**) ABR (= *Excelentíssimo*) Dear

êxodo ['ezodu] M exodus

exorcista [ezor'sista] M/F exorcist

exótico, -a [e'zɔtʃiku, a] ADJ exotic

expandir [ispã'dʒir] VT to expand; (*espalhar*) to spread; **expandir-se** VR to expand; **~-se com alguém** to be frank with sb

expansão [ispã'sãw] F expansion, spread; (*de alegria*) effusiveness

expansivo, -a [ispã'sivu, a] ADJ (*pessoa*) outgoing

expeça [is'pɛsa] VB *ver* **expedir**

expectativa [ispekta'tʃiva] F expectation

expedição [ispedʒi'sãw] (*pl* -**ões**) F (*viagem*) expedition; (*de mercadorias*) despatch; (*por navio*) shipment; (*de passaporte etc*) issue

expediente [ispe'dʒẽtʃi] M means; (*serviço*) working day; (*correspondência*) correspondence ▶ ADJ expedient; **~ bancário** banking hours *pl*; **~ do escritório** office hours *pl*

expedir [ispe'dʒir] VT to send, despatch; (*bilhete, passaporte, decreto*) to issue

expelir [ispe'lir] VT to expel; (*sangue*) to spit

experiência [ispe'rjẽsja] F experience; (*prova*) experiment, test; **em ~** on trial

experimentar [isperimẽ'tar] VT (*comida*) to taste; (*vestido*) to try on; (*pôr à prova*) to try out, test; (*conhecer pela experiência*) to experience; (*sofrer*) to suffer, undergo; **experimento** [isperi'mẽtu] M experiment

expilo [is'pilu] VB *ver* **expelir**

expirar [ispi'rar] VT to exhale, breathe out ▶ VI to die; (*terminar*) to end

explicação [isplika'sãw] (*pl* -**ões**) F explanation

explicar [ispli'kar] VT, VI to explain; **explicar-se** VR to explain o.s.

explícito, -a [is'plisitu, a] ADJ explicit, clear

explodir [isplo'dʒir] VT, VI to explode

exploração [isplora'sãw] F exploration; (*abuso*) exploitation; (*de uma mina*) running

explorador, a [isplora'dor(a)] M/F explorer; (*de outros*) exploiter

explorar [isplo'rar] VT (região) to explore; (mina) to work, run; (ferida) to probe; (trabalhadores etc) to exploit

explosão [isplo'zãw] (pl -ões) F explosion; (fig) outburst; **explosivo, -a** [isplo'zivu, a] ADJ explosive; (pessoa) hot-headed ▶ M explosive

expor [is'por] (irreg: como **pôr**) VT to expose; (a vida) to risk; (teoria) to explain; (revelar) to reveal; (mercadorias) to display; (quadros) to exhibit; **expor-se** VR to expose o.s.

exportação [isporta'sãw] F (ato) export(ing); (mercadorias) exports pl

exportador, a [isporta'dor(a)] ADJ exporting ▶ M/F exporter

exportar [ispor'tar] VT to export

exposição [ispozi'sãw] (pl -ões) F exhibition; (explicação) explanation; (declaração) statement; (narração) account; (Foto) exposure

exposto, -a [is'postu, 'posta] ADJ (lugar) exposed; (quadro, mercadoria) on show ou display ▶ M: **o acima ~** the above

expressão [ispre'sãw] (pl -ões) F expression

expressar [ispre'sar] VT to express; **expressivo, -a** [ispre'sivu, a] ADJ expressive; (pessoa) demonstrative

expresso, -a [is'presu, a] PP de **exprimir** ▶ ADJ definite, clear; (trem, ordem, carta) express ▶ M express

expressões [ispre'sõjs] FPL de **expressão**

exprimir [ispri'mir] VT to express

expulsão [ispu'sãw] (pl -ões) F expulsion; (Esporte) sending off

expulsar [ispuw'sar] VT to expel; (de uma festa, clube etc) to throw out; (inimigo) to drive out; (estrangeiro) to expel, deport; (jogador) to send off

expulso, -a [is'puwsu, a] PP de **expulsar**

expulsões [ispul'sõjs] FPL de **expulsão**

êxtase ['estazi] M ecstasy

extenso, -a [is'tēsu, a] ADJ extensive; (comprido) long; (artigo) full, comprehensive; **por ~** in full

extenuante [iste'nwãtʃi] ADJ exhausting; (debilitante) debilitating

exterior [iste'rjor] ADJ (de fora) outside, exterior; (aparência) outward; (comércio) foreign ▶ M (da casa) outside; (aspecto) outward appearance; **do ~** (do estrangeiro) from abroad; **no ~** abroad

exterminar [istermi'nar] VT (inimigo) to wipe out, exterminate; (acabar com) to do away with

externo, -a [is'tɛrnu, a] ADJ external; (aparente) outward; **aluno ~** day pupil

extinguir [istʃĩ'gir] VT (fogo) to put out, extinguish; (um povo) to wipe out; **extinguir-se** VR (fogo, luz) to go out; (Bio) to become extinct

extinto, -a [is'tʃĩtu, a] ADJ (fogo) extinguished; (língua) dead; (animal, vulcão) extinct; (associação etc) defunct; **extintor** [istʃĩ'tor] M (fire) extinguisher

extorsão [istor'sãw] F extortion

extra ['estra] ADJ extra ▶ M/F extra person; (Teatro) extra

extração [istra'sãw] (pl -ões) F extraction; (de loteria) draw

extrair [istra'jir] VT to extract, take out

extraordinário, -a [istraordʒi'narju, a] ADJ extraordinary; (despesa) extra; (reunião) special

extrato [is'tratu] M extract; (resumo) summary; **~ (bancário)** (bank) statement

extravagância [istrava'gãsja] F extravagance; **extravagante** [istrava'gãtʃi] ADJ extravagant; (roupa) outlandish; (conduta) wild

extravasar [istrava'zar] VI to overflow

extraviado, -a [istra'vjadu, a] ADJ lost, missing

extraviar [istra'vjar] VT to mislay; (pessoa) to lead astray; (dinheiro) to embezzle; **extraviar-se** VR to get lost; **extravio** [istra'viu] M loss; (roubo) embezzlement; (fig) deviation

extremado, -a [istre'madu, a] ADJ extreme

extremidade [istremi'dadʒi] F extremity; (do dedo) tip; (ponta) end; (beira) edge

extremo, -a [is'tɛemu, a] ADJ extreme ▶ M extreme; **ao ~** extremely

extrovertido, -a [estrover'tʃidu, a] ADJ extrovert, outgoing ▶ M/F extrovert

exultante [ezuw'tãtʃi] ADJ jubilant, exultant

f

The best-known musical form in Portugal is the melancholic **fado**, which is traditionally sung by a soloist (known as a *fadista*) accompanied by the Portuguese *guitarra*. There are two main types of **fado**: Coimbra **fado** is traditionally sung by men, and is considered to be more cerebral than the **fado** from Lisbon, which is sung by both men and women. The theme is nearly always one of deep nostalgia known as *saudade*, and the harsh reality of life.

fã [fã] (col) M/F fan
fábrica ['fabrika] F factory; **~ de cerveja** brewery; **a preço de ~** wholesale
fabricação [fabrika'sãw] F manufacture; **~ em série** mass production
fabuloso, -a [fabu'lozu, ɔza] ADJ fabulous
faca ['faka] F knife; **facada** [fa'kada] F stab, cut
façanha [fa'saɲa] F exploit, deed
facção [fak'sãw] (pl **-ões**) F faction
face ['fasi] F face; (bochecha) cheek; **em ~ de** in view of; **fazer ~ a** to face up to
fáceis ['fasejs] ADJ PL de **fácil**
faceta [fa'seta] F facet
fachada [fa'ʃada] F façade, front
fácil ['fasiw] (pl **-eis**) ADJ easy; (temperamento, pessoa) easy-going ▶ ADV easily; **facilidade** [fasili'dadʒi] F ease; (jeito) facility; **facilidades** FPL (recursos) facilities; **ter facilidade para algo** to have a talent ou a facility for sth
facilitar [fasili'tar] VT to facilitate, make easy; (fornecer): **~ algo a alguém** to provide sb with sth
fã-clube [fã'klubi] (pl **-s**) M fan club
faço ['fasu] VB ver **fazer**
facto ['faktu] (PT) M = **fato**
factual [fak'twaw] (pl **-ais**) ADJ factual
faculdade [fakuw'dadʒi] F faculty; (poder) power
facultativo, -a [fakuwta'tʃivu, a] ADJ optional ▶ M/F doctor
fadado, -a [fa'dadu, a] ADJ destined
fadiga [fa'dʒiga] F fatigue
fadista [fa'dʒista] M/F "fado" singer ▶ M (PT) ruffian
fado ['fadu] M fate; (canção) traditional song of Portugal

faia ['faja] F beech (tree)
faisão [faj'zãw] (pl **-ões**) M pheasant
faísca [fa'iska] F spark; (brilho) flash
faisões [faj'zõjs] MPL de **faisão**
faixa ['fajʃa] F (cinto, Judô) belt; (tira) strip; (área) zone; (Auto: pista) lane; (BR: para pedestres) zebra crossing (BRIT), crosswalk (US); (Med) bandage; (num disco) track
fala ['fala] F speech; **chamar às ~s** to call to account; **sem ~** speechless
falante [fa'lãtʃi] ADJ talkative
falar [fa'lar] VT (língua) to speak; (besteira etc) to talk; (dizer) to say; (verdade, mentira) to tell ▶ VI to speak; **~ algo a alguém** to tell sb sth; **~ de ou em algo** to talk about sth; **~ com alguém** to talk to sb; **por ~ em** speaking of; **sem ~ em** not to mention; **falou!**, **'tá falado!** (col) OK!
falcão [faw'kãw] (pl **-ões**) M falcon
falcatrua [fawka'trua] F (col) scam
falecer [fale'ser] VI to die; **falecimento** [falesi'mẽtu] M death
falência [fa'lẽsja] F bankruptcy; **abrir ~** to declare o.s. bankrupt; **ir à ~** to go bankrupt; **levar à ~** to bankrupt
falésia [fa'lɛzja] F cliff
falha ['faʎa] F fault; (lacuna) omission; (de caráter) flaw
falhar [fa'ʎar] VI to fail; (não acertar) to miss; (errar) to be wrong; **sua voz está falhando** you're breaking up
falho, -a ['faʎu, a] ADJ faulty; (deficiente) wanting
falido, -a [fa'lidu, a] ADJ, M/F bankrupt
falir [fa'lir] VI to fail; (Com) to go bankrupt
falsário, -a [faw'sarju, a] M/F forger
falsidade [fawsi'dadʒi] F falsehood; (fingimento) pretence (BRIT), pretense (US)
falsificar [fawsifi'kar] VT (forjar) to forge; (falsear) to falsify; (adulterar) to adulterate; (desvirtuar) to misrepresent

falso, -a ['fawsu, a] ADJ false; (*fraudulento*) dishonest; (*errôneo*) wrong; (*joia, moeda, quadro*) fake; **pisar em ~** to blunder

falta ['fawta] F (*carência*) lack; (*ausência*) absence; (*defeito, culpa*) fault; (*Futebol*) foul; **por ou na ~ de** for lack of; **sem ~** without fail; **fazer ~** to be lacking, be needed; **sentir ~ de alguém/algo** to miss sb/sth; **ter ~ de** to lack, be in need of

faltar [faw'tar] VI to be lacking, be wanting; (*pessoa*) to be absent; (*falhar*) to fail; **~ ao trabalho** to be absent from work; **~ à palavra** to break one's word; **falta pouco para ...** it won't be long until ...

fama ['fama] F (*renome*) fame; (*reputação*) reputation

família [fa'milja] F family

familiar [fami'ljar] ADJ (*da família*) family atr; (*conhecido*) familiar ▶ M/F relation, relative; **familiaridade** [familjari'daʒi] F familiarity; (*sem-cerimônia*) informality

famoso, -a [fa'mozu, ɔza] ADJ famous

fanático, -a [fa'natʃiku, a] ADJ fanatical ▶ M/F fanatic

fantasia [fāta'zia] F fantasy; (*imaginação*) imagination; (*capricho*) fancy; (*traje*) fancy dress

fantasiar [fāta'zjar] VT to imagine ▶ VI to daydream; **fantasiar-se** VR to dress up (in fancy dress)

fantasma [fā'tazma] M ghost; (*alucinação*) illusion

fantástico, -a [fā'tastʃiku, a] ADJ fantastic; (*ilusório*) imaginary; (*incrível*) unbelievable

fantoche [fā'tɔʃi] M puppet

farda ['farda] F uniform

farei [fa'rej] VB ver **fazer**

farinha [fa'riɲa] F: **~ (de mesa)** (manioc) flour; **~ de rosca** breadcrumbs pl; **~ de trigo** plain flour

farmacêutico, -a [farma'sewtʃiku, a] ADJ pharmaceutical ▶ M/F pharmacist, chemist (BRIT)

farmácia [far'masja] F pharmacy, chemist's (shop) (BRIT)

faro ['faru] M sense of smell; (*fig*) flair

farofa [fa'rɔfa] F (*Culin*) side dish based on manioc flour

farol [fa'rɔw] (*pl* -**óis**) M lighthouse; (*Auto*) headlight; **~ alto** (*Auto*) full (BRIT) ou high (US) beam; **~ baixo** dipped headlights pl (BRIT), dimmed beam (US)

farra ['faha] F binge, spree

farrapo [fa'hapu] M rag

farsa ['farsa] F farce; **farsante** [far'sātʃi] M/F joker

fartar [far'tar] VT to satiate; (*encher*) to fill up; **fartar-se** VR to gorge o.s.

farto, -a ['fartu, a] ADJ full, satiated; (*abundante*) plentiful; (*aborrecido*) fed up

fartura [far'tura] F abundance

fascinante [fasi'nātʃi] ADJ fascinating

fascinar [fasi'nar] VT to fascinate; (*encantar*) to charm; **fascínio** [fa'sinju] M fascination

fase ['fazi] F phase

fashion ['fɛfjõ] (*col*) ADJ trendy

fatal [fa'taw] (*pl* -**ais**) ADJ (*mortal*) fatal; (*inevitável*) fateful; **fatalidade** [fatali'dadʒi] F fate; (*desgraça*) disaster

fatia [fa'tʃia] F slice

fatigante [fatʃi'gātʃi] ADJ tiring; (*aborrecido*) tiresome

fatigar [fatʃi'gar] VT to tire; (*aborrecer*) to bore; **fatigar-se** VR to get tired

Fátima ['fatima] F see note

> **Fátima**, situated in central Portugal, is known worldwide as a site of pilgrimage for Catholics. It is said that, in 1917, the Virgin Mary appeared six times to three shepherd children (*os três pastorinhos*). Millions of pilgrims visit Fátima every year.

fato ['fatu] M fact; (*acontecimento*) event; (*PT: traje*) suit; **~ de banho** (PT) swimming costume (BRIT), bathing suit (US); **de ~** in fact, really

fator [fa'tor] M factor

fatura [fa'tura] F bill, invoice; **faturar** [fatu'rar] VT to invoice; (*dinheiro*) to make ▶ VI (*col: ganhar dinheiro*): **faturar (alto)** to rake it in

fava ['fava] F broad bean; **mandar alguém às ~s** to send sb packing

favela [fa'vɛla] F slum

favor [fa'vor] M favour (BRIT), favor (US); **a ~ de** in favo(u)r of; **por ~** please; **se faz ~** (PT) please; **faça** ou **faz o ~ de ...** would you be so good as to ..., kindly ...; **favorável** [favo'ravew] (*pl* -**eis**) ADJ: **favorável (a)** favourable (BRIT) ou favorable (US) (to); **favorecer** [favore'ser] VT to favour (BRIT), favor (US); (*beneficiar*) to benefit; (*suj: vestido*) to suit; (: *retrato*) to flatter; **favorito, -a** [favo'ritu, a] ADJ, M/F (*tb Comput*) favourite (BRIT), favorite (US)

fax [faks] M fax; **enviar por ~** to fax

faxina [fa'ʃina] F: **fazer ~** to clean up; **faxineiro, -a** [faʃi'nejru, a] M/F cleaner

fazenda [fa'zẽda] F farm; (de café)
plantation; (de gado) ranch; (pano) cloth,
fabric; (Econ) treasury; **fazendeiro**
[fazẽ'dejru] M farmer; (de café)
plantation-owner; (de gado) rancher,
ranch-owner

(PALAVRA-CHAVE)

fazer [fa'zer] VT
1 (fabricar, produzir) to make; (construir) to
build; (pergunta) to ask; (poema, música)
to write; **fazer um filme/ruído** to make
a film/noise
2 (executar) to do; **o que você está
fazendo?** what are you doing?; **fazer a
comida** to do the cooking; **fazer o
papel de** (Teatro) to play
3 (estudos, alguns esportes) to do; **fazer
medicina/direito** to do ou study
medicine/law; **fazer ioga/ginástica** to
do yoga/keep-fit
4 (transformar, tornar): **sair o fará sentir
melhor** going out will make him feel
better; **sua partida fará o trabalho
mais difícil** his departure will make
work more difficult
5 (como substituto de vb): **ele bebeu e eu
fiz o mesmo** he drank and I did likewise
6: **ele faz anos hoje** it's his birthday
today; **fiz 30 anos ontem** I was 30
yesterday
▶ VI **1** (portar-se) to act, behave; **fazer
bem/mal** to do the right/wrong thing;
não fiz por mal I didn't mean it; **faz
como quem não sabe** act as if you don't
know anything
2: **fazer com que alguém faça algo** to
make sb do sth
▶ VB IMPESS **1**: **faz calor/frio** it's hot/cold
2 (tempo): **faz um ano** a year ago; **faz
dois anos que ele se formou** it's two
years since he graduated; **faz três
meses que ele está aqui** he's been here
for three months
3: **não faz mal** never mind; **tanto faz**
it's all the same
fazer-se VR **1**: **fazer-se de
desentendido** to pretend not to
understand
2: **faz-se com ovos e leite** it's made
with eggs and milk; **isso não se faz**
that's not done

fé [fɛ] F faith; (crença) belief; (confiança)
trust; **de boa/má fé** in good/bad faith
febre ['fɛbri] F fever; (fig) excitement;
~ do feno hay fever; **febril** [fe'briw]
(pl **-is**) ADJ feverish

fechado, -a [fe'ʃadu, a] ADJ shut, closed;
(pessoa) reserved; (sinal) red; (luz,
torneira) off; (tempo) overcast; (cara)
stern
fechadura [feʃa'dura] F (de porta) lock
fechar [fe'ʃar] VT to close, shut; (concluir)
to finish, conclude; (luz, torneira) to turn
off; (rua) to close off; (ferida) to close up;
(bar, loja) to close down ▶ VI to close (up),
shut; to close down; (tempo) to cloud
over; **fechar-se** VR to close, shut;
(pessoa) to withdraw; **~ à chave** to lock
fecho ['feʃu] M fastening; (trinco) latch;
(término) close; **~ ecler** zip fastener
(BRIT), zipper (US)
fécula ['fɛkula] F starch
feder [fe'der] VI to stink
federação [federa'sãw] (pl **-ões**) F
federation
federal [fede'raw] (pl **-ais**) ADJ federal;
(col: grande) huge
fedor [fe'dor] M stench
feijão [fej'ʒãw] (pl **-ões**) M bean(s) (pl);
(preto) black bean(s) (pl); **feijoada**
[fej'ʒwada] F (Culin) meat, rice and black
beans
feio, -a ['feju, a] ADJ ugly; (situação) grim;
(atitude) bad; (tempo) horrible ▶ ADV
(perder) badly
feira ['fejra] F fair; (mercado) market
feiticeira [fejtʃi'sejra] F witch
feiticeiro, -a [fejtʃi'sejru, a] ADJ
bewitching, enchanting ▶ M wizard
feitiço [fej'tʃisu] M charm, spell
feitio [fej'tʃiu] M shape, pattern; (caráter)
nature, manner; (Tec) workmanship
feito, -a ['fejtu, a] PP de **fazer** ▶ ADJ
finished, ready ▶ M act, deed; (façanha)
feat ▶ CONJ like; **~ a mão** hand-made;
homem ~ grown man
feiura [fe'jura] F ugliness
felicidade [felisi'dadʒi] F happiness;
(sorte) good luck; (êxito) success;
felicidades FPL (congratulações)
congratulations
felicitações [felisita'sõjs] FPL
congratulations, best wishes
feliz [fe'liz] ADJ happy; (afortunado) lucky;
felizmente [feliz'mẽtʃi] ADV
fortunately
feltro ['fewtru] M felt
fêmea ['femja] F female
feminino, -a [femi'ninu, a] ADJ
feminine; (sexo) female; (equipe, roupa)
women's ▶ M (Ling) feminine
feminista [femi'nista] ADJ, M/F
feminist
feno ['fenu] M hay

fenomenal [fenome'naw] (pl **-ais**) ADJ phenomenal; (*espantoso*) amazing; (*pessoa*) brilliant

fenômeno [fe'nomenu] M phenomenon

fera ['fɛra] F wild animal

feriado [fe'rjadu] M (public) holiday (BRIT), vacation (US)

férias ['fɛrjas] FPL holiday(s) (BRIT), vacation sg (US); **de ~** on holiday (BRIT) ou vacation (US); **tirar ~** to have ou take a holiday (BRIT) ou vacation (US)

ferida [fe'rida] F wound, injury; ver tb **ferido**

ferido, -a [fe'ridu, a] ADJ injured; (*em batalha*) wounded; (*magoado*) hurt ▸ M/F casualty

ferimento [feri'mẽtu] M injury; (*em batalha*) wound

ferir [fe'rir] VT to injure; (tb fig) to hurt; (*em batalha*) to wound; (*ofender*) to offend

fermentar [fermẽ'tar] VI to ferment

fermento [fer'mẽtu] M yeast; **~ em pó** baking powder

feroz [fe'rɔz] ADJ fierce, ferocious; (*cruel*) cruel

ferragem [fe'haʒẽ] (pl **-ns**) F (*peças*) hardware; (*guarnição*) metalwork; **loja de ferragens** ironmonger's (BRIT), hardware store (US)

ferramenta [feha'mẽta] F tool; (*caixa de ferramentas*) tool kit

ferrão [fe'hãw] (pl **-ões**) M goad; (*de inseto*) sting

ferrenho, -a [fe'heɲu, a] ADJ (*vontade*) iron

ferro ['fɛhu] M iron; **ferros** MPL (*algemas*) shackles, chains; **~ de passar** iron; **~ batido** wrought iron; **~ fundido** cast iron; **~ ondulado** corrugated iron

ferrões [fe'hõjs] MPL de **ferrão**

ferrolho [fe'hoʎu] M (*trinco*) bolt

ferrovia [feho'via] F railway (BRIT), railroad (US); **ferroviário, -a** [feho'vjarju, a] ADJ railway atr (BRIT), railroad atr (US) ▸ M/F railway ou railroad worker

ferrugem [fe'huʒẽ] F rust

fértil ['fɛrtʃiw] (pl **-eis**) ADJ fertile; **fertilizante** [fertʃili'zãtʃi] M fertilizer; **fertilizar** [fertʃili'zar] VT to fertilize

ferver [fer'ver] VT, VI to boil; **~ de raiva/ indignação** to seethe with rage/ indignation; **~ em fogo baixo** (*Culin*) to simmer

fervilhar [fervi'ʎar] VI to simmer; (*com atividade*) to hum; (*pulular*): **~ de** to swarm with

fervor [fer'vor] M fervour (BRIT), fervor (US)

festa ['fɛsta] F (*reunião*) party; (*conjunto de ceremônias*) festival; **festas** FPL (*carícia*) embrace; **boas ~s** Merry Christmas and a Happy New Year; **dia de ~** public holiday

festejar [feste'ʒar] VT to celebrate; (*acolher*) to welcome, greet; **festejo** [fes'teʒu] M festivity; (*ato*) celebration

festival [festʃi'vaw] (pl **-ais**) M festival

festividade [festʃivi'dadʒi] F festivity

festivo, -a [fes'tʃivu, a] ADJ festive

fetiche [fe'tʃiʃi] M fetish

feto ['fɛtu] M (*Med*) foetus (BRIT), fetus (US)

fevereiro [feve'rejru] M February

fez [fez] VB ver **fazer**

fezes ['fɛzis] FPL faeces (BRIT), feces (US)

fiado, -a ['fjadu, a] ADV: **comprar/ vender ~** to buy/sell on credit

fiador, a [fja'dor(a)] M/F (*Jur*) guarantor; (*Com*) backer

fiambre ['fjãbri] M cold meat; (*presunto*) ham

fiança ['fjãsa] F guarantee; (*Jur*) bail; **prestar ~ por** to stand bail for; **sob ~** on bail

fiar ['fjar] VT (*algodão etc*) to spin; (*confiar*) to entrust; (*vender a crédito*) to sell on credit; **fiar-se** VR: **~-se em** to trust

fibra ['fibra] F fibre (BRIT), fiber (US)

(PALAVRA-CHAVE)

ficar [fi'kar] VI **1** (*permanecer*) to stay; (*sobrar*) to be left; **ficar perguntando/ olhando** etc to keep asking/looking etc; **ficar por fazer** to have still to be done; **ficar para trás** to be left behind
2 (*tornar-se*) to become; **ficar cego/ surdo/louco** to go blind/deaf/mad; **fiquei contente ao saber da notícia** I was happy when I heard the news; **ficar com raiva/medo** to get angry/ frightened; **ficar de bem/mal com alguém** (*col*) to make up/fall out with sb
3 (*posição*) to be; **a casa fica ao lado da igreja** the house is next to the church; **ficar sentado/deitado** to be sitting down/lying down
4 (*tempo: durar*): **ele ficou duas horas para resolver** he took two hours to decide; (: *ser adiado*): **a reunião ficou para amanhã** the meeting has been postponed until tomorrow
5 (*comportamento*): **sua atitude não ficou bem** his (*ou* her *etc*) behaviour was inappropriate; (*cor*): **você fica bem em azul** blue suits you, you look good in blue; (*roupa*): **ficar bem para** to suit

6: **ficar bom** (de saúde) to be cured; (trabalho, foto etc) to turn out well
7: **ficar de fazer algo** (combinar) to arrange to do sth; (prometer) to promise to do sth
8: **ficar de pé** to stand up

ficção [fik'sãw] F fiction
ficha ['fiʃa] F (tb: ~ **de telefone**) token; (tb: ~ **de jogo**) chip; (de fichário) (index) card; (Polícia) record; (PT Elet) plug; (em loja, lanchonete) ticket
fichário [fi'ʃarju] M filing cabinet; (caixa) card index; (caderno) file
ficheiro [fi'ʃejru] (PT) M = **fichário**
fidelidade [fideli'dadʒi] F fidelity, loyalty; (exatidão) accuracy
fiel [fjew] ADJ (leal) faithful, loyal; (acurado) accurate; (que não falha) reliable
figa ['figa] F talisman; **fazer uma ~** to make a figa, ≈ cross one's fingers; **de uma ~** (col) damned
fígado ['figadu] M liver
figo ['figu] M fig; **figueira** [fi'gejra] F fig tree
figura [fi'gura] F figure; (forma) form, shape; (Ling) figure of speech; (aspecto) appearance
figurino [figu'rinu] M model; (revista) fashion magazine
fila ['fila] F row, line; (BR: fileira de pessoas) queue (BRIT), line (US); (num teatro, cinema) row; **em ~** in a row; **fazer ~** to form a line, queue; **~ indiana** single file
filé [fi'lɛ] M (bife) steak; (peixe) fillet
fileira [fi'lejra] F row, line; **fileiras** FPL (serviço militar) military service sg
filho, -a ['fiʎu, a] M/F son/daughter; **filhos** MPL children; (de animais) young; **~ da mãe, ~ da puta** (!) bastard (!)
filhote [fi'ʎɔtʃi] M (de leão, urso etc) cub; (cachorro) pup(py)
filial [fi'ljaw] (pl **-ais**) F (sucursal) branch
filipeta [fili'peta] F flyer
Filipinas [fili'pinas] FPL: **as ~** the Philippines
filmadora [fiwma'dora] F video camera
filmar [fiw'mar] VT, VI to film
filme ['fiwmi] M film (BRIT), movie (US)
filosofia [filozo'fia] F philosophy; **filósofo, -a** [fi'lɔzofu, a] M/F philosopher
filtrar [fiw'trar] VT to filter; **filtrar-se** VR to filter; (infiltrar-se) to infiltrate
filtro ['fiwtru] M (Tec) filter
fim [fĩ] (pl **-ns**) M end; (motivo) aim, purpose; (de história, filme) ending; **a ~ de** in order to; **no ~ das contas** after all;

por ~ finally; **sem ~** endless; **levar ao ~** to carry through; **pôr** ou **dar ~ a** to put an end to; **ter ~** to come to an end; **~ de semana** weekend
finado, -a [fi'nadu, a] ADJ, M/F deceased

> The day of **Finados**, 2 November, a holiday throughout Brazil, is dedicated to remembering the dead. On this day, people usually gather in cemeteries to remember their family dead, and also to worship at the graves of popular figures from Brazilian culture and society, such as singers, actors and other personalities. It is popularly believed that these people can work miracles.

final [fi'naw] ADJ final, last ▶ M end; (Mús) finale ▶ F (Esporte) final; **finalista** [fina'lista] M/F finalist; **finalizar** [finali'zar] VT to finish, conclude
finanças [fi'nãsas] FPL finance sg; **financeiro, -a** [finã'sejru, a] ADJ financial ▶ M/F financier; **financiar** [finã'sjar] VT to finance
fingimento [fiʒi'mẽtu] M pretence (BRIT), pretense (US)
fingir [fi'ʒir] VT to feign ▶ VI to pretend; **fingir-se** VR: **~-se de** to pretend to be
finito, -a [fi'nitu, a] ADJ finite
finlandês, -esa [filã'des, eza] ADJ Finnish ▶ M/F Finn ▶ M (Ling) Finnish
Finlândia [fi'lãdʒja] F: **a ~** Finland
fino, -a ['finu, a] ADJ fine; (delgado) slender; (educado) polite; (som, voz) shrill; (elegante) refined ▶ ADV: **falar ~** to talk in a high voice
fins [fĩs] MPL de **fim**
fio ['fiu] M thread; (Bot) fibre (BRIT), fiber (US); (Elet) wire; (Tel) line; (de líquido) trickle; (gume) edge; (encadeamento) series; **horas/dias a ~** hours/days on end; **sem ~** (Comput) wireless
firewall [faja'waw] M firewall
firma ['firma] F signature; (Com) firm, company
firmar [fir'mar] VT to secure, make firm; (assinar) to sign; (estabelecer) to establish; (basear) to base ▶ VI (tempo) to settle; **firmar-se** VR: **~-se em** (basear-se) to rest on, be based on
firme ['firmi] ADJ firm; (estável) stable; (sólido) solid; (tempo) settled ▶ ADV firmly; **firmeza** [fir'meza] F firmness; (estabilidade) stability; (solidez) solidity
fiscal [fis'kaw] (pl **-ais**) M/F supervisor; (aduaneiro) customs officer; (de impostos)

tax inspector; **fiscalizar** [fiskali'zar] VT to supervise; (*examinar*) to inspect, check

fisco ['fisku] M: **o ~** ≈ the Inland Revenue (*BRIT*), ≈ the Internal Revenue Service (*US*)

física ['fizika] F physics *sg*; *ver tb* **físico**

físico, -a ['fiziku, a] ADJ physical ► M/F (*cientista*) physicist ► M (*corpo*) physique

fisionomia [fizjono'mia] F (*rosto*) face; (*ar*) expression, look; (*aspecto de algo*) appearance

fissura [fi'sura] F crack

fita ['fita] F (*tira*) strip, band; (*filme*) film; (*para máquina de escrever*) ribbon; (*magnética, adesiva*) tape; **~ durex**® adhesive tape, Sellotape® (*BRIT*), Scotch tape® (*US*); **~ métrica** tape measure

fitar [fi'tar] VT to stare at, gaze at

fivela [fi'vela] F buckle

fixar [fik'sar] VT to fix; (*colar, prender*) to stick; (*data, prazo, regras*) to set; (*atenção*) to concentrate; **fixar-se** VR: **~-se em** (*assunto*) to concentrate on; (*detalhe*) to fix on; (*apegar-se a*) to be attached to; **~ os olhos em** to stare at; **~ residência** to set up house

fixo, -a ['fiksu, a] ADJ fixed; (*firme*) firm; (*permanente*) permanent; (*cor*) fast ► M (*tb*: **telefone ~**) landline

fiz [fiz] VB *ver* **fazer**

flagelado, -a [flaʒe'ladu, a] M/F: **os ~s** the afflicted, the victims

flagrante [fla'grãtʃi] ADJ flagrant; **apanhar em ~ (delito)** to catch red-handed *ou* in the act

flagrar [fla'grar] VT to catch

flanela [fla'nɛla] F flannel

flash [flaʃ] M (*Foto*) flash

flauta ['flawta] F flute

flecha ['flɛʃa] F arrow

fleuma ['flewma] F phlegm

floco ['flɔku] M flake; **~ de milho** cornflake; **~ de neve** snowflake

flor [flor] F flower; (*o melhor*) cream, pick; **em ~** in bloom; **à ~ da pele** on edge

florescente [flore'sẽtʃi] ADJ (*Bot*) in flower; (*próspero*) flourishing

florescer [flore'ser] VI (*Bot*) to flower; (*prosperar*) to flourish

floresta [flo'rɛsta] F forest; **florestal** [flores'taw] (*pl* **florestais**) ADJ forest *atr*

florido, -a [flo'ridu, a] ADJ (*jardim*) in flower

fluente [flu'ẽtʃi] ADJ fluent

fluido, -a ['flwidu, a] ADJ fluid ► M fluid

fluir [flwir] VI to flow

fluminense [flumi'nẽsi] ADJ from the state of Rio de Janeiro ► M/F native *ou* inhabitant of the state of Rio de Janeiro

flutuar [flu'twar] VI to float; (*bandeira*) to flutter; (*fig: vacilar*) to waver

fluvial [flu'vjaw] (*pl* **-ais**) ADJ river *atr*

fluxo ['fluksu] M (*corrente*) flow; (*Elet*) flux; **~ de caixa** (*Com*) cash flow

fobia [fo'bia] F phobia

foca ['fɔka] F seal

foco ['fɔku] M focus; (*Med, fig*) seat, centre (*BRIT*), center (*US*); **fora de ~** out of focus

fofo, -a ['fofu, a] ADJ soft; (*col: pessoa*) cute

fofoca [fo'fɔka] F piece of gossip; **fofocas** FPL (*mexericos*) gossip *sg*; **fofocar** [fofo'kar] VI to gossip

fogão [fo'gãw] (*pl* **-ões**) M stove, cooker

fogareiro [foga'rejru] M stove

foge ['fɔʒi] VB *ver* **fugir**

fogo ['fogu] M fire; (*fig*) ardour (*BRIT*), ardor (*US*); **você tem ~?** have you got a light?; **~ de artifício** fireworks; **pôr ~ a** to set fire to

fogões [fo'gõjs] MPL *de* **fogão**

fogueira [fo'gejra] F bonfire

foguete [fo'getʃi] M rocket

foi [foj] VB *ver* **ir**, **ser**

folclore [fowk'lori] M folklore

folclórico, -a [fowk'lɔriku, a] ADJ (*música etc*) folk *atr*; (*comida, roupa*) ethnic

fôlego ['folegu] M breath; (*folga*) breathing space; **perder o ~** to get out of breath

folga ['fɔwga] F rest, break; (*espaço livre*) clearance; (*ócio*) inactivity; (*col: atrevimento*) cheek; **dia de ~** day off; **folgado, -a** [fow'gadu, a] ADJ (*roupa*) loose; (*vida*) leisurely; (*col: atrevido*) cheeky; **folgar** [fow'gar] VT to loosen ► VI (*descansar*) to rest; (*divertir-se*) to have fun

folha ['foʎa] F leaf; (*de papel, de metal*) sheet; (*página*) page; (*de faca*) blade; (*jornal*) paper; **novo em ~** brand new; **~ de estanho** tinfoil (*BRIT*), aluminum foil (*US*); **~ de exercícios** worksheet

folhagem [fo'ʎaʒẽ] F foliage

folheto [fo'ʎetu] M booklet, pamphlet

fome ['fɔmi] F hunger; (*escassez*) famine; (*fig: avidez*) longing; **passar ~** to go hungry; **estar com** *ou* **ter ~** to be hungry

fone ['fɔni] M telephone, phone; (*peça do telefone*) receiver

fonte ['fõtʃi] F (*nascente*) spring; (*chafariz*) fountain; (*origem*) source; (*Anat*) temple

for [for] VB *ver* **ir**, **ser**

fora¹ ['fɔra] ADV out, outside ► PREP (*além de*) apart from ► M: **dar o ~** (*bateria, radio*) to give out; (*pessoa*) to leave, be off;

dar um ~ to slip up; **dar um ~ em alguém** (*namorado*) to chuck sb, dump sb; (*esnobar*) to snub sb; **levar um ~** (*de namorado*) to be given the boot; (*ser esnobado*) to get the brush-off; **~ de** outside; **~ de si** beside o.s.; **estar ~** (*viajando*) to be away; **estar ~ (de casa)** to be out; **lá ~** outside; (*no exterior*) abroad; **jantar ~** to eat out; **com os braços de ~** with bare arms; **ser de ~** to be from out of town; **ficar de ~** not to join in; **lá para ~** outside; **ir para ~** (*viajar*) to go out of town; **com a cabeça para ~ da janela** with one's head sticking out of the window; **costurar/cozinhar para ~** to do sewing/cooking for other people; **por ~** on the outside; **cobrar por ~** to charge extra; **~ de dúvida** beyond doubt; **~ de propósito** irrelevant

fora² VB *ver* **ir, ser**
foragido, -a [fora'ʒidu, a] ADJ, M/F fugitive; **estar ~** to be on the run
forasteiro, -a [foras'tejru, a] M/F outsider, stranger; (*de outro país*) foreigner
força ['forsa] F strength; (*Tec, Elet*) power; (*esforço*) effort; (*coerção*) force; **à ~** by force; **à ~ de** by dint of; **com ~** hard; **por ~** of necessity; **fazer ~** to try (hard); **~ de trabalho** workforce
forçado, -a [for'sadu, a] ADJ forced; (*afetado*) false
forçar [for'sar] VT to force; (*olhos, voz*) to strain
forma ['forma] F form; (*de um objeto*) shape; (*físico*) figure; (*maneira*) way; (*Med*) fitness; **desta ~** in this way; **de qualquer ~** anyway; **manter a ~** to keep fit
fôrma ['forma] F (*Culin*) cake tin; (*molde*) mould (BRIT), mold (US)
formação [forma'sãw] (*pl* -**ões**) F formation; (*antecedentes*) background; (*caráter*) make-up; (*profissional*) training
formado, -a [for'madu, a] ADJ (*modelado*): **ser ~ de** to consist of ▶ M/F graduate
formal [for'maw] (*pl* -**ais**) ADJ formal; **formalidade** [formali'dadʒi] F formality
formar [for'mar] VT to form; (*constituir*) to constitute, make up; (*educar*) to train; **formar-se** VR to form; (*Educ*) to graduate
formatar [forma'tar] VT (*Comput*) to format
formidável [formi'davew] (*pl* -**eis**) ADJ tremendous, great
formiga [for'miga] F ant

formigar [formi'gar] VI to abound; (*sentir comichão*) to itch
formoso, -a [for'mozu, ɔza] ADJ beautiful; (*esplêndido*) superb
fórmula ['fɔrmula] F formula
formular [formu'lar] VT to formulate; (*queixas*) to voice
formulário [formu'larju] M form; **formulários** MPL: **~s contínuos** (*Comput*) continuous stationery *sg*
fornecedor, a [fornese'dor(a)] M/F supplier ▶ F (*empresa*) supplier
fornecer [forne'ser] VT to supply, provide; **fornecimento** [fornesi'mẽtu] M supply
forno ['fornu] M (*Culin*) oven; (*Tec*) furnace; (*para cerâmica*) kiln; **alto ~** blast furnace
foro ['foru] M forum; (*Jur*) Court of Justice; **foros** MPL (*privilégios*) privileges
forro ['fohu] M covering; (*interior*) lining
forró [fo'hɔ] M *see note*

> **Forró** is a style of popular music and dance that originated in the north-east of Brazil, but which is now popular all over the country. The instruments which feature in **forró** are the accordion, the bass drum and the triangle, and it is danced with a partner. There are a number of different styles of **forró**, such as the faster-paced *forró universitário*, which has attracted a considerable following among the younger generation in Brazil's cities.

fortalecer [fortale'ser] VT to strengthen
fortaleza [forta'leza] F fortress; (*força*) strength; (*moral*) fortitude
forte ['fɔrtʃi] ADJ strong; (*pancada*) hard; (*chuva*) heavy; (*som*) loud; (*dor*) sharp ▶ ADV strongly; (*som*) loud(ly) ▶ M fort; (*talento*) strength; **ser ~ em algo** (*versado*) to be good at sth *ou* strong in sth
fortuito, -a [for'twitu, a] ADJ accidental
fortuna [for'tuna] F fortune, (good) luck; (*riqueza*) fortune, wealth
fórum ['fɔrũ] (*pl* -**ns**) M (*Comput*) forum; **~ de discussão** discussion forum, message board
fosco, -a ['fosku, a] ADJ dull; (*opaco*) opaque
fósforo ['fɔsforu] M match
fossa ['fɔsa] F pit
fosse ['fosi] VB *ver* **ir, ser**
fóssil ['fɔsiw] (*pl* -**eis**) M fossil
fosso ['fosu] M trench, ditch
foto ['fɔtu] F photo

fotocópia [foto'kɔpja] F photocopy; **fotocopiadora** [fotokopja'dora] F photocopier; **fotocopiar** [fotoko'pjar] VT to photocopy

fotografar [fotogra'far] VT to photograph

fotografia [fotogra'fia] F photography; (*uma foto*) photograph

fotógrafo, -a [fo'tɔgrafu, a] M/F photographer

foz [fɔz] F mouth (*of river*)

fração [fra'sãw] (*pl* **-ões**) F fraction

fracassar [fraka'sar] VI to fail; **fracasso** [fra'kasu] M failure

fraco, -a ['fraku, a] ADJ weak; (*sol, som*) faint

frágil ['fraʒiw] (*pl* **-eis**) ADJ (*débil*) fragile; (*Com*) breakable; (*pessoa*) frail; (*saúde*) delicate, poor

fragmento [frag'mẽtu] M fragment

fragrância [fra'grãsja] F fragrance, perfume

fralda ['frawda] F (*da camisa*) shirt tail; (*para bebê*) nappy (BRIT), diaper (US); (*de montanha*) foot

framboesa [frãbo'eza] F raspberry

França ['frãsa] F France

francamente [frãka'mẽtʃi] ADV (*abertamente*) frankly; (*realmente*) really

francês, -esa [frã'ses, eza] ADJ French ▶ M/F Frenchman/woman ▶ M (*Ling*) French

franco, -a ['frãku, a] ADJ frank; (*isento de pagamento*) free; (*óbvio*) clear ▶ M franc; **entrada franca** free admission

frango ['frãgu] M chicken

franja ['frãʒa] F fringe (BRIT), bangs *pl* (US)

franquia [frã'kia] F (*Com*) franchise; (*isenção*) exemption

franzino, -a [frã'zinu, a] ADJ skinny

fraqueza [fra'keza] F weakness

frasco ['frasku] M bottle

frase ['frazi] F sentence; **~ feita** set phrase

fratura [fra'tura] F fracture, break; **fraturar** [fratu'rar] VT to fracture

freada [fre'ada] (BR) F: **dar uma ~** to slam on the brakes

frear [fre'ar] (BR) VT to curb, restrain; (*veículo*) to stop ▶ VI (*veículo*) to brake

freezer ['frizer] M freezer

freguês, -guesa ['fre'ges, 'geza] M/F customer; (PT) parishioner; **freguesia** [frege'zia] F customers *pl*; (PT) parish

freio ['freju] M (BR: *veículo*) brake; (*de cavalo*) bridle; (*bocado do freio*) bit; **~ de mão** handbrake

freira ['frejra] F nun

frenesi [frene'zi] M frenzy; **frenético, -a** [fre'netʃiku, a] ADJ frantic, frenzied

frente ['frẽtʃi] F front; (*rosto*) face; (*fachada*) façade; **~ a ~** face to face; **de ~ para** facing; **em ~ de** in front of; (*de fronte a*) opposite; **para a ~** ahead, forward; **porta da ~** front door; **seguir em ~** to go straight on; **na minha** (*ou* **sua** *etc*) **~** in front of me (*ou* you *etc*); **sair da ~** to get out of the way; **pra ~** (*col*) fashionable, trendy

frequência [fre'kwẽsja] F frequency; **com ~** often, frequently

frequentar [frekwẽ'tar] VT to frequent

frequente [fre'kwẽtʃi] ADJ frequent

fresco, -a ['fresku, a] ADJ fresh; (*vento, tempo*) cool; (*col: efeminado*) camp; (: *afetado*) pretentious; (: *cheio de luxo*) fussy ▶ M (*ar*) fresh air

frescobol [fresko'bɔw] M (kind of) racketball (*played mainly on the beach*)

frescura [fres'kura] F freshness; (*frialdade*) coolness; (*col: luxo*) fussiness; (: *afetaçao*) pretentiousness

frete ['frɛtʃi] M (*carregamento*) freight, cargo; (*tarifa*) freightage

frevo ['frevu] M *improvised Carnival dance*

fria ['fria] F: **dar uma ~ em alguém** to give sb the cold shoulder; **estar/entrar numa ~** (*col*) to be in/get into a mess

fricção [frik'sãw] F friction; (*ato*) rubbing; (*Med*) massage; **friccionar** [friksjo'nar] VT to rub

frieza ['frjeza] F coldness; (*indiferença*) coolness

frigideira [friʒi'dejra] F frying pan

frigorífico [frigo'rifiku] M refrigerator; (*congelador*) freezer

frio, -a ['friu, a] ADJ cold ▶ M coldness; **frios** MPL (*Culin*) cold meats; **estou com ~** I'm cold; **faz** *ou* **está ~** it's cold

frisar [fri'zar] VT (*encrespar*) to curl; (*salientar*) to emphasize

fritar [fri'tar] VT to fry

fritas ['fritas] FPL French fries, chips (BRIT)

frito, -a ['fritu, a] ADJ fried; (*col*): **estar ~** to be done for

frívolo, -a ['frivolu, a] ADJ frivolous

fronha ['frona] F pillowcase

fronteira [frõ'tejra] F frontier, border

frota ['frota] F fleet

frouxo, -a ['frofu, a] ADJ loose; (*corda*) slack; (*fraco*) weak; (*col: condescendente*) soft

frustrar [frus'trar] VT to frustrate

fruta ['fruta] F fruit; **frutífero, -a** [fru'tʃiferu, a] ADJ (*proveitoso*) fruitful; (*árvore*) fruit-bearing

fruto ['frutu] M (*Bot*) fruit; (*resultado*) result, product; **dar ~** (*fig*) to bear fruit

fubá [fu'ba] M corn meal

fugir [fu'ʒir] VI to flee, escape; (*prisioneiro*) to escape

fui [fuj] VB *ver* **ir, ser**

fulano, -a [fu'lanu, a] M/F so-and-so

fulminante [fuwmi'nãtʃi] ADJ devastating; (*palavras*) scathing

fulo, -a ['fulu, a] ADJ: **estar** *ou* **ficar ~ de raiva** to be furious

fumaça [fu'masa] (BR) F (*de fogo*) smoke; (*de gás*) fumes *pl*

fumador, a [fuma'dor(a)] (PT) M/F smoker

fumante [fu'mãtʃi] M/F smoker

fumar [fu'mar] VT, VI to smoke

fumo ['fumu] M (PT: *de fogo*) smoke; (: *de gás*) fumes *pl*; (BR: *tabaco*) tobacco; (*fumar*) smoking

função [fũ'sãw] (*pl* **-ões**) F function; (*ofício*) duty; (*papel*) role; (*espetáculo*) performance

funcionalismo [fũsjona'lizmu] M: **~ público** civil service

funcionamento [fũsjona'mẽtu] M functioning, working; **pôr em ~** to set going, start

funcionar [fũsjo'nar] VI to function; (*máquina*) to work, run; (*dar bom resultado*) to work

funcionário, -a [fũsjo'narju, a] M/F official; **~ (público)** civil servant

funções [fũ'sõjs] FPL *de* **função**

fundação [fũda'sãw] (*pl* **-ões**) F foundation

fundamental [fũdamẽ'taw] (*pl* **-ais**) ADJ fundamental, basic

fundamento [fũda'mẽtu] M (*fig*) foundation, basis; (*motivo*) motive

fundar [fũ'dar] VT to establish, found; (*basear*) to base; **fundar-se** VR: **~-se em** to be based on

fundir [fũ'dʒir] VT to fuse; (*metal*) to smelt, melt down; (*Com: empresas*) to merge; (*em molde*) to cast; **fundir-se** VR to melt; (*juntar-se*) to merge

fundo, -a ['fũdu, a] ADJ deep; (*fig*) profound ▶ M (*do mar, jardim*) bottom; (*profundidade*) depth; (*base*) basis; (*da loja, casa, do papel*) back; (*de quadro*) background; (*de dinheiro*) fund ▶ ADV deeply; **fundos** MPL (*Com*) funds; (*da casa etc*) back *sg*; **a ~** thoroughly; **no ~** at the bottom; (*da casa etc*) at the back; (*fig*) basically

fúnebre ['funebri] ADJ funeral *atr*, funereal; (*fig*) gloomy

funeral [fune'raw] (*pl* **-ais**) M funeral

funil [fu'niw] (*pl* **-is**) M funnel

furacão [fura'kãw] (*pl* **-ões**) M hurricane

furado, -a [fu'radu, a] ADJ perforated; (*pneu*) flat; (*orelha*) pierced

furão, -rona [fu'rãw, 'rɔna] (*pl* **-ões/-s**) M ferret ▶ M/F (*col*) go-getter ▶ ADJ (*col*) hard-working, dynamic

furar [fu'rar] VT to perforate; (*penetrar*) to penetrate; (*frustrar*) to foil; (*fila*) to jump ▶ VI (*col: programa*) to fall through

fúria ['furja] F fury, rage; **furioso, -a** [fu'rjozu, ɔza] ADJ furious

furo ['furu] M hole; (*num pneu*) puncture

furões [fu'rõjs] MPL *de* **furão**

furona [fu'rɔna] F *de* **furão**

furor [fu'ror] M fury, rage; **fazer ~** to be all the rage

furtar [fur'tar] VT, VI to steal; **furtar-se** VR: **~-se a** to avoid

furtivo, -a [fur'tʃivu, a] ADJ furtive, stealthy

furto ['furtu] M theft

fusível [fu'zivew] (*pl* **-eis**) M (*Elet*) fuse

fuso ['fuzu] M (*Tec*) spindle; **~ horário** time zone

futebol [futʃi'bɔw] M football; **~ de salão** indoor football

futevôlei [futʃi'volej] M *see note*

> **Futevôlei** is a type of volleyball in which the ball is allowed to touch only the feet, legs, trunk and head of the players. It is very popular on the beaches of Rio de Janeiro, where tournaments take place during the summer, in which many famous footballers take part.

fútil ['futʃiw] (*pl* **-eis**) ADJ (*pessoa*) shallow; (*insignificante*) trivial

futilidade [futʃili'dadʒi] F (*de pessoa*) shallowness; (*insignificância*) triviality; (*coisa fútil*) trivial thing

futuro, -a [fu'turu, a] ADJ future ▶ M future; **no ~** in the future

fuzil [fu'ziw] (*pl* **-is**) M rifle; **fuzilar** [fuzi'lar] VT to shoot

fuzis [fu'zis] MPL *de* **fuzil**

g ABR (= *grama*) gr.

gabar [ga'bar] vт to praise; **gabar-se** vʀ: **~-se de** to boast about

gabinete [gabi'netʃi] м (*Com*) office; (*escritório*) study; (*Pol*) cabinet

gado ['gadu] м livestock; (*bovino*) cattle; **~ leiteiro** dairy cattle; **~ suíno** pigs *pl*

gafanhoto [gafa'ɲotu] м grasshopper

gafe ['gafi] ꜰ gaffe, faux pas

gagueira [ga'gejra] ꜰ stutter

gaguejar [gage'ʒar] vi to stammer, stutter

gaiato, -a [ga'jatu, a] ADJ funny

gaiola [ga'jɔla] ꜰ cage; (*cadeia*) jail ▶ м (*barco*) riverboat

gaita ['gajta] ꜰ harmonica; **~ de foles** bagpipes *pl*

gaivota [gaj'vɔta] ꜰ seagull

gajo ['gaʒu] (ᴘᴛ *col*) м guy, fellow

gala ['gala] ꜰ: **traje de ~** evening dress; **festa de ~** gala

galão [ga'lãw] (*pl* **-ões**) м (*Mil*) stripe; (*medida*) gallon; (ᴘᴛ: *café*) white coffee; (*passamanaria*) braid

Galápagos [ga'lapagus] N: **(as) Ilhas ~** (the) Galapagos Islands

galáxia [ga'laksja] м galaxy

galera [ga'lera] ꜰ (*Náut*) galley; (*col: pessoas, público*) crowd

galeria [gale'ria] ꜰ gallery; (*Teatro*) circle

Gales ['galis] м: **País de ~** Wales

galho ['gaʎu] м (*de árvore*) branch

galinha [ga'liɲa] ꜰ hen; (*Culin*) chicken; **galinheiro** [gali'ɲejru] м hen-house

galo ['galu] м cock, rooster; (*inchação*) bump; **missa do ~** midnight mass

galões [ga'lõjs] мᴘʟ *de* **galão**

galopar [galo'par] vi to gallop; **galope** [ga'lɔpi] м gallop

gama ['gama] ꜰ (*Mús*) scale; (*fig*) range; (*Zool*) doe

gambá [gã'ba] м (*Zool*) opossum

game ['geimi] м computer game

Gana ['gana] м Ghana

gana ['gana] ꜰ craving, desire; (*ódio*) hate; **ter ~s de (fazer) algo** to feel like (doing) sth; **ter ~ de alguém** to hate sb

ganância [ga'nãsja] ꜰ greed; **ganancioso, -a** [ganã'sjozu, ɔza] ADJ greedy

gancho ['gãʃu] м hook; (*de calça*) crotch

gangue ['gãgi] (*col*) ꜰ gang

ganhador, a [gaɲa'dor(a)] ADJ winning ▶ м/ꜰ winner

ganha-pão ['gaɲa-] (*pl* **-pães**) м living, livelihood

ganhar [ga'ɲar] vт to win; (*salário*) to earn; (*adquirir*) to get; (*lugar*) to reach; (*lucrar*) to gain ▶ vi to win; **~ de alguém** (*num jogo*) to beat sb; **ganho** ['gaɲu] ᴘᴘ *de* **ganhar** ▶ м profit, gain; **ganhos** мᴘʟ (*ao jogo*) winnings

ganso, -a ['gãsu, a] м/ꜰ goose

garagem [ga'raʒẽ] (*pl* **-ns**) ꜰ garage

garantia [garã'tʃia] ꜰ guarantee; (*de dívida*) surety

garçom [gar'sõ] (ʙʀ) (*pl* **-ns**) м waiter

garçonete [garso'netʃi] (ʙʀ) ꜰ waitress

garçons [gar'sõs] мᴘʟ *de* **garçom**

garfo ['garfu] м fork

gargalhada [garga'ʎada] ꜰ burst of laughter; **rir às ~s** to roar with laughter; **dar** *ou* **soltar uma ~** to burst out laughing

gargalo [gar'galu] м (*tb fig*) bottleneck

garganta [gar'gãta] ꜰ throat; (*Geo*) gorge, ravine

gargarejo [garga'reʒu] м (*ato*) gargling; (*líquido*) gargle

gari [ga'ri] м/ꜰ (*na rua*) road sweeper (ʙʀɪᴛ), street sweeper (ᴜs); (*lixeiro*) dustman (ʙʀɪᴛ), garbage man (ᴜs)

garoa [ga'roa] ꜰ drizzle; **garoar** [ga'rwar] vi to drizzle

garotada [garo'tada] ꜰ: **a ~** the kids *pl*

garoto, -a [ga'rotu, a] м/ꜰ boy/girl ▶ м (ʙʀ: *chope*) small beer; (ᴘᴛ: *café*) coffee with milk

garoupa [ga'ropa] ꜰ (*peixe*) grouper

garrafa [ga'hafa] ꜰ bottle

garupa [ga'rupa] ꜰ (*de cavalo*) hindquarters *pl*; (*de moto*) back seat; **andar na ~** (*de moto*) to ride pillion

gás [gajs] м gas; **gases** мᴘʟ (*do intestino*) wind *sg*; **~ natural** natural gas; **~ de efeito estufa** greenhouse gas

gasóleo [ga'zɔlju] м diesel oil

gasolina [gazo'lina] ꜰ petrol (ʙʀɪᴛ), gas(oline) (ᴜs)

gasosa [ga'zɔza] F fizzy drink
gasoso, -a [ga'zozu, ɔza] ADJ (água) sparkling; (bebida) fizzy
gastador, -deira [gasta'dor, 'dejra] ADJ, M/F spendthrift
gastar [gas'tar] VT to spend; (gasolina, electricidade) to use; (roupa, sapato) to wear out; (salto, piso etc) to wear down; (saúde) to damage; (desperdiçar) to waste ▶ VI to spend; to wear out; to wear down; **gastar-se** VR to wear out; to wear down
gástrico, -a ['gastriku, a] ADJ gastric
gata ['gata] F (she-)cat
gatilho [ga'tiʎu] M trigger
gato ['gatu] M cat; **~ montês** wild cat
gatuno, -a [ga'tunu, a] ADJ thieving ▶ M/F thief
gaveta [ga'veta] F drawer
geada ['ʒjada] F frost
geladeira [ʒela'dejra] (BR) F refrigerator, icebox (US)
gelado, -a [ʒe'ladu, a] ADJ frozen ▶ M (PT: sorvete) ice cream
gelar [ʒe'lar] VT to freeze; (vinho etc) to chill ▶ VI to freeze
gelatina [ʒela'tʃina] F gelatine; (sobremesa) jelly (BRIT), Jell-O® (US)
geleia [ʒe'lɛja] F jam
gélido, -a ['ʒɛlidu, a] ADJ chill, icy
gelo ['ʒelu] ADJ INV light grey (BRIT) ou gray (US) ▶ M ice; (cor) light grey (BRIT) ou gray (US)
gema ['ʒema] F yolk; (pedra preciosa) gem
gêmeo, -a ['ʒemju, a] ADJ, M/F twin; **Gêmeos** MPL (Astrologia) Gemini sg
gemer [ʒe'mer] VI (de dor) to groan, moan; (lamentar-se) to wail; (animal) to whine; (vento) to howl; **gemido** [ʒe'midu] M groan, moan; (lamento) wail; (de animal) whine
gene ['ʒɛni] M gene
Genebra [ʒe'nɛbra] N Geneva
general [ʒene'raw] (pl -ais) M general
generalizar [ʒenerali'zar] VT to propagate ▶ VI to generalize; **generalizar-se** VR to become general, spread
gênero ['ʒeneru] M type, kind; (Bio) genus; (Ling) gender; **gêneros** MPL (produtos) goods; **~s alimentícios** foodstuffs; **~ humano** humankind, human race
generosidade [ʒenerozi'dadʒi] F generosity
generoso, -a [ʒene'rozu, ɔza] ADJ generous
genética [ʒe'nɛtʃika] F genetics sg

gengibre [ʒẽ'ʒibri] M ginger
gengiva [ʒẽ'ʒiva] F (Anat) gum
genial [ʒe'njaw] (pl -ais) ADJ inspired, brilliant; (col) terrific, fantastic
gênio ['ʒenju] M (temperamento) nature; (irascibilidade) temper; (talento, pessoa) genius; **de bom ~** good-natured; **de mau ~** bad-tempered
genital [ʒeni'taw] (pl -ais) ADJ: **órgãos genitais** genitals pl
genoma [ʒe'noma] M genome
genro ['ʒẽhu] M son-in-law
gente ['ʒẽtʃi] F people pl; (col) folks pl; (col: alguém): **tem ~ batendo à porta** there's somebody battering at the door; **a ~** (nós: suj) we; (: obj) us; **a casa da ~** our house; **toda a ~** everybody; **~ grande** grown-ups pl
gentil [ʒẽ'tʃiw] (pl -is) ADJ kind; **gentileza** [ʒẽtʃi'leza] F kindness; **por gentileza** if you please; **tenha a gentileza de fazer ...** would you be so kind as to do ...?
genuíno, -a [ʒe'nwinu, a] ADJ genuine
geografia [ʒeogra'fia] F geography
geometria [ʒeome'tria] F geometry
geração [ʒera'sãw] (pl -ões) F generation
gerador, a [ʒera'dor(a)] M/F (produtor) creator ▶ M (Tec) generator
geral [ʒe'raw] (pl -ais) ADJ general ▶ F (Teatro) gallery; **em ~** in general, generally; **de um modo ~** on the whole; **geralmente** [ʒeraw'mẽtʃi] ADV generally, usually
gerânio [ʒe'ranju] M geranium
gerar [ʒe'rar] VT to produce; (eletricidade) to generate
gerência [ʒe'rẽsja] F management; **gerenciar** [ʒerẽ'sjar] VT, VI to manage
gerente [ʒe'rẽtʃi] ADJ managing ▶ M/F manager
gerir [ʒe'rir] VT to manage, run
germe ['ʒermi] M (embrião) embryo; (micróbio) germ
gesso ['ʒesu] M plaster (of Paris)
gesticular [ʒestʃiku'lar] VI to make gestures, gesture
gesto ['ʒɛstu] M gesture
Gibraltar [ʒibraw'tar] F Gibraltar
gigabyte [ʒiga'bajtʃi] M gigabyte
gigante, -a [ʒi'gãtʃi, a] ADJ gigantic, huge ▶ M giant; **gigantesco, -a** [ʒigã'tesku, a] ADJ gigantic
gim [ʒĩ] (pl -ns) M gin
ginásio [ʒi'nazju] M gymnasium; (escola) secondary (BRIT) ou high (US) school
ginástica [ʒi'nastʃika] F gymnastics sg; (para fortalecer o corpo) keep-fit

ginecologia [ʒinekolo'ʒia] F
gynaecology (BRIT), gynecology (US)
ginecologista [ʒinekolo'ʒista] M/F
gynaecologist (BRIT), gynecologist (US)
ginjinha [ʒi'ʒiɲa] (PT) F cherry brandy
gira-discos (PT) M INV record-player
girafa [ʒi'rafa] F giraffe
girar [ʒi'rar] VT to turn, rotate; (*como
pião*) to spin ▶ VI to go round; to spin;
(*vaguear*) to wander
girassol [ʒira'sɔw] (*pl* -**óis**) M sunflower
gíria ['ʒirja] F (*calão*) slang; (*jargão*) jargon
giro[1] ['ʒiru] M turn; **dar um ~** to go for a
wander; (*em veículo*) to go for a spin;
que ~! (PT) great!
giro[2] VB *ver* **gerir**
giz [ʒiz] M chalk
glacê [gla'se] M icing
glacial [gla'sjaw] (*pl* -**ais**) ADJ icy
glamouroso, -a [glamu'rozu, ɔza] ADJ
glamorous
glândula ['glãdula] F gland
global [glo'baw] (*pl* -**ais**) ADJ global;
(*total*) overall; **quantia ~** lump sum;
globalização [globaliza'sãw] F
globalization
globo ['globu] M globe; **~ ocular** eyeball
glória ['glɔrja] F glory; **glorificar**
[glorifi'kar] VT to glorify; **glorioso, -a**
[glo'rjozu, ɔza] ADJ glorious
glossário [glo'sarju] M glossary
gnomo ['gnomu] M gnome
goiaba [go'jaba] F guava; **goiabada**
[goja'bada] F guava jelly
gol [gow] (*pl* **gols**) M goal
gola ['gɔla] F collar
gole ['gɔli] M gulp, swallow; (*pequeno*)
sip; **dar um ~** to have a sip
goleiro [go'lejru] (BR) M goalkeeper; (*col*)
goalie
golfe ['gowfi] M golf; **campo de ~** golf
course
golfinho [gow'fiɲu] M (*Zool*) dolphin
golfo ['gowfu] M gulf
golinho [go'liɲu] M sip; **beber algo
aos ~s** to sip sth
golo ['golu] (PT) M = **gol**
golpe ['gɔwpi] M (*tb fig*) blow; (*de mão*)
smack; (*de punho*) punch; (*manobra*) ploy;
(*de vento*) gust; **de um só ~** at a stroke;
dar um ~ em alguém to hit sb; (*fig:
trapacear*) to trick sb; **~ (de estado)** coup
(d'état); **~ de mestre** masterstroke;
golpear [gow'pjar] VT to hit; (*com
navalha*) to stab; (*com o punho*) to punch
goma ['gɔma] F gum, glue; (*de roupa*)
starch; **~ de mascar** chewing gum
gomo ['gomu] M (*de laranja*) slice

gordo, -a ['gordu, a] ADJ fat; (*gordurento*)
greasy; (*carne*) fatty; (*fig: quantia*)
considerable, ample ▶ M/F fat man/
woman
gordura [gor'dura] F fat; (*derretida*)
grease; (*obesidade*) fatness; **gorduroso,
-a** [gordu'rozu, ɔza] ADJ (*pele*) greasy;
(*comida*) fatty
gorila [go'rila] M gorilla
gorjeta [gor'ʒeta] F tip, gratuity
gorro ['gohu] M cap; (*de lã*) hat
gosma ['gɔzma] F spittle; (*fig*) slime
gostar [gos'tar] VI: **~ de** to like; (*férias,
viagem etc*) to enjoy; **gostar-se** VR to like
each other; **~ mais de ...** to prefer ..., to
like ... better
gosto ['gostu] M taste; (*prazer*) pleasure;
a seu ~ to your liking; **com ~** willingly;
(*vestir-se*) tastefully; (*comer*) heartily; **de
bom/mau ~** in good/bad taste; **ter ~ de**
to taste of; **gostoso, -a** [gos'tozu, ɔza]
ADJ tasty; (*agradável*) pleasant; (*cheiro*)
lovely; (*risada*) good; (*col: pessoa*)
gorgeous
gota ['gota] F drop; (*de suor*) bead; (*Med*)
gout; **~ a ~** drop by drop
goteira [go'tejra] F (*cano*) gutter;
(*buraco*) leak
gourmet [gur'me] (*pl* -**s**) M/F gourmet
governador, a [governador(a)] M/F
governor
governamental [governamẽ'taw]
(*pl* -**ais**) ADJ government atr
governante [gover'nãtʃi] ADJ ruling
▶ M/F ruler ▶ F governess
governar [gover'nar] VT to govern, rule;
(*barco*) to steer
governo [go'vernu] M government;
(*controle*) control
gozação [goza'sãw] (*pl* -**ões**) F
enjoyment; (*zombaria*) teasing; (*uma
gozação*) joke
gozado, -a [go'zadu, a] ADJ funny;
(*estranho*) strange, odd
gozar [go'zar] VT to enjoy; (*col: rir de*) to
make fun of ▶ VI to enjoy o.s.; **~ de** to
enjoy; to make fun of; **gozo** ['gozu] M
(*prazer*) pleasure; (*uso*) enjoyment, use;
(*orgasmo*) orgasm
GPS ABR M (= *global positioning system*) GPS
Grã-Bretanha [grã-bre'taɲa] F Great
Britain
graça ['grasa] F (*Rel*) grace; (*charme*)
charm; (*gracejo*) joke; (*Jur*) pardon; **de ~**
(*grátis*) for nothing; (*sem motivo*) for no
reason; **sem ~** dull, boring; **fazer ou ter ~**
to be funny; **ficar sem ~** to be
embarrassed; **~s a** thanks to

gracejar [grase'ʒar] vi to joke; **gracejo** [gra'seʒu] m joke

gracioso, -a [gra'sjozu, ɔza] ADJ (*pessoa*) charming; (*gestos*) gracious

grade ['gradʒi] F (*no chão*) grating; (*grelha*) grill; (*na janela*) bars pl; (*col: cadeia*) prison

gradear [gra'dʒjar] vt (*janela*) to put bars up at; (*jardim*) to fence off

graduação [gradwa'sãw] (*pl* **-ões**) F (*classificação*) grading; (*Educ*) graduation; (*Mil*) rank

gradual [gra'dwaw] (*pl* **-ais**) ADJ gradual

graduar [gra'dwar] vt (*classificar*) to grade; (*luz, fogo*) to regulate; **graduar-se** vr to graduate

gráfica ['grafika] F graphics sg; *ver tb* **gráfico**

gráfico, -a ['grafiku, a] ADJ graphic ▶ M/F printer ▶ M (*Mat*) graph; (*diagrama*) diagram, chart; **gráficos** MPL (*Comput*) graphics; **~ de barras** bar chart

grã-fino, -a [grã'finu, a] (*col*) ADJ posh ▶ M/F nob, toff

grama ['grama] M gram ▶ F (BR: *capim*) grass

gramado [gra'madu] (BR) M lawn; (*Futebol*) pitch

gramática [gra'matʃika] F grammar

grampear [grã'pjar] vt to staple

grampo ['grãpu] M staple; (*no cabelo*) hairgrip; (*de carpinteiro*) clamp; (*de chapéu*) hatpin

grande ['grãdʒi] ADJ big, large; (*alto*) tall; (*notável, intenso*) great; (*longo*) long; (*adulto*) grown-up; **mulher ~** big woman; **~ mulher** great woman; **grandeza** [grã'deza] F size; (*fig*) greatness; (*ostentação*) grandeur

grandioso, -a [grã'dʒjozu, ɔza] ADJ magnificent, grand

granito [gra'nitu] M granite

granizo [gra'nizu] M hailstone; **chover ~** to hail; **chuva de ~** hailstorm

granulado, -a [granu'ladu, a] ADJ grainy; (*açúcar*) granulated

grão ['grãw] (*pl* **grãos**) M grain; (*semente*) seed; (*de café*) bean; **grão-de-bico** (*pl* **grãos-de-bico**) M chickpea

gratidão [gratʃi'dãw] F gratitude

gratificar [gratʃifi'kar] vt to tip; (*dar bônus a*) to give a bonus to; (*recompensar*) to reward

grátis ['gratʃis] ADJ free

grato, -a ['gratu, a] ADJ grateful; (*agradável*) pleasant

gratuito, -a [gra'twitu, a] ADJ (*grátis*) free; (*infundado*) gratuitous

grau [graw] M degree; (*nível*) level; (*Educ*) class; **em alto ~** to a high degree; **ensino de primeiro/segundo ~** primary (BRIT) *ou* elementary (US) / secondary education

gravação [grava'sãw] F (*em madeira*) carving; (*em disco, fita*) recording

gravador, a [grava'dor(a)] M tape recorder ▶ M/F engraver; **~ de CD/DVD** CD/DVD burner, CD/DVD writer

gravar [gra'var] vt to carve; (*metal, pedra*) to engrave; (*na memória*) to fix; (*disco, fita*) to record

gravata [gra'vata] F tie; **~ borboleta** bow tie

grave ['gravi] ADJ serious; (*tom*) deep; **gravemente** [grave'mētʃi] ADV (*doente, ferido*) seriously

grávida ['gravida] ADJ pregnant

gravidade [gravi'dadʒi] F gravity

gravidez [gravi'dez] F pregnancy

gravura [gra'vura] F (*em madeira*) engraving; (*estampa*) print

graxa ['graʃa] F (*para sapatos*) polish; (*lubrificante*) grease

Grécia ['grɛsja] F: **a ~** Greece; **grego, -a** ['gregu, a] ADJ, M/F Greek ▶ M (*Ling*) Greek

grelha ['grɛʎa] F grill; (*de fornalha*) grate; **bife na ~** grilled steak; **grelhado, -a** [gre'ʎadu, a] ADJ grilled ▶ M (*prato*) grill

grêmio ['gremju] M (*associação*) guild; (*clube*) club

grená [gre'na] ADJ, M dark red

greve ['grevi] F strike; **fazer ~** to go on strike; **~ branca** go-slow; **grevista** [gre'vista] M/F striker

grilo ['grilu] M cricket; (*Auto*) squeak; (*col: de pessoa*) hang-up; **qual é o ~?** what's the matter?; **não tem ~!** (*col*) (there's) no problem!

gringo, -a ['grĩgu, a] (*col, pej*) M/F foreigner

gripado, -a [gri'padu, a] ADJ: **estar/ ficar ~** to have/get a cold

gripe ['gripi] F flu, influenza; **~ aviária** bird flu; **~ suína** swine flu

grisalho, -a [gri'zaʎu, a] ADJ (*cabelo*) grey (BRIT), gray (US)

gritante [gri'tãtʃi] ADJ (*hipocrisia*) glaring; (*desigualdade*) gross; (*mentira*) blatant; (*cor*) loud, garish

gritar [gri'tar] vt to shout, yell ▶ vi to shout; (*de dor, medo*) to scream; **~ com alguém** to shout at sb; **gritaria** [grita'ria] F shouting, din; **grito** ['gritu] M shout; (*de medo*) scream; (*de dor*) cry; (*de animal*) call; **dar um grito** to cry out;

falar/protestar aos gritos to shout/
shout protests
Groenlândia [grwẽ'lãdʒja] F: **a ~**
Greenland
grosseiro, -a [gro'sejɾu, a] ADJ rude;
(*piada*) crude; (*modos*) coarse; **grosseria**
[grose'ria] F rudeness; (*ato*): **fazer uma
grosseria** to be rude; (*dito*): **dizer uma
grosseria** to be rude, say something
rude
grosso, -a ['grosu, 'grɔsa] ADJ thick;
(*áspero*) rough; (*voz*) deep; (*col: pessoa,
piada*) rude ► M: **o ~ de** the bulk of;
grossura [gro'sura] F thickness
grotesco, -a [gro'tesku, a] ADJ
grotesque
grudar [gru'dar] VT to glue, stick ► VI to
stick
grude ['grudʒi] F glue; **grudento, -a**
[gru'dẽtu, a] ADJ sticky
grunhir [gru'ɲir] VI (*porco*) to grunt;
(*tigre*) to growl; (*resmungar*) to grumble
grupo ['grupu] M group
guarda ['gwarda] M/F police officer ► F
(*vigilância*) guarding; (*de objeto*)
safekeeping ► M (*Mil*) guard; **estar de ~**
to be on guard; **pôr-se em ~** to be on
one's guard; **a G~ Civil** the Civil Guard;
guarda-chuva (*pl* **-s**) M umbrella;
guarda-costas M INV (*Náut*) coastguard
boat; (*capanga*) bodyguard; **guardados**
[gwar'dadus] MPL keepsakes, valuables;
guarda-fogo (*pl* **-s**) M fireguard;
guarda-louça [gwarda'losa] (*pl* **-s**) M
sideboard; **guardanapo** [gwarda'napu]
M napkin; **guarda-noturno** (*pl*
guardas-noturnos) M night watchman;
guardar [gwar'dar] VT to put away;
(*zelar por*) to guard; (*lembrança, segredo*)
to keep; **guardar-se** VR (*defender-se*) to
protect o.s.; **guardar-se de** (*acautelar-se*)
to guard against; **guarda-redes** (PT) M
INV goalkeeper; **guarda-roupa** (*pl* **-s**) M
wardrobe; **guarda-sol** (*pl* **-sóis**) M
sunshade, parasol
guardião, -diã [gwar'dʒjãw, 'dʒjã] (*pl*
-ães/-s) M/F guardian
guarnição [gwarni'sãw] (*pl* **-ões**) F (*Mil*)
garrison; (*Náut*) crew; (*Culin*) garnish
Guatemala [gwate'mala] F: **a ~**
Guatemala
gude ['gudʒi] M: **bola de ~** marble; (*jogo*)
marbles *pl*
guerra ['gɛha] F war; **em ~** at war;
fazer ~ to wage war; **~ civil** civil war;
~ mundial world war; **guerreiro, -a**
[ge'hejɾu, a] ADJ (*espírito*) fighting;
(*belicoso*) warlike ► M warrior

guerrilha [ge'hiʎa] F (*luta*) guerrilla
warfare; (*tropa*) guerrilla band;
guerrilheiro, -a [gehi'ʎejɾu, a] M/F
guerrilla
guia ['gia] F guidance; (*Com*) permit, bill
of lading; (*formulário*) advice slip ► M
(*livro*) guide(book) ► M/F (*pessoa*) guide
Guiana ['gjana] F: **a ~** Guyana
guiar [gjar] VT to guide; (*Auto*) to drive
► VI to drive; **guiar-se** VR: **~-se por** to
go by
guichê [gi'ʃe] M ticket window; (*em
banco, repartição*) window, counter
guinada [gi'nada] F: **dar uma ~** (*com o
carro*) to swerve
guindaste [gĩ'dastʃi] M hoist, crane
guisado [gi'zadu] M stew
guitarra [gi'taha] F (electric) guitar
guloso, -a [gu'lozu, ɔza] ADJ greedy

h

há [a] VB *ver* **haver**

hábil ['abiw] (*pl* **-eis**) ADJ competent, capable; (*astucioso, esperto*) clever; (*sutil*) diplomatic; **em tempo ~** in reasonable time; **habilidade** [abili'dadʒi] F skill, ability; (*astúcia, esperteza*) shrewdness; (*tato*) discretion; **habilidoso, -a** [abili'dozu, ɔza] ADJ skilful (*BRIT*), skillful (*US*), clever

habilitação [abilita'sãw] (*pl* **-ões**) F competence; (*ato*) qualification; **habilitações** FPL (*conhecimentos*) qualifications

habilitar [abili'tar] VT to enable; (*dar direito a*) to qualify, entitle; (*preparar*) to prepare

habitação [abita'sãw] (*pl* **-ões**) F dwelling, residence; (*alojamento*) housing

habitante [abi'tãtʃi] M/F inhabitant

habitar [abi'tar] VT to live in; (*povoar*) to inhabit ▶ VI to live

hábito ['abitu] M habit; (*social*) custom; (*Rel: traje*) habit

habituado, -a [abi'twadu, a] ADJ: **~ a (fazer) algo** used to (doing) sth

habituar [abi'twar] VT: **~ alguém a** to get sb used to, accustom sb to; **habituar-se** VR: **~-se a** to get used to

hacker ['haker] (*pl* **-s**) M (*Comput*) hacker

Haia ['aja] N the Hague

haja ['aʒa] VB *ver* **haver**

hálito ['alitu] M breath

hall [hɔw] (*pl* **halls**) M hall; (*de teatro, hotel*) foyer; **~ de entrada** entrance hall

hambúrguer [ã'burger] (*pl* **-s**) M hamburger

hão [ãw] VB *ver* **haver**

hardware ['hadwer] M (*Comput*) hardware

harmonia [armo'nia] F harmony

harmonioso, -a [armo'njozu, ɔza] ADJ harmonious

harmonizar [armoni'zar] VT (*Mús*) to harmonize; (*conciliar*): **~ algo (com algo)** to reconcile sth (with sth); **harmonizar-se** VR: **~(-se) (com algo)** (*ideias etc*) to coincide (with sth); (*pessoas*) to be in agreement (with sth)

harpa ['arpa] F harp

Havaí [avaj'i] M: **o ~** Hawaii

(PALAVRA-CHAVE)

haver [a'ver] VB AUX **1** (*ter*) to have; **ele havia saído/comido** he had left/eaten

2: **quem haveria de dizer que ...** who would have thought that ...

▶ VB IMPESS **1** (*existência*): **há** (*sg*) there is; (*pl*) there are; **o que é que há?** what's the matter?; **o que é que houve?** what happened?, what was that?; **não há de quê** don't mention it, you're welcome; **haja o que houver** come what may

2 (*tempo*): **há séculos/cinco dias que não o vejo** I haven't seen him for ages/five days; **há um ano que ela chegou** it's a year since she arrived; **há cinco dias (atrás)** five days ago

haver-se VR: **haver-se com alguém** to sort things out with sb

▶ M (*Com*) credit; **haveres** MPL (*pertences*) property *sg*, possessions; (*riqueza*) wealth *sg*

---

haxixe [a'ʃiʃi] M hashish

hebraico, -a [e'brajku, a] ADJ Hebrew ▶ M (*Ling*) Hebrew

Hébridas ['ɛbridas] FPL: **as (ilhas) ~** the Hebrides

hediondo, -a [e'dʒjõdu, a] ADJ vile, revolting; (*crime*) heinous

hei [ej] VB *ver* **haver**

hélice ['ɛlisi] F propeller

helicóptero [eli'kɔpteru] M helicopter

hematoma [ema'tɔma] M bruise

hemorragia [emoha'ʒia] F haemorrhage (*BRIT*), hemorrhage (*US*); **~ nasal** nosebleed

hemorróidas [emo'hɔjdas] FPL haemorrhoids (*BRIT*), hemorrhoids (*US*), piles

hepatite [epa'tʃitʃi] F hepatitis

hera ['ɛra] F ivy

herança [e'rãsa] F inheritance; (*fig*) heritage

herdar [er'dar] VT: **~ algo (de)** to inherit sth (from); **~ a** to bequeath to

herdeiro, -a [er'dejru, a] M/F heir(ess)

herói [e'rɔi] M hero

heroína [ero'ina] F heroine; (*droga*) heroin

hesitação [ezita'sãw] (*pl* -ões) F hesitation

hesitante [ezi'tãtʃi] ADJ hesitant

hesitar [ezi'tar] VI to hesitate

heterossexual [eterosek'swaw] (*pl* -ais) ADJ, M/F heterosexual

híbrido, -a ['ibridu, a] ADJ hybrid

hidratante [idra'tãtʃi] M moisturizer

hidrato [i'dratu] M: ~ **de carbono** carbohydrate

hidráulico, -a [i'drawliku, a] ADJ hydraulic

hidrelétrico, -a [idre'lɛtriku, a] ADJ hydroelectric

hidro... [idru] PREFIXO hydro..., water... *atr*

hidrogênio [idro'ʒenju] M hydrogen

hidroginástica [idroʒi'nastʃika] F aquaerobics

hífen ['ifẽ] (*pl* **hífens**) M hyphen

higiene [i'ʒjeni] F hygiene; **higiênico, -a** [i'ʒjeniku, a] ADJ hygienic; (*pessoa*) clean; **papel higiênico** toilet paper

hindu [ĩ'du] ADJ, M/F Hindu

hino ['inu] M hymn; ~ **nacional** national anthem

hipermercado [ipermer'kadu] M hypermarket

hipertensão [ipertẽ'sãw] F high blood pressure

hipismo [i'pizmu] M (*turfe*) horse racing; (*equitação*) (horse) riding

hipocrisia [ipokri'zia] F hypocrisy; **hipócrita** [i'pɔkrita] ADJ hypocritical ▶ M/F hypocrite

hipódromo [i'pɔdromu] M racecourse

hipopótamo [ipo'pɔtamu] M hippopotamus

hipoteca [ipo'tɛka] F mortgage; **hipotecar** [ipote'kar] VT to mortgage

hipótese [i'pɔtezi] F hypothesis; **na** ~ **de** in the event of; **em** ~ **alguma** under no circumstances; **na melhor/pior das** ~**s** at best/worst

hispânico, -a [is'paniku, a] ADJ Hispanic

histeria [iste'ria] F hysteria; **histérico, -a** [is'tɛriku, a] ADJ hysterical

história [is'tɔrja] F history; (*conto*) story; **histórias** FPL (*chateação*) bother *sg*, fuss *sg*; **isso é outra** ~ that's a different matter; **que** ~ **é essa?** what's going on?; **historiador, a** [istorja'dor(a)] M/F historian; **histórico, -a** [is'tɔriku, a] ADJ historical; (*fig: notável*) historic ▶ M history

hobby ['hɔbi] (*pl* -bies) M hobby

hoje ['oʒi] ADV today; (*atualmente*) now(adays); ~ **à noite** tonight

Holanda [o'lãda] F: **a** ~ Holland; **holandês, -esa** [olã'des, eza] ADJ Dutch ▶ M/F Dutchman/woman ▶ M (*Ling*) Dutch

holocausto [olo'kawstu] M holocaust

homem ['omẽ] (*pl* -ns) M man; (*a humanidade*) mankind; ~ **de empresa** *ou* **negócios** businessman; ~ **de estado** statesman; **homem-bomba** (*pl* **homens-bomba**) M suicide bomber

homenagear [omena'ʒjar] VT (*pessoa*) to pay tribute to, honour (BRIT), honor (US)

homenagem [ome'naʒẽ] F tribute; (*Rel*) homage; **prestar** ~ **a alguém** to pay tribute to sb

homens ['omẽs] MPL *de* **homem**

homeopático, -a [omjo'patʃiku, a] ADJ homoeopathic (BRIT), homeopathic (US)

homicida [omi'sida] ADJ homicidal ▶ M/F murderer; **homicídio** [omi'sidʒju] M murder; **homicídio involuntário** manslaughter

homologar [omolo'gar] VT to ratify

homólogo, -a [o'mɔlogu, a] ADJ homologous; (*fig*) equivalent ▶ M/F opposite number

homossexual [omosek'swaw] (*pl* -ais) ADJ, M/F homosexual

Honduras [õ'duras] F Honduras

honestidade [onestʃi'dadʒi] F honesty; (*decência*) decency; (*justeza*) fairness

honesto, -a [o'nɛstu, a] ADJ honest; (*decente*) decent; (*justo*) fair, just

honorário, -a [ono'rarju, a] ADJ honorary; **honorários** [ono'rarjus] MPL fees

honra ['õha] F honour (BRIT), honor (US); **em** ~ **de** in hono(u)r of

honrado, -a [õ'hadu, a] ADJ honest; (*respeitado*) honourable (BRIT), honorable (US)

honrar [õ'har] VT to honour (BRIT), honor (US)

honroso, -a [õ'hozu, ɔza] ADJ honourable (BRIT), honorable (US)

hóquei ['hɔkej] M hockey; ~ **sobre gelo** ice hockey

hora ['ɔra] F (*60 minutos*) hour; (*momento*) time; **a que** ~**s?** (at) what time?; **que** ~**s são?** what time is it?; **são duas** ~**s** it's two o'clock; **você tem as** ~**s?** have you got the time?; **fazer** ~ to kill time; **de** ~ **em** ~ every hour; **na** ~ on the spot; **chegar na** ~ to be on time; **de última** ~ *adj* last-minute; *adv* at the last minute; ~ **do almoço** lunch hour; **meia** ~ half an

hour; **~s extras** overtime *sg*; **horário, -a**
[o'rarju, a] ADJ: **100 km horários** 100 km
an hour ▸ M timetable; (*hora*) time;
horário de expediente working hours
pl; (*de um escritório*) office hours *pl*

horizontal [orizõ'taw] (*pl* **-ais**) ADJ
horizontal

horizonte [ori'zõtʃi] M horizon

horóscopo [o'rɔskopu] M horoscope

horrível [o'hivew] (*pl* **-eis**) ADJ awful,
horrible

horror [o'hor] M horror; **que ~!** how
awful!; **ter ~ a algo** to hate sth;
horrorizar [ohori'zar] VT to horrify,
frighten; **horroroso, -a** [oho'rozu, ɔza]
ADJ horrible, ghastly

hortaliças [orta'lisas] FPL vegetables

hortelã [orte'lã] F mint; **~ pimenta**
peppermint

horticultor, a [ortʃikuw'tor(a)] M/F
market gardener (*BRIT*), truck farmer (*US*)

hortifrutigranjeiros
[ortʃifrutʃigrã'ʒejrus] MPL fruit and
vegetables

horto ['ortu] M market garden (*BRIT*),
truck farm (*US*)

hospedagem [ospe'daʒẽ] F guest house

hospedar [ospe'dar] VT to put up;
hospedar-se VR to stay, lodge;
hospedaria [ospeda'ria] F guest house

hóspede ['ɔspedʒi] M (*amigo*) guest;
(*estranho*) lodger

hospedeira [ospe'dejra] F landlady; (*PT*:
de bordo) stewardess, air hostess (*BRIT*)

hospício [os'pisju] M psychiatric
hospital

hospital [ospi'taw] (*pl* **-ais**) M hospital

hospitalidade [ospitali'dadʒi] F
hospitality

hostil [os'tʃiw] (*pl* **-is**) ADJ hostile;
hostilizar [ostʃili'zar] VT to antagonize;
(*Mil*) to wage war on

hotel [o'tɛw] (*pl* **-éis**) M hotel;
hoteleiro, -a [ote'lejru, a] M/F hotelier

houve ['ovi] VB *ver* **haver**

humanidade [umani'dadʒi] F (*os homens*)
man(kind); (*compaixão*) humanity

humanitário, -a [umani'tarju, a] ADJ
humane

humano, -a [u'manu, a] ADJ human;
(*bondoso*) humane

humildade [umiw'dadʒi] F humility;
(*pobreza*) poverty

humilde [u'miwdʒi] ADJ humble; (*pobre*)
poor

humilhar [umi'ʎar] VT to humiliate

humor [u'mor] M mood, temper; (*graça*)
humour (*BRIT*), humor (*US*); **de bom/**
mau ~ in a good/bad mood; **humorista**
[umo'rista] M/F comedian;
humorístico, -a [umo'ristʃiku, a] ADJ
humorous

húngaro, -a ['ũgaru, a] ADJ, M/F
Hungarian

Hungria [ũ'gria] F: **a ~** Hungary

hurra ['uha] M cheer ▸ EXCL hurrah!

I

ia ['ia] VB ver **ir**

iate ['jatʃi] M yacht; **~ clube** yacht club

ibérico, -a [i'bɛriku, a] ADJ, M/F Iberian

ibero-americano, -a [ibɛru-] ADJ, M/F Ibero-American

ICMS (BR) ABR M (= Imposto sobre Circulação de Mercadorias e Prestação de Serviços) ≈ VAT

icone ['ikoni] M (ger, Comput) icon

ida ['ida] F going, departure; **~ e volta** round trip, return; **a (viagem de) ~** the outward journey; **na ~** on the way there

idade [i'dadʒi] F age; **ter cinco anos de ~** to be five (years old); **de meia ~** middle-aged; **qual é a ~ dele?** how old is he?; **na minha ~** at my age; **ser menor/ maior de ~** to be under/of age; **pessoa de ~** elderly person; **I~ Média** Middle Ages pl

ideal [ide'jaw] (pl -ais) ADJ, M ideal; **idealista** [idea'lista] ADJ idealistic ▶ M/F idealist

ideia [i'dɛja] F idea; (mente) mind; **mudar de ~** to change one's mind; **não ter a mínima ~** to have no idea; **não faço~** I can't imagine; **estar com ~ de fazer** to plan to do

idem ['idẽ] PRON ditto

idêntico, -a [i'dẽtʃiku, a] ADJ identical

identidade [idẽtʃi'dadʒi] F identity

identificação [idẽtʃifika'sãw] F identification

identificar [idẽtʃifi'kar] VT to identify; **identificar-se** VR: **~-se com** to identify with

idioma [i'dʒoma] M language

idiota [i'dʒɔta] ADJ idiotic ▶ M/F idiot

ido, -a ['idu, a] ADJ past

ídolo ['idolu] M idol

idoso, -a [i'dozu, ɔza] ADJ elderly, old

ignorado, -a [igno'radu, a] ADJ unknown

ignorância [igno'rãsja] F ignorance; **ignorante** [igno'rãtʃi] ADJ ignorant, uneducated ▶ M/F ignoramus

ignorar [igno'rar] VT not to know; (não dar atenção a) to ignore

igreja [i'greʒa] F church

igual [i'gwaw] (pl -ais) ADJ equal; (superfície) even ▶ M/F equal

igualar [igwa'lar] VT to equal; (fazer igual) to make equal; (nivelar) to level ▶ VI: **~ a** ou **com** to be equal to, be the same as; (ficar no mesmo nível) to be level with; **igualar-se** VR: **~-se a alguém** to be sb's equal

igualdade [igwaw'dadʒi] F equality; (uniformidade) uniformity

igualmente [igwaw'mẽtʃi] ADV equally; (também) likewise, also; **~!** (saudação) the same to you!

ilegal [ile'gaw] (pl -ais) ADJ illegal

ilegítimo, -a [ile'ʒitʃimu, a] ADJ illegitimate; (ilegal) unlawful

ilegível [ile'ʒivew] (pl -eis) ADJ illegible

iletrado, -a [ile'tradu, a] ADJ illiterate

ilha ['iʎa] F island; **ilhéu, ilhoa** [i'ʎɛw, i'ʎoa] M/F islander

ilícito, -a [i'lisitu, a] ADJ illicit

ilimitado, -a [ilimi'tadu, a] ADJ unlimited

iluminar [ilumi'nar] VT to light up; (estádio etc) to floodlight; (fig) to enlighten

ilusão [ilu'zãw] (pl -ões) F illusion; (quimera) delusion; **ilusório, -a** [ilu'zɔrju, a] ADJ deceptive

ilustração [ilustra'sãw] (pl -ões) F illustration

ilustrado, -a [ilus'tradu, a] ADJ illustrated; (instruído) learned

ilustrar [ilus'trar] VT to illustrate; (instruir) to instruct

ilustre [i'lustri] ADJ illustrious; **um ~ desconhecido** a complete stranger

ímã ['imã] M magnet

imagem [i'maʒẽ] (pl -ns) F image; (semelhança) likeness; (TV) picture; **imagens** FPL (Literatura) imagery sg

imaginação [imaʒina'sãw] (pl -ões) F imagination

imaginar [imaʒi'nar] VT to imagine; (supor) to suppose; **imaginar-se** VR to imagine o.s.; **imagine só!** just imagine!; **imaginário, -a** [imaʒi'narju, a] ADJ imaginary

imaturo, -a [ima'turu, a] ADJ immature

imbatível [ĩba'tʃívew] (pl **-eis**) ADJ
invincible

imbecil [ĩbe'siw] (pl **-is**) ADJ stupid ▶ M/F
imbecile; **imbecilidade** [ĩbesili'dadʒi] F
stupidity

imediações [imedʒa'sõjs] FPL vicinity
sg, neighbourhood sg (BRIT),
neighborhood sg (US)

imediatamente [imedʒata'mẽtʃi] ADV
immediately, right away

imediato, -a [ime'dʒatu, a] ADJ
immediate; (seguinte) next; **~ a** next to;
de ~ straight away

imenso, -a [i'mẽsu, a] ADJ immense,
huge; (ódio, amor) great

imigração [imigra'sãw] (pl **-ões**) F
immigration

imigrante [imi'grãtʃi] ADJ, M/F
immigrant

iminente [imi'nẽtʃi] ADJ imminent

imitação [imita'sãw] (pl **-ões**) F
imitation

imitar [imi'tar] VT to imitate;
(assinatura) to copy

imobiliária [imobi'ljarja] F estate
agent's (BRIT), real estate broker's (US)

imobiliário, -a [imobi'ljarju, a] ADJ
property atr

imobilizar [imobili'zar] VT to
immobilize; (fig) to bring to a standstill

imoral [imo'raw] (pl **-ais**) ADJ immoral

imortal [imor'taw] (pl **-ais**) ADJ immortal

imóvel [i'mɔvew] (pl **-eis**) ADJ
motionless, still; (não movediço)
immovable ▶ M property; (edifício)
building; **imóveis** MPL (propriedade) real
estate sg, property sg

impaciência [ĩpa'sjẽsja] F impatience;
impacientar-se [ĩpasjẽ'tarsi] VR to lose
one's patience; **impaciente** [ĩpa'sjẽtʃi]
ADJ impatient

impacto [ĩ'paktu], (PT) **impacte** M
impact

ímpar [ĩpar] ADJ (número) odd; (sem igual)
unique, unequalled

imparcial [ĩpar'sjaw] (pl **-ais**) ADJ fair,
impartial

impecável [ĩpe'kavew] (pl **-eis**) ADJ
perfect, impeccable

impeço [ĩ'pɛsu] VB ver **impedir**

impedido, -a [ĩpe'dʒidu, a] ADJ (Futebol)
offside; (PT Tel) engaged (BRIT), busy (US)

impedimento [ĩpedʒi'mẽtu] M
impediment

impedir [ĩpe'dʒir] VT to obstruct;
(estrada, passagem, tráfego) to block;
(movimento, execução, progresso) to
impede; **~ alguém de fazer algo** to

prevent sb from doing sth; (proibir) to
forbid sb to do sth; **~ (que aconteça)
algo** to prevent sth (happening)

impenetrável [ĩpene'travew] (pl **-eis**)
ADJ impenetrable

impensado, -a [ĩpẽ'sadu, a] ADJ
thoughtless; (não calculado)
unpremeditated; (imprevisto)
unforeseen

imperador [ĩpera'dor] M emperor

imperativo, -a [ĩpera'tʃivu, a] ADJ
imperative ▶ M imperative

imperatriz [ĩpera'triz] F empress

imperdoável [ĩper'dwavew] (pl **-eis**) ADJ
unforgivable, inexcusable

imperfeito, -a [ĩper'fejtu, a] ADJ
imperfect ▶ M (Ling) imperfect (tense)

imperial [ĩpe'rjaw] (pl **-ais**) ADJ imperial

imperícia [ĩpe'risja] F inability;
(inexperiência) inexperience

império [ĩ'pɛrju] M empire

impermeável [ĩper'mjavew] (pl **-eis**)
ADJ: **~ a** (tb fig) impervious to; (à água)
waterproof ▶ M raincoat

impessoal [ĩpe'swaw] (pl **-ais**) ADJ
impersonal

ímpeto ['ĩpetu] M (Tec) impetus;
(movimento súbito) start; (de cólera) fit;
(de emoção) surge; (de chamas) fury; **agir
com ~** to act on impulse; **levantar-se
num ~** to get up with a start

impiedoso, -a [ĩpje'dozu, ɔza] ADJ
merciless, cruel

implacável [ĩpla'kavew] (pl **-eis**) ADJ
(pessoa) unforgiving

implantação [ĩplãta'sãw] (pl **-ões**) F
introduction; (Med) implant

implementar [ĩplemẽ'tar] VT to
implement

implicar [ĩpli'kar] VT (envolver) to
implicate; (pressupor) to imply ▶ VI:
~ com alguém (chatear) to tease sb, pick
on sb; **implicar-se** VR to get involved;
~ (em) algo to involve sth

implícito, -a [ĩ'plisitu, a] ADJ implicit

implorar [ĩplo'rar] VT: **~ (algo a
alguém)** to beg ou implore (sb for sth)

impopular [ĩpopu'lar] ADJ unpopular;
impopularidade [ĩpopulari'dadʒi] F
unpopularity

impor [ĩ'por] (irreg: como **pôr**) VT to
impose; (respeito) to command;
impor-se VR to assert o.s.; **~ algo a
alguém** to impose sth on sb

importação [importa'sãw] (pl **-ões**) F
(ato) importing; (mercadoria) import

importador, a [ĩporta'dor(a)] ADJ
import atr ▶ M/F importer

importância [ĩporˈtãsja] F importance; (*de dinheiro*) sum, amount; **não tem ~** it doesn't matter, never mind; **ter ~** to be important; **sem ~** unimportant; **importante** [ĩporˈtãtʃi] ADJ important ▶ M: **o (mais) importante** the (most) important thing

importar [ĩporˈtar] VT (*Com*) to import; (*trazer*) to bring in; (*causar: prejuízos etc*) to cause; (*implicar*) to imply, involve ▶ VI to matter, be important; **importar-se** VR: **~-se com algo** to mind sth; **não me importo** I don't care

importunar [ĩportuˈnar] VT to bother, annoy

importuno, -a [ĩporˈtunu, a] ADJ annoying; (*inoportuno*) inopportune ▶ M/F nuisance

impossibilitado, -a [ĩposibiliˈtadu, a] ADJ: **~ de fazer** unable to do

impossibilitar [ĩposibiliˈtar] VT: **~ algo** to make sth impossible; **~ alguém de fazer, ~ a alguém fazer** to prevent sb doing; **~ algo a alguém, ~ alguém para algo** to make sth impossible for sb

impossível [ĩpoˈsivew] (*pl* -**eis**) ADJ impossible; (*insuportável: pessoa*) insufferable; (*incrível*) incredible

imposto [ĩˈpostu] M tax; **antes/depois de ~s** before/after tax; **~ ambiental** green tax, environmental tax; **~ de renda** (BR) income tax; **~ predial** rates *pl*; **I~ sobre Circulação de Mercadorias (e Serviços)** (BR), **~ sobre valor agregado** value added tax (BRIT), sales tax (US)

impotente [ĩpoˈtẽtʃi] ADJ powerless; (*Med*) impotent

impraticável [ĩpratʃiˈkavew] (*pl* -**eis**) ADJ impracticable; (*rua, rio etc*) impassable

impreciso, -a [ĩpreˈsizu, a] ADJ vague; (*falto de rigor*) inaccurate

imprensa [ĩˈprẽsa] F printing; (*máquina, jornais*) press

imprescindível [ĩpresĩˈdʒivew] (*pl* -**eis**) ADJ essential, indispensable

impressão [ĩpreˈsãw] (*pl* -**ões**) F impression; (*de livros*) printing; (*marca*) imprint; **causar boa ~** to make a good impression; **ficar com/ter a ~ (de) que** to get/have the impression that

impressionante [ĩpresjoˈnãtʃi] ADJ impressive

impressionar [ĩpresjoˈnar] VT to affect ▶ VI to be impressive; (*pessoa*) to make an impression; **impressionar-se** VR:

~-se (com algo) (*comover-se*) to be moved (by sth)

impresso, -a [ĩˈpresu, a] PP *de* **imprimir** ▶ ADJ printed ▶ M (*para preencher*) form; (*folheto*) leaflet; **impressos** MPL (*formulário*) printed matter *sg*

impressões [ĩpreˈsõjs] FPL *de* **impressão**

impressora [ĩpreˈsora] F (*Comput*) printer; **~ jato de tinta** ink-jet printer

imprestável [ĩpresˈtavew] (*pl* -**eis**) ADJ (*inútil*) useless; (*pessoa*) unhelpful

imprevisível [ĩpreviˈzivew] (*pl* -**eis**) ADJ unforeseeable

imprevisto, -a [ĩpreˈvistu, a] ADJ unexpected, unforeseen ▶ M: **um ~** something unexpected

imprimir [ĩpriˈmir] VT to print; (*marca*) to stamp; (*infundir*) to instil (BRIT), instill (US)

impróprio, -a [ĩˈprɔprju, a] ADJ inappropriate; (*indecente*) improper

improvável [ĩproˈvavew] (*pl* -**eis**) ADJ unlikely

improviso [ĩproˈvizu] M: **de ~** (*de repente*) suddenly; (*sem preparação*) without preparation

imprudente [ĩpruˈdẽtʃi] ADJ (*irrefletido*) rash; (*motorista*) careless

impulsivo, -a [ĩpuwˈsivu, a] ADJ impulsive

impulso [ĩˈpuwsu] M impulse; (*fig: estímulo*) urge, impulse

impune [ĩˈpuni] ADJ unpunished; **impunidade** [ĩpuniˈdadʒi] F impunity

imundície [imũˈdʒisji] F filth; **imundo, -a** [iˈmũdu, a] ADJ filthy; (*obsceno*) dirty

imune [iˈmuni] ADJ: **~ a** immune to; **imunidade** [imuniˈdadʒi] F immunity

inábil [iˈnabiw] (*pl* -**eis**) ADJ incapable; (*desajeitado*) clumsy

inabitado, -a [inabiˈtadu, a] ADJ uninhabited

inacabado, -a [inakaˈbadu, a] ADJ unfinished

inacreditável [inakredʒiˈtavew] (*pl* -**eis**) ADJ unbelievable, incredible

inadequado, -a [inadeˈkwadu, a] ADJ inadequate; (*impróprio*) unsuitable

inadiável [inaˈdʒjavew] (*pl* -**eis**) ADJ pressing

inadimplência [inadʒĩˈplẽsja] F (*Jur*) breach of contract, default

inaptidão [inaptʃiˈdãw] (*pl* -**ões**) F inability

inatingível [inatʃĩˈʒivew] (*pl* -**eis**) ADJ unattainable

inativo, -a [ina'tʃivu, a] ADJ inactive; (*aposentado, reformado*) retired

inauguração [inawgura'sãw] (*pl* **-ões**) F inauguration; (*de exposição*) opening; **inaugural** [inawgu'raw] (*pl* **-ais**) ADJ inaugural; **inaugurar** [inawgu'rar] VT to inaugurate; (*exposição*) to open

incapacidade [ĩkapasi'dadʒi] F incapacity; (*incompetência*) incompetence

incapacitado, -a [ĩkapasi'tadu, a] ADJ (*inválido*) disabled ▶ M/F person with a disability; **estar ~ de fazer** to be unable to do

incapaz [ĩka'pajʒ] ADJ, M/F incompetent; **~ de fazer** incapable of doing; **~ para** unfit for

incendiar [ĩsẽ'dʒjar] VT to set fire to; (*fig*) to inflame; **incendiar-se** VR to catch fire

incêndio [ĩ'sẽdʒju] M fire; **~ criminoso** *ou* **premeditado** arson

incenso [ĩ'sẽsu] M incense

incentivar [ĩsẽtʃi'var] VT to stimulate, encourage

incentivo [ĩsẽ'tʃivu] M incentive; **~ fiscal** tax incentive

incerteza [ĩser'teza] F uncertainty

incerto, -a [ĩ'sɛrtu, a] ADJ uncertain

incesto [ĩ'sɛstu] M incest

inchado, -a [ĩ'ʃadu, a] ADJ swollen; (*fig*) conceited

inchar [ĩ'ʃar] VT, VI to swell

incidência [ĩsi'dẽsja] F incidence, occurrence

incidente [ĩsi'dẽtʃi] M incident

incisivo, -a [ĩsi'zivu, a] ADJ cutting, sharp; (*fig*) incisive

incitar [ĩsi'tar] VT to incite; (*pessoa, animal*) to drive on

inclinação [ĩklina'sãw] (*pl* **-ões**) F inclination; **~ da cabeça** nod

inclinar [ĩkli'nar] VT to tilt; (*cabeça*) to nod ▶ VI to slope; (*objeto*) to tilt; **inclinar-se** VR to tilt; (*dobrar o corpo*) to bow, stoop; **~-se sobre algo** to lean over sth

incluir [ĩ'klwir] VT to include; (*em carta*) to enclose; **incluir-se** VR to be included

inclusão [ĩklu'zãw] F inclusion; **inclusive** [ĩklu'zivi] PREP including ▶ ADV inclusive; (*até mesmo*) even

incoerente [ĩkoe'rẽtʃi] ADJ incoherent; (*contraditório*) inconsistent

incógnita [ĩ'kɔgnita] F (*Mat*) unknown; (*fato incógnito*) mystery

incógnito, -a [ĩ'kɔgnitu, a] ADJ unknown ▶ ADV incognito

incolor [ĩko'lor] ADJ colourless (*BRIT*), colorless (*US*)

incomodar [ĩkomo'dar] VT to bother, trouble; (*aborrecer*) to annoy ▶ VI to be bothersome; **incomodar-se** VR to bother, put o.s. out; **~-se com algo** to be bothered by sth, mind sth; **não se incomode!** don't worry!

incômodo, -a [ĩ'komodu, a] ADJ uncomfortable; (*incomodativo*) troublesome; (*inoportuno*) inconvenient

incompetente [ĩkõpe'tẽtʃi] ADJ, M/F incompetent

incompreendido, -a [ĩkõprjẽ'dʒidu, a] ADJ misunderstood

incomum [ĩko'mũ] ADJ uncommon

incomunicável [ĩkomuni'kavew] (*pl* **-eis**) ADJ cut off; (*privado de comunicação, fig*) incommunicado; (*preso*) in solitary confinement

inconformado, -a [ĩkõfor'madu, a] ADJ bitter; **~ com** unreconciled to

inconfundível [ĩkõfũ'dʒivew] (*pl* **-eis**) ADJ unmistakeable

inconsciência [ĩkõ'sjẽsja] F (*Med*) unconsciousness; (*irreflexão*) thoughtlessness

inconsciente [ĩkõ'sjẽtʃi] ADJ unconscious ▶ M unconscious

inconsequente [ĩkõse'kwẽtʃi] ADJ inconsistent; (*contraditório*) illogical; (*irresponsável*) irresponsible

inconsistente [ĩkõsis'tẽtʃi] ADJ inconsistent; (*sem solidez*) runny

inconstante [ĩkõs'tãtʃi] ADJ fickle; (*tempo*) changeable

incontrolável [ĩkõtro'lavew] (*pl* **-eis**) ADJ uncontrollable

inconveniência [ĩkõve'njẽsja] F inconvenience; (*impropriedade*) inappropriateness

inconveniente [ĩkõve'njẽtʃi] ADJ inconvenient; (*inoportuno*) awkward; (*grosseiro*) rude; (*importuno*) annoying ▶ M disadvantage; (*obstáculo*) difficulty, problem

incorreto, -a [ĩko'hɛtu, a] ADJ incorrect; (*desonesto*) dishonest

incrédulo, -a [ĩ'krɛdulu, a] ADJ incredulous; (*cético*) sceptical (*BRIT*), skeptical (*US*) ▶ M/F sceptic (*BRIT*), skeptic (*US*)

incrível [ĩ'krivew] (*pl* **-eis**) ADJ incredible

incumbência [ĩkũ'bẽsja] F task, duty

incumbir [ĩkũ'bir] **~ alguém de algo** *ou* **algo a alguém** to put sb in charge of sth ▶ VI: **~ a alguém** to be sb's duty; **incumbir-se** VR: **~-se de** to undertake, take charge of

indagação [ĩdaga'sãw] (pl -ões) F investigation; (pergunta) inquiry, question

indagar [ĩda'gar] VT to investigate ▶ VI to inquire; **indagar-se** VR: **~-se a si mesmo** to ask o.s.; **~ algo de alguém** to ask sb about sth

indecente [ĩde'sẽtʃi] ADJ indecent, improper; (obsceno) rude, vulgar

indecoroso, -a [ĩdeko'rozu, ɔza] ADJ indecent, improper

indefinido, -a [ĩdefi'nidu, a] ADJ indefinite; (vago) vague, undefined; **por tempo ~** indefinitely

indelicado, -a [ĩdeli'kadu, a] ADJ impolite, rude

indenização [ĩdeniza'sãw], (PT) **indemnização** (pl -ões) F compensation; (Com) indemnity

indenizar [ĩdeni'zar], (PT) **indemnizar** VT: **~ alguém por** ou **de algo** (compensar) to compensate sb for sth; (por gastos) to reimburse sb for sth

independência [ĩdepẽ'dẽsja] F independence; **independente** [ĩdepẽ'dẽtʃi] ADJ independent

indesejável [ĩdeze'ʒavew] (pl -eis) ADJ undesirable

indevido, -a [ĩde'vidu, a] ADJ (imerecido) unjust; (impróprio) inappropriate

Índia [ˈĩdʒa] F: **a ~** India; **as ~s Ocidentais** the West Indies; **indiano, -a** [ĩˈdʒjanu, a] ADJ, M/F Indian

indicação [ĩdʒika'sãw] (pl -ões) F indication; (de termômetro) reading; (para um cargo, prêmio) nomination; (recomendação) recommendation; (de um caminho) directions pl

indicado, -a [ĩdʒi'kadu, a] ADJ appropriate

indicador, a [ĩdʒika'dor(a)] ADJ: **~ de** indicative of ▶ M indicator; (Tec) gauge; (dedo) index finger; (ponteiro) pointer

indicar [ĩdʒi'kar] VT to indicate; (apontar) to point to; (temperatura) to register; (recomendar) to recommend; (para um cargo) to nominate; (determinar) to determine; **~ o caminho a alguém** to give sb directions

índice [ˈĩdʒisi] M (de livro) index; (taxa) rate

indício [ĩ'dʒisju] M (sinal) sign; (vestígio) trace; (Jur) clue

indiferença [ĩdʒife'rẽsa] F indifference; **indiferente** [ĩdʒife'rẽtʃi] ADJ:

indiferente (a) indifferent (to); **isso me é indiferente** it's all the same to me

indígena [ĩ'dʒiʒena] ADJ, M/F native; (índio: da América) Indian

indigência [ĩdʒi'ʒẽsja] F poverty; (fig) lack, need

indigestão [ĩdʒiʒes'tãw] F indigestion

indigesto, -a [ĩdʒi'ʒɛstu, a] ADJ indigestible

indignação [ĩdʒigna'sãw] F indignation; **indignado, -a** [ĩdʒig'nadu, a] ADJ indignant

indignar [ĩdʒig'nar] VT to anger, incense; **indignar-se** VR to get angry

índio, -a [ˈĩdʒju, a] ADJ, M/F (da América) Indian; **o Oceano Í~** the Indian Ocean

indireto, -a [ĩdʒi'rɛtu, a] ADJ indirect

indiscreto, -a [ĩdʒis'krɛtu, a] ADJ indiscreet

indiscutível [ĩdʒisku'tʃivew] (pl -eis) ADJ indisputable

indispensável [ĩdʒispẽ'savew] (pl -eis) ADJ essential, vital ▶ M: **o ~** the essentials pl

indispor [ĩdʒis'por] (irreg: como **pôr**) VT (de saúde) to make ill; (aborrecer) to upset; **indisposto, -a** [ĩdʒis'postu, 'pɔsta] ADJ unwell, poorly

indistinto, -a [ĩdʒis'tʃĩtu, a] ADJ indistinct

individual [ĩdʒivi'dwaw] (pl -ais) ADJ individual

indivíduo [ĩdʒi'vidwu] M individual; (col: sujeito) person

indócil [ĩ'dɔsiw] (pl -eis) ADJ unruly, wayward; (impaciente) restless

índole [ˈĩdoli] F (temperamento) nature; (tipo) sort, type

indolor [ĩdo'lor] ADJ painless

Indonésia [ĩdo'nɛzja] F: **a ~** Indonesia

indústria [ĩ'dustrja] F industry; **industrial** [ĩdus'trjaw] (pl -ais) ADJ industrial ▶ M/F industrialist; **industrializar** [ĩdustrjali'zar] VT (país) to industrialize; (aproveitar) to process

induzir [ĩdu'zir] VT to induce; (persuadir): **~ alguém a fazer** to persuade sb to do

inédito, -a [i'nɛdʒitu, a] ADJ (livro) unpublished; (incomum) unheard-of, rare

inegável [ine'gavew] (pl -eis) ADJ undeniable

inelutável [inelu'tavew] (pl -eis) ADJ inescapable

inepto, -a [i'nɛptu, a] ADJ inept, incompetent

inequívoco, -a [ine'kivoku, a] ADJ (evidente) clear; (inconfundível) unmistakeable

inércia [i'nɛrsja] F lethargy; (Fís) inertia

inerente [ine'rētʃi] ADJ: **~ a** inherent in ou to

inerte [i'nɛrtʃi] ADJ lethargic; (Fís) inert

inesgotável [inezgo'tavew] (pl **-eis**) ADJ inexhaustible; (superabundante) boundless

inesperado, -a [inespe'radu, a] ADJ unexpected, unforeseen ▸ M: **o ~** the unexpected

inesquecível [ineske'sivew] (pl **-eis**) ADJ unforgettable

inestimável [inestʃi'mavew] (pl **-eis**) ADJ invaluable

inexato, -a [ine'zatu, a] ADJ inaccurate

inexistência [inezis'tēsja] F lack

inexperiência [inespe'rjēsja] F inexperience; **inexperiente** [inespe'rjētʃi] ADJ inexperienced; (ingênuo) naive

inexpressivo, -a [inespre'sivu, a] ADJ expressionless

infância [ī'fāsja] F childhood

infantil [īfã'tʃiw] (pl **-is**) ADJ (ingênuo) childlike; (pueril) childish; (para crianças) children's

infarto [ī'fartu] M heart attack

infecção [īfek'sãw] (pl **-ões**) F infection; **infeccionar** [īfeksjo'nar] VT (ferida) to infect; **infeccioso, -a** [īfek'sjozu, ɔza] ADJ infectious

infelicidade [īfelisi'dadʒi] F unhappiness; (desgraça) misfortune

infeliz [īfe'liz] ADJ unhappy; (infausto) unlucky; (ação, medida) unfortunate; (sugestão, ideia) inappropriate ▸ M/F unhappy person; **infelizmente** [īfeliz'mētʃi] ADV unfortunately

inferior [īfe'rjor] ADJ: **~ (a)** (em valor, qualidade) inferior (to); (mais baixo) lower (than) ▸ M/F inferior, subordinate; **inferioridade** [īferjori'dadʒi] F inferiority

infernal [īfer'naw] (pl **-ais**) ADJ infernal

inferno [ī'fɛrnu] M hell; **vá pro ~!** (col) go to hell!

infetar [īfe'tar] VT to infect

infiel [ī'fjew] (pl **-éis**) ADJ disloyal; (marido) unfaithful; (texto) inaccurate ▸ M/F (Rel) non-believer

ínfimo, -a [ī'fimu, a] ADJ lowest; (qualidade) poorest

infindável [īfī'davew] (pl **-eis**) ADJ unending, constant

infinidade [īfini'dadʒi] F infinity; **uma ~ de** countless

infinitivo, -a [īfini'tʃivu, a] ADJ, M (Ling) infinitive

inflação [īfla'sãw] F inflation; **inflacionário, -a** [īflasjo'narju, a] ADJ inflationary

inflamação [īflama'sãw] (pl **-ões**) F inflammation; **inflamado, -a** [īfla'madu, a] ADJ (Med) inflamed; (discurso) heated

inflamar [īfla'mar] VT (madeira, pólvora) to set fire to; (Med, fig) to inflame; **inflamar-se** VR to catch fire; (fig) to get worked up; **~-se de algo** to be consumed with sth

inflamável [īfla'mavew] (pl **-eis**) ADJ inflammable

inflar [ī'flar] VT to inflate, blow up; **inflar-se** VR to swell (up)

inflexível [īflek'sivew] (pl **-eis**) ADJ stiff, rigid; (fig) unyielding

influência [ī'flwēsja] F influence; **sob a ~ de** under the influence of; **influenciar** [īflwē'sjar] VT to influence ▸ VI: **influenciar em algo** to influence sth, have an influence on sth; **influenciar-se** VR: **influenciar-se por** to be influenced by; **influente** [ī'flwētʃi] ADJ influential; **influir** [ī'flwir] VI to matter, be important; **influir em** ou **sobre** to influence, have an influence on

informação [īforma'sãw] (pl **-ões**) F (piece of) information; (notícia) news; **informações** FPL (detalhes) information sg; **Informações** FPL (Tel) directory enquiries (BRIT), information (US); **pedir informações sobre** to ask about, inquire about

informal [īfor'maw] (pl **-ais**) ADJ informal

informar [īfor'mar] VT: **~ alguém (de/ sobre algo)** to inform sb (of/about sth) ▸ VI to inform, be informative; **informar-se** VR: **~-se de** to find out about, inquire about; **~ de** to report on

informática [īfor'matʃika] F IT, information technology

informativo, -a [īforma'tʃivu, a] ADJ informative

informatizar [īformatʃi'zar] VT to computerize

infortúnio [īfor'tunju] M misfortune

infração [īfra'sãw] (pl **-ões**) F breach, infringement; (Esporte) foul

infrator, a [īfra'tor(a)] M/F offender

infrutífero, -a [īfru'tʃiferu, a] ADJ fruitless

ingênuo, -a [ĩ'ʒenwu, a] ADJ ingenuous, naïve; (comentário) harmless ▸ M/F naïve person

ingerir [ĩʒe'rir] VT to ingest; (*engolir*) to swallow

Inglaterra [ĩgla'tɛha] F: **a ~** England; **inglês, -esa** [ĩ'gles, eza] ADJ English ▶ M/F Englishman/woman ▶ M (*Ling*) English; **os ingleses** MPL the English

ingrediente [ĩgre'dʒjẽtʃi] M ingredient

íngreme ['ĩgremi] ADJ steep

ingressar [ĩgre'sar] VI: **~ em** to enter, go into; (*um clube*) to join

ingresso [ĩ'grɛsu] M (*entrada*) entry; (*admissão*) admission; (*bilhete*) ticket

inibição [inibi'sãw] (*pl* **-ões**) F inhibition

inibido, -a [ini'bidu, a] ADJ inhibited

inibir [ini'bir] VT to inhibit

inicial [ini'sjaw] (*pl* **-ais**) ADJ, F initial

iniciar [ini'sjar] VT, VI (*começar*) to begin, start; **~ alguém em algo** (*arte, seita*) to initiate sb into sth

iniciativa [inisja'tʃiva] F initiative; **a ~ privada** (*Econ*) private enterprise

início [i'nisju] M beginning, start; **no ~** at the start

inimigo, -a [ini'migu, a] ADJ, M/F enemy

injeção [ĩʒe'sãw] (*pl* **-ões**) F injection

injetar [ĩʒe'tar] VT to inject

injúria [ĩ'ʒurja] F insult

injustiça [ĩʒus'tʃisa] F injustice

inocência [ino'sẽsja] F innocence

inocentar [inosẽ'tar] VT: **~ alguém (de algo)** to clear sb (of sth)

inocente [ino'sẽtʃi] ADJ innocent ▶ M/F innocent man/woman

inofensivo, -a [inofẽ'sivu, a] ADJ harmless, inoffensive

inovação [inova'sãw] (*pl* **-ões**) F innovation

inquérito [ĩ'kɛritu] M inquiry; (*Jur*) inquest

inquietação [ĩkjeta'sãw] F anxiety, uneasiness; (*agitação*) restlessness

inquietante [ĩkje'tãtʃi] ADJ worrying, disturbing

inquietar [ĩkje'tar] VT to worry, disturb; **inquietar-se** VR to worry, bother; **inquieto, -a** [ĩ'kjetu, a] ADJ anxious, worried; (*agitado*) restless

inquilino, -a [ĩki'linu, a] M/F tenant

insalubre [ĩsa'lubri] ADJ unhealthy

insanidade [ĩsani'dadʒi] F madness, insanity; **insano, -a** [ĩ'sanu, a] ADJ insane

insatisfatório, -a [ĩsatʃisfa'tɔrju, a] ADJ unsatisfactory

insatisfeito, -a [ĩsatʃis'fejtu, a] ADJ dissatisfied, unhappy

inscrever [ĩskre'ver] VT to inscribe; (*aluno*) to enrol (BRIT), enroll (US); (*em registro*) to register

inscrito, -a [ĩ'skritu, a] PP *de* **inscrever**

insegurança [ĩsegu'rãsa] F insecurity; **inseguro, -a** [ĩse'guru, a] ADJ insecure

insensato, -a [ĩsẽ'satu, a] ADJ unreasonable, foolish

inserir [ĩse'rir] VT to insert, put in; (*Comput: dados*) to enter

inseticida [ĩsetʃi'sida] M insecticide

inseto [ĩ'setu] M insect

insípido, -a [ĩ'sipidu, a] ADJ insipid

insiro [ĩ'siru] VB *ver* **inserir**

insistência [ĩsis'tẽsja] F: **~ (em)** insistence (on); (*obstinação*) persistence (in); **insistente** [ĩsis'tẽtʃi] ADJ (*pessoa*) insistent; (*apelo*) urgent

insistir [ĩsis'tʃir] VI: **~ (em)** to insist (on); (*perseverar*) to persist (in); **~ (em) que** to insist that

insolação [ĩsola'sãw] F sunstroke; **pegar uma ~** to get sunstroke

insólito, -a [ĩ'sɔlitu, a] ADJ unusual

insônia [ĩ'sonja] F insomnia

insosso, -a [ĩ'sosu, a] ADJ unsalted; (*sem sabor*) tasteless; (*pessoa*) uninteresting, dull

inspeção [ĩspe'sãw] (*pl* **-ões**) F inspection, check; **inspecionar** [ĩspesjo'nar] VT to inspect

inspetor, a [ĩspe'tor(a)] M/F inspector

inspirar [ĩspi'rar] VT to inspire; (*Med*) to inhale; **inspirar-se** VR to be inspired

INSS (BR) ABR M (= *Instituto Nacional do Seguro Social*) ≈ DSS (BRIT), ≈ Welfare Dept (US)

instalação [ĩstala'sãw] (*pl* **-ões**) F installation; **~ elétrica** (*de casa*) wiring

instalar [ĩsta'lar] VT to install; (*estabelecer*) to set up; **instalar-se** VR (*numa cadeira*) to settle down

instantâneo, -a [ĩstã'tanju, a] ADJ instant, instantaneous ▶ M (*Foto*) snap

instante [ĩs'tãtʃi] ADJ urgent ▶ M moment; **num ~** in an instant, quickly; **só um ~!** just a moment!

instável [ĩs'tavew] (*pl* **-eis**) ADJ unstable; (*tempo*) unsettled

instintivo, -a [ĩstʃĩ'tʃivu, a] ADJ instinctive

instinto [ĩs'tʃĩtu] M instinct; **por ~** instinctively

instituição [ĩstʃitwi'sãw] (*pl* **-ões**) F institution

instituto [ĩstʃi'tutu] M (*escola*) institute; (*instituição*) institution; **~ de beleza** beauty salon

instrução [ĩstru'sãw] (pl -ões) F
education; (erudição) learning; (diretriz)
instruction; (Mil) training; **instruções**
FPL (para o uso) instructions (for use)

instruído, -a [ĩs'trwidu, a] ADJ educated

instruir [ĩs'trwir] VT to instruct; (Mil) to
train; **instruir-se** VR: **~-se em algo** to
learn sth; **~ alguém de** ou **sobre algo** to
inform sb about sth

instrumento [ĩstru'mẽtu] M
instrument; (ferramenta) implement;
(Jur) deed, document; **~ de cordas/
percussão/sopro** stringed/percussion/
wind instrument; **~ de trabalho** tool

instrutivo, -a [ĩstru'tʃivu, a] ADJ
instructive

instrutor, a [ĩstru'tor(a)] M/F
instructor; (Esporte) coach

insubordinação [ĩsuboɾdʒina'sãw] F
rebellion; (Mil) insubordination

insubstituível [ĩsubistʃi'twivew]
(pl -eis) ADJ irreplaceable

insuficiência [ĩsufi'sjẽsja] F
inadequacy; (carência) shortage; (Med)
deficiency; **~ cardíaca** heart failure;
insuficiente [ĩsufi'sjẽtʃi] ADJ
insufficient; (Educ: nota) ≈ fail; (pessoa)
incompetent

insulina [ĩsu'lina] F insulin

insultar [ĩsuw'tar] VT to insult; **insulto**
[ĩ'suwtu] M insult

insuportável [ĩsupor'tavew] (pl -eis)
ADJ unbearable

insurgir-se [ĩsur'ʒirsi] VR to rebel, revolt

insurreição [ĩsuhej'sãw] (pl -ões) F
rebellion, insurrection

intato, -a [ĩ'tatu, a] ADJ intact

íntegra ['ĩtegra] F: **na ~** in full

integral [ĩte'graw] (pl -ais) ADJ whole
▶ F (Mat) integral; **pão ~** wholemeal
(BRIT) ou wholewheat (US) bread;
integralmente [ĩtegraw'mẽtʃi] ADV in
full, fully

integrar [ĩte'grar] VT to unite, combine;
(completar) to form, make up; (Mat, raças)
to integrate; **integrar-se** VR to become
complete; **~-se em** ou **a algo** to join sth;
(adaptar-se) to integrate into sth

integridade [ĩtegri'dadʒi] F entirety;
(fig: de pessoa) integrity

íntegro, -a [ĩtegru, a] ADJ entire;
(honesto) upright, honest

inteiramente [ĩtejra'mẽtʃi] ADV
completely

inteirar [ĩtej'rar] VT (completar) to
complete; **inteirar-se** VR: **~-se de** to
find out about; **~ alguém de** to inform
sb of

inteiro, -a [ĩ'tejru, a] ADJ whole, entire;
(ileso) unharmed; (não quebrado)
undamaged

intelecto [ĩte'lɛktu] M intellect;
intelectual [ĩtelek'twaw] (pl -ais) ADJ,
M/F intellectual

inteligência [ĩteli'ʒẽsja] F intelligence;
inteligente [ĩteli'ʒẽtʃi] ADJ intelligent;
(Tel) smart

inteligível [ĩteli'ʒivew] (pl -eis) ADJ
intelligible

intenção [ĩtẽ'sãw] (pl -ões) F intention;
segundas intenções ulterior motives;
ter a ~ de to intend to; **intencionado,
-a** [ĩtẽsjo'nadu, a] ADJ: **bem
intencionado** well-meaning; **mal
intencionado** spiteful; **intencional**
[ĩtẽsjo'naw] (pl -ais) ADJ intentional,
deliberate; **intencionar** [ĩtẽsjo'nar] VT
to intend

intensificar [ĩtẽsifi'kar] VT to intensify;
intensificar-se VR to intensify

intensivo, -a [ĩtẽ'sivu, a] ADJ intensive

intenso, -a [ĩ'tẽsu, a] ADJ intense;
(emoção) deep; (impressão) vivid; (vida
social) full

interação [ĩtera'sãw] F interaction

interativo, -a [ĩtera'tʃivu, a] ADJ
(Comput) interactive

intercâmbio [ĩter'kãbju] M exchange

interdição [ĩterdʒi'sãw] (pl -ões) F (de
estrada, porta) closure; (Jur) injunction

interditar [ĩterdʒi'tar] VT (importação
etc) to ban; (estrada, praia) to close off;
(cinema etc) to close down

interessado, -a [ĩtere'sadu, a] ADJ
interested; (amizade) self-seeking

interessante [ĩtere'sãtʃi] ADJ
interesting

interessar [ĩtere'sar] VT to interest ▶ VI
to be interesting; **interessar-se** VR: **~-se
em** ou **por** to take an interest in, be
interested in; **a quem possa ~** to whom
it may concern

interesse [ĩte'resi] M interest; (próprio)
self-interest; (proveito) advantage; **no ~
de** for the sake of; **por ~ (próprio)** for
one's own ends; **interesseiro, -a**
[ĩtere'sejru, a] ADJ self-seeking

interface [ĩter'fasi] F (Comput)
interface

interferência [ĩterfe'rẽsja] F
interference

interferir [ĩterfe'rir] VI: **~ em** to
interfere in; (rádio) to jam

interfone [ĩter'fɔni] M intercom

interior [ĩte'rjor] ADJ inner, inside; (Com)
domestic, internal ▶ M inside, interior;

(do país): **no ~** inland; **Ministério do I~** ≈ Home Office (BRIT), ≈ Department of the Interior (US)

interjeição [īterʒej'sãw] (pl **-ões**) F interjection

interlocutor, a [īterloku'tor(a)] M/F speaker; **meu ~** the person I was speaking to

intermediário, -a [īterme'dʒjarju, a] ADJ intermediary ▶ M/F (Com) middleman; (mediador) intermediary, mediator

intermédio [īter'mɛdʒu] M: **por ~ de** through

internação [īterna'sãw] (pl **-ões**) F (de doente) admission

internacional [īternasjo'naw] (pl **-ais**) ADJ international

internações [īterna'sõjs] FPL de **internação**

internar [īter'nar] VT (aluno) to put into boarding school; (doente) to take into hospital; (Mil, Pol) to intern

internauta [īter'nawta] M/F internet user, web ou net surfer (col)

Internet [īter'netʃi] F internet

interno, -a [ī'tɛrnu, a] ADJ internal; (Pol) domestic ▶ M/F (tb: **aluno ~**) boarder; (Med: estudante) houseman (BRIT), intern (US); **de uso ~** (Med) for internal use

interpretação [īterpreta'sãw] (pl **-ões**) F interpretation; (Teatro) performance

interpretar [īterpre'tar] VT to interpret; (um papel) to play; **intérprete** [ī'tɛrpretʃi] M/F interpreter; (Teatro) performer, artist

interrogação [ītehoga'sãw] (pl **-ões**) F interrogation; **ponto de ~** question mark

interrogar [īteho'gar] VT to question, interrogate; (Jur) to cross-examine

interromper [ītehõ'per] VT to interrupt; (parar) to stop; (Elet) to cut off

interruptor [ītehup'tor] M (Elet) switch

interseção [īterse'sãw] (pl **-ões**) F intersection

interurbano, -a [īterur'banu, a] ADJ (Tel) long-distance ▶ M long-distance ou trunk call

intervalo [īter'valu] M interval; (descanso) break; **a ~s** every now and then

intervir [īter'vir] (irreg: como **vir**) VI to intervene; (sobrevir) to come up

intimação [ītʃima'sãw] (pl **-ões**) F (ordem) order; (Jur) summons

intimar [ītʃi'mar] VT (Jur) to summon; **~ alguém a fazer** ou **a alguém que faça** to order sb to do

íntimo, -a [ī'tʃimu, a] ADJ intimate; (sentimentos) innermost; (amigo) close; (vida) private ▶ M/F close friend; **no ~** at heart

intolerante [ītole'ratʃi] ADJ intolerant

intolerável [ītole'ravew] (pl **-eis**) ADJ intolerable, unbearable

intoxicação [ītoksika'sãw] F poisoning; **~ alimentar** food poisoning

intoxicar [ītoksi'kar] VT to poison

intranet [ītra'netʃi] F intranet

intransitável [ītrãsi'tavew] (pl **-eis**) ADJ impassable

intratável [ītra'tavew] (pl **-eis**) ADJ (pessoa) contrary, awkward; (doença) untreatable; (problema) insurmountable

intriga [ī'triga] F intrigue; (enredo) plot; (fofoca) piece of gossip; **intrigas** FPL (fofocas) gossip sg; **~ amorosa** (PT) love affair; **intrigante** [ītri'gãtʃi] M/F troublemaker ▶ ADJ intriguing; **intrigar** [ītri'gar] VT to intrigue ▶ VI to be intriguing

introdução [ītrodu'sãw] (pl **-ões**) F introduction

introduzir [ītrodu'zir] VT to introduce

intrometer-se [ītrome'tersi] VR to interfere, meddle; **intrometido, -a** [ītrome'tʃidu, a] ADJ interfering; (col) nosey ▶ M/F busybody

introvertido, -a [ītrover'tʃidu, a] ADJ introverted ▶ M/F introvert

intruso, -a [ī'truzu, a] M/F intruder

intuição [ītwi'sãw] (pl **-ões**) F intuition

intuito [ī'tuito] M intention, aim

inúmero, -a [i'numeru, a] ADJ countless, innumerable

inundação [inũda'sãw] (pl **-ões**) F (enchente) flood; (ato) flooding

inundar [inũ'dar] VT to flood; (fig) to inundate ▶ VI to flood

inusitado, -a [inuzi'tadu, a] ADJ unusual

inútil [i'nutʃiw] (pl **-eis**) ADJ useless; (esforço) futile; (desnecessário) pointless; **inutilizar** [inutʃili'zar] VT to make useless, render useless; (incapacitar) to put out of action; (danificar) to ruin; (esforços) to thwart; **inutilmente** [inutʃiw'mẽtʃi] ADV in vain

invadir [īva'dʒir] VT to invade; (suj: água) to overrun; (: sentimento) to overcome

inválido, -a [ī'validu, a] ADJ, M/F invalid

invasão [īva'zãw] (pl **-ões**) F invasion

inveja [ĩ'veʒa] F envy; **invejar** [ĩve'ʒar] vt to envy; (*cobiçar*) to covet ▶ vi to be envious; **invejoso, -a** [ĩve'ʒozu, ɔza] ADJ envious

invenção [ĩvẽ'sãw] (*pl* **-ões**) F invention

inventado, -a [ĩvẽ'tadu, a] ADJ (*história, personagem*) made-up

inventar [ĩvẽ'tar] vt to invent

inventivo, -a [ĩvẽ'tʃivu, a] ADJ inventive

inventor, a [ĩvẽ'tor(a)] M/F inventor

inverno [ĩ'vɛrnu] M winter

inverossímil [ĩvero'simiw], (*PT*) **inverosímil** (*pl* **-eis**) ADJ unlikely, improbable; (*inacreditável*) implausible

invés [ĩ'vɛs] M: **ao ~ de** instead of

investigação [ĩvestʃiga'sãw] (*pl* **-ões**) F investigation; (*pesquisa*) research

investigar [ĩvestʃi'gar] vt to investigate; (*examinar*) to examine

investimento [ĩvestʃi'mẽtu] M investment

investir [ĩves'tʃir] vt (*dinheiro*) to invest

inviável [ĩ'vjavew] (*pl* **-eis**) ADJ impracticable

invisível [ĩvi'zivew] (*pl* **-eis**) ADJ invisible

invisto [ĩ'vistu] vʙ *ver* **investir**

invocar [ĩvo'kar] vt to invoke

ioga ['jɔga] F yoga

iogurte [jo'gurtʃi] M yogurt

IR (*BR*) ABR M **= imposto de renda**

PALAVRA-CHAVE

ir [ir] vɪ **1** to go; (*a pé*) to walk; (*a cavalo*) to ride; (*viajar*) to travel; **ir caminhando** to walk; **fui de trem** I went *ou* travelled by train; **vamos (embora)!, vamos nessa!** (*col*) let's go!; **já vou!** I'm coming!; **ir atrás de alguém** (*seguir*) to follow sb; (*confiar*) to take sb's word for it
2 (*progredir: pessoa, coisa*) to go; **o trabalho vai muito bem** work is going very well; **como vão as coisas?** how are things going?; **vou muito bem** I'm very well; (*na escola etc*) I'm getting on very well
▶ vʙ AUX **1** (+ *infin*): **vou fazer** I will do, I am going to do
2 (+ *gerúndio*): **ir fazendo** to keep on doing
ir-se vʀ to go away, leave

ira ['ira] F anger, rage

Irã [i'rã] M: **o ~** Iran

iraniano, -a [ira'njanu, a] ADJ, M/F Iranian

Irão [i'rãw] (*PT*) M = **Irã**

Iraque [i'raki] M: **o ~** Iraq; **iraquiano, -a** [ira'kjanu, a] ADJ, M/F Iraqi

ir e vir M INV comings and goings *pl*

Irlanda [ir'lãda] F: **a ~** Ireland; **a ~ do Norte** Northern Ireland; **irlandês, -esa** [irlã'des, eza] ADJ Irish ▶ M/F Irishman/woman ▶ M (*Ling*) Irish

irmã [ir'mã] F sister; **~ gêmea** twin sister; **~ de criação** adoptive sister

irmão [ir'mãw] (*pl* **irmãos**) M brother; (*fig: similar*) twin; (*col: companheiro*) mate; **~ de criação** adoptive brother; **~ gêmeo** twin brother

ironia [iro'nia] F irony

irra! ['iha] (*PT*) EXCL damn!

irracional [ihasjo'naw] (*pl* **-ais**) ADJ irrational

irreal [ihe'aw] (*pl* **-ais**) ADJ unreal

irregular [ihegu'lar] ADJ irregular; (*vida*) unconventional; (*feições*) unusual; (*aluno, gênio*) erratic

irremediável [iheme'dʒjavew] (*pl* **-eis**) ADJ irremediable; (*sem remédio*) incurable

irrequieto, -a [ihe'kjɛtu, a] ADJ restless

irresistível [ihezis'tʃivew] (*pl* **-eis**) ADJ irresistible

irresponsável [ihespõ'savew] (*pl* **-eis**) ADJ irresponsible

irrigar [ihi'gar] vt to irrigate

irritação [ihita'sãw] (*pl* **-ões**) F irritation

irritadiço, -a [ihita'dʒisu, a] ADJ irritable

irritante [ihi'tãtʃi] ADJ irritating, annoying

irritar [ihi'tar] vt to irritate; **irritar-se** vʀ to get angry, get annoyed

irromper [ihõ'per] vɪ (*entrar subitamente*): **~ (em)** to burst in(to)

isca ['iska] F (*Pesca*) bait; (*fig*) lure, bait

isenção [izẽ'sãw] (*pl* **-ões**) F exemption

isentar [izẽ'tar] vt to exempt; (*livrar*) to free

Islã [iz'lã] M Islam

Islândia [iz'lãdʒa] F: **a ~** Iceland

isolado, -a [izo'ladu, a] ADJ isolated; (*solitário*) lonely

isolamento [izola'mẽtu] M isolation; (*Elet*) insulation

isotônico, -a [izo'toniku, a] ADJ isotonic

isqueiro [is'kejru] M (cigarette) lighter

Israel [izha'ɛw] M Israel; **israelense** [izhae'lẽsi] ADJ, M/F Israeli

isso ['isu] PRON that; (*col: isto*) this; **~ mesmo** exactly; **por ~** therefore, so; **por ~ mesmo** for that very reason; **só ~?** is that all?

isto ['istu] PRON this; **~ é** that is, namely

Itália [i'talja] F: **a ~** Italy; **italiano, -a** [ita'ljanu, a] ADJ, M/F Italian ▶ M (*Ling*) Italian

Itamarati [itamara'tʃi] M: **o ~** the Brazilian Foreign Ministry

The Palace of **Itamarati** was built in 1855 in Rio de Janeiro. It became the seat of government when Brazil became a republic in 1889, and was later the Foreign Ministry. It ceased to be this when the Brazilian capital was transferred to Brasília, but **Itamarati** is still used to refer to the Foreign Ministry.

item ['itẽ] (pl **-ns**) M item
itinerário [itʃine'rarju] M itinerary; (caminho) route

J

já [ʒa] ADV already; (em perguntas) yet; (agora) now; (imediatamente) right away; (agora mesmo) right now ▶ CONJ on the other hand; **até já** bye; **desde já** from now on; **já não** no longer; **já que** as, since; **já se vê** of course; **já vou** I'm coming; **já até** even; **já, já** right away
jabuti [ʒabu'tʃi] M giant tortoise
jabuticaba [ʒabutʃi'kaba] F jaboticaba (type of berry)
jaca ['ʒaka] F jackfruit
jacaré [ʒaka'rɛ] (BR) M alligator
jaguar [ʒa'gwar] M jaguar
jaguatirica [ʒagwatʃi'rika] F leopard cat
Jamaica [ʒa'majka] F: **a ~** Jamaica
jamais [ʒa'majs] ADV never; (com palavra negativa) ever
janeiro [ʒa'nejru] M January
janela [ʒa'nɛla] F window
jangada [ʒã'gada] F raft
jantar [ʒã'tar] M dinner ▶ VT to have for dinner ▶ VI to have dinner
Japão [ʒa'pãw] M: **o ~** Japan; **japonês, -esa** [ʒapo'nes, eza] ADJ, M/F Japanese ▶ M (Ling) Japanese
jararaca [ʒara'raka] F jararaca (snake)
jardim [ʒar'dʒĩ] (pl **-ns**) M garden; **~ de infância** kindergarten; **~ zoológico** zoo; **jardinagem** [ʒardʒi'naʒẽ] F gardening
jardineira [ʒardʒi'nejra] F (caixa) trough; (calça) dungarees pl; ver tb **jardineiro**
jardineiro, -a [ʒardʒi'nejru, a] M/F gardener
jardins [ʒar'dʒĩs] MPL de **jardim**
jargão [ʒar'gãw] M jargon
jarra ['ʒaha] F pot
jarro ['ʒahu] M jug
jasmim [ʒaz'mĩ] M jasmine

jato ['ʒatu] M jet; (*de luz*) flash; (*de ar*) blast; **a ~** at top speed

jaula ['ʒawla] F cage

jazigo [ʒa'zigu] M grave; (*monumento*) tomb

jazz [dʒɛz] M jazz

jeito ['ʒejtu] M (*maneira*) way; (*aspecto*) appearance; (*aptidão, habilidade*) skill, knack; (*modos pessoais*) manner; **ter ~ de** to look like; **não ter ~** (*pessoa*) to be awkward; (*situação*) to be hopeless; **dar um ~ em algo** (*pé*) to twist sth; (*quarto, casa, papéis*) to tidy sth up; (*consertar*) to fix sth; **dar um ~** to find a way; **o ~ é ...** the thing to do is ...; **é o ~** it's the best way; **ao ~ de** in the style of; **com ~** tactfully; **daquele ~** (in) that way; (*col: em desordem, mal*) anyhow; **de qualquer ~** anyway; **de ~ nenhum!** no way!

jejuar [ʒe'ʒwar] vi to fast

jejum [ʒe'ʒũ] (*pl* **-ns**) M fast; **em ~** fasting

Jesus [ʒe'zus] M Jesus ▶ EXCL heavens!

jiboia [ʒi'bɔja] F boa (constrictor)

jihad [dʒi'ha:d] F jihad

jiló [ʒi'lɔ] M *kind of vegetable*

jingle ['dʒĩgew] M jingle

joalheria [ʒoaʎe'ria] F jeweller's (shop) (*BRIT*), jewelry store (*US*)

joaninha [ʒwa'niɲa] F ladybird (*BRIT*), ladybug (*US*)

joelho [ʒo'eʎu] M knee; **de ~s** kneeling; **ficar de ~s** to kneel down

jogada [ʒo'gada] F move; (*lanço*) throw; (*negócio*) scheme; move

jogador, a [ʒoga'dor(a)] M/F player; (*de jogo de azar*) gambler

jogar [ʒo'gar] vt to play; (*em jogo de azar*) to gamble; (*atirar*) to throw; (*indiretas*) to drop ▶ vi to play; to gamble; (*barco*) to pitch; **~ fora** to throw away

jogging ['ʒɔgĩ] M jogging; (*roupa*) track suit; **fazer ~** to go jogging, jog

jogo ['ʒogu] M game; (*jogar*) play; (*de azar*) gambling; (*conjunto*) set; (*artimanha*) trick; **~ de computador** computer game; **J~s Olímpicos** Olympic Games®

joia ['ʒɔja] F jewel

Jordânia [ʒor'danja] F: **a ~** Jordan; **Jordão** [ʒor'dãw] M: **o (rio) Jordão** the (River) Jordan

jornada [ʒor'nada] F journey; **~ de trabalho** working day

jornal [ʒor'naw] (*pl* **-ais**) M newspaper; (*TV, Rádio*) news *sg*; **jornaleiro, -a** [ʒorna'lejru, a] M/F newsagent (*BRIT*), newsdealer (*US*)

jornalismo [ʒorna'lizmu] M journalism; **jornalista** [ʒorna'lista] M/F journalist

jovem ['ʒɔvẽ] (*pl* **-ns**) ADJ young ▶ M/F young person

jovial [ʒo'vjaw] (*pl* **-ais**) ADJ jovial, cheerful

Jr ABR = **Júnior**

judaico, -a [ʒu'dajku, a] ADJ Jewish

judeu, judia [ʒu'dew, ʒu'dʒia] ADJ Jewish ▶ M/F Jew

judiar [ʒu'dʒjar] vi: **~ de alguém/algo** to ill-treat sb/sth

judicial [ʒudʒi'sjaw] (*pl* **-ais**) ADJ judicial

judiciário, -a [ʒudʒi'sjarju, a] ADJ judicial; **o (poder) ~** the judiciary

judô [ʒu'do] M judo

juiz, juíza [ʒwiz, -'iza] M/F judge; (*em jogos*) referee; **~ de paz** justice of the peace; **juizado** [ʒwi'zado] M court

juízo ['ʒwizu] M judgement; (*parecer*) opinion; (*siso*) common sense; (*foro*) court; **perder o ~** to lose one's mind; **não ter ~** to be foolish; **tomar** *ou* **criar ~** to come to one's senses; **chamar/levar a ~** to summon/take to court; **~!** behave yourself!

julgamento [ʒuwga'mẽtu] M judgement; (*audiência*) trial; (*sentença*) sentence

julgar [ʒuw'gar] vt to judge; (*achar*) to think; (*Jur: sentenciar*) to sentence; **julgar-se** vr: **~-se algo** to consider o.s. sth, think of o.s. as sth

julho ['ʒuʎu] M July

jumento, -a [ʒu'mẽtu, a] M/F donkey

junção [ʒũ'sãw] (*pl* **-ões**) F (*ato*) joining; (*junta*) join

junco ['ʒũku] M reed, rush

junções [ʒũ'sõjs] FPL *de* **junção**

junho ['ʒuɲu] M June

júnior ['ʒunjor] (*pl* **juniores**) ADJ younger, junior ▶ M/F (*Esporte*) junior; **Eduardo Autran J~** Eduardo Autran Junior

juntar [ʒũ'tar] vt to join; (*reunir*) to bring together; (*aglomerar*) to gather together; (*recolher*) to collect up; (*acrescentar*) to add; (*dinheiro*) to save up ▶ vi to gather; **juntar-se** vr to gather; (*associar-se*) to join up; **~-se a alguém** to join sb

junto, -a ['ʒũtu, a] ADJ joined; (*chegado*) near; **ir ~s** to go together; **~ a/de** near/next to; **segue ~** (*Com*) please find enclosed

jura ['ʒura] F vow

jurado, -a [ʒu'radu, a] ADJ sworn ▶ M/F juror

juramento [ʒura'mẽtu] M oath

jurar [ʒu'rar] vt, vi to swear; **jura?** really?

júri ['ʒuri] M jury

jurídico, -a [ʒu'ridʒiku, a] ADJ legal

juros ['ʒurus] MPL (*Econ*) interest *sg*;
~ **simples/compostos** simple/
compound interest

justamente [ʒusta'mẽtʃi] ADV fairly,
justly; (*precisamente*) exactly

justiça [ʒus'tʃisa] F justice; (*poder judiciário*)
judiciary; (*equidade*) fairness; (*tribunal*)
court; **com ~** justly, fairly; **ir à ~** to go
to court

justificar [ʒustʃifi'kar] VT to justify

justo, -a ['ʒustu, a] ADJ just, fair;
(*legítimo: queixa*) legitimate, justified;
(*exato*) exact; (*apertado*) tight ▶ ADV just

juvenil [ʒuve'niw] (*pl* **-is**) ADJ youthful;
(*roupa*) young; (*livro*) for young people;
(*Esporte: equipe, campeonato*) youth *atr*,
junior

juventude [ʒuvẽ'tudʒi] F youth;
(*jovialidade*) youthfulness; (*jovens*) young
people *pl*, youth

k

kg ABR (= *quilograma*) kg

kit ['kitʃi] (*pl* **-s**) M kit

kitchenette [kitʃe'nɛtʃi] F studio flat

km ABR (= *quilômetro*) km

km/h ABR (= *quilômetros por hora*) km/h

lá [la] ADV there ▶ M (*Mús*) A; **lá fora** outside; **lá em baixo** down there; **por lá** (*direção*) that way; (*situação*) over there; **até lá** (*no espaço*) there; (*no tempo*) until then

lã [lã] F wool

-la [la] PRON her; (*você*) you; (*coisa*) it

labia ['labja] F (*astúcia*) cunning; **ter ~** to have the gift of the gab

lábio ['labju] M lip

labirinto [labi'rĩtu] M labyrinth, maze

laboratório [labora'tɔrju] M laboratory

laca ['laka] F lacquer

laçar [la'sar] VT to bind, tie

laço ['lasu] M bow; (*de gravata*) knot; (*armadilha*) snare; (*fig*) bond, tie; **dar um ~** to tie a bow

lacrar [la'krar] VT to seal (with wax); **lacre** ['lakri] M sealing wax

lacuna [la'kuna] F gap; (*omissão*) omission; (*espaço em branco*) blank

ladeira [la'dejra] F slope

lado ['ladu] M side; (*Mil*) flank; (*rumo*) direction; **ao ~** (*perto*) close by; **a casa ao ~** the house next door; **ao ~ de** beside; **deixar de ~** to set aside; (*fig*) to leave out; **de um ~ para outro** back and forth

ladra ['ladra] F thief, robber; (*picareta*) crook

ladrão, -ona [la'drãw, ɔna] (*pl* **-ões/-s**) ADJ thieving ▶ M/F thief, robber; (*picareta*) crook

ladrilho [la'driʎu] M tile; (*chão*) tiled floor, tiles *pl*

ladrões [la'drõjs] MPL *de* **ladrão**

lagarta [la'garta] F caterpillar

lagartixa [lagar'tʃiʃa] F gecko

lagarto [la'gartu] M lizard

lago ['lagu] M lake; (*de jardim*) pond

lagoa [la'goa] F pool, pond; (*lago*) lake

lagosta [la'gosta] F lobster

lagostim [lagos'tʃĩ] (*pl* **-ns**) M crayfish

lágrima ['lagrima] F tear

lama ['lama] F mud

lamaçal [lama'saw] (*pl* **-ais**) M quagmire; (*pântano*) bog, marsh

lamber [lã'ber] VT to lick; **lambida** [lã'bida] F: **dar uma lambida em algo** to lick sth

lambuzar [lãbu'zar] VT to smear

lamentar [lamẽ'tar] VT to lament; (*sentir*) to regret; **lamentar-se** VR: **~-se (de algo)** to lament (sth); **~ (que)** to be sorry (that); **lamentável** [lamẽ'tavew] (*pl* **-eis**) ADJ regrettable; (*deplorável*) deplorable; **lamento** [la'mẽtu] M lament; (*gemido*) moan

lâmina ['lamina] F (*chapa*) sheet; (*placa*) plate; (*de faca*) blade; (*de persiana*) slat

lâmpada ['lãpada] F lamp; (*tb*: **~ elétrica**) light bulb; **~ de mesa** table lamp

lançar [lã'sar] VT to throw; (*navio, produto, campanha*) to launch; (*disco, filme*) to release; (*Com: em livro*) to enter; (*em leilão*) to bid

lancha ['lãʃa] F launch; **~ torpedeira** torpedo boat

lanchar [lã'ʃar] VI to have a snack ▶ VT to have as a snack; **lanche** ['lãʃi] M snack

lanchonete [lãʃo'nɛtʃi] (*BR*) F snack bar

LAN house [lã'hawzi] F internet café

lanterna [lã'tɛrna] F lantern; (*portátil*) torch (*BRIT*), flashlight (*US*)

lápide ['lapidʒi] F (*tumular*) tombstone; (*comemorativa*) memorial stone

lápis ['lapis] M INV pencil; **~ de cor** coloured (*BRIT*) *ou* colored (*US*) pencil, crayon; **~ de olho** eyebrow pencil; **lapiseira** [lapi'zejra] F propelling (*BRIT*) *ou* mechanical (*US*) pencil; (*caixa*) pencil case

lapso ['lapsu] M lapse; (*de tempo*) interval; (*erro*) slip

lar [lar] M home

laranja [la'rãʒa] ADJ INV orange ▶ F orange ▶ M (*cor*) orange; **laranjada** [larã'ʒada] F orangeade; **laranjeira** [larã'ʒejra] F orange tree

lareira [la'rejra] F hearth, fireside

larga ['larga] F: **à ~** lavishly; **dar ~s a** to give free rein to; **viver à ~** to lead a lavish life

largada [lar'gada] F start; **dar a ~** to start; (*fig*) to make a start

largar [lar'gar] VT to let go of, release; (*deixar*) to leave; (*deixar cair*) to drop; (*risada*) to let out; (*velas*) to unfurl; (*piada*) to tell; (*pôr em liberdade*) to let go ▶ VI (*Náut*) to set sail; **largar-se** VR (*desprender-se*) to free o.s.; (*ir-se*) to go off; (*pôr-se*) to proceed

largo, -a ['largu, a] ADJ wide, broad; (*amplo*) extensive; (*roupa*) loose, baggy; (*conversa*) long ▶ M (*praça*) square; (*alto-mar*) open sea; **ao ~** at a distance, far off; **passar de ~ sobre um assunto** to gloss over a subject; **passar ao ~ de algo** (*fig*) to sidestep sth; **largura** [lar'gura] F width, breadth

laringite [larĩ'ʒitʃi] F laryngitis

lasanha [la'zaɲa] F lasagna

laser ['lejzer] M laser; **raio ~** laser beam

lástima ['lastʃima] F pity, compassion; (*infortúnio*) misfortune; **é uma ~ (que)** it's a shame (that); **lastimar** [lastʃi'mar] VT to lament; **lastimar-se** VR to complain, feel sorry for o.s.

lata ['lata] F can, tin (BRIT); (*material*) tin-plate; **~ de lixo** rubbish bin (BRIT), garbage can (US); **~ velha** (*col: carro*) old banger (BRIT) *ou* clunker (US)

latão [la'tãw] M brass

lataria [lata'ria] F (*Auto*) bodywork; (*enlatados*) canned food

latejar [late'ʒar] VI to throb

latente [la'tẽtʃi] ADJ latent

lateral [late'raw] (*pl* -**ais**) ADJ side, lateral ▶ F (*Futebol*) sideline ▶ M (*Futebol*) throw-in

latido [la'tʃidu] M bark(ing), yelp(ing)

latifundiário, -a [latʃifũ'dʒjarju, a] M/F landowner

latifúndio [latʃi'fũdʒju] M large estate

latim [la'tʃĩ] M (*Ling*) Latin; **gastar o seu ~** to waste one's breath

latino, -a [la'tʃinu, a] ADJ Latin; **latino-americano, -a** ADJ, M/F Latin-American

latir [la'tʃir] VI to bark, yelp

latitude [latʃi'tudʒi] F latitude; (*largura*) breadth; (*fig*) scope

latrocínio [latro'sinju] M armed robbery

laudo ['lawdu] M (*Jur*) decision; (*resultados*) findings pl; (*peça escrita*) report

lava ['lava] F lava

lavabo [la'vabu] M toilet

lavadeira [lava'dejra] F washerwoman

lavagem [la'vaʒẽ] F washing; **~ a seco** dry cleaning; **~ cerebral** brainwashing

lavanda [la'vãda] F (*Bot*) lavender; (*colônia*) lavender water; (*para lavar os dedos*) finger bowl

lavar [la'var] VT to wash; (*culpa*) to wash away; **~ a seco** to dry-clean

lavatório [lava'tɔrju] M washbasin; (*aposento*) toilet

lavoura [la'vora] F tilling; (*agricultura*) farming; (*terreno*) plantation

laxativo, -a [laʃa'tʃivu, a] ADJ, M laxative

lazer [la'zer] M leisure

leal [le'aw] (*pl* -**ais**) ADJ loyal; **lealdade** [leaw'dadʒi] F loyalty

leão [le'ãw] (*pl* -**ões**) M lion; **L~** (*Astrologia*) Leo

lebre ['lebri] F hare

lecionar [lesjo'nar] VT, VI to teach

legal [le'gaw] (*pl* -**ais**) ADJ legal, lawful; (*col*) fine; (: *pessoa*) nice ▶ ADV (*col*) well; **(tá) ~!** OK!; **legalidade** [legali'dadʒi] F legality, lawfulness; **legalizar** [legali'zar] VT to legalize; (*documento*) to authenticate

legendado, -a [leʒẽ'dadu, a] ADJ (*filme*) subtitled

legendário, -a [leʒẽ'darju, a] ADJ legendary

legislação [leʒizla'sãw] F legislation

legislar [leʒiz'lar] VI to legislate ▶ VT to pass

legislativo, -a [leʒizla'tʃivu, a] ADJ legislative ▶ M legislature

legitimar [leʒitʃi'mar] VT to legitimize; (*justificar*) to legitimate

legume [le'gumi] M vegetable

lei [lej] F law; (*regra*) rule; (*metal*) standard

leigo, -a ['lejgu, a] ADJ (*Rel*) lay, secular ▶ M layman; **ser ~ em algo** (*fig*) to be no expert at sth, be unversed in sth

leilão [lej'lãw] (*pl* -**ões**) M auction; **vender em ~** to sell by auction, auction off; **leiloar** [lej'lwar] VT to auction

leio ['leju] VB *ver* **ler**

leitão, -toa [lej'tãw, 'toa] (*pl* -**ões**/-**s**) M/F sucking (BRIT) *ou* suckling (US) pig

leite ['lejtʃi] M milk; **~ em pó** powdered milk; **~ desnatado** *ou* **magro** skimmed milk; **~ de magnésia** milk of magnesia; **~ semidesnatado** semi-skimmed milk; **leiteira** [lej'tejra] F (*para ferver*) milk pan; (*para servir*) milk jug; **leiteiro, -a** [lej'tejru, a] ADJ (*vaca, gado*) dairy ▶ M/F milkman/woman

leitões [lej'tõjs] MPL *de* **leitão**

leitor, a [lej'tor(a)] M/F (*pessoa*) reader; (*professor*) lector ▶ M (*objeto*) reader; **~ de livros digitais** e-reader

leitura [lej'tura] F reading; (*livro etc*) reading matter

lema ['lɛma] M motto; (*Pol*) slogan

lembrança [lẽ'brãsa] F recollection, memory; (*presente*) souvenir; **lembranças** FPL (*recomendações*): **~s a sua mãe!** regards to your mother!

lembrar [lẽ'brar] VT, VI to remember; **lembrar-se** VR: **~(-se) de** to remember; **~(-se) (de) que** to remember that; **~ algo a alguém, ~ alguém de algo** to remind sb of sth; **~ alguém de que, ~ a alguém que** to remind sb that; **ele lembra meu irmão** he reminds me of my brother, he is like my brother; **lembrete** [lẽ'bretʃi] M reminder

leme ['lɛmi] M rudder; (*Náut*) helm; (*fig*) control

lenço ['lẽsu] M handkerchief; (*de pescoço*) scarf; (*de cabeça*) headscarf; **~ de papel** tissue; **~ umedecido** baby wipe

lençol [lẽ'sɔw] (*pl* **-óis**) M sheet; **estar em maus lençóis** to be in a fix

lenda ['lẽda] F legend; (*fig: mentira*) lie; **lendário, -a** [lẽ'darju, a] ADJ legendary

lenha ['lɛɲa] F firewood

lente ['lẽtʃi] F lens *sg*; **~ de aumento** magnifying glass; **~s de contato** contact lenses

lentidão [lẽtʃi'dãw] F slowness

lento, -a ['lẽtu, a] ADJ slow

leoa [le'oa] F lioness

leões [le'õjs] MPL *de* **leão**

leopardo [ljo'pardu] M leopard

lepra ['lɛpra] F leprosy

leque ['lɛki] M fan; (*fig*) array

ler [ler] VT, VI to read

lesão [le'zãw] (*pl* **-ões**) F harm, injury; (*Jur*) violation; (*Med*) lesion; **~ corporal** (*Jur*) bodily harm

lesar [le'zar] VT to harm, damage; (*direitos*) to violate

lésbica ['lɛzbika] F lesbian

lesma ['lezma] F slug; (*fig: pessoa*) slowcoach

lesões [le'zõjs] FPL *de* **lesão**

lesse ['lesi] VB *ver* **ler**

leste ['lɛstʃi] M east

letal [le'taw] (*pl* **-ais**) ADJ lethal

letargia [letar'ʒia] F lethargy

letivo, -a [le'tʃivu, a] ADJ school *atr*; **ano ~** academic year

letra ['letra] F letter; (*caligrafia*) handwriting; (*de canção*) lyrics *pl*; **Letras** FPL (*curso*) language and literature; **à ~** literally; **ao pé da ~** literally, word for word; **~ de câmbio** (*Com*) bill of exchange; **~ de imprensa** print;

letrado, -a [le'tradu, a] ADJ learned, erudite ▶ M/F scholar; **letreiro** [le'trejru] M sign, notice; (*inscrição*) inscription; (*Cinema*) subtitle

leu [lew] VB *ver* **ler**

léu [lɛw] M: **ao ~** (*à toa*) aimlessly; (*à mostra*) uncovered

leucemia [lewse'mia] F leukaemia (BRIT), leukemia (US)

levado, -a [le'vadu, a] ADJ mischievous; (*criança*) naughty

levantador, a [levãta'dor(a)] ADJ lifting ▶ M/F: **~ de pesos** weightlifter

levantamento [levãta'mẽtu] M lifting, raising; (*revolta*) uprising, rebellion; (*arrolamento*) survey

levantar [levã'tar] VT to lift, raise; (*voz, capital*) to raise; (*apanhar*) to pick up; (*suscitar*) to arouse; (*ambiente*) to brighten up ▶ VI to stand up; (*da cama*) to get up; (*dar vida*) to brighten; **levantar-se** VR to stand up; (*da cama*) to get up; (*rebelar-se*) to rebel

levar [le'var] VT to take; (*portar*) to carry; (*tempo*) to pass, spend; (*roupa*) to wear; (*lidar com*) to handle; (*induzir*) to lead; (*filme*) to show; (*peça teatral*) to do, put on; (*vida*) to lead ▶ VI to get a beating; **~ a** to lead to; **~ a mal** to take amiss

leve ['lɛvi] ADJ light; (*insignificante*) slight; **de ~** lightly, softly

leviandade [levjã'dadʒi] F frivolity

leviano, -a [le'vjanu, a] ADJ frivolous

lha [ʎa] = **lhe + a**

lhas [ʎas] = **lhe + as**

lhe [ʎi] PRON (*a ele*) to him; (*a ela*) to her; (*a você*) to you

lhes [ʎis] PRON PL (*a eles/elas*) to them; (*a vocês*) to you

lho [ʎu] = **lhe + o**

lhos [ʎus] = **lhe + os**

li [li] VB *ver* **ler**

Líbano ['libanu] M: **o ~** Lebanon

libélula [li'bɛlula] F dragonfly

liberação [libera'sãw] F liberation

liberal [libe'raw] (*pl* **-ais**) ADJ, M/F liberal

liberar [libe'rar] VT to release; (*permitir*) to allow

liberdade [liber'dadʒi] F freedom; **liberdades** FPL (*direitos*) liberties; **pôr alguém em ~** to set sb free; **~ condicional** probation; **~ de palavra** freedom of speech; **~ sob palavra** parole

libertação [liberta'sãw] F release

libertino, -a [liber'tʃinu, a] ADJ loose-living ▶ M/F libertine

Líbia ['libja] F: **a ~** Libya

libidinoso, -a [libidʒi'nozu, ɔza] ADJ lecherous, lustful

líbio, -a ['libju, a] ADJ, M/F Libyan

libra ['libra] F pound; **L~** (*Astrologia*) Libra

lição [li'sãw] (*pl* **-ões**) F lesson

licença [li'sẽsa] F licence (BRIT), license (US); (*permissão*) permission; (*do trabalho, Mil*) leave; **com ~** excuse me; **estar de ~** to be on leave; **dá ~?** may I?

licenciado, -a [lisẽ'sjadu, a] M/F graduate

licenciar [lisẽ'sjar] VT to license; **licenciar-se** VR (*Educ*) to graduate; (*ficar de licença*) to take leave; **licenciatura** [lisẽsja'tura] F (*título*) degree; (*curso*) degree course

liceu [li'sew] (*PT*) M secondary (BRIT) ou high (US) school

lições [li'sõjs] FPL *de* **lição**

licor [li'kor] M liqueur

lidar [li'dar] VI: **~ com** (*ocupar-se*) to deal with; (*combater*) to struggle against; **~ em algo** to work in sth

líder ['lider] M/F leader; **liderança** [lide'rãsa] F leadership; (*Esporte*) lead; **liderar** [lide'rar] VT to lead

ligado, -a [li'gadu, a] ADJ (*Tec*) connected; (*luz, rádio etc*) on; (*metal*) alloy

ligadura [liga'dura] F bandage

ligamento [liga'mẽtu] M ligament

ligar [li'gar] VT to tie, bind; (*unir*) to join, connect; (*luz, TV*) to switch on; (*afetivamente*) to bind together; (*carro*) to start (up) ▸ VI (*telefonar*) to ring; **ligar-se** VR to join; **~-se com alguém** to join with sb; **~-se a algo** to be connected with sth; **~ para alguém** to ring sb up; **~ para** ou **a algo** (*dar atenção*) to take notice of sth; (*dar importância*) to care about sth; **eu nem ligo** it doesn't bother me; **não ligo a mínima (para)** I couldn't care less (about)

ligeiro, -a [li'ʒejru, a] ADJ light; (*ferimento*) slight; (*referência*) passing; (*conhecimentos*) scant; (*rápido*) quick, swift; (*ágil*) nimble ▸ ADV swiftly, nimbly

lilás [li'las] ADJ, M lilac

lima ['lima] F (*laranja*) type of orange; (*ferramenta*) file; **~ de unhas** nailfile

limão [li'mãw] (*pl* **-ões**) M lime; (*tb:* **~-galego**) lemon

limiar [li'mjar] M threshold

limitação [limita'sãw] (*pl* **-ões**) F limitation, restriction

limitar [limi'tar] VT to limit, restrict; **limitar-se** VR: **~-se a** to limit o.s. to;

~(-se) com to border on; **limite** [li'mitʃi] M limit, boundary; (*fig*) limit; **passar dos limites** to go too far

limo ['limu] M (*Bot*) water weed; (*lodo*) slime

limoeiro [li'mwejru] M lemon tree

limões [li'mõjs] MPL *de* **limão**

limonada [limo'nada] F lemonade (BRIT), lemon soda (US)

limpar [lĩ'par] VT to clean; (*lágrimas, suor*) to wipe away; (*polir*) to shine, polish; (*fig*) to clean up; (*roubar*) to rob

limpo, -a ['lĩpu, a] PP *de* **limpar** ▸ ADJ clean; (*céu, consciência*) clear; (*Com*) net; (*fig*) pure; (*col: pronto*) ready; **passar a ~** to make a fair copy; **tirar a ~** to find out the truth about, clear up; **estar ~ com alguém** (*col*) to be in with sb

linchar [lĩ'ʃar] VT to lynch

lindo, -a ['lĩdu, a] ADJ lovely

lingerie [lĩʒe'ri] M lingerie

língua ['lĩgwa] F tongue; (*linguagem*) language; **botar a ~ para fora** to stick out one's tongue; **dar com a ~ nos dentes** to let the cat out of the bag; **estar na ponta da ~** to be on the tip of one's tongue

linguado [lĩ'gwadu] M (*peixe*) sole

linguagem [lĩ'gwaʒẽ] (*pl* **-ns**) F (*tb: Comput*) language; **~ de máquina** (*Comput*) machine language

linguarudo, -a [lĩgwa'rudu, a] ADJ gossiping ▸ M/F gossip

linguiça [lĩ'gwisa] F sausage

linha ['liɲa] F line; (*para costura*) thread; (*barbante*) string, cord; **linhas** FPL (*carta*) letter *sg*; **em ~** in line, in a row; (*Comput*) on line; **fora de ~** out of production; **manter/perder a ~** to keep/lose one's cool; **o telefone não deu ~** the line was dead; **~ aérea** airline; (*PT*) helpline; **~ de apoio** (*PT*) helpline; **~ de mira** sights *pl*; **~ de montagem** assembly line; **~ férrea** railway (BRIT), railroad (US)

linho ['liɲu] M linen; (*planta*) flax

liquidação [likida'sãw] (*pl* **-ões**) F liquidation; (*em loja*) (clearance) sale; (*de conta*) settlement; **em ~** on sale

liquidar [liki'dar] VT to liquidate; (*conta*) to settle; (*mercadoria*) to sell off; (*assunto*) to lay to rest ▸ VI (*loja*) to have a sale; **liquidar-se** VR (*destruir-se*) to be destroyed; **~ (com) alguém** (*fig: arrasar*) to destroy sb; (: *matar*) to do away with sb

liquidificador [likwidʒifika'dor] M liquidizer

líquido, -a ['likidu, a] ADJ liquid, fluid; (*Com*) net ▸ M liquid

lira ['lira] F lyre; (*moeda*) lira
lírio ['lirju] M lily
Lisboa [liz'boa] N Lisbon; **lisboeta** [liz'bweta] ADJ Lisbon *atr* ▶ M/F inhabitant *ou* native of Lisbon
liso, -a ['lizu, a] ADJ smooth; (*tecido*) plain; (*cabelo*) straight; (*col: sem dinheiro*) broke
lisonjear [lizõ'ʒjar] VT to flatter
lista ['lista] F list; (*listra*) stripe; (*PT: menu*) menu; ~ **negra** blacklist; ~ **telefônica** telephone directory; **listar** [lis'tar] VT to list
listra ['listra] F stripe; **listrado, -a** [lis'tradu, a] ADJ striped
literal [lite'raw] (*pl* **-ais**) ADJ literal
literário, -a [lite'rarju, a] ADJ literary
literatura [litera'tura] F literature;
Literatura de cordel *see note*

> **Literatura de cordel** is a type of literature typical of the north-east of Brazil, and published in the form of cheaply printed booklets. Their authors hang these booklets from wires attached to walls in the street so that people can look at them. While they do this, the authors sing their stories aloud. **Literatura de cordel** deals both with local events and people, and with everyday public life, almost always in an irreverent manner.

litoral [lito'raw] (*pl* **-ais**) ADJ coastal ▶ M coast, seaboard
litro ['litru] M litre (BRIT), liter (US)
livrar [li'vrar] VT to release, liberate; (*salvar*) to save; **livrar-se** VR to escape; **~-se de** to get rid of; (*compromisso*) to get out of; **Deus me livre!** Heaven forbid!
livraria [livra'ria] F bookshop (BRIT), bookstore (US)
livre ['livri] ADJ free; (*lugar*) unoccupied; (*desimpedido*) clear, open; ~ **de impostos** tax-free; **livre-arbítrio** M free will
livro ['livru] M book; ~ **brochado** paperback; ~ **de bolso** pocket-sized book; ~ **de cheques** cheque book (BRIT), check book (US); ~ **de consulta** reference book; ~ **eletrônico** e-book; ~ **encadernado** *ou* **de capa dura** hardback
lixa ['liʃa] F sandpaper; (*de unhas*) nailfile; (*peixe*) dogfish; **lixar** [li'ʃar] VT to sand
lixeira [li'ʃejra] F dustbin (BRIT), garbage can (US)
lixeiro [li'ʃejru] M dustman (BRIT), garbage man (US)

lixo ['liʃu] M rubbish, garbage (US); **ser um ~** (*col*) to be rubbish; ~ **atômico** nuclear waste
-lo [lu] PRON him; (*você*) you; (*coisa*) it
lobo ['lobu] M wolf
locação [loka'sãw] (*pl* **-ões**) F lease; (*de vídeo etc*) rental
locador, a [loka'dor(a)] M/F (*de casa*) landlord; (*de carro, filme*) rental agent ▶ F rental company; ~ **a de vídeo** video rental shop
local [lo'kaw] (*pl* **-ais**) ADJ local ▶ M site, place ▶ F (*notícia*) story; **localidade** [lokali'dadʒi] F (*lugar*) locality; (*povoação*) town; **localização** [lokaliza'sãw] (*pl* **-ões**) F location; **localizar** [lokali'zar] VT to locate; (*situar*) to place; **localizar-se** VR to be located; (*orientar-se*) to get one's bearings
loção [lo'sãw] (*pl* **-ões**) F lotion; ~ **após-barba** aftershave (lotion)
locatário, -a [loka'tarju, a] M/F (*de casa*) tenant; (*de carro, filme*) hirer
loções [lo'sõjs] FPL *de* **loção**
locomotiva [lokomo'tʃiva] F railway (BRIT) *ou* railroad (US) engine, locomotive
locomover-se [lokomo'versi] VR to move around
locutor, a [loku'tor(a)] M/F (*TV, Rádio*) announcer
lógica ['lɔʒika] F logic; **lógico, -a** ['lɔʒiku, a] ADJ logical; **(é) lógico!** of course!
logo ['lɔgu] ADV (*imediatamente*) right away, at once; (*em breve*) soon; (*justamente*) just, right; (*mais tarde*) later; ~, ~ in no time; ~ **mais** later; ~ **no começo** right at the start; ~ **que, tão ~** as soon as; **até ~!** bye!; ~ **antes/depois** just before/shortly afterwards; ~ **de saída** *ou* **de cara** straightaway, right away
logotipo [logo'tʃipu] M logo
lograr [lo'grar] VT (*alcançar*) to achieve; (*obter*) to get, obtain; (*enganar*) to cheat; ~ **fazer** to manage to do
loiro, -a ['lojru, a] ADJ = **louro**
loja ['lɔʒa] F shop; ~ **de presentes** gift shop (BRIT), gift store (US); **lojista** [lo'ʒista] M/F shopkeeper
lombo ['lõbu] M back; (*carne*) loin
lona ['lɔna] F canvas
Londres ['lõdris] N London; **londrino, -a** [lõ'drinu, a] ADJ London *atr* ▶ M/F Londoner
longa-metragem (*pl* **longas-metragens**) M: **(filme de) ~** feature (film)

longe ['lõʒi] ADV far, far away ▸ ADJ
distant; **ao ~** in the distance; **de ~** from
far away; (sem dúvida) by a long way; **~ de**
a long way ou far from; **~ disso** far from
it; **ir ~ demais** (fig) to go too far

longínquo, -a [lõ'ʒĩkwu, a] ADJ distant,
remote

longitude [lõʒi'tudʒi] F (Geo) longitude

longo, -a ['lõgu, a] ADJ long ▸ M (vestido)
long dress, evening dress; **ao ~ de** along,
alongside

lotação [lota'sãw] F capacity; (de
funcionários) complement; (BR: ônibus)
bus; **~ completa** ou **esgotada** (Teatro)
sold out

lotado, -a [lo'tadu, a] ADJ (Teatro) full;
(ônibus) full up; (bar, praia) packed,
crowded

lotar [lo'tar] VT to fill, pack; (funcionário)
to place ▸ VI to fill up

lote ['lɔtʃi] M portion, share; (em leilão)
lot; (terreno) plot; (de ações) parcel, batch

loteria [lote'ria] F lottery; **~ esportiva**
football pools pl (BRIT), lottery (US)

louça ['losa] F china; (conjunto) crockery;
(tb: **~ sanitária**) bathroom suite; **de ~**
china atr; **~ de barro** earthenware; **~ de
jantar** dinner service; **lavar a ~** to do
the washing up (BRIT) ou the dishes

louco, -a ['loku, a] ADJ crazy, mad;
(sucesso) runaway; (frio) freezing ▸ M/F
lunatic (pej); **~ varrido** raving mad; **~ de
fome/raiva** ravenous/hopping mad;
~ por crazy about; **deixar alguém ~** to
drive sb crazy; **loucura** [lo'kura] F
madness; (ato) crazy thing; **ser loucura
(fazer)** to be crazy (to do); **ser uma
loucura** to be crazy; (col: ser muito bom)
to be fantastic

louro, -a ['loru, a] ADJ blond, fair ▸ M
laurel; (Culin) bay leaf; (papagaio) parrot;
louros MPL (fig) laurels

louva-a-deus ['lova-] M INV praying
mantis

louvar [lo'var] VT, VI: **~ (a)** to praise;
louvável [lo'vavew] (pl -**eis**) ADJ
praiseworthy

louvor [lo'vor] M praise

LP ABR M LP (record)

Ltda. ABR (= Limitada) Ltd

lua ['lua] F moon; **estar** ou **viver no
mundo da ~** to have one's head in the
clouds; **estar de ~** (col) to be in a mood;
ser de ~ (col) to be moody; **~ cheia/
nova** full/new moon; **~ de mel**
honeymoon

luar ['lwar] M moonlight

lubrificante [lubrifi'kãtʃi] M lubricant

lúcido, -a ['lusidu, a] ADJ lucid

lúcio ['lusju] M (peixe) pike

lucrar [lu'krar] VT (tirar proveito) to profit
from ou by; (dinheiro) to make; (gozar) to
enjoy ▸ VI to make a profit; **~ com** ou **em**
to profit by

lucrativo, -a [lukra'tʃivu, a] ADJ
lucrative, profitable

lucro ['lukru] M gain; (Com) profit; **~s e
perdas** (Com) profit and loss

lugar [lu'gar] M place; (espaço) space,
room; (para sentar) seat; (emprego) job;
(ocasião) opportunity; **em ~ de** instead
of; **dar ~ a** (causar) to give rise to;
~ comum commonplace; **em
primeiro ~** in the first place; **em algum/
nenhum/todo ~** somewhere/
nowhere/everywhere; **em outro ~**
somewhere else, elsewhere; **ter ~**
(acontecer) to take place; **~ de
nascimento** place of birth; **lugarejo**
[luga'reʒu] M village

lula ['lula] F squid

lume ['lumi] M fire; (luz) light

luminária [lumi'narja] F lamp;
luminárias FPL (iluminações)
illuminations

luminosidade [luminozi'dadʒi] F
brightness

luminoso, -a [lumi'nozu, ɔza] ADJ
luminous; (fig: raciocínio) clear; (: ideia,
talento) brilliant; (letreiro) illuminated

lunar [lu'nar] ADJ lunar ▸ M (na pele) mole

lunático, -a [lu'natʃiku, a] ADJ mad

lusitano, -a [luzi'tanu, a] ADJ
Portuguese, Lusitanian

luso, -a ['luzu, a] ADJ Portuguese;
luso-brasileiro, -a (pl **luso-brasileiros**)
ADJ Luso-Brazilian

lustre ['lustri] M gloss, sheen; (fig) lustre
(BRIT), luster (US); (luminária) chandelier

luta ['luta] F fight, struggle; **~ de boxe**
boxing; **~ livre** wrestling; **lutador, a**
[luta'dor(a)] M/F fighter; (atleta)
wrestler; **lutar** [lu'tar] VI to fight,
struggle; (luta livre) to wrestle ▸ VT
(caratê, judô) to do; **lutar contra/por
algo** to fight against/for sth; **lutar para
fazer algo** to fight ou struggle to do sth;
lutar com (dificuldades) to struggle
against; (competir) to fight with

luto ['lutu] M mourning; (tristeza) grief;
de ~ in mourning; **pôr ~** to go into
mourning

luva ['luva] F glove; **luvas** FPL (pagamento)
payment sg; (ao locador) fee sg

Luxemburgo [luʃẽ'burgu] M: **o ~**
Luxembourg

luxo ['luʃu] M luxury; **de ~** luxury *atr*;
dar-se ao ~ de to allow o.s. to; **luxuoso,**
-a [lu'ʃwozu, ɔza] ADJ luxurious
luxúria [lu'ʃurja] F lust
luz [luz] F light; (*eletricidade*) electricity;
à ~ de by the light of; (*fig*) in the light of;
a meia ~ with subdued lighting; **dar à ~**
(um filho) to give birth (to a son);
deu-me uma ~ I had an idea

ma [ma] PRON = **me + a**
má [ma] ADJ F *de* **mau**
maca ['maka] F stretcher
maçã [ma'sã] F apple; **~ do rosto**
cheekbone
macabro, -a [ma'kabru, a] ADJ
macabre
macacão [maka'kãw] (*pl* **-ões**) M (*de*
trabalhador) overalls *pl* (BRIT), coveralls *pl*
(US); (*da moda*) jump-suit
macaco, -a [ma'kaku, a] M/F monkey
▶ M (*Mecânica*) jack; **(fato) ~** (PT) overalls
pl (BRIT), coveralls *pl* (US); **~ velho** (*fig*)
old hand
macacões [maka'kõjs] MPL *de*
macacão
maçador, a [masa'dor(a)] (PT) ADJ
boring
maçaneta [masa'neta] F knob
maçante [ma'sãtʃi] (BR) ADJ boring
macarrão [maka'hãw] M pasta; (*em*
forma de canudo) spaghetti;
macarronada [makaho'nada] F pasta
with cheese and tomato sauce
macete [ma'setʃi] M mallet
machado [ma'ʃadu] M axe (BRIT),
ax (US)
machista [ma'ʃista] ADJ chauvinistic,
macho ▶ M male chauvinist
macho ['maʃu] ADJ male; (*fig*) virile,
manly; (*valentão*) tough ▶ M male;
(*Tec*) tap
machucado, -a [maʃu'kadu, a] ADJ
hurt; (*pé, braço*) bad ▶ M injury; (*área*
machucada) sore patch
machucar [maʃu'kar] VT to hurt;
(*produzir contusão*) to bruise ▶ VI to hurt;
machucar-se VR to hurt o.s.
maciço, -a [ma'sisu, a] ADJ solid;
(*espesso*) thick; (*quantidade*) massive

macio, -a [ma'siu, a] ADJ soft; (liso) smooth

maço ['masu] M (de folhas, notas) bundle; (de cigarros) packet

maçom [ma'sõ] (pl **-ns**) M (free)mason

maconha [ma'kɔɲa] F dope; **cigarro de ~** joint

maçons [ma'sõs] MPL de **maçom**

má-criação (pl **-ões**) F rudeness; (ato, dito) rude thing

mácula ['makula] F stain, blemish

macumba [ma'kũba] F ≈ voodoo; (despacho) macumba offering; **macumbeiro, -a** [makũ'bejru, a] ADJ ≈ voodoo atr ▶ M/F follower of macumba

madama [ma'dama] F = **madame**

madame [ma'dami] F (senhora) lady; (col: dona de casa) lady of the house

madeira [ma'dejra] F wood ▶ M Madeira (wine); **de ~** wooden; **bater na ~** (fig) to touch (BRIT) ou knock on (US) wood; **~ compensada** plywood

madeirense [madej'rẽsi] ADJ, M/F Madeiran

madeixa [ma'dejʃa] F (de cabelo) lock

madrasta [ma'drasta] F stepmother

madrepérola [madre'pɛrola] F mother of pearl

Madri [ma'dri] N Madrid

Madrid [ma'drid] (PT) N Madrid

madrinha [ma'driɲa] F godmother

madrugada [madru'gada] F (early) morning; (alvorada) dawn, daybreak

madrugar [madru'gar] VI to get up early; (aparecer cedo) to be early

maduro, -a [ma'duro, a] ADJ ripe; (fig) mature; (: prudente) prudent

mãe [mãj] F mother; **~ adotiva** ou **de criação** adoptive mother

maestro, -trina [ma'estru, 'trina] M/F conductor

má-fé F malicious intent

magia [ma'ʒia] F magic

mágica ['maʒika] F magic; (truque) magic trick; ver tb **mágico**

mágico, -a ['maʒiku, a] ADJ magic ▶ M/F magician

magistério [maʒis'tɛrju] M (ensino) teaching; (profissão) teaching profession; (professorado) teachers pl

magnético, -a [mag'nɛtʃiku, a] ADJ magnetic

magnífico, -a [mag'nifiku, a] ADJ splendid, magnificent

mago ['magu] M magician; **os reis ~s** the Three Wise Men, the Three Kings

mágoa ['magwa] F (tristeza) sorrow, grief; (fig: desagrado) hurt

magoado, -a [ma'gwadu, a] ADJ hurt

magoar [ma'gwar] VT, VI to hurt; **magoar-se** VR: **~-se com algo** to be hurt by sth

magro, -a ['magru, a] ADJ (pessoa) slim; (carne) lean; (fig: parco) meagre (BRIT), meager (US); (leite) skimmed

maio ['maju] M May

maiô [ma'jo] (BR) M swimsuit

maionese [majo'nezi] F mayonnaise

maior [ma'jɔr] ADJ (compar: de tamanho) bigger; (: de importância) greater; (superl: de tamanho) biggest; (: de importância) greatest ▶ M/F adult; **~ de idade** of age, adult; **~ de 21 anos** over 21; **maioria** [majo'ria] F majority; **a maioria de** most of; **maioridade** [majori'dadʒi] F adulthood

PALAVRA-CHAVE

mais [majs] ADV **1** (compar): **mais magro/inteligente (do que)** thinner/more intelligent (than); **ele trabalha mais (do que eu)** he works more (than me)

2 (superl): **o mais ...** the most ...; **o mais magro/inteligente** the thinnest/most intelligent

3 (negativo): **ele não trabalha mais aqui** he doesn't work here any more; **nunca mais** never again

4 (+ adj, valor intensivo): **que livro mais chato!** what a boring book!

5: **por mais que** however much; **por mais que se esforce ...** no matter how hard you try ...; **por mais que eu quisesse ...** much as I should like to ...

6: **a mais: temos um a mais** we've got one extra

7 (tempo): **mais cedo ou mais tarde** sooner or later; **a mais tempo** sooner; **logo mais** later on; **no mais tardar** at the latest

8 (frases): **mais ou menos** more or less; **mais uma vez** once more; **cada vez mais** more and more; **sem mais nem menos** out of the blue

▶ ADJ **1** (compar): **mais (do que)** more (than); **ele tem mais dinheiro (do que o irmão)** he's got more money (than his brother)

2 (superl): **ele é quem tem mais dinheiro** he's got most money

3 (+ números): **ela tem mais de dez bolsas** she's got more than ten bags

4 (negativo): **não tenho mais dinheiro** I haven't got any more money

5 (*adicional*) else; **mais alguma coisa?** anything else?; **nada/ninguém mais** nothing/no-one else
▶ PREP: **2 mais 2 são 4** 2 and 2 *ou* plus 2 is 4
▶ M: **o mais** the rest

maisena [maj'zena] F cornflour (*BRIT*), corn starch (*US*)

maiúscula [ma'juskula] F capital letter

majestade [maʒes'tadʒi] F majesty; **majestoso, -a** [maʒes'tozu, ɔza] ADJ majestic

major [ma'ʒɔr] M (*Mil*) major

majoritário, -a [maʒori'tarju, a] ADJ majority *atr*

mal [maw] (*pl* **males**) M harm; (*Med*) illness ▶ ADV badly; (*quase não*) hardly ▶ CONJ hardly; **~ desliguei o fone, a campainha tocou** I had hardly put the phone down when the doorbell rang; **falar ~ de alguém** to speak ill of sb, run sb down; **não faz ~** never mind; **estar ~** (*doente*) to be ill; **passar ~** to be sick; **estar de ~ com alguém** not to be speaking to sb; **~ de Alzheimer** Alzheimer's (disease)

mal- [maw] PREFIXO badly, mis-

mala ['mala] F suitcase; (*BR Auto*) boot, trunk (*US*); **malas** FPL (*bagagem*) luggage *sg*; **fazer as ~s** to pack

malabarismo [malaba'rizmu] M juggling; **malabarista** [malaba'rista] M/F juggler

mal-acabado, -a ADJ badly finished; (*pessoa*) deformed

malagueta [mala'geta] F chilli (*BRIT*) *ou* chili (*US*) pepper

Malaísia [mala'izja] F: **a ~** Malaysia

malandragem [malã'draʒē] F (*patifaria*) double-dealing; (*preguiça*) idleness; (*esperteza*) cunning

malária [ma'larja] F malaria

mal-arrumado, -a [-ahu'madu, a] ADJ untidy

malcomportado, -a [mawkõpor'tadu, a] ADJ badly behaved

malcriado, -a [maw'krjadu, a] ADJ rude ▶ M/F slob

maldade [maw'dadʒi] F cruelty; (*malícia*) malice

maldição [mawdʒi'sãw] (*pl* **-ões**) F curse

maldizer [mawdʒi'zer] (*irreg: como* **dizer**) VT to curse

maldoso, -a [maw'dozu, ɔza] ADJ wicked; (*malicioso*) malicious

maledicência [maledʒi'sẽsja] F slander

mal-educado, -a ADJ rude ▶ M/F slob

malefício [male'fisju] M harm; **maléfico, -a** [ma'lɛfiku, a] ADJ (*pessoa*) malicious; (*prejudicial*) harmful

mal-entendido, -a ADJ misunderstood ▶ M misunderstanding

mal-estar M indisposition; (*embaraço*) awkward situation

malfeito, -a [maw'fejtu, a] ADJ (*roupa*) poorly made; (*corpo*) misshapen

malfeitor, -a [mawfej'tor(a)] M/F wrongdoer

malha ['maʎa] F (*de rede*) mesh; (*tecido*) jersey; (*suéter*) sweater; (*de ginástica*) leotard; **fazer ~** (*PT*) to knit; **artigos de ~** knitwear; **vestido de ~** jersey dress

malhar [ma'ʎar] VT (*bater*) to beat; (*cereais*) to thresh; (*col: criticar*) to knock, run down

mal-humorado, -a [-umo'radu, a] ADJ grumpy, sullen

maligno, -a [ma'lignu, a] ADJ evil, malicious; (*danoso*) harmful; (*Med*) malignant

malograr [malo'grar] VT (*planos*) to upset; (*frustrar*) to thwart, frustrate ▶ VI (*planos*) to fall through; (*fracassar*) to fail; **malograr-se** VR to fall through; to fail

malpassado, -a [mawpa'sadu, a] ADJ underdone; (*bife*) rare

malsucedido, -a [mawsuse'dʒidu, a] ADJ unsuccessful

Malta ['mawta] F Malta

malta ['mawta] (*PT*) F gang, mob

maltrapilho, -a [mawtra'piʎu, a] ADJ in rags, ragged ▶ M/F ragamuffin

maluco, -a [ma'luku, a] ADJ crazy, daft ▶ M/F madman/woman

malvadeza [mawva'deza] F wickedness; (*ato*) wicked thing

malvado, -a [maw'vadu, a] ADJ wicked

Malvinas [maw'vinas] FPL: **as (ilhas) ~** the Falklands, the Falkland Islands

mama ['mama] F breast

mamadeira [mama'dejra] (*BR*) F feeding bottle

mamãe [ma'mãj] F mum, mummy

mamão [ma'mãw] (*pl* **-ões**) M papaya

mamar [ma'mar] VT to suck; (*dinheiro*) to extort ▶ VI to be breastfed; **dar de ~ a um bebê** to (breast)feed a baby

mamífero [ma'miferu] M mammal

mamilo [ma'milu] M nipple

mamões [ma'mõjs] MPL *de* **mamão**

manada [ma'nada] F herd, drove

mancada [mã'kada] F (*erro*) mistake; (*gafe*) blunder; **dar uma ~** to blunder

mancar [mã'kar] VT to cripple ▶ VI to limp; **mancar-se** VR (*col*) to get the message, take the hint

Mancha ['mãʃa] F: **o canal da ~** the English Channel

mancha ['mãʃa] F stain; (*na pele*) mark, spot; **sem ~s** (*reputação*) spotless; **manchado, -a** [mã'ʃadu, a] ADJ soiled; (*malhado*) mottled, spotted; **manchar** [mã'ʃar] VT to stain, mark; (*reputação*) to soil

manchete [mã'ʃetʃi] F headline

manco, -a ['mãku, a] ADJ crippled, lame

mandado [mã'dadu] M order; (*Jur*) writ; (*tb:* **~ de segurança**) injunction; **~ de prisão/busca** arrest/search warrant; **~ de segurança** injunction

mandão, -dona [mã'dãw, 'dɔna] (*pl* **-ões/-s**) ADJ bossy, domineering

mandar [mã'dar] VT (*ordenar*) to order; (*enviar*) to send ▸ VI to be in charge; **mandar-se** VR (*col: partir*) to make tracks, get going; (*fugir*) to take off; **~ buscar** *ou* **chamar** to send for; **~ fazer um vestido** to have a dress made; **~ que alguém faça, ~ alguém fazer** to tell sb to do; **o que é que você manda?** (*col*) what can I do for you?; **~ em alguém** to boss sb around

mandato [mã'datu] M mandate; (*ordem*) order; (*Pol*) term of office

mandioca [mã'dʒjɔka] F cassava, manioc

mandões [mã'dõjs] MPL *de* **mandão**

mandona [mã'dɔna] F *de* **mandão**

maneira [ma'nejra] F (*modo*) way; (*estilo*) style, manner; **maneiras** FPL (*modos*) manners; **à ~ de** like; **de ~ que** so that; **de ~ alguma** *ou* **nenhuma** not at all; **desta ~** in this way; **de qualquer ~** anyway; **não houve ~ de convencê-lo** it was impossible to convince him

maneiro, -a [ma'nejru, a] ADJ (*ferramenta*) easy to use; (*roupa*) attractive; (*trabalho*) easy; (*pessoa*) capable; (*col: bacana*) great, brilliant

manejar [mane'ʒar] VT (*instrumento*) to handle; (*máquina*) to work; **manejo** [ma'neʒu] M handling

manequim [mane'kĩ] (*pl* **-ns**) M (*boneco*) dummy ▸ M/F model

manga ['mãga] F sleeve; (*fruta*) mango; **em ~s de camisa** in (one's) shirt sleeves

mangueira [mã'gejra] F hose(pipe); (*árvore*) mango tree

manha ['maɲa] F guile, craftiness; (*destreza*) skill; (*ardil*) trick; (*birra*) tantrum; **fazer ~** to have a tantrum

manhã [ma'ɲã] F morning; **de** *ou* **pela ~** in the morning; **amanhã/hoje de ~** tomorrow/this morning

manhoso, -a [ma'ɲozu, ɔza] ADJ crafty, sly; (*criança*) whining

mania [ma'nia] F (*Med*) mania; (*obsessão*) craze; **estar com ~ de ...** to have a thing about ...; **maníaco, -a** [ma'niaku, a] ADJ manic ▸ M/F maniac

manicômio [mani'komju] M psychiatric hospital

manifestação [manifesta'sãw] (*pl* **-ões**) F show, display; (*expressão*) expression, declaration; (*política*) demonstration

manifestante [manifes'tãtʃi] M/F demonstrator

manifestar [manifes'tar] VT to show, display; (*declarar*) to express, declare

manifesto, -a [mani'fɛstu, a] ADJ obvious, clear ▸ M manifesto

manipulação [manipula'sãw] F handling; (*fig*) manipulation

manipular [manipu'lar] VT to manipulate; (*manejar*) to handle

manjericão [mãʒeri'kãw] M basil

manobra [ma'nɔbra] F manoeuvre (BRIT), maneuver (US); (*de mecanismo*) operation; (*de trens*) shunting; **manobrar** [mano'brar] VT to manoeuvre (BRIT), maneuver (US); (*mecanismo*) to operate, work; (*governar*) to take charge of; (*manipular*) to manipulate ▸ VI to manoeuvre *ou* maneuver

manso, -a ['mãsu, a] ADJ gentle; (*mar*) calm; (*animal*) tame

manta ['mãta] F blanket; (*xale*) shawl; (*agasalho*) cloak

manteiga [mã'tejga] F butter; **~ de cacau** cocoa butter

manter [mã'ter] (*irreg: como* **ter**) VT to maintain; (*num lugar*) to keep; (*uma família*) to support; (*a palavra*) to keep; (*princípios*) to abide by; **manter-se** VR to support o.s.; (*permanecer*) to remain; **mantimento** [mãtʃi'mẽtu] M maintenance; **mantimentos** MPL (*alimentos*) provisions

manual [ma'nwaw] (*pl* **-ais**) ADJ manual ▸ M handbook, manual

manufatura [manufa'tura] F manufacture; **manufaturar** [manufatu'rar] VT to manufacture

manusear [manu'zjar] VT to handle; (*livro*) to leaf through

mão [mãw] (*pl* **mãos**) F hand; (*de animal*) paw; (*de pintura*) coat; (*de direção*) flow of traffic; **à ~** by hand; (*perto*) at hand; **de segunda ~** second-hand; **em ~** by hand; **dar a ~ a alguém** to hold sb's hand;

(cumprimentar) to shake hands with sb;
dar uma ~ a alguém to give sb a hand,
help sb out; **~ única/dupla** one-way/
two-way traffic; **rua de duas ~s** two-way
street; **~ de obra** labour (BRIT), labor (US)

mapa ['mapa] M map; *(gráfico)* chart

maquiagem [ma'kjaʒẽ] F
= **maquilagem**

maquiar [ma'kjar] VT to make up;
maquiar-se VR to make o.s. up, put on
one's make-up

maquilagem [maki'laʒẽ], (PT)
maquilhagem F make-up; *(ato)*
making up

máquina ['makina] F machine; *(de trem)*
engine; *(fig)* machinery; **~ de costura**
sewing machine; **~ fotográfica** camera;
~ de lavar (roupa) washing machine;
~ de lavar louça dishwasher; **escrito à ~**
typewritten

maquinar [maki'nar] VT to plot ▸ VI to
conspire

maquinista [maki'nista] M *(Ferro)*
engine driver; *(Náut)* engineer

mar [mar] M sea; **por ~** by sea; **fazer-se
ao ~** to set sail; **pleno ~, ~ alto** high sea;
o ~ Morto the Dead Sea; **o ~ Negro** the
Black Sea

maracujá [maraku'ʒa] M passion fruit;
pé de ~ passion flower

maratona [mara'tona] F marathon

maravilha [mara'viʎa] F marvel,
wonder; **maravilhoso, -a**
[maravi'ʎozu, ɔza] ADJ wonderful

marca ['marka] F mark; *(Com)* make,
brand; *(carimbo)* stamp; **~ de fábrica**
trademark; **~ registrada** registered
trademark

marcação [marka'sãw] *(pl -ões)* F
marking; *(em jogo)* scoring; *(de
instrumento)* reading; *(Teatro)* action; *(PT
Tel)* dialling

marcador [marka'dor] M marker; *(de
livro)* bookmark; *(Esporte: quadro)*
scoreboard; *(: jogador)* scorer

marca-passo [marka'pasu] *(pl -s)* M
(Med) pacemaker

marcar [mar'kar] VT to mark; *(hora,
data)* to fix, set; *(PT Tel)* to dial; *(gol,
ponto)* to score ▸ VI to make one's mark;
~ uma consulta, ~ hora to make an
appointment; **~ um encontro com
alguém** to arrange to meet sb

marcha ['marʃa] F march; *(de
acontecimentos)* course; *(passo)* pace;
(Auto) gear; *(progresso)* progress; **~ à ré
(BR), ~ atrás (PT)** reverse (gear); **pôr-se
em ~** to set off

marchar [mar'ʃar] VI to go; *(andar a pé)*
to walk; *(Mil)* to march

marco ['marku] M landmark; *(de janela)*
frame; *(fig)* frontier; *(moeda)* mark

março ['marsu] M March

maré [ma'rɛ] F tide

marechal [mare'ʃaw] *(pl -ais)* M
marshal

maremoto [mare'mɔtu] M tidal wave

marfim [mar'fĩ] M ivory

margarida [marga'rida] F daisy

margarina [marga'rina] F margarine

margem ['marʒẽ] *(pl -ns)* F *(borda)* edge;
(de rio) bank; *(litoral)* shore; *(de impresso)*
margin; *(fig: tempo)* time; *(: lugar)* space;
à ~ de alongside

marginal [marʒi'naw] *(pl -ais)* ADJ
marginal ▸ M/F delinquent

marido [ma'ridu] M husband

marimbondo [marĩ'bõdu] M hornet

marinha [ma'riɲa] F *(tb: ~ de guerra)*
navy; **~ mercante** merchant navy;
marinheiro [mari'ɲejru] M seaman,
sailor

marinho, -a [ma'riɲu, a] ADJ sea atr,
marine

mariposa [mari'poza] F moth

marítimo, -a [ma'ritʃimu, a] ADJ sea atr

marketing ['marketʃĩ] M marketing

marmelada [marme'lada] F quince jam

marmelo [mar'mɛlu] M quince

marmita [mar'mita] F *(vasilha)* pot

mármore [mar'mori] M marble

marquês, -quesa [mar'kes, 'keza] M/F
marquis/marchioness

marqueteiro, -a [marke'tejru, a] M/F
(col) spin doctor

marquise [mar'kizi] F awning, canopy

Marrocos [ma'hɔkus] M: **o ~** Morocco

marrom [ma'hõ] *(pl -ns)* ADJ, M brown

martelar [marte'lar] VT to hammer;
(amolar) to bother ▸ VI to hammer;
(insistir): **~ (em algo)** to keep ou harp on
(about) sth; **martelo** [mar'tɛlu] M
hammer

mártir ['martʃir] M/F martyr; **martírio**
[mar'tʃirju] M martyrdom; *(fig)* torment

marxista [mar'ksista] ADJ, M/F Marxist

mas [ma(j)s] CONJ but ▸ PRON = **me + as**

mascar [mas'kar] VT to chew

máscara ['maskara] F mask; *(para
limpeza de pele)* face pack; **sob a ~ de**
under the guise of; **mascarar**
[maska'rar] VT to mask; *(disfarçar)* to
disguise; *(encobrir)* to cover up

mascote [mas'kɔtʃi] F mascot

masculino, -a [masku'linu, a] ADJ
masculine; *(Bio)* male

massa ['masa] F (*Fís, fig*) mass; (*de tomate*) paste; (*Culin: de pão*) dough; (: *macarrão etc*) pasta

massacrar [masa'krar] VT to massacre; **massacre** [ma'sakri] F massacre

massagear [masa'ʒjar] VT to massage; **massagem** [ma'saʒẽ] (*pl* **-ns**) F massage

mastigar [mastʃi'gar] VT to chew

mastro ['mastru] M (*Náut*) mast; (*para bandeira*) flagpole

masturbar-se [mastur'barsi] VR to masturbate

mata ['mata] F forest, wood

matadouro [mata'doru] M slaughterhouse

matança [ma'tãsa] F massacre; (*de reses*) slaughter(ing)

matar [ma'tar] VT to kill; (*sede*) to quench; (*fome*) to satisfy; (*aula*) to skip; (*trabalho: não aparecer*) to skive off; (: *fazer rápido*) to dash off; (*adivinhar*) to guess ▶ VI to kill; **matar-se** VR to kill o.s.; (*esfalfar-se*) to wear o.s. out; **um calor/ uma dor de ~** stifling heat/excruciating pain

mate ['matʃi] ADJ matt ▶ M (*chá*) maté tea; (*xeque-mate*) checkmate

matemática [mate'matʃika] F mathematics *sg*, maths *sg* (BRIT), math (US); **matemático, -a** [mate'matʃiku, a] ADJ mathematical ▶ M/F mathematician

matéria [ma'tɛrja] F matter; (*Tec*) material; (*Educ: assunto*) subject; (*tema*) topic; (*jornalística*) story, article; **em ~ de** on the subject of

material [mate'rjaw] (*pl* **-ais**) ADJ material; (*físico*) physical ▶ M material; (*Tec*) equipment; **materialista** [materja'lista] ADJ materialistic; **materializar** [materjali'zar] VT to materialize; **materializar-se** VR to materialize

maternal [mater'naw] (*pl* **-ais**) ADJ motherly, maternal; **escola ~** nursery (school); **maternidade** [materni'dadʒi] F motherhood, maternity; (*hospital*) maternity hospital

materno, -a [ma'tɛrnu, a] ADJ motherly, maternal; (*língua*) native

matinê [matʃi'ne] F matinée

matiz [ma'tʃiz] M (*de cor*) shade

mato ['matu] M scrubland, bush; (*plantas agrestes*) scrub; (*o campo*) country

matraca [ma'traka] F rattle

matrícula [ma'trikula] F (*lista*) register; (*inscrição*) registration; (*pagamento*) enrolment (BRIT) *ou* enrollment (US) fee;

(PT *Auto*) registration number (BRIT), license number (US); **fazer a ~** to enrol (BRIT), enroll (US)

matrimonial [matrimo'njaw] (*pl* **-ais**) ADJ marriage *atr*, matrimonial

matrimônio [matri'monju] M marriage

matriz [ma'triz] F (*Med*) womb; (*fonte*) source; (*molde*) mould (BRIT), mold (US); (*Com*) head office

maturidade [maturi'dadʒi] F maturity

mau, má [maw, ma] ADJ bad; (*malvado*) evil, wicked ▶ M bad; (*Rel*) evil; **os ~s** bad people; (*num filme*) the baddies

maus-tratos MPL ill-treatment *sg*

maxila [mak'sila] F jawbone

maxilar [maksi'lar] M jawbone

máxima ['masima] F maxim

máximo, -a ['masimu, a] ADJ (*maior que todos*) greatest; (*o maior possível*) maximum ▶ M maximum; (*o cúmulo*) peak; (*temperature*) high; **no ~** at most; **ao ~** to the utmost

me [mi] PRON (*direto*) me; (*indireto*) (to) me; (*reflexivo*) (to) myself

meado ['mjadu] M middle; **em** *ou* **nos ~s de julho** in mid-July

Meca ['mɛka] N Mecca

mecânica [me'kanika] F (*ciência*) mechanics *sg*; (*mecanismo*) mechanism; *ver tb* **mecânico**

mecânico, -a [me'kaniku, a] ADJ mechanical ▶ M/F mechanic

mecanismo [meka'nizmu] M mechanism

meço ['mɛsu] VB *ver* **medir**

medalha [me'daʎa] F medal; **medalhão** [meda'ʎãw] (*pl* **-ões**) M medallion

média ['mɛdʒja] F average; (*café*) coffee with milk; **em ~** on average

mediano, -a [me'dʒjanu, a] ADJ medium; (*médio*) average; (*medíocre*) mediocre

mediante [me'dʒjãtʃi] PREP by (means of), through; (*a troco de*) in return for

medicamento [medʒika'mẽtu] M medicine

medicina [medʒi'sina] F medicine

médico, -a ['mɛdʒiku, a] ADJ medical ▶ M/F doctor; **receita médica** prescription

medida [me'dʒida] F measure; (*providência*) step; (*medição*) measurement; (*moderação*) prudence; **à ~ que** while, as; **na ~ em que** in so far as; **feito sob ~** made to measure; **ir além da ~** to go too far; **tirar as ~s de alguém** to take sb's measurements; **tomar ~s** to take steps; **tomar as ~s de** to measure

medieval [medʒje'vaw] (pl **-ais**) ADJ medieval

médio, -a ['mɛdʒju, a] ADJ (dedo, classe) middle; (tamanho, estatura) medium; (mediano) average; **ensino ~** secondary education

medir [me'dʒir] VT to measure; (atos, palavras) to weigh; (avaliar: consequências, distâncias) to weigh up ▸ VI to measure; **quanto você mede? — meço 1.60 m** how tall are you? — I'm 1.60 m (tall)

meditar [medʒi'tar] VI to meditate; **~ sobre algo** to ponder (on) sth

mediterrâneo, -a [medʒite'hanju, a] ADJ Mediterranean ▸ M: **o M~** the Mediterranean

medo ['medu] M fear; **com ~** afraid; **meter ~ em alguém** to frighten sb; **ter ~ de** to be afraid of

medonho, -a [me'doɲu, a] ADJ terrible, awful

medroso, -a [me'drozu, ɔza] ADJ (com medo) frightened; (tímido) timid

megabyte [mega'bajtʃi] M megabyte

meia ['meja] F stocking; (curta) sock; (meia-entrada) half-price ticket ▸ NUM six; **meia-idade** F middle age; **pessoa de meia-idade** middle-aged person; **meia-noite** F midnight

meigo, -a ['mejgu, a] ADJ sweet

meio, -a ['meju, a] ADJ half ▸ ADV a bit, rather ▸ M middle; (recurso) means; (social, profissional) environment; (tb: **~ ambiente**) environment; **meios** MPL (recursos) means pl; **~ quilo** half a kilo; **um mês e ~** one and a half months; **cortar ao ~** to cut in half; **dividir algo ~ a ~** to divide sth in half ou fifty-fifty; **em ~ a** amid; **no ~ (de)** in the middle (of); **~s de comunicação (de massa)** (mass) media pl; **~s de comunicação social** social media pl; **por ~ de** through; **meio-dia** M midday, noon; **meio-fio** (pl **meios-fios**) M kerb (BRIT), curb (US); **meio-termo** (pl **meios-termos**) M (fig) compromise

mel [mɛw] M honey

melaço [me'lasu] M treacle (BRIT), molasses sg (US)

melancia [melã'sia] F watermelon

melancolia [melãko'lia] F melancholy, sadness; **melancólico, -a** [melã'kɔliku, a] ADJ melancholy, sad

melão [me'lãw] (pl **-ões**) M melon

melhor [me'ʎɔr] ADJ, ADV (compar) better; (superl) best; **~ que nunca** better than ever; **quanto mais ~** the more the better; **seria ~ começarmos** we had

better begin; **tanto ~** so much the better; **ou ~ ...** (ou antes) or rather ...; **melhora** [me'ʎɔra] F improvement; **melhoras!** get well soon!; **melhorar** [meʎo'rar] VT to improve, make better; (doente) to cure ▸ VI to improve, get better

melodia [melo'dʒia] F melody; (composição) tune

melões [me'lõjs] MPL de **melão**

melro ['mɛwhu] M blackbird

membro ['mẽbru] M member; (Anat: braço, perna) limb

meme ['meme] M (Comput) meme

memória [me'mɔrja] F memory; **memórias** FPL (de autor) memoirs; **de ~** by heart

memorizar [memori'zar] VT to memorize

mencionar [mẽsjo'nar] VT to mention

mendigar [mẽdʒi'gar] VT to beg for ▸ VI to beg; **mendigo, -a** [mẽ'dʒigu, a] M/F beggar

menina [me'nina] F: **~ do olho** pupil; **ser a ~ dos olhos de alguém** (fig) to be the apple of sb's eye; ver tb **menino**

meninada [meni'nada] F kids pl

menino, -a [me'ninu, a] M/F boy/girl

menopausa [meno'pawza] F menopause

menor [me'nɔr] ADJ (mais pequeno: compar) smaller; (: superl) smallest; (mais jovem: compar) younger; (: superl) youngest; (o mínimo) least, slightest; (tb: **~ de idade**) under age ▸ M/F juvenile, young person; (Jur) minor; **não tenho a ~ ideia** I haven't the slightest idea

PALAVRA-CHAVE

menos ['menus] ADJ **1** (compar): **menos (do que)** (quantidade) less (than); (número) fewer (than); **com menos entusiasmo** with less enthusiasm; **menos gente** fewer people
2 (superl) least; **é o que tem menos culpa** he is the least to blame
▸ ADV **1** (compar): **menos (do que)** less (than); **gostei menos do que do outro** I liked it less than the other one
2 (superl): **é o menos inteligente da classe** he is the least bright in his class; **de todas elas é a que menos me agrada** out of all of them she's the one I like least; **pelo menos** at (the very) least
3 (frases): **temos sete a menos** we are seven short; **não é para menos** it's no wonder; **isso é o de menos** that's nothing
▸ PREP (exceção) except; (números) minus;

todos menos eu everyone except (for) me; **5 menos 2** 5 minus 2
▶ CONJ: **a menos que** unless; **a menos que ele venha amanhã** unless he comes tomorrow
▶ M: **o menos** the least

menosprezar [menuspre'zar] VT (*subestimar*) to underrate; (*desprezar*) to despise, scorn

mensageiro, -a [mẽsa'ʒejru, a] M/F messenger

mensagem [mẽ'saʒẽ] (*pl* **-ns**) F message; **~ de texto** text (message); **mandar uma ~ de texto para alguém** to text sb

mensal [mẽ'saw] (*pl* **-ais**) ADJ monthly; **ele ganha £2000 mensais** he earns £2000 a month; **mensalidade** [mẽsali'dadʒi] F monthly payment; **mensalmente** [mẽsaw'mẽtʃi] ADV monthly

menstruação [mẽstrwa'sãw] F period; (*Med*) menstruation

menta ['mẽta] F mint

mental [mẽ'taw] (*pl* **-ais**) ADJ mental; **mentalidade** [mẽtali'dadʒi] F mentality

mente ['mẽtʃi] F mind; **de boa ~** willingly; **ter em ~** to bear in mind

mentir [mẽ'tʃir] VI to lie

mentira [mẽ'tʃira] F lie; (*ato*) lying; **parece ~ que** it seems incredible that; **de ~** not for real; **~!** (*acusação*) that's a lie!, you're lying; (*de surpresa*) you don't say!, no!; **mentiroso, -a** [mẽtʃi'rozu, ɔza] ADJ lying ▶ M/F liar

menu [me'nu] M (*tb: Comput*) menu

mercado [mer'kadu] M market; **M~ Comum** Common Market; **~ negro** *ou* **paralelo** black market

mercadoria [merkado'ria] F commodity; **mercadorias** FPL (*produtos*) goods

mercearia [mersja'ria] F grocer's (shop) (*BRIT*), grocery store

mercúrio [mer'kurju] M mercury

merda ['mɛrda] (!) F shit (!) ▶ M/F (*pessoa*) jerk; **a ~ do carro** the bloody (*BRIT*) *ou* goddamn (*US*) car (!)

merecer [mere'ser] VT to deserve; (*consideração*) to merit; (*valer*) to be worth ▶ VI to be worthy; **merecido, -a** [mere'sidu, a] ADJ deserved; (*castigo, prêmio*) just

merenda [me'rẽda] F packed lunch

merengue [me'rẽgi] M meringue

mergulhador, a [merguʎa'dor(a)] M/F diver

mergulhar [mergu'ʎar] VI to dive; (*penetrar*) to plunge ▶ VT: **~ algo em algo** (*num líquido*) to dip sth into sth; (*na terra etc*) to plunge sth into sth; **mergulho** [mer'guʎu] M dip(ping), immersion; (*em natação*) dive; **dar um mergulho** (*na praia*) to go for a dip

mérito ['mɛritu] M merit

mero, -a ['mɛru, a] ADJ mere

mês [mes] M month

mesa ['meza] F table; (*de trabalho*) desk; (*comitê*) board; (*numa reunião*) panel; **pôr/tirar a ~** to lay/clear the table; **à ~** at the table; **~ de cabeceira** bedside table; **~ de toalete** dressing table; **~ telefônica** switchboard

mesada [me'zada] F monthly allowance; (*de criança*) pocket money

mesmo, -a ['mezmu, a] ADJ same; (*enfático*) very ▶ ADV (*exatamente*) right; (*até*) even; (*realmente*) really ▶ M/F: **o ~/a mesma** the same (one); **o ~** (*a mesma coisa*) the same (thing); **este ~ homem** this very man; **ele ~ o fez** he did it himself; **dá no ~** *ou* **na mesma** it's all the same; **aqui/agora/hoje ~** right here/right now/this very day; **~ que** even if; **é ~** it's true; **é ~?** really?; **(é) isso ~!** exactly!; **por isso ~** that's why; **nem ~** not even; **só ~** only; **por si ~** by oneself

mesquinho, -a [mes'kiɲu, a] ADJ mean

mesquita [mes'kita] F mosque

mestre, -a ['mɛstri, a] ADJ (*chave, viga*) master; (*linha, estrada*) main ▶ M/F master/mistress; (*professor*) teacher; **obra mestra** masterpiece

meta ['mɛta] F (*em corrida*) finishing post; (*gol*) goal; (*objetivo*) aim

metade [me'tadʒi] F half; (*meio*) middle

metáfora [me'tafora] F metaphor

metal [me'taw] (*pl* **-ais**) M metal; **metais** MPL (*Mús*) brass *sg*; **metálico, -a** [me'taliku, a] ADJ metallic; (*de metal*) metal *atr*

meteorologia [meteorolo'ʒia] F meteorology; **meteorologista** [meteorolo'ʒista] M/F meteorologist; (*TV, Rádio*) weather forecaster

meter [me'ter] VT (*colocar*) to put; (*envolver*) to involve; (*introduzir*) to introduce; **meter-se** VR (*esconder-se*) to hide; **~-se a fazer algo** to decide to have a go at sth; **~-se com** (*provocar*) to pick a quarrel with; (*associar-se*) to get involved with; **~-se em** to get involved in; (*intrometer-se*) to interfere in

meticuloso, -a [metʃiku'lozu, ɔza] ADJ meticulous

metido, -a [me'tʃidu, a] ADJ (*envolvido*) involved; (*intrometido*) meddling; **~ (a besta)** snobbish

metódico, -a [me'tɔdʒiku, a] ADJ methodical

método ['mɛtodu] M method

metralhadora [metraʎa'dora] F machine gun

métrico, -a ['mɛtriku, a] ADJ metric

metro ['mɛtru] M metre (BRIT), meter (US); (PT: *metropolitano*) underground (BRIT), subway (US)

metrô [me'tro] (BR) M underground (BRIT), subway (US)

metrópole [me'trɔpoli] F metropolis; (*capital*) capital

meu, minha [mew, 'miɲa] ADJ my ▶ PRON mine; **os meus** MPL (*minha família*) my family ou folks (col); **um amigo ~** a friend of mine

mexer [me'ʃer] VT to move; (*cabeça: dizendo sim*) to nod; (: *dizendo não*) to shake; (*misturar*) to stir; (*ovos*) to scramble ▶ VI to move; **mexer-se** VR to move; (*apressar-se*) to get a move on; **~ em algo** to touch sth; **mexa-se!** get going!, move yourself!

mexerico [meʃe'riku] M piece of gossip; **mexericos** MPL (*fofocas*) gossip sg

México ['mɛʃiku] M: **o ~** Mexico

mexido, -a [me'ʃidu, a] ADJ (*papéis*) mixed up; (*ovos*) scrambled

mexilhão [meʃi'ʎãw] (*pl* **-ões**) M mussel

mi [mi] M (*Mús*) E

miau [mjaw] M miaow

micro... [mikru] PREFIXO micro...; **microblog, microblogue** [mikro'blɔgi] M microblog; **microcefalia** [mikro'sefalia] F (*Med*) microcephaly; **microfone** [mikro'fɔni] M microphone; **micro-ondas** [mikro'õdas] M INV microwave; **microprocessador** [mikroprosesa'dor] M microprocessor; **microscópio** [mikro'skɔpju] M microscope

mídia ['midʒja] F media pl; **~s sociais** social media pl

migalha [mi'gaʎa] F crumb; **migalhas** FPL (*restos, sobras*) scraps

migrar [mi'grar] VI to migrate

mijar [mi'ʒar] (col) VI to pee; **mijar-se** VR to wet o.s.

mil [miw] NUM thousand; **dois ~** two thousand

milagre [mi'lagri] M miracle; **por ~** miraculously; **milagroso, -a** [mila'grozu, ɔza] ADJ miraculous

milhão [mi'ʎãw] (*pl* **-ões**) M million; **um ~ de vezes** hundreds of times

milhar [mi'ʎar] M thousand; **turistas aos ~es** tourists in their thousands

milho ['miʎu] M maize (BRIT), corn (US)

milhões [mi'ʎõjs] MPL *de* **milhão**

miligrama [mili'grama] M milligram(me)

milionário, -a [miljo'narju, a] M/F millionaire

milionésimo, -a [miljo'nɛzimu, a] NUM millionth

militar [mili'tar] ADJ military ▶ M soldier ▶ VI to fight; **~ em** (*Mil: regimento*) to serve in; (*Pol: partido*) to belong to, be active in; (*profissão*) to work in

mim [mĩ] PRON me; (*reflexivo*) myself; **de ~ para ~** to myself

mímica ['mimika] F mime

mimo ['mimu] M gift; (*pessoa, coisa encantadora*) delight; (*carinho*) tenderness; (*gentileza*) kindness; **cheio de ~s** (*criança*) spoiled, spoilt (BRIT); **mimoso, -a** [mi'mozu, ɔza] ADJ (*delicado*) delicate; (*carinhoso*) tender, loving; (*encantador*) delightful

mina ['mina] F mine

mindinho [mĩ'dʒiɲu] M (*tb:* **dedo ~**) little finger

mineiro, -a [mi'nejru, a] ADJ mining atr ▶ M/F miner

mineral [mine'raw] (*pl* **-ais**) ADJ, M mineral

minério [mi'nerju] M ore

míngua ['mĩgwa] F lack; **à ~ de** for want of; **viver à ~** to live in poverty; **minguado, -a** [mĩ'gwadu, a] ADJ scant; (*criança*) stunted; **minguado de algo** short of sth

minguar [mĩ'gwar] VI (*diminuir*) to decrease, dwindle; (*faltar*) to run short

minha ['miɲa] F *de* **meu**

minhoca [mi'ɲɔka] F (earth)worm

mini... [mini] PREFIXO mini...

miniatura [minja'tura] ADJ, F miniature

mínima ['minima] F (*temperatura*) low; (*Mús*) minim

mínimo, -a ['minimu, a] ADJ minimum ▶ M minimum; (*tb:* **dedo ~**) little finger; **não dou** ou **ligo a mínima para isso** I couldn't care less about it; **a mínima importância/ideia** the slightest importance/idea; **no ~** at least

minissaia [mini'saja] F miniskirt

ministério [mini'sterju] M ministry; **M~ da Fazenda** ≈ Treasury (BRIT), ≈ Treasury Department (US); **M~ das Relações Exteriores** ≈ Foreign Office (BRIT), ≈ State Department (US)

ministro, -a [mi'nistru, a] M/F minister

minoria [mino'ria] F minority

minto ['mītu] VB ver **mentir**

minucioso, -a [minu'sjozu, ɔza] ADJ (*indivíduo, busca*) thorough; (*explicação*) detailed

minúsculo, -a [mi'nuskulu, a] ADJ minute, tiny; **letra minúscula** lower case letter

minuta [mi'nuta] F draft

minuto [mi'nutu] M minute

miolo ['mjolu] M inside; (*polpa*) pulp; (*de maçã*) core; **miolos** MPL (*cérebro, inteligência*) brains

míope ['mjopi] ADJ short-sighted

mira ['mira] F (*de fuzil*) sight; (*pontaria*) aim; (*fig*) aim, purpose; **à ~ de** on the lookout for; **ter em ~** to have one's eye on

miragem [mi'raʒē] (*pl* **-ns**) F mirage

miserável [mize'ravew] (*pl* **-eis**) ADJ (*digno de compaixão*) wretched; (*pobre*) impoverished; (*avaro*) stingy, mean; (*insignificante*) paltry; (*lugar*) squalid; (*infame*) despicable ▶ M wretch; (*coitado*) poor thing; (*pessoa infame*) rotter

miséria [mi'zɛrja] F misery; (*pobreza*) poverty; (*avareza*) stinginess

misericórdia [mizeri'kɔrdʒja] F (*compaixão*) pity, compassion; (*graça*) mercy

missa ['misa] F (*Rel*) mass

missão [mi'sãw] (*pl* **-ões**) F mission; (*dever*) duty

míssil ['misiw] (*pl* **-eis**) M missile

missionário, -a [misjo'narju, a] M/F missionary

missões [mi'sõjs] FPL *de* **missão**

mistério [mis'tɛrju] M mystery; **misterioso, -a** [miste'rjozu, ɔza] ADJ mysterious

mistificar [mistʃifi'kar] VT, VI to fool

misto, -a ['mistu, a] ADJ mixed; (*confuso*) mixed up ▶ M mixture; **misto-quente** (*pl* **mistos-quentes**) M toasted cheese and ham sandwich

mistura [mis'tura] F mixture; (*ato*) mixing; **misturar** [mistu'rar] VT to mix; (*confundir*) to mix up; **misturar-se** VR: **misturar-se com** to mingle with

mito ['mitu] M myth

miudezas [mju'dezas] FPL minutiae; (*bugigangas*) odds and ends; (*objetos pequenos*) trinkets

miúdo, -a [mi'mjudu, a] ADJ tiny, minute ▶ M/F (PT: *criança*) youngster, kid; **miúdos** MPL (*dinheiro*) change *sg*; (*de aves*) giblets; **dinheiro ~** small change

mm ABR (= *milímetro*) mm

mo [mu] PRON = **me + o**

moa ['moa] VB ver **moer**

móbil ['mɔbiw] (*pl* **-eis**) ADJ = **móvel**

móbile ['mɔbili] M mobile

mobília [mo'bilja] F furniture; **mobiliar** [mobi'ljar] (BR) VT to furnish; **mobiliário** [mobi'ljarju] M furnishings *pl*

moça ['mosa] F girl, young woman

Moçambique [mosã'biki] M Mozambique

moção [mo'sãw] (*pl* **-ões**) F motion

mochila [mo'ʃila] F rucksack

mochilão [moʃi'lãw] M backpacking trip; **mochileiro, -a** [moʃi'ljru] M/F backpacker

mocidade [mosi'dadʒi] F youth; (*os moços*) young people *pl*

moço, -a ['mosu, a] ADJ young ▶ M young man, lad

moções [mo'sõjs] FPL *de* **moção**

moda ['mɔda] F fashion; **estar na ~** to be in fashion, be all the rage; **fora da ~** old-fashioned; **sair da** *ou* **cair de ~** to go out of fashion

modalidade [modali'dadʒi] F kind; (*Esporte*) event

modelo [mo'delu] M model; (*criação de estilista*) design; (*pessoa admirada*) role-model ▶ M/F (*manequim*) model

modem ['modē] (*pl* **-ns**) M modem

moderar [mode'rar] VT to moderate; (*violência*) to control, restrain; (*velocidade*) to reduce; (*voz*) to lower; (*gastos*) to cut down

modernizar [moderni'zar] VT to modernize; **modernizar-se** VR to modernize

moderno, -a [mo'dɛrnu, a] ADJ modern; (*atual*) present-day

modéstia [mo'dɛstʃja] F modesty

módico, -a ['mɔdʒiku, a] ADJ moderate; (*preço*) reasonable; (*bens*) scant

modificar [modʒifi'kar] VT to modify, alter

modista [mo'dʒista] F dressmaker

modo ['mɔdu] M (*maneira*) way, manner; (*método*) way; (*Mús*) mode; **modos** MPL (*comportamento*) manners; **de (tal) ~ que** so (that); **de ~ nenhum** in no way; **de qualquer ~** anyway, anyhow; **~ de emprego** instructions *pl* for use

módulo ['mɔdulu] M module

moeda ['mwɛda] F (*uma moeda*) coin; (*dinheiro*) currency; **uma ~ de 50p** a 50p piece; **~ corrente** currency; **Casa da M~** ≈ the (Royal) Mint (BRIT), ≈ the (US) Mint (US)

moedor [moe'dor] M (de café) grinder; (de carne) mincer

moer [mwer] VT (café) to grind; (cana) to crush

mofado, -a [mo'fadu, a] ADJ mouldy (BRIT), moldy (US)

mofo ['mofu] M (Bot) mould (BRIT), mold (US); **cheiro de ~** musty smell

mogno ['mɔgnu] M mahogany

mói [mɔj] VB ver **moer**

moía [mo'ia] VB ver **moer**

moído, -a [mo'idu, a] ADJ (café) ground; (carne) minced (BRIT), ground (US); (cansado) tired out; (corpo) aching

moinho ['mwiɲu] M mill; (de café) grinder; **~ de vento** windmill

mola ['mɔla] F (Tec) spring; (fig) motive, motivation

moldar [mow'dar] VT to mould (BRIT), mold (US); (metal) to cast; **molde** ['mɔwdʒi] M mould (BRIT), mold (US); (de papel) pattern; (fig) model; **molde de vestido** dress pattern

moldura [mow'dura] F (de pintura) frame

mole ['mɔli] ADJ soft; (sem energia) listless; (carnes) flabby; (col: fácil) easy; (lento) slow; (preguiçoso) sluggish ▶ ADV (lentamente) slowly

moleque [mo'lɛki] M (de rua) urchin; (menino) youngster; (pessoa sem palavra) unreliable person; (canalha) scoundrel ▶ ADJ (levado) mischievous; (brincalhão) funny

molestar [moles'tar] VT to upset; (enfadar) to annoy; (importunar) to bother

moléstia [mo'lestʃia] F illness

moleza [mo'leza] F softness; (falta de energia) listlessness; (falta de força) weakness; **ser (uma) ~** (col) to be easy; **na ~** without exerting oneself

molhado, -a [mo'ʎadu, a] ADJ wet, damp

molhar [mo'ʎar] VT to wet; (de leve) to moisten, dampen; (mergulhar) to dip; **molhar-se** VR to get wet

molho¹ ['mɔʎu] M (de chaves) bunch; (de trigo) sheaf

molho² [mo'ʎu] M (Culin) sauce; (: de salada) dressing; (: de carne) gravy; **pôr de ~** to soak; **estar/deixar de ~** (roupa etc) to be/leave to soak

momentâneo, -a [momẽ'tanju, a] ADJ momentary

momento [mo'mẽtu] M moment; (Tec) momentum; **a todo ~** constantly; **de um ~ para outro** suddenly; **no ~ em que** just as

Mônaco ['monaku] M Monaco

monarquia [monar'kia] F monarchy

monitor [moni'tor] M monitor

monopólio [mono'pɔlju] M monopoly; **monopolizar** [monopoli'zar] VT to monopolize

monotonia [monoto'nia] F monotony; **monótono, -a** [mo'nɔtonu, a] ADJ monotonous

monstro, -a ['mõstru, a] ADJ INV giant ▶ M (tb fig) monster; **monstruoso, -a** [mõ'strwozu, ɔza] ADJ monstrous; (enorme) gigantic, huge

montagem [mõ'taʒẽ] (pl -ns) F assembly; (Arq) erection; (Cinema) editing; (Teatro) production

montanha [mõ'taɲa] F mountain; **montanha-russa** F roller coaster

montante [mõ'tãtʃi] M amount, sum; **a ~** (nadar) upstream

montar [mõ'tar] VT (cavalo) to mount, get on; (colocar em) to put on; (cavalgar) to ride; (peças) to assemble, put together; (loja, máquina) to set up; (casa) to put up; (peça teatral) to put on ▶ VI to ride; **~ a ou em** (animal) to get on; (cavalgar) to ride; (despesa) to come to

monte ['mõtʃi] M hill; (pilha) heap, pile; **um ~ de** (muitos) a lot of, lots of; **gente aos ~s** loads of people

montra ['mõtra] (PT) F shop window

monumento [monu'mẽtu] M monument

moqueca [mo'kɛka] F fish or seafood simmered in coconut cream and palm oil; **~ de camarão** prawn moqueca

morada [mo'rada] F home, residence; (PT: endereço) address; **moradia** [mora'dʒia] F home, dwelling; **morador, a** [mora'dor(a)] M/F resident; (de casa alugada) tenant

moral [mo'raw] (pl -ais) ADJ moral ▶ F (ética) ethics pl; (conclusão) moral ▶ M (de pessoa) sense of morality; (ânimo) morale; **moralidade** [morali'dadʒi] F morality

morango [mo'rãgu] M strawberry

morar [mo'rar] VI to live, reside

mórbido, -a ['mɔrbidu, a] ADJ morbid

morcego [mor'segu] M (Bio) bat

mordaça [mor'dasa] F (de animal) muzzle; (fig) gag

morder [mor'der] VT to bite; (corroer) to corrode; **mordida** [mor'dʒida] F bite

mordomia [mordo'mia] F (de executivos) perk; (col: regalia) luxury, comfort

mordomo [mor'dɔmu] M butler

moreno, -a [mo'rɛnu, a] ADJ
dark(-skinned); (de cabelos)
dark(-haired); (de tomar sol) brown
▶ M/F dark person

mormaço [mor'masu] M sultry
weather

morno, -a ['mornu, 'mɔrna] ADJ
lukewarm, tepid

morrer [mo'her] VI to die; (luz, cor) to
fade; (fogo) to die down; (Auto) to stall

morro ['mohu] M hill; (favela) slum

mortadela [morta'dɛla] F salami

mortal [mor'taw] (pl -ais) ADJ mortal;
(letal, insuportável) deadly ▶ M mortal

mortalidade [mortali'dadʒi] F
mortality

morte ['mɔrtʃi] F death

mortífero, -a [mor'tʃiferu, a] ADJ
deadly, lethal

morto, -a ['mortu, 'mɔrta] PP de **matar,
morrer** ▶ ADJ dead; (cor) dull; (exausto)
exhausted; (inexpressivo) lifeless ▶ M/F
dead man/woman; **estar ~** to be dead;
ser ~ to be killed; **estar ~ de inveja** to
be green with envy; **estar ~ de vontade
de** to be dying to

mos [mus] PRON = **me + os**

mosca ['moska] F fly; **estar às ~s** (bar
etc) to be deserted

Moscou [mos'kow] (BR) N Moscow

Moscovo [mos'kovu] (PT) N Moscow

mosquito [mos'kitu] M mosquito

mostarda [mos'tarda] F mustard

mosteiro [mos'tejru] M monastery; (de
monjas) convent

mostrador [mostra'dor] M (de relógio)
face, dial

mostrar [mos'trar] VT to show;
(mercadorias) to display; (provar) to
demonstrate, prove; **mostrar-se** VR to
show o.s. to be; (exibir-se) to show off

motel [mo'tɛw] (pl -éis) M motel

motivar [motʃi'var] VT (causar) to cause,
bring about; (estimular) to motivate;
motivo [mo'tʃivu] M (causa): **motivo
(de ou para)** cause (of), reason (for);
(fim) motive; (Arte, Mús) motif; **por
motivo de** because of, owing to

moto ['mɔtu] F motorbike ▶ M (lema)
motto

motoboy [moto'bɔj] M motorcycle
courier

motocicleta [motosi'kleta] F
motorcycle, motorbike

motociclista [motosi'klista] M/F
motorcyclist

motociclo [moto'siklu] (PT) M
= **motocicleta**

motor, motriz [mo'tor, mo'triz] ADJ, M
motor; (de carro, avião) engine; **força
motriz** driving force; **~ de explosão**
internal combustion engine; **~ diesel**
diesel engine; **~ de pesquisa** (PT Comput)
search engine

motorista [moto'rista] M/F driver

móvel ['mɔvew] (pl -eis) ADJ movable
▶ M piece of furniture; **móveis** MPL
(mobília) furniture sg

mover [mo'ver] VT to move; (cabeça) to
shake; (mecanismo) to drive; (campanha)
to start (up); **mover-se** VR to move

movimentado, -a [movimẽ'tadu, a]
ADJ (rua, lugar) busy; (pessoa) active;
(show, música) up-tempo

movimentar [movimẽ'tar] VT to move;
(animar) to liven up

movimento [movi'mẽtu] M movement;
(Tec) motion; (na rua) activity, bustle; **de
muito ~** busy

MST (BR) ABR M (= Movimento dos
Trabalhadores Rurais Sem Terra) pressure
group for land reform

muamba ['mwãba] (col) F (contrabando)
contraband; (objetos roubados) loot

muçulmano, -a [musuw'manu, a] ADJ,
M/F Moslem

muda ['muda] F (planta) seedling; (vestuário)
outfit; **~ de roupa** change of clothes

mudança [mu'dãsa] F change; (de casa)
move; (Auto) gear; **~s climáticas**
climate change

mudar [mu'dar] VT to change; (deslocar)
to move ▶ VI to change; (ave) to moult
(BRIT), molt (US); **mudar-se** VR (de casa)
to move (away); **~ de roupa/de
assunto** to change clothes/the subject;
~ de casa to move (house); **~ de ideia**
to change one's mind

mudo, -a ['mudu, a] ADJ with a speech
impairment; (calado, filme) silent;
(telefone) dead ▶ M/F person with a
speech impairment

PALAVRA-CHAVE

muito, -a ['mwĩtu, a] ADJ (quantidade) a
lot of; (em frase negativa ou interrogativa)
much; (número) lots of, a lot of, many;
muito esforço a lot of effort; **faz muito
calor** it's very hot; **muito tempo** a long
time; **muitas amigas** lots ou a lot of
friends; **muitas vezes** often
▶ PRON a lot; (em frase negativa ou
interrogativa: sg) much; (: pl) many;
tenho muito que fazer I've got a lot to
do; **muitos dizem que ...** a lot of people
say that ...

▶ADV **1** a lot; (+*adj*) very; (+*compar*):
muito melhor much *ou* far *ou* a lot
better; **gosto muito disto** I like it a lot;
sinto muito I'm very sorry; **muito
interessante** very interesting
2 (*resposta*) very; **está cansado? —
muito** are you tired? — very
3 (*tempo*): **muito depois** long after; **há
muito** a long time ago; **não demorou
muito** it didn't take long

mula ['mula] F mule
muleta [mu'leta] F crutch; (*fig*) support
mulher [mu'ʎer] F woman; (*esposa*)
wife; **mulher-bomba** (*pl* **mulheres-
bomba**) F suicide bomber
multa ['muwta] F fine; **levar uma ~** to
be fined; **multar** [muw'tar] VT to fine;
multar alguém em $1000 to fine sb
$1000
multi... [muwtʃi] PREFIXO multi...
multidão [muwtʃi'dãw] (*pl* **-ões**) F
crowd; **uma ~ de** (*muitos*) lots of
multimídia [muwtʃi'midʒja] ADJ
multimedia
multinacional [muwtʃinasjo'naw] (*pl*
-ais) ADJ, F multinational
multiplicar [muwtʃipli'kar] VT to
multiply; (*aumentar*) to increase
múltiplo, -a ['muwtʃiplu, a] ADJ, M
multiple
múmia ['mumja] F mummy
mundial [mũ'dʒjaw] (*pl* **-ais**) ADJ
worldwide; (*guerra, recorde*) world *atr* ▶ M
world championship
mundo ['mũdu] M world; **todo o ~**
everybody; **um ~ de** lots of, a great
many
munição [muni'sãw] (*pl* **-ões**) F (*de
armas*) ammunition; (*chumbo*) shot; (*Mil*)
munitions *pl*, supplies *pl*
municipal [munisi'paw] (*pl* **-ais**) ADJ
municipal
município [muni'sipju] M local
authority; (*cidade*) town; (*condado*)
county
munições [muni'sõjs] FPL *de* **munição**
munir [mu'nir] VT: **~ de** to provide with,
supply with; **munir-se** VR: **~-se de**
(*provisões*) to equip o.s. with
muralha [mu'raʎa] F (*de fortaleza*)
rampart; (*muro*) wall
murchar [mur'ʃar] VT (*Bot*) to wither;
(*sentimentos*) to dull; (*pessoa*) to sadden
▶ VI to wither, wilt; (*fig*) to fade
murmurar [murmu'rar] VI to murmur,
whisper; (*queixar-se*) to mutter, grumble;
(*água*) to ripple; (*folhagem*) to rustle ▶ VT

to murmur; **murmúrio** [mur'murju] M
murmuring, whispering; (*queixa*)
grumbling; (*de água*) rippling; (*de
folhagem*) rustling
muro ['muru] M wall
murro ['muhu] M punch; **dar um ~ em
alguém** to punch sb
musa ['muza] F muse
musculação [muskula'sãw] F weight
training
músculo ['muskulu] M muscle;
musculoso, -a [musku'lozu, ɔza] ADJ
muscular
museu [mu'zew] M museum; (*de pintura*)
gallery
musgo ['muzgu] M moss
música ['muzika] F music; (*canção*)
song; *ver tb* **músico**; **músico, -a**
['muziku, a] ADJ musical ▶ M/F musician
mútuo, -a ['mutwu, a] ADJ mutual

n

N ABR (= *norte*) N

na [na] = **em** + **a**

-na [na] PRON her; (*coisa*) it

nabo ['nabu] M turnip

nação [na'sãw] (*pl* **-ões**) F nation

nacional [nasjo'naw] (*pl* **-ais**) ADJ national; (*carro, vinho etc*) domestic, home-produced; **nacionalidade** [nasjonali'dadʒi] F nationality; **nacionalismo** [nasjona'lizmu] M nationalism; **nacionalista** [nasjona'lista] ADJ, M/F nationalist

nações [na'sõjs] FPL *de* **nação**

nada ['nada] PRON nothing ▶ ADV at all; **antes de mais ~** first of all; **não é ~ difícil** it's not at all hard, it's not hard at all; **~ mais** nothing else; **~ de novo** nothing new; **obrigado — de ~** thank you — not at all *ou* don't mention it

nadador, a [nada'dor(a)] M/F swimmer

nadar [na'dar] VI to swim

nádegas ['nadegas] FPL buttocks

nado ['nadu] M: **atravessar a ~** to swim across; **~ borboleta** butterfly (stroke); **~ de costas** backstroke; **~ de peito** breaststroke

naipe ['najpi] M (*cartas*) suit

namorado, -a [namo'radu, a] M/F boyfriend/girlfriend

namorar [namo'rar] VT (*ser namorado de*) to be going out with

namoro [na'moru] M relationship

não [nãw] ADV not; (*resposta*) no ▶ M no; **~ sei** I don't know; **~ muito** not much; **~ só ... mas também** not only ... but also; **agora ~** not now; **~ tem de quê** don't mention it; **~ é?** isn't it?, won't you?; **eles são brasileiros, ~ é?** they're Brazilian, aren't they?

não... [nãw] PREFIXO non-

naquele(s), naquela(s) [na'keli(s), na'kɛla(s)] = **em** + **aquele(s), aquela(s)**

naquilo [na'kilu] = **em** + **aquilo**

narina [na'rina] F nostril

nariz [na'riz] M nose

narração [naha'sãw] (*pl* **-ões**) F narration; (*relato*) account

narrar [na'har] VT to narrate

narrativa [naha'tʃiva] F narrative; (*história*) story

nas [nas] = **em** + **as**

-nas [nas] PRON them

nascença [na'sẽsa] F birth; **de ~** by birth; **ele é surdo de ~** he was born deaf

nascente [na'sẽtʃi] M East, Orient ▶ F (*fonte*) spring

nascer [na'ser] VI to be born; (*plantas*) to sprout; (*o sol*) to rise; (*ave*) to hatch; (*fig: ter origem*) to come into being ▶ M: **~ do sol** sunrise; **ele nasceu para médico *etc*** he was born to be a doctor *etc*; **nascimento** [nasi'mẽtu] M birth; (*fig*) origin; (*estirpe*) descent

nata ['nata] F cream

natação [nata'sãw] F swimming

natais [na'tajs] ADJ PL *de* **natal**

Natal [na'taw] M Christmas; **Feliz ~!** Merry Christmas!

natal [na'taw] (*pl* **-ais**) ADJ (*relativo ao nascimento*) natal; (*país*) native; **cidade ~** home town

natalino, -a [nata'linu, a] ADJ Christmas *atr*

nativo, -a [na'tʃivu, a] ADJ, M/F native

natural [natu'raw] (*pl* **-ais**) ADJ natural; (*nativo*) native ▶ M/F native; **ao ~** (*Culin*) fresh, uncooked; **naturalidade** [naturali'dadʒi] F naturalness; **de naturalidade paulista** *etc* born in São Paulo *etc*; **naturalizar** [naturali'zar] VT to naturalize; **naturalizar-se** VR to become naturalized; **naturalmente** [naturaw'mẽtʃi] ADV naturally; **naturalmente!** of course!

natureza [natu'reza] F nature; (*espécie*) kind, type

nau [naw] F (*literário*) ship

náusea ['nawzea] F nausea; **dar ~s a alguém** to make sb feel sick; **sentir ~s** to feel sick

náutico, -a [na'wtʃiku, a] ADJ nautical

naval [na'vaw] (*pl* **-ais**) ADJ naval; **construção ~** shipbuilding

navalha [na'vaʎa] F (*de barba*) razor; (*faca*) knife

nave ['navi] F (*de igreja*) nave

navegação [navega'sãw] F navigation, sailing; **~ aérea** air traffic; **companhia de ~** shipping line

navegar [nave'gar] VT to navigate; (*mares*) to sail ▶ VI to sail; (*dirigir o rumo*) to navigate

navio [na'viu] M ship; **~ cargueiro** cargo ship, freighter; **~ de guerra** warship; **~ petroleiro** oil tanker

nazi [na'zi] (PT) ADJ, M/F = **nazista**

nazista [na'zista] (BR) ADJ, M/F Nazi

NB ABR (= *note bem*) NB

neblina [ne'blina] F fog, mist

nebuloso, -a [nebu'lozu, ɔza] ADJ foggy, misty; (*céu*) cloudy; (*fig*) vague

necessário, -a [nese'sarju, a] ADJ necessary ▶ M: **o ~** the necessities *pl*

necessidade [nesesi'dadʒi] F need, necessity; (*o que se necessita*) need; (*pobreza*) poverty, need; **ter ~ de** to need; **em caso de ~** if need be

necessitado, -a [nesesi'tadu, a] ADJ needy, poor; **~ de** in need of

necessitar [nesesi'tar] VT to need, require ▶ VI: **~ de** to need

neerlandês, -esa [neerlã'des, eza] ADJ Dutch ▶ M/F Dutchman/woman

Neerlândia [neer'lãdʒa] F the Netherlands *pl*

negar [ne'gar] VT to deny; (*recusar*) to refuse; **negar-se** VR: **~-se a** to refuse to

negativa [nega'tʃiva] F (*Ling*) negative; (*recusa*) denial

negativo, -a [nega'tʃivu, a] ADJ negative ▶ M (*Tec, Foto*) negative ▶ EXCL (*col*) nope!

negligência [negli'ʒẽsja] F negligence, carelessness; **negligente** [negli'ʒẽtʃi] ADJ negligent, careless

negociação [negosja'sãw] (*pl* **-ões**) F negotiation

negociante [nego'sjãtʃi] M/F businessman/woman

negociar [nego'sjar] VT to negotiate; (*Com*) to trade ▶ VI: **~ (com)** to trade *ou* deal (in); to negotiate (with)

negócio [ne'gɔsju] M (*Com*) business; (*transação*) deal; (*questão*) matter; (*col: troço*) thing; (*assunto*) affair, business; **homem de ~s** businessman; **a ~s** on business; **fechar um ~** to make a deal

negro, -a ['negru, a] ADJ black; (*fig: lúgubre*) black, gloomy ▶ M/F black man/woman

nele(s), nela(s) ['neli(s), 'nɛla(s)] = **em + ele(s), ela(s)**

nem [nẽj] CONJ nor, neither; **~ (sequer)** not even; **~ que** even if; **~ bem** hardly; **~ um só** not a single one; **~ estuda ~ trabalha** he neither studies nor works;

~ eu nor me; **sem ~** without even; **~ todos** not all; **~ tanto** not so much; **~ sempre** not always

nenê [ne'ne] M/F baby

neném [ne'nẽj] (*pl* **-ns**) M/F = **nenê**

nenhum, a [ne'nũ, 'ɲuma] ADJ no, not any ▶ PRON (*nem um só*) none, not one; (*de dois*) neither; **~ lugar** nowhere

nervo ['nervu] M (*Anat*) nerve; (*fig*) energy, strength; (*em carne*) sinew; **nervosismo** [nervo'zizmu] M (*nervosidade*) nervousness; (*irritabilidade*) irritability; **nervoso, -a** [ner'vozu, ɔza] ADJ nervous; (*irritável*) touchy, on edge; (*exaltado*) worked up; **isso/ele me deixa nervoso** he gets on my nerves

nesse(s), nessa(s) ['nesi(s), 'nɛsa(s)] = **em + esse(s), essa(s)**

neste(s), nesta(s) ['nestʃi(s), 'nɛsta(s)] = **em + este(s), esta(s)**

netbanking [nɛt'bãkin] M online banking

neto, -a ['nɛtu, a] M/F grandson/ daughter; **netos** MPL grandchildren

neurose [new'rɔzi] F neurosis; **neurótico, -a** [new'rɔtʃiku, a] ADJ, M/F neurotic

neutro, -a ['newtru, a] ADJ (*Ling*) neuter; (*imparcial*) neutral

nevar [ne'var] VI to snow; **nevasca** [ne'vaska] F snowstorm; **neve** ['nɛvi] F snow

névoa ['nɛvoa] F fog; **nevoeiro** [nevo'ejru] M thick fog

nexo ['nɛksu] M connection, link; **sem ~** disconnected, incoherent

Nicarágua [nika'ragwa] F: **a ~** Nicaragua

nicotina [niko'tʃina] F nicotine

Nigéria [ni'ʒɛrja] F: **a ~** Nigeria

Nilo ['nilu] M: **o ~** the Nile

ninguém [nĩ'gẽj] PRON nobody, no-one

ninho ['niɲu] M nest; (*toca*) lair; (*lar*) home

nisso ['nisu] = **em + isso**

nisto ['nistu] = **em + isto**

nitidez [nitʃi'dez] F (*clareza*) clarity; (*brilho*) brightness; (*imagem*) sharpness

nítido, -a ['nitʃidu, a] ADJ clear, distinct; (*brilhante*) bright; (*imagem*) sharp, clear

nível ['nivew] (*pl* **-eis**) M level; (*fig: padrão*) standard; (: *ponto*) point, pitch; **~ de vida** standard of living

nº ABR (= *número*) no.

no [nu] = **em + o**

nó [nɔ] M knot; (*de uma questão*) crux; **nós dos dedos** knuckles; **dar um nó** to tie a knot

-no [nu] PRON him; (*coisa*) it

nobre ['nɔbri] ADJ, M/F noble; **horário ~** prime time; **nobreza** [no'breza] F nobility

noção [no'sãw] (*pl* **-ões**) F notion; **noções** FPL (*rudimentos*) rudiments, basics; **~ vaga** inkling; **não ter a menor ~ de algo** not to have the slightest idea about sth

nocaute [no'kawtʃi] M knockout ▸ ADV: **pôr alguém ~** to knock sb out

nocivo, -a [no'sivu, a] ADJ harmful

noções [no'sõjs] FPL *de* **noção**

nódoa ['nɔdwa] F spot; (*mancha*) stain

nogueira [no'gejra] F (*árvore*) walnut tree; (*madeira*) walnut

noite ['nojtʃi] F night; **à** *ou* **de ~** at night, in the evening; **boa ~** good evening; (*despedida*) good night; **da ~ para o dia** overnight; **tarde da ~** late at night

noivado [noj'vadu] M engagement

noivo, -a ['nojvu, a] M/F (*prometido*) fiancé/fiancée; (*no casamento*) bridegroom/bride; **os noivos** MPL (*prometidos*) the engaged couple; (*no casamento*) the bride and groom; (*recém-casados*) the newly-weds

nojento, -a [no'ʒẽtu, a] ADJ disgusting

nojo ['noʒu] M nausea; (*repulsão*) disgust, loathing; **ela é um ~** she's horrible; **este trabalho está um ~** this work is messy

no-la(s) = nos + a(s)

no-lo(s) = nos + o(s)

nome ['nɔmi] M name; (*fama*) fame; **de ~** by name; **escritor de ~** famous writer; **um restaurante de ~** a restaurant with a good reputation; **em ~ de** in the name of; **~ de batismo** Christian name; **~ de usuário** (BR) *ou* **utilizador** (PT) (*Comput*) username

nomear [no'mjar] VT to nominate; (*conferir um cargo a*) to appoint; (*dar nome a*) to name

nono, -a ['nonu, a] NUM ninth

nora ['nɔra] F daughter-in-law

nordeste [nor'dɛstʃi] M, ADJ northeast

norma ['nɔrma] F standard, norm; (*regra*) rule; **como ~** as a rule

normal [nor'maw] (*pl* **-ais**) ADJ normal; (*habitual*) usual; **normalizar** [normali'zar] VT to bring back to normal; **normalizar-se** VR to return to normal

noroeste [nor'wɛstʃi] ADJ northwest, northwestern ▸ M northwest

norte ['nɔrtʃi] ADJ northern, north; (*vento, direção*) northerly ▸ M north; **norte-americano, -a** ADJ, M/F (North) American

Noruega [nor'wɛga] F Norway; **norueguês, -esa** [norwe'ges, geza] ADJ, M/F Norwegian ▸ M (*Ling*) Norwegian

nos¹ [nus] = em + os

nos² [nus] PRON (*direto*) us; (*indireto*) us, to us, for us; (*reflexivo*) (to) ourselves; (*recíproco*) (to) each other

nós [nɔs] PRON we; (*depois de prep*) us; **~ mesmos** we ourselves

-nos [nus] PRON them

nosso, -a ['nɔsu, a] ADJ our ▸ PRON ours; **um amigo ~** a friend of ours; **Nossa Senhora** (*Rel*) Our Lady

nostalgia [nostaw'ʒia] F nostalgia; **nostálgico, -a** [nos'tawʒiku, a] ADJ nostalgic

nota ['nɔta] F note; (*Educ*) mark; (*conta*) bill; (*cédula*) banknote; **~ de venda** sales receipt; **~ fiscal** receipt

notar [no'tar] VT to notice, note; **notar-se** VR to be obvious; **fazer ~** to call attention to; **notável** [no'tavew] (*pl* **-eis**) ADJ notable, remarkable

notícia [no'tʃisja] F (*uma notícia*) piece of news; (*TV etc*) news item; **notícias** FPL (*informações*) news *sg*; **pedir ~s de** to inquire about; **ter ~s de** to hear from; **noticiário** [notʃi'sjarju] M (*de jornal*) news section; (*Cinema*) newsreel; (*TV, Rádio*) news bulletin

notório, -a [no'tɔrju, a] ADJ well-known

noturno, -a [no'turnu, a] ADJ nocturnal, nightly; (*trabalho*) night atr ▸ M (*trem*) night train

nova ['nɔva] F piece of news; **novas** FPL (*novidades*) news *sg*

novamente [nova'mẽtʃi] ADV again

novato, -a [no'vatu, a] ADJ inexperienced, raw ▸ M/F beginner, novice; (*Educ*) fresher

nove ['nɔvi] NUM nine

novela [no'vɛla] F short novel, novella; (*Rádio, TV*) soap opera

novelo [no'velu] M ball of thread

novembro [no'vẽbru] M November

noventa [no'vẽta] NUM ninety

novidade [novi'dadʒi] F novelty; (*notícia*) piece of news; **novidades** FPL (*notícias*) news *sg*

novilho, -a [no'viʎu, a] M/F young bull/heifer

novo, -a ['novu, 'nɔva] ADJ new; (*jovem*) young; (*adicional*) further; **de ~** again

noz [nɔs] F nut; (*da nogueira*) walnut; **~ moscada** nutmeg

nu, a [nu, 'nua] ADJ naked; (*braço, arvore, sala, parede*) bare ▸ M nude

nublado, -a [nu'bladu, a] ADJ cloudy, overcast

nuclear [nu'kljar] ADJ nuclear

núcleo ['nuklju] M nucleus sg; (centro)
centre (BRIT), center (US)

nudez [nu'dez] F nakedness, nudity; (de
paredes etc) bareness

nudista [nu'dʒista] ADJ, M/F nudist

nulo, -a ['nulu, a] ADJ (Jur) null, void;
(nenhum) non-existent; (sem valor)
worthless; (esforço) vain, useless

num [nũ] = **em + um**

numa(s) ['numa(s)] = **em + uma(s)**

numeral [nume'raw] (pl -**ais**) M numeral

numerar [nume'rar] VT to number

numérico, -a [nu'mɛriku, a] ADJ
numerical

número ['numeru] M number; (de jornal)
issue; (Teatro etc) act; (de sapatos, roupa)
size; **sem ~** countless; **~ de matrícula**
registration (BRIT) ou license plate (US)
number; **numeroso, -a** [nume'rozu,
ɔza] ADJ numerous

nunca ['nũka] ADV never; **~ mais** never
again; **quase ~** hardly ever; **mais que ~**
more than ever

nuns [nũs] = **em + uns**

núpcias ['nupsjas] FPL nuptials,
wedding sg

nutrição [nutri'sãw] F nutrition

nuvem ['nuvẽj] (pl -**ns**) F cloud; (de
insetos) swarm

o, a [u, a] ART DEF **1** the; **o livro/a mesa/
os estudantes** the book/table/students
2 (com n abstrato, não se traduz): **o amor/a
juventude** love/youth
3 (posse, traduz-se muitas vezes por adj
possessivo): **quebrar o braço** to break
one's arm; **ele levantou a mão** he put
his hand up; **ela colocou o chapéu** she
put her hat on
4 (valor descritivo): **ter a boca grande/
os olhos azuis** to have a big mouth/
blue eyes
▶ PRON DEMOSTRATIVO: **meu livro e o
seu** my book and yours; **as de Pedro
são melhores** Pedro's are better; **não
a(s) branca(s) mas a(s) verde(s)** not
the white one(s) but the green one(s);
o que (etc) ▶ PRON RELATIVO **1** (indef):
os que quiserem podem sair anyone
who wants to can leave; **leve o que
mais gostar** take the one you like best
2 (def): **o que comprei ontem** the one
I bought yesterday; **os que sairam**
those who left
3: **o que** what; **o que eu acho/mais
gosto** what I think/like most
▶ PRON PESSOAL **1** (pessoa: m): him; (: f)
her; (: pl) them; **não consigo vê-lo(s)**
I can't see him/them; **vemo-la todas as
semanas** we see her every week
2 (animal, coisa: sg) it; (: pl) them; **não
consigo vê-lo(s)** I can't see it/them;
acharam-nos na praia they found
them on the beach

obedecer [obede'ser] VI: **~ a** to obey;
obediência [obe'dʒẽsja] F obedience;
obediente [obe'dʒẽtʃi] ADJ obedient

óbito ['ɔbitu] M death; **atestado de ~** death certificate

objeção [obʒe'sãw] (pl **-ões**) F objection; **fazer** ou **pôr objeções a** to object to

objetivo, -a [obʒe'tʃivu, a] ADJ objective ▶ M objective

objeto [ob'ʒɛtu] M object

obra ['ɔbra] F work; (Arq) building, construction; (Teatro) play; **em ~s** under repair; **ser ~ de alguém** to be the work of sb; **~ de arte** work of art; **~s públicas** public works; **obra-prima** (pl **obras-primas**) F masterpiece

obrigação [obriga'sãw] (pl **-ões**) F obligation; (Com) bond

obrigado, -a [obri'gadu, a] ADJ obliged, compelled ▶ EXCL thank you; (recusa) no, thank you

obrigar [obri'gar] VT to oblige, compel; **obrigar-se** VR: **~-se a fazer algo** to undertake to do sth; **obrigatório, -a** [obriga'tɔrju, a] ADJ compulsory, obligatory

obsceno, -a [obi'sɛnu, a] ADJ obscene

obscurecer [obiskure'ser] VT to darken; (entendimento, verdade etc) to obscure ▶ VI to get dark

obscuro, -a [obi'skuru, a] ADJ dark; (fig) obscure

observação [obiserva'sãw] (pl **-ões**) F observation; (comentário) remark, comment; (de leis, regras) observance

observador, a [obiserva'dor(a)] M/F observer

observar [obiser'var] VT to observe; (notar) to notice; **~ algo a alguém** to point sth out to sb

observatório [obiserva'tɔrju] M observatory

obsessão [obise'sãw] (pl **-ões**) F obsession; **obsessivo, -a** [obise'sivu, a] ADJ obsessive

obsoleto, -a [obiso'lɛtu, a] ADJ obsolete

obstinado, -a [obistʃi'nadu, a] ADJ obstinate, stubborn

obstrução [obistru'sãw] (pl **-ões**) F obstruction; **obstruir** [obi'strwir] VT to obstruct; (impedir) to impede

obter [obi'ter] (irreg: como **ter**) VT to obtain, get; (alcançar) to gain

obturação [obitura'sãw] (pl **-ões**) F (de dente) filling

obtuso, -a [obi'tuzu, a] ADJ (ger) obtuse; (fig: pessoa) thick

óbvio, -a ['ɔbvju, a] ADJ obvious; **(é) ~!** of course!

ocasião [oka'zjãw] (pl **-ões**) F opportunity, chance; (momento, tempo) occasion; **ocasionar** [okazjo'nar] VT to cause, bring about

oceano [o'sjanu] M ocean

ocidental [oside'taw] (pl **-ais**) ADJ western ▶ M/F westerner

ocidente [osi'dẽtʃi] M west

ócio ['ɔsju] M (lazer) leisure; (inação) idleness; **ocioso, -a** [o'sjozu, ɔza] ADJ idle; (vaga) unfilled

oco, -a ['oku, a] ADJ hollow, empty

ocorrência [oko'hẽsja] F incident, event; (circunstância) circumstance

ocorrer [oko'her] VI to happen, occur; (vir ao pensamento) to come to mind; **~ a alguém** to happen to sb; (vir ao pensamento) to occur to sb

octogésimo, -a [okto'ʒɛzimu, a] NUM eightieth

oculista [oku'lista] M/F optician

óculo ['ɔkulu] M spyglass; **óculos** MPL glasses, spectacles; **~s de proteção** goggles

ocultar [okuw'tar] VT to hide, conceal; **oculto, -a** [o'kuwtu, a] ADJ hidden; (desconhecido) unknown; (secreto) secret; (sobrenatural) occult

ocupação [okupa'sãw] (pl **-ões**) F occupation

ocupado, -a [oku'padu, a] ADJ (pessoa) busy; (lugar) taken, occupied; (BR: telefone) engaged (BRIT), busy (US); **sinal de ~** (BR Tel) engaged tone (BRIT), busy signal (US)

ocupar [oku'par] VT to occupy; (tempo) to take up; (pessoa) to keep busy; **ocupar-se** VR: **~-se com** ou **de** ou **em algo** (cuidar de) to look after sth; (passar seu tempo com) to occupy o.s. with sth

odiar [o'dʒjar] VT to hate; **ódio** ['ɔdʒju] M hate, hatred; **odioso, -a** [o'dʒjozu, ɔza] ADJ hateful

odor [o'dor] M smell

oeste ['wɛstʃi] M west ▶ ADJ INV (região) western; (direção, vento) westerly

ofegante [ofe'gãtʃi] ADJ breathless, panting

ofender [ofẽ'der] VT to offend; **ofender-se** VR to take offence (BRIT) ou offense (US)

ofensa [o'fẽsa] F insult; (à lei, moral) offence (BRIT), offense (US); **ofensiva** [ofẽ'siva] F offensive; **ofensivo, -a** [ofẽ'sivu, a] ADJ offensive

oferecer [ofere'ser] VT to offer; (dar) to give; (jantar) to give; (propor) to propose; (dedicar) to dedicate; **oferecer-se** VR (pessoa) to offer o.s., volunteer; (oportunidade) to present itself, arise;

~-se para fazer to offer to do;
oferecimento [oferesi'mẽtu] M offer;
oferta [o'fɛrta] F offer; (*dádiva*) gift;
(*Com*) bid; (*em loja*) special offer
oficial [ofi'sjaw] (*pl* **-ais**) ADJ official
▶ M/F official; (*Mil*) officer; **~ de justiça**
bailiff
oficina [ofi'sina] F workshop;
~ mecânica garage
ofício [o'fisju] M trade; (*Rel*) service;
(*carta*) official letter; (*função*) function;
(*encargo*) job, task
oitavo, -a [oj'tavu, a] NUM eighth
oitenta [oj'tẽta] NUM eighty
oito ['ojtu] NUM eight
olá [o'la] EXCL hello!
olaria [ola'ria] F (*fábrica: de louças de
barro*) pottery; (*: de tijolos*) brickworks *sg*
óleo ['ɔlju] M (*lubricante*) oil; **~ de
bronzear** suntan oil; **~ diesel** diesel oil;
oleoso, -a [o'ljozu, ɔza] ADJ oily;
(*gorduroso*) greasy
olfato [ow'fatu] M sense of smell
olhada [o'ʎada] F glance, look; **dar uma
~** to have a look
olhadela [oʎa'dɛla] F peep
olhar [o'ʎar] VT to look at; (*observar*) to
watch; (*ponderar*) to consider; (*cuidar de*)
to look after ▶ VI to look ▶ M look;
olhar-se VR to look at o.s.; (*duas pessoas*)
to look at each other; **~ fixamente** to
stare at; **~ para** to look at; **~ por** to look
after; **~ fixo** stare
olho ['oʎu] M (*Anat, de agulha*) eye; (*vista*)
eyesight; **~ nele!** watch him!; **~ vivo!**
keep your eyes open!; **a ~** (*medir, calcular
etc*) by eye; **~ mágico** (*na porta*)
peephole; **~ roxo** black eye; **num abrir
e fechar de ~s** in a flash
olimpíada [olĩ'piada] F: **as O~s** the
Olympics®
oliveira [oli'vejra] F olive tree
ombro ['õbru] M shoulder; **encolher os
~s, dar de ~s** to shrug one's shoulders
omelete [ome'letʃi] F omelette (*BRIT*),
omelet (*US*)
omissão [omi'sãw] (*pl* **-ões**) F omission;
(*negligência*) negligence
omitir [omi'tʃir] VT to omit
omoplata [omo'plata] F shoulder blade
onça ['õsa] F ounce; (*animal*) jaguar
onda ['õda] F wave; (*moda*) fashion;
~ curta/média/longa short/medium/
long wave; **~ de calor** heat wave
onde ['õdʒi] ADV where ▶ CONJ where, in
which; (*para onde*) where; **de ~ você é?** where are you
from?; **por ~** through which; **por ~?**
which way?; **~ quer que** wherever

ondulado, -a [õdu'ladu, a] ADJ wavy
ônibus ['onibus] (*BR*) M INV bus; **ponto
de ~** bus stop
ontem ['õtẽ] ADV yesterday; **~ à noite**
last night
ONU ['onu] ABR F (= *Organização das
Nações Unidas*) UNO
ônus ['onus] M INV onus; (*obrigação*)
obligation; (*Com*) charge; (*encargo
desagradável*) burden
onze ['õzi] NUM eleven
opaco, -a [o'paku, a] ADJ opaque;
(*obscuro*) dark
opção [op'sãw] (*pl* **-ões**) F option, choice;
(*preferência*) first claim, right
ópera ['ɔpera] F opera
operação [opera'sãw] (*pl* **-ões**) F
operation; (*Com*) transaction; (*Pol*) **~ lava
jato** corruption
operador, a [opera'dor(a)] M/F
operator; (*cirurgião*) surgeon; (*num
cinema*) projectionist
operar [ope'rar] VT to operate; (*produzir*)
to effect, bring about; (*Med*) to operate
on ▶ VI to operate; (*agir*) to act, function;
operar-se VR (*suceder*) to take place;
(*Med*) to have an operation
operário, -a [ope'rarju, a] ADJ working
▶ M/F worker; **classe operária** working
class
opinar [opi'nar] VT to think ▶ VI to give
one's opinion
opinião [opi'njãw] (*pl* **-ões**) F opinion;
mudar de ~ to change one's mind
oponente [opo'nẽtʃi] ADJ opposing
▶ M/F opponent
opor [o'por] (*irreg: como* **pôr**) VT to
oppose; (*resistência*) to put up, offer;
(*objeção, dificuldade*) to raise; **opor-se**
VR: **~-se a** to object to; (*resistir*) to
oppose
oportunidade [oportuni'dadʒi] F
opportunity
oportunista [oportu'nista] ADJ, M/F
opportunist
oportuno, -a [opor'tunu, a] ADJ
(*momento*) opportune, right; (*oferta de
ajuda*) well-timed; (*conveniente*)
convenient, suitable
oposição [opozi'sãw] F opposition; **em
~ a** against; **fazer ~ a** to oppose
opressão [opre'sãw] (*pl* **-ões**) F
oppression; **opressivo, -a** [opre'sivu, a]
ADJ oppressive
oprimir [opri'mir] VT to oppress;
(*comprimir*) to press
optar [op'tar] VI to choose; **~ por** to opt
for; **~ por fazer** to opt to do

ora ['ɔra] ADV now ▶ CONJ well; **por ~** for the time being; **~ ...** , **~ ...** one moment ..., the next ...; **~ bem** now then

oração [ora'sãw] (pl **-ões**) F prayer; (discurso) speech; (Ling) clause

oral [o'raw] (pl **-ais**) ADJ oral ▶ F oral (exam)

orar [o'rar] VI (Rel) to pray

órbita ['ɔrbita] F orbit; (do olho) socket

Órcades ['ɔrkadʒis] FPL: **as ~** the Orkneys

orçamento [orsa'mẽtu] M (do estado etc) budget; (avaliação) estimate

orçar [or'sar] VT to value, estimate ▶ VI: **~ em** (gastos etc) to be valued at, be put at

ordem ['ɔrdẽ] (pl **-ns**) F order; **até nova ~** until further notice; **de primeira ~** first-rate; **estar em ~** to be tidy; **por ~** in order, in turn; **~ do dia** agenda; **~ pública** public order, law and order

ordenado, -a [orde'nadu, a] ADJ (posto em ordem) in order; (metódico) orderly ▶ M salary, wages pl

ordens ['ɔrdẽs] FPL de **ordem**

ordinário, -a [ordʒi'narju, a] ADJ ordinary; (comum) usual; (medíocre) mediocre; (grosseiro) coarse, vulgar; (de má qualidade) inferior; **de ~** usually

orelha [o'reʎa] F ear; (aba) flap

orelhão [ore'ʎãw] (pl **-ões**) M payphone

órfão, -fã ['ɔrfãw, fã] (pl **-s/-s**) ADJ, M/F orphan

orgânico, -a [or'ganiku, a] ADJ organic

organismo [orga'nizmu] M organism; (entidade) organization

organização [organiza'sãw] (pl **-ões**) F organization; **organizar** [organi'zar] VT to organize

órgão ['ɔrgãw] (pl **-s**) M organ; (governamental etc) institution, body

orgasmo [or'gazmu] M orgasm

orgia [or'ʒia] F orgy

orgulho [or'guʎu] M pride; **orgulhoso, -a** [orgu'ʎozu, ɔza] ADJ proud

orientação [orjẽta'sãw] F guidance; (posição) position; **~ educacional** training, guidance

oriental [orjẽ'taw] (pl **-ais**) ADJ eastern; (do Extremo Oriente) oriental

orientar [orjẽ'tar] VT to orientate; (indicar o rumo) to direct; (aconselhar) to guide; **orientar-se** VR to get one's bearings; **~-se por algo** to follow sth

oriente [o'rjẽtʃi] M: **o O~** the East; **Extremo O~** Far East; **O~ Médio** Middle East

origem [o'riʒẽ] (pl **-ns**) F origin; (ascendência) lineage, descent; **lugar de ~** birthplace

original [oriʒi'naw] (pl **-ais**) ADJ original; (estranho) strange, odd ▶ M original; **originalidade** [oriʒinali'dadʒi] F originality; (excentricidade) eccentricity

originar [oriʒi'nar] VT to give rise to, start; **originar-se** VR to arise; **~-se de** to originate from

oriundo, -a [o'rjũdu, a] ADJ: **~ de** arising from; (natural) native of

orla ['ɔrla] F: **~ marítima** seafront

ornamento [orna'mẽtu] M adornment, decoration

orquestra [or'kɛstra], (PT) **orquesta** F orchestra

orquídea [or'kidʒja] F orchid

ortodoxo, -a [orto'dɔksu, a] ADJ orthodox

ortografia [ortogra'fia] F spelling

orvalho [or'vaʎu] M dew

os [us] ART DEF ver **o**

osso ['osu] M bone

ostensivo, -a [ostẽ'sivu, a] ADJ ostensible

ostentar [ostẽ'tar] VT to show; (alardear) to show off, flaunt

ostra ['ostra] F oyster

OTAN ['otã] ABR F (= Organização do Tratado do Atlântico Norte) NATO

ótica ['ɔtʃika] F optics sg; (loja) optician's; (fig: ponto de vista) viewpoint; ver tb **ótico**

ótico, -a ['ɔtʃiku, a] ADJ optical ▶ M/F optician

otimista [otʃi'mista] ADJ optimistic ▶ M/F optimist

ótimo, -a ['ɔtʃimu, a] ADJ excellent, splendid ▶ EXCL great!, super!

ou [o] CONJ or; **ou este ou aquele** either this one or that one; **ou seja** in other words

ouço ['osu] VB ver **ouvir**

ouriço [o'risu] M (europeu) hedgehog; (casca) shell

ouro ['oru] M gold; **ouros** MPL (Cartas) diamonds

ousadia [oza'dʒia] F daring; **ousado, -a** [o'zadu, a] ADJ daring, bold

ousar [o'zar] VT, VI to dare

outono [o'tonu] M autumn

(**PALAVRA-CHAVE**)

outro, -a ['otru, a] ADJ **1** (distinto: sg) another; (: pl) other; **outra coisa** something else; **de outro modo, de outra maneira** otherwise; **no outro**

dia the next day; **ela está outra** (*mudada*) she's changed
2 (*adicional*): **quer outro café?** would you like another coffee?; **outra vez** again
▶ PRON **1**: **o outro** the other one; **(os) outros** (the) others; **de outro** somebody else's
2 (*recíproco*): **odeiam-se uns aos outros** they hate one another *ou* each other
3: **outro tanto** the same again; **comer outro tanto** to eat the same *ou* as much again; **ele recebeu uma dezena de telegramas e outras tantas chamadas** he got about ten telegrams and as many calls

outubro [o'tubru] M October
ouvido [o'vidu] M (*Anat*) ear; (*sentido*) hearing; **de ~** by ear; **dar ~s a** to listen to
ouvinte [o'vĩtʃi] M/F listener; (*estudante*) auditor
ouvir [o'vir] VT to hear; (*com atenção*) to listen to; (*missa*) to attend ▶ VI to hear; to listen; **~ dizer que ...** to hear that ...; **~ falar de** to hear of
ova ['ɔva] F roe
oval [o'vaw] (*pl* **-ais**) ADJ, F oval
ovário [o'varju] M ovary
ovelha [o'veʎa] F sheep
óvni ['ɔvni] M flying saucer
ovo ['ovu] M egg; **~ pochê** (BR) *ou* **escalfado** (PT) poached egg; **~ estrelado** *ou* **frito** fried egg; **~s mexidos** scrambled eggs; **~ cozido** *ou* **quente** boiled egg; **~s de granja** free-range eggs
oxidar [oksi'dar] VT to rust; **oxidar-se** VR to rust, go rusty
oxigenado, -a [oksiʒe'nadu, a] ADJ (*cabelo*) bleached; **água oxigenada** peroxide
oxigênio [oksi'ʒenju] M oxygen
ozônio [o'zonju] M ozone; **camada de ~** ozone layer

P. ABR (= *Praça*) Sq.
pá [pa] F shovel; (*de remo, hélice*) blade
▶ M (PT) pal, mate; **pá de lixo** dustpan
paca ['paka] F (*Zool*) paca
pacato, -a [pa'katu, a] ADJ (*pessoa*) quiet; (*lugar*) peaceful
paciência [pa'sjēsja] F patience; **paciente** [pa'sjētʃi] ADJ, M/F patient
pacífico, -a [pa'sifiku, a] ADJ (*pessoa*) peace-loving; (*aceito sem discussão*) undisputed; (*sossegado*) peaceful; **o (Oceano) P~** the Pacific (Ocean)
pacote [pa'kɔtʃi] M packet; (*embrulho*) parcel; (*Econ, Comput, Turismo*) package
pacto ['paktu] M pact; (*ajuste*) agreement
padaria [pada'ria] F bakery, baker's (shop)
padeiro [pa'dejru] M baker
padiola [pa'dʒjɔla] F stretcher
padrão [pa'drãw] (*pl* **-ões**) M standard; (*medida*) gauge; (*desenho*) pattern; (*fig: modelo*) model; **~ de vida** standard of living
padrasto [pa'drastu] M stepfather
padre ['padri] M priest
padrinho [pa'driɲu] M godfather; (*de noivo*) best man; (*patrono*) sponsor
padroeiro, -a [pa'drwejru, a] M/F patron; (*santo*) patron saint
padrões [pa'drõjs] MPL *de* **padrão**
pães [pãjs] MPL *de* **pão**
pagador, a [paga'dor(a)] ADJ paying ▶ M/F payer; (*de salário*) pay clerk; (*de banco*) teller
pagamento [paga'mẽtu] M payment; **~ a prazo** *ou* **em prestações** payment in instal(l)ments; **~ à vista** cash payment; **~ contra entrega** (*Com*) COD, cash on delivery

pagar [pa'gar] VT to pay; (*compras, pecados*) to pay for; (*o que devia*) to pay back; (*retribuir*) to repay ► VI to pay; **~ por algo** (*tb fig*) to pay for sth; **~ a prestações** to pay in instal(l)ments; **~ de contado** (*PT*) to pay cash

página ['paʒina] F page; **~ (da) web** web page; **~ inicial** home page; **P~s Amarelas** Yellow Pages®

pago, -a ['pagu, a] PP *de* **pagar** ► ADJ paid; (*fig*) even ► M pay

pai [paj] M father; **pais** MPL parents

painel [paj'nɛw] (*pl* **-éis**) M panel; (*quadro*) picture; (*Auto*) dashboard; (*de avião*) instrument panel; **~ solar** solar panel

país [pa'jis] M country; (*região*) land; **~ natal** native land

paisagem [paj'zaʒẽ] (*pl* **-ns**) F scenery; landscape

paisano, -a [paj'zanu, a] ADJ civilian ► M/F (*não militar*) civilian; (*compatriota*) fellow countryman

Países Baixos MPL: **os ~** the Netherlands

paixão [paj'ʃãw] (*pl* **-ões**) F passion

palácio [pa'lasju] M palace; **~ da justiça** courthouse; **Palácio do Planalto** *see note*

> **Palácio de Planalto** is the seat of the Brazilian government, in Brasília. The name comes from the fact that the Brazilian capital is situated on a plateau. It has come to be a byword for central government.

paladar [pala'dar] M taste; (*Anat*) palate

palafita [pala'fita] F (*estacaria*) stilts *pl*; (*habitação*) stilt house

palavra [pa'lavra] F word; (*fala*) speech; (*promessa*) promise; (*direito de falar*) right to speak; **dar a ~ a alguém** to give sb the chance to speak; **ter ~** (*pessoa*) to be reliable; **~s cruzadas** crossword (puzzle) *sg*; **palavrão** [pala'vrãw] (*pl* **-ões**) M swearword

palco ['pawku] M (*Teatro*) stage; (*fig: local*) scene

Palestina [pales'tʃina] F: **a ~** Palestine; **palestino, -a** [pales'tʃinu, a] ADJ, M/F Palestinian

palestra [pa'lɛstra] F chat, talk; (*conferência*) lecture

paletó [pale'tɔ] M jacket

palha ['paʎa] F straw

palhaço [pa'ʎasu] M clown

pálido, -a ['palidu, a] ADJ pale

palito [pa'litu] M stick; (*para os dentes*) toothpick

palma ['pawma] F (*folha*) palm leaf; (*da mão*) palm; **bater ~s** to clap; **palmada** [paw'mada] F slap

palmeira [paw'mejra] F palm tree

palmo ['pawmu] M span; **~ a ~** inch by inch

palpável [paw'pavew] (*pl* **-eis**) ADJ tangible; (*fig*) obvious

pálpebra ['pawpebra] F eyelid

palpitação [pawpita'sãw] (*pl* **-ões**) F beating, throbbing; **palpitações** FPL (*batimentos cardíacos*) palpitations

palpitante [pawpi'tãtʃi] ADJ beating, throbbing; (*fig: emocionante*) thrilling; (: *de interesse atual*) sensational

palpitar [pawpi'tar] VI (*coração*) to beat

palpite [paw'pitʃi] M (*intuição*) hunch; (*Jogo, Turfe*) tip; (*opinião*) opinion

pampa ['pãpa] F pampas

Panamá [pana'ma] M: **o ~** Panama; **o canal do ~** the Panama Canal

pancada [pã'kada] F (*no corpo*) blow, hit; (*choque*) knock; (*de relógio*) stroke; **dar ~ em alguém** to hit sb; **pancadaria** [pãkada'ria] F (*surra*) beating; (*tumulto*) fight

pandeiro [pã'dejru] M tambourine

pandemia [pãde'mia] F pandemic

pane ['pani] F breakdown

panela [pa'nɛla] F (*de barro*) pot; (*de metal*) pan; (*de cozinhar*) saucepan; (*no dente*) hole; **~ de pressão** pressure cooker

panfleto [pã'fletu] M pamphlet

pânico ['paniku] M panic; **entrar em ~** to panic

pano ['panu] M cloth; (*Teatro*) curtain; (*vela*) sheet, sail; **~ de pratos** tea towel; **~ de pó** duster; **~ de fundo** (*tb fig*) backdrop

panorama [pano'rama] M view

panqueca [pã'kɛka] F pancake

pantanal [pãta'naw] (*pl* **-ais**) M swampland

pântano ['pãtanu] M marsh, swamp

pantera [pã'tɛra] F panther

pão [pãw] (*pl* **pães**) M bread; **o P~ de Açúcar** (*no Rio*) Sugarloaf Mountain; **~ árabe** pitta (*BRIT*) *ou* pita (*US*) bread; **~ torrado** toast; **pão-duro** (*pl* **pães-duros**) (*col*) ADJ mean, stingy ► M/F miser; **pãozinho** [pãw'ziɲu] M roll

papa ['papa] M Pope

papagaio [papa'gaju] M parrot; (*pipa*) kite

papai [pa'paj] M dad, daddy; **P~ Noel** Santa Claus, Father Christmas

papel [pa'pɛw] (*pl* **-éis**) M paper; (*Teatro*) part; (*função*) role; **~ de embrulho** wrapping paper; **~ de escrever/de alumínio** writing paper/tinfoil; **~ de parede** wallpaper; **~ de seda/ transparente** tissue paper/tracing paper; **~ filme** Clingfilm® (BRIT), Saran Wrap® (US); **~ higiênico** toilet paper; **papelada** [pape'lada] F pile of papers; (*burocracia*) paperwork, red tape; **papelão** [pape'lãw] M cardboard; (*fig*) fiasco; **papelaria** [papela'ria] F stationer's (shop); **papel-carbono** M carbon paper

papinha [pa'piɲa] F: **~ de bebê** baby food

papo ['papu] M (*col*) double chin; (: *conversa*) chat; (: *papo furado*) hot air; **bater** *ou* **levar um ~** (*col*) to have a chat; **bater ~** (*col*) to chat (*also internet*); **ficar de ~ para o ar** (*fig*) to laze around

paquerar [pake'rar] (*col*) VI to flirt ▶ VT to chat up

paquistanês, -esa [pakista'nes, eza] ADJ, M/F Pakistani

Paquistão [pakis'tãw] M: **o ~** Pakistan

par [par] ADJ (*igual*) equal; (*número*) even ▶ M pair; (*casal*) couple; (*pessoa na dança*) partner; **~ a ~** side by side, level; **sem ~** incomparable

para ['para] PREP for; (*direção*) to, towards; **~ que** so that, in order that; **~ quê?** what for?, why?; **ir ~ casa** to go home; **~ com** (*atitude*) towards; **de lá ~ cá** since then; **~ a semana** next week; **estar ~** to be about to; **é ~ nós ficarmos aqui?** should we stay here?

parabéns [para'bẽjs] MPL congratulations; (*no aniversário*) happy birthday; **dar ~ a** to congratulate

para-brisa ['para-] (*pl* **-s**) M windscreen (BRIT), windshield (US)

para-choque ['para-] (*pl* **-s**) M (*Auto*) bumper

parada [pa'rada] F stop; (*Com*) stoppage; (*militar, colegial*) parade

parado, -a [pa'radu, a] ADJ (*imóvel*) standing still; (*sem vida*) lifeless; (*carro*) stationary; (*máquina*) out of action; (*olhar*) fixed; (*trabalhador, fábrica*) idle

paradoxo [para'dɔksu] M paradox

parafuso [para'fuzu] M screw

paragem [pa'raʒẽ] (*pl* **-ns**) F (PT) stop; **paragens** FPL (*lugares*) parts; **~ de elétrico** (PT) tram (BRIT) *ou* streetcar (US) stop

parágrafo [pa'ragrafu] M paragraph

Paraguai [para'gwaj] M: **o ~** Paraguay; **paraguaio, -a** [para'gwaju, a] ADJ, M/F Paraguayan

paraíso [para'izu] M paradise

para-lama ['para-] (*pl* **-s**) M wing (BRIT), fender (US); (*de bicicleta*) mudguard

paralelepípedo [paralele'pipedu] M cobblestone

paralelo, -a [para'lɛlu, a] ADJ

parapeito [para'pejtu] M wall, parapet; (*da janela*) windowsill

parapente [para'pẽtʃi] M (*Esporte*) paragliding; (*equipamento*) paraglider

paraquedas [para'kɛdas] M INV parachute

parar [pa'rar] VI to stop; (*ficar*) to stay ▶ VT to stop; **fazer ~** (*deter*) to stop; **~ na cadeia** to end up in jail; **~ de fazer** to stop doing

para-raios ['para-] M INV lightning conductor

parasita [para'zita] M parasite

parceiro, -a [par'sejru, a] ADJ matching ▶ M/F partner

parcela [par'sɛla] F piece, bit; (*de pagamento*) instalment (BRIT), installment (US); (*de terra*) plot; (*do eleitorado etc*) section; (*Mat*) item

parceria [parse'ria] F partnership

parcial [par'sjaw] (*pl* **-ais**) ADJ partial; (*feito por partes*) in parts; (*pessoa*) biased; (*Pol*) partisan; **parcialidade** [parsjali'dadʒi] F bias, partiality

pardal [par'daw] (*pl* **-ais**) M sparrow

pardieiro [par'dʒjejru] M ruin, heap

pardo, -a ['pardu, a] ADJ (*cinzento*) grey (BRIT), gray (US); (*castanho*) brown

parecer [pare'ser] VI (*ter a aparência de*) to look, seem; **parecer-se** VR: **~-se com alguém** to look like sb; **~ alguém/algo** to look like sb/sth; **ao que parece** apparently; **parece-me que** I think that, it seems to me that; **que lhe parece?** what do you think?; **parece que** (*pelo visto*) it looks as if; (*segundo dizem*) apparently

parecido, -a [pare'sidu, a] ADJ alike, similar; **~ com** like

parede [pa'redʒi] F wall

parente [pa'rẽtʃi] M/F relative, relation; **parentesco** [parẽ'tesku] M relationship; (*fig*) connection

parêntese [pa'rẽtezi] M parenthesis; (*na escrita*) bracket; (*fig: digressão*) digression

páreo ['pareu] M race; (*fig*) competition

parir [pa'rir] VT to give birth to ▶ VI to give birth; (*mulher*) to have a baby

Paris ['paris] N Paris; **parisiense**
[pari'zjɛsi] ADJ, M/F Parisian
parlamentar [parlamẽ'tar] ADJ
parliamentary ▶ M/F member of
parliament
parlamento [parla'mẽtu] M parliament
paróquia [pa'rɔkja] F (*Rel*) parish
parque ['parki] M park; **~ industrial**
industrial estate; **~ nacional** national
park; **~ de diversões** amusement park
parte ['partʃi] F part; (*quinhão*) share;
(*lado*) side; (*ponto*) point; (*Jur*) party;
(*papel*) role; **a maior ~** most of; **à ~**
aside; (*separado*) separate;
(*separadamente*) separately; (*além de*)
apart from; **da ~ de alguém** on sb's
part; **em alguma/qualquer ~**
somewhere/anywhere; **em ~ alguma**
nowhere; **por toda (a) ~** everywhere;
pôr de ~ to set aside; **tomar ~ em** to
take part in; **dar ~ de alguém à polícia**
to report sb to the police
participar [partʃisi'par] VT to announce,
notify of ▶ VI: **~ de** *ou* **em** to participate
in, take part in; (*compartilhar*) to share in
particípio [partʃi'sipju] M participle
particular [partʃiku'lar] ADJ particular,
special; (*privativo, pessoal*) private ▶ M
particular; (*indivíduo*) individual;
particulares MPL (*pormenores*) details;
em ~ in private; **particularmente**
[partʃikular'mẽtʃi] ADV privately;
(*especialmente*) particularly
partida [par'tʃida] F (*saída*) departure;
(*Esporte*) game, match
partidário, -a [partʃi'darju, a] ADJ
supporting ▶ M/F supporter, follower
partido, -a [par'tʃidu, a] ADJ broken ▶ M
(*Pol*) party; **tirar ~ de** to profit from;
tomar o ~ de to side with
partilhar [partʃi'ʎar] VT to share;
(*distribuir*) to share out
partir [par'tʃir] VT to break; (*dividir*) to
split ▶ VI (*pôr-se a caminho*) to set off, set
out; (*ir-se embora*) to leave, depart;
partir-se VR to break; **a ~ de** (starting)
from; **~ para outra** (*col*) to move on
parto ['partu] M (child)birth; **estar em
trabalho de ~** to be in labour (*BRIT*) *ou*
labor (*US*)
Páscoa ['paskwa] F Easter; (*dos judeus*)
Passover
pasmo, -a ['pazmu, a] ADJ astonished
▶ M amazement
passa ['pasa] F raisin
passadeira [pasa'dejra] F (*tapete*) stair
carpet; (*mulher*) ironing lady; (*PT: para
peões*) zebra crossing (*BRIT*), crosswalk (*US*)

passado, -a [pa'sadu, a] ADJ past;
(*antiquado*) old-fashioned; (*fruta*) bad;
(*peixe*) off ▶ M past; **o ano ~** last year;
bem ~ (*carne*) well done
passageiro, -a [pasa'ʒejru, a] ADJ
passing ▶ M/F passenger
passagem [pa'saʒẽj] (*pl* **-ns**) F passage;
(*preço de condução*) fare; (*bilhete*) ticket;
~ de ida e volta return ticket, round trip
ticket (*US*); **~ de nível** level (*BRIT*) *ou*
grade (*US*) crossing; **~ de pedestres**
pedestrian crossing (*BRIT*), crosswalk
(*US*); **~ subterrânea** underpass,
subway (*BRIT*)
passaporte [pasa'pɔrtʃi] M passport
passar [pa'sar] VT to pass; (*exceder*) to go
beyond, exceed; (*a ferro*) to iron; (*o tempo*)
to spend; (*Comput*) to swipe; (*a outra
pessoa*) to pass on; (*pomada*) to put on
▶ VI to pass; (*na rua*) to go past; (*tempo*)
to go by; (*dor*) to wear off; (*terminar*) to
be over; **passar-se** VR (*acontecer*) to go
on, happen; **~ bem** (*de saúde*) to be well;
passava das dez horas it was past ten
o'clock; **~ alguém para trás** to con sb;
(*cônjuge*) to cheat on sb; **~ por algo** (*sofrer*)
to go through sth; (*transitar, estrada*) to
go along sth; (*ser considerado como*) to be
thought of as sth; **~ sem** to do without
passarela [pasa'rɛla] F footbridge
pássaro ['pasaru] M bird
passatempo [pasa'tẽpu] M pastime
passe ['pasi] M pass
passear [pa'sjar] VT to take for a walk
▶ VI (*a pé*) to go for a walk; (*sair*) to go out;
~ a cavalo/de carro to go for a ride/a
drive; **passeata** [pa'sjata] F (*marcha
coletiva*) protest march; **passeio**
[pa'seju] M walk; (*de carro*) drive, ride;
(*excursão*) outing; (*calçada*) pavement
(*BRIT*), sidewalk (*US*); **dar um passeio**
to go for a walk; (*de carro*) to go for a drive
ou ride
passível [pa'sivew] (*pl* **-eis**) ADJ: **~ de** (*dor
etc*) susceptible to; (*pena, multa*) subject
to
passivo, -a [pa'sivu, a] ADJ passive ▶ M
(*Com*) liabilities *pl*
passo ['pasu] M step; (*medida*) pace;
(*modo de andar*) walk; (*ruído dos passos*)
footstep; (*sinal de pé*) footprint; **ao ~
que** while; **ceder o ~ a** to give way to
pasta ['pasta] F paste; (*de couro*)
briefcase; (*de cartolina*) folder; (*de
ministro*) portfolio; **~ dentifrícia** *ou* **de
dentes** toothpaste
pastar [pas'tar] VT to graze on ▶ VI to
graze

pastel [pas'tɛw] (pl -**éis**) ADJ INV (cor) pastel ▸ M samosa

pastelão [paste'lãw] M slapstick

pastelaria [pastela'ria] F cake shop; (comida) pastry

pasteurizado, -a [pastewri'zadu, a] ADJ pasteurized

pastilha [pas'tʃiʎa] F (Med) tablet; (doce) pastille

pastor, a [pas'tor(a)] M/F shepherd(ess) ▸ M (Rel) clergyman, pastor

pata ['pata] F (pé de animal) foot, paw; (ave) duck; (col: pé) foot

patamar [pata'mar] M (de escada) landing; (fig) level

pateta [pa'tɛta] ADJ stupid, daft ▸ M/F idiot

patético, -a [pa'tɛtʃiku, a] ADJ pathetic, moving

patife [pa'tʃifi] M scoundrel, rogue

patim [pa'tʃĩ] (pl -**ns**) M skate; ~ **de rodas** roller skate; **patins em linha** Rollerblades®; **patinar** [patʃi'nar] VI to skate; (Auto: derrapar) to skid

patins [pa'tʃĩs] MPL de **patim**

pátio ['patʃju] M (de uma casa) patio, backyard; (espaço cercado de edifícios) courtyard; (tb: ~ **de recreio**) playground; (Mil) parade ground

pato ['patu] M duck; (macho) drake

patologia [patolo'ʒia] F pathology; **patológico, -a** [pato'lɔʒiku, a] ADJ pathological

patrão [pa'trãw] (pl -**ões**) M (Com) boss; (dono de casa) master; (proprietário) landlord; (Náut) skipper

pátria ['patrja] F homeland

patrimônio [patri'monju] M (herança) inheritance; (fig) heritage; (bens) property

patriota [pa'trjɔta] M/F patriot

patrocinar [patrosi'nar] VT to sponsor; (proteger) to support; **patrocínio** [patro'sinju] M sponsorship, backing; (proteção) support

patrões [pa'trõjs] MPL de **patrão**

patrulha [pa'truʎa] F patrol; **patrulhar** [patru'ʎar] VT, VI to patrol

pau [paw] M (madeira) wood; (vara) stick; **paus** MPL (Cartas) clubs; ~ **a** ~ neck and neck; ~ **de bandeira** flagpole; ~ **de selfie** selfie stick

pausa ['pawza] F pause; (intervalo) break; (descanso) rest

pauta ['pawta] F (linha) (guide)line; (ordem do dia) agenda; (indicações) guidelines pl; **sem** ~ (papel) plain; **em** ~ on the agenda

pavão, -voa [pa'vãw, 'voa] (pl -**ões/-s**) M/F peacock/peahen

pavilhão [pavi'ʎãw] (pl -**ões**) M tent; (de madeira) hut; (no jardim) summerhouse; (em exposição) pavilion; (bandeira) flag

pavimento [pavi'mẽtu] M (chão, andar) floor; (da rua) road surface

pavões [pa'võjs] MPL de **pavão**

pavor [pa'vor] M dread, terror; **ter** ~ **de** to be terrified of; **pavoroso, -a** [pavo'rozu, ɔza] ADJ dreadful, terrible

paywall ['pejwɔ] M (Comput) paywall

paz [pajz] F peace; **fazer as** ~**es** to make up, be friends again

PC ABR M PC

Pça. ABR (= Praça) Sq.

pé [pɛ] M foot; (da mesa) leg; (fig: base) footing; (de milho, café) plant; **ir a pé** to walk, go on foot; **ao pé de** near, by; **ao pé da letra** literally; **estar de pé** (festa etc) to be on; **em** ou **de pé** standing (up); **dar no pé** (col) to run away, take off; **não ter pé nem cabeça** (fig) to make no sense

peão [pjãw] (pl -**ões**) M (PT) pedestrian

peça ['pɛsa] F piece; (Auto) part; (aposento) room; (Teatro) play; ~ **de reposição** spare part; ~ **de roupa** garment

pecado [pe'kadu] M sin

pecar [pe'kar] VI to sin; ~ **por excesso de zelo** to be over-zealous

pechincha [pe'ʃĩʃa] F (vantagem) godsend; (coisa barata) bargain; **pechinchar** [peʃĩ'ʃar] VI to bargain, haggle

peço ['pɛsu] VB ver **pedir**

peculiar [peku'ljar] ADJ special, peculiar; (particular) particular; **peculiaridade** [pekuljari'dadʒi] F peculiarity

pedaço [pe'dasu] M piece; (fig: trecho) bit; **aos** ~**s** in pieces

pedágio [pe'daʒju] M (BR) (pagamento) toll

pedal [pe'daw] (pl -**ais**) M pedal; **pedalar** [peda'lar] VT, VI to pedal

pedante [pe'dãtʃi] ADJ pretentious ▸ M/F pseud

pedestre [pe'dɛstri] (BR) M pedestrian

pedicuro, -a [pedʒi'kuru, a] M/F chiropodist (BRIT), podiatrist (US)

pedido [pe'dʒidu] M request; (Com) order; ~ **de demissão** resignation; ~ **de desculpa** apology

pedinte [pe'dʒĩtʃi] M/F beggar

pedir [pe'dʒir] VT to ask for; (Com, comida) to order; (exigir) to demand ▸ VI to ask;

(*num restaurante*) to order; **~ algo a alguém** to ask sb for sth; **~ a alguém que faça, ~ para alguém fazer** to ask sb to do

pedófilo, -a [pe'dɔfilu, a] M/F paedophile (BRIT), pedophile (US)

pedra ['pɛdra] F stone; (*rochedo*) rock; (*de granizo*) hailstone; (*de açúcar*) lump; (*quadro-negro*) slate; **~ de gelo** ice cube; **pedreiro** [pe'drejru] M stonemason

pegada [pe'gada] F (*de pé*) footprint; (*Futebol*) save; **~ de carbono** carbon footprint

pegado, -a [pe'gadu, a] ADJ stuck; (*unido*) together

pegajoso, -a [pega'ʒozu, ɔza] ADJ sticky

pegar [pe'gar] VT to catch; (*selos*) to stick (on); (*segurar*) to take hold of; (*hábito, mania*) to get into; (*compreender*) to take in; (*trabalho*) to take on; (*estação de rádio*) to pick up, get ▸ VI to stick; (*planta*) to take; (*moda*) to catch on; (*doença*) to be catching; (*motor*) to start; **~ em** (*segurar*) to grab, pick up; **ir ~** (*buscar*) to go and get; **~ um emprego** to get a job; **~ fogo a algo** to set fire to sth; **~ no sono** to get to sleep

pego, -a ['pɛgu, a] PP de **pegar**

peito ['pejtu] M (*Anat*) chest; (*de ave, mulher*) breast; (*fig*) courage

peitoril [pejto'riw] (*pl* -**is**) M windowsill

peixada [pej'ʃada] F *fish cooked in a seafood sauce*

peixaria [pejʃa'ria] F fish shop, fishmonger's (BRIT)

peixe ['pejʃi] M fish; **Peixes** MPL (*Astrologia*) Pisces sg

pela ['pɛla] = **por + a**

pelada [pe'lada] F football game

> **Pelada** is an improvised, generally short, game of football, which in the past was played with a ball made out of socks, or an inflatable rubber ball. It is still played today on any piece of open land, or even in the street.

pelado, -a [pe'ladu, a] ADJ (*sem pele*) skinned; (*sem pelo, cabelo*) shorn; (*nu*) naked, in the nude; (*sem dinheiro*) broke

pelar [pe'lar] VT (*tirar a pele*) to skin; (*tirar o pelo*) to shear

pelas ['pɛlas] = **por + as**

pele ['pɛli] F skin; (*couro*) leather; (*como agasalho*) fur; (*de animal*) hide

película [pe'likula] F film

pelo¹ ['pelu] = **por + o**

pelo² ['pelu] M hair; (*de animal*) fur, coat; **nu em ~** stark naked

pelos ['pɛlus] = **por + os**

peludo, -a [pe'ludu, a] ADJ hairy; (*animal*) furry

pena ['pena] F feather; (*de caneta*) nib; (*escrita*) writing; (*Jur*) penalty, punishment; (*sofrimento*) suffering; (*piedade*) pity; **que ~!** what a shame!; **dar ~** to be upsetting; **ter ~ de** to feel sorry for; **~ de morte** death penalty

pênalti ['penawtʃi] M (*Futebol*) penalty (kick)

penar [pe'nar] VT to grieve ▸ VI to suffer

pendência [pẽ'dẽsja] F dispute, quarrel

pendente [pẽ'dẽtʃi] ADJ hanging; (*por decidir*) pending; (*inclinado*) sloping; (*dependent*): **~ de** dependent on ▸ M pendant

pêndulo ['pẽdulu] M pendulum

pendurar [pẽdu'rar] VT to hang

penedo [pe'nedu] M rock, boulder

peneira [pe'nejra] F sieve; **peneirar** [penej'rar] VT to sift, sieve ▸ VI (*chover*) to drizzle

penetrar [pene'trar] VT to get into, penetrate; (*compreender*) to understand ▸ VI: **~ em** ou **por** ou **entre** to penetrate

penhasco [pe'ɲasku] M cliff, crag

penhorar [peɲo'rar] VT (*dar em penhor*) to pledge, pawn

penicilina [penisi'lina] F penicillin

península [pe'nĩsula] F peninsula

pênis ['penis] M INV penis

penitência [peni'tẽsja] F penitence; (*expiação*) penance; **penitenciária** [penitẽ'sjarja] F prison

penoso, -a [pe'nozu, ɔza] ADJ (*assunto, tratamento*) painful; (*trabalho*) hard

pensamento [pẽsa'mẽtu] M thought; (*mente*) mind; (*opinião*) way of thinking; (*ideia*) idea

pensão [pẽ'sãw] (*pl* -**ões**) F (*tb*: **casa de ~**) boarding house; (*comida*) board; **~ completa** full board; **~ de aposentadoria** (*retirement*) pension

pensar [pẽ'sar] VI to think; (*imaginar*) to imagine; **~ em** to think of ou about; **~ fazer** to intend to do; **pensativo, -a** [pẽsa'tʃivu, a] ADJ thoughtful, pensive

pensionista [pẽsjo'nista] M/F pensioner

pensões [pẽ'sõjs] FPL de **pensão**

pente ['pẽtʃi] M comb; **penteado, -a** [pẽ'tʃjadu, a] ADJ (*cabelo*) in place; (*pessoa*) smart ▸ M hairdo, hairstyle; **pentear** [pẽ'tʃjar] VT to comb; (*arranjar o cabelo*) to do, style; **pentear-se** VR to comb one's hair; to do one's hair

penúltimo, -a [pe'nuwtʃimu, a] ADJ last but one, penultimate

penumbra [pe'nũbra] F twilight, dusk; (*sombra*) shadow; (*meia-luz*) half-light
penúria [pe'nurja] F poverty
peões [pjõjs] MPL *de* **peão**
pepino [pe'pinu] M cucumber
pequeno, -a [pe'kenu, a] ADJ small; (*mesquinho*) petty ▶ M boy
Pequim [pe'kĩ] N Beijing
pera ['pera] F pear
perambular [perãbu'lar] VI to wander
perante [pe'rãtʃi] PREP before, in the presence of
per capita [pɛr'kapita] ADV, ADJ per capita
perceber [perse'ber] VT to realize; (*por meio dos sentidos*) to perceive; (*compreender*) to understand; (*ver*) to see; (*ouvir*) to hear; (*ver ao longe*) to make out; (*dinheiro: receber*) to receive
percentagem [persẽ'taʒẽj] F percentage
percepção [persep'sãw] F perception; **perceptível** [persep'tʃivew] (*pl* **-eis**) ADJ perceptible, noticeable; (*som*) audible
percevejo [perse'veʒu] M (*inseto*) bug; (*prego*) drawing pin (BRIT), thumbtack (US)
perco ['perku] VB *ver* **perder**
percorrer [perko'her] VT (*viajar por*) to travel (across *ou* over); (*passar por*) to go through, traverse; (*investigar*) to search through
percurso [per'kursu] M (*espaço percorrido*) distance (covered); (*trajeto*) route; (*viagem*) journey
percussão [perku'sãw] F (*Mús*) percussion
perda ['perda] F loss; (*desperdício*) waste; **~s e danos** damages, losses
perdão [per'dãw] M pardon, forgiveness; **~!** sorry!, I beg your pardon!
perder [per'der] VT to lose; (*tempo*) to waste; (*trem, show, oportunidade*) to miss ▶ VI to lose; **perder-se** VR to get lost; (*arruinar-se*) to be ruined; (*desaparecer*) to disappear; **~-se de alguém** to lose sb
perdido, -a [per'dʒidu, a] ADJ lost; **~s e achados** lost and found, lost property
perdiz [per'dʒiz] F partridge
perdoar [per'dwar] VT to forgive
perdurar [perdu'rar] VI to last a long time; (*continuar a existir*) to still exist
perecível [pere'sivew] (*pl* **-eis**) ADJ perishable
peregrinação [peregrina'sãw] (*pl* **-ões**) F (*viagem*) travels *pl*; (*Rel*) pilgrimage
peregrino, -a [pere'grinu, a] M/F pilgrim
peremptório, -a [perẽp'tɔrju, a] ADJ final; (*decisivo*) decisive

perene [pe'rɛni] ADJ everlasting; (*Bot*) perennial
perfeição [perfej'sãw] F perfection
perfeitamente [perfejta'mẽtʃi] ADV perfectly ▶ EXCL exactly!
perfeito, -a [per'fejtu, a] ADJ perfect ▶ M (*Ling*) perfect
perfil [per'fiw] (*pl* **-is**) M profile; (*silhueta*) silhouette, outline; (*Arq*) (cross) section
perfume [per'fumi] M perfume; scent
perfurar [perfu'rar] VT (*o chão*) to drill a hole in; (*papel*) to punch (a hole in)
pergunta [per'gũta] F question; **fazer uma ~ a alguém** to ask sb a question; **perguntar** [pergũ'tar] VT to ask; (*interrogar*) to question ▶ VI: **perguntar por alguém** to ask after sb; **perguntar-se** VR to wonder; **perguntar algo a alguém** to ask sb sth
perícia [pe'risja] F expertise; (*destreza*) skill; (*exame*) investigation
periferia [perife'ria] F periphery; (*da cidade*) outskirts *pl*
perigo [pe'rigu] M danger; **perigoso, -a** [peri'gozu, ɔza] ADJ dangerous; (*arriscado*) risky
período [pe'riodu] M period; (*estação*) season
periquito [peri'kitu] M parakeet
perito, -a [pe'ritu, a] ADJ expert ▶ M/F expert; (*quem faz perícia*) investigator
permanecer [permane'ser] VI to remain; (*num lugar*) to stay; (*continuar a ser*) to remain, keep; **~ parado** to keep still
permanência [perma'nẽsja] F permanence; (*estada*) stay; **permanente** [perma'nẽtʃi] ADJ (*dor*) constant; (*cor*) fast; (*residência, pregas*) permanent ▶ M (*cartão*) pass ▶ F perm
permissão [permi'sãw] F permission, consent; **permissivo, -a** [permi'sivu, a] ADJ permissive
permitir [permi'tʃir] VT to allow, permit
perna ['pɛrna] F leg; **~s tortas** bow legs
pernil [per'niw] (*pl* **-is**) M (*de animal*) haunch; (*Culin*) leg
pernilongo [perni'lõgu] M mosquito
pernis [per'nis] MPL *de* **pernil**
pernoitar [pernoj'tar] VI to spend the night
pérola ['pɛrola] F pearl
perpendicular [perpẽdʒiku'lar] ADJ, F perpendicular
perpetuar [perpe'twar] VT to perpetuate; **perpétuo, -a** [per'pɛtwu, a] ADJ perpetual
persa ['pɛrsa] ADJ, M/F Persian

perseguição [persegi'sãw] F pursuit; (Rel, Pol) persecution

perseguir [perse'gir] VT to pursue; (correr atrás) to chase (after); (Rel, Pol) to persecute; (importunar) to harass, pester

perseverante [perseve'rãtʃi] ADJ persistent

perseverar [perseve'rar] VI to persevere

Pérsia ['pɛrsja] F: **a ~** Persia

persiana [per'sjana] F blind

Pérsico, -a ['pɛrsiku, a] ADJ: **o golfo ~** the Persian Gulf

persigo [per'sigu] VB ver **perseguir**

persistir [persis'tʃir] VI to persist

personagem [perso'naʒē] (pl -ns) M/F famous person, celebrity; (num livro, filme) character

personalidade [personali'dadʒi] F personality

perspectiva [perspek'tʃiva] F perspective; (panorama) view; (probabilidade) prospect

perspicácia [perspi'kasja] F insight, perceptiveness; **perspicaz** [perspi'kajz] ADJ perceptive; (sagaz) shrewd

persuadir [perswa'dʒir] VT to persuade; **persuadir-se** VR to convince o.s.; **persuasão** [perswa'zãw] F persuasion; **persuasivo, -a** [perswa'zivu, a] ADJ persuasive

pertencente [pertē'sētʃi] ADJ: **~ a** pertaining to

pertencer [pertē'ser] VI: **~ a** to belong to; (referir-se) to concern

pertences [per'tēsis] MPL (de uma pessoa) belongings

pertinência [pertʃi'nēsja] F relevance; **pertinente** [pertʃi'nētʃi] ADJ relevant; (apropriado) appropriate

perto, -a ['pɛrtu, a] ADJ nearby ▶ ADV near; **~ de** near to; (em comparação com) next to; **de ~** closely; (ver) close up; (conhecer) very well

perturbar [pertur'bar] VT to disturb; (abalar) to upset, trouble; (atrapalhar) to put off; (andamento, trânsito) to disrupt; (envergonhar) to embarrass; (alterar) to affect

Peru [pe'ru] M: **o ~** Peru

peru, a [pe'ru(a)] M/F turkey

peruca [pe'ruka] F wig

perverso, -a [per'vɛrsu, a] ADJ perverse; (malvado) wicked

perverter [perver'ter] VT to corrupt, pervert; **pervertido, -a** [perver'tʃidu, a] ADJ perverted ▶ M/F pervert

pesadelo [peza'delu] M nightmare

pesado, -a [pe'zadu, a] ADJ heavy; (ambiente) tense; (trabalho) hard; (estilo) dull, boring; (andar) slow; (piada) coarse; (comida) stodgy; (tempo) sultry ▶ ADV heavily

pêsames ['pezamis] MPL condolences, sympathy sg

pesar [pe'zar] VT to weigh; (fig) to weigh up ▶ VI to weigh; (ser pesado) to be heavy; (influir) to carry weight; (causar mágoa): **~ a** to hurt, grieve ▶ M grief; **~ sobre** (recair) to fall upon

pesaroso, -a [peza'rozu, ɔza] ADJ sorrowful, sad; (arrependido) regretful, sorry

pesca ['pɛska] F fishing; (os peixes) catch; **ir à ~** to go fishing

pescada [pes'kada] F whiting

pescado [pes'kadu] M fish

pescador, a [peska'dor(a)] M/F fisherman/woman; **~ à linha** angler

pescar [pes'kar] VT (peixe) to catch; (tentar apanhar) to fish for; (retirar da água) to fish out ▶ VI to fish

pescoço [pes'kosu] M neck

peso ['pezu] M weight; (fig: ônus) burden; (importância) importance; **~ bruto/líquido** gross/net weight

pesquisa [pes'kiza] F research; **uma ~** a study; **pesquisar** [peski'zar] VT, VI to research

pêssego ['pesegu] M peach

pessimista [pesi'mista] ADJ pessimistic ▶ M/F pessimist

péssimo, -a ['pɛsimu, a] ADJ very bad, awful

pessoa [pe'soa] F person; **pessoas** FPL people; **pessoal** [pe'swaw] (pl -ais) ADJ personal ▶ M personnel pl, staff pl; (col) people pl, folks pl

pestana [pes'tana] F eyelash

peste ['pɛstʃi] F epidemic; (bubônica) plague; (fig) pest, nuisance

pétala ['pɛtala] F petal

petição [petʃi'sãw] (pl -ões) F request; (documento) petition

petisco [pe'tʃisku] M savoury (BRIT), savory (US), titbit (BRIT), tidbit (US)

petróleo [pe'trɔlju] M oil, petroleum; **~ bruto** crude oil

peúga ['pjuga] (PT) F sock

pevide [pe'vidʒi] (PT) F (de melão) seed; (de maçã) pip

p. ex. ABR (= por exemplo) e.g.

pia ['pia] F wash basin; (da cozinha) sink; **~ batismal** font

piada ['pjada] F joke

pianista [pja'nista] M/F pianist

piano ['pjanu] M piano

piar [pjar] VI (*pinto*) to cheep; (*coruja*) to hoot

picada [pi'kada] F (*de agulha etc*) prick; (*de abelha*) sting; (*de mosquito, cobra*) bite; (*de avião*) dive; (*de navalha*) stab; (*atalho*) path, trail

picante [pi'kãtʃi] ADJ (*tempero*) hot

picar [pi'kar] VT to prick; (*suj: abelha*) to sting; (: *mosquito*) to bite; (: *pássaro*) to peck; (*um animal*) to goad; (*carne*) to mince; (*papel*) to shred; (*fruta*) to chop up ▶ VI (*comichar*) to prickle

picareta [pika'reta] F pickaxe (BRIT), pickax (US) ▶ M/F crook

pico ['piku] M (*cume*) peak; (*ponta aguda*) sharp point; (PT: *um pouco*) a bit; **mil e ~** just over a thousand

picolé [piko'lɛ] M lolly

picotar [piko'tar] VT to perforate; (*bilhete*) to punch

piedade [pje'dadʒi] F piety; (*compaixão*) pity; **ter ~ de** to have pity on; **piedoso, -a** [pje'dozu, ɔza] ADJ pious; (*compassivo*) merciful

piercing ['pirsi] (*pl* -**s**) M piercing

pifar [pi'far] (col) VI (*carro*) to break down; (*rádio etc*) to go wrong; (*plano, programa*) to fall through

pijama [pi'ʒama] M pyjamas *pl* (BRIT), pajamas *pl* (US)

pilantra [pi'lãtra] (col) M/F crook

pilar [pi'lar] VT to pound, crush ▶ M pillar

pilha ['piʎa] F (Elet) battery; (*monte*) pile, heap

pilhar [pi'ʎar] VT to plunder, pillage; (*roubar*) to rob; (*surpreender*) to catch

pilotar [pilo'tar] VT (*avião*) to fly

piloto [pi'lotu] M pilot; (*motorista*) (racing) driver; (*bico de gás*) pilot light ▶ ADJ INV (*usina, plano*) pilot; (*peça*) sample *atr*

pílula ['pilula] F pill; **a ~ (anticoncepcional)** the pill

pimenta [pi'mẽta] F (Culin) pepper; **~ de Caiena** cayenne pepper; **pimenta-do-reino** F black pepper; **pimenta-malagueta** (*pl* **pimentas-malagueta**) F chilli (BRIT) *ou* chili (US) pepper; **pimentão** [pimẽ'tãw] (*pl* -**ões**) M (Bot) pepper

pinça ['pĩsa] F (*de sobrancelhas*) tweezers *pl*; (*de casa*) tongs *pl*; (Med) callipers *pl* (BRIT), calipers *pl* (US)

pincel [pĩ'sew] (*pl* -**éis**) M brush; (*para pintar*) paintbrush; **pincelar** [pĩse'lar] VT to paint

pinga ['pĩga] F (*cachaça*) rum; (PT: *trago*) drink

pingar [pĩ'gar] VI to drip

pingo ['pĩgu] M (*gota*) drop

pingue-pongue [pĩgi-'põgi] M ping-pong

pinguim [pĩ'gwĩ] (*pl* -**ns**) M penguin

pinheiro [pi'nejru] M pine (tree)

pinho ['pinu] M pine

pino ['pinu] M (*peça*) pin; (Auto: *na porta*) lock; **a ~** upright

pinta ['pĩta] F (*mancha*) spot

pintar [pĩ'tar] VT to paint; (*cabelo*) to dye; (*rosto*) to make up; (*descrever*) to describe; (*imaginar*) to picture ▶ VI to paint; **pintar-se** VR to make o.s. up

pintarroxo [pĩta'hoʃu] M (BR) linnet; (PT) robin

pinto ['pĩtu] M chick; (!) prick (!)

pintor, a [pĩ'tor(a)] M/F painter

pintura [pĩ'tura] F painting; (*maquiagem*) make-up

piolho ['pjoʎu] M louse

pioneiro, -a [pjo'nejru, a] M/F pioneer

pior ['pjɔr] ADJ, ADV (*compar*) worse; (*superl*) worst ▶ M: **o ~** worst of all; **piorar** [pjo'rar] VT to make worse, worsen ▶ VI to get worse

pipa ['pipa] F barrel, cask; (*de papel*) kite

pipi [pi'pi] (col) M pee; **fazer ~** to have a pee

pipoca [pi'pɔka] F popcorn

pipocar [pipo'kar] VI to pop up

piquenique [piki'niki] M picnic

pirâmide [pi'ramidʒi] F pyramid

piranha [pi'rana] F piranha (fish)

pirata [pi'rata] M pirate

pires ['piris] M INV saucer

Pirineus [piri'news] MPL: **os ~** the Pyrenees

pirulito [piru'litu] (BR) M lollipop

pisar [pi'zar] VT to tread on; (*esmagar, subjugar*) to crush ▶ VI to step, tread

pisca-pisca [piska-'piska] (*pl* -**s**) M (Auto) indicator

piscar [pis'kar] VT to blink; (*dar sinal*) to wink; (*estrelas*) to twinkle ▶ M: **num ~ de olhos** in a flash

piscina [pi'sina] F swimming pool

piso ['pizu] M floor

pisotear [pizo'tʃiar] VT to trample (on)

pista ['pista] F (*vestígio*) trace; (*indicação*) clue; (*de corridas*) track; (Aer) runway; (*de estrada*) lane; (*de dança*) (dance) floor

pistola [pis'tɔla] F pistol

pitada [pi'tada] F (*porção*) pinch

pivete [pi'vetʃi] M child thief

pivô [pi'vo] M pivot; (*fig*) central figure, prime mover

pizza ['pitsa] F pizza

placa ['plaka] F plate; (*Auto*) number plate (*BRIT*), license plate (*US*); (*comemorativa*) plaque; (*na pele*) blotch; **~ de sinalização** road sign

placar [pla'kar] M scoreboard

plácido, -a ['plasidu, a] ADJ calm; (*manso*) placid

plágio ['plaʒu] M plagiarism

planalto [pla'nawtu] M tableland, plateau

planar [pla'nar] VI to glide

planear [pla'njar] (*PT*) VT = **planejar**

planejamento [planeʒa'mẽtu] M planning; **~ familiar** family planning

planejar [plane'ʒar] (*BR*) VT to plan; (*edifício*) to design

planeta [pla'neta] M planet

planície [pla'nisi] F plain

planilha [pla'niʎa] F spreadsheet

plano, -a ['planu, a] ADJ flat, level; (*liso*) smooth ▶ M plan; **~ de saúde** health insurance; **em primeiro/em último ~** in the foreground/background

planta ['plãta] F plant; (*de pé*) sole; (*Arq*) plan

plantação [plãta'sãw] F (*ato*) planting; (*terreno*) planted land; (*safra*) crops *pl*

plantão [plã'tãw] (*pl* **-ões**) M duty; (*noturno*) night duty; (*plantonista*) person on duty; (*Mil: serviço*) sentry duty; (: *pessoa*) sentry; **estar de ~** to be on duty

plantar [plã'tar] VT to plant; (*estaca*) to drive in; (*estabelecer*) to set up

plantões [plã'tõjs] MPL *de* **plantão**

plástico, -a ['plastʃiku, a] ADJ, M plastic

plataforma [plata'fɔrma] F platform; **~ de exploração de petróleo** oil rig; **~ de lançamento** launch pad

plateia [pla'teja] F (*Teatro etc*) stalls *pl* (*BRIT*), orchestra (*US*); (*espectadores*) audience

platina [pla'tʃina] F platinum

platinados [platʃi'nadus] MPL (*Auto*) points

plausível [plaw'zivew] (*pl* **-eis**) ADJ credible, plausible

playground [plej'grãwdʒi] (*pl* **-s**) M play area

plenamente [plena'mẽtʃi] ADV fully, completely

pleno, -a ['plenu, a] ADJ full; (*completo*) complete; **em ~ dia** in broad daylight; **em ~ inverno** in the middle *ou* depths of winter

plural [plu'raw] (*pl* **-ais**) ADJ, M plural

pneu ['pnew] M tyre (*BRIT*), tire (*US*)

pneumonia [pnewmo'nia] F pneumonia

pó [pɔ] M powder; (*sujeira*) dust; **pó de arroz** face powder; **sabão em pó** soap powder; **tirar o pó (de algo)** to dust (sth)

pobre ['pɔbri] ADJ poor ▶ M/F poor person; **pobreza** [po'breza] F poverty

poça ['posa] F puddle, pool

poção [po'sãw] (*pl* **-ões**) F potion

poço ['posu] M well; (*de mina, elevador*) shaft

poções [po'sõjs] FPL *de* **poção**

pôde ['podʒi] VB *ver* **poder**

poder [po'der] VI **1** (*capacidade*) can, be able to; **não posso fazê-lo** I can't do it, I'm unable to do it
2 (*ter o direito de*) can, may, be allowed to; **posso fumar aqui?** can I smoke here?; **pode entrar?** (*posso?*) can I come in?
3 (*possibilidade*) may, might, could; **pode ser** maybe; **pode ser que** it may be that; **ele poderá vir amanhã** he might come tomorrow
4: **não poder com: não posso com ele** I cannot cope with him
5 (*col: indignação*): **pudera!** no wonder!; **como é que pode?** you're joking!
▶ M power; (*autoridade*) authority; **poder aquisitivo** purchasing power; **estar no poder** to be in power; **em poder de alguém** in sb's hands

poderoso, -a [pode'rozu, ɔza] ADJ powerful

podre ['pɔdri] ADJ rotten; **podridão** [podri'dãw] F decay, rottenness; (*fig*) corruption

põe [põj] VB *ver* **pôr**

poeira ['pwejra] F dust; **~ radioativa** fall-out; **poeirento, -a** [pwej'rẽtu, a] ADJ dusty

poema ['pwɛma] M poem

poesia [poe'zia] F poetry; (*poema*) poem

poeta ['pwɛta] M poet; **poético, -a** ['pwɛtʃiku, a] ADJ poetic; **poetisa** [pwe'tʃiza] F (woman) poet

pois [pojs] ADV (*portanto*) so; (*PT: assentimento*) yes ▶ CONJ as, since; (*mas*) but; **~ bem** well then; **~ é** that's right; **~ não!** (*BR*) of course!; **~ não?** (*BR: numa loja*) can I help you?; (*PT*) isn't it?, aren't you?, didn't they? *etc*; **~ sim!** certainly not!; **~ (então)** then

polaco, -a [po'laku, a] ADJ Polish ▶ M/F
Pole ▶ M (*Ling*) Polish

polar [po'lar] ADJ polar

polegada [pole'gada] F inch

polegar [pole'gar] M (*tb*: **dedo ~**) thumb

polêmica [po'lemika] F controversy;
polêmico, -a [po'lemiku, a] ADJ
controversial

pólen ['polē] M pollen

polícia [po'lisja] F police, police force
▶ M/F police officer; **policial** [poli'sjaw]
(*pl* **-ais**) ADJ police *atr* ▶ M/F (BR) police
officer; **novela** *ou* **romance policial**
detective novel; **policiar** [poli'sjar] VT to
police; (*instintos, modos*) to control, keep
in check

polidez [poli'dez] F good manners *pl*,
politeness

polido, -a [po'lidu, a] ADJ polished,
shiny; (*cortês*) well-mannered, polite

pólio ['polju] F polio

polir [po'lir] VT to polish

política [po'litʃika] F politics *sg*;
(*programa*) policy; **político, -a**
[po'litʃiku, a] ADJ political ▶ M/F
politician

polo ['polu] M pole; (*Esporte*) polo; **P~
Norte/Sul** North/South Pole

polonês, -esa [polo'nes, eza] ADJ Polish
▶ M/F Pole ▶ M (*Ling*) Polish

Polônia [po'lonja] F: **a ~** Poland

polpa ['powpa] F pulp

poltrona [pow'trona] F armchair

poluição [polwi'sãw] F pollution; **poluir**
[po'lwir] VT to pollute

polvo ['powvu] M octopus

pólvora ['powvora] F gunpowder

pomada [po'mada] F ointment

pomar [po'mar] M orchard

pomba ['põba] F dove

pombo ['põbu] M pigeon

ponderação [põdera'sãw] F
consideration, meditation; (*prudência*)
prudence

ponderado, -a [põde'radu, a] ADJ
prudent

ponderar [põde'rar] VT to consider,
weigh up ▶ VI to meditate, muse

ponho ['poɲu] VB ver **pôr**

ponta ['põta] F tip; (*de faca*) point; (*de
sapato*) toe; (*extremidade*) end; (*Futebol:
posição*) wing; **uma ~
de** (*um pouco*) a touch of; **~ do dedo**
fingertip; **de ~** (*tecnologia*) cutting-edge

pontapé [põta'pɛ] M kick; **dar ~s em
alguém** to kick sb

pontaria [põta'ria] F aim; **fazer ~** to
take aim

ponte ['põtʃi] F bridge; **~ aérea** air
shuttle, airlift; **~ de safena** (*heart*)
bypass operation

ponteiro [põ'tejru] M (*indicador*) pointer;
(*de relógio*) hand

pontiagudo, -a [põtʃja'gudu, a] ADJ
sharp, pointed

ponto ['põtu] M point; (*Med, Costura,
Tricô*) stitch; (*pequeno sinal, do i*) dot; (*na
pontuação*) full stop (BRIT), period (US);
(*na pele*) spot; (*de ônibus*) stop; (*de táxi*)
rank (BRIT), stand (US); (*matéria escolar*)
subject; **estar a ~ de fazer** to be on the
point of doing; **às cinco em ~** at five
o'clock on the dot; **dois ~s** colon *sg*; **~ de
admiração** (PT) exclamation mark; **~ de
exclamação/interrogação**
exclamation/question mark; **~ de vista**
point of view, viewpoint; **~ e vírgula**
semicolon

pontuação [põtwa'sãw] F punctuation

pontual [põ'twaw] (*pl* **-ais**) ADJ punctual

pontudo, -a [põ'tudu, a] ADJ pointed

popa ['popa] F stern

população [popula'sãw] (*pl* **-ões**) F
population

popular [popu'lar] ADJ popular;
popularidade [populari'dadʒi] F
popularity

pôquer ['poker] M poker

(PALAVRA-CHAVE)

por [por] (*por + o(s)/a(s) = pelo(s)/a(s)*)
PREP **1** (*objetivo*) for; **lutar pela pátria** to
fight for one's country

2 (*+ infin*): **está por acontecer** it is about
to happen, it is yet to happen; **está por
fazer** it is still to be done

3 (*causa*) out of, because of; **por falta de
fundos** through lack of funds; **por
hábito/natureza** out of habit/by
nature; **faço isso por ela** I do it for her;
por isso therefore; **a razão pela qual ...**
the reason why ...; **pelo amor de Deus!**
for Heaven's sake!

4 (*tempo*): **pela manhã** in the morning;
por volta das duas horas at about two
o'clock; **ele vai ficar por uma semana**
he's staying for a week

5 (*lugar*): **por aqui** this way; **viemos
pelo parque** we came through the park;
passar por São Paulo to pass through
São Paulo; **por fora/dentro** outside/
inside

6 (*troca, preço*) for; **trocar o velho pelo
novo** to change old for new; **comprei o
livro por dez libras** I bought the book
for ten pounds

7 (*valor proporcional*): **por cento** per cent; **por hora/dia/semana/mês/ano** hourly/daily/weekly/monthly/yearly; **por cabeça** a ou per head; **por mais difícil** *etc* **que seja** however difficult *etc* it is
8 (*modo, meio*) by; **por correio/avião** by post/air; **por sí** by o.s.; **por escrito** in writing; **entrar pela entrada principal** to go in through the main entrance
9: **por que** why; **por quê?** why?
10: **por mim tudo bem** as far as I'm concerned that's OK

(PALAVRA-CHAVE)

pôr [por] VT **1** (*colocar*) to put; (*roupas*) to put on; (*objeções, dúvidas*) to raise; (*ovos, mesa*) to lay; (*defeito*) to find; **põe mais forte** turn it up; **você põe açúcar?** do you take sugar?; **pôr de lado** to set aside **2** (+ *adj*) to make; **você está me pondo nervoso** you're making me nervous
pôr-se VR **1** (*sol*) to set
2 (*colocar-se*): **pôr-se de pé** to stand up; **ponha-se no meu lugar** put yourself in my position
3: **pôr-se a** to start to; **ela pôs-se a chorar** she started crying
▶ M: **o pôr do sol** sunset

porão [po'rãw] (*pl* **-ões**) M (*de casa*) basement; (: *armazém*) cellar
porca ['porka] F (*animal*) sow
porção [por'sãw] (*pl* **-ões**) F portion, piece; **uma ~ de** a lot of
porcaria [porka'ria] F filth; (*dito sujo*) obscenity; (*coisa ruim*) piece of junk
porcelana [porse'lana] F porcelain
porcentagem [porse'taʒẽ] (*pl* **-ns**) F percentage
porco, -a ['porku, 'porka] ADJ filthy ▶ M (*animal*) pig; (*carne*) pork
porções [por'sõjs] FPL *de* **porção**
porém [po'rẽ] CONJ however
pormenor [porme'nor] M detail
pornografia [pornogra'fia] F pornography
poro ['poru] M pore
porões [po'rõjs] MPL *de* **porão**
porque [por'ke] CONJ because; (*interrogativo*: PT) why
porquê [por'ke] ADV (PT) why ▶ M reason, motive; **~?** (PT) why?
porrete [po'hetʃi] M club
porta ['porta] F door; (*vão da porta*) doorway; (*de um jardim*) gate
portador, a [porta'dor(a)] M/F bearer
portagem [por'taʒẽ] (PT) (*pl* **-ns**) F toll

portal [por'taw] (*pl* **-ais**) M doorway
porta-luvas M INV (*Auto*) glove compartment
porta-malas M INV (*Auto*) boot (BRIT), trunk (US)
porta-níqueis M INV purse
portanto [por'tãtu] CONJ so, therefore
portão [por'tãw] (*pl* **-ões**) M gate
portar [por'tar] VT to carry; **portar-se** VR to behave
portaria [porta'ria] F (*de um edifício*) entrance hall; (*recepção*) reception desk; (*do governo*) edict, decree
portátil [por'tatʃiw] (*pl* **-eis**) ADJ portable
porta-voz (*pl* **-es**) M/F (*pessoa*) spokesman, spokesperson
porte ['portʃi] M transport; (*custo*) freight charge, carriage; **~ pago** post paid; **de grande ~** far-reaching, important
porteiro, -a [por'tejru, a] M/F caretaker; **~ eletrônico** entry phone
pórtico ['portʃiku] M porch, portico
porto ['portu] M (*do mar*) port, harbour (BRIT), harbor (US); (*vinho*) port; **o P~** Oporto
portões [por'tõjs] MPL *de* **portão**
Portugal [portu'gaw] M Portugal; **português, -guesa** [portu'ges, 'geza] ADJ Portuguese ▶ M/F Portuguese *inv* ▶ M (*Ling*) Portuguese
porventura [porvẽ'tura] ADJ by chance; **se ~ você ...** if you happen to ...
pôs [pos] VB *ver* **pôr**
posar [po'zar] VI (*Foto*) to pose
posição [pozi'sãw] (*pl* **-ões**) F position; (*social*) standing, status; **posicionar** [pozisjo'nar] VT to position
positivo, -a [pozi'tʃivu, a] ADJ positive
possante [po'sãtʃi] ADJ powerful, strong; (*carro*) flashy
possessão [pose'sãw] F possession; **possessivo, -a** [pose'sivu, a] ADJ possessive
possibilidade [posibili'dadʒi] F possibility; **possibilidades** FPL (*recursos*) means
possibilitar [posibili'tar] VT to make possible, permit
possível [po'sivew] (*pl* **-eis**) ADJ possible; **fazer todo o ~** to do one's best
posso ['posu] VB *ver* **poder**
possuidor, a [poswi'dor(a)] M/F owner
possuir [po'swir] VT (*casa, livro etc*) to own; (*dinheiro, talento*) to possess
post [post] (*pl* **-s**) M (*Comput*) post; **~ de blog** blogpost
postal [pos'taw] (*pl* **-ais**) ADJ postal ▶ M postcard

postar [pos'tar] VT to place, post;
(Comput) to post

poste ['pɔstʃi] M pole, post

posterior [poste'rjor] ADJ (mais tarde)
subsequent, later; (traseiro) rear, back;
posteriormente [posterjor'mētʃi] ADV
later, subsequently

postiço, -a [pos'tʃisu, a] ADJ false,
artificial

posto, -a ['postu, 'posta] PP de pôr ▶ M
post, position; (emprego) job; **~ de
gasolina** service ou petrol station; **~ que**
although; **~ de saúde** health centre ou
center

póstumo, -a ['pɔstumu, a] ADJ
posthumous

postura [pos'tura] F posture; (aspecto
físico) appearance

potável [po'tavew] (pl -eis) ADJ
drinkable; **água ~** drinking water

pote ['pɔtʃi] M jug, pitcher; (de geleia) jar;
(de creme) pot; **chover a ~s** (PT) to rain
cats and dogs

potência [po'tēsja] F power

potencial [potē'sjaw] (pl -ais) ADJ, M
potential

potente [po'tētʃi] ADJ powerful, potent

(PALAVRA-CHAVE)

pouco, -a ['poku, a] ADJ 1 (sg) little, not
much; **pouco tempo** little ou not much
time; **de pouco interesse** of little
interest, not very interesting; **pouca
coisa** not much
2 (pl) few, not many; **uns poucos** a few,
some; **poucas vezes** rarely; **poucas
crianças comem o que devem** few
children eat what they should
▶ ADV 1 little, not much; **custa pouco** it
doesn't cost much; **dentro em pouco,
daqui a pouco** shortly; **pouco antes**
shortly before
2 (+ adj, negativo): **ela é pouco
inteligente/simpática** she's not very
bright/friendly
3: **por pouco eu não morri** I almost
died
4: **pouco a pouco** little by little
5: **aos poucos** gradually
▶ M: **um pouco** a little, a bit; **nem um
pouco** not at all

poupador, a [popa'dor(a)] ADJ thrifty
poupança [po'pāsa] F thrift; (economias)
savings pl; (tb: **caderneta de ~**) savings
bank
poupar [po'par] VT to save; (vida) to
spare

pousada [po'zada] F (hospedagem)
lodging; (hospedaria) inn
pousar [po'zar] VT to place; (mão) to rest
▶ VI (avião, pássaro) to land; (pernoitar) to
spend the night
povo ['povu] M people; (raça) people pl,
race; (plebe) common people pl;
(multidão) crowd
povoação [povwa'sãw] (pl -ões) F
(aldeia) village, settlement; (habitantes)
population
povoado [po'vwadu] M village
povoar [po'vwar] VT (de habitantes) to
people, populate; (de animais etc) to
stock
pra [pra] (col) PREP = **para a**; ver **para**
praça ['prasa] F (largo) square; (mercado)
marketplace; (soldado) soldier; **~ de
touros** bullring
praga ['praga] F nuisance; (maldição)
curse; (desgraça) misfortune; (erva
daninha) weed
pragmático, -a [prag'matʃiku, a] ADJ
pragmatic
praia ['praja] F beach
prancha ['prãʃa] F plank; (de surfe) board
prata ['prata] F silver; (col: cruzeiro) ≈ quid
(BRIT), ≈ buck (US)
prateleira [prate'lejra] F shelf
prática ['pratʃika] F practice;
(experiência) experience, know-how;
(costume) habit, custom; ver tb **prático**
praticante [pratʃi'kãtʃi] ADJ practising
(BRIT), practicing (US) ▶ M/F apprentice;
(de esporte) practitioner
praticar [pratʃi'kar] VT to practise (BRIT),
practice (US); (roubo, operação) to carry
out; **prático, -a** ['pratʃiku, a] ADJ
practical ▶ M/F expert
prato ['pratu] M plate; (comida) dish; (de
uma refeição) course; (de toca-discos)
turntable; **pratos** MPL (Mús) cymbals
praxe ['praʃi] F custom, usage; **de ~**
usually; **ser de ~** to be the norm
> Student life in Portugal follows the
traditions set out in a written set of
rules known as the 'código da **praxe**'. It
begins in freshman's week, where
first-year students are jeered at by
their seniors, and are subjected to a
number of humiliating practical jokes,
such as having their hair cut against
their will and being made to walk
around town in fancy dress.

prazer [pra'zer] M pleasure; **muito ~ em
conhecê-lo** pleased to meet you
prazo ['prazu] M term, period; (vencimento)
expiry date, time limit; **a curto/médio/**

precário |

longo ~ in the short/medium/long term; **comprar a ~** to buy on hire purchase (BRIT) ou on the installment plan (US)
precário, -a [pre'karju, a] ADJ precarious; (escasso) failing
precaução [prekaw'sãw] (pl -ões) F precaution
precaver-se [preka'versi] VR: **~ (contra ou de)** to be on one's guard (against); **precavido, -a** [preka'vidu, a] ADJ cautious
prece ['presi] F prayer; (súplica) entreaty
precedente [prese'dẽtʃi] ADJ preceding ▶ M precedent
preceder [prese'der] VT, VI to precede; **~ a algo** to precede sth; (ter primazia) to take precedence over sth
precioso, -a [pre'sjozu, ɔza] ADJ precious
precipício [presi'pisju] M precipice; (fig) abyss
precipitação [presipita'sãw] F haste; (imprudência) rashness
precipitado, -a [presipi'tadu, a] ADJ hasty; (imprudente) rash
precisamente [presiza'mẽtʃi] ADV precisely
precisar [presi'zar] VT to need; (especificar) to specify; **precisar-se** VR: **"precisa-se"** "needed"; **~ de** to need; **não precisa você se preocupar** you needn't worry
preciso, -a [pre'sizu, a] ADJ precise, accurate; (necessário) necessary; (claro) concise; **é ~ você ir** you must go
preço ['presu] M price; (custo) cost; (valor) value; **a ~ de banana** (BR) ou **de chuva** (PT) dirt cheap
preconceito [prekõ'sejtu] M prejudice
predador [preda'dor] M predator
predileto, -a [predʒi'lɛtu, a] ADJ favourite (BRIT), favorite (US)
prédio ['predʒju] M building; **~ de apartamentos** block of flats (BRIT), apartment house (US)
predispor [predʒis'por] (irreg: como pôr) VT: **~ alguém contra** to prejudice sb against; **predispor-se** VR: **~-se a/para** to get o.s. in the mood to/for
predominar [predomi'nar] VI to predominate, prevail
preencher [preẽ'fer] VT (formulário) to fill in (BRIT) ou out, complete; (requisitos) to fulfil (BRIT), fulfill (US), meet; (espaço, vaga, tempo, cargo) to fill
prefácio [pre'fasju] M preface
prefeito, -a [pre'fejtu, a] M/F mayor; **prefeitura** [prefej'tura] F town hall

preferência [prefe'rẽsja] F preference; (Auto) priority; **de ~** preferably; **ter ~ por** to have a preference for; **preferencial** [preferẽ'sjaw] (pl -ais) ADJ (rua) main ▶ F main road (with priority)
preferido, -a [prefe'ridu, a] ADJ favourite (BRIT), favorite (US)
preferir [prefe'rir] VT to prefer
prefiro [pre'firu] VB ver **preferir**
prefixo [pre'fiksu] M (Ling) prefix; (Tel) code
prega ['prega] F pleat, fold
pregar¹ [pre'gar] VT, VI to preach
pregar² [pre'gar] VT (com prego) to nail; (fixar) to pin, fasten; (cosendo) to sew on; **~ uma peça** to play a trick; **~ um susto em alguém** to give sb a fright
prego ['pregu] M nail; (col: casa de penhor) pawn shop
preguiça [pre'gisa] F laziness; (animal) sloth; **estar com ~** to feel lazy; **preguiçoso, -a** [pregi'sozu, ɔza] ADJ lazy
pré-histórico, -a ADJ prehistoric
preia-mar (PT) F high tide
prejuízo [pre'ʒwizu] M damage, harm; (em dinheiro) loss; **em ~ de** to the detriment of
prematuro, -a [prema'turu, a] ADJ premature
premiado, -a [pre'mjadu, a] ADJ prize-winning; (bilhete) winning ▶ M/F prize-winner
premiar [pre'mjar] VT to award a prize to; (recompensar) to reward
prêmio ['premju] M prize; (recompensa) reward; (Seguros) premium
prenda ['prẽda] F gift, present; (em jogo) forfeit; **~s domésticas** housework sg
prendedor [prẽde'dor] M fastener; (de cabelo, gravata) clip; **~ de roupa** clothes peg; **~ de papéis** paper clip
prender [prẽ'der] VT to fasten, fix; (roupa) to pin; (cabelo) to tie back; (capturar) to arrest; (atar, ligar) to tie; (atenção) to catch; (afetivamente) to tie, bind; (reter: doença, compromisso) to keep; (movimentos) to restrict; **prender-se** VR to get caught, stick; **~-se a alguém** (por amizade) to be attached to sb
preocupação [preokupa'sãw] (pl -ões) F preoccupation; (inquietação) worry, concern
preocupar [preoku'par] VT to preoccupy; (inquietar) to worry; **preocupar-se** VR: **~-se com** to worry about, be worried about
preparação [prepara'sãw] (pl -ões) F preparation

preparar [prepa'rar] VT to prepare;
preparar-se VR to get ready;
preparativos [prepara'tʃivus] MPL
preparations, arrangements

preponderante [prepõde'rãtʃi] ADJ
predominant

preposição [prepozi'sãw] (pl **-ões**) F
preposition

prepotente [prepo'tẽtʃi] ADJ
predominant; (despótico) despotic;
(atitude) overbearing

prescrever [preskre'ver] VT to prescribe;
(prazo) to set

presença [pre'zẽsa] F presence;
(frequência) attendance; **ter boa ~** to be
presentable; **presenciar** [prezẽ'sjar] VT
to be present at; (testemunhar) to
witness

presente [pre'zẽtʃi] ADJ present; (fig:
interessado) attentive; (: evidente) clear,
obvious ▶ M present ▶ F (Com: carta): **a ~**
this letter; **os presentes** MPL (pessoas)
those present; **presentear** [prezẽ'tʃjar]
VT: **presentear alguém (com algo)** to
give sb (sth as) a present

preservação [prezerva'sãw] F
preservation

presidente, -a [prezi'dẽtʃi, ta] M/F
president

presidiário, -a [prezi'dʒjarju, a] M/F
convict

presídio [pre'zidʒju] M prison

presidir [prezi'dʒir] VT, VI: **~ (a)** to
preside over; (reunião) to chair; (suj: leis,
critérios) to govern

preso, -a ['prezu, a] ADJ imprisoned;
(capturado) under arrest; (atado) tied
▶ M/F prisoner; **estar ~ a alguém** to be
attached to sb

pressa ['presa] F haste, hurry; (rapidez)
speed; (urgência) urgency; **às ~s**
hurriedly; **estar com ~** to be in a
hurry; **ter ~ de** ou **em fazer** to be in a
hurry to do

presságio [pre'saʒu] M omen, sign;
(pressentimento) premonition

pressão [pre'sãw] (pl **-ões**) F pressure;
(colchete de) **~** press stud, popper

pressentimento [presẽtʃi'mẽtu] M
premonition

pressentir [presẽ'tʃir] VT to foresee;
(suspeitar) to sense

pressionar [presjo'nar] VT (botão) to
press; (coagir) to pressure ▶ VI to press,
put on pressure

pressões [pre'sõjs] FPL de **pressão**

pressupor [presu'por] (irreg: como **pôr**)
VT to presuppose

prestação [presta'sãw] (pl **-ões**) F
instalment (BRIT), installment (US); (por
uma casa) repayment

prestar [pres'tar] VT (cuidados) to give;
(favores, serviços) to do; (contas) to render;
(informações) to supply; (uma qualidade a
algo) to lend ▶ VI: **~ a alguém para algo**
to be of use to sb for sth; **prestar-se** VR:
~-se a to be suitable for; (admitir) to lend
o.s. to; (dispor-se) to be willing to;
~ atenção to pay attention

prestes ['prestʃis] ADJ INV ready; (a ponto
de): **~ a partir** about to leave

prestígio [pres'tʃiʒu] M prestige

presunção [prezũ'sãw] (pl **-ões**) F
presumption; (vaidade) conceit,
self-importance; **presunçoso, -a**
[prezũ'sozu, ɔza] ADJ vain, self-
important

presunto [pre'zũtu] M ham

pretender [pretẽ'der] VT to claim;
(cargo, emprego) to go for; **~ fazer** to
intend to do

pretensão [pretẽ'sãw] (pl **-ões**) F claim;
(vaidade) pretension; (propósito) aim;
(aspiração) aspiration; **pretensioso, -a**
[pretẽ'sjozu, ɔza] ADJ pretentious

pretérito [pre'teritu] M (Ling) preterite

pretexto [pre'testu] M pretext

preto, -a ['pretu, a] ADJ black

prevalecer [prevale'ser] VI to prevail;
prevalecer-se VR: **~-se de** (aproveitar-se)
to take advantage of

prevenção [prevẽ'sãw] (pl **-ões**) F
prevention; (preconceito) prejudice;
(cautela) caution; **estar de ~ com** ou
contra alguém to be bias(s)ed
against sb

prevenido, -a [preve'nidu, a] ADJ
cautious, wary

prevenir [preve'nir] VT to prevent;
(avisar) to warn; (preparar) to prepare

prever [pre'ver] (irreg: como **ver**) VT to
predict, foresee; (pressupor) to
presuppose

prévio, -a ['prɛvju, a] ADJ prior;
(preliminar) preliminary

previsão [previ'zãw] (pl **-ões**) F
foresight; (prognóstico) prediction,
forecast; **~ do tempo** weather forecast

previsível [previ'zivew] (pl **-eis**) ADJ
predictable

previsões [previ'zõjs] FPL de **previsão**

prezado, -a [pre'zadu, a] ADJ esteemed;
(numa carta) dear

prezar [pre'zar] VT (amigos) to value
highly; (autoridade) to respect; (gostar de)
to appreciate

primário, -a [pri'marju, a] ADJ primary;
(*elementar*) basic, rudimentary;
(*primitivo*) primitive ▶ M (*curso*)
elementary education

primavera [prima'vɛra] F spring;
(*planta*) primrose

primeira [pri'mejra] F (*Auto*) first (gear)

primeiro, -a [pri'mejru, a] ADJ, ADV first;
de primeira first-class

primo, -a ['primu, a] M/F cousin;
~ irmão first cousin

princesa [prĩ'seza] F princess

principal [prĩsi'paw] (*pl* **-ais**) ADJ
principal; (*entrada, razão, rua*) main ▶ M
head, principal; (*essencial, de dívida*)
principal

príncipe ['prĩsipi] M prince

principiante [prĩsi'pjãtʃi] M/F beginner

principiar [prĩsi'pjar] VT, VI to begin

princípio [prĩ'sipju] M beginning, start;
(*origem*) origin; (*legal, moral*) principle;
princípios MPL (*de matéria*) rudiments

prioridade [prjori'dadʒi] F priority

prisão [pri'zãw] (*pl* **-ões**) F
imprisonment; (*cadeia*) prison, jail;
(*detenção*) arrest; **~ de ventre**
constipation; **prisioneiro, -a**
[prizjo'nejru, a] M/F prisoner

privacidade [privasi'dadʒi] F privacy

privada [pri'vada] F toilet

privado, -a [pri'vadu, a] ADJ private;
(*carente*) deprived

privar [pri'var] VT to deprive

privativo, -a [priva'tʃivu, a] ADJ
(*particular*) private; **~ de** peculiar to

privilegiado, -a [privile'ʒjadu, a] ADJ
privileged; (*excepcional*) unique,
exceptional

privilegiar [privile'ʒjar] VT to privilege;
(*favorecer*) to favour (BRIT), favor (US)

privilégio [privi'lɛʒu] M privilege

pró [prɔ] ADV for, in favour (BRIT) *ou* favor
(US) ▶ M advantage; **os ~s e os
contras** the pros and cons; **em ~ de** in
favo(u)r of

pró- [prɔ] PREFIXO pro-

proa ['proa] F prow, bow

probabilidade [probabili'dadʒi] F
probability; **probabilidades** FPL
(*chances*) odds

problema [prob'lɛma] M problem

procedência [prose'dẽsja] F origin,
source; (*lugar de saída*) point of
departure

proceder [prose'der] VI to proceed;
(*comportar-se*) to behave; (*agir*) to act
▶ M conduct; **procedimento**
[prosedʒi'mẽtu] M conduct, behaviour

(BRIT), behavior (US); (*processo*)
procedure; (*Jur*) proceedings *pl*

processamento [prosesa'mẽtu] M
processing; (*Jur*) prosecution;
(*verificação*) verification; **~ de texto**
word processing

processar [prose'sar] VT (*Jur*) to take
proceedings against, prosecute;
(*requerimentos, dados*) to process

processo [pro'sɛsu] M process;
(*procedimento*) procedure; (*Jur*) lawsuit,
legal proceedings *pl*; (: *autos*) record;
(*conjunto de documentos*) documents *pl*

procissão [prosi'sãw] (*pl* **-ões**) F
procession

Proclamação da República *see note*
Commemorated on 15 November,
which is a public holiday, the
proclamation of the republic in 1889
was a military coup led by Marshal
Deodoro da Fonseca. It brought down
the empire which had been
established after independence and
installed a federal republic in Brazil.

proclamar [prokla'mar] VT to proclaim

procura [pro'kura] F search; (*Com*)
demand

procuração [prokura'sãw] (*pl* **-ões**) F:
por ~ by proxy

procurador, a [prokura'dor(a)] M/F
attorney; **P~ Geral da República**
Attorney General

procurar [proku'rar] VT to look for, seek;
(*emprego*) to apply for; (*ir visitar*) to call
on; (*contatar*) to get in touch with;
~ fazer to try to do

produção [produ'sãw] (*pl* **-ões**) F
production; (*volume de produção*) output;
(*produto*) product; **~ em massa** *ou* **série**
mass production

produtivo, -a [produ'tʃivu, a] ADJ
productive; (*rendoso*) profitable

produto [pro'dutu] M product; (*renda*)
proceeds *pl*, profit

produtor, a [produ'tor(a)] ADJ
producing ▶ M/F producer

produzir [produ'zir] VT to produce;
(*ocasionar*) to cause, bring about; (*render*)
to bring in

proeminente [proemi'nẽtʃi] ADJ
prominent

proeza [pro'eza] F achievement, feat

profanar [profa'nar] VT to desecrate,
profane; **profano, -a** [pro'fanu, a] ADJ
profane ▶ M/F layman/woman

profecia [profe'sia] F prophecy

professor, a [profe'sor(a)] M/F teacher;
(*universitário*) lecturer

profeta, -tisa [proˈfɛta, profeˈtʃiza] M/F
prophet; **profetizar** [profetʃiˈzar] VT, VI
to prophesy, predict
profissão [profiˈsãw] (pl **-ões**) F
profession; **profissional** [profisjoˈnaw]
(pl **-ais**) ADJ, M/F professional;
profissionalizante [profisjonaliˈzãtʃi]
ADJ (ensino) vocational
profundidade [profũdʒiˈdadʒi] F depth
profundo, -a [proˈfũdu, a] ADJ deep;
(fig) profound
profusão [profuˈzãw] F profusion,
abundance
prognóstico [progˈnɔstʃiku] M
prediction, forecast
programa [proˈgrama] M programme
(BRIT), program (US); (Comput) program;
(plano) plan; (diversão) thing to do; (de um
curso) syllabus; **programação**
[programaˈsãw] F planning; (TV, Rádio,
Comput) programming; **programador, a**
[programaˈdor(a)] M/F programmer;
programar [progaˈmar] VT to plan;
(Comput) to program
progredir [progreˈdʒir] VI to progress;
(avançar) to move forward; (infecção) to
progress
progressista [progreˈsista] ADJ, M/F
progressive
progressivo, -a [progreˈsivu, a] ADJ
progressive; (gradual) gradual
progresso [proˈgresu] M progress
progrido [proˈgridu] VB ver **progredir**
proibição [proibiˈsãw] (pl **-ões**) F
prohibition, ban
proibir [proiˈbir] VT to prohibit; (livro,
espetáculo) to ban; **"é proibido fumar"**
"no smoking"; **~ alguém de fazer, ~ que
alguém faça** to forbid sb to do
projeção [proʒeˈsãw] (pl **-ões**) F
projection
projetar [proʒeˈtar] VT to project
projétil [proˈʒɛtʃiw] (pl **-eis**) M projectile,
missile
projeto [proˈʒɛtu] M project; (plano)
plan; (Tec) design; **~ de lei** bill
projetor [proʒeˈtor] M (Cinema)
projector
proliferar [prolifeˈrar] VI to proliferate
prolongação [prolõgaˈsãw] F extension
prolongado, -a [prolõˈgadu, a] ADJ
prolonged; (alongado) extended
prolongar [prolõˈgar] VT to extend,
lengthen; (decisão etc) to postpone;
(vida) to prolong; **prolongar-se** VR to
extend; (durar) to last
promessa [proˈmɛsa] F promise
prometer [promeˈter] VT, VI to promise

promíscuo, -a [proˈmiskwu, a] ADJ
disorderly, mixed up; (comportamento
sexual) promiscuous
promissor, a [promiˈsor(a)] ADJ
promising
promoção [promoˈsãw] (pl **-ões**) F
promotion; **fazer ~ de alguém/algo** to
promote sb/sth
promotor, a [promoˈtor(a)] M/F
promoter; (Jur) prosecutor
promover [promoˈver] VT to promote;
(causar) to bring about
pronome [proˈnɔmi] M pronoun
pronto, -a [ˈprõtu, a] ADJ ready; (rápido)
quick, speedy; (imediato) prompt ▶ ADV
promptly; **de ~** promptly; **estar ~ a ...**
to be prepared ou willing to ...;
pronto-socorro (pl **prontos-socorros**)
M (BR) casualty (BRIT), emergency room
(US); (PT: reboque) tow truck
pronúncia [proˈnũsja] F pronunciation;
(Jur) indictment
pronunciar [pronũˈsjar] VT to
pronounce; (discurso) to make, deliver;
(Jur: réu) to indict; (: sentença) to pass
propaganda [propaˈgãda] F (Pol)
propaganda; (Com) advertising; (: uma
propaganda) advert, advertisement;
fazer ~ de to advertise
propagar [propaˈgar] VT to propagate;
(fig: difundir) to disseminate
propensão [propẽˈsãw] (pl **-ões**) F
inclination, tendency; **propenso, -a**
[proˈpẽsu, a] ADJ: **propenso a** inclined
to; **ser propenso a** to be inclined to,
have a tendency to
propina [proˈpina] F (gorjeta) tip; (PT:
cota) fee
propor [proˈpor] (irreg: como **pôr**) VT to
propose; (oferecer) to offer; (um problema)
to pose; **propor-se** VR: **~-se (a) fazer**
(pretender) to intend to do; (visar) to aim
to do; (dispor-se) to decide to do;
(oferecer-se) to offer to do
proporção [proporˈsãw] (pl **-ões**) F
proportion; **proporções** FPL (dimensões)
dimensions; **proporcional**
[proporsjoˈnaw] (pl **-ais**) ADJ
proportional; **proporcionar**
[proporsjoˈnar] VT to provide, give;
(adaptar) to adjust, adapt
proposição [propoziˈsãw] (pl **-ões**) F
proposition, proposal
proposital [propoziˈtaw] (pl **-ais**) ADJ
intentional
propósito [proˈpɔzitu] M (intenção)
purpose; (objetivo) aim; **a ~** by the way;
a ~ de with regard to; **de ~** on purpose

proposta [pro'pɔsta] F proposal; (*oferecimento*) offer

propriamente [proprja'mētʃi] ADV properly, exactly; **~ falando** *ou* **dito** strictly speaking

propriedade [proprje'dadʒi] F property; (*direito de proprietário*) ownership; (*o que é apropriado*) propriety

proprietário, -a [proprje'tarju, a] M/F owner, proprietor

próprio, -a ['prɔprju, a] ADJ own, of one's own; (*mesmo*) very, selfsame; (*hora, momento*) opportune, right; (*nome*) proper; (*característico*) characteristic; (*sentido*) proper, true; (*depois de pronome*) -self; **~ (para)** suitable (for); **eu ~** I myself; **por si ~** of one's own accord; **ele é o ~ inglês** he's a typical Englishman; **é o ~** it's him himself

prorrogação [prohoga'sāw] (*pl* **-ões**) F extension

prosa ['prɔza] F prose; (*conversa*) chatter; (*fanfarrice*) boasting, bragging ▶ ADJ full of oneself

prospecto [pros'pɛktu] M leaflet; (*em forma de livro*) brochure

prosperar [prospe'rar] VI to prosper, thrive; **prosperidade** [prosperi'dadʒi] F prosperity; (*bom êxito*) success; **próspero, -a** ['prɔsperu, a] ADJ prosperous; (*bem sucedido*) successful; (*favorável*) favourable (BRIT), favorable (US)

prosseguir [prose'gir] VT, VI to continue; **~ em** to continue (with)

prostíbulo [pros'tʃibulu] M brothel

prostituta [prostʃi'tuta] F prostitute

prostrado, -a [pros'tradu, a] ADJ prostrate

protagonista [protago'nista] M/F protagonist

proteção [prote'sāw] F protection

proteger [prote'ʒer] VT to protect; **protegido, -a** [prote'ʒidu, a] M/F protégé(e)

proteína [prote'ina] F protein

protejo [pro'teʒu] VB *ver* **proteger**

protestante [protes'tātʃi] ADJ, M/F Protestant

protestar [protes'tar] VT, VI to protest; **protesto** [pro'tɛstu] M protest

protetor, a [prote'tor(a)] ADJ protective ▶ M/F protector; **~ solar** sunscreen; **~ de tela** (*Comput*) screensaver

protuberância [protube'rãsja] F bump; **protuberante** [protube'rãtʃi] ADJ sticking out

prova ['prɔva] F proof; (*Tec: teste*) test, trial; (*Educ: exame*) examination; (*sinal*) sign; (*de comida, bebida*) taste; (*de roupa*) fitting; (*Esporte*) competition; (*Tip*) proof; **prova(s)** F(PL)(*Jur*) evidence *sg*; **à ~ de bala/fogo/água** bulletproof/ fireproof/waterproof; **pôr à ~** to put to the test

provar [pro'var] VT to prove; (*comida*) to taste, try; (*roupa*) to try on ▶ VI to try

provável [pro'vavew] (*pl* **-eis**) ADJ probable, likely

provedor, a [prove'dor(a)] M/F provider; **~ de acesso à Internet** internet service provider

proveito [pro'vejtu] M advantage; (*ganho*) profit; **em ~ de** for the benefit of; **fazer ~ de** to make use of; **proveitoso, -a** [provej'tozu, ɔza] ADJ profitable, advantageous; (*útil*) useful

proveniente [prove'njētʃi] ADJ: **~ de** originating from; (*que resulta de*) arising from

prover [pro'ver] (*irreg: como* **ver**) VT to provide, supply; (*vaga*) to fill ▶ VI: **~ a** to take care of, see to

provérbio [pro'vɛrbju] M proverb

providência [provi'dēsja] F providence; **providências** FPL (*medidas*) measures, steps; **providencial** [providē'sjaw] (*pl* **-ais**) ADJ opportune; **providenciar** [providē'sjar] VT to provide; (*tomar providências*) to arrange ▶ VI to make arrangements, take steps; **providenciar para que** to see to it that

província [pro'vīsja] F province; **provinciano, -a** [provī'sjanu, a] ADJ provincial

provisório, -a [provi'zɔrju, a] ADJ provisional, temporary

provocador, a [provoka'dor(a)] ADJ provocative

provocante [provo'kātʃi] ADJ provocative

provocar [provo'kar] VT to provoke; (*ocasionar*) to cause; (*atrair*) to tempt, attract; (*estimular*) to rouse, stimulate

próximo, -a ['prɔsimu, a] ADJ (*no espaço*) near, close; (*no tempo*) close; (*seguinte*) next; (*amigo, parente*) close; (*vizinho*) neighbouring (BRIT), neighboring (US) ▶ ADV near ▶ M fellow man; **~ a** *ou* **de** near (to), close to; **até a próxima!** see you again soon!

prudência [pru'dēsja] F care, prudence; **prudente** [pru'dētʃi] ADJ prudent

prurido [pru'ridu] M itch

psicanálise [psika'nalizi] F psychoanalysis

psicologia [psikolo'ʒia] F psychology;
psicológico, -a [psiko'lɔʒiku, a] ADJ
psychological; **psicólogo, -a**
[psi'kɔlogu, a] M/F psychologist
psique ['psiki] F psyche
psiquiatra [psi'kjatra] M/F psychiatrist
psiquiatria [psikja'tria] F psychiatry
psíquico, -a ['psikiku, a] ADJ
psychological
puberdade [puber'dadʒi] F puberty
publicação [publika'sãw] F
publication
publicar [publi'kar] VT to publish;
(*divulgar*) to divulge; (*proclamar*) to
announce
publicidade [publisi'dadʒi] F publicity;
(*Com*) advertising; **publicitário, -a**
[publisi'tarju, a] ADJ publicity atr; (*Com*)
advertising atr
público, -a ['publiku, a] ADJ public ▶ M
public; (*Cinema, Teatro etc*) audience
pude ['pudʒi] VB ver **poder**
pudera [pu'dɛra] VB ver **poder**
pudim [pu'dʒĩ] (*pl* -**ns**) M pudding
pudor [pu'dor] M bashfulness, modesty;
(*moral*) decency
pular [pu'lar] VI to jump; (*no Carnaval*) to
celebrate ▶ VT to jump (over); (*páginas,
trechos*) to skip; **~ Carnaval** to celebrate
Carnival; **~ corda** to skip
pulga ['puwga] F flea
pulmão [puw'mãw] (*pl* -**ões**) M lung
pulo¹ ['pulu] M jump; **dar um ~ em** to
stop off at
pulo² VB ver **polir**
pulôver [pu'lover] (BR) M pullover
pulsação [puwsa'sãw] F pulsation,
beating; (*Med*) pulse
pulseira [puw'sejra] F bracelet; (*de
sapato*) strap
pulso ['puwsu] M (*Anat*) wrist; (*Med*)
pulse; (*fig*) vigour (BRIT), vigor (US),
energy
punha ['puɲa] VB ver **pôr**
punhado [pu'ɲadu] M handful
punhal [pu'ɲaw] (*pl* -**ais**) M dagger
punho ['puɲu] M fist; (*de manga*) cuff;
(*de espada*) hilt
punição [puni'sãw] (*pl* -**ões**) F
punishment
punir [pu'nir] VT to punish
pupila [pu'pila] F (*Anat*) pupil
purê [pu're] M purée; **~ de batatas**
mashed potatoes
pureza [pu'reza] F purity
purificar [purifi'kar] VT to purify
puritano, -a [puri'tanu, a] ADJ
puritanical; (*seita*) puritan ▶ M/F puritan

puro, -a ['puru, a] ADJ pure; (*uísque etc*)
neat; (*verdade*) plain; (*intenções*)
honourable (BRIT), honorable (US);
(*estilo*) clear
pus¹ [pus] M pus
pus² [pujs] VB ver **pôr**
puser [pu'zer] VB ver **pôr**
puta ['puta] (!) F whore (!); ver tb **puto**
puto, -a ['putu, a] (!) M/F (*sem-vergonha*)
bastard ▶ ADJ (*zangado*) furious; (*incrível*):
um ~ ... a hell of a ...; **o ~ de ...** the
bloody ...
pútrido, -a ['putridu, a] ADJ putrid,
rotten
puxador [puʃa'dor] M handle, knob
puxão [pu'ʃãw] (*pl* -**ões**) M tug, jerk
puxar [pu'ʃar] VT to pull; (*sacar*) to pull
out; (*assunto*) to bring up; (*conversa*) to
strike up; (*briga*) to pick ▶ VI: **~ de uma
perna** to limp; **~ a** to take after
puxões [pu'ʃõjs] MPL de **puxão**

q

QG ABR M (= *Quartel-General*) HQ
QI ABR M (= *Quociente de Inteligência*) IQ
quadra ['kwadra] F (*quarteirão*) block; (*de tênis etc*) court; (*período*) time, period
quadrado, -a [kwa'dradu, a] ADJ square ▶ M square ▶ M/F (*col*) square
quadril [kwa'driw] (*pl* -**is**) M hip
quadrinho [kwa'driɲu] M: **história em ~s** (BR) cartoon, comic strip
quadris [kwa'dris] MPL *de* **quadril**
quadro ['kwadru] M painting; (*gravura, foto*) picture; (*lista*) list; (*tabela*) chart, table; (*Tec: painel*) panel; (*pessoal*) staff; (*time*) team; (*Teatro, fig*) scene; **~ branco** whiteboard; **~ interativo** interactive whiteboard; **quadro-negro** (*pl* **quadros-negros**) M blackboard
quadruplicar [kwadrupli'kar] VT, VI to quadruple
qual [kwaw] (*pl* -**ais**) PRON which ▶ CONJ as, like ▶ EXCL what!; **o ~** which; (*pessoa: suj*) who; (: *objeto*) whom; **seja ~ for** whatever *ou* whichever it may be; **cada ~** each one
qualidade [kwali'dadʒi] F quality
qualificação [kwalifika'sãw] (*pl* -**ões**) F qualification
qualificado, -a [kwalifi'kadu, a] ADJ qualified
qualificar [kwalifi'kar] VT to qualify; (*avaliar*) to evaluate; **qualificar-se** VR to qualify; **~ de** *ou* **como** to classify as
qualquer [kwaw'ker] (*pl* **quaisquer**) ADJ, PRON any; **~ pessoa** anyone, anybody; **~ um dos dois** either; **~ que seja** whichever it may be; **a ~ momento** at any moment
quando ['kwãdu] ADV when ▶ CONJ when; (*interrogativo*) when?; (*ao passo que*) whilst; **~ muito** at most

quantia [kwã'tʃia] F sum, amount
quantidade [kwãtʃi'dadʒi] F quantity, amount

quanto, -a ['kwãtu, a] ADJ **1** (*interrogativo: sg*) how much?; (: *pl*) how many?; **quanto tempo?** how long?
2 (*o que for necessário*) all that, as much as; **daremos quantos exemplares ele precisar** we'll give him as many copies as *ou* all the copies he needs
3: **tanto/tantos … quanto** as much/many … as
▶ PRON **1** how much?; how many?; **quanto custa?** how much is it?; **a quanto está o jogo?** what's the score?
2: **tudo quanto** everything that, as much as
3: **tanto/tantos quanto …** as much/as many as …
4: **um tanto quanto** somewhat, rather
▶ ADV **1**: **quanto a** as regards; **quanto a mim** as for me
2: **quanto antes** as soon as possible
3: **quanto mais** (*principalmente*) especially; (*muito menos*) let alone; **quanto mais cedo melhor** the sooner the better
4: **tanto quanto possível** as much as possible; **tão … quanto …** as … as …
▶ CONJ: **quanto mais trabalha, mais ele ganha** the more he works, the more he earns; **quanto mais, (tanto) melhor** the more, the better

quarenta [kwa'rẽta] NUM forty
quarentena [kwarẽ'tena] F quarantine
quaresma [kwa'rezma] F Lent
quarta ['kwarta] F (*tb*: **~-feira**) Wednesday; (*parte*) quarter; (*Auto*) fourth (gear); **quarta-feira** (*pl* **quartas-feiras**) F Wednesday; **quarta-feira de cinzas** Ash Wednesday
quarteirão [kwartej'rãw] (*pl* -**ões**) M (*de casas*) block
quartel [kwar'tew] (*pl* -**éis**) M barracks *sg*; **quartel-general** M headquarters *pl*
quarteto [kwar'tetu] M quartet(te)
quarto, -a ['kwartu, a] NUM fourth ▶ M quarter; (*aposento*) bedroom; **~ de banho** bathroom; **~ de dormir** bedroom; **três ~s de hora** three quarters of an hour
quase ['kwazi] ADV almost, nearly; **~ nunca** hardly ever
quatorze [kwa'torzi] NUM fourteen
quatro ['kwatru] NUM four

que [ki] CONJ **1** (*com oração subordinada: muitas vezes não se traduz*) that; **ele disse que viria** he said (that) he would come; **não há nada que fazer** there's nothing to be done; **espero que sim/não** I hope so/not; **dizer que sim/não** to say yes/no

2 (*consecutivo: muitas vezes não se traduz*) that; **é tão pesado que não consigo levantá-lo** it's so heavy (that) I can't lift it

3 (*comparações*): **(do) que** than; *ver tb* **mais, menos, mesmo**

▶ PRON **1** (*coisa*) which, that; (+ *prep*) which; **o chapéu que você comprou** the hat (that ou which) you bought

2 (*pessoa: suj*) who, that; (: *complemento*) whom, that; **o amigo que me levou ao museu** the friend who took me to the museum; **a moça que eu convidei** the girl (that ou whom) I invited

3 (*interrogativo*) what?; **o que você disse?** what did you say?

4 (*exclamação*) what!; **que pena!** what a pity!; **que lindo!** how lovely!

quê [ke] M (*col*) something ▶ PRON what; **~!** what!; **não tem de ~** don't mention it; **para ~?** what for?; **por ~?** why?

quebra ['kɛbra] F break, rupture; (*falência*) bankruptcy; (*de energia elétrica*) cut; **de ~** in addition; **quebra-cabeça** (*pl* **quebra-cabeças**) M puzzle, problem; (*jogo*) jigsaw puzzle

quebrado, -a [ke'bradu, a] ADJ broken; (*cansado*) exhausted; (*falido*) bankrupt; (*carro, máquina*) broken down; (*telefone*) out of order

quebrar [ke'brar] VT to break ▶ VI to break; (*carro*) to break down; (*Com*) to go bankrupt; (*ficar sem dinheiro*) to go broke

queda ['kɛda] F fall; (*fig*) downfall; **ter ~ para algo** to have a bent for sth; **~ de barreira** landslide; **queda-d'água** (*pl* **quedas-d'água**) F waterfall

queijo ['kejʒu] M cheese

queimado, -a [kej'madu, a] ADJ burnt; (*de sol: machucado*) sunburnt; (: *bronzeado*) brown, tanned; (*plantas, folhas*) dried up

queimadura [kejma'dura] F burn; (*de sol*) sunburn

queimar [kej'mar] VT to burn; (*roupa*) to scorch; (*com líquido*) to scald; (*bronzear a pele*) to tan; (*planta, folha*) to wither ▶ VI to burn; **queimar-se** VR (*pessoa*) to burn o.s.; (*bronzear-se*) to tan

queima-roupa F: **à ~** point-blank, at point-blank range

queira ['kejra] VB *ver* **querer**

queixa ['kejʃa] F complaint; (*lamentação*) lament; **fazer ~ de alguém** to complain about sb

queixar-se [kej'farsi] VR to complain; **~ de** to complain about; (*dores etc*) to complain of

queixo ['kejʃu] M chin; (*maxilar*) jaw; **bater o ~** to shiver

quem [kẽj] PRON who; (*como objeto*) who(m); **de ~ é isto?** whose is this?; **~ diria!** who would have thought (it)!; **~ sabe** (*talvez*) perhaps

Quênia ['kenja] M: **o ~** Kenya

quente ['kẽtʃi] ADJ hot; (*roupa*) warm

quentinha [kẽ'tʃiɲa] F heatproof carton (*for food*); (*de restaurante*) doggy bag

quer [ker] CONJ: **~ ... ~ ...** whether ... or ...; **~ chova ~ não** whether it rains or not; **onde/quando/quem ~ que** wherever/whenever/whoever; **o que ~ que seja** whatever it is

querer [ke'rer] VT **1** (*desejar*) to want; **quero mais dinheiro** I want more money; **queria um chá** I'd like a cup of tea; **quero ajudar/que vá** I want to help/you to go; **você vai querer sair amanhã?** do you want to go out tomorrow?; **eu vou querer uma cerveja** (*num bar etc*) I'd like a beer; **por/sem querer** intentionally/unintentionally; **como queira** as you wish

2 (*perguntas para pedir algo*): **você quer fechar a janela?** will you shut the window?; **quer me dar uma mão?** can you give me a hand?

3 (*amar*) to love

4 (*convite*): **quer entrar/sentar** do come in/sit down

5: **querer dizer** (*significar*) to mean; (*pretender dizer*) to mean to say; **quero dizer** I mean; **quer dizer** (*com outras palavras*) in other words

▶ VI: **querer bem a** to be fond of

querer-se VR to love one another

▶ M (*vontade*) wish; (*afeto*) affection

querido, -a [ke'ridu, a] ADJ dear ▶ M/F darling; **Q~ João** Dear John

querosene [kero'zɛni] M kerosene

questão [kes'tãw] (*pl* **-ões**) F question; (*problema*) issue, question; (*Jur*) case; (*contenda*) dispute, quarrel; **fazer ~ (de)**

to insist (on); **em ~** in question; **há ~ de um ano** about a year ago; **questionar** [kestʃo'nar] vi to question ▶ vt to question, call into question; **questionário** [kestʃjo'narju] m questionnaire; **questionável** [kestʃjo'navew] (pl **-eis**) adj questionable

quicar [ki'kar] vt, vi to bounce

quieto, -a ['kjɛtu, a] adj quiet; (imóvel) still; **quietude** [kje'tudʒi] f calm, tranquillity

quilate [ki'latʃi] m carat

quilo ['kilu] m kilo; **quilobyte** [kilo'bajtʃi] m kilobyte; **quilograma** [kilo'grama] m kilogram; **quilometragem** [kilome'traʒẽ] f number of kilometres ou kilometers travelled, ≈ mileage; **quilômetro** [ki'lometru] m kilometre (BRIT), kilometer (US); **quilowatt** [kilo'watʃi] m kilowatt

química ['kimika] f chemistry

químico, -a ['kimiku, a] adj chemical ▶ m/f chemist

quina ['kina] f corner; (de mesa etc) edge; **de ~** edgeways (BRIT), edgewise (US)

quindim [kĩ'dʒĩ] m sweet made of egg yolks, coconut and sugar

quinhão [ki'ɲãw] (pl **-ões**) m share, portion

quinhentos, -as [ki'ɲẽtus, as] num five hundred

quinhões [ki'ɲõjs] mpl de **quinhão**

quinquilharias [kĩkiʎa'rias] fpl odds and ends; (miudezas) knick-knacks, trinkets

quinta ['kĩta] f (tb: **~-feira**) Thursday; (propriedade) estate; (PT) farm; **quinta-feira** ['kĩta-'fejra] (pl **quintas-feiras**) f Thursday

quintal [kĩ'taw] (pl **-ais**) m back yard

quinteto [kĩ'tetu] m quintet(te)

quinto, -a ['kĩtu, a] num fifth

quinze ['kĩzi] num fifteen; **duas e ~** a quarter past (BRIT) ou after (US) two; **~ para as sete** a quarter to (BRIT) ou of (US) seven

quinzena [kĩ'zena] f two weeks, fortnight (BRIT); **quinzenal** [kĩze'naw] (pl **-ais**) adj fortnightly; **quinzenalmente** [kĩzenaw'mẽtʃi] adv fortnightly

quiosque ['kjɔski] m kiosk

quis [kiz] vb ver **querer**

quiser [ki'zer] vb ver **querer**

quisto ['kistu] m cyst

quitanda [ki'tãda] f grocer's (shop) (BRIT), grocery store (US)

quitar [ki'tar] vt (dívida: pagar) to pay off; (: perdoar) to cancel; (devedor) to release

quite ['kitʃi] adj (livre) free; (com um credor) squared up; (igualado) even; **estar ~ (com alguém)** to be quits (with sb)

quitute [ki'tutʃi] m titbit (BRIT), tidbit (US)

quota ['kwɔta] f quota; (porção) share, portion

quotidiano, -a [kwotʃi'dʒjanu, a] adj everyday

r

R ABR (= *rua*) St

R$ ABR = **real**

rã [hã] F frog

rabanete [haba'netʃi] M radish

rabiscar [habis'kar] VT to scribble; (*papel*) to scribble on ▶ VI to scribble; (*desenhar*) to doodle; **rabisco** [ha'bisku] M scribble

rabo ['habu] M tail

rabugento, -a [habu'ʒẽtu, a] ADJ grumpy

raça ['hasa] F breed; (*grupo étnico*) race; **cão/cavalo de ~** pedigree dog/ thoroughbred horse

racha ['haʃa] F (*fenda*) split; (*greta*) crack; **rachadura** [haʃa'dura] F crack; **rachar** [ha'ʃar] VT to crack; (*objeto, despesas*) to split; (*lenha*) to chop ▶ VI to split; (*cristal*) to crack; **rachar-se** VR to split; to crack

racial [ha'sjaw] (*pl* -**ais**) ADJ racial

raciocínio [hasjo'sinju] M reasoning

racional [hasjo'naw] (*pl* -**ais**) ADJ rational; **racionalizar** [hasjonali'zar] VT to rationalize

racionamento [hasjona'mẽtu] M rationing

racismo [ha'sizmu] M racism; **racista** [ha'sista] ADJ, M/F racist

radar [ha'dar] M radar

radiação [hadʒja'sãw] F radiation

radiador [hadʒja'dor] M radiator

radical [hadʒi'kaw] (*pl* -**ais**) ADJ radical

radicar-se [hadʒi'karsi] VR to take root; (*fixar residência*) to settle

rádio ['hadʒju] M radio; (*Quím*) radium; **radioativo, -a** [hadʒjua'tʃivu, a] ADJ radioactive; **radiodifusão** [hadʒjodʒifu'zãw] F broadcasting; **radiografar** [hadʒjogra'far] VT to X-ray; **radiografia** [hadʒjogra'fia] F X-ray

raia ['haja] F (*risca*) line; (*fronteira*) boundary; (*limite*) limit; (*de corrida*) lane; (*peixe*) ray

raiar [ha'jar] VI to shine

rainha [ha'iɲa] F queen

raio ['haju] M (*de sol*) ray; (*de luz*) beam; (*de roda*) spoke; (*relâmpago*) flash of lightning; (*distância*) range; (*Mat*) radius; **~ X** X-rays

raiva ['hajva] F rage, fury; (*Med*) rabies sg; **estar/ficar com ~ (de)** to be/get angry (with); **ter ~ de** to hate; **raivoso, -a** [haj'vozu, ɔza] ADJ furious

raiz [ha'iz] F root; (*origem*) source; **~ quadrada** square root

rajada [ha'ʒada] F (*vento*) gust

ralado, -a [ha'ladu, a] ADJ grated; **ralador** [hala'dor] M grater

ralar [ha'lar] VT to grate

ralhar [ha'ʎar] VI to scold; **~ com alguém** to tell sb off

rali [ha'li] M rally

ralo, -a ['halu, a] ADJ (*cabelo*) thinning; (*tecido*) flimsy; (*vegetação*) sparse; (*sopa*) thin, watery; (*café*) weak ▶ M (*de regador*) rose, nozzle; (*de pia, banheiro*) drain

rama ['hama] F branches *pl*, foliage; **pela ~** superficially; **ramagem** [ha'maʒẽ] F branches *pl*, foliage; **ramal** [ha'maw] (*pl* -**ais**) M (*Ferro*) branch line; (*Tel*) extension; (*Auto*) side road

ramificar-se [hamifi'karsi] VR to branch out

ramo ['hamu] M branch; (*profissão, negócios*) line; (*de flores*) bunch; **Domingo de R~s** Palm Sunday

rampa ['hãpa] F ramp; (*ladeira*) slope

ranger [hã'ʒer] VI to creak ▶ VT: **~ os dentes** to grind one's teeth

ranhura [ha'ɲura] F groove; (*para moeda*) slot

rapar [ha'par] VT to scrape; (*a barba*) to shave; (*o cabelo*) to shave off

rapariga [hapa'riga] F girl

rapaz [ha'pajz] M boy; (*col*) lad

rapidez [hapi'dez] F speed

rápido, -a ['hapidu, a] ADJ quick, fast ▶ ADV fast, quickly ▶ M (*trem*) express

rapina [ha'pina] F robbery; **ave de ~** bird of prey

raptar [hap'tar] VT to kidnap; **rapto** ['haptu] M kidnapping; **raptor** [hap'tor] M kidnapper

raquete [ha'ketʃi] F racquet

raquítico, -a [ha'kitʃiku, a] ADJ (*franzino*) puny; (*vegetação*) poor

raramente [hara'mẽtʃi] ADV rarely, seldom

raro, -a ['haru, a] ADJ rare ▶ ADV rarely, seldom

rasgado, -a [haz'gadu, a] ADJ (roupa) torn, ripped

rasgão [haz'gãw] (pl -ões) M tear, rip

rasgar [haz'gar] VT to tear, rip; (destruir) to tear up, rip up; **rasgar-se** VR to split; **rasgo** ['hazgu] M tear, rip

rasgões [haz'gõjs] MPL de **rasgão**

raso, -a ['hazu, a] ADJ (liso) flat, level; (não fundo) shallow; (baixo) low; **soldado ~** private

raspa ['haspa] F (de madeira) shaving; (de metal) filing

raspão [has'pãw] (pl -ões) M scratch, graze

raspar [has'par] VT to scrape; (alisar) to file; (tocar de raspão) to graze; (arranhar) to scratch; (pelos, cabeça) to shave; (apagar) to rub out ▶ VI: **~ em** to scrape

raspões [has'põjs] MPL de **raspão**

rasteira [has'tejra] F: **dar uma ~ em alguém** to trip sb up

rasteiro, -a [has'tejru, a] ADJ crawling; (planta) creeping

rastejar [haste'ʒar] VI to crawl; (furtivamente) to creep; (fig: rebaixar-se) to grovel ▶ VT (fugitivo etc) to track

rasto ['hastu] M (pegada) track; (de veículo) trail; (fig) sign, trace; **andar de ~s** to crawl

rastro ['hastru] M = **rasto**

rata ['hata] F rat; (pequena) mouse

ratificar [hatʃifi'kar] VT to ratify

rato ['hatu] M rat; (rato pequeno) mouse; **~ de hotel/praia** hotel/beach thief; **ratoeira** [ha'twejra] F rat trap; (pequena) mousetrap

ravina [ha'vina] F ravine

razão [ha'zãw] (pl -ões) F reason; (argumento) reasoning; (Mat) ratio ▶ M (Com) ledger; **à ~ de** at the rate of; **em ~ de** on account of; **dar ~ a alguém** to support sb; **ter/não ter ~** to be right/wrong; **razoável** [ha'zwavew] (pl -eis) ADJ reasonable

r/c (PT) ABR = **rés do chão**

ré [hɛ] F (Auto) reverse (gear); **dar (marcha à) ré** to reverse, back up; ver tb **réu**

reabastecer [heabaste'ser] VT (avião) to refuel; (carro) to fill up; **reabastecer-se** VR: **~-se de** to replenish one's supply of

reação [hea'sãw] (pl -ões) F reaction

reagir [hea'ʒir] VI to react; (doente, time perdedor) to fight back; **~ a** (resistir) to resist; (protestar) to rebel against

reais [he'ajs] ADJ PL de **real**

reaja [he'aʒa] VB ver **reagir**

reajuste [hea'ʒustʃi] M adjustment

real [he'aw] (pl -ais) ADJ real; (relativo à realeza) royal ▶ M (moeda) real

The Brazilian currency, the **real**, was introduced in 1994 as part of a comprehensive economic stabilization package known as the **Plano Real**. This brought an end to some thirty years of hyperinflation which saw successive devaluations and name-changes to the Brazilian currency, from cruzeiro to cruzado (1986), to cruzado novo (1989), back to cruzeiro (1990), to cruzeiro real (1993) and finally to real (1994). The real is subdivided into 100 centavos. The currency symbol is R$ and a comma is used to separate reais and centavos, e.g. R$ 2,40 (two reais and forty centavos).

realçar [heaw'sar] VT to highlight; **realce** [he'awsi] M emphasis; (mais brilho) highlight; **dar realce a** to enhance

realeza [hea'leza] F royalty

realidade [heali'dadʒi] F reality; **na ~** actually, in fact; **~ virtual** virtual reality

realista [hea'lista] ADJ realistic ▶ M/F realist

realização [healiza'sãw] F fulfilment (BRIT), fulfillment (US), realization; (de projeto) execution, carrying out

realizador, a [healiza'dor(a)] ADJ enterprising

realizar [heali'zar] VT to achieve; (projeto) to carry out; (ambições, sonho) to fulfil (BRIT), fulfill (US), realize; (negócios) to transact; (perceber, convertir en dinheiro) to realize; **realizar-se** VR to take place; (ambições) to be realized; (sonhos) to come true

realmente [heaw'mẽtʃi] ADV really; (de fato) actually

reanimar [heani'mar] VT to revive; (encorajar) to encourage; **reanimar-se** VR to cheer up

reatar [hea'tar] VT to resume, take up again

reaver [hea'ver] VT to recover, get back

rebaixar [hebaj'ʃar] VT to lower; (reduzir) to reduce; (time) to relegate; (funcionário) to demote; (humilhar) to put down ▶ VI to drop; **rebaixar-se** VR to demean o.s.

rebanho [he'baɲu] M (de carneiros, fig) flock; (de gado, elefantes) herd

rebelar-se [hebe'larsi] VR to rebel; **rebelde** [he'bɛwdʒi] ADJ rebellious;

(*indisciplinado*) unruly, wild ▶ M/F rebel;
rebeldia [hebew'dʒia] F rebelliousness;
(*fig: obstinação*) stubbornness;
(: *oposição*) defiance
rebelião [hebe'ljãw] (*pl* -**ões**) F
rebellion
rebentar [hebē'tar] VI (*guerra*) to break
out; (*louça*) to smash; (*corda*) to snap;
(*represa*) to burst; (*ondas*) to break ▶ VT
to smash; to snap; (*porta, ponte*) to
break down
rebocador [heboka'dor] M tug (boat)
rebocar [hebo'kar] VT (*paredes*) to
plaster; (*dar reboque a*) to tow
rebolar [hebo'lar] VT to swing ▶ VI to
sway
reboque¹ [he'bɔki] M tow; (*veículo: tb:*
carro ~) trailer; (*cabo*) towrope; (BR: *de*
socorro) tow truck; **a** ~ on *ou* in (US) tow
reboque² VB *ver* **rebocar**
rebuçado [hebu'sadu] (PT) M sweet,
candy (US)
recado [he'kadu] M message; **deixar** ~
to leave a message
recair [heka'ir] VI (*doente*) to relapse
recalcar [hekaw'kar] VT to repress
recalque VB *ver* **recalcar**
recanto [he'kãtu] M corner, nook
recapitular [hekapitu'lar] VT to sum
up, recapitulate; (*fatos*) to review;
(*matéria escolar*) to revise
recarga [he'karga] F (*de celular*) top-up;
preciso fazer a ~ do meu celular I need
to top up my mobile
recarregar [hekahe'gar] VT (*celular*) to
top up; (*bateria*) to recharge; (*cartucho*)
to refill
recatado, -a [heka'tadu, a] ADJ
(*modesto*) modest; (*reservado*) reserved
recauchutado, -a [hekawʃu'tadu, a]
ADJ: **pneu** ~ (*Auto*) retread, remould
(BRIT)
recear [he'sjar] VT to fear ▶ VI: ~ **por** to
fear for; ~ **fazer/que** to be afraid to
do/that
receber [hese'ber] VT to receive; (*ganhar*)
to earn, get; (*hóspedes*) to take in;
(*convidados*) to entertain; (*acolher bem*) to
welcome ▶ VI (*receber convidados*) to
entertain; **recebimento** [hesebi'mẽtu]
(BR) M reception; (*de uma carta*) receipt;
acusar o recebimento de to
acknowledge receipt of
receio [he'seju] M fear; **ter** ~ **de que** to
fear that
receita [he'sejta] F income; (*do Estado*)
revenue; (*Med*) prescription; (*culinária*)
recipe; **R~ Federal** ≈ Inland Revenue

(BRIT), ≈ IRS (US); **receitar** [hesej'tar] VT
to prescribe
recém [he'sē] ADV recently, newly;
recém-casado, -a ADJ: **os recém-**
casados the newlyweds; **recém-**
chegado, -a M/F newcomer;
recém-nascido, -a M/F newborn child
recente [he'sētʃi] ADJ recent; (*novo*) new
▶ ADV recently; **recentemente**
[hesētʃi'mẽtʃi] ADV recently
receoso, -a [he'sjozu, ɔza] ADJ
frightened, fearful; **estar ~ de (fazer)** to
be afraid of (doing)
recepção [hesep'sãw] (*pl* -**ões**) F
reception; (PT: *de uma carta*) receipt;
acusar a ~ de (PT) to acknowledge
receipt of; **recepcionista**
[hesepsjo'nista] M/F receptionist
receptivo, -a [hesep'tʃivu, a] ADJ
receptive; (*acolhedor*) welcoming
receptor [hesep'tor] M receiver
recessão [hese'sãw] (*pl* -**ões**) F recession
recessões [hese'sõjs] FPL *de* **recessão**
recheado, -a [he'ʃjadu, a] ADJ (*ave, carne*)
stuffed; (*empada, bolo*) filled; (*cheio*) full,
crammed
rechear [he'ʃjar] VT to fill; (*ave, carne*) to
stuff; **recheio** [he'ʃeju] M stuffing; (*de*
empada, de bolo) filling; (*o conteúdo*)
contents *pl*
rechonchudo, -a [heʃõ'ʃudu, a] ADJ
chubby, plump
recibo [he'sibu] M receipt
reciclar [hesi'klar] VT to recycle
reciclável [hesi'klavew] (*pl* -**eis**) ADJ
recyclable
recinto [he'sĩtu] M enclosure; (*lugar*)
area
recipiente [hesi'pjētʃi] M container,
receptacle
recíproco, -a [he'siproku, a] ADJ
reciprocal
recitar [hesi'tar] VT to recite
reclamação [heklama'sãw] (*pl* -**ões**) F
complaint
reclamar [hekla'mar] VT to demand;
(*herança*) to claim ▶ VI: ~ (**de**) (*comida etc*)
to complain (about)
reclinar [hekli'nar] VT to rest, lean;
reclinar-se VR to lie back; (*deitar-se*) to lie
down
recobrar [heko'brar] VT to recover, get
back; **recobrar-se** VR to recover
recolher [heko'ʎer] VT to collect; (*gado,*
roupa do varal) to bring in; (*juntar*) to
collect up; **recolhido, -a** [heko'ʎidu, a]
ADJ (*lugar*) secluded; (*pessoa*) withdrawn;
recolhimento [hekoʎi'mẽtu] M

retirement; (*arrecadação*) collection; (*ato de levar*) taking

recomeçar [hekome'sar] VT, VI to restart

recomendação [hekomẽda'sãw] (*pl -ões*) F recommendation; **recomendações** FPL (*cumprimentos*) regards

recomendar [hekomẽ'dar] VT to recommend; **recomendável** [hekomẽ'davew] (*pl -eis*) ADJ advisable

recompensa [hekõ'pẽsa] F reward; **recompensar** [hekõpẽ'sar] VT to reward

recompor [hekõ'por] (*irreg: como* **pôr**) VT to reorganize; (*restabelecer*) to restore

reconciliar [hekõsi'ljar] VT to reconcile

reconhecer [hekoɲe'ser] VT to recognize; (*Mil*) to reconnoitre (*BRIT*), reconnoiter (*US*); **reconhecido, -a** [hekoɲe'sidu, a] ADJ recognized; (*agradecido*) grateful, thankful; **reconhecimento** [hekoɲesi'mẽtu] M recognition; (*admissão*) admission; (*gratidão*) gratitude; (*Mil*) reconnaissance; **reconhecível** [hekoɲe'sivew] (*pl -eis*) ADJ recognizable

reconstruir [hekõs'trwir] VT to rebuild

recordação [hekorda'sãw] (*pl -ões*) F (*reminiscência*) memory; (*objeto*) memento

recordar [hekor'dar] VT to remember; **recordar-se** VR: **~-se de** to remember; **~ algo a alguém** to remind sb of sth

recorde [he'kɔrdʒi] ADJ INV record *atr* ▶ M record

recorrer [heko'her] VI: **~ a** to turn to; (*valer-se de*) to resort to

recortar [hekor'tar] VT to cut out; **recorte** [he'kɔrtʃi] M (*ato*) cutting out; (*de jornal*) cutting, clipping

recreação [hekrja'sãw] F recreation

recreio [he'kreju] M recreation

recriminar [hekrimi'nar] VT to reproach, reprove

recrutamento [hekruta'mẽtu] M recruitment

recrutar [hekru'tar] VT to recruit

recuar [he'kwar] VT to move back ▶ VI to move back; (*exército*) to retreat

recuperar [hekupe'rar] VT to recover; (*tempo perdido*) to make up for; (*reabilitar*) to rehabilitate; **recuperar-se** VR to recover

recurso [he'kursu] M resource; (*Jur*) appeal; **recursos** MPL (*financeiros*) resources

recusa [he'kuza] F refusal; (*negação*) denial; **recusar** [heku'zar] VT to refuse;

to deny; **recusar-se** VR: **recusar-se a** to refuse to

redação [heda'sãw] (*pl -ões*) F (*ato*) writing; (*Educ*) composition, essay; (*redatores*) editorial staff

redator, a [heda'tor(a)] M/F editor

rede ['hedʒi] F net; (*de dormir*) hammock; (*Ferro, Tec, Comput, TV, fig*) network; (*Tel*) signal; **a ~** (*a Internet*) the web; **~ de área local** local area network; **~ sem fio** wireless network; **~ social** social network, social networking site

rédea ['hɛdʒja] F rein

redentor, a [hedẽ'tor(a)] ADJ redeeming

redigir [hedʒi'ʒir] VT, VI to write

redobrar [hedo'brar] VT (*aumentar*) to increase; (*esforços*) to redouble

redondamente [hedõda'mẽtʃi] ADV (*completamente*) completely

redondeza [hedõ'deza] F roundness; **redondezas** FPL surroundings

redondo, -a [he'dõdu, a] ADJ round

redor [he'dor] M: **ao** *ou* **em ~ (de)** around, round about

redução [hedu'sãw] (*pl -ões*) F reduction

redundância [hedũ'dãsja] F redundancy; **redundante** [hedũ'dãtʃi] ADJ redundant

reduzido, -a [hedu'zidu, a] ADJ reduced; (*limitado*) limited; (*pequeno*) small

reduzir [hedu'zir] VT to reduce; **reduzir-se** VR: **~-se a** to be reduced to; (*fig: resumir-se em*) to come down to

reembolsar [heẽbow'sar] VT to recover; (*restituir*) to reimburse; (*depósito*) to refund; **reembolso** [heẽ'bowsu] M (*de depósito*) refund; (*de despesa*) reimbursement

reencontro [heẽ'kõtru] M reunion

refeição [hefej'sãw] (*pl -ões*) F meal; **refeitório** [hefej'tɔrju] M refectory

refém [he'fẽ] (*pl -ns*) M hostage

referência [hefe'rẽsja] F reference; **referências** FPL (*informações para emprego*) references; **fazer ~ a** to make reference to, refer to

referente [hefe'rẽtʃi] ADJ: **~ a** concerning, regarding

referir [hefe'rir] VT to relate, tell; **referir-se** VR: **~-se a** to refer to

REFESA F (= *Rede Ferroviária SA*) Brazilian rail network

refinamento [hefina'mẽtu] M refinement

refinaria [hefina'ria] F refinery

refiro [he'firu] VB *ver* **referir**

refletir [hefle'tʃir] VT to reflect ▶ VI: **~ em** *ou* **sobre** to consider, think about

reflexão [heflek'sãw] (pl **-ões**) F
reflection

reflexo, -a [he'flɛksu, a] ADJ (luz)
reflected; (ação) reflex ▶ M reflection;
(Anat) reflex; (no cabelo) streak

reflexões [heflek'sõjs] FPL de **reflexão**

reflito [he'flitu] VB ver **refletir**

reforçado, -a [hefor'sadu, a] ADJ
reinforced; (pessoa) strong; (café da
manhã, jantar) hearty

reforçar [hefor'sar] VT to reinforce;
(revigorar) to invigorate; **reforço**
[he'forsu] M reinforcement

reforma [he'fɔrma] F reform; (Arq)
renovation; **reformado, -a**
[hefor'madu, a] ADJ reformed;
renovated; (Mil) retired; **reformar**
[hefor'mar] VT to reform; to renovate;
reformar-se VR to reform

refrão [he'frãw] (pl **-ões**) M chorus,
refrain; (provérbio) saying

refratário, -a [hefra'tarju, a] ADJ (Tec)
heat-resistant; (Culin) ovenproof

refrear [hefre'ar] VT (cavalo) to rein in;
(inimigo) to contain, check; (paixões,
raiva) to control; **refrear-se** VR to
restrain o.s.

refrescante [hefres'kãtʃi] ADJ refreshing

refrescar [hefres'kar] VT (ar, ambiente) to
cool; (pessoa) to refresh ▶ VI to cool down

refresco [he'fresku] M cool fruit drink,
squash; **refrescos** MPL (refrigerantes)
refreshments

refrigerador [hefriʒera'dor] M
refrigerator, fridge (BRIT)

refrigerante [hefriʒe'rãtʃi] M soft drink

refugiado, -a [hefu'ʒjadu, a] ADJ, M/F
refugee

refugiar-se [hefu'ʒjarsi] VR to take
refuge; **refúgio** [he'fuʒju] M refuge

refugo [he'fugu] M rubbish, garbage
(US); (mercadoria) reject

rega ['hɛga] F (PT) irrigation

regador [hega'dor] M watering can

regalia [hega'lia] F privilege

regar [he'gar] VT (plantas, jardim) to
water; (umedecer) to sprinkle

regatear [hega'tʃjar] VT (o preço) to
haggle over, bargain for ▶ VI to haggle

regenerar [heʒene'rar] VT to regenerate

reger [he'ʒer] VT to govern; (orquestra) to
conduct; (empresa) to run ▶ VI to rule;
(maestro) to conduct

região [he'ʒjãw] (pl **-ões**) F region, area

regime [he'ʒimi] M (Pol) regime; (dieta)
diet; (maneira) way; **estar de ~** to be on
a diet

regimento [heʒi'mẽtu] M regiment

regiões [he'ʒjõjs] FPL de **região**

regional [heʒjo'naw] (pl **-ais**) ADJ
regional

registrar [heʒis'trar], (PT) **registar** VT
to register; (anotar) to record

registro [he'ʒistru], (PT) **registo** M (ato)
registration; (: anotação) recording; (livro,
Ling) register; (histórico, Comput) record;
~ civil registry office

regra ['hɛgra] F rule; **regras** FPL (Med)
periods

regravável [hegra'vavew] (pl **-eis**) ADJ
rewritable

regressar [hegre'sar] VI to come (ou go)
back, return; **regresso** [he'grɛsu] M
return

régua ['hɛgwa] F ruler; **~ de calcular**
slide rule

regulador [hegula'dor] M regulator

regulamento [hegula'mẽtu] M rules pl,
regulations pl

regular [hegu'lar] ADJ regular; (estatura)
average, medium; (tamanho) normal;
(razoável) not bad ▶ VT to regulate; (reger)
to govern; (máquina) to adjust; (carro,
motor) to tune ▶ VI to work, function;
regularidade [hegulari'dadʒi] F
regularity

rei [hej] M king; **Dia de R~s** Epiphany;
R~ Momo carnival king

reinado [hej'nadu] M reign

reinar [hej'nar] VI to reign

reino ['hejnu] M kingdom; (fig) realm;
o R~ Unido the United Kingdom

reivindicação [hejvĩdʒika'sãw] (pl **-ões**)
F claim, demand

reivindicar [hejvĩdʒi'kar] VT to claim;
(aumento salarial, direitos) to demand

rejeição [heʒej'sãw] (pl **-ões**) F rejection

rejeitar [heʒej'tar] VT to reject; (recusar)
to refuse

rejo ['heʒu] VB ver **reger**

rejuvenescer [heʒuvene'ser] VT to
rejuvenate

relação [hela'sãw] (pl **-ões**) F relation;
(conexão) connection; (relacionamento)
relationship; (Mat) ratio; (lista) list; **com
ou em ~ a** regarding, with reference to;
relações públicas public relations;
relacionamento [helasjona'mẽtu] M
relationship; **relacionar** [helasjo'nar]
VT to make a list of; (ligar): **relacionar
algo com algo** to connect sth with sth,
relate sth to sth; **relacionar-se** VR to be
connected ou related

relâmpago [he'lãpagu] M flash of
lightning; **relâmpagos** MPL (clarões)
lightning sg

relance [he'lãsi] M glance; **olhar de ~ to** glance at

relapso, -a [he'lapsu, a] ADJ (*negligente*) negligent

relatar [hela'tar] VT to give an account of

relativo, -a [hela'tʃivu, a] ADJ relative

relato [he'latu] M account

relatório [hela'tɔrju] M report

relaxado, -a [hela'ʃadu, a] ADJ relaxed; (*desleixado*) slovenly, sloppy; (*relapso*) negligent

relaxante [hela'ʃãtʃi] ADJ relaxing

relaxar [hela'ʃar] VT, VI to relax

relegar [hele'gar] VT to relegate

relembrar [helē'brar] VT to recall

relevante [hele'vãtʃi] ADJ relevant

relevo [he'levu] M relief

religião [heli'ʒãw] (*pl* **-ões**) F religion; **religioso, -a** [heli'ʒozu, ɔza] ADJ religious ▶ M/F religious person; (*frade/freira*) monk/nun

relíquia [he'likja] F relic; **~ de família** family heirloom

relógio [he'lɔʒu] M clock; (*de gás*) meter; **~ (de pulso)** (wrist)watch; **~ de sol** sundial

relutante [helu'tãtʃi] ADJ reluctant

relva ['hɛwva] F grass; (*terreno gramado*) lawn

relvado [hew'vadu] (*PT*) M lawn

remar [he'mar] VT, VI to row

rematar [hema'tar] VT to finish off; **remate** [he'matʃi] M (*fim*) end; (*acabamento*) finishing touch

remediar [heme'dʒjar] VT to put right, remedy

remédio [he'mɛdʒju] M (*medicamento*) medicine; (*recurso, solução*) remedy; (*Jur*) recourse; **não tem ~** there's no way

remendar [hemē'dar] VT to mend; (*com pano*) to patch; **remendo** [he'mēdu] M repair; patch

remessa [he'mɛsa] F shipment; (*de dinheiro*) remittance

remetente [heme'tētʃi] M/F sender

remexer [heme'ʃer] VT (*papéis*) to shuffle; (*sacudir: braços*) to wave; (*folhas*) to shake; (*revolver: areia, lama*) to stir up ▶ VI: **~ em** to rummage through

reminiscência [hemini'sēsja] F reminiscence

remo ['hɛmu] M oar; (*Esporte*) rowing

remoção [hemo'sãw] F removal

remorso [he'mɔrsu] M remorse

remover [hemo'ver] VT to move; (*transferir*) to transfer; (*demitir*) to dismiss; (*retirar, afastar*) to remove; (*terra*) to churn up

renal [he'naw] (*pl* **-ais**) ADJ renal, kidney *atr*

Renascença [hena'sēsa] F: **a ~ the** Renaissance

renascer [hena'ser] VI to be reborn; (*fig*) to revive

renascimento [henasi'mētu] M rebirth; (*fig*) revival; **o R~** the Renaissance

renda ['hēda] F income; (*nacional*) revenue; (*de aplicação, locação*) yield; (*tecido*) lace

render [hē'der] VT (*lucro, dinheiro*) to bring in, yield; (*preço*) to fetch; (*homenagem*) to pay; (*graças*) to give; (*serviços*) to render; (*armas*) to surrender; (*guarda*) to relieve; (*causar*) to bring ▶ VI (*dar lucro*) to pay; **render-se** VR to surrender; **rendição** [hēdʒi'sãw] F surrender

rendimento [hēdʒi'mētu] M income; (*lucro*) profit; (*juro*) yield, interest

renegar [hene'gar] VT (*crença*) to renounce; (*detestar*) to hate; (*trair*) to betray; (*negar*) to deny; (*desprezar*) to reject

renomado, -a [heno'madu, a] ADJ renowned

renovar [heno'var] VT to renew; (*Arq*) to renovate

rentabilidade [hētabili'dadʒi] F profitability

rentável [hē'tavew] (*pl* **-eis**) ADJ profitable

renúncia [he'nũsja] F resignation

renunciar [henũ'sjar] VT to give up, renounce ▶ VI to resign; (*abandonar*): **~ a algo** to give sth up

reouve [he'ovi] VB *ver* **reaver**

reouver [heo'ver] VB *ver* **reaver**

reparação [hepara'sãw] (*pl* **-ões**) F mending, repairing; (*de mal, erros*) remedying; (*fig*) amends *pl*, reparation

reparar [hepa'rar] VT to repair; (*forças*) to restore; (*mal, erros*) to remedy; (*prejuizo, danos, ofensa*) to make amends for; (*notar*) to notice ▶ VI: **~ em** to notice; **reparo** [he'paru] M repair; (*crítica*) criticism; (*observação*) observation

repartição [hepartʃi'sãw] (*pl* **-ões**) F distribution

repartir [hepar'tʃir] VT (*distribuir*) to distribute; (*dividir entre vários*) to share out; (*dividir em várias porções*) to divide up

repelente [hepe'lētʃi] ADJ, M repellent

repente [he'pētʃi] M outburst; **de ~** suddenly; (*col: talvez*) maybe

repentino, -a [hepẽ'tʃinu, a] ADJ
sudden

repercussão [heperku'sãw] (pl **-ões**) F
repercussion

repercutir [heperku'tʃir] VT to echo ▶ VI
to reverberate, echo; (fig): **~ (em)** to
have repercussions (on)

repertório [heper'tɔrju] M list; (coleção)
collection; (Mús) repertoire

repetidamente [hepetʃida'mẽtʃi] ADV
repeatedly

repetir [hepe'tʃir] VT to repeat ▶ VI (ao
comer) to have seconds; **repetir-se** VR to
happen again; (pessoa) to repeat o.s.;
repetitivo, -a [hepetʃi'tʃivu, a] ADJ
repetitive

repito [he'pitu] VB ver **repetir**

repleto, -a [he'plɛtu, a] ADJ replete,
full up

réplica ['hɛplika] F replica; (contestação)
reply, retort

replicar [hepli'kar] VT to answer, reply to
▶ VI to reply, answer back

repolho [he'poʎu] M cabbage

repor [he'por] (irreg: como **pôr**) VT to put
back, replace; (restituir) to return;
repor-se VR to recover

reportagem [hepor'taʒẽ] (pl **-ns**) F
reporting; (notícia) report

repórter [he'pɔrter] M/F reporter

repousar [hepo'zar] VI to rest; **repouso**
[he'pozu] M rest

representação [heprezẽta'sãw] (pl
-ões) F representation; (Teatro)
performance; **representante**
[heprezẽ'tãtʃi] M/F representative

representar [heprezẽ'tar] VT to
represent; (Teatro: papel) to play ▶ VI to
act; **representativo, -a**
[heprezẽta'tʃivu, a] ADJ representative

repressão [hepre'sãw] (pl **-ões**) F
repression

reprimir [hepri'mir] VT to repress

reprodução [heprodu'sãw] (pl **-ões**) F
reproduction

reproduzir [heprodu'zir] VT to
reproduce; (repetir) to repeat;
reproduzir-se VR to breed

reprovar [hepro'var] VT to disapprove
of; (aluno) to fail

réptil ['hɛptʃiw] (pl **-eis**) M reptile

república [he'publika] F republic;
republicano, -a [hepubli'kanu, a] ADJ,
M/F republican

repudiar [hepu'dʒjar] VT to repudiate;
repúdio [he'pudʒju] M repudiation

repulsivo, -a [hepuw'sivu, a] ADJ
repulsive

reputação [reputa'sãw] (pl **-ões**) F
reputation

requeijão [hekej'ʒãw] M cheese spread

requerer [heke'rer] VT (emprego) to
apply for; (pedir) to request; (exigir) to
require; **requerimento** [hekeri'mẽtu]
M application; request; (petição)
petition

requintado, -a [hekĩ'tadu, a] ADJ
refined, elegant

requinte [he'kĩtʃi] M refinement,
elegance; (cúmulo) height

requisito [heki'zitu] M requirement

rés do chão [hɛzdu'ʃãw] (PT) M INV
ground floor (BRIT), first floor (US)

reserva [he'zerva] F reserve; (para hotel,
fig) reservation ▶ M/F (Esporte) reserve

reservado, -a [hezer'vadu, a] ADJ
reserved

reservar [hezer'var] VT to reserve;
(guardar de reserva) to keep; (forças) to
conserve; **reservar-se** VR to save o.s.

reservatório [hezerva'tɔrju] M
reservoir

resfriado, -a [hes'frjadu, a] (BR) ADJ:
estar ~ to have a cold ▶ M cold, chill;
ficar ~ to catch (a) cold

resgatar [hezga'tar] VT (salvar) to
rescue; (retomar) to get back, recover;
resgate [hez'gatʃi] M rescue; (para livrar
reféns) ransom

residência [hezi'dẽsja] F residence;
residencial [hezidẽ'sjaw] (pl **-ais**) ADJ
residential; (computador, telefone etc)
home atr; **residente** [hezi'dẽtʃi] ADJ,
M/F resident

residir [hezi'dʒir] VI to live, reside

resíduo [he'zidwu] M residue

resignação [hezigna'sãw] (pl **-ões**) F
resignation

resignar-se [hezig'narsi] VR: **~ com** to
resign o.s. to

resina [he'zina] F resin

resistente [hezis'tẽtʃi] ADJ resistant;
(material, objeto) hard-wearing, strong

resistir [hezis'tʃir] VI to hold; (pessoa) to
hold out; **~ a** to resist; (sobreviver) to
survive

resmungar [hezmũ'gar] VT, VI to
mutter, mumble

resolução [hezolu'sãw] (pl **-ões**) F
resolution; (de um problema) solution;
resoluto, -a [hezo'lutu, a] ADJ decisive

resolver [hezow'ver] VT to sort out;
(problema) to solve; (questão) to resolve;
(decidir) to decide; **resolver-se** VR: **~-se
(a fazer)** to make up one's mind (to do),
decide (to do)

respectivo, -a [heʃpek'tʃivu, a] ADJ
respective

respeitar [heʃpej'tar] VT to respect;
respeitável [heʃpej'tavew] (pl **-eis**) ADJ
respectable; (considerável) considerable

respeito [heʃ'pejtu] M: **~ (a** ou **por)**
respect (for); **respeitos** MPL
(cumprimentos) regards; **a ~ de, com ~ a**
as to, as regards; (sobre) about; **dizer ~ a**
to concern; **em ~ a** with respect to

respiração [heʃpira'sãw] F breathing

respirar [heʃpi'rar] VT, VI to breathe

respiro [heʃ'piru] M breath

resplandecente [heʃplãde'sẽtʃi] ADJ
resplendent

responder [heʃpõ'der] VT to answer
▶ VI to answer; (ser respondão) to answer
back; **~ por** to be responsible for,
answer for

responsabilidade [heʃpõsabili'dadʒi]
F responsibility

responsabilizar [heʃpõsabili'zar] VT:
~ alguém (por algo) to hold sb
responsible (for sth); **responsabilizar-
se** VR: **~-se por** to take responsibility for

responsável [heʃpõ'savew] (pl **-eis**) ADJ:
~ (por) responsible (for); **~ a** answerable
to, accountable to

resposta [heʃ'poʃta] F answer, reply

resquício [heʃ'kisju] M (vestígio) trace

ressabiado, -a [hesa'bjadu, a] ADJ
wary; (ressentido) resentful

ressaca [he'saka] F undertow; (mar
bravo) rough sea; (fig: de quem bebeu)
hangover

ressalva [he'sawva] F safeguard

ressentido, -a [hesẽ'tʃidu, a] ADJ
resentful

ressentimento [hesẽtʃi'mẽtu] M
resentment

ressentir-se [hesẽ'tʃirsi] VR: **~ de**
(ofender-se) to resent; (magoar-se) to be
hurt by; (sofrer) to suffer from, feel the
effects of

ressurgimento [hesurʒi'mẽtu] M
resurgence, revival

ressuscitar [hesusi'tar] VT, VI to revive

restabelecer [heʃtabele'ser] VT to
re-establish, restore; **restabelecer-se**
VR to recover, recuperate;
restabelecimento [heʃtabelesi'mẽtu]
M re-establishment; restoration;
recovery

restante [heʃ'tãtʃi] ADJ remaining ▶ M
rest

restar [heʃ'tar] VI to remain, be left

restauração [heʃtawra'sãw] (pl **-ões**) F
restoration; (de costumes, usos) revival

restaurante [heʃtaw'rãtʃi] M
restaurant

restaurar [heʃtaw'rar] VT to restore

restituição [heʃtʃitwi'sãw] (pl **-ões**) F
restitution, return; (de dinheiro) repayment

restituir [heʃtʃi'twir] VT to return;
(dinheiro) to repay; (forças, saúde) to
restore; (usos) to revive; (reempossar) to
reinstate

resto ['heʃtu] M rest; (Mat) remainder;
restos MPL (sobras) remains; (de comida)
scraps

restrição [heʃtri'sãw] (pl **-ões**) F
restriction

resultado [hezuw'tadu] M result

resultante [hezuw'tãtʃi] ADJ resultant;
~ de resulting from

resultar [hezuw'tar] VI: **~ (de/em)** to
result (from/in) ▶ VI (vira ser) to turn out
to be

resumir [hezu'mir] VT to summarize;
(livro) to abridge; (reduzir) to reduce;
(conter em resumo) to sum up; **resumo**
[he'zumu] M summary, résumé; **em
resumo** in short, briefly

retaguarda [heta'gwarda] F rearguard;
(posição) rear

retaliação [hetalja'sãw] (pl **-ões**) F
retaliation

retângulo [he'tãgulu] M rectangle

retardar [hetar'dar] VT to hold up, delay;
(adiar) to postpone

reter [he'ter] (irreg: como **ter**) VT (guardar,
manter) to keep; (deter) to stop; (segurar)
to hold; (ladrão, suspeito) to detain;
(na memória) to retain; (lágrimas,
impulsos) to hold back; (impedir de sair)
to keep back

reticente [hetʃi'sẽtʃi] ADJ reticent

retificar [hetʃifi'kar] VT to rectify

retirada [hetʃi'rada] F (Mil) retreat;
(salário, saque) withdrawal

reto, -a ['hɛtu, a] ADJ straight; (fig: justo)
fair; (: honesto) honest, upright ▶ M (Anat)
rectum

retorcer [hetor'ser] VT to twist;
retorcer-se VR to wriggle, writhe

retornar [hetor'nar] VI to return, go
back; **retorno** [he'tornu] M return;
dar retorno to do a U-turn; **retorno
(do carro)** (Comput) (carriage) return

retraído, -a [hetra'idu, a] ADJ (tímido)
reserved, timid

retrair [hetra'ir] VT to withdraw; (contrair)
to contract; (pessoa) to make reserved

retrato [he'tratu] M portrait; (Foto)
photo; (fig: efígie) likeness; (: representação)
portrayal; **~ falado** Identikit® picture

retribuir [hetri'bwir] VT to reward,
recompense; (*pagar*) to remunerate;
(*hospitalidade, favor, sentimento, visita*) to
return
retroceder [hetrose'der] VI to retreat,
fall back; **retrocesso** [hetro'sɛsu] M
retreat; (*ao passado*) return
retrógrado, -a [he'trɔgradu, a] ADJ
retrograde; (*reacionário*) reactionary
retrospecto [hetro'spɛktu] M: **em ~** in
retrospect
retrovisor [hetrovi'zor] ADJ, M:
(espelho) ~ rear-view mirror
réu, ré [hɛw, hɛ] M/F defendant;
(*culpado*) culprit, criminal
reumatismo [hewma'tʃizmu] M
rheumatism
reunião [heu'njãw] (*pl* **-ões**) F meeting;
(*ato, reencontro*) reunion; (*festa*)
get-together, party; **~ de cúpula**
summit (meeting)
revanche [he'vãʃi] F revenge
reveillon [heve'jõ] M New Year's Eve
revelação [hevela'sãw] (*pl* **-ões**) F
revelation
revelar [heve'lar] VT to reveal; (*Foto*) to
develop; **revelar-se** VR to turn out to be
revelia [heve'lia] F default; **à ~** by
default; **à ~ de** without the knowledge
ou consent of
revendedor, a [hevẽde'dor(a)] M/F
dealer
rever [he'ver] (*irreg: como* **ver**) VT to see
again; (*examinar*) to check; (*revisar*) to
revise
reverência [heve'rẽsja] F reverence,
respect; (*ato*) bow; (*: de mulher*) curtsey;
fazer uma ~ to bow; to curtsey
reverso [he'vɛrsu] M reverse
reverter [hever'ter] VT to revert
revestir [heves'tʃir] VT (*paredes etc*) to
cover; (*interior de uma caixa etc*) to line
revezar [heve'zar] VT to take turns with
▶ VI to take turns; **revezar-se** VR to take
it in turns
revidar [hevi'dar] VT (*soco, insulto*) to
return; (*retrucar*) to answer; (*crítica*) to
rise to, respond to ▶ VI to hit back;
(*retrucar*) to respond
revirar [hevi'rar] VT to turn round;
(*gaveta*) to turn out, go through
revisão [hevi'zãw] (*pl* **-ões**) F revision;
(*de máquina*) overhaul; (*de carro*) service;
(*Jur*) appeal
revisar [hevi'zar] VT to revise
revisões [hevi'zõjs] FPL *de* **revisão**
revista [he'vista] F (*busca*) search; (*Mil,
exame*) inspection; (*publicação*)

magazine; (*: profissional, erudita*) journal;
(*Teatro*) revue
revisto [he'vistu] VB *ver* **revestir**
revogar [hevo'gar] VT to revoke
revolta [he'vowta] F revolt; (*fig:
indignação*) disgust; **revoltado, -a**
[hevow'tadu, a] ADJ in revolt; (*indignado*)
disgusted; (*amargo*) bitter; **revoltante**
[hevow'tãtʃi] ADJ disgusting; revolting
revoltar [hevow'tar] VT to disgust;
revoltar-se VR to rebel, revolt;
(*indignar-se*) to be disgusted
revolto, -a [he'vowtu, a] PP *de* **revolver**
▶ ADJ (*década*) turbulent; (*mundo*)
troubled; (*cabelo*) dishevelled; (*mar*)
rough; (*desarrumado*) untidy
revolução [hevolu'sãw] (*pl* **-ões**) F
revolution; **revolucionar**
[hevolusjo'nar] VT to revolutionize;
revolucionário, -a [hevolusjo'narju, a]
ADJ, M/F revolutionary
revolver [hevow'ver] VI to revolve,
rotate
revólver [he'vɔwver] M revolver
reza ['hɛza] F prayer; **rezar** [he'zar] VI to
pray
riacho ['hjaʃu] M stream, brook
ribeiro [hi'bejru] M brook, stream
rico, -a ['hiku, a] ADJ rich; (PT: *lindo*)
beautiful; (*: excelente*) splendid ▶ M/F rich
man/woman
ridicularizar [hidʒikulari'zar] VT to
ridicule
ridículo, -a [hi'dʒikulu, a] ADJ
ridiculous
rifa ['hifa] F raffle
rifle ['hifli] M rifle
rigidez [hiʒi'dez] F rigidity, stiffness;
(*austeridade*) severity, strictness
rígido, -a ['hiʒidu, a] ADJ rigid, stiff; (*fig*)
strict
rigor [hi'gor] M rigidity; (*meticulosidade*)
rigour (BRIT), rigor (US); (*severidade*)
harshness, severity; (*exatidão*) precision;
ser de ~ to be essential *ou* obligatory;
rigoroso, -a [higo'rozu, ɔza] ADJ
rigorous; (*severo*) strict; (*exigente*)
demanding; (*minucioso*) precise,
accurate; (*inverno*) hard, harsh
rijo, -a ['hiʒu, a] ADJ tough, hard; (*severo*)
harsh, severe
rim [hĩ] (*pl* **-ns**) M kidney; **rins** MPL (*parte
inferior das costas*) small *sg* of the back
rima ['hima] F rhyme; (*poema*) verse,
poem; **rimar** [hi'mar] VT, VI to rhyme
rímel® ['himew] (*pl* **-eis**) M mascara
ringue ['hĩgi] M ring
rins [hĩs] MPL *de* **rim**

Rio ['hiu] M: **o ~ (de Janeiro)** Rio (de Janeiro)

rio ['hiu] M river

riqueza [hi'keza] F wealth, riches pl; (qualidade) richness

rir [hir] VI to laugh; **~ de** to laugh at

risada [hi'zada] F laughter

risca ['hiska] F stroke; (listra) stripe; (no cabelo) parting

riscar [his'kar] VT (marcar) to mark; (apagar) to cross out; (desenhar) to outline

risco ['hisku] M (marca) mark, scratch; (traço) stroke; (desenho) drawing, sketch; (perigo) risk; **correr o ~ de** to run the risk of

riso ['hizu] M laughter; **risonho, -a** [hi'zoɲu, a] ADJ smiling; (contente) cheerful

ríspido, -a ['hispidu, a] ADJ brusque; (áspero) harsh

ritmo ['hitʃmu] M rhythm

rito ['hitu] M rite

ritual [hi'twaw] (pl **-ais**) ADJ, M ritual

rival [hi'vaw] (pl **-ais**) ADJ, M/F rival; **rivalidade** [hivali'dadʒi] F rivalry; **rivalizar** [hivali'zar] VT to rival ▶ VI: **rivalizar com** to compete with, vie with

roa ['hoa] VB ver **roer**

robô [ho'bo] M robot

roça ['hɔsa] F plantation; (no mato) clearing; (campo) country

rocha ['hɔʃa] F rock; (penedo) crag

rochedo [ho'ʃedu] M crag, cliff

rock-and-roll [-ã'hɔw] M rock and roll

roda ['hɔda] F wheel; (círculo, grupo de pessoas) circle; **~ dentada** cog(wheel); **em** ou **à ~ de** round, around

rodada [ho'dada] F (de bebidas, Esporte) round

rodar [ho'dar] VT to turn, spin; (viajar por) to tour, travel round; (quilômetros) to do; (filme) to make; (imprimir) to print; (Comput: programa) to run ▶ VI to turn round; (Auto) to drive around; **~ por** (a pé) to wander around; (de carro) to drive around

rodela [ho'dɛla] F (pedaço) slice

rodízio [ho'dʒizju] M rota; **em ~** on a rota basis

rodopiar [hodo'pjar] VI to whirl around, swirl

rodovia [hodo'via] F highway, ≈ motorway (BRIT), ≈ interstate (US)

rodoviária [hodo'vjarja] F (tb: **estação ~**) bus station; ver tb **rodoviário**

rodoviário, -a [hodo'vjarju, a] ADJ road atr; (polícia) traffic atr

roer [hwer] VT to gnaw, nibble; (enferrujar) to corrode; (afligir) to eat away

rogar [ho'gar] VI to ask, request; **~ a alguém que faça** to beg sb to do

rói [hɔj] VB ver **roer**

roía [ho'ia] VB ver **roer**

rolar [ho'lar] VT, VI to roll

roleta [ho'leta] F roulette; (borboleta) turnstile

rolha ['hoʎa] F cork

roliço, -a [ho'lisu, a] ADJ (pessoa) plump, chubby; (objeto) round, cylindrical

rolo ['holu] M (de papel etc) roll; (para nivelar o solo, para pintura) roller; (para cabelo) curler; (col: briga) brawl, fight; **cortina de ~** roller blind; **~ compressor** steamroller

Roma ['homa] N Rome

romã [ho'mã] F pomegranate

romance [ho'mãsi] M novel; (caso amoroso) romance; **~ policial** detective story

romano, -a [ho'manu, a] ADJ, M/F Roman

romântico, -a [ho'mãtʃiku, a] ADJ romantic

rombo ['hõbu] M (buraco) hole; (fig: desfalque) embezzlement; (: prejuízo) loss, shortfall

Romênia [ho'menja] F: **a ~** Romania; **romeno, -a** [ho'menu, a] ADJ, M/F Romanian ▶ M (Ling) Romanian

romper [hõ'per] VT to break; (rasgar) to tear; (relações) to break off ▶ VI: **~ em pranto** ou **lágrimas** to burst into tears; **rompimento** [hõpi'mẽtu] M breakage; (fenda) break; (de relações) breaking off

roncar [hõ'kar] VI to snore; **ronco** ['hõku] M snore

ronda ['hõda] F patrol, beat; **fazer a ~** to go the rounds; **rondar** [hõ'dar] VT to patrol; (espreitar) to prowl ▶ VI to prowl, lurk; (fazer a ronda) to patrol; **a inflação ronda os 10% ao ano** inflation is in the region of 10% a year

rosa ['hɔza] ADJ INV pink ▶ F rose; **rosado, -a** [ho'zadu, a] ADJ rosy, pink

rosário [ho'zarju] M rosary

rosbife [hoz'bifi] M roast beef

roseira [ho'zejra] F rosebush

rosnar [hoz'nar] VI (cão) to growl, snarl; (murmurar) to mutter, mumble

rosto ['hostu] M face

rota ['hɔta] F route, course

roteador [hotea'dor] M (BR: Comput) router

roteiro [ho'tejru] M itinerary; (ordem) schedule; (guia) guidebook; (de filme) script

rotina [ho'tʃina] F routine; **rotineiro, -a** [hotʃi'nejru, a] ADJ routine

roto, -a ['hotu, a] ADJ broken; (*rasgado*) torn

rotular [hotu'lar] VT to label; **rótulo** ['hotulu] M label

roubar [ho'bar] VT to steal; (*loja, casa, pessoa*) to rob ▶ VI to steal; (*em jogo, no preço*) to cheat; **~ algo a alguém** to steal sth from sb; **roubo** ['hobu] M theft, robbery

rouco, -a ['roku, a] ADJ hoarse

round ['hāwdʒi] (*pl* **-s**) M (*Boxe*) round

roupa ['hopa] F clothes *pl*, clothing; **~ de baixo** underwear; **~ de cama** bedclothes *pl*, bed linen

roupão [ho'pãw] (*pl* **-ões**) M dressing gown

rouxinol [hoʃi'nɔw] (*pl* **-óis**) M nightingale

roxo, -a ['hoʃu, a] ADJ purple, violet

royalty ['hɔjawtʃi] (*pl* **-ies**) M royalty

rua ['hua] F street; **~ principal** main street; **~ sem saída** no through road, cul-de-sac

rubéola [hu'bɛola] F (*Med*) German measles

rubi [hu'bi] M ruby

rubor [hu'bor] M blush; (*fig*) shyness, bashfulness

ruborizar-se [hubori'zarsi] VR to blush

rubrica [hu'brika] F (signed) initials *pl*

rubro, -a ['hubru, a] ADJ (*faces*) rosy, ruddy

ruço, -a ['husu, a] ADJ grey (*BRIT*), gray (*US*), dun; (*desbotado*) faded

rúcula ['hukula] F rocket (*BRIT*), arugula (*US*)

ruela ['hwɛla] F lane, alley

ruga ['huga] F (*na pele*) wrinkle; (*na roupa*) crease

ruge ['huʒi] M rouge

rugido [hu'ʒidu] M roar

rugir [hu'ʒir] VI to roar

ruído ['hwidu] M noise; **ruidoso, -a** [hwi'dozu, ɔza] ADJ noisy

ruim [hu'ĩ] (*pl* **-ns**) ADJ bad; (*defeituoso*) defective

ruína ['hwina] F ruin; (*decadência*) downfall

ruins [hu'ĩs] ADJ PL *de* **ruim**

ruir ['hwir] VI to collapse, go to ruin

ruivo, -a ['hwivu, a] ADJ red-haired ▶ M/F redhead

rum [hũ] M rum

rumo ['humu] M course, bearing; (*fig*) course; **~ a** bound for; **sem ~** adrift

rumor [hu'mor] M noise; (*notícia*) rumour (*BRIT*), rumor (*US*), report

ruptura [hup'tura] F break, rupture

rural [hu'raw] (*pl* **-ais**) ADJ rural

rush [hʌʃ] M rush; **(a hora do) ~** rush hour

Rússia ['husja] F: **a ~** Russia; **russo, -a** ['husu, a] ADJ, M/F Russian ▶ M (*Ling*) Russian

S

S. ABR (= *Santo/a, São*) St

SA ABR (= *Sociedade Anônima*) plc (BRIT), Inc. (US)

sã [sã] F *de* **são**

Saara [sa'ara] M: **o ~** the Sahara

sábado ['sabadu] M Saturday

sabão [sa'bãw] (*pl* **-ões**) M soap

sabedoria [sabedo'ria] F wisdom; (*erudição*) learning

saber [sa'ber] VT, VI to know; (*descobrir*) to find out ▶ M knowledge; **a ~** namely; **~ fazer** to know how to do, be able to do; **que eu saiba** as far as I know

sabiá [sa'bja] M/F thrush

sabido, -a [sa'bidu, a] ADJ knowledgeable; (*esperto*) shrewd

sabões [sa'bõjs] MPL *de* **sabão**

sabonete [sabo'netʃi] M toilet soap

sabor [sa'bor] M taste, flavour; flavor (US); **saborear** [sabo'rjar] VT to taste, savour (BRIT), savor (US); **saboroso, -a** [sabo'rozu, ɔza] ADJ tasty, delicious

sabotagem [sabo'taʒẽ] F sabotage

sabotar [sabo'tar] VT to sabotage

SAC ['saki] ABR M (= *serviço de atendimento ao cliente*) customer service

saca ['saka] F sack

sacar [sa'kar] VT to take out; (*dinheiro*) to withdraw; (*arma, cheque*) to draw; (*Esporte*) to serve; (*col: entender*) to understand ▶ VI (*col: entender*) to understand

saca-rolhas M INV corkscrew

sacerdote [saser'dɔtʃi] M priest

saciar [sa'sjar] VT (*fome etc*) to satisfy; (*sede*) to quench

saco ['saku] M bag; (*enseada*) inlet; **~ de café** coffee filter; **~ de dormir** sleeping bag

sacode [sa'kɔdʒi] VB *ver* **sacudir**

sacola [sa'kɔla] F bag

sacramento [sakra'mẽtu] M sacrament

sacrificar [sakrifi'kar] VT to sacrifice; **sacrificar-se** VR to sacrifice o.s.; **sacrifício** [sakri'fisju] M sacrifice

sacrilégio [sakri'lɛʒju] M sacrilege

sacro, -a ['sakru, a] ADJ sacred

sacudida [saku'dʒida] F shake

sacudir [saku'dʒir] VT to shake; **sacudir-se** VR to shake

sádico, -a ['sadʒiku, a] ADJ sadistic

sadio, -a [sa'dʒiu, a] ADJ healthy

safado, -a [sa'fadu, a] ADJ shameless; (*imoral*) dirty; (*travesso*) mischievous ▶ M rogue

safira [sa'fira] F sapphire

safra ['safra] F harvest

Sagitário [saʒi'tarju] M Sagittarius

sagrado, -a [sa'gradu, a] ADJ sacred, holy

saia ['saja] F skirt

saiba ['sajba] VB *ver* **saber**

saída [sa'ida] F exit, way out; (*partida*) departure; (*ato: de pessoa*) going out; (*fig: solução*) way out; (*Comput: de programa*) exit; (: *de dados*) output; **~ de emergência** emergency exit

sair [sa'ir] VI to go (*ou* come) out; (*partir*) to leave; (*realizar-se*) to turn out; (*Comput*) to exit; **sair-se** VR: **~-se bem/ mal de** to be successful/unsuccessful in

sal [saw] (*pl* **sais**) M salt; **sem ~** (*comida*) salt-free; (*pessoa*) lacklustre (BRIT), lackluster (US)

sala ['sala] F room; (*num edifício público*) hall; (*classe, turma*) class; **~ (de aula)** classroom; **~ de bate-papo** (*Internet*) chatroom; **~ de espera** waiting room; **~ (de estar)** living room; **~ de jantar** dining room; **~ de operação** (*Med*) operating theatre (BRIT) *ou* theater (US)

salada [sa'lada] F salad; (*fig*) confusion, jumble

sala e quarto (*pl* **-s, salas e quarto**) M two-room flat (BRIT) *ou* apartment (US)

salão [sa'lãw] (*pl* **-ões**) M large room, hall; (*exposição*) show; **~ de beleza** beauty salon

salário [sa'larju] M wages *pl*, salary

saldo ['sawdu] M balance; (*sobra*) surplus

saleiro [sa'lejru] M salt cellar

salgadinho [sawga'dʒiɲu] M savoury (BRIT), savory (US), snack

salgado, -a [saw'gadu, a] ADJ salty, salted

salgueiro [saw'gejru] M willow; **~ chorão** weeping willow

salientar [saljẽ'tar] vt to point out; (acentuar) to stress, emphasize; **saliente** [sa'ljẽtʃi] ADJ prominent; (evidente) clear, conspicuous; (importante) outstanding; (assanhado) forward

saliva [sa'liva] F saliva

salmão [saw'mãw] (pl -ões) M salmon

salmoura [saw'mora] F brine

salões [sa'lõjs] MPL de **salão**

salsa ['sawsa] F parsley

salsicha [saw'siʃa] F sausage; **salsichão** [sawsi'ʃãw] (pl -ões) M sausage

saltar [saw'tar] vt to jump (over), leap (over); (omitir) to skip ▶ vi to jump, leap; (sangue) to spurt out; (de ônibus, cavalo): **~ de** to get off

salto ['sawtu] M jump, leap; (de calçado) heel; **~ de vara** pole vault; **~ em altura** high jump; **~ em distância** long jump

salubre [sa'lubri] ADJ healthy, salubrious

salvamento [sawva'mẽtu] M rescue; (de naufrágio) salvage

salvar [saw'var] vt to save; (resgatar) to rescue; (objetos, de ruína) to salvage; (honra) to defend; **salvar-se** vr to escape

salva-vidas M INV (boia) lifebuoy ▶ M/F INV (pessoa) lifeguard; **barco ~** lifeboat

salvo, -a ['sawvu, a] ADJ safe ▶ PREP except, saving; **a ~** in safety

samba ['sãba] M samba

The greatest form of musical expression of the Brazilian people, the **samba** is a type of music and dance of African origin. It embraces a number of rhythmic styles, such as samba de breque, samba-enredo, samba-canção and pagode, among others. Officially, the first samba, entitled Pelo telefone, was written in Rio in 1917.

SAMU (BR) ABR M (= Serviço de Atendimento Móvel de Urgência) emergency ambulance service

sanar [sa'nar] vt to cure; (remediar) to remedy

sanção [sã'sãw] (pl -ões) F sanction; **sancionar** [sansjo'nar] vt to sanction

sandália [sã'dalja] F sandal

sandes ['sãdəs] (PT) F INV sandwich

sanduíche [sand'wiʃi] (BR) M sandwich

saneamento [sanja'mẽtu] M sanitation

sanear [sa'njar] vt to clean up

sangrar [sã'grar] vt, vi to bleed; **sangrento, -a** [sã'grẽtu, a] ADJ bloody; (Culin: carne) rare

sangue ['sãgi] M blood

sanguinário, -a [sãgi'narju, a] ADJ bloodthirsty

sanguíneo, -a [sã'ginju, a] ADJ: **grupo ~** blood group; **pressão sanguínea** blood pressure; **vaso ~** blood vessel

sanidade [sani'dadʒi] F (saúde) health; (mental) sanity

sanita [sa'nita] (PT) F toilet, lavatory

sanitário, -a [sani'tarju, a] ADJ sanitary; **vaso ~** toilet, lavatory (bowl); **sanitários** [sani'tarjus] MPL toilets

santo, -a ['sãtu, a] ADJ holy ▶ M/F saint

santuário [sã'twarju] M shrine, sanctuary

São [sãw] M Saint

são, sã [sãw, sã] (pl -s/-s) ADJ healthy; (conselho) sound; (mentalmente) sane; **~ e salvo** safe and sound

São Paulo [-'pawlu] N São Paulo

sapataria [sapata'ria] F shoe shop

sapateiro [sapa'tejru] M shoemaker; (vendedor) shoe salesman; (que conserta) shoe repairer; (loja) shoe repairer's

sapatilha [sapa'tʃiʎa] F (de balé) shoe; (sapato) pump; (de atleta) running shoe

sapato [sa'patu] M shoe

sapo ['sapu] M toad

saque¹ ['saki] M (de dinheiro) withdrawal; (Com) draft, bill; (Esporte) serve; (pilhagem) plunder, pillage; **~ a descoberto** (Com) overdraft

saque² VB ver **sacar**

saquear [sa'kjar] vt to pillage, plunder

sarampo [sa'rãpu] M measles sg

sarar [sa'rar] vt to cure; (ferida) to heal ▶ vi to recover

sarcasmo [sar'kazmu] M sarcasm

sarda ['sarda] F freckle

Sardenha [sar'deɲa] F: **a ~** Sardinia

sardinha [sar'dʒiɲa] F sardine

sargento [sar'ʒẽtu] M sergeant

sarjeta [sar'ʒeta] F gutter

Satã [sa'tã] M Satan

Satanás [sata'nas] M Satan

satélite [sa'tɛlitʃi] M satellite

sátira [ˈsatʃira] F satire

satisfazer [satʃisfa'zer] (irreg: como **fazer**) vt to satisfy ▶ vi to be satisfactory; **satisfazer-se** vr to be satisfied; (saciar-se) to fill o.s. up; **~ a** to satisfy; **satisfeito, -a** [satʃis'fejtu, a] ADJ satisfied; (saciado) full; **dar-se por satisfeito com algo** to be content with sth

saudação [sawda'sãw] (pl -ões) F greeting

saudade [saw'dadʒi] F longing, yearning; (lembrança nostálgica) nostalgia; **deixar ~s** to be greatly missed; **ter ~s de** (desejar) to long for;

(*sentir falta de*) to miss; **~s (de casa** *ou* **da família** *ou* **da pátria)** homesickness *sg*

saudar [saw'dar] VT to greet; (*dar as boas vindas*) to welcome; (*aclamar*) to acclaim

saudável [saw'davew] (*pl* **-eis**) ADJ healthy; (*moralmente*) wholesome

saúde [sa'udʒi] F health; (*brinde*) toast; **~!** (*brindando*) cheers!; (*quando se espirra*) bless you!; **beber à ~ de** to drink to, toast; **estar bem/mal de ~** to be well/ill

saudosismo [sawdo'zizmu] M nostalgia

saudoso, -a [saw'dozu, ɔza] ADJ (*nostálgico*) nostalgic; (*da família ou terra natal*) homesick; (*de uma pessoa*) longing; (*que causa saudades*) much-missed

sauna ['sawna] F sauna

saxofone [sakso'fɔni] M saxophone

sazonal [sazo'naw] (*pl* **-ais**) ADJ seasonal

scanner ['skaner] M scanner

PALAVRA-CHAVE

se [si] PRON **1** (*reflexivo: impess*) oneself; (: *m*) himself; (: *f*) herself; (: *coisa*) itself; (: *você*) yourself; (: *pl*) themselves; (: *vocês*) yourselves; **ela está se vestindo** she's getting dressed
2 (*uso recíproco*) each other, one another; **olharam-se** they looked at each other
3 (*impess*): **come-se bem aqui** you can eat well here; **sabe-se que ...** it is known that ...; **vende(m)-se jornais naquela loja** they sell newspapers in that shop
▶ CONJ if; (*em pergunta indireta*) whether; **se bem que** even though

sê [se] VB *ver* **ser**

sebe ['sɛbi] (*PT*) F fence; **~ viva** hedge

sebo ['sebu] M tallow; **seboso, -a** [se'bozu, ɔza] ADJ greasy; (*sujo*) dirty

seca ['seka] F drought

secador [seka'dor] M: **~ de cabelo/roupa** hairdryer/clothes horse

seção [se'sãw] (*pl* **-ões**) F section; (*em loja, repartição*) department

secar [se'kar] VT to dry; (*planta*) to parch ▶ VI to dry; to wither; (*fonte*) to dry up

seco, -a ['seku, a] ADJ dry; (*ríspido*) curt, brusque; (*magro*) thin; (*pessoa: frio*) cold; (: *sério*) serious

seções [se'sõjs] FPL *de* **seção**

secretaria [sekreta'ria] F general office; (*de secretário*) secretary's office; (*ministério*) ministry

secretária [sekre'tarja] F writing desk; **~ eletrônica** answering machine; *ver tb* **secretário**

secretário, -a [sekre'tarju, a] M/F secretary; **S~ de Estado de ...** Secretary of State for ...

século ['sɛkulu] M century; (*época*) age

secundário, -a [sekũ'darju, a] ADJ secondary

seda ['seda] F silk

sedativo [seda'tʃivu] M sedative

sede¹ ['sɛdʒi] F (*de empresa, instituição*) headquarters *sg*; (*de governo*) seat; (*Rel*) see, diocese

sede² ['sedʒi] F thirst; **estar com** *ou* **ter ~** to be thirsty; **sedento, -a** [se'dẽtu, a] ADJ thirsty

sediar [se'dʒjar] VT to base

sedução [sedu'sãw] (*pl* **-ões**) F seduction

sedutor, a [sedu'tor(a)] ADJ seductive; (*oferta etc*) tempting

seduzir [sedu'zir] VT to seduce; (*fascinar*) to fascinate

segmento [seg'mẽtu] M segment

segredo [se'gredu] M secret; (*sigilo*) secrecy; (*de fechadura*) combination

segregar [segre'gar] VT to segregate

seguidamente [segida'mẽtʃi] ADV (*sem parar*) continuously; (*logo depois*) soon afterwards

seguido, -a [se'gidu, a] ADJ following; (*contínuo*) continuous, consecutive; **~ de** *ou* **por** followed by; **três dias ~s** three days running; **horas seguidas** for hours on end; **em seguida** next; (*logo depois*) soon afterwards; (*imediatamente*) immediately, right away; **seguidor, a** M/F (*Mídias Soc*) follower

seguimento [segi'mẽtu] M continuation; **dar ~ a** to proceed with; **em ~ de** after

seguinte [se'gĩtʃi] ADJ following, next; **eu lhe disse o ~** this is what I said to him

seguir [se'gir] VT (*tb: Mídias Soc*) to follow; (*continuar*) to continue ▶ VI to follow; (*continuar*) to continue, carry on; (*ir*) to go; **seguir-se** VR: **~-se (a)** to follow; **logo a ~** next; **~-se (de)** to result (from)

segunda [se'gũda] F (*tb*: **~-feira**) Monday; (*Auto*) second (gear); **de ~** second-rate; **segunda-feira** (*pl* **segundas-feiras**) F Monday

segundo, -a [se'gũdu, a] ADJ second ▶ PREP according to ▶ CONJ as, from what ▶ ADV secondly ▶ M second; **de segunda mão** second-hand; **segunda (classe)** second-class; **~ ele disse** according to what he said; **~ dizem** apparently; **~ me consta** as far as I know; **segundas intenções** ulterior motives

seguramente [segura'metʃi] ADV certainly; (*muito provavelmente*) surely

segurança [segu'rãsa] F security; (*ausência de perigo*) safety; (*confiança*) confidence ▶ M/F security guard; **com ~** assuredly

segurar [segu'rar] VT to hold; (*amparar*) to hold up; (*Com: bens*) to insure ▶ VI: **~ em** to hold; **segurar-se** VR: **~-se em** to hold on to

seguro, -a [se'guru, a] ADJ safe; (*livre de risco, firme*) secure; (*certo*) certain, assured; (*confiável*) reliable; (*de si mesmo*) confident; (*tempo*) settled ▶ ADV confidently ▶ M (*Com*) insurance; **estar ~ de/de que** to be sure of/that; **fazer ~** to take out an insurance policy; **~ contra acidentes/incêndio** accident/fire insurance; **seguro-saúde** (*pl* **seguros-saúde**) M health insurance

sei [sej] VB *ver* **saber**

seio ['seju] M breast, bosom; (*âmago*) heart; **~ paranasal** sinus

seis [sejs] NUM six

seita ['sejta] F sect

seixo ['sejʃu] M pebble

seja ['seʒa] VB *ver* **ser**

sela ['sɛla] F saddle

selar [se'lar] VT (*carta*) to stamp; (*documento oficial, pacto*) to seal; (*cavalo*) to saddle

seleção [sele'sãw] (*pl* **-ões**) F selection; (*Esporte*) team

selecionar [selesjo'nar] VT to select

seleções [sele'sõjs] FPL *de* **seleção**

seleto, -a [se'lɛtu, a] ADJ select

selfie [selfi] F (*Tel*) selfie

selim [se'lĩ] (*pl* **-ns**) M saddle

selo ['selu] M stamp; (*carimbo, sinete*) seal

selva ['sewva] F jungle

selvagem [sew'vaʒẽ] (*pl* **-ns**) ADJ wild; (*feroz*) fierce; (*povo*) savage; **selvageria** [sewvaʒe'ria] F savagery

sem [sẽ] PREP without ▶ CONJ: **~ que eu peça** without my asking; **estar/ficar ~ dinheiro/gasolina** to have no/have run out of money/petrol

semáforo [se'maforu] M (*Auto*) traffic lights *pl*; (*Ferro*) signal

semana [se'mana] F week; **semanal** [sema'naw] (*pl* **-ais**) ADJ weekly; **semanário** [sema'narju] M weekly (publication)

semear [se'mjar] VT to sow; **semelhante** [seme'ʎãtʃi] ADJ similar; (*tal*) such ▶ M fellow creature

sêmen ['semẽ] M semen

semente [se'mẽtʃi] F seed

semestral [semes'traw] (*pl* **-ais**) ADJ half-yearly, bi-annual

semestre [se'mɛstri] M six months; (*Educ*) semester

semi... [semi] PREFIXO semi..., half...; **semicírculo** [semi'sirkulu] M semicircle; **semifinal** [semi'finaw] (*pl* **-ais**) F semi-final

seminário [semi'narju] M seminar; (*Rel*) seminary

sem-número M: **um ~ de coisas** loads of things

sempre ['sẽpri] ADV always; **você ~ vai?** (*PT*) are you still going?; **~ que** whenever; **como ~** as usual; **a comida/hora** *etc* **de ~** the usual food/time *etc*

sem-terra ADJ INV landless ▶ M/F INV landless labourer (BRIT) *ou* laborer (US)

sem-teto ADJ INV homeless ▶ M/F INV homeless person; **os ~** the homeless

sem-vergonha ADJ INV shameless ▶ M/F INV (*pessoa*) rogue

senado [se'nadu] M senate; **senador, a** [sena'dor(a)] M/F senator

senão [se'nãw] (*pl* **-ões**) CONJ otherwise; (*mas sim*) but, but rather ▶ PREP except ▶ M flaw, defect

senha ['sɛɲa] F sign; (*palavra de passe, Comput*) password; (*de caixa eletrônico*) PIN number; (*recibo*) receipt; (*passe*) pass

senhor, a [se'ɲor(a)] M (*homem*) man; (*formal*) gentleman; (*homem idoso*) elderly man; (*Rel*) lord; (*dono*) owner; (*tratamento*) Mr(.); (*tratamento respeitoso*) sir ▶ F (*mulher*) lady; (*esposa*) wife; (*mulher idosa*) elderly lady; (*dona*) owner; (*tratamento*) Mrs(.), Ms(.); (*tratamento respeitoso*) madam; **o ~/a ~a** (*você*) you; **nossa ~a!** (*col*) gosh; **sim, ~(a)!** yes indeed

senhorita [seɲo'rita] F young lady; (*tratamento*) Miss, Ms(.); **a ~** (*você*) you

senil [se'niw] (*pl* **-is**) ADJ senile

senões [se'nõjs] MPL *de* **senão**

sensação [sẽsa'sãw] (*pl* **-ões**) F sensation; **sensacional** [sẽsasjo'naw] (*pl* **-ais**) ADJ sensational

sensível [sẽ'sivew] (*pl* **-eis**) ADJ sensitive; (*visível*) noticeable; (*considerável*) considerable; (*dolorido*) tender

senso ['sẽsu] M sense; (*juízo*) judgement

sensual [sẽ'swaw] (*pl* **-ais**) ADJ sensual

sentado, -a [sẽ'tadu, a] ADJ sitting

sentar [sẽ'tar] VT to seat ▶ VI to sit; **sentar-se** VR to sit down

sentença [sẽ'tẽsa] F (*Jur*) sentence; **sentenciar** [sẽtẽ'sjar] VT (*julgar*) to pass judgement on; (*condenar por sentença*) to sentence

sentido, -a [sẽ'tʃidu, a] ADJ (*magoado*) hurt; (*choro, queixa*) heartfelt ▶ M sense; (*direção*) direction; (*atenção*) attention; (*aspecto*) respect; **~!** (*Mil*) attention!; **em certo ~** in a sense; **"~ único"** (PT: *sinal*) "one-way"

sentimental [sẽtʃimẽ'taw] (*pl* **-ais**) ADJ sentimental; **vida ~** love life

sentimento [sẽtʃi'mẽtu] M feeling; (*senso*) sense; **sentimentos** MPL (*pêsames*) condolences

sentinela [sẽtʃi'nɛla] F sentry, guard

sentir [sẽ'tʃir] VT to feel; (*perceber, pressentir*) to sense; (*ser afetado por*) to be affected by; (*magoar-se*) to be upset by ▶ VI to feel; (*sofrer*) to suffer; **sentir-se** VR to feel; (*julgar-se*) to consider o.s. (to be); **~ (a) falta de** to miss; **~ cheiro/gosto (de)** to smell/taste; **~ vontade de** to feel like; **sinto muito** I am very sorry

separação [separa'sãw] (*pl* **-ões**) F separation

separado, -a [sepa'radu, a] ADJ separate; **em ~** separately, apart

separar [sepa'rar] VT to separate; (*dividir*) to divide; (*pôr de lado*) to put aside; **separar-se** VR to separate; to be divided

sepultamento [sepuwta'mẽtu] M burial

sepultar [sepuw'tar] VT to bury; **sepultura** [sepuw'tura] F grave, tomb

sequência [se'kwẽsja] F sequence

sequer [se'kɛr] ADV at least; **(nem) ~** not even

sequestrar [sekwes'trar] VT (*bens*) to seize, confiscate; (*raptar*) to kidnap; (*avião etc*) to hijack; **sequestro** [se'kwɛstru] M seizure; (*rapto*) abduction, kidnapping; (*de avião etc*) hijack

(PALAVRA-CHAVE)

ser [ser] VI **1** (*descrição*) to be; **ela é médica/muito alta** she's a doctor/very tall; **é Ana** (*Tel*) Ana speaking *ou* here; **ela é de uma bondade incrível** she's incredibly kind; **ele está é danado** he's really angry; **ser de mentir/briga** to be the sort to lie/fight
2 (*horas, datas, números*): **é uma hora** it's one o'clock; **são seis e meia** it's half past six; **é dia 1º de junho** it's the first of June; **somos/são seis** there are six of us/them

3 (*origem, material*): **ser de** to be *ou* come from; (*feito de*) to be made of; (*pertencer*) to belong to; **sua família é da Bahia** his (*ou* her *etc*) family is from Bahia; **a mesa é de mármore** the table is made of marble; **é de Pedro** it's Pedro's, it belongs to Pedro

4 (*em orações passivas*): **já foi descoberto** it had already been discovered

5 (*locuções com subjun*): **ou seja** that is to say; **seja quem for** whoever it may be; **se eu fosse você** if I were you; **se não fosse você, ...** if it hadn't been for you ...

6 (*locuções*): **a não ser** except; **a não ser que** unless; **é** (*resposta afirmativa*) yes; **..., não é?** isn't it?, don't you? *etc*; **ah, é?** really?; **que foi?** (*o que aconteceu?*) what happened?; (*qual é o problema?*) what's the problem?; **será que ...?** I wonder if ...?
▶ M being; **seres** MPL (*criaturas*) creatures

sereia [se'reja] F mermaid

série ['sɛri] F series; (*sequência*) sequence, succession; (*Educ*) grade; (*categoria*) category; **fora de ~** out of order; (*fig*) extraordinary

seriedade [serje'dadʒi] F seriousness; (*honestidade*) honesty

seringa [se'rĩga] F syringe

sério, -a ['sɛrju, a] ADJ serious; (*honesto*) honest, decent; (*responsável*) responsible; (*confiável*) reliable; (*roupa*) sober ▶ ADV seriously; **a ~** seriously; **~?** really?

sermão [ser'mãw] (*pl* **-ões**) M sermon; (*fig*) telling-off

serpente [ser'pẽtʃi] F snake

serra ['sɛha] F (*montanhas*) mountains *pl*; (*Tec*) saw

serralheiro, -a [seha'ʎejru, a] M/F locksmith

serrano, -a [se'hanu, a] ADJ highland *atr* ▶ M/F highlander

serrar [se'har] VT to saw

sertanejo, -a [serta'neʒu, a] ADJ rustic, country ▶ M/F inhabitant of the *sertão*

sertão [ser'tãw] (*pl* **-ões**) M backwoods *pl*, bush (country)

servente [ser'vẽtʃi] M/F servant; (*operário*) labourer (BRIT), laborer (US)

serviçal [servi'saw] (*pl* **-ais**) ADJ obliging, helpful ▶ M/F servant; (*trabalhador*) wage earner

serviço [ser'visu] M service; (*de chá etc*) set; **estar de ~** to be on duty; **prestar ~** to help

servidor, a [servi'dor(a)] M/F servant; (*funcionário*) employee ▶ M (*Comput*) server; **~ público** civil servant

servil [ser'viw] (*pl* **-is**) ADJ servile

servir [ser'vir] VT to serve ▶ VI to serve; (*ser útil*) to be useful; (*ajudar*) to help; (*roupa: caber*) to fit; **servir-se** VR: **~-se (de)** (*comida, café*) to help o.s. (to); **~-se de** (*meios*) to use, make use of; **~ de** (*prover*) to supply with, provide with; **você está servido?** (*num bar*) are you all right for a drink?; **~ de algo** to serve as sth; **qualquer ônibus serve** any bus will do

servis [ser'vis] ADJ PL **de servil**

sessão [se'sãw] (*pl* **-ões**) F (*do parlamento etc*) session; (*reunião*) meeting; (*de cinema*) showing

sessenta [se'sẽta] NUM sixty

sessões [se'sõjs] FPL **de sessão**

sesta ['sɛsta] F siesta, nap

seta ['sɛta] F arrow

sete ['sɛtʃi] NUM seven

setembro [se'tẽbru] M September

Brazil's independence from Portugal is commemorated on 7 September (**7 de setembro**). Independence was declared in 1822 by the Portuguese prince regent, Dom Pedro, who rebelled against several orders from the Portuguese crown, among them the order to swear loyalty to the Portuguese constitution. It is a national holiday and the occasion for processions and military parades through the main cities.

setenta [se'tẽta] NUM seventy

sétimo, -a ['sɛtʃimu, a] NUM seventh

setor [se'tor] M sector

seu, sua [sew, 'sua] ADJ (*dele*) his; (*dela*) her; (*de coisa*) its; (*deles, delas*) their; (*de você, vocês*) your ▶ PRON (*dele*) his; (*dela*) hers; (*deles, delas*) theirs; (*de você, vocês*) yours ▶ M (*senhor*) Mr(.)

severidade [severi'dadʒi] F severity

severo, -a [se'vɛru, a] ADJ severe

sexo ['sɛksu] M sex

sexta ['sesta] F (*tb*: **~-feira**) Friday; **sexta-feira** (*pl* **sextas-feiras**) F Friday; **Sexta-feira Santa** Good Friday

sexto, -a ['sestu, a] NUM sixth

sexual [se'kswaw] (*pl* **-ais**) ADJ sexual; (*vida, ato*) sex *atr*

sexualidade [sekswali'dadʒi] F sexuality

sexy ['sɛksi] (*pl* **-s**) ADJ sexy

s.f.f. (*PT*) ABR = **se faz favor**

short ['ʃortʃi] M (pair of) shorts *pl*

si [si] PRON oneself; (*ele*) himself; (*ela*) herself; (*coisa*) itself; (*PT: você*) yourself, you; (: *vocês*) yourselves; (*eles, elas*) themselves

SIDA ['sida] (*PT*) ABR F (= *síndrome de deficiência imunológica adquirida*) AIDS

siderúrgica [side'ruʒika] F steel industry

sigilo [si'ʒilu] M secrecy

sigla ['sigla] F acronym; (*abreviação*) abbreviation

significado [signifi'kadu] M meaning

significar [signifi'kar] VT to mean, signify; **significativo, -a** [signifika'tʃivu, a] ADJ significant

signo ['signu] M sign

sigo ['sigu] VB *ver* **seguir**

sílaba ['silaba] F syllable

silenciar [silẽ'sjar] VT to silence

silêncio [si'lẽsju] M silence, quiet; **silencioso, -a** [silẽ'sjozu, ɔza] ADJ silent, quiet ▶ M (*Auto*) silencer (*BRIT*), muffler (*US*)

silhueta [si'ʎweta] F silhouette

silvestre [siw'vestri] ADJ wild

sim [sĩ] ADV yes; **creio que ~** I think so

símbolo ['sĩbolu] M symbol

simetria [sime'tria] F symmetry

similar [simi'lar] ADJ similar

simpatia [sĩpa'tʃia] F liking; (*afeto*) affection; (*afinidade, solidariedade*) sympathy; **simpatias** FPL (*inclinações*) sympathies; **simpático, -a** [sĩ'patʃiku, a] ADJ (*pessoa, decoração etc*) nice; (*lugar*) pleasant, nice; (*amável*) kind; **simpatizante** [sĩpatʃi'zãtʃi] ADJ sympathetic ▶ M/F sympathizer; **simpatizar** [sĩpatʃi'zar] VI: **simpatizar com** (*pessoa*) to like; (*causa*) to sympathize with

simples ['sĩplis] ADJ INV simple; (*único*) single; (*fácil*) easy; (*mero*) mere; (*ingênuo*) naïve ▶ ADV simply; **simplicidade** [sĩplisi'dadʒi] F simplicity; **simplificar** [sĩplifi'kar] VT to simplify

simular [simu'lar] VT to simulate

simultaneamente [simuwtanja'mẽtʃi] ADV simultaneously

simultâneo, -a [simuw'tanju, a] ADJ simultaneous

sinagoga [sina'gɔga] F synagogue

sinal [si'naw] (*pl* **-ais**) M sign; (*gesto, Tel*) signal; (*na pele*) mole; (: *de nascença*) birthmark; (*depósito*) deposit; (*tb*: **~ de tráfego luminoso**) traffic light; **por ~** (*por falar nisso*) by the way; (*aliás*) as a matter of fact; **~ de chamada** (*Tel*) ringing tone; **~ de discar** (BR) *ou* **de marcar** (PT) dialling tone (BRIT), dial tone (US); **~ de ocupado** (BR) *ou* **de impedido** (PT) engaged tone (BRIT), busy signal (US); **sinalização** [sinaliza'sãw] F (*ato*) signalling; (*para motoristas*) traffic signs pl

sincero, -a [sī'sɛru, a] ADJ sincere

sindicalista [sīdʒika'lista] M/F trade unionist

sindicato [sīdʒi'katu] M trade union; (*financeiro*) syndicate

síndrome ['sīdromi] F syndrome; **~ de Down** Down's syndrome

sinfonia [sīfo'nia] F symphony

singular [sīgu'lar] ADJ singular; (*extraordinário*) exceptional; (*bizarro*) odd, peculiar

sino ['sinu] M bell

sintaxe [sī'tasi] F syntax

síntese ['sītezi] F synthesis; **sintético, -a** [sī'tɛtʃiku, a] ADJ synthetic; **sintetizar** [sītetʃi'zar] VT to synthesize

sinto ['sītu] VB *ver* **sentir**

sintoma [sī'tɔma] M symptom

sinuca [si'nuka] F snooker

sinuoso, -a [si'nwozu, ɔza] ADJ (*caminho*) winding; (*linha*) wavy

siri [si'ri] M crab

sirvo ['sirvu] VB *ver* **servir**

sistema [sis'tema] M system; (*método*) method; **~ imunológico** immune system

site ['sajtʃi] M (*na Internet*) website; **~ de relacionamentos** social networking site

sítio ['sitʃju] M (*Mil*) siege; (*propriedade rural*) small farm; (PT: *lugar*) place

situação [sitwa'sãw] (*pl* **-ões**) F situation; (*posição*) position

situado, -a [si'twadu, a] ADJ situated

situar [si'twar] VT to place, put; (*edifício*) to situate, locate; **situar-se** VR to position o.s.; (*estar situado*) to be situated

slogan [iz'lɔgã] (*pl* **-s**) M slogan

smoking [iz'mokīs] (*pl* **-s**) M dinner jacket (BRIT), tuxedo (US)

só [sɔ] ADJ alone; (*único*) single; (*solitário*) solitary ▶ ADV only; **a sós** alone

soar [swar] VI to sound ▶ VT (*horas*) to strike; (*instrumento*) to play; **~ a** to sound like; **~ bem/mal** (*fig*) to go down well/badly

sob [sob] PREP under; **~ juramento** on oath; **~ medida** (*roupa*) made to measure

sobe ['sɔbi] VB *ver* **subir**

soberano, -a [sobe'ranu, a] ADJ sovereign; (*fig: supremo*) supreme ▶ M/F sovereign

sobra ['sɔbra] F surplus, remnant; **sobras** FPL remains; (*de tecido*) remnants; (*de comida*) leftovers; **ter algo de ~** to have sth extra; (*tempo, comida, motivos*) to have plenty of sth; **ficar de ~** to be left over

sobrado [so'bradu] M (*andar*) floor; (*casa*) house (*of two or more storeys*)

sobrancelha [sobrã'seʎa] F eyebrow

sobrar [so'brar] VI to be left; (*dúvidas*) to remain

sobre ['sobri] PREP on; (*por cima de*) over; (*acima de*) above; (*a respeito de*) about

sobrecarregar [sobrikahe'gar] VT to overload

sobremesa [sobri'meza] F dessert

sobrenatural [sobrinatu'raw] (*pl* **-ais**) ADJ supernatural

sobrenome [sobri'nɔmi] (BR) M surname, family name

sobrepor [sobri'por] (*irreg: como* **pôr**) VT: **~ algo a algo** to put sth on top of sth

sobressair [sobrisa'ir] VI to stand out; **sobressair-se** VR to stand out

sobressalente [sobrisa'lẽtʃi] ADJ, M spare

sobressalto [sobri'sawtu] M start; (*temor*) trepidation; **de ~** suddenly

sobretaxa [sobri'taʃa] F surcharge

sobretudo [sobri'tudu] M overcoat ▶ ADV above all, especially

sobrevivência [sobrivi'vẽsja] F survival; **sobrevivente** [sobrivi'vẽtʃi] ADJ surviving ▶ M/F survivor

sobreviver [sobrivi'ver] VI: **~ (a)** to survive

sobrinho, -a [so'briɲu, a] M/F nephew/niece

sóbrio, -a ['sɔbrju, a] ADJ sober; (*moderado*) moderate, restrained

socar [so'kar] VT (*esmurrar*) to hit, strike; (*calcar*) to crush, pound; (*massa de pão*) to knead

social [so'sjaw] (*pl* **-ais**) ADJ social; **socialista** [sosja'lista] ADJ, M/F socialist

sociedade [sosje'dadʒi] F society; (*Com: empresa*) company; (*associação*) association; **~ anônima** limited company (BRIT), incorporated company (US)

sócio, -a ['sɔsju, a] M/F (*Com*) partner; (*de clube*) member

soco ['soku] M punch; **dar um ~ em** to punch

socorrer [soko'her] VT to help, assist; (*salvar*) to rescue; **socorrer-se** VR:

~-se de to resort to, have recourse to;
socorro [so'kohu] M help, assistance;
(*reboque*) breakdown (BRIT) ou tow (US)
truck; **socorro!** help!; **primeiros
socorros** first aid *sg*

soda ['sɔda] F soda (water)

sofá [so'fa] M sofa, settee; **sofá-cama**
(*pl* **sofás-camas**) M sofa-bed

sofisticado, -a [sofistʃi'kadu, a] ADJ
sophisticated; (*afetado*) pretentious

sofrer [so'frer] VT to suffer; (*acidente*) to
have; (*aguentar*) to bear, put up with;
(*experimentar*) to undergo ▶ VI to suffer;
sofrido, -a [so'fridu, a] ADJ long-suffering;
sofrimento [sofri'mẽtu] M suffering

software [sof'twer] M (*Comput*) software

sogro, -a ['sogru, 'sɔgra] M/F
father-in-law/mother-in-law

sóis [sɔjs] MPL *de* **sol**

soja ['sɔʒa] F soya (BRIT), soy (US)

sol [sɔw] (*pl* **sóis**) M sun; (*luz*) sunshine,
sunlight; **fazer ~** to be sunny; **pegar ~**
to get the sun

sola ['sɔla] F sole

solar [so'lar] ADJ solar; **energia/painel ~**
solar energy/panel

soldado [sow'dadu] M soldier

soleira [so'lejra] F doorstep

solene [so'leni] ADJ solemn; **solenidade**
[soleni'dadʒi] F solemnity; (*cerimônia*)
ceremony

soletrar [sole'trar] VT to spell

solicitar [solisi'tar] VT to ask for;
(*emprego etc*) to apply for; (*amizade,
atenção*) to seek; **~ algo a alguém** to ask
sb for sth

solícito, -a [so'lisitu, a] ADJ helpful

solidão [soli'dãw] F solitude; (*sensação*)
loneliness

solidariedade [solidarje'dadʒi] F
solidarity

solidário, -a [soli'darju, a] ADJ (*pessoa*)
supportive; **ser ~ a** ou **com** (*pessoa*) to
stand by; (*causa*) to be sympathetic to,
sympathize with

sólido, -a ['sɔlidu, a] ADJ solid

solitário, -a [soli'tarju, a] ADJ lonely,
solitary ▶ M hermit

solo ['sɔlu] M ground, earth; (*Mús*) solo

soltar [sow'tar] VT to set free; (*desatar*) to
loosen; (*largar*) to let go of; (*emitir*) to
emit; (*grito, risada*) to let out; (*cabelo*) to
let down; (*freio, animais*) to release;
soltar-se VR to come loose; (*desinibir-se*)
to let o.s. go

solteirão, -rona [sowtej'rãw, rɔna]
(*pl* **-ões/-s**) ADJ unmarried ▶ M/F
bachelor/spinster

solteiro, -a [sow'tejru, a] ADJ single
▶ M/F single man/woman

solteirões [sowtej'rõjs] MPL *de*
solteirão

solto, -a ['sowtu, a] PP *de* **soltar** ▶ ADJ
loose; (*livre*) free; (*sozinho*) alone

solução [solu'sãw] (*pl* **-ões**) F solution

soluçar [solu'sar] VI (*chorar*) to sob;
(*Med*) to hiccup

solucionar [solusjo'nar] VT to solve;
(*decidir*) to resolve

soluço [so'lusu] M sob; (*Med*) hiccup

soluções [solu'sõjs] FPL *de* **solução**

som [sõ] (*pl* **-ns**) M sound; **~ cd** compact
disc player

soma ['sɔma] F sum; **somar** [so'mar] VT
(*adicionar*) to add (up); (*chegar a*) to add
up to, amount to ▶ VI to add up

sombra ['sõbra] F shadow; (*proteção*)
shade; (*indício*) trace, sign

sombrinha [sõ'briɲa] F parasol,
sunshade

some ['sɔmi] VB *ver* **sumir**

somente [sɔ'mẽtʃi] ADV only

somos ['somos] VB *ver* **ser**

sonâmbulo, -a [so'nãbulu, a] M/F
sleepwalker

sondar [sõ'dar] VT to probe; (*opinião etc*)
to sound out

soneca [so'nɛka] F nap, snooze

sonegar [sone'gar] VT (*dinheiro, valores*)
to conceal, withhold; (*furtar*) to steal,
pilfer; (*impostos*) to dodge, evade;
(*informações, dados*) to withhold

soneto [so'netu] M sonnet

sonhar [so'ɲar] VT, VI to dream; **~ com**
to dream about; **sonho** ['sɔɲu] M dream;
(*Culin*) doughnut

sono ['sɔnu] M sleep; **estar com** ou **ter ~**
to be sleepy

sonolento, -a [sono'lẽtu, a] ADJ sleepy,
drowsy

sonoro, -a [so'nɔru, a] ADJ resonant

sons [sõs] MPL *de* **som**

sonso, -a ['sõsu, a] ADJ sly, artful

sopa ['sopa] F soup

soporífero, -a [sopo'riferu, a] ADJ
soporific ▶ M sleeping drug

soprar [so'prar] VT to blow; (*balão*) to
blow up; (*vela*) to blow out; (*dizer em voz
baixa*) to whisper ▶ VI to blow; **sopro**
['sopru] M blow, puff; (*de vento*) gust

sórdido, -a ['sɔrdʒidu, a] ADJ sordid;
(*imundo*) squalid

soro ['soru] M (*Med*) serum

sorridente [sohi'dẽtʃi] ADJ smiling

sorrir [so'hir] VI to smile; **sorriso**
[so'hizu] M smile .

sorte ['sɔrtʃi] F luck; (casualidade) chance; (destino) fate, destiny; (condição) lot; (espécie) sort, kind; **de ~ que** so that; **dar ~** (trazer sorte) to bring good luck; (ter sorte) to be lucky; **estar com** ou **ter ~** to be lucky

sortear [sor'tʃjar] VT to draw lots for; (rifar) to raffle; (Mil) to draft; **sorteio** [sor'teju] M draw; (rifa) raffle; (Mil) draft

sortido, -a [sor'tʃidu, a] ADJ (abastecido) supplied, stocked; (variado) assorted; (loja) well-stocked

sortudo, -a [sor'tudu, a] (col) ADJ lucky

sorvete [sor'vetʃi] (BR) M ice cream

SOS ABR SOS

sossegado, -a [sose'gadu, a] ADJ peaceful, calm

sossegar [sose'gar] VT to calm, quieten ▶ VI to quieten down

sossego [so'segu] M peace (and quiet)

sótão ['sɔtãw] (pl **-s**) M attic, loft

sotaque [so'taki] M accent

soterrar [sote'har] VT to bury

sou [so] VB ver **ser**

soube ['sobi] VB ver **saber**

soutien [su'tʃjã] M = **sutiã**

sova ['sova] F beating, thrashing

sovaco [so'vaku] M armpit

sovina [so'vina] ADJ mean, stingy ▶ M/F miser

sozinho, -a [sɔ'ziɲu, a] ADJ (all) alone, by oneself; (por si mesmo) by oneself

spam [is'pã] (pl **-s**) M (Comput) spam

squash [is'kwɛʃ] M squash

Sr. ABR (= senhor) Mr

Sra. (BR), **Sr.a** (PT) ABR (= senhora) Mrs

Srta. (BR), **Sr.ta** (PT) ABR (= senhorita) Miss

sua ['sua] F de **seu**

suar [swar] VT, VI to sweat

suave ['swavi] ADJ gentle; (música, voz) soft; (sabor, vinho) smooth; (cheiro) delicate; (dor) mild; (trabalho) light; **suavidade** [suavi'dadʒi] F gentleness; softness

subalterno, -a [subaw'tɛrnu, a] ADJ, M/F subordinate

subconsciente [subkõ'sjetʃi] ADJ, M subconscious

subdesenvolvido, -a [subdʒizẽvow'vidu, a] ADJ underdeveloped

subentender [subẽtẽ'der] VT to understand, assume; **subentendido, -a** [subẽtẽ'dʒidu, a] ADJ implied ▶ M implication

subestimar [subestʃi'mar] VT to underestimate

subida [su'bida] F ascent, climb; (ladeira) slope; (de preços) rise

subir [su'bir] VI to go up; (preço, de posto etc) to rise ▶ VT to raise; (ladeira, escada, rio) to climb, go up; **~ em** to climb, go up; (cadeira, palanque) to climb onto, get up onto; (ônibus) to get on

súbito, -a ['subitu, a] ADJ sudden ▶ ADV (tb: **de ~**) suddenly

subjetivo, -a [subʒe'tʃivu, a] ADJ subjective

subjuntivo, -a [subʒũ'tʃivu, a] ADJ, M subjunctive

sublime [su'blimi] ADJ sublime

sublinhar [subli'ɲar] VT to underline; (destacar) to emphasize, stress

submarino, -a [subma'rinu, a] ADJ underwater ▶ M submarine

submeter [subme'ter] VT to subdue; (plano) to submit; (sujeitar) **~ a** to subject to; **submeter-se** VR: **~-se a** to submit to; (operação) to undergo

submisso, -a [sub'misu, a] ADJ submissive

subnutrição [subnutri'sãw] F malnutrition

subornar [subor'nar] VT to bribe; **suborno** [su'bornu] M bribery

subsequente [subse'kwẽtʃi] ADJ subsequent

subserviente [subser'vjẽtʃi] ADJ obsequious, servile

subsidiária [subsi'dʒjarja] F (Com) subsidiary (company)

subsidiário, -a [subsi'dʒjarju, a] ADJ subsidiary

subsídio [sub'sidʒu] M subsidy; (ajuda) aid

subsistência [subsis'tẽsja] F subsistence

subsistir [subsis'tʃir] VI to exist; (viver) to subsist

subsolo [sub'sɔlu] M (de prédio) basement

substância [sub'stãsja] F substance; **substancial** [substã'sjaw] (pl **-ais**) ADJ substantial

substantivo, -a [substã'tʃivu, a] ADJ substantive ▶ M noun

substituir [substʃi'twir] VT to substitute

subtil [sub'tiw] (PT) = **sutil** etc

subtrair [subtra'ir] VT to steal; (deduzir) to subtract ▶ VI to subtract

subumano, -a [subu'manu, a] ADJ subhuman; (desumano) inhuman

suburbano, -a [subur'banu, a] ADJ suburban

subúrbio [su'burbju] M suburb

subvenção [subvẽ'sãw] (pl -ões) F
subsidy, grant
subversivo, -a [subver'sivu, a] ADJ, M/F
subversive
sucata [su'kata] F scrap metal
sucção [suk'sãw] F suction
suceder [suse'der] VI to happen ▶ VT to
succeed; **~ a** (num cargo) to succeed;
(seguir) to follow
sucessão [suse'sãw] (pl -ões) F
succession; **sucessivo, -a** [suse'sivu, a]
ADJ successive
sucesso [su'sɛsu] M success; (música,
filme) hit; **fazer ou ter ~** to be successful
sucinto, -a [su'sĩtu, a] ADJ succinct
suco ['suku] (BR) M juice
suculento, -a [suku'lẽtu, a] ADJ
succulent
sucumbir [sukũ'bir] VI to succumb;
(morrer) to die, perish
sucursal [sukur'saw] (pl -ais) F (Com)
branch
Sudão [su'dãw] M: **o ~** (the) Sudan
sudeste [su'dɛstʃi] M south-east
súdito ['sudʒitu] M (de rei etc) subject
sudoeste [sud'wɛstʃi] M south-west
Suécia ['swɛsja] F: **a ~** Sweden;
sueco, -a ['swɛku, a] ADJ Swedish ▶ M/F
Swede ▶ M (Ling) Swedish
suéter ['swɛter] (BR) M ou F sweater
suficiente [sufi'sjẽtʃi] ADJ sufficient,
enough
sufixo [su'fiksu] M suffix
sufocar [sufo'kar] VT, VI to suffocate
sugar [su'gar] VT to suck
sugerir [suʒe'rir] VT to suggest
sugestão [suʒes'tãw] (pl -ões) F
suggestion; **dar uma ~** to make a
suggestion; **sugestivo, -a** [suʒes'tʃivu,
a] ADJ suggestive
sugiro [su'ʒiru] VB ver **sugerir**
Suíça ['swisa] F: **a ~** Switzerland
suíças ['swisas] FPL sideburns; ver tb
suíço
suicida [swi'sida] ADJ suicidal ▶ M/F
suicidal person; (morto) suicide;
suicidar-se [swisi'darsi] VR to commit
suicide; **suicídio** [swi'sidʒju] M suicide
suíço, -a ['swisu, a] ADJ, M/F Swiss
suíte ['switʃi] F (Mús, em hotel) suite
sujar [su'ʒar] VT to dirty ▶ VI to make a
mess; **sujar-se** VR to get dirty
sujeira [su'ʒejra] F dirt; (estado)
dirtiness; (col) dirty trick
sujeito, -a [su'ʒejtu, a] ADJ: **~ a** subject
to ▶ M (Ling) subject ▶ M/F man/woman
sujo, -a ['suʒu, a] ADJ dirty; (fig:
desonesto) dishonest ▶ M dirt

sul [suw] ADJ INV south, southern ▶ M:
o ~ the south; **sul-africano, -a** ADJ, M/F
South African; **sul-americano, -a** ADJ,
M/F South American
sulco [suw'ku] M furrow
suma ['suma] F: **em ~** in short
sumário, -a [su'marju, a] ADJ (breve)
brief, concise; (Jur) summary; (biquíni)
skimpy ▶ M summary
sumiço [su'misu] M disappearance
sumir [su'mir] VI to disappear, vanish
sumo, -a ['sumu, a] ADJ (importância)
extreme; (qualidade) supreme ▶ M (PT)
juice
sunga ['sũga] F swimming trunks pl
suor [swɔr] M sweat
super... [super-] PREFIXO super-, over-
superado, -a [supe'radu, a] ADJ (ideias)
outmoded
superalimento [super'alimẽtu] M
superfood
superar [supe'rar] VT (rival) to surpass;
(inimigo, dificuldade) to overcome;
(expectativa) to exceed
superfície [super'fisi] F surface;
(extensão) area; (fig: aparência)
appearance
supérfluo, -a [su'pɛrflwu, a] ADJ
superfluous
superior [supe'rjor] ADJ superior; (mais
elevado) higher; (quantidade) greater;
(mais acima) upper ▶ M superior;
superioridade [superjori'dadʒi] F
superiority
superlotado, -a [superlo'tadu, a] ADJ
crowded; (excessivamente cheio)
overcrowded
supermercado [supermer'kadu] M
supermarket
superpotência [superpo'tẽsja] F
superpower
superstição [superstʃi'sãw] (pl -ões) F
superstition; **supersticioso, -a**
[superstʃi'sjozu, ɔza] ADJ superstitious
supervisão [supervi'zãw] F supervision;
supervisionar [supervizjo'nar] VT to
supervise; **supervisor, a**
[supervi'zor(a)] M/F supervisor
suplemento [suple'mẽtu] M supplement
súplica ['suplika] F supplication, plea;
suplicar [supli'kar] VT, VI to plead, beg
suplício [su'plisju] M torture
supor [su'por] (irreg: como **pôr**) VT to
suppose; (julgar) to think
suportar [supor'tar] VT to hold up,
support; (tolerar) to bear, tolerate;
suportável [supor'tavew] (pl -eis) ADJ
bearable; **suporte** [su'portʃi] M support

suposto, -a [su'postu, 'pɔstu] ADJ
supposed ▶ M assumption, supposition
supremo, -a [su'prɛmu, a] ADJ supreme
suprimir [supri'mir] VT to suppress
surdo, -a ['surdu, a] ADJ deaf; (som)
muffled, dull ▶ M/F deaf person;
surdo-mudo, surda-muda ADJ hearing
and speech impaired ▶ M/F person with a
hearing and speech impairment
surfe ['surfi] M surfing
surfista [sur'fista] M/F surfer
surgir [sur'ʒir] VI to appear; (problema,
dificuldade) to arise
surjo ['surʒu] VB ver **surgir**
surpreendente [surprjẽ'dẽtʃi] ADJ
surprising
surpreender [surprjẽ'der] VT to
surprise; **surpreender-se** VR: **~-se (de)**
to be surprised (at); **surpresa**
[sur'preza] F surprise; **surpreso, -a**
[sur'prezu, a] PP de **surpreender** ▶ ADJ
surprised
surra ['suha] F: **dar uma ~ em** to thrash;
levar uma ~ (de) to get thrashed (by);
surrar [su'har] VT to beat, thrash
surtar [sur'tar] VI to freak out
surtir [sur'tʃir] VT to produce, bring
about
surto ['surtu] M (de doença) outbreak;
(ataque) outburst
SUS [sus] (BR) ABR M (= Sistema Único de
Saúde) national health service
suspeita [sus'pejta] F suspicion;
suspeitar [suspej'tar] VT to suspect ▶ VI:
suspeitar de algo to suspect sth;
suspeito, -a [sus'pejtu, a] ADJ, M/F
suspect
suspender [suspẽ'der] VT (levantar) to
lift; (pendurar) to hang; (trabalho,
pagamento etc) to suspend; (encomenda)
to cancel; (sessão) to adjourn, defer;
(viagem) to put off; **suspensão**
[suspẽ'sãw] (pl **-ões**) F (ger, Auto)
suspension; (de trabalho, pagamento)
stoppage; (de viagem, sessão) deferment;
(de encomenda) cancellation; **suspense**
[sus'pẽsi] M suspense; **filme de
suspense** thriller; **suspenso, -a**
[sus'pẽsu, a] PP de **suspender**
suspensórios [suspẽ'sɔrjus] MPL braces
(BRIT), suspenders (US)
suspirar [suspi'rar] VI to sigh; **suspiro**
[sus'piru] M sigh; (doce) meringue
sussurrar [susu'har] VT, VI to whisper;
sussurro [su'suhu] M whisper
sustentar [sustẽ'tar] VT to sustain;
(prédio) to hold up; (padrão) to maintain;
(financeiramente, acusação) to support;

sustentável [sustẽ'tavew] (pl **-eis**) ADJ
sustainable; **sustento** [sus'tẽtu] M
sustenance; (subsistência) livelihood;
(amparo) support
susto ['sustu] M fright, scare
sutiã [su'tʃjã] M bra(ssiere)
sutil [su'tʃiw] (pl **-is**) ADJ subtle; **sutileza**
[sutʃi'leza] F subtlety.

t

ta [ta] = **te** + **a**

tabacaria [tabaka'ria] F tobacconist's (shop)

tabaco [ta'baku] M tobacco

tabela [ta'bɛla] F table, chart; (*lista*) list; **por ~** indirectly

taberna [ta'bɛrna] F tavern, bar

tablet ['tablitʃ] (*pl* -**s**) M (*Comput*) tablet

tablete [ta'blɛtʃi] M (*de chocolate*) bar

tabu [ta'bu] ADJ, M taboo

tábua ['tabwa] F plank, board; (*Mat*) table; **~ de passar roupa** ironing board

tabuleiro [tabu'lejru] M tray; (*Xadrez*) board

tabuleta [tabu'leta] F (*letreiro*) sign, signboard

taça ['tasa] F cup

tacha ['taʃa] F tack

tachinha [ta'ʃiɲa] F drawing pin (*BRIT*), thumb tack (*US*)

taco ['taku] M (*Bilhar*) cue; (*Golfe*) club

tagarela [taga'rɛla] ADJ talkative ▶ M/F chatterbox; **tagarelar** [tagare'lar] VI to chatter

Tailândia [taj'lãdʒja] F: **a ~** Thailand

tal [taw] (*pl* **tais**) ADJ such; **~ e coisa** this and that; **um ~ de Sr. X** a certain Mr. X; **que ~?** what do you think?; (*PT*) how are things?; **que ~ um cafezinho?** what about a coffee?; **que ~ nós irmos ao cinema?** what about (us) going to the cinema?; **~ pai, ~ filho** like father, like son; **~ como** such as; (*da maneira que*) just as; **~ qual** just like; **o ~ professor** that teacher; **a ~ ponto** to such an extent; **de ~ maneira** in such a way; **e ~** and so on; **o/a ~** (*col*) the greatest; **o Pedro de ~** Peter what's-his-name; **na rua ~** in such and such a street; **foi um ~ de gente ligar lá para casa**

there were people ringing home non-stop

talão [ta'lãw] (*pl* -**ões**) M (*de recibo*) stub; **~ de cheques** cheque book (*BRIT*), check book (*US*)

talco ['tawku] M talcum powder; **pó de ~** (*PT*) talcum powder

talento [ta'lẽtu] M talent; (*aptidão*) ability

talha ['taʎa] F carving; (*vaso*) pitcher; (*Náut*) tackle

talher [ta'ʎer] M set of cutlery; **talheres** MPL cutlery *sg*

talo ['talu] M stalk, stem

talões [ta'lõjs] MPL *de* **talão**

talvez [taw'vez] ADV perhaps, maybe

tamanco [ta'mãku] M clog, wooden shoe

tamanduá [tamã'dwa] M anteater

tamanho, -a [ta'maɲu, a] ADJ such (a) great ▶ M size

tâmara ['tamara] F date

também [tã'bẽj] ADV also, too, as well; (*além disso*) besides; **~ não** not ... either, nor

tambor [tã'bor] M drum

tamborim [tãbo'rĩ] (*pl* -**ns**) M tambourine

Tâmisa ['tamiza] M: **o ~** the Thames

tampa ['tãpa] F lid; (*de garrafa*) cap

tampão [tã'pãw] (*pl* -**ões**) M tampon

tampar [tã'par] VT (*lata, garrafa*) to put the lid on; (*cobrir*) to cover

tampinha [tã'piɲa] F lid, top

tampo ['tãpu] M lid

tampões [tã'põjs] MPL *de* **tampão**

tampouco [tã'poku] ADV nor, neither

tangerina [tãʒe'rina] F tangerine

tanque ['tãki] M tank; (*de lavar roupa*) sink

tanto, -a ['tãtu, a] ADJ, PRON (*sg*) so much; (: + *interrogativa/negativa*) as much; (*pl*) so many; (: + *interrogativa/negativa*) as many ▶ ADV so much; **~ ... como ...** both ... and ...; **~ ...quanto ...** as much ... as ...; **~ tempo** so long; **quarenta e ~s anos** forty-odd years; **~ faz** it's all the same to me, I don't mind; **um ~ (quanto)** (*como adv*) rather, somewhat; **~ (assim) que** so much so that

tão [tãw] ADV so; **~ rico quanto** as rich as; **~ só** only

tapa ['tapa] M slap

tapar [ta'par] VT to cover; (*garrafa*) to cork; (*caixa*) to put the lid on; (*orifício*) to block up; (*encobrir*) to block out

tapear [ta'pjar] VT, VI to cheat

tapeçaria [tapesa'ria] F tapestry

tapete [ta'petʃi] M carpet, rug
tardar [tar'dar] VI to delay; (chegar tarde) to be late ▶ VT to delay; **sem mais ~** without delay; **~ a ou em fazer** to take a long time to do; **o mais ~** at the latest
tarde ['tardʒi] F afternoon ▶ ADV late; **mais cedo ou mais ~** sooner or later; **antes ~ do que nunca** better late than never; **boa ~!** good afternoon!; **à ou de ~** in the afternoon
tardio, -a [tar'dʒiu, a] ADJ late
tarefa [ta'rɛfa] F task, job; (faina) chore
tarifa [ta'rifa] F tariff; (para transportes) fare; (lista de preços) price list; **~ alfandegária** customs duty
tartaruga [tarta'ruga] F turtle
tasca ['taska] (PT) F cheap eating place
tática ['tatʃika] F tactics pl
tático, -a ['tatʃiku, a] ADJ tactical
tato ['tatu] M touch; (fig: diplomacia) tact
tatu [ta'tu] M armadillo
tatuagem [ta'twaʒẽ] (pl **-ns**) F tattoo
taxa ['taʃa] F (imposto) tax; (preço) fee; (índice) rate; **~ de câmbio** exchange rate; **~ de juros** interest rate; **taxação** [taʃa'sãw] F taxation; **taxar** [ta'ʃar] VT (fixar o preço de) to fix the price of; (lançar impostos sobre) to tax
táxi ['taksi] M taxi
taxista [tak'sista] M/F taxi driver
tchau [tʃaw] EXCL bye!
tcheco, -a ['tʃɛku, a] ADJ, M/F Czech; **a República Tcheca** the Czech Republic
te [tʃi] PRON you; (para você) (to) you
teatro ['tʃjatru] M theatre (BRIT), theater (US); (obras) plays pl, dramatic works pl; (gênero, curso) drama; **peça de ~** play
tecer [te'ser] VT, VI to weave; **tecido** [te'sidu] M cloth, material; (Anat) tissue
tecla ['tɛkla] F key; **teclado** [tek'ladu] M keyboard
técnica ['tɛknika] F technique; ver tb **técnico**
técnico, -a ['tɛkniku, a] ADJ technical ▶ M/F technician; (especialista) expert
tecnologia [teknolo'ʒia] F technology; **tecnológico, -a** [tekno'lɔʒiku, a] ADJ technological
tédio ['tɛdʒju] M tedium, boredom; **tedioso, -a** [te'dʒjozu, ɔza] ADJ tedious, boring
teia ['teja] F web; **~ de aranha** cobweb
teimar [tej'mar] VI to insist, keep on; **~ em** to insist on
teimosia [tejmo'zia] F stubbornness; **~ em fazer** insistence on doing
teimoso, -a [tej'mozu, ɔza] ADJ obstinate; (criança) wilful (BRIT), willful (US)

Tejo ['teʒu] M: **o (rio) ~** the (river) Tagus
tela ['tɛla] F fabric, material; (de pintar) canvas; (Cinema, TV) screen
tele... ['tele] PREFIXO tele...; **telecomunicações** [telekomunika'sõjs] FPL telecommunications; **teleconferência** [telekõfe'rẽsja] F teleconference
teleférico [tele'fɛriku] M cable car
telefonar [telefo'nar] VI: **~ para alguém** to (tele)phone sb
telefone [tele'fɔni] M phone, telephone; (número) (tele)phone number; (telefonema) phone call; **~ celular** cellphone, mobile phone; **~ de carro** carphone; **~ fixo** landline; **telefonema** [telefo'nɛma] M phone call; **dar um telefonema** to make a phone call; **telefônico, -a** [tele'foniku, a] ADJ telephone atr; **telefonista** [telefo'nista] M/F telephonist; (na companhia telefônica) operator
tele...: telegrama [tele'grama] M telegram, cable; **telejornal** [teleʒor'naw] (pl **-ais**) M television news sg; **telemóvel** [tele'mɔvel] (PT) (pl **-eis**) M mobile (phone) (BRIT), cellphone (US); **telenovela** [teleno'vɛla] F (TV) soap opera; **telescópio** [tele'skɔpju] M telescope; **telespectador, a** [telespekta'dor(a)] M/F viewer
televendas [tele'vẽdas] FPL telesales; **televisão** [televi'zãw] F television; **~ por assinatura** pay television; **~ a cabo** cable television; **~ a cores** colo(u)r television; **~ digital** digital television; **~ via satélite** satellite television; **aparelho de ~** television set; **televisionar** [televizjo'nar] VT to televise; **televisivo, -a** [televi'zivu, a] ADJ television atr; **televisor** [televi'zor] M (aparelho) television (set), TV (set)
telha ['teʎa] F tile; (col: cabeça) head; **ter uma ~ de menos** to have a screw loose
telhado [te'ʎadu] M roof
tema ['tema] M theme; (assunto) subject; **temática** [te'matʃika] F theme
temer [te'mer] VT to fear, be afraid of ▶ VI to be afraid
temeroso, -a [teme'rozu, ɔza] ADJ fearful, afraid; (pavoroso) dreadful
temido, -a [te'midu, a] ADJ fearsome, frightening
temível [te'mivew] (pl **-eis**) ADJ = **temido**
temor [te'mor] M fear
temperado, -a [tẽpe'radu, a] ADJ (clima) temperate; (comida) seasoned

temperamento [tẽpera'mẽtu] M
temperament, nature

temperar [tẽpe'rar] VT to season

temperatura [tẽpera'tura] F
temperature

tempero [tẽ'peru] M seasoning,
flavouring (BRIT), flavoring (US)

tempestade [tẽpes'tadʒi] F storm;
tempestuoso, -a [tẽpes'twozu, ɔza] ADJ
stormy

templo ['tẽplu] M temple; (igreja) church

tempo ['tẽpu] M time; (meteorológico)
weather; (Ling) tense; **o ~ todo** the
whole time; **a ~** on time; **ao mesmo ~**
at the same time; **a um ~** at once; **com
~** in good time; **de ~ em ~** from time to
time; **nesse meio ~** in the meantime;
quanto ~? how long?; **mais ~** longer;
há ~s for ages; (atrás) ages ago; **~ livre**
spare time; **primeiro/segundo ~**
(Esporte) first/second half

temporada [tẽpo'rada] F season;
(tempo) spell

temporal [tẽpo'raw] (pl **-ais**) M storm,
gale

temporário, -a [tẽpo'rarju, a] ADJ
temporary, provisional

tenacidade [tenasi'dadʒi] F tenacity

tencionar [tẽsjo'nar] VT to intend, plan

tenda ['tẽda] F tent

tendão [tẽ'dãw] (pl **-ões**) M tendon

tendões [tẽ'dõjs] MPL de **tendão**

tenebroso, -a [tene'brozu, ɔza] ADJ
dark, gloomy; (fig) horrible

tenho ['teɲu] VB ver **ter**

tênis ['tenis] M INV tennis; (sapatos)
training shoes pl; (um sapato) training
shoe; **~ de mesa** table tennis; **tenista**
[te'nista] M/F tennis player

tenor [te'nor] M (Mús) tenor

tenro, -a ['tẽhu, a] ADJ tender; (macio)
soft; (delicado) delicate; (novo) young

tensão [tẽ'sãw] F tension; (pressão)
pressure, strain; (rigidez) tightness; (Elet:
voltagem) voltage

tenso, -a ['tẽsu, a] ADJ tense; (sob
pressão) under stress, strained

tentação [tẽta'sãw] F temptation

tentáculo [tẽ'takulu] M tentacle

tentar [tẽ'tar] VT to try; (seduzir) to
tempt ▶ VI to try; **tentativa** [tẽta'tʃiva]
F attempt; **tentativa de homicídio/
suicídio/roubo** attempted murder/
suicide/robbery; **por tentativas** by trial
and error

tênue ['tenwi] ADJ tenuous; (fino) thin;
(delicado) delicate; (luz, voz) faint;
(pequeníssimo) minute

teor [te'or] M (conteúdo) tenor; (sentido)
meaning, drift

teoria [teo'ria] F theory; **teoricamente**
[teorika'mẽtʃi] ADV theoretically, in
theory; **teórico, -a** [te'ɔriku, a] ADJ
theoretical ▶ M/F theoretician

tépido, -a ['tɛpidu, a] ADJ tepid

PALAVRA-CHAVE

ter [ter] VT **1** (possuir, ger) to have; (na
mão) to hold; **você tem uma caneta?**
have you got a pen?; **ela vai ter neném**
she is going to have a baby

2 (idade, medidas, estado) to be; **ela tem
7 anos** she's 7 (years old); **a mesa tem
1 metro de comprimento** the table is
1 metre long; **ter fome/sorte** to be
hungry/lucky; **ter frio/calor** to be
cold/hot

3 (conter) to hold, contain; **a caixa tem
um quilo de chocolates** the box holds
one kilo of chocolates

4: **ter que** ou **de fazer** to have to do

5: **ter a ver com** to have to do with

6: **ir ter com** to (go and) meet

▶ VB IMPESS **1**: **tem** (sg) there is; (pl) there
are; **tem 3 dias que não saio de casa** I
haven't been out for 3 days

2: **não tem de quê** don't mention it

terapeuta [tera'pewta] M/F therapist

terapia [tera'pia] F therapy

terça ['tersa] F (tb: **~-feira**) Tuesday;
terça-feira (pl **terças-feiras**) F
Tuesday; **terça-feira gorda** Shrove
Tuesday

terceiro, -a [ter'sejru, a] NUM third;
terceiros MPL (os outros) outsiders; ver tb
quinto

terço ['tersu] M third (part)

termas ['termas] FPL bathhouse sg

térmico, -a ['termiku, a] ADJ thermal;
garrafa térmica (Thermos®) flask

terminal [termi'naw] (pl **-ais**) ADJ
terminal ▶ M (de rede, Elet, Comput)
terminal ▶ F terminal; **~ (de vídeo)**
monitor, visual display unit

terminar [termi'nar] VT to finish ▶ VI
(pessoa) to finish; (coisa) to end; **~ de
fazer** to finish doing; (ter feito há pouco)
to have just done; **~ por algo/fazer algo**
to end with sth/end up doing sth

término ['terminu] M end, termination

termo ['termu] M term; (fim) end,
termination; (limite) limit, boundary;
(prazo) period; (PT: garrafa) (Thermos®)
flask; **meio ~** compromise; **em ~s (de)**
in terms (of)

termômetro [ter'mometru] M
thermometer

terno, -a ['ternu, a] ADJ gentle, tender
▶ M (BR: *roupa*) suit; **ternura** [ter'nura] F
gentleness, tenderness

terra ['tɛha] F earth, world; (*Agr,
propriedade*) land; (*pátria*) country; (*chão*)
ground; (*Geo*) soil; (*pó*) dirt

terraço [te'hasu] M terrace

terramoto [teha'mɔtu] (PT) M
= **terremoto**

terreiro [te'hejru] M yard, square

terremoto [tehe'mɔtu] M earthquake

terreno, -a [te'henu, a] M ground, land;
(*porção de terra*) plot of land ▶ ADJ earthly

térreo, -a ['tɛhju, a] ADJ: **andar ~** (BR)
ground floor (BRIT), first floor (US)

terrestre [te'hɛstri] ADJ land *atr*

território [tehi'tɔrju] M territory

terrível [te'hivew] (*pl* **-eis**) ADJ terrible,
dreadful

terror [te'hoh] M terror, dread;
terrorista [teho'rista] ADJ, M/F terrorist;
terrorista suicida suicide bomber

tese ['tɛzi] F proposition, theory; (*Educ*)
thesis; **em ~** in theory

teso, -a ['tezu, a] ADJ (*cabo*) taut; (*rígido*)
stiff

tesouraria [tezora'ria] F treasury

tesouro [te'zoru] M treasure; (*erário*)
treasury, exchequer; (*livro*) thesaurus

testa ['tɛsta] F brow, forehead

testar [tes'tar] VT to test; (*deixar em
testamento*) to bequeath

teste ['tɛstʃi] M test

testemunha [teste'muɲa] F witness;
testemunhar [testemu'ɲar] VI to
testify ▶ VT to give evidence about;
(*presenciar*) to witness; (*confirmar*) to
demonstrate; **testemunho**
[teste'muɲu] M evidence

testículo [tes'tʃikulu] M testicle

teta ['tɛta] F teat

tétano ['tɛtanu] M tetanus

teto ['tɛtu] M ceiling; (*telhado*) roof;
(*habitação*) home

teu, tua [tew, 'tua] ADJ your ▶ PRON
yours

teve ['tevi] VB *ver* **ter**

têxtil ['testʃiw] (*pl* **-eis**) M textile

texto ['testu] M text

textura [tes'tura] F texture

thriller ['triler] (*pl* **-s**) M thriller

ti [tʃi] PRON you

tia ['tʃia] F aunt

Tibete [tʃi'bɛtʃi] M: **o ~** Tibet

TIC [tʃik] ABR F (= *Tecnologia de Informação
e Comunicação*) ICT

tido, -a ['tʃidu, a] PP *de* **ter** ▶ ADJ: **~ como
ou por** considered to be

tigela [tʃi'ʒɛla] F bowl

tigre ['tʃigri] M tiger

tijolo [tʃi'ʒolu] M brick

til [tʃiw] (*pl* **tis**) M tilde

timbre ['tʃibri] M insignia, emblem;
(*selo*) stamp; (*Mús*) tone, timbre; (*de voz*)
tone; (*em papel de carta*) heading

time ['tʃimi] (BR) M team; **de segundo ~**
(*fig*) second-rate

tímido, -a ['tʃimidu, a] ADJ shy, timid

tímpano ['tʃipanu] M eardrum; (*Mús*)
kettledrum

tingir [tʃi'ʒir] VT to dye; (*fig*) to tinge

tinha ['tʃiɲa] VB *ver* **ter**

tinjo ['tʃiʒu] VB *ver* **tingir**

tinta ['tʃita] F (*de pintar*) paint; (*de
escrever*) ink; (*para tingir*) dye; (*fig:
vestígio*) shade, tinge

tinto, -a ['tʃitu, a] ADJ dyed; (*fig*) stained;
vinho ~ red wine

tintura [tʃi'tura] F dye; (*ato*) dyeing; (*fig*)
tinge, hint

tinturaria [tʃitura'ria] F dry-cleaner's

tio ['tʃiu] M uncle

típico, -a ['tʃipiku, a] ADJ typical

tipo ['tʃipu] M type; (*de imprensa*) print;
(*de impressora*) typeface; (*col: sujeito*) guy,
chap; (*pessoa*) person

tipografia [tʃipogra'fia] F printing;
(*estabelecimento*) printer's

tíquete ['tʃiketʃi] M ticket

tira ['tʃira] F strip ▶ M (BR *col*) cop

tira-gosto (*pl* **-s**) M snack, savoury (BRIT)

tirano, -a [tʃi'ranu, a] ADJ tyrannical
▶ M/F tyrant

tirar [tʃi'rar] VT to take away; (*de dentro*)
to take out; (*de cima*) to take off; (*roupa,
sapatos*) to take off; (*arrancar*) to pull out;
(*férias*) to take, have; (*boas notas*) to get;
(*salário*) to earn; (*curso*) to do, take;
(*mancha*) to remove; (*foto, cópia*) to take;
(*mesa*) to clear; **~ algo a alguém** to take
sth from sb

tiritar [tʃiri'tar] VI to shiver

tiro ['tʃiru] M shot; (*ato de disparar*)
shooting; **~ ao alvo** target practice;
trocar ~s to fire at one another

tiroteio [tʃiro'teju] M shooting,
exchange of shots

tis [tʃis] MPL *de* **til**

titular [tʃitu'lar] ADJ titular ▶ M/F holder

título ['tʃitulu] M title; (*Com*) bond;
(*universitário*) degree; **~ de propriedade**
title deed

tive ['tʃivi] VB *ver* **ter**

to [tu] = **te** + **o**

toa ['toa] F towrope; **à ~** at random; (*sem motivo*) for no reason; (*inutilmente*) for nothing

toalete [twa'lɛtʃi] M (*banheiro*) toilet
▶ F: **fazer a ~** to have a wash

toalha [to'aʎa] F towel

toca ['tɔka] F burrow, hole

toca-discos (BR) M INV record-player

tocador [toka'dor] M player; **~ MP3** MP3 player

toca-fitas M INV cassette player

tocaia [to'kaja] F ambush

tocante [to'kãtʃi] ADJ moving, touching; **no ~ a** regarding, concerning

tocar [to'kar] VT to touch; (*Mús*) to play
▶ VI to touch; (*Mús*) to play; (*campainha, sino, telefone*) to ring; **tocar-se** VR to touch (each other); **~ a** (*dizer respeito a*) to concern, affect; **~ em** to touch; (*assunto*) to touch upon; **~ para alguém** (*telefonar*) to ring sb (up), call sb (up); **pelo que me toca** as far as I am concerned

tocha ['tɔʃa] F torch

todavia [toda'via] ADV yet, still, however

(PALAVRA-CHAVE)

todo, -a ['todu, 'tɔda] ADJ **1** (*com artigo sg*) all; **toda a carne** all the meat; **toda a noite** all night, the whole night; **todo o Brasil** the whole of Brazil; **a toda (velocidade)** at full speed; **todo o mundo** (BR), **toda a gente** (PT) everybody, everyone; **em toda (a) parte** everywhere

2 (*com artigo pl*) all; (: *cada*) every; **todos os livros** all the books; **todos os dias/ todas as noites** every day/night; **todos os que querem sair** all those who want to leave; **todos nós** all of us
▶ ADV: **ao todo** altogether; (*no total*) in all; **de todo** completely
▶ PRON: **todos** everybody *sg*, everyone *sg*

todo-poderoso, -a ADJ all-powerful
▶ M: **o T~** the Almighty

toicinho [toj'siɲu] M bacon fat

tolerância [tole'rãsja] F tolerance; **tolerante** [tole'rãtʃi] ADJ tolerant

tolerar [tole'rar] VT to tolerate; **tolerável** [tole'ravew] (*pl* **-eis**) ADJ tolerable, bearable; (*satisfatório*) passable; (*falta*) excusable

tolice [to'lisi] F stupidity, foolishness; (*ato, dito*) stupid thing

tom [tõ] (*pl* **-ns**) M tone; (*Mús: altura*) pitch; (: *escala*) key; (*cor*) shade

tomada [to'mada] F capture; (*Elet*) socket

tomar [to'mar] VT to take; (*capturar*) to capture, seize; (*decisão*) to make; (*bebida*) to drink; **~ café** (*de manhã*) to have breakfast

tomara [to'mara] EXCL: **~!** if only!; **~ que venha hoje** I hope he comes today

tomate [to'matʃi] M tomato

tombadilho [tõba'dʒiʎu] M deck

tombar [tõ'bar] VI to fall down, tumble down ▶ VT to knock down, knock over; **tombo** ['tõbu] M tumble, fall

tomilho [to'miʎu] M thyme

tona ['tɔna] F surface; **vir à ~** to come to the surface; (*fig*) to emerge; **trazer à ~** to bring up; (*recordações*) to bring back

tonalidade [tonali'dadʒi] F (*de cor*) shade

tonelada [tone'lada] F ton

tônica ['tonika] F (*água*) tonic (water); (*fig*) keynote

tônico, -a ['toniku, a] ADJ tonic ▶ M tonic; **acento ~** stress

tons [tõs] MPL *de* **tom**

tonteira [tõ'tejra] F dizziness

tonto, -a ['tõtu, a] ADJ stupid, silly; (*zonzo*) dizzy, lightheaded; (*atarantado*) flustered

topar [to'par] VT to agree to ▶ VI: **~ com** to come across; **topar-se** VR (*duas pessoas*) to run into one another; **~ em** (*tropeçar*) to stub one's toe on; (*esbarrar*) to run into; (*tocar*) to touch

tópico, -a ['tɔpiku, a] ADJ topical ▶ M topic

topless [tɔp'lɛs] ADJ INV topless

topo ['topu] M top; (*extremidade*) end, extremity

toque VB *ver* **tocar**

Tóquio ['tɔkju] N Tokyo

tora ['tɔra] F (*pedaço*) piece; (*de madeira*) log; (*sesta*) nap

toranja [to'rãʒa] F grapefruit

torção [tor'sãw] (*pl* **-ões**) M twist; (*Med*) sprain

torcedor, a [torse'dor(a)] M/F supporter, fan

torcer [tor'ser] VT to twist; (*Med*) to sprain; (*desvirtuar*) to distort, misconstrue; (*roupa: espremer*) to wring; (: *na máquina*) to spin; (*vergar*) to bend
▶ VI: **~ por** (*time*) to support; **torcer-se** VR to squirm, writhe

torcicolo [torsi'kɔlu] M stiff neck

torcida [tor'sida] F (*pavio*) wick; (*Esporte: ato de torcer*) cheering; (: *torcedores*) supporters *pl*

torções [tor'sõjs] MPL *de* **torção**

tormenta [tor'mẽta] F storm

tormento [tor'mẽtu] M torment; (*angústia*) anguish

tornar [tor'nar] VI to return, go back ▶ VT: **~ algo em algo** to turn *ou* make sth into sth; **tornar-se** VR to become; **~ a fazer algo** to do sth again

torneio [tor'neju] M tournament

torneira [tor'nejra] F tap (*BRIT*), faucet (*US*)

tornozelo [torno'zelu] M ankle

torpedo [tor'pedu] M (*bomba*) torpedo; (*col: mensagem*) text (message)

torrada [to'hada] F toast; **uma ~** a piece of toast; **torradeira** [toha'dejra] F toaster

torrão [to'hãw] (*pl -ões*) M turf, sod; (*terra*) soil, land; (*de açúcar*) lump

torrar [to'har] VT to toast; (*café*) to roast

torre ['tohi] F tower; (*Xadrez*) castle, rook; (*Elet*) pylon; **~ de controle** (*Aer*) control tower

tórrido, -a ['tɔhidu, a] ADJ torrid

torrões [to'hõjs] MPL *de* **torrão**

torso ['torsu] M torso

torta ['tɔrta] F pie, tart

torto, -a ['tortu, 'tɔrta] ADJ twisted, crooked; **a ~ e a direito** indiscriminately

tortuoso, -a [tor'twozu, ɔza] ADJ winding

tortura [tor'tura] F torture; (*fig*) anguish; **torturar** [tortu'rar] VT to torture; to torment

tos [tus] = **te + os**

tosco, -a ['tosku, a] ADJ rough, unpolished; (*grosseiro*) coarse, crude

tosse ['tɔsi] F cough; **~ de cachorro** whooping cough; **tossir** [to'sir] VI to cough

tosta ['tɔsta] (*PT*) F toast; **~ mista** toasted cheese and ham sandwich

tostão [tos'tãw] M cash

tostar [tos'tar] VT to toast; (*pele, pessoa*) to tan; **tostar-se** VR to get tanned

total [to'taw] (*pl -ais*) ADJ, M total

touca ['toka] F bonnet; **~ de banho** bathing cap

tourada [to'rada] F bullfight; **toureiro** [to'rejru] M bullfighter

touro ['toru] M bull; **T~** (*Astrologia*) Taurus

tóxico, -a ['tɔksiku, a] ADJ toxic ▶ M poison; (*droga*) drug; **toxicômano, -a** [toksi'komanu, a] M/F drug addict

TPM ABR F (= *tensão pré-menstrual*) PMT

trabalhador, a [trabaʎa'dor(a)] ADJ hard-working, industrious; (*Pol: classe*) working ▶ M/F worker

trabalhar [traba'ʎar] VI to work ▶ VT (*terra*) to till; (*madeira, metal*) to work; (*texto*) to work on; **~ com** (*comerciar*) to deal in; **~ de** *ou* **como** to work as; **trabalhista** [traba'ʎista] ADJ labour *atr* (*BRIT*), labor *atr* (*US*); **trabalho** [tra'baʎu] M work; (*emprego, tarefa*) job; (*Educ: tarefa*) assignment; **trabalho braçal** manual work; **trabalho doméstico** housework; **trabalhoso, -a** [traba'ʎozu, ɔza] ADJ laborious, arduous

traça ['trasa] F moth

traçado [tra'sadu] M sketch, plan

tração [tra'sãw] F traction

traçar [tra'sar] VT to draw; (*determinar*) to set out, outline; (*planos*) to draw up; (*escrever*) to compose

tradição [tradʒi'sãw] (*pl -ões*) F tradition; **tradicional** [tradʒisjo'naw] (*pl -ais*) ADJ traditional

tradução [tradu'sãw] (*pl -ões*) F translation

tradutor, a [tradu'tor(a)] M/F translator

traduzir [tradu'zir] VT to translate

trafegar [trafe'gar] VI to move, go

tráfego ['trafegu] M traffic

traficante [trafi'kãtʃi] M/F trafficker, dealer

traficar [trafi'kar] VI: **~ (com)** to deal (in)

tráfico ['trafiku] M traffic

tragar [tra'gar] VT to swallow; (*fumaça*) to inhale; (*suportar*) to tolerate ▶ VI to inhale

tragédia [tra'ʒɛdʒja] F tragedy; **trágico, -a** ['traʒiku, a] ADJ tragic

trago¹ ['tragu] M mouthful

trago² VB *ver* **trazer**

traiçoeiro, -a [traj'swejru, a] ADJ treacherous

traidor, a [traj'dor(a)] M/F traitor

trailer ['trejler] (*pl -s*) M trailer; (*tipo casa*) caravan (*BRIT*), trailer (*US*)

trair [tra'ir] VT to betray; (*mulher, marido*) to be unfaithful to; (*esperanças*) not to live up to; **trair-se** VR to give o.s. away

trajar [tra'ʒar] VT to wear

traje ['traʒi] M dress, clothes *pl*; **~ de banho** swimsuit

trajeto [tra'ʒɛtu] M course, path

trajetória [traʒe'tɔrja] F trajectory, path; (*fig*) course

tralha ['traʎa] F fishing net

trama ['trama] F (*tecido*) weft (*BRIT*), woof (*US*); (*enredo, conspiração*) plot

tramar [tra'mar] VT (*tecer*) to weave; (*maquinar*) to plot ▶ VI: **~ contra** to conspire against

trâmites ['tramitʃis] MPL procedure *sg*, channels

trampolim [trãpo'lĩ] (*pl* **-ns**) M trampoline; (*de piscina*) diving board; (*fig*) springboard

tranca ['trãka] F (*de porta*) bolt; (*de carro*) lock

trança ['trãsa] F (*cabelo*) plait; (*galão*) braid

trancar [trã'kar] VT to lock

tranquilidade [trãkwili'dadʒi] F tranquillity; (*paz*) peace

tranquilizante [trãkwili'zãtʃi] M (*Med*) tranquillizer

tranquilizar [trãkwili'zar] VT to calm, quieten; (*despreocupar*) **~ alguém** to reassure sb, put sb's mind at rest; **tranquilizar-se** VR to calm down

tranquilo, -a [trã'kwilu, a] ADJ peaceful; (*mar, pessoa*) calm; (*criança*) quiet; (*consciência*) clear; (*seguro*) sure, certain

transação [trãza'sãw] (*pl* **-ões**) F transaction

transar [trã'zar] (BR col) VI (*ter relação sexual*) to have sex

transbordar [trãzbor'dar] VI to overflow

transbordo [trãz'bordu] M (*de viajantes*) change, transfer

transe ['trãzi] M ordeal; (*lance*) plight; (*hipnótico*) trance

transeunte [trã'zjũtʃi] M/F passer-by

transferência [trãsfe'rẽsja] F transfer

transferir [trãsfe'rir] VT to transfer; (*adiar*) to postpone

transformação [trãsforma'sãw] (*pl* **-ões**) F transformation

transformador [trãsforma'dor] M (*Elet*) transformer

transformar [trãsfor'mar] VT to transform; **transformar-se** VR to turn

transfusão [trãsfu'zãw] (*pl* **-ões**) F transfusion

transgênico, -a [trãz'ʒeniku, a] ADJ (*planta, alimento*) genetically modified, GM

transição [trãzi'sãw] (*pl* **-ões**) F transition

transitivo, -a [trãzi'tʃivu, a] ADJ (*Ling*) transitive

trânsito ['trãzitu] M transit, passage; (*na rua: veículos*) traffic; (: *pessoas*) flow; **transitório, -a** [trãzi'tɔrju, a] ADJ transitory; (*período*) transitional

transmissão [trãzmi'sãw] (*pl* **-ões**) F transmission; (*transferência*) transfer; **~ ao vivo** live broadcast

transmissor, a [trãzmi'sor(a)] ADJ transmitting ▶ M transmitter

transmitir [trãzmi'tʃir] VT to transmit; (*Rádio, TV*) to broadcast; (*transferir*) to transfer; (*recado, notícia*) to pass on

transparente [trãspa'rẽtʃi] ADJ transparent; (*roupa*) see-through; clear

transpirar [trãspi'rar] VI to perspire; (*divulgar-se*) to become known; (*verdade*) to come out ▶ VT to exude

transplante [trãs'plãtʃi] M transplant

transportar [trãspor'tar] VT to transport; (*levar*) to carry; (*enlevar*) to entrance, enrapture

transporte [trãs'pɔrtʃi] M transport; (*Com*) haulage

transtorno [trãs'tornu] M upset, disruption

trapalhão, -lhona [trapa'ʎãw, 'ʎona] (*pl* **-ões/-s**) M/F bungler, blunderer

trapo ['trapu] M rag

trarei [tra'rej] VB *ver* **trazer**

trás [trajs] PREP, ADV: **para ~** backwards; **por ~ de** behind; **de ~** from behind

traseira [tra'zejra] F rear; (*Anat*) bottom

traste ['trastʃi] M thing; (*coisa sem valor*) piece of junk

tratado [tra'tadu] M treaty

tratamento [trata'mẽtu] M treatment

tratar [tra'tar] VT to treat; (*tema*) to deal with; (*combinar*) to agree ▶ VI: **~ com** to deal with; (*combinar*) to agree with; **~ de** to deal with; **de que se trata?** what is it about?

trato ['tratu] M treatment; (*contrato*) agreement, contract; **tratos** MPL (*relações*) dealings

trator [tra'tor] M tractor

trauma ['trawma] M trauma

travão [tra'vãw] (PT) (*pl* **-ões**) M brake

travar [tra'var] VT (*roda*) to lock; (*iniciar*) to engage in; (*conversa*) to strike up; (*luta*) to wage; (*carro*) to stop; (*passagem*) to block; (*movimentos*) to hinder ▶ VI (PT) to brake

trave ['travi] F beam; (*Esporte*) crossbar

través [tra'vɛs] M slant, incline; **de ~** across, sideways

travessa [tra'vɛsa] F crossbeam, crossbar; (*rua*) lane, alley; (*prato*) dish; (*para o cabelo*) comb, slide

travessão [trave'sãw] (*pl* **-ões**) M (*de balança*) bar, beam; (*pontuação*) dash

travesseiro [trave'sejru] M pillow

travessia [trave'sia] F (*viagem*) journey, crossing

travessões [trave'sõjs] MPL *de* **travessão**

travessura [trave'sura] F mischief, prank

travões [tra'võjʃ] MPL de **travão**

trazer [tra'zer] VT to bring

trecho ['treʃu] M passage; (de rua, caminho) stretch; (espaço) space

trégua ['trɛgwa] F truce; (descanso) respite

treinador, a [trejna'dor(a)] M/F trainer

treinamento [trejna'mētu] M training

treinar [trej'nar] VT to train; **treinar-se** VR to train; **treino** ['trejnu] M training

trejeito [tre'ʒejtu] M gesture; (careta) grimace, face

trem [trēj] (pl -ns) M train; **~ de aterrissagem** (avião) landing gear

tremendo, -a [tre'mēdu, a] ADJ tremendous; (terrível) terrible, awful

tremer [tre'mer] VI to shudder, quake; (terra) to shake; (de frio, medo) to shiver

trêmulo, -a ['tremulu, a] ADJ shaky, trembling

trenó [tre'nɔ] M sledge, sleigh (BRIT), sled (US)

trens [trējʃ] MPL de **trem**

trepar [tre'par] VT to climb ▶ VI: **~ em** to climb

trepidar [trepi'dar] VI to tremble, shake

três [tres] NUM three; ver tb **cinco**

trevas ['trɛvaʃ] FPL darkness sg

treze ['trezi] NUM thirteen

triângulo ['trjãgulu] M triangle

tribal [tri'baw] (pl -ais) ADJ tribal

tribo ['tribu] F tribe

tribuna [tri'buna] F platform, rostrum; (Rel) pulpit

tribunal [tribu'naw] (pl -ais) M court; (comissão) tribunal

tributo [tri'butu] M tribute; (imposto) tax

tricô [tri'ko] M knitting; **tricotar** [triko'tar] VT, VI to knit

trigo ['trigu] M wheat

trilha ['triʎa] F (caminho) path; (rasto) track, trail; **~ sonora** soundtrack

trilhão [tri'ʎãw] (pl -ões) M billion (BRIT), trillion (US)

trilho ['triʎu] M (BR Ferro) rail; (vereda) path, track

trilhões [tri'ʎõjʃ] MPL de **trilhão**

trimestral [trimeʃ'traw] (pl -ais) ADJ quarterly; **trimestralmente** [trimeʃtraw'mētʃi] ADV quarterly

trimestre [tri'meʃtri] M (Educ) term; (Com) quarter

trincar [trī'kar] VT to crunch; (morder) to bite; (dentes) to grit ▶ VI to crunch

trinco ['trīku] M latch

trinta ['trīta] NUM thirty

trio ['triu] M trio; **~ elétrico** see note

> **Trios elétricos** are trucks, carrying floats equipped for sound and/or live music, which parade through the streets during carnaval, especially in Bahia. Bands and popular performers on the floats draw crowds by giving frenzied performances of various types of music.

tripa ['tripa] F gut, intestine; **tripas** FPL (intestinos) bowels; (vísceras) guts; (Culin) tripe sg

tripé [tri'pɛ] M tripod

triplicar [tripli'kar] VT, VI to treble; **triplicar-se** VR to treble

tripulação [tripula'sãw] (pl -ões) F crew

tripulante [tripu'lãtʃi] M/F crew member

triste ['triʃtʃi] ADJ sad; (lugar) depressing

tristeza [triʃ'teza] F sadness; (de lugar) gloominess

triturar [tritu'rar] VT to grind

triunfar [trjũ'far] VI to triumph; **triunfo** ['trjũfu] M triumph

trivial [tri'vjaw] (pl -ais) ADJ common(place), ordinary; (insignificante) trivial

triz [triz] M: **por um ~** by a hair's breadth

troca ['trɔka] F exchange, swap

trocadilho [troka'dʒiʎu] M pun, play on words

trocado [tro'kadu] M: **~(s)** (small) change

trocador, a [troka'dor(a)] M/F (em ônibus) conductor

trocar [tro'kar] VT to exchange, swap; (mudar) to change; (inverter) to change ou swap round; (confundir) to mix up; **trocar-se** VR to change; **~ dinheiro** to change money

troco ['trɔku] M (dinheiro) change; (revide) retort, rejoinder

troféu [tro'fɛw] M trophy

tromba ['trõba] F (do elefante) trunk; (de outro animal) snout

trombeta [trõ'beta] F trumpet

trombone [trõ'boni] M trombone

trombose [trõ'bozi] F thrombosis

tronco ['trõku] M trunk; (ramo) branch; (de corpo) torso, trunk

trono ['trɔnu] M throne

tropa ['trɔpa] F troop; (exército) army; **ir para a ~** (PT) to join the army

tropeçar [trope'sar] VI to stumble, trip; (fig) to blunder

tropical [tropi'kaw] (pl -ais) ADJ tropical

trotar [tro'tar] vi to trot; **trote** ['trɔtʃi] M trot; (por telefone etc) hoax call

trouxe ['trosi] vB ver **trazer**

trovão [tro'vãw] (pl **-ões**) M clap of thunder; (trovoada) thunder; **trovejar** [trove'ʒar] vi to thunder; **trovoada** [tro'vwada] F thunderstorm

truque ['truki] M trick; (publicitário) gimmick

truta ['truta] F trout

tu [tu] PRON you

tua ['tua] F de **teu**

tuba ['tuba] F tuba

tubarão [tuba'rãw] (pl **-ões**) M shark

tuberculose [tuberku'lɔzi] F tuberculosis

tubo ['tubu] M tube, pipe; **~ de ensaio** test tube

tucano [tu'kanu] M toucan

tudo ['tudu] PRON everything; **~ quanto** everything that; **antes de ~** first of all; **acima de ~** above all

tufão [tu'fãw] (pl **-ões**) M typhoon

tuitar [twi'tar] vT, vi to tweet

tulipa [tu'lipa] F tulip

tumba ['tũba] F tomb; (lápide) tombstone

tumor [tu'mor] M tumour (BRIT), tumor (US)

túmulo ['tumulu] M tomb; (sepultura) burial

tumulto [tu'muwtu] M uproar, trouble; (grande movimento) bustle; (balbúrdia) hubbub; (motim) riot; **tumultuado, -a** [tumuw'twadu, a] ADJ riotous, heated; **tumultuar** [tumuw'twar] vT to disrupt; (amotinar) to rouse, incite

túnel ['tunew] (pl **-eis**) M tunnel

túnica ['tunika] F tunic

Tunísia [tu'nizja] F: **a ~** Tunisia

tupi [tu'pi] M Tupi (tribe); (Ling) Tupi ▸ M/F Tupi Indian

tupi-guarani [-gwara'ni] M see note

> **Tupi-guarani** is an important branch of indigenous languages from the tropical region of South America. It takes in thirty indigenous peoples and includes Tupi, Guarani, and other languages. Before Brazil was discovered by the Portuguese it had 1,300 indigenous languages, 87% of which are now extinct due to the extermination of indigenous peoples and the loss of territory.

tupiniquim [tupini'kĩ] (pej) (pl **-ns**) ADJ Brazilian (Indian)

turbilhão [turbi'ʎãw] (pl **-ões**) M (de vento) whirlwind; (de água) whirlpool

turbina [tur'bina] F turbine; **~ eólica** wind turbine

turbulência [turbu'lẽsja] F turbulence; **turbulento, -a** [turbu'lẽtu, a] ADJ turbulent

turco, -a ['turku, a] ADJ Turkish ▸ M/F Turk ▸ M (Ling) Turkish

turismo [tu'rizmu] M tourism; **turista** [tu'rista] M/F tourist ▸ ADJ (classe) tourist atr

turma ['turma] F group; (Educ) class

turquesa [tur'keza] ADJ INV turquoise

Turquia [tur'kia] F: **a ~** Turkey

tusso ['tusu] vB ver **tossir**

tutela [tu'tɛla] F protection; (Jur) guardianship

tutor, a [tu'tor(a)] M/F guardian

tutu [tu'tu] M (Culin) beans, bacon and manioc flour

TV [te've] ABR F (= televisão) TV

u

2 (*dando ênfase*): **estou com uma fome!**
I'm so hungry!; **ela é de uma beleza
incrível** she's incredibly beautiful
3: **um ao outro** one another; (*entre dois*)
each other

umbigo [ũ'bigu] M navel
umbilical [ũbili'kaw] (*pl* **-ais**) ADJ:
cordão ~ umbilical cord
umedecer [umede'ser] VT to moisten,
wet; **umedecer-se** VR to get wet
umidade [umi'dadʒi] F dampness;
(*clima*) humidity
úmido, -a ['umidu, a] ADJ wet, moist;
(*roupa*) damp; (*clima*) humid
unânime [u'nanimi] ADJ unanimous
unha ['uɲa] F nail; (*garra*) claw; **unhada**
[u'ɲada] F scratch
união [u'njãw] (*pl* **-ões**) F union; (*ato*)
joining; (*unidade, solidariedade*) unity;
(*casamento*) marriage; (*Tec*) joint; **a U~
Europeia** the European Union
unicamente [unika'mẽtʃi] ADV only
único, -a ['uniku, a] ADJ only; (*sem igual*)
unique; (*um só*) single
unidade [uni'dadʒi] F unity; (*Tec, Com*)
unit; **~ central de processamento**
(*Comput*) central processing unit; **~ de
disco** (*Comput*) disk drive
unido, -a [u'nidu, a] ADJ joined, linked;
(*fig*) united
unificar [unifi'kar] VT to unite; **unificar-
se** VR to join together
uniforme [uni'fɔrmi] ADJ uniform;
(*semelhante*) alike, similar; (*superfície*)
even ▶ M uniform; **uniformizado, -a**
[uniformi'zadu, a] ADJ uniform,
standardized; (*vestido de uniforme*) in
uniform; **uniformizar** [uniformi'zar] VT
to standardize
uniões [u'njõjs] FPL *de* **união**
unir [u'nir] VT to join together; (*ligar*) to
link; (*pessoas, fig*) to unite; (*misturar*) to
mix together; **unir-se** VR to come
together; (*povos etc*) to unite
uníssono [u'nisonu] M: **em ~** in unison
universal [univer'saw] (*pl* **-ais**) ADJ
universal; (*mundial*) worldwide
universidade [universi'dadʒi] F
university; **universitário, -a**
[universi'tarju, a] ADJ university *atr*
▶ M/F (*professor*) lecturer; (*aluno*)
university student
universo [uni'vɛrsu] M universe;
(*mundo*) world
uns [ũs] MPL *de* **um**
untar [ũ'tar] VT (*esfregar*) to rub; (*com óleo,
manteiga*) to grease

UE ABR F (= *União Europeia*) EU
Uganda [u'gãda] M Uganda
uísque ['wiski] M whisky (BRIT),
whiskey (US)
uivar [wi'var] VI to howl; (*berrar*) to yell;
uivo ['wivu] M howl; (*fig*) yell
úlcera ['uwsera] F ulcer
ultimamente [uwtʃima'mẽtʃi] ADV lately
ultimato [uwtʃi'matu] M ultimatum
último, -a ['uwtʃimu, a] ADJ last; (*mais
recente*) latest; (*qualidade*) lowest; (*fig*)
final; **por ~** finally; **nos ~s anos** in recent
years; **a última** (*notícia*) the latest (news)
ultra... [uwtra-] PREFIXO ultra-
ultrajar [uwtra'ʒar] VT to outrage;
(*insultar*) to insult, offend; **ultraje**
[uw'traʒi] M outrage; (*insulto*) insult,
offence (BRIT), offense (US)
ultramar [uwtra'mar] M overseas
ultrapassado, -a [uwtrapa'sadu, a] ADJ
(*ideias etc*) outmoded
ultrapassar [uwtrapa'sar] VT
(*atravessar*) to cross, go beyond; (*ir além
de*) to exceed; (*transgredir*) to overstep;
(*Auto*) to overtake (BRIT), pass (US); (*ser
superior a*) to surpass ▶ VI (*Auto*) to
overtake (BRIT), pass (US)
ultrassom [uwtra'sõ] M ultrasound
ultravioleta [uwtravjo'leta] ADJ
ultraviolet

(PALAVRA-CHAVE)

um, a [ũ, 'uma] (*pl* **uns/umas**) NUM one;
um e outro both; **um a um** one by one;
à uma (hora) at one (o'clock)
▶ ADJ: **uns cinco** about five; **uns poucos**
a few
▶ ART INDEF **1** (*sg*) a; (*antes de vogal ou 'h'
mudo*) an; (*pl*) some; **um livro** a book;
uma maçã an apple

urbanismo [urba'nizmu] M town planning

urbano, -a [ur'banu, a] ADJ (da cidade) urban; (fig) urbane

urgência [ur'ʒẽsja] F urgency; **com toda ~** as quickly as possible; **urgente** [ur'ʒẽtʃi] ADJ urgent

urina [u'rina] F urine; **urinar** [uri'nar] VI to urinate ▶ VT (sangue) to pass; (cama) to wet; **urinar-se** VR to wet o.s.; **urinol** [uri'nɔw] (pl **-óis**) M chamber pot

urna ['urna] F urn; **~ eleitoral** ballot box

urrar [u'har] VT, VI to roar; (de dor) to yell

ursa ['ursa] F bear

urso ['ursu] M bear

urtiga [ur'tʃiga] F nettle

Uruguai [uru'gwaj] M: **o ~** Uruguay

urze ['urzi] M heather

usado, -a [u'zadu, a] ADJ used; (comum) common; (roupa) worn; (gasto) worn out; (de segunda mão) second-hand

usar [u'zar] VT (servir-se de) to use; (vestir) to wear; (gastar com o uso) to wear out; (barba, cabelo curto) to have, wear ▶ VI: **~ de** to use; **modo de ~** directions pl

usina [u'zina] F (fábrica) factory; (de energia) plant

uso ['uzu] M use; (utilização) usage; (prática) practice

usual [u'zwaw] (pl **-ais**) ADJ usual; (comum) common

usuário, -a [uzu'warju, a] M/F user

usufruir [uzu'frwir] VT to enjoy ▶ VI: **~ de** to enjoy

úteis ['utejs] PL de **útil**

utensílio [utẽ'silju] M utensil

útero ['uteru] M womb, uterus

útil ['utʃiw] (pl **-eis**) ADJ useful; (vantajoso) profitable, worthwhile; **utilidade** [utʃili'dadʒi] F usefulness; **utilização** [utʃiliza'sãw] F use; **utilizador, a** [utʃiliza'dor(a)] (PT) M/F user; **utilizar** [utʃili'zar] VT to use; **utilizar-se** VR: **utilizar-se de** to make use of

uva ['uva] F grape

V

v ABR (= volt) v

vá [va] VB ver **ir**

vã [vã] F de **vão²**

vaca ['vaka] F COW; **carne de ~** beef

vacina [va'sina] F vaccine; **vacinar** [vasi'nar] VT to vaccinate

vácuo ['vakwu] M vacuum; (fig) void; (espaço) space

vaga ['vaga] F wave; (em hotel, trabalho) vacancy

vagão [va'gãw] (pl **-ões**) M (de passageiros) carriage; (de cargas) wagon; **vagão-leito** (pl **vagões-leitos**) (PT) M sleeping car; **vagão-restaurante** (pl **vagões-restaurantes**) M buffet car

vagar [va'gar] VI to wander about; (barco) to drift; (ficar vago) to be vacant

vagaroso, -a [vaga'rozu, ɔza] ADJ slow

vagina [va'ʒina] F vagina

vago, -a ['vagu, a] ADJ vague; (desocupado) vacant, free

vagões [va'gõjs] MPL de **vagão**

vai [vaj] VB ver **ir**

vaia ['vaja] F booing; **vaiar** [va'jar] VT, VI to boo, hiss

vaidade [vaj'dadʒi] F vanity; (futilidade) futility

vaidoso, -a [vaj'dozu, ɔza] ADJ vain

vaivém [vaj'vẽj] M to-ing and fro-ing

vala ['vala] F ditch

vale ['vali] M valley; (escrito) voucher; **~ postal** postal order

valer [va'ler] VI to be worth; (ser válido) to be valid; (ter influência) to carry weight; (servir) to serve; (ser proveitoso) to be useful; **valer-se** VR: **~-se de** to use, make use of; **~ a pena** to be worthwhile; **~ por** (equivaler) to be worth the same as; **para ~** (muito) very much, a lot; (realmente) for real, properly; **vale dizer** in other words; **mais vale ... (do que ...)** it would be better to ... (than ...)

valeta [va'leta] F gutter

valha ['vaʎa] VB ver **valer**

validade [vali'dadʒi] F validity; (de cartão de crédito) expiry date (BRIT), expiration date (US); (de alimento) best-before date

validar [vali'dar] VT to validate; **válido, -a** ['validu, a] ADJ valid

valioso, -a [va'ljozu, ɔza] ADJ valuable

valise [va'lizi] F case, grip

valor [va'lor] M value; (mérito) merit; (coragem) courage; (preço) price; (importância) importance; **valores** MPL (morais) values; (num exame) marks; (Com) securities; **dar ~ a** to value; **valorizar** [valori'zar] VT to value

valsa ['vawsa] F waltz

válvula ['vawvula] F valve

vampiro, -a [vã'piru, a] M/F vampire

vandalismo [vãda'lizmu] M vandalism

vândalo, -a [a'vãdalu, a] M/F vandal

vangloriar-se [vãglo'rjarsi] VR: **~ de** to boast of ou about

vanguarda [vã'gwarda] F vanguard; (arte) avant-garde

vantagem [vã'taʒẽ] (pl **-ns**) F advantage; (ganho) profit, benefit; **tirar ~ de** to take advantage of; **vantajoso, -a** [vãta'ʒozu, ɔza] ADJ advantageous; (lucrativo) profitable; (proveitoso) beneficial

vão¹ [vãw] VB ver **ir**

vão², vã [vãw, vã] (pl **-s/-s**) ADJ vain; (fútil) futile ▶ M (intervalo) space; (de porta etc) opening

vaqueiro [va'kejru] M cowboy

vara ['vara] F stick; (Tec) rod; (Jur) jurisdiction; (de porcos) herd; **salto de ~** pole vault; **~ de condão** magic wand

varal [va'raw] (pl **-ais**) M clothes line

varanda [va'rãda] F verandah; (balcão) balcony

varar [va'rar] VT to pierce; (passar) to cross

varejista [vare'ʒista] (BR) M/F retailer ▶ ADJ (mercado) retail

varejo [va'reʒu] (BR) M (Com) retail trade; **a ~** retail

variação [varja'sãw] (pl **-ões**) F variation

variado, -a [va'rjadu, a] ADJ varied; (sortido) assorted

variar [va'rjar] VT, VI to vary; **variável** [va'rjavew] (pl **-eis**) ADJ variable; (tempo, humor) changeable

varicela [vari'sela] F chickenpox

variedade [varje'dadʒi] F variety

varinha [va'riɲa] F wand; **~ de condão** magic wand

vário, -a ['varju, a] ADJ (diverso) varied; (pl) various, several; (Com) sundry

varizes [va'rizis] FPL varicose veins

varrer [va'her] VT to sweep; (fig) to sweep away

vaselina® [vaze'lina] F Vaseline®

vasilha [va'ziʎa] F (para líquidos) jug; (para alimentos) dish; (barril) barrel

vaso ['vazu] M pot; (para flores) vase

vassoura [va'sora] F broom

vasto, -a ['vastu, a] ADJ vast

vatapá [vata'pa] M fish or chicken with coconut milk, shrimps, peanuts, palm oil and spices

Vaticano [vatʃi'kanu] M: **o ~** the Vatican

vazamento [vaza'mẽtu] M leak

vazão [va'zãw] (pl **-ões**) F flow; (venda) sale; **dar ~ a** (expressar) to give vent to; (atender) to deal with; (resolver) to attend to

vazar [va'zar] VT to empty; (derramar) to spill; (verter) to pour out ▶ VI to leak

vazio, -a [va'ziu, a] ADJ empty; (pessoa) empty-headed, frivolous; (cidade) deserted ▶ M emptiness; (deixado por alguém/algo) void

vazões [va'zõjs] FPL de **vazão**

vê [ve] VB ver **ver**

veado ['vjadu] M deer; **carne de ~** venison

vedado, -a [ve'dadu, a] ADJ (proibido) forbidden; (fechado) enclosed

vedar [ve'dar] VT to ban, prohibit; (buraco) to stop up; (entrada, passagem) to block; (terreno) to close off

vegetação [veʒeta'sãw] F vegetation

vegetal [veʒe'taw] (pl **-ais**) ADJ vegetable atr; (reino, vida) plant atr ▶ M vegetable

vegetalista [veʒeta'lista] ADJ, M/F vegan

vegetariano, -a [veʒeta'rjanu, a] ADJ, M/F vegetarian

veia ['veja] F vein

veículo [ve'ikulu] M (tb: fig) vehicle

veio¹ ['veju] M (de rocha) vein; (na mina) seam; (de madeira) grain

veio² VB ver **vir**

vejo ['veʒu] VB ver **ver**

vela ['vela] F candle; (Auto) spark plug; (Náut) sail; **barco à ~** sailing boat

velar [ve'lar] VT to veil; (ocultar) to hide; (vigiar) to keep watch over; (um doente) to sit up with ▶ VI (não dormir) to stay up; (vigiar) to keep watch; **~ por** to look after

veleiro [ve'lejru] M sailing boat

velejar [vele'ʒar] VI to sail

velhaco, -a [ve'ʎaku, a] ADJ crooked ▶ M/F crook

velhice [ve'ʎisi] F old age

velho, -a ['vɛʎu, a] ADJ old ▶ M/F old man/woman

velocidade [velosi'dadʒi] F speed, velocity; (PT Auto) gear

velório [ve'lɔrju] M wake

veloz [ve'lɔz] ADJ fast

vem [vẽj] VB ver **vir¹**

vêm [vẽj] VB ver **vir¹**

vencedor, a [vẽse'dor(a)] ADJ winning ▶ M/F winner

vencer [vẽ'ser] VT (num jogo) to beat; (competição) to win; (inimigo) to defeat; (exceder) to surpass; (obstáculos) to overcome; (percorrer) to pass ▶ VI (num jogo) to win; **vencido, -a** [vẽ'sidu, a] ADJ: **dar-se por vencido** to give in; **vencimento** [vẽsi'mẽtu] M (Com) expiry; (data) expiry date; (salário) salary; (de gêneros alimentícios etc) sell-by date; **vencimentos** MPL (ganhos) earnings

venda ['vẽda] F sale; (pano) blindfold; (mercearia) general store; **à ~** on sale, for sale

vendaval [vẽda'vaw] (pl -ais) M gale

vendedor, a [vẽde'dor(a)] M/F seller; (em loja) sales assistant; (de imóvel) vendor; **~ ambulante** street vendor

vender [vẽ'der] VT, VI to sell; **~ por atacado/a varejo** to sell wholesale/retail

veneno [ve'nenu] M poison; **venenoso, -a** [vene'nozu, ɔza] ADJ poisonous

venerar [vene'rar] VT to revere; (Rel) to worship

venéreo, -a [ve'nɛrju, a] ADJ: **doença venérea** venereal disease

Venezuela [vene'zwɛla] F: **a ~** Venezuela

venha ['vẽɲa] VB ver **vir¹**

ventania [vẽta'nia] F gale

ventar [vẽ'tar] VI: **está ventando** it is windy

ventilação [vẽtʃila'saw] F ventilation

ventilador [vẽtʃila'dor] M ventilator; (elétrico) fan

vento ['vẽtu] M wind; (brisa) breeze; **ventoinha** [vẽ'twiɲa] F weathercock, weather vane; (PT Auto) fan

ventre ['vẽtri] M belly

ver [ver] VT to see; (olhar para, examinar) to look at; (televisão) to watch ▶ VI to see ▶ M: **a meu ~** in my opinion; **vai ~ que ...** maybe ...; **não tem nada a ~ (com)** it has nothing to do (with)

veracidade [verasi'dadʒi] F truthfulness

veraneio [vera'neju] M summer holidays pl (BRIT) ou vacation (US)

verão [ve'raw] (pl -ões) M summer

verba ['vɛrba] F allowance; **verba(s)** F(PL) (recursos) funds pl

verbal [ver'baw] (pl -ais) ADJ verbal

verbete [ver'betʃi] M (num dicionário) entry

verbo ['vɛrbu] M verb

verdade [ver'dadʒi] F truth; **na ~** in fact; **de ~** (falar) truthfully; (ameaçar etc) really; **para falar a ~** to tell the truth; **verdadeiro, -a** [verda'dejru, a] ADJ true; (genuíno) real; (pessoa) truthful

verde ['verdʒi] ADJ green; (fruta) unripe ▶ M green; (plantas etc) greenery

verdura [ver'dura] F (hortaliça) greens pl; (Bot) greenery; (cor verde) greenness

verdureiro, -a [verdu'rejru, a] M/F greengrocer (BRIT), produce dealer (US)

vereador, a [verja'dor(a)] M/F councillor (BRIT), councilor (US)

veredicto [vere'dʒiktu] M verdict

verga ['verga] F (vara) stick; (de metal) rod

vergonha [ver'goɲa] F shame; (timidez) embarrassment; (humilhação) humiliation; (ato indecoroso) indecency; (brio) self-respect; **ter ~** to be ashamed; (tímido) to be shy; **vergonhoso, -a** [vergo'nozu, ɔza] ADJ shameful; (indecoroso) disgraceful

verídico, -a [ve'ridʒiku, a] ADJ true, truthful

verificar [verifi'kar] VT to check; (confirmar, Comput) to verify

verme ['vɛrmi] M worm

vermelho, -a [ver'meʎu, a] ADJ red ▶ M red

verniz [ver'niz] M varnish; (couro) patent leather

verões [ve'rõjs] MPL de **verão**

verossímil [vero'simiw], (PT) **verosímil** (pl -eis) ADJ likely, probable; (crível) credible

verruga [ve'huga] F wart

versão [ver'saw] (pl -ões) F version; (tradução) translation

versátil [ver'satʃiw] (pl -eis) ADJ versatile

verso ['versu] M verse; (linha) line of poetry

versões [ver'sõjs] FPL de **versão**

verter [ver'ter] VT to pour; (por acaso) to spill; (traduzir) to translate; (lágrimas, sangue) to shed ▶ VI: **~ de** to spring from; **~ em** (rio) to flow into

vertical [vertʃi'kaw] (pl -ais) ADJ vertical; (de pé) upright, standing ▶ F vertical

vespa ['vespa] F wasp

véspera ['vespera] F: **a ~ (de)** the day before; **a ~ de Natal** Christmas Eve

vestiário [ves'tʃjarju] M (em casa, teatro) cloakroom; (Esporte) changing room (BRIT), locker-room (US); (de ator) dressing room

vestíbulo [ves'tʃibulu] M hall(way), vestibule; (Teatro) foyer

vestido, -a [ves'tʃidu, a] ADJ: ~ de **branco** etc dressed in white etc ▶ M dress

vestígio [ves'tʃiʒju] M (rastro) track; (fig) sign, trace

vestimenta [vestʃi'mẽta] F garment

vestir [ves'tʃir] VT (uma criança) to dress; (pôr sobre si) to put on; (trajar) to wear; (comprar, dar roupa para) to clothe; (fazer roupa para) to make clothes for; **vestir-se** VR to get dressed

vestível [vestibel] ADJ (Comput) wearable

vestuário [ves'twarju] M clothing

veterano, -a [vete'ranu, a] ADJ, M/F veteran

veterinário, -a [veteri'narju, a] M/F vet(erinary surgeon)

veto ['vetu] M veto

véu [vɛw] M veil

vexame [ve'ʃami] F shame, disgrace; (tormento) affliction; (humilhação) humiliation; (afronta) insult

vez [vez] F time; (turno) turn; **uma ~ once**; (algumas ~es, às ~es sometimes; ~ por outra sometimes; cada ~ (que) every time; de ~ em quando from time to time; em ~ de instead of; uma ~ que since; **3 ~es 6** 3 times 6; de uma ~ por todas once and for all; muitas ~es many times; (frequentemente) often; toda ~ que every time; um de cada ~ one at a time; uma ~ ou outra once in a while

vi [vi] VB ver **ver**

via¹ ['via] F road, route; (meio) way; (documento) copy; (conduto) channel ▶ PREP via, by way of; em ~s de in the process of; por ~ terrestre/marítima by land/sea

via² VB ver **ver**

viaduto [vja'dutu] M viaduct

viagem ['vjaʒẽ] (pl -ns) F journey, trip; (o viajar) travel; (Náut) voyage; **viagens** FPL (jornadas) travels; ~ de ida e volta return trip, round trip

viajante [vja'ʒãtʃi] ADJ travelling (BRIT), traveling (US) ▶ M traveller (BRIT), traveler (US)

viajar [vja'ʒar] VI to travel

viável ['vjavew] (pl -eis) ADJ feasible, viable

víbora ['vibora] F viper

vibração [vibra'sãw] (pl -ões) F vibration; (fig) thrill

vibrante [vi'brãtʃi] ADJ vibrant; (discurso) stirring

vibrar [vi'brar] VT to brandish; (fazer estremecer) to vibrate; (cordas) to strike ▶ VI to vibrate; (som) to echo

vice ['visi] M/F deputy

vice- [visi-] PREFIXO vice-; **vice-presidente, -a** M/F vice president; **vice-versa** [-'vɛrsa] ADV vice versa

viciado, -a [vi'sjadu, a] ADJ addicted; (ar) foul ▶ M/F addict; ~ em algo addicted to sth

viciar [vi'sjar] VT (falsificar) to falsify; **viciar-se** VR: ~-se em algo to become addicted to sth

vício ['visju] M vice; (defeito) failing; (costume) bad habit; (em entorpecentes) addiction

viço ['visu] M vigour (BRIT), vigor (US); (da pele) freshness

vida ['vida] F life; (duração) lifetime; (fig) vitality; **com ~ alive**; **ganhar a ~ to earn** one's living; **modo de ~ way of life**; **dar a ~ por algo/por fazer algo** to give one's right arm for sth/to do sth; **estar bem de ~** to be well off

videira [vi'dejra] F grapevine

vidente [vi'dẽtʃi] M/F clairvoyant

vídeo ['vidʒju] M video; **videocassete** [vidʒjuka'setʃi] M video cassette ou tape; (aparelho) video (recorder); **videoteipe** [vidʒju'tejpi] M video tape

vidraça [vi'drasa] F window pane

vidrado, -a [vi'dradu, a] ADJ glazed; (porta) glass atr; (olhos) glassy

vidro ['vidru] M glass; (frasco) bottle; **fibra de ~** fibreglass (BRIT), fiberglass (US); ~ de aumento magnifying glass

vier [vjer] VB ver **vir¹**

viés [vjɛs] M slant; ao ou de ~ diagonally

vieste ['vjestʃi] VB ver **vir¹**

Vietnã [vjet'nã] M: o ~ Vietnam; **vietnamita** [vjetna'mita] ADJ, M/F Vietnamese

vigiar [vi'ʒjar] VT to watch; (ocultamente) to spy on; (presos, fronteira) to guard ▶ VI to be on the lookout

vigilância [viʒi'lãsja] F vigilance; **vigilante** [viʒi'lãtʃi] ADJ vigilant; (atento) alert

vigor [vi'gor] M energy; **em ~** in force; **entrar/pôr em ~** to take effect/put into effect; **vigoroso, -a** [vigo'rozu, ɔza] ADJ vigorous

vil [viw] (pl **vis**) ADJ vile

vila ['vila] F town; (casa) villa

vilão, -lã [vi'lãw, 'lã] (*pl* **-ões/-s**) M/F
villain

vilarejo [vila'reʒu] M village

vim [vĩ] VB *ver* **vir¹**

vime ['vimi] M wicker

vinagre [vi'nagri] M vinegar

vinco ['vĩku] M crease; (*sulco*) furrow;
(*no rosto*) line

vincular [vĩku'lar] VT to link, tie;
vínculo ['vĩkulu] M bond, tie; (*relação*)
link

vinda ['vĩda] F arrival; (*regresso*) return;
dar as boas ~ s a to welcome

vingança [vĩ'gãsa] F vengeance,
revenge; **vingar** [vĩ'gar] VT to avenge;
vingar-se VR: **vingar-se de** to take
revenge on; **vingativo, -a** [vĩga'tʃivu, a]
ADJ vindictive

vinha¹ ['viɲa] F vineyard; (*planta*) vine

vinha² VB *ver* **vir¹**

vinho ['viɲu] M wine; **~ branco/
rosado/tinto** white/rosé/red wine;
~ seco/doce dry/sweet wine; **~ do
Porto** port

vinte ['vĩtʃi] NUM twenty

viola ['vjɔla] F viola

violão [vjo'lãw] (*pl* **-ões**) M guitar

violar [vjo'lar] VT to violate; (*a lei*) to
break

violência [vjo'lẽsja] F violence;
violentar [vjolẽ'tar] VT to force; (*mulher*)
to rape; **violento, -a** [vjo'lẽtu, a] ADJ
violent

violeta [vjo'leta] F violet

violino [vjo'linu] M violin

violões [vjo'lõjs] MPL *de* **violão**

violoncelo [vjolõ'sɛlu] M cello

vir¹ [vir] VI to come; **~ a ser** to turn out to
be; **a semana que vem** next week

vir² VB *ver* **ver**

viral [vi'raw] ADJ (*tb: Comput*) viral

vira-lata ['vira-] (*pl* **vira-latas**) M (*cão*)
mongrel

virar [vi'rar] VT to turn; (*página, disco,
barco*) to turn over; (*copo*) to empty;
(*transformar-se em*) to become ▶ VI to
turn; (*barco*) to capsize; (*mudar*) to
change; **virar-se** VR to turn; (*voltar-se*) to
turn round; (*defender-se*) to fend for o.s.

virgem ['virʒẽ] (*pl* **-ns**) F virgin; **V~**
(*Astrologia*) Virgo

vírgula ['virgula] F comma; (*decimal*)
point

viril [vi'riw] (*pl* **-is**) ADJ virile

virilha [vi'riʎa] F groin

viris [vi'ris] ADJ PL *de* **viril**

virtual [vir'twaw] (*pl* **-ais**) ADJ virtual;
(*potencial*) potential

virtude [vir'tudʒi] F virtue; **em ~ de**
owing to, because of; **virtuoso, -a**
[vir'twozu, ɔza] ADJ virtuous

virulento, -a [viru'lẽtu, a] ADJ virulent

vírus ['virus] M INV (*tb: Comput*) virus; **~
Ébola** (*PT*) Ebola virus; **~ Zika** Zika virus

vis [vis] ADJ PL *de* **vil**

visão [vi'zãw] (*pl* **-ões**) F vision; (*Anat*)
eyesight; (*vista*) sight; (*maneira de
perceber*) view

visar [vi'zar] VT (*alvo*) to aim at; (*ter em
vista*) to have in view; (*ter como objetivo*)
to aim for

vísceras ['viseras] FPL innards, bowels

visita [vi'zita] F visit, call; (*pessoa*) visitor;
(*na Internet*) hit; **fazer uma ~ a** to visit;
~ guiada guided tour; **visitante**
[vizi'tãtʃi] ADJ visiting ▶ M/F visitor;
visitar [vizi'tar] VT to visit

visível [vi'zivew] (*pl* **-eis**) ADJ visible

vislumbrar [vizlũ'brar] VT to glimpse,
catch a glimpse of; **vislumbre** [viz'lũbri]
M glimpse

visões [vi'zõjs] FPL *de* **visão**

visse ['visi] VB *ver* **ver**

vista ['vista] F sight; (*Med*) eyesight;
(*panorama*) view; **à** *ou* **em ~ de** in view of;
dar na ~ to attract attention; **dar uma
~ de olhos em** to glance at; **fazer ~
grossa (a)** to turn a blind eye (to); **ter
em ~** to have in mind; **à ~** visible,
showing; (*Com*) in cash; **até a ~!** see you!

visto¹, -a ['vistu, a] PP *de* **ver** ▶ ADJ seen
▶ M (*em passaporte*) visa; (*em documento*)
stamp; **pelo ~** by the looks of things

visto² VB *ver* **vestir**

vistoria [visto'ria] F inspection

vistoso, -a [vis'tozu, ɔza] ADJ
eye-catching

visual [vi'zwaw] (*pl* **-ais**) ADJ visual;
visualizar [vizwali'zar] VT to visualize

vital [vi'taw] (*pl* **-ais**) ADJ vital; **vitalício,
-a** [vita'lisju, a] ADJ for life

vitamina [vita'mina] F vitamin; (*para
beber*) fruit crush

vitela [vi'tɛla] F calf; (*carne*) veal

vítima ['vitʃima] F victim

vitória [vi'tɔrja] F victory; **vitorioso, -a**
[vito'rjozu, ɔza] ADJ victorious

vitrina [vi'trina] F = **vitrine**

vitrine [vi'trini] F shop window;
(*armário*) display case

viúvo, -a ['vjuvu, a] M/F widower/
widow

viva ['viva] M cheer; **~!** hurray!

viva-voz [viva'vɔz] M (*BR Tel: em telefone*)
speakerphone; (*para celular*) hands-free kit

viveiro [vi'vejru] M nursery

vivência [vi'vēsja] F existence; (*experiência*) experience

vivenda [vi'vēda] F (*casa*) residence

viver [vi'ver] vi, vt to live ▶ M life; ~ **de** to live on

vívido, -a ['vividu, a] ADJ vivid

vivo, -a ['vivu, a] ADJ living; (*esperto*) clever; (*cor*) bright; (*criança, debate*) lively ▶ M: **os ~s** the living

vizinhança [vizi'nãsa] F neighbourhood (BRIT), neighborhood (US)

vizinho, -a [vi'ziɲu, a] ADJ neighbouring (BRIT), neighboring (US); (*perto*) nearby ▶ M/F neighbour (BRIT), neighbor (US)

vó [vɔ] (*col*) F gran

vô [vo] (*col*) M grandad, grandpa

voar [vo'ar] vi to fly; (*explodir*) to blow up, explode

vocabulário [vokabu'larju] M vocabulary

vocábulo [vo'kabulu] M word

vocal [vo'kaw] (*pl* -**ais**) ADJ vocal

você [vo'se] PRON you

vocês [vo'ses] PRON PL you

vodca ['vɔdʒka] F vodka

vogal [vo'gaw] (*pl* -**ais**) F (*Ling*) vowel

vol. ABR (= *volume*) vol

volante [vo'lãtʃi] M steering wheel

vôlei ['volej] M volleyball

voleibol [volej'bɔw] M = **vôlei**

volt ['vɔwtʃi] (*pl* -**s**) M volt

volta ['vɔwta] F turn; (*regresso*) return; (*curva*) bend, curve; (*circuito*) lap; (*resposta*) retort; **dar uma** ~ (*a pé*) to go for a walk; (*de carro*) to go for a drive; **estar de** ~ to be back; **na** ~ **do correio** by return (post); **por** ~ **de** about, around; **à** *ou* **em** ~ **de** around; **na** ~ (*no caminho de volta*) on the way back

voltagem [vow'taʒē] F voltage

voltar [vow'tar] vt to turn ▶ vi to return, go (*ou* come) back; **voltar-se** vr to turn round; ~ **a fazer** to do again; ~ **a si** to come to; ~-**se para** to turn to; ~-**se contra** to turn against

volume [vo'lumi] M volume; (*pacote*) package; **volumoso, -a** [volu'mozu, ɔza] ADJ bulky, big

voluntário, -a [volũ'tarju, a] ADJ voluntary ▶ M/F volunteer

volúvel [vo'luvew] (*pl* -**eis**) ADJ fickle

vomitar [vomi'tar] vt, vi to vomit; **vômito** ['vomitu] M (*ato*) vomiting; (*efeito*) vomit

vontade [võ'tadʒi] F will; (*desejo*) wish; **com** ~ (*com prazer*) with pleasure; (*com gana*) with gusto; **estar com** *ou* **ter** ~ **de fazer** to feel like doing

voo ['vou] M flight; **levantar** ~ to take off; ~ **livre** (*Esporte*) hang-gliding

voraz [vo'rajz] ADJ voracious

vos [vus] PRON you

vós [vɔs] PRON you

vosso, -a ['vɔsu, a] ADJ your ▶ PRON: **(o)** ~ yours

votação [vota'sãw] (*pl* -**ões**) F vote, ballot; (*ato*) voting

votar [vo'tar] vt (*eleger*) to vote for; (*aprovar*) to pass; (*submeter a votação*) to vote on ▶ vi to vote; **voto** ['vɔtu] M vote; (*promessa*) vow; **votos** MPL (*desejos*) wishes

vou [vo] VB ver **ir**

vovó [vo'vɔ] F grandma

vovô [vo'vo] M grandad

voz [vɔz] F voice; (*clamor*) cry; **a meia** ~ in a whisper; **de viva** ~ orally; **ter** ~ **ativa** to have a say; **em** ~ **baixa** in a low voice; **em** ~ **alta** aloud; ~ **de comando** command

vulcão [vuw'kãw] (*pl* -**ões**) M volcano

vulgar [vuw'gar] ADJ common; (*pej*: *pessoa etc*) vulgar

vulnerável [vuwne'ravew] (*pl* -**eis**) ADJ vulnerable

vulto ['vuwtu] M figure; (*volume*) mass; (*fig*) importance; (*pessoa importante*) important person

W X

walkie-talkie [wɔki'tɔki] (*pl* **-s**) M
walkie-talkie
watt ['wɔtʃi] (*pl* **-s**) M watt
web ['wɛbi] F, ADJ (*Comput*) web
webcam [wɛb'cã] F webcam
windsurfe M windsurfing

xadrez [ʃa'dɾez] M chess; (*tabuleiro*)
chessboard; (*tecido*) checked cloth
xampu [ʃã'pu] M shampoo
xarope [ʃa'ɾɔpi] M syrup; (*para a tosse*)
cough syrup
xeque ['ʃɛki] M (*soberano*) sheikh; **pôr
em ~** (*fig*) to call into question;
xeque-mate (*pl* **xeques-mate**) M
checkmate
xerocar [ʃeɾo'kar] VT to photocopy,
Xerox®
xerox® [ʃe'ɾɔks] M (*cópia*) photocopy;
(*máquina*) photocopier
xícara ['ʃikaɾa] (BR) F cup
xingar [ʃĩ'gar] VT to swear at ▶ VI to
swear
Xingu [ʃĩ'gu] M *see note*

> The **Xingu** National Park was created
> in 1961 by the federal government and
> directed by the brothers Orlando and
> Cláudio Vilasboas, who were known
> internationally for their efforts to
> preserve Brazil's indigenous people.
> Situated in the north of the state of
> Mato Grosso, it aims to preserve
> indigenous culture. It brings together
> sixteen communities, a total of two
> thousand Indians.

Z

zagueiro [za'gejɾu] M (*Futebol*) fullback
Zâmbia ['zãbja] F Zambia
zangado, -a [zã'gadu, a] ADJ angry;
annoyed; (*irritadiço*) bad-tempered
zangar [zã'gar] VT to annoy, irritate ▶ VI to
get angry; **zangar-se** VR (*aborrecer-se*) to
get annoyed; **~-se com** to get cross with
zarpar [zar'par] VI (*navio*) to set sail;
(*ir-se*) to set off; (*fugir*) to run away
zebra ['zebra] F zebra

zelador, a [zela'dor(a)] M/F caretaker
zelar [ze'lar] VT, VI: **~ (por)** to look after
zerar [ze'rar] VT (*conta, inflação*) to reduce
to zero; (*déficit*) to pay off, wipe out
zero ['zɛru] M zero; (*Esporte*) nil;
zero-quilômetro ADJ INV brand new
ziguezague [zigi'zagi] M zigzag
Zimbábue [zĩ'babwi] M: **o ~** Zimbabwe
-zinho, -a [-'ziɲu, a] SUFIXO little;
florzinha little flower
zíper ['ziper] M zip (BRIT), zipper (US)
zodíaco [zo'dʒiaku] M zodiac
zoeira ['zwejra] F din
zombar [zõ'bar] VI to mock; **~ de** to
make fun of; **zombaria** [zõba'ria] F
mockery, ridicule
zona ['zona] F area; (*de cidade*) district;
(*Geo*) zone; (*col: local de meretrício*)
red-light district; (: *confusão*) mess;
(: *tumulto*) free-for-all; **~ eleitoral**
electoral district, constituency
zonzo, -a ['zõzu, a] ADJ dizzy
zoo ['zou] M zoo
zoológico, -a [zo'lɔʒiku, a] ADJ
zoological; **jardim ~** zoo
zumbido [zũ'bidu] M buzz(ing); (*de
tráfego*) hum
zunzum [zũ'zũ] M buzz(ing)